April 18–20, 2017
Pittsburgh, PA, USA

Association for Computing Machinery

Advancing Computing as a Science & Profession

HSCC'17

Proceedings of the 20th International Conference on Hybrid Systems: Computation and Control (part of CPS Week)

Sponsored by:

ACM SIGBED

Supported by:

CSS, Denso, and Toyota

Association for
Computing Machinery

Advancing Computing as a Science & Profession

The Association for Computing Machinery
2 Penn Plaza, Suite 701
New York, New York 10121-0701

ISBN: 978-1-4503-4590-3 (Digital)

ISBN: 978-1-4503-4590-3 (Print)

Additional copies may be ordered prepaid from:

ACM Order Department
PO Box 30777
New York, NY 10087-0777, USA

Phone: 1-800-342-6626 (USA and Canada)
+1-212-626-0500 (Global)
Fax: +1-212-944-1318
E-mail: acmhelp@acm.org
Hours of Operation: 8:30 am – 4:30 pm ET

Printed in the USA

Welcome Remarks from HSCC 2017 Program Committee Chairs

Welcome to the proceedings of the 20th ACM International Conference on *Hybrid Systems: Computation and Control* (HSCC'17), held in Pittsburgh, Pennsylvania. HSCC is the premier research conference on foundations of Cyber-Physical Systems. It covers design, analysis, control synthesis techniques and their applications in various domains such as autonomous vehicles, robotics, mixed signal circuits, infrastructure networks, as well as in biochemical models that demonstrate hybrid behavior.

HSCC'17 is held as part of the 10th Cyber Physical Systems Week (CPS Week'17), and located with the International Conference on Cyber-Physical Systems (ICCPS), the International Conference on Information Processing in Sensor Networks (IPSN), the Real-Time and Embedded Technology and Applications Symposium (RTAS), the International Conference on Internet-of-things: Design and Implementation (IOTDI), and several CPSWeek Workshops.

There were 76 submissions to HSCC 2017—a number that is comparable to recent HSCCs held in the United States. 25 regular papers and 4 tool and case study papers were accepted for inclusion in the conference program. The overall acceptance rate for the conference is 38%; for regular papers the acceptance rate is 39%. More information about previous editions of HSCC can be found at http://www.hscc-conference.org.

This year we introduced a light version of double blind reviewing to improve the quality and integrity of the review process. The process is time-tested in other conferences like SIGCOMM, PLDI, and CAV. The policies and process were disseminated in the HSCC 2017 website (http://hscc2017.ece.illinois.edu) as well as in the Calls For Papers. Author's names were omitted from submissions and authors had to cite their own papers in the third person. Fifty Program Committee (PC) members and their sub-reviewers provided at least 4 reviews for each of the anonymized submissions. The reviews were sent to authors for a 5-day rebuttal period. For the rebuttal, author identities were disclosed to the reviewers, and optional auxiliary material from the authors (proofs etc.) were made available to the PC. The final decisions were made after two weeks of vigorous on-line discussions amongst the PC members.

Most of the technical program committee members provided excellent, in-depth reviews. We checked that all reviews provided the appropriate level of detail, gave actionable feedback to authors, and struck the right tone. In addition, reviewers were directed to read and respond to author responses, and a summary of the on-line discussions was included to provide feedback to the authors.

In addition to the papers appearing in the proceedings, HSCC demos and posters were presented at the joint CPSWeek Poster and Demo session. The Demo and Poster session for HSCC was chaired by Akshay Rajhans.

Since 2014, HSCC features a Repeatability Evaluation (RE) process, which draws upon several similar efforts at other conferences (SIGMOD, SAS, CAV, ECOOP, OOPSLA, all of them having an emphasis on "artifacts"). Re-creation of computational elements presented in research papers is challenging because details of the implementation are unavoidably absent in the paper. The goal of the HSCC RE process is to improve the reproducibility of computational results in the papers selected for the conference. The effort was led by Sergiy Bogomolov, aided by an RE Committee of 21 researchers, providing at least 3 evaluations to each of the 14 submitted RE packages. The papers that have passed the RE process are highlighted in the proceedings with an RE stamp on their first page.

HSCC 2017 features three awards: a best student paper award, a best poster/demo award, and a best RE award. These awards have been administered by the Awards Committee, headed by Ricardo Sanfelice. A significant highlight of HSCC 2017 is the 20th Anniversary Invited Talk by Russ Tedrake of MIT, in addition to several CPSWeek'17 plenary talks.

HSCC 2017 is the result of the combined efforts of many individuals to whom we are deeply grateful. We thank the PC chairs of HSCC`16, Alessandro Abate and Georgios Fainekos, for prompt and valuable advice. Thanks to Sergiy Bogomolov for leading the RE process, Necmiye Ozay for help with publicity, Akshay Rajhans for chairing the Demos and Posters session, Hussein M. Sibai for managing the website, and Ricardo Sanfelice for leading the Awards Committee. We would also like to thank the HSCC Steering Committee: Rajeev Alur, Werner Damm, John Lygeros, Oded Maler, Paulo Tabuada, and Claire Tomlin. Special thanks to the CPSWeek organizers for their tremendous support. We especially thank ACM Program Coordinator Abbi Sumandal, and Lisa Tolles of Sheridan Printing. We gratefully acknowledge our industrial sponsors Denso Corporation and Toyota Motor Engineering & Manufacturing North America. Finally, we thank the PC members and the sub-reviewers for their hard work in ensuring the quality of the contributions, the authors for entrusting their research to the HSCC review process, and the participants for contributing in the discussions. We hope that you find HSCC 2017 to be inspiring, thought provoking, and memorable.

Goran Frehse and Sayan Mitra

HSCC'17 Program Committee Chairs

Table of Contents

HSCC 2017 Conference Organization

Program Chairs: Goran Frehse *(Univ. Grenoble Alpes)*
Sayan Mitra *(University of Illinois at Urbana Champaign)*

Awards Chair: Ricardo Sanfelice *(University of Arizona)*

Publicity Chair: Necmiye Ozay *(University of Michigan)*

Demo & Poster Session Chair: Akshay Rajhans *(The MathWorks)*

Repeatability Evaluation Chair: Sergiy Bogomolov *(Australian National University)*

Webmaster: Hussein Sibai *(University of Illinois at Urbana-Champaign)*

Steering Committee: Rajeev Alur *(University of Pennsylvania)*
Werner Damm *(OFFIS)*
John Lygeros *(ETH Zurich)*
Oded Maler *(Verimag)*
Paulo Tabuada *(UCLA)*
Claire Tomlin *(University of California Berkeley)*

Program Committee: Alessandro Abate *(Oxford University)*
Erika Abraham *(RWTH Aachen University)*
Matthias Althoff *(TU München)*
Saurabh Amin *(MIT)*
Murat Arcak *(UC Berkeley)*
Shun-Ichi Azuma *(Kyoto University)*
Hamsa Balakrishnan *(MIT)*
Ezio Bartocci *(TU Wien)*
Calin Belta *(Boston University)*
Sergiy Bogomolov *(Australian National University)*
Alessandro Cimatti *(Fondazione Bruno Kessler)*
Alessandro D'Innocenzo *(University of L'Aquila)*
Thao Dang *(VERIMAG, France)*
Anupam Datta *(Carnegie Mellon University)*
Jyotirmoy Deshmukh *(Toyota)*
Arvind Easwaran *(Nanyang Technological University)*
Georgios Fainekos *(Arizona State University)*
Lu Feng *(University of Virginia)*
Martin Fränzle *(Carl von Ossietzky Universität Oldenburg)*
Sicun Gao *(MIT)*
Antoine Girard *(Laboratoire des Signaux et Systèmes - CNRS)*
Ichiro Hasuo *(University of Tokyo)*
Franjo Ivancic *(Google)*Taylor T Johnson *(Vanderbilt University)*

Program Committee (continued):

Taylor T Johnson *(Vanderbilt University)*
James Kapinski *(Toyota)*
Hadas Kress-Gazit *(Cornell University)*
Marta Kwiatkowska *(Oxford University)*
Mircea Lazar *(Eindhoven University of Technology)*
Jun Liu *(University of Waterloo)*
Daniele Magazzeni *(King's College London)*
Manuel Mazo Jr. *(TU Delft)*
Ian Mitchell *(University of British Columbia)*
Meeko Oishi *(University of New Mexico)*
Necmiye Ozay *(University of Michigan)*
André Platzer *(Carnegie Mellon University)*
Vinayak Prabhu *(MPI-SWS)*
Maria Prandini *(Politecnico di Milano)*
Akshay Rajhans *(MathWorks)*
S Ramesh *(General Motors)*
Grigore Rosu *(University of Illinois at Urbana-Champaign)*
Indranil Saha *(Indian Institute of Technology Kanpur)*
Ricardo Sanfelice *(University of Arizona)*
Scott Smolka *(Stony Brook Universtiy)*
Oleg Sokolsky *(University of Pennsylvania)*
Herbert Tanner *(University of Delaware)*
Ashish Tiwari *(SRI)*
Ufuk Topcu *(University of Texas at Austin)*
Jana Tumova *(Royal Institute of Technology)*
Ram Vasudevan *(University of Michigan)*

Additional reviewers:

Arvind Adimoolam
Mohd Ashraf Ahmad
Francisco Penedo Alvarez
Kyungmin Bae
Stanley Bak
Ayca Balkan
Nicolas Basset
Mohamed Amin Ben Sassi
Brandon Bohrer
Giuseppe Bombara
Dimitris Boskos
Marco Bozzano
Manuela Bujorianu
Pedro Casau
Xiaohong Chen
Samuel Coogan
Sankar Narayan Das
Tommaso Dreossi
Chuchu Fan
Anqi Fu
Marco Gario
Daniel Gburek
Sebastian Gerwinn
Khalil Ghorbal
Joseph Gleason
Karthik Gopalakrishnan
Alberto Griggio
Meng Guo
Shuo Han
Everett Hildenbrandt
Baisravan Homchaudhuri
Xiaowei Huang
Ahmed Irfan
Ran Ji
Xiaoqing Jin
Li Jin
Jesper Karlsson
Eric Kim

Additional reviewers (continued):

Koichi Kobayashi
Hui Kong
Gereon Kremer
Tanmoy Kundu
Morteza Lahijanian
Luca Laurenti
Kevin Leahy
Kendra Lesser
Hai Lin
Curtis Madsen
Igor Melatti
Pierre-Jean Meyer
Andrea Micheli
Stefan Mitsch
Swarup Mohalik
Ryosuke Morita
Peter Nazier Mosaad
Nedialko Nedialkov
Dejan Nickovic
Petter Nilsson
Gregor Nitsche
Masahiro Ono
Nicola Paoletti
Ivan Papusha
Daejun Park
Dung Phan
Vasumathi Raman
Rajarshi Ray
Alexandre Rocca
Marco Roveri
Sadra Sadraddini
Manoranjan Satpathy
Stefan Schupp
Matt Shubert
Hussein Sibaie
Andrew Sogokon
Sadegh Soudjani
David Spivak
Adam Stager
Vijayakumar Sundar
Mária Svoreňová
Stefano Tonetta
Natsuki Urabe
Cristian-Ioan Vasile
Marcell Vazquez-Chanlatte
Cees Verdier
Abraham Vinod
Yu Wang
Edmund Widl
Eric Wolff
Xiangru Xu
Guosong Yang
Junxing Yang
Wei Zhang

Repeatability Evaluation Committee:

Nikos Arechiga
Stanley Bak
Sergiy Bogomolov
Milan Ceska
Xin Chen
Marcelo Forets
Khalil Ghorbal
Mirco Giacobbe
Ernst Moritz Hahn
Bardh Hoxha
Ievgen Ivanov
Umang Mathur
Marius Mikučionis
Ian Mitchell
Nicola Paoletti
Junkil Park
Carna Radojicic
Rajarshi Ray
Matthias Rungger
Christian Schilling
Fedor Shmarov
Sadegh Soudjani

HSCC 2017 Sponsor & Supporters

Sponsor: ACM SIGBED

Technical Supporter: CSS

Donors: DENSO TOYOTA

Forward Inner-Approximated Reachability of Non-Linear Continuous Systems

Eric Goubault
LIX, Ecole Polytechnique, CNRS,
Université Paris-Saclay, 91128 Palaiseau,
France
goubault@lix.polytechnique.fr

Sylvie Putot
LIX, Ecole Polytechnique, CNRS,
Université Paris-Saclay, 91128 Palaiseau,
France
putot@lix.polytechnique.fr

ABSTRACT

We propose an approach for computing inner-approximations (also called under-approximations) of reachable sets of dynamical systems defined by non-linear, uncertain, ordinary differential equations. This is a notoriously difficult problem, much more intricate than outer-approximations (also called over-approximations), for which there exist well known solutions, mostly based on Taylor models. The few methods developed recently for inner-approximation mostly rely on backward flowmaps, and extra ingredients, either coming from optimization, or involving topological criteria, are required. Our solution, in comparison, builds on rather inexpensive set-based methods, namely a generalized mean-value theorem combined with Taylor models outer-approximations of the flow and its Jacobian with respect to the uncertain inputs and parameters. We demonstrate with a C/C++ prototype implementation that our method is both efficient and precise on classical examples. The combination of such forward inner and outer Taylor-model based approximations can be used as a basis for the verification and falsification of properties of cyber-physical systems.

Keywords

Inner-approximation; Taylor models; affine arithmetic; modal intervals; reachability

1. INTRODUCTION

We propose an approach to compute inner-approximating flowpipes, that under-approximate reachable sets of uncertain continuous systems described by ordinary differential equations, which are widely used for modeling all sorts of physical, biological and even economic or social systems.

While outer-approximations describe states that may be reached, inner-approximations represent states that are actually reachable from one of the initial states. They are thus a very useful complement to the more classical outer-approximations, since they allow to show that some executions of the system will actually reach a target or a bad state. Also, the combination of inner and outer-approximations allows for judging the quality of the abstractions involved. But methods for inner-approximated reachability are far less developed, and especially in the non-linear case, since most methods in the non-linear case rely on conservative linearizations, which necessarily produce outer approximations.

In this work, we concentrate on the inner-approximation of the reachable sets of the continuous part of hybrid systems. We consider general systems of parametric ODEs, i.e. possibly non-linear, or even non-polynomial, of the form :

$$\dot{x}(t) = f(x, p, t) \tag{1}$$

where the continuous variables x belong to a state-space domain $\mathcal{D} \subseteq \mathbb{R}^n$, the (constant) parameters p belong to the uncertainty domain $\mathcal{P} \subseteq \mathbb{R}^p$, and $f : \mathcal{D} \times \mathcal{P} \times \mathbb{R}^+ \to \mathcal{D}$ is assumed sufficiently smooth on $\mathcal{D} \subseteq \mathbb{R}^n$ (at least $\mathcal{C}^1$, and sometimes more when we will use higher Taylor models, see Section 2.4).

Introducing the new state variable $z = (x, p, t)$ with $\dot{z} = (\dot{x}, 0, 1)$, and defining $\mathcal{Z} = \mathcal{D} \times \mathcal{P} \times \mathbb{R}^+$, the equation (1) can be rewritten with all uncertainties embedded in the initial state vector :

$$\dot{z}(t) = f(z) \tag{2}$$

In the sequel, we will write x_i and f_i for the ith component $(i = 1, \ldots, n)$ of the state vector x and of the function f.

Contributions:.
This paper extends the work of [13, 14], where were proposed an approach for direct forward inner-approximated reachability of discrete dynamical systems, and a few hints to handle continuous and hybrid systems. We are computing here inner-approximations of the flow of uncertain initial value problems, as defined in Section 2. There are two main ingredients involved in our method. The first ingredient is that in order to derive inner-approximations, we only need forward outer-approximations of some dynamics, which we can compute using classical Taylor models, introduced in Section 2.4. But we need to outer-approximate not only the set of reachable states of the dynamics but also of the variational equations, including the dynamics of the Jacobian of the flow with respect to the uncertain initial values.

The second main ingredient of our method is a generalized mean value theorem, that we introduce in Section 2.3, applied to the flow of the uncertain ODE. The generalized mean value theorem relies itself on modal intervals, a simple extension of classical interval arithmetic (see Section 2.2), to inner-approximate the image of an input set by a

HSCC'17, April 18 - 20, 2017, Pittsburgh, PA, USA
ACM ISBN 978-1-4503-4590-3/17/04...$15.00
DOI: http://dx.doi.org/10.1145/3049797.3049811

non-linear vector-valued function. Note that (Kaucher) interval methods, known to be conservative, are locally used to derive inner ranges, but that this conservatism does not propagate: the inner range is always computed from the outer-approximated Taylor models.

In many ways, all this is remarkably simple, with respect to other existing methods (using backward propagation of the flow of the dynamics), that we discuss in the paragraph devoted to related work. Our method is not much more complex than a classical Taylor model approach for outer-approximations. But we have to consider a larger dynamical system, since we have to consider also the dynamics of the Jacobian with respect to the initial values. Thus, if the original system contains n equations, we must compute Taylor models for n^2 equations. However, the Taylor coefficients of the Jacobian can easily be derived from the Taylor models of the original equations, as we show in Section 3.

Finally, we carry out some experiments with our prototype implementation and provide comparisons to existing work.

Related work:.

There are numerous methods for the computation of outer-approximating (or over-approximating) flowpipes and reachable sets of ODEs, either linear [9], or non-linear [6, 25, 26], linear in the presence of uncertain parameters [8] or non-linear with uncertain parameters [1]. This is also supported by several tools, that can often also consider hybrid systems, see e.g. NLToolBox [27], SpaceEx [7], Flow* [3], CORA [2] and VNODE-LP [24] to mention but a few.

Inner-approximations have been far less studied, except in the case of linear systems, see e.g. [9], or using ellipsoidal methods [21] (and the corresponding tool [20]). In [18], the authors compute inner-approximations of the viability kernel by iterating backward (inner-approximated) reachability problems, using the ellipsoidal methods of [21]. The methods we propose here for inner-approximating reachable sets can be used for inner-approximating viability kernels as well.

The main existing method for under-approximating (or inner-approximating as we put it here) flowpipes of non-linear systems is a backward method, described in [4]. The method starts with a general compact and connected set of states X_0 described by a system of polynomial inequalities, and constructs a Taylor model for the backward flowmap Φ of the dynamics. Then, any *connected* set Ω which contains a point x which is mapped by Φ into X_0 is an inner-approximation of the reachable set of states X if Ω does not intersect the boundary of X. The method of [4] relies then on two computational ingredients. First, it builds a Taylor model for the backward flowmap (it is of the same order of complexity as for any forward outer-approximation, or for our inner-approximation method). Then, a candidate inner-approximation Ω that does not intersect the boundary of X is given by a set of polynomial constraints, derived from the Taylor model for the backward flowmap, and the constraints defining the initial set of states X_0. The method of [4] has then to test connectedness, which is intractable in general but can be semi-decided using clever interval methods.

A similar backward approach has been proposed in [28]. It is similar in that it also constructs an outer-approximation of the backward flowmap. But their authors construct an outer-approximation of the boundary of the reachable set to find inner-approximations. This is done using interval methods and a careful subdivision of the state-space, which might be very costly given that the boundary of the reachable set of highly non-linear ODEs might be extremely complicated to approximate.

Finally, the authors have recently discovered Section 4 of the work [11], which contains ideas that look similar to ours. The main differences seem to be that we are considering more general parameterized dynamical systems, which will later allow us to handle guard conditions for hybrid systems, and that we have a different scheme for bounding the remainder in our inner-approximated Taylor models. But we could not assess the practical differences since the description in [11] is sketchy, and contains no real experiment.

2. PRELIMINARIES

We introduce here the main ingredients used in our approach. Section 2.2 is devoted to generalized intervals and Kaucher arithmetic, which are instrumental in extending the mean-value theorem to obtain an inner-approximation of the range of a function over interval inputs, as described in Section 2.3. Finally briefly introduce Taylor methods for enclosing flows of ODEs in Section 2.4.

2.1 Outer and inner interval approximations

Classical intervals [23] are used in many situations to rigorously compute with interval domains instead of reals, usually leading to outer approximations of function ranges over boxes. We denote the set of classical intervals by $\mathbb{IR} = \{[\underline{x}, \overline{x}],\ \underline{x} \in \mathbb{R}, \overline{x} \in \mathbb{R}, \underline{x} \leqslant \overline{x}\}$

In what follows, uncertain quantities defined in intervals (inputs) are noted in bold, outer-approximating interval enclosures are noted in bold and enclosed within inward facing brackets, and inner-approximating intervals are noted in bold and enclosed within outward facing brackets.

An outer-approximating extension of a function $f : \mathbb{R}^n \rightarrow \mathbb{R}$ is a function $[\boldsymbol{f}] : \mathbb{IR}^n \rightarrow \mathbb{IR}$ such that for all $\boldsymbol{x}$ in $\mathbb{IR}^n$, $\text{range}(f, \boldsymbol{x}) = \{f(x), x \in \boldsymbol{x}\} \subseteq [\boldsymbol{f}](\boldsymbol{x})$. The natural interval extension consists in replacing real operations by their interval counterparts in the expression of the function. A generally more accurate extension relies on the mean-value theorem, linearizing the function to compute. Suppose the function f is differentiable over the interval $\boldsymbol{x} = [a, b]$. Then, the mean-value theorem implies that for any choice of $x_0 \in \boldsymbol{x}$, then we have $\forall x \in \boldsymbol{x},\ \exists c \in \boldsymbol{x},\ f(x) = f(x_0) + f'(c)(x - x_0)$.

If we can bound the range of the gradient of f over $\boldsymbol{x}$, by $\text{range}(f', \boldsymbol{x}) \subseteq [\boldsymbol{f}'](\boldsymbol{x})$, then we can derive the following interval enclosure, usually called the mean-value extension: for any $x_0 \in \boldsymbol{x}$, $\text{range}(f, \boldsymbol{x}) \subseteq f(x_0) + [\boldsymbol{f}'](\boldsymbol{x})(\boldsymbol{x} - x_0)$.

Classical interval computations can be interpreted as quantified propositions. Consider for example $f(x) = x^2 - x$, its exact range over $x = [2, 3]$ is $[2, 6]$. The natural interval extension of f, evaluated on $[2, 3]$, is $[\boldsymbol{f}]([2, 3]) = [2, 3]^2 - [2, 3] = [1, 7]$, which can be interpreted as the proposition $(\forall x \in [2, 3])\,(\exists z \in [1, 7])\,(f(x) = z)$. The mean-value extension gives $f(2.5) + [\boldsymbol{f}']([2, 3]) \times ([2, 3] - 2.5) = [1.25, 6.25]$, and can be interpreted similarly as an outer-aproximation.

Inner-approximations determine a set of values proved to belong to the range of the function over some input box. The fact that some $]\boldsymbol{z}[\in \mathbb{IR}$ satisfies $]\boldsymbol{z}[\subseteq \text{range}(f, \boldsymbol{x})$, i.e., is an inner-approximation of the range of f over $\boldsymbol{x}$, can again be written using quantifiers : $(\forall z \in]\boldsymbol{z}[)\,(\exists x \in \boldsymbol{x})\,(f(x) = z)$.

2.2 Modal intervals and Kaucher arithmetic

The results and notations introduced in this section are mostly based on the work of Goldsztejn *et al.* on modal intervals [10]. Let us first introduce generalized intervals, i.e., intervals whose bounds are not ordered, and Kaucher arithmetic [17] on these intervals.

The set of generalized intervals is denoted by $\mathbb{IK} = \{\boldsymbol{x} = [\underline{x}, \overline{x}],\ \underline{x} \in \mathbb{R}, \overline{x} \in \mathbb{R}\}$. Related to a set of real numbers $\{x_0 \in \mathbb{R},\ \underline{x} \leqslant x_0 \leqslant \overline{x}\}$, one can consider two generalized intervals, $[\underline{x}, \overline{x}]$, which is called *proper*, and $[\overline{x}, \underline{x}]$, which is called *improper*. We define the operations dual $[a, b] = [b, a]$ and pro $[a, b] = [\min(a, b), \max(a, b)]$.

Definition 1 ([10]). *Let $f : \mathbb{R}^n \to \mathbb{R}$ be a continuous function and $\boldsymbol{x} \in \mathbb{IK}^n$, which we can decompose in $\boldsymbol{x}_{\mathcal{A}} \in \mathbb{IR}^p$ and $\boldsymbol{x}_{\mathcal{E}} \in (\text{dual } \mathbb{IR})^q$ with $p + q = n$. A generalized interval $\boldsymbol{z} \in \mathbb{IK}$ is $(f, \boldsymbol{x})$-interpretable if*

$$(\forall x_{\mathcal{A}} \in \boldsymbol{x}_{\mathcal{A}})\,(Q_z z \in pro\ \boldsymbol{z})\,(\exists x_{\mathcal{E}} \in pro\ \boldsymbol{x}_{\mathcal{E}}), (f(x) = z) \quad (3)$$

where $Q_z = \exists$ if $(\boldsymbol{z})$ is proper, and $Q_z = \forall$ otherwise.

When all intervals in (3) are proper, we retrieve the interpretation of classical interval computation, which gives an outer approximation of range$(f, \boldsymbol{x})$, that is $(\forall x \in \boldsymbol{x})\,(\exists z \in [\boldsymbol{z}])\,(f(x) = z)$. When all intervals are improper, (3) becomes an inner-approximation of range$(f, \boldsymbol{x})$, that is $(\forall z \in]\text{pro } \boldsymbol{z}[)\,(\exists x \in \text{pro } \boldsymbol{x})\,(f(x) = z)$.

Kaucher arithmetic [17] returns intervals that are interpretable as inner-approximations in some simple cases. Kaucher addition extends addition on classical intervals by $\boldsymbol{x} + \boldsymbol{y} = [\underline{x} + \underline{y}, \overline{x} + \overline{y}]$ and $\boldsymbol{x} - \boldsymbol{y} = [\underline{x} - \overline{y}, \overline{x} - \underline{y}]$.

For multiplication, let us decompose $\mathbb{IK}$ in $\mathcal{P} = \{\boldsymbol{x} = [\underline{x}, \overline{x}],\ \underline{x} \geqslant 0 \land \overline{x} \geqslant 0\}$, $-\mathcal{P} = \{\boldsymbol{x} = [\underline{x}, \overline{x}],\ \underline{x} \leqslant 0 \land \overline{x} \leqslant 0\}$, $\mathcal{Z} = \{\boldsymbol{x} = [\underline{x}, \overline{x}],\ \underline{x} \leqslant 0 \leqslant \overline{x}\}$, and dual $\mathcal{Z} = \{\boldsymbol{x} = [\underline{x}, \overline{x}],\ \underline{x} \geqslant 0 \geqslant \overline{x}\}$. When restricted to proper intervals, the Kaucher multiplication coincides with the classical interval multiplication. Kaucher multiplication $\boldsymbol{x} \times \boldsymbol{y}$ extends the classical multiplication for all possible combinations of $\boldsymbol{x}$ and $\boldsymbol{y}$ belonging to these sets. We refer to [17] for full details, and only give below an intuitive explanation of one of these cases. Let us interpret the result of the multiplication $\boldsymbol{z} = \boldsymbol{x} \times \boldsymbol{y}$ when $\boldsymbol{y} \in$ dual $\mathcal{Z}$, and $\boldsymbol{x} \in \mathcal{Z}$, which is $\boldsymbol{z} = \boldsymbol{x} \times \boldsymbol{y} = 0$. Proposition 1 will express the fact that the result can be interpreted as in Definition 1. Interval $\boldsymbol{z}$ can a priori either be proper or improper, let us consider the improper case. We obtain an inner-approximation of the range of the multiplication: according to the quantifiers in Definition 1, computing $\boldsymbol{z} = \boldsymbol{x} \times \boldsymbol{y}$ consists in finding $\boldsymbol{z}$ such that for all $x \in \boldsymbol{x}$, for all $z \in$ pro $\boldsymbol{z}$, there exists $y \in$ pro $\boldsymbol{y}$ such that $z = x \times y$. If $\boldsymbol{x}$ contains zero, which is the case when $\boldsymbol{x} \in \mathcal{Z}$, then $\boldsymbol{z}$ is necessarily 0. Indeed, a property that holds for all $x \in \boldsymbol{x}$, holds in particular for $x = 0$, from which we deduce that for all $z \in$ pro $\boldsymbol{z}$, (there exists $y \in$ pro $\boldsymbol{y}$) $z = 0$.

The important feature of Kaucher arithmetic is that it defines a generalized interval natural extension (see [10]) :

Proposition 1. *Let $f : \mathbb{R}^n \to \mathbb{R}$ be a function, given by an arithmetic expression where each variable appears syntactically only once (and with dregree 1). Then for $\boldsymbol{x} \in \mathbb{IK}^n$, $f(\boldsymbol{x})$, computed using Kaucher arithmetic, is $(f, \boldsymbol{x})$-interpretable.*

Kaucher arithmetic can thus be used in some cases to compute an inner-approximation of range$(f, \boldsymbol{x})$. But the restriction to functions f with single occurrences of variables, that is with no dependency, prevents its direct use. A mean-value extension allows us to overcome this limitation.

2.3 Generalized interval mean value extension

In the general case of a differentiable function f, the mean-value theorem can be extended to define a generalized interval mean value extension (see [10]) :

Theorem 1. *Let $f : \mathbb{R}^n \to \mathbb{R}$ be differentiable, $\boldsymbol{x} \in \mathbb{IK}^n$ an improper interval, and suppose that for each $i \in \{1, \ldots, n\}$, we can compute $[\boldsymbol{\Delta}_i] \in \mathbb{IR}$ such that*

$$\left\{ \frac{\partial f}{\partial x_i}(x),\ x \in pro\ \boldsymbol{x} \right\} \subseteq [\boldsymbol{\Delta}_i]. \quad (4)$$

Then, for any $\tilde{x} \in$ pro $\boldsymbol{x}$, the following interval, evaluated with Kaucher arithmetic, is $(f, \boldsymbol{x})$-interpretable :

$$\tilde{f}(\boldsymbol{x}) = f(\tilde{x}) + \sum_{i=1}^{n} [\boldsymbol{\Delta}_i](\boldsymbol{x}_i - \tilde{x}_i). \quad (5)$$

When using (5) for inner-approximation, we can only get a subset of all possible cases in the Kaucher multiplication, we list them and the corresponding multiplication rules below: $(\boldsymbol{x} \in \mathcal{P}) \times (\boldsymbol{y} \in \text{dual } \mathcal{Z}) = [\underline{x}\underline{y}, \underline{x}\overline{y}]$, $(\boldsymbol{x} \in -\mathcal{P}) \times (\boldsymbol{y} \in \text{dual } \mathcal{Z}) = [\overline{x}\overline{y}, \overline{x}\underline{y}]$, and $(\boldsymbol{x} \in \mathcal{Z}) \times (\boldsymbol{y} \in \text{dual } \mathcal{Z}) = 0$. Indeed, for an improper $\boldsymbol{x}$ and $\tilde{x} \in$ pro $\boldsymbol{x}$, then $(\boldsymbol{x} - \tilde{x})$ is in dual $\mathcal{Z}$. The outer-approximation $[\boldsymbol{\Delta}_i]$ of the Jacobian is a proper interval, thus in $\mathcal{P}$, $-\mathcal{P}$ or $\mathcal{Z}$, and we can deduce from the multiplication rules that the inner-approximation is non empty only when $[\boldsymbol{\Delta}_i]$ does not contain 0.

Example 1. *Let f be defined by $f(x) = x^2 - x$, for which we want to compute an inner-approximation of the range over $\boldsymbol{x} = [2, 3]$. Due to the two occurrences of x, $f(dual\boldsymbol{x})$, computed with Kaucher arithmetic, is not $(f, \boldsymbol{x})$-interpretable. The interval $\tilde{f}(\boldsymbol{x}) = f(2.5) + \boldsymbol{f}'([2, 3])(\boldsymbol{x} - 2.5) = 3.75 + [3, 5](\boldsymbol{x} - 2.5)$ given by its mean-value extension, computed with Kaucher arithmetic, is $(f, \boldsymbol{x})$-interpretable. For $\boldsymbol{x} = [3, 2]$, using the multiplication rule for $\mathcal{P} \times$ dual $\mathcal{Z}$, we get $\tilde{f}(\boldsymbol{x}) = 3.75 + [3, 5]([3, 2] - 2.5) = 3.75 + [3, 5][0.5, -0.5] = 3.75 + [1.5, -1.5] = [5.25, 2.25]$, that can be interpreted as: $\forall z \in [2.25, 5.25]$, $\exists x \in [2, 3]$, $z = f(x)$. Thus, $[2.25, 5.25]$ is an inner-approximation of* range$(f, [2, 3])$.

In Section 3, we will be using Theorem 1 with f being the solution of the uncertain dynamical system (2): for this, we need to be able to outer-approximate, at any time t, $f(\tilde{x}), \tilde{x} \in$ pro $\boldsymbol{x}$, and its Jacobian with respect to the (uncertain) initial value of the system, $\left\{ \frac{\partial f}{\partial x_i}(x),\ x \in \text{pro } \boldsymbol{x} \right\}$. Computing an enclosure of the solution of an initial value problem is the objective of Section 2.4.

2.4 Enclosing the flow of an uncertain ODE with interval Taylor methods

Consider the uncertain dynamical system (2), where $z = (x, p, t)$ and with initial condition $z(t_0) \in \mathcal{Z}_I$ at time $t_0 \geq 0$. Let us denote $\mathcal{Z}(t; t_0, \mathcal{Z}_I)$ the set of solutions of (2) at time t for initial conditions in $\mathcal{Z}_I$ at t_0. We define a time grid $t_0 < t_1 < \ldots < t_N$, and assume $\mathcal{Z}_I = \boldsymbol{z}_0 = [\underline{z}_0, \overline{z}_0]$ at time $t_0 \geq 0$.

Interval Taylor methods for guaranteed set integration, see [25] for a review, compute flowpipes that are guaranteed to contain the reachable set of solutions $\mathcal{Z}(t; t_0, \mathcal{Z}_I)$ of (2) for all time t in $[t_j, t_{j+1}]$. They first verify the existence and uniqueness of the solution using the Banach fixed point theorem and the Picard-Lindelöf operator, and compute an a priori rough enclosure $[r_{j+1}]$ of $\mathcal{Z}(t)$ for all t in $[t_j, t_{j+1}]$. A tighter enclosure for the set of reachable values for t in $[t_j, t_{j+1}]$ is then computed using a Taylor series expansion of order k of the solution at t_j, where $[r_{j+1}]$ is used to enclose the remaining term :

$$[z](t, t_j, [z_j]) = [z_j] + \sum_{i=1}^{k-1} \frac{(t-t_j)^i}{i!} f^{[i]}([z_j]) + \frac{(t-t_j)^k}{k!} f^{[k]}([r_{j+1}]), \quad (6)$$

where the Taylor coefficients $f^{[i]}$, which are the $i-1$th Lie derivative of f along vector field f, are defined inductively, and can be computed by automatic differentiation as follows (for all $k = 1, \dots, n$) :

$$f_k^{[1]} = f_k \quad (7)$$

$$f_k^{[i+1]} = \sum_{j=1}^{n} \frac{\partial f_k^{[i]}}{\partial z_j} f_j \quad (8)$$

Let us quickly recall how Equation (6) is obtained. Let $z(t)$ be a solution to Equation (2) starting at time 0 at point z_0. By definition :

$$\tfrac{dz}{dt}(t) = f(z(t)) = f^{[1]}(z(t))$$

and more generally, we can prove by induction on l that $\frac{d^{(l+1)}z}{dt^{(l+1)}}(t) = f^{[l+1]}(z(t))$, since by induction hypothesis :

$$\begin{aligned}\tfrac{d^{(l+1)}z}{dt^{(l+1)}}(t) &= \tfrac{d}{dt}\left(t \mapsto f^{[l]}(z(t))\right) \\ &= \sum_{j=1}^{n} \dot{z}_j(t) \tfrac{\partial f^{[l]}}{\partial z_j}(z(t)) \\ &= \sum_{j=1}^{n} f_j(z(t)) \tfrac{\partial f^{[l]}}{\partial z_j}(z(t)) = f^{[l+1]}(z(t))\end{aligned}$$

Equation (6) is then a direct consequence from Taylor-Lagrange expansion, for sufficiently smooth functions f.

Finally, we use enclosure $[z_{j+1}] = [z](t_{j+1}, t_j, [z_j])$ as initial solution set at time t_{j+1} to derive the interval Taylor model on the next time step.

If evaluated plainly in interval arithmetic, scheme (6) yields enclosures of increasing width. A classical way to control the loss of accuracy due to the loss of correlation in interval arithmetic, called wrapping effect, is a method introduced by Lohner, that uses QR-factorization [25]. Alternatively, we choose here to control wrapping using affine arithmetic [5] instead of interval arithmetic in this evaluation.

3. FORWARD INNER REACHABILITY

As in Section 2.4, we consider the uncertain dynamical system (2), where $z = (x, p, t)$ and with initial condition $z(t_0) \in \mathcal{Z}_I = \boldsymbol{z}_0 = [\underline{z}_0, \overline{z}_0]$ at time $t_0 \geq 0$, and we denote $\mathcal{Z}(t; t_0, \boldsymbol{z}_0)$ the set of solutions $\{z(t, z_0),\ z_0(t_0) \in \boldsymbol{z}_0\}$ of (2) at time t. We have seen in Section 2.4, that for a time grid $t_0 < t_1 < \dots < t_N$, we can compute on each time interval $[t_j, t_{j+1}]$, a flowpipe (6) that is guaranteed to contain the reachable set of solutions of (2) for all time t in $[t_j, t_{j+1}]$. We now want to compute also an inner-approximating flowpipe of this reachable set, that is for all t in $[t_j, t_{j+1}]$, a range $]z[(t, t_j, [z_j])$ such that all values inside that range are sure to be reached at time t by an execution of system (2). For that, we will apply Theorem 1, at all time t, to the function $z_0 \mapsto z(t, z_0)$ from $\mathbb{R}^n$ to $\mathbb{R}^n$ solution of the IVP (2).

In Section 3.1, we give the main lines of the computation of inner-approximated flowpipes, and state the algorithm. We then detail and comment each of its steps. In Section 3.2, we show how we use the classical interval Picard-Lindelöf iteration method to get rough enclosures of the solution and its Jacobian on each time step, that we use for computing the remainders of the Taylor models. In Section 3.3, we build the Taylor models, and show that we can compute the Taylor model of the Jacobian as if we were simply deriving the Taylor model for the solution of the initial ODE, which makes its construction very simple and efficient. Finally, in Section 3.4, we comment the actual computation of the inner-approximating flow-pipe, and show how a loss of accuracy in the outer-approximation results in a loss of accuracy in the inner-approximation, and even possibly to an empty inner-approximation.

3.1 Principle of the algorithm

On each time interval, in order to compute an inner range of the solution of the uncertain system, we need an outer-enclosure of the solution starting from a point in the initial set, $z(t, \tilde{z_0})$ for some $\tilde{z_0} \in \boldsymbol{z}_0$ (Equation (15) in Algorithm 1), an enclosure of the solution by the system $z(t, z_0)$ over range $z_0 in \boldsymbol{z}_0$ (Equation (16)), and an enclosure of its Jacobian with respect to z_0, evaluated over range $\boldsymbol{z}_0$ (Equation (17)). The Jacobian is defined $J_{ij}(t, \boldsymbol{z}_0) = \frac{\partial z_i}{\partial z_{0,j}}(t, \boldsymbol{z}_0)$, for i and j between 1 and n, and where z_i is the i-th component of the vector flow function z, and $z_{0,j}$ the j-th component of the vector of initial conditions z_0.

We compute these outer-approximations by applying the Taylor method of Section 2.4 to $z(t, \tilde{z_0})$ and $J(t, z_0)$ where $z_0 \in \boldsymbol{z}_0$ and with initial condition $J(t_0) = Id$ the identity matrix : $z(t, \tilde{z_0})$ satisfies system (2) with $z(t_0) = \tilde{z_0} \in \boldsymbol{z}_0$, so that we can directly use the Taylor expansion (6) on each time interval $[t_j, t_{j+1}]$ to compute $\mathcal{Z}(t; t_0, \tilde{z_0})$. The coefficients of the Jacobian matrix of the flow satisfy :

$$\dot{J}_{ij}(t, z_0) = \sum_{k=1}^{n} \frac{\partial f_i}{\partial z_k}(z).J_{kj}(t, z_0) \quad (9)$$

that can be rewritten

$$\dot{J}(t, z_0) = \mathrm{Jac}_z f(z(t, z_0)).J(t, z_0). \quad (10)$$

with $J(t_0) = Id$ (these are the "variational equations" used in particular in [29] for improving outer-approximations of continuous dynamical systems). We will denote by $\nabla_z f$ the function of variables z_i and J_{ij} (linear in J_{ij}) which is the right hand side of Equation 10. Hence, its *pq* entry is :

$$(\nabla_z f)_{pq}(z, J) = \sum_{k=1}^{n} \frac{\partial f_p}{\partial z_k}(z) J_{kq} \quad (11)$$

A Taylor expansion can thus be used to outer-approximate the solution of (10) noted $\mathcal{J}(t; t_0, \boldsymbol{z}_0)$ on each time interval $[t_j, t_{j+1}]$, using the outer-approximation for $z(t, z_0)$ given by Taylor expansion (6). Equations (9) together with Equations (1) define a system of $n(n+1)$ ordinary differential equations in $n(n+1)$ variables (z and J). We call the corresponding vector field F and write similarly, by an abuse of notation, for H a function in variables z and J, $H^{[i]}$ the $i-1$th Lie derivative of H along the (augmented) vector field H. More explicitly, it is defined inductively as follows :

$$H^{[1]} = H \quad (12)$$

$$H^{[i+1]} = (H^{[i]})^{[2]} \quad (13)$$

where the first Lie derivative is :

$$H^{[2]} = \sum_{i=1}^{n} \frac{\partial H}{\partial z_i} f_i + \sum_{k,l=1}^{n} \frac{\partial H}{\partial J_{kl}} \left(\sum_{s=1}^{n} \frac{\partial f_k}{\partial z_s} J_{sl} \right) \quad (14)$$

Let us briefly detail how we obtained Equation (14). Consider a solution $t \mapsto z_i(t)$ and $t \mapsto J_{ij}(t)$ of Equations (9) and (1). The Lie derivative of H is the time derivative of $\tilde{H}(t) = H(z_1(t), \ldots, z_n(t), J_{11}(t), \ldots, J_{nn}(t))$:

$$\dot{\tilde{H}}(t) = \sum_{i=1}^{n} \frac{\partial H}{\partial z_i}(t)\dot{z}_i(t) + \sum_{k,l=1}^{n} \frac{\partial H}{\partial J_{kl}}(t)\dot{J}_{kl}(t)$$

We get the formula (14) by replacing $\dot{z}_i$ by its expression in Equation (1) and $\dot{J}_{kl}$ by its expression in Equation (9).

We summarize the procedure for computing the inner and outer reachable sets in pseudo-Algorithm 1.

In the next sections, we detail the different steps of Algorithm 1 and illustrate them on a running example:

EXAMPLE 2. *We consider the Brusselator equation:*

$$f(x) = \begin{pmatrix} 1 - 2x_1 + \frac{3}{2}x_1^2 x_2 \\ x_1 - \frac{3}{2}x_1^2 x_2 \end{pmatrix}$$

with $x = (x_1, x_2)$, *over the time interval* $[0, h]$ $\left(h = \frac{1}{20}\right)$, *and with initial conditions* $[x_0] = ([2, 2.15], [0.1, 0.15])$.

The Jacobian that appears in Equation (10) is :

$$Jac_z f(z(t, z_0)) = \begin{pmatrix} -2 + 3x_1x_2 & \frac{3}{2}x_1^2 \\ 1 - 3x_1x_2 & -\frac{3}{2}x_1^2 \end{pmatrix}$$

3.2 Step 1: computing the rough enclosures

In order to compute the kth term in Equations (15) and (16) we need to compute $[\boldsymbol{r}_j]$ (respectively $[\boldsymbol{R}_j]$), i.e. a priori enclosures of the components of the solutions z and J over the time interval $[t_j, t_{j+1}]$. This is done following the classical approach [25] relying on the interval Picard-Lindelöf method. This goes as follows. First note that Equation (1) can be rewritten as the integral equation

$$z(t) = z_0 + \int_{t_j}^{t_{j+1}} f(z(s))\mathrm{d}s \quad (19)$$

and define F the functional which to function z associates the right-hand side of Equation (19). Under the condition that f is Lipschitz, F admits a unique fixpoint, solution to Equations (1) and (19). The interval version $F^\sharp$ of the Picard-Lindelöf operator F enjoys the same property and is derived using the obvious rough interval approximation of the integral : $F^\sharp([z]) = z_0 + [t_j, t_{j+1}][\boldsymbol{f}]([z])$ (where $[z]$ will denote ultimately the "rough" enclosure of the solutions to Equation (1) and $[\boldsymbol{f}]$ denotes the interval extension of function f). Simple Jacobi like iteration suffices to reach the fixpoint of $F^\sharp$: $[z]_0 = z_0$, $[z]_{i+1} = F^\sharp([z]_i)$ for all $i \in \boldsymbol{N}$. Convergence can be ensured using outwards rounding in finite precision, numerical acceleration techniques etc.

EXAMPLE 3. *We carry on with the computation of outer-approximations for solutions and Jacobians for the Brusselator on the first time step. We will write* $[x_i](t)$ *instead of* $[x_i](t, 0, [x_0])$ *as we are only considering the first time step. We first need to determine the rough enclosures* $[\boldsymbol{r}_1]_i$ *and* $[\boldsymbol{R}_1]_{i,j}$ *of the* $x_i(t)$ *and* $J_{ij}(t)$ *over* $t \in [0, h]$, $x \in [x_0]$ *using the interval Picard-Lindelöf method of Section 3.2 :* $[\boldsymbol{r}_1] = \begin{pmatrix} [1.86, 2.15] \\ [0.10, 0.23] \end{pmatrix}$, $[\boldsymbol{R}_1] = \begin{pmatrix} [0.92, 1.00] & [0.00, 0.35] \\ [-0.025, 0.022] & [0.65, 1.00] \end{pmatrix}$.

The remainders for $k = 2$ *(first order Taylor model for Equations (15) and (17)) will be determined in Example 4.*

Data: a time grid $t_0 < t_1 < \ldots < t_N$, an initial range $\boldsymbol{z}_0$, and some $\tilde{z}_0 \in \boldsymbol{z}_0$
Result: $[\boldsymbol{z}](t, \boldsymbol{z}_0)$ and $]\boldsymbol{z}[(t, \boldsymbol{z}_0)$ over $t = [t_0, t_N]$
Init: $j = 0$, $t_j = t_0$, $[\boldsymbol{z}_j] = \boldsymbol{z}_0$, $[\tilde{z}_j] = \tilde{z}_0$, $[\boldsymbol{J}_j] = Id$
while $j < N - 1$ **do**

Step 1. compute a priori enclosures $[\boldsymbol{r}_{j+1}]$ of $\mathcal{Z}(t; t_j, \boldsymbol{z}_j)$ for all t in $[t_j, t_{j+1}]$, $[\tilde{\boldsymbol{r}}_{j+1}]$ of $\mathcal{Z}(t; t_j, \tilde{z}_j)$ for all t in $[t_j, t_{j+1}]$, and $[\boldsymbol{R}_{j+1}]$ of $\mathcal{J}(t; t_j, \boldsymbol{z}_j)$

Step 2. build the Taylor Models valid on $[t_j, t_{j+1}]$:

$$[\boldsymbol{z}](t, t_j, [\boldsymbol{z}_j]) = [\boldsymbol{z}_j] + \sum_{i=1}^{k-1} \frac{(t - t_j)^i}{i!} f^{[i]}([\boldsymbol{z}_j]) + \frac{(t - t_j)^k}{k!} f^{[k]}([\boldsymbol{r}_{j+1}]). \quad (15)$$

$$[\tilde{\boldsymbol{z}}](t, t_j, [\tilde{\boldsymbol{z}}_j]) = [\tilde{\boldsymbol{z}}_j] + \sum_{i=1}^{k-1} \frac{(t - t_j)^i}{i!} f^{[i]}([\tilde{\boldsymbol{z}}_j]) + \frac{(t - t_j)^k}{k!} f^{[k]}([\tilde{\boldsymbol{r}}_{j+1}]). \quad (16)$$

$$[\boldsymbol{J}](t, t_j, [\boldsymbol{z}_j]) = [\boldsymbol{J}_j] + \sum_{i=1}^{k-1} \frac{(t - t_j)^i}{i!} \mathrm{Jac}_z f^{[i]}([\boldsymbol{z}_j]).[\boldsymbol{J}_j] + \frac{(t - t_j)^k}{k!} \mathrm{Jac}_z f^{[k]}([\boldsymbol{r}_{j+1}]).[\boldsymbol{R}_{j+1}] \quad (17)$$

Step 3. deduce an inner-approximation valid for t in $[t_j, t_{j+1}]$: if $]\boldsymbol{z}(t, t_j)$ defined by Equation (18) is an improper interval

$$]\boldsymbol{z}[(t, t_j) = [\tilde{\boldsymbol{z}}](t, t_j, [\tilde{\boldsymbol{z}}_j]) + [\boldsymbol{J}](t, t_j, [\boldsymbol{z}_j]) * ([\overline{z_0}, \underline{z_0}] - \tilde{z}_0) \quad (18)$$

then interval pro $]\boldsymbol{z}[(t, t_j)$ is an inner-approximation of the set of solutions $\{z(t, z_0),\ z_0(t_0) \in \boldsymbol{z}_0\}$ of (2) at time t, otherwise the inner-approximation is empty.

Step 4. $[\boldsymbol{z}_{j+1}] = [\boldsymbol{z}](t_{j+1}, t_j, [\boldsymbol{z}_j])$, $[\tilde{\boldsymbol{z}}_{j+1}] = [\tilde{\boldsymbol{z}}](t_{j+1}, t_j, [\tilde{\boldsymbol{z}}_j])$, $[\boldsymbol{J}_{j+1}] = [\boldsymbol{J}](t, t_j, [\boldsymbol{z}_j])$

end

Algorithm 1: Computing inner and outer reachable sets

3.3 Step 2: building the Taylor models

Building the Lie derivatives of the Jacobian.

The formulation of Equation (17) relies on the possibility to commute the ith Lie derivative with the calculation of the Jacobian. Without this, we would have written:

$$[\boldsymbol{J}](t,t_j,[\boldsymbol{z}_j]) = [\boldsymbol{J}_j] + \sum_{i=1}^{k-1} \frac{(t-t_j)^i}{i!}(\mathrm{Jac}_z(f))^{[i]}([\boldsymbol{z}_j]).[\boldsymbol{J}_j] + \frac{(t-t_j)^k}{k!}(\mathrm{Jac}_z(f))^{[k]}([\boldsymbol{r}_{j+1}]).[\boldsymbol{R}_{j+1}] \quad (20)$$

$\mathrm{Jac}_z(f)$ being seen as a function of variables z_i and J_{ij}, which is linear in the J_{ij} as in Equation (11). Equations (17) and (20) are equivalent since the two derivatives (the Jacobian calculation and the Lie derivative) commute.

We prove this equivalence by induction on the number of Lie derivations. For $i=1$, we have, by definition $\nabla_z(f^{[1]}) = \nabla_z(f) = (\nabla_z(f))^{[1]}$. Suppose now we have, as an induction step $\nabla_z(f^{[i]}) = (\nabla_z(f))^{[i]}$. We now write :

$$\nabla_z(f^{[i+1]})_{pq} = \sum_{k=1}^{n} \frac{\partial f_p^{[i+1]}}{\partial z_k} J_{kq} = \sum_{k=1}^{n} \frac{\partial}{\partial z_k}\left(\sum_{l=1}^{n} \frac{\partial f_p^{[i]}}{\partial z_l} f_l\right) J_{kq}$$

hence,

$$\nabla_z(f^{[i+1]})_{pq} = \sum_{k,l=1}^{n} \left(\frac{\partial^2 f_p^{[i]}}{\partial z_k \partial z_l} f_l + \frac{\partial f_p^{[i]}}{\partial z_l}\frac{\partial f_l}{\partial z_k}\right) J_{kq} \quad (21)$$

On the other hand we have :

$$(\nabla_z(f)_{pq})^{[i+1]} = (\nabla_z(f^{[i]})_{pq})^{[2]}$$

by Definition (14) and by the induction step. Using now Equation (14), and Equation (11) recalled below:

$$(\nabla_z(f^{[i]}))_{pq} = \sum_{k=1}^{n} \frac{\partial f_p^{[i]}}{\partial z_k} J_{kq}$$

we have :

$$(\nabla_z(f)_{pq})^{[i+1]} = \sum_{k,l=1}^{n} \frac{\partial^2 f_p^{[i]}}{\partial z_k \partial z_l} f_l J_{kq} + \sum_{r=1}^{n} \frac{\partial f_p^{[i]}}{\partial z_r}\left(\sum_{t=1}^{n} \frac{\partial f_r}{\partial z_t} J_{tq}\right) \quad (22)$$

which is thus seen to be equal to $\nabla_z(f^{[i+1]})_{pq}$ by Equation (21).

Equation (17) is simpler to compute since we already computed the Lie derivative of f, in Equation (16), the Jacobian calculation being by itself rather inexpensive.

Computing the coefficients of the Taylor models.

We need to outer-approximate the values of some functions, and in particular, all Lie derivatives, which are coefficients in the Taylor models, in Equations (15-17). We have a wide choice from the existing set-based methods, is polynomial. We will use in our running example affine arithmetic [5], as in our prototype. Affine arithmetic was also used in [13] for inner-approximations of discrete dynamical systems. One interest is that we can use the results from [12] to also get good estimates of the joint inner range of the state variables z_j, altogether, when needed.

EXAMPLE 4. *We compute a first-order Taylor model for the Brusselator, using Equation (6) with $k=2$, and using affine arithmetic to compute $Jac_z(f^{[i]})([\boldsymbol{r}_{j+1}])[\boldsymbol{J}_j]$ and $f^{[i]}([\boldsymbol{z}_j])$. We start with $[x_0] = ([2,2.5],[0.1,0.15])$, hence, in affine arithmetic, $[x_0] = \left(\frac{83}{40}+\frac{3}{40}\epsilon_1, \frac{1}{8}+\frac{1}{40}\epsilon_2\right)$. We evaluate $f^{[1]} = f$ using simple rules from affine arithmetic, e.g. :*

$$f^{[1]}([x_0]) = -\frac{119919}{51200} - \frac{1173}{12800}\epsilon_1 + \frac{41361}{256000}\epsilon_2 + \frac{27}{51200}\eta_1 + \frac{3015}{256000}\eta_2 \quad (23)$$

and, e.g. $Jac_z(f^{[1]})([x_0])_{11} = -\frac{391}{320} + \frac{9}{320}\epsilon_1 + \frac{249}{1600}\epsilon_2 + \frac{9}{1600}\eta_3$. The non-linearity of f and its Jacobian produces new symbols in the evaluation with affine arithmetic than ϵ_1, ϵ_2 : we note them using the η letter, instead of ϵ, to make apparent the uncertainty produced by the interpretation in affine arithmetic. Equation (23) evaluates in interval $[-2.6077, -2.0766]$.

To obtain the remainders, we compute $f_i^{[2]}$ and $Jac_z(f_i^{[2]})$:

$$f_1^{[2]} = -2 + 4x_1 + 3x_1x_2 + \frac{3}{2}x_1^3 - 9x_1^2x_2 + \frac{9}{2}x_1^3x_2^2 - \frac{9}{4}x_1^4x_2 \quad (24)$$

$$\begin{aligned} Jac_z(f^{[2]})_{11}(x_1,x_2)(J_{11},J_{21}) &= (3x_2f_1 + 3x_1f_2)J_{11} \\ &+ (-2+3x_1x_2)Jac_z(f^{[1]})_{11}(x_1,x_2)(J_{11},J_{21}) \\ &+ 3x_1f_1J_{21} + \frac{3}{2}x_1^2 Jac_z(f^{[1]})_{21}(x_1,x_2)(J_{11},J_{21}) \end{aligned} \quad (25)$$

where $Jac_z(f^{[1]})_{11}$ and $Jac_z(f^{[1]})_{21}$ are just $Jac_z f(z(t,z_0))_{11}$ and $Jac_z f(z(t,z_0))_{21}$ given in Example 2.

Now again, we are applying affine arithmetic to compute $f^{[2]}([\boldsymbol{r}_1])$ and $Jac_z(f^{[2]})([\boldsymbol{r}_1])[\boldsymbol{R}_1]$ given the rough enclosures $\boldsymbol{r}_1$ and $\boldsymbol{R}_1$ computed in Example 3 and we find :

$$f^{[2]}([\boldsymbol{r}_1]) = \begin{pmatrix} [3.5371, 13.7617] \\ [-11.1499, -1.5368] \end{pmatrix} \quad (26)$$

and $Jac_z(f^{[2]})([\boldsymbol{r}_1])[\boldsymbol{R}_1]$ is the matrix :

$$\begin{pmatrix} [-3.1897, 15.7653] & [-74.8884, -19.3243] \\ [-14.0978, 3.5433] & [16.4500, 68.0696] \end{pmatrix}$$

As a direct consequence, we can evaluate Equations (15) and (17) to get the outer-approximation of z and J at time h :

$$[\boldsymbol{z}](h,t_0,[\boldsymbol{z}_0]) = ([1.88320, 2.05421], [0.15728, 0.20358]) \quad (27)$$

$$[\boldsymbol{J}](h,t_0,[\boldsymbol{z}_0]) = \begin{pmatrix} [0.92545, 0.96808] & [0.20597, 0.32253] \\ [-0.016, 0.02499] & [0.67388, 0.78551] \end{pmatrix} \quad (28)$$

For instance, the first component in Equation (27) is found by using Equation (15) with $k=2$ and by instantiating the constant coefficient with $[x_0] = ([2,2.5],[0.1,0.15])$, the Taylor coefficient in degree one in t with the result of Equation (23), and in degree two with the result of Equation (26). Using a coarser interval abstraction of coefficients in degree zero and one, we indeed find an outer-approximation of the flowpipe until time h : $[\boldsymbol{z}_1](h,t_0,[\boldsymbol{z}_0]) = [2,2.5] + [-2.6077,-2.0766]\,t + [3.5371,13.7617]\,\frac{t^2}{2}$ equal at time h to $[1.8740, 2.0634]$, which slightly over-approximates the result of Equation (27) with affine arithmetic.

Computing the center of the inner-approximation.

Equation (16) is required to evaluate Equation (18) and get inner-approximations: we need to propagate a (center) point in the set of initial values through the flowpipe of solutions of ODE (1), at each time step t_j in our time grid.

This center solution is certainly not derivable from the outer-approximation of the flowpipe, e.g. as its midpoint: in order to soundly use the mean-value theorem, this solution must outer-approximate the image by the flow of the initial point.

We use the same Taylor expansion, but with different initial conditions, to compute in (15) an outer-approximation of the solution of system (2) with $z(t_0) = \tilde{z_0}$, used as the center in inner-approximation (18), and in (16) an outer-approximation of the solution of the same system but with uncertain $z(t_0) \in \boldsymbol{z}_0$, used to compute the Taylor coefficients in Equation (17).

EXAMPLE 5. *Starting with the center $\tilde{x}_0 = (2.075, 0.125)$ of the initial condition $[x_0] = ([2, 2.15], [0.1, 0.15])$, and applying the interval Picard-Lindelöf method of Section 3.2, we find $x = ([1.9655, 1.9718], [0.1774, 0.1831])$ at time h.*

3.4 Step 3: computing the inner-approximation

The algorithm described in Section 3.1 fully relies on outer-approximations at each step, to deduce an inner-approximation at Step 3. This means that we can soundly compute and implement most of our approach using interval-based methods with outward rounding as classically: outward rounding should be used for the outer approximations of flows and Jacobians (the larger these, the tighter the inner-approx), but the computation by Kaucher aithmetic of improper intervals should be done with inward rounding.

Also, the wider the outer-approximation in Taylor models (15-17), the tighter thus the less accurate the inner-approximation (18): it can even lead to an empty inner-approximation if the result of Equation (18) in Kaucher arithmetic is not an improper interval.

The phenomenon we mentioned above can occur in two ways. First, $[\overline{z_0}, \underline{z_0}] - \tilde{z_0}$ is an improper interval that belongs to dual $\mathbb{Z}$ as defined in Section 2.2. The outer-approximation of the Jacobian matrix, $[\boldsymbol{J}](t, t_j, [\boldsymbol{z}_j])$ is a proper interval. The Kaucher multiplication, as mentioned in Section 2.3, will yield a non-zero improper interval only if $[\boldsymbol{J}](t, t_j, [\boldsymbol{z}_j])$ does not contain 0. And, in this case, the result of this multiplication will depend on the lower bound of the absolute value of the Jacobian (while the same mean-value theorem used for outer-approximation would imply a multiplication of proper intervals that would depend on the upper bound of the absolute value of the Jacobian). The larger this lower bound, the wider the inner-approximation.

Suppose that the Kaucher multiplication yields an improper interval. It is added to proper outer-approximation $[\tilde{\boldsymbol{z}}](t, t_j, [\tilde{\boldsymbol{z}}_j])$ of the solution at time t of the system starting from point $\tilde{\boldsymbol{z}}_0$. Ideally, this should be tight, but if this interval is wider than the improper interval resulting from the Kaucher multiplication, then the sum of the two intervals - computed using the extension of interval addition - will be proper, and the inner-approximation empty.

The quality of the inner-approximation is strongly linked to the quality of the outer-approximation. We can if necessary locally improve the quality by using higher-order Taylor models. Indeed, as we know that the exact reachable set of the uncertain system lies between the inner and outer-approximated flows, we can bound the approximation error at each instant, and use this information to dynamically refine the approximation.

EXAMPLE 6. *Now we can instantiate Equation (18) as follows, for e.g. the first component of x and time $t = h$, using the result of Example 5 for the outer-approximation of the center at time h and Equation (28) for the outer-approximation of the Jacobian at time h :*

$$]\boldsymbol{z}[(h,0) = [1.9655, 1.9718] + [0.9254, 0.9680]\,[0.075, -0.075] + [0.2059, 0.3225]\,[0.025, -0.025] \quad (29)$$

Finally, using Kaucher arithmetic (see Section 2.2), we find

$$]\boldsymbol{z}[(h,0) \;=\; [1.9655 + 0.92545 \times 0.075 + 0.20597 \times 0.025, \; 1.9718 - 0.9254 \times 0.075 - 0.20597 \times 0.025]$$

whose proper counterpart is $[1.8973, 2.0400]$. We thus efficiently find a quite tight characterization of the reachable set with a very low order scheme, for the Brusselator at time h :

$$[1.8973, 2.0400] \subseteq z(h, 0, [z_0]) \subseteq [1.88320, 2.05421]$$

Of course, similarly to Example 4 for the outer-approximation of z, Equation (18) is valid for all times t in $[0, h]$, hence gives an inner-approximation of the flowpipe for the Brusselator. This is what we will be doing in Section 4.1.

4. EXPERIMENTS AND BENCHMARKS

We implemented[1] our method relying on the **FILIB++** C++ library [22] for interval computations, the **FADBAD++** package (http://www.fadbad.com) for automatic differentiation, and (a slightly modified version of) the **aaflib** library (http://aaflib.sourceforge.net) for affine arithmetic. Affine arithmetic is used for the coefficients of the Taylor models in order to limit the wrapping effect. Matrix preconditioning is a more classical alternative, but affine arithmetic proved to be both efficient, if we limit the number of noise symbols used, and accurate. It is also very convenient for prototyping, as we rely on the **aaflib** library.

We first demonstrate in Section 4.1 the good behavior of our inner-approximated flowpipes on the quite difficult Brusselator model. Then, in Section 4.2, we provide some comparison to the experimental results of the related work.

4.1 Brusselator

We consider in this section another instance of the Brusselator system, slightly different from the version of Example 2, which has been used in e.g. [4, 28] :

$$\begin{cases} \dot{x}_1 &= 1 + x_1^2 x_2 - 2.5 x_1 \\ \dot{x}_2 &= 1.5 x_1 - x_1^2 x_2 \end{cases}$$

with $x_1(0) \in [0.9, 1]$ and $x_2(0) \in [0, 0.1]$.

We use Taylor models of order 4 in time, and represent in Figure 1, the inner and outer approximated flowpipes for variables x_1 and x_2, up to a maximum time $t = 10$. The inner-approximations are represented in dashed lines, and the outer-approximations in plain lines.

We can note that the width of the inner-approximation (internal dashed lines) decreases at times, and the inner-approximation even becomes empty (for example for variable x_2 around $t = 4$), but the width can still later be non-zero again. This is not a bug: this phenomenon is an illustration of the fact detailed in Section 3.4, that when adding an improper with a proper interval to get the inner range of a variable, we can get a proper interval, which results in an empty inner-approximation (of the variable of interest

[1]available from http://www.lix.polytechnique.fr/Labo/Sylvie.Putot/software.html

- actually, you can note that on this example, the inner-approximations of the two variables do not become empty at the same time). This does not prevent us from carrying on with the computation of the Taylor models : non-empty inner-approximations will be obtained at later times, depending on the behavior of the Jacobian of the flow.

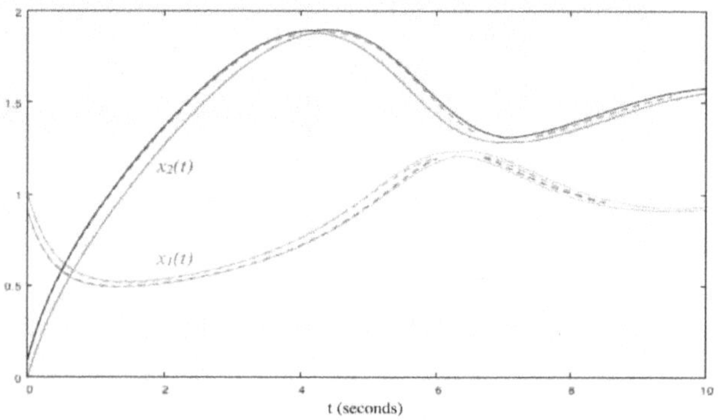

Figure 1: Brusselator (x_1 and x_2), Taylor models order 4

4.2 Comparisons to the related work

We provide in this section some elements of comparisons to the experimental results given in [4,28]. Let us highlight that it is difficult to compare these methods in a fair manner, as evaluating the compared accuracy of these methods is difficult. Also, our implementation is preliminary (using fixed step of integration for instance), while some of the related work relies on the highly optimized interval solver for initial value problem `VNODE-LP` [24].

Among the examples studied in both [4] and [28], we first selected the version of the Brusselator introduced in Section 4.1 as a representative of the systems of low degree. We chose as second example a biological system of higher degree (7), so as to demonstrate the way our approach scales.

$$\dot{\begin{pmatrix} x_1 \\ x_2 \\ x_3 \\ x_4 \\ x_5 \\ x_6 \\ x_7 \end{pmatrix}} = \begin{pmatrix} -0.4x_1 + ax_3x_4 \\ 0.4x_1 - x_2 \\ x_2 - ax_3x_4 \\ ax_5x_6 - ax_3x_4 \\ -ax_5x_6 + ax_3x_4 \\ 0.5x_7 - ax_5x_6 \\ -0.5x_7 + ax_5x_6 \end{pmatrix} \tag{30}$$

In this system, a is a parameter which is taken equal to 50 in [4] and to 5 in [28]. We will use the corresponding value of the parameter when comparing to the related work.

4.2.1 Comparison to [4]

In [4], the accuracy of computations is measured by the minimum width ratio

$$\gamma_{\min} = \min \frac{\gamma_u(v)}{\gamma_o(v)}, v \in V$$

where V is a set of vectors, and $\gamma_u(v)$ and $\gamma_o(v)$ measure respectively the width of the inner-approximation and outer-approximation in direction $v \in V$. Intuitively, the larger this ratio, the better the approximation. Our method naturally gives inner ranges for the projection of the flow system on its state variables. We thus measure in our case the minimum over the state variables x_i of our system of this ratio. We believe this corresponds to the measure that was used for experiments in [4], as they mention that the vectors are selected along the dimensions (axis-aligned).

Comparison on the Brusselator.

The initial set taken in [4], defined by $x_1 \geq 0.9$, $x_2 \geq 0$, $x_1 + x_2 - 1 \leq 0$, can be projected on $1 \geq x_1 \geq 0.9$, $0.1 \geq x_2 \geq 0$. This outer-approximation of the initial set is quite inaccurate, which results in a lower quality of the inner-approximation that must be taken into account in the comparison to the results of [4]. We could actually also consider initial sets that are not given as boxes but for instance as zonotopes, but we did not investigate this here.

In [4], the authors study the result for $t = 3$ and $t = 4$, with 4th order Taylor models and integration time step $h = 0.02$. We choose, as they do, 4th order Taylor models, and time step $h = 0.02$. Our implementation until $t = 4$ takes a total of 3.2 seconds (to compute both outer and inner approximations), where [4] takes 89 seconds. Our implementation is thus more than an order of magnitude quicker. Note also that with our approach, taking order 3 Taylor models and a larger time step of 0.1, we still obtain results of very similar quality on $\gamma_{\min}$, in 0.25 seconds. Further decreasing the precision starts degrading the quality of results.

In Figure 2, we represent $\gamma_{\min}$ as a function of time, for a time range extended to a maximum time of 10. We observe that at $t = 3$, the relative width of the inner-approximation over the outer-approximation is of order 0.7, which is equal to the value given in Table 1 of [4]. However, this ratio decreases quickly, mostly due to the x_2 component, and at $t = 4$, we get a ratio very close to 0.1, instead of 0.55 as in [4]. Indeed, $t = 4$ is a time at which, as already noted in Section 4.1, our inner-approximation of variable x_2 is temporarily of lower quality, even though the x_1 inner estimate is still of high quality. It is only temporary, as at further times the quality improves, before degrading again.

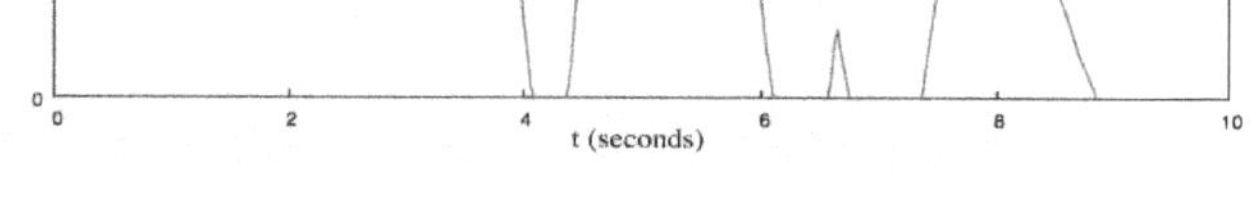

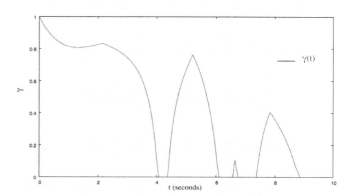

Figure 2: Evolution of $\gamma_{\min}$ with time

In Figure 3, we represent the evolution with time of the widths of the inner- and outer-approximations of x_2, the component that makes $\gamma_{\min}$ decrease drastically around $t = 4$. Whenever the width of the inner-approximation on x_2 decreases to zero, the width of the outer-approximation is also strongly decreasing: the difference between these widths remains almost stable. We also note again that the inner-approximation becoming empty at some point does not impact the behavior of the inner-approximation at further times. Finally, we note that this system looks quite stable, with solution widths that tend to decrease with time. This is a difficult case for the inner-approximation, as its width naturally tends towards 0 due to the problem, as we note on Figure 3. We advocate that inner and outer-approximations should be considered jointly in order to assess the behavior of a system.

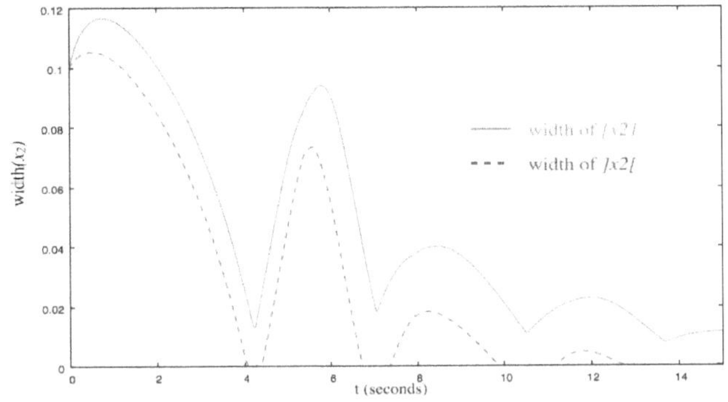

Figure 3: Evolution with time of the width of inner- and outer-approximations on x_2

Comparison on the biological system.

We now consider the biological system, with initial condition $\boldsymbol{x}_0 \in [0.1, 0.1175] \times ... \times [0.1, 0.1175]$, which is an outer-approximation of the simplex taken in [4]. We compute inner and outer approximated flowpipes for time in [0,0.2], with order 5 Taylor Models and a step size of 0.01. The computation completes in 4.7 seconds, and we get as a measure of quality of the approximation $\gamma_{\min}(t = 0.2) \approx 0.65$, which is this time a much better accuracy than the $\gamma_{\min}(t = 0.2) = 0.25$ obtained in 632 seconds in [4]. This seems to confirm that our approaches scales very well to high dimensional systems, with a very good accuracy.

We also measure as an indication of the accuracy the mean value on the components x_i of the distance between the inner and outer approximations x_i^{in} and x_i^{out}, computed as

$$\sum_{i=1}^{n} \frac{\max(\sup(x_i^{out}) - \sup(x_i^{in}), \inf(x_i^{in}) - \inf(x_i^{out}))}{n}.$$

It gives an over-estimation of the error between the inner-approximation and the exact reachable state at time t: this value for $t = 0.2$ is 4.10^{-3}.

4.2.2 *Comparison to [28]*

Comparison on the Brusselator.

In [28] the authors take $X = [0.3, 0.4] \times [0.5, 0.7]$ for a time frame in [0,1.1], and a time step h=0.05. We compute the inner and outer-approximations, for same time step and with order 3 Taylor Models. In [28], the accuracy of the result is estimated by a parameter ϵ_M that bounds the size of the boxes used to approximated the boundary of the exact reachable set, inside which they will look for an inner-approximation. We believe this parameter comparable in spirit to our measure of the maximum distance between the inner and the outer approximations. We can point 2 differences. First, in our case we compute the distance to the outer-approximation, which will always be greater than the distance to the exact reachable set. Also, our understanding is that there are no guarantees in the method of [28] on the actual distance from the inner-approximation itself to the reachable set, whereas our bounds are guaranteed.

We obtain in 0.8 seconds a distance equal to 0.005 for x_1, and 0.01 for x_2, which is 10 times larger than the estimation 0.001 obtained in 55 seconds in [28].

Comparison on the biological system.

We now consider the biological system, with, as in [28], a box initial condition $\boldsymbol{x}_0 \in [-0.015, 0.001] \times ... \times [-0.015, 0.001]$. In order to compare our results to their backward estimate, we consider the reverse flow, for time in [0,0.2] , and use order 3 Taylor Models and a step size of 0.02. Our computation of the inner and outer approximated flowpipes takes 0.2 seconds. We get inner-approximations that always strictly contain the ones of [28], which takes 0.67 seconds. Our analysis is thus both faster and with better accuracy.

Using as quality measure the measure of [4] that computes the ratio γ of the width of the inner-approximation over the width of the outer-approximation, here componentwise on the variables, and using our outer-approximation in both cases, we obtain for our approximation $(\gamma_1, \ldots, \gamma_n) = (0.970, 0.999, 0.973, 0.938, 0.938, 0.970, 0.971)$, while with the results of [28] we get the lower quality results $(\gamma_1, \ldots, \gamma_n) = (0.85, 0.86, 0.22, 0.84, 0.84, 0.85, 0.85)$.

We also compare our results with the outer-approximation computed by VNODE with a Taylor model of order 5. We represent on Figure 4 the upper bound for each of the 7 variables x_i on the outer-approximation by VNode, our outer-approximation, our inner-approximation, and that of [28], in that order, from left to right. The results confirm that

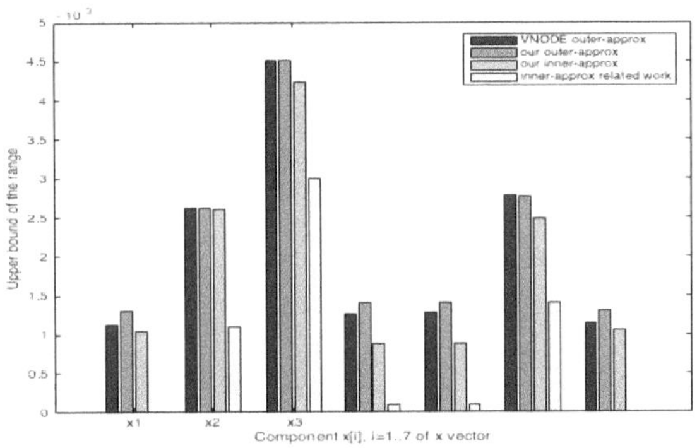

Figure 4: Upper bounds on inner and outer-approximations on the 7 variables of the biological system

our inner-approximation (third bar of each group in the Figure) is generally very close to the outer-approximations (first two bars in each group), while the inner-approximation of the related work (fourth bar) is of lower quality, and on some variables even absent (upper bound equal to zero).

5. CONCLUSION AND FUTURE WORK

We presented an approach to compute inner-approximating flowpipes of uncertain ODEs, that extends in a simple way Taylor-based methods for outer-approximation. The joint computation of the inner and outer-approximating flowpipes gives us a bound on the error to the exact reachable set at each instant, that we can use if needed to dynamically refine the approximation by using higher order Taylor models or smaller step sizes. Indeed, accurate error estimation, which is usually a difficult task, is a direct outcome of our computation. A natural future extension of the present work, is the inner-approximation of reachable sets in presence of guards and constraints, so as to handle general hybrid systems. Our approach allows us to inner-approximate not only the variables as demonstrated here, but also the projection on whatever function of these variables, not only at specific times like the related work, but as flowpipes, that can be used for detection of intersection. The symbolic information included in our model when we evaluate the Taylor models with affine arithmetic, will allow us to use existing work on the inner-approximation of joint range of functions and constraint solving, as e.g. [15].

Among the interests of inner-approximation is the possibility to falsify properties. Our objective in that respect, is to use the combination of inner and outer approximations to tackle the verification and falsification of temporal properties of uncertain hybrid systems, along the lines of [16,30].

Finally, this work can be applied to other, related problems. First, this can be applied to backward reachability problems, such as the ones treated in e.g. [28], by considering the opposite vector field. Secondly, this can be applied to a particular backward reachability problem : the inner-approximation of region of attractions, for which we should compare our method with existing work [19].

6. ACKNOWLEDGMENTS

The authors were supported by ANR project MALTHY, ANR-13-INSE-0003, DGA project "Complex Robotics Systems Safety" and the academic chair "Complex Systems Engineering" of Ecole polytechnique-ENSTA-Télécom-Thalès-Dassault-DCNS-DGA-FX-FDO-Fondation ParisTech.

7. REFERENCES

[1] M. Althoff. Reachability analysis of nonlinear systems using conservative polynomialization and non-convex sets. In *HSCC'13*, pages 173–182. ACM, 2013.

[2] M. Althoff. An introduction to CORA 2015. In *In ARCH 2014 and ARCH 2015*, pages 120–151, 2015.

[3] X. Chen, E. Ábrahám, and S. Sankaranarayanan. Flow*: An analyzer for non-linear hybrid systems. In *CAV*, pages 258–263, 2013.

[4] X. Chen, S. Sankaranarayanan, and E. Abraham. Under-approximate flowpipes for non-linear continuous systems. In *FMCAD*, pages 59–66. IEEE/ACM, 2014.

[5] J. Comba and J. Stolfi. Affine arithmetic and its applications to computer graphics. *In SIBGRAPI*, 1993.

[6] T. Dang, O. Maler, and R. Testylier. Accurate hybridization of nonlinear systems. In *HSCC*, 2010.

[7] G. Frehse, C. L. Guernic, A. Donzé, S. Cotton, R. Ray, O. Lebeltel, R. Ripado, A. Girard, T. Dang, and O. Maler. Spaceex: Scalable verification of hybrid systems. In *CAV*, pages 379–395, 2011.

[8] A. Girard. Reachability of uncertain linear systems using zonotopes. In *HSCC'05*. Springer, 2005.

[9] A. Girard, C. L. Guernic, and O. Maler. Efficient computation of reachable sets of linear time-invariant systems with inputs. In *HSCC*, pages 257–271, 2006.

[10] A. Goldsztejn, D. Daney, M. Rueher, and P. Taillibert. Modal intervals revisited: a mean-value extension to generalized intervals. In *QCP'05*, 2005.

[11] A. Goldsztejng and W. Hayes. Rigorous inner approximation of the range of functions. In *SCAN*. IEEE Computer Society, 2006.

[12] E. Goubault, M. Kieffer, O. Mullier, and S. Putot. General inner approximation of vector-valued functions. *Reliable Computing*, 18:117–143, 2013.

[13] E. Goubault, O. Mullier, S. Putot, and M. Kieffer. Inner approximated reachability analysis. In *HSCC*, pages 163–172, 2014.

[14] E. Goubault and S. Putot. Under-approximations of computations in real numbers based on generalized affine arithmetic. In *SAS*, pages 137–152, 2007.

[15] D. Ishii, A. Goldsztejn, and C. Jermann. Interval-based projection method for under-constrained numerical systems. *Constraints*, 17(4):432–460, 2012.

[16] D. Ishii, N. Yonezaki, and A. Goldsztejn. Monitoring temporal properties using interval analysis. *IEICE Transactions*, 2016.

[17] E. Kaucher. Interval analysis in the extended interval space IR. *Comput. (Supplementum) 2*, 1980.

[18] S. Kaynama, J. Maidens, M. Oishi, I. M. Mitchell, and G. A. Dumont. Computing the viability kernel using maximal reachable sets. In *HSCC'12*. ACM, 2012.

[19] M. Korda, D. Henrion, and C. N. Jones. Inner approximations of the region of attraction for polynomial dynamical systems. In *NOLCOS*, 2013.

[20] A. B. Kurzhanski and P. Varaiya. Ellipsoidal toolbox. Technical report, EECS, Berkeley, May.

[21] A. B. Kurzhanski and P. Varaiya. Ellipsoidal techniques for reachability analysis: internal approximation. *Systems & control letters*, 2000.

[22] M. Lerch, G. Tischler, J. W. von Gudenberg, W. Hofschuster, and W. Kramer. filib++, a fast interval library supporting containment computations. *ACM Trans. Math. Soft.*, 2006.

[23] R. E. Moore. *Interval analysis.* 1966.

[24] N. S. Nedialkov. An interval solver for initial value problems in ordinary differential equations.

[25] N. S. Nedialkov, K. Jackson, and G. Corliss. Validated solutions of initial value problems for ordinary differential equations. *Appl. Math. Comp.*, 1999.

[26] M. A. B. Sassi, R. Testylier, T. Dang, and A. Girard. Reachability analysis of polynomial systems using linear programming relaxations. In *ATVA*, 2012.

[27] R. Testylier and T. Dang. NLTOOLBOX: A library for reachability computation of nonlinear dynamical systems. In *ATVA*, pages 469–473, 2013.

[28] B. Xue, Z. She, and A. Easwaran. Under-approximating backward reachable sets by polytopes. In *CAV*, 2016.

[29] P. Zgliczynski. C^1 Lohner algorithm. *Foundations of Computational Mathematics*, 2(4):429–465, 2002.

[30] A. Zutshi, S. Sankaranarayanan, J. V. Deshmukh, J. Kapinski, and X. Jin. Falsification of safety properties for closed loop control systems. In *HSCC*, pages 299–300, 2015.

On the Polytope Escape Problem for Continuous Linear Dynamical Systems

Joël Ouaknine [*†]
MPI-SWS and Oxford U.
joel@mpi-sws.org

João Sousa-Pinto [*‡]
Oxford U.
jspinto@cs.ox.ac.uk

James Worrell [*]
Oxford U.
jbw@cs.ox.ac.uk

ABSTRACT

The Polytope Escape Problem for continuous linear dynamical systems consists of deciding, given an affine function $f : \mathbb{R}^d \to \mathbb{R}^d$ and a convex polytope $\mathcal{P} \subseteq \mathbb{R}^d$, both with rational descriptions, whether there exists an initial point $\boldsymbol{x}_0$ in $\mathcal{P}$ such that the trajectory of the unique solution to the differential equation

$$\begin{cases} \dot{\boldsymbol{x}}(t) = f(\boldsymbol{x}(t)) \\ \boldsymbol{x}(0) = \boldsymbol{x}_0 \end{cases}$$

is entirely contained in $\mathcal{P}$. We show that this problem is reducible in polynomial time to the decision version of linear programming with real algebraic coefficients. The latter is a special case of the decision problem for the existential theory of real closed fields, which is known to lie between **NP** and **PSPACE**. Our algorithm makes use of spectral techniques and relies, among others, on tools from Diophantine approximation.

CCS Concepts

•**Theory of computation → Timed and hybrid models;**

Keywords

Orbit Problem; Continuous Linear Dynamical Systems

1. INTRODUCTION

In ambient space $\mathbb{R}^d$, a *continuous linear dynamical system* is a trajectory $\boldsymbol{x}(t)$, where t ranges over the non-negative reals, defined by a differential equation $\dot{\boldsymbol{x}}(t) = f(\boldsymbol{x}(t))$ in which the function f is *affine* or *linear*. If the initial point $\boldsymbol{x}(0)$ is given, the differential equation uniquely defines the entire trajectory. (Linear) dynamical systems have been extensively studied in Mathematics, Physics, and Engineering, and more recently have played an increasingly important role in Computer Science, notably in the modelling and analysis of cyber-physical systems; a recent and authoritative textbook on the matter is [2].

In the study of dynamical systems, particularly from the perspective of control theory, considerable attention has been given to the study of *invariant sets*, i.e., subsets of $\mathbb{R}^d$ from which no trajectory can escape; see, e.g., [10, 5, 3, 20]. Our focus in the present chapter is on sets with the dual property that *no trajectory remains trapped.* Such sets play a key role in analysing *liveness* properties in cyber-physical systems (see, for instance, [2]): discrete progress is ensured by guaranteeing that all trajectories (i.e., from any initial starting point) must eventually reach a point at which they 'escape' (temporarily or permanently) the set in question.

More precisely, given an affine function $f : \mathbb{R}^d \to \mathbb{R}^d$ and a convex polytope $\mathcal{P} \subseteq \mathbb{R}^d$, both specified using rational coefficients encoded in binary, we consider the *Polytope Escape Problem* which asks whether there is some point $\boldsymbol{x}_0$ in $\mathcal{P}$ for which the corresponding trajectory of the solution to the differential equation

$$\begin{cases} \dot{\boldsymbol{x}}(t) = f(\boldsymbol{x}(t)) \\ \boldsymbol{x}(0) = \boldsymbol{x}_0 \end{cases}$$

is entirely contained in $\mathcal{P}$. Our main result is to show that this problem is decidable by reducing it in polynomial time to the decision version of linear programming with real algebraic coefficients, which itself reduces in polynomial time to deciding the truth of a sentence in the first-order theory of the reals: a problem whose complexity is known to lie between **NP** and **PSPACE** [9]. Our algorithm makes use of spectral techniques and relies among others on tools from Diophantine approximation.

It is interesting to note that a seemingly closely related problem, that of determining whether a given trajectory of a linear dynamical system ever hits a given hyperplane (also known as the *continuous Skolem Problem*), is not known to be decidable; see, in particular, [4, 12, 11]. When the target is instead taken to be a single point (rather than a hyperplane), the corresponding reachability question (known as

*Supported by the EPSRC.
†Supported by the ERC grant AVS-ISS (648701).
‡Supported by the ERC grant ALGAME (321171).

HSCC'17 April 18-20, 2017, Pittsburgh, PA, USA

ACM ISBN 978-1-4503-4590-3/17/04.

DOI: http://dx.doi.org/10.1145/3049797.3054956

the *continuous Orbit Problem*) can be decided in polynomial time [14].

2. MATHEMATICAL BACKGROUND

2.1 Kronecker's Theorem

Let $\mathbb{T}$ denote the group of complex numbers of modulus 1, with multiplication as group operation. Then the function $\phi : \mathbb{R} \to \mathbb{T}$ given by $\phi(x) = \exp(2\pi i x)$ is a homomorphism from the additive group of real numbers to $\mathbb{T}$, with kernel the subgroup of integers.

Recall from [15] the following classical theorem of Kronecker on simultaneous inhomogeneous Diophantine approximation.

THEOREM 1 (KRONECKER). *Let $\theta_1, \ldots, \theta_s$ be real numbers such that the set $\{\theta_1, \ldots, \theta_s, 1\}$ is linearly independent over $\mathbb{Q}$. Then for all $\psi_1, \ldots, \psi_s \in \mathbb{R}$ and $\varepsilon > 0$, there exists a positive integer n and integers $n_1, \ldots, n_s$ such that*

$$|n\theta_1 - \psi_1 - n_1| < \varepsilon, \ldots, |n\theta_s - \psi_s - n_s| < \varepsilon\,.$$

We obtain the following simple corollary:

COROLLARY 2. *Let $\theta_1, \ldots, \theta_s$ be real numbers such that the set $\{\theta_1, \ldots, \theta_s, 1\}$ is linearly independent over $\mathbb{Q}$. Then*

$$\{(\phi(n\theta_1), \ldots, \phi(n\theta_s)) : n \in \mathbb{N}\}$$

is a dense subset of $\mathbb{T}^s$.

PROOF. Since ϕ is surjective, an arbitrary element of $\mathbb{T}^s$ can be written in the form $(\phi(\psi_1), \ldots, \phi(\psi_s))$ for some real numbers $\psi_1, \ldots, \psi_s$. Applying Kronecker's Theorem, we get that for all $\varepsilon > 0$, there exists a positive integer n and integers $n_1, \ldots, n_s$ such that

$$|n\theta_1 - \psi_1 - n_1| < \varepsilon, \ldots, |n\theta_s - \psi_s - n_s| < \varepsilon\,.$$

By continuity of ϕ it follows that $(\phi(\psi_1), \ldots, \phi(\psi_s))$ is a limit point of $\{(\phi(n\theta_1), \ldots, \phi(n\theta_s)) : n \in \mathbb{N}\}$. This establishes the result. □

2.2 Laurent polynomials

A multivariate *Laurent polynomial* is a polynomial in positive and negative powers of variables $z_1, \ldots, z_s$ with complex coefficients. We are interested in Laurent polynomials of the special form

$$g = \sum_{j=1}^{k} \left(c_j {z_1}^{n_{1,j}} \ldots {z_s}^{n_{s,j}} + \overline{c_j} {z_1}^{-n_{1,j}} \ldots {z_s}^{-n_{s,j}} \right),$$

where $c_1, \ldots, c_k \in \mathbb{C}$ and $n_{1,1}, \ldots, n_{s,k} \in \mathbb{Z}$. We call such g *self-conjugate Laurent polynomials.* Notice that if $a_1, \ldots, a_s \in \mathbb{T}$ then $g(a_1, \ldots, a_s)$ is a real number, so we may regard g as a function from $\mathbb{T}^s$ to $\mathbb{R}$.

LEMMA 3. *Let $g \in \mathbb{C}[z_1^{\pm 1}, \ldots, z_s^{\pm 1}]$ be a self-conjugate Laurent polynomial that has no constant term. Given real numbers $\theta_1, \ldots, \theta_s \in \mathbb{R}$ such that $\theta_1, \ldots, \theta_s, 1$ are linearly independent over $\mathbb{Q}$, define a function $f : \mathbb{R}_{\geq 0} \to \mathbb{R}$ by*

$$f(t) = g(\phi(t\theta_1), \ldots, \phi(t\theta_s))\,.$$

Then either f is identically zero, or

$$\liminf_{n\to\infty} f(n) < 0\,,$$

where n ranges over the nonnegative integers.

PROOF. Recall that we may regard g as a function from $\mathbb{T}^s$ to $\mathbb{R}$. Now we consider the function $g \circ \phi^s : \mathbb{R}^s \to \mathbb{R}$,

$$(x_1, \ldots, x_s) \mapsto g(\phi(x_1), \ldots, \phi(x_s))\,.$$

We use an averaging argument to establish that either $g \circ \phi^s$ is identically zero on $\mathbb{R}^s$ or there exist $x_1^*, \ldots, x_s^* \in [0, 1]$ such that $g(\phi(x_1^*), \ldots, \phi(x_s^*)) < 0$.

Since $\int_0^1 \exp(2\pi i n x)dx = 0$ for all non-zero integers n, it holds that

$$\int_0^1 \cdots \int_0^1 g(\phi(x_1), \ldots, \phi(x_s))dx_1 \ldots dx_s = 0\,.$$

Suppose that $g \circ \phi^s$ is not identically zero over $\mathbb{R}^s$ and hence not identically zero over $[0, 1]^s$. Then $g \circ \phi^s$ cannot be nonnegative on $[0, 1]^s$, since the integral over a set of positive measure of a continuous nonnegative function that is not identically zero must be strictly positive. We conclude that there must exist $(x_1^*, \ldots, x_s^*) \in [0, 1]^s$ such that $g(\phi(x_1^*), \ldots, \phi(x_s^*)) < 0$.

By assumption, $\theta_1, \ldots, \theta_s, 1$ are linearly independent over $\mathbb{Q}$. By Corollary 2 it follows that

$$\{(\phi(n\theta_1), \ldots, \phi(n\theta_s)) : n \in \mathbb{N}\}$$

is dense in $\mathbb{T}^s$ and hence has $(\phi(x_1^*), \ldots, \phi(x_s^*))$ as a limit point. Since $g \circ \phi^s$ is continuous, there are arbitrarily large $n \in \mathbb{N}$ for which

$$f(n) = g(\phi(n\theta_1), \ldots, \phi(n\theta_s)) \leq \tfrac{1}{2} g(\phi(x_1^*), \ldots, \phi(x_s^*)) < 0\,,$$

which proves the result. □

Note that this proof could be made constructive by using an effective version of Kronecker's Theorem, as studied in [7] and [17], although we do not make use of this fact in the present paper.

We say that a self-conjugate Laurent polynomial g is *simple* if it has no constant term and each monomial mentions only a single variable. More precisely, g is simple if it can be written in the form

$$g = \sum_{j=1}^{k} c_j z_{i_j}^{n_j} + \overline{c_j} z_{i_j}^{-n_j}\,,$$

where $c_1, \ldots, c_k \in \mathbb{C}$, $i_1, \ldots, i_k \in \{1, \ldots, s\}$, and $n_1, \ldots, n_k \in \mathbb{Z}$.

The following consequence of Lemma 3 will be key to proving decidability of the problem at hand. It is an extension of Lemma 4 from [6].

THEOREM 4. *Let $g \in \mathbb{C}[z_1^{\pm 1}, \ldots, z_s^{\pm 1}]$ be a simple self-conjugate Laurent polynomial and $\theta_1, \ldots, \theta_s$ non-zero real numbers. Then either*

$$g(\phi(t\theta_1), \ldots, \phi(t\theta_s)) = 0 \text{ for all } t \in \mathbb{R}$$

or

$$\liminf_{n\to\infty} g(\phi(n\theta_1), \ldots, \phi(n\theta_s)) < 0\,,$$

where n ranges over the nonnegative integers.

PROOF. Note that if $1, \theta_1, \ldots, \theta_s$ are linearly independent over $\mathbb{Q}$ then the result follows from Lemma 3. Otherwise, let $\{\theta_{i_1}, \ldots, \theta_{i_k}\}$ be a maximal subset of $\{\theta_1, \ldots, \theta_s\}$ such that $1, \theta_{i_1}, \ldots, \theta_{i_k}$ are linearly independent over $\mathbb{Q}$.

Then, for some $N \in \mathbb{N}$ and each j, one can write

$$N\theta_j = \left(m + \sum_{l=1}^{k} n_l \theta_{i_l} \right) ,$$

where $m, n_1, \ldots, n_k$ are integers that depend on j, whilst N does not depend on j. It follows that for all j and $t \in \mathbb{R}$,

$$\begin{aligned} \phi(N\theta_j t) &= \phi(mt) \cdot \prod_{l=1}^{k} \phi(n_l \theta_{i_l} t) \\ &= \phi(t)^m \cdot \prod_{l=1}^{k} \phi(\theta_{i_l} t)^{n_l} . \end{aligned}$$

In other words, for all $j \geq k+1$, $\phi(N\theta_j t)$ can be written as a product of positive and negative powers of the terms

$$\phi(t), \phi(\theta_{i_1} t), \ldots, \phi(\theta_{i_k} t) .$$

It follows that there exists a self-conjugate Laurent polynomial $h \in \mathbb{C}[z_1^{\pm 1}, \ldots, z_k^{\pm 1}]$, not necessarily simple, but with zero constant term, such that for all $t \in \mathbb{R}$,

$$g(\phi(N\theta_1 t), \ldots, \phi(N\theta_s t)) = h(\phi(\theta_{i_1} t), \ldots, \phi(\theta_{i_k} t)) .$$

Since $1, \theta_{i_1}, \ldots, \theta_{i_k}$ are linearly independent over $\mathbb{Q}$, the result follows by applying Lemma 3 to h. □

2.3 Jordan Canonical Forms

Let $A \in \mathbb{Q}^{d \times d}$ be a square matrix with rational entries. The *minimal polynomial* of A is the unique monic polynomial $m(x) \in \mathbb{Q}[x]$ of least degree such that $m(A) = 0$. By the Cayley-Hamilton Theorem the degree of m is at most the dimension d of A. The set $\sigma(A)$ of eigenvalues is the set of roots of m. The *index* of an eigenvalue λ, denoted by $\nu(\lambda)$, is its multiplicity as a root of m. We use $\nu(A)$ to denote $\max_{\lambda \in \sigma(A)} \nu(\lambda)$: the maximum index over all eigenvalues of A. Given an eigenvalue $\lambda \in \sigma(A)$, we say that $\boldsymbol{v} \in \mathbb{C}^d$ is a *generalised eigenvector* of A if $\boldsymbol{v} \in \ker(A - \lambda I)^k$, for some $k \in \mathbb{N}$.

We denote by $\mathcal{V}_\lambda$ the subspace of $\mathbb{C}^d$ spanned by the set of generalised eigenvectors associated with some eigenvalue λ of A. We denote the subspace of $\mathbb{C}^d$ spanned by the set of generalised eigenvectors associated with some real eigenvalue by $\mathcal{V}^r$. We likewise denote the subspace of $\mathbb{C}^d$ spanned by the set of generalised eigenvectors associated to eigenvalues with non-zero imaginary part by $\mathcal{V}^c$.

It is well known that each vector $\boldsymbol{v} \in \mathbb{C}^d$ can be written uniquely as $\boldsymbol{v} = \sum_{\lambda \in \sigma(A)} \boldsymbol{v}_\lambda$, where $\boldsymbol{v}_\lambda \in \mathcal{V}_\lambda$. It follows that $\boldsymbol{v}$ can also be uniquely written as $\boldsymbol{v} = \boldsymbol{v}^r + \boldsymbol{v}^c$, where $\boldsymbol{v}^r \in \mathcal{V}^r$ and $\boldsymbol{v}^c \in \mathcal{V}^c$.

We can write any matrix $A \in \mathbb{C}^{d \times d}$ as $A = Q^{-1}JQ$ for some invertible matrix Q and block diagonal Jordan matrix $J = \text{diag}(J_1, \ldots, J_N)$, with each block J_i having the following form:

$$\begin{pmatrix} \lambda & 1 & 0 & \cdots & 0 \\ 0 & \lambda & 1 & \cdots & 0 \\ \vdots & \vdots & \vdots & \ddots & \vdots \\ 0 & 0 & 0 & \cdots & 1 \\ 0 & 0 & 0 & \cdots & \lambda \end{pmatrix}$$

Given a rational matrix A, its Jordan Normal Form $A = Q^{-1}JQ$ can be computed in polynomial time, as shown in [8].

Note that each vector $\boldsymbol{v}$ appearing as a column of the matrix Q^{-1} is a generalised eigenvector of A. We also note that the index $\nu(\lambda)$ of some eigenvalue λ corresponds to the dimension of the largest Jordan block associated with it.

One can obtain a closed-form expression for powers of block diagonal Jordan matrices, and use this to get a closed-form expression for exponential block diagonal Jordan matrices. In fact, if J_i is a $k \times k$ Jordan block associated with some eigenvalue λ, then

$$J_i^n = \begin{pmatrix} \lambda^n & n\lambda^{n-1} & \binom{n}{2}\lambda^{n-1} & \cdots & \binom{n}{k-1}\lambda^{n-k+1} \\ 0 & \lambda^n & n\lambda^{n-1} & \cdots & \binom{n}{k-2}\lambda^{n-k+2} \\ \vdots & \vdots & \vdots & \ddots & \vdots \\ 0 & 0 & 0 & \cdots & n\lambda^{n-1} \\ 0 & 0 & 0 & \cdots & \lambda^n \end{pmatrix}$$

and

$$\exp(J_i t) = \exp(\lambda t) \begin{pmatrix} 1 & t & \cdots & \frac{t^{k-1}}{(k-1)!} \\ 0 & 1 & \cdots & \frac{t^{k-2}}{(k-2)!} \\ \vdots & \vdots & \ddots & \vdots \\ 0 & 0 & \cdots & t \\ 0 & 0 & \cdots & 1 \end{pmatrix}$$

In the above, $\binom{n}{j}$ is defined to be 0 when $n < j$.

Proposition 5. *Let $\boldsymbol{v}$ lie in the generalised eigenspace $\mathcal{V}_\lambda$ for some $\lambda \in \sigma(A)$. Then $\boldsymbol{b}^T \exp(At)\boldsymbol{v}$ is a linear combination of terms of the form $t^n \exp(\lambda t)$.*

Proof. Note that, if $A = Q^{-1}JQ$ and $J = diag(J_1, \ldots, J_N)$ is a block diagonal Jordan matrix, then

$$\exp(At) = Q^{-1} \exp(Jt) Q$$

and

$$\exp(Jt) = \text{diag}(\exp(J_1 t), \ldots, \exp(J_N t)) .$$

The result follows by observing that $Q\boldsymbol{v}$ is zero in every component other than those pertaining the block corresponding to the eigenspace $\mathcal{V}_\lambda$. □

In order to compare the asymptotic growth of expressions of the form $t^n \exp(\lambda t)$, for $\lambda \in \mathbb{R}$ and $n \in \mathbb{N}_0$, we define $\prec$ to be the lexicographic order on $\mathbb{R} \times \mathbb{N}_0$, that is,

$$(\eta, j) \prec (\rho, m) \quad \text{iff} \quad \eta < \rho \text{ or } (\eta = \rho \text{ and } j < m) .$$

Clearly $\exp(\eta t) t^j = o(\exp(\rho t) t^m)$ as $t \to \infty$ if and only if $(\eta, j) \prec (\rho, m)$.

Definition 1. *If $\boldsymbol{b}^T \exp(At)\boldsymbol{v}$ is not identically zero, the maximal $(\rho, m) \in \mathbb{R} \times \mathbb{N}_0$ (with respect to $\prec$) for which there is a term $t^m \exp(\lambda t)$ with $\Re(\lambda) = \rho$ in the closed-form expression for $\boldsymbol{b}^T \exp(At)\boldsymbol{v}$ is called* dominant *for $\boldsymbol{b}^T \exp(At)\boldsymbol{v}$.*

Before we can proceed, we shall need the following auxiliary result:

Proposition 6. *Suppose that $\boldsymbol{v} \in \mathbb{R}^d$ and that*

$$\boldsymbol{v} = \sum_{\lambda \in \sigma(A)} \boldsymbol{v}_\lambda ,$$

where $\boldsymbol{v}_\lambda \in \mathcal{V}_\lambda$. Then $\boldsymbol{v}_{\overline{\lambda}}$ and $\boldsymbol{v}_\lambda$ are component-wise complex conjugates.

PROOF. We start by observing that

$$\mathbf{0} = \boldsymbol{v} - \overline{\boldsymbol{v}} = \sum_{\lambda \in \sigma(A)} (\boldsymbol{v}_\lambda - \overline{\boldsymbol{v}_{\overline{\lambda}}}) . \tag{1}$$

But if $\boldsymbol{v}_\lambda \in \ker(A - \lambda I)^k$ then $\overline{\boldsymbol{v}_{\overline{\lambda}}} \in \ker(A - \overline{\lambda} I)^k$, and hence $\overline{\boldsymbol{v}_{\overline{\lambda}}} \in \mathcal{V}_\lambda$. Thus each summand $\boldsymbol{v}_\lambda - \overline{\boldsymbol{v}_{\overline{\lambda}}}$ in (1) lies in $\mathcal{V}_\lambda$. Since $\mathbb{C}^d$ is a direct sum of the generalised eigenspaces of A, we must have $\boldsymbol{v}_\lambda = \overline{\boldsymbol{v}_{\overline{\lambda}}}$ for all $\lambda \in \sigma(A)$. □

We now derive a corollary of Theorem 4.

COROLLARY 7. *Consider a function of the form* $h(t) = \boldsymbol{b}^T \exp(At)\boldsymbol{v}^c$*, where* $\boldsymbol{v}^c \in \mathcal{V}^c$*, with* $(\rho, m) \in \mathbb{R} \times \mathbb{N}_0$ *dominant. If* $h(t) \not\equiv 0$*, then we have*

$$-\infty < \liminf_{t\to\infty} \frac{h(t)}{\exp(\rho t) t^m} < 0 .$$

PROOF. Let

$$\Re(\sigma(A)) = \{\eta \in \mathbb{R} : \eta + i\theta \in \sigma(A), \text{ for some } \theta \in \mathbb{R}\} .$$

For each $\eta \in \Re(\sigma(A))$ define $\boldsymbol{\theta}_\eta = \{\theta \in \mathbb{R}_{>0} : \eta + i\theta \in \sigma(A)\}$. By abuse of notation, we also use $\boldsymbol{\theta}_\eta$ to refer to the vector whose coordinates are exactly the members of this set, ordered in an increasing way. We note that, due to Proposition 6 and Proposition 5, the following holds:

$$\begin{aligned}
\boldsymbol{b}^T \exp(At)\boldsymbol{v}^c &= \boldsymbol{b}^T \exp(At) \sum_{\eta \in \Re(\sigma(A))} \sum_{\theta \in \boldsymbol{\theta}_\eta} \boldsymbol{v}_{\eta+i\theta} + \boldsymbol{v}_{\eta-i\theta} \\
&= \sum_{\eta \in \Re(\sigma(A))} \sum_{\theta \in \boldsymbol{\theta}_\eta} \boldsymbol{b}^T \exp(At)\boldsymbol{v}_{\eta+i\theta} \\
&\qquad + \overline{\boldsymbol{b}^T \exp(At)\boldsymbol{v}_{\eta+i\theta}} \\
&= \sum_{\eta \in \Re(\sigma(A))} \sum_{j=0}^{\nu(A)-1} t^j \exp(\eta t) g_{(\eta,j)}(\exp(i\boldsymbol{\theta}_\eta t))
\end{aligned}$$

for some simple self-conjugate Laurent polynomials $g_{(\eta,j)}$. Note that

$$(\rho, m) = \max_{\prec}\{(\eta, j) \in \mathbb{R} \times \mathbb{N}_0 : g_{(\eta,j)}(\exp(i\boldsymbol{\theta}_\eta t)) \not\equiv 0\} .$$

The result then follows from Theorem 4 and the fact that

$$\liminf_{t\to\infty} \frac{h(t)}{\exp(\rho t) t^m} = \liminf_{t\to\infty} g_{(\rho,m)}(\exp(i\boldsymbol{\theta}_\rho t)) .$$

□

2.4 Computation with Algebraic Numbers

In this section, we briefly explain how one can represent and manipulate algebraic numbers efficiently.

Any given algebraic number α can be represented as a tuple (p, a, ε), where $p \in \mathbb{Q}[x]$ is its minimal polynomial, $a = a_1 + a_2 i$, with $a_1, a_2 \in \mathbb{Q}$, is an approximation of α, and $\varepsilon \in \mathbb{Q}$ is sufficiently small that α is the unique root of p within distance ε of a. This is referred to as the standard or canonical representation of an algebraic number.

Let $f \in \mathbb{Z}[x]$ be a polynomial. The following root-separation bound, due to Mignotte [18], can be used to give a value of ε such that any disk of radius ε in the complex plane contains at most one root of f.

PROPOSITION 8. *Let* $f \in \mathbb{Z}[x]$*. If* α_1 *and* α_2 *are distinct roots of* f*, then*

$$|\alpha_1 - \alpha_2| > \frac{\sqrt{6}}{d^{(d+1)/2} H^{d-1}}$$

where d *and* H *are respectively the degree and height (maximum absolute value of the coefficients) of* f*.*

It follows that in the canonical representation (p, a, ε) of an algebraic number α, where p has degree d and height H, we may choose a_1, a_2, ϵ to have bit length polynomial in d and $\log H$.

Given canonical representations of two algebraic numbers α and β, one can compute canonical representations of $\alpha+\beta$, $\alpha\beta$, and α/β, all in polynomial time. More specifically, one can:

- factor an arbitrary polynomial with rational coefficients as a product of irreducible polynomials in polynomial time using the LLL algorithm, described in [16];
- compute an approximation of an arbitrary algebraic number accurate up to polynomially many bits in polynomial time, due to the work in [19];
- use the sub-resultant algorithm (see Algorithm 3.3.7 in [13]) and the two aforementioned procedures to compute canonical representations of sums, differences, multiplications, and quotient of two canonically represented algebraic numbers.

3. EXISTENTIAL FIRST-ORDER THEORY OF THE REALS

Let $\boldsymbol{x} = (x_1, \ldots, x_m)$ be a list of m real-valued variables, and let $\sigma(\boldsymbol{x})$ be a Boolean combination of atomic predicates of the form $g(\boldsymbol{x}) \sim 0$, where each $g(\boldsymbol{x})$ is a polynomial with integer coefficients in the variables $\boldsymbol{x}$, and $\sim$ is either $>$ or $=$. Tarski has famously shown that we can decide the truth over the field $\mathbb{R}$ of sentences of the form $\phi = Q_1 x_1 \cdots Q_m x_m \sigma(\boldsymbol{x})$, where Q_i is either $\exists$ or $\forall$. He did so by showing that this theory admits quantifier elimination (Tarski-Seidenberg Theorem [21]). The set of all true sentences of such form is called the first-order theory of the reals, and the set of all true sentences where only existential quantification is allowed is called the existential first-order theory of the reals. The complexity class $\exists\mathbb{R}$ is defined as the set of problems having a polynomial-time many-one reduction to the existential theory of the reals. It was shown in [9] that $\exists\mathbb{R} \subseteq PSPACE$.

We also remark that our standard representation of algebraic numbers allows us to write them explicitly in the first-order theory of the reals, that is, given $\alpha \in \mathbb{A}$, there exists a sentence $\sigma(x)$ such that $\sigma(x)$ is true if and only if $x = \alpha$. Thus, we allow their use when writing sentences in the first-order theory of the reals, for simplicity.

The decision version of linear programming with canonically-defined algebraic coefficients is in $\exists\mathbb{R}$, as the emptiness of a convex polytope can easily be described by a sentence of the form $\exists x_1 \cdots \exists x_n \sigma(\boldsymbol{x})$.

Finally, we note that even though the decision version of linear programming with rational coefficients is in P, allowing algebraic coefficients makes things more complicated. While it has been shown in [1] that this is solvable in time polynomial in the size of the problem instance and on the degree of the smallest number field containing all algebraic numbers in each instance, it turns out that in the problem at hand the degree of that extension can be exponential in the size of the input. In other words, the splitting field of the characteristic polynomial of a matrix can have a degree which is exponential in the degree of the characteristic polynomial.

4. THE POLYTOPE ESCAPE PROBLEM

The Polytope Escape Problem for continuous linear dynamical systems consists of deciding, given an affine function $f : \mathbb{R}^d \to \mathbb{R}^d$ and a convex polytope $\mathcal{P} \subseteq \mathbb{R}^d$, whether there exists an initial point $\boldsymbol{x}_0 \in \mathcal{P}$ for which the trajectory of the unique solution to the differential equation $\dot{\boldsymbol{x}}(t) = f(\boldsymbol{x}(t)), \boldsymbol{x}(0) = \boldsymbol{x}_0, t \geq 0$, is entirely contained in $\mathcal{P}$. A starting point $\boldsymbol{x}_0 \in \mathcal{P}$ is said to be *trapped* if the trajectory of the corresponding solution is contained in $\mathcal{P}$, and *eventually trapped* if the trajectory of the corresponding solution contains a trapped point. Therefore, the Polytope Escape Problem amounts to deciding whether a trapped point exists, which in turn is equivalent to deciding whether an eventually trapped point exists.

The goal of this section is to prove the following result:

THEOREM 9. *The Polytope Escape Problem is polynomial-time reducible to the decision version of linear programming with algebraic coefficients.*

A d-dimensional instance of the Polytope Escape Problem is a pair $(f, \mathcal{P})$, where $f : \mathbb{R}^d \to \mathbb{R}^d$ is an affine function and $\mathcal{P} \subseteq \mathbb{R}^d$ is a convex polytope. In this formulation we assume that all numbers involved in the definition of f and $\mathcal{P}$ are rational.[1]

An instance $(f, \mathcal{P})$ of the Polytope Escape Problem is said to be *homogeneous* if f is a linear function and $\mathcal{P}$ is a convex polytope cone (in particular, $\boldsymbol{x} \in \mathcal{P}, \alpha > 0 \Rightarrow \alpha\boldsymbol{x} \in \mathcal{P}$).

The restriction of the Polytope Escape Problem to homogeneous instances is called the homogeneous Polytope Escape Problem.

LEMMA 10. *The Polytope Escape Problem is polynomial-time reducible to the homogeneous Polytope Escape Problem.*

PROOF. Let $(f, \mathcal{P})$ be an instance of the Polytope Escape Problem in $\mathbb{R}^d$, and write

$$f(\boldsymbol{x}) = A\boldsymbol{x} + \boldsymbol{a} \text{ and } \mathcal{P} = \{\boldsymbol{x} \in \mathbb{R}^d : B_1\boldsymbol{x} > \boldsymbol{b}_1 \wedge B_2\boldsymbol{x} \geq \boldsymbol{b}_2\}.$$

Now define

$$A' = \begin{pmatrix} A & \boldsymbol{a} \\ \boldsymbol{0}^T & 0 \end{pmatrix}, B_1' = \begin{pmatrix} B_1 & -\boldsymbol{b}_1 \\ \boldsymbol{0}^T & 1 \end{pmatrix}, B_2' = \begin{pmatrix} B_2 & -\boldsymbol{b}_2 \end{pmatrix},$$

$$\mathcal{P}' = \left\{ \begin{pmatrix} \boldsymbol{x} \\ y \end{pmatrix} \in \mathbb{R}^{d+1} : B_1' \begin{pmatrix} \boldsymbol{x} \\ y \end{pmatrix} > \boldsymbol{0} \wedge B_2' \begin{pmatrix} \boldsymbol{x} \\ y \end{pmatrix} \geq \boldsymbol{0} \right\},$$

and

$$g\begin{pmatrix} \boldsymbol{x} \\ y \end{pmatrix} = A' \begin{pmatrix} \boldsymbol{x} \\ y \end{pmatrix}.$$

[1]The assumption of rationality is required to justify some of our complexity claims (e.g., Jordan Canonical Forms are only known to be polynomial-time computable for matrices with rational coordinates). Nevertheless, our procedure remains valid in a more general setting, and in fact, the overall $\exists\mathbb{R}$ complexity of our algorithm would not be affected if one allowed real algebraic numbers when defining problem instances.

Then $(g, \mathcal{P}')$ is a homogeneous instance of the Polytope Escape Problem.

It is clear that $\boldsymbol{x}(t)$ satisfies the differential equation $\dot{\boldsymbol{x}}(t) = f(\boldsymbol{x}(t))$ if and only if $\begin{pmatrix} \boldsymbol{x}(t) \\ 1 \end{pmatrix}$ satisfies the differential equation $\begin{pmatrix} \dot{\boldsymbol{x}} \\ \dot{y} \end{pmatrix} = g\begin{pmatrix} \boldsymbol{x} \\ y \end{pmatrix} == \begin{pmatrix} A\boldsymbol{x} + y\boldsymbol{a} \\ 0 \end{pmatrix}$. In general, in any trajectory $\begin{pmatrix} \boldsymbol{x} \\ y \end{pmatrix}$ that satisfies this last differential equation, the y-component must be constant.

We claim that $(f, \mathcal{P})$ is a positive instance of the Polytope Escape Problem if and only if $(g, \mathcal{P}')$ is a positive instance. Indeed, if the point $\boldsymbol{x}_0 \in \mathbb{R}^d$ is trapped in $(f, \mathcal{P})$ then the point $\begin{pmatrix} \boldsymbol{x}_0 \\ 1 \end{pmatrix}$ is trapped in $(g, \mathcal{P}')$. Conversely, suppose that $\begin{pmatrix} \boldsymbol{x}_0 \\ y_0 \end{pmatrix}$ is trapped in $(g, \mathcal{P}')$. Then, since $B_1' \begin{pmatrix} \boldsymbol{x}_0 \\ y_0 \end{pmatrix} > \boldsymbol{0}$, we must have $y_0 > 0$. Scaling, it follows that $\begin{pmatrix} y_0^{-1}\boldsymbol{x}_0 \\ 1 \end{pmatrix}$ is also trapped in $(g, \mathcal{P}')$. This implies that $y_0^{-1}\boldsymbol{x}_0$ is trapped in $(f, \mathcal{P})$. □

We remind the reader that the unique solution of the differential equation $\dot{\boldsymbol{x}}(t) = f(\boldsymbol{x}(t)), \boldsymbol{x}(0) = \boldsymbol{x}_0, t \geq 0$, where $f(\boldsymbol{x}) = A\boldsymbol{x}$, is given by $\boldsymbol{x}(t) = \exp(At)\boldsymbol{x}_0$. In this setting, the sets of trapped and eventually trapped points are, respectively:

$$T = \{\boldsymbol{x}_0 \in \mathbb{R}^d : \forall t \geq 0, \exp(At)\boldsymbol{x}_0 \in \mathcal{P}\}$$
$$ET = \{\boldsymbol{x}_0 \in \mathbb{R}^d : \exists t \geq 0, \exp(At)\boldsymbol{x}_0 \in T\}$$

Note that both T and ET are convex subsets of $\mathbb{R}^d$.

LEMMA 11. *The homogeneous Polytope Escape Problem is polynomial-time reducible to the decision version of linear programming with algebraic coefficients.*

PROOF. Let $\boldsymbol{x}_0 = \boldsymbol{x}_0^r + \boldsymbol{x}_0^c$, where $\boldsymbol{x}_0^r \in \mathcal{V}^r$ and $\boldsymbol{x}_0^c \in \mathcal{V}^c$. We start by showing that if $\boldsymbol{x}_0$ lies in the set T of trapped points then its component $\boldsymbol{x}_0^r$ in the real eigenspace $\mathcal{V}^r$ lies in the set ET of eventually trapped points. Due to the fact that the intersection of finitely many convex polytopes is still a convex polytope, it suffices to prove this claim for the case when $\mathcal{P}$ is defined by a single inequality—say $\mathcal{P} = \{\boldsymbol{x} \in \mathbb{R}^d : \boldsymbol{b}^T\boldsymbol{x} \rhd 0\}$, where $\rhd$ is either $>$ or $\geq$.

We may assume that $\boldsymbol{b}^T \exp(At)\boldsymbol{x}_0^c$ is not identically zero, as in that case

$$\boldsymbol{b}^T \exp(At)\boldsymbol{x}_0 \equiv \boldsymbol{b}^T \exp(At)\boldsymbol{x}_0^r$$

and our claim holds trivially. Also, if $\boldsymbol{x}_0 \in T$, it cannot hold that

$$\boldsymbol{b}^T \exp(At)\boldsymbol{x}_0^r \equiv 0,$$

since $\boldsymbol{b}^T \exp(At)\boldsymbol{x}_0^c$ is negative infinitely often by Corollary 7.

Suppose that $\boldsymbol{x}_0 \in T$ and let (ρ, m) and (η, j) be the dominant indices for $\boldsymbol{b}^T \exp(At)\boldsymbol{x}_0^r$ and $\boldsymbol{b}^T \exp(At)\boldsymbol{x}_0^c$ respectively. Then by Proposition 5 we have

$$\boldsymbol{b}^T \exp(At)\boldsymbol{x}_0^r = \exp(\rho t)t^m(c + o(1)) \quad (2)$$

as $t \to \infty$, where c is a non-zero real number. We will show that $c > 0$, from which it follows that $\boldsymbol{x}_0^r \in ET$.

It must hold that $(\eta, j) \preceq (\rho, m)$. Indeed, if $(\eta, j) \succ (\rho, m)$, then, as $t \to \infty$,

$$\boldsymbol{b}^T \exp(At)\boldsymbol{x}_0 = \exp(\eta t)t^j \left(\underbrace{\frac{\boldsymbol{b}^T \exp(At)\boldsymbol{x}_0^c}{\exp(\eta t)t^j}}_{\text{A}} + o(1) \right),$$

but the limit inferior of the term A above is strictly negative by Corollary 7, contradicting the fact that $\boldsymbol{x}_0 \in T$.

If $(\eta, j) = (\rho, m)$, then, as $t \to \infty$,

$$\boldsymbol{b}^T \exp(At)\boldsymbol{x}_0 = \exp(\rho t)t^m \left(c + \frac{\boldsymbol{b}^T \exp(At)\boldsymbol{x}_0^c}{\exp(\rho t)t^m} + o(1) \right),$$

and by invoking Corollary 7 as above, it follows that $c > 0$.

Finally, if $(\eta, j) \prec (\rho, m)$, then, as $t \to \infty$,

$$\boldsymbol{b}^T \exp(At)\boldsymbol{x}_0^c = \exp(\rho t)t^m \cdot o(1), \qquad (3)$$

and hence, by (2) and (3), it follows that

$$\boldsymbol{b}^T \exp(At)\boldsymbol{x}_0 = \exp(\rho t)t^m \left(c + o(1) \right).$$

From the fact that $\boldsymbol{x}_0 \in T$ and that $c \neq 0$ we must have $c > 0$.

In all cases it holds that $c > 0$ and hence $\boldsymbol{x}_0^r \in ET$.

Having argued that $ET \neq \emptyset$ iff $ET \cap \mathcal{V}^r \neq \emptyset$, we will now show that the set $ET \cap \mathcal{V}^r$ is a convex polytope that we can efficiently compute. As before, it suffices to prove this claim for the case when $\mathcal{P} = \{\boldsymbol{x} \in \mathbb{R}^d : \boldsymbol{b}^T\boldsymbol{x} \rhd 0\}$ (where $\rhd$ is either $>$ or $\geq$).

In what follows, we let $[K]$ denote the set $\{0, \ldots, K-1\}$. We can write

$$\boldsymbol{b}^T \exp(At) = \sum_{(\eta,j)\in\sigma(A)\times[\nu(A)]} \exp(\eta t)t^j \boldsymbol{u}_{(\eta,j)}^T,$$

where $\boldsymbol{u}_{(\eta,j)}^T$ is a vector of coefficients.

Note that if $\boldsymbol{x} \in \mathcal{V}^r$ and $(\eta, j) \in (\sigma(A) \setminus \mathbb{R}) \times \mathbb{N}_0$, then $\boldsymbol{u}_{(\eta,j)}^T\boldsymbol{x} = 0$, as $\boldsymbol{u}_{(\eta,j)}^T\boldsymbol{x}$ is the coefficient of $t^j \exp(\eta t)$ in $\boldsymbol{b}^T \exp(At)\boldsymbol{x}$, and $\mathcal{V}^r$ is invariant under $\exp(At)$. Moreover,

$$ET \cap \mathcal{V}^r = (\mathcal{B} \cap \mathcal{C}) \cup \begin{cases} \{\mathbf{0}\} & \text{if } \rhd \text{ is } \geq \\ \emptyset & \text{if } \rhd \text{ is } > \end{cases}$$

where

$$\mathcal{B} = \bigcap_{(\eta,j)\in(\sigma(A)\setminus\mathbb{R})\times[\nu(A)]} \{\boldsymbol{x} \in \mathbb{R}^d : \boldsymbol{u}_{(\eta,j)}^T\boldsymbol{x} = 0\}$$

$$\mathcal{C} = \bigcup_{(\eta,j)\in(\sigma(A)\cap\mathbb{R})\times[\nu(A)]} \left[\{\boldsymbol{x} \in \mathbb{R}^d : \boldsymbol{u}_{(\eta,j)}^T\boldsymbol{x} > 0\} \cap \bigcap_{(\rho,m)\succ(\eta,j)} \{\boldsymbol{x} \in \mathbb{R}^d : \boldsymbol{u}_{(\rho,m)}^T\boldsymbol{x} = 0\} \right]$$

The set $ET \cap \mathcal{V}^r$ can be seen to be convex from the above characterisation. Alternatively, note that ET can be shown to be convex from its definition and that $\mathcal{V}^r$ is convex, therefore so must be their intersection. Thus $ET \cap \mathcal{V}^r$ must be a convex polytope whose definition possibly involves canonically-represented real algebraic numbers, and the Polytope Escape Problem reduces to testing this polytope for non-emptiness. □

5. CONCLUSION

We have shown that the Polytope Escape Problem for continuous-time linear dynamical systems is decidable, and in fact, polynomial-time reducible to the decision problem for the existential theory of real closed fields. Given an instance of the problem $(f, \mathcal{P})$, with f an affine map, our decision procedure involves analysing the real eigenstructure of the linear operator $g(\boldsymbol{x}) := f(\boldsymbol{x}) - f(\mathbf{0})$. In fact, we showed that all complex eigenvalues could essentially be ignored for the purposes of deciding this problem.

Interestingly, the seemingly closely related question of whether a given single trajectory of a linear dynamical system remains trapped within a given polytope appears to be considerably more challenging and is not known to be decidable. In that instance, it seems that the influence of the complex eigenstructure cannot simply be discarded.

6. REFERENCES

[1] I. Adler and P. Beling. Polynomial algorithms for linear programming over the algebraic numbers. *Algorithmica*, 12(6):436–457, 1994.

[2] R. Alur. *Principles of Cyber-Physical Systems.* MIT Press, 2015.

[3] A. Bacciotti and L. Mazzi. Stability of dynamical polysystems via families of Lyapunov functions. *Jour. Nonlin. Analysis*, 67:2167–2179, 2007.

[4] P. C. Bell, J. Delvenne, R. M. Jungers, and V. D. Blondel. The continuous Skolem-Pisot problem. *Theor. Comput. Sci.*, 411(40-42):3625–3634, 2010.

[5] V. Blondel and J. Tsitsiklis. A survey of computational complexity results in systems and control. *Automatica*, 36(9):1249–1274, 2000.

[6] M. Braverman. Termination of integer linear programs. In *Proc. Intern. Conf. on Computer Aided Verification (CAV)*, volume 4144 of *LNCS*. Springer, 2006.

[7] D. Bridges and P. Schuster. A simple constructive proof of Kronecker's density theorem. *Elemente der Mathematik*, 61:152–154, 2006.

[8] J.-Y. Cai. Computing Jordan normal forms exactly for commuting matrices in polynomial time. *Int. J. Found. Comput. Sci.*, 5(3/4):293–302, 1994.

[9] J. Canny. Some algebraic and geometric computations in PSPACE. In *Proceedings of STOC'88*, pages 460–467. ACM, 1988.

[10] E. B. Castelan and J.-C. Hennet. On invariant polyhedra of continuous-time linear systems. *IEEE Transactions on Automatic Control*, 38(11):1680–85, 1993.

[11] V. Chonev, J. Ouaknine, and J. Worrell. On recurrent reachability for continuous linear dynamical systems. In *Proceedings of the 31st Annual ACM/IEEE Symposium on Logic in Computer Science, LICS '16, New York, NY, USA, July 5-8, 2016*, pages 515–524, 2016.

[12] V. Chonev, J. Ouaknine, and J. Worrell. On the Skolem Problem for continuous linear dynamical systems. In *43rd International Colloquium on Automata, Languages, and Programming, ICALP 2016, July 11-15, 2016, Rome, Italy*, pages 100:1–100:13, 2016.

[13] H. Cohen. *A Course in Computational Algebraic Number Theory.* Springer-Verlag, 1993.

[14] E. Hainry. Reachability in linear dynamical systems. In *Logic and Theory of Algorithms, 4th Conference on*

Computability in Europe, CiE 2008, Athens, Greece, June 15-20, 2008, Proceedings, pages 241–250, 2008.
[15] G. H. Hardy and E. M. Wright. *An Introduction to the Theory of Numbers*. Oxford University Press, 1938.
[16] A. Lenstra, H. L. Jr., and L. Lovász. Factoring polynomials with rational coefficients. *Math. Ann.*, 261:515–534, 1982.
[17] G. Malajovich. An effective version of Kronecker's theorem on simultaneous diophantine approximation. Technical report, UFRJ, 1996.
[18] M. Mignotte. Some useful bounds. In *Computer Algebra*, 1982.
[19] V. Pan. Optimal and nearly optimal algorithms for approximating polynomial zeros. *Computers & Mathematics with Applications*, 31(12), 1996.
[20] S. Sankaranarayanan, T. Dang, and F. Ivancic. A policy iteration technique for time elapse over template polyhedra. In *Proceedings of HSCC*, volume 4981 of *LNCS*. Springer, 2008.
[21] A. Tarski. *A Decision Method for Elementary Algebra and Geometry*. University of California Press, 1951.

SMC: Satisfiability Modulo Convex Optimization

Yasser Shoukry[§†] Pierluigi Nuzzo[*] Alberto L. Sangiovanni-Vincentelli[†]
Sanjit A. Seshia[†] George J. Pappas[**] Paulo Tabuada[§]

[†]Department of Electrical Engineering and Computer Sciences, University of California, Berkeley, CA
[§]Department of Electrical Engineering, University of California, Los Angeles, CA
[*] Ming Hsieh Department of Electrical Engineering, University of Southern California, Los Angeles, CA
[**]Department of Electrical and Systems Engineering, University of Pennsylvania, Philadelphia, PA

ABSTRACT

We address the problem of determining the satisfiability of a Boolean combination of convex constraints over the real numbers, which is common in the context of hybrid system verification and control. We first show that a special type of logic formulas, termed monotone Satisfiability Modulo Convex (SMC) formulas, is the most general class of formulas over Boolean and nonlinear real predicates that reduce to convex programs for any satisfying assignment of the Boolean variables. For this class of formulas, we develop a new satisfiability modulo convex optimization procedure that uses a lazy combination of SAT solving and convex programming to provide a satisfying assignment or determine that the formula is unsatisfiable. Our approach can then leverage the efficiency and the formal guarantees of state-of-the-art algorithms in both the Boolean and convex analysis domains. A key step in lazy satisfiability solving is the generation of succinct infeasibility proofs that can support conflict-driven learning and decrease the number of iterations between the SAT and the theory solver. For this purpose, we propose a suite of algorithms that can trade complexity with the minimality of the generated infeasibility certificates. Remarkably, we show that a minimal infeasibility certificate can be generated by simply solving one convex program for a sub-class of SMC formulas, namely ordered positive unate SMC formulas, that have additional monotonicity properties. Perhaps surprisingly, ordered positive unate formulas appear themselves very frequently in a variety of practical applications. By exploiting the properties of monotone SMC formulas, we can then build and demonstrate effective and scalable decision procedures for problems in hybrid system verification and control, including secure state estimation and robotic motion planning.

1. INTRODUCTION

The central difficulty in analyzing and designing hybrid systems is the very different nature of the technical tools used to analyze continuous dynamics (e.g., real analysis) and discrete dynamics (e.g., combinatorics). The same difficulty arises in the context of optimization and feasibility problems involving continuous and discrete variables. In fact, some of these problems arise from the analysis of hybrid systems. In complex, high-dimensional systems, a vast discrete/continuous space must be searched under constraints that are often nonlinear. Developing efficient techniques to perform this task is, therefore, crucial to substantially enhance our ability to design and analyze hybrid systems.

Constraint Programming (CP) and Mixed Integer Programming (MIP) have emerged over the years as means for addressing many of the challenges posed by hybrid systems and hybrid optimization problems [1]. Rooted in Satisfiability (SAT) solving and, more recently, Satisfiability Modulo Theory (SMT) solving, CP relies on logic-based methods such as domain reduction and constraint propagation to accelerate the search. Modern SAT and SMT solvers [2] can efficiently find satisfying valuations of very large propositional formulas with complex Boolean structure, including combinations of atoms from various decidable theories, such as lists, arrays, bit vectors, linear integer arithmetic, and linear real arithmetic. However, while SMT solving for generic nonlinear theories over the reals is undecidable in general [3, 4], algorithms and tools that can address useful fragments of these theories with solid guarantees of correctness and scalability have only recently started to appear.

MIP-based approaches encode, instead, a Boolean combination of nonlinear constraints into a conjunction of mixed integer constraints and solve it by leveraging numerical algorithms based on branch-and-bound and cutting-plane methods. When applied to mixed integer convex constraints, optimization-based techniques tend to be efficient if the Boolean structure of the problem is simple. Moreover, convex programming is extensively used as the core engine in a variety of applications, ranging from control design to communications, from electronic design to data analysis and modeling [5]. However, encoding some logic operations, such as disjunction and implication, into mixed integer constraints usually requires approximations and heuristic techniques, such as the well-known "big-M" method [1], which may eventually affect the correctness of the solution.

In this paper, we aim at bridging the gap between CP and MIP based techniques, which have shown superior performance in handling, respectively, complex Boolean structures and large sets of convex constraints. While attempts at combining logic-based inference with optimization trace back to the 1950s [1], they were mostly limited to "prepro-

HSCC'17, April 18 - 20, 2017, Pittsburgh, PA, USA

ISBN 978-1-4503-4590-3/17/04...$15.00
DOI: http://dx.doi.org/10.1145/3049797.3049819

cessing" and "implicit enumeration" schemes, doomed soon to be outperformed by branch-and-bound or cutting-plane methods. As the effectiveness of CP techniques has steadily increased over the years, their integration with optimization has been the subject of increasing research activity. However, devising a robust and widely acceptable integration scheme is still largely an open issue. We tackle this challenge by focusing on the satisfiability problem for a class of formulas over Boolean variables and convex constraints. We target this special class of problems because of their pervasiveness as well as the efficiency and robustness of the solution methods made available by convex programming [5].

The first contribution of this paper is to identify a special type of logic formulas, termed monotone Satisfiability Modulo Convex (SMC) formulas, and to show that it is the most general class of formulas over Boolean and nonlinear real arithmetic predicates that can be solved via a finite number of convex programs. For monotone SMC formulas, we develop a new procedure, which we call Satisfiability Modulo Convex Optimization, that uses a lazy combination of SAT solving and convex programming to provide a satisfying assignment or determine that the formula is unsatisfiable. As in the lazy SMT paradigm [2], a classic SAT solving algorithm [6] interacts with a theory solver. The SAT solver efficiently reasons about combinations of Boolean constraints to suggest possible assignments. The theory solver only checks the consistency of the given assignments, i.e., conjunctions of theory predicates, and provides the reason for the conflict, an UNSAT certificate, whenever inconsistencies are found.

Checking the feasibility of a set of convex constraints can be performed efficiently, with a complexity that is polynomial in the number of constraints and real variables. A key step is, however, the generation of compact certificates to support conflict-driven learning and decrease the number of iterations between the SAT and the theory solver. The second contribution of this paper is to propose a suite of algorithms that can trade complexity with the minimality of the generated certificates. Remarkably, we show that a minimal infeasibility certificate can be generated by simply solving one convex program for a sub-class of monotone SMC formulas, namely Ordered Positive Unate (OPU) formulas, that present additional monotonicity properties. Since monotone SMC and OPU formulas appear frequently in practical applications, we can then build and demonstrate effective and scalable decision procedures for several problems in hybrid system verification and control. Experimental results show that our approach outperforms state-of-the-art SMT and MICP solvers on problems with complex Boolean structure and a large number of real variables.

Related Work. Our work focuses on feasibility problems and leverages optimization methods to accelerate the search task. In this respect, it differs from other research efforts such as the "optimization modulo theories" [7] or "symbolic optimization" [8] approaches, which propose SMT-based techniques to solve optimization problems. The ABSOLVER tool [9] adopts a similar lazy SMT approach as in our work, by leveraging a generic nonlinear optimization tool to solve Boolean combinations of polynomial arithmetic constraints. However, generic nonlinear optimization techniques may produce incomplete or possibly incorrect results, due to their "local" nature, explicitly requiring upper and lower bounds to all the real variables. The Z3 [10] solver can also provide support for nonlinear polynomial arithmetic, while still being subject to incompleteness or termination issues[1]. The iSAT algorithm builds on a unification of SAT-solving and Interval Constraint Propagation (ICP) [11] to efficiently address arbitrary smooth, possibly transcendental, functions. The integration of SAT solving with ICP is also used in dREAL to build a δ-complete decision procedure which solves SMT problems over the reals with nonlinear functions, such as polynomials, sine, exponentiation, or logarithms [12], but with limited support for Boolean combinations of nonlinear constraints. By targeting the special classes of convex constraints and monotone SMC formulas, we are able to leverage the efficiency, robustness, and correctness guarantees of state-of-the-art convex optimization algorithms. Moreover, we can efficiently generate UNSAT certificates that are more compact, or even minimal.

Our results build upon the seminal work of CALCS, which pioneered the integration of SAT solving and optimization algorithms for convex SMT formulas [13]. Differently from CALCS, we focus on the satisfiability problem for monotone SMC formulas, which do not require approximation techniques to handle negated convex constraints and are rich enough to capture several problem instances in hybrid system verification and control. For SMC formulas, we provide formal correctness guarantees for our algorithms in terms of δ-completeness [4]. Moreover, we propose new algorithms to generate UNSAT certificates that improve on the efficiency or minimality guarantees of the previous ones, which were based on the sensitivity of the objective of a convex optimization problem to its constraints.

We have also recently developed specialized SMT-based algorithms for applications in secure state estimation, IMHOTEP-SMT [14], and robotic motion planning [15]. We show that the approach detailed in this paper subsumes these results. Finally, our decision procedure encompasses Mixed Integer Convex Programming (MICP) based techniques. In fact, we show that any feasibility problem on MIC constraints can be posed as a satisfiability problem on a monotone SMC formula. While an MICP formulation can execute faster on problems with simpler Boolean structure, our algorithms outperform MICP-based techniques on problems with large numbers of Boolean variables and constraints.

2. MOTIVATING EXAMPLE

We illustrate the practical relevance of the logic addressed in this paper using a representative hybrid system control problem inspired by robotic motion planning [15]. To develop algorithmic techniques for robotic motion planning, we need to reason about the tight integration of discrete abstractions (as in *task planning*) with continuous motions (*motion planning*) [16]. Task planning relies on specifications of temporal goals that are usually captured by logics such as Linear Temporal Logic (LTL) [17]. Motion planning deals with complex geometries, motion dynamics, and collision avoidance constraints that can only be accurately captured by continuous models. Ideally, we wish to combine effective discrete planning techniques with effective methods for generating collision-free and dynamically-feasible trajectories to satisfy both the dynamics and task planner constraints.

[1]As reported by the official Z3 website, http://research.microsoft.com/en-us/um/redmond/projects/z3/arith-tutorial/.

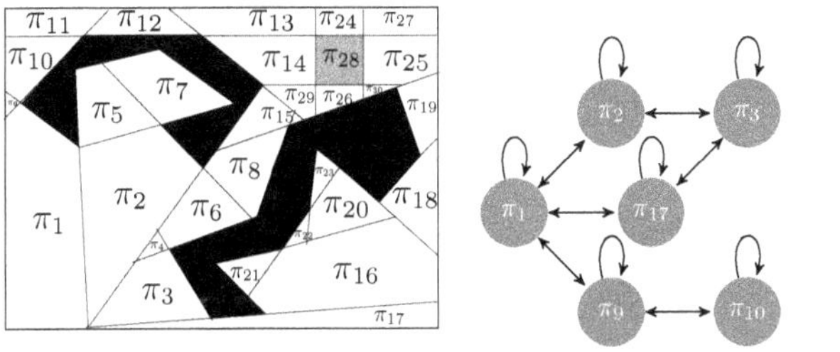

Figure 1: Obstacle-based discretization of the workspace for the motion planning problem (left), and transition system describing the adjacency relation between regions in the workspace (right).

For simplicity, we present below an encoding for the basic reach-avoid problem. We assume a discrete-time, linear model of the robot dynamics and a description of a workspace in terms of a set of obstacles and a target region, where both the obstacles and the region are polyhedra. The goal is to construct a trajectory, and the associated control strategy, that steers the robot from its initial point to the target while avoiding obstacles. We further assume that the workspace is partitioned into a set of regions, as in Figure 1 (left), which can also be described by polyhedra and captured by linear constraints of the form $(Px + q \leq 0)$, where $x \in \mathbb{R}^n$ represents the state variables of the robot, including its coordinates in the workspace. For a fixed horizon L, the controller design problem translates into *finding a sequence of regions of length L (discrete plan) that brings the robot from the initial point to the target and is compatible with the continuous dynamics.*

It is convenient to capture the adjacency relation between regions via a transition system as in Figure 1 (right). A valid trajectory for the robot can then be represented by a run of the transition system. Let b_i^j be a Boolean variable that is asserted if and only if the robot is in region i at time j. We can then encode the constraints for the controller using the following *logic formula* φ:

$$\varphi ::= b^0_{\text{start}} \qquad \text{(Initial partition)}$$

$$\wedge\, b^L_{\text{goal}} \qquad \text{(Goal partition)}$$

$$\wedge \left(b_i^j \rightarrow \bigvee_{i' \in \Pi(i)} b_{i'}^{j+1} \right) \qquad \forall\, j \in \{0, \dots, L-1\}, i \in \{1, \dots, m\}$$

$$\text{(Adjacency constraints)}$$

$$\wedge \left(\sum_{i=1}^{m} b_i^j = 1 \right) \qquad \forall j \in \{0, \dots, L-1\}$$

$$\text{(Mutual exclusion)}$$

$$\wedge\, (x^{j+1} = Ax^j + Bu^j) \qquad \forall j \in \{0, \dots, L-1\}$$

$$\text{(Robot dynamics)}$$

$$\wedge\, (\|u^j\| \leq \bar{u}) \qquad \forall j \in \{0, \dots, L-1\}$$

$$\text{(Input constraints)}$$

$$\wedge\, (x^0 = \bar{x}) \qquad \text{(Initial state)}$$

$$\wedge \left(b_i^j \rightarrow P_i x + q_i \leq 0 \right) \qquad \forall j \in \{0, \dots, L-1\}, i \in \{1, \dots, m\}$$

$$\text{(Region constraints)}$$

where $\Pi(i)$ is the set of regions that are adjacent to region i, m is the total number of regions, A and B are the state and input matrices governing the robot dynamics, and $\bar{u}$ is the maximum feasible magnitude $\|u^j\|$ (e.g., ℓ_2 or ℓ_∞ norm) of the control input at time j.

The formula φ captures the constraints of a reach-avoid problem as a conjunction of logic clauses, possibly including pseudo-Boolean predicates (e.g., mutual exclusion or cardinality constraints), and where some of the literals are convex constraints (e.g., in the dynamics, input, and region constraints). We call such a formula a *monotone SMC formula* since none of the convex constraints are negated. The formal definition is in Section 3. We further observe that the satisfying assignments of the "purely Boolean" portion of φ are characterized by an ordering imposed by the feasible runs of the transition system in Figure 1. If a sequence of regions σ is feasible, then so is any prefix sequence of σ. We will call the formulas encoding such a scenario *OPU formulas* and provide the formal definition in Section 5.3. OPU formulas are by no means specific to the encoding of motion planning constraints. They appear in several applications; for example, whenever Boolean variables are used to capture the occurrence of events (or modes) that are sequentially concatenated. This is the case for the variables encoding the states in a finite state machine or for switched systems in which modes are captured by a finite state automaton and dynamics are expressed by convex constraints.

We will show that *Boolean solving can be effectively combined with convex optimization to determine the satisfiability of monotone SMC and OPU formulas. Scalable decision procedures can be developed based on efficient methods for detecting minimal sets of conflicting convex constraints. In particular, this task reduces to solving only one convex program in OPU formulas.* To formalize these categories of decision problems, we first define the syntax and semantics of monotone SMC formulas.

3. MONOTONE SMC FORMULAS

3.1 Notation

We denote as $b = (b_1, b_2, \dots, b_m)$ the set of Boolean variables in a formula, with $b_i \in \mathbb{B}$, and with $x = (x_1, x_2, \dots, x_n)$ the set of real-valued variables, where $x_i \in \mathbb{R}$. When not directly inferred from the context, we adopt the notation $\varphi(x, b)$ to highlight the set of variables over which a formula φ is defined. A valuation μ is a function that associates each variable in b to a truth value in $\mathbb{B}$. We denote as $[\![b]\!]_\mu \in \mathbb{B}^m$ the set of values assigned to each variable in b by μ.

A *convex constraint* is a constraint of the form $f(x)\ \{<, \leq\}\ 0$ or $h(x) = 0$, where $f(x)$ and $h(x)$ are convex and affine (linear) functions, respectively, of their real variables $x \in \mathcal{D} \subseteq \mathbb{R}^n$, $\mathcal{D}$ being a convex set. In what follows, we will compactly denote a generic convex constraint as $(g(x) \lhd 0)$. A convex constraint is associated with a set $\mathcal{C} = \{x \in \mathcal{D} : g(x) \lhd 0\}$, i.e., the set of points in the domain of the convex function g that satisfy the constraint. The set $\mathcal{C}$ is also convex[2]. We further denote the negation of a convex constraint, expressed in the form $f(x) \geq 0$ $(f(x) > 0)$, as *reverse convex* constraint. A reverse convex constraint is, in general, non-convex and so is its satisfying set. For a formal definition of convex function, we refer the reader to the literature [5].

[2]In fact, given a representation of the convex domain $\mathcal{D}$ as a convex constraint $(d(x) \leq 0)$, we can directly account for the domain by directly embedding it into the expression of the convex constraint, e.g., by defining $(\tilde{g}(x) \lhd 0) = (g(x) \lhd 0) \wedge (d(x) \leq 0)$.

To be able to capture linear constraints on Boolean variables in a compact way, we also use pseudo-Boolean predicates. A *pseudo-Boolean predicate pB_predicate* is an affine constraint over Boolean variables with integer coefficients.

3.2 Syntax and Semantics

We represent *monotone Satisfiability Modulo Convex (SMC) formulas* to be quantifier-free formulas in conjunctive normal form, with atomic propositions ranging over propositional variables and convex constraints. Formally,

DEFINITION 3.1 (MONOTONE SMC FORMULA). *A monotone SMC formula is any formula that can be represented using the following syntax:*

$$\begin{aligned} formula &::= \{clause\ \wedge\}^* clause \\ clause &::= (\{literal\ \vee\}^* literal) \mid pB\_predicate \\ literal &::= bool\_var \mid \neg bool\_var \mid \top \mid \bot \mid \\ & \quad conv\_constraint \qquad (1) \\ conv\_constraint &::= equation \mid inequality \\ equation &::= affine\_function = 0 \\ inequality &::= convex\_function\ relation\ 0 \\ relation &::= < \mid \leq \end{aligned}$$

In the grammar above, *bool_var* denotes a Boolean variable, and *affine_function* and *convex_function* denote affine and convex functions, respectively. Monotone SMC formulas can only admit convex constraints as theory atoms. Differently from generic (non-monotone) SMC formulas, i.e., generic SMT formulas over convex constraints [13], reverse convex constraints are not allowed. The monotonicity property is key to guarantee that a *model*, i.e., a satisfying assignment, can always be found by solving one (or more) optimization problems that are convex, as we further discuss below. We rely on the disciplined convex programming approach [5, 18] as an effective method to specify the syntax of convex constraints out of a library of atomic functions and automatically ensure the convexity of a constraint.

Formulas are interpreted over valuations μ (i.e., $[\![b, x]\!]_\mu \in \mathbb{B}^m \times \mathbb{R}^n$). A formula φ is satisfied by a valuation μ ($\mu \models \varphi$) if and only if all its clauses are satisfied, that is, if and only if at least one literal is satisfied in any clause. A Boolean literal l is satisfied if $[\![l]\!]_\mu = \top$. Satisfaction of real constraints is with respect to the standard interpretation of the arithmetic operators and the ordering relations over the reals.

Aiming at a scalable solver architecture, we exploit efficient numerical algorithms based on convex programming to decide the satisfiability of convex constraints and provide a model when the constraints are feasible. However, convex solvers usually perform floating point (hence inexact) calculations, although the numerical error can be bounded by a constant that can be made arbitrarily small. Therefore, to provide correctness guarantees for our algorithms, we resort to similar notions of δ-satisfaction and δ-completeness as the ones previously proposed by Gao et al. [4], which we define below on generic SMC formulas.

DEFINITION 3.2 (δ-RELAXATION). *Given an SMC formula φ, let $|C|$ be the number of convex constraints in φ and $\delta \in \mathbb{Q}^+ \cup \{0\}$ any non-negative rational number δ. We define the δ-relaxation of φ as the formula obtained by replacing any convex constraints of the forms $(f_i(x) \leq 0)$ and $(h_j(x) = 0)$ in φ with their perturbed versions $(f_i(x) \leq \delta_i)$ and $(|h_j(x)| \leq \delta_j)$, respectively, where $\delta_k \in \mathbb{Q}^+ \cup \{0\}$ for all $k \in \{1, \dots, |C|\}$, and such that $\sum_{k=1}^{|C|} \delta_k \leq \delta$. We denote the newly obtained formula as φ^δ.*

DEFINITION 3.3 (δ-SATISFACTION). *Given an SMC formula φ and $\delta \in \mathbb{Q}^+$, we say that φ is δ-SAT when φ^δ is satisfiable. Otherwise, we say that φ is UNSAT.*

We simply say that φ is SAT when there is no ambiguity about the choice of δ. If $\varphi = \varphi^0$ is satisfiable, then φ^δ is satisfiable for all $\delta \in \mathbb{Q}^+$, i.e., $\varphi \rightarrow \varphi^\delta$. The opposite is, however, not true. In fact, depending on the value of δ, φ^0 and φ^δ can be made, respectively, false and true at the same time. When this happens, we admit both the SAT and UNSAT answers. This outcome is acceptable in practical applications, since small perturbations capable of modifying the truth value of a formula usually denote lack of robustness either in the system or in the model. Finally, we say that an algorithm is *δ-complete* if it can correctly solve the satisfiability problem for an SMC formula in the sense of Definition 3.3.

3.3 Properties

Monotone SMC formulas have the desirable property that they can always be solved via a finite set of convex feasibility problems. To show this, we introduce the following proposition and the related definitions of *Boolean abstraction* and *monotone convex expansion* of a convex formula.

DEFINITION 3.4 (MONOTONE CONVEX EXPANSION). *Let φ be an SMC formula, C be the set of convex constraints, and $|C|$ its cardinality. We define* propositional abstraction *of φ a formula φ_B obtained from φ by replacing each convex constraint with a Boolean variable a_i, $i \in \{1, \dots, |C|\}$. We further define* monotone convex expansion *of φ the formula φ' defined as:*

$$\varphi' = \varphi_B \wedge \bigwedge_{i=1}^{|C|} (a_i \rightarrow (g_i(x) \lhd 0)), \qquad (2)$$

where $(g_i(x) \lhd 0)$ denotes a convex constraint as defined in Section 3.1.

PROPOSITION 3.5. *Let φ' be the monotone convex expansion of a monotone SMC formula φ, defined as in (2), where φ_B is the propositional abstraction of φ. Then, the following properties hold:*

1. *φ and φ' are equisatisfiable, i.e., if (b^*, x^*, a^*) is a model (a satisfying assignment) for φ', then (b^*, x^*) is a model for φ; if φ' is unsatisfiable, then so is φ;*
2. *any satisfying Boolean assignment for φ_B turns φ' into a conjunction of convex constraints;*
3. *the satisfiability problem for φ', hence φ, can always be cast as the feasibility problem for a finite disjunction of convex programs.*

Proposition 3.5 directly descends from the monotonicity of φ. Its proof as well as the proofs of all the results in this paper can be found in an extended version of the paper [19]. By Proposition 3.5, any monotone SMC formula φ can be solved by casting and solving a disjunction of convex programs. We will use this property to construct our decision procedure in Section 4. It is possible to show that monotone convex formulas are also the only class of formulas over

Boolean propositions, pseudo-Boolean predicates, and predicates in the nonlinear theories over the reals, to present this property. This is formally stated by the following theorem.

Theorem 3.6. *Let φ be a formula over Boolean propositions, pseudo-Boolean predicates, and predicates in the nonlinear theories over the reals, and such that the satisfiability problem can be posed as the feasibility problem for a finite disjunction of convex programs. Then, φ can be posed as a monotone SMC formula.*

Finally, the following corollary is an immediate consequence of the results above.

COROLLARY 3.7. *Monotone SMC formulas include any Boolean Satisfiability (SAT) problem instance and any Mixed Integer Convex (MIC) feasibility problem instance as a particular case.*

Any MIC formulation can be translated into an equisatisfiable SMC formula, but the opposite is not true. Often, disjunctions of predicates, such as the one in $\varphi := \neg b \vee (x-3<0)$, cannot be expressed as a conjunction of MIC constraints unless relaxations (approximations) are used [1]. For instance, φ is typically encoded with the constraint $c := x-3 < (1-b)\cdot M$, using the "big-M" method. However, for any value of M, the assignment $(b,x) = (0, M+3)$ is a satisfying assignment for φ, but violates c.

4. ALGORITHM ARCHITECTURE

Our decision procedure combines a SAT solver (SAT-SOLVE) and a theory solver ($\mathcal{C}$-SOLVE) for convex constraints on real numbers by following the *lazy* SMT paradigm [2]. The SAT solver efficiently reasons about combinations of Boolean and pseudo-Boolean constraints, using the David-Putnam-Logemann-Loveland (DPLL) algorithm [6], to suggest possible assignments for the convex constraints. The theory solver checks the consistency of the given assignments and provides the reason for a conflict, i.e., an UNSAT *certificate*, whenever inconsistencies are found. Each certificate results in learning new constraints which will be used by the SAT solver to prune the search space. Because the monotone convex expansion φ' of a monotone formula φ translates into a conjunction of convex constraints for any Boolean assignments by Proposition 3.5, we are assured that we can solve for φ using a lazy SMT approach, since we are guaranteed to generate queries to the theory solver that are always in the form of conjunctions of convex constraints and, therefore, can be efficiently solved by convex programming. Our decision task is thus broken into two simpler tasks, respectively, over the Boolean and convex domains.

As illustrated in Algorithm 4, we start by generating the propositional abstraction $\varphi_B(b,a)$ of φ. We denote as $\mathcal{M}$ the map that associates each convex constraint in φ to an auxiliary variable a_i. By only relying on the Boolean structure of φ_B, SAT-SOLVE may either return UNSAT or propose a satisfying assignment μ for the variables b and a, thus hypothesizing which convex constraints should be jointly satisfied.

Let a^* be the assignment proposed by SAT-SOLVE for the auxiliary Boolean variables a in φ_B; we denote as $\mathrm{supp}(a^*)$ the set of indices of auxiliary variables a_i which are asserted in a^*, i.e., such that $[\![a_i]\!]_\mu = \top$. This Boolean assignment is then used by $\mathcal{C}$-SOLVE to determine whether there exist

Algorithm 1 SMC
Input: φ, δ **Output:** $\eta(b,x)$

$(\varphi_B(b,a), \mathcal{M}) :=$ ABSTRACT(φ);
while TRUE **do**
  (status, $\mu(b,a)$) := SAT-SOLVE(φ_B);
  if status == UNSAT **then**
    return
  else
    (status, x) := $\mathcal{C}$-SOLVE.CHECK($\mu, \mathcal{M}, \delta$);
    if status == SAT **then**
      return $\eta(b,x)$
    else
      $\varphi_{\text{ce}} := \mathcal{C}$-SOLVE.CERT($\mu, \mathcal{M}, \delta$);
      $\varphi_B := \varphi_B \wedge \varphi_{\text{ce}}$;

real variables $x \in \mathbb{R}^n$ which satisfy all the convex constraints related to asserted auxiliary variables. Formally, we are interested in the following problem

$$\text{find} \quad x \quad \text{s.t.} \quad g_i(x) \lhd 0 \quad \forall\, i \in \mathrm{supp}(a^*) \tag{3}$$

which we denote as feasibility problem associated with a^*. The above problem can be efficiently cast as the following optimization problem with the addition of slack variables, which we call a *sum-of-slacks feasibility* (*SSF*) problem:

$$\min_{\substack{s_1,\ldots,s_L \in \mathbb{R} \\ x \in \mathbb{R}^n}} \sum_{i=1}^{L} |s_i| \quad \text{s.t.} \quad g_{j_i}(x) \lhd s_i, \quad i = 1,\ldots,L \tag{4}$$

where L is the cardinality of $\mathrm{supp}(a^*)$ and j_i spans $\mathrm{supp}(a^*)$ as i varies in $\{1,\ldots,L\}$. Problem 4 is equivalent to (3), as it tries to minimize the infeasibilities of the constraints by pushing each slack variable to be as much as possible close to zero. The optimum is zero and is achieved if and only if the original set of constraints in (3) is feasible. Therefore, if the cost at optimum is zero (in practice, the condition $\sum_{i=1}^{L} |s_i| \le \delta$ is satisfied for a "small" $\delta \in \mathbb{Q}^+$), then μ is indeed a valid assignment, an optimum x^* is found, and our algorithm terminates with SAT and provides the solution (x^*, b). Otherwise, an UNSAT certificate φ_{ce} is generated in terms of a new Boolean clause explaining which auxiliary variables should be negated since the associated convex constraints are conflicting. A trivial certificate can always be provided in the form of:

$$\varphi_{\text{trivial-ce}} = \bigvee_{i \in \mathrm{supp}(a^*)} \neg a_i, \tag{5}$$

which encodes the fact that at least one of the auxiliary variables indexed by an element in $\mathrm{supp}(a^*)$ should actually be negated. The augmented Boolean problem consisting of the original formula φ_B and the generated certificate φ_{ce} is then fed back to SAT-SOLVE to produce a new assignment. The sequence of new SAT queries is then repeated until either $\mathcal{C}$-SOLVE terminates with SAT or SAT-SOLVE terminates with UNSAT. The following statement summarizes the formal guarantees of Algorithm 4 with the trivial certificate (5).

PROPOSITION 4.1. *Let φ be a monotone SMC formula and $\delta \in \mathbb{Q}^+$ a user-defined tolerance used in $\mathcal{C}$-SOLVE.CHECK in Algorithm 4 to accommodate numerical errors. Algorithm 4 with the UNSAT certificate φ_{ce} in (5) is δ-complete.*

The worst case bound on the number of iterations in Algorithm 4 is exponential in the number of convex constraints

Certificate	# Convex Programs	Length ℓ
Trivial	1	$\lvert S\rvert$
IIS-Based	Exponential in $\lvert S\rvert$	$\lvert I\rvert$ (minimal)
SSF-Based	Linear in $\lvert S\rvert$	$\lvert I\rvert \leq \ell \leq \lvert S\rvert$
Prefix-Based	1	$\lvert I\rvert \leq \ell \leq \lvert S\rvert$

Table 1: Proposed algorithms for certificate generation: number of convex programs needed to generate the certificate and length of the generated certificate. |S| is the number of constraints in the convex program.

$|C|$. To help the SAT solver quickly find a correct assignment, a central problem in the lazy SMT paradigm is to generate *succinct certificates*, possibly highlighting the minimum set of conflicting assignments, i.e., the "reason" for the inconsistency. The smaller the *conflict clause*, the larger is the region that is excluded from the search space of the SAT solver. Moreover, certificates should be generated *efficiently*, ideally in polynomial time, to provide a negligible overhead with respect to the exponential complexity of SAT solving. In the following, we discuss efficient algorithms to generate smaller conflict clauses.

5. GENERATING SMALL CERTIFICATES

5.1 IIS-Based Certificates

When $\mathcal{C}$-SOLVE.CHECK finds an infeasible problem, a minimal certificate can be generated by providing an *Irreducibly Inconsistent Set* (IIS) [20] of constraints, defined as follows.

DEFINITION 5.1 (IRREDUCIBLY INCONSISTENT SET). *Given a feasibility problem with constraint set S, an* Irreducibly Inconsistent Set *I is a subset of constraints $I \subseteq S$ such that: (i) the feasibility problem with constraint set I is infeasible; (ii) $\forall\ c \in I$, the feasibility problem with constraint set $I \setminus \{c\}$ is feasible.*

In other words, an IIS is an infeasible subset of constraints that becomes feasible if any single constraint is removed. Let $\mathcal{I}$ be set of indices of auxiliary Boolean variables in φ_B that are associated to a convex constraint in an IIS I. Then, once I is found, a minimal certificate can be generated as

$$\varphi_{\text{IIS-ce}} = \bigvee_{i \in \mathcal{I}} \neg a_i. \tag{6}$$

Most of the techniques proposed in the literature to isolate IISs are based on either adding constraints, one by one or in groups, or by deleting them from the original problem [20]. An IIS guarantees that the length of the certificate is minimal, which can dramatically reduce the search space in Algorithm 4. However, isolating one IIS is expensive, especially for nonlinear programs. In the worst case, as shown in Table 1, finding an IIS can require solving a feasibility problem for each subset of constraints in S, which is exponential in the size $|S|$. The following proposition summarizes the correctness guarantees of Algorithm 4 with the IIS-based certificate (6).

PROPOSITION 5.2. *Let φ be a monotone SMC formula and $\delta \in \mathbb{Q}^+$ a user-defined tolerance used in $\mathcal{C}$-SOLVE.CHECK in Algorithm 4 to accommodate numerical errors. Algorithm 4 with the UNSAT certificate in (6) is δ-complete.*

In the following, we describe an algorithm that can generate a small, albeit non minimal, set of conflicting constraints by solving a number of convex programs that is linear in $|S|$.

Algorithm 2 $\mathcal{C}$-SOLVE.CERT-SSF$(\mu, \mathcal{M}, \delta)$

Compute optimal slack variables and sort them
  $s^* :=$ SOLVE-SSF$(\mu, \mathcal{M}, \delta)$;
  $s' :=$ SORTASCENDINGLY(s^*);
Pick index for minimum slack
  $\mathcal{I}\_min :=$ INDEX(s'_1);
  $\mathcal{I}\_max :=$ INDEX$(s'_{\{|s|,|s|-1,\ldots,2\}})$;
Search linearly for the UNSAT certificate
  status = SAT; counter = 1;
  $\mathcal{I}\_temp := \mathcal{I}\_min \cup \mathcal{I}\_max_{counter}$;
while status == SAT **do**
  (status, x) := $\mathcal{C}$-SOLVE.CHECK$(\mu_{\mathcal{I}_temp}, \mathcal{M}, \delta)$;
  if status == UNSAT **then**
    $\varphi_{\text{ce-SSF}} := \bigvee_{i \in \mathcal{I}\_temp} \neg a_i$;
  else
    counter := counter + 1;
    $\mathcal{I}\_temp := \mathcal{I}\_temp \cup \mathcal{I}\_max\_r_{counter}$;
return $\varphi_{\text{ce-SSF}}$

5.2 SSF-Based Certificates

A computationally more efficient alternative to IIS-based certificates is to directly exploit the information in the slacks of the SSF problem (4). If a constraint k is associated with a non-zero optimal slack, $|s^*_k| > 0$, then it is a member of one of the IIS in problem (3). However, the set of all the constraints with a non-zero slack does not necessarily include all the constraints of at least one IIS. Therefore, we propose a search procedure over the constraint set S, which guarantees that at least one IIS is included in the returned set of conflicting constraints by solving a number of convex programs that is linear in the number of constraints $|S|$ in (3), even if the returned conflict set may not be minimal. In fact, the cardinality of the returned conflict set, hence the length of the proposed certificate, can be as large as $|S|$ in the worst case, as shown in Table 1.

The conjecture behind the search strategy is that the constraints with the highest slack values are most likely to be in at least one IIS and conflict with the constraint with the lowest (possible zero) slack. We can then generate a small conflict set including the lowest slack constraint in conjunction with the highest slack constraints, added one-by-one, until a conflict is detected. At each step we solve a convex feasibility problem to detect the occurrence of a conflict. The earlier a conflict is detected, the earlier our search terminates and the shorter the certificate will be. Based on this intuition, our procedure is summarized in Algorithm 2.

We first compute the optimal slacks s^* and sort them in ascending order. We then pick the constraint corresponding to the minimum slack, indexed by $\mathcal{I}\_min$, and generate a new set of indexes $\mathcal{I}\_temp$ by searching for one more constraint that leads to a conflict with the minimum slack constraint, starting with the constraint related to the maximum slack. $\mathcal{I}\_max$ is the set of all slack indexes except the index of the minimum slack in $\mathcal{I}\_min$. If the constraints indexed by $\mathcal{I}\_temp$ are infeasible, then we obtain a conflict set of two elements, and can immediately generate the UNSAT certificate. Otherwise, we repeat the same process by adding the constraint associated with the second largest slack variable in the sorted list of slacks, till we reach a conflicting set. Once the set is discovered, we stop and generate the compact certificate using the auxiliary variables indexed by $\mathcal{I}\_temp$. The following proposition summarizes the correctness guarantees of Algorithm 4 with the SSF-based certificate.

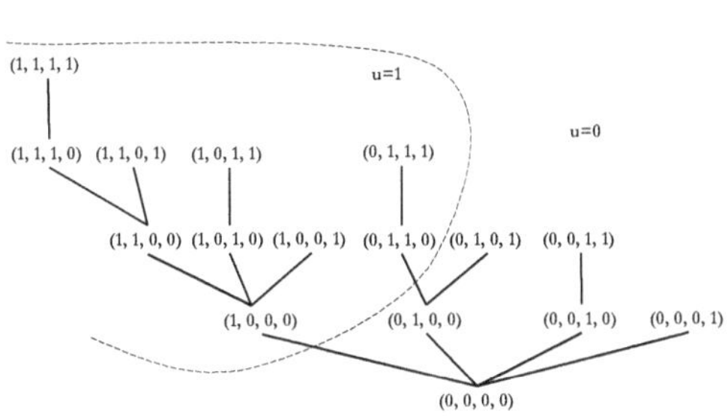

Figure 2: Pictorial representation of the partial order over the assignments for an OPU function u.

PROPOSITION 5.3. *Let φ be a monotone SMC formula and $\delta \in \mathbb{Q}^+$ a user-defined tolerance used in $\mathcal{C}$-SOLVE.CHECK in Algorithm 4 to accommodate numerical errors. Algorithm 4 with the certificate from Algorithm 2 is δ-complete.*

5.3 Prefix-Based Certificate

Under additional monotonicity assumptions on the structure of φ we are able to construct UNSAT certificates that are "minimal" by solving only one convex program. To formalize these monotonicity assumptions and the related notion of minimality, we introduce the concept of *Ordered Positive Unate (OPU) function* as an extension of the classical definition of positive unite function below. For convenience, we also use the notation $b = 1(0)$ to indicate that b is asserted (negated).

DEFINITION 5.4 (POSITIVE UNATE FUNCTION). *A Boolean function $u(b_1, b_2, \dots, b_m)$ is said to be* positive unate *in b_i if, for all possible values of b_j, $j \neq i$, we have*

$$u(b_1, \dots, b_{i-1}, 0, b_{i+1}, \dots, b_m) \leq u(b_1, \dots, b_{i-1}, 1, b_{i+1}, \dots, b_m),$$

i.e., by only switching b_i from 0 to 1 we do not decrease the value of u.

DEFINITION 5.5 (OPU FUNCTION). *A Boolean function $u(b_1, b_2, \dots, b_m)$ is said to be* ordered positive unate *with respect to an ordering $(b_1, \dots, b_m)$ of its Boolean variables if, for all possible values of b_i, we have*

$$u(0, \dots, 0) \leq u(b_1, 0, \dots, 0) \leq u(b_1, b_2, 0, \dots, 0) \leq \dots$$
$$\dots \leq u(b_1, b_2, \dots, b_{m-1}, 0) \leq u(b_1, b_2, \dots, b_{m-1}, b_m).$$

In other words, given a valuation over the ordered set $b = (b_1, \dots, b_m)$, and such that there is a suffix of variables assigned to zero, i.e., $b_i = b_{i+1} = \dots = b_{m-1} = b_m = 0$, $i \in \{1, \dots, m\}$, switching the first variable b_i in the suffix from 0 to 1 does not decrease the value of u.

By Definition 5.5, OPU functions determine a partial order over the set of Boolean assignments based on their prefixes, and such that $(0, \dots, 0)$ is the bottom element. A pictorial representation of such an order is offered in Figure 2 when $m = 4$. All the assignments for $(b_1, \dots, b_4)$ form a tree; each vertex in the tree shares a prefix with its ancestor and differs from it only in the first variable of the suffix, which is set to 1. We also show in Figure 2 a possible scenario for the values of u. If u evaluates to 1 at a certain vertex v in the tree, then the value of u over all the upper vertices along the path from v to a leaf is also bounded to be 1. Similarly, if u evaluates to 0 at v, then this will be the case over all the lower vertices along the path from v to the root. We now extend this notion of monotonicity to a sub-class of convex formulas of our interest, which we denote as *ordered positive unate formulas.*

DEFINITION 5.6 (OPU FORMULAS). *Let φ be a monotone SMC formula, φ_B its propositional abstraction, and $\chi_\varphi(a_1, a_2, \dots, a_{|C|})$ be the restriction of the characteristic function for the valid assignments of φ_B to the auxiliary variables a, i.e.,*

$$\chi_\varphi([\![a]\!]_\mu) = \begin{cases} 1 & \text{if} \quad \exists\, b \text{ s.t.} \quad \mu(b, a) \models \varphi_B \\ 0 & \text{otherwise.} \end{cases}$$

We say that φ is an ordered positive unate formula *with respect to κ if there exists an ordering (renaming) $\kappa \colon \mathcal{I} \to \mathcal{I}$ over the index set $\mathcal{I} = \{1, \dots, |C|\}$ such that χ_φ is ordered positive unate with respect to a', where $a' = (a'_1, \dots, a'_{|C|}) = (a_{\kappa(1)}, \dots, a_{\kappa(|C|)})$.*

An OPU formula φ introduces a partial order over the assignments for a that can drastically simplify the task of finding a minimal UNSAT certificate. In fact, once the set of variables a is ordered according to κ to obtain a', the assignments over a' can also be ordered based on their prefix as in Definition 5.5. A similar scenario as the one in Figure 2 will then occur, where, in this case, u represents the characteristic function χ_φ, which evaluates to 1 on a subset of vertices of the tree. It is according to this prefix-based ordering and the resulting tree that we define a "minimal" UNSAT certificate for φ.

Let us assume, for instance, that the assignment $(1, 1, 1, 0)$ is generated by SAT-SOLVE in Algorithm 4, but is found to be infeasible by $\mathcal{C}$-SOLVE. Then, an effective UNSAT certificate should maximally prune the search space of SAT-SOLVE and minimize the amount of backtracking along the branches of the tree. To find such a conflicting assignment, we must look for the closest vertex to the root of the tree, e.g., the assignment $(1, 0, 0, 0)$ in our example, such that the associated convex set of constraints is still inconsistent. The lower the vertex, the higher the number of discarded assignments from the search tree. We observe that, since the number of zeros in the assignments increases as we move backward towards the root of the tree, a minimal certificate with respect to the prefix order pictured in Figure 2 would usually produce a small clause. However, such a clause does not necessarily correspond, in general, to a minimal IIS for the associated set of convex constraints in the sense of Definition 5.1.

Based on the discussion above, finding a minimal certificate for OPU formulas amounts to looking for the longest prefix associated with a set of consistent constraints before an inconsistent constraint is reached along a path of the tree. To formalize this objective, we proceed as follows. Given an OPU formula φ with respect to an ordering κ, let $a'_\mu = (a'_{\mu,1}, \dots, a'_{\mu,L})$ be the set of variables in $a' = (a_{\kappa(1)}, \dots, a_{\kappa(|C|)})$ that are asserted by the valuation $\mu(b, a)$ of SAT-SOLVE, taken in the same order as in a'. We also denote as $\{(g'_{\mu,1}(x) \lhd 0), \dots, (g'_{\mu,L}(x) \lhd 0)\}$ the set of convex constraints in φ associated with the variables a'_μ. Then, for a constant $\delta \in \mathbb{Q}^+$, we define the function $\text{ZEROPREFIX}_\delta : \mathbb{R}^L_+ \to \mathbb{N}$ as:

$$\text{ZEROPREFIX}_\delta(s_1, \dots, s_L) = \min k \;\; \text{s.t.} \;\; \sum_{i=1}^{k} |s_i| > \delta.$$

Intuitively, for small δ, ZEROPREFIX_δ returns the first nonzero element of the sequence $s = (s_1, \ldots, s_L)$, and practically the length of its "zero prefix." Using this function, we can then look for sequences of slack variables that maximize the number of initial elements set to zero before the first nonzero element is introduced, by casting the following optimization problem:

PROBLEM 1.

$$\max_{\substack{s_1,\ldots,s_L \in \mathbb{R} \\ x \in \mathcal{W} \subseteq \mathbb{R}^n}} \quad \text{ZEROPREFIX}_\delta(s_1, \ldots, s_L)$$

$$\text{s.t.} \quad g'_{\mu,i}(x) \lhd s_i, \qquad i = 1, \ldots, L$$

where $\mathcal{W}$ is the domain of real variables x and $g'_{\mu,i}$, for all i, are defined as above. Problem 1 is a modified version of a conventional feasibility problem, where convex constraints are perturbed by adding slack variables s_i. By looking at the longest prefix of zero slack variables, Problem 1 is able to find the longest sequence of convex constraints that are consistent before the first "stretched" inconsistent constraint appears according to the ordering induced by κ. If the optimum prefix length is k^*, then k^* is also the length of the resulting UNSAT certificate.

A remaining drawback is the possible intractability of Problem 1 whose objective function, basically counting the number of zero elements in the prefix of a sequence, is non-convex. *It is, however, possible to still find the optimum k^* from Problem 1 using a convex program.* To state this result, at the heart of our efficient decision procedure,we consider formulas $\varphi(b, x)$ such that the domain $\mathcal{W} \in \mathbb{R}^n$ of its real variables x is bounded. Under this assumption, we are guaranteed that there is always an upper bound to the minimum sum of slack values that can make any conjunction of convex constraints in φ feasible. We can define such a bound $\bar{s}$ as follows.

DEFINITION 5.7. *Let $\mathcal{W} \in \mathbb{R}^n$ be a bounded convex set, and $\{(g_1(x) \lhd 0), \ldots, (g_{|C|}(x) \lhd 0)\}$ the set of convex constraints in the monotone SMC formula φ. We define as $\bar{s}$ the solution of the following convex optimization problem:*

$$\max_{x \in \mathcal{W}} \min_{s_1,\ldots,s_{|C|} \in \mathbb{R}} \sum_{i=1}^{|C|} |s_i| \quad \text{s.t.} \quad g_i(x) \lhd s_i, \quad i = 1, \ldots, |C|$$

The bound $\bar{s}$ can be easily pre-computed offline for a given φ. Then, for a given tolerance $\delta \in \mathbb{Q}^+$, we can use the following problem to find the maximum length of the zero-prefix of a sequence of slacks:

PROBLEM 2.

$$\min_{\substack{s_1,\ldots,s_L \in \mathbb{R} \\ x \in \mathcal{W} \subseteq \mathbb{R}^n}} \sum_{i=1}^{L} |s_i|$$

$$\text{s.t.} \quad g'_{\mu,i}(x) \lhd s_i, \qquad i = 1, \ldots, L$$

$$\frac{\bar{s}}{\delta}\left(\sum_{k=1}^{i-1} |s_k|\right) \leq |s_i| \qquad i = 2, \ldots, L \qquad (7)$$

Problem 2 is a modified version of the SSF problem because of the addition of constraints (7)[3]. However, we observe

[3]While constraints (7) are non-convex, they can translated into linear constraints using standard transformations dealing with the minimization of the sum of absolute values.

Algorithm 3
$(\text{CSTATUS}, x, \varphi_{\text{ce}}) = \mathcal{C}\text{-SOLVE.PREFIX}(\mu, \mathcal{M}, \kappa, \delta)$

$s^* := \text{SOLVE-PROBLEM2}(\mu, \mathcal{M}, \kappa, \delta)$;
if $\sum_{i=1}^{L} s_i^* \leq \delta$ **then**
  CSTATUS = SAT;
  return $(\text{CSTATUS}, x^*, 1)$
else
  CSTATUS = UNSAT;
  $k^* := \text{ZEROPREFIX}_\delta(s_1^* \ldots s_L^*)$;
  $\varphi_{\text{ce}} := \bigvee_{i=1}^{k^*} \neg a'_{\mu,i}$;
  return $(\text{CSTATUS}, x^*, \varphi_{\text{ce}})$;

that, if the problem is feasible, constraints (7) become redundant. Therefore, if the sum of slacks at optimum is zero (in practice, the condition $\sum_{i=1}^{L} |s_i| \leq \delta$ is satisfied), then μ is indeed a valid assignment. If, instead, this is not the case, constraints (7) induce an ordering over the non-zero slack variables which can be used to generate the prefix-based minimal certificate. It is therefore sufficient to solve Problem 2, as established by the following result.

Theorem 5.8 (PREFIX-BASED CERTIFICATE). *Let φ be a OPU formula with respect to an ordering κ and defined over a bounded real variable domain $\mathcal{W}$. Let μ be a satisfying assignment for the propositional abstraction φ_B, $\delta \in \mathbb{Q}^+$, and $\bar{s} \in \mathbb{R}^+$, defined as in Definition 5.7, with $\bar{s} \geq \delta$. Let Problem 2 be the feasibility problem associated with μ, $\bar{s}$, and δ. Then, the following hold:*

- *If Problem 2 is feasible and x^* is the optimum for x, then $([\![b]\!]_\mu, x^*) \models \varphi$;*
- *If Problem 2 is infeasible and k^* is the minimum index such that $s_k^* > 0$, then, the following clause:*

$$\varphi_{ce} := \bigvee_{i=1}^{k^*} \neg a'_{\mu,i}, \qquad (8)$$

is an UNSAT certificate for μ which is minimal with respect to κ.

The prefix-based certificate generation procedure can then implemented as in Algorithm 3. By Theorem 5.8 we can then state the following guarantees of Algorithm 4 with the generation of UNSAT certificates in Algorithm 3.

PROPOSITION 5.9. *Let φ be a monotone SMC formula and $\delta \in \mathbb{Q}^+$ a user-defined tolerance used in $\mathcal{C}$-SOLVE.CHECK in Algorithm 4 to accommodate numerical errors. Algorithm 4 with the certificate from Algorithm 3 is δ-complete.*

Overall, as summarized in Table 1, IIS-based certificates are generally the shortest and most effective, but also the most expensive to compute. IIS-based and SSF-based certificates can be used with any monotone SMC formula, while prefix-based certificates are the most efficient to compute for OPU formulas. As an example, OPU formulas can be used to encode the runs of a finite-state transition system, which would also form a tree, as in in Figure 2. Coupled with continuous dynamics, this pattern arises in several systems, including switched system, linear hybrid systems, piecewise affine systems, and mixed logical dynamical systems [21].

6. RESULTS

We implemented all our algorithms in the prototype solver SATEX. We use Z3 [10] as a SAT solver and CPLEX [22] as a convex optimization solver. To validate our approach, we first compare the scalability of the proposed SMC procedure with respect to state-of-art SMT and MIP solvers, such as Z3 and CPLEX, on a set of synthetically generated monotone SMC formulas. We then demonstrate the performance of SATEX and different UNSAT certificates on two hybrid system problems that both generate SMC instances: secure state estimation and robotic motion planning. All the experiments were executed on an Intel Core i7 2.5-GHz processor with 16 GB of memory. CPLEX was configured to utilize 1,2,3, or 4 processor cores.

6.1 Scalability

To test the scalability of our algorithm, we generate SMC problem instances as follows. We consider purely Boolean problem instances from the 2014 SAT competition (application track) [23] and selectively include Boolean clauses from these instances to create SMC problems with an increasing number of Boolean constraints, from 1000 to 130,000, over a maximum number of 4,288 Boolean variables. We then augment the Boolean instance with clauses of the form $\neg b_i \vee h_i(x) \leq 0$ where b_i is a pre-existing Boolean variable and h_i is a randomly generated affine function. Affine constraints are all generated in such a way that the whole SMC formula is always satisfiable. SATEX will then terminate after at most one iteration.

Figure 3 (left) reports the execution time of SATEX as the number of Boolean constraints in an SMC instance increases for a fixed number of real variables. For instances with a relatively small number of Boolean constraints (less than 15,000), MIP techniques, based on branch-and-bound and cutting plane methods, show a superior performance. However, as the number of Boolean constraints increases, the performance of SATEX, relying on SAT solving, exceeds the one of MIP techniques by 4-5 orders of magnitude in execution time. The performance gap between the lazy procedure of SATEX and Z3 is also observed to increase with the number of Boolean constraints, and reach more than one order of magnitude. On the other hand, when the number of continuous variables in the affine constraints increases, as shown on the right side of Figure 3, Z3 reaches a 600-s timeout on problem instances with more than 1500 continuous variables, while optimization-based algorithms show the expected polynomial degradation, with SATEX running approximately twice as faster as MIP.

Next, we consider SMC formulas that are certified to be unsatisfiable, since they are directly created using UNSAT Boolean instances from the SAT 2014 competition, augmented with linear constraints as above. As shown in Figure 4, again, when relying on SAT solving to detect unsatisfiability, SATEX runs faster by two orders of magnitude with respect to MIP based techniques. Its performance is, in this case, comparable with the one of Z3.

6.2 Application to Secure State Estimation

Given a set of p sensor measurements $Y_1, Y_2, \ldots, Y_p$ out of a linear dynamical system, the secure state estimation problem consists in reconstructing the state x of the dynamical system even if up to k sensors are maliciously corrupted [14]. The sensor measurements are a function of the system state, where

$$Y_i = \begin{cases} H_i x & \text{if sensor } i \text{ is attack-free} \\ H_i x + \alpha_i & \text{if sensor } i \text{ is under attack} \end{cases}$$

and α_i models the attack injection. It is possible to encode the secure state estimation problem as an SMC instance by introducing indicator variables b_i that are assigned to 1 if and only if the sensor is attacked. We therefore obtain the following monotone SMC formula:

$$\varphi ::= \left(\sum_{i=1}^{p} b_i \leq k \right) \wedge \bigwedge_{i=1}^{p} \left(\neg b_i \rightarrow (\|Y_i - H_i x\|_2^2 \leq \nu) \right)$$

where the first constraint is a pseudo-Boolean predicate that requires that no more than k sensors be under attack, while the other constraints establish that the state x is linearly related with the measurements in the case of attack-free sensors, except for an error bounded by $\nu \in \mathbb{R}^+$.

As shown in Figure 5, SATEX outperforms the MIP solver by up to 1 order of magnitude as the number of sensors (hence the number of Boolean variables and constraints) increases. Moreover, IIS-based certificates are often not better than SSF-based certificates, even if they are minimal, because of the cost paid for constructing them. In all our benchmarks, Z3 exceeds the 600-s timeout, possibly because of the longer run times of the nonlinear real arithmetic theory required by the quadratic constraints.

6.3 Application to Motion Planning

The reach-avoid problem examined in Section 2 reduces to an OPU formula, as suggested by the ordering of the Boolean variables associated with the different regions according to the transition system in Figure 1. We can, therefore, exploit our results on prefix-based UNSAT certificates.

Figure 6 shows the runtime performance of SATEX with respect to a MIP solver on instances of the motion planning problem. We assume that we operate with the linearized dynamics of a quadrotor (having 14 continuous states) moving in a 3-dimensional workspace. Moreover, we partition the workspace into cubes of size $1m \times 1m \times 1m$ and randomly select some of them to be obstacles. We then keep fixed to 4 m the workspace width and height and let its length increase (along the x axis). This translates into increasing both the number of Boolean and continuous variables in φ, since L must also increase in order to reach the target. Consistently with our previous observations, increasing the number of Boolean variables directly maps into a larger performance gap associated with prefix-based UNSAT certificates, which outperform both the IIS-based and MIP-based approaches.

7. CONCLUSIONS

We demonstrated a procedure for determining the satisfiability of two special, yet common, types of logic formulas over Boolean and convex constraints. By leveraging the strengths of both SAT solving and convex programming as well as efficient conflict-driven learning strategies, our approach outperforms state-of-the-art SMT and MICP solvers on problems with complex Boolean structure and a large number of real variables. The proposed satisfiability modulo convex optimization scheme can then be used to build effective and scalable decision procedures for problems in hybrid system verification and control.

Acknowledgments

This work was partially sponsored by TerraSwarm, one of six centers of STARnet, a Semiconductor Research Corporation program sponsored by MARCO and DARPA, by the NSF project

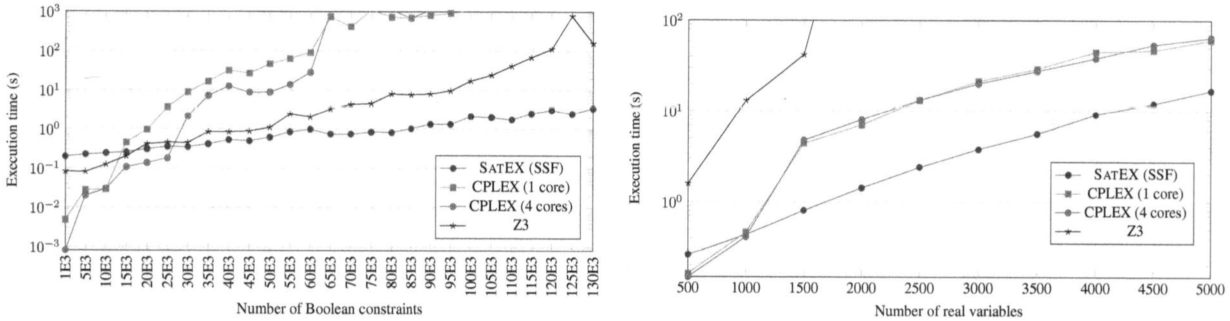

Figure 3: Execution time on SMC problem instances, when the number of Boolean constraints increases for a fixed number of 100 real variables (left side) and when the number of real variables increases for a fixed number of 7000 Boolean constraints (right side).

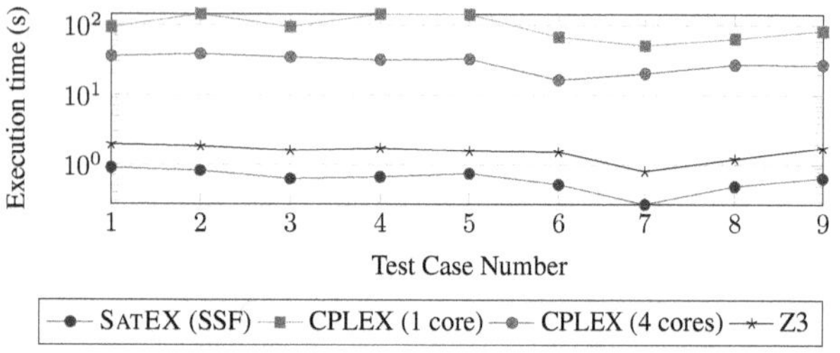

Figure 4: Execution time on UNSAT SMC instances due to UNSAT Boolean constraints: the number of Boolean clauses varies from 225 to 960, while the number of real variables is fixed to 500.

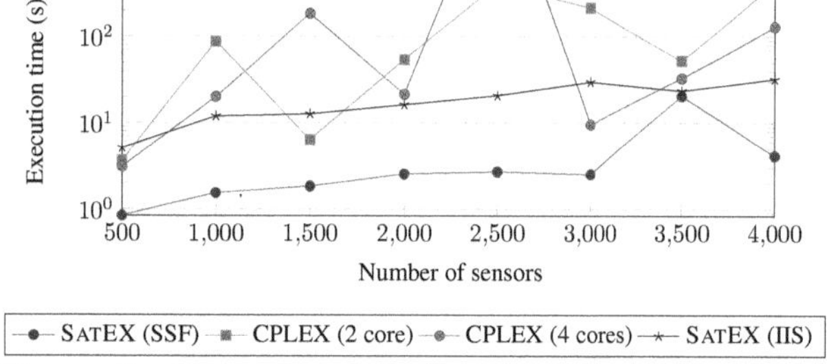

Figure 5: Execution time on instances of the secure state estimation problem when the number of sensors increase. Z3 exceeds a 600-s timeout in all benchmarks.

ExCAPE: Expeditions in Computer Augmented Program Engineering, and by the NSF award 1239085.

8. REFERENCES

[1] J. N. Hooker, "Logic, optimization, and constraint programming," *INFORMS Journal on Computing*, vol. 14, no. 4, pp. 295–321, 2002.

[2] C. Barrett, R. Sebastiani, S. A. Seshia, and C. Tinelli, *Satisfiability Modulo Theories, Chapter in Handbook of Satisfiability.* IOS Press, 2009.

[3] S. Ratschan, "Efficient solving of quantified inequality constraints over the real numbers," *ACM Trans. Comput. Logic*, vol. 7, no. 4, pp. 723–748, 2006.

[4] S. Gao, J. Avigad, and E. M. Clarke, "δ-complete decision procedures for satisfiability over the reals," in *Proc. Int. Joint Conf. Automated Reasoning*, 2012, pp. 286–300.

[5] S. Boyd and L. Vandenberghe, *Convex Optimization.* Cambridge Univesity Press, 2004.

[6] R. Nieuwenhuis, A. Oliveras, and C. Tinelli, "Solving SAT and SAT Modulo Theories: From an abstract Davis–Putnam–Logemann–Loveland procedure to DPLL(T)," *J. ACM*, vol. 53, no. 6, pp. 937–977, Nov. 2006.

[7] A. Cimatti *et al.*, "Satisfiability modulo the theory of costs: Foundations and applications," in *Proc. TACAS*, 2010.

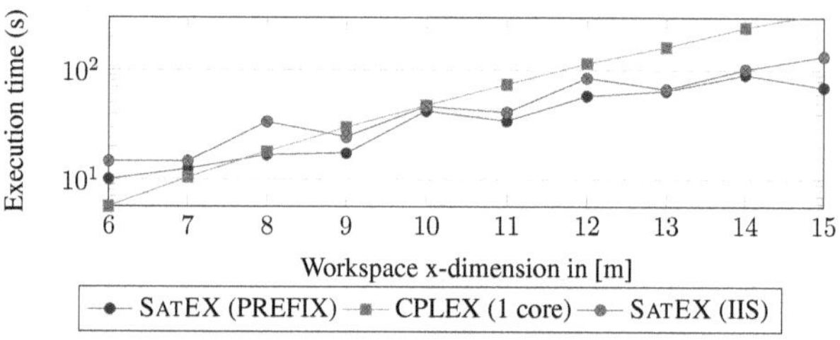

Figure 6: Execution time on a set of SMC instances for the motion planning problem as the size of the workspace increases.

[8] Y. Li *et al.*, "Symbolic optimization with SMT solvers," in *ACM SIGPLAN Notices*, vol. 49, no. 1, 2014, pp. 607–618.

[9] A. Bauer, M. Pister, and M. Tautschnig, "Tool-support for the analysis of hybrid systems and models," in *Proc. of DATE*, 2007.

[10] L. De Moura and N. Björner, "Z3: An efficient SMT solver," in *Proc. Int. Conf. Tools and Algorithms for the Construction and Analysis of Systems*, 2008, pp. 337–340.

[11] M. Franzle *et al.*, "Efficient solving of large non-linear arithmetic constraint systems with complex Boolean structure," in *JSAT Special Issue on SAT/CP Integration*, 2007.

[12] S. Gao, S. Kong, and E. M. Clarke, "dReal: An SMT solver for nonlinear theories over the reals," 2013, vol. 7898, pp. 208–214.

[13] P. Nuzzo *et al.*, "CalCS: SMT solving for non-linear convex constraints," in *Proc. Formal Methods in Computer-Aided Design*, Oct. 2010, pp. 71–79.

[14] Y. Shoukry *et al.*, "Sound and complete state estimation for linear dynamical systems under sensor attack using satisfiability modulo theory solving," in *Proc. American Control Conference*, 2015, pp. 3818–3823.

[15] Y. Shoukry *et al.*, "Scalable lazy SMT-based motion planning," in *Proc. Int. Conf. Decision and Control*, 2016, pp. 6683–6688.

[16] E. Plaku and S. Karaman, "Motion planning with temporal-logic specifications: Progress and challenges," *AI Communications*, no. Preprint, pp. 1–12.

[17] A. Pnueli, "The temporal logic of programs," in *FOCS*, 1977, pp. 46–57.

[18] M. Grant, S. Boyd, and Y. Ye, "Disciplined convex programming," in *Global optimization.* Springer, 2006, pp. 155–210.

[19] Y. Shoukry, P. Nuzzo, A. Sangiovanni-Vincentelli, S. Seshia, G. Pappas, and P. Tabuada, "SMC: Satisfiability modulo convex optimization," *ArXiv e-prints*, 2017.

[20] J. W. Chinneck and E. W. Dravnieks, "Locating minimal infeasible constraint sets in linear programs," *ORSA Journal on Computing*, vol. 3, no. 2, pp. 157–168, 1991.

[21] A. Bemporad and M. Morari, "Control of systems integrating logic, dynamics, and constraints," *Automatica*, vol. 35, 1999.

[22] (2012, Feb.) IBM ILOG CPLEX Optimizer. [Online]. Available: www.ibm.com/software/integration/optimization/cplex-optimizer/

[23] "The international SAT competitions web page." http://www.satcompetition.org/, accessed: 2016-10-01.

Sapo: Reachability Computation and Parameter Synthesis of Polynomial Dynamical Systems[*]

Tommaso Dreossi
UC Berkeley
Berkeley, CA, USA
dreossi@berkeley.edu

ABSTRACT

Sapo is a tool for the formal analysis of polynomial dynamical systems. Its main features are 1) *Reachability computation*, i.e., the calculation of the set of states reachable from a set of initial conditions, and 2) *Parameter synthesis*, i.e., the refinement of a set of parameters so that the system satisfies a given specification. Sapo can represent reachable sets as unions of boxes, parallelotopes, or parallelotope bundles (symbolic representation of polytopes). Sets of parameters are represented with polytopes while specifications are formalized as Signal Temporal Logic (STL) formulas.

Keywords

Reachability; parameter synthesis; dynamical systems; Bernstein

1. INTRODUCTION

Formal verification involves the strict and exhaustive study of systems using mathematically based techniques. The development and application of formal methods are motivated by the fact that the formal study of a model implies the reliability and robustness of the abstracted system.

Formal analysis of dynamical systems involves two fundamental problems: *reachability computation* and *parameter synthesis*. In the first case, for a given set of initial conditions, it is asked to compute the set of states reachable by the dynamical system. In the second case, an initial set of conditions together with a set of parameters and a specification are provided, and it is asked to refine the set of parameters in such a way that the system satisfies the specification. Reachability computation can be used, for instance, to determine whether a system reaches some undesired states or remains within a particular subset of the state space, while synthesis of parameters can be used to design dynamical systems and tune their parameters so that to fit experimental observations or satisfy requirements.

Despite numerous tools available for the analysis of linear dynamical systems (i.e., systems whose dynamics are linear functions), not many tools for the study of nonlinear systems are available. The main difficulties arising from nonlinearity concern the transformation of sets with respect to nonlinear functions. This operation, in general, does not preserve critical properties of the sets (e.g., convexity), and thus approximation techniques are necessary.

In this work, we present Sapo[1], a scalable tool that targets discrete-time polynomial dynamical systems (possibly parametric) and deals with both the reachability computation and parameter synthesis problems. Sapo can be used either to generate flowpipes that over-approximate reachable sets over bounded time horizons or to refine sets of parameters in such a way that the system satisfies a Signal Temporal Logic (STL) [20] specification.

The tool allows the construction of flowpipes using boxes (i.e., hyperrectangles), parallelotopes (i.e., n-dimensional parallelograms), or parallelotope bundles (i.e., sets of parallelotopes whose intersections symbolically represent polytopes), and the refinement of parameter sets represented by polytopes. Sapo's underlying algorithms exploit some properties of Bernstein coefficients of polynomials. Intuitively, the Bernstein coefficients can be used to bound a polynomial over the unit box domain (i.e., $[0,1]^n$). The core idea on which Sapo relies is the transformation of unit boxes into generic sets. With this trick, Sapo exploits Bernstein coefficients to maximize polynomials and determine sets that over-approximate the trajectories of the system. A similar approach is also used to reduce the parameter synthesis problem into linear programs, where the linear systems, constructed through parameterized Bernstein coefficients, represent sets of valid parameters. The algorithms implemented in Sapo are based on the theoretical results and methods proposed by [9, 12, 7, 8, 13, 11].

The herein paper is organized as follows: Section 2 defines the reachability and parameter synthesis problems for discrete-time dynamical systems; Section 3 summarizes the techniques used by Sapo to compute reachable sets and refine parameter sets; in Section 4 the tool structure and some of its applications are shown; Section 5 concludes the paper with some remarks.

[*]This work is funded in part by the DARPA BRASS program under agreement number FA8750-16-C-0043 and NSF grants CNS-1646208 and CCF-1139138.

HSCC'17, April 18-20, 2017, Pittsburgh, PA, USA

DOI: http://dx.doi.org/10.1145/3049797.3049824

[1] https://github.com/tommasodreossi/sapo

2. REACHABILITY AND PARAMETER SYNTHESIS

Sapo deals with discrete-time parametric polynomial dynamical systems described by difference equations of the form:

$$x_{k+1} = f(x_k, p) \tag{1}$$

where $f : \mathbb{R}^n \times \mathbb{R}^m \to \mathbb{R}^n$ is a polynomial linear in p, $x_k \in \mathbb{R}^n$ is the state of the system at time $k \in \mathbb{N}$, and $p \in \mathbb{R}^m$ are the parameters. Given an initial condition $x_0 \in \mathbb{R}^n$ and parameters $p \in \mathbb{R}^m$, the trajectory $x_0, x_1, x_2, \dots$ describing the evolution of the system, can be obtained by iterating the function (1).

The problems addressed by Sapo are:

- *Reachability computation*: Given a set of initial conditions $X_0 \subset \mathbb{R}^n$, a set of parameters $P \subset \mathbb{R}^m$, and a time instant $T \in \mathbb{N}$, determine a sequence of tight sets $X_0, X_1, X_2, \dots X_T$, called flowpipe, such that all the trajectories of length T with initial conditions in X_0 and parameters in P are included in the constructed flowpipe;
- *Parameter synthesis*: Given a set of initial conditions $X_0 \subset \mathbb{R}^n$, a set of parameters $P \subset \mathbb{R}^m$, and a specification φ, determine the largest set $P_\varphi \subseteq P$ such that all the trajectories with initial conditions in X_0 and parameters in P_φ satisfy φ.

3. MAIN FEATURES

3.1 Bernstein Coefficients

At the core of Sapo for both reachability computation and parameter synthesis, there are Bernstein coefficients of polynomials. Intuitively, Bernstein coefficients can be used to represent a polynomial in Bernstein form, i.e., as the linear combination of Bernstein basis and coefficients. Given a polynomial $\pi : \mathbb{R}^n \to \mathbb{R}$:

$$\pi(x) = \sum_{i \in I^\pi} a_i x^i \tag{2}$$

where $i = (i_1, \dots, i_n) \in \mathbb{N}^n$ is a multi-index, $x^i = x_1^{i_1} \dots x_n^{i_n}$ is a monomial, $a_i \in \mathbb{R}$ is a coefficient, and $I^\pi \subset \mathbb{N}^n$ is the multi-index set of π, the i-th *Bernstein coefficient* is:

$$b_i = \sum_{j \le i} \frac{\binom{i}{j}}{\binom{d}{j}} a_j \tag{3}$$

where $i \le j$ if $i_k \le j_k$ for $k = 1, \dots, n$, $\binom{i}{j}$ is the product of the binomial coefficients $\binom{i_1}{j_1} \dots \binom{i_n}{j_n}$, and d is the smallest multi-index such that $i \le d$ for all $i \in I^\pi$.

One of the interesting properties of Bernstein coefficients is the *range enclosure property* [5] stating that $\min_{i \in I^\pi} b_i \le \pi(x) \le \max_{i \in I^\pi} b_i$ for $x \in [0,1]^n$. This implies that the maximum Bernstein coefficient is an upper bound of the maximum of π over the unit box domain. Thus, to optimize a polynomial, instead of using nonlinear/nonconvex optimization techniques, one can compute the Bernstein coefficients and extract their maximum. The main drawback of this approach is that the enclosure property holds only on the unit box domain.

In [11] the range enclosure property has been extended to parametric polynomials of the form $\pi : \mathbb{R}^n \times \mathbb{R}^m \to \mathbb{R}$, showing that $\min_{i \in I^\pi} \min_{p \in P} b_i(p) \le \pi(x,p) \le \max_{i \in I^\pi} \max_{p \in P} b_i(p)$ for all $x \in [0,1]^n$ and parameters $p \in P$. This property, with a slight adaptation of the treated polynomial, is the key element of Sapo's reachability and parameter synthesis algorithms.

3.2 Reachability Computation

The flowpipe $X_0, X_1, \dots, X_T$ that includes the reachable set can be obtained as a sequence of set image transformations $X_{k+1} = f(X_k, P)$. Unluckily, this operation is difficult when f is nonlinear, since many properties of sets (e.g., convexity) can be lost. A common method to circumvent this problem consists in over-approximating the image of sets with simpler objects such as *polytopes*.

A polytope $X \subset \mathbb{R}^n$ is a convex set that can be represented by the solutions of a linear system $Dx \le c$, where $D \in \mathbb{R}^{m \times n}$ and $c \in \mathbb{R}^m$. The matrix D and vector c are called *template* and *offset*, and the polytope generated by D and c is denoted by $\langle D, c \rangle$. Given a template D, the offset c such that the set $\langle D, c \rangle$ over-approximates the set $f(X_k, P)$ can be determined by solving optimization problems of the form:

$$c_i \ge \max_{x \in X_k, p \in P} D_i f(x,p) \tag{4}$$

for $i = 1, \dots, m$. An upper-bound of the maximum of $D_i f(x,p)$ over the unit box can be found computing its Bernstein coefficients and maximizing them over the set P. However, in order to apply this technique to generic domains, a slight adjustment of the treated polynomial is needed.

A method that combines Bernstein coefficients and parameter synthesis on generic box domains has been proposed in [12]. Intuitively, for a given box X_k, we can compute a map $v : [0,1]^n \to X_k$ that transforms the unit box into X_k. It is easy to see that $f(X_k, P) = f(v([0,1]^n), P)$, which implies that an upper bound of $D_i f(x,p)$, with $x \in X_k$ and $p \in P$, can be established determining the maximum Bernstein coefficient of $D_i f(v(x), p)$. Repeating this operation for all the directions of the template D, we can obtain a new offset c that leads to an over-approximating box $\langle D, c \rangle \supseteq f(X_k, P)$ (see Figure 1a).

By changing the map v, we can alter the shape of the over-approximation set and define reachability algorithms based on sets different from boxes. For instance, [7] shows how the map v can be defined to transform unit boxes into parallelotopes. In doing so, we can define a parallelotope-based set image approximation technique that is more flexible in the choice of the initial set and more precise than the box-based one (see Figure 1b).

The transformation of a unit box into a generic polytope is in general difficult. However, [13] defined a new way or representing polytopes as finite intersections of polytopes (see Figure 1c). These sets are called *parallelotope bundles.* Once that a polytope is decomposed in a collection of parallelotopes, we can reason separately on each of its parallelotopes and, using the Bernstein coefficients, we can determine a new parallelotope bundle that over-approximates the image of the starting polytope. This method significantly increases the accuracy of the over-approximation flowpipes at the cost of a higher number of optimizations.

In summary, for reachability computation, Sapo supports the construction of flowpipes based on boxes, parallelotopes,

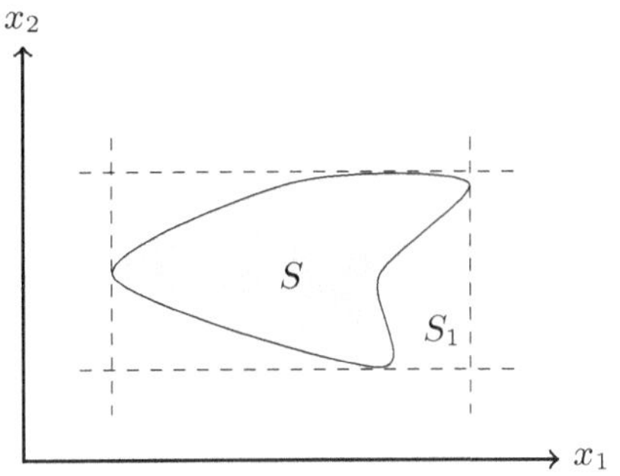

(a) Box-based over-approximation.

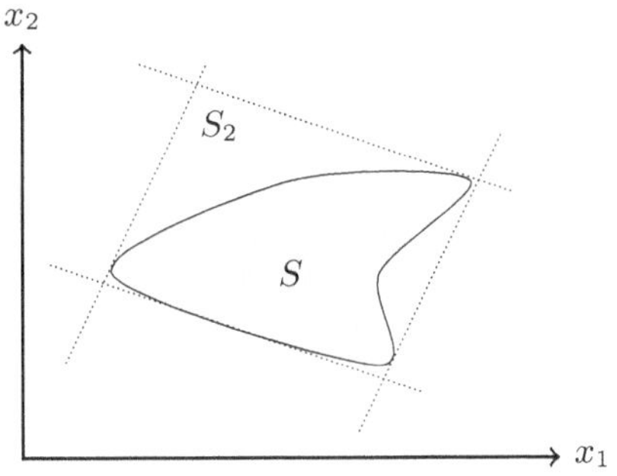

(b) Parallelotope-based over-approximation.

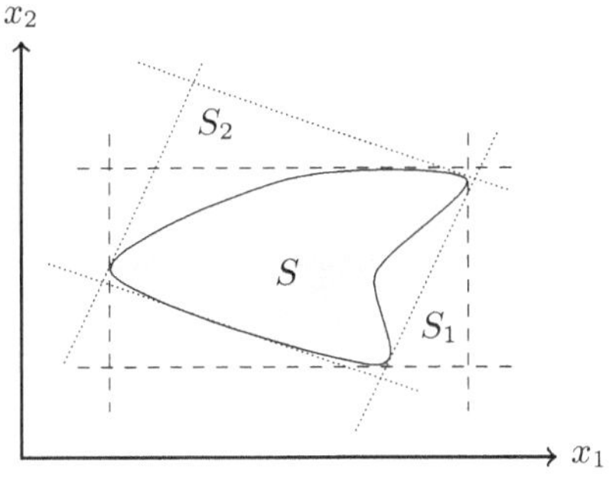

(c) Bundle-based over-approximation.

Figure 1: Set over-approximation techniques adopted by Sapo.

and parallelotope bundles. All these objects are represented by Sapo as both solutions of linear systems (constraint representation) and affine transformations of unit boxes (generator representation). Sapo uses either of these representations depending on the operation to perform on the set.

3.3 Parameter Synthesis

Given a set of initial conditions X_0, a set of parameters P, and a specification φ, we want to determine the largest set $P_\varphi \subseteq P$ such that the reachable set starting in $f(X_0, P_\varphi)$ satisfies φ.

Sapo allows the user to formalize the specifications in terms of STL formulas [20] in positive normal form, i.e., formulas generated by the following grammar:

$$\varphi := \sigma \mid \varphi \wedge \varphi \mid \varphi \vee \varphi \mid \varphi \mathcal{U}_I \varphi \qquad (5)$$

with $\sigma = g(x_1, \ldots, x_n) \leq 0$, where $g : \mathbb{R}^n \to \mathbb{R}$, and $I \subset \mathbb{N}$ is an interval.

Similarly to the reachability computation, also the parameter synthesis algorithm implemented in Sapo exploits the Bernstein coefficients. Given the sets X_k, P and a predicate $\sigma = g(x_1, \ldots, x_n) \leq 0$, the set P is a valid parameter set if $g(f(x,p)) \leq 0$ holds for all $x \in X_k$ and $p \in P$. This constraint can be verified by determining a map $v : [0,1]^n \to X_k$, computing the Bernstein coefficients of the function $g(f(v(x),p))$, and checking that $b_i(p) \leq 0$ for all $b_i(p) \in I^{g \circ f \circ v}$ and $p \in P$. In particular, a refinement P_σ of the set P with respect to the predicate σ can be obtained by adding the linear constraints $b_i(p) \leq 0$ to the linear system representing P. The solutions of the new linear system are the valid parameters. This condition can be verified solving a single linear program.

Reasoning by structural induction on the given specification, it is possible to reduce the parameter synthesis problem into a collection of refinements over predicates. The partial results are then combined accordingly with the treated formula. The refinement of the until formula requires also the computation of the evolution of the system, a task that can be achieved by the reachability methods previously introduced. The parameter synthesis algorithm, its correctness, and its complexity are presented in detail in [8, 11].

In summary, for the parameter synthesis, Sapo receives in input a set of initial conditions representable with a box or a parallelotope, a polytopic set of parameters specified as a linear system, an STL formula, and it produces a collection of polytopes representing the set of parameters under which the system satisfies the specification.

4. STRUCTURE AND USAGE

4.1 Tool Architecture

Sapo is available at https://github.com/tommasodreossi/sapo. The tool is implemented in C++ and it consists in around 5k lines of code. It relies on the external libraries GiNaC[2] for symbolically manipulating polynomials and on GLPK[3] for solving linear programs.

Figure 2 summarizes the structure of the tool, showing its main modules and the association relationships (uses, interacts-with) between them. The user can specify a dynamical system and a possible specification using the `Model` and `STL` modules, respectively. The set of initial conditions and possible parameters can be specified using the modules `Bundle` and `LinearSystemSet`, respectively, that in turn make use of the modules `Parallelotope` and `LinearSystem` to internally represent sets. Note that a single box or parallelotope can be seen as a bundle with a single template.

With these elements, the user can analyze the dynamical system invoking the main module `SapoCore`. This block implements the reachability and parameter synthesis algorithms and returns the computed results. An important module with which `SapoCore` interacts is the `BaseConverter`. This block computes Bernstein coefficients of polynomial functions heavily exploited by our algorithms. The `BaseConverter` symbolically computes the Bernstein coefficients of a polynomial only once. The symbolic coefficients are stored in a data structure from which they are fetched and numerically instantiated whenever needed. This trick allows the tool to save computations and sensibly speeds up the analysis. Bernstein coefficients are computed by default using the improved matrix method presented in [12].

To visualize the results, Sapo gives the possibility to generate a Matlab script that displays 2/3-dimensional sets or projections of higher dimensional sets.

4.2 Experimental Evaluation

As a demonstration, we apply Sapo to the SIR epidemic model, a 3d nonlinear system that describes the progress of a disease in a population. The model considers three groups

[2] http://www.ginac.de

[3] https://www.gnu.org/software/glpk/

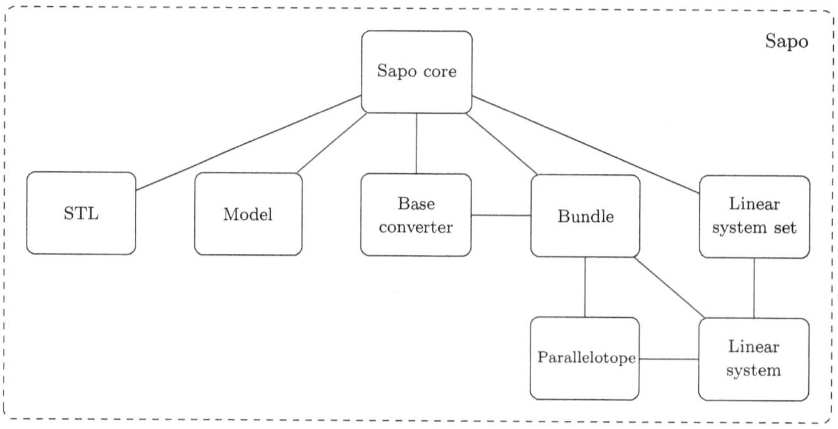

Figure 2: Overview of Sapo's architecture.

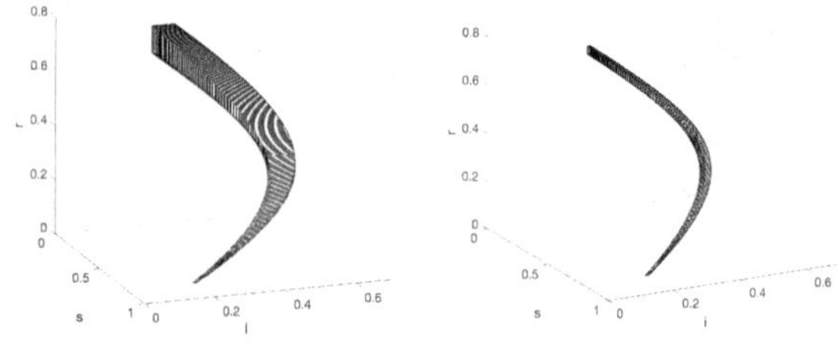

(a) Box-based (b) Bundle-based

Figure 3: Reachable sets of SIR model (300 steps)

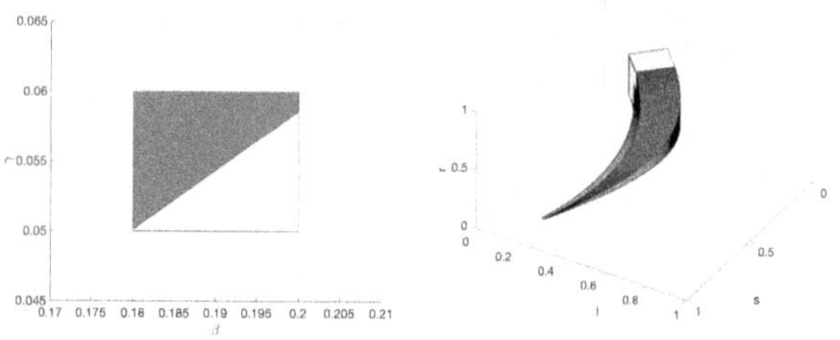

(a) Synthesized parameters (b) Constrained evolution

Figure 4: Parameter synthesis of SIR ($G_{[50,100]}(i \leq 0.44)$)

of individuals: s the susceptible healthy, i the infected, and r the removed from the system (e.g., the recovered ones). Two parameters regulate the system's evolution: β the contraction rate and γ, where $1/\gamma$ is the mean infective period.

We used Sapo to compute the bounded time reachable set of the SIR model with different configurations. At first, with parameters $\beta = 0.34, \gamma = 0.05$, and set of initial conditions $s_0 \in [0.79, 0.80], i_0 \in [0.19, 0.20]$, and $r_0 \in [0.00, 0.00]$, we computed in 0.12s the reachable set for 300 steps using a single box (see Figure 3a). Then, by adding two surrounding parallelotopes to the set of initial conditions, we obtained in 2.83s a bundle-based flowpipe that better over-approximates the reachable set (see Figure 3b). Notice how, for the same initial set, the bundle-based flowpipe is more accurate than the box-based one.

Sapo can also be used to synthesize sets of valid parameters. For instance, considering the set of initial conditions $s_0 \in [0.79, 0.80]$, $i_0 \in [0.19, 0.20]$, and $r_0 = [0.00, 0.00]$, and the initial set of parameters $\beta \in [0.18, 0.20]$ and $\gamma \in [0.05, 0.06]$, we can ask Sapo to refine the parameter set so that the STL formula $G_{[50,100]}(i \leq 0.44)$ holds. Figure 4a shows the original parameter set (in white) and the synthesized one (in gray) computed in 0.83s, while Figure 4b depicts the evolution of the system under the synthesized parameter set.

Sapo's reachability and parameter synthesis algorithms have been applied to several dynamical systems. Tables 1 and 2 give an intuition of the scalability of the implemented methods. In particular, Table 1 shows the running times for the reachability analysis of a number of dynamical systems that span from 2 to 17 dimensions. The table reports the number of directions and templates adopted in the construction of the flowpipes (computed with the AFO set transformation method; for details see [11, 13]).

Table 2 shows the running times for the parameter synthesis of some epidemic models with 3 to 5 variables and 2 to 4 parameters. The parameters of each model have been refined with respect to the STL specifications reported in Table 2.

These illustrative examples demonstrate that Sapo scales well in the system's dimensions and parameters, handling models larger than those treated by the state-of-the-art tools (which treat around 10 variables). However, recall that Sapo deals exclusively with discrete-time polynomial dynamics while other tools are specialized on continuous-time or broader classes of dynamics. Some reachability analysis comparisons of Sapo with other tools are reported in [14].

5. CONCLUSION

5.1 Related Work

In the last two decades, numerous tools have been developed for the reachability analysis of linear dynamical systems and hybrid automata. Some examples are SpaceEx [16], HyTech [17], or d/dt [3]. Unlike for the linear case, not many tools for nonlinear analysis are available. Some tools, such as Breach [10], S-TaLiRo [1], or C2E2 [15] address nonlinearity using a finite number of simulations. Other works, such as [2,

Model	Vars	Steps	Dirs/Temps	Time
Van der Pol	2	300	4/6	1.45
Rössler	3	250	5/3	0.42
SIR	3	300	5/3	0.79
Lotka-Volterra	5	500	7/3	51.52
Phosphorelay	7	200	10/3	8.13
Quadcopter	17	300	18/2	7.65

Table 1: Reachability benchmark. Model: model's name; Vars: number of variables; Steps: reachability steps; Dirs/Temps: number of used directions and templates; Time: computation time (sec).

Model	Vars	Params	Spec	Time
SIR	3	2	$\mathcal{G}_{[50,100]}(i \leq 0.44)$	0.42
Influenza	4	2	$\mathcal{G}_{[0,50]}(i \leq 0.43)$	2.12
Ebola	5	4	$(q > 0.04)\mathcal{U}_{[10,15]}(i > 0.27)$	0.0007

Table 2: Parameter synthesis benchmark. Model: model's name; Vars: number of variables; Params: number of parameters; Spec: STL specification; Time: computation time (sec).

4, 18], face nonlinearity using linearization, hybridization, or abstraction techniques. Tools that directly deal with nonlinear systems are dReach [19], KeYmaera [21], and Flow*[6]. The latter is probably the closest tool to Sapo in terms of both problem formulation and provided results. The main difference between Flow* and Sapo is that the former considers continuous-time models and produces flowpipes grouping collections of Taylor models, while the latter produces a collection of polytopes computed using Bernestein coefficients. Another difference is that Flow* can work on hybrid automata, while Sapo, at the moment, focuses only on dynamical systems.

5.2 Future Developments

Sapo is still under development. It is our intention to extend the reachability computation to polynomial hybrid automata, where invariants and guards need to be considered. An interesting aspect of operations on parallelotope bundles is that they can be easily parallelized. It could be interesting to implement a parallel version of the tool and investigate its scalability.

6. REFERENCES

[1] Yashwanth Annpureddy, Che Liu, Georgios E. Fainekos, and Sriram Sankaranarayanan. S-TaLiRo: A tool for temporal logic falsification for hybrid systems. In *Tools and Algorithms for the Construction and Analysis of Systems, TACAS*, pages 254–257, 2011.

[2] Eugene Asarin, Thao Dang, and Antoine Girard. Reachability analysis of nonlinear systems using conservative approximation. In *International Workshop on Hybrid Systems: Computation and Control*, pages 20–35. Springer, 2003.

[3] Eugene Asarin, Thao Dang, and Oded Maler. The d/dt tool for verification of hybrid systems. In *International Conference on Computer Aided Verification*, pages 365–370. Springer, 2002.

[4] Stanley Bak, Sergiy Bogomolov, Thomas A Henzinger, Taylor T Johnson, and Pradyot Prakash. Scalable static hybridization methods for analysis of nonlinear systems. In *Proceedings of the 19th International Conference on Hybrid Systems: Computation and Control*, pages 155–164. ACM, 2016.

[5] GT Cargo and Oved Shisha. The bernstein form of a polynomial. *Journal of Research*, 70:79–81, 1966.

[6] Xin Chen, Erika Ábrahám, and Sriram Sankaranarayanan. Flow*: An analyzer for non-linear hybrid systems. In *Computer Aided Verification, CAV*, pages 258–263, 2013.

[7] Thao Dang, Tommaso Dreossi, and Carla Piazza. Parameter synthesis using parallelotopic enclosure and applications to epidemic models. In *Hybrid Systems and Biology, HSB*, pages 67–82, 2014.

[8] Thao Dang, Tommaso Dreossi, and Carla Piazza. Parameter synthesis through temporal logic specifications. In *International Synmposium on Formal Methods, FM*, pages 213–230, 2015.

[9] Thao Dang and Romain Testylier. Reachability analysis for polynomial dynamical systems using the Bernstein expansion. *Reliable Computing*, 17(2):128–152, 2012.

[10] Alexandre Donzé. Breach, a toolbox for verification and parameter synthesis of hybrid systems. In *Computer Aided Verification, CAV*, pages 167–170. Springer, 2010.

[11] Tommaso Dreossi. *Reachability Computation and Parameter Synthesis for Polynomial Dynamical Systems*. PhD thesis, 2016.

[12] Tommaso Dreossi and Thao Dang. Parameter synthesis for polynomial biological models. In *Hybrid Systems: Computation and Control, HSCC*, pages 233–242, 2014.

[13] Tommaso Dreossi, Thao Dang, and Carla Piazza. Parallelotope bundles for polynomial reachability. In *Hybrid Systems: Computation and Control, HSCC*, pages 297–306, 2016.

[14] Tommaso Dreossi, Thao Dang, and Carla Piazza. Reachability computation for polynomial dynamical systems. *Formal Methods in System Design*, pages 1–38, 2017.

[15] Parasara Sridhar Duggirala, Sayan Mitra, Mahesh Viswanathan, and Matthew Potok. C2e2: a verification tool for stateflow models. In *International Conference on Tools and Algorithms for the Construction and Analysis of Systems*, pages 68–82. Springer, 2015.

[16] Goran Frehse, Colas Le Guernic, Alexandre Donzé, Scott Cotton, Rajarshi Ray, Olivier Lebeltel, Rodolfo Ripado, Antoine Girard, Thao Dang, and Oded Maler. Spaceex: Scalable verification of hybrid systems. In *Computer Aided Verification, CAV*, pages 379–395. Springer, 2011.

[17] Thomas A Henzinger, Pei-Hsin Ho, and Howard Wong-Toi. Hytech: A model checker for hybrid systems. In *Computer Aided Verification, CAV*, pages 460–463. Springer, 1997.

[18] Hui Kong, Ezio Bartocci, Sergiy Bogomolov, Radu Grosu, Thomas A Henzinger, Yu Jiang, and Christian Schilling. Discrete abstraction of multiaffine systems. In *International Workshop on Hybrid Systems Biology*, pages 128–144. Springer, 2016.

[19] Soonho Kong, Sicun Gao, Wei Chen, and Edmund Clarke. dreach: δ-reachability analysis for hybrid systems. In *Tools and Algorithms for the Construction and Analysis of Systems, TACAS*, pages 200–205. Springer, 2015.

[20] Oded Maler and Dejan Nickovic. Monitoring temporal properties of continuous signals. In *Formal Techniques, Modelling and Analysis of Timed and Fault-Tolerant Systems*, pages 152–166. Springer, 2004.

[21] André Platzer and Jan-David Quesel. Keymaera: A hybrid theorem prover for hybrid systems (system description). In *International Joint Conference on Automated Reasoning, IJCAR*, pages 171–178, 2008.

Forward Stochastic Reachability Analysis for Uncontrolled Linear Systems using Fourier Transforms

Abraham P. Vinod
Electrical & Comp. Eng.
University of New Mexico
Albuquerque, NM 87131, USA
aby.vinod@gmail.com

Baisravan HomChaudhuri
Electrical & Comp. Eng.
University of New Mexico
Albuquerque, NM 87131, USA
baisravan.hc@gmail.com

Meeko M. K. Oishi
Electrical & Comp. Eng.
University of New Mexico
Albuquerque, NM 87131, USA
oishi@unm.edu

ABSTRACT

We propose a scalable method for forward stochastic reachability analysis for uncontrolled linear systems with affine disturbance. Our method uses Fourier transforms to efficiently compute the forward stochastic reach probability measure (density) and the forward stochastic reach set. This method is applicable to systems with bounded or unbounded disturbance sets. We also examine the convexity properties of the forward stochastic reach set and its probability density. Motivated by the problem of a robot attempting to capture a stochastically moving, non-adversarial target, we demonstrate our method on two simple examples. Where traditional approaches provide approximations, our method provides exact analytical expressions for the densities and probability of capture.

CCS Concepts

•**Theory of computation** → **Stochastic control and optimization;** *Convex optimization;* •**Computing methodologies** → *Control methods;* Computational control theory;

Keywords

Stochastic reachability; Fourier transform; Convex optimization

1. INTRODUCTION

Reachability analysis of discrete-time dynamical systems with stochastic disturbance input is an established tool to provide probabilistic assurances of safety or performance and has been applied in several domains, including motion planning in robotics [1, 2], spacecraft docking [3], fishery management and mathematical finance [4], and autonomous surveilliance [5]. The computation of stochastic reachable and viable sets has been formulated within a dynamic programming framework [4, 6] that generalizes to discrete-time stochastic hybrid systems, and suffers from the well-known curse of dimensionality [7]. Recent work in computing stochastic reachable and viable sets aims to circumvent these computational challenges, through approximate dynamic programming [8–10], Gaussian mixtures [9], particle filters [3, 10], and convex chance-constrained optimization [3,5]. These methods have been applied to systems that are at most 6-dimensional [8] – far beyond the scope of what is possible with dynamic programming, but are not scalable to larger and more realistic scenarios.

We focus in particular on the forward stochastic reachable set, defined as the smallest closed set that covers all the reachable states. For LTI systems with bounded disturbances, established verification methods [11–13] can be adapted to overapproximate the forward stochastic reachable set. However, these methods return a trivial result with unbounded disturbances and do not address the forward stochastic reach probability measure, which provides the likelihood of reaching a given set of states.

We present a scalable method to perform forward stochastic reachability analysis of LTI systems with stochastic dynamics, that is, a method to compute the forward stochastic reachable set as well as its probability measure. We show that Fourier transforms can be used to provide exact reachability analysis, for systems with bounded or unbounded disturbances. We provide both iterative and analytical expressions for the probability density, and show that explicit expressions can be derived in some cases.

We are motivated by a particular application: pursuit of a dynamic, non-adversarial target [14]. Such a scenario may arise in e.g., the rescue of a lost first responder in a building on fire [15], capture of a non-aggressive UAV in an urban environment [16], or other non-antagonistic situations. Solutions for an adversarial target, based in a two-person, zero-sum differential game, can accommodate bounded disturbances with unknown stochasticity [17–21], but will be conservative for a non-adversarial target. We seek scalable solutions that synthesize an optimal controller for the non-adversarial scenario, by exploiting the forward reachable set and probability measure for the target. We analyze the convexity properties of the forward stochastic reach probability density and sets, and propose a convex optimization problem to provide the exact probabilistic guarantee of success and the corresponding optimal controller.

The main contributions of this paper are: 1) a method to efficiently compute the forward stochastic reach sets and the corresponding probability measure for linear systems with

HSCC '17, April 18–20, 2017, Pittsburgh, PA, USA

DOI: http://dx.doi.org/10.1145/3049797.3049818

uncertainty using Fourier transforms, 2) the convexity properties of the forward stochastic reach probability measure and sets, and 3) a convex formulation to maximize the probability of capture of a non-adversarial target with stochastic dynamics using the forward stochastic reachability analysis.

The paper is organized as follows: We define the forward stochastic reachability problem and review some properties from probability theory and Fourier analysis in Section 2. Section 3 formulates the forward stochastic reachability analysis for linear systems using Fourier transforms and provides convexity results for the probability measure and the stochastic reachable set. We apply the proposed method to solve the controller synthesis problem in Section 4, and provide conclusions and possible future work in Section 5.

2. PRELIMINARIES AND PROBLEM FORMULATION

In this section, we review some properties from probability theory and Fourier analysis relevant for our discussion and setup the problems. For detailed discussions on probability theory, see [22–25], and on Fourier analysis, see [26]. We denote random vectors with bold case and non-random vectors with an overline.

2.1 Preliminaries

A random vector $\boldsymbol{w} \in \mathbb{R}^p$ is defined in a probability space $(\mathcal{W}, \sigma(\mathcal{W}), \mathbb{P}_{\boldsymbol{w}})$. Given a sample space $\mathcal{W}$, the sigma-algebra $\sigma(\mathcal{W})$ provides a collection of measurable sets defined over $\mathcal{W}$. The sample space can be either countable (discrete random vector $\boldsymbol{w}$) or uncountable (continuous random vector $\boldsymbol{w}$). In this paper, we focus only on absolutely continuous random variables. For an absolutely continuous random vector, the probability measure defines a probability density function $\psi_{\boldsymbol{w}} : \mathbb{R}^p \rightarrow \mathbb{R}$ such that given a (Borel) set $\mathcal{B} \in \sigma(\mathcal{W})$, we have $\mathbb{P}_{\boldsymbol{w}}\{\boldsymbol{w} \in \mathcal{B}\} = \int_{\mathcal{B}} \psi_{\boldsymbol{w}}(\bar{z})d\bar{z}$. Here, $d\bar{z}$ is short for $dz_1 dz_2 \ldots dz_p$.

We will use the concept of support to define the forward stochastic reach set. The support of a random vector is the smallest closed set that will occur almost surely. Formally, the support of a random vector $\boldsymbol{w}$ is a unique *minimal* closed set $\mathrm{supp}(\boldsymbol{w}) \in \sigma(\mathcal{W})$ such that 1) $\mathbb{P}_{\boldsymbol{w}}\{\boldsymbol{w} \in \mathrm{supp}(\boldsymbol{w})\} = 1$, and 2) if $\mathcal{D} \in \sigma(\mathcal{W})$ such that $\mathbb{P}_{\boldsymbol{w}}\{\boldsymbol{w} \in \mathcal{D}\} = 1$, then $\mathrm{supp}(\boldsymbol{w}) \subseteq \mathcal{D}$ [22, Section 10, Ex. 12.9]. Alternatively, denoting the Euclidean ball of radius δ centered at $\bar{z}$ as $\mathrm{Ball}(\bar{z}, \delta)$, we have (1) which is equivalent to (2) via [27, Proposition 19.3.2],

$$\mathrm{supp}(\boldsymbol{w}) = \left\{ \bar{z} \in \mathcal{W} \middle| \forall \delta > 0, \int_{\mathrm{Ball}(\bar{z},\delta)} \psi_{\boldsymbol{w}}(\bar{z})d\bar{z} > 0 \right\} \tag{1}$$

$$= \mathcal{W} \setminus \{\bar{z} \in \mathcal{W} | \exists \delta > 0, \psi_{\boldsymbol{w}}(\bar{z}) = 0 \text{ a.e. in } \mathrm{Ball}(\bar{z}, \delta)\} \tag{2}$$

For a continuous $\psi_{\boldsymbol{w}}$, (2) is the support of the density [28, Section 8.8]. Denoting the closure of a set using $\mathrm{cl}(\cdot)$,

$$\mathrm{supp}(\boldsymbol{w}) = \mathrm{support}(\psi_{\boldsymbol{w}}) = \mathrm{cl}(\{\bar{z} \in \mathcal{W} | \psi_{\boldsymbol{w}}(\bar{z}) > 0\}). \tag{3}$$

The characteristic function (CF) of a random vector $\boldsymbol{w} \in \mathbb{R}^p$ with probability density function $\psi_{\boldsymbol{w}}(\bar{z})$ is

$$\Psi_{\boldsymbol{w}}(\bar{\alpha}) \triangleq \mathbb{E}_{\boldsymbol{w}}\left[\exp\left(j\bar{\alpha}^\top \boldsymbol{w}\right)\right] = \int_{\mathbb{R}^p} e^{j\bar{\alpha}^\top \bar{z}} \psi_{\boldsymbol{w}}(\bar{z})d\bar{z} = \mathscr{F}\left\{\psi_{\boldsymbol{w}}(\cdot)\right\}(-\bar{\alpha}) \tag{4}$$

where $\mathscr{F}\{\cdot\}$ denotes the Fourier transformation operator and $\bar{\alpha} \in \mathbb{R}^p$. Given a CF $\Psi_{\boldsymbol{w}}(\bar{\alpha})$, the density function can be computed as

$$\psi_{\boldsymbol{w}}(\bar{z}) = \mathscr{F}^{-1}\left\{\Psi_{\boldsymbol{w}}(\cdot)\right\}(-\bar{z}) = \left(\frac{1}{2\pi}\right)^p \int_{\mathbb{R}^p} e^{-j\bar{\alpha}^\top \bar{z}} \Psi_{\boldsymbol{w}}(\bar{\alpha})d\bar{\alpha} \tag{5}$$

where $\mathscr{F}^{-1}\{\cdot\}$ denotes the inverse Fourier transformation operator and $d\bar{\alpha}$ is short for $d\alpha_1 d\alpha_2 \ldots d\alpha_p$.

We define the $L^d(\mathbb{R}^p)$ spaces, $1 \leq d < \infty$, of measurable real-valued functions with finite L^d norm. The L^d norm of a density $\psi_{\boldsymbol{w}}$ is $\|\psi_{\boldsymbol{w}}\|_d \triangleq \left(\int_{\mathbb{R}^d} |\psi_{\boldsymbol{w}}(\bar{z})|^d d\bar{z}\right)^{1/d}$ where $|\cdot|$ denotes the absolute value. Here, $L^1(\mathbb{R}^p)$ is the space of absolutely integrable functions, and $L^2(\mathbb{R}^p)$ is the space of square-integrable functions. The Fourier transformation is defined for all functions in $L^1(\mathbb{R}^p)$ and all functions in $L^2(\mathbb{R}^p)$. Since probability densities are, by definition, in $L^1(\mathbb{R}^p)$, CFs exist for every probability density [26, Section 1]. Let $\boldsymbol{w}_1, \boldsymbol{w}_2 \in \mathbb{R}^p$ be random vectors with densities $\psi_{\boldsymbol{w}_1}$ and $\psi_{\boldsymbol{w}_2}$ and CFs $\Psi_{\boldsymbol{w}_1}$ and $\Psi_{\boldsymbol{w}_2}$ respectively. By definition, $\psi_{\boldsymbol{w}_1}, \psi_{\boldsymbol{w}_2} \in L^1(\mathbb{R}^p)$. Let $\bar{z}, \bar{z}_1, \bar{z}_2, \bar{\alpha}, \bar{\alpha}_1, \bar{\alpha}_2 \in \mathbb{R}^p, \bar{\beta} \in \mathbb{R}^n$.

P1) If $\boldsymbol{x} = \boldsymbol{w}_1 + \boldsymbol{w}_2$, then $\psi_{\boldsymbol{x}}(\bar{z}) = (\psi_{\boldsymbol{w}_1}(\cdot) * \psi_{\boldsymbol{w}_2}(\cdot))(\bar{z})$ and $\Psi_{\boldsymbol{x}}(\bar{\alpha}) = \Psi_{\boldsymbol{w}_1}(\bar{\alpha})\Psi_{\boldsymbol{w}_2}(\bar{\alpha})$ [24, Section 21.11]. Also, $\mathrm{supp}(\boldsymbol{x}) \subseteq \mathrm{cl}(\mathrm{supp}(\boldsymbol{w}_1) \oplus \mathrm{supp}(\boldsymbol{w}_2))$ [28, Lemma 8.15]. Here, $*$ denotes convolution and $\oplus$ Minkowski sum.

P2) If $\boldsymbol{x} = F\boldsymbol{w}_1 + G$ where $F \in \mathbb{R}^{n \times p}, G \in \mathbb{R}^n$ are matrices, $\Psi_{\boldsymbol{x}}(\bar{\beta}) = \exp\left(j\bar{\beta}^\top G\right)\Psi_{\boldsymbol{w}_1}(F^\top \bar{\beta})$ (from [24, Section 22.6] and [26, Equation 1.5]).

P3) If $\boldsymbol{w}_1$ and $\boldsymbol{w}_2$ are independent vectors, then $\boldsymbol{x} = [\boldsymbol{w}_1^\top\ \boldsymbol{w}_2^\top]^\top$ has probability density $\psi_{\boldsymbol{x}}(\bar{z}) = \psi_{\boldsymbol{w}_1}(\bar{z}_1)\psi_{\boldsymbol{w}_2}(\bar{z}_2), \bar{z} = [\bar{z}_1^\top\ \bar{z}_2^\top]^\top \in \mathbb{R}^{2p}$ and CF $\Psi_{\boldsymbol{x}}(\bar{\gamma}) = \Psi_{\boldsymbol{w}_1}(\bar{\alpha}_1)\Psi_{\boldsymbol{w}_2}(\bar{\alpha}_2), \bar{\gamma} = [\bar{\alpha}_1^\top\ \bar{\alpha}_2^\top]^\top \in \mathbb{R}^{2p}$ [24, Section 22.4].

P4) The marginal probability density of any group of k components selected from the random vector $\boldsymbol{w}_1$ is obtained by setting the remaining $p-k$ Fourier variables in the CF to zero [24, Section 22.4].

An additional assumption of square-integrability of the probability density of the random variable $\boldsymbol{w}_3 \in \mathbb{R}^p$ results in $\psi_{\boldsymbol{w}_3} \in L^1(\mathbb{R}^p) \cap L^2(\mathbb{R}^p)$. Along with Properties P1-P4, $\psi_{\boldsymbol{w}_3}$ satisfies the following property:

P5) The Fourier transform preserves the inner product in $L^2(\mathbb{R}^p)$ [26, Theorem 2.3]. Given a square-integrable function $h(\bar{z})$ with Fourier transform $H(\bar{\alpha}) = \mathscr{F}\{h(\cdot)\}(\bar{\alpha})$ and a square-integrable probability density $\psi_{\boldsymbol{w}_3}$,

$$\int_{\mathbb{R}^p} \psi_{\boldsymbol{w}_3}(\bar{z})^\dagger h(\bar{z})d\bar{z} = \left(\frac{1}{2\pi}\right)^p \int_{\mathbb{R}^p} \left(\mathscr{F}\left\{\psi_{\boldsymbol{w}_3}(\cdot)\right\}(\bar{\alpha})\right)^\dagger \times H(\bar{\alpha})d\bar{\alpha}$$

Here, $\dagger$ denotes complex conjugation.

Lemma 1. *For square-integrable $\psi_{\boldsymbol{w}_3}$ and h,*

$$\int_{\mathbb{R}^p} \psi_{\boldsymbol{w}_3}(\bar{z})h(\bar{z})d\bar{z} = \left(\frac{1}{2\pi}\right)^p \int_{\mathbb{R}^p} \Psi_{\boldsymbol{w}_3}(\bar{\alpha})H(\bar{\alpha})d\bar{\alpha}. \tag{6}$$

Proof: Follows from Property P5, (5), and [24, Section 10.6]. Since probability densities are real functions, $(\psi_{\boldsymbol{w}_3}(\bar{z}))^\dagger = \psi_{\boldsymbol{w}_3}(\bar{z})$ and $(\mathscr{F}\{\psi_{\boldsymbol{w}_3}(\cdot)\}(\bar{\alpha}))^\dagger = \Psi_{\boldsymbol{w}_3}(\bar{\alpha})$. ■

2.2 Problem formulation

Consider the discrete-time linear time-invariant system,

$$\boldsymbol{x}[t+1] = A\boldsymbol{x}[t] + B\boldsymbol{w}[t] \tag{7}$$

with state $\boldsymbol{x}[t] \in \mathcal{X} \subseteq \mathbb{R}^n$, disturbance $\boldsymbol{w}[t] \in \mathcal{W} \subseteq \mathbb{R}^p$, and matrices A, B of appropriate dimensions. Let $\bar{x}_0 \in \mathcal{X}$ be the given initial state and T be the finite time horizon. The disturbance set $\mathcal{W}$ is an uncountable set which can be either bounded or unbounded, and the random vector $\boldsymbol{w}[t]$ is defined in a probability space $(\mathcal{W}, \sigma(\mathcal{W}), \mathbb{P}_{\boldsymbol{w}})$. The random vector $\boldsymbol{w}[t]$ is assumed to be absolutely continuous with a known density function $\psi_{\boldsymbol{w}}$. The disturbance process $\boldsymbol{w}[\cdot]$ is assumed to be a random process with an independent and identical distribution (IID).

The dynamics in (7) are quite general and includes affine noise perturbed LTI discrete-time systems with known state-feedback based inputs. An additional affine term in (7) can include affine noise perturbed LTI discrete-time systems with known open-loop controllers. For time $\tau \in [1, T]$,

$$\boldsymbol{x}[\tau] = A^\tau \bar{x}_0 + \mathscr{C}_{n\times(\tau p)}\boldsymbol{W} \tag{8}$$

with $\mathscr{C}_{n\times(\tau p)} = [B\ AB\ A^2B\ \ldots\ A^{\tau-1}B] \in \mathbb{R}^{n\times(\tau p)}$ and $\boldsymbol{W} = [\boldsymbol{w}^\top[\tau-1]\ \boldsymbol{w}^\top[\tau-2]\ \ldots\ \boldsymbol{w}^\top[0]]^\top$ as a random vector defined by the sequence of random vectors $\{\boldsymbol{w}[t]\}_{t=0}^{t=\tau-1}$. For any given τ, the random vector $\boldsymbol{W}$ is defined in the product space $(\mathcal{W}^\tau, \sigma(\mathcal{W}^\tau), \mathbb{P}_{\boldsymbol{W}})$ where $\mathcal{W}^\tau = \bigtimes_{t=0}^{\tau} \mathcal{W}$ and $\mathbb{P}_{\boldsymbol{W}} = \prod_{t=0}^{\tau} \mathbb{P}_{\boldsymbol{w}}$, $\psi_{\boldsymbol{W}} = \prod_{t=0}^{\tau} \psi_{\boldsymbol{w}}$ by the IID assumption of the random process $\boldsymbol{w}[\cdot]$. From (8), the state $\boldsymbol{x}[\cdot]$ is a random process with the random vector at each instant $\boldsymbol{x}[t]$ defined in the probability space $(\mathcal{X}, \sigma(\mathcal{X}), \mathbb{P}_{\boldsymbol{x}}^{t,\bar{x}_0})$ where the probability measure $\mathbb{P}_{\boldsymbol{x}}^{t,\bar{x}_0}$ is induced from $\mathbb{P}_{\boldsymbol{W}}$. We denote the random process originating from $\bar{x}_0$ as $\boldsymbol{\xi}[\cdot;\bar{x}_0]$ where for all t, $\boldsymbol{\xi}[t;\bar{x}_0] = \boldsymbol{x}[t]$, and let $\bar{Z} = [\bar{z}^\top[\tau-1]\ \bar{z}^\top[\tau-2]\ \ldots\ \bar{z}^\top[0]]^\top \in \mathbb{R}^{\tau p}$ denote a realization of the random vector $\boldsymbol{W}$.

An iterative method for the forward stochastic reachability analysis (FSR analysis) is given in [1] [29, Section 10.5]. However, for systems perturbed by continuous random variables, the numerical implementation of the iterative approach becomes erroneous for larger time instants due to the iterative numerical evaluation of improper integrals, motivating the need for an alternative implementable approach.

Problem 1. *Given the dynamics (7) with initial state $\bar{x}_0$, construct analytical expressions at time instant τ for*

1. *the smallest closed set that covers all the reachable states (i.e., the forward stochastic reach set), and*
2. *the probability measure over the forward stochastic reach set (i.e., the forward stochastic reach probability measure)*

that do not require an iterative approach.

We are additionally interested in applying the forward stochastic reachable set (FSR set) and probability measure (FSRPM) to the problem of capturing a non-adversarial target. Specifically, we seek a convex formulation to the problem of capturing a non-adversarial target. This requires convexity of the FSR set and concavity of the objective function defined on the probability of successful capture.

Problem 2. *For a finite time horizon, find a) a convex formulation for the maximization of the probability of capture of a non-adversarial target with known stochastic dynamics and initial state, and b) the resulting optimal controller that a deterministic robot must employ when there is a non-zero probability of capture.*

Problem 2.a. *Characterize the sufficient conditions for log-concavity of the FSRPM and convexity of the FSR set.*

3. FORWARD STOCHASTIC REACHABILITY ANALYSIS

The existence of forward stochastic reach probability density (FSRPD) for systems of the form (7) has been demonstrated in [29, Section 10.5]. For any $\tau \in [1, T]$, the probability of the state reaching a set $\mathcal{S} \in \sigma(\mathcal{X})$ at time τ starting at $\bar{x}_0$ is defined using the FSRPM $\mathbb{P}_{\boldsymbol{x}}^{\tau,\bar{x}_0}$,

$$\mathbb{P}_{\boldsymbol{x}}^{\tau,\bar{x}_0}\{\boldsymbol{x}[\tau] \in \mathcal{S}\} = \int_{\mathcal{S}} \psi_{\boldsymbol{x}}(\bar{y};\tau,\bar{x}_0)d\bar{y}, \quad \bar{y} \in \mathbb{R}^n. \tag{9}$$

Since the disturbance set $\mathcal{W}$ is uncountable, we focus on the computation of the FSRPD $\psi_{\boldsymbol{x}}$, and use (9) to link it to the FSRPM. We have discussed the countable case in [1].

We define the forward stochastic reach set (FSR set) as the support of the random vector $\boldsymbol{\xi}[\tau;\bar{x}_0] = \boldsymbol{x}[\tau]$ at $\tau \in [1, T]$ when the initial condition is $\bar{x}_0 \in \mathcal{X}$. From (3), for a continuous FSRPD,

$$\mathrm{FSReach}(\tau, \bar{x}_0) = \mathrm{cl}(\{\bar{y} \in \mathcal{X} | \psi_{\boldsymbol{x}}(\bar{y};\tau,\bar{x}_0) > 0\}) \subseteq \mathcal{X}. \tag{10}$$

Lemma 2. $\mathcal{S} \cap \mathrm{FSReach}(\tau, \bar{x}_0) = \emptyset \Rightarrow \mathbb{P}_{\boldsymbol{x}}^{\tau,\bar{x}_0}\{\boldsymbol{x}[\tau] \in \mathcal{S}\} = 0.$

Proof: Follows from (2). ■

Note that when the disturbance set $\mathcal{W}$ is unbounded, the definition of the FSR set (10) might trivially become $\mathbb{R}^n$. Also, for uncountable $\mathcal{W}$, the probability of the state taking a particular value is zero, and therefore, the superlevel sets of the FSRPD do not have the same interpretation as in the countable case [1]. However, given the FSRPD, we can obtain the likelihood that the state of (7) will reach a particular set of interest via (9) and the FSR set via (10).

3.1 Iterative method for reachability analysis

We extend the iterative approach for the FSR analysis proposed in [1] for a nonlinear discrete-time systems with discrete random variables to a linear discrete-time system with continuous random variables. This discussion, inspired in part by [29, Section 10.5], helps to develop proofs presented later.

Assume that the system matrix A of (7) is invertible. This assumption holds for continuous-time systems which have been discretized via Euler method. For $\tau \in [0, T-1]$, we have from (7) and Property P1,

$$\psi_{\boldsymbol{x}}(\bar{y};\tau+1,\bar{x}_0) = \left(\psi_{A\boldsymbol{x}}(\cdot;\tau,\bar{x}_0) * \psi_{B\boldsymbol{w}}(\cdot)\right)(\bar{y}) \tag{11}$$

with

$$\psi_{A\boldsymbol{x}}(\bar{y};\tau,\bar{x}_0) = |A|^{-1}\psi_{\boldsymbol{x}}(A^{-1}\bar{y};\tau,\bar{x}_0) \tag{12}$$

$\psi_{A\boldsymbol{x}}(\bar{y};\tau,\bar{x}_0) = (\det A)^{-1}\psi_{\boldsymbol{x}}(A^{-1}\bar{y};\tau,\bar{x}_0)$ from [23, Example 8.9] for $\tau \geq 1$, $\psi_{A\boldsymbol{x}}(\bar{y};0,\bar{x}_0) = \delta(\bar{y} - A\bar{x}_0)$ where $\delta(\cdot)$ is the Dirac-delta function [30, Chapter 5], and $\psi_{B\boldsymbol{w}}$ as the probability density of the random vector $B\boldsymbol{w}$. We use Property P2 and (5) to obtain $\psi_{B\boldsymbol{w}}$ [26, Corollary 1]. Equation (11) is a special case of the result in [29, Section 10.5]. We extend the FSR set computation presented in [1] in the following lemma.

Lemma 3. *For $\tau \in [1,T]$, closed disturbance set $\mathcal{W}$, and the system in (7) with initial condition $\bar{x}_0$,* $\mathrm{FSReach}(\tau,\bar{x}_0) \subseteq A(\mathrm{FSReach}(\tau-1,\bar{x}_0)) \oplus B\mathcal{W} = \{A^\tau \bar{x}_0\} \oplus \mathscr{C}_{n\times(\tau p)}\mathcal{W}^\tau$.

Proof: Follows from (7), (8), and Property P1. ■

Lemma 3 allows the use of existing reachability analysis schemes designed for bounded non-stochastic disturbance models [11–13] for overapproximating FSR sets. Also, (10) and (11) provide an iterative method for exact FSR analysis.

Note that (11) is an improper integral which must be solved iteratively. For densities whose convolution integrals are difficult to obtain analytically, we would need to rely on numerical integration (quadrature) techniques. Numerical evaluation of multi-dimensional improper integrals is computationally expensive [31, Section 4.8]. Moreover, the quadratures in this method will become increasingly erroneous for larger values of $\tau \in [1,T]$ due to the iterative definition. These disadvantages motivate the need to solve Problem 1 — an approach that provides analytical expressions of the FSRPD, and thereby reduce the number of quadratures required. The iterative method performs well with discrete random vectors as in [1] because discretization for computation can be exact, however, this is clearly not true when the disturbance set is uncountable.

3.2 Efficient reachability analysis via characteristic functions

We employ Fourier transformation to provide analytical expressions of the FSRPD at any instant $\tau \in [1,T]$. This method involves computing a single integral for the time instant of interest τ as opposed to the iterative approach in Subsection 3.1. We also show that for certain disturbance distributions like the Gaussian distribution, an explicit expression for the FSRPD can be obtained.

By Property P3 and the IID assumption on the random process $\boldsymbol{w}[\cdot]$, the CF of the random vector $\boldsymbol{W}$ is

$$\Psi_{\boldsymbol{W}}(\bar{\alpha}) = \prod_{t=0}^{t=\tau-1} \Psi_{\boldsymbol{w}}(\bar{\alpha}_t) \tag{13}$$

where $\bar{\alpha} = [\bar{\alpha}_0^\top\ \bar{\alpha}_1^\top\ \ldots\ \bar{\alpha}_{\tau-1}^\top]^\top \in \mathbb{R}^{(\tau p)}$, $\bar{\alpha}_t \in \mathbb{R}^p$ for all $\tau \in [0,\tau-1]$. As seen in (8), the random vector $\boldsymbol{W}$ concatenates the disturbance random process $\boldsymbol{w}[t]$ over $t \in [0,\tau-1]$.

Theorem 1. *For any time instant $\tau \in [1,T]$ and an initial state $\bar{x}_0 \in \mathcal{X}$, the FSRPD $\psi_{\boldsymbol{x}}(\cdot;\tau,\bar{x}_0)$ of (7) is given by*

$$\Psi_{\boldsymbol{x}}(\bar{\alpha};\tau,\bar{x}_0) = \exp\left(j\bar{\alpha}^\top(A^\tau\bar{x}_0)\right)\Psi_{\boldsymbol{W}}(\mathscr{C}_{n\times(\tau p)}^\top\bar{\alpha}) \tag{14}$$

$$\psi_{\boldsymbol{x}}(\bar{y};\tau,\bar{x}_0) = \mathscr{F}^{-1}\left\{\Psi_{\boldsymbol{x}}(\bar{\alpha};\tau,\bar{x}_0)\right\}(-\bar{y}) \tag{15}$$

where $\bar{y} \in \mathcal{X}, \bar{\alpha} \in \mathbb{R}^{n\times 1}$.

Proof: Follows from Property P2, (5), and (8). ■

Theorem 1 provides an analytical expression for the FSRPD. Theorem 1 holds even if we relax the identical distribution assumption on the random process $\boldsymbol{w}[t]$ to a time-varying independent disturbance process, provided $\Psi_{\boldsymbol{w}[t]}(\cdot)$ is known for all $t \in [0,\tau-1]$. Using Property P2, Theorem 1 can also be easily extended to include affine noise perturbed LTI discrete-time systems with known open-loop controllers.

Note that the computation of the FSRPD via Theorem 1 does not require gridding of the state space, hence mitigating the curse of dimensionality associated with the traditional gridding-based approaches. When the CF $\Psi_{\boldsymbol{x}}(\bar{\alpha};\tau,\bar{x}_0)$ has the structure of known Fourier transforms, Theorem 1 can be used to provide explicit expressions for the FSRPD (see Proposition 1). In systems where the inverse Fourier transform is not known, the evaluation of (15) can be done via any quadrature techniques that can handle improper integrals. Alternatively, the improper integral can be approximated by the quadrature of an appropriately defined proper integral [31, Chapter 4]. For high-dimensional systems, performance is affected by the scalability of quadrature schemes with dimension. However, Theorem 1 still requires only a single n-dimensional quadrature for any time instant of interest $\tau \in [1,T]$. On the other hand, the iterative method proposed in Subsection 3.1 requires τ quadratures, each n-dimensional, resulting in higher computational costs and degradation in accuracy as τ increases.

One example of a CF with known Fourier transforms arises in Gaussian distributions. We use Theorem 1 to derive an explicit expression for the FSRPD of (7) when perturbed by a Gaussian random vector. Note that the FSRPD in this case can also be computed using the well-known properties on linear combination of Gaussian random vectors [23, Section 9] or the theory of Kalman-Bucy filter [32].

Proposition 1. *The system trajectory of (7) with initial condition $\bar{x}_0$ and noise process $\boldsymbol{w} \sim \mathcal{N}(\bar{\mu}_{\boldsymbol{w}},\Sigma_{\boldsymbol{w}}) \in \mathbb{R}^p$ is*

$$\boldsymbol{\xi}[\tau;\bar{x}_0] \sim \mathcal{N}(\bar{\mu}[\tau],\Sigma[\tau]) \tag{16}$$

where $\tau \in [1,T]$ and

$$\bar{\mu}[\tau] = A^\tau\bar{x}_0 + \mathscr{C}_{n\times(\tau p)}(\bar{1}_{\tau\times 1}\otimes\bar{\mu}_{\boldsymbol{w}}), \tag{17}$$

$$\Sigma[\tau] = \mathscr{C}_{n\times(\tau p)}(I_\tau\otimes\Sigma_{\boldsymbol{w}})\mathscr{C}_{n\times(\tau p)}^\top. \tag{18}$$

Proof: For $\bar{\alpha} \in \mathbb{R}^p$, the CF of a multivariate Gaussian random vector $\boldsymbol{w}$ is [23, Section 9.3]

$$\Psi_{\boldsymbol{w}}(\bar{\alpha}) = \exp\left(j\bar{\alpha}^\top\bar{\mu}_{\boldsymbol{w}} - \frac{\bar{\alpha}^\top\Sigma_{\boldsymbol{w}}\bar{\alpha}}{2}\right). \tag{19}$$

From the IID assumption of $\boldsymbol{w}[\cdot]$, Property P3, and (19), the CF of $\boldsymbol{W}$ is

$$\begin{aligned}\Psi_{\boldsymbol{W}}(\bar{\alpha}) &= \prod_{t=0}^{t=\tau-1}\exp\left(j\bar{\alpha}_t^\top\bar{\mu}_{\boldsymbol{w}} - \frac{\bar{\alpha}_t^\top\Sigma_{\boldsymbol{w}}\bar{\alpha}_t}{2}\right)\\ &= \exp\left(j\bar{\alpha}^\top(\bar{1}_{\tau\times 1}\otimes\bar{\mu}_{\boldsymbol{w}}) - \frac{\bar{\alpha}^\top(I_\tau\otimes\Sigma_{\boldsymbol{w}})\bar{\alpha}}{2}\right)\end{aligned}$$

where $\bar{\alpha} = (\bar{\alpha}_0,\bar{\alpha}_1,\ldots,\bar{\alpha}_{\tau-1}) \in \mathbb{R}^{(\tau p)}$ with $\bar{\alpha}_t \in \mathbb{R}^p$. Here, $\bar{1}_{p\times q} \in \mathbb{R}^{p\times q}$ is a matrix with all entries as 1, and I_n is the identity matrix of dimension n. By (15) and (19), $\boldsymbol{W} \sim \mathcal{N}(\bar{1}_{\tau\times 1}\otimes\bar{\mu}_{\boldsymbol{w}}, I_\tau\otimes\Sigma_{\boldsymbol{w}})$ [26, Corollary 1.22]. From (14), we see that for $\bar{\beta} \in \mathbb{R}^n$,

$$\begin{aligned}\Psi_{\boldsymbol{x}}(\bar{\beta};\tau,\bar{x}_0) &= \exp\left(j\bar{\beta}^\top(A^\tau\bar{x}_0)\right)\Psi_{\boldsymbol{W}}(\mathscr{C}_{n\times(\tau p)}^\top\bar{\beta}))\\ &= \exp\left(j\bar{\beta}^\top(A^\tau\bar{x}_0 + \mathscr{C}_{n\times(\tau p)}(\bar{1}_{\tau\times 1}\otimes\bar{\mu}_{\boldsymbol{w}}))\right)\times\\ &\exp\left(-\frac{\bar{\beta}^\top\mathscr{C}_{n\times(\tau p)}(I_\tau\otimes\Sigma_{\boldsymbol{w}})\mathscr{C}_{n\times(\tau p)}^\top\bar{\beta}}{2}\right).\end{aligned} \tag{20}$$

Equation (20) is the CF of a multivariate Gaussian random vector [26, Corollary 1.22], and we obtain $\mu_G[\tau]$ and $\Sigma_G[\tau]$ using (19). ■

Depending on the system dynamics and time instant of interest τ, we can have $\mathrm{rank}(\mathscr{C}_{n\times(\tau p)}) < n$. In such cases, the support of the random vector $\boldsymbol{x}[\tau]$ will be restricted to sets of lower dimension than n [33, Section 8.5], and certain marginal densities can be Dirac-delta functions. For example, we see that turning off the effect of disturbance in (7) (setting $B = 0 \Rightarrow \mathscr{C}_{n\times(\tau p)} = 0$ in Theorem 1) yields $\psi_{\boldsymbol{x}}(\bar{y};\tau,\bar{x}_0) = \delta(\bar{y} - A^{\tau}\bar{x}_0)$, the trajectory of the corresponding deterministic system. We have used the relation $\mathscr{F}\{\delta(\bar{y}-\bar{y}_0)\}(\bar{\alpha}) = \exp(j\bar{\alpha}^\top \bar{y}_0)$ [30, Chapters 5,6].

Theorem 1 and (10) provide an analytical expression for the FSRPD and the FSR set respectively, and thereby solve Problem 1 for any density function describing the stochastics of the perturbation $\boldsymbol{w}[t]$ in (7).

3.3 Convexity results for reachability analysis

For computational tractability, it is useful to study the convexity properties of the FSRPD and the FSR sets. We define the random vector $\boldsymbol{w}_B = B\boldsymbol{w}$ with density $\psi_{\boldsymbol{w}_B}$.

Lemma 4. *[25, Lemma 2.1] If $\psi_{\boldsymbol{w}}$ is a log-concave distribution, then $\psi_{\boldsymbol{w}_B}$ is a log-concave distribution.*

Theorem 2. *If $\psi_{\boldsymbol{w}}$ is a log-concave distribution, and A in (7) is invertible, then the FSRPD $\psi_{\boldsymbol{x}}(\bar{y};\tau,\bar{x}_0)$ of (7) is log-concave in $\bar{y}$ for every $\tau \in [1, T]$.*

Proof: We prove this theorem via induction. First, we need to show that the base case is true, i.e, we need to show that $\psi_{\boldsymbol{x}}(\bar{y}; 1, \bar{x}_0)$ is log-concave in $\bar{y}$. From (7) and Lemma 4, we have a log-concave density $\psi_{\boldsymbol{x}}(\bar{y}; 1, \bar{x}_0) = \psi_{\boldsymbol{w}_B}(\bar{y} - A\bar{x}_0)$ since affine transformations preserve log-concavity [34, Section 3.2.4]. Assume for induction, $\psi_{\boldsymbol{x}}(\bar{y};\tau,\bar{x}_0)$ is log-concave in $\bar{y}$ for some $\tau \in [1, T]$. We have log-concave $\psi_{A\boldsymbol{x}}(\bar{y};\tau,\bar{x}_0)$ from (12). Since convolution preserves log-concavity [34, Section 3.5.2], Lemma 4 and (11) complete the proof. ∎

Corollary 1. *If $\psi_{\boldsymbol{w}}$ is a log-concave distribution,* $\mathrm{FSReach}(\tau, \bar{x}_0)$ *of the system (7) is convex for every $\tau \in [1, T]$, $\bar{x}_0 \in \mathcal{X}$.*

Proof: Follows from (10) and [25, Theorem 2.5]. ∎

Theorem 2 and Corollary 1 solve Problem 2.a.

4. REACHING A NON-ADVERSARIAL TARGET WITH STOCHASTIC DYNAMICS

In this section, we will leverage the theory developed in this paper to solve Problem 2 efficiently.

We consider the problem of a controlled robot (R) having to capture a stochastically moving non-adversarial target, denoted here by a goal robot (G). The robot R has controllable linear dynamics while the robot G has uncontrollable linear dynamics, perturbed by an absolutely continuous random vector. The robot R is said to capture robot G if the robot G is inside a pre-determined set defined around the current position of robot R. We seek an *open-loop* controller (independent of the current state of robot G) for the robot R which maximizes the probability of capturing robot G within the time horizon T. The information available to solve this problem are the position of the robots R and G at $t = 0$, the deterministic dynamics of the robot R, the perturbed dynamics of the robot G, and the density of the perturbation. We consider a 2-D environment, but our approach can be easily extended to higher dimensions. We perform the FSR analysis in the inertial coordinate frame.

We model the robot R as a point mass system discretized in time,

$$\bar{x}_R[t+1] = \bar{x}_R[t] + B_R\bar{u}_R[t] \tag{21}$$

with state (position) $\bar{x}_R[t] \in \mathbb{R}^2$, input $\bar{u}_R[t] \in \mathcal{U} \subseteq \mathbb{R}^2$, input matrix $B_R = T_s I_2$ and sampling time T_s. We define an open-loop control policy $\bar{u}_R[t] = \pi_{\mathrm{open},\bar{x}_R[0]}[t]$ where $\pi_{\mathrm{open},\bar{x}_R[0]}[t]$ depends on the initial condition, that is, $\pi_{\mathrm{open},\bar{x}_R[0]} : [0, T-1] \to \mathcal{U}$ is a sequence of control actions for a given initial condition $\bar{x}_R[0]$. Let $\mathcal{M}$ denote the set of all feasible control policies $\pi_{\mathrm{open},\bar{x}_R[0]}$. From (8),

$$\bar{x}_R[\tau+1] = \bar{x}_R[0] + (\bar{1}_{1\times\tau} \otimes B_R)\bar{\pi}_\tau,\ \tau \in [0, T-1] \tag{22}$$

with the input vector $\bar{\pi}_\tau = [\bar{u}_R^\top[\tau-1]\ \bar{u}_R^\top[\tau-2]\ \ldots\ \bar{u}_R^\top[0]]^\top$, $\bar{\pi}_\tau \in \overline{\mathcal{M}}_\tau \subseteq \mathbb{R}^{(2\tau)}$, and $\bar{u}_R[t] = \pi_{\mathrm{open},\bar{x}_R[0]}[t]$.

We consider two cases for the dynamics of the robot G: 1) point mass dynamics, and 2) double integrator dynamics, both discretized in time and perturbed by an absolutely continuous random vector. In the former case, we presume that the velocity is drawn from a bivariate Gaussian distribution,

$$\boldsymbol{x}_G[t+1] = \boldsymbol{x}_G[t] + B_{\mathrm{G,PM}}\boldsymbol{v}_G[t] \tag{23a}$$

$$\boldsymbol{v}_G[t] \sim \mathcal{N}(\bar{\mu}_G^{\boldsymbol{v}}, \Sigma_G). \tag{23b}$$

The state (position) is the random vector $\boldsymbol{x}_G[t]$ in the probability space $(\mathcal{X}, \sigma(\mathcal{X}), \mathbb{P}_{\boldsymbol{x}_G}^{t,\bar{x}_G[0]})$ with $\mathcal{X} = \mathbb{R}^2$, disturbance matrix $B_{\mathrm{G,PM}} = B_R$, and $\bar{x}_G[0]$ as the known initial state of the robot G. The stochastic velocity $\boldsymbol{v}_G[t] \in \mathbb{R}^2$ has mean vector $\bar{\mu}_G^{\boldsymbol{v}}$, covariance matrix Σ_G and the CF with $\bar{\alpha} \in \mathbb{R}^2$ is given in (19). In the latter case, acceleration in each direction is an independent exponential random variable,

$$\boldsymbol{x}_G[t+1] = A_{\mathrm{G,DI}}\boldsymbol{x}_G[t] + B_{\mathrm{G,DI}}\boldsymbol{a}[t] \tag{24a}$$

$$(\boldsymbol{a}[t])_{\mathrm{x}} \sim \mathrm{Exp}(\lambda_{\mathrm{ax}}),\quad (\boldsymbol{a}[t])_{\mathrm{y}} \sim \mathrm{Exp}(\lambda_{\mathrm{ay}}) \tag{24b}$$

$$A_{\mathrm{G,DI}} = I_2 \otimes \begin{bmatrix} 1 & T_s \\ 0 & 1 \end{bmatrix}, B_{\mathrm{G,DI}} = I_2 \otimes \begin{bmatrix} \frac{T_s^2}{2} \\ T_s \end{bmatrix}.$$

The state (position and velocity) is the random vector $\boldsymbol{x}_G[t]$ in the probability space $(\mathcal{X}_{\mathrm{DI}}, \sigma(\mathcal{X}_{\mathrm{DI}}), \mathbb{P}_{\boldsymbol{x}_G}^{t,\bar{x}_G[0]})$ with $\mathcal{X}_{\mathrm{DI}} = \mathbb{R}^4$ and $\bar{x}_G[0]$ as the known initial state of the robot G. The stochastic acceleration $\boldsymbol{a}[t] = [(\boldsymbol{a}[t])_{\mathrm{x}}\ (\boldsymbol{a}[t])_{\mathrm{y}}]^\top \in \mathbb{R}_+^2 = [0,\infty) \times [0,\infty)$ has the following probability density and CF ($\bar{z} = [z_1\ z_2]^\top \in \mathbb{R}_+^2 = [0,\infty)\times[0,\infty), \bar{\alpha} = [\alpha_1\ \alpha_2]^\top \in \mathbb{R}^2$),

$$\psi_{\boldsymbol{a}}(\bar{z}) = \lambda_{\mathrm{ax}}\lambda_{\mathrm{ay}}\exp(-\lambda_{\mathrm{ax}}z_1 - \lambda_{\mathrm{ay}}z_2) \tag{25}$$

$$\Psi_{\boldsymbol{a}}(\bar{\alpha}) = \frac{\lambda_{\mathrm{ax}}\lambda_{\mathrm{ay}}}{(\lambda_{\mathrm{ax}} - j\alpha_1)(\lambda_{\mathrm{ay}} - j\alpha_2)}. \tag{26}$$

The CF $\Psi_{\boldsymbol{a}}(\bar{\alpha})$ is defined using Property P3 and the CF of the exponential given in [22, Section 26].

Formally, the robot R captures robot G at time τ if $\boldsymbol{x}_G[\tau] \in \mathrm{CaptureSet}(\bar{x}_R[\tau])$. In other words, the capture region of the robot R is the $\mathrm{CaptureSet}(\bar{y}) \subseteq \mathbb{R}^2$ when robot R is at $\bar{y} \in \mathbb{R}^2$. The optimization problem to solve Problem 2 is

$$\mathrm{ProbA}: \quad \begin{array}{ll} \text{maximize} & \mathrm{CapturePr}_{\bar{\pi}}(\tau, \bar{\pi}_\tau; \bar{x}_R[0], \bar{x}_G[0]) \\ \text{subject to} & (\tau, \bar{\pi}_\tau) \in [1, T] \times \overline{\mathcal{M}}_\tau \end{array}$$

where the decision variables are the time of capture τ and the control policy $\bar{\pi}$, and the objective function $\mathrm{CapturePr}_{\bar{\pi}}(\cdot)$ gives the probability of robot R capturing robot G. By (22), an initial state $\bar{x}_R[0]$ and the control policy $\bar{\pi}_t$ determines a unique $\bar{x}_R[\tau]$ for every τ. Using this observation, we define the objective function $\mathrm{CapturePr}_{\bar{\pi}}(\cdot)$ in (27). We obtain $\psi_{\boldsymbol{x}_G}$ in (27) using our solution to Problem 1, Theorem 1.

$$\text{CapturePr}_{\bar{\pi}}(\tau,\bar{\pi}_\tau;\bar{x}_R[0],\bar{x}_G[0]) = \text{CapturePr}_{\bar{x}_R}(\tau,\bar{x}_R[\tau];\bar{x}_G[0]) = \mathbb{P}^{\tau,\bar{x}_G[0]}_{\boldsymbol{x}_G}\{\boldsymbol{x}_G[\tau]\in \text{CaptureSet}(\bar{x}_R[\tau])\}$$
$$= \int_{\text{CaptureSet}(\bar{x}_R[\tau])} \psi_{\boldsymbol{x}_G}(\bar{y};\tau,\bar{x}_G[0])d\bar{y}. \quad (27)$$

Problem ProbA is equivalent (see [34, Section 4.1.3]) to

$$\text{ProbB}: \quad \begin{array}{ll} \text{maximize} & \text{CapturePr}_{\bar{x}_R}(\tau,\bar{x}_R[\tau];\bar{x}_G[0]) \\ \text{subject to} & \left\{ \begin{array}{ll} \tau & \in [1,T] \\ \bar{x}_R[\tau] & \in \text{Reach}_R(\tau;\bar{x}_R[0]) \end{array}\right. \end{array}$$

where the decision variables are the time of capture τ and the position of the robot R $\bar{x}_R[\tau]$ at time τ. From (22), we define the reach set for the robot R at time τ as

$$\text{Reach}_R(\tau;\bar{x}_R[0]) = \{\bar{y}\in\mathcal{X} | \exists \bar{\pi}_\tau \in \overline{\mathcal{M}}_\tau \text{ s.t. } \bar{x}_R[\tau]=\bar{y}\}.$$

Several deterministic reachability computation tools are available for the computation of $\text{Reach}_R(\tau;\bar{x}_R[0])$, like MPT [35] and ET [12]. We will now formulate Problem ProbB as a convex optimization problem based on the results developed in Subsection 3.3.

Lemma 5. *[11] If the input space $\mathcal{U}$ is convex, the forward reach set $\text{Reach}_R(\tau;\bar{x}_R[0])$ is convex.*

Proposition 2. *If $\psi_{\boldsymbol{w}}$ is a log-concave distributions and $\text{CaptureSet}(\bar{y})$ is convex for all $\bar{y}\in\mathcal{X}$, then $\text{CapturePr}_{\bar{x}_R}(\tau,\bar{y};\bar{x}_G[0])$ is log-concave in $\bar{y}$ for all τ.*

Proof: From Theorem 2, we know that $\psi_{\boldsymbol{x}}(\bar{y};\tau,\bar{x}_R[0])$ is log-concave in $\bar{y}$ for every τ. The proof follows from (27) since the integration of a log-concave function over a convex set is log-concave [34, Section 3.5.2]. ■

Remark 1. *The densities $\psi_{\boldsymbol{v}}$ and $\psi_{\boldsymbol{a}}$ are log-concave since multivariate Gaussian density and exponential distribution (gamma distribution with shape parameter $p=1$) are log-concave, and log-concavity is preserved for products [25, Sections 1.4, 2.3] [34, Section 3.5.2].*

For any $\tau\in[1,T]$, Proposition 2 and Lemma 5 ensure

$$\text{ProbC}: \quad \begin{array}{ll} \text{minimize} & -\log(\text{CapturePr}_{\bar{x}_R}(\tau,\bar{x}_R[\tau];\bar{x}_G[0])) \\ \text{subject to} & \bar{x}_R[\tau]\in\text{Reach}_R(\tau;\bar{x}_R[0]) \end{array}$$

is convex with the decision variable $\bar{x}_R[\tau]$. Problem ProbC is an equivalent convex optimization problem of the partial maximization with respect to $\bar{x}_R[\tau]$ of Problem ProbB since we have transformed the original objective function with a monotone function to yield a convex objective and the constraint sets are identical [34, Section 4.1.3].

We solve Problem ProbB by solving Problem ProbC for each time instant $\tau\in[1,T]$ to obtain $\bar{x}^*_R[\tau]$ and compute the maximum of the resulting finite set to get $(\tau^*,\bar{x}^*_R[\tau^*])$. Since Problem ProbB could be non-convex, this approach ensures a global optimum is found. Note that in order to prevent taking the logarithm of zero, we add an additional constraint to Problem ProbC

$$\text{CapturePr}_{\bar{x}_R}(\tau,\cdot;\bar{x}_G[0]) \geq \epsilon. \quad (28)$$

The constraint (28) does not affect its convexity (ϵ is a small positive number) from Proposition 2 and the fact that log-concave functions are quasiconcave. Quasiconcave functions have convex superlevel sets [34, Sections 3.4, 3.5].

Using the optimal solution of Problem ProbB, we can compute the open-loop controller to drive the robot R from $\bar{x}_R[0]$ to $\bar{x}^*_R[\tau^*]$ by solving Problem ProbD. Defining $\mathscr{C}_R = (\bar{1}_{1\times(\tau^*-1)}\otimes B_R)$ from (22),

$$\text{ProbD}: \quad \begin{array}{ll} \text{minimize} & J_\pi(\bar{\pi}_{\tau^*}) \\ \text{subject to} & \left\{ \begin{array}{ll} \bar{\pi}_{\tau^*} & \in \overline{\mathcal{M}}_{\tau^*} \\ \mathscr{C}_R\bar{\pi}_{\tau^*} & = \bar{x}_R[\tau^*]-\bar{x}_R[0] \end{array}\right. \end{array}$$

where the decision variable is $\bar{\pi}_{\tau^*}$. The objective function $J_\pi(\bar{\pi}_{\tau^*})=0$ provides a feasible open-loop controller, and $J_\pi(\bar{\pi}_{\tau^*})=\bar{\pi}^\top_{\tau^*}\bar{R}\bar{\pi}_{\tau^*}$, $\bar{R}\in\mathbb{R}^{(2\tau^*)\times(2\tau^*)}$ provides an open-loop controller policy that minimizes the control effort while ensuring that maximum probability of robot R capturing robot G is achieved. Solving the optimization problems ProbB and ProbD answers Problem 2.

Our approach to solving Problem 2 is based on our solution to Problem 1, the Fourier transform based FSR analysis, and Problem 2.a, the convexity results of the FSRPD and the FSR sets presented in this paper. In contrast, the iterative approach for the FSR analysis, presented in Subsection 3.1, would yield erroneous $\text{CapturePr}_{\bar{x}_R}(\tau,\cdot;\bar{x}_G[0])$ for larger values of τ due to the heavy reliance on quadrature techniques. Additionally, the traditional approach of dynamic programming based computations [4] would be prohibitively costly for the large FSR sets encountered in this problem due to unbounded disturbances. The numerical implementation of this work is discussed in Subsection 4.3.

4.1 Robot G with point mass dynamics

We solve Problem ProbB for the system given by (23). Here, the disturbance set is $\mathcal{W}=\mathbb{R}^2$.

Lemma 6. *For the system given in (23) and initial state of the robot G as $\bar{x}_G[0]\in\mathbb{R}^2$, $\text{FSReach}_G(\tau,\bar{x}_G[0])=\mathbb{R}^2$ for every $\tau\in[1,T]$.*

Proof: Follows from Proposition 1 and (10). ■

Proposition 1 provides the FSRPD and Lemma 6 provides the FSR set for the system (23). The probability of successful capture of the robot G can be computed using (27) since the FSRPD $\psi_{\boldsymbol{x}_G}(\cdot;\tau,\bar{x}_G[0])$ is available.

We implement the problem with the following parameters: $T_s=0.2$, $T=20$, $\bar{\mu}^{\boldsymbol{v}}_G=[1.3\ 0.3]^\top$, $\Sigma_G=\begin{bmatrix}0.5 & 0.8\\ 0.8 & 2\end{bmatrix}$, $\bar{x}_G[0]=[-3\ 0]^\top$, $\bar{x}_R[0]=[-3\ -2]^\top$ and $\mathcal{U}=[1,2]^2$. The capture region of the robot R is a box centered about the position of the robot $\bar{y}$ with edge length $2a$ ($a=0.25$) and edges parallel to the axes — $\text{CaptureSet}(\bar{y})=\text{Box}(\bar{y},a)$, a convex set. We use $J_\pi(\bar{\pi})=0$ in Problem ProbD.

Figure 1 shows the evolution of the mean position of the robot G and the optimal capture position for the robot R at time instants $4,5,8,14$, and 20. The contour plots of $\psi_{\boldsymbol{x}_G}(\cdot;\tau,\bar{x}_G[0])$ are rotated ellipses since Σ_E is not a diagonal matrix. From (17), the mean position of the robot G moves in a straight line $\mu_G[\tau]$, as it is the trajectory of (23a) when the input is always $\bar{\mu}^{\boldsymbol{v}}_G$. The optimal time of capture is $\tau^*=5$, the optimal capture position is $\bar{x}^*_R[\tau^*]=[-1.8\ 0]^\top$, and

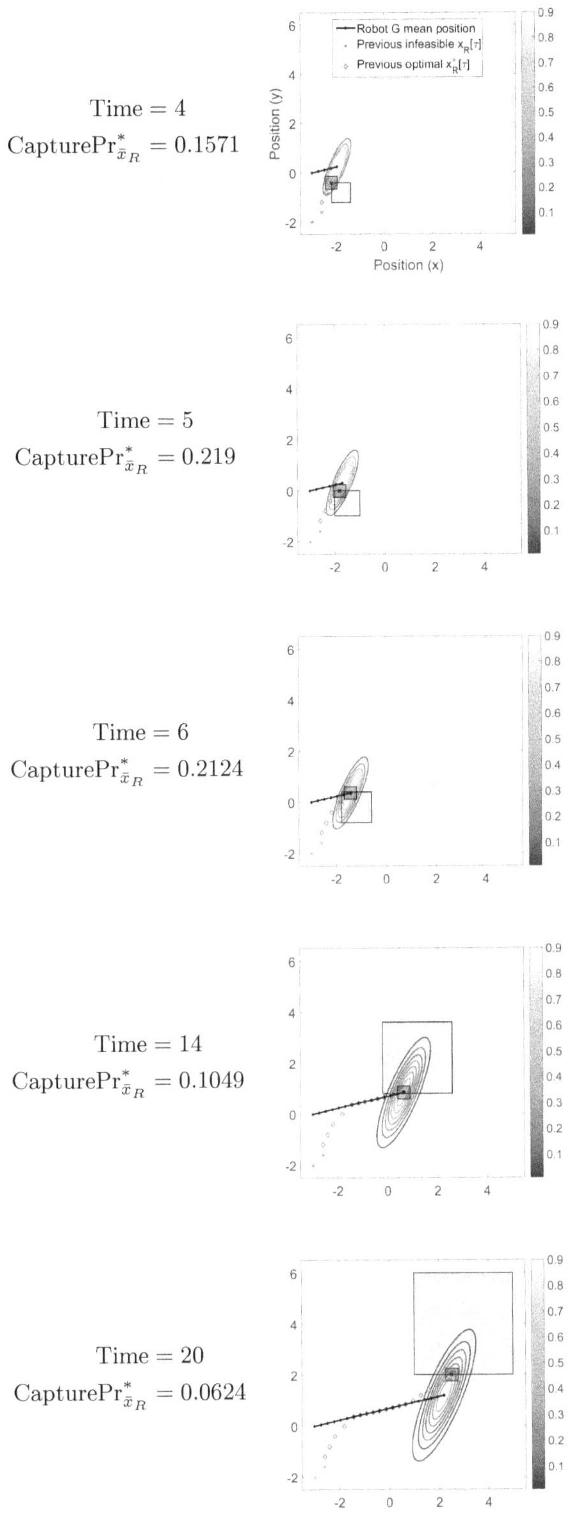

Figure 1: Snapshots of optimal capture positions of the robots G and R when G has point mass dynamics (23). The blue line shows the mean position trajectory of robot G $\mu_G[\tau]$, the contour plot characterizes $\psi_{\boldsymbol{x}_G}(\cdot;\tau,\bar{x}_G[0])$, the blue box shows the reach set of the robot R at time τ $\mathrm{Reach}_R(\tau,\bar{x}_R[0])$, and the red box shows the capture region centered at $\bar{x}^*_R[\tau]$ $\mathrm{CaptureSet}(\bar{x}^*_R[\tau])$.

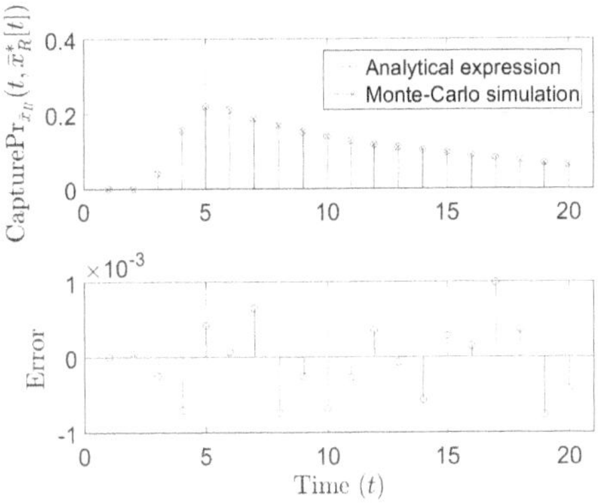

Figure 2: Solution to Problem ProbC for robot G dynamics in (23), and validation of $\mathrm{CapturePr}_{\bar{x}_R}(\tau,\bar{x}^*_R[\tau];\bar{x}_G[0])$ via Monte-Carlo simulations. The optimal capture time is $\tau^* = 5$ and the likelihood of capture is $\mathrm{CapturePr}_{\bar{x}_R}(\tau^*,\bar{x}^*_R[\tau^*];\bar{x}_G[0]) = 0.219$.

the corresponding probability of robot R capturing robot G is 0.219. Note that at this instant, the reach set of the robot R does not cover the current mean position of the robot G, $\bar{\mu}[\tau^*] = [-1.7\ 0.3]^\top$ (Figure 1b). While the reach set covers the mean position of robot G at the next time instant $t = 6$, the uncertainty in (23) causes the probability of successful capture to further reduce (Figure 1c). Counterintuitively, attempting to reach the mean $\mu_G[\tau]$ is not always best. Figure 2 shows the optimal capture probabilities obtained when solving Problem ProbC for the dynamics (23).

4.2 Robot G with double integrator dynamics

We now consider a more complicated capture problem, in which the disturbance is exponential (hence tracking the mean has little relevance because it is not the mode, the global maxima of the density), and the robot dynamics are more realistic. We solve Problem ProbB for the system given by (24). Here, the disturbance set is $\mathcal{W} = \mathbb{R}^2_+$. Based on the mean of the stochastic acceleration $\boldsymbol{a}[t]$, the mean position of robot G has a parabolic trajectory due to the double integrator dynamics, as opposed to the linear trajectory seen in Subsection 4.1. Also, in this case, we do not have an explicit expression for the FSRPD like Proposition 1. Using Theorem 1, we obtain an explicit expression for the CF of the FSRPD. We utilize Lemma 1 to evaluate $\mathrm{CapturePr}(\cdot)$.

Analogous to Lemma 6 and Proposition 1, we characterize the FSR set in Lemma 7 and the FSRPD in Proposition 3. We use Lemma 3 to obtain an overapproximation of the FSR set due to the unavailability of FSRPD to use (10).

Lemma 7. *For the system given in* (24) *with initial state* $\bar{x}_G[0] \in \mathbb{R}^4$ *of the robot G, we have* $\mathrm{FSReach}_G(\tau,\bar{x}_G[0]) \subseteq \{A^\tau_{\mathrm{G,DI}}\bar{x}_G[0]\} \oplus \mathbb{R}^4_+$ *for every* $2 \le \tau \le T$, *and* $\mathrm{FSReach}_G(1,\bar{x}_G[0]) \subseteq \{A_{\mathrm{G,DI}}\bar{x}_G[0]\} \oplus B_{\mathrm{G,DI}}\mathbb{R}^2_+$.

Proof: For the dynamics in (24), $\mathscr{C}^\top_{4\times(2\tau)}\mathbb{R}^{2\tau}_+ = \mathbb{R}^4_+$ since the rank of $\mathscr{C}^\top_{4\times(2\tau)}$ is 4 for every $\tau \ge 2$, and elements of $\mathscr{C}^\top_{4\times(2\tau)}$ are nonnegative. For $\tau = 1$, $\mathscr{C}^\top_{4\times(2\tau)} = B_{\mathrm{G,DI}}$. Lemma 3 completes the proof. ■

Time = 1
$\text{CapturePr}^*_{\bar{x}_R} = 0$
(Infeasible)

Time = 2
$\text{CapturePr}^*_{\bar{x}_R} = 0.6044$

Time = 3
$\text{CapturePr}^*_{\bar{x}_R} = 0.3885$

Time = 6
$\text{CapturePr}^*_{\bar{x}_R} = 0.0495$

Time = 9
$\text{CapturePr}^*_{\bar{x}_R} = 0.0091$

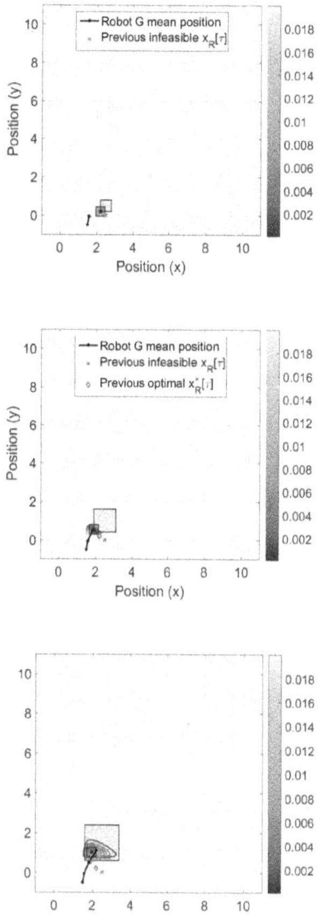

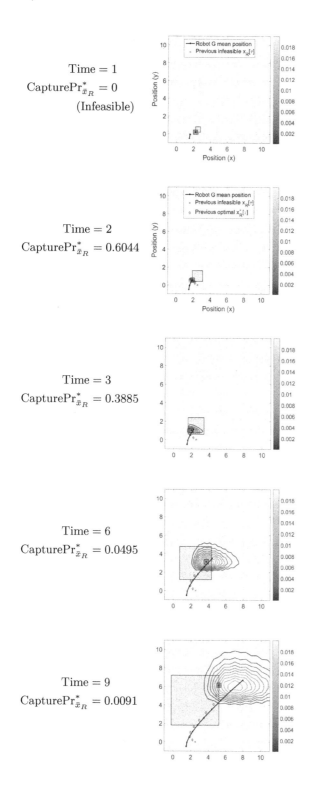

Figure 3: Snapshots of optimal capture positions of the robots G and R when G has double integrator dynamics (24). The blue line shows the mean position trajectory of robot G $\mu_G[\tau]$, the contour plot characterizes $\psi^{\text{pos}}_{\boldsymbol{x}_G}(\cdot;\tau,\bar{x}_G[0])$ via Monte-Carlo simulation, the blue box shows the reach set of the robot R at time τ, $\text{Reach}_R(\tau,\bar{x}_R[0])$, and the red box shows the capture region centered at $\bar{x}^*_R[\tau]$, $\text{CaptureSet}(\bar{x}^*_R[\tau])$.

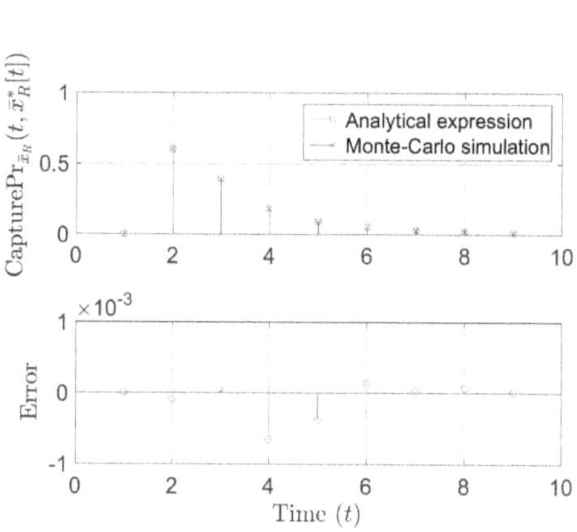

Figure 4: Solution to Problem ProbC for robot G dynamics in (24), and validation of $\text{CapturePr}_{\bar{x}_R}(\tau,\bar{x}^*_R[\tau];\bar{x}_G[0])$ via Monte-Carlo simulations. The optimal capture time is $\tau^* = 2$ and the capture probability is $\text{CapturePr}_{\bar{x}_R}(\tau^*,\bar{x}^*_R[\tau^*];\bar{x}_G[0]) = 0.6044$.

Proposition 3. *The CF of the FSRPD of the robot G for dynamics (24) is*

$$\Psi_{\boldsymbol{x}_G}(\bar{\beta};\tau,\bar{x}_G[0]) = \exp(j\bar{\beta}^\top(A^\tau_{\text{G,DI}}\bar{x}_G[0]))\times \prod_{t=0}^{\tau-1}\frac{\lambda_{\text{ax}}\lambda_{\text{ay}}}{(\lambda_{\text{ax}}-j\bar{\alpha}_{2t})(\lambda_{\text{ay}}-j\bar{\alpha}_{2t+1})} \tag{29}$$

where $\bar{\alpha} = \mathscr{C}^\top_{4\times(2\tau)}\bar{\beta}\in\mathbb{R}^{(2\tau)}$ and $\bar{\beta}\in\mathbb{R}^4$. The FSRPD of the robot G is $\psi_{\boldsymbol{x}_G}(\bar{x};\tau,\bar{x}_G[0]) = \mathscr{F}^{-1}\{\Psi_{\boldsymbol{x}_G}(\cdot;\tau,\bar{x}_G[0])\}(-\bar{x})$.

Proof: Apply Theorem 1 to the dynamics (24). ∎

To solve Problem ProbB, we define $\text{CapturePr}_{\bar{x}_R}(\cdot)$ as in (27). Since we are interested in just the position of robot G, we require only the marginal density of the FSRPD over the position subspace of robot G, $\psi^{\text{pos}}_{\boldsymbol{x}_G}$. By Property P4, we have for $\bar{\gamma} = [\gamma_1\ \gamma_2]\in\mathbb{R}^2$,

$$\Psi^{\text{pos}}_{\boldsymbol{x}_G}(\bar{\gamma};\tau,\bar{x}_G[0]) = \Psi_{\boldsymbol{x}_G}([\gamma_1\ 0\ \gamma_2\ 0]^\top;\tau,\bar{x}_G[0]). \tag{30}$$

Unlike the case with Gaussian disturbance, explicit expressions for the FSRPD $\psi_{\boldsymbol{x}_G}$ or its marginal density $\psi^{\text{pos}}_{\boldsymbol{x}_G}$ are unavailable since the Fourier transform (29) is not standard.

Lemma 8. $\psi_{B_{\text{G,DI}}\boldsymbol{a}}$, $\psi_{\boldsymbol{x}_G}\in L^1(\mathbb{R}^4)\cap L^2(\mathbb{R}^4)$.

Proof: *(For $\psi_{B_{\text{G,DI}}\boldsymbol{a}}$)* By Hölder's inequality [22, Section 19], $\psi_{\boldsymbol{a}}\in L^1(\mathbb{R}^2)\cap L^2(\mathbb{R}^2)$. We also have $\psi_{B_{\text{G,DI}}\boldsymbol{a}}(z_1,z_2,z_3,z_4) = \delta(z_3-\frac{T_s z_4}{2})\delta(z_1-\frac{T_s z_2}{2})\psi_{\boldsymbol{z}_{24}}(z_2,z_4)$ where $\boldsymbol{z}_{24} = [z_2\ z_4]^\top = T_s\boldsymbol{a}\in\mathbb{R}^2$ and $\psi_{\boldsymbol{z}_{24}}(z_2,z_4) = T_s^{-2}\psi_{\boldsymbol{a}}(\frac{z_2}{T_s},\frac{z_4}{T_s})$ from (12). For $i=\{1,2\}$, $\|\psi_{B_{\text{G,DI}}\boldsymbol{a}}\|_i = \|\psi_{\boldsymbol{z}_{24}}\|_i = T_s^{2-2i}\|\psi_{\boldsymbol{a}}\|_i<\infty$ completing the proof.

(For $\psi_{\boldsymbol{x}_G}$) Via induction using (11) (similar to the proof of Theorem 2). Note that functions in $L^1(\mathbb{R}^4)\cap L^2(\mathbb{R}^4)$ are closed under convolution [26, Theorem 1.3]. ∎

Lemma 9. $\psi^{\text{pos}}_{\boldsymbol{x}_G}(\bar{x};\tau,\bar{x}_G[0])\in L^1(\mathbb{R}^2)\cap L^2(\mathbb{R}^2)$.

Proof: For $i=\{1,2\}$, we have from (30), $\|\psi^{\text{pos}}_{\boldsymbol{x}_G}\|_i = \|\psi_{\boldsymbol{x}_G}\|_i$, and from Lemma 8, $\|\psi_{\boldsymbol{x}_G}\|_i<\infty$. ∎

Similar to Subsection 4.1, we define a convex capture region $\text{CaptureSet}(\bar{y}_R) = \text{Box}(\bar{y}_R,a)\subseteq\mathbb{R}^2$ where $\bar{y}_R\in\mathbb{R}^2$ is the state of the robot R. We define $h(\bar{y};\bar{y}_R,a) = \mathbf{1}_{\text{Box}(\bar{y}_R,a)}(\bar{y})$ as the indicator function corresponding to a 2-D box centered at $\bar{y}_R$ with edge length $2a>0$ with $h(\bar{y})=1$

if $\bar{y} \in \text{CaptureSet}(\bar{y}_R)$ and zero otherwise. The Fourier transform of h is a product of *sinc* functions shifted by $\bar{y}_R$ (follows from Property P2 and [30, Chapter 13])

$$\begin{aligned} H(\bar{\gamma}; \bar{y}_R, a) &= \mathscr{F}\{h(\cdot; \bar{y}_R, a)\}(\bar{\gamma}) \\ &= 4a^2 \exp\left(-j\bar{y}_R^\top \bar{\gamma}\right) \frac{\sin(a\gamma_1)\sin(a\gamma_2)}{\gamma_1\gamma_2}. \end{aligned} \quad (31)$$

Clearly, h is square-integrable, and from Lemmas 1 and 9, we define $\text{CapturePr}_{\bar{x}_R}(\cdot)$ in (33). Equation (33) is evaluated using (29), (30), and (31). We use (33) as opposed (32) due to the unavailability of an explicit expression for $\psi^{\text{pos}}_{\bar{\boldsymbol{x}}_G}$. The numerical evaluation of the inverse Fourier transform of $\Psi^{\text{pos}}_{\bar{\boldsymbol{x}}_G}$ to compute (32) will require two quadratures, resulting in a higher approximation error as compared to (33).

We implement the problem with the following parameters: $T_s = 0.2$, $T = 9$, $a = 0.25$, $\lambda_{\text{ax}} = 0.25$, $\lambda_{\text{ay}} = 0.45$, $\bar{x}_G[0] = [1.5\ 0\ \ -0.5\ 2]^\top$, $\bar{x}_R[0] = [2.5\ 0]^\top$, and $\mathcal{U} = [-1.5, 1.5] \times [1, 4]$. We use $J_\pi(\bar{\pi}) = 0$ in Problem ProbD.

Figure 3 shows the evolution of the mean position of the robot G and the optimal capture position for the robot R at time instants $1, 2, 3, 6$, and 9. For every $\tau \in [1, T]$, the contour plots of $\psi^{\text{pos}}_{\bar{\boldsymbol{x}}_G}(\cdot; \tau, \bar{x}_G[0])$ were estimated via Monte-Carlo simulation since evaluating $\psi^{\text{pos}}_{\bar{\boldsymbol{x}}_G}(\cdot; \tau, \bar{x}_G[0])$ via (5) over a grid is computationally expensive. Note that the mean position of the robot G does not coincide with the mode of $\psi^{\text{pos}}_{\bar{\boldsymbol{x}}_G}(\cdot; \tau, \bar{x}_G[0])$ in contrast to the problem discussed in Subsection 4.1. The optimal time of capture is at $\tau^* = 2$, the optimal capture position is $\bar{x}_R^*[\tau^*] = [1.9\ 0.55]^\top$, and the corresponding probability of robot R capturing robot G is 0.6044 (Figure 3b). Figure 4 shows the optimal capture probabilities obtained when solving Problem ProbC for the dynamics (24), and the validation of the results.

4.3 Numerical implementation and analysis

All computations in this paper were performed using MATLAB on an Intel Core i7 CPU with 3.4GHz clock rate and 16 GB RAM. The MATLAB code for this work is available at http://hscl.unm.edu/files/code/HSCC17.zip.

We solved Problem ProbC using MATLAB's built-in functions — *fmincon* for the optimization, *mvncdf* to compute the objective (27) for the case in Subsection 4.1, *integral* to compute the objective (33) for the case in Subsection 4.2, and *max* to compute the global optimum of Problem ProbB. In both the sections, we used MPT for the reachable set calculation and solved Problem ProbD using CVX [36]. Using Lemma 2, the FSR sets restrict the search while solving Problem ProbC. All geometric computations were done in the facet representation. We computed the initial guess for the optimization of Problem ProbC by performing Euclidean projection of the mean to the feasible set using CVX [34, Section 8.1.1]. Since computing the objective was costly, this operation saved significant computational time. The Monte-Carlo simulation used 500,000 particles. No offline computations were done in either of the cases.

The overall computation of Problem ProbB and ProbD for the case in Subsection 4.1 took 5.32 seconds for $T = 20$. Since Proposition 1 provides explicit expressions for the FSRPD, the evaluation of the FSRPD for any given point $\bar{y} \in \mathcal{X}$ takes 1.6 milliseconds on average. For the case in Subsection 4.2, the overall computation took 488.55 seconds ($\sim$ 8 minutes) for $T = 9$. The numerical evaluation of the improper integral (33) is the major cause of increase in runtime. The evaluation of the FSRPD for any given point $\bar{y} \in \mathcal{X}$ using (5) takes about 10.5 seconds, and the runtime and the accuracy depend heavily on the point $\bar{y}$ as well as the bounds used for the integral approximation. However, the evaluation of $\text{CapturePr}_{\bar{x}_R}(\cdot)$ using (33) is much faster (0.81 seconds) because $H(\bar{\gamma}; \bar{y}_R, a)$ is a decaying, 2-D sinc function (decaying much faster than the CF).

The decaying properties of the integrand in (33) and CFs in general permits approximating the improper integrals in (5) and (33) by as a proper integral with suitably defined finite bounds. The tradeoff between accuracy and computational speed, common in quadrature techniques, dictates the choice of the bound. A detailed analysis of various quadrature techniques, their computational complexity, and their error analysis can be found in [31, Chapter 4].

5. CONCLUSIONS AND FUTURE WORK

This paper provides a method for forward stochastic reachability analysis using Fourier transforms. The method is applicable to uncontrolled stochastic linear systems. Fourier transforms simplify the computation and mitigate the curse of dimensionality associated with gridding the state space. We also analyze several convexity results associated with the FSRPD and FSR sets. We demonstrate our method on the problem of controller synthesis for a controlled robot pursuing a stochastically moving non-adversarial target.

Future work includes exploration of various quadrature techniques like particle filters for high-dimensional quadratures and extension to a model predictive control framework and to discrete random vectors (countable disturbance sets). Multiple pursuer applications will also be investigated.

6. ACKNOWLEDGEMENTS

The authors thank Prof. M. Hayat for discussions on Fourier transforms in probability theory and the reviewers for their insightful comments.

This material is based upon work supported by the National Science Foundation, under Grant Numbers CMMI-1254990, CNS-1329878, and IIS-1528047. Any opinions, findings, and conclusions or recommendations expressed in this material are those of the authors and do not necessarily reflect the views of the National Science Foundation.

7. REFERENCES

[1] Baisravan HomChaudhuri, Abraham P. Vinod, and Meeko M. K. Oishi. Computation of forward stochastic reach sets: Application to stochastic, dynamic obstacle avoidance. In *Proc. American Control Conf.*, 2017. (accepted).

[2] Nick Malone, Kendra Lesser, Meeko Oishi, and Lydia Tapia. Stochastic reachability based motion planning for multiple moving obstacle avoidance. In *Proc. Hybrid Syst.: Comput. and Control*, pages 51–60, 2014.

[3] Kendra Lesser, Meeko Oishi, and R. Scott Erwin. Stochastic reachability for control of spacecraft relative motion. In *Proc. IEEE Conf. on Decision and Control*, pages 4705–4712, 2013.

[4] Sean Summers and John Lygeros. Verification of discrete time stochastic hybrid systems: A stochastic reach-avoid decision problem. *Automatica*, 46(12):1951–1961, 2010.

[5] Nikolaos Kariotoglou, Davide M Raimondo, Sean Summers, and John Lygeros. A stochastic reachability

$$\text{CapturePr}_{\bar{x}_R}(\tau, \bar{x}_R[\tau]; \bar{x}_G[0]) = \int_{\mathbb{R}^2} \psi^{\text{pos}}_{\bar{\boldsymbol{x}}_G}(\bar{x}; \tau, \bar{x}_G[0]) h(\bar{x}; \bar{x}_R[\tau], a) d\bar{x} \tag{32}$$

$$= \left(\frac{1}{2\pi}\right)^2 \int_{\mathbb{R}^2} \Psi^{\text{pos}}_{\bar{\boldsymbol{x}}_G}(\bar{\gamma}; \tau, \bar{x}_G[0]) H(\bar{\gamma}; \bar{x}_R[\tau], a) d\bar{\gamma}. \tag{33}$$

framework for autonomous surveillance with pan-tilt-zoom cameras. In *European Control Conf.*, pages 1411–1416, 2011.

[6] Alessandro Abate, Maria Prandini, John Lygeros, and Shankar Sastry. Probabilistic reachability and safety for controlled discrete time stochastic hybrid systems. *Automatica*, 44(11):2724–2734, 2008.

[7] Alessandro Abate, Saurabh Amin, Maria Prandini, John Lygeros, and Shankar Sastry. Computational approaches to reachability analysis of stochastic hybrid systems. In *Proc. Hybrid Syst.: Comput. and Control*, pages 4–17, 2007.

[8] Nikolaos Kariotoglou, Sean Summers, Tyler Summers, Maryam Kamgarpour, and John Lygeros. Approximate dynamic programming for stochastic reachability. In *European Control Conf.*, pages 584–589, 2013.

[9] Nikolaos Kariotoglou, Kostas Margellos, and John Lygeros. On the computational complexity and generalization properties of multi-stage and stage-wise coupled scenario programs. *Syst. and Control Lett.*, 94:63–69, 2016.

[10] Giorgio Manganini, Matteo Pirotta, Marcello Restelli, Luigi Piroddi, and Maria Prandini. Policy search for the optimal control of Markov Decision Processes: A novel particle-based iterative scheme. *IEEE Trans. Cybern.*, pages 1–13, 2015.

[11] Michal Kvasnica, Bálint Takács, Juraj Holaza, and Deepak Ingole. Reachability analysis and control synthesis for uncertain linear systems in MPT. *IFAC Symp. on Robust Control D.*, 48(14):302–307, 2015.

[12] Alex A. Kurzhanskiy and Pravin Varaiya. Ellipsoidal toolbox. Technical Report UCB/EECS-2006-46, EECS Department, University of California, Berkeley, 2006.

[13] Antoine Girard. Reachability of uncertain linear systems using zonotopes. In *Proc. Hybrid Syst.: Comput. and Control*, pages 291–305, 2005.

[14] Geoffrey Hollinger, Sanjiv Singh, Joseph Djugash, and Athanasios Kehagias. Efficient multi-robot search for a moving target. *Int'l J. Robotics and Research*, 28(2):201–219, 2009.

[15] Vijay Kumar, Daniela Rus, and Sanjiv Singh. Robot and sensor networks for first responders. *IEEE Pervasive computing*, 3(4):24–33, 2004.

[16] Christopher Geyer. Active target search from UAVs in urban environments. In *Proc. IEEE Int'l Conf. Robotics and Autom.*, pages 2366–2371, 2008.

[17] Ian Mitchell and Claire J. Tomlin. Level set methods for computation in hybrid systems. In *Proc. Hybrid Syst.: Comput. and Control*, pages 310–323, 2000.

[18] Claire J. Tomlin, John Lygeros, and Shankar Sastry. A game theoretic approach to controller design for hybrid systems. *Proc. IEEE*, 88(7):949–970, 2000.

[19] Claire J. Tomlin, Ian Mitchell, Alexandre M. Bayen, and Meeko Oishi. Computational techniques for the verification of hybrid systems. *Proc. IEEE*, 91(7):986–1001, 2003.

[20] Olivier Bokanowski, Nicolas Forcadel, and Hasnaa Zidani. Reachability and Minimal Times for State Constrained Nonlinear Problems without Any Controllability Assumption. *SIAM J. of Control and Optimization*, 48(7):4292–4316, 2010.

[21] Haomiao Huang, Jerry Ding, Wei Zhang, and Claire J. Tomlin. Automation-assisted capture-the-flag: A differential game approach. *IEEE Trans. Control Syst. Technol.*, 23:1014–1028, 2015.

[22] Patrick Billingsley. *Probability and measure.* Wiley, New York, 3 edition, 1995.

[23] John A Gubner. *Probability and random processes for electrical and computer engineers.* Cambridge University Press, New York; Cambridge, 2006.

[24] Harald Cramér. *Mathematical methods of statistics (PMS-9).* Princeton university press, 9 edition, 1961.

[25] Sudhakar Dharmadhikari and Kumar Joag-Dev. *Unimodality, convexity, and applications.* Elsevier, 1988.

[26] Elias M Stein and Guido L Weiss. *Introduction to Fourier analysis on Euclidean spaces*, volume 1. Princeton University Press, 1971.

[27] Terence Tao. *Analysis II.* Hindustan Book Agency, 2 edition, 2009.

[28] Jean-Paul Penot. *Analysis: From Concepts to Applications.* Springer, 1 edition, 2016.

[29] Andrzej Lasota and Michael C Mackey. *Chaos, fractals, and noise: stochastic aspects of dynamics*, volume 97. Springer Science & Business Media, 2013.

[30] Ron Bracewell. *The Fourier transform and its applications.* McGraw-Hill, Inc., 1986.

[31] William H. Press, Saul A. Teukolsky, William T. Vetterling, and Brian P. Flannery. *Numerical recipes: The art of scientific computing.* Cambridge University Press, New York, NY, USA, 3 edition, 2007.

[32] Peter Dorato, Vito Cerone, and Chaouki Abdallah. *Linear-quadratic control: An introduction.* Simon & Schuster, 1994.

[33] Y.S. Chow and H. Teicher. *Probability Theory: Independence, Interchangeability, Martingales.* Springer Texts in Statistics. Springer New York, 1997.

[34] Stephen P. Boyd and Lieven Vandenberghe. *Convex optimization.* Cambridge University Press, Cambridge, UK ; New York, 2004.

[35] Martin Herceg, Michal Kvasnica, Colin N. Jones, and Manfred Morari. Multi-Parametric Toolbox 3.0. In *European Control Conf.*, pages 502–510, 2013. http://control.ee.ethz.ch/~mpt.

[36] Michael Grant and Stephen Boyd. CVX: MATLAB software for disciplined convex programming, version 2.1. http://cvxr.com/cvx, 2014.

Controller Synthesis for Reward Collecting Markov Processes in Continuous Space

Sadegh Esmaeil Zadeh Soudjani
Max Planck Institute for Software Systems
Kaiserslautern, Germany
sadegh@mpi-sws.org

Rupak Majumdar
Max Planck Institute for Software Systems
Kaiserslautern, Germany
rupak@mpi-sws.org

ABSTRACT

We propose and analyze a generic mathematical model for optimizing rewards in continuous-space, dynamic environments, called Reward Collecting Markov Processes. Our model is motivated by request-serving applications in robotics, where the objective is to control a dynamical system to respond to stochastically generated environment requests, while minimizing wait times. Our model departs from usual discounted reward Markov decision processes in that the reward function is not determined by the current state and action. Instead, a background process generates rewards whose values depend on the number of steps between generation and collection. For example, a reward is declared whenever there is a new request for a robot and the robot gets higher reward the sooner it is able to serve the request. A policy in this setting is a sequence of control actions which determines a (random) trajectory over the continuous state space. The reward achieved by the trajectory is the cumulative sum of all rewards obtained along the way in the finite horizon case and the long run average of all rewards in the infinite horizon case.

We study both the finite horizon and infinite horizon problems for maximizing the expected (respectively, the long run average expected) collected reward. We characterize these problems as solutions to dynamic programs over an augmented hybrid space, which gives history-dependent optimal policies. Second, we provide a computational method for these problems which abstracts the continuous-space problem into a discrete-space collecting reward Markov decision process. Under assumptions of Lipschitz continuity of the Markov process and uniform bounds on the discounting, we show that we can bound the error in computing optimal solutions on the finite-state approximation. Finally, we provide a fixed point characterization of the optimal expected collected reward in the infinite case, and show how the fixed point can be obtained by value iteration.

HSCC'17, April 18 - 20, 2017, Pittsburgh, PA, USA

ISBN 978-1-4503-4590-3/17/04. . . $15.00

DOI: http://dx.doi.org/10.1145/3049797.3049827

Keywords Reward collecting Markov processes; formal controller synthesis; continuous-space stochastic systems

1. INTRODUCTION

Consider a mobile robot in an environment. The robot receives requests from different users and must serve these requests by traveling to the location of the request. The aim of the robot is to respond to each request as soon as possible. How should the robot plan its actions?

This scenario generalizes many problems studied in the robotics, control, and combinatorial optimization literatures. In the most general form, these problems incorporate: (a) control of continuous-state dynamical systems w.r.t. temporal requirements (the robot must navigate to different locations while maintaining safety), (b) dynamic requests from a stochastic environment (user requests can be modeled as a stochastic process), (c) cumulative reward collection (the robot gets a reward on serving a request, depending on the wait time, and the overall reward is cumulative).

We propose and analyze a generic mathematical model for optimizing rewards in continuous-space, dynamic environments, called Reward Collecting Controlled Markov Processes (RCCMP). Our model is motivated by the above request-serving applications, where the objective is to control a dynamical system to respond to environment requests that are generated stochastically, while minimizing wait times. An RCCMP is defined using (a) a controlled Markov process, (b) a reward process, and (c) a reward functional. The controlled Markov process is defined over a continuous state space in discrete time. That is, the states and inputs form Borel spaces, and the transitions are defined by a conditional stochastic kernel which associates with each state and control input a probability measure over the next states. The reward process is defined over a given finite partition of the state space, and assigns a random reward to the partition at each time step. Finally, we use discounted reward as the classic way to ensure low latency for each request: if the Markov process visits a particular region consecutively at two time instances $t = k$ and $t = k'$, then the cumulative reward is collected, which is the sum of all the rewards associated with the requests generated at this region between times k and k' each discounted depending on the time the request is generated and the time it is served (i.e., k').

A *policy* ascribes a control action to the controlled Markov process at each time step. It determines a random trajectory. The reward achieved by the trajectory is the cumulative sum of all rewards obtained along the trajectory. We study both the finite horizon and infinite horizon problems for maximizing the expected cumulative reward for finite horizon and the long run average expected cumulative reward for the infinite horizon. We also study how to design a policy that maximizes the expected rewards.

Our first result characterizes these problems as solutions to dynamic programs. Second, we provide a computational method which abstracts the continuous-space problem into a discrete-space cumulative reward Markov decision process. Under assumptions of Lipschitz continuity of the Markov process and uniform bounds on the discounting, we show that we can bound the error in computing optimal solutions on the finite-state approximation. Finally, we provide a fixed point characterization of the optimal expected cumulative reward in the finite case, and show how the fixed point can be obtained by value iteration. We illustrate our results with a simple request-serving robot example.

Related Work. A number of models studied in the optimization and control literature are close to ours. For example, (dynamic) traveling salesman problems, and their analogues such as the stochastic orienteering problem or the vehicle routing problem, study strategies to optimize path costs in a finite graph. In contrast, our model is defined over a general continuous-state stochastic process and defines rewards dynamically and cumulatively.

A second related model is Markov reward models (MRMs) [8] in which the model is deterministic (i.e., with no input) and the reward is a function of state $r(x_t)$. Another related model is Markov decision process (MDPs) over finite or infinite state spaces, in which the rewards are usually defined as fixed functions of the current state and action taken at that state $r(x_t, u_t)$. The reinforcement learning community sometimes works with rewards defined as functions of the tuple (current state, action, next state) $r(x_t, u_t, x_{t+1})$ [15, Chapter 3.6].

Infinite-horizon performance evaluation in MRMs and optimization in MDPs are performed via the following measures: total reward, discounted reward, and average reward. The first measure is just the infinite sum of all rewards associated to the paths of the process, which may not be bounded in general. The other two measures ensures boundedness of the measure by considering respectively the infinite sum of discounted and long-run average rewards. Such problems are throughly studied in [12] for finite and countable space models and in [10] for continuous uncountable space models. The third measure is in fact the long-run average expected value of the rewards, while the paper [3] and related works study a stronger infinite-horizon optimization in MDPs, which is the expected long-run average (the difference is in the position of the expected value operator).

Our model departs from MDPs in that the reward function is not deterministically determined for each state and action once and for all. Instead, a background stochastic process repeatedly generates rewards in the state space, and each generated reward decays over time through a discount factor. The treatment of accumulating rewards through a "double summation" over consecutive visits to a location introduces differences from the MDP model: for an RCCMP, we show that memoryless policies are no longer optimal. The work [13] studies MDPs with functional rewards, in which the reward is also a function of previously collected rewards. However, we cannot define our rewards in their framework: our rewards depend on the time since of the last visit.

Finite-state approximations of continuous-space Markov processes with guarantees on error bounds was studied before [1, 4, 6, 14, 16]. In comparison with [4], the main challenge in our context is that the state space has a countable, unbounded, component tracking the time steps since the last visit to each region. Second, approximations studied in [1, 6, 14] consider finite-horizon temporal specifications with extensions to infinite-horizon ones [16]. These approximations benefit from the fact that the associated value functions are bounded by one uniformly. We study cumulative reward problems over finite and infinite horizons and must modify the approximation construction due to the lack of this bound. Our work is also distinct from the previous related work in that we give such approximation and the error analysis for long-run average criterion.

2. CONTROLLED MARKOV PROCESSES

2.1 Preliminaries

We consider a probability space $(\Omega, \mathcal{F}_\Omega, P_\Omega)$, where Ω is the sample space, $\mathcal{F}_\Omega$ is a sigma-algebra on Ω comprising subsets of Ω as events, and P_Ω is a probability measure than assigns probabilities to events. We assume that random variables introduced in this article are measurable functions of the form $X : (\Omega, \mathcal{F}_\Omega) \to (S_X, \mathcal{F}_X)$. Any random variable X induces a probability measure on its space $(S_X, \mathcal{F}_X)$ as $Prob\{A\} = P_\Omega\{X^{-1}(A)\}$ for any $A \in \mathcal{F}_X$. We often directly discuss the probability measure on $(S_X, \mathcal{F}_X)$ without explicitly mentioning the underlying probability space and the function X itself.

A topological space S is called a Borel space if it is homeomorphic to a Borel subset of a Polish space (i.e., a separable and completely metrizable space). Examples of a Borel space are the Euclidean spaces $\mathbb{R}^n$, its Borel subsets endowed with a subspace topology, as well as hybrid spaces. Any Borel space S is assumed to be endowed with a Borel sigma-algebra, which is denoted by $\mathcal{B}(S)$. We say that a map $f : S \to Y$ is measurable whenever it is Borel measurable.

The following notation is used throughout the paper. We denote the set of nonnegative integers by $\mathbb{N} := \{0, 1, 2, \ldots\}$ and the set of positive integers by $\mathbb{Z}_+ := \{1, 2, 3, \ldots\}$. The bounded set of integers is indicated by $\mathbb{N}[a, b] := \{a, a + 1, \ldots, b\}$ for any $a, b \in \mathbb{N}$, $a \leq b$. For any set A we denote by $A^{\mathbb{N}}$ the Cartesian product of a countable number of copies of A, i.e., $A^{\mathbb{N}} = \prod_{k=0}^{\infty} A$. We denote with $\mathbb{I}(\cdot)$ the indicator function which takes a Boolean-valued expression as an argument and gives 1 if this expression evaluates to true and 0 when it is false.

2.2 Controlled Markov Processes

We adopt the notation from [10] and consider controlled Markov processes (CMP) in discrete time defined over a general state space, characterized by a tuple

$$\mathfrak{S} = (\mathcal{S}, \mathcal{U}, \{\mathcal{U}(s) | s \in \mathcal{S}\}, T_{\mathfrak{s}}),$$

where $\mathcal{S}$ is a Borel space as the state space of the process. We denote by $(\mathcal{S}, \mathcal{B}(\mathcal{S}))$ as the measurable space with $\mathcal{B}(\mathcal{S})$ being the Borel sigma-algebra on the state space. $\mathcal{U}$ is a Borel space as the input space of the process. The set $\{\mathcal{U}(s) | s \in \mathcal{S}\}$ is a family of non-empty measurable subsets of $\mathcal{U}$ with the property that

$$\mathcal{K} := \{(s, u) : s \in \mathcal{S}, u \in \mathcal{U}(s)\}$$

is measurable in $\mathcal{S} \times \mathcal{U}$. Intuitively, $\mathcal{U}(s)$ is the set of inputs that are feasible at state $s \in \mathcal{S}$. $T_{\mathfrak{s}} : \mathcal{B}(\mathcal{S}) \times \mathcal{S} \times \mathcal{U} \to [0,1]$, is a conditional stochastic kernel that assigns to any $s \in \mathcal{S}$ and $u \in \mathcal{U}(s)$ a probability measure $T_{\mathfrak{s}}(\cdot|s,u)$ on the measurable space $(\mathcal{S}, \mathcal{B}(\mathcal{S}))$ so that for any set $A \in \mathcal{B}(\mathcal{S}), P_{s,u}(A) = \int_A T_s(ds|s,u)$, where $P_{s,u}$ denotes the conditional probability $P(\cdot|s,u)$.

2.3 Semantics

The semantics of a CMP is characterized by its *paths* or executions, which reflect both the history of previous states of the system and of implemented control inputs. Paths are used to measure the performance of the system.

DEFINITION 1. *Given a CMP $\mathfrak{S}$, a* finite path *is a sequence*

$$w_n = (s_0, u_0, \ldots, s_{n-1}, u_{n-1}, s_n), \quad n \in \mathbb{N},$$

where $s_i \in \mathcal{S}$ are state coordinates and $u_i \in \mathcal{U}(s_i)$ are control input coordinates of the path. The space of all paths of length n is denoted by $\mathsf{PATH}_n := \mathcal{K}^n \times \mathcal{S}$. Further, we denote projections by $w_n[i] := s_i$ and $w_n(i) := u_i$. An infinite path *of the CMP $\mathfrak{S}$ is the sequence $w = (s_0, u_0, s_1, u_1, \ldots)$, where $s_i \in \mathcal{S}$ and $u_i \in \mathcal{U}(s_i)$ for all $i \in \mathbb{N}$. As above, let us introduce $w[i] := s_i$ and $w(i) := u_i$. The space of all infinite paths is denoted by $\mathsf{PATH}_\infty := \mathcal{K}^\infty$.*

Given an infinite path w or a finite path w_n, we assume below that s_i and u_i are their state and control coordinates respectively, unless otherwise stated. For any infinite path $w \in \mathsf{PATH}_\infty$, its n-prefix (ending in a state) w_n is a finite path of length n, which we also call *n-history*. We are now ready to introduce the notion of control policy.

DEFINITION 2. *A* policy *is a sequence $\rho = (\rho_0, \rho_1, \rho_2, \ldots)$ of universally measurable stochastic kernels ρ_n [2], each defined on the input space $\mathcal{U}$ given PATH_n and such that for all $w_n \in \mathsf{PATH}_n$ with $n \in \mathbb{N}$, $\rho_n(\mathcal{U}(s_n)|w_n) = 1$. The set of all policies is denoted by Π.*

Given a policy $\rho \in \Pi$ and a finite path $w_n \in \mathsf{PATH}_n$, the distribution of the next control input u_n given by $\rho_n(\cdot|w_n)$ is supported on $\mathcal{U}(s_n)$. A policy ρ is *deterministic* if all stochastic kernels ρ_i, $i \in \mathbb{N}$, are Dirac delta measures, otherwise it is called *randomized*. Among the class of all possible policies, special interest is shown in the literature towards those with a simple structure in that they depend only on the current state, rather than on the whole history.

DEFINITION 3. *A policy $\rho \in \Pi$ is called a Markov policy if for any $n \in \mathbb{N}$ it holds that $\rho_n(\cdot|w_n) = \rho_n(\cdot|s_n)$, i.e., ρ_n depends on the history w_n only through the current state s_n. The class of all Markov policies is denoted by $\Pi_M \subset \Pi$.*

A more restrictive set of policies, which will be used in Section 5, is the class of *stationary* policies $\Pi_S \subset \Pi_M$, which are Markov, deterministic, and time-independent. Namely, there is a function $d : \mathcal{S} \to \mathcal{U}$ such that at any time epoch $n \in \mathbb{N}$, the input u_n is taken to be $d(s_n) \in \mathcal{U}(s_n)$. We denote stationary policies just by $d \in \Pi_S$.

For a CMP $\mathfrak{S}$, any policy $\rho \in \Pi$ together with an initial probability measure $\alpha : \mathcal{B}(\mathcal{S}) \to [0,1]$ of the CMP induce a unique probability measure on the canonical sample space of paths [10] denoted by P^ρ_α with the expectation $\mathbb{E}^\rho_\alpha$. In the case when the initial probability measure is supported on a single point, i.e., $\alpha(s) = 1$, we write P^ρ_s and $\mathbb{E}^\rho_s$ in place of P^ρ_α and $\mathbb{E}^\rho_\alpha$, respectively. We denote the set of probability measures on $(\mathcal{S}, \mathcal{B}(\mathcal{S}))$ by $\mathfrak{D}$.

EXAMPLE 1. *Consider a robot moving in a 2-dimensional environment $\mathcal{S} = [0,a] \times [0,b]$, surrounded by walls, according to the dynamics:*

$$s_{t+1} = s_t + \alpha_0 g_{\mathsf{m}}(u_t) + \eta_t, \quad t \in \mathbb{N}, \tag{1}$$

where $\{\eta_t, t \in \mathbb{N}\}$ are independent identically-distributed (iid) random variables with η_t having normal distribution $\mathcal{N}(0, \Sigma_{\mathsf{r}})$ and models the uncertainty in the movement of the robot. The input space is $\mathcal{U} = \{\mathit{left}, \mathit{right}, \mathit{up}, \mathit{down}\}$. The parameter α_0 is the length of the nominal move of the robot and the function $g_{\mathsf{m}} : \mathcal{U} \to \mathbb{R}^2$ indicates the move direction:

$$g_{\mathsf{m}}(\mathit{left}) = \begin{bmatrix}-1\\0\end{bmatrix}, g_{\mathsf{m}}(\mathit{right}) = \begin{bmatrix}1\\0\end{bmatrix}, g_{\mathsf{m}}(\mathit{up}) = \begin{bmatrix}0\\1\end{bmatrix}, g_{\mathsf{m}}(\mathit{down}) = \begin{bmatrix}0\\-1\end{bmatrix}.$$

The stochastic kernel of the dynamical system (1) is also normal $T_{\mathfrak{s}}(ds_{t+1}|s_t, u_t) \sim \mathcal{N}(s_t + \alpha_0 g_{\mathsf{m}}(u_t), \Sigma_{\mathsf{r}})$.

3. PROBLEM DEFINITION

3.1 Cumulative Discounted Rewards

A measurable partition of the state space $\mathcal{S}$ is a finite set $\mathcal{D} := \{D_1, \ldots, D_m\}$ such that each D_j is a non-empty measurable subset of $\mathcal{S}$, the sets are pairwise disjoint, i.e., $D_i \cap D_j =$ for $i \neq j$, and the union of the sets is $\mathcal{S}$, i.e., $\mathcal{S} = \cup_i D_i$. We refer to the subsets D_j as *regions*.

Fix a measurable partition $\mathcal{D}$. We associate the following functions with $\mathcal{D}$. A *reward function* $r : \Omega \times \mathbb{N} \times \mathcal{D} \to \mathbb{R}$ is a stochastic process assigning real random reward $r(\cdot, t, D)$ to any region $D \in \mathcal{D}$ at any time $t \in \mathbb{N}$. The *discounting function* $\gamma : \mathcal{D} \to (0,1)$ associates with each region D a discounting factor $\gamma(D)$, which is a real number in the open interval $(0,1)$.

Each state $s \in \mathcal{S}$ belongs to exactly one $D \in \mathcal{D}$. We define the map $\Xi : \mathcal{S} \to \mathcal{D}$ that maps $s \in \mathcal{S}$ with the (unique) region $D \in \mathcal{D}$ s.t. $s \in D$. We also use $\xi : \mathcal{S} \to \{0,1\}^m$ with $\xi(s)$ being a row vector of dimension m with elements $\mathbb{I}(s \in D_i)$, $i \in \mathbb{N}[1,m]$.

For a finite path $w_n = (s_0, u_0, \ldots, s_{n-1}, u_{n-1}, s_n)$, a region $D \in \mathcal{D}$, and an index $k \leq n$, we define $\mathsf{Last}(w_n, D, k)$ as the last time epoch before k that the path w_n visits region D, defining it to be -1 in case w_n does not visit D before time epoch k:

$$\mathsf{Last}(w_n, D, k) := \max\left\{\{j | j < k, w_n[j] \in D\} \cup \{-1\}\right\}.$$

The finite-horizon *cumulative discounted reward* (CDR) is defined as a map from the set of policies Π and set of measures $\mathfrak{D}$ to $\mathbb{R}$ as follows:

$$\mathsf{CDR}_n(\rho, \alpha) = \mathbb{E}\left[\sum_{k=0}^{n} \sum_{t=\mathsf{Last}(w_n, \Xi(s_k), k)+1}^{k} \gamma(\Xi(s_k))^{k-t} r(\varsigma, t, \Xi(s_k))\right], \tag{2}$$

for any $\rho \in \Pi$ and $\alpha \in \mathfrak{D}$, with s_k being the state visited at time epoch k by w_n. Intuitively, the path w_n visits the region $\Xi(s_k)$ at time epoch k. The inner sum gives the discounted reward accumulated at region $\Xi(s_k)$ since the last visit of the region: the reward $r(\varsigma, t, \Xi(s_k))$ generated at time epoch t is discounted by multiplying it with the factor $\gamma(\Xi(s_k))^{k-t}$, which depends on the difference $k - t$ between the time the reward is generated and the time it is collected.

The expected value in (2) is respect to both the canonical sample space of paths and the underlying probability space of the generated rewards $\varsigma \in \Omega$.

We assume that the random variables $r(\cdot, t, D)$ are stochastically independent of the $\mathfrak{S}$ dynamics and their expected value exists, is non-negative, and is denoted by $\lambda(t, D)$. Due to the additive nature of CDR, we can write

$$\mathsf{CDR}_n(\rho,\alpha) = \mathbb{E}^{\rho}_{\alpha}\left[\sum_{k=0}^{n}\ \sum_{t=\mathsf{Last}(w_n,\Xi(s_k),k)+1}^{k} \gamma(\Xi(s_k))^{k-t}\lambda(t,\Xi(s_k))\right],$$

for all $\rho \in \Pi$ and $\alpha \in \mathfrak{D}$. We define the infinite-horizon CDR as

$$\mathsf{CDR}_\infty(\rho,\alpha) = \liminf_{n\to\infty} \frac{1}{n+1}\,\mathsf{CDR}_n(\rho,\alpha), \qquad (3)$$

which is the *liminf average* of the finite-horizon CDR. Note that limit average does not necessarily exist, thus we have selected the worst case limiting reward accumulated along the path. Alternatively, one may opt for best case limiting reward, i.e *limsup average*. The analysis and results of this paper are valid for both cases with minor modifications.

DEFINITION 4. *A RCCMP is a pair $(\mathfrak{S},\mathfrak{R})$ with CMP $\mathfrak{S}$ defined in Section 2.2 and the tuple $\mathfrak{R} := (\mathcal{D}, \lambda, \gamma)$, where $\mathcal{D}$ is a measurable partition of the state space, $\lambda : \mathbb{N}\times\mathcal{D} \to \mathbb{R}_{\geq 0}$ is the expected generated rewards, and $\gamma : \mathcal{D} \to (0,1)$ is the discounting function.*

REMARK 1. *The definition of CDR relies on having geometrically discounting factors for each region, i.e., the sequence*

$$\{1, \gamma(D), \gamma(D)^2, \gamma(D)^3, \ldots\},$$

the larger discount the longer takes to collect the reward (the term $\gamma(D)^{k-t}$ in (2)). While we present our results using this familiar notion of discounting, such geometric discounting factors may not be appropriate for applications in which the required time to serve customers takes multiple time steps. The whole analysis of this paper is valid if the discounting is performed with any other non-negative sequence $\{a_t,\ t \in \mathbb{N}\}$ with bounded total sum $\sum_{t=0}^{\infty} a_t < \infty$.

Example 1 (continued). Suppose that the 2-dimensional state space is partitioned into two offices and one hallway as depicted in Figure 1. Consider discounting factors $\gamma(D_i) := \gamma_i$ in $(0,1)$ and expected generated reward $\lambda(t, D_i) := \lambda_i$ for all $i \in \{1,2,3\}$ and $t \in \mathbb{N}$, such that $\lambda_2 = 0$ and $\lambda_1, \lambda_3 > 0$. For a policy ρ generating a sample path that visits the following regions consecutively:

$$D_2, D_2, D_3, D_2, D_1, D_2, D_2, \ldots,$$

the expected collected reward is

$$\lambda_2 + \lambda_2 + \lambda_3(1+\gamma_3+\gamma_3^2) + \lambda_2(1+\gamma_2) +$$
$$+\lambda_1(1+\gamma_1+\gamma_1^2+\gamma_1^3+\gamma_1^4) + \lambda_2(1+\gamma_2) + \lambda_2 + \ldots.$$

This sum goes to infinity if the path visits either of the regions D_1, D_3 infinitely often. The long-run average reward for the path that visits the regions $(D_2, D_2, D_3, D_2, D_1)$ periodically is

$$\frac{1}{5}\left[\lambda_2(1+\gamma_2) + \lambda_2 + \frac{\lambda_3(1-\gamma_3^5)}{1-\gamma_3} + \lambda_2(1+\gamma_2) + \frac{\lambda_1(1-\gamma_1^5)}{1-\gamma_1}\right].$$

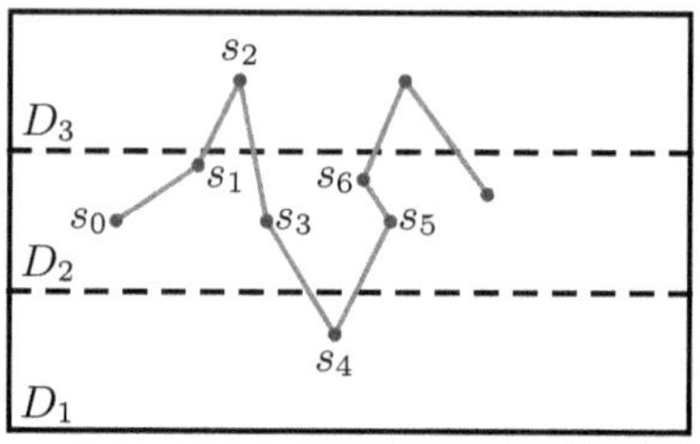

Figure 1: Layout of the 2-dimensional space for the robot's move in Example 1. D_1 and D_3 are offices and D_2 is the hallway. A sample path of the robot is sketched.

3.2 Optimal Policy and Value Problems

For the RCCMP $(\mathfrak{S},\mathfrak{R})$ described in Section 3.1, we can define different problems depending on whether we are interested in computing optimal collected reward, deciding on the existence of policies generating a minimum collected reward, or synthesizing optimal policies. These problems can be defined for both finite and infinite horizon, and also features exact and approximate versions.

DEFINITION 5. **[Optimal policy problems]** *Let $(\mathfrak{S},\mathfrak{R})$ be the RCCMP defined in Section 3.1.*

1. *Given $n \in \mathbb{N}$ and initial probability measure $\alpha \in \mathfrak{D}$, the* finite horizon optimal policy problem *asks to compute a policy $\rho = (\rho_0, \rho_1, \ldots, \rho_{n-1})$ of length n, such that for every policy ρ' of length n it holds that $\mathsf{CDR}_n(\rho,\alpha) \geq \mathsf{CDR}_n(\rho',\alpha)$.*

2. *Given an initial probability measure $\alpha \in \mathfrak{D}$, the* infinite horizon optimal policy problem *asks to compute an infinite policy $\rho = (\rho_0, \rho_1, \rho_2, \ldots)$, such that for every infinite policy ρ' in Π it holds that $\mathsf{CDR}_\infty(\rho,\alpha) \geq \mathsf{CDR}_\infty(\rho',\alpha)$.*

In the ϵ-optimal policy problem *we require computation of a policy ρ such that for all ρ', we have respectively for finite and infinite horizon, $\mathsf{CDR}_n(\rho,\alpha) \geq \mathsf{CDR}_n(\rho',\alpha) - \epsilon$ and $\mathsf{CDR}_\infty(\rho,\alpha) \geq \mathsf{CDR}_\infty(\rho',\alpha) - \epsilon$.*

DEFINITION 6. **[Value computation problems]** *Let $(\mathfrak{S},\mathfrak{R})$ be the RCCMP defined in Section 3.1.*

1. *Given $n \in \mathbb{N}$ and initial probability measure $\alpha \in \mathfrak{D}$, the* finite horizon value computation problem *asks to compute the value*
$$\mathsf{CDR}^*_n(\alpha) := \sup_{\rho\in\Pi} \mathsf{CDR}_n(\rho,\alpha). \qquad (4)$$

2. *Given an initial probability measure $\alpha \in \mathfrak{D}$, the* infinite horizon value computation problem *asks to compute the value*
$$\mathsf{CDR}^*_\infty(\alpha) := \sup_{\rho\in\Pi} \mathsf{CDR}_\infty(\rho,\alpha). \qquad (5)$$

In the ϵ-optimal value problem *we require computation of quantities $\mathsf{CDR}^\epsilon_n(\alpha)$ and $\mathsf{CDR}^\epsilon_\infty(\alpha)$ such that $|\mathsf{CDR}^\epsilon_n(\alpha) - \mathsf{CDR}^*_n(\alpha)| \leq \epsilon$ and $|\mathsf{CDR}^\epsilon_\infty(\alpha) - \mathsf{CDR}^*_\infty(\alpha)| \leq \epsilon$.*

DEFINITION 7. **[Value decision problems]** *Let $(\mathfrak{S},\mathfrak{R})$ be a RCCMP defined in Section 3.1 and $\mathsf{r_d} \in \mathbb{R}$.*

1. *Given $n \in \mathbb{N}$ and initial probability measure $\alpha \in \mathfrak{D}$, the* finite horizon value decision problem *asks to decide if* $\mathsf{CDR}^*_n(\alpha) \geq \mathsf{r_d}$.

2. *Given an initial probability measure $\alpha \in \mathfrak{D}$, the* infinite horizon value decision problem *asks to decide if* $\mathsf{CDR}^*_\infty(\alpha) \geq \mathsf{r_d}$.

In this paper we formulate the solution of optimal policy and value computation problems. Moreover, we discuss abstraction methods for the ϵ-optimal value computation problem[1]. The usual performance measures in the literature (e.g. total, discounted, or long-run average rewards) have an additive structure that results in *dynamic programming* (DP) procedures. Thus Markov policies are sufficient for the optimization under very mild assumptions [2]. The definition of CDR indicates that in general the computation of $\mathsf{CDR}_n, \mathsf{CDR}_\infty$ (and therefore that of $\mathsf{CDR}^*_n, \mathsf{CDR}^*_\infty$) requires the knowledge of history, thus Markov policies are not sufficient for optimizing the expected CDR. Take for instance the robot dynamics in Example 1. The robot should visit both regions D_1 and D_3 to collect the rewards generated in these regions, so the robot's move from D_2 will be towards either of the regions depending not only on its current location but also on the previously visited regions. To tackle this difficulty, we reformulate the optimization problem via an additive reward function in an augmented state space, for which the theory of DP is rather rich. We study finite and infinite horizon cases in Sections 4 and 5, respectively.

4. FINITE-HORIZON CDR

4.1 Dynamic Programming Formulation

Given the RCCMP $(\mathfrak{S}, \mathfrak{R})$ with the reward structure $\mathfrak{R} = (\mathcal{D}, \lambda, \gamma)$, we consider a new CMP

$$\hat{\mathfrak{S}} = \left(\hat{\mathcal{S}}, \mathcal{U}, \{\hat{\mathcal{U}}(s,y) | (s,y) \in \hat{\mathcal{S}}\}, \hat{T}_{\mathfrak{s}}\right)$$

with an augmented state space $\hat{\mathcal{S}} = \mathcal{S} \times \mathbb{Z}^m_+$, where m is the cardinality of $\mathcal{D}$. The states are of the form (s, y) with coordinates being $s \in \mathcal{S}$, $y \in \mathbb{Z}^m_+$. For a given finite path w_n, the ith element of y is in fact the length of the path starting at the previous occurrence of a state being in set D_i, $y_k(i) := k - \mathsf{Last}(w_n, D_i, k)$. The control space $\mathcal{U}$ is the same and we further define $\hat{\mathcal{U}}(s, y) = \mathcal{U}(s)$. The dynamics of $\hat{\mathfrak{S}}$ are given as follows:

$$\begin{cases} s_{n+1} & \sim \quad T_{\mathfrak{s}}(\cdot | s_n, u_n) \\ y_{n+1} & = \quad g_{\mathfrak{d}}(s_n, y_n), \end{cases} \tag{6}$$

where $g_{\mathfrak{d}}(s, y) := y + \mathbf{1}_m - \xi(s).y$ with $\mathbf{1}_m$ being a row vector of dimension m with all elements equal to one. $\xi(s)$ is a row vector of dimension m with elements $\mathbb{I}(s \in D_i)$, $i \in \mathbb{N}[1, m]$. The dot in $\xi(s).y$ indicates the element-wise product. Hence the corresponding transition kernel $\hat{T}_{\mathfrak{s}}$ is given by

$$\hat{T}_{\mathfrak{s}}(B \times \{y'\} | s, y, u) := T_{\mathfrak{s}}(B | s, u) \mathbb{I}\left(y' = g_{\mathfrak{d}}(s, y)\right), \tag{7}$$

for all $B \in \mathcal{B}(\mathcal{S})$. In words, the state s is updated stochastically according to $T_{\mathfrak{s}}$ while the state y is updated deterministically by incrementing all its elements by one except the ith element which is set to one.

[1]The proposed methods can be used iteratively to answer the value decision problem in Definition 7 with termination guarantees for any $\mathsf{r_d} \neq \mathsf{CDR}^*_n, \mathsf{CDR}^*_\infty$.

We construct a space of policies $\hat{\Pi}$ and for each $\hat{\rho} \in \hat{\Pi}$, a probability measure $\hat{P}^{\hat{\rho}}$ with the expectation $\hat{\mathbb{E}}^{\hat{\rho}}$. We denote by $\hat{\Pi}_M \subset \hat{\Pi}$ the corresponding class of Markov policies for $\hat{\mathfrak{S}}$. The reward structure consists of reward functions $\mathsf{rew} : \mathbb{N} \times \hat{\mathcal{S}} \to \mathbb{R}$, given by

$$\mathsf{rew}(k, s, y) := \sum_{t=0}^{\xi(s) y^T - 1} \gamma(\Xi(s))^t \lambda(k - t, \Xi(s)), \tag{8}$$

and additive functional $\widehat{\mathsf{CDR}}^{\hat{\rho}}_n(s, y) := \hat{\mathbb{E}}^{\hat{\rho}}_{s,y}\left[\sum_{k=0}^{n} \mathsf{rew}(k, s_k, y_k)\right]$

and its long-run average $\widehat{\mathsf{CDR}}^{\hat{\rho}}_\infty(s, y) := \liminf_{n \to \infty} \frac{1}{n+1} \widehat{\mathsf{CDR}}^{\hat{\rho}}_n(s, y)$.

In order to relate $(\hat{\mathfrak{S}}, \mathsf{rew})$ to the original formulation defined over the RCCMP $(\mathfrak{S}, \mathfrak{R})$, we first have to establish an explicit relationship between classes of strategies Π and $\hat{\Pi}$. Clearly, we can treat Π as a subset of $\hat{\Pi}$ as any policy $\rho \in \Pi$ for the CMP $\mathfrak{S}$ serves also as a policy for the CMP $\hat{\mathfrak{S}}$. We let $\iota : \Pi \to \hat{\Pi}$ be the inclusion map. On the other hand, we define the projection map $\theta : \hat{\Pi} \to \Pi$ by

$$\theta_j(\rho)(du_j | w_j) := \hat{\rho}_j(du_j | s_0, y_0, u_0, \ldots, s_j, y_j), \tag{9}$$

with $w_j = (s_0, u_0, s_1, u_1, \ldots, s_j)$, $y_k(i) = k - \mathsf{Last}(w_j, D_i, k)$, for all $i \in \mathbb{N}[1, m]$ and $k \in \mathbb{N}[0, j]$. The following result relates the two optimization problems.

THEOREM 1. *For any $n \in \mathbb{N}$, $\rho \in \Pi$ and $\hat{\rho} \in \hat{\Pi}$, it holds that*

$$\widehat{\mathsf{CDR}}^{\hat{\rho}}_n(s, \mathbf{1}_m) = \mathsf{CDR}_n(\theta(\hat{\rho}), s),\ \mathsf{CDR}_n(\rho, s) = \widehat{\mathsf{CDR}}^{\iota(\rho)}_n(s, \mathbf{1}_m),$$

$$\widehat{\mathsf{CDR}}^{\hat{\rho}}_\infty(s, \mathbf{1}_m) = \mathsf{CDR}_\infty(\theta(\hat{\rho}), s),\ \mathsf{CDR}_\infty(\rho, s) = \widehat{\mathsf{CDR}}^{\iota(\rho)}_\infty(s, \mathbf{1}_m).$$

□

Theorem 1 has several important corollaries. First of all, it can be used to prove that Markov policies $\hat{\Pi}_M$ are sufficient for the finite-horizon optimal value problem of RCCMP $(\mathfrak{S}, \mathfrak{R})$ in the *augmented* state space $\hat{\mathcal{S}}$. At the same time, the optimal policy may depend on time and thus is not necessary stationary. Let us further define $\widehat{\mathsf{CDR}}^*_n(s, y) := \sup_{\hat{\rho} \in \hat{\Pi}} \widehat{\mathsf{CDR}}^{\hat{\rho}}_n(s, y)$ and $\widehat{\mathsf{CDR}}^*_\infty(s, y) := \sup_{\hat{\rho} \in \hat{\Pi}} \widehat{\mathsf{CDR}}^{\hat{\rho}}_\infty(s, y)$.

COROLLARY 1. *For any $n \in \mathbb{N}$ and $s \in \mathcal{S}$, it holds that $\mathsf{CDR}^*_n(s) = \widehat{\mathsf{CDR}}^*_n(s, \mathbf{1}_m)$ and $\mathsf{CDR}^*_\infty(s) = \widehat{\mathsf{CDR}}^*_\infty(s, \mathbf{1}_m)$.* □

Finally, we can exploit DP recursions for the additive functionals $\widehat{\mathsf{CDR}}^*_n$ to compute the finite-horizon optimal value problem of RCCMP $(\mathfrak{S}, \mathfrak{R})$. Let us introduce the following time-dependent operators

$$\mathfrak{J}_k f(s, y, u) := \mathsf{rew}(k, s, y) + $$
$$+ \sum_{y' \in \mathbb{Z}^m_+} \int_{\mathcal{S}} f(s', y') \hat{T}_{\mathfrak{s}}(ds' \times \{y'\} | s, y, u), \tag{10}$$

and $\mathfrak{J}^*_k f(s, y) = \sup_{u \in \hat{\mathcal{U}}(s,y)} \mathfrak{J}_k f(s, y, u)$, which act on the space of bounded universally measurable functions. These operators can be used to compute optimal value functions recursively, as the following result states.

COROLLARY 2. *For any $n \in \mathbb{N}$, consider value functions $V_k : \hat{\mathcal{S}} \to \mathbb{R}$, $k \in \mathbb{N}[0, n]$ defined recursively as*

$$V_k = \mathfrak{J}^*_k V_{k+1}, \quad V_n(s, y) = \mathsf{rew}(n, s, y).$$

These value functions are universally measurable. Moreover, $\widehat{\mathsf{CDR}}^*_n(s, y) = V_0(s, y)$. □

Note that the operators in (10) can be further simplified to

$$\mathfrak{J}_k f(s,y,u) := \mathsf{rew}(k,s,y) + \int_{\mathcal{S}} f(s', g_{\mathfrak{d}}(s,y)) T_{\mathfrak{s}}(ds'|s,u). \tag{11}$$

4.2 Approximate Abstractions

Since the recursion in Corollary 2 does not admit a closed-form solution, we introduce an abstraction procedure, which results in numerical methods for the computation of such functions. Moreover, we provide an explicit upper bound on the error caused by the abstraction. We focus on finite-horizon optimal value problem in this section and then present the results for the infinite-horizon case in Section 5.

The abstraction algorithm initially proposed in [1] and further developed in [5, 17] are not directly applicable to our problem. First, in these works the state space of the process is considered to be continuous or hybrid. Applying such techniques to our problem that has $\mathcal{S} \times \mathbb{Z}_+^m$ as its state space results in a *countable unbounded* abstract space, which is difficult to deal with computationally. Second, the error of these abstraction algorithms are computed with respect to formal synthesis of policies for satisfaction of a given specification, while in our case we are optimizing collected rewards. In this section we present the abstraction algorithm adapted to our problem and then show how to solve the ϵ-optimal value problem.

Algorithm 1 presents the procedure for abstracting RC-CMP $(\mathfrak{S}, \mathfrak{R})$ to a finite-state RCCMP $(\mathfrak{M}, \mathfrak{R}_{\mathfrak{d}})$. It works directly on the CMP $\mathfrak{S}$ and computes MDP $\mathfrak{M}$ as its abstraction. It also gives the construction of collecting reward structure $\mathfrak{R}_{\mathfrak{d}}$ on the MDP $\mathfrak{M}$. Here the state space $\mathcal{S}$ is partitioned such that the partition refines $\mathcal{D}$, i.e., for any $i \in \mathbb{N}[1, m_{\mathfrak{s}}]$ there is a $D \in \mathcal{D}$ such that $S_i \subset D$. Then representative points z_i are selected and the state space of $\mathfrak{M}$ is constructed in Step 3. The input sets $\mathcal{U}(z_i)$ are also partitioned in Step 4 and arbitrary representative points are selected in Step 5. Step 6 defines the set of valid discrete inputs at each state and finally Step 7 gives the transition probabilities of the MDP $\mathfrak{M}$.

In this algorithm $\Xi_{\mathfrak{s}} : \mathcal{S} \to 2^{\mathcal{S}}$ is a set-valued map that assigns any state $s \in \mathcal{S}$ to the partition set it belongs to, i.e., $\Xi_{\mathfrak{s}}(s) = S_i$ whenever $s \in S_i$. Step 8 constructs the collecting reward structure by defining discrete regions $\mathcal{D}_{\mathfrak{d}}$ (intersection of elements of $\mathcal{D}$ with the discrete space $\mathcal{S}_{\mathfrak{d}}$) and then restricting functions λ, γ to $\mathcal{D}_{\mathfrak{d}}$. Moreover, it selects a different discounting sequence in which the power of discounting factor is saturated with a constant $\ell \in \mathbb{N}$.

The DP formulation in Section 4.1 is also applicable to the RCCMP $(\mathfrak{M}, \mathfrak{R}_{\mathfrak{d}})$. Due to the particular choice of discounting sequence $\gamma_{\mathfrak{d}}$ in Step 8 of Algorithm 1, the augmented MDP $\hat{\mathfrak{M}}$ will have the finite state space $\hat{\mathcal{S}}_{\mathfrak{d}} = \mathcal{S}_{\mathfrak{d}} \times \mathbb{N}[1,\ell]^m$. Its transition probabilities are also defined as

$$\hat{T}_{\mathfrak{d}}(z', w'|z, w, v) = T_{\mathfrak{d}}(z'|z,v)\mathbb{I}(w' = g_\ell(z,w)),$$

which requires that the second coordinate of the state $(z, w) \in \hat{\mathcal{S}}_{\mathfrak{d}}$ is deterministically updated according to $w' = g_\ell(z,w)$ with

$$g_\ell(z,w) := \min\{w + \mathbf{1}_m - \xi(z).w, \ell\}.$$

Next we present the DP recursion for computation of ϵ-value and policy problem. Define operators

---

Algorithm 1 Abstraction of RCCMP $(\mathfrak{S}, \mathfrak{R})$ by finite-state RCCMP $(\mathfrak{M}, \mathfrak{R}_{\mathfrak{d}})$

Require: input model $\mathfrak{S} = (\mathcal{S}, \mathcal{U}, \{\mathcal{U}(s) | s \in \mathcal{S}\}, T_{\mathfrak{s}})$ and reward structure $\mathfrak{R} = (\mathcal{D}, \lambda, \gamma)$

1: Select a finite partition $\{S_1, \ldots, S_{m_{\mathfrak{s}}}\}$ of $\mathcal{S}$ which refines $\mathcal{D}$
2: For each S_i, select a single representative point $z_i \in S_i$
3: Define $\mathcal{S}_{\mathfrak{d}} = \{z_i \mid i \in \mathbb{N}[1, m_{\mathfrak{s}}]\}$ as the state space of the MDP $\mathfrak{M}$
4: For each $i \in \mathbb{N}[1, m_{\mathfrak{s}}]$, select a finite partition of the input set $\mathcal{U}(z_i)$ as $\mathcal{U}(z_i) = \cup_{j=1}^{m_{\mathfrak{u}_i}} U_{ij}$ where $m_{\mathfrak{u}_i}$ represents the cardinality of the partition of $\mathcal{U}(z_i)$
5: For each U_{ij}, select single representative point $v_{ij} \in U_{ij}$
6: Define $\mathcal{U}_{\mathfrak{d}} = \{v_{ij} \mid j \in \mathbb{N}[1, m_{\mathfrak{u}_i}], i \in \mathbb{N}[1, m_{\mathfrak{s}}]\}$ as the finite input space of the MDP $\mathfrak{M}$, $\mathcal{U}_{\mathfrak{d}}(z_i) = \{v_{ij} \mid j \in \mathbb{N}[1, m_{\mathfrak{u}_i}]\}$ as the set of feasible inputs when $\mathfrak{M}$ is at any state $z_i \in \mathcal{S}_{\mathfrak{d}}$
7: Compute the state transition matrix $\hat{T}_{\mathfrak{d}}$ for $\mathfrak{M}$ as:
$$T_{\mathfrak{d}}(z'|z,v) = \hat{T}_{\mathfrak{s}}(\Xi_{\mathfrak{s}}(z')|z,v), \tag{12}$$
for any $z, z' \in \mathcal{S}_{\mathfrak{d}}$ and $v \in \mathcal{U}_{\mathfrak{d}}(z)$
8: Define discrete regions $\mathcal{D}_{\mathfrak{d}} := \{D_i \cap \mathcal{S}_{\mathfrak{d}} \mid i \in \mathbb{N}[1, m]\}$, discounting sequence $\gamma_{\mathfrak{d}} := \{1, \gamma, \gamma^2, \ldots, \gamma^{\ell-1}, \gamma^\ell, \gamma^\ell, \ldots\}$, and $\lambda_{\mathfrak{d}} := \lambda|_{\mathcal{D}_{\mathfrak{d}}}$

Ensure: output finite-state RCCMP $(\mathfrak{M}, \mathfrak{R}_{\mathfrak{d}})$ with $\mathfrak{M} = (\mathcal{S}_{\mathfrak{d}}, \mathcal{U}_{\mathfrak{d}}, \{\mathcal{U}_{\mathfrak{d}}(z) | (z) \in \mathcal{S}_{\mathfrak{d}}\}, T_{\mathfrak{d}})$ and $\mathfrak{R}_{\mathfrak{d}} = (\mathcal{D}_{\mathfrak{d}}, \lambda_{\mathfrak{d}}, \gamma_{\mathfrak{d}})$

$$\bar{\mathfrak{J}}_k f_{\mathfrak{d}}(z,w,v) := \mathsf{rew}_{\mathsf{a}}(k,z,w) + \sum_{(z',w') \in \hat{\mathcal{S}}_{\mathfrak{d}}} f_{\mathfrak{d}}(z',w') \hat{T}_{\mathfrak{d}}(z',w'|z,w,v),$$

and $\bar{\mathfrak{J}}_k^* f_{\mathfrak{d}}(z,w) = \max_{v \in \hat{\mathcal{U}}_{\mathfrak{d}}(z,w)} \bar{\mathfrak{J}}_k f_{\mathfrak{d}}(z,w,v)$. The functions $\mathsf{rew}_{\mathsf{a}}$ are defined as

$$\mathsf{rew}_{\mathsf{a}}(k,z,w) = \sum_{t=0}^{\xi(z)w^T - 1} \gamma(\Xi_{\mathfrak{d}}(z))^t \lambda(k-t, \Xi_{\mathfrak{d}}(z)),$$

where the function $\Xi_{\mathfrak{d}} : \mathcal{S}_{\mathfrak{d}} \to \mathcal{D}_{\mathfrak{d}}$ assigns to any discrete state $z \in D_i$ the discrete region $\Xi_{\mathfrak{d}}(z) = D_i \cap \mathcal{S}_{\mathfrak{d}}$. (cf. the reward function in (8)).

The discrete value functions are computed using the recursion $\bar{V}_k = \bar{\mathfrak{J}}_k^* \bar{V}_{k+1}$ with $\bar{V}_n(z,w) = \mathsf{rew}_{\mathsf{a}}(n,z,w)$. Then the approximate solution of the finite-horizon CDR will be $\overline{\mathsf{CDR}}^*(z,w) = \bar{V}_0(z,w)$. The finite-state MDP $\mathfrak{M}$ can be computed using software tool FAUST^2 [7] and the value functions can be computed with numerically efficient methods [11]. We discuss in the next section how the error of the abstraction algorithm 1 can be quantified based on suitable assumptions on the RCMCP.

4.3 Error Computation

Since $\mathcal{S}$ and $\mathcal{U}$ are Borel spaces they are metrizable topological spaces. Let $d_{\mathfrak{s}}$ and $d_{\mathfrak{u}}$ be metrics on $\mathcal{S}$ and $\mathcal{U}$ respectively, which are consistent with the given topologies of the underlying spaces. Define the *diameter* of a set $A \subset \mathcal{S}$ as

$$\mathrm{diam}_{\mathfrak{s}}(A) := \sup\{d_{\mathfrak{s}}(s,s') |\ s, s' \in \mathcal{S}\},$$

likewise for subsets of $\mathcal{U}$. Also define diameter of the partition $\mathcal{S} = \cup_{i=1}^{m_{\mathfrak{s}}} S_i$ as the maximum diameter of its elements $\delta_{\mathfrak{s}} := \max_i \mathrm{diam}_{\mathfrak{s}}(S_i)$, and $\delta_{\mathfrak{u}} := \max_{i,j} \mathrm{diam}_{\mathfrak{u}}(U_{ij})$. We assume that the selected partition sets S_i refine $\mathcal{D}$, i.e., for any $i \in \mathbb{N}[1, m_{\mathfrak{s}}]$ and $D \in \mathcal{D}$ either $S_i \subset D$ or $S_i \cap D = \emptyset$.

The error quantification of the MDP abstraction approach, presented in Algorithm 1, requires the study of the family of sets $\mathcal{U}(s)$ as a function of state. For this purpose, we assign the Hausdorff distance to the family of non-empty subsets of $\mathcal{U}$, which is defined as

$$d_H(X, Y) := \max\left\{\sup_{x\in X}\inf_{y\in Y} d_{\mathfrak{u}}(x, y),\ \sup_{y\in Y}\inf_{x\in X} d_{\mathfrak{u}}(x, y)\right\},$$

for all $X, Y \subset \mathcal{U}$. The next assumption poses a regularity condition on state-dependent input sets.

Assumption 1. *There exists a constant $h_{\mathfrak{u}} \in \mathbb{R}$ such that the family of state-dependent input sets $\{\mathcal{U}(s) | s \in \mathcal{S}\}$ satisfies the Lipschitz inequality*

$$d_H(\mathcal{U}(s), \mathcal{U}(s')) \le h_{\mathfrak{u}} d_{\mathfrak{s}}(s, s') \quad \forall s, s' \in \mathcal{S}.$$

The error quantification also requires a regularity assumption on the stochastic kernel $T_{\mathfrak{s}}(\bar{s}|s, u)$. Given a function $f : \mathcal{S} \to \mathbb{R}$, we define $T_{\mathfrak{s}} f : \mathcal{K} \to \mathbb{R}$ as

$$T_{\mathfrak{s}} f(s, u) = \int_{\mathcal{S}} f(\bar{s}) T_{\mathfrak{s}}(\bar{s}|s, u),$$

provided that the corresponding integrals are well defined and finite. We pose the following assumption on the stochastic kernel $T_{\mathfrak{s}}$ of the process.

Assumption 2. *There exists a constant $h_{\mathfrak{T}} > 0$ such that for every (s, u) and (s', u') in $\mathcal{K}$, and bounded function $f : \mathcal{S} \to \mathbb{R}$, with Lipschitz constant h_f,*

$$|T_{\mathfrak{s}} f(s, u) - T_{\mathfrak{s}} f(s', u')| \le h_{\mathfrak{T}} h_f \left[d_{\mathfrak{s}}(s, s') + d_{\mathfrak{u}}(u, u')\right].$$

The kernel $T_{\mathfrak{s}}$ is said to be $h_{\mathfrak{T}}$-Lipschitz continuous. We also assume that $T_{\mathfrak{s}}(D_i|s, u)$ is Lipschitz continuous, i.e., there exists a constant $h_{\mathfrak{c}} > 0$ such that for all $i \in \mathbb{N}[1, m]$,

$$|T_{\mathfrak{s}}(D_i|s, u) - T_{\mathfrak{s}}(D_i|s', u')| \le h_{\mathfrak{c}} \left[d_{\mathfrak{s}}(s, s') + d_{\mathfrak{u}}(u, u')\right].$$

The following lemma (1) provides an upper bound on the value functions V_k, $k \in \mathbb{N}[0, n]$ and (2) under Assumptions 1 and 2, establishes piecewise continuity properties of the value functions. Note that the reward functions $\mathsf{rew}(k, s, y)$ are piecewise constant with continuity regions $D_i \in \mathcal{D}, i \in \mathbb{N}[1, m]$.

Lemma 1. *1. Assume there is a constant $\lambda_{\mathrm{m}} \in \mathbb{R}_{\ge 0}$ such that $\lambda(t, D) \le \lambda_{\mathrm{m}}$ for all $D \in \mathcal{D}$ and $t \in \mathbb{N}$. Let $\kappa := \lambda_{\mathrm{m}}/(1 - \gamma_{\mathrm{m}})$ with $\gamma_{\mathrm{m}} := \max_i \gamma(D_i)$. Then the reward functions are bounded $\mathsf{rew}(k, s, y) \le \kappa$ and the value functions are bounded by*

$$V_k(s, y) \le (n + 1 - k)\kappa, \quad \forall (s, y) \in \hat{\mathcal{S}},\ k \in \mathbb{N}[0, n],$$

2. Under Assumptions 1 and 2, the value functions V_k are piecewise Lipschitz continuous with continuity regions D_i, and their Lipschitz constants are L_k, computed recursively with $L_n = 0$ and

$$L_k = (1 + h_{\mathfrak{u}}) \left[h_{\mathfrak{T}} L_{k+1} + m h_{\mathfrak{c}} \kappa\right],\ k \in \mathbb{N}[0, n-1], \quad (13)$$

where m is the cardinality of $\mathcal{D}$ and κ and γ_{m} are defined as above.

□

Piecewise continuous value functions enable us to quantify the abstraction error of Algorithm 1 induced on the respective value functions. Define the function $\xi_{\mathfrak{d}}$ on $\hat{\mathcal{S}}$ such that $\xi_{\mathfrak{d}}(s, y)$ assigns the associated representative point (z, w) to (s, y) as selected in Algorithm 1. Then we have the following theorem.

Theorem 2. **[Finite-horizon ε-optimal value problem]** *Suppose Assumptions 1 and 2 hold. Define $\mathcal{L}_{\mathfrak{u}} := \sum_{k=0}^{n-1} L_k$, $\mathcal{L}_{\mathfrak{s}} := h_{\mathfrak{T}} \sum_{k=1}^{n} L_k$, and $\epsilon(\ell) := (n+1)\kappa\gamma_{\mathrm{m}}^{\ell}$, where L_k, κ, and γ_{m} are defined as in Lemma 1. The abstraction error of Algorithm 1 on the computed optimal finite-horizon CDR is*

$$|\widehat{\mathsf{CDR}}_n^*(s, y) - \overline{\mathsf{CDR}}_n^*(\xi_{\mathfrak{d}}(s, y))| \le \mathcal{L}_{\mathfrak{u}}\delta_{\mathfrak{u}} + \mathcal{L}_{\mathfrak{s}}\delta_{\mathfrak{s}} + \epsilon(\ell), \quad (14)$$

for all $(s, y) \in \hat{\mathcal{S}}$. □

The error bound in Theorem 2 can be used to solve the ε-optimal policy problem as follows.

Corollary 3. **[Finite-horizon ε-optimal policy problem]** *Suppose Assumptions 1 and 2 hold. If we synthesize an optimal policy $\bar{\rho}^* = (\bar{\rho}_0^*, \bar{\rho}_1^*, \ldots)$ for $\mathfrak{M}$ and apply the policy $\rho = (\rho_0, \rho_1, \ldots)$ with $\rho = \theta\bar{\rho}^*\xi_{\mathfrak{d}}(\cdot)$ to $\mathfrak{S}$, with θ being the policy projection map defined in (9), then the error will be*

$$|\mathsf{CDR}_n(\rho, s) - \mathsf{CDR}_n^*(s)| \le 2(\mathcal{L}_{\mathfrak{u}}\delta_{\mathfrak{u}} + \mathcal{L}_{\mathfrak{s}}\delta_{\mathfrak{s}} + \epsilon(\ell)).$$

Note that the approximate optimal policy is computed as follows: compute (s_j, y_j) for a given path $(s_0, u_0, \ldots, s_j)$; find the discrete representative state $(z_j, w_j) \in \hat{\mathcal{S}}_{\mathfrak{d}}$; compute $v_j = \bar{\rho}_j^*(z_j, w_j) \in \mathcal{U}(s_j)$ and apply it to $\mathfrak{S}$.

The abstraction error in (14) has three terms: the first term is related to discretization of the input space; the second term reflects the effect of discretizing the state space; and the last term is related to the choice of discounting sequence in step 8 of the abstraction algorithm. The error can be tuned by proper selection of partition diameters $\delta_{\mathfrak{u}}$ and $\delta_{\mathfrak{s}}$ and the choice of ℓ.

Remark 2. *The above error computation is distinct from the one from [1, 6, 16] in there is no requirement on having a bounded state space or on value functions being in the interval $[0, 1]$.*

Example 2. *Consider a nonlinear dynamical system with additive noise*

$$s_{t+1} = f_{\mathrm{m}}(s_t, u_t) + \eta_t,$$

where $\{\eta_t,\ t \in \mathbb{N}\}$ are iid with the distribution $\eta_t \sim T_\eta(\cdot)$. Suppose f_{m} is Lipschitz continuous with constant $h_{f_{\mathrm{m}}}$. Then Assumption 2 holds for this system with the same constant $h_{\mathfrak{T}} = h_{f_{\mathrm{m}}}$ no matter what the distribution of noise $T_\eta(\cdot)$ is. In contrast, previous error analysis in [1, 6] requires continuity of $T_\eta(\cdot)$.

The behavior of the error in Theorem 2(2) as a function of horizon n depends on the constant $(1 + h_{\mathfrak{u}})h_{\mathfrak{T}}$ in recursion (13): the error grows exponentially if $(1 + h_{\mathfrak{u}})h_{\mathfrak{T}} > 1$; it grows quadratically if $(1 + h_{\mathfrak{u}})h_{\mathfrak{T}} = 1$; and it diverges linearly if $(1 + h_{\mathfrak{u}})h_{\mathfrak{T}} < 1$. Thus the error analysis of the abstraction method is useful for the infinite-horizon CDR only in the last case, i.e., $(1 + h_{\mathfrak{u}})h_{\mathfrak{T}} < 1$: the linearly growing error will be normalized by the horizon and gives a bounded tunable error. We study the infinite-horizon CDR in the next section based on the limiting behavior of the CMP.

5. INFINITE-HORIZON CDR

Recall the definition of infinite-horizon CDR $\mathsf{CDR}_\infty(\rho,\alpha)$ in (3) for a policy $\rho \in \Pi$ and initial distribution $\alpha \in \mathfrak{D}$. For the sake of succinct presentation of the theoretical results, with a slight abuse of notation, we construct the augmented process $\hat{\mathfrak{S}}$ based on the modified discounting sequence $\{1,\gamma,\gamma^2,\ldots,\gamma^{\ell-1},\gamma^\ell,\gamma^\ell,\ldots\}$. Thus the dynamics of $\hat{\mathfrak{S}}$ are

$$\begin{cases} s_{n+1} & \sim & T_{\mathfrak{s}}(\cdot|s_n,u_n) \\ y_{n+1} & = & g_\ell(s_n,y_n), \end{cases} \tag{15}$$

where $g_\ell(s,y) := \min\{y+\mathbf{1}_m - \xi(s).y,\ell\}$ (cf. dynamics in (6)) with ℓ being a properly chosen value (cf. Theorem 5). Based on our discussion in Section 4.3, the induced error on the infinite-horizon CDR is upper bounded by

$$|\,\mathsf{CDR}^*_\infty(s) - \widehat{\mathsf{CDR}}^*_\infty(s,\mathbf{1}_m)| \le \epsilon_1 := \kappa\gamma^\ell_{\mathrm{m}},$$

where $\widehat{\mathsf{CDR}}^*_\infty(s,y)$ is the optimal long-run average reward function over the augmented process $\hat{\mathfrak{S}}$ with dynamics (15),

$$\widehat{\mathsf{CDR}}^*_\infty(s,y) = \sup_{\hat\rho}\liminf_{n\to\infty}\frac{1}{n+1}\hat{\mathbb{E}}^{\hat\rho}_{s,y}\left[\sum_{k=0}^{n}\mathsf{rew}(k,s_k,y_k)\right],$$

and the reward function $\mathsf{rew}(k,s_k,y_k)$ is defined in (8). We also assume that the expected reward λ is stationary (it is only a function of regions and does not depend on time). Therefore $\mathsf{rew}(k,s,y)$ will be denoted by $\mathsf{rew}(s,y)$. The quantity $\widehat{\mathsf{CDR}}^*_\infty(s,y)$ depends on the limiting behavior of the process $\hat{\mathfrak{S}}$ and its computational aspect varies depending on the structural properties of the process [10, 12]. For instance ergodicity of the process under any stationary policy ensures that the optimal average reward $\widehat{\mathsf{CDR}}^*_\infty(s,y)$ is independent of the initial state (s,y). We present in Section 5.1 an optimality equation whose solution gives the optimal average reward. We provide an assumption on the original process $\mathfrak{S}$ under which the optimality equation has a solution. In Section 5.2, we discuss value iteration for the computation of the solution of the optimality equation and provide an approximation procedure based on abstraction with guaranteed error bounds.

5.1 Optimality Equation

Define $\mathbb{B}(\hat{\mathcal{S}})$ as the Banach space of real-valued bounded measurable functions $f:\hat{\mathcal{S}}\to\mathbb{R}$ with the supremum norm $\|f\| := \sup_{\hat s\in\hat{\mathcal{S}}}|f(\hat s)|$. Under the assumption of generated reward being stationary in expectation (thus having bounded time-independent $\mathsf{rew}(s,y)$), the following theorem presents optimality equation for the infinite-horizon CDR.

THEOREM 3. *Suppose the generated reward is stationary in expectation. If there is a constant g and a function v^* in $\mathbb{B}(\hat{\mathcal{S}})$ such that for all $(s,y)\in\hat{\mathcal{S}}$,*

$$g+v^*(s,y) = \sup_{u\in\mathcal{U}(s)}\left\{\mathsf{rew}(s,y) + \int_{\hat{\mathcal{S}}} v^*(s',y')\hat T_{\mathfrak{s}}(ds',dy'|s,y,u)\right\}, \tag{16}$$

then $\widehat{\mathsf{CDR}}^*_\infty(s,y) \le g$ for all $(s,y)\in\hat{\mathcal{S}}$. If $d^*\in\hat\Pi_S$ is a stationary policy such that $d^*:\hat{\mathcal{S}}\to\mathcal{U}$ and $d^*(s,y)\in\mathcal{U}(s)$ maximizes the right-hand side of optimality equation (16), then d^* is optimal and $\widehat{\mathsf{CDR}}^{d^*}_\infty(s,y) = g$ for all $(s,y)\in\hat{\mathcal{S}}$. □

If g and $v^*\in\mathbb{B}(\hat{\mathcal{S}})$ are as in Theorem 3, it is then said that $\{g,v^*\}$ is a *solution* to the optimality equation (OE) (16). The OE (16) is sometimes called the average-reward dynamic programming equation [10]. We also define the DP operator

$$\mathfrak{J}^*f(s,y) := \mathsf{rew}(s,y) + \sup_{u\in\mathcal{U}(s)}\int_{\mathcal{S}} f(s',g_\ell(s,y))T_{\mathfrak{s}}(ds'|s,u), \tag{17}$$

which is the time-independent version of (11) adapted to the dynamics (15). Using the DP operator $\mathfrak{J}^*$ in (17) we can write the OE (16) as

$$g+v^*(s,y) = \mathfrak{J}^*v^*(s,y),\quad \forall (s,y)\in\hat{\mathcal{S}}.$$

Note that the solution of OE is not unique in general if it exists at all. In fact, if $\{g,v^*\}$ is a solution to the OE, so if $\{g,v^*+\varrho\}$ for any $\varrho\in\mathbb{R}$. Even if there is a solution $\{g,v^*\}$, it is not guaranteed to get a stationary policy maximizing the right-hand side of OE. The following lemma guarantees existence of such a policy.

LEMMA 2. *Suppose $\mathcal{U}(s)$ is a (non-empty) compact subset of $\mathcal{U}$ for each state $s\in\mathcal{S}$ and the generated reward is stationary in expectation. Then under Assumption 2, if the OE (16) has a solution, there exists a stationary policy $d^*\in\hat\Pi_S$ that achieves the optimal value g.* □

The next thing to look at is the existence of a solution for the OE (16). Ergodicity conditions for continuous space processes are discussed in [9] and structural conditions for countable space processes are presented in [12]. We adapt the assumption from [9] to the CMP $\hat{\mathfrak{S}}$.

ASSUMPTION 3. *For any stationary policy $\hat d\in\hat\Pi_S$ with $\hat d:\hat{\mathcal{S}}\to\mathcal{U}$ there exists a probability measure $\hat p_{\hat d}$ on $\hat{\mathcal{S}}$ such that*

$$\|\hat T^k_{\hat d}(\cdot|s,y) - \hat p_{\hat d}(\cdot)\| \le \hat{\mathfrak{c}}_k,\quad \forall (s,y)\in\hat{\mathcal{S}},\ k\in\mathbb{N},$$

where the sequence $\{\hat{\mathfrak{c}}_k,\ k\in\mathbb{N}\}$ is independent of (s,y) and of $\hat d$, and $\sum_k\hat{\mathfrak{c}}_k<\infty$. Here $\hat T^k_{\hat d}(\cdot|s,y)$ denotes the $k-$step transition probability measure of the Markov process $\hat{\mathfrak{S}}$ when the stationary policy $\hat d\in\hat\Pi_S$ is used, given that the initial state is (s,y). The norm $\|\cdot\|$ denotes the total variation norm for signed measures.

For probability measures P_1 and P_2 on $(\hat{\mathcal{S}},\mathcal{B}(\hat{\mathcal{S}}))$, recall that P_1-P_2 is a finite signed measure and its total variation is given by

$$\|P_1-P_2\| = 2\sup_{B\in\mathcal{B}(\hat{\mathcal{S}})}|P_1(B)-P_2(B)|.$$

If P_1 and P_2 have densities p_1 and p_2 with respect to some sigma-finite measure μ on $\hat{\mathcal{S}}$, then

$$\|P_1-P_2\| = \int_{\hat{\mathcal{S}}}|p_1-p_2|d\mu.$$

THEOREM 4. *Under Assumption 3, the optimal average reward $\widehat{\mathsf{CDR}}^*_\infty(s,y)$ is independent of the initial state (s,y) and the optimality equation (16) has a solution.* □

Assumption 3 puts a restriction on the augmented CMP $\hat{\mathfrak{S}}$. It is possible to check satisfaction of this assumption by looking at the CMP $\mathfrak{S}$. More precisely, Assumption 3 holds if the same condition is true for $\mathfrak{S}$ with a larger class of policies, namely history-dependent policies with finite memory:

$$\|T_d^k(\cdot|s) - p_d(\cdot)\| \leq \mathfrak{c}_k, \quad \forall s \in \mathcal{S},\ k \in \mathbb{N},$$

for all deterministic policies $(d, d, \ldots) \in \Pi$ with $d(w_n)$ being only a function of $(s_{n-\ell+1}, \ldots, s_{n-1}, s_n)$.

Existence of a solution for the OE (16) is ensured by Assumption 3. In the next section we study value iteration method for the approximate computation of the solution with guaranteed error bounds.

5.2 Value Iteration

In this section we discuss how the solution of OE (16) can be obtained using value iteration under proper assumptions on the operator $\mathfrak{J}^*$. We define the value iteration functions $W_k \in \mathbb{B}(\hat{\mathcal{S}})$ by

$$W_{n+1} = \mathfrak{J}^* W_n = \mathfrak{J}^{*n+1} W_0,\ n \in \mathbb{N}, \tag{18}$$

where $W_0(s, y) \in \mathbb{B}(\hat{\mathcal{S}})$ is arbitrary. As we observed in Section 4, $W_n(s, y)$ can be interpreted as the maximal expected reward for finite horizon n when the initial state is $(s_0, y_0) = (s, y)$ if the initial value function $W_0(s, y) = \mathsf{rew}(s, y)$ is selected. Clearly, as $n \to \infty$, W_n might not converge to a function in $\mathbb{B}(\hat{\mathcal{S}})$. We put the following assumption that ensures appropriate transformations of W_n do converge.

ASSUMPTION 4. *The DP operator* (17) *is a span-contraction operator, i.e.,*

$$sp(\mathfrak{J}^* f_1 - \mathfrak{J}^* f_2) \leq \alpha_{\mathfrak{J}}\, sp(f_1 - f_2), \quad \forall f_1, f_2 \in \mathcal{B}(\hat{\mathcal{S}}),$$

for some $\alpha_{\mathfrak{J}} < 1$. The span semi-norm *of a function is defined as* $sp(f) := \sup_{\hat{s}} f(\hat{s}) - \inf_{\hat{s}} f(\hat{s})$.

Banach's fixed point theorem for contraction operators on complete metric spaces [9] implies that under Assumption 4, $\mathfrak{J}^*$ has a span-fixed-point, i.e., there is a function $v^* \in \mathbb{B}(\hat{\mathcal{S}})$ such that $sp(\mathfrak{J}^* v^* - v^*) = 0$. Equivalently, $\mathfrak{J}^* v^* - v^*$ is a constant function. Thus, the OE has a solution.

REMARK 3. *Assumption 4 may be generalized by requiring multi-step span-contraction, i.e., there exists an positive integer ϑ such that $\mathfrak{J}^{*\vartheta}$ is a span-contraction operator. The following results are also valid for such operators.*

Let us define a sequence of functions e_n in $\mathbb{B}(\hat{\mathcal{S}})$ by

$$e_n(s, y) := \mathfrak{J}^{*n} W_0(s, y) - \mathfrak{J}^{*n} v^*(s, y) = W_n(s, y) - v^*(s, y) - ng,$$

for all $(s, y) \in \hat{\mathcal{S}}$ and $n \in \mathbb{N}$. We also define $v_n^+ := \sup(W_n - W_{n-1})$ and $v_n^- := \inf(W_n - W_{n-1})$.

LEMMA 3. *The sequence v_n^+ is non-increasing, v_n^- is non-decreasing, and both sequences converge exponentially fast to g; namely, for all $n \in \mathbb{Z}_+$,*

$$-\alpha_{\mathfrak{J}}^{n-1} sp(e_0) \leq v_n^- - g \leq v_n^+ - g \leq \alpha_{\mathfrak{J}}^{n-1} sp(e_0). \qquad \square$$

Lemma 3 provides a uniform approximation to the optimal average reward g.

THEOREM 5. *Suppose we select $\ell \in \mathbb{N}$ sufficiently large such that Assumption 4 is still valid and $\kappa\gamma_{\mathfrak{m}}^{\ell} \leq \epsilon_1$. Suppose the horizon $n \in \mathbb{N}$ is also sufficiently large, such that $4\kappa\alpha_{\mathfrak{J}}^{n-1} \leq \epsilon_2$. If we compute $\overline{\mathsf{CDR}}_n^*(z, w)$ using abstraction algorithm in Section 4.2 with error ϵ_3, then*

$$|\,\overline{\mathsf{CDR}}_n^*(z, w) - \overline{\mathsf{CDR}}_{n-1}^*(z, w) - g| \leq \epsilon_1 + \epsilon_2 + 2\epsilon_3,$$

which gives $\overline{\mathsf{CDR}}_n^*(z, w) - \overline{\mathsf{CDR}}_{n-1}^*(z, w)$ as an approximation of $g = \widehat{\mathsf{CDR}}_\infty^*(s, y)$ with error $\epsilon_1 + \epsilon_2 + 2\epsilon_3$. $\square$

6. CASE STUDY

We apply our results to the model of the robot in Example 1. The state space $\mathcal{S} = [0, 4] \times [0, 9]$ is partitioned into three regions, $D_i = [0, 4] \times [3(i-1), 3i]$, $i = 1, 2, 3$, as depicted in Figure 1. The process noise is normally distributed with covariance matrix $\Sigma_{\mathfrak{r}} = \mathrm{diag}(\sigma_1^2, \sigma_2^2)$. With this selection, the dynamics of the robot in each dimension are independent and the layout is symmetric. Therefore the solution of the problem should only depend on the dynamics along the vertical axis, i.e., the actions should be either up or down independent of the history of the robot's horizontal locations. This fact is confirmed by the simulations.

Since the set of valid inputs to the system is independent from the current state, Assumption 1 holds with $h_{\mathfrak{u}} = 0$. The input set is already discrete thus there is no need for discretization and so $\delta_{\mathfrak{u}} = 0$. As we discussed in Example 2, Assumption 2 holds with $h_{\mathfrak{T}} = 1$ and also $h_{\mathfrak{c}} = 1/\sigma_2\sqrt{2\pi}$. Therefore, the Lipschitz constants in Lemma 2 are $L_k = 3(n-k)h_{\mathfrak{c}}\kappa$ and the error grows quadratically with n as

$$\varepsilon = \kappa\left[\frac{n(n-1)}{2} 3h_{\mathfrak{c}}\delta_{\mathfrak{s}} + (n+1)\gamma_{\mathfrak{m}}^{\ell}\right].$$

The required memory usage and the computational complexity of the proposed approach depend on the size of the CMP $\mathfrak{M}$, i.e., the number of discrete inputs and states, and on the parameter ℓ for truncating the required history. Suppose state and input spaces of CMP $\mathfrak{S}$ has dimensions $d_{\mathfrak{s}}$ and $d_{\mathfrak{u}}$, respectively, and we take $n_{\mathfrak{s}}$ and $n_{\mathfrak{u}}$ partition sets along each dimension. Then the augmented MDP $\hat{\mathfrak{M}}$ has $n_{\mathfrak{s}}^{d_{\mathfrak{s}}}\ell^m$ discrete states with $n_{\mathfrak{u}}^{d_{\mathfrak{u}}}$ discrete actions, which are exponential is dimension of the process and in ℓ but polynomial is the required accuracy ε. This complexity can be reduced in the following ways. First, we do not need the whole state space $\hat{S}_{\mathfrak{d}} = S_{\mathfrak{d}} \times \mathbb{N}[1, \ell]^m$ but its subset that is reachable from $\xi_{\mathfrak{d}}(s, \mathbf{1}_m)$ for any s in the set of initial states of the CMP $\mathfrak{S}$. Second, the transition probability matrix of $\hat{\mathfrak{M}}$ is quite sparse, which enables us to utilize more efficient data structures to have a tradeoff between computational time and memory usage. Finally, adaptive girdding techniques proposed in [6] can also be used in this setting to reduce the required number of discrete states for a given accuracy.

The expected generated rewards $\lambda_1 = 5$ and $\lambda_3 = 7$ are chosen. The discounting factors are $\gamma_1 = 0.99 = \gamma_3 = 0.99$. For the hallway the expected generated reward is zero $\lambda_2 = 0$ and the discounting factor can be any quantity with no influence on the outcome: we set $\gamma_2 = 0.9$. We select $n_{\mathfrak{s}} = 45$ partition sets and $\ell = 6$. Standard deviation of the process noise is $\sigma_2 = 1.2$ and step size of the robot $\alpha_0 = 1.5$.

Figure 2 shows the approximate computation of $\mathsf{CDR}_n^*(s)$ as a function of initial state s and for different values of horizon n. As it is expected, these functions are piecewise continuous with continuity regions D_1, D_2, D_3. The difference $\mathsf{CDR}_n^*(s) - \mathsf{CDR}_{n-1}^*(s)$ converges to 10.30 after 30 iterations, which gives an approximation for $\mathsf{CDR}_\infty^*(s)$. Sample paths of the robot under the approximate optimal policy is shown in Figure 3 with the robot being initially in the hallway. Despite the robot being initially closer to region D_1, it decides to move up to visit D_3 since the expected value of the generated reward at D_3 is higher. After visiting D_3 the robot takes the action down to visit D_1. This clearly shows that the actions taken by the robot depend not only on its current location but also on the previously visited regions.

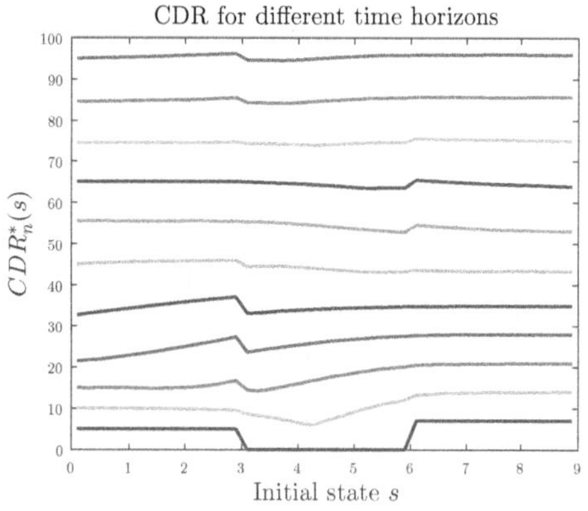

Figure 2: Approximate computation of CDR $\mathsf{CDR}_n^*(s)$ as a function of initial state s and for different values of horizon n in Example 1.

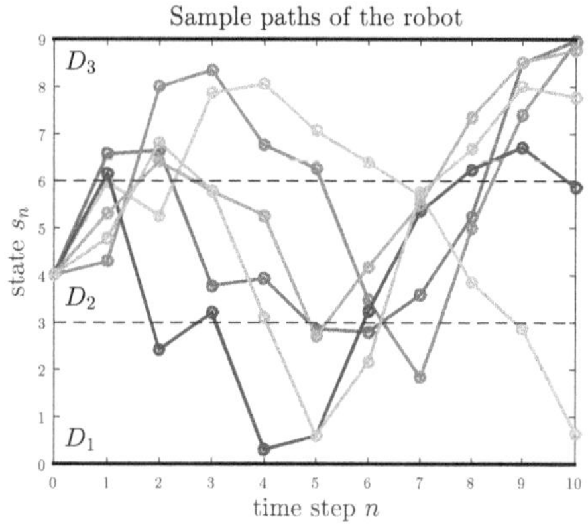

Figure 3: Sample paths of the robot in Example 1 as a function of time. The robot is initially in the hallway and moves towards the region with higher expected generated reward.

7. CONCLUDING REMARKS

We have proposed a mathematical model for optimizing rewards in dynamic environments, called *Reward Collecting Markov Processes*. Our model is motivated by request-serving applications, where a background process generates rewards whose values depend on the number of steps between generation and collection. We studied both the finite and infinite horizon synthesis problems for maximizing the collected reward. We characterized these problems as solutions to dynamic programs over an augmented hybrid space. We also provided a computational method for these problems with guaranteed error bounds based on abstracting the continuous-space problem into a discrete one.

8. REFERENCES

[1] A. Abate, J.-P. Katoen, J. Lygeros, and M. Prandini. Approximate model checking of stochastic hybrid systems. *European J. Control*, 6:624–641, 2010.

[2] D. Bertsekas and S. Shreve. *Stochastic Optimal Control: The Discrete-Time Case.* Athena Scientific, 1996.

[3] T. Brázdil, V. Brozek, K. Chatterjee, V. Forejt, and A. Kucera. Two views on multiple mean-payoff objectives in Markov decision processes. In *LICS*, pages 33–42, 2011.

[4] F. Dufour and T. Prieto-Rumeau. Approximation of Markov decision processes with general state space. *Journal of Mathematical Analysis and Applications*, 388(2):1254 – 1267, 2012.

[5] S. Esmaeil Zadeh Soudjani. *Formal Abstractions for Automated Verification and Synthesis of Stochastic Systems.* PhD thesis, Technische Universiteit Delft, The Netherlands, November 2014.

[6] S. Esmaeil Zadeh Soudjani and A. Abate. Adaptive and sequential gridding procedures for the abstraction and verification of stochastic processes. *SIAM Journal on Applied Dynamical Systems*, 12(2):921–956, 2013.

[7] S. Esmaeil Zadeh Soudjani, C. Gevaerts, and A. Abate. FAUST^2: Formal abstractions of uncountable-state stochastic processes. In *TACAS'15*, volume 9035 of *Lecture Notes in Computer Science*, pages 272–286. Springer, 2015.

[8] A. Gouberman and M. Siegle. Markov reward models and Markov decision processes in discrete and continuous time: Performance evaluation and optimization. In *Stochastic Model Checking. Rigorous Dependability Analysis Using Model Checking Techniques for Stochastic Systems: International Autumn School, ROCKS 2012*, pages 156–241. Springer, 2014.

[9] O. Hernández-Lerma. *Adaptive Markov control processes.* Applied mathematical sciences. Springer, New York, 1989.

[10] O. Hernández-Lerma and J. B. Lasserre. *Discrete-time Markov control processes*, volume 30 of *Applications of Mathematics.* Springer, 1996.

[11] A. Hinton, M. Kwiatkowska, G. Norman, and D. Parker. PRISM: A tool for automatic verification of probabilistic systems. In *TACAS*, volume 3920 of *Lecture Notes in Computer Science*, pages 441–444. Springer, 2006.

[12] M. L. Puterman. *Markov Decision Processes: Discrete Stochastic Dynamic Programming.* John Wiley & Sons, Inc., New York, NY, USA, 1st edition, 1994.

[13] O. Spanjaard and P. Weng. Markov decision processes with functional rewards. In *Multi-disciplinary Trends in Artificial Intelligence MIWAI 2013*, pages 269–280. Springer, 2013.

[14] S. Summers and J. Lygeros. Verification of discrete time stochastic hybrid systems: A stochastic reach-avoid decision problem. *Automatica*, 46(12):1951–1961, 2010.

[15] R. S. Sutton and A. G. Barto. *Reinforcement Learning: An Introduction.* MIT Press, 1998.

[16] I. Tkachev and A. Abate. Characterization and computation of infinite-horizon specifications over Markov processes. *Theoretical Computer Science*, 515(0):1–18, 2014.

[17] I. Tkachev, A. Mereacre, J. Katoen, and A. Abate. Quantitative automata-based controller synthesis for non-autonomous stochastic hybrid systems. In *Hybrid Systems: Computation and Control*, pages 293–302. ACM, 2013.

Reachability Computation for Switching Diffusions: Finite Abstractions with Certifiable and Tuneable Precision

Luca Laurenti
Department of Computer Science
University of Oxford

Alessandro Abate
Department of Computer Science
University of Oxford

Luca Bortolussi
Department of Mathematics and Geosciences
University of Trieste

Luca Cardelli
Microsoft Research &
University of Oxford

Milan Ceska
Faculty of Information Technology
Brno University of Technology

Marta Kwiatkowska
Department of Computer Science
University of Oxford

ABSTRACT

We consider continuous time stochastic hybrid systems with no resets and continuous dynamics described by linear stochastic differential equations – models also known as switching diffusions. We show that for this class of models reachability (and dually, safety) properties can be studied on an abstraction defined in terms of a discrete time and finite space Markov chain (DTMC), with provable error bounds. The technical contribution of the paper is a characterization of the uniform convergence of the time discretization of such stochastic processes with respect to safety properties. This allows us to newly provide a complete and sound numerical procedure for reachability and safety computation over switching diffusions.

Keywords

Switching diffusions; stochastic hybrid models; reachability and safety analysis; finite abstractions; time and space discretisation; numerical computations

1. INTRODUCTION

Hybrid models are natural in the context of cyber-physical systems applications, where continuous dynamics of physical variables are interleaved with discrete updates of finite-state models. In many engineering and natural systems, noise or uncertainty structured via probabilistic laws are relevant, which leads to stochastic models. In this context stochastic hybrid models encompass all these features, and their properties have been recently investigated [17, 10, 18, 3].

In this work we consider switching diffusions [27, 38, 6], models that are characterised by dynamics over a hybrid state space: continuous-time flows are determined by the solution of a mode-dependent linear diffusion process, whereas mode updates (over finitely many locations) hinge on events triggered by Poisson processes, with rates that depend on the continuous variables. As such, switching diffusions can be regarded as special instances of stochastic hybrid models, the latter dealing also with probabilistic resets between discrete-mode commutations. The models considered in this work are fully observable and not subject to any form of non-determinism (such as control inputs, as discussed in [27, 6]).

This paper investigates the problem of reachability analysis for switching diffusions, a central problem due to the duality between reachability and safety problems, and its role in the verification of many other specifications (thanks to product constructions). Whilst this is a widely investigated problem, contributions in the literature have been limited to the characterisation of this problem, with computational aspects that have been relegated to the use of approximation techniques often resorting to state-space gridding with no guarantees.

Contribution

This work provides a formal computational procedure for the reachability analysis problem over switching diffusions. As such, we address an open problem also for the special case of linear stochastic differential equations. More precisely, we provide approximation algorithms with certificates on their precision, which reduce the problem to the computation over a finite-state Markov chain. In other words, we show that probabilistic reachability can be formally computed over finite abstractions, obtained by discretising the continuous components of the models (time and space).

Related work

Stochastic hybrid models (SHS) are extensively discussed in [18, 10], and switching diffusions investigated in [27, 38, 1, 6]. The characterisation of probabilistic reachability for SHS is elaborated in [13] by means of a number of techniques, but not under the lens of computations. [13] leverages and extends theory developed for piecewise deterministic Markov processes in [20]. Further, [29] has characterised probabilistic reachability for SHS as a solution of a PDE (HJI partial differential equation), but only provided weak convergence results for its computation, based on the approximation the-

HSCC '17, April 18–20, 2017, Pittsburgh, PA, USA.

DOI: http://dx.doi.org/10.1145/3049797.3054964

ory in [30]. A similar approach has been pursued in [34], but again without a numerical scheme with certifiable errors. It appears that the application of numerical schemes for time discretisation of SDE [28] are not helpful. [22] has extended the characterisation to constrained reachability problems. In [11, 16, 12] numerical algorithms for verification of linear SDE, obtained for Markov population processes in the limit of high population, have been given with just weak convergence results.

For discrete-time stochastic hybrid models, probabilistic reachability (and safety) have been fully characterised [3], connected with verification procedures [2, 37], formally computed via software tools [23] leveraging finite abstractions, and indeed extended to general specifications [36].

An alternative approach towards formal, finite approximations of continuous-time stochastic models is discussed in [40] and extended in [39] to switching diffusions. Noteworthy are also techniques and tools for verification of related probabilistic models based on abstractions [41], measurability conditions [24], and SMT technology [25] approaches. These techniques, alongside that of this work, are clearly distinct from statistical model checking approaches [15].

2. STOCHASTIC HYBRID PROCESSES

We consider the following class of continuous time stochastic hybrid systems with no guards or resets, which are also commonly denoted as switching diffusions. We refer the reader to [10, 18] for technical details on the measure theoretical aspects underlying these processes.

DEFINITION 1. *A switching diffusion $\mathcal{H}$ is a tuple $\mathcal{H} = (\mathcal{Q}, K, F, G, W, \Lambda)$, where*

- $\mathcal{Q} = \{q_1, ..., q_{|\mathcal{Q}|}\}$ *is the set of* discrete modes
- $K \subseteq \mathbb{R}^m$, *for $m > 0$, is the state space of the* continuous dynamics. *The hybrid state space is defined as* $\mathcal{D} = \cup_{q\in\mathcal{Q}}\{q\} \times K$
- $F : \mathcal{Q} \to \mathbb{R}^{m\times m}$ *is the* drift term *for the continuous dynamics*
- $G : \mathcal{Q} \to \mathbb{R}^{m\times q}$ *is the* diffusion *associated to the continuous dynamics*
- *W is a $q-$dimensional Wiener process*
- $\Lambda : \mathcal{D} \times \mathcal{Q} \to \mathbb{R}_{\geq 0}$ *is an* intensity function, *where for* $(q_i, x) \in \mathcal{D}, q_j \in \mathcal{Q}$, *we define* $\Lambda((q_i, x), q_j) = \lambda_{i,j}(x)$

Let W be defined in the probability space $(\Omega, \mathcal{F}, P)$ with filtration $\mathcal{F}_t$, where a filtration is a family of $\sigma-$algebras representing the information available at time t. Then, given $\mathcal{H}$ and an initial condition $y_0 = (x_0, q_0) \in \mathcal{D}$, the stochastic process $Y = (X, \alpha)$, defined on the hybrid state space $\mathcal{D} = \cup_{q\in\mathcal{Q}}\{q\} \times K$ is a solution of $\mathcal{H}$ if it satisfies

$$dX(t) = F(\alpha(t)) \cdot X(t)dt + G(\alpha(t)) \cdot dW(t), \quad (1)$$

and for $i \neq j$

$$P\left(\alpha(t + \Delta t) = q_j | Y(t) = (q_i, x)\right) = \lambda_{i,j}(x)\Delta t + o(\Delta t) \quad (2)$$

with $(X(0), \alpha(0)) = (x_0, q_0)$.

The discrete dynamics of Y, described by the variable α, evolves as a jump process over the discrete state space $\mathcal{Q}$, with jump rate dependent on the continuous part. The continuous dynamics of Y evolves according to a linear diffusion. That is, when the discrete system is in a particular state, X evolves according to a linear SDE driven by a Wiener process. Then, when the discrete system hits a change in its state, X continues to evolve according to a different SDE without resetting its state.

ASSUMPTION 1. *We introduce the following assumptions, which are standard in the literature [33, 38]:*

- *$\lambda_{i,j}(x)$ is a bounded and locally Lipschitz continuous function in x, for all $q_i, q_j \in \mathcal{Q}$*
- *$|F(q)x| + |G(q)| \leq C(1 + |x|)$ for all $q \in \mathcal{Q}$, for some constant C where $|G(q)| = \sum_{i,j} |G(q)(i,j)|$*
- *$|F(q)x - F(q)x'| \leq D|x - x'|$ for all $q \in \mathcal{Q}$, for some constant D*

The first condition guarantees that, over any finite time interval, α almost surely jumps only a finite number of times, thus excluding Zeno behaviours. The second and third conditions guarantee that the continuous solution X exists and is unique, and that it remains bounded over a finite time interval [33].

EXAMPLE 1. *Consider the stochastic process X described by the following SDE*

$$dX(t) = F \cdot X(t)dt + G \cdot dW(t) \quad (3)$$

with initial condition $X(0) = x_0 \in \mathbb{R}^m$. That is, X is the solution of a hybrid process $\mathcal{H}$ with a singleton discrete state space ($\mathcal{Q} = \{q\}$). It is well known that the evolution of the probability distribution of the solution of a SDE over time satisfies the following Fokker-Planck equation [26]:

$$\frac{\partial p(\mathbf{x}, t)}{\partial t} = -\sum_{i=1}^{N} \frac{\partial}{\partial x_i}\left[(F(t) \cdot x)_i p(\mathbf{x}, t)\right] + \frac{1}{2}\sum_{i=1}^{N}\sum_{j=1}^{N} \frac{\partial^2}{\partial x_i \partial x_j}\left[D_{ij} p(\mathbf{x}, t)\right],$$

with diffusion tensor $D_{ij} = \sum_{k=1}^{q} G_{ik}G_{jk}$.

The following lemma guarantees that X, process solution of Equation 3, is a Gaussian process.

LEMMA 1. *[7, 35] Let $X(0)$ be a normally distributed random variable with expected value $E[X(0)] = E_{x_0}$ and covariance matrix $C_X(0) = E[X(0)X(0)] = C_{x_0}$. Then, X, as defined in (3), is a Gaussian Markov process with expected value and covariance matrix given by*

$$\begin{cases} \frac{dE[X(t)]}{dt} &= FE[X(t)] \\ E[X(0)] &= E_{x_0}, \end{cases} \quad (4)$$

$$\begin{cases} \frac{dC_X(t)}{dt} &= FC_X(t) + C_X(t)^T F + G(G^T) \\ dC_X(0) &= C_{x_0}. \end{cases} \quad (5)$$

Lemma 1 allows us to derive the analytical solution for the expectation and variance of the solution of a linear SDE as

$$E[X(t)] = e^{Ft}E_{x_0},$$

$$C_X(t) = e^{Ft}C_{x_0}\left(e^{Ft}\right)^T + \int_0^t \left(e^{F(t-s)}\right) GG^T \left(e^{F(t-s)}\right)^T ds.$$

3. PROBLEM DEFINITION

Given a stochastic process Y with state space $\mathcal{D}$, a *target set* $\mathcal{S} \subseteq \mathcal{D}$, which is assumed to be measurable, and a time interval $I \subseteq \mathbb{R}_{\geq 0}$, the reachability problem is defined as the search for the characterisation and computation of the probability that Y will reach $\mathcal{S}$ during I from any point in $\mathcal{D}$. This problem is dual to the safety problem, that is, computing the probability that the system will remain in a given, measurable safe region, over a given time interval. The characterisation of the two problems is thus interchangeable [2]. Reachability analysis is one of the fundamental problems in the quantitative analysis of models, and it is likewise key for the analysis of stochastic hybrid processes [14]. Model checking of Continuous Stochastic Logic (CSL) [8] reduces to computing reachability problems. Similarly, for discrete-time stochastic hybrid systems, reachability and safety play a pivotal role for model checking PCTL formulae [31] and more complex properties via the product construction [36].

PROBLEM 1. *(Probabilistic Reachability) Let $\mathcal{H}$ be a hybrid process, and $Y = (X, \alpha)$ its solution with state space $\mathcal{D}$. Let $\mathcal{S} \subseteq \mathcal{D}$ be a measurable set and $I = [t_1, t_2]$ a time interval. The reachability probability for Y to reach $\mathcal{S}$ in I is defined as*

$$P_{reach}(Y, \mathcal{S}, I) = Prob\{\exists t \in I \; s.t. \, Y(t) \in \mathcal{S}\}. \quad (6)$$

The safety problem is introduced as

$$P_{safe}(Y, \mathcal{S}, I) = Prob\{\forall t \in I, Y(t) \in \mathcal{S}\}$$

and is the dual of the reachability problem, namely

$$P_{safe}(Y, \mathcal{S}, I) = 1 - P_{reach}(Y, \mathcal{S}^c, I)$$

where $\mathcal{S}^c$ is the complement of set $\mathcal{S}$.

Analytic solutions of Problem 1 for the class of hybrid systems we consider are in general infeasible, as they would be tantamount to viscosity solutions of systems of Hamilton-Jacobi-Bellman equations [29]. In this work we instead introduce a numerical algorithm that employs time- and space discretization to solve Problem 1 – in particular the time discretisation part of the scheme is new. We further show that for the class of processes considered in this paper, the safety value computed on the discrete time and finite space Markov chain (DTMC) abstraction, obtained from the overall procedure, converges uniformly to the safety value associated to the given (continuous) switching diffusion as the discretisation parameters become zero. We also offer explicit error bounds quantifying this approximation level.

In the following illustrative example, we consider a simple SDE model, for which analytical solutions to the probabilistic safety problem exist.

EXAMPLE 2. *Consider the stochastic process X described by the SDE $dX(t) = GdW(t)$, where $G \in \mathbb{R}_{\geq 0}$ and W is a uni-dimensional Brownian motion. Assume there is no discrete switching (and a single discrete location), then the probability density function of process X is described by the following diffusion equation*

$$\frac{\partial p(x, t \mid x_0)}{\partial t} = \frac{G^2}{2} \frac{\partial^2 p(x, t \mid x_0)}{\partial x^2},$$

with initial condition $p(x, 0 \mid x_0) = \delta(x - x_0)$. For $\bar{x} \in \mathbb{R}$, we consider the safe set $\mathcal{S}_{\bar{X}} = \{x \in \mathbb{R} : x \leq \bar{x}\}$. In order to solve $P_{safe}(X, S_{\bar{X}}, [0, 1])$, we need to integrate $p(x, t; x_0)$ with the boundary condition $P(\bar{x}, t) = 0$: this leads to the following density function for, $x < \bar{x}$,

$$p(x, t; x_0, \bar{x}) = \frac{1}{\sqrt{2\pi G t}} \left(e^{-\frac{(x-x_0)^2}{2Gt}} - e^{-\frac{(x-(2\bar{x}-x_0))^2}{2Gt}} \right).$$

We then obtain

$$P_{safe}(X, S_{\bar{X}}, [0, 1]) = \int_{-\infty}^{\bar{x}} p(x, 1; x_0, \bar{x}) dx = erf\left(\frac{\bar{x} - x_0}{\sqrt{2G}}\right),$$

where erf() is the Gaussian error function.

4. TIME DISCRETIZATION

Given a hybrid system $\mathcal{H}$, its solution, $Y = (X, \alpha)$, is a continuous time Markov process defined on the hybrid space $\mathcal{D} = \cup_{q \in \mathcal{Q}} \{q\} \times K$, where $K \subseteq \mathbb{R}^m, m > 0$. By sampling Y with a fixed interval $h > 0$, we obtain a discrete-time Markov process $\bar{Y} = (\bar{X}, \bar{\alpha})$ defined on the same hybrid state space $\mathcal{D}$ and such that $\bar{Y}(k) = Y(h \cdot k), k \in \mathbb{N}$.

DEFINITION 2. *For $k \in \mathbb{N}$, the discrete-time Markov process (DTMP) $(\bar{Y}(k) = (\bar{X}(k), \bar{\alpha}(k))$ is a time homogeneous hybrid model, uniquely defined by a quadruple $(\mathcal{D}, \sigma, T^c, T^d)$, where $(\mathcal{D}, \sigma)$ is the measurable space inherited from $\mathcal{H}$; $T^c : A \times \mathcal{D} \to [0, 1]$, for $A \subseteq \mathbb{R}^m$, is a continuous transition kernel; and $T^d : \mathcal{Q} \times \mathcal{D} \to [0, 1]$ is a discrete transition kernel.*

T^c and T^d describe the probability that the continuous and discrete components of the process transition onto a measurable set at the next discrete step, given the current state of the process. More precisely, for state $(q, x) \in \mathcal{D}$ and Borel-measurable set $(q', A) \subseteq \mathcal{D}$, we have that

$$T^c(A, x, q) = Prob(\bar{X}(k+1) \in A | \bar{X}(k) = x, \bar{\alpha}(k) = q)$$
$$T^d(q', x, q) = Prob(\bar{\alpha}(k+1) = q' | \bar{X}(k) = x, \bar{\alpha}(k) = q).$$

T^c and T^d fully characterize $\bar{Y} = (\bar{X}, \bar{\alpha})$. In the following proposition we derive an analytical form for such kernels. To simplify the presentation, for the following theorem only we make a further restriction that the jump rates do not depend on the continuous state $x \in K$: $\lambda_{ij}(x) = \lambda_{ij}$. This assumption allows us to have a simpler form of the kernel. In order to deal with more general rate functions, we can assume that they are piecewise constant in each considered interval of time, and fix the value of λ_{ij} at the initial state for each time interval. As rate functions are locally Lipschitz, the distance between the true rate and the obtained λ_{ij} will be bounded by a term of order $O(h)$, whose error contribution can be lifted to the kernel level.

THEOREM 1. *Let $\mathcal{H} = (\mathcal{Q}, K, F, G, W, \Lambda)$ be a hybrid process and $Y = (X, \alpha)$ its solution. Assume the jump rates do not depend on the continuous state. Let $h > 0$ be a sampling time and $\mathcal{N}(\bar{x}|E, C)$ the normal distribution with mean E and covariance C. Introduce terms*

$$\Gamma(i, t) = \int_0^t \left(e^{F(q_i)(t-m)}\right) G(q_i) G(q_i)^T \left(e^{F(q_i)(t-m)}\right)^T dm,$$

$$\Omega_{\lambda_i, \lambda_j, t}(s) = (\lambda_j - \lambda_i) \frac{e^{(\lambda_j s - \lambda_j t - \lambda_i s)}}{e^{(-\lambda_i t)} - e^{(-\lambda_j t)}},$$

and for $x \in \mathbb{R}^m$ define $\lambda_i(x) = \sum_{j \neq i} \lambda_{i,j}(x)$. Then, given $(q, x) \in \mathcal{D}$ and a measurable set (q', A), for the resulting DTMP $\bar{Y} = (\bar{X}, \bar{\alpha})$ it holds that

$$T^c(A,x,q_i) = \int_A \mathcal{N}\left(\bar{x}|e^{F(q_i)\cdot h}x, \Gamma(i,h)\right) d\bar{x} \cdot e^{-\lambda_i h} +$$
$$\sum_{q_j \neq q_i} \int_A \left(\int_0^h \mathcal{N}\left(\bar{x}|E^{\mathcal{H}}_{q_i,x}(s), C^{\mathcal{H}}_{q_i,x}(s)\right) \cdot \Omega_{\lambda_i,\lambda_j,h}(s) ds\right) \cdot$$
$$\frac{\lambda_{ij}}{\lambda_i} \cdot \lambda_i h \cdot e^{-\lambda_i h}\, d\bar{x} + \epsilon$$

and

$$T^d(q_j,x,q_i) = \begin{cases} e^{-\lambda_i h} + \epsilon & \textit{if } q_i = q_j \\ \lambda_i h \cdot e^{-\lambda_i h} \cdot \frac{\lambda_{ij}}{\lambda_i} + \epsilon & \textit{if } q_i \neq q_j \end{cases},$$

where

$$E^{\mathcal{H}}_{q_i,x}(s) = e^{F(q_i)s} e^{F(q_i)(h-s)} x,$$
$$C^{\mathcal{H}}_{q_i,x,s} = e^{F(q_i)s}\Gamma(i,s)(e^{F(q_i)s})^T + \Gamma(j,h-s),$$
$$0 \leq \epsilon \leq 1 - e^{-\lambda_i h} - \lambda_i h \cdot e^{-\lambda_i h}.$$

The full derivation of the continuous kernel, $T^c(A,x,q_i)$, is shown in Section 9. Each integral over A quantifies the probability that the continuous component of the model enters set A, conditional on the discrete part of the process performing either 0 or 1 jumps during the sampling interval h. Assuming to be in the discrete location q_i, the probability of these events is respectively $e^{-\lambda_i h}$ and $\lambda_i h \cdot e^{-\lambda_i h}$ [19], where x is the state at time kh. If the discrete system makes no jumps within $[0,h]$, then, because of the memory-less property of the SDE, during this interval X evolves according to equations as in Lemma 1 and specific to location q_i. As a consequence, at time h, X is normally distributed, with mean $e^{F(q_i)\cdot h}x$ and variance $\Gamma(i,h)$. If instead the system jumps once within $[0,h]$, after marginalizing over the jump time and the state where this event happens, we end up with a *linear Gaussian model* [9]. This process is still Gaussian with mean and covariance matrix that can be derived from the equations in Lemma 1. Finally, parameter ϵ takes into account the probability associated to paths with more than one jump within $[kh,(k+1)h]$: based on the provided upper bound on ϵ, it is clear that the probability of such event becomes negligible as h gets small enough.

The discrete kernel $T^d(q_j,x,q_i)$ has a much simpler derivation. If we assume that the system makes at most one jump during h, then the probability that $q_j = q_i$ amounts to the probability that the system does not jump within $[0,h]$. Instead, for the condition $q_j \neq q_i$ the resulting probability is obtained as the probability of making a jump once, multiplied by the probability of jumping to the specific state q_j.

From T^c and T^d, it is easy to calculate the following transition kernel for $(x,q_i) \in \mathcal{D}$ and a measurable set $(A,q_j) \subseteq \mathcal{D}$

$$T((A,q_j),(x,q_i)) =$$
$$Prob(Y((k+1)h) \in (A,x_j)|Y((k)h) = (q,x_i), k \in \mathbb{N}).$$

In fact, from Theorem 1, we have

$$T((A,q_j),(x,q_i)) =$$
$$\begin{cases} \int_A \mathcal{N}\left(\bar{x}|e^{F(q_i)\cdot h}x, \Gamma(i,h)\right) d\bar{x} \cdot e^{-\lambda_i h} & \text{if } q_i = q_j \\ \int_A \left(\int_0^h \mathcal{N}\left(\bar{x}|E^{\mathcal{H}}_{q_i,x}(s), C^{\mathcal{H}}_{q_i,x}(s)\right) \cdot \Omega_{\lambda_i,\lambda_j,h}(s) ds\right) \cdot & \\ \quad d\bar{x} \cdot \frac{\lambda_{ij}}{\lambda_i} \lambda_i h e^{-\lambda_i h} & \text{if } q_i \neq q_j \end{cases}$$

Note that the derived kernels are time homogeneous: from a numerical point of view this is a key property that facilitates the practical computation of the resulting DTMP, which is also time homogeneous.

4.1 Error Bounds for Time Discretization

In this section we quantify the approximation level introduced by the discretisation procedure. More precisely, we characterize the error associated to the computation of reachability properties with the DTMP over a discrete set of sampling points, with sampling time $h > 0$: by deriving formal error bounds, we show uniform convergence as $h \to 0$.

ASSUMPTION 2. *Assume that the target set $\mathcal{S}$ is independent of the locations, namely select $S \subseteq \mathbb{R}^m$ so that $\mathcal{S} = \cup_{q \in \mathcal{Q}} \{q\} \times S$.*

Note that, although this assumption limits the class of properties that can be expressed, there are many applications where target sets independent of discrete locations are of great interest. For example, in the context of controlling room temperature in smart buildings, often the focus is on checking the temperature (continuous variable) regardless of the discrete state of the thermostats (locations). At the end of the section we briefly discuss how this assumption can be relaxed.

Let $\mathcal{H} = (\mathcal{Q}, K, F, G, W, \Lambda)$ be a hybrid system and $Y = (X, \alpha)$ its solution. Let $I \subseteq \mathbb{R}_{\geq 0}$ be a finite time interval. For any $q \in \mathcal{Q}$, call X_q the solution of the SDE:

$$dX_q(t) = F(q)X_q(t)dt + G(q)dW(t).$$

In this section we assume that X_q is a uni-dimensional, zero mean Gaussian process (GP). In the next subsection, we show how to generalize the results derived here for general GPs and multi-dimensional processes.

X_q is almost surely bounded within the interval I by Assumption 1. Set $h = min\{\frac{2^{-n}}{2\sqrt{2}K^2 K_d}, 2^{-n}\}$ and $\epsilon_n = 2^{-\frac{n}{2}}$, where $n \in \mathbb{N}$, and K_d is a constant such that for any $t_1, t_2 \in I$

$$\max_{q \in \mathcal{Q}} \{d_q(t_1,t_2)\} \leq K_d \cdot |t_2 - t_1|,$$

where d_q is a pseudometric defined as

$$d_q(t_1,t_2) = \sqrt{E[(X_q(t_2) - X_q(t_1))^2]},$$

and $K \geq 12$ is the universal constant in the Dudley's metric entropy integral [32]. Fix a set of sampling times $\Sigma = \{t_1, ..., t_{|\Sigma_n|}\}$, with step distance h. Call

$$S^{\epsilon_n} = \{x \in S \;:\; |x - \partial S| \geq \epsilon_n\},$$

where ∂S is the boundary of S and $|\cdot|$ is the Euclidean distance metrics between a point and a set. Define the events

$$\mathcal{A}^n = \{\forall t_i \in \Sigma,\; X(t_i) \in S^{\epsilon_n}\}$$

and

$$\mathcal{B} = \{\exists t \in [0,T] \; s.t. \; X(t) \notin S\}.$$

As $S \subseteq \mathbb{R}$, we have that $P_{\mathsf{safe}}(Y, \mathcal{S}, I) = P_{\mathsf{safe}}(X, S, I)$, where $P_{\mathsf{safe}}(X,S,I)$ is the probability that the continuous component X of Y, stays in S during I. It is easy to see that

$$P_{\mathsf{safe}}(X,S,I) = \lim_{n \to \infty} P(\mathcal{A}^n \wedge \mathcal{B}^c).$$

For a finite $n > 0$, $P(\mathcal{A}^n \wedge \mathcal{B}^c)$ is the lower bound for the safety probability computed on $\mathcal{S}$, since it requires the system to be inside $S^{\epsilon_n} \subseteq S$ at sampling times in Σ. Notice that for n big enough S and S^{ϵ_n} become indistinguishable. As a consequence, we can compute the reachability on S^{ϵ_n} instead of S, assuming n is big enough. Let us define as $P(\mathcal{A}^n)$ the reachability probability computed considering only the discrete times in Σ.

THEOREM 2. *Under Assumption 1, it holds that for $n \geq 3$ and over a finite time interval $I \subseteq \mathbb{R}_{\geq 0}$*

$$P(\mathcal{A}^n) \geq P(\mathcal{A}^n \wedge \mathcal{B}^c) \geq P(\mathcal{A}^n) \cdot \left(1 - \frac{I}{h} \exp^{-\left(2^n - 2^{\frac{n}{2}} + 1\right)}\right),$$

where $h = min\{\frac{2^{-n}}{2\sqrt{2}K^2 K_d}, 2^{-n}\}$.

COROLLARY 1. *Under Assumption 1, it holds that*

$$\lim_{n\to\infty} P(\mathcal{A}^n \wedge \mathcal{B}^c) = \lim_{n\to\infty} P(\mathcal{A}^n).$$

Theorem 2 guarantees that for any $n \geq 3$, we obtain

$$|P(\mathcal{A}^n) - P(\mathcal{A}^n \wedge \mathcal{B}^c)| \leq \frac{I}{h} \exp^{-\left(2^n - 2^{\frac{n}{2}} + 1\right)}.$$

This enables choosing, a priori, a sampling interval h that guarantees meeting a chosen error on the precision. The proof of Theorem 2 is given in the Appendix. Here, we explain the main ideas. The proof of Theorem 2 is based on the fact that, for any $q \in \mathcal{Q}$, X_q is a Gaussian process, which is almost surely bounded in T. It is possible to show that the supremum of X_q is still distributed as a Gaussian [4]. Then, the use of the entropy Dudley's integral [21] allows to bound the probability that each X_q stays in a ϵ_n-neighbourhood between two sampling points. The fact that S^{ϵ_n} depends on the sampling interval concludes the proof. Note that a key feature enabling this approach is the absence of resets of the continuous state upon mode change. As a consequence, we can simply assume that we can find constants for the "worst behaving X_q" in a particular interval, without worrying about the discrete mode changes.

Discussion on the error and extensions

In the derivation of Theorem 2 we have assumed that the continuous component of Y, solution of $\mathcal{H}$, is zero mean and uni-dimensional. This is not a limitation: Lemma 1 guarantees that for any $q \in \mathcal{Q}$, the variance of the solution X_q is independent of the particular continuous location, depending exclusively on time. Moreover, given a set $S \subseteq \mathbb{R}$ and $h > 0$, for $E[X(0)] = x \in S$ from Equation (4), it is possible to derive a constant $K_{h,S}^m$ such that

$$sup_{q\in\mathbb{Q},t_1,t_2\in[0,h]}\{|E[X_q(t_2) - E[X_q(t_1)]|\} \leq K_{h,S}^m \cdot h.$$

Then, we can simply consider as target for the continuous components the set

$$S' = S \cup \{x \in \mathbb{R} - S : |x - \partial S| \leq K_{h,S}^m \cdot h\}.$$

The bound computed for $X - E[X]$ on $\mathcal{S} = \cup_{q\in\mathcal{Q}} q \times S$ still holds for X on $\mathcal{S}' = \cup_{q\in\mathcal{Q}} q \times S'$. One of the key properties of a multivariate Gaussian Process (mGP) is that each of its components is itself a Gaussian process. Moreover, the Euclidean metric distance for X at time t can be defined as

$$|X(t)| = \sqrt{\sum_{i=1}^{m} |X_i(t)|^2},$$

where X_i is the $i-th$ component of X. As a consequence,

$$P\left(|X(t)| < \epsilon\right) \leq P\left(sup_{i\in[1,n]}|X_i(t)| < \sqrt{\frac{\epsilon^2}{n}}\right).$$

These observations allow us to derive the following theorem, which generalizes Theorem 2 to multi-dimensional continuous components.

THEOREM 3. *Let $\mathcal{H}$ be a hybrid process and $Y = (X, \alpha)$ its solution, with X m-dimensional process, for $m > 0$. Define $K_{d,i}$, the K_d constant relative to X_i, as introduced in Section 4.1. Then, it holds that for $n \geq 3$ and over a finite time interval $I \subseteq \mathbb{R}_{\geq 0}$*

$$P(\mathcal{A}^n) \geq P(\mathcal{A}^n \wedge \mathcal{B}^c) \geq P(\mathcal{A}^n) \cdot \left(1 - \frac{I}{h} \exp^{-\left(2^n - 2^{\frac{n}{2}} + 1\right)}\right),$$

where $h = min\left\{\frac{2^{-n}}{2\sqrt{2}K^2 \bar{K}_d}, 2^{-n}\right\}$, for $K \geq 12$ and $\bar{K}_d = sup_{i\in1,\ldots,m}(K_{d,i})$.

Finally, it is important to stress that Assumption 2 can be relaxed by modifying the time discretization error and including a term encompassing the probability that the system jumps more than once during the time interval $[0, h]$. Moreover, as explained next, Theorem 3 can still be used to get lower bounds of cases where the target set depends on the discrete mode. However, the bounds we obtain can be quite conservative if the target sets corresponding to different modes greatly differ.

OBSERVATION 1. *Consider a hybrid system $\mathcal{H}$ with solution $Y = (X, \alpha)$, where X takes values in $\mathbb{R}^m$ and α takes values in a finite set of discrete states $\mathcal{Q}$. Given a measurable set $\mathcal{S} = \cup_{q_i\in\mathcal{Q}}(q_i, S_i) \subseteq \mathcal{D}$, we can define $S' = \cap_{q_i\in\mathcal{Q}} S_i$ and $\mathcal{S}' = \cup_{q_i\in\mathcal{Q}}(q_i, S'$. Then, we have that for a general time interval I, $P_{safe}(Y, \mathcal{S}, I) \geq P_{safe}(Y, \mathcal{S}', I)$. That is, if we need to compute probabilistic safety on a set that depends on the discrete modes, then we can always compute a lower bound of this safety considering a target set that is independent of the locations.*

5. STATE SPACE DISCRETIZATION

In order to complete the procedure leading to a model where we can numerically compute safety or reachability properties, we introduce a numerical scheme inspired by the results of [2, 23]. The numerical scheme is based on a discrete-time Markov chain (DTMC) approximation of the DTMP that results from the time discretization of the original switching diffusion process $\mathcal{H}$. We discuss convergence results and relative error bounds both of this second (state space) approximation step, and of the combined (time- and state approximation) procedure.

Let $\mathcal{S} = \cup_{q\in\mathcal{Q}}\{q\} \times A_q$ be the safe set, where $A_q \subseteq \mathbb{R}^m$. We assume $\mathcal{S}$ to be measurable and compact. Given $dx \in \mathbb{R}_{\geq 0}$, we define the grid

$$\mathcal{G}_{dx} = \cup_{q\in\mathbb{Q}} \cup_{i\in m_q} \{q\} \times A_{i,q},$$

where $A_{i,q}$ are pairwise disjoint measurable sets, such that for $q \in \mathcal{Q}$ $\cup_{i\in m_q} A_{i,q} = A_q$, for $i \neq j$ $A_{i,q} \cap A_{j,q} = \emptyset$, and

$$A_{i,q} = \{x, x' \in A_q : |x - x'| \leq dx\}.$$

In other words, $\mathcal{G}_{dx}$ is a partition of $\mathcal{S}$ in sets of diameter dx. For each $(q, A_{i,q}) \in \mathcal{G}_{dx}$, we consider a representative point $(q, x_i) \in \{q\} \times A_{i,q}$. The set of representative points $\mathcal{S}_{dx} = \{(q, x_i), i \in \{1, ...m_q\}, q \in \mathcal{Q}\}$ makes up the finite state space of the DTMC, a discrete version of the set $\mathcal{S}$. Let us introduce $\xi : \mathcal{S} \to \mathcal{S}_{dx}$, a map that associates to any $(q, x) \in \mathcal{S}$ the corresponding representative point. Similarly, the set-valued map $\Xi : \mathcal{S} \to \mathcal{G}_{dx}$ relates any representative point to the concrete $A_{i,q}$ partition.

We define the discrete state space $\mathcal{Z}_{dx} = \mathcal{S}_{dx} \cup \phi$, where ϕ is a discrete state modeling all the states outside $\mathcal{S}$. Note that the compactness of $\mathcal{S}$ guarantees that $\mathcal{Z}$ is finite. The resulting DTMC is completely characterized by its transition kernel $T_{dx} : \mathcal{Z}_{dx} \times \mathcal{Z}_{dx} \to \mathbb{R}_{\geq 0}$, such that for $z_1 = (x_1, q_1), z_2 = (x_2, q_2) \in \mathcal{Z}_{dx}$, $T_{dx}(z_1, z_2)$ describes the probability of going in z_1 in the next discrete step, being in z_2 at the current time. T_{dx} can be easily computed from kernel T presented in Section 4 as $T_{dx}(z_1, z_2) =$

$$\begin{cases} T(z_1, z_2), & \text{if } z_1, z_2 \in \mathcal{S}_{dx} \\ 1 - \sum_{z_j \in \mathcal{S}_{dx^r}} T(z_1, \Xi(z_j)), & \text{if } z_1 \in \mathcal{S}_{dx}, z_2 \in \phi \\ 1, & \text{if } z_1, z_2 \in \phi \\ 0, & \text{if } z_1 \in \phi, z_2 \in \mathcal{S}_{dx}. \end{cases}$$

5.1 Error Bounds for Space Discretization

Let $\bar{Y}$ the discrete time continuous space hybrid process derived through time discretization of Y, solution of the hybrid process $\mathcal{H}$, with initial condition $(x, q) \in \mathcal{S}$. Call Y^D the approximated DTMC with state space $\mathcal{Z}_{dx}$ and initial condition $(x^D, q^D) = \xi((x, q))$. We show that, for $I \subseteq \mathbb{R}_{\geq 0}$, under Assumption 1, the property$P_{\text{safe}}(Y^D, \mathcal{S}_{dx}, I)$ converges uniformly to $P_{\text{safe}}(\bar{Y}, S, I)$, which also allows us to derive uniform convergence on the original continuous time stochastic process, and to derive error bounds on the global approximation procedure.

DEFINITION 3. *Let us introduce the following Lipschitz constants $h_1, h_2 \in \mathbb{R}_{\geq 0}$, which are such that*

$$|T^d(q', x_1, q) - T^d(q', x_2, q)| \leq h_1 \cdot |x_2 - x_1|,$$
for all $(q, x_1), (q, x_2) \in \mathcal{S}, q' \in \mathcal{Q}$,
$$|t^c(x', x_1, q) - t^c(x', x_2, q)| \leq h_2 \cdot |x_2 - x_1|,$$
for all $(q, x_1), (q, x_2) \in \mathcal{S}, x' \in K \cap \mathcal{S}$,

where t^c is the density function of the continuous kernel T^c.

THEOREM 4. *[2] Let $\bar{Y}$ be the discrete-time continuous space hybrid process with initial condition $(x, q) \in \mathcal{S}$, where $\mathcal{S}$ is a measurable set. Call Y^D the approximated DTMC with state space $\mathcal{Z}_{dx}$, where $dx > 0$ is the discretization parameter, and initial condition $(x^D, q^D) = \xi(x, q)$. Then, given $[0, N] \subseteq \mathbb{N}$, it holds that*

$$|P_{safe}(Y^D, \mathcal{S}_{dx}, N) - P_{safe}(\bar{Y}, \mathcal{S}, N)| \leq N \cdot \mathcal{K} \cdot dx,$$

where $\mathcal{K} = mh_1 + Lh_2$, with L the Lebesque measure of the continuous set $\mathcal{S}$, and m cardinality of the discrete set $\mathcal{Q}$.

Notice that, as $dx \downarrow 0$, the two probabilities collapse.

6. GLOBAL ALGORITHM AND ERRORS

Using the results in Theorem 4, we can derive the uniform convergence between $P_{\text{safe}}(Y^D, \mathcal{S}_{dx}, N)$ and $P_{\text{safe}}(Y, S, I)$ for $h, dx \to 0$ and N discretized version of I.

THEOREM 5. *Let Y be the solution of a switching diffusion process $\mathcal{H}$ with initial condition $(x, q) \in \mathcal{S}$. Call Y^D the approximated DTMC, with $h, dx > 0$ time and space discretization parameters, and with initial condition $(x^D, q^D) = \xi((x, q))$. Then, given $I = [0, t] \subseteq \mathbb{R}_{\geq 0}$, it holds that:*

$$\left| P_{safe}\left(Y^D, \mathcal{S}_{dx}, \left\lceil \frac{I}{h} \right\rceil\right) - P_{safe}(Y, \mathcal{S}, I) \right| \leq$$
$$\frac{I}{h} \cdot \left(\mathcal{K}dx + e^{-\left(2^n - 2^{\frac{n}{2}} + 1\right)} \right)$$

where $h = min\left\{\frac{2^{-n}}{2\sqrt{2}K^2\bar{K}_d}, 2^{-n}\right\}$ for $n \geq 3$, with $K \geq 12$ and $\bar{K}_d$ constant introduced in Section 4.

PROOF. By triangular inequality we have

$$\left| P_{\text{safe}}(Y^D, \mathcal{S}_{dx}, \left\lceil \frac{I}{h} \right\rceil) - P_{\text{safe}}(Y, \mathcal{S}, I) \right| \leq$$
$$\left| P_{\text{safe}}(Y^D, \mathcal{S}_{dx}, \left\lceil \frac{I}{h} \right\rceil) - P_{\text{safe}}(\bar{Y}, \mathcal{S}, \left\lceil \frac{I}{h} \right\rceil) \right| +$$
$$|P_{\text{safe}}(\bar{Y}, \mathcal{S}, I) - P_{\text{safe}}(Y, \mathcal{I}, I)|.$$

The proof results from the application of Theorem 4 and Theorem 2. □

Algorithm 1 Probabilistic safety computation by finite DTMC abstraction

---

Require: $Y = (X, \alpha)$ solution of $\mathcal{H}$ with initial condition (x, q), safe set $\mathcal{S}$, finite time interval $I = [0, t]$, and parameters $dx, h = min\left\{\frac{2^{-n}}{2\sqrt{2}K^2\bar{K}_d}, 2^{-n}\right\}$;

1: Select the partition $\mathcal{G}_{dx} = \cup_{q \in \mathcal{Q}} \cup_{i \in m_q} \{q\} \times A_{i,q}$;

2: Select the set of representative points, leading to $\mathcal{S}_{dx}$;

3: Define the DTMC Y^D with state space $\mathcal{Z}_{dx} = \mathcal{S}_{dx} \cup \phi$, initial condition z_0 equals to 1 for the entry corresponding to $\xi((x, q))$ and 0 otherwise, and transition matrix P_{dx} such that $P_{dx}(i, j) = T_{dx}(z_i, z_j)$;

4: Compute $z^t = z_0 \cdot P_{dx}^{(\lceil \frac{I}{h} \rceil)}$;

5: Return $P_{\text{safe}}(Y, \mathcal{S}, I) = 1 - z^t(\phi)$ with the error given as $\frac{I}{h} \cdot (\mathcal{K}dx + e^{-(2^n - 2^{\frac{n}{2}} + 1)})$.

In Algorithm 1 we present a numerical routine to compute safety properties over continuous-time hybrid systems. The inputs of the algorithm are $Y = (X, \alpha)$, solution of the continuous time hybrid process $\mathcal{H}$ with a given initial condition, a finite time interval I, the sampling time h, the grid parameter dx and the target set $\mathcal{S}$. (In the case study presented in the next section we consider parameters $h = 0.1$, $dx = 0.2$ and $I = [0, 2]$.) Theorem 5 allows us to compute a bound on the error as a function of parameters dx and h. Moreover, such parameters can be selected to meet a required precision error. That is, given the maximum error that is tolerated, Theorem 5 returns possible h and dx that guarantee such an error. In Lines 1, 2, 3 the algorithm computes the DTMC abstraction from Y and $\mathcal{S}$, as described in the previous section: P_{dx} is the transition probability matrix of the resulting DTMC [31], namely $P_{dx}(i, j)$ describes the probability of going from the discrete state z_i to the discrete state z_j at the next time step. Line 4 computes the transient evolution of the DTMC Y^D. This is done by multiplying the initial state z_0 for P_{dx} $\lceil \frac{I}{h} \rceil$ times, where $\lceil \frac{I}{h} \rceil$ are the number of discrete steps: $P_{\text{safe}}(Y, \mathcal{S}, I)$ is just the probability of not being in the sink state ϕ. A bound on the error is computed using Theorem 5.

7. CASE STUDY

We consider a continuous-time switching diffusion process studied in [1]. The discrete state space is composed of two locations $\mathcal{Q} = \{on, off\}$, and the continuous process takes values in $\mathbb{R}^2$, so that the hybrid state space is $\mathcal{D} = \mathcal{Q} \times \mathbb{R}^2$. The drift is given by the following two matrices

$$F(on) = \begin{pmatrix} -0.6 & 0.3 \\ -0.6 & 0.15 \end{pmatrix}, \quad F(off) = \begin{pmatrix} -0.35 & 0 \\ 0.1 & -0.25 \end{pmatrix}.$$

The continuous dynamics are further affected by a 1−dimensional Wiener process scaled by matrices

$$G(on) = \begin{pmatrix} 0.2 \\ 0.2 \end{pmatrix}, \quad G(off) = \begin{pmatrix} 0.3 \\ 0.3 \end{pmatrix}.$$

The Poisson measures are independent of the continuous component of the process and are given by the following rates: $\lambda_{on,off} = 0.41$ and $\lambda_{off,on} = 0.38$. We consider the Borel sigma algebra over $\mathcal{D}$ and a measurable set A. As the rates are independent of the continuous components, for $A \subseteq \mathbb{R}^2, q_i, q_j \in \{on, off\}$ with $q_i \neq q_j$, $x \in \mathbb{R}^2$ and $h \in \mathbb{R}_{\geq 0}$ small enough, we have the following transition kernels (see Theorem 1):

$$T^c(A, x, q_i, k) = \int_A \mathcal{N}\left(\bar{x} | e^{F(q_i)\cdot h} x, \Gamma(i,h)\right) d\bar{x} \cdot e^{-\lambda_{i,j} h} +$$
$$\int_A \left(\int_0^h \mathcal{N}\left(\bar{x} | E^{\mathcal{H}}_{q_i,x}(s), C^{\mathcal{H}}_{q_i,x,s}\right) \cdot \Omega_{i,j,h}(s) ds \right) \cdot$$
$(\lambda_{i,j}\, h\, e^{-\lambda_{i,j} h}) d\bar{x}$, where
$$E^{\mathcal{H}}_{q_i,x}(s) = e^{F(q_i)\cdot s} e^{F(q_i)(h-s)} x,$$
$$C^{\mathcal{H}}_{q_i,x,s} = e^{F(q_i)\cdot s} \Gamma(i,s) \left(e^{F(q_i)\cdot s}\right)^T + \Gamma(j, h-s), \text{ and}$$
$$T^d(q_j, x, q_i, k) = \begin{cases} e^{-\lambda_{i,j} h} & \text{if } q_i = q_j \\ \lambda_{i,j} h \cdot e^{-\lambda_{i,j} h} & \text{if } q_i \neq q_j \end{cases}$$

In order to choose h, we need to compute constants K_d, h_1, and h_2. As the rate coefficients are independent of the continuous components we have $h_1 = 0$. It can be further derived that

$$h_2 \leq \max_{x \in \mathbb{R}^2} \left\{ \left| \frac{\partial t^c(x'|x, q_i)}{\partial x} \right| \right\},$$

where t^c is the density function of the kernel T^C. Further, $\bar{K}_d$ can be computed as

$$\bar{K}_d = \max_{q_i \in \{on,off\}, j \in \{1,2\}} \left\{ \sqrt{\Gamma(i,h)(j,j)} \right\},$$

where $\Gamma(i,h)(j,j)$ is the component (j,j) of matrix $\Gamma(i,h)$. Note that K_d is also independent of the continuous component of the process.

In order to demonstrate the soundness of our method we implement Algorithm 1 in Matlab, and compare the numerical implementation with empirical results obtained by simulations. We consider the following safe region

$$\mathcal{S} = \left\{ x \in \mathbb{R}^2 \text{ s.t. for } i \in \{1,2\}, -0.2 \leq x_i \leq 1 \right\},$$

where x_i is the $i-$th component of vector x. We select the time interval $I = [0, 2]$. Firstly, we consider $h = 0.1$ and $dx = 0.2$. For such values, the resulting abstract DTMC is made up of 5184 states. We consider different initial conditions and we compare the safety computed on the abstraction with the same property computed on the original continuous-time model using 1000 simulations. As expected, for any initial condition, the abstraction provides a safety value that is a lower bound of the empirical one. We observe a maximal error of 0.11. Note that, for $h = 0.1$ and $dx = 0.2$, Theorem 5 guarantees a theoretical time discretization error bound of 0.2, and an uninformative space discretization error bound (e.g. > 1). This is because, for small values of h, the value of the constant h_2 tends to increase, requiring a finer space grid.

In order to increase the precision it is possible to decrease h and dx at the price of more computational effort (a larger DTMC abstraction). To guarantee a theoretical error ≤ 0.1, we can select $h = 0.03$, which results in a theoretical time discretization error $\leq 4 \cdot 10^{-4}$. However, for such small h, t^c has very small variance, rendering h_2 large. As a consequence, in order to keep the error small, we would need $dx < 10^{-3}$) and the resulting DTMC would be composed of $> 10^6$ states. This dimensionality issue arises also because we are considering a uniform grid (dx constant). As a consequence, we use the same space resolution both for states with no probability mass and for states with large probability mass, which are the great minority for h small. In fact, as described in the next Section, the use of more advanced, adaptive grid techniques [23] would allow us to meet the given precision with a much smaller resulting DTMC – this is targeted as future work.

8. CONCLUSIONS

We have presented a novel and formal approach to compute probabilistic reachability (and dually safety) for continuous time hybrid processes with no guards and no resets, and with continuous dynamics that can be described by linear stochastic differential equations. We have considered an approach based on space and time discretization of the original process, and derived uniform convergence of the algorithm, as well as error bounds that can be used to tune and control the approximation error.

The main contributions of the paper are the characterization of the kernels for the time discretizion of such processes and the error bound for the time discretization process. Finding formal bounds for the time discretization of stochastic hybrid processes has been an open problem, and, to our knowledge, only limited to results of weak convergence of the approximation. We have first presented the bound for uni-dimensional target sets, and then have shown how to extend it to multidimensional processes.

For the space discretization we have considered an approach based on uniform gridding of the state space, insipred by the work in [2]. Although formally correct, this approach in combination with time discretization may result in large DTMC abstractions. In fact, as shown in a case study, the diameter of each grid location tends to grow as the sampling time of the time discretization process decreases. A much better solution would be to consider adaptive gridding tecniques [23]. These would be extremely beneficial, since, when the sampling time is small, the distribution of the continuous kernel has very small variance. As a consequence, only a very small set of states has non-negligible probability mass. This is exactly the scenario where adaptive techniques perform better. As a future work, we plan to merge our time discretization approach with adaptive gridding techniques and to release a tool based on that.

9. PROOFS

PROOF OF THEOREM 1. We show the derivation of the continuous kernel. Note that the discrete kernel can be derived similarly. By definition we have

$$T^c(A, x, q_i) = \int_A t^c(\bar{x}|x, q_i)d\bar{x},$$

where $t^c(\bar{x}|x, q_i)$ is the density function of X, continuous component of Y, assuming $X(0) = x$ and $\alpha(0) = \lambda_i$. We define $Num^h_\alpha = k$ as the event such that α, discrete component of Y, jumps k times between $[0, h]$. By marginalizing with respect to the number of times that α jumps during $[0, h]$, we have

$$T^c(A, x, q_i) = \int_A t^c(\bar{x}|x, q_i)d\bar{x} =$$

$$\int_A \Big(t^c(\bar{x}|x, q_i, Num^h_\alpha = 0) \cdot Prob(Num^h_\alpha = 0|x, q_i) +$$

$$t^c(\bar{x}|x, q_i, Num^h_\alpha = 1) \cdot Prob(Num^h_\alpha = 1|x, q_i) + \epsilon\Big)\, d\bar{x}$$

where $\epsilon \leq Prob(Num^h_\alpha > 1|x, q_i) =$

$$1 - \sum_{i\in\{0,1\}} Prob(Num^h_\alpha = i|x, q_i).$$

$t^c(\bar{x}|x, q_i, Num^h_\alpha = 0)$ is the normal distribution derived from solving the linear SDE corresponding to mode q_i from initial condition x for the interval $[0, h]$ because the solution of a SDE is Markov. The properties of Poisson processes give us

$$Prob(Num^h_\alpha = 0|x, q_i) = e^{-\lambda_i h},$$

and similarly

$$Prob(Num^h_\alpha = 1|x, q_i) = \lambda_i h e^{-\lambda_i h}.$$

We further define $Jump_{i,j}$ and $Jump^s_{i,j}$ as the events such that α jumps from state q_i in state q_j, and α jumps from state q_i in state q_j at time s, respectively. By marginalizing $t^c(\bar{x}|x, q_i, Num^h_\alpha = 1)$ with respect to the discrete location where we jump and the time when α jumps we get:

$$t^c(\bar{x}|x, q_i, Num^h_\alpha = 1) =$$

$$\sum_{q_j \neq q_i} \int_0^h t^c\left(\bar{x}|x, q_i, Num^h_\alpha = 1, Jump^s_{i,j}\right) \cdot$$

$$f(s|x, q_i, Num^h_\alpha = 1, Jump_{i,j})Prob(Jump_{i,j})ds$$

The first term is a linear Gaussian model. This class of models has been extensively studied in literature [9]. More specifically, it has a Gaussian distribution whose variance and expectation can be derived from Lemma 3. As a conseqeunce, we have

$$t^c(\bar{x}|x, q_i, Jump^s_{i,j}) = \mathcal{N}(\bar{x}|E, C), \text{ where}$$

$$E = e^{F(q_i)\cdot s} e^{F(q_i)(h-s)} x, \text{ and}$$

$$C = e^{F(q_i)\cdot s}\Gamma(i, s)\left(e^{F(q_i)\cdot s}\right)^T + \Gamma(j, h - s)).$$

$Prob(Jump_{i,j}) = \frac{\lambda_{ij}}{\lambda_i}$ is the probability of jumping in q_j at the next jump. and $f(s|x, q, Num^h_\alpha = 1, Jump_{i,j})$ is the density function of the jumping time conditioned on the fact that we jump in $[0, h]$. This can be derived from properties of Poisson processes as

$$f(s|x, q, Num^h_\alpha = 1, Jump_{i,j}) = (\lambda_j - \lambda_i)\frac{e^{(\lambda_j s - \lambda_j t - \lambda_i s)}}{e^{(-\lambda_i t)} - e^{(-\lambda_j t)}}.$$

□

PROOF OF THEOREM 2. For each $q \in \mathcal{Q}$, X_q is an almost surely bounded and uniformly continuous GP in I, time interval of interest. This guarantees the existence of a sequence $\{\delta_n\}$ with $\delta_n \to 0$ such that $\phi(\delta_n) \leq 2^{-n}$ (see Theorem 2.1.3 of [5]), where

$$\phi(\delta_n) = E\left[\max_{q\in\mathcal{Q}}\left\{\sup_{s,s'\in I:|s'-s|\leq\delta_n}(X(s) - X(s'))\right\}\right].$$

Set $h = min\{\delta_n, 2^{-n}\}$and $\epsilon_n = 2^{-\frac{n}{2}}$. For a set of a sampling times $\Sigma = \{t_1, ..., t_{|\Sigma_n|}\}$, with step distance $h > 0$, call $S \subseteq \mathbb{R}^n$ the *safe set* and,

$$S^{\epsilon_n} = \{x \in S \ : \ |x - \partial S| \leq \epsilon_n\},$$

where ∂S is the boundary of S, and $|\cdot|$ stands for euclidean metric distance. Define the events

$$\mathcal{A}^n = \{\forall t_i \in \Sigma_n, . \ X(t_i) \in S^{\epsilon_n}\}$$

and

$$\mathcal{B} = \{\exists t \in I \ s.t. \ X(t) \notin \mathcal{S}\}.$$

Using the rules of probability we get

$$P(\mathcal{A}^n \wedge \mathcal{B}^c) = P(\mathcal{A}^n) \cdot (1 - P(\mathcal{B}|\mathcal{A}^n))$$

By definition of probability we have that

$$\begin{aligned}
&0 \leq P(\mathcal{B}|\mathcal{A}^n)\\
&\leq P(\exists t_i \in \Sigma_n \, s.t. \sup_{t\in[t_i,t_i+h]}(X(t) - X(i)) > \epsilon_n)\\
&\leq P(\exists t_i \in \Sigma_n \, s.t. \sup_{t\in[t_i,t_i+h]}(X(t) - X(i)) > \epsilon_n)\\
&\leq \sum_{i=1}^{|\Sigma_n|} P\left(\sup_{t\in[t_i,t_i+h]}(X(t) - X(i)) > \epsilon_n\right),
\end{aligned}$$

with $X(t_i) \in S^{\epsilon_n}$.

In order to bound $P(\sup_{t\in[t_i,t_i+h]}(X(t) - X(i)) > \epsilon_n)$ we need to take into account that during $[t_i, t_i + h]$ the discrete state may hit a transition. However, there is no reset for the continuous components. As a consequence, it is enough to assume that, during $[t_i, t_i + h]$, X always evolves accoridng to the "worst" behaving X_q. Then, being X_q a GP, we can make use of the Borell's bound [4, 5]. Given an interval I and a centered and bounded Guassian process X_q with $\sigma_I = \sup_{t\in I}(\sigma(t))$, supremum of the standard deviation of the process, the Borrell bound guarantees that

$$Prob\left(\sup_{t\in I} X_q(t) > u\right) \leq \exp^{-\left(u - E\left[sup_{t\in I} X_q(t)\right]\right)^2/(\sigma_I^2)}$$

Applying this result to our case for intervals of the type $[t_i, t_i + h]$, and for $u = \epsilon_n = 2^{-\frac{n}{2}}$, where $n \geq 3$ we have that

$$\sum_{i}^{|\Sigma_n|} P\left(\sup_{t\in[t_i,t_i+h]} (X(t) - X(t_i))\right) > \epsilon_n)$$

$$\leq |\Sigma_n| \exp^{-\frac{\left(2^{-\frac{n}{2}}-2^{-n}\right)^2}{2^{-2n}}} \leq |\Sigma_n| \exp^{-\left(2^n - 2^{\frac{n}{2}}+1\right)}$$

At this point, the last, and non-trivial, step in order to derive our convergence results and relative error bounds is to show that

$$\lim_{n\to\infty} |\Sigma_n| \exp^{-\left(2^n - 2^{\frac{n}{2}}+1\right)} = 0.$$

In fact, as

$$0 \leq P(\mathcal{B}|A^n) \leq |\Sigma_n| \exp^{-\left(2^n - 2^{\frac{n}{2}}+1\right)},$$

this would guarantee that

$$P_{\text{safe}}(X,S,I) = \lim_{n\to\infty} P(\mathcal{A}^n \wedge \mathcal{B}^c) = \lim_{n\to\infty} P(\mathcal{A}^n).$$

To do that, it is sufficient to show that $h = \frac{2^{-n}}{C}$, for some constant C. In fact, this implies $|\Sigma_n| = \frac{I \cdot C}{2^{-n}}$.

Recall that we chose h such that for all $t_i \in \Sigma_n$,

$$E\left[\sup_{t\in[t_i,t_i+h]} (X(t) - X(t_i))\right] \leq 2^{-n}.$$

As a consequence, it is enough to take h as the greatest interval smaller than 2^{-n} such that this condition is verified. For $t_i \in \Sigma_n$ call $\bar{X}_i = X(t) - X(t_i)$. We can now make use of the *Dudley integral (or entropy integral)* [4], which guarantees that for $t_i \in \Sigma_n$,

$$E[\sup_{t\in[t_i,t_i+h]} (\bar{X}_i)] \leq$$

$$K \int_0^{\frac{diam([t_i,t_i+h])}{2}} \sqrt{\ln(N([t_i,t_i+h],d,\epsilon))} d\epsilon,$$

where $K \geq 12$ is a constant and d is a pseudo-metric defined as

$$d(t,t+dt) = \sqrt{E[(X(t+dt)-X(t))^2]}.$$

$N([t_i,t_i+h],d,\epsilon)$ represents the smallest number of balls of radius ϵ, which covers $[t_i,t_i+h]$, under metric d, where $diam([t_i,t_i+h])$ is defined as

$$diam([t_i,t_i+h]) = sup_{s',s\in[t_i,t_i+h]} d(s',s)$$

and with our assumptions, it is possible to show that there exists a constant K_d such that

$$d(t,t+h) \leq K_d \cdot h$$

Moreover, for $\bar{T}_i = [t_i, t_i+h] \subseteq \mathbb{R}_{\geq 0}$ we have

$$N(\bar{T}_i, d, \epsilon) \leq \frac{K_d h}{2\epsilon} + 1,$$

This can be easily understood thinking at the geometry of the problem. As a consequence, we have

$$E\left[\sup_{t\in\bar{T}_i}(\bar{X}_i(t))\right] \leq K \int_0^{\sqrt{2}\cdot 2^{-n-1}} \sqrt{ln\left(\frac{K_d h}{2\epsilon}+1\right)} d\epsilon$$

Now, our property is satisfied if we chose h such that

$$K \int_0^{\sqrt{2}\cdot 2^{-n}} \sqrt{\ln\left(\frac{K_d h}{2\epsilon}+1\right)} d\epsilon \leq 2^{-n}.$$

The integral inequality we need to solve cannot be solved analytically. However, as $K_d h > 0$, we can write

$$K \int_0^{\sqrt{2}\cdot 2^{-n}} \sqrt{\ln\left(\frac{K_d h}{2\epsilon}+1\right)} d\epsilon \leq K \int_0^{\sqrt{2}\cdot 2^{-n}} \sqrt{\frac{K_d h}{2\epsilon}} d\epsilon$$

$$= K\sqrt{\frac{K_d h}{2}} \int_0^{\sqrt{2}\cdot 2^{-n}} \sqrt{\frac{1}{\epsilon}} d\epsilon = K\sqrt{\frac{K_d h}{2}} 2\sqrt{\sqrt{2}2^{-n}}.$$

Asking for this quantity to be smaller than 2^{-n}, we obtain the following bound for the sampling time h :

$$h \leq min\left\{\frac{2^{-n}}{2\sqrt{2}K^2K_d}, 2^{-n}\right\}.$$

□

Acknowledgments

This work has been supported by the Royal Society Professorship (L.Cardelli), the Czech Grant Agency grants GA16-24707Y (M. Češka), the EU-FET project QUANTICOL (nr. 600708) and by FRA-UniTS (L. Bortolussi).

10. REFERENCES

[1] A. Abate. Probabilistic bisimulations of switching and resetting diffusions. In *CDC*, pages 5918–5923. IEEE, 2010.

[2] A. Abate, J.-P. Katoen, J. Lygeros, and M. Prandini. Approximate model checking of stochastic hybrid systems. *Eur. J. Control*, 6:624–641, 2010.

[3] A. Abate, M. Prandini, J. Lygeros, and S. Sastry. Probabilistic reachability and safety for controlled discrete time stochastic hybrid systems. *Automatica*, 44(11):2724–2734, November 2008.

[4] R. J. Adler. *The geometry of random fields*, volume 62. Siam, 2010.

[5] R. J. Adler and J. E. Taylor. *Random fields and geometry*. Springer Science & Business Media, 2009.

[6] A. Arapostathis, V. Borkar, and M. Ghosh. *Ergodic Control of Diffusion Processes*. Cambridge University Press, 2012.

[7] L. Arnold. Stochastic differential equations. *New York*, 1974.

[8] A. Aziz, K. Sanwal, V. Singhal, and R. Brayton. Model-checking continuous-time Markov chains. *ACM Transactions on Computational Logic*, 1(1):162–170, 2000.

[9] C. M. Bishop. *Neural networks for pattern recognition*. Oxford university press, 1995.

[10] H. Blom and J. Lygeros (Eds.). *Stochastic Hybrid Systems: Theory and Safety Critical Applications*. Number 337 in Lecture Notes in Control and Information Sciences. Springer Verlag, Berlin Heidelberg, 2006.

[11] L. Bortolussi, L. Cardelli, M. Kwiatkowska, and L. Laurenti. Approximation of probabilistic reachability for chemical reaction networks using the

linear noise approximation. In *QEST*, pages 72–88. Springer, 2016.

[12] L. Bortolussi and R. Lanciani. Model checking markov population models by central limit approximation. In *QEST*, pages 123–138. Springer, 2013.

[13] L. Bujorianu. *Stochastic Reachability Analysis of Hybrid Systems*. Springer-Verlag, London, 2012.

[14] L. M. Bujorianu. *Stochastic reachability analysis of hybrid systems*. Springer Science & Business Media, 2012.

[15] P. Bulychev, A. David, K. Guldstrand Larsen, A. Legay, M. Mikučionis, and D. Bøgsted Poulsen. *Checking and Distributing Statistical Model Checking*, pages 449–463. Springer Berlin Heidelberg, 2012.

[16] L. Cardelli, M. Kwiatkowska, and L. Laurenti. Stochastic analysis of chemical reaction networks using linear noise approximation. In *CMSB*, pages 64–76. Springer, 2015.

[17] L. Cardelli, M. Kwiatkowska, and L. Laurenti. A stochastic hybrid approximation for chemical kinetics based on the linear noise approximation. In *CMSB*, pages 147–167. Springer, 2016.

[18] C. Cassandras and J. Lygeros (Eds.). *Stochastic Hybrid Systems*. Number 24 in Control Engineering. CRC Press, Boca Raton, 2006.

[19] D. J. Daley and D. Vere-Jones. *An introduction to the theory of point processes: volume II: general theory and structure*. Springer Science & Business Media, 2007.

[20] M. Davis. *Markov Models and Optimization*. Chapman & Hall/CRC Press, London, 1993.

[21] R. M. Dudley. The sizes of compact subsets of hilbert space and continuity of gaussian processes. *Journal of Functional Analysis*, 1(3):290–330, 1967.

[22] P. M. Esfahani, D. Chatterjee, and J. Lygeros. The stochastic reach-avoid problem and set characterization for diffusions. *Automatica*, 70:43–56, 2016.

[23] S. Esmaeil Zadeh Soudjani and A. Abate. Adaptive and sequential gridding procedures for the abstraction and verification of stochastic processes. *SIAM Journal on Applied Dynamical Systems*, 12(2):921–956, 2013.

[24] M. Fränzle, E. M. Hahn, H. Hermanns, N. Wolovick, and L. Zhang. Measurability and safety verification for stochastic hybrid systems. In *HSCC*, pages 43–52, 2011.

[25] M. Fränzle, H. Hermanns, and T. Teige. Stochastic satisfiability modulo theory: A novel technique for the analysis of probabilistic hybrid systems. In M. Egerstedt and B. Misra, editors, *HSCC*, volume 4981 of *Lecture Notes in Computer Science*, pages 172–186. Springer Verlag, Berlin Heidelberg, 2008.

[26] C. W. Gardiner et al. *Handbook of stochastic methods*, volume 3. Springer-Verlag, 1985.

[27] M. K. Ghosh, A. Arapostathis, and S. I. Marcus. Optimal control of switching diffusions with application to flexible manufacturing systems. *SIAM Journal on Control and Optimization*, 31(5):1183–1204, 1993.

[28] P. E. Kloeden and E. Platen. *Numerical Solution of Stochastic Differential Equations*. Springer Science & Business Media, 2011.

[29] K. Koutsoukos and D. Riley. Computational methods for reachability analysis of stochastic hybrid systems. In J. Hespanha and A. Tiwari, editors, *HSCC*, volume 3927 of *Lecture Notes in Computer Science*, pages 377–391. Springer Verlag, Berlin Heidelberg, 2006.

[30] H. J. Kushner and P. Dupuis. *Numerical Methods for Stochastic Control Problems in Continuous Time*. Springer-Verlag, New York, 2001.

[31] M. Kwiatkowska, G. Norman, and D. Parker. Stochastic model checking. In *Formal methods for performance evaluation*, pages 220–270. Springer, 2007.

[32] P. Massart. *Concentration inequalities and model selection*, volume 6. Springer, 2007.

[33] B. Øksendal. *Stochastic differential equations*. Springer, 2003.

[34] M. Prandini and J. Hu. Stochastic reachability: Theory and numerical approximation. In C. Cassandras and J. Lygeros, editors, *Stochastic hybrid systems*, Automation and Control Engineering Series 24, pages 107–138. Taylor & Francis Group/CRC Press, 2006.

[35] S. Särkkä et al. *Recursive Bayesian inference on stochastic differential equations*. Helsinki University of Technology, 2006.

[36] I. Tkachev, A. Mereacre, J.-P. Katoen, and A. Abate. Quantitative automata-based controller synthesis for non-autonomous stochastic hybrid systems. In *HSCC*, pages 293–302, 2013.

[37] Y. Wang, N. Roohi, M. West, M. Viswanathan, and G. E. Dullerud. Statistical verification of dynamical systems using set oriented methods. In *HSCC*, pages 169–178. ACM, 2015.

[38] G. G. Yin and C. Zhu. *Hybrid switching diffusions: properties and applications*, volume 63. Springer Science & Business Media, 2009.

[39] M. Zamani and A. Abate. Symbolic models for randomly switched stochastic systems. *Systems & Control Letters*, 69:38–46, 2014.

[40] M. Zamani, P. M. Esfahani, R. Majumdar, A. Abate, and J. Lygeros. Symbolic control of stochastic systems via approximately bisimilar finite abstractions. *IEEE Transactions on Automatic Control*, 59(12):2825–2830, 2014.

[41] L. Zhang, Z. She, S. Ratschan, H. Hermanns, and E. M. Hahn. *Safety Verification for Probabilistic Hybrid Systems*, pages 196–211. Springer Berlin Heidelberg, Berlin, Heidelberg, 2010.

Statistical Verification of the Toyota Powertrain Control Verification Benchmark

Nima Roohi
Dep. of Computer Science
University of Illinois at Urbana-Champaign, USA
roohi2@illinois.edu

Yu Wang
Coordinated Science Laboratory
University of Illinois at Urbana-Champaign, USA
yuwang8@illinois.edu

Matthew West
Department of Mechanical Science and Engineering
University of Illinois at Urbana-Champaign, USA
mwest@illinois.edu

Geir E. Dullerud
Coordinated Science Laboratory
University of Illinois at Urbana-Champaign, USA
dullerud@illinois.edu

Mahesh Viswanathan
Department of Computer Science
University of Illinois at Urbana-Champaign, USA
vmahesh@illinois.edu

ABSTRACT

The Toyota Powertrain Control Verification Benchmark has been recently proposed as challenge problems that capture features of realistic automotive designs. In this paper we statistically verify the most complicated of the powertrain control models proposed, that includes features like delayed differential and difference equations, look-up tables, and highly non-linear dynamics, by simulating the C++ code generated from the `Simulink`™ model of the design. Our results show that for at least 98% of the possible initial operating conditions the desired properties hold. These are the first verification results for this model, statistical or otherwise.

1. INTRODUCTION

The powertrain control problem is one of regulating the air-to-fuel ratio in a automotive engine. A series of models of such controllers, with increasing levels of sophistication and fidelity to real-world designs, have been recently proposed by Toyota researchers [6] as challenge problems for today's verification technologies. Ever since these models were proposed 2 years back, they have served as a high water mark for evaluating verification tools and techniques for cyber-physical systems. When the models were first proposed [6], the authors used the tool `S-Taliro` [1] to search for counter-examples in each of the controller models. While the search for counter-examples was unsuccessful, this analysis did not establish any formal statements of correctness for the designs. This is because `S-Taliro` is a *falsification* tool rather than a verification tool. Last year [4], the first (and to date, only) proof of correctness for one of the designs was established. Duggirala et. al. [4] used the tool `C2E2` to prove the correctness of Model 3, the simplest of the 3 models proposed by Toyota researchers. While Model 3 is a challenging non-linear hybrid system model, it is nonetheless extremely simple when compared with the most realistic Toyota model. All dynamics in Model 3 are described by polynomial differential equations.

In this paper we present our results in verifying the most complicated of the models proposed in [6] (Model 1, Section 3.1) that has features like delayed differential and difference equations, look-up tables, in addition to highly non-linear continuous dynamics for the state variables. Like `S-Taliro` and `C2E2`, our verification approach is also simulation-based, where the `Simulink`™ model (or, in our case, the C++ code generated from the `Simulink`™ model) provided by the authors of [6] is executed to generate traces which are then analyzed. However, unlike previous approaches, in this paper, we use *statistical model checking* [8, 13] to analyze the traces.

Statistical model checking is an approach to check if a stochastic model satisfies certain quantitative properties. One example of a very simple quantitative property is that "75% of all system executions are safe". To check such a requirement, statistical model checking would probabilistic sample executions of the system, and see if the generated sample provides sufficient *statistical evidence* that 75% of the execution are indeed safe; this is determined based on the size of the sample, the evidence of the sample, and using statistical tests like Chernoff bounds or sequential probability ratio test. Since statistical model checking is a randomized algorithm, it can have both false positive and false negative errors. These are usually characterized by the Type I and Type II errors of hypothesis testing, and can be made as small as desired by increasing the number of samples drawn.

The power train control model (Model 1 in [6]) is not stochastic. In fact, if we fix the values of the input parameters, namely, engine speed and throttle angle signal profile, the model is completely deterministic. So how can we justify the use of statistical model checking which works only for stochastic models? The goal of verification is to show that for every setting of the input parameters, the execution of the controller satisfies the correctness requirements specified as *Signal Temporal Logic (STL)* properties given in [6]. In

HSCC'17, April 18-20, 2017, Pittsburgh, PA, USA

DOI: http://dx.doi.org/10.1145/3049797.3049804

this paper, our goal is to establish a weaker statement about correctness. Instead of proving that executions for *every* setting of initial parameters are correct, we aim to show that the system behaves correctly for *most* settings of the initial parameters. If the values of initial parameters are set *uniformly at random* from the input space, then we could view the powertrain controller as a stochastic model (where the only stochastic step is the choice of initial parameter values), and statistical model checking would indeed provide the relaxed correctness goals we are aiming for. Our experimental results show that Model 1 is correct for *at least* 98% of the settings for the input parameters; our probability of false positive and false negative errors were bounded to be at most 0.01.

While the statistical techniques we use to bound sample sizes are standard, we need a couple of ideas to enable checking whether a single sample execution satisfies the prescribed STL property. Mathematically, an execution of the powertrain controller is a function that specifies for each time instant, the state of the system. Clearly, such a "continuous" function cannot be sampled/simulated. Instead, what the simulation can generate, and what we can hope to analyze, is the sequence of system states sampled at discrete time points. But can analyzing the execution sampled at discrete time points determine the correctness of the actual, continuous execution? This is a standard problem that confronts all simulation-based verification methods for cyber-physical systems. We use ideas similar to those outlined in [5] to come up with a list of conditions on how finely the execution must be sampled (based on the correctness property) and an approximate satisfaction relation that together guarantee that if the discretely sampled execution satisfies an STL property then so does the actual, continuous execution. However, for such a property preservation result to go through, one needs to know the Lipschitz constant for the functions used to define the basic atomic propositions of the STL properties, over the set of reachable states of the systems. Determining such a Lipschitz bound for the powertrain controller is not easy because of its complicated dynamics. We overcome this through an innovative technique. The sampling algorithm starts with some value for the Lipschitz constant (which maybe wrong). We add a monitor to the Simulink™ model that *continuously* checks the derivative of the function whose Lipschitz bound we need, raising an "alarm" when this exceeds the guessed bound. When an execution generated by the Simulink™ model + monitor has no alarms, then the sample execution can be checked against the STL property because the Lipschitz bound holds for this execution, and if an alarm is raised then we need to abandon the execution, change the Lipschitz bound in the monitor, and resimulate.

The rest of the paper is organized as follows. In Section 2, we introduce the basic mathematical notation we use, and an introduction to statistical model checking; we assume that the reader is comfortable with the model hybrid automata, but for completeness it is defined in the Appendix. Section 3 describes in detail Model 1 of [6] that we analyze statistically. Our approach to verifying the model is described in Section 4. Our experimental results are in Section 5. Finally, we present our conclusions in Section 6.

2. PRELIMINARIES

The sets of *natural*, *real*, *non-negative real*, and *positive real* numbers are represented by $\mathbb{N}$, $\mathbb{R}$, $\mathbb{R}_{\geq 0}$, and $\mathbb{R}_{+}$, respectively. For an element x and a set A, we use $x : A$ to denote that x is "of type" A or $x \in A$. For any two sets A and B, the set of functions from B to A is represented by A^B. In order to make the notations simpler, we denote $A^{\{0,1,\dots,n-1\}}$ by A^n. Furthermore, *the set of subsets* of A is represented by 2^A. $A \times B$ is the *Cartesian product* of A and B. For any function $f : A \to B$ and a set C, by $f\downharpoonright_C$ we mean a function from $A \cap C$ to B that maps a to $f(a)$. Also, by $\mathsf{range}(f)$ we mean $\{b : B \mid \exists a : A \bullet b = f(a)\}$. For any two metric spaces (M_1, ρ_1) and (M_2, ρ_2), and a function $f : M_1 \to M_2$, function f is called *Lipschitz continuous* if there is a constant $c : \mathbb{R}$ such that $\forall \epsilon : \mathbb{R}_+ \bullet x, y : M_1 \bullet \rho_1(x, y) < \epsilon \Rightarrow \rho_2(f(x), f(y)) < c\epsilon$. For any two sets $A, B \subseteq \mathbb{R}$ we define $A + B$ to be $\{x + y \mid x \in A \wedge y \in B\}$. Finally, $\mathcal{I}$ is the set of non-empty intervals over $\mathbb{R}_{\geq 0}$, and for any $I : \mathcal{I}$, infimum (supremum) of I is denoted by $\inf I$ ($\sup I$).

2.1 Signal Temporal Logic

Signal Temporal Logic (STL) is used to specify predicates over real-time signal. The most basic ingredient of STL is its atomic propositions. Each atomic proposition is a predicate over valuation of the state variables expressed as an inequality. Let $f : \mathbb{R}^{\mathsf{x}} \to \mathbb{R}$ be any Lipschitz continuous real valued function. An atomic proposition is then of the form $f > 0$. Syntax of a STL formula ϕ is defined using the following BNF grammar:

$$\phi := \top \mid f > 0 \mid \neg\phi \mid \phi \vee \phi \mid \phi \mathcal{U}_{\mathcal{I}} \phi$$

For a STL formula ϕ, duration $T : \mathbb{R}_{\geq 0}$, a signal $\tau : [0, T] \to \mathbb{R}^{\mathsf{x}}$, and a time $t : [0, T]$, satisfaction of ϕ by τ at time t is shown by $(\tau, t) \models \phi$ are defined using the following inductive rules. If $t > T$ then $(\tau, t) \models \phi$ is undefined. Otherwise,

$$\begin{array}{lll}
(\tau, t) \models \top & & \\
(\tau, t) \models f > 0 & \text{iff} & f(\tau(t)) > 0 \\
(\tau, t) \models \neg\phi & \text{iff} & (\tau, t) \not\models \phi \\
(\tau, t) \models \phi \vee \psi & \text{iff} & (\tau, t) \models \phi \text{ or } (\tau, t) \models \psi \\
(\tau, t) \models \phi \mathcal{U}_I \psi & \text{iff} & \exists r : I \bullet (\tau, t + r) \models \psi \wedge \\
& & \quad \forall r' : [0, r) \bullet (\tau, t + r') \models \phi
\end{array}$$

Other connectives can be defined as well. $\bot := \neg\top$, $\phi \wedge \psi := \neg(\neg\phi \vee \neg\psi)$, $\phi \mathcal{R}_I \psi := \neg(\neg\phi \mathcal{U}_I \neg\psi)$, $\Diamond_I \phi := \top \mathcal{U}_I \phi$, and $\Box_I \phi := \neg(\Diamond_I \neg\phi)$. Intuitively, $\phi \mathcal{U}_I \psi$ means there is a time in I such that ψ is true at that time and ϕ is true up until that time. $\phi \mathcal{R}_I \psi$ means that ψ should always be true during the time interval I, a requirement which is released when ϕ becomes true. $\Diamond_I \phi$ means there is a time in I such that ϕ is true at that time. $\Box_I \phi$ means ϕ is always true during I. Finally, $\tau \models \phi$ is defined as $(\tau, 0) \models \phi$. Note that since we want to do statistical model checking, we won't be able to distinguish $f > 0$ from $f \geq 0$. Therefore, we only consider the strict form of inequality. Furthermore, having negation ($\neg$), disjunction ($\vee$) and conjunction ($\wedge$), among the set of STL operators, we know $f \leq 0$, $f < 0$, $f \geq 0$, $f = 0$, and $f \neq 0$ can be defined using $\neg(f > 0)$, $-f > 0$, $\neg(f < 0)$, $(f \geq 0) \wedge (f \leq 0)$, and $(f > 0) \vee (f < 0)$. Note that with the help of $\bot$, $\wedge$, and $\mathcal{R}$ operators, one can always push the negations to the front of atomic formulas and have a formula in negated normal form.

2.2 Sampling Based Algorithms

Statistical model checking [13] is a technique to verify stochastic systems against quantitative properties expressed in a temporal logic. The approach draws sample trajectories from the model by discrete-event simulations, and uses hypothesis testing to infer whether the samples provide statistical evidence for the satisfaction or violation of the specification. The crux of this approach is that sample runs of a stochastic system are drawn according to the distribution defined by the system, and hence can be used to get estimates of the probability measure of executions.

In this paper, the properties we need to check are very simple quantitative properties and so here we outline the broad ideas behind checking such properties. Suppose the actual probability that executions of a system satisfy a STL property ϕ is θ'. Let H_0 be $\theta' < 1$ and H_1 be $\theta' \geq \theta$ for any value $\theta : (0,1)$. Our goal is to determine which of the two hypotheses is true (with a small error probability); that is, the probability of saying H_0 (similarly H_1) is true while it is false should be small. Now every time we sample an execution, with probability θ' the execution will satisfy ϕ, and this can be thought of as a Bernoulli variable. Therefore, in n samples the number of executions satisfying ϕ is expected to be $n\theta'$. Though we don't know what θ' is, the fraction of executions satisfying ϕ is statistically a good estimate for θ', especially if the number of samples is large. This is the basis of statistical model checking algorithm. If θ and θ' are equal to each other then no matter how large of a sample we take, statistically we will not be able to decide whether $\theta' \geq \theta$ is true or not. Therefore, statistical tests work only when θ' is δ-away from θ for some arbitrarily small $\delta : \mathbb{R}_+$. Under this condition, several algorithms have been proposed using either Chernoff bounds, or sequential probability ratio test [8, 11, 12] that determine how many samples need to be drawn in order to ensure that the likelihood of our making a mistake is small. Taking S to be a Bernoulli random variable with mean θ', a typical algorithm $\mathcal{A}^\delta(S, t, \alpha, \beta, \gamma)$ takes the indifference parameter δ, and error bounds α, β, and γ as parameters and outputs either H_1, H_0, or **unknown**. The answer **unknown** is returned when $|\theta - \theta'| \leq \delta$. The algorithm is such that parameters δ, α, β, and γ can be made arbitrary small at the cost of more samples. It guarantees the following.

$$\mathbb{P}[result = H_0 \mid H_0 \text{ is false}] \leq \alpha \quad (1)$$
$$\mathbb{P}[result = H_1 \mid H_1 \text{ is false}] \leq \beta \quad (2)$$
$$\mathbb{P}[result = \texttt{unknown} \mid |\theta - \theta'| > \delta] \leq \gamma \quad (3)$$

Formula 1 (respectively Formula 2) guarantees that the probability of returning a wrong hypothesis is bounded by α (and β). Formula 3 guarantees that the probability of returning **unknown** when θ is δ-away from θ' is bounded by γ. Notice that α, β, and γ are parameters and can be made as small as desired; the number of samples needed will grow proportionally. Second, the algorithm requires δ as a parameter as well, and this might seem difficult to obtain. However, observe that even if δ is given incorrectly (i.e., $|\theta - \theta'| < \delta$) the answers of the algorithm are not incorrect; it is just more likely to return **unknown**. In Section 4 we show that in the case of specific H_0 and H_1 defined here, we can set indifference and some of the error probabilities to zero while still guaranteeing conditions 1 through 3.

3. POWERTRAIN CONTROL PROBLEM

The goal of the powertrain control system is to maintain the air-fuel ratio at a desired value for optimal function of the internal combustion engine under different driving behaviors and conditions. It is modeled in Simulink™. Intuitively, the model takes input from a driver (input throttle angle θ_{in}) and from the environment (engine speed ω and **failed** event) and controls the behavior of the engine. It is a non-linear hybrid model with 4 control modes and around 15 state and intermediate variables defined as parallel composition of two hybrid i/o automaton (HIOA): a controller (A_c) and a plant (A_p). [6] introduced 3 different models of this controller, with increasing fidelity to the real world. In this paper, we analyzed the most complicated model. Dynamics of both controller and plant are non-linear. Furthermore, plant's dynamics are highly non-linear and involve delayed differential equation. Table 1 briefly describes different variables used in the specification of the system.

State	Unit	Description
p	bar	Intake Manifold Pressure
λ_c	-	A/F Ratio in Cylinder
λ_m	-	Transfer Function Output
p_e	bar	Estimated Manifold Pressure
i	-	Integrator State, PI
$\dot{m}_{af}$	g/s	Inlet Air Mass Flow Rate
$\dot{m}_c$	g/s	Air Flow Rate to Cylinder
$\dot{m}_\phi$	g/s	Fuel Mass Aspirated into the Cylinder
$\dot{m}_\psi$	g/s	Fuel Mass Injected into Intake Manifold
θ_{in}	degrees	Throttle Angle Input
θ	degrees	Delay-Filtered Throttle Angle
$\hat{\theta}$	-	O/P of Throttle Polynomial
F_c	g/s	Command fuel
ω	rad/sec	Engine Speed
n	round/sec	Engine Speed ($\frac{\omega}{2\pi}$)

Table 1: States and Indeterminate Variables

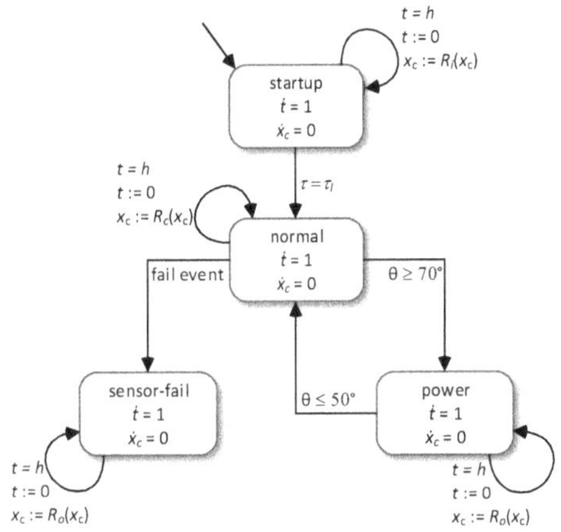

Figure 1: Hybrid automaton A_c Modeling the Controller Part of the Powertrain System

The hybrid automaton $A = A_c || A_p$ has two inputs: 1. the engine speed (ω) which is a constant value in $[900, 1100]$. 2. the throttle angle (θ_{in}) signal profile, which is the set of pulse train signals (with pulse width equal to half the period). In this work, we verify the model when the period (ζ) is in $[10, 30]$ and amplitude (a) is in $[8.8, 70]$.

Properties that need to be verified are specified using Signal Temporal Logic (STL) [3]. The following two formulas are used to specify points in time that input signal θ_{in} is

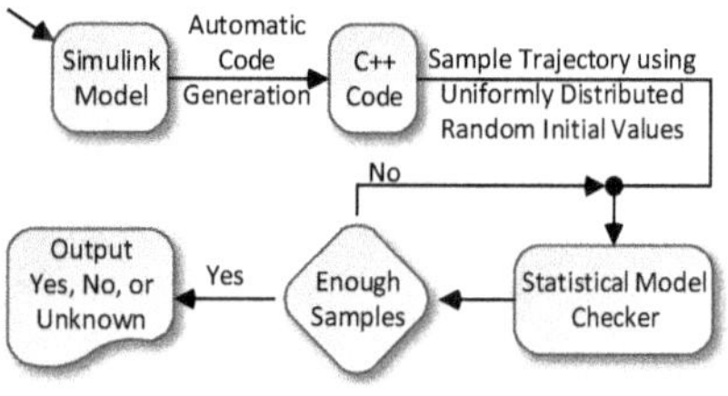

Figure 2: Steps of Our Approach to Model Check Powertrain Controller Verification Problem

about to go up or down:

$$\texttt{rise}(a) := (\theta_{in} = 8.8) \wedge \Diamond_{(0,\epsilon)}(\theta_{in} = a) \tag{4}$$

$$\texttt{fall}(a) := (\theta_{in} = a) \wedge \Diamond_{(0,\epsilon)}(\theta_{in} = 8.8) \tag{5}$$

A normalized error signal μ that measures the error in A/F Ratio (λ_m) (a state variable of the system) from the reference stoichiometric value λ_{ref} is defined as follows:

$$\mu(t) = \frac{\lambda_m(t) - \lambda_{ref}}{\lambda_{ref}} \tag{6}$$

Finally, we want to check the following two properties [1]:

$$\Box_{(\tau_s,T)}|\mu| < 0.05 \tag{7}$$

$$\Box_{(\tau_s,T)}\big(\texttt{rise}(a) \vee \texttt{fall}(a) \Rightarrow \Box_{(\eta,5)}|\mu| < 0.02\big) \tag{8}$$

Formula 7 specifies the maximum allowed overshoot or undershoot. Formula 8 specifies that η seconds after a signal rises or falls, the signal settles and remains in the settling region for at least 4 seconds. Parameters ϵ, λ_{ref}, τ_s, η, and T are set to 0.02, 14.7, 11, 1, and 50, respectively [2].

4. OUR APPROACH

We statistically model check [9,13] the powertrain control design. More precisely, given a model M, STL formula ϕ, and threshold θ, the goal of the verification procedure is to check that the measure of initial states satisfying formula ϕ is less that 1 (hypothesis H_0) or larger than θ (hypothesis H_1). Our algorithm randomly simulates the model (or more precisely the `C++` code automatically generated from the `Simulink`™ model) from different uniformly chosen initial states. On any sampled execution τ, our algorithm first checks if τ satisfies ϕ (see Section 4.1). If the answer is `unknown` or `no`, our algorithm immediately returns `unknown` or H_0, respectively. If τ satisfies ϕ, our algorithm returns H_1 if the number of sampled executions is $> \frac{\ln(\beta)}{\ln(\theta)}$. Otherwise, it draws another sample and repeats the whole process. Figure 2 depicts the high level steps of our approach.

If we ever find an execution that does not satisfy ϕ, then clearly H_0 is true and there will be no error in returning it. When number of samples, n, is larger than $\frac{\ln(\beta)}{\ln(\theta)}$ it means $\theta^n < \beta$. If H_1 is false, it means that the measure of initial states satisfying ϕ (θ') is less than or equal to θ. Therefore, $\theta'^n \leq \theta^n < \beta$. Hence, the probability of sampling n executions all satisfying ϕ will be less than the error probability β. Therefore, our algorithm guarantees the two conditions given by inequalities (1) and (2). Note that we do not have any indifference region (*i.e.* δ is zero). β the only parameter to our algorithm (the number of samples will increase as β becomes smaller). Thus our algorithm ensures

$$\mathbb{P}[result = H_0 \mid H_0 \text{ is false}] = 0 \tag{9}$$

$$\mathbb{P}[result = H_1 \mid H_1 \text{ is false}] \leq \beta \tag{10}$$

In Section 4.1, we define a robustness condition and show that our algorithm also guarantees the following condition:

$$\mathbb{P}[result = \texttt{unknown} \mid \text{sampled executions are robust}] = 0 \tag{11}$$

4.1 Checking Executions against STL Specification

To complete the description of our model checking algorithm, we need to describe how to check if a sampled execution satisfies an STL specification. Now the model of an STL formula is a signal which is function that gives for each time instant the system state. Clearly such an execution must be represented in some finite, computationally tractable manner. Simulation will result in an execution that is sampled at discrete time points, and the system state is only known at the sample time points.

Given a time step $\Delta : \mathbb{R}_+$, an execution sampled at discrete time points, will be a sequence of systems states at times $n\Delta$, where $n : \mathbb{N}$. Because the execution only gives the state at times of the form $n\Delta$, the challenge is discover conditions when we can conclude the satisfaction of the STL property ϕ at *all* times. The problem has been considered previously, and we borrow ideas from [5] to overcome this challenge.

The key to addressing this issue is to introduce a new "approximate satisfaction" relation. Let $\Delta : \mathbb{R}_+$ be a time step. Table 2 defines a ternary discrete semantics we use in our approach. In this table ΔI is defined to be $\{n : \mathbb{N} \mid n\Delta \in I\}$, and ΔI^- is defined to be $\{n : \mathbb{N} \mid \forall r : \Delta I \bullet n < r\}$. Thus, ΔI is the set of all natural numbers n such that $n\Delta$ is in I and, ΔI^- is the set of all natural numbers n that are smaller than all numbers in ΔI.

Intuitvely, the semantics in Table 2 tries to achieve the following: $((\tau, n) \models_\Delta \phi)$ is $\top$ if we can conclude that $(\tau, t) \models \phi$ for all $t \in [(n-1)\Delta, (n+1)\Delta]$ based on the state at time $n\Delta$; similarly, $((\tau, n) \models_\Delta \phi)$ is $\bot$ if we can conclude that $(\tau, t) \not\models \phi$ for all $t \in [(n-1)\Delta, (n+1)\Delta]$ based on the state at time $n\Delta$; and finally, $((\tau, n) \models_\Delta \phi)$ is `unknown` otherwise. The semantics can be understood being built up from the case of atomic propositions. If for any $t = n\Delta$, $f(\tau(t)) > c\Delta$, where c is the Lipschitz constant for f, then one can conclude that $f(\tau(t')) > 0$ for all $t' : [t - \Delta, t + \Delta]$. Similarly, if $f(\tau(t)) < -c\Delta$, then one can conclude that $f(\tau(t')) < 0$ for all $t' : [t - \Delta, t + \Delta]$. On the other hand, if $|f(\tau(t))| \leq c\Delta$ then by just looking at $f(\tau(t))$ we cannot conclude whether $f(\tau(t'))$ is above or below 0 for all $t' : [t - \Delta, t + \Delta]$; hence we define this to be `unknown`. The rest of the semantics is built naturally from this observation. The main result of this section is that this property holds for the approximate semantics we have defined above.

Theorem 1. *Consider a signal $\tau : [0, T] \to \mathbb{R}^{\mathrm{X}}$, an STL formula ϕ, and sampling time Δ that satisfy the following conditions.*

[1] Formulas 7 and 8 are required to be true only when the controller is in the `normal` mode. But in our case, the input signals guarantee that the controller mode us normal for all times in (τ_s, T).

[2] T is the default value set in [2]. Other parameters are directly from [6].

$((\tau,n) \models_\Delta \top)$	$:= \top$	iff	always true
$((\tau,n) \models_\Delta f > 0)$	$:= \top$	iff	$f(\tau(n\Delta)) > c\Delta$
$((\tau,n) \models_\Delta f > 0)$	$:= \bot$	iff	$f(\tau(n\Delta)) < -c\Delta$
$((\tau,n) \models_\Delta f > 0)$	$:=$ `unknown`	iff	otherwise
$((\tau,n) \models_\Delta \neg(f > 0))$	$:= \top$	iff	$f(\tau(n\Delta)) < -c\Delta$
$((\tau,n) \models_\Delta \neg(f > 0))$	$:= \bot$	iff	$f(\tau(n\Delta)) > c\Delta$
$((\tau,n) \models_\Delta \neg(f > 0))$	$:=$ `unknown`	iff	otherwise
$((\tau,n) \models_\Delta \phi \vee \psi)$	$:= \top$	iff	$((\tau,n) \models_\Delta \phi) = \top$ or $((\tau,n) \models_\Delta \psi) = \top$
$((\tau,n) \models_\Delta \phi \vee \psi)$	$:= \bot$	iff	$((\tau,n) \models_\Delta \phi) = \bot$ and $((\tau,n) \models_\Delta \psi) = \bot$
$((\tau,n) \models_\Delta \phi \vee \psi)$	$:=$ `unknown`	iff	otherwise
$((\tau,n) \models_\Delta \phi \wedge \psi)$	$:= \top$	iff	$((\tau,n) \models_\Delta \phi) = \top$ and $((\tau,n) \models_\Delta \psi) = \top$
$((\tau,n) \models_\Delta \phi \wedge \psi)$	$:= \bot$	iff	$((\tau,n) \models_\Delta \phi) = \bot$ or $((\tau,n) \models_\Delta \psi) = \bot$
$((\tau,n) \models_\Delta \phi \wedge \psi)$	$:=$ `unknown`	iff	otherwise
$((\tau,n) \models_\Delta \phi\mathcal{U}_I\psi)$	$:= \top$	iff	$\exists r : \Delta I \bullet ((\tau, n+r) \models_\Delta \psi) = \top \wedge$
			$\forall r' : \{0,\ldots,r\} \bullet ((\tau, n+r') \models_\Delta \phi) = \top$
$((\tau,n) \models_\Delta \phi\mathcal{U}_I\psi)$	$:= \bot$	iff	$\forall r : \Delta I + \{-\Delta, 0, \Delta\} \bullet ((\tau, n+r) \models_\Delta \psi) = \bot$ or
			$\exists r : \Delta I^- \bullet ((\tau, n+r) \models_\Delta \phi) = \bot$ or
			$\exists r : \Delta I \bullet ((\tau, n+r) \models_\Delta \phi) = \bot \wedge$
			$\forall r' : \Delta I \cap \{0,\ldots,r\} \bullet ((\tau, n+r') \models_\Delta \psi) = \bot$
$((\tau,n) \models_\Delta \phi\mathcal{U}_I\psi)$	$:=$ `unknown`	iff	otherwise
$((\tau,n) \models_\Delta \phi\mathcal{R}_I\psi)$	$:= \top$	iff	$\forall r : \Delta I + \{-\Delta, 0, \Delta\} \bullet ((\tau, n+r) \models_\Delta \psi) = \top$ or
			$(\exists r : \Delta I \bullet ((\tau, n+r) \models_\Delta \phi) = \top \wedge$
			$\forall r' : \{0,\ldots,r\} \cap \Delta I \bullet ((\tau, n+r') \models_\Delta \psi) = \top)$
$((\tau,n) \models_\Delta \phi\mathcal{R}_I\psi)$	$:= \bot$	iff	$\exists r : \Delta I \bullet ((\tau, n+r) \models_\Delta \psi) = \bot \wedge$
			$\forall r' : \Delta I \cap \{0,\ldots,r\} \bullet ((\tau, n+r') \models_\Delta \phi) = \bot$
$((\tau,n) \models_\Delta \phi\mathcal{R}_I\psi)$	$:=$ `unknown`	iff	otherwise

Table 2: Semantic Rules for Ternary $\models_\Delta$. Parameters $\Delta : \mathbb{R}_+$ is a time step and $c : \mathbb{R}_+$ is a *guessed* Lipschitz Constant.

1. There is $c : \mathbb{R}_+$ such that all functions used in atomic formulas of ϕ are c-Lipschitz continuous in the domain of τ.

2. The sampling time Δ is such that for any interval I appearing in ϕ, $\Delta \leq \frac{1}{2}(\sup I - \inf I)$. This condition ensures that there will be at least one sample point inside each interval appearing in ϕ.

3. All intervals appearing in ϕ are bounded [3].

4. Let $M = \sum_{I:\phi} \sup I$. Then $T > |\phi|\Delta + M$.

Then, the semantics in Table 2 guarantees

$$\forall n : \mathbb{N} \bullet (((\tau,n) \models_\Delta \phi) = \top) \Rightarrow$$
$$\forall t : [(n-1)\Delta, (n+1)\Delta] \cap [0,\infty) \bullet (\tau, t) \models \phi$$
and
$$\forall n : \mathbb{N} \bullet (((\tau,n) \models_\Delta \phi) = \bot) \Rightarrow$$
$$\forall t : [(n-1)\Delta, (n+1)\Delta] \cap [0,\infty) \bullet (\tau, t) \not\models \phi$$

Corollary 2. *Under the conditions of Theorem 1 we have:*

$$((\tau \models_\Delta \phi) = \top) \Rightarrow \tau \models \phi$$
$$((\tau \models_\Delta \phi) = \bot) \Rightarrow \tau \not\models \phi$$

[3]Note that since τ is a signal over bounded time $[0, T]$, this is not a restriction.

4.2 Checking Lipschitzness

As mentioned in Section 4.1, we are using discrete time sampling. Therefore, we need to make sure that the conditions in Theorem 1 are satisfied. The main problem is that dynamics of the input system is too complex and we cannot analytically find a Lipschitz constant for the functions in atomic formulas. In order to solve this problem we guess a Lipschitz constant and augment the `Simulink`™ model (before generating C++ code) such that if our guess ever falsified a flag will be set. Note, that the flag will be set if our guess for the Lipschitz constant is violated at *any time*, and not just at the sampled times. Then after simulating a trajectory we check the flag. If it indicates our guess was wrong, we guess a new value for the constant and repeat the whole process. We use simulations in `Simulink`™ as a source for our guess. In our experiment Lipschitz constant $c = 2$ was never falsified. So we use $c = 2$ as our final guess. The correctness of our guess for the Lischtiz constant relies on the correctness of the zero finder algorithms implemented in C++ libraries of `Simulink`™.

Finally, if we want to prove a probability is larger than the given threshold, we treat $(\tau \models_\Delta \phi) =$ `unknown` as $(\tau \models_\Delta \phi) = \bot$. And similarly, if we want to prove a probability is smaller than the given threshold, we treat $(\tau \models_\Delta \phi) =$ `unknown` as $(\tau \models_\Delta \phi) = \top$.

5. EXPERIMENTAL RESULTS

We used EmbeddedCoder of Simulink™ to generate C++ code from the model files in [2]. "Sample Rate" (Δ for us) is fixed to 0.0001 seconds. "Device Vendor" is set to Intel™, and "Device Type" is set to x86 − 64 (Mac OS X). We also set for "Execution efficiency". ODE solver is set to be selected automatically by Simulink™. Finally, we used C++03 (ISO) for "Standard math library". Note that automatic code generation is only for simulation. The model checker was written manually in C++. All executions ran on an iMac with 3.5 GHz Intel Core i7 processor and 32 GB 1600 MHz DDR3 memory.

In our experiment, we set $\beta = 0.001$ and $t = 0.98$. Both Formulas 7 and 8 could be verified after an average of 453 samples. Verification of Formula 7 takes about 2.2 minutes and verification of Formula 8 takes about 2.8 minutes.

5.1 Other Requirements

There are other requirements specified in [6], specially regarding the power mode and when the controller switches between power and normal multiple times. We failed to verify these requirements. The main reason is that since neither Simulink™ nor C++ has formal semantics, there is no guarantee that the translation from Simulink™ to C++ preserves the behavior of the modeled system. The requirement in this case, demands that when the amplitude is set to 80 degrees in the input throttle, the controller mode switches between modes normal and power periodically. This behavior can be easily observed in simulations performed by Simulink™. However, the C++ code that is *automatically generated* from the model does not exhibit such a behavior.

6. CONCLUSION AND PLANNED FUTURE WORK

The results presented here are the first results providing mathematical guarantees of correctness for Model 1, the most complex design, presented in [6]. It relied on statistically model checking, discretely sampled executions of the C++ code generated from the Simulink™ model of the controller. Our approach did not account for any errors introduced due to numerical integration. Our take here was that the C++ program generated automatically from the Simulink™ model is the artifact to be checked as it may be directly running on an embedded chip. If such errors are important and can be quantified, future analyses of this model will need to account for them.

Currently, our results certify that with high probability more than 98% of the initial states satisfy the correctness requirements. We would like to push our analysis closer towards 100%. Naïve sampling becomes infeasible in this case. We believe this problem can be solved in two complementary ways: 1. anti-correlated sampling [7] 2. importance sampling [10].

7. ACKNOWLEDGEMENT

The authors acknowledge partial support for this work from grants NSF CPS 1329991 and NSF CCF 1422798.

8. REFERENCES

[1] Y. Annpureddy, C. Liu, G. Fainekos, and S. Sankaranarayanan. S-taliro: A tool for temporal logic falsification for hybrid systems. In *Tools and Algorithms for the Construction and Analysis of Systems: 17th International Conference, TACAS*, pages 254–257, 2011.

[2] J. V. Deshmukh. Simulink/Stateflow models of the Powertrain Controller Verification Benchmark. Personal Communication.

[3] A. Donzé and O. Maler. Robust satisfaction of temporal logic over real-valued signals. In *Formal Modeling and Analysis of Timed Systems: 8th International Conference, FORMATS*, pages 92–106, 2010.

[4] P. S. Duggirala, C. Fan, S. Mitra, and M. Viswanathan. Meeting a powertrain verification challenge. In *Computer Aided Verification: 27th International Conference, CAV*, pages 536–543. Springer International Publishing, 2015.

[5] G. E. Fainekos and G. J. Pappas. Robust Sampling for MITL Specifications. In *Formal Modeling and Analysis of Timed Systems: 5th International Conference, FORMATS*, pages 147–162, 2007.

[6] X. Jin, J. V. Deshmukh, J. Kapinski, K. Ueda, and K. Butts. Powertrain control verification benchmark. In *Proceedings of the 17th International Conference on Hybrid Systems: Computation and Control, HSCC*, pages 253–262, New York, NY, USA, 2014. ACM.

[7] P. A. Maginnis, M. West, and G. E. Dullerud. Anticorrelated discrete-time stochastic simulation. In *Decision and Control (CDC), IEEE 52nd Annual Conference on*, pages 618–623, 2013.

[8] K. Sen, M. Viswanathan, and G. Agha. On statistical model checking of stochastic systems. In K. Etessami and S. K. Rajamani, editors, *Computer Aided Verification*, number 3576 in Lecture Notes in Computer Science, pages 266–280. Springer Berlin Heidelberg, 2005.

[9] K. Sen, M. Viswanathan, and G. Agha. On statistical model checking of stochastic systems. In *Computer Aided Verification: 17th International Conference, CAV*, pages 266–280, 2005.

[10] R. Srinivasan. *Importance sampling : applications in communications and detection.* Springer, Berlin, New York, 2002.

[11] A. Wald. Sequential tests of statistical hypotheses. *The Annals of Mathematical Statistics*, 16(2):pp. 117–186, 1945.

[12] H. L. S. Younes. Error control for probabilistic model checking. In *Verification, Model Checking, and Abstract Interpretation, 7th International Conference, VMCAI*, pages 142–156, 2006.

[13] H. L. S. Younes and R. G. Simmons. Probabilistic verification of discrete event systems using acceptance sampling. In *Computer Aided Verification: 14th International Conference, CAV*, pages 223–235, 2002.

Optimal Data Rate for State Estimation of Switched Nonlinear Systems*

Hussein Sibai and Sayan Mitra
{sibai2, mitras}@illinois.edu
Coordinate Science Laboratory
University of Illinois at Urbana Champaign
Urbana, IL 61801

ABSTRACT

State estimation is a fundamental problem for monitoring and controlling systems. Engineering systems interconnect sensing and computing devices over a shared bandwidth-limited channels, and therefore, estimation algorithms should strive to use bandwidth optimally. We present a notion of entropy for state estimation of switched nonlinear dynamical systems, an upper bound for it and a state estimation algorithm for the case when the switching signal is unobservable. Our approach relies on the notion of topological entropy and uses techniques from the theory for control under limited information. We show that the average bit rate used is optimal in the sense that, the efficiency gap of the algorithm is within an additive constant of the gap between estimation entropy of the system and its known upper-bound. We apply the algorithm to two system models and discuss the performance implications of the number of tracked modes.

Keywords

State Estimation; Switched Systems; Data Rate; Entropy

1. INTRODUCTION

This paper deals with monitoring continuous time dynamical systems with optimal usage of network resources. The key problem is to compute approximations of the state of the system from a small number of bits coming from quantized sensor measurements. This is the *state estimation* problem. The related problem of *mode detection* arises when the plant dynamics itself is unknown or changing. Contemporary engineering systems interconnect sensing and computing devices over shared communication channel for monitoring and control. For example, more than 70 embedded computing units communicate over shared 1 MBps CAN bus in cars [1]. Large number of machines, conveyor belts, and robotic manipulators need to be monitored in warehouses and factory floors—-again over a shared network backbone [14]. Such bandwidth constraints call for optimal allocation of network resources for estimation and detection.

In the stochastic setting, Kalman and particle filtering are used for solving these problems; in some cases using neural networks (see, for example [16, 17, 15]). Our approach relies on the theory of topological entropy for dynamical systems. The measure-theoretic notion of entropy plays a central role in information theory, estimation and detection. In the theory of dynamical systems, the analogous topological notion of entropy plays a fundamental role in describing the rate of growth of uncertainty about system state ([6, 3, 11, 2, 10, 13]). It also relates to the rate at which information about the system should be collected for state estimation. Drawing this connection, the notion of *estimation entropy* has been defined in [8, 12] for nonlinear systems. For a dynamical system of the form: $\dot{x}(t) = f(x(t))$, roughly, it is the minimum bit rate needed to construct state estimates from quantized measurements, that converge to the actual state of the system at a desired exponential rate of α. Estimation entropy is in general hard to compute exactly, but can be upper-bounded by $(C+\alpha)n/\ln 2$; where n is the dimension of system and C is either the Lipschitz constant L of f [8] or an upper-bound on the matrix measure of the Jacobian of f [9]. In [8] an algorithm for state estimation is given which uses an average bit rate of $(L+\alpha)n/\ln 2$. This is optimal in the sense that, the efficiency gap of the algorithm is no more than the gap between estimation entropy and its upper-bound.

In this paper, we study state estimation of switched nonlinear dynamical system $\dot{x} = f_{\sigma(t)}(x(t))$ where the switches between N modes are brought about by an unknown switching signal $\sigma : \mathbb{R}_{\geq 0} \to [N]$. Each mode $\dot{x} = f_p(x(t))$, $p \in [N]$, where $[N]$ is the set of integers from 0 to $N-1$, could capture, for example, uncertainties in the plant, different operating regimes–nominal and failure dynamics, and parameter values.

Since the mode information is not available to the estimator, exponential convergence of state estimates may be impossible immediately after a mode switch. We relax the notion of estimation entropy of [8] by allowing a period of time $\tau > 0$ following a mode switch, during which the estimation error is only bounded by a constant ε; and thereafter the error decays exponentially as usual. We show that for a large enough ε—determined by the minimum dwell time of σ and the difference in the dynamics of the different modes—the estimation entropy is upper-bounded by $\frac{(L+\alpha)n}{\ln 2} + \frac{\log N}{T_e}$. Here

*This research was supported in part by the NSF grant CAREER-1054247 and the Science of Security Lablet, Maryland Procurement Office under Contract No. H98230-14-C-0141.

HSCC'17, April 18-20, 2017, Pittsburgh, PA, USA
© 2017 ACM. ISBN 978-1-4503-4590-3/17/04...$15.00
DOI: http://dx.doi.org/10.1145/3049797.3049799

L is the largest between the Lipschitz constants of all f_p's and T_e is a positive constant less than or equal to τ.

We present an algorithm for state estimation for switched systems. The interdependence of the uncertainties in the state and the mode requires this algorithm to simultaneously solve the estimation and mode detection problems: Unless a mode $f_p, p \in [N]$ is detected, it may be impossible to get exponentially converging estimates, and (b) unless an accurate enough estimate for the state is known, it may not be possible to distinguish between two candidate modes.

Our algorithm keeps track of $\hat{N}$ possible modes of the switched system, where $\hat{N}$ is a parameter between 1 and N. If the actual mode of the system is one of the tracked modes, then, owing to a shrinking quantized measurement strategy, the state estimate converges at the desired exponential rate. If the actual mode is not tracked, then the actual state of the system may *escape* the constructed state estimate bounds. In this case, the algorithm expands the estimate and captures the state. When a mode switch happens, there may be a burst of escapes, but we prove that if the rate of switches is slow enough and the modes are different enough, then the correct mode is detected, and thereafter, the state estimates converge exponentially.

We establish worst case estimation error bounds and time bounds on mode detection. We also show that the average bit rate used is within $\frac{\hat{N}}{T_p} - \frac{\log N}{T_e}$ from the upper bound on the entropy, i.e. the upper bound on the optimal bit-rate; where T_p is the sampling time of the algorithm. We present preliminary experimental results on applying the algorithm to linear and nonlinear switched systems, and discuss the implications of the choice of the key parameter $\hat{N}$.

2. SWITCHED SYSTEMS AND ENTROPY

A *switched system* is a standard way for describing control systems with several different modes (see, for example, the book [7]). Suppose we are given a family $f_p, p \in [N]$, of functions from $\mathbb{R}^n$ to $\mathbb{R}^n$. Assuming that the functions f_p are Lipschitz continuous with Lipschitz constant L_p, the above gives rise to a family of dynamical system modes:

$$\dot{x} = f_p(x), p \in [N] \tag{1}$$

evolving on $\mathbb{R}^n$. If the mode $p \in [N]$ is known, then the solution of the differential equation is the function $\xi_p : \mathbb{R}^n \times \mathbb{R}_{\geq 0} \to \mathbb{R}^n$. If in addition the initial state x_0 is known, then for any point in time t the state $\xi_p(x_0, t)$ can be approximated using numerical integration. However, for the state estimation problem we are interested in, both the initial state and the mode are unknown.

The time varying mode is modeled as a *switching signal.* This is a not observable piecewise constant function $\sigma : [0, \infty) \to [N]$ which specifies at each time instant t, the index $\sigma(t) \in [N]$ of the function from the family (1) that is currently being followed. The points of discontinuity in σ are called *switching times.* Thus, the switched system with a time-dependent switching signal σ can be described by:

$$\dot{x} = f_{\sigma(t)}(x). \tag{2}$$

For a fixed switching signal σ the solution of the above switched system is defined in the standard way and denoted by the function $\xi_\sigma : \mathbb{R}^n \times \mathbb{R}_{\geq 0} \to \mathbb{R}^n$. Moreover, $f_{\sigma(t)}$ is Lipschitz continuous with Lipschitz constant $L = \max_{p \in [N]} L_p$.

The switching signal σ models the adversary (or the environment) changing the underlying mode of the system. In general, it may have arbitrary discontinuities, however, to prove stability or in our case correctness of state estimation, typically one assumes bounds on switching speed [7, 5, 18].

Covers, dwell-times, and reachable sets.

A switching signal σ has a *minimum dwell time* $T_d > 0$ if at least T_d time units elapses between consecutive switches. For any point $x \in \mathbb{R}^n$ and $\delta > 0$, $B(x, \delta)$ is a δ-ball—closed hypercube of radius δ—centered at x. For a hyperrectangle $S \subseteq \mathbb{R}^n$ and $\delta > 0$, $grid(S, \delta)$, is a collection of 2δ-separated points along axis parallel planes such that the δ-balls around these points cover S. We denote $\Sigma(T_d)$ the family of switching signals with minimum dwell-time T_d switching between the N modes. Moreover, we define $Reach(\Sigma, K)$ to be the set of *reachable states* by system (2) with any $\sigma \in \Sigma(T_d)$ from the compact initial set K. More formally, $Reach(\Sigma, K) = \{x \in \mathbb{R}^n \mid \exists\, \sigma \in \Sigma(T_d),\ x_0 \in K,\ t \in [0, \infty) : \xi_\sigma(x_0, t) = x\}$.

2.1 State Estimation, bit-rate, and entropy

Let us fix throughout the paper a compact set K of possible initial states of (2), the family of switching signals $\Sigma(T_d)$, two estimation accuracy related constants $\varepsilon, \alpha > 0$ and a time constant τ ($\tau \leq T_d$). Consider a setup in which a sensor has access to the actual current state of the system $\xi_\sigma(x_0, t)$ (and not the switching signal σ), and it needs to send bits across a bandwidth-constrained channel such that: for any initial state $x_0 \in K$ and for any (unknown) switching signal $\sigma \in \Sigma(T_d)$, the estimator would be able to construct a function $z : \mathbb{R}_{\geq 0} \to \mathbb{R}^n$, where for all $j \geq 0$ and for all $t \in [s_j, s_{j+1})$,

$$|z(t) - \xi_\sigma(x_0, t)| \leq \begin{cases} \varepsilon & t \in [s_j, s_j + \tau), \\ \varepsilon e^{-\alpha(t-(s_j+\tau))} & otherwise, \end{cases} \tag{3}$$

where $s_0 = 0, s_1, \ldots$ are the switching times in σ. The norm in inequality (3) can be arbitrary. We call such a function $z(.)$ an $(\varepsilon, \alpha, \tau)$-*approximation* of $\xi_\sigma(x_0, \cdot)$. The second bound gives the ideal behavior in which the estimate converges to the actual trajectory $\xi_\sigma(x_0, \cdot)$ exponentially at the rate α as in [8] and [2]. Since this exponential convergence may be unrealistic after a mode switch that may completely change the dynamics, the first condition allows a "lenient" period of duration τ, during which the error is bounded by ε.

A finite set of functions $\hat{X} = \{\hat{x}_1, \ldots, \hat{x}_M\}$ from $[0, T]$ to $\mathbb{R}^n$ is $(T, \varepsilon, \alpha, \tau)$-*approximating* if for every initial state $x \in K$ and every switching signal $\sigma \in \Sigma(T_d)$ there exists some $\hat{x}_i \in \hat{X}$ such that for all $t \in [0, T]$, $\hat{x}_i$ is an $(\varepsilon, \alpha, \tau)$-approximating function for $\xi_\sigma(x_0, t)$. Note that $\hat{X}$ depends on K, T_d and the N modes but we are suppressing these parameters for brevity.

Let $s_{\text{est}}(T, \varepsilon, \alpha, \tau)$ denote the minimal cardinality of such a $(T, \varepsilon, \alpha, \tau)$-approximating set. The *estimation entropy* of the system is defined as

$$h_{\text{est}}(\varepsilon, \alpha, \tau) := \limsup_{T \to \infty} \frac{1}{T} \log s_{\text{est}}(T, \varepsilon, \alpha, \tau).$$

Intuitively, since s_{est} corresponds to the minimal number of functions needed to approximate the state with desired accuracy, h_{est} is the minimum average number of bits needed to identify these approximating functions. The lim sup extracts the base-2 exponential growth rate of s_{est} with time.

Then, s_{est} corresponds to the number of different quantization points needed to identify the trajectories, and h_{est} gives a measure of the long-term bit rate needed for communicating sensor measurements to the estimator.

Later on, we will bound the error in state estimates when the system evolves according to two *different* dynamics, from the same state. To this end we introduce the function:

$$d(t) := \max_{p,r \in [N]} \sup_{x \in Reach(\Sigma,K)} \int_0^t \|f_p(\xi_p(x,s)) - f_r(\xi_r(x,s))\| ds.$$

In this paper, we will assume that the supremum exists for all $t \leq \tau$. This condition can be checked, for example, if the reach set $Reach(\Sigma, K)$ is compact.

2.2 Entropy upper bound

In this section, we will establish an upper-bound on the estimation entropy h_{est} for switched systems. First, we fix a time horizon $T > 0$ and prove an upper bound on s_{est} using an inductive construction of approximating functions. Now let us present the following proposition which will be used in the proof.

Proposition 1 *There exists $T_e \in (0, \tau]$ such that $d(T_e) \leq \varepsilon(1 - e^{-\alpha(T_d - T_e)})$.*

$d(t)$ is a monotonically increasing continuous function for $t \geq 0$ and equal to zero at $t = 0$. Moreover, the right hand side of the inequality increases as T_e decreases. Therefore, we can always find a T_e small enough that satisfies the inequality. Let us fix a trajectory $\xi_\sigma(x_0, \cdot)$ of the switched system (2). We define an inductive procedure that constructs a corresponding approximating function $z(\cdot)$. It follows that the set of all functions that can be computed by this procedure is a $(T, \varepsilon, \alpha, \tau)$-*approximating set*. Then, the cardinality of the set of all functions that can be computed by this procedure gives us an upper bound.

Let $s_0 = 0, s_1, \ldots$ be the sequence of switching times in the switching signal σ generating $\xi_\sigma(x_0, \cdot)$. The approximating function $z(\cdot)$ is constructed in time steps of size T_e ($T_e \leq \tau$), where T_e is the largest one that satisfy the inequality in Proposition 1. We start by choosing an open cover C_0 of K with balls of radii $\varepsilon e^{-(L+\alpha)T_e}$. Let q_0 be the center of a ball that contains x_0. We construct $z(t) := \xi_{\sigma(0)}(q_0, t)$ for $t \in [0, T_e]$. Since $\sigma(t) = \sigma(0)$ for $t \in [0, T_e)$ (recall, $T_d \geq \tau \geq T_e$), the estimation error over that interval would be $\|z(t) - \xi_\sigma(x_0, t)\| \leq e^{Lt}\|x_0 - q_0\| \leq e^{Lt}\varepsilon e^{-(L+\alpha)T_e} \leq \varepsilon e^{-\alpha t}$ (by Bellman-Grownall inequality).

Next, for each integer $1 \leq i \leq \lfloor \frac{T}{T_e} \rfloor$, we compute an n-dimensional ball over-approximating the reachable set of states at $t = iT_e$ given the difference between the actual state x_{i-1} and the quantized one q_{i-1} at $t = (i-1)T_e$, and $\sigma((i-1)T_e)$. Then, we construct a grid with a predefined resolution over that ball. Next, we quantize the actual state at $t = iT_e$ with respect to the grid to get q_i. After that, we compute the trajectory which results from running the actual mode at $t = iT_e$ over the time interval $(iT_e, (i+1)T_e]$ starting from q_i. Finally, we bound the difference between the actual trajectory $\xi_\sigma(x_0, \cdot)$ and the constructed one $z(\cdot)$ and we prove that the ball computed at the $(i+1)^{th}$ iteration does contain the actual state at $t = (i+1)T_e$.

Formally, let s_j be the time of the last switch before iT_e. We construct C_i to be an open cover of $B(z(iT_e), R_i)$, where

$$R_i = \begin{cases} R_{i-1}e^{-\alpha T_e} + d(T_e) & \text{if } s_j \in ((i-1)T_e, iT_e), \\ R_{i-1}e^{-\alpha T_e} & \text{otherwise,} \end{cases}$$

and $R_0 = \varepsilon$, with balls of radii equal to $r_i = R_i e^{-(L+\alpha)T_e}$. Then, we let q_i to be any of the centers of the balls in C_i that contain $\xi_\sigma(x_0, iT_e)$. Note that $\xi_\sigma(x_0, T_e) \in B(z(T_e), R_1)$. Next, we construct $z(t) := \xi_{\sigma(iT_e)}(q_i, t - iT_e)$ for $t \in (iT_e, (i+1)T_e]$.

Lemma 1 *$z(\cdot)$ is an $(\varepsilon, \alpha, \tau)$-approximating function of $\xi_\sigma(x_0, \cdot)$.*

Proof. Based on where the next switching time s_{j+1} falls with respect to the interval $[iT_e, (i+1)T_e]$, there are two cases here: (a) $s_{j+1} = iT_e$ or $s_{j+1} \geq (i+1)T_e$ and (b) $s_{j+1} \in (iT_e, (i+1)T_e)$. For (a),

$$\begin{aligned}
&\|\xi_\sigma(x_0,t) - z(t)\| = \|\xi_\sigma(x_0,t) - \xi_{\sigma(iT_e)}(q_i, t - iT_e)\| \\
&= \|\xi_{\sigma(iT_e)}(\xi_\sigma(x_0, iT_e), t - iT_e) - \xi_{\sigma(iT_e)}(q_i, t - iT_e)\| \\
&\qquad [\text{since } \sigma(t) = \sigma(iT_e) \text{ for } t \in [iT_e, (i+1)T_e)] \\
&\leq e^{L_{\sigma(iT_e)}(t - iT_e)}\|\xi_\sigma(x_0, iT_e) - q_i\| \\
&\qquad [\text{Bellman-Gronwall inequality}] \\
&\leq e^{L(t-iT_e)} r_i \\
&\qquad [L_{\sigma(iT_e)} \leq L; \text{ by the definition of } q_i \in C_i] \\
&= e^{L(t-iT_e)} R_i e^{-(L+\alpha)T_e} \\
&\qquad [\text{substituting } r_i] \\
&\leq e^{L(t-iT_e)} R_i e^{-(L+\alpha)(t-iT_e)} \\
&\qquad [\text{since } t - iT_e \leq T_e] \\
&= R_i e^{-\alpha(t-iT_e)}.
\end{aligned}$$

For (b), we can repeat the same steps of part (a) for any $t \in (iT_e, s_{j+1})$ to get $\|z(t) - \xi_\sigma(x_0, t)\| \leq R_i e^{-\alpha(t-iT_e)}$. After the switch at s_{j+1}, that is, for any $t \in [s_{j+1}, (i+1)T_e]$,

$$\begin{aligned}
&\|\xi_\sigma(x_0,t) - z(t)\| = \|\xi_\sigma(x_0,t) - \xi_{\sigma(iT_e)}(q_i, t - iT_e)\| \\
&= \|\xi_\sigma(\xi_\sigma(x_0, s_{j+1}), t - s_{j+1}) - \xi_{\sigma(iT_e)}(q_i, t - iT_e)\| \\
&\leq \|\xi_\sigma(\xi_\sigma(x_0, s_{j+1}), t - s_{j+1}) - \xi_\sigma(q_i, t - iT_e)\| \\
&\quad + \|\xi_\sigma(q_i, t - iT_e) - \xi_{\sigma(iT_e)}(q_i, t - iT_e)\| \\
&\qquad [\text{by triangular inequality}] \\
&\leq e^{L(t-s_{j+1})}\|\xi_\sigma(x_0, s_{j+1}) - \xi_\sigma(q_i, s_{j+1} - iT_e)\| \\
&\quad + \|\int_0^{t-iT_e} (f_\sigma(\xi_\sigma(q_i, t')) - f_{\sigma(iT_e)}(\xi_{\sigma(iT_e)}(q_i, t')))dt'\| \\
&\qquad [\text{by Bellman-Gronwall inequality}] \\
&\leq e^{L(t-s_{j+1})}\|\xi_\sigma(x_0, s_{j+1}) - \xi_\sigma(q_i, s_{j+1} - iT_e)\| \\
&\quad + \int_0^{t-iT_e} \|f_\sigma(\xi_\sigma(q_i, t')) - f_{\sigma(iT_e)}(\xi_{\sigma(iT_e)}(q_i, t'))\|dt' \\
&\leq e^{L(t-s_{j+1})} e^{L(s_{j+1} - iT_e)}\|\xi_\sigma(x_0, iT_e) - q_i\| + d(t - iT_e) \\
&\qquad [\text{using the definition of } d(\cdot)] \\
&\leq e^{L(t-iT_e)} R_i e^{-(L+\alpha)T_e} + d(t - iT_e) \\
&\qquad [\text{substituting } \|\xi_\sigma(x_0, iT_e) - q_i\| \text{ with } r_i\text{'s value}] \\
&\leq R_i e^{-\alpha(t-iT_e)} + d(T_e) \\
&\qquad [\text{since } d(t) \text{ is an increasing function}].
\end{aligned}$$

In both cases, $\xi_\sigma(x_0, (i+1)T_e) \in B(z((i+1)T_e), R_{i+1})$. Now we want to prove that $z(\cdot)$ is an approximation function to

$\xi_\sigma(x_0, \cdot)$. First, note that $R_i = \varepsilon e^{-\alpha i T_e}$ for all i before the first switch s_1. Hence, $\|z(\cdot) - \xi_\sigma(x_0, \cdot)\| \leq \varepsilon e^{-\alpha t}$ for all $t \in [0, s_1]$ by part (a) above. Therefore, $z(\cdot)$ satisfies inequality (3) between time 0 and s_1. Next, we let $i_1 = \lceil s_1/T_e \rceil$ (the first iteration after the first switch). We know from the previous argument that $R_{i_1} \leq \varepsilon e^{-\alpha i_1 T_e} + d(T_e) \leq \varepsilon e^{-\alpha T_d} + d(T_e)$. Thus, $R_{i_1} \leq \varepsilon$ by our choice of T_e that satisfies the inequality in Proposition 1. Then, $\|z(\cdot) - \xi_\sigma(x_0, \cdot)\| \leq \varepsilon e^{-\alpha t} + d(t - s_1) \leq \varepsilon e^{-\alpha T_d} + d(T_e) \leq \varepsilon$ for $t \in [s_1, i_1 T_e]$ by part (b) above. Moreover, we know that $T_e \leq \tau$, then $z(\cdot)$ satisfies the first part of inequality (3) for $t \in [s_1, i_1 T_e]$. Now, the same argument done before for $t \in [0, s_1]$ can be repeated for the time interval $t \in [i_1 T_e, s_2]$ which has a size greater than or equal to $T_d - T_e$. Finally, by induction on all switches, $z(\cdot)$ satisfy the properties in (3). Therefore, $z(\cdot)$ is an approximating function to $\xi_\sigma(x_0, \cdot)$. □

Lemma 2 *$s_{est}(T, \varepsilon, \alpha, \tau)$ is upper-bounded by $\#C_0 N(HN)^{\lfloor T/T_e \rfloor}$, where $H = \lceil e^{(L+\alpha)T_e} \rceil^n$ and $\#C_0$ is the cardinality of C_0.*

PROOF. We count the number of functions that can be computed by the above procedure. First, note that a function $z(.)$ is defined by the quantization points and the modes chosen at multiples of T_e. Moreover, the cardinality of C_0 is $\#C_0 = \lceil \frac{diam(K)}{2\varepsilon e^{-(L+\alpha)T_e}} \rceil^n$, where $diam(K)$ is the diameter of K. The upper bound on the cardinality of C_i, for $i \geq 1$, is $\#C_i = \lceil \frac{R_i}{R_i e^{-(L+\alpha)T_e}} \rceil^n = \lceil e^{(L+\alpha)T_e} \rceil^n$, which is independent of R_i. At each iteration $0 \leq i \leq \lfloor T/T_e \rfloor$, we are choosing one from the N modes and a quantization point in the cover C_i. We can conclude that the number of functions that can be computed using the above procedure is upper bounded by $(\#C_0) H^{\lfloor T/T_e \rfloor} N^{\lfloor T/T_e \rfloor + 1}$. □

Theorem 1 *$h_{est}(\varepsilon, \alpha, \tau) \leq (L + \alpha)n/\ln 2 + (\log N)/T_e$, where T_e is as chosen in Section 2.2.*

PROOF. This proof is along the lines of the proof of Proposition 2 in [8].

$$
\begin{aligned}
&\limsup_{T\to\infty} \frac{1}{T} \log s_{\text{est}}(T, \varepsilon, \alpha, \tau) \\
&\leq \limsup_{T\to\infty} \frac{1}{T} \log (\#C_0)(HN)^{\lfloor \frac{T}{T_e} \rfloor + 1} \\
&= \limsup_{T\to\infty} \frac{1}{T} \log \#C_0 \\
&\qquad + \limsup_{T\to\infty} \frac{1 + T_e/T}{T_e} (\log \lceil e^{(L+\alpha)T_e} \rceil^n + \log N) \\
&\leq \frac{(L+\alpha)n}{\ln 2} + \frac{\log N}{T_e}.
\end{aligned}
$$

The last step is follows from the fact that $\limsup_{T\to\infty} \frac{1}{T} \log \lceil \frac{diam(K)}{2\varepsilon e^{-(L+\alpha)T_e}} \rceil^n = 0$. □

Note that, if $N = 1$, we get the previous bound on entropy given in [8].

Remark 1 (Relationship between parameters) Larger values of the parameters ε or τ allow T_e to be larger. This decreases the upper bound on entropy. However, having a larger α may increase or decrease the upper bound since while it decreases the second term by allowing a larger T_e, it increases the first term.

2.3 Relation between entropy and the bit rate of estimation algorithms

In the following proposition we prove that no bit rate less than h_{est} can be achieved by any algorithm that constructs an $(\varepsilon, \tau, \alpha)$-approximating function given any trajectory $\xi_\sigma(x_0, t)$ while having a fixed bit rate. Assume that the sampling time of the algorithm is T_p time units. The bit rate of the algorithm is defined as

$$b_r(\varepsilon, \tau, \alpha) := \limsup_{j\to\infty} \frac{1}{jT_p} \sum_{i=0}^{j} \log Q_i$$

where $\log Q_i$ is the number of bits sent at $t = iT_p$. Having a fixed bit rate means $\log Q_i = \log Q$ for all i. Hence, $b_r(\varepsilon, \tau, \alpha) = 1/T_p \log Q$.

Proposition 2 *Consider an algorithm with fixed bit rate at each iteration i. If for each trajectory of the system $\xi_\sigma(x, t)$, the trajectory constructed by the algorithm satisfies the properties in (3) for any ε, τ and $\alpha > 0$, then the algorithm's bit rate cannot be smaller than $h_{est}(\varepsilon, \alpha, \tau)$.*

PROOF. The proof is similar to the proof of Proposition 5 in [8]. Arguing for contradiction, assume that there exists such an algorithm that satisfies the properties and has a bit rate less than $h_{est}(\varepsilon, \alpha, \tau)$. Recall that $h_{\text{est}}(\varepsilon, \alpha, \tau) = \limsup_{T\to\infty} 1/T \log s_{\text{est}}(T, \varepsilon, \alpha, \tau)$. Then, there exists l large enough where $b_r(\varepsilon, \tau, \alpha)$ is less than $1/lT_p \log s_{\text{est}}(lT_p, \varepsilon, \alpha, \tau)$. Substituting $b_r(\varepsilon, \tau, \alpha)$ with $1/T_p \log Q$ leads to the inequality $Q^l < s_{\text{est}}(lT_p, \varepsilon, \alpha, \tau)$. Q^l is the number of possible sequences of quantized states q_i's of length l and the right hand side is the minimal cardinality of an $(lT_p, \varepsilon, \alpha, \tau)$-approximating set. Then, the set of trajectories that can be constructed by the algorithm defines an $(lT_p, \varepsilon, \alpha, \tau)$-approximating set which has a cardinality less than s_{est} which contradicts the assumption that s_{est} has the minimum cardinality. □

2.4 Separation of modes

In order for an algorithm to distinguish two modes $p, r \in [N]$, $p \neq r$, it is necessary for the solutions generated by the two modes to be separable in some sense. The following notion of *exponential separation* is proposed in [8]. For $L_s, T_s > 0$ we say that the two modes $p, r \in [N]$ are (L_s, T_s)-*exponentially separated* if there exists a constant $\epsilon_{\min} > 0$ such that for any $\varepsilon \leq \epsilon_{\min}$, for any two nearby initial states $x_1, x_2 \in \mathbb{R}^n$ with $|x_1 - x_2| \leq \varepsilon$,

$$\xi_p(x_1, T_s) - \xi_r(x_2, T_s) > \varepsilon e^{L_s T_s}.$$

That is, trajectories separate out exponentially if they start from a sufficiently small neighborhood. The exponential separation holds if, for example, (1) the two vector fields have a positive separation angle, and (2) at least one of them has a positive velocity. It is believed that this property is generic in the sense that it holds for almost all pairs of systems. We assume (without loss of generality) that the modes are mutually (L, T_p)-exponentially separated (see Remark 2). Also, ϵ_{min} is assumed to be global for all pairs of the exponentially separated modes.

Remark 2 (Similar modes) If there are two modes $p, r \in [N]$ such that for all $x \in Reach(\Sigma, K)$ and for all $t \in [0, T_p]$, $\|\xi_p(x_1, t) - \xi_r(x_2, t)\|_\infty \leq \|x_1 - x_2\|_\infty e^{Lt}$, then they will not be exponentially separated. However, although they will

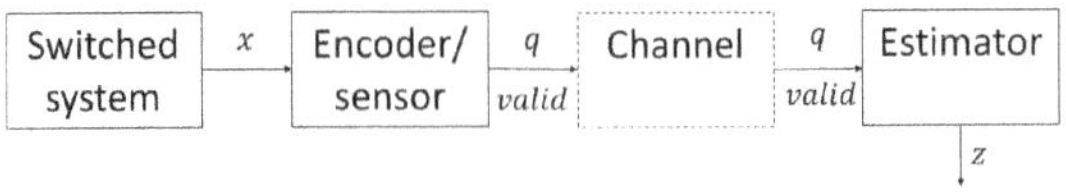

Figure 1: Block diagram showing the flow of information from the switched system to the sensor to the estimator.

not be distinguished by the algorithm presented in the next section, this does *not* influence the correctness of the state estimation. An example would be modes that are exponentially stable, with convergence rate larger than α, to a common equilibrium point.

3. STATE ESTIMATION

We consider a setup where a sensor is sampling the state of the switched system each T_p time units without being able to sense the mode. It sends a quantized version of the state along with other few bits over a communication channel to the estimator. In turn, the estimator needs to compute $(\varepsilon, \alpha, \tau)$-approximating function of the trajectory of the system using the measurements received from the sensor (see Figure 1).

3.1 Estimation algorithm overview

First, we briefly discuss the basic principle of constant bit-rate state estimation for a single dynamical system (see for example [8]). In this case, the system evolves as $\dot{x}(t) = f_p(x(t))$, for a given $p \in [N]$, $x_0 \in K$, and there is no uncertainty about the mode. Suppose at a given time t the estimator has somehow computed a certain estimate for the state of the system, say represented by a hypercube S. In the absence of any new measurement information, the uncertainty in a state estimate or the size of S blows-up exponentially with time as $e^{L_p t}$, where L_p is the Lipschitz constant of f_p. In order to obtain the required exponentially shrinking state estimates, i.e., S shrinking as $e^{-\alpha t}$, the sensor has to send new measurements to the estimator.

One strategy is for the sensor to send information every $T_p > 0$ time units as follows: it partitions S, which has a radius r, into a grid with cells of radii $re^{-(L_p+\alpha)T_p}$, makes a quantized measurement of the state of the system $\xi(x_0, t)$ according to this grid and sends a few bits to the estimator so that the algorithm running at the estimator can identify the correct cell in which state resides (see Figure 1). At this point, the uncertainty in the state reduces by a factor of $e^{(L_p+\alpha)T_p}$ so that after T_p time units when the uncertainty grows by a multiple of $e^{L_p T_p}$ there is still a net reduction in uncertainty by a factor of $e^{\alpha T_p}$. It can also be seen that the number of bits the sensor needs to send (for identifying one grid cell out of $e^{(L_p+\alpha)T_p n}$) is $O(n(L_p+\alpha)T_p)$ and this gives the average bit rate of $n(L_p+\alpha)/\ln 2$.

Algorithm 1 which runs on the sensor side extends this strategy to work with switched systems. The basic idea is to track a number $(1 \leq \hat{N} \leq N)$ of possible modes that the system could be in, and run the above algorithm of quantization-based estimation, for each of these $\hat{N}$ modes. The set of tracked modes is stored in the vector m. A mode $m_i[r]$, $r \in [\hat{N}]$, is valid ($valid_i[r] = 1$) if the current state $\xi_\sigma(x_0, iT_p)$ is contained in the corresponding state estimate $S_i[r]$ at line 9 and $m_i[r] \neq -1$. However, it is possible that none of the $\hat{N}$ tracked modes are valid. In particular, the mode may switch and the state may evolve to fall outside of the estimates of the tracked modes or it may be that none of the $\hat{N}$ tracked modes in m_i is the actual mode of the system over $[(i-1)T_p, iT_p]$. This scenario where none of the modes are valid, the state is said to have *escaped* (line 15). In the case of an escape, the algorithm replaces all modes from the vector m and considers a new set of modes from $[N]$. If the rate of actual mode switches is slow enough (Lemma 4) then it is guaranteed to include the actual mode of the system in m before the next switch. And once the actual mode is tracked in m, the estimation error converges exponentially.

In the above description of the algorithm, we suggested that each tracked mode $m_i[r]$ maintains its own corresponding state estimate $S_i[r]$ and quantization grid $C_i[r]$. This not only uses excessive memory, but also implies that $\hat{N}$ different quantized measurements of the state has to be sent by the sensor. In Algorithm 1, at any iteration $i \geq 1$, only a single state estimate S_i is maintained, a single grid C_i is computed according to which a single measurement is sent by the sensor. That is S_i and C_i are actually $S_i[mode_{i-1}]$ and $C_i[mode_{i-1}]$ where $mode_{i-1}$ is some $r \in [\hat{N}]$ agreed on between the sensor and the estimator. In our case we consider it the valid mode with the minimum index in m_i (line 11). In order to check the validity of the other tracked modes in m_i, the actual state is shifted with vectors which are computed according to the dynamics of these modes. That is, $v_i[r]$ represents the center of hypercube $S_i[r]$ which is the state estimate of the system corresponding to the dynamics $\dot{x} = f_{m_i[r]}(x)$. To check if $x_i \in S_i[r]$, x_i is shifted with the vector $v_i[mode_{i-1}] - v_i[r]$ and then checked if it belongs to S_i.

If there is an escape at a certain iteration, S_i is constructed as a hyperrectangle centered at $v_i[mode_{i-1}]$ with radius δ_i plus $d(T_p)$. Recall, that δ_i is the radius used for computing S_i assuming that there is no escape (line 34) and $d(T_p)$ is the additional factor that capture maximum deviation between two trajectories of two different modes in $[N]$ starting from the same state in $Reach(\Sigma, K)$, the reachable states by (2), and running for T_p seconds. Next, q_i will be the quantization of x_i with respect to the new C_i computed in line 19.

The NextMode() function cycles through all the $[N]$ modes in the following two-phase fashion. For a sequence of N calls in phase I, it returns the modes in $[N]$ in some arbitrary order. Then, it returns -1 for the next $\hat{N}-1$ calls in Phase II and then goes back to Phase I. Phase I is used by the estimation algorithm to cycle through all the modes fairly in discovering the actual mode after a switch. Phase II is used to keep the actual mode as the only mode tracked in m_i while the rest of m_i is equal to -1.

Estimator side algorithm.

On the estimator side, a similar algorithm to 1 is executed with small changes: instead of taking x_i as input (line 7), q_i, a quantized version of x_i, and the $valid_i$ vector are taken. Hence, the estimator knows if $x_i \in S_i[r]$ or not for a certain $r \in [N]$ by examining the $valid_i$ vector sent from the sensor. In addition, line 14 is replaced by "true". Finally, lines 8 to 10, line 20 and line 22 are omitted. These lines only compute values which are sent by the sensor.

Reading the pseudo-code.

$B(x_c, r_c)$ defines an over approximation of the initial set K as a hypercube of radius r_c centered at x_c. The **input** x_i (Line 7) executed at time t, reads the current state of the system $\xi_\sigma(x_0, iT_p)$ into the program variable x_i. In the next line $x_i \in S_i[r]$ is assumed to be computed by checking if $x_i + (v_i[mode_{i-1}] - v_i[r]) \in S_i$ if $i \geq 1$ and $x_i + (v_i[0] - v_i[r]) \in S_i$ if $i = 0$. In Line 11, the minimum index of a valid mode is assigned to $mode_i$ but this could be any arbitrary choice. It is set to $\perp$ if there is no valid mode.

Comparison with upper bound construction.

This algorithm is similar to the construction of an approximating function used in the proof of the upper bound in Section 2.2. However, the mode is known at the sampling times in the upper bound while it is not in the Algorithm. Thus, the construction used in the upper bound knows the iterations where the switch happens. That makes us being able to increase the size of the ball representing the state estimate in the iteration following a switch. However, because it is assumed that the mode is not known, Algorithm 1 needs to wait till the state x_i leaves the state estimate S_i to know that a switch happened or that a mode considered in m_i is different from the actual mode. That required the additional assumption that the modes are exponentially separated to bound the number of iterations needed for the state to leave a state estimate constructed based on a wrong mode. That required us to sample faster ($T_p \leq T_e$) and track several modes in parallel to figure out the actual mode and upper-bound the error by ε between a switch and its following τ time units.

4. ANALYSIS OF ESTIMATION ALGORITHM

In this section, we prove a sequence of error bounds on the state estimate for different cases that arise from considering a mode which is different from the actual mode over a time interval of size T_p. Then in Section 4.2 we establish bounds on the maximum number of possible escapes between switches. The main Theorem in Section 4.3 uses these results together with an upper bound on the speed of mode switches to give detailed bounds on the state estimation error. Finally, in Section 4.4 we analyze the average bit rate and compare it to the upper bound on h_{est} defined in Theorem 1.

Notations.

We fix all the parameters of the algorithm including the sampling period T_p and the mode window size $\hat{N}$. We also fix a particular (unknown) initial state $x_0 \in K$ and a particular (unknown) switching signal σ for the system described by Equation (2). This defines a particular solution $\xi_\sigma(x_0, \cdot)$ of the switched system and the sequence of states $\xi_\sigma(x_0, T_p), \xi(x_0, 2T_p), \ldots,$ sampled by Algorithm 1 which runs on the sensor side. We abbreviate $\xi_\sigma(x_0, iT_p)$ as x_i and the quantized measurement of x_i that is sent by the sensor as q_i. Moreover, δ_i, S_i, C_i, etc., denote the valuations of the variables δ, S, C, etc. at line 22 in the ith iteration of the algorithm. However, the modes in m_{i+1} are the modes considered over the interval $(iT_p, (i+1)T_p]$. The switching times in σ are denoted by $s_0 = 0, s_1, \ldots$ For a given switching time s_j, we define $last(j) := \lfloor s_j/T_p \rfloor$ and $next(j) := \lceil s_j/T_p \rceil$ as the last iterations of the algorithm before the jth switch and the first iteration after the jth switch respectively.

Recall, that an escape occurs when the state of the system $\xi(x_0, iT_p)$ is not in any of the state estimates $S_i[r]$'s at line 9, i.e., it occurs when the **else** branch in Line 15 is taken.

4.1 Error bounds across a single iteration

In this section, we establish how the error in state estimation, $\|\xi_\sigma(x_0,t) - z(t)\|_\infty$, evolves over a single iteration of the algorithm, that is, over $t \in [iT_p, (i+1)T_p]$. The estimate $z(t)$ over $[iT_p, (i+1)T_p]$ is $\xi_{m_{i+1}}[r](q_i, \cdot)$ for some r, and therefore, we track the error by bounding $\|\xi_\sigma(x_0,t) - \xi_{m_{i+1}[r]}(q_i,t)\|_\infty$, for all $r \in [\hat{N}]$ with $m_{i+1}[r] \neq -1$.

There are several sub-cases to consider based on (a) whether there is a switch, and (b) whether the tracked mode $m_{i+1}[r]$ matches the actual mode at a given time, over the considered interval between the iterations. For each of these cases, we establish a bound on $\|\xi_\sigma(x_0,t) - z(t)\|_\infty$ using (a) Bellman-Gronwall inequality to bound $\|\xi_u(x,t) - \xi_u(x',t)\|_\infty$, and (b) triangular inequality to bound $\|\xi_u(x,t) - \xi_p(x',t)\|_\infty$, where $u \neq p \in [\hat{N}]$ and $x \neq x' \in \mathbb{R}^n$. Recall that $T_p \leq \tau \leq T_d$, so no more than one switch can occur between iT_p and $(i+1)T_p$.

Each of the following propositions covers one of the above cases. Proposition 3 considers the case when there is a switch between iT_p and $(i+1)T_p$, the considered mode $m_{i+1}[r]$ is the same as the actual mode $\sigma(iT_p)$ at $t = iT_p$, and there exists a state estimate $S_i[p]$ that contains the actual state $\xi_\sigma(x_0, iT_p)$ at $t = iT_p$. It shows that the estimate converges

Algorithm 1 Procedure for estimating the state of a switched system (sensor side).

1: input: T_p, α, δ_0, $K \subset B(x_c, r_c)$, $\hat{N}$
2: $m_0 \leftarrow \langle 0, 1, \ldots \hat{N}-1 \rangle$;
3: $S_0 \leftarrow B(x_c, r_c)$;
4: $C_0 \leftarrow grid(S_0, \delta_0 e^{-(L+\alpha)T_p})$;
5: $mode_0 \leftarrow 0$; $i \leftarrow 0$;
6: **while** true **do** {i^{th} iteration}
7:   input x_i;
8:   **for** $r \in [\hat{N}]$ **do**
9:     $valid_i[r] \leftarrow [x_i \in S_i[r]$ *and* $m_i[r] \neq -1]$;
10:   **end for**
11:   $mode_i \leftarrow \min\{r \mid valid_i[r]\}$;
12:   $escape \leftarrow mode_i \neq \perp$;
13:   **if** not *escape* **then** {no escape}
14:     $q_i \leftarrow quantize(x_i, C_i[mode_i])$;
15:   **else** {escape}
16:     $mode_i \leftarrow mode_{i-1}$;
17:     $\delta_i \leftarrow d(T_p) + \delta_i$;
18:     $S_i \leftarrow B(z_i(T_p), \delta_i)$;
19:     $C_i \leftarrow grid(S_i, \delta_i e^{-(L+\alpha)T_p})$;
20:     $q_i \leftarrow quantize(x_i, C_i[mode_i])$;
21:   **end if**
22:   send $\langle q_i, valid_i \rangle$;
23:   i++; {parameters for next iteration}
24:   $m_i \leftarrow m_{i-1}$;
25:   **for** $r \in [\hat{N}]$ **do**
26:     **if** *escape* or (not $valid_{i-1}[r]$ and $m_i[r] \neq -1$) **then**
27:       $m_i[r] \leftarrow NextMode()$;
28:     **end if**
29:     **if** $m_i[r] \neq -1$ **then**
30:       $v_i[r] \leftarrow \xi_{m_i[r]}(q_{i-1}, T_p)$;
31:     **end if**
32:   **end for**
33:   $\delta_i \leftarrow e^{-\alpha T_p}\delta_{i-1}$;
34:   $S_i \leftarrow B(v_i[mode_{i-1}], \delta_i)$;
35:   $C_i \leftarrow grid(S_i, \delta_i e^{-(L+\alpha)T_p})$;
36:   $z_i(.) \leftarrow \xi_{m_i[mode_{i-1}]}(q_{i-1}, \cdot)$;
37:   wait(T_p);
38: **end while**

exponentially until the switch, and after that it accumulates an additive factor of $d(T_p)$.

Proposition 3 *Fix an iteration i, a switching time $s_j \in (iT_p, (i+1)T_p)$, and an index $r \in [\hat{N}]$. If $m_{i+1}[r] = \sigma(iT_p)$ and $x_i \in S_i[p]$ for some $p \in [\hat{N}]$, then for all $t \in [iT_p, (i+1)T_p]$, $\|\xi_\sigma(x_0, t) - \xi_{m_{i+1}[r]}(q_i, t - iT_p)\|_\infty \le$*

$$\begin{cases} \delta_i e^{-\alpha(t-iT_p)} & \text{if } t < s_j \quad (4) \\ d(T_p) + \delta_i e^{-\alpha(t-iT_p)} & \text{otherwise.} \quad (5) \end{cases}$$

PROOF. For (4), $\|x_i - q_i\|_\infty \le \delta_i e^{-(L+\alpha)T_p}$ since $x_i \in S_i[p]$ for some $p \in [\hat{N}]$ and the boxes in $C_i[p]$ are of radii $\delta_i e^{-(L+\alpha)T_p}$. Then, $\|\xi_\sigma(x_0, t) - \xi_{m_{i+1}[r]}(q_i, t - iT_p)\|_\infty$

$$= \|\xi_\sigma(x_i, t - iT_p) - \xi_{m_{i+1}[r]}(q_i, t - iT_p)\|_\infty$$
$$[\text{since } \xi_\sigma(x_0, t) = \xi_\sigma(\xi_\sigma(x_0, iT_p), t - iT_p)]$$
$$= \|\xi_{m_{i+1}[r]}(x_i, t - iT_p) - \xi_{m_{i+1}[r]}(q_i, t - iT_p)\|_\infty$$
$$[\sigma(iT_p) = m_{i+1}[r]]$$
$$\le e^{L_{m_{i+1}[r]}(t-iT_p)} \|x_i - q_i\|_\infty$$
$$[\text{Bellman-Gronwall inequality}]$$
$$\le \delta_i e^{L_{m_{i+1}[r]}(t-iT_p)} e^{-(L+\alpha)T_p}$$
$$[q_i \text{ is quantization of } x_i]$$
$$\le \delta_i e^{-\alpha(t-iT_p)}.$$

The last inequality follows because $L_{m_{i+1}[r]} \le L$ and $t - iT_p \le T_p$. For (5), we assume without loss of generality that $m_{i+1}[r] = \sigma(t) = 1$ for $t \in [iT_p, s_j)$, $\sigma(t) = 2$ for $t \in [s_j, (i+1)T_p]$. Then, $\|\xi_\sigma(x_0, t) - \xi_{m_{i+1}[r]}(q_i, t - iT_p)\|_\infty$

$$= \|\xi_2(\xi_1(x_0, s_j), t - s_j) - \xi_1(\xi_1(q_i, s_j - iT_p), t - s_j)\|_\infty$$
$$\le \|\xi_2(\xi_1(x_0, s_j), t - s_j) - \xi_1(\xi_1(x_0, s_j), t - s_j)\|_\infty$$
$$+ \|\xi_1(\xi_1(x_0, s_j), t - s_j) - \xi_1(\xi_1(q_i, s_j - iT_p), t - s_j)\|_\infty$$
$$[\text{by triangle inequality}]$$
$$\le \| \int_0^{t-s_j} (f_2(\xi_2(\xi_1(x_0, s_j), t')) - f_1(\xi_1(\xi_1(x_0, s_j), t')))dt' \|$$
$$+ \|\xi_1(\xi_1(x_0, s_j), t - s_j) - \xi_1(\xi_1(q_i, s_j - iT_p), t - s_j)\|_\infty$$
$$\le d(t - s_j) + e^{L_1(t-iT_p)} \|x_i - q_i\|_\infty$$
$$[\text{by Bellman-Gronwall inequality}]$$
$$\le d(T_p) + \delta_i e^{-\alpha(t-iT_p)}.$$

□

The next proposition holds under the same conditions as Proposition 3 except that the considered mode $m_{i+1}[r]$ matches the mode of the switched system $\sigma((i+1)T_p)$ at $t = (i+1)T_p$ iteration, but it is not the same as $\sigma(iT_p)$. The proof of (6) is analogous to the proof of (5).

Proposition 4 *Fix an iteration i, a switching time $s_j \in (iT_p, (i+1)T_p)$, and an index $r \in [\hat{N}]$. If $m_{i+1}[r] \ne \sigma(iT_p)$, $m_{i+1}[r] = \sigma((i+1)T_p)$ and $x_i \in S_i[p]$ for some $p \in [\hat{N}]$, then, for all $t \in [iT_p, (i+1)T_p]$,*
$\|\xi_\sigma(x_0, t) - \xi_{m_{i+1}[r]}(q_i, t - iT_p)\|_\infty \le$

$$\begin{cases} d(T_p) + \delta_i e^{-\alpha(t-iT_p)} & \text{if } t < s_j \quad (6) \\ 2d(T_p) + \delta_i e^{-\alpha(t-iT_p)} & \text{otherwise.} \quad (7) \end{cases}$$

PROOF. For (7), $\|\xi_\sigma(x_0, t) - \xi_{m_{i+1}[r]}(q_i, t - iT_p)\|_\infty$

$$\le \|\xi_\sigma(x_0, t) - \xi_{\sigma(iT_p)}(x_i, t - iT_p)\|_\infty$$
$$+ \|\xi_{\sigma(iT_p)}(x_i, t - iT_p) - \xi_{m_{i+1}[r]}(q_i, t - iT_p)\|_\infty$$
$$[\text{by triangle inequality}]$$
$$\le \|\xi_\sigma(\xi_\sigma(x_0, s_j), t - s_j) - \xi_{\sigma(iT_p)}(\xi_\sigma(x_0, s_j), t - s_j)\|_\infty$$
$$+ \|\xi_{\sigma(iT_p)}(x_i, t - iT_p) - \xi_{m_{i+1}[r]}(q_i, t - iT_p)\|_\infty$$
$$\le d(t - s_j) + d(T_p) + \delta_i e^{-\alpha(t-iT_p)}$$
$$[\text{by similar argument to (5)}]$$
$$\le 2d(T_p) + \delta_i e^{-\alpha(t-iT_p)}.$$

□

Proposition 5 also holds under the same conditions as Proposition 3 except that the considered mode $m_{i+1}[r]$, the actual mode $\sigma(iT_p)$ at the ith iteration and $\sigma((i+1)T_p)$ at the $(i+1)^{st}$ iteration are all distinct. Inequality (8) is the same as (6). Also, the proof of (9) is analogous to the proof of (7).

Proposition 5 *Fix an iteration i, a switching time $s_j \in (iT_p, (i+1)T_p)$, and an index $r \in [\hat{N}]$. If $m_{i+1}[r] \ne \sigma(iT_p)$, $m_{i+1}[r] \ne \sigma((i+1)T_p)$, $m_{i+1} \ne -1$ and $x_i \in S_i[p]$ for some $p \in [\hat{N}]$, then, for all $t \in [iT_p, (i+1)T_p]$,*
$\|\xi_\sigma(x_0, t) - \xi_{m_{i+1}[r]}(q_i, t - iT_p)\|_\infty \le$

$$\begin{cases} d(T_p) + \delta_i e^{-\alpha(t-iT_p)} & \text{if } t < s_j \quad (8) \\ 2d(T_p) + \delta_i e^{-\alpha(t-iT_p)} & \text{otherwise.} \quad (9) \end{cases}$$

From the above Propositions, it follows immediately that if there is no switch between the ith and the $(i+1)^{st}$ iteration, then the bounds given by inequalities (4), (6) and (8) will continue to hold for the entire period between the iterations.

The following assumption will be used to prove several intermediate results about the estimation algorithm detecting the right mode and estimation bounds. Then, in Lemma 4 in Section 4.2, we will establish a lower bound on the dwell-time T_d which guarantees this assumption.

Assumption 1 For each switching time s_j other than $s_0 = 0$, let $i = last(j)$. Then, there exists $r \in [\hat{N}]$ where $m_{i+1}[r]$ is the actual mode of the system $\sigma(iT_p)$ and $m_{i+1}[p] = -1$ for all $p \ne r$ and $\delta_i \le \min\{\delta_0, \epsilon_{min}\}$.

Proposition 6 *Under Assumption 1, for each i there exists $r \in [\hat{N}]$ with $x_i \in S_i[r]$.*

PROOF. If there is an escape at iteration i, then the state x_i is not in any of the $S_i[r]$'s at line 9, however, it is still guaranteed to be in all the expanded (corrected) estimates $S_i[r]$'s computed at line 18 based on δ_i and $d(T_p)$. That is because, under Assumption 1, inequalities (7) and (9) in Propositions 4 an 5, are not relevant (they are useful for analyzing the error bounds for faster switching signals). Therefore, line 17 takes care of the worst case scenario in the estimation error over a single iteration. □

4.2 Bounding escapes between switches

Proposition 7 upper bounds the number of escapes that can happen between two consecutive switches to $\lceil N/\hat{N} \rceil$.

Proposition 7 *Under Assumption 1, the maximum number of escapes between two consecutive switches is* $\lceil N/\hat{N} \rceil$.

PROOF. First, note that at an escape, all the $\hat{N}$ invalid modes are dropped from the vector m_i and new candidate modes are added fairly by the *NextMode*() function. Hence, all the N modes would have been considered after $\lceil N/\hat{N} \rceil$ escapes. Thus, the correct mode $\sigma(t)$ would have been in m at some iteration i. Then, let $m_{i+1}[r] = \sigma(iT_p)$. Second, we know that $x_i \in S_i[p]$ for some $p \in [\hat{N}]$ by Proposition 6. Therefore, we can apply the estimation error bound given by (4) in Proposition 3 to conclude that in the next iteration $valid_i[r]$ will be set to 1 and will remain thereafter until a new switch occur. Thus, there will be no more escapes till the next switch. □

Because of the exponential separation property, we can show that if the dwell time of the switching signal is large enough, then after some maximum number of iterations after a switch, the actual mode $\sigma(t)$ still remains unchanged and the size of the state estimate S_i will be small enough to the point that all incorrect modes in m_i will be invalidated. We define $i_{inv}(\delta)$ to be an upper bound on the number of iterations needed to invalidate a mode when the current radius of the ball representing the state estimate S is δ. Let us define: for any $\delta > 0$,

$$i_{inv}(\delta) := \max\{\lceil \frac{1}{\alpha T_p} \ln(\frac{\delta}{\epsilon_{min}}) - \frac{L}{\alpha} \rceil, 1\}.$$

Proposition 8 *Under Assumption 1, if at a given iteration* $i \geq 0$, $-1 \neq m_{i+1}[r] \neq \sigma(t)$, *then* $m_{i+1}[r]$ *will be replaced with a different mode after a maximum of* $i_{inv}(\delta_i)$ *iterations.*

PROOF. Let $c = \lceil \frac{1}{\alpha T_p} \ln(\frac{\delta_i}{\epsilon_{min}}) - \frac{L+\alpha}{\alpha} \rceil$. First, note that until $m_{i+1}[r]$ is replaced, δ_i will be decreasing by a $e^{\alpha T_p}$ factor in each iteration (because there is no escape if it is not replaced). Then, $\delta_{i+c} e^{-(L+\alpha)T_p} = \delta_i e^{-((i+c)-i)\alpha T_p} e^{-(L+\alpha)T_p} < \epsilon_{min}$. Thus, by the exponential separation property:

$$\begin{aligned}
&\|\xi_\sigma(x_i, (c+1)T_p) - \xi_{m_{i+c+1}[r]}(q_{i+c}, T_p)\|_\infty \\
&= \|\xi_\sigma(x_{i+c}, T_p) - \xi_{m_{i+c+1}[r]}(q_{i+c}, T_p)\|_\infty > \delta_{i+c} e^{-(L+\alpha)T_p} e^{LT_p} \\
&= \delta_{i+c+1}. \qquad \text{[computed at line 33]}
\end{aligned}$$

Thus, the actual state will not belong to $S_{i+c+1}[r]$ computed at line 34 and $m_{i+c+2}[r] \neq m_{i+c+1}[r]$. □

We upper bound the radius δ_i of the state estimate S_i at iteration i with,

$$\delta_{max} := \max_{i \in [1, \lceil N/\hat{N} \rceil]} \{\delta_0 e^{-i\alpha T_p} + d(T_p) \frac{1 - e^{-i\alpha T_p}}{1 - e^{-\alpha T_p}}\}.$$

Note that the first term decays geometrically with i and the second term increases, and the max value could be attained somewhere in the middle.

Proposition 9 *Under Assumption 1,* $\delta_i \leq \delta_{max}$ *for all* i.

PROOF. The radius δ_i of S_i decreases between two escapes and possibly increase at an escape. Therefore, the maximum of δ_i would achieved if some number of escapes (less than or equal to $\lceil N/\hat{N} \rceil$) happened in consecutive iterations immediately after a switch. Assumption 1 is used to make sure that $\delta_i \leq \delta_0$ at $i = last(j)$. □

The following definitions and two lemmas are used to compute the minimum dwell-time that suffices for Assumption 1 to be true. The following i_{det} represents the maximum number of iterations needed after a switch for the actual mode to be detected, all other modes be invalidated and $\delta_i \leq \epsilon_{min}$.

$$\begin{aligned}
i_{det} &:= \sum_{i=1}^{\lceil N/\hat{N} \rceil} i_{inv}(\delta_0 e^{-i\alpha T_p} + d(T_p) \sum_{j=0}^{i-1} e^{-j\alpha T_p}) + 2 \\
&\leq \lceil \frac{N}{\hat{N}} \rceil i_{inv}(\delta_{max}) + 2
\end{aligned}$$

Lemma 3 *Under Assumption 1, after a maximum of* i_{det} *iterations of any switch* s_j, $m_{i+1}[r] = \sigma(t)$, *for some* $r \in [\hat{N}]$, $m_{i+1}[u] = -1$ *for all* $u \neq r$ *and* $\delta_i \leq \epsilon_{min}$.

PROOF. (sketch) After a switch, the only mode considered in m_i will no longer be the correct mode. In the worst case, $\sigma(t)$ will be considered in the last set of modes m_{i+1}. Each set of modes m_{i+1} needs a maximum of $i_{inv}(\delta_i)$ iterations to be invalidated. Moreover, there is a maximum of $\lceil N/\hat{N} \rceil$ escapes. The first escape will happen after a maximum of 2 iterations after the switch to invalidate $m_{i+1}[r]$ by the exponential separation assumption since $\delta_i \leq \epsilon_{min}$ before the switch. Since i_{inv} is monotonically increasing w.r.t δ, we summed the values of i_{inv} when evaluated on the $\lceil N/\hat{N} \rceil$ maximum possible values of δ_i. The last $i_{inv}(\delta_{max})$ in i_{det} is to invalidate all wrong modes (and replace them with -1) and keep the actual one in m_i. It will also make $\delta_i \leq \epsilon_{min}$ by the definition of $i_{inv}(\delta_{max})$. □

Finally, we define the following to upper bound the number of iterations, with no escapes, needed to decrease δ_i from ϵ_{min} to less than δ_0:

$$i_{est} := \max(\lceil \frac{1}{\alpha T_p} \ln(\frac{\epsilon_{min}}{\delta_0}) \rceil, 0).$$

Lemma 4 *If the minimum dwell-time of* σ *is greater than* $(i_{det} + i_{est} + 1)T_p$, *then Assumption 1 is true.*

PROOF. Lemma 3 holds between $s_0 = 0$ and s_1 given the minimum dwell time and the fact that $\epsilon_{min}\, e^{-\alpha T_p (i_{est})} \leq \delta_0$ without Assumption 1. Then, the argument holds inductively for the rest of the intervals. □

4.3 Estimation error

Combining the above we derive bounds on the estimation error in Theorem 2. It shows that after a switch, the algorithm will be in four possible "phases". The estimation error will increase in the first few iterations after a switch where escapes occur, until the correct mode is found in m, and thereafter, the estimate converges exponentially, provided the dwell time is large enough.

Let the iterations of the algorithm when escapes occur between two consecutive switches s_j and s_{j+1} be numbered $w_1, \ldots w_k$. Fixing j we avoid indexing the w's and k with j.

Theorem 2 *If* σ *has dwell time* $T_d \geq (i_{det} + i_{est} + 1)T_p$, *then for any* $t \in [s_j, s_{j+1})$, *the estimation error*

$\|\xi_\sigma(x_0,t) - z(t)\|_\infty \leq$

$$\begin{cases} d(T_p) + \delta_0 e^{-\alpha(t - last(j)T_p)} & \text{if } t \in [s_j, w_1 T_p] \quad (10) \\ d(T_p) + \delta_{w_h} e^{-\alpha(t - w_h T_p)} & (11) \\ \quad \text{if } \exists\, h \in \{1,\ldots,k\}, t \in [w_h T_p, w_{h+1} T_p] & \\ d(T_p) + \delta_{w_k} e^{-\alpha(t - w_k T_p)} & (12) \\ \quad \text{if } t \in [w_k T_p, (w_k + i_{inv}(\delta_{w_k}))T_p] & \\ \delta_{w_k} e^{-\alpha(t - w_k T_p)} \quad \text{otherwise}. & (13) \end{cases}$$

PROOF. We start by proving (10): By Lemma 4, $\delta_{last(j)} \leq \epsilon_{min}$, $\delta_{last(j)} \leq \delta_0$ and $z(t) = \xi_\sigma(q_{last(j)}, t - last(j)T_p)$ for $t \in [last(j)T_p, s_j)$. Then, by inequality (5) in Proposition 3 , the inequality is satisfied for $t \in [s_j, next(j)T_p]$. Moreover, if w_1, the first escape after s_j, was not at $next(j)$ then it will be at $next(j)+1$, since, by the exponential separation property, $\|z(t) - \xi_\sigma(x_0,t)\| \geq \delta_0 e^{LT_p}$, so $w_1 = next(j)+1$. If that is the case, then the inequality holds for $t \in [next(j)T_p, (next(j)+1)T_p]$ as a result of inequality (6) in Proposition 4 and the fact that $\delta_{next(j)} \leq \delta_0 e^{-\alpha T_p} \leq \delta_0$.

Inequalities (11) and (12) have similar proofs as (10) but instead of δ_0 we have δ_{w_h}. Inequality (13) follows from the fact that at $t = (w_k + i_{inv}(\delta_{w_k})T_p)$ there is $r \in [\hat{N}]$ with $m[r] = \sigma(s_j)$ and $m[p] = -1$ for $p \neq r$, and the repeated application of inequality (4) in proposition 3. □

Corollary 1 summarizes the error bounds in Theorem 2.

Corollary 1 *Under the assumptions of Lemma 4, consider the time between the two consecutive switches s_j and s_{j+1}. Then, for all $t \in [s_j, s_{j+1})$, $\|\xi_\sigma(x_0,t) - z(t)\|_\infty \leq$*

$$\begin{cases} \delta_{max} + d(T_p) & t \in [s_j, w_k T_p] \quad (14) \\ \delta_{w_k} e^{-\alpha(t - w_k T_p)} & \text{otherwise}. \quad (15) \end{cases}$$

Thus, for a given ε, τ and α defined as for Theorem 1, we can choose δ_0, T_p and $\hat{N}$ to control the variables i_{det}, $d(T_p)$ and δ_{max} so as to achieve the inequalities in (3).

4.4 Optimal network usage

We show that the estimation algorithm uses network bandwidth optimally in the following sense: An analysis similar to that of Proposition 4 of [8] shows that the average bit rate used by our algorithm is $(L+\alpha)n/\ln 2 + \hat{N}/T_p$. The sensor needs to send (a) q_i: the quantization of x_i with respect to one of the $\hat{N}$ $S_i[r]$'s and (b) the $valid_i$ bit vector: for each $r \in [\hat{N}]$ one bit indicating whether or not x_i belongs to $S_i[r]$. The quantized state q_0 requires $\#C_0 = \lceil \frac{diam(K)}{2\delta_0 e^{-(L+\alpha)T_p}} \rceil^n$ bits to be sent. For $i \geq 1$, the number of bits required to represent q_i is $\#C_i = \lceil \frac{\delta_i}{\delta_i e^{-(L+\alpha)T_p}} \rceil^n = \lceil e^{(L+\alpha)T_p} \rceil^n$. Hence, the average bit rate used by the algorithm is $b_r(\varepsilon, \alpha, T_p) = \lim_{i\to\infty} 1/T_p \log(\#C_i \hat{N}) = \frac{(L+\alpha)n}{\ln 2} + \frac{\hat{N}}{T_p}$.

Theorem 3 *Average bit rate of Algorithm 1 is $\frac{(L+\alpha)}{\ln 2} + \frac{\hat{N}}{T_p}$.* Hence, it follows that the bit-rate used by the estimation algorithm is larger than the upper bound on the estimation entropy by at most $\frac{\hat{N}}{T_p} - \frac{\log N}{T_e}$ bits. Therefore, the efficiency gap between the bit-rate used by our algorithm and the bit rate (h_{est}) used by the best possible algorithm, is at most $\frac{\hat{N}}{T_p} - \frac{\log N}{T_e}$ bits more than the gap between h_{est} and its upper-bound. The unobservability of the switching signal and the switching times contributes to the gap.

5. EXPERIMENTS

We implemented Algorithm 1 and experimented on two switched systems [1]. We used Python 2.7 and ODEint package to generate the trajectories. The running time of each iteration of the algorithm is $O(n+N)$, assuming $O(1)$ time computation of trajectories. In practice, it took milliseconds on a laptop with 2 GHz Intel Core i7 processor, which suggests that the algorithm can be used in real-time.

Switched linear systems.

In a switched linear system, the dynamics of all the modes are of the form: $\dot{x} = A_p x + B_p u$. We present estimation of a five dimensional switched linear system with five modes. For each $p \in [5] = \{0, \ldots 4\}$ the matrix A_p and the column vector B_p are generated randomly, and the input u is also a random constant. In the presented results, the settling time for the first mode is 11.89 and the others are unstable. The maximum Lipschitz constant was $L = 28.28$. We work with switching signals that satisfy Assumption 1. We chose the following parameters $\alpha = 1$, $T_p = 0.1s$, $\varepsilon = 2$ and $\hat{N} = 2$. Two state components of the system are shown in Figure 2 (Left). Observe that the state estimates (yellow and blue) enlarge after escapes and that the state and the mode eventually converge to the correct values. $d(T_p)$ was approximated at each escape by computing the distance between all possible pairs of modes starting from the actual state of the system (can be replaced with the estimated state) at the time of that escape. It was around 2. The bit rate used here is $(L+\alpha)n/\ln 2 + \hat{N}/T_p = 231$ bps. The maximum time needed to detect the correct mode is 2.2 seconds and the maximum radius of a bounding box δ was around 3. So, if $\tau \geq 2.2s$ and $\varepsilon \geq 5$, the parameters of the algorithm in this experiment satisfy the properties in (3).

Nonlinear glycemic index model.

Estimating the blood glucose level is an important problem for administering controlling insulin for diabetes patients given [4]. We consider a polynomial switched system model of plasma glucose concentration [2]. The model has nine modes representing different control inputs. The state consists of three variables: G, I and X. In this model, the switching between different modes are brought about by certain threshold based rules depending on the state variables. In the span of $150s$ of each execution, 6 switches happened. Although Assumption 1 was not always satisfied, it was still able to do state estimation. The Lipschitz constant of each of the modes is estimated through sampling. The parameters of the algorithm are chosen as $\alpha = 1$ and $T_p = 1s$. For each value of $\hat{N} \in [1, 9]$, 100 initial states x_0 are drawn randomly and the algorithm is executed on the resulting solutions $\xi_\sigma(x_0, \cdot)$. Two sample executions are shown in Figure 2 and the average results are shown in the table below.

As the number of modes tracked $\hat{N}$ increases, as expected, the number of escapes decreases. In fact, beyond $\hat{N} = 5$, the marginal benefit to sending more bits is small as far as the worst case error estimate (δ_{max}) is concerned. In practice, the choice for d_0, $\hat{N}$ and T_p should be chosen to satisfy the convergence parameters specified.

[1]Code available at: https://github.com/HusseinSibai/SwitchedSystemsStateEstimation

[2]Switched system benchmark available from: https://ths.rwth-aachen.de/research/projects/hypro/glycemic-control/

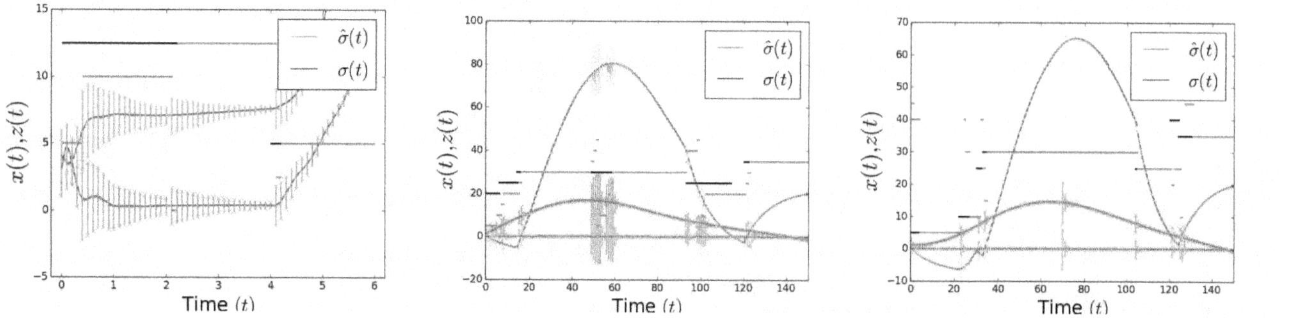

Figure 2: Execution of estimation algorithm. Actual mode (black), mode estimate (red), the values of the other variables are shown by the continuous plots. The vertical cut lines show the error estimates (δ) on those variables. Linear five dimensional system (*left*), Glycemic nonlinear control system, $\hat{N} = 1$ (*center*) and $\hat{N} = 9$ (*right*). Figure with $\hat{N} = 9$ has much less escapes than that with $\hat{N} = 1$.

$\hat{N}$	δ_{max}	Escps.
1	14.17	25
2	12.97	12.92
3	12.3	8.95
4	10.16	6.95
5	9.67	6.38
6	10.12	6.5
7	9.67	6.06
8	9.66	6.0
9	9.59	5.81

6. CONCLUSION

We have presented an algorithm for state estimation of switched nonlinear systems with finite number of modes and unobservable switching signal using quantized measurements with optimality guarantees on the number of bits needed to be sent from the sensor to the estimator. These results suggest several future research directions including extensions to hybrid models with partially known switching structure, models with input disturbances, and developing lower-bounds on corresponding notions of estimation entropy.

7. REFERENCES

[1] Bosch. CAN specification version 1.0. Technical report, Robert Bosch Gmbh, Postfach 50, Stuttgart, September 1991.

[2] F. Colonius and C. Kawan. Invariance entropy for control systems. *SIAM J. Control Optim.*, 48:1701–1721, 2009.

[3] T. M. Cover and J. A. Thomas. *Elements of Information Theory.* Wiley, New York, 1991.

[4] S. Furler, E. Kraegen, R. Smallwood, and D. Chisholm. Blood glucose control by intermittent loop closure in the basal mode: computer simulation studies with a diabetic model. *Diabetes Care*, 8:553???–561, 1985.

[5] J. Hespanha and A. Morse. Stability of switched systems with average dwell-time. In *Proceedings of 38th IEEE Conference on Decision and Control*, pages 2655–2660, 1999.

[6] A. Katok and B. Hasselblatt. *Introduction to the Modern Theory of Dynamical Systems.* Cambridge University Press, 1995.

[7] D. Liberzon. *Switching in Systems and Control.* Systems and Control: Foundations and Applications. Birkhauser, Boston, June 2003.

[8] D. Liberzon and S. Mitra. Entropy and minimal data rates for state estimation and model detections. In *HSCC 2016*, Vienna, April 2016. ACM.

[9] D. Liberzon and S. Mitra. Entropy notions for state estimation and model detection with finite-data-rate measurements. In *CDC*, Las Vegas, 2016.

[10] G. N. Nair. A nonstochastic information theory for communication and state estimation. *IEEE Transactions on automatic control*, 58(6):1497–1510, 2013.

[11] G. N. Nair and R. J. Evans. Stabilization with data-rate-limited feedback: tightest attainable bounds. *Systems Control Lett.*, 41:49–56, 2000.

[12] A. V. Savkin. Analysis and synthesis of networked control systems: Topological entropy, observability, robustness and optimal control. *Automatica*, 42:51–62, 2006.

[13] J. Schmidt. Topological Entropy Bounds for Switched Linear Systems with Lie Structure. *ArXiv e-prints*, Oct. 2016.

[14] C. Steiner. Bot in the delivery:kiva systems. *Forbes Magazine*, March 2009. http://www.forbes.com/forbes/2009/0316/040_bot_time_saves_nine.html.

[15] R. Van Der Merwe, A. Doucet, N. De Freitas, and E. Wan. The unscented particle filter. In *NIPS*, volume 2000, pages 584–590, 2000.

[16] E. A. Wan and A. T. Nelson. Dual kalman filtering methods for nonlinear prediction, smoothing and estimation. In *NIPS 9, Denver, CO, USA, December 2-5, 1996*, pages 793–799, 1996.

[17] R. Wilson and L. Finkel. A neural implementation of the kalman filter. In Y. Bengio, D. Schuurmans, J. D. Lafferty, C. K. I. Williams, and A. Culotta, editors, *NIPS 22*, pages 2062–2070. Curran Associates, Inc., 2009.

[18] G. Yang and D. Liberzon. Stabilizing a switched linear system with disturbance by sampled-data quantized feedback. In *American Control Conference (ACC), 2015*, pages 2193–2198. IEEE, 2015.

Path-Complete Graphs and Common Lyapunov Functions*

David Angeli
Dept. of Electrical and Electronic Engineering, Imperial College London, UK
Dept. of Information Engineering, University of Florence, Italy.
d.angeli@imperial.ac.uk

Nikolaos Athanasopoulos Raphaël M. Jungers[†] Matthew Philippe
ICTEAM, Applied Mathematics Dept., Université catholique de Louvain, Louvain-la-Neuve, Belgium
{matthew.philippe, nikolaos.athanasopoulos,raphael.jungers}@uclouvain.be

ABSTRACT

A Path-Complete Lyapunov Function is an algebraic criterion composed of a finite number of functions, called pieces, and a directed, labeled graph defining *Lyapunov inequalities* between these pieces. It provides a stability certificate for discrete-time arbitrary switching systems.
In this paper, we prove that the satisfiability of such a criterion implies the existence of a Common Lyapunov Function, expressed as the composition of minima and maxima of the pieces of the Path-Complete Lyapunov function. The converse however is not true even for discrete-time linear systems: we present such a system where a max-of-2 quadratics Lyapunov function exists while no corresponding Path-Complete Lyapunov function with 2 quadratic pieces exists. In light of this, we investigate when it is possible to decide if a Path-Complete Lyapunov function is less conservative than another. By analyzing the combinatorial and algebraic structure of the graph and the pieces respectively, we provide simple tools to decide when the existence of such a Lyapunov function implies that of another.

CCS Concepts

•Computing methodologies → Symbolic and algebraic algorithms;

Keywords

Discrete-time switching systems, Lyapunov Function, Path-Complete graphs, Observer Automaton.

*N.A., R.M.J. and M.P. are supported by the French Community of Belgium and by the IAP network DYSCO. M.P. if a F.N.R.S./F.R.I.A. Fellow. R.J. is a Fulbright Fellow and a F.N.R.S. Fellow.

[†]Currently visiting UCLA, Department of Electrical Engineering, Los Angeles, USA.

HSCC'17, April 18-20, 2017, Pittsburgh, PA, USA

DOI: http://dx.doi.org/10.1145/3049797.3049817

1. INTRODUCTION

Switching systems are dynamical systems for which the state dynamics varies between different operating modes. They find application in several applications and theoretical fields, see e.g. [1, 11, 16, 19]. They take the form

$$x(t+1) = f_{\sigma(t)}(x(t)) \qquad (1)$$

where the state $x(t)$ evolves in $\mathbb{R}^n$. The *mode* $\sigma(t)$ of the system at time t takes value in $\{1, \dots, M\}$ for some integer M. Each mode $i \in \{1, \dots, M\}$ of the system is described by a continuous map $f_i(x) : \mathbb{R}^n \to \mathbb{R}^n$. We assume that $f_i(x) = 0 \Leftrightarrow x = 0$ for all modes.

In this paper, we study criteria guaranteeing that the system (1) is stable under *arbitrary switching*, i.e. when the function $\sigma(\cdot)$, called the switching sequence, may take any value in $\{1, \dots, M\}$ at any time t. This analysis can be extended to the more general *constrained switching* setting of [19] (see [14], [19, Section 3.5]). We study the following notions of stability, where $x(t, \sigma(\cdot), x_0)$ is the state of the system (1) at time t with a switching sequence $\sigma(\cdot)$ and an initial condition $x_0 \in \mathbb{R}^n$.

Definition 1. *The system (1) is Globally Uniformly Stable if there is a $\mathcal{K}_\infty$-function[1] $\alpha : \mathbb{R}^+ \mapsto \mathbb{R}^+$ such that for all $x_0 \in \mathbb{R}^n$, for all switching sequences $\sigma(\cdot)$ and for all $t \geq 0$,*

$$\|x(t, \sigma(\cdot), x_0)\| \leq \alpha(\|x_0\|).$$

The system is Globally Uniformly Asymptotically Stable if there is a $\mathcal{KL}$-function[2] $\beta : \mathbb{R}^+ \times \mathbb{R}^+ \mapsto \mathbb{R}^+$ such that for all $x_0 \in \mathbb{R}^n$, for all switching sequences $\sigma(\cdot)$ and for all $t \geq 0$,

$$\|x(t, \sigma(\cdot), x_0)\| \leq \beta(\|x_0\|, t).$$

The stability analysis of switching systems is a central and challenging question in control (see [17] for a description of several approaches on the topic). The question of whether or not a system is uniformly globally stable is in general undecidable, even when the dynamics are *linear* at each mode (see e.g. [4, 11]).

[1]A function $\alpha(z)$ is of class $\mathcal{K}$ if it is continuous, strictly increasing, with $\alpha(0) = 0$. It is of class $\mathcal{K}_\infty$ if it is unbounded as well.

[2]A function $\beta(z, t)$ is of class $\mathcal{KL}$ if, for each fixed t, $\beta(z, t)$ is a $\mathcal{K}$-function in z, and for each fixed z, $\beta(z, t)$ is a continuous function of t, strictly decreasing with $\lim_{t\to\infty} \beta(z, t) = 0$.

A way to assess stability for switching systems is to use Lyapunov methods, with the drawback that they often provide conservative stability certificates. For example, for *linear* discrete-time switching systems of the form

$$x(t+1) = A_{\sigma(t)}x(t),$$

it is easy to check for the existence of a *common quadratic* Lyapunov function (see e.g. [17, Section II-A]). However, such a Lyapunov function may not exist, even though the system is asymptotically stable (see e.g. [16, 17]). Less conservative parameterizations of candidate Lyapunov functions have been proposed, at the cost of greater computational effort (e.g. for linear switching systems, [18] uses sum-of-squares polynomials, [9] uses max-of-quadratics Lyapunov functions, and [2] uses polytopic Lyapunov functions). *Multiple Lyapunov functions* (see [5, 10, 20]) arise as an alternative to common Lyapunov functions. In the case of linear systems, the multiple *quadratic* Lyapunov functions such as those introduced in [3, 7, 8, 15] hold special interest as checking for their existence boils down to solving a set of LMIs. The general framework of *Path-Complete* Lyapunov functions was recently introduced in [1] in this context, for analyzing and unifying the approaches cited above.
A Path-Complete Lyapunov function is a multiple Lyapunov function composed of a finite set of *pieces* $\mathcal{V} = (V_i)_{i=1,\dots,N}$, with $V_i : \mathbb{R}^n \mapsto \mathbb{R}^+$, and a set of *valid Lyapunov inequalities* between these pieces. We assume there exist two $\mathcal{K}_\infty$-functions α_1 and α_2 such that

$$\forall x \in \mathbb{R}^n,\ \forall i \in \{1,\dots,N\},\ \alpha_1(\|x\|) \le V_i(x) \le \alpha_2(\|x\|). \quad (2)$$

Lyapunov inequalities between pieces are represented by a directed and labeled graph $\mathbf{G} = (S, E)$, where S is the set of nodes, and E the set of edges of the graph. There is one node in the graph for each one of the pieces $(V_i)_{i\in\{1,\dots,N\}}$ of the Lyapunov function. An edge takes the form $(p, q, w) \in E$, where $p, q \in S$ are respectively its source and destination nodes, and where w is the *label* of the edge. Such a label is a finite sequence of modes of the system (1) of the form $w = \sigma_1 \dots \sigma_k$, with $\sigma_i \in \{1,\dots,M\}$, $1 \le i \le k$.
An edge as described above encodes the Lyapunov inequality[3]

$$(p, q, w) \in E \Rightarrow \forall x \in \mathbb{R}^n,\ V_q(f_w(x)) \le V_p(x), \quad (3)$$

where $1 \le p, q \le P$ and for $w = \sigma_1 \dots \sigma_k$, with $\sigma_i \in \{1,\dots,M\}$, and $f_w = f_{\sigma_k} \circ \dots \circ f_{\sigma_1}$ (see Figure 1). By tran-

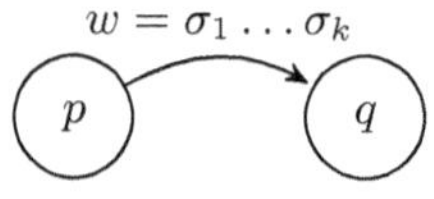

Figure 1: The edge encodes $V_q(f_w(x)) \le V_p(x)$.

sitivity, paths in the graph $\mathbf{G}$ encode Lyapunov inequalities as well. Given a path $p = (s_i, s_{i+1}, w_i)_{i=1,\dots,k}$ of length k, we define the *label* of the path as the sequence $w_1 \dots w_k$ (i.e. the concatenation of the sequences on the k edges). Such a path encodes the inequality $V_{s_{k+1}}(f_{w_k} \circ \dots \circ f_{w_1}(x)) = V_{s_{k+1}}(f_{w_1 \dots w_K}(x)) \le V_{s_1}(x)$.
The graph $\mathbf{G}$ defining a Path-Complete Lyapunov function has a special structure defined below (see Figure 2).

[3]We consider here certificates for Global Uniform Stability. Analogous criteria for Global Uniform Asymptotic Stability can be obtained by making the inequalities in (3) strict.

Definition 2 (Path-Complete Graph). *Consider a directed and labeled graph* $\mathbf{G} = (S, E)$, *with edges* $(s, d, w) \in E$ *where* $s, d \in S$ *and where the label* w *is a finite sequence over* $\{1,\dots,M\}$. *The graph is* path-complete *if for any finite sequence* w *on* $\{1,\dots,M\}$, *there is a* path *in the graph with a label* w' *such that* w *is contained in* w'.

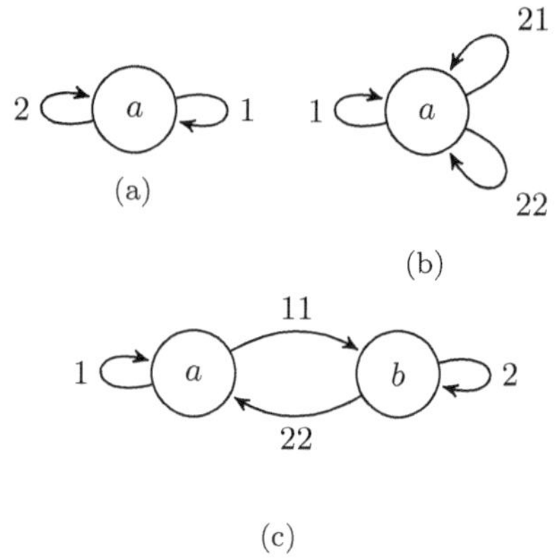

Figure 2: The graphs on Figure 2a and 2b are both path-complete, but the graph on Figure 2c is not as there are no paths containing the finite sequence 1212.

It is shown in [1, Theorem 2.4] that a Path-Complete Lyapunov function is indeed a sufficient stability certificate for a switching system[4]. Interestingly, it was recently shown in [12] that, for linear systems, given a candidate multiple Lyapunov function with quadratic pieces $(V_i)_{i=1,\dots,N}$ and with Lyapunov inequalities encoded by a graph $\mathbf{G}$, we cannot conclude stability *unless* $\mathbf{G}$ is path-complete.
In this paper we first ask a natural question which aims at revealing the connection to classic Lyapunov theory: *Can we extract a Common Lyapunov function for the system (1) from a Path-Complete Lyapunov function*? We answer this question affirmatively in Section 3, and show that we can always extract a Lyapunov function which is of the form

$$V(x) = \min_{S_1,\dots,S_k \subseteq S} \left(\max_{s \in S_i} V_s(x) \right), \quad (4)$$

for some finite integer k. Our proof is constructive and makes use of a classical tool from automata theory, namely the *observer automaton*, to form subsets of nodes in $\mathbf{G}$ that interact in a well defined manner. Next, we show in Subsection 3.2 that the converse does not hold. In detail, we show that there is an asymptotically stable linear system that has a max-of-2-quadratics Lyapunov function, but for which no Path-Complete max-of-2-quadratics Lyapunov function exists. In Section 4 we turn our attention to the problem of deciding a priori when a candidate Path-Complete Lyapunov function provides less conservative stability certificates than another. By analyzing the combinatorial and algebraic structure of the graph and the pieces respectively, we provide tools in Subsections 4.1 and 4.2 to decide when the existence of such a Lyapunov function implies that of another. We illustrate our results numerically in Section 5, and draw the conclusions in Section 6.

[4]While the cited result relates to linear systems and homogeneous Lyapunov functions, it extends directly to the more general setup studied here.

2. PRELIMINARIES

Given any integer $M \geq 1$, we write $[M] = \{1, \ldots, M\}$. For the sake of exposition, the directed graphs $\mathbf{G} = (S, E)$ considered herein have the following property: the labels on their edges are of length 1, i.e., for $(i, j, w) \in E$, $w \in [M]$ (which is not the case, e.g. for the graph of Figure 2b). It is easy to extend our results to the more general case (see Remark 2).
We use several tools and concepts from *Automata theory* (see e.g. [6, Chapter 2]).

DEFINITION 3. *(Connected graph) The graph $G = (S, E)$ is strongly connected if for all pairs $p, q \in S$, there is a directed path from p to q.*

DEFINITION 4 ((CO)-DETERMINISTIC GRAPH).
A graph $G = (S, E)$ is deterministic *if for all $s \in S$, and all $\sigma \in [M]$, there is* at most one *edge $(s, q, \sigma) \in E$.*
The graph is co-deterministic *if for all $q \in S$, and all $\sigma \in [M]$, there is at most one edge $(s, q, \sigma) \in E$.*

DEFINITION 5 ((CO)-COMPLETE GRAPH).
A graph $G = (S, E)$ is complete *if for all $s \in S$, for all $\sigma \in [M]$ there exists* at least one *edge $(s, q, \sigma) \in E$.*
The graph is co-complete *if for all $q \in S$, for all $\sigma \in [M]$, there exists at least one edge $(s, q, \sigma) \in E$.*

A (co)-complete graph is also path-complete [1, Proposition 3.3]. The following allows us to dissociate the graph of a Path-Complete Lyapunov function from its pieces:

DEFINITION 6. *Given a system* (1)*, a graph $\mathbf{G} = (S, E)$ and a set of functions $\mathcal{V} = (V_s)_{s \in S}$, we say that $\mathcal{V}$ is a* solution *for $\mathbf{G}$, or equivalently, $\mathbf{G}$ is feasible for $\mathcal{V}$, if for all $(p, q, \sigma) \in E$, $V_q(f_\sigma(x)) \leq V_p(x)$.*

Whenever clear from the context, we will make all references to the system (1) implicit.

3. INDUCED COMMON LYAPUNOV FUNCTIONS

As defined in the introduction, a Path-Complete Lyapunov function is a type of multiple Lyapunov function with a path-complete graph $\mathbf{G} = (S, E)$ describing Lyapunov inequalities of the form (3) between its pieces $(V_s)_{s \in S}$.
In this section, we show that we can always extract from a Path-Complete Lyapunov function an *induced common Lyapunov function* $V(x)$ for the system, that satisfies

$$\forall x \in \mathbb{R}^n, \forall \sigma \in [M], V(f_\sigma(x)) \leq V(x).$$

To do so, we use the concept of *observer automaton* [6, Section 2.3.4], adapted from general automata to directed and labeled graphs (see Remark 1). The *observer graph* is defined as follows, and its construction is illustrated in Example 1.

DEFINITION 7 (OBSERVER GRAPH). *Consider a graph $\mathbf{G} = (S, E)$. The* observer *graph $O(\mathbf{G}) = (S_O, E_O)$ is a graph where each state corresponds to a subset of S, i.e. $S_O \subseteq 2^S$, and is constructed as follows:*

1. *Let $S_O := \{S\}$ and $E_O := \emptyset$.*
2. *Let $X := \emptyset$. For each pair $(P, \sigma) \in S_O \times [M]$:*
   (a) Compute $Q := \bigcup_{p \in P} \{q | (p, q, \sigma) \in E\}$.
   (b) If $Q \neq \emptyset$, set $E_O := E_O \cup \{(P, Q, \sigma)\}$ then $X := X \cup Q$.
3. *If $X \subseteq S_O$, then the observer is given by $O(\mathbf{G}) = (S_O, E_O)$. Else, let $S_O := S_O \cup X$ and go to step 2.*

We stress that the nodes of the observer graph $O(\mathbf{G})$ correspond to *sets of nodes* of the graph $\mathbf{G}$.

EXAMPLE 1. *Consider the graph $\mathbf{G}$ of Figure 3. The*

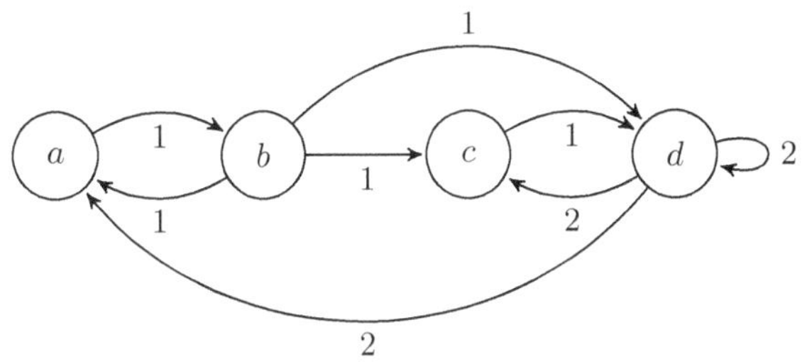

Figure 3: A path-complete graph on 4 nodes a,b,c,d and 2 modes, for Example 1.

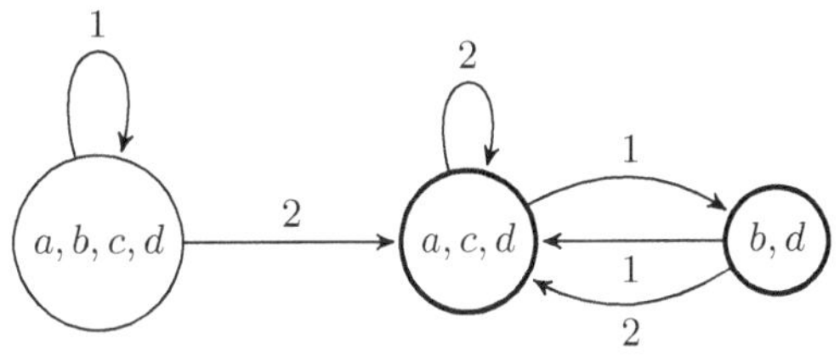

Figure 4: Observer graph constructed from the graph $\mathbf{G}$ on Figure 3. Each node of the observer $O(\mathbf{G})$ is associated to a set of nodes of $\mathbf{G}$. Notice that the subgraph on the nodes $\{a, c, d\}$, $\{b, d\}$ is itself a *complete* graph.

observer graph $O(\mathbf{G})$ is given on Figure 4. The first run through step 2 in Definition 7 is as follows. We have $P = S$. For $\sigma = 1$ the set Q is again S itself: indeed, each node $s \in S$ has at least one inbound edge with the label 1. For $\sigma = 2$, since node b has no inbound edge labeled 2, we get $Q = \{a, c, d\}$. This set is then added to S_O in step 3, and the algorithm repeats step 2 with the updated S_O.

REMARK 1. *The* observer automaton *is presented in [6, Section 2.3.4]. Generally, an automaton is represented by a directed labeled graph with a* start state *and one or more* accepting *states. The graphs considered here can be easily transformed into non-deterministic automata by using the so-called ϵ-transitions (see [6, Section 2.2.4] for definitions). Given a graph $\mathbf{G} = (S, E)$, one can add ϵ-transitions from a new node "a" to all node in S and from all nodes in S to a new node "b". The automaton we obtain has the node "a" as the start state and the node "b" as the (single) accepting state. If we then construct the observer automaton, we obtain the observer graph of Definition 7, where all states are accepting, and $S \in S_O$ is the start state.*

Observe that in Figure 4 the subgraph of $O(\mathbf{G})$ with two nodes $\{a, c, d\}$ and $\{b, d\}$ is complete and strongly connected. This is due to a key property of the observer graph. We suspect that this property is known (maybe in the automata theory literature) but we have not been able to find a reference.

LEMMA 1. *The observer graph $O(\mathbf{G}) = (S_O, E_O)$ of any path-complete graph $\mathbf{G} = (S, E)$ contains a* unique *sub-graph $O^\star(\mathbf{G}) = (S_O^\star, E_O^\star)$ which is* strongly connected, deterministic and complete.

PROOF. The fact that the observer automaton has a complete, deterministic, connected component is well known [6, p.90]. From Remark 1, the result extends as well to the observer graph.
We prove that this component is unique. For the sake of contradiction, we assume that the observer graph has two complete and deterministic connected components $\mathbf{G}_1 = (S_{O,1}, E_{O,1})$ and $\mathbf{G}_2 = (S_{O,2}, E_{O,2})$. Each component is itself a path-complete graph. Moreover, since they are deterministic and complete, there can never be a path from one component to another.

For any sequence w of elements in $[M]$, there exists a *unique* path in $O(\mathbf{G})$ with source $S \in S_O$ and label w. Since $\mathbf{G}_1$, $\mathbf{G}_2$ are in $O(\mathbf{G})$, then by construction, there exist two sequences w_1 and w_2 such that there is a path from $S \in S_O$ with label w_1 that ends in a node in $\mathbf{G}_1$ and a path with label w_2 that ends in a node in $\mathbf{G}_2$.

We now consider two paths of infinite length which start from $S \in S_O$. The first has the label $w_1 w_2 w_1 \ldots$, illustrated below,

$$S \to_{w_1} P^1 \to_{w_2} Q^1 \to_{w_1} P^2 \to_{w_2} Q^2 \cdots$$

and visits the nodes $P^i \in S_{O,1}$ and $Q^i \in S_{O,1}$ after the *ith* occurrence of the sequences w_1 and w_2 respectively. The second path has the label $w_2 w_1 w_2 \ldots$, illustrated below,

$$S \to_{w_2} R^1 \to_{w_1} T^1 \to_{w_2} R^2 \to_{w_2} T^2 \cdots$$

and visits $R^i \in S_{O,2}$ and $T^i \in S_{O,2}$ after the i-th occurrence of the word w_2 and w_1 respectively.

Since $\mathbf{G}_1$ and $\mathbf{G}_2$ are disconnected, we know that $S \neq P^i \neq T^i$ and $S \neq Q^i \neq R^i$. Thus, $P^1 \subset S$ which in turn implies $Q^1 \subset R^1$, $P^2 \subset T^1$ and so on. More generally, for all i, it holds that $Q^i \subset R^i$ and $P^{i+1} \subset T^i$ for all i. By symmetry, we have that $T^i \subset P^i$ and $R^{i+1} \subset Q^i$. Consequently, we observe that[5] $|P^{i+1}| \leq |P^i| - 2$, thus, necessarily, $|P^{|S|-1}| = 0$, which is a contradiction since $O(\mathbf{G})$ by construction cannot have empty nodes. Thus, $O(\mathbf{G})$ has a unique, strongly connected, deterministic and complete sub-graph.n □

We are now in position to introduce our main result.

THEOREM 1 (INDUCED COMMON LYAPUNOV FUNCTION). *Consider Path-Complete Lyapunov function with graph $\mathbf{G} = (S, E)$ and pieces $\mathcal{V} = (V_s)_{s \in S}$ for the system (1). Let $O^\star(\mathbf{G}) = (S_O^\star, E_O^\star)$ be the complete and connected sub-graph of the observer $O(\mathbf{G})$. Then, the function*

$$V(x) = \min_{Q \in S_O^\star} \left(\max_{s \in Q} V_s(x) \right) \tag{5}$$

is a Common Lyapunov function *for the system* (1).

[5]We denote the cardinality of a discrete set P by $|P|$.

The result is illustrated in the following example, and its proof is provided in Subsection 3.1.

EXAMPLE 2. *Consider the graph $\mathbf{G}$ of Figure 3 and its observer graph in Figure 4. For this observer graph, the unique, strongly connected, deterministic and complete component $O^\star(\mathbf{G}) = (S_O^\star, E_O^\star)$ has $S_O^\star = \{\{a, c, d\}, \{b, d\}\}$. Thus, if $\mathbf{G}$ is feasible for a set of functions $\mathcal{V} = \{V_a, V_b, V_c, V_d\}$, from Theorem 1, we conclude that*

$$V(x) = \min \{\max (V_a(x), V_c(x), V_d(x)), \max (V_b(x), V_d(x))\} \tag{6}$$

is a Common Lyapunov function. Figure 5a presents an example of the level sets of such a function (6) when each piece is a quadratic function. Note that this level set is not convex, which shows the expressive power of path-complete criteria. A geometric illustration of the Lyapunov inequalities inferred by the graph $\mathbf{G}$, and in particular the effect of mode f_1 and that $V(f_1(x)) \leq V(x)$, is presented in Figure 5b. Note that these figures do not necessarily match a system, their purpose is illustrative.

3.1 Existence of an induced Common Lyapunov Function

In order to extract a common Lyapunov function from a Path-Complete one, we investigate its graph to highlight new Lyapunov valid inequalities. The following results expose relations between subsets of states of a graph $\mathbf{G} = (S, E)$ that lead to Lyapunov inequalities between the corresponding subsets of pieces of a Path-Complete Lyapunov function. These intermediate results are central to the proof of Theorem 1.

PROPOSITION 1. *Consider the system* (1) *and a graph $\mathbf{G} = (S, E)$ which is feasible for a set of functions $(V_s)_{s \in S}$. Take two subsets P and Q of S. If there is a label σ such that*

$$\forall p \in P, \exists q \in Q : (p, q, \sigma) \in E, \tag{7}$$

then

$$\min_{q \in Q} V_q(f_\sigma(x)) \leq \min_{p \in P} V_p(x).$$

PROOF. Take any $x \in \mathbb{R}^n$. There exists a node $p^\star \in P$ such that $\min_{p \in P} V_p(x) = V_{p^\star}(x)$. Also, there is at least one edge $(p^\star, q^\star, \sigma) \in E$, with $q^\star \in Q$. Thus, $V_{q^\star}(f_\sigma(x)) \leq V_{p^\star}(x)$ and taking into account that $\min_{q \in Q} V_q(f_\sigma(x)) \leq V_{q^\star}(f_\sigma(x))$ the result follows. □

Proposition 1 generalizes the following result, first stated in [1, Corollary 3.4].

COROLLARY 1. *If $\mathbf{G} = (S, E)$ is* complete *and feasible for a set $(V_s)_{s \in S}$, then $\min_{s \in S} V_s(x)$ is a common Lyapunov function for the system (1).*

PROOF. Proposition 1 holds here for $P = Q = S$, and all modes $\sigma \in [M]$. □

PROPOSITION 2. *Consider the system* (1) *and a graph $\mathbf{G} = (S, E)$ which is feasible for a set of functions $(V_s)_{s \in S}$. Take two sets of nodes P and Q. If there is a label σ such that,*

$$\forall q \in Q, \exists p \in P : (p, q, \sigma) \in E, \tag{8}$$

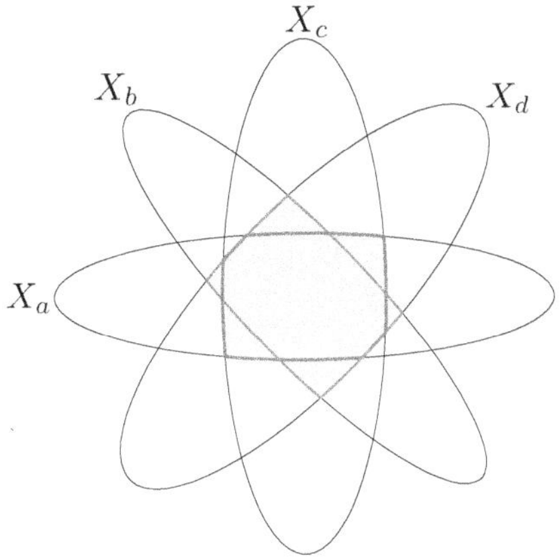

(a) A graphical illustration of the level set of V at Eq. (6) in Example Example 2. The unit sublevel sets X_s, $s \in \{a, b, c, d\}$ of the functions $(V_s)_{s \in S}$ are ellipsoids. The level set of $V(x)$ is the union of two sets: the set $X_a \cap X_c \cap X_d$ (in blue) and the set $X_b \cap X_d$ (in orange).

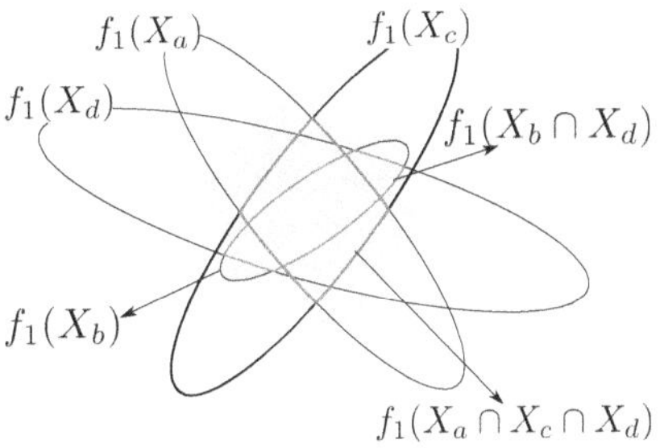

(b) A graphical illustration of the Lyapunov inequalities for Example 2. Let $(X_s)_{s \in S}$, the level sets of the functions $(V_s)_{s \in S}$ be such as in Figure 5a. The image of the set X_s set through f_1 is $f_1(X_s) = \{f_1(x),\, x \in X_s\}$. From an edge $(s, d, 1) \in E$ of the graph $\mathbf{G}$, we can infer that $f_1(X_s) \subseteq X_d$ since $V_s(x) \geq V_d(f_1(x))$. We can infer more refined relations by taking several edges. For example, from the edges $(b, a, 1)$, $(b, c, 1)$, and $(b, d, 1)$, we infer that $f_1(X_b) \subseteq X_a \cap X_c \cap X_d$. Taking all edges of the form $(s, d, 1)$ into account, we observe that the level set of $V(x)$ (in gray) at Eq. (4) is mapped into itself through f_1.

Figure 5: Illustrations for Example 2.

then

$$\max_{q \in Q} V_q(f_\sigma(x)) \leq \max_{p \in P} V_p(x).$$

PROOF. Take any $x \in \mathbb{R}^n$. There exists a node $q^\star \in Q$ such that $\max_{q \in Q} V_q(f_\sigma(x)) = V_{q^\star}(f_\sigma(x))$. Also, since there exists a node $p^\star \in P$ such that $(p^\star, q^\star, \sigma) \in E$, it holds that $V_{q^\star}(f_\sigma(x)) \leq V_{p^\star}(x) \leq \max_{p \in P} V_p(x)$ and the result follows. $\square$

Proposition 2 generalizes the following result, first stated in [1, Corollary 3.5].

COROLLARY 2. *If* $\mathbf{G} = (S, E)$ *is* co-complete *and feasible for a set* $(V_s)_{s \in S}$, *then* $\max_{s \in S} V_s(x)$ *is a common Lyapunov function for the system.*

PROOF. Proposition 2 holds here for $P = Q = S$, and all modes $\sigma \in [M]$. $\square$

We are in the position to prove Theorem 1.

PROOF PROOF OF THEOREM 1. Take a Path-Complete Lyapunov function with a graph $\mathbf{G} = (S, E)$ and pieces $(V_s)_{s \in S}$. Then, construct the *observer graph* $O(\mathbf{G}) = (S_O, E_O)$. By definition, there is an edge $(P, Q, \sigma) \in E_O$ if and only if $Q = \cup_{p \in P}\{q | (p, q, \sigma) \in E\}$, and therefore, the following property holds for such edges: $\forall q \in Q$, $\exists p \in P$ such that $(p, q, \sigma) \in E$. Consequently, from Proposition 2, we have that

$$(P, Q, \sigma) \in E_O \Rightarrow \max_{q \in Q} V_q(f_\sigma(x)) \leq \max_{p \in P} V_p(x).$$

Therefore, the graph $O(\mathbf{G})$ is *feasible* for the set of functions $\mathcal{W} = \{W_P(x)\}_{P \in S_O}$, where

$$W_P(x) = \max_{p \in P} V_p(x), \quad \forall P \in S_O.$$

From Lemma 1, there exists a sub-graph $O^\star(\mathbf{G}) = (S_O^\star, E_O^\star)$ of $O(\mathbf{G})$ (with $S_O^\star \subseteq S_O$) which is complete and strongly connected. Since $O(\mathbf{G})$ is feasible for $\mathcal{W}$, its subgraph $O^\star(\mathbf{G})$ is feasible for the $\{W_P\}_{P \in S_O^\star}$. Finally, since by Lemma 1 $O^\star(\mathbf{G})$ is complete, we apply Corollary 1 and deduce that the function $W(x) = \min_{P \in S_O^\star} W_P(x)$ is a common Lyapunov function for the system. $\square$

REMARK 2. *Our results extend to graphs* $\mathbf{G} = (S, E)$ *where the labels are finite sequences of elements in* $[M]$ *(e.g., as in Figure 2b, 2c) as follows. One can apply the results on the so-called* expanded form *of these graphs [1, Definition 2.1]. The idea there is the following: if an edge* $(p, q, w) \in E$ *has a label* $w = \sigma_1, \ldots, \sigma_k$ *of length* $k \geq 2$, *then it is replaced by a path of length* k, $(s_i, s_{i+1}, \sigma_i)_{i=1,\ldots,k}$ *where* $\sigma_1 = p$, $\sigma_{k+1} = q$, *by adding the nodes* $s_2, \ldots, s_k$ *to the graph. The expanded form is obtained by repeating the process until all labels in the graph are of size 1 (see Figure 6).*

If the graph $\mathbf{G} = (S, E)$ *is feasible for a set* $\mathcal{V}$, *we can always construct a set of functions* $\mathcal{W}$ *such that the expanded graph* $\mathbf{G}_e = (S_e, E_e)$ *of* $\mathbf{G}$ *is feasible for* $\mathcal{W}$. *For example, for a path* $(s_i, s_{i+1}, \sigma_i)_{i=1,\ldots,k}$ *in the expanded form corresponding to an edge* (p, q, w) *in* $\mathbf{G}$ *with* $w = \sigma_1 \ldots \sigma_k$, *we set* $W_p = V_p$, $W_q = V_q$, *and* $W_{s_i}(x) = V_j(f_{\sigma_{i+1} \ldots \sigma_k}(x))$. *In Figure 6, we would have* $W_{s_2}(x) = V_j(f_{\sigma_2}(x))$.

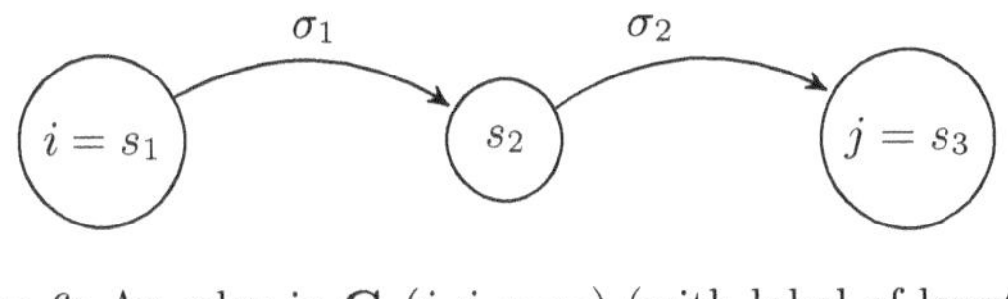

Figure 6: An edge in $\mathbf{G}$ $(i, j, \sigma_1\sigma_2)$ (with label of length 2), is replaced by a path of length 2 in the extended form.

REMARK 3. *We can establish a* 'dual' *version of the Theorem 1. In specific, given the graph* $\mathbf{G}$, *we reverse the direction of the edges obtaining a graph* $\mathbf{G}^\top$, *construct its observer* $O(\mathbf{G}^\top)$ *and reverse the direction of its edges again, obtaining a graph* $O(\mathbf{G}^\top)^\top$. *This graph is co-deterministic and contains a unique, strongly-connected, co-complete subgraph that induces a Lyapunov function of the form*

$$V(x) = \max_{S_1, \ldots, S_k \subseteq S} \left(\min_{s \in S_i} V_s(x) \right),$$

which is, in general, not *equal to the common Lyapunov function obtained through Theorem 1.*

3.2 The converse does not hold

In this subsection we investigate whether or not *any* Lyapunov function of the form (4) can be induced from a path-complete graph with as many nodes as the number of pieces of the function itself. We give a negative answer to this question by providing a counter example from [9, Example 11]. Consider the discrete-time linear switching system on two modes $x(t+1) = A_{\sigma(t)}x(t)$ with

$$A_1 = \begin{pmatrix} 0.3 & 1 & 0 \\ 0 & 0.6 & 1 \\ 0 & 0 & 0.7 \end{pmatrix}, A_2 = \begin{pmatrix} 0.3 & 0 & 0 \\ -0.5 & 0.7 & 0 \\ -0.2 & -0.5 & 0.7 \end{pmatrix}. \quad (9)$$

The system has a max-of-quadratics Lyapunov function $V(x) = \max\{V_1(x), V_2(x)\}$, with $V_i(x) = (x^\top Q_i x)$, Q_i being positive definite matrices. An explicit Lyapunov function is given by[6]

$$Q_1 = \begin{pmatrix} 36.95 & -36.91 & -5.58 \\ \cdot & 84.11 & -38.47 \\ \cdot & \cdot & 49.32 \end{pmatrix},$$

$$Q_2 = \begin{pmatrix} 13.80 & -6.69 & 4.80 \\ \cdot & 21.87 & 10.11 \\ \cdot & \cdot & 82.74 \end{pmatrix}.$$

We first observe that these quadratic functions cannot be the solution of a path-complete stability criterion for our example. Indeed, let us draw the graph of all the valid Lyapunov inequalities. More precisely, we define the graph $\mathbf{G} = (\{1, 2\}, E)$ with two nodes and

$$(i, j, \sigma) \in E \Leftrightarrow A_\sigma^\top Q_j A_\sigma - Q_i \preceq 0, \quad (10)$$

i.e. the matrix $A_\sigma^\top Q_j A_\sigma - Q_i$ is negative semi-definite. The graph obtained is presented on Figure 7. This graph is not path-complete, and thus we cannot form a Common Lyapunov Function, as done in the previous section, with these two particular pieces.

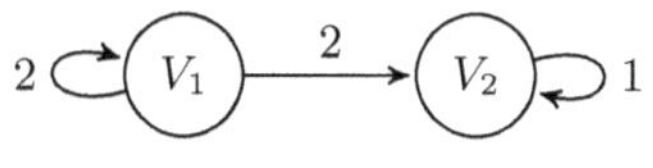

Figure 7: The valid Lyapunov inequalities for the quadratic functions for the system and the Lyapunov function in [9, Example 11] are represented by the graph above. The graph is not path complete.

However, we can go further and investigate whether *another* pair of quadratic functions would exist, which we could find by solving a path-complete criterion, and such that their maximum would be a valid CLF. Recall that co-complete graphs induce Lyapunov functions of the form $\max_{v \in S} V_v(x)$ (see Corollary 2).

PROPOSITION 3. *Consider the discrete-time linear system with two modes (9). The system does not have a Path-Complete Lyapunov function with quadratic pieces defined on co-complete graphs with 2 nodes.*

PROOF. From Definition 5, there is a total of 16 graphs that are co-complete and consist of two nodes and four edges (1 edge per mode and per state). We do not examine co-complete graphs with more than four edges since satisfaction of the Lyapunov conditions for these graphs would imply that of the conditions for at least one graph with four edges. For each graph, the existence of a feasible set of quadratic functions can be tested by solving the LMIs (10).
For the system under consideration, none of the 16 sets of LMIs have a solution. Thus, no induced Lyapunov function of the type $\max\{V_1(x), V_2(x)\}$ exists. □

REMARK 4. *In fact, for the Proof of Proposition 3, we need only to test four graphs. Three are co-complete with two nodes:*

$$G_1 = (\{a, b\}, \{(a, a, 1), (a, b, 1), (b, a, 2), (b, b, 2)\}),$$
$$G_2 = (\{a, b\}, \{(a, a, 1), (a, b, 1), (a, b, 2), (b, a, 2)\}),$$
$$G_3 = (\{a, b\}, \{(a, a, 2), (a, b, 1), (a, b, 2), (b, a, 1)\}),$$

and the last one corresponds to the common quadratic Lyapunov function

$$G_4 = (\{a\}, \{(a, a, 1), (a, a, 2)\}).$$

One can show that each one of the 13 *remaining co-complete graph is equivalent to one of these four graphs (either isomorphic, or satisfying the conditions of Corollary 3 which will be presented later).*

REMARK 5. *For linear systems and for the assessment of asymptotic stability, Path-Complete Lyapunov functions have been shown to be* universal. *In particular, [15] show this for the so-called Path-Dependent Lyapunov functions, which are Path-Complete Lyapunov functions with a particular choice of complete graphs, specifically, the so-called* De Bruijn *graphs. The system concerned by Proposition 3 is actually asymptotically stable (see [9]). The interest of Proposition 3 lies in the fact that there do not exist necessarily Path-Complete Lyapunov functions with* the same number of pieces *as a* max-*type common Lyapunov function. This is a limitation imposed by the combinatorial structure of the Path-Complete Lyapunov function.*

The proof of Proposition 3 highlights an interesting fact. Several different path-complete graphs may induce the same common Lyapunov function (4). However, the strength of the stability certificate they provide may differ. This has a practical implication: if we are given a system of the form (1), it is unclear which graph $\mathbf{G}$ we should use to form a Path-Complete Lyapunov function for some number of pieces satisfying a given template (e.g., quadratic functions). We present, in Section 4, a first attempt for analyzing the relative strength of Path-Complete Lyapunov functions based on their graphs and the algebraic properties of the set of functions defining their pieces.

4. PARTIAL ORDER ON PATH-COMPLETE GRAPHS

We now provide tools for establishing an *ordering* between Lyapunov functions defined on general path-complete graphs, extending the work of [1, Section 4.2] on *complete* graphs. In the following definition, we introduce $\mathcal{U}$ as a *template* or *family* of functions to which the pieces of Path-Complete Lyapunov functions belong. For example, $\mathcal{U}$ could be the set of quadratic functions: $\mathcal{U} = \{x \mapsto x^\top Qx, Q \succ 0\}$. We assume that (2) holds for any finite subset of $\mathcal{U}$.

[6]Such a function can be found numerically by solving the inequalities of [9, Section 5] for a choice of $\lambda_{:,:,1} = \left(\begin{smallmatrix} .627 & 0 \\ 1 & 1 \end{smallmatrix}\right)$.

Definition 8. *(Ordering). For two path-complete graphs* $\mathbf{G}_1 = (S_1, E_1)$, $\mathbf{G}_2 = (S_2, E_2)$ *and a template* $\mathcal{U}$, *we write* $\mathbf{G}_1 \leq_{\mathcal{U}} \mathbf{G}_2$ *if the existence of a Path-Complete Lyapunov function on the graph* $\mathbf{G}_1$ *with pieces* $(V_s)_{s \in S_1}$, $V_s \in \mathcal{U}$ *implies that of a Path-Complete Lyapunov function on the graph* $\mathbf{G}_2$ *with pieces* $(W_s)_{s \in S_2}$, $W_s \in \mathcal{U}$.

For each family of functions $\mathcal{U}$, this defines a partial order on path-complete graphs. A minimal element of the ordering, independent of the choice of $\mathcal{U}$, is given by (see Figure 2a)

$$\mathbf{G}^{\star} = (\{a\}, \{(a, a, \sigma)_{\sigma \in [M]}\}). \tag{11}$$

A Path-Complete Lyapunov function on this graph corresponds to the existence of a common Lyapunov function from $\mathcal{U}$ for the system. Thus, $\mathbf{G}^{*} \leq_{\mathcal{U}} \mathbf{G}$ for any $\mathcal{U}$.

Remark 6. *We highlight that the properties of the set* $\mathcal{U}$ *influence the ordering relation defined in Definition 8. For example, if* $\mathcal{U}$ *is a singleton, then it is not difficult to see that* $\mathbf{G}_1 \leq_{\mathcal{U}} \mathbf{G}_2$ *for any two path-complete graphs. From Theorem 1, one can show that this holds as well for a set* $\mathcal{U}$ *closed under* min *and* max *operations.*

4.1 Bijections between sets of states

We present a sufficient condition under which a graph $\mathbf{G}$ satisfies $\mathbf{G} \leq_{\mathcal{U}} \mathbf{G}^{\star}$. It is similar in nature to those of Subsection 3.1, and requires as well that the set $\mathcal{U}$ is *closed under addition*, an algebraic property satisfied, e.g., by the set of quadratic functions.

Proposition 4 (Bijection). *Consider a graph* $\mathbf{G} = (S, E)$ *feasible for a set of functions* $(V_s)_{s \in S}$. *Take two subsets* P *and* Q *of* S. *If for* $\sigma \in [M]$, *there is a subset* E' *of* E *such that,*

$$\forall p \in P, \exists!\, q \in Q : (p, q, \sigma) \in E',$$
$$\forall q \in Q, \exists!\, p \in P : (p, q, \sigma) \in E',$$

then

$$\sum_{q \in Q} V_q(f_\sigma(x)) \leq \sum_{p \in P} V_p(x),\ \forall x \in \mathbb{R}^n.$$

Proof. The result is obtained by first enumerating the $|P| = |Q|$ Lyapunov inequalities encoded in E', and then summing them up. □

Example 3. *Consider the graphs* $\mathbf{G}_1 = (S_1, E_1)$ *and* $\mathbf{G}_2 = (S_2, E_2)$ *of Figure 8a and 8b respectively.*
Observe that in $\mathbf{G}_1$, *if we take the two subsets of nodes* $R_1 = \{a, b\}$ *and* $R_2 = \{a, c\}$, *then we have that Proposition 4 holds for* $P = Q = R_1$ *and* $\sigma = 1$; $P = Q = R_2$ *and* $\sigma = 2$; $P = R_1, Q = R_2$ *and* $\sigma = 1$; *and* $P = R_2, Q = R_1$ *and* $\sigma = 2$.
Putting together these new Lyapunov inequalities, this allows us to conclude that if $\{V_a, V_b, V_c\}$ *is a solution for* $\mathbf{G}_1$, *then* $W_{a'} = V_a + V_b$ *and* $W_{b'} = V_a + V_c$ *is a solution for* $\mathbf{G}_2$. *Thus, if* $\mathcal{U}$ *is closed under addition, then it follows that* $\mathbf{G}_1 \leq_{\mathcal{U}} \mathbf{G}_2$.

Corollary 3. *For a graph* $\mathbf{G} = (S, E)$, *if for all* $\sigma \in [M]$, *there exists a subset* $E_\sigma \subset E$ *such that*

$$\forall p \in S, \exists!\, q \in S : (p, q, \sigma) \in E_\sigma,$$
$$\forall q \in S, \exists!\, p \in S : (p, q, \sigma) \in E_\sigma,$$

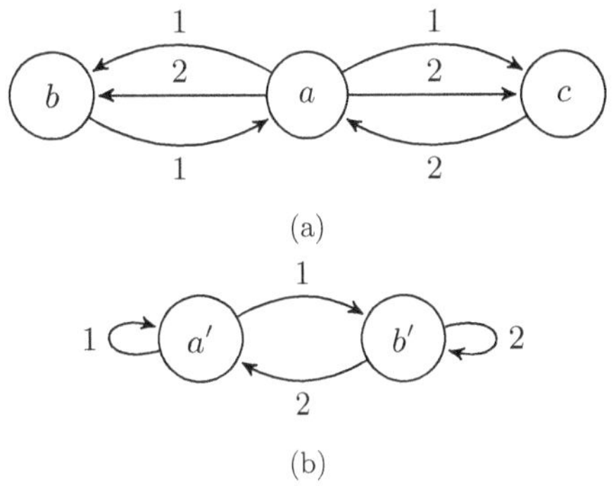

Figure 8: Example 4.1, the graph $\mathbf{G}_1$ (8a) and the graph $\mathbf{G}_2$ (8b).

then if $\mathbf{G}$ *is feasible for* $(V_s)_{s \in S}$, *the sum* $\sum_{s \in S} V_s$ *is a common Lyapunov function for the system.*

Proof. Proposition 4 holds for $P = Q = S$ and all $\sigma \in [M]$. □

Example 4. *Consider the graph* $\mathbf{G}$ *of Figure 9 on four nodes and two modes. If* $\mathbf{G}$ *is feasible for a set* $\{V_a, V_b, V_c, V_d\}$, *then the system has a common Lyapunov function given by* $V_a + V_b + V_c + V_d$.

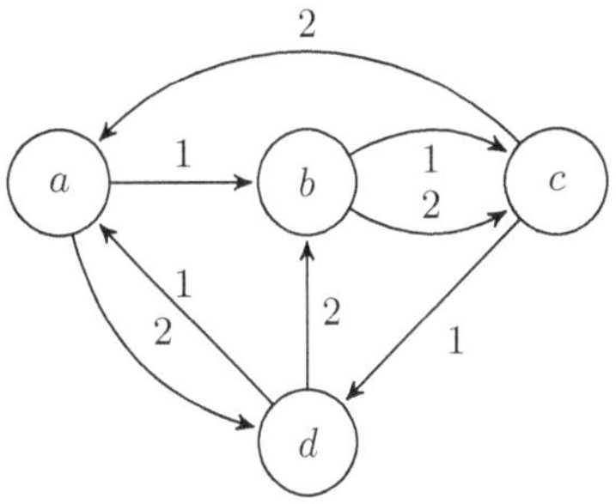

Figure 9: A graph $\mathbf{G}$ whose feasibility implies that of $\mathbf{G}^{\star}$ (Example 4).

If e.g. $\mathcal{U}$ *is the set of quadratic functions, then* $\mathbf{G} \leq_{\mathcal{U}} \mathbf{G}^{\star}$.

4.2 Ordering by simulation

This next criterion for ordering is actually independent of the choice of $\mathcal{U}$. It is inspired by the concept of *simulation* between two automata [6, pp. 91–92].

Definition 9. *(Simulation) Consider two path-complete graphs* $\mathbf{G}_1 = (S_1, E_1)$ *and* $\mathbf{G}_2 = (S_2, E_2)$ *with a same labels* $[M]$. *We say that* $\mathbf{G}_1$ simulates $\mathbf{G}_2$ *if there exists a function* $F(\cdot) : S_2 \to S_1$ *such that for any edge* $(s_2, d_2, \sigma) \in E_2$ *there exists an edge* $(s_1, d_1, \sigma) \in E_1$ *with* $F(s_2) = s_1$, $F(d_2) = d_1$.

Remark 7. *The notion of simulation we use here is actually stronger than the classical one defined for automata, which defines a* relation *between the states of the two automata rather than a* function.

Proposition 5. *Consider two graphs* $\mathbf{G}_1 = (S_1, E_1)$ *and* $\mathbf{G}_2 = (S_2, E_2)$. *If* $\mathbf{G}_1$ *is feasible for* $(V_s)_{s \in S_1}$, *and* $\mathbf{G}_1$ *simulates* $\mathbf{G}_2$ *through the function* $F : S_2 \to S_1$, *then* $\mathbf{G}_2$ *is feasible for* $(W_s)_{s\in S_2}$, *with*

$$W_s = V_{F(s)}, \quad \forall s \in S_2.$$

PROOF. Taking any edge $(s, d, \sigma) \in E_2$, we get

$$W_d(f_\sigma(x)) = V_{F(d)}(f_\sigma(x)) \leq V_{F(s)}(x) = W_s(x).$$

□

EXAMPLE 5. *Consider the graphs on three modes* $\mathbf{G}_1 = (S_1, E_1)$ *and* $\mathbf{G}_2 = (S_2, E_2)$ *on three modes with the first depicted on Fig. 10a and the second on Fig. 10b. Proposition 5 applies here with* $F(\cdot) : S_2 \to S_1$ *defined as* $F(a') = a$, $F(b_1') = F(b_2') = b$, $F(c') = c$.

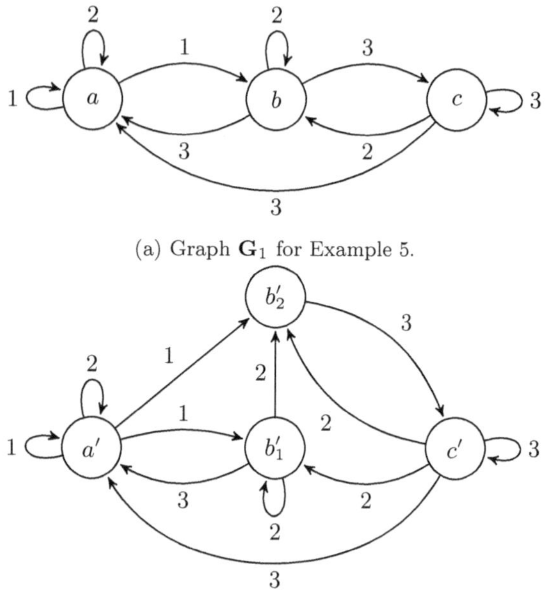

(a) Graph $\mathbf{G}_1$ for Example 5.

(b) Graph $\mathbf{G}_2$ for Example 5.

Figure 10: $\mathbf{G}_1$ simulates $\mathbf{G}_2$.

5. EXAMPLE AND EXPERIMENT

In this section, we provide an illustration of our results. First, we present a practically motivated example, where we extract a common Lyapunov function from a Path-Complete Lyapunov function for a given discrete-time linear switching systems on three modes. We next present a numerical experiment comparing the performance of three particular path-complete graphs on a testbench of randomly generated systems, similar to that presented in [1, Section 4].

Our focus is on *linear switching systems*, and Path-Complete Lyapunov functions with *quadratic pieces*. The existence of such Lyapunov functions can then be checked by solving the LMIs (10)[7].

5.1 Extracting a Common Lyapunov function.

The scenario considered here is similar to that of [19, Section 4], and deals with the stability analysis of closed-loop linear time-invariant systems subject to failures in a communication channel of a *networked control system* (see e.g. [13] for more on the topic). We are given a linear-time invariant system of the form

$$x(t+1) = (A + BK)x(t),$$

with

$$A = \begin{pmatrix} 0.97 & 0.58 \\ 0.17 & 0.5 \end{pmatrix}, \; B = \begin{pmatrix} 0 \\ 1 \end{pmatrix}, K = \begin{pmatrix} -0.55, 0.24 \end{pmatrix}.$$

When a communication failure occurs, no signal arrives at the plant, and the control input is automatically set to zero. In this case, the communication channel needs to be fixed before any feedback signal can reach the plant. In order to prevent the impact of failures, periodic inspections of the channel are foreseen every M steps. However, the inspection of the communication channel is costly, and we would like to compute the largest M such that an inspection of the plant at every M steps is sufficient to ensure its stability.
Given $M \geq 1$, we model the failing plant as a switching system with M modes:

$$x(t+M) = \tilde{A}_{\sigma(t)}x(t), \tag{12}$$

where

$$\forall \sigma \in \{1, \ldots, M\}, \tilde{A}_\sigma = A^{\sigma-1}(A + BK)^{M-\sigma+1}.$$

In other words, for $\sigma(t) = k$, the communication channel will function properly from time t up until time $t + (M - k)$ included, and will then be down from time $t + (M - k) + 1$ until time $t + M - 1$ included. This assumes that the channel always functions properly at the very first step after inspection.

For $M = 1$, the stability analysis is direct as $(A + BK)$ is stable. For $M = 2$ we can verify that the system has a *Path-Complete Lyapunov function* for the graph of Figure 8b. The case $M = 4$ is straightforward: the matrix $\tilde{A}_4 = A^3(A + BK)$ is unstable, and thus the system is unstable in view of Definition 1.

For the case when $M = 3$, we verify numerically that the system does not have a common quadratic Lyapunov function. Furthermore, it does not have a Path-Complete Lyapunov function with quadratic pieces for $\mathbf{G}_2$ on four nodes represented at Figure 10b. Note that since $\mathbf{G}_1$ simulates $\mathbf{G}_2$ (see Example 5), this allows us to conclude that $\mathbf{G}_1$ will not provide us with a Path-Complete Lyapunov function as well (that would contradict Proposition 5).

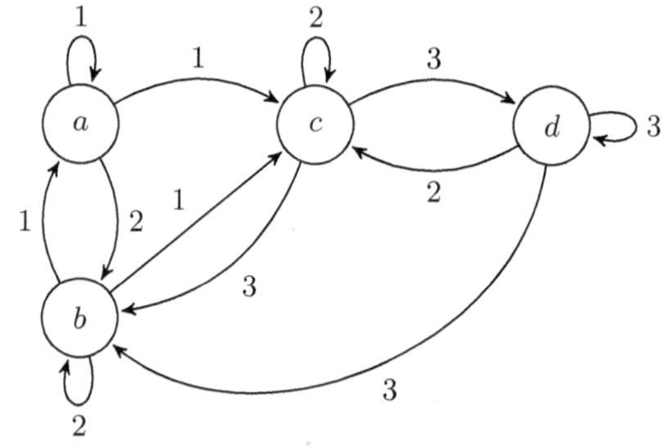

Figure 11: Graph $\mathbf{G}_3$, for the example of Section 5.

However, the graph $\mathbf{G}_3$ on four nodes represented at Figure 11, which alike $\mathbf{G}_2$ is simulated by $\mathbf{G}_1$, does provide us

[7]A Matlab implementation for this example can be found at http://sites.uclouvain.be/scsse/HSCC17_PCLF-AND-CLF.zip.

with a Path-Complete Lyapunov function with four quadratic pieces. By applying Theorem 1, after computing the observer graph of $\mathbf{G}_3$ (see Figure 12), we obtain a common Lyapunov function $V(x)$ of the form (4) for the system,

$$V(x) = \min_{S \in \{\{a,c\},\{b,c\},\{b,d\}\}} \left(\max_{s \in S} V_s(x) \right).$$

whose level set is represented in Figure 13.

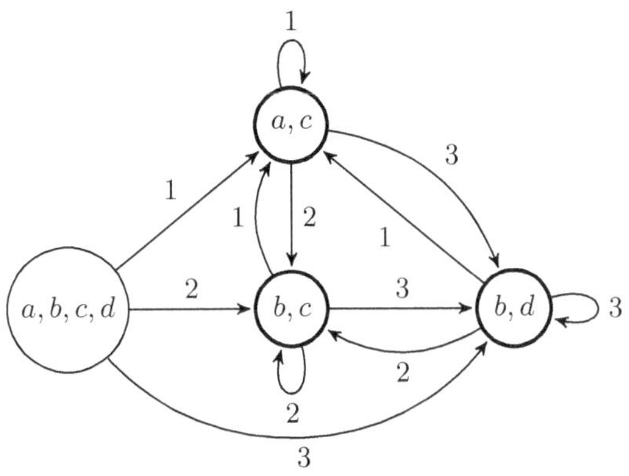

Figure 12: Observer graph for $\mathbf{G}_3$ at Figure 11. The subgraph on the nodes $\{a,c\}$, $\{b,c\}$ and $\{b,d\}$ is complete.

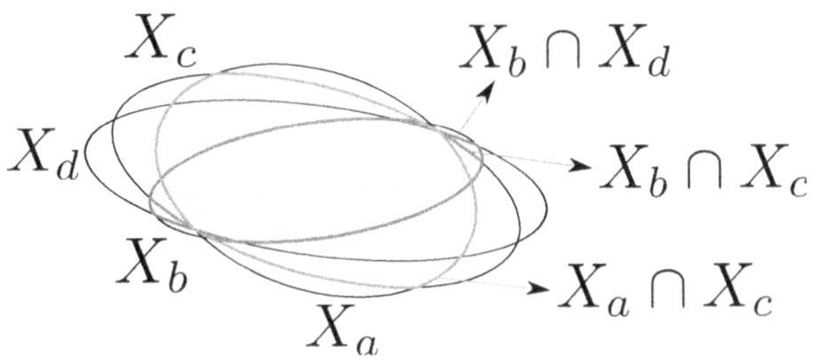

Figure 13: The sets X_a, X_b, X_c and X_d are the level sets of the pieces of the Path-Complete Lyapunov function for the system (12). The grey set is a level set of a Common Lyapunov function for the system, obtained from the Path-Complete Lyapunov function through Theorem 1.

5.2 Numerical experiment.

In Section 5.1 we presented a linear switching system for which a Path-Complete Lyapunov function with quadratic pieces exists for the graph $\mathbf{G}_3$ of Figure 11, but not for $\mathbf{G}_1$ of Figure 10a and $\mathbf{G}_2$ of Figure 10b. However for another system with three modes, it could be $\mathbf{G}_2$ that provides a stability certificate, and not $\mathbf{G}_3$. It is therefore natural to ask which case is the more likely to occur for random systems.

To this purpose[8] we generate triplets of random matrices $M = \{A_1, A_2, A_3\}$[9]. Then, for each triplet and for each

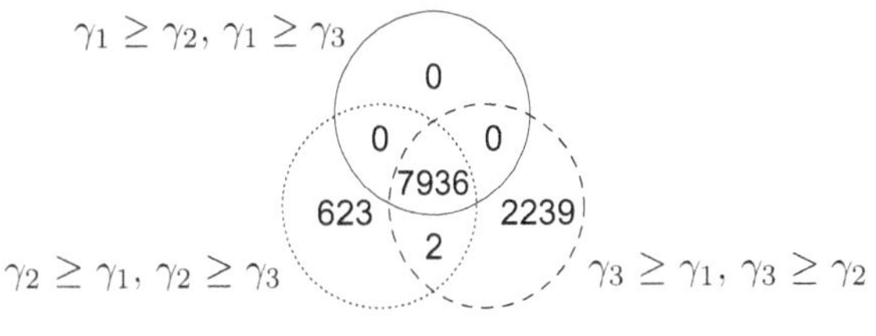

Figure 14: Visualization of the outcome of the numerical experiment. As expected, whenever $\mathbf{G}_1$ provides a stability certificate, so do $\mathbf{G}_2$ and $\mathbf{G}_3$. There are more systems for which $\mathbf{G}_3$ provides a certificate and not $\mathbf{G}_2$ than the reverse. Interestingly, it appears unusual that a system has a stability certificate for $\mathbf{G}_2$ and $\mathbf{G}_3$ but not $\mathbf{G}_1$.

graph $\mathbf{G}_i = (S_i, E_i)$, $i = 1,2,3$, we compute[10] the quantity

$$\gamma_i = \sup_{\gamma,\,(Q_s \succ 0)_{s \in S_i}} \gamma : \begin{cases} \forall (s,d,\sigma) \in E_i, \\ \gamma^2 A_\sigma^\top Q_d A_\sigma - Q_s \preceq 0, \end{cases}$$

that is, the higher number γ such that $\mathbf{G}_i$ provides a stability certificate for the system $x(t+1) = \gamma A_{\sigma(t)} x(t)$, $A_\sigma \in M$. For a given triplet $M = \{A_1, A_2, A_3\}$, the fact that $\gamma_i \geq \gamma_j$, $i \neq j$, translates as follows: whenever $\mathbf{G}_j$ induces a Lyapunov function so does $\mathbf{G}_i$. Note that it is possible that for a triplet M, we get $\gamma_i = \gamma_j$.

The results are presented in the Venn diagram of Figure 14 for 10800 triplets with matrices of dimension $n = 2$.

We observe that the results are in agreement with Proposition 5, when $\mathbf{G}_1$ provides a stability certificate, so do $\mathbf{G}_2$ and $\mathbf{G}_3$. Also, it appears that a random triplet of matrices is more likely to have a Lyapunov function induced by $\mathbf{G}_3$ ($\sim$ 94% of the cases) rather than by $\mathbf{G}_2$ ($\sim$ 79% of the cases). Interestingly, there appear to be very few instances for which $\gamma_2 = \gamma_3 > \gamma_1$, which deserves further attention.

6. CONCLUSION

Path-complete criteria are promising tools for the analysis of hybrid or cyber-physical systems. They encapsulate several powerful and popular techniques for the stability analysis of swiching systems. However, their range of application seems much wider, as for instance 1) they can handle switching nonlinear systems as well, as it is the case herein, 2) they are not limited to LMIs and quadratic pieces and 3) they have been used to analyze systems where the switching signal is constrained [19]. On top of this, we are investigating the possibility of studying other problems than stability analysis with these tools.

However, already for the simplest particular case of multiple quadratic Lyapunov functions for switching linear systems, many questions still need to be clarified. In this paper we first gave a clear interpretation of these criteria in terms of common Lyapunov function: each criterion implies the existence of a common Lyapunov function which can be expressed as the minimum of maxima of sets of functions. We then studied the problem of comparing the (worst-case) performance of these criteria, and provided two results that help to partly understand when one criterion is better than another. We leave open the problem of deciding, given two path-complete graphs, whether one is better than the other.

[8]For a similar study with other graphs, see [1, Section 4].

[9]Each entry of each matrix is the sum of a Gaussian random variable with zero mean and unit variance, and of a uniformly distributed random variable on $[-1, 1]$

[10]This is a quasi-convex optimization program, solved using the numerical tools established in e.g. [1].

References

[1] Amir Ali Ahmadi, Raphaël M Jungers, Pablo A Parrilo, and Mardavij Roozbehani. Joint spectral radius and path-complete graph lyapunov functions. *SIAM Journal on Control and Optimization*, 52(1):687–717, 2014.

[2] Nikolaos Athanasopoulos and Mircea Lazar. Alternative stability conditions for switched discrete time linear systems. In *IFAC World Congress*, pages 6007–6012, 2014.

[3] Pierre-Alexandre Bliman and Giancarlo Ferrari-Trecate. Stability analysis of discrete-time switched systems through lyapunov functions with nonminimal state. In *Proceedings of IFAC Conference on the Analysis and Design of Hybrid Systems*, pages 325–330, 2003.

[4] Vincent D Blondel and John N Tsitsiklis. The boundedness of all products of a pair of matrices is undecidable. *Systems & Control Letters*, 41(2):135–140, 2000.

[5] Michael S Branicky. Multiple lyapunov functions and other analysis tools for switched and hybrid systems. *IEEE Transactions on Automatic Control*, 43(4):475–482, 1998.

[6] Christos G Cassandras and Stephane Lafortune. *Introduction to discrete event systems*. Springer Science & Business Media, 2009.

[7] Jamal Daafouz, Pierre Riedinger, and Claude Iung. Stability analysis and control synthesis for switched systems: a switched lyapunov function approach. *IEEE Transactions on Automatic Control*, 47(11):1883–1887, 2002.

[8] Ray Essick, Ji-Woong Lee, and Geir E Dullerud. Control of linear switched systems with receding horizon modal information. *IEEE Transactions on Automatic Control*, 59(9):2340–2352, 2014.

[9] Rafal Goebel, Tingshu Hu, and Andrew R Teel. Dual matrix inequalities in stability and performance analysis of linear differential/difference inclusions. In *Current trends in nonlinear systems and control*, pages 103–122. Springer, 2006.

[10] Mikael Johansson, Anders Rantzer, et al. Computation of piecewise quadratic lyapunov functions for hybrid systems. *IEEE transactions on automatic control*, 43(4):555–559, 1998.

[11] Raphaël Jungers. The joint spectral radius. *Lecture Notes in Control and Information Sciences*, 385, 2009.

[12] Raphael M Jungers, Amirali Ahmadi, Pablo Parrilo, and Mardavij Roozbehani. A characterization of lyapunov inequalities for stability of switched systems. *arXiv preprint arXiv:1608.08311*, 2016.

[13] Raphael M Jungers, WPMH Heemels, and Atreyee Kundu. Observability and controllability analysis of linear systems subject to data losses. *arXiv preprint arXiv:1609.05840*, 2016.

[14] Victor Kozyakin. The Berger–Wang formula for the markovian joint spectral radius. *Linear Algebra and its Applications*, 448:315–328, 2014.

[15] Ji-Woong Lee and Geir E Dullerud. Uniform stabilization of discrete-time switched and markovian jump linear systems. *Automatica, 42(2), 205-218*, 2006.

[16] Daniel Liberzon and Stephen A Morse. Basic problems in stability and design of switched systems. *IEEE Control Systems Magazine*, 19(5):59–70, 1999.

[17] Hai Lin and Panos J Antsaklis. Stability and stabilizability of switched linear systems: a survey of recent results. *IEEE Transactions on Automatic control*, 54(2):308–322, 2009.

[18] Pablo A Parrilo and Ali Jadbabaie. Approximation of the joint spectral radius using sum of squares. *Linear Algebra and its Applications*, 428(10):2385–2402, 2008.

[19] Matthew Philippe, Ray Essick, Geir Dullerud, and Raphaël M Jungers. Stability of discrete-time switching systems with constrained switching sequences. *Automatica*, 72:242–250, 2016.

[20] Robert Shorten, Fabian Wirth, Oliver Mason, Kai Wulff, and Christopher King. Stability criteria for switched and hybrid systems. *SIAM review*, 49(4):545–592, 2007.

Invariance Feedback Entropy of Nondeterministic Control Systems

Matthias Rungger
Hybrid Control Systems Group
Technical University of Munich
Munich, Germany
matthias.rungger@tum.de

Majid Zamani
Hybrid Control Systems Group
Technical University of Munich
Munich, Germany
zamani@tum.de

ABSTRACT

We introduce a notion of invariance feedback entropy for discrete-time, nondeterministic control systems as a measure of necessary state information to enforce a given subset of the state space to be invariant. We provide conditions that guarantee finiteness and show that the well-known notion of invariance feedback entropy for deterministic systems is recovered in the deterministic case. We establish the data rate theorem which shows that the entropy equals the largest lower bound on the data rate of any coder-controller that achieves invariance. For finite systems, the invariance feedback entropy is characterized by the value function of an appropriately designed mean-payoff game. We use several examples throughout the paper to instantiate the various definitions and results.

1. INTRODUCTION

Networked control systems are spatially distributed systems, where the state information collected by the sensors needs to be send through a digital communication network to the controllers and actuators in order to close the control loop [1]. In this context, one of the most fundamental question is: What is the minimal bit rate of the digital channel between sensor and controller to be able to implement a certain control task? Or equivalently, what state information is required to achieve a given control goal?

For the situation illustrated in Figure 1, in which the state information is encoded at the sensor side and transmitted via a noiseless digital channel to the controller that is assumed to be located next to the actuator, this question has been successfully answered for the stabilizability of linear systems without disturbances, with stochastic disturbances or bounded disturbances. Remarkably, for various different notions of data rate and independent of the particular disturbance model, the critical data rate below which stabilizability is not possible, is characterized as an intrinsic system property in terms of the unstable eigenvalues of the system, see e.g. [2].

HSCC'17, April 18 - 20, 2017, Pittsburgh, PA, USA

ISBN 978-1-4503-4590-3/17/04...$15.00
DOI: http://dx.doi.org/10.1145/3049797.3049801

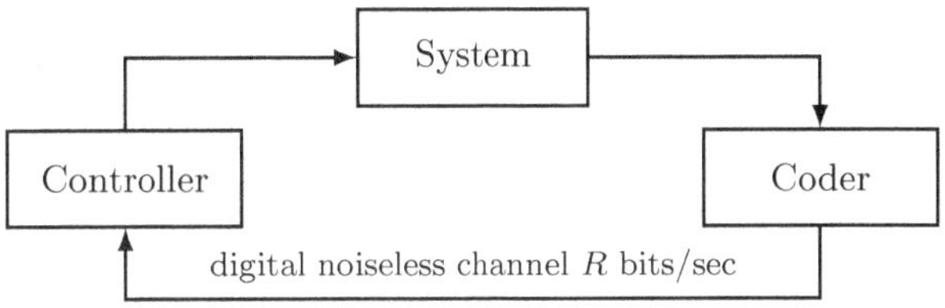

Figure 1: Code-controller feedback loop.

We are interested in minimal data rates of a coder-controller to render a given subset Q of the state space invariant. In the seminal paper [3], Nair et al., inspired by the notion of entropy of dynamical systems, introduced the notion of entropy for discrete-time, deterministic, nonlinear control systems to characterize the critical data rate to achieve invariance for Q. In [4] Colonius and Kawan introduced different definitions of entropy of continuous-time nonlinear control systems, one of which recovers the notion of Nair et al. in the discrete-time case [5]. All entropy notions are defined in terms of open-loop control functions. In [3] the open-loop control functions are defined on an open-cover, while in [4, 5] the growth rate of the number of open-loop control functions necessary to render Q invariant over a growing time horizon is directly used as a measure for the data rate to achieve invariance.

We continue this line of research and introduce a notion of entropy for discrete-time, nondeterministic control systems to characterize the critical asymptotic average data rate necessary to achieve invariance. Similar to [3, 4] the introduced notion of entropy does not involve any assumption on the particular coder or controller and can be regarded as an intrinsic system property. However, since the considered systems are nondeterministic, we cannot employ open-loop control functions but introduce invariant covers as a basis for the entropy definition. We provide conditions that guarantee the finiteness and show its equivalence with the entropy in [5] in the deterministic case. We establish the data rate theorem and discuss different candidate data rate definitions. Afterwards, we focus on finite systems and characterize the entropy by the value function of an appropriately designed mean-payoff game (MPG) [6, 7] – a result which is unparalleled in the data rate limited feedback control literature. Although, this result provides an algorithm to compute the entropy, in the worst-case the size of the MPG increases double exponentially with the number of system states. Further research is required to determine whether better complexity bounds are attainable or not.

2. NOTATION

We denote by $\mathbb{N}$, $\mathbb{Z}$ and $\mathbb{R}$ the set of natural, integer and real numbers, respectively. We annotate those symbols with subscripts to restrict the sets in the obvious way, e.g. $\mathbb{R}_{>0}$ denotes the positive real numbers. We denote the closed, open and half-open intervals in $\mathbb{R}$ with endpoints a and b by $[a,b]$, $]a,b[$, $[a,b[$, and $]a,b]$, respectively. The corresponding intervals in $\mathbb{Z}$ are denoted by $[a;b]$, $]a;b[$, $[a;b[$, and $]a;b]$, i.e., $[a;b] = [a,b] \cap \mathbb{Z}$ and $[0;0[= \varnothing$.

For a set A, we use $\#A \in \mathbb{Z}_{\geq 0} \cup \{\infty\}$ to denote the number of elements of A, i.e., if A is finite we have $\#A \in \mathbb{Z}_{\geq 0}$ and $\#A = \infty$ otherwise. Given two sets A and B, we say that A is smaller (larger) than B if $\#A \leq \#B$ ($\#A \geq \#B$) holds. A set $(U_\alpha)_{\alpha \in A}$ of subsets of A, is said to *cover* B, where $B \subseteq A$, if B is a subset of the union of the U_α's. A *cover* of B, is a set of subsets of B that covers B. An *enumeration* of a finite set A is a function $e : [1;\#A] \to A$ such that $e([1;\#A]) = A$. We say that A is a topological space if it is endowed with some topology $\mathcal{T}$.

Given two sets $A, B \subseteq \mathbb{R}^n$, we define the Minkowski set addition by $A + B = \{x \in \mathbb{R}^n \mid \exists_{a \in A}, \exists_{b \in B}\ x = a + b\}$. If $A = \{a\}$, we slightly abuse notation and use $a + B = \{a\} + B$.

We follow [8] and use $f\colon A \rightrightarrows B$ to denote a *set-valued map* from A into B, whereas $f\colon A \to B$ denotes an ordinary map. If f is set-valued, then f is *strict* if for every $a \in A$ we have $f(a) \neq \varnothing$. The inverse mapping $f^{-1}\colon B \rightrightarrows A$ is defined by $f^{-1}(b) = \{a \in A \mid b \in f(a)\}$. The restriction of f to a subset $M \subseteq A$ is denoted by $f|_M$. By convention we set $f|_\varnothing := \varnothing$. The composition of $f : A \rightrightarrows B$ and $g : C \rightrightarrows A$, $(f \circ g)(x) = f(g(x))$ is denoted by $f \circ g$. We use B^A to denote the set of all functions $f : A \to B$.

The concatenation of two functions $x : [0;\tau_1[\to X$ and $y : [0;\tau_2[\to X$ with $\tau_1 \in \mathbb{N}$ and $\tau_2 \in \mathbb{N} \cup \{\infty\}$ is simply denoted by xy which we define by $xy(t) := x(t)$ for $t \in [0;\tau_1[$ and $xy(t) := y(t - \tau_1)$ for $t \in [\tau_1, \tau_1 + \tau_2[$.

We use $\inf \varnothing = \infty$ and $\log_2 \infty = \infty$.

3. THE CONTROL SYSTEM

In this work we analyze discrete-time, nondeterministic control systems described by difference inclusions of the form

$$\xi(t+1) \in F(\xi(t), \nu(t)) \tag{1}$$

where $\xi(t) \in X$ is the *state signal* and $\nu(t) \in U$ is the *input signal*. The sets X and U are referred to as *state alphabet* and *input alphabet* respectively. The map F is called the *transition function*.

As already outlined in the introduction, we are interested in coder-controllers that control a nonempty set Q of the state alphabet X invariant, i.e., every state signal ξ of the closed-loop illustrated in Figure 1 with $\xi(0) \in Q$ satisfies $\xi(t) \in Q$ for all $t \in \mathbb{Z}_{\geq 0}$. Specifically, we are interested in the average data rate of such coder-controllers, i.e., the data rate of the digital channel that connects the coder with the controller.

Notably, our system description is rather general and, depending on the structure of alphabets X and U, we can represent a variety of commonly used system models. If we assume X and U to be discrete, we can use (1) to represent discrete event systems[1] [9] and digital/embedded systems [10]. Let us present a simple example.

[1]If (1) represents a discrete event system, the data rate unit is given in bits/event.

EXAMPLE 1. Consider a system with state alphabet and input alphabet given by $X := \{0,1,2\}$ and $U := \{a,b\}$ respectively. The transition function is illustrated by

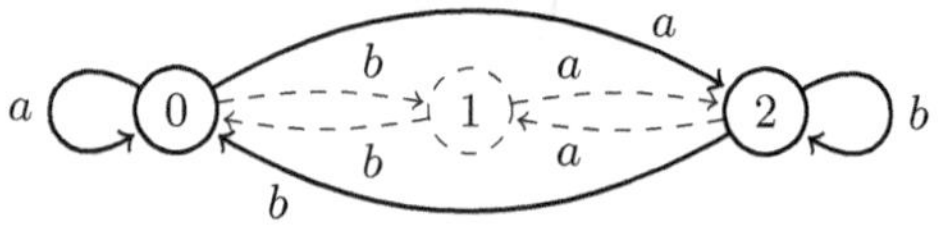

The set of interest is defined to $Q := \{0,2\}$. The transitions and states that lead, respectively, are outside Q are indicated by dashed lines. When the system is in state 0 the only valid input is given by a. Similarly, if the system is in state 2 the only valid input is given by b. If the input a is applied at 0 at time t, the system can either be in 0 or 2 at time $t+1$. Note that the valid control inputs for the states 0 and 2 differ and the controller is required to have exact state information at every point in time. Due to the nondeterministic transition function, it is not possible to determine the current state of the system based on the knowledge of the past states, the past control inputs and the transition function. Therefore, the controller can obtain the state information only through measurement, which implies that at least one bit needs to be transmitted at every time step. □

Current theories [3, 4, 11] cannot explain the data rate constraint encountered in Example 1.

If we allow X and U to be (subsets of) Euclidean spaces, we are able to recover one of the most fundamental system models in control theory, i.e., the class of nonlinear control systems with bounded disturbances [12, 13]. If the system description is given in continuous-time, we can use (1) to represent the sampled-data system [14] with sampling time $\tau \in \mathbb{R}_{>0}$ as illustrated in Fig. 2. The disturbance signal

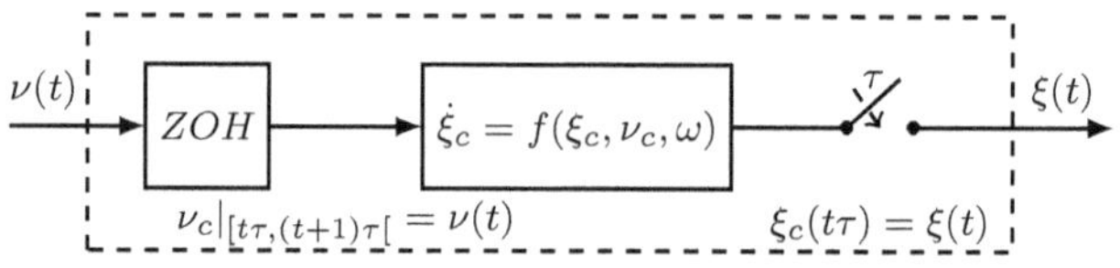

Figure 2: Sampled-data discrete-time system.

ω is assumed to be bounded $\omega(s) \in W \subseteq \mathbb{R}^p$ for all times $s \in \mathbb{R}_{\geq 0}$. The transition function $F(x,u)$ is defined as the set of states that are reachable by the continuous-time system at time τ from initial state x under constant input signal $\nu_c(s) = u$ and a bounded disturbance signal ω. If the continuous-time dynamics is linear, the sampled-data system results in a discrete-time system of the form

$$\xi(t+1) \in A\xi(t) + B\nu(t) + W$$

where A and B are matrices of appropriate dimension and W is a nonempty, bounded subset of the state space. An example is given below.

EXAMPLE 2. Consider an instance of (1) with $X := \mathbb{R}$, $U := [-1,1]$ and

$$F(x,u) := x + u + W$$

where $W := [-1,1]$ and the set of interest is $Q := [-2,2]$. □

For Example 2, we establish in Section 4, that the smallest possible data rate of a coder-controller that enforces Q

to be invariant must be greater than zero. This is in stark contrast to what is known for data rate constraints of feedback control of linear systems with bounded disturbances in the context of asymptotic stabilization (or norm boundedness) [3, Thm. 1], or for data rates of coder-controllers for controlled invariance for unperturbed linear systems [4, Thm. 5.1]. Both results suggest that the data rate should be zero, since the system in Example 2 is stable.

4. INVARIANCE FEEDBACK ENTROPY

In this section, we introduce a notion of invariance feedback entropy, provide conditions that guarantee its finiteness and establish the connection to the notion of entropy in [3–5] for the deterministic case.

4.1 The Entropy

Formally, we define a *system* as triple

$$\Sigma := (X, U, F) \tag{2}$$

where X and U are nonempty sets and $F : X \times U \rightrightarrows X$ is assumed to be strict. A *trajectory* of (2) on $[0;\tau[$ with $\tau \in \mathbb{N} \cup \{\infty\}$ is a pair of sequences (ξ, ν), consisting of a state signal $\xi : [0; \tau + 1[\to X$ and an input signal $\nu : [0;\tau[\to U$, that satisfies (1) for all $t \in [0;\tau[$. We denote the set of all trajectories on $[0;\infty[$ by $\mathcal{B}(\Sigma)$.

Throughout the paper, we call a system (X, U, F) *finite* if X and U are finite. We call (X, U, F) *topological* if X is a topological space.

We follow [3] and [4, Sec. 6] and define the invariance feedback entropy with the help of covers of Q.

Consider the system $\Sigma = (X, U, F)$ and a nonempty set $Q \subseteq X$. A cover $\mathcal{A}$ of Q and a function $G : \mathcal{A} \to U$ is called an *invariant cover* $(\mathcal{A}, G)$ of Σ and Q if $\mathcal{A}$ is finite and for all $A \in \mathcal{A}$ we have $F(A, G(A)) \subseteq Q$.

Consider an invariant cover $(\mathcal{A}, G)$ of Σ and Q, fix $\tau \in \mathbb{N}$ and let $\mathcal{S} \subseteq \mathcal{A}^{[0;\tau[}$ be a set of sequences in $\mathcal{A}$. For $\alpha \in \mathcal{S}$ and $t \in [0;\tau-1[$ we define

$$P(\alpha|_{[0;t]}) := \{A \in \mathcal{A} \mid \exists_{\hat{\alpha} \in \mathcal{S}}\ \hat{\alpha}|_{[0;t]} = \alpha|_{[0;t]} \wedge A = \hat{\alpha}(t+1)\}.$$

The set $P(\alpha|_{[0;t]})$ contains the cover elements A so that the sequence $\alpha|_{[0;t]}A$ can be extended to a sequence in $\mathcal{S}$. For $t = \tau - 1$ we have $\alpha|_{[0;\tau-1]} = \alpha$ and we define for notational convenience the set

$$P(\alpha) := \{A \in \mathcal{A} \mid \exists_{\hat{\alpha} \in \mathcal{S}}\ A = \hat{\alpha}(0)\}$$

which is actually independent of $\alpha \in \mathcal{S}$ and corresponds to the "initial" cover elements A in $\mathcal{S}$, i.e., there exists $\alpha \in \mathcal{S}$ with $A = \alpha(0)$. A set $\mathcal{S} \subseteq \mathcal{A}^{[0;\tau[}$ is called (τ, Q)*-spanning* in $(\mathcal{A}, G)$ if the set $P(\alpha)$ with $\alpha \in \mathcal{S}$ covers Q and we have

$$\forall_{\alpha \in \mathcal{S}} \forall_{t \in [0;\tau-1[} \quad F(\alpha(t), G(\alpha(t))) \subseteq \bigcup_{A' \in P(\alpha|_{[0;t]})} A'. \tag{3}$$

We associate with every (τ, Q)-spanning set $\mathcal{S}$ the *expansion number* $N(\mathcal{S})$, which we define by

$$N(\mathcal{S}) := \max_{\alpha \in \mathcal{S}} \prod_{t=0}^{\tau-1} \#P(\alpha|_{[0;t]}).$$

A tight lower bound on the expansion number of any (τ, Q)-spanning set $\mathcal{S}$ in $(\mathcal{A}, G)$ is given by

$$r_{\text{inv}}(\tau, Q) := \min\{N(\mathcal{S}) \mid \mathcal{S} \text{ is } (\tau, Q)\text{-spanning in } (\mathcal{A}, G)\}.$$

We define the *entropy* of an invariant cover $(\mathcal{A}, G)$ by

$$h(\mathcal{A}, G) := \lim_{\tau \to \infty} \frac{1}{\tau} \log_2 r_{\text{inv}}(\tau, Q). \tag{4}$$

As shown in Lemma 1 (stated below), the limit of the sequence in (4) exists so that the entropy of an invariant cover $(\mathcal{A}, G)$ is well-defined.

The *invariance feedback entropy* of Σ and Q follows by

$$h_{\text{inv}} := \inf_{(\mathcal{A}, G)} h(\mathcal{A}, G) \tag{5}$$

where we take the infimum over all $(\mathcal{A}, G)$ invariant covers of Σ and Q. Let us revisit the examples from the previous section to illustrate the various definitions.

Example 1 (Continued). First, we determine an invariant cover $(\mathcal{A}, G)$ of the system in Example 1 and Q. Since the system is finite, we can set $\mathcal{A} := \{\{x\} \mid x \in Q\}$. Recall that $Q = \{0, 2\}$ and a suitable function G is given by $G(\{0\}) := a$ and $G(\{2\}) := b$. Suppose that $\mathcal{S} \subseteq \mathcal{A}^{[0;\tau[}$ is (τ, Q)-spanning with $\tau \in \mathbb{N}$. Let us check condition (3) for $t \in [0;\tau-1[$ and $\alpha \in \mathcal{S}$. If $\alpha(t) = \{0\}$, we have $P(\alpha) = \{\{0\}, \{2\}\}$ since $F(\{0\}, G(\{0\})) = F(0, a) = \{0, 2\}$. If $\alpha(t) = \{2\}$ the same reasoning leads to $P(\alpha) = \{\{0\}, \{2\}\}$. Also for $\alpha \in \mathcal{S}$ we have $P(\alpha) = \{\{0\}, \{2\}\}$ since $P(\alpha)$ is required to be a cover of Q. It follows that $\mathcal{S} = \mathcal{A}^{[0;\tau[}$ and the expansion number $N(\mathcal{S}) = r_{\text{inv}}(\mathcal{A}, G) = 2^\tau$ so that the entropy of the $(\mathcal{A}, G)$ follows to $h(\mathcal{A}, G) = 1$. Since $(\mathcal{A}, G)$ is the only invariant cover we obtain $h_{\text{inv}} = 1$. □

Example 2 (Continued). Let us recall the perturbed, linear system in Example 2. An invariant cover $(\mathcal{A}, G)$ is given by $\mathcal{A} := \{a_0, a_1\}$ with $a_0 := [-2, 0]$, $a_1 := [0, 2]$ and $G(a_0) := 1$, $G(a_1) := -1$. We use a similar reasoning as in Example 1 to see that for every $\tau \in \mathbb{N}$ the only (τ, Q)-spanning set is $\mathcal{S} := \mathcal{A}^{[0;\tau[}$. Since $\#\mathcal{A} = 2$ we obtain for the entropy of the invariant cover $h(\mathcal{A}, G) = 1$.

It is also easy to see that $h_{\text{inv}} > 0$, since for each $x \in Q$ we have $Q \subseteq F(F(x, u_0), u_1)$ independent of $u_0, u_1 \in U$. Hence, every information on the initial state is lost after two steps, so that the state information needs to be updated by new sensor information at least every three time steps.

In the remaining part of this subsection, we show the subadditivity of $\log_2 r_{\text{inv}}(\cdot, Q)$.

Lemma 1. *Consider the system $\Sigma = (X, U, F)$ and a nonempty set $Q \subseteq X$. Let $(\mathcal{A}, G)$ be an invariant cover of Σ and Q, then the function $\tau \mapsto \log_2 r_{\text{inv}}(\tau, Q)$, $\mathbb{N} \to \mathbb{R}_{\geq 0}$ is subadditive, i.e., for all $\tau_1, \tau_2 \in \mathbb{N}$ the inequality*

$$\log_2 r_{\text{inv}}(\tau_1 + \tau_2, Q) \leq \log_2 r_{\text{inv}}(\tau_1, Q) + \log_2 r_{\text{inv}}(\tau_2, Q)$$

holds and we have

$$\lim_{\tau \to \infty} \frac{1}{\tau} \log_2 r_{\text{inv}}(\tau, Q) = \inf_{\tau \in \mathbb{N}} \frac{1}{\tau} \log_2 r_{\text{inv}}(\tau, Q). \tag{6}$$

The following lemma might be of independent interest. We use it in the proof of Theorem 3.

Lemma 2. *Consider an invariant cover $(\mathcal{A}, G)$ of (2) and some nonempty set $Q \subseteq X$. Let $\mathcal{S}$ be a (τ, Q)-spanning set, then we have $\#\mathcal{S} \leq N(\mathcal{S})$.*

The proofs of both lemmas are given in the appendix.

4.2 Conditions for Finiteness

We analyze two particular instances of systems – finite systems and topological systems – and provide conditions ensuring that the invariance entropy is finite. The results are based on the following lemma.

LEMMA 3. *Consider a system* $\Sigma = (X, U, F)$ *and a nonempty set* $Q \subseteq X$. *If there exists an invariant cover* $(\mathcal{A}, G)$ *of* Σ *and* Q *then* $h_{\text{inv}} < \infty$.

PROOF. For the reverse direction, we assume that $(\mathcal{A}, G)$ is an invariant cover of Σ and Q. We fix $\tau \in \mathbb{N}$ and define $\mathcal{S} := \{\alpha \in \mathcal{A}^{[0;\tau[} \mid \alpha(0) \in \mathcal{A} \wedge \forall_{t \in [0;\tau-1[}\ \alpha(t+1) \cap F(\alpha(t), G(\alpha(t)) \neq \varnothing\}$. It is easy to verify that $\mathcal{S}$ is (τ, Q)-spanning and $N(\mathcal{S}) \leq (\#\mathcal{A})^\tau$. An upper bound on h_{inv} follows by $\log_2 \#\mathcal{A}$. □

If Σ is finite, it is rather straightforward to show that the controlled invariance of Q w.r.t. Σ is necessary and sufficient for h_{inv} to be finite. Let us recall the notion of controlled invariance [13].

We call $Q \subseteq X$ *controlled invariant* with respect to a system $\Sigma = (X, U, F)$, if for all $x \in Q$ there exists $u \in U$ so that $F(x, u) \subseteq Q$.

THEOREM 1. *Consider a finite system* $\Sigma = (X, U, F)$ *and a nonempty set* $Q \subseteq X$. *Then* $h_{\text{inv}} < \infty$ *if and only if* Q *is controlled invariant.*

PROOF. Let h_{inv} be finite. Then there exists an invariant cover $(\mathcal{A}, G)$ so that $h(\mathcal{A}, G) < \infty$. Hence, for every $x \in Q$ we can pick an $A \in \mathcal{A}$ with $x \in A$, so that $F(x, G(A)) \subseteq F(A, G(A)) \subseteq Q$. Hence Q is controlled invariant w.r.t. Σ.

Assume Q is controlled invariant w.r.t. Σ. For $x \in Q$, let $u_x \in U$ be such that $F(x, u_x) \subseteq Q$. It is easy to check that $(\mathcal{A}, G)$ with $\mathcal{A} := \{\{x\} \mid x \in Q\}$ and $G(\{x\}) := u_x$ is an invariant cover of Σ and Q, so that the assertion follows from Lemma 3. □

In general controlled invariance of Q is not sufficient to guarantee finiteness of the invariance feedback entropy.

EXAMPLE 3. Consider $\Sigma = (\mathbb{R}, [-1, 1], F)$ with the dynamics given by $F(x, u) := x + u + [-1, 1]$. Let $Q := [-1, 1]$, then for every $x \in Q$ we can pick $u = -x$ so that $F(x, u) = [-1, 1] \subseteq Q$, which shows that Q is controlled invariant. Now suppose that h_{inv} is finite. Then according to Lemma 3 there exists an invariant cover $(\mathcal{A}, G)$ of Σ and Q. Since $\mathcal{A}$ is required to be finite, there exists $A \in \mathcal{A}$ with an infinite number of elements and therefore we can pick two different states in A, i.e., $x, x' \in A$ with $x \neq x'$. However, there does not exist a single $u \in U$ so that $F(x, u) \subseteq Q$ and $F(x', u) \subseteq Q$. Hence, $(\mathcal{A}, G)$ cannot be an invariant cover, which implies $h_{\text{inv}} = \infty$. □

In the subsequent theorem we present some conditions for topological systems, which imply the finiteness of the invariance entropy. With this conditions, we follow closely the assumptions based on continuity and strong invariance used in [2, 5] to ensure finiteness of the invariance entropy for deterministic systems. We use the following notion of continuity of set-valued maps [15].

Let A and B be topological spaces and $f : A \rightrightarrows B$. We say that f is *upper semi-continuous*, if for every $a \in A$ and every open set $V \subseteq B$ containing $f(a)$ there exists an open set $U \subseteq A$ with $a \in U$ so that $f(U) \subseteq V$.

THEOREM 2. *Consider a topological system* $\Sigma = (X, U, F)$ *and a nonempty compact subset* Q *of* X. *If* $F(\cdot, u)$ *is upper semi-continuous for every* $u \in U$ *and* Q *is strongly controlled invariant, i.e., for all* $x \in Q$ *there exists* $u \in U$ *so that* $F(x, u) \subseteq \operatorname{int} Q$, *then* $h_{\text{inv}} < \infty$.

PROOF. For each $x \in Q$, we pick an input $u_x \in U$ so that $F(x, u_x) \subseteq \operatorname{int} Q$. Since $F(\cdot, u_x)$ is upper semi-continuous and $\operatorname{int} Q$ is open, there exists an open subset A_x of X, so that $x \in A_x$ and $F(A_x, u_x) \subseteq \operatorname{int} Q$. Hence, the set $\{A_x \mid x \in Q\}$ of open subsets of X covers Q. Since Q is a compact subset of X, there exist a finite set $\{A_{x_1}, \ldots, A_{x_m}\}$ so that $Q \subseteq \cup_{i \in [1;m]} A_{x_i}$ [16, Ch. 2.6]. Let $\mathcal{A} := \{A_{x_1} \cap Q, \ldots, A_{x_m} \cap Q\}$ and define for every $i \in [1; m]$ the function $G(A_{x_i}) := u_{x_i}$. Then $(\mathcal{A}, G)$ is an invariant cover of Σ and Q, and the assertion follows from Lemma 3. □

EXAMPLE 3 (CONTINUED). Let $\varepsilon > 0$, consider Σ from Example 3 with the modified input set $U_\varepsilon := [-1 - \varepsilon, 1 + \varepsilon]$. Let $Q_\varepsilon := [-1 - \varepsilon, 1 + \varepsilon]$ then we see that Q_ε is strongly controlled invariant. We construct an invariant cover for Σ and Q_ε as follows. We define n as the smallest integer lager than $\frac{1}{2\varepsilon}$ and introduce $\{x_{-n}, \ldots, x_0, \ldots x_n\}$ with $x_i := 2i\varepsilon$ and set $A_i := (x_i + [-\varepsilon, \varepsilon]) \cap Q_\varepsilon$. For each $i \in [-n; n]$ we define $G(A_i) := -x_i$ so that $F(A_i, G(A_i)) = Q_\varepsilon$. By definition of n we have $x_{-n} \leq -1$ and $1 \leq x_n$ and we see that $(\mathcal{A}, G)$ with $\mathcal{A} := \{A_i \mid i \in [-n; n]\}$ is an invariant cover of Σ and Q_ε. Hence, it follows from Lemma 3 that h_{inv} is finite. □

4.3 Deterministic Systems

For deterministic systems we recover the notion of invariance feedback entropy in [3, 5].

Let us consider the map $f : X \times U \to X$ representing a deterministic system

$$\xi(t+1) = f(\xi(t), \nu(t)). \tag{7}$$

We can interpret (7) as special instance of (2), where F is given by $F(x, u) := \{f(x, u)\}$ for all $x \in X$ and $u \in U$ and the notions of a trajectory of (2) extend to (7) in the obvious way. Given an input $u \in U$, we introduce $f_u : X \to X$ by $f_u(x) := f(x, u)$ and extend this notation to sequences $\nu \in U^{[0;t]}$, $t \in \mathbb{N}$ by

$$f_\nu(x) := f_{\nu(t)} \circ \cdots \circ f_{\nu(0)}(x).$$

We follow [5] to define the entropy of (7). Consider a nonempty set $Q \subseteq X$ and fix $\tau \in \mathbb{N}$. A set $\mathcal{S} \subseteq U^{[0;\tau[}$ is called (τ, Q)-*spanning* for f and Q, if for every $x \in Q$ there exists $\nu \in \mathcal{S}$ so that the associated trajectory (ξ, ν) on $[0; \tau[$ of (7) with $\xi(0) = x$ satisfies $\xi([0; \tau]) \subseteq Q$. We use $r_{\text{det}}(\tau, Q)$ to denote the number of elements of the smallest (τ, Q)-spanning set

$$r_{\text{det}}(\tau, Q) := \inf\{\#\mathcal{S} \mid \mathcal{S} \text{ is } (\tau, Q)\text{-spanning}\}. \tag{8}$$

The *(deterministic) invariance entropy* of (X, U, f) and Q is defined by

$$h_{\text{det}} := \lim_{\tau \to \infty} \frac{1}{\tau} \log_2 r_{\text{det}}(\tau, Q). \tag{9}$$

Again the function $\tau \mapsto \frac{1}{\tau} \log_2 r_{\text{det}}(\tau, Q)$ is subadditive [5, Prop. 2.2] which ensures that the limit in (9) exists.

We have the following theorem.

THEOREM 3. *Consider the system $\Sigma = (X, U, F)$ and a nonempty set $Q \subseteq X$. Suppose F satisfy $F(x, u) = \{f(x, u)\}$ for all $x \in X$, $u \in U$ for some $f : X \times U \to X$. Then the invariance feedback entropy of Σ and Q equals the deterministic invariance entropy of (X, U, f) and Q, i.e.,*

$$h_{\mathrm{inv}} = h_{\mathrm{det}}. \qquad (10)$$

PROOF. We begin with the inequality $h_{\mathrm{det}} \geq h_{\mathrm{inv}}$. If $h_{\mathrm{det}} = \infty$ the inequality trivially holds and subsequently we assume that h_{det} is finite. We fix $\varepsilon > 0$ and pick $\tau \in \mathbb{N}$ so that $\frac{1}{\tau}\log_2 r_{\mathrm{det}}(\tau, Q) \leq h_{\mathrm{det}} + \varepsilon$. We chose a (τ, Q)-spanning set $\mathcal{S}_{\mathrm{det}}$ for f and Q with $\#\mathcal{S}_{\mathrm{det}} = r_{\mathrm{det}}(\tau, Q)$. For every $\nu \in \mathcal{S}_{\mathrm{det}}$ we define the sets

$$A_0(\nu) := Q \cap \bigcap_{t=0}^{\tau-1} f^{-1}_{\nu|_{[0;t]}}(Q)$$

and for $t \in [0; \tau-1[$ the sets $A_{t+1}(\nu) := f(A_t(\nu), \nu(t))$. The minimality of $\mathcal{S}_{\mathrm{det}}$ implies that $A_0(\nu) \neq \varnothing$ for all $\nu \in \mathcal{S}_{\mathrm{det}}$. Let $\mathcal{A}$ be the set of all sets $A_t(\nu)$ for $t \in [0; \tau[$ and $\nu \in \mathcal{S}_{\mathrm{det}}$ and set $G(A_t(\nu)) := \nu(t)$. By definition of $A_t(\nu)$, it is easy to see that $f(A_t(\nu), G(A_t(\nu))) \subseteq Q$ for all $t \in [0; \tau[$ and $\nu \in \mathcal{S}_{\mathrm{det}}$. Moreover, since $\mathcal{S}_{\mathrm{det}}$ is (τ, Q)-spanning, for every $x \in Q$ there is $\nu \in \mathcal{S}_{\mathrm{det}}$ so that for all $t \in [0; \tau[$ we have $f_{\nu|_{[0;t]}}(x) \in Q$ which implies $x \in A_0(\nu)$ and we see that $\{A_0(\nu) \mid \nu \in \mathcal{S}_{\mathrm{det}}\}$ covers Q. It follows that $(\mathcal{A}, G)$ is an invariant cover of (X, U, F) and Q. For every $\nu \in \mathcal{S}_{\mathrm{det}}$ we define the function $\alpha_\nu : [0; \tau[\to \mathcal{A}$ by $\alpha_\nu(t) := A_t(\nu)$ and introduce $\mathcal{S}_{\mathrm{inv}} := \{\alpha_\nu \mid \nu \in \mathcal{S}_{\mathrm{det}}\}$. Since $\alpha_\nu(0) = A_0(\nu)$, we see that $P(\alpha_\nu) = \{A_0(\nu) \mid \nu \in \mathcal{S}_{\mathrm{det}}\}$, which shows that $P(\alpha_\nu)$ covers Q. Also for every $t \in [0; \tau-1[$ and $\alpha_\nu \in \mathcal{S}_{\mathrm{inv}}$ we have $f(\alpha_\nu(t), G(\alpha_\nu(t))) = f(\alpha_\nu(t), \nu(t)) = \alpha_\nu(t+1)$ so that $\mathcal{S}_{\mathrm{inv}}$ satisfies (3). Therefore, $\mathcal{S}_{\mathrm{inv}}$ is (τ, Q)-spanning in $(\mathcal{A}, G)$. Moreover, for all $\alpha_\nu \in \mathcal{S}_{\mathrm{inv}}$ we have $\#P(\alpha_\nu|_{[0;t]}) = 1$ for all $t \in [0; \tau-1[$ and $\#P(\alpha_\nu) = \#\mathcal{S}_{\mathrm{det}}$. Hence, $r_{\mathrm{inv}}(\tau, Q) \leq N(\mathcal{S}_{\mathrm{inv}}) = \#\mathcal{S}_{\mathrm{det}} = r_{\mathrm{det}}(\tau, Q)$. Due to Lemma 1, we have $\log_2 r_{\mathrm{inv}}(n\tau, Q) \leq n \log_2 r_{\mathrm{inv}}(\tau, Q)$ and we see that $\frac{1}{\tau}\log_2 r_{\mathrm{inv}}(\tau, Q)$ (and therefore $\frac{1}{\tau}\log_2 r_{\mathrm{det}}(\tau, Q)$) provides an upper bound for $h(\mathcal{A}, Q)$ so that we obtain $h_{\mathrm{inv}} \leq h(\mathcal{A}, Q) \leq h_{\mathrm{det}} + \varepsilon$. Since this holds for any $\varepsilon > 0$ we obtain the desired inequality.
We continue with the inequality $h_{\mathrm{det}} \leq h_{\mathrm{inv}}$. If $h_{\mathrm{inv}} = \infty$ the inequality trivially holds and subsequently we assume $h_{\mathrm{inv}} < \infty$. We fix $\varepsilon > 0$ and pick an invariant cover $(\mathcal{A}, G)$ of Σ and Q so that $h(\mathcal{A}, G) \leq h_{\mathrm{inv}} + \varepsilon$. We fix $\tau \in \mathbb{N}$ and pick a (τ, Q)-spanning set $\mathcal{S}_{\mathrm{inv}}$ in $(\mathcal{A}, G)$ so that $N(\mathcal{S}_{\mathrm{inv}}) = r_{\mathrm{inv}}(\tau, Q)$. We define for every $\alpha \in \mathcal{S}_{\mathrm{inv}}$ the input sequence $\nu_\alpha : [0; \tau[\to U$ by $\nu_\alpha(t) := G(\alpha(t))$ and introduce the set $\mathcal{S}_{\mathrm{det}} := \{\nu_\alpha \mid \alpha \in \mathcal{S}_{\mathrm{inv}}\}$. For $x \in Q$ we iteratively construct $\alpha \in \mathcal{A}^{[0;\tau[}$ and $\nu \in U^{[0;\tau[}$ as follows: for $t = 0$ we pick $\alpha_0 \in \mathcal{S}_{\mathrm{inv}}$ so that $x \in \alpha_0(0)$ and set $\nu(0) := G(\alpha_0(0))$. For $t \in [0; \tau-1[$ we pick $\alpha_{t+1} \in \mathcal{S}_{\mathrm{inv}}$ so that $\alpha_{t+1}|_{[0;t]} = \alpha_t$ and $f_{\nu|_{[0;t]}}(x) \in \alpha_{t+1}(t+1)$ and set $\nu(t+1) := G(\alpha_{t+1}(t+1))$. Since $(\mathcal{A}, G)$ is an invariant cover of (X, U, F) and Q, it is easy to show that $f_{\nu|_{[0;t]}}(x) \in Q$ holds for all $t \in [0; \tau[$, which implies that $\mathcal{S}_{\mathrm{det}}$ is (τ, Q)-spanning for f and Q and we obtain $r_{\mathrm{det}}(\tau, Q) \leq \#\mathcal{S}_{\mathrm{det}} \leq \#\mathcal{S}_{\mathrm{inv}} \leq N(\mathcal{S}_{\mathrm{inv}}) = r_{\mathrm{inv}}(\tau, Q)$, where the inequality $\#\mathcal{S}_{\mathrm{inv}} \leq N(\mathcal{S}_{\mathrm{inv}})$ follows from Lemma 2. Since this holds for any $\tau \in \mathbb{N}$, we obtain the inequality $\varepsilon + h_{\mathrm{inv}} \geq h(\mathcal{A}, G) \geq h_{\mathrm{det}}$ for arbitrary $\varepsilon > 0$ which shows $h_{\mathrm{inv}} \geq h_{\mathrm{det}}$. □

5. DATA-RATE-LIMITED FEEDBACK

Let us recall the feedback loop illustrated in Fig. 1. The state information from the sensor side is transmitted via a discrete noiseless channel to the controller using a so called coder-controller. In this section, we show that the invariance feedback entropy provides a lower bound on the data rate for any admissible coder-controller. Moreover, we show that the lower bound on the data rate given by the invariance feedback entropy is achievable by an admissible coder-controller with arbitrary precision.

Compared to the other nonstochastic approaches, which use time-invariant [2] or time-variant [3, 4] notions of transmission data rates, we use a worst-case, dynamic notion of data rate, which we interpret as a nonstochastic variant of the notion of data rate used e.g. in [17, Def. 4.1] for noisy linear systems, defined as the average of the expected length of the transmitted symbols in the closed-loop. We motivate the particular notion of data rate by two examples; one which illustrates that the time-varying definition [3] results in too large data rates and one that shows that the notion of data rate based on the framework of nonstochastic information theory, used in [18, 19] for estimation [19] and control [18] of linear systems, leads to too small data rates.

5.1 The Coder-Controller

We assume that the coder is located at the sensor side (see Fig. 1), which at every time step, encodes the current state of the system using the finite *coding alphabet* S. It transmits a symbol $s_t \in S$ via the discrete noiseless channel to the controller. The transmitted symbol $s_t \in S$ might depend on all past states and is determined by the *coder function*

$$\gamma : \bigcup_{t \in \mathbb{Z}_{\geq 0}} X^{[0;t]} \to S.$$

At time $t \in \mathbb{Z}_{\geq 0}$, the controller received $t+1$ symbols $s_0 \ldots s_t$, which are used to determine the control input given by the *controller function*

$$\delta : \bigcup_{t \in \mathbb{Z}_{\geq 0}} S^{[0;t]} \to U.$$

A *coder-controller* for (2) is a triple $H := (S, \gamma, \delta)$, where S is a coding alphabet and γ and δ is a compatible coder function and controller function, respectively.

Given a coder-controller (S, γ, δ) for (2) and $\xi \in X^{[0;t]}$ with $t \in \mathbb{Z}_{\geq 0}$, let us use the mapping $\Gamma_t : X^{[0;t]} \to S^{[0;t]}$ to denote the sequence $\zeta = \Gamma_t(\xi)$ of coder symbols generated by ξ, i.e., $\zeta(t') = \gamma(\xi|_{[0;t']})$ holds for all $t' \in [0; t]$. Subsequently, for $\zeta \in S^{[0;t[}$ with $t \in \mathbb{N}$, we use

$$Z(\zeta) := \{s \in S \mid \exists_{(\xi,\nu) \in \mathcal{B}(\Sigma)}\, \zeta s = \Gamma(\xi|_{[0;t]}) \wedge \nu|_{[0;t[} = \delta \circ \zeta\} \qquad (11)$$

to denote the possible successor coder symbols s of the symbol sequence ζ in the closed-loop illustrated in Fig. 1. For notational convenience, let us use the convention $Z(\varnothing) := S$, so that $Z(\zeta|_{[0;0[}) = S$ for any sequence ζ in S. For $\tau \in \mathbb{N} \cup \{\infty\}$, we introduce the set

$$\mathcal{Z}_\tau := \{\zeta \in S^{[0;\tau[} \mid \zeta(0) \in \gamma(X) \wedge \forall_{t \in]0;\tau[}\, \zeta(t) \in Z(\zeta|_{[0;t[})\}$$

and define the *transmission data rate* of a coder-controller H by

$$R(H) := \limsup_{\tau \to \infty} \max_{\zeta \in \mathcal{Z}_\tau} \frac{1}{\tau} \sum_{t=0}^{\tau-1} \log_2 \#Z(\zeta|_{[0;t[}) \qquad (12)$$

as the asymptotic average numbers of symbols in $Z(\zeta)$ considering the worst-case of possible symbol sequences $\zeta \in \mathcal{Z}_\tau$.

A coder-controller $H = (S, \gamma, \delta)$ for (2) is called *Q-admissible* where Q is a nonempty subset of X, if for every trajectory (ξ, ν) on $[0; \infty[$ of (2) that satisfies

$$\xi(0) \in Q \quad \text{and} \quad \forall_{t \in \mathbb{Z}_{\geq 0}}\ \nu(t) = \delta(\Gamma_t(\xi|_{[0;t]})) \tag{13}$$

we have $\xi(\mathbb{Z}_{\geq 0}) \subseteq Q$. Let us use $\mathcal{B}_Q(H)$ to denote the set of all trajectories (ξ, ν) on $[0; \infty[$ of (2) that satisfy (13).

5.1.1 Time-varying data rate definition

We follow [3] and introduce a time-varying notion of data rate for a coder-controller $H = (S, \gamma, \delta)$ for (2). Let $(S_t)_{t \geq 0}$ be the sequence in S that for each $t \in Z_{\geq 0}$ contains the smallest number of symbols so that $\gamma(\xi) \in S_t$ holds for all $\xi \in X^{[0;t]}$. Then the time-varying data rate of H follows by

$$R_{\text{tv}}(H) := \liminf_{\tau \to \infty} \frac{1}{\tau} \sum_{t=0}^{\tau - 1} \log_2 \# S_t.$$

In the following we use an example to show that there exists a Q-admissible coder-controller H, which satisfies $R(H) < R_{\text{tv}}(\bar{H})$ for any other $\bar{H}$ which is Q-admissible coder-controller. Note that this inequality is purely a nondeterministic phenomenon: if the control system is deterministic, it follows from the deterministic and the nondeterministic data rate theorem ([3, Thm. 1] and Theorem 4 below) and the equivalence $h_{\text{det}} = h_{\text{inv}}$ (Theorem 3) that the different notions of data rates coincide in the sense that $\inf_H R(H) = \inf_H R_{\text{tv}}(H)$ (at least if the strong invariance condition in [3, Thm. 1] holds).

Example 4. Consider an instance of (2) with $U := \{a, b\}$, $X := \{0, 1, 2, 3\}$ and F illustrated by

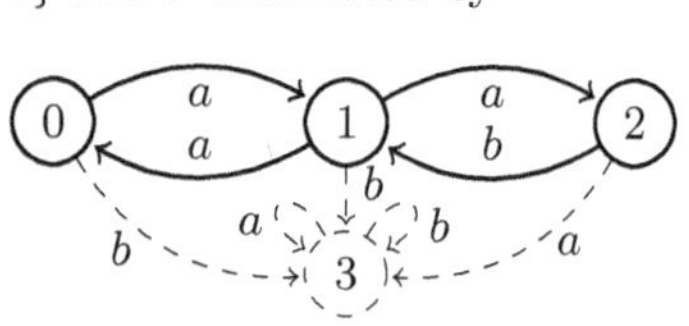

Let $Q := \{0, 1, 2\}$. The transitions that lead outside Q and the states that are outside Q are marked by dashed lines. Consider the coder-controller $H = (S, \gamma, \delta)$ with $S := X$ and γ and δ are given for $\xi \in X^{[0;t]}$, $t \in \mathbb{Z}_{\geq 0}$, by $\gamma(\xi) := \xi(t)$ and $\delta(\xi) := a$ if $\xi(t) \in \{0, 1, 3\}$ and $\delta(\xi) := b$ if $\xi(t) = 2$. We compute the number of possible successor symbols $Z(\xi)$ for $\xi \in X^{[0;t]}$, $t \in \mathbb{Z}_{\geq 0}$, by $\#Z(\xi) = 1$ if $\xi(t) \in \{0, 2, 3\}$ and $\#Z(\xi) = 2$ if $\xi(t) = 1$. It is easy to verify that H is Q-admissible. Since the state $\xi(t) = 1$ occurs only every other time step for any element (ξ, ν) of the closed-loop, we compute the data rate to $R(H) = 1/2$. Consider a time-varying Q-admissible coder-controller $\bar{H} = (\bar{S}, \bar{\gamma}, \bar{\delta})$. Initially, the states $\{0, 1\}$ and $\{2\}$ need to be distinguishable at the controller side in order to confine the system to Q so that $\#\bar{S}_0 \geq 2$ follows. At time $t = 1$, the system is possibly again in any of the states $\{0, 1, 2\}$ (depending on the initial condition) and we have $\#\bar{S}_1 \geq 2$. By continuing this argument we see that $\#\bar{S}_t \geq 2$ for all $t \in \mathbb{Z}_{\geq 0}$ and $R_{\text{tv}}(\bar{H}) \geq 1$ follows. □

5.1.2 Zero-error capacity of uncertain channels

Alternatively to the definition of the data rate of a coder-controller in (12) we could follow [18, 19] and define the data rate of a coder-controller as the zero-error capacity C_0 of an *ideal stationary memoryless uncertain channel* (SMUC) in the nonstochastic information theory framework presented in [19, Def. 4.1]. The input alphabet of the SMUC equals the output alphabet and is given by S. The channel is ideal and does not introduce any errors in the transmission. Hence, the transition function is the identity, i.e., $T(s) = s$ holds for all $s \in S$. The input function space $\mathcal{Z}_\infty \subseteq S^{[0;\infty[}$ is the set of all possible symbol sequences that are generated by the closed-loop, which represents the total amount of information that needs to be transmitted by the channel. For the ideal SMUC the zero-error capacity [18, Eq. (25)], for a coder-controller H results in

$$C_0(H) := \lim_{\tau \to \infty} \frac{1}{\tau} \log_2 \# \mathcal{Z}_\tau.$$

We use the following example to demonstrate that the zero-error capacity is too conservative, i.e., $C_0(H) = 0$ while $R(H) \geq 1$.

Example 5. Consider an instance of (2) with $U := \{a, b\}$, $X := \{0, 1, 2, 3\}$ and F illustrated by

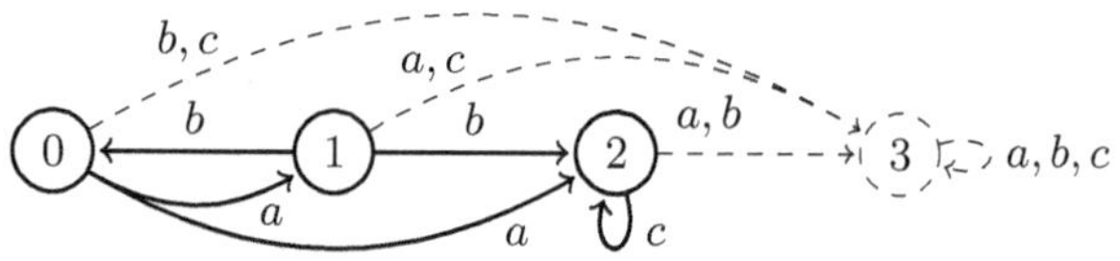

The transitions and states that lead, respectively, are outside the set of interest $Q := \{0, 1, 2\}$ are dashed. Consider the Q-admissible coder-controller $H = (S, \gamma, \delta)$ with $S := X$ and γ and δ are given for $\xi \in X^{[0;t]}$, $t \in \mathbb{Z}_{\geq 0}$ by $\gamma(\xi) := \xi(t)$ and

$$\delta(\xi) := \begin{cases} a & \text{if } \xi(t) \in \{0, 3\} \\ b & \text{if } \xi(t) = 1 \\ c & \text{if } \xi(t) = 2 \end{cases}$$

We pick the trajectory $(\xi, \nu) \in \mathcal{B}_Q(H)$ given for $t \in \mathbb{Z}_{\geq 0}$ by $\xi(2t) = 0$ and $\xi(2t+1) = 1$. We obtain $Z(\xi|_{[0;t]}) = \{1, 2\}$ if $\xi(t) = 0$ and $Z(\xi|_{[0;t]}) = \{0, 2\}$ if $\xi(t) = 1$. Since $\#F(x, u) \leq 2$ for all $x \in X$ and $u \in U$, its straightforward to see that $\sum_{t=0}^{\tau-1} \log_2 \#Z(\xi|_{[0;t[}) = \max_{\zeta \in \mathcal{Z}_\tau} \sum_{t=0}^{\tau-1} \log_2 \#Z(\zeta|_{[0;t[})$ holds for all $\tau \in \mathbb{N}$. Hence, we obtain $R(H) = 1$.

We are going to derive $C_0(H)$. Consider the set $\mathcal{Z}_\tau \subseteq X^{[0;\tau[}$ and the hypothesis for $\tau \in \mathbb{N}$: there exists at most one $\xi \in \mathcal{Z}_\tau$ with $\xi(\tau - 1) = 1$ and there exists at most one $\xi \in \mathcal{Z}_\tau$ with $\xi(\tau - 1) = 0$. For $\tau = 1$ we have $\mathcal{Z}_1 = X$ and the hypothesis holds. Suppose the hypothesis holds for $\tau \in \mathbb{N}$ and let $\xi \in \mathcal{Z}_\tau$. We have $Z(\xi) = \{0, 2\}$ if $\xi(t) = 1$, $Z(\xi) = \{1, 2\}$ if $\xi(t) = 0$, $Z(\xi) = \{2\}$ if $\xi(t) = 2$ and $Z(\xi) = \{3\}$ if $\xi(t) = 3$, so that the hypothesis holds for $\tau + 1$, which shows that the hypothesis holds for every $\tau \in \mathbb{N}$. Therefore, we obtain a bound of the number of elements in $\mathcal{Z}_\tau$ by $4 + 2(\tau - 1)$ and the zero-error capacity of H follows by $C_0(H) = 0$. □

Example 5 shows that even though, the asymptotic average of the total amount of information that needs to be transmitted (= symbol sequences generated by the closed-loop) via the channel is zero, the necessary (and sufficient) data rate to confine the system Σ within Q is one. The discrepancy results from the causality constraints that are imposed on the coder-controller structure by the invariance condition, i.e., at each instant in time the controller needs to be able to produce a control input so that all successor states are inside Q see e.g. [17]. Contrary to this observation, the zero-error capacity is an adequate measure for data rate constraints for linear systems (without disturbances) [18, 19].

5.1.3 Periodic coder-controllers

In the proof of the data rate theorem, we work with periodic coder-controllers. Given $\tau \in \mathbb{N}$ and a coder-controller $H = (S, \gamma, \delta)$, we say that H is *τ-periodic* if for all $t \in \mathbb{Z}_{\geq 0}$, $\zeta \in S^{[0;t]}$ and $\xi \in X^{[0;t]}$ we have

$$\begin{aligned}\gamma(\xi) &= \gamma(\xi|_{[\tau\lfloor t/\tau \rfloor;t]}),\\ \delta(\zeta) &= \delta(\zeta|_{[\tau\lfloor t/\tau \rfloor;t]}).\end{aligned} \tag{14}$$

LEMMA 4. *The transmission data rate of a τ-periodic coder-controller $H = (S, \gamma, \delta)$ for (2) is given by*

$$R(H) = \max_{\zeta \in \mathcal{Z}_\tau} \frac{1}{\tau} \sum_{t=0}^{\tau-1} \log_2 \#Z(\zeta|_{[0;t]}). \tag{15}$$

PROOF. Let L denote the right-hand-side of (15). Consider $T \in \mathbb{N}$, $\zeta \in \mathcal{Z}_T$ and set $a := \lfloor T/\tau \rfloor$ and $\bar{\tau} := T - \tau a$. We define $\zeta_i := \zeta|_{[i\tau;(i+1)\tau[}$ for $i \in [0; a[$ and $\zeta_a := \zeta|_{[a\tau;T[}$. Since γ is τ-periodic, we see that each ζ_i with $i \in [0; a[$ is an element of $\mathcal{Z}_\tau$, and we obtain for $N_i := \sum_{t=0}^{\tau-1} \log_2 \#Z(\zeta_i|_{[0;t]})$ the bound $N_i \leq L\tau$ for all $i \in [0; a[$. We define $N_a := \sum_{t=0}^{\bar{\tau}-1} \log_2 \#Z(\zeta_a|_{[0;t]})$ which is bounded by $N_a \leq \tau \log_2 \#S$. Note that $(a-1)\tau + \bar{\tau} = T$, so that for $C := -\bar{\tau}L + \tau \log_2 \#S$ we have

$$\begin{aligned}\tfrac{1}{T}\textstyle\sum_{t=0}^{T-1} \log_2 \#Z(\zeta|_{[0;t]}) &= \tfrac{1}{T}(\textstyle\sum_{i=0}^{a-1} N_i + N_a)\\ &\leq \tfrac{1}{T}((a-1)L\tau + L\bar{\tau} + C) = L + \tfrac{C}{T}\end{aligned}$$

Since C is independent of T the assertion follows. □

LEMMA 5. *For every coder-controller $H = (S, \delta, \gamma)$ for (2) and $\varepsilon > 0$, there exists a τ-periodic coder-controller $\hat{H} = (S, \hat{\delta}, \hat{\gamma})$ that satisfies*

$$R(\hat{H}) \leq \varepsilon + R(H).$$

PROOF. For $\varepsilon > 0$ we pick $\tau \in \mathbb{N}$ so that $\log_2 \#\mathcal{Z}_0/\tau \leq \varepsilon/2$ and $\max_{\zeta \in \mathcal{Z}_\tau} \frac{1}{\tau} \sum_{t=0}^{\tau-1} \log_2 \#Z(\zeta|_{[0;t]}) \leq R(H) + \varepsilon/2$. We define $\hat{\gamma}$ and $\hat{\delta}$ for all $\xi \in X^{[0;t]}$, $\zeta \in S^{[0;t]}$ with $t \in \mathbb{Z}_{\geq 0}$ by

$$\hat{\gamma}(\xi) := \gamma(\xi|_{[\tau\lfloor t/\tau \rfloor;t]}) \quad \text{and} \quad \hat{\delta}(\zeta) := \delta(\zeta|_{[\tau\lfloor t/\tau \rfloor;t]}).$$

Let $\hat{Z}$ be defined in (11) w.r.t. $\hat{\gamma}$. Then we have for all $\zeta \in S^{[0;t]}$ with $t \in [0; \tau - 1[$ the equality $Z(\zeta) = \hat{Z}(\zeta)$ and for every $\zeta \in S^{[0;\tau[}$ we have $\hat{Z}(\zeta) = \mathcal{Z}_0$ which follows from the fact that $\hat{\gamma}$ is τ-periodic. The transmission data rate of $\hat{H}$ follows by (15) which is bounded by

$$\max_{\zeta \in \hat{\mathcal{Z}}_\tau} \frac{1}{\tau}\Big(\sum_{t=0}^{\tau-2} \log_2 \#\hat{Z}(\zeta|_{[0;t]}) + \log_2 \#\mathcal{Z}_0\Big) \leq R(H) + \varepsilon \quad \square$$

5.2 The Data Rate Theorem

THEOREM 4. *Consider the system $\Sigma = (X, U, F)$ and a nonempty set $Q \subseteq X$. The invariance feedback entropy of Σ and Q satisfies*

$$h_{\text{inv}} = \inf_{H \in \mathcal{H}} R(H) \tag{16}$$

where $\mathcal{H}$ is the set of all Q-admissible coder-controllers for Σ.

We use the following two technical lemmas to show the theorem.

LEMMA 6. *Let $H = (S, \gamma, \delta)$ be Q-admissible τ-periodic coder-controller for $\Sigma = (X, U, F)$. Then there exists an invariant cover $(\mathcal{A}, G)$ of Σ and Q and a (τ, Q)-spanning set $\mathcal{S}$ in $(\mathcal{A}, G)$ so that*

$$\frac{1}{\tau} \log_2 N(\mathcal{S}) \leq R(H).$$

PROOF. For every $t \in [0; \tau[$ and every $\zeta \in \mathcal{Z}_{t+1}$ we define $A(\zeta) := \{x \in Q \mid \exists_{(\xi,\nu) \in \mathcal{B}_Q(H)}\ \zeta = \Gamma_t(\xi|_{[0;t]}) \wedge \xi(t) = x\}$, $G(A(\zeta)) := \delta(\zeta)$ and $\mathcal{A} := \{A(\zeta) \mid \zeta \in \mathcal{Z}_{t+1} \wedge t \in [0; \tau[\}$. We show that $(\mathcal{A}, G)$ is an invariant cover of Σ and Q. Clearly $\mathcal{A}$ is finite and every element of $\mathcal{A}$ is a subset of Q. Since H is Q-admissible, for every $x \in Q$ there exists $(\xi, \nu) \in \mathcal{B}_Q(H)$ so that $\xi(0) = x$. Hence, $\{A(s) \mid s \in \mathcal{Z}_1\}$ covers Q and we see that $\mathcal{A}$ covers Q. Let $A \in \mathcal{A}$ and suppose that there exists $x \in A$ so that $F(x, G(A)) \not\subseteq Q$. Since $A \in \mathcal{A}$, there exists $t \in [0; \tau[$, $\zeta \in \mathcal{Z}_{t+1}$ and $(\xi, \nu) \in \mathcal{B}_Q(H)$ so that $A = A(\zeta)$, $\zeta = \Gamma_t(\xi|_{[0;t]})$ and $x = \xi(t)$. Note that ν satisfies (13) so that $\nu(t) = G(A(\zeta))$ holds. We fix $x' \in F(x, G(A)) \setminus Q$ and pick a trajectory (ξ', ν') of Σ on $[0; \infty[$ such that $\xi'(0) = x'$ and $\nu'(t') = \delta(\Gamma_t((\xi|_{[0;t]}\xi')|_{[t;t+t'+1]}))$ holds for all $t' \in \mathbb{Z}_{\geq 0}$. We define $(\bar{\xi}, \bar{\nu})$ by $\bar{\xi} := \xi|_{[0;t]}\xi'$ and $\bar{\nu} := \nu|_{[0;t]}\nu'$, which by construction is a trajectory of Σ on $[0; \infty[$ which satisfies (13) but $\bar{\xi}([0; \infty[) \not\subseteq Q$. This contradicts the Q-admissibility of H and we can deduce that $F(A, G(A)) \subseteq Q$ for all $A \in \mathcal{A}$, which shows that $(\mathcal{A}, G)$ is an invariant cover of Σ and Q.
We are going to construct a (τ, Q)-spanning set $\mathcal{S} \subseteq \mathcal{A}^{[0;\tau[}$ with the help of $\mathcal{Z}_\tau$. For each $\zeta \in \mathcal{Z}_\tau$ we define a sequence $\alpha_\zeta : [0; \tau[\to \mathcal{A}$ by $\alpha_\zeta(t) := A(\zeta|_{[0;t]})$ for all $t \in [0; \tau[$ and use $\mathcal{S}$ to denote the set of all such sequences $\{\alpha_\zeta \mid \zeta \in \mathcal{Z}_\tau\}$. Note that $P(\alpha_\zeta) = \{A(s) \mid s \in \mathcal{Z}_1\}$ holds for all $\alpha_\zeta \in \mathcal{S}$, and we see that $P(\alpha_\zeta)$ covers Q. Let us show (3). Let $\alpha_\zeta \in \mathcal{S}$, $t \in [0; \tau - 1[$ so that $\alpha_\zeta(t) = A(\zeta|_{[0;t]})$. We define $\zeta_t := \zeta|_{[0;t]}$ and fix $x_0 \in A(\zeta_t)$ and $x_1 \in F(x_0, G(A(\zeta_t)))$. Since $x_0 \in A(\zeta_t)$ there exists $(\xi, \nu) \in \mathcal{B}_Q(H)$ so that $\zeta_t = \Gamma_t(\xi|_{[0;t]})$ with $\xi(t) = x_0$ and we use (13) to see that $G(A(\zeta_t)) = \delta(\zeta_t) = \nu(t)$. Therefore, $(\xi, \nu)|_{[0;t]}$ can be extended to a trajectory in $(\bar{\xi}, \bar{\nu}) \in \mathcal{B}_Q(H)$ with $\bar{\xi}(t+1) = x_1$. Let $s = \gamma(\bar{\xi}|_{[0;t+1]})$, then we have $s \in Z(\zeta_t)$ and $\zeta_{t+1} := \zeta_t s \in \mathcal{Z}_{t+2}$ holds. Moreover, $\zeta_{t+1} = \Gamma_{t+1}(\bar{\xi}|_{[0;t+1]})$ and we conclude that $x_1 \in A(\zeta_{t+1})$. We repeat this process for $x_i \in F(A(\zeta_{t+i}), G(A(\zeta_{t+i})), i \in [0; k]$ until $t + k = \tau - 1$ at which point we arrive at $\zeta_{t+k} \in \mathcal{Z}_\tau$ and we see that the associated sequence $\alpha_{\zeta_{t+k}}$ is an element of $\mathcal{S}$ that satisfies $x_1 \in \alpha_{\zeta_{t+k}}(t+1)$ and $\alpha_{\zeta_{t+k}}|_{[0;t]} = \alpha_\zeta|_{[0;t]}$. Since such a sequence can be constructed for every $x_1 \in F(x_0, G(A(\zeta_t)))$ and $x_0 \in A(\zeta_t)$, we see that (3) holds and it follows that $\mathcal{S}$ is (τ, Q)-spanning in $(\mathcal{A}, G)$.
We claim that $\#P(\alpha_\zeta|_{[0;t]}) \leq \#Z(\zeta|_{[0;t]})$ for every $\alpha_\zeta \in \mathcal{S}$ and $t \in [0; \tau - 1[$. Let $A \in P(\alpha_\zeta|_{[0;t]})$, then there exists $\alpha_{\zeta'} \in \mathcal{S}$ such that $A = \alpha_{\zeta'}(t+1)$ and $\zeta'|_{[0;t]} = \zeta_{[0;t]}$. Hence $\zeta'(t+1) \in Z(\zeta|_{[0;t]})$. Moreover, for $A, A' \in P(\alpha_\zeta|_{[0;t]})$ with $A \neq \bar{A}$ there exists $\alpha_{\zeta'}, \alpha_{\bar{\zeta}'} \in \mathcal{S}$ such that $A = A(\zeta'|_{[0;t+1]})$ and $\bar{A} = A(\bar{\zeta}'|_{[0;t+1]})$, which shows that $\zeta'(t+1) \neq \bar{\zeta}'(t+1)$ and $\zeta'(t+1), \bar{\zeta}'(t+1) \in Z(\zeta|_{[0;t]})$ and we obtain $\#P(\alpha_\zeta|_{[0;t]}) \leq \#Z(\zeta|_{[0;t]})$ for all $t \in [0; \tau - 1[$ and $\zeta \in \mathcal{Z}_\tau$. For $t = \tau - 1$ we have $P(\zeta) = \{A(s) \mid s \in \mathcal{Z}_1\}$. For $Z(\zeta)$ we have $Z(\zeta) = S$, since H is τ-periodic and we obtain $\#P(\alpha_\zeta) \leq \#Z(\zeta)$ for every $\zeta \in \mathcal{Z}_\tau$. Hence, $N(\mathcal{S}) \leq \max_{\zeta \in \mathcal{Z}_\tau} \prod_{t=0}^{\tau-1} \#Z(\zeta|_{[0;t]})$ follows and we obtain $\frac{1}{\tau} \log_2 N(\mathcal{S}) \leq R(H)$. □

LEMMA 7. *Consider an invariant cover* $(\mathcal{A}, G)$ *of* $\Sigma = (X, U, F)$ *and some nonempty set* $Q \subseteq X$. *Let* $\mathcal{S}$ *be a* (τ, Q)-*spanning set in* $(\mathcal{A}, G)$. *Then there exists a* Q-*admissible* τ-*periodic coder-controller* $H = (S, \gamma, \delta)$ *for* Σ *so that*

$$\frac{1}{\tau}\log_2 N(\mathcal{S}) \geq R(H).$$

PROOF. We define $\mathcal{S}_t := \{\alpha \in \mathcal{A}^{[0;t]} \mid \exists_{\hat{\alpha}\in\mathcal{S}}\ \hat{\alpha}|_{[0;t]} = \alpha\}$ for $t \in [0;\tau[$ and observe that $\mathcal{S}_\tau = \mathcal{S}$ and for every $\alpha \in \mathcal{S}$ we have $P(\alpha) = \mathcal{S}_0$. For $\alpha \in \mathcal{S}_t$ with $t \in [0; \tau - 1[$ let $e(\alpha)$ be an enumeration of $P(\alpha)$. We slightly abuse the notation, and use $e(\varnothing)$ to denote an enumeration of $\mathcal{S}_0$ so that $e(\alpha|_{[0;0[}) = e(\varnothing)$ for all $\alpha \in \mathcal{S}$. Let $m \in \mathbb{N}$ be the smallest number so that every co-domain of $e(\alpha)$ is a subset of $[1; m]$. We use this interval to define the set of symbols $S := [1; m]$. We are going to define $\gamma(\xi)$ and $\delta(\zeta)$ for all sequences $\xi \in X^{[0;t]}$, respectively, $\zeta \in S^{[0;t]}$ with $t \in [0; \tau[$, which determines γ and δ for all elements in their domain, since γ and δ are τ-periodic. We begin with γ, which we define iteratively. For $t = 0$ and $x \in X$ we set $\gamma(x) := e(\varnothing)(A)$ if there exists $A \in \mathcal{S}_0$ with $x \in A$. If there are several $A \in \mathcal{S}_0$ that contain x we simply pick one. If there does not exist any $A \in \mathcal{S}_0$ with $x \in A$ we set $\gamma(x) := 1$. For $t \in]0; \tau[$ and $\xi \in X^{[0;t]}$ we define $\gamma(\xi) := e(\alpha|_{[0;t[})(\alpha(t))$ if there exists $\alpha \in \mathcal{S}_t$ so that i) $\xi(t) \in \alpha(t)$ and ii) $\gamma(\xi|_{[0;t']}) = e(\alpha|_{[0;t'[})(\alpha(t'))$ holds for all $t' \in [0; t[$. Again, if there are several such $\alpha \in \mathcal{S}_t$ we simply pick one. If there does not exist any α in $\mathcal{S}_t$ that satisfies i) and ii), we set $\gamma(\xi) := 1$. We define δ for $t \in [0; \tau[$ and $\zeta \in S^{[0;t]}$ as follows: if there exists $\alpha \in \mathcal{S}_t$ that satisfies $e(\alpha|_{[0;t'[})(\alpha(t')) = \zeta(t')$ for all $t' \in [0; t]$, we set $\delta(\zeta) := G(\alpha(t))$, otherwise we set $\delta(\zeta) := u$ for some $u \in U$. Let us show that the coder-controller is Q-admissible. We fix $(\xi, \nu) \in \mathcal{B}_Q(H)$ and proceed by induction with the hypothesis parameterized by $t \in [0; \tau[$: there exists $\alpha \in \mathcal{S}_t$ so that $\xi(t) \in \alpha(t)$, $\gamma(\xi|_{[0;t']}) = e(\alpha|_{[0;t'[})(\alpha(t'))$ and $\nu(t') = G(\alpha(t'))$ holds for all $t' \in [0; t]$. For $t = 0$, we know that $\mathcal{S}_0$ covers Q so that for $\xi(0) \in Q$ there exists $A \in \mathcal{S}_0$ with $x \in A$ and it follows from the definition of γ and δ that $\gamma(\xi(0)) = e(\varnothing)(\bar{A})$ for some $\bar{A} \in \mathcal{S}_0$ with $\xi(0) \in \bar{A}$ and $\nu(0) = \delta(\gamma(\bar{A})) = G(\bar{A})$. Now suppose that the induction hypothesis holds for $t \in]0; \tau - 1[$. Since $\xi(t) \in \alpha(t)$ and $\nu(t) = G(\alpha(t))$ for some $\alpha \in \mathcal{S}_t$, we use (3) to see that there exists $\bar{\alpha} \in \mathcal{S}$ so that $\bar{\alpha}|_{[0;t]} = \alpha$ and $\xi(t+1) \in \bar{\alpha}(t+1)$, so that $\bar{\alpha}$ satisfies i) and ii) in the definition of γ and we have $\gamma(\xi|_{[0;t+1]}) = e(\alpha)(\hat{\alpha}(t+1))$ for some $\hat{\alpha} \in \mathcal{S}_{t+1}$ with $\xi(t+1) \in \hat{\alpha}(t+1)$ and $\hat{\alpha}|_{[0;t]} = \alpha$. Since $\hat{\alpha}$ is uniquely determined by the symbol sequence $\zeta \in S^{[0;t+1]}$ given by $\zeta(t') = e(\hat{\alpha}|_{[0;t'[})(\hat{\alpha}(t'))$ for all $t' \in [0; t+1]$, we have $\nu(t+1) = \delta(\zeta) = G(\hat{\alpha}(t+1))$, which completes the induction. Note that the induction hypothesis implies that $F(\xi(t), \nu(t)) \subseteq Q$ for all $t \in [0; \tau[$, since $\xi(t) \in \alpha(t)$ and $\nu(t) = G(\alpha(t))$. We obtain $\xi([0; \infty[) \subseteq Q$ from the τ-periodicity of H and the Q-admissibility follows.

We derive a bound for $R(H)$. Since H is τ-periodic, we have for any $\zeta \in \mathcal{Z}_\tau$ the equality $Z(\zeta) = e(\varnothing)(\mathcal{S}_0)$ and we see that $\#Z(\zeta) = \#e(\varnothing)(\mathcal{S}_0) = \#P(\alpha)$ for any $\alpha \in \mathcal{S}$. We fix $\zeta \in \mathcal{Z}_\tau$ and pick $\alpha \in \mathcal{S}$ with $\alpha(t) = e^{-1}(\alpha|_{[0;t[})(\zeta(t))$ holds for all $t \in [0; \tau[$. By definition, the set $Z(\zeta|_{[0;t]})$ is the co-domain of an enumeration of $P(\alpha|_{[0;t]})$, which shows $\#Z(\zeta|_{[0;t]}) = \#P(\alpha|_{[0;t]})$. Therefore, we have $\max_{\zeta\in\mathcal{Z}_\tau}\prod_{t=0}^{\tau-1}\#Z(\zeta|_{[0;t]}) \leq \max_{\alpha\in\mathcal{S}}\prod_{t=0}^{\tau-1}\#P(\alpha|_{[0;t]})$ and the assertion follows by (15). □

PROOF OF THEOREM 4. Let us first prove the inequality $h_{\text{inv}} \leq \inf_{H\in\mathcal{H}} R(H)$. If the right-hand-side of (16) equals infinity the inequality trivially holds and subsequently we assume that the right-hand side of (16) is finite. We fix $\varepsilon > 0$ and pick a coder-controller $\bar{H} = (S, \bar{\gamma}, \bar{\delta})$ so that $R(\bar{H}) \leq \inf_{H\in\mathcal{H}} R(H) + \varepsilon$. According to Lemma 5 there exists a τ-periodic coder-controller $H = (S, \gamma, \delta)$ so that $R(H) \leq R(\bar{H}) + \varepsilon$. It is straightforward to see that for every $(\xi, \nu) \in \mathcal{B}_Q(H)$ and $\xi_i := \xi|_{[i\tau;(i+1)\tau[}$, $i \in \mathbb{Z}_{\geq 0}$, there exists $(\bar{\xi}, \bar{\nu}) \in \mathcal{B}_Q(\bar{H})$, so that $\xi_i = \bar{\xi}|_{[0;\tau[}$, which shows that H is Q-admissible. From Lemma 6 follows that there exists an $(\mathcal{A}, G)$ of Σ and Q and a (τ, Q)-spanning set in $(\mathcal{A}, G)$ so that $\frac{1}{\tau}\log_2 N(\mathcal{S}) \leq R(H)$. We use Lemma 1 to see that $r_{\text{inv}}(n\tau, Q) \leq n r_{\text{inv}}(\tau, Q)$ so that $h(\mathcal{A}, G) = \lim_{n\to\infty}\frac{1}{n\tau}\log_2 r_{\text{inv}}(n\tau, Q) \leq \frac{1}{\tau}\log_2 r_{\text{inv}}(\tau, Q) \leq \frac{1}{\tau}\log_2 N(\mathcal{S})$. By the choice H we obtain $2\varepsilon + \inf_{H\in\mathcal{H}} R(H) \geq R(H) \geq h_{\text{inv}}$. Since this holds for arbitrary $\varepsilon > 0$ we arrive at the desired inequality.

We continue with the inequality $h_{\text{inv}} \geq \inf_{H\in\mathcal{H}} R(H)$. If $h_{\text{inv}} = \infty$ the inequality trivially holds and subsequently we assume that $h_{\text{inv}} < \infty$. We fix $\varepsilon > 0$ and pick an invariant cover $(\mathcal{A}, G)$ of Σ and Q so that $h(\mathcal{A}, G) < h_{\text{inv}} + \varepsilon$. We pick $\tau \in \mathbb{N}$ so that $\frac{1}{\tau}\log_2 r_{\text{inv}}(\tau, Q) < h(\mathcal{A}, G) + \varepsilon$. Let $\mathcal{S}$ be (τ, Q)-spanning set that satisfies $r_{\text{inv}}(\tau, Q) = N(\mathcal{S})$. It follows from Lemma 7 that there exists a Q-admissible coder-controller H so that $\frac{1}{\tau}\log_2 N(\mathcal{S}) \geq R(H)$ holds, so that we obtain $2\varepsilon + h_{\text{inv}} \geq R(H)$. This inequality holds for any $\varepsilon > 0$, which implies that $h_{\text{inv}} \geq \inf_{H\in\mathcal{H}} R(H)$. □

6. FINITE SYSTEMS

In this section, we characterize the invariance feedback entropy of finite systems in terms of the value function of mean-payoff games [6, 7].

6.1 Mean-Payoff Games

A *mean-payoff game* (MPG) is played by two players, player 1 and player 2, on a finite, directed, edge-weighted graph $G = (V, E, w)$, where $V := V_1 \cup V_2$, $V_1 \cap V_2 = \varnothing$ with V_i, $i \in \{1, 2\}$ being two nonempty sets, $E \subseteq V \times V$, $w : E \to \mathbb{Z}$ and for every $v \in V$ there exists $v' \in V$ so that $(v, v') \in E$. The vertices V are also referred to as *positions* of the game. Starting from an initial position $v_0 \in V$, player 1 and player 2 take turns in picking the next position depending on the current position of the game: given $v_0 \in V_i$ for $i \in \{1, 2\}$ player i picks the successor vertex $v_1 \in V$ so that $(v_0, v_1) \in E$ and the play continues with $v_1 \in V$. The duration of the game is infinite and the resulting infinite sequence of edges $e_0e_1e_2\ldots$ is called a *play*. Player 1 wants to minimize the payoff

$$\nu_{\min}(e_0e_1e_2\ldots) := \limsup_{k\to\infty}\frac{1}{k}\sum_{j=0}^{k-1} w(e_j)$$

while player 2 wants to maximize the payoff

$$\nu_{\max}(e_0e_1e_2\ldots) := \liminf_{k\to\infty}\frac{1}{k}\sum_{j=0}^{k-1} w(e_j).$$

A *positional strategy* for player i is a function $\sigma_i : V_i \to V$ so that $(v, \sigma_i(v)) \in E$ holds for all $v \in V_i$. Given a positional strategy σ_i for player i and a position $v \in V$, let us use $\mathcal{P}_i(v, \sigma_i) \subseteq E^{[0;\infty[}$ to denote the set of all plays $((v_k, v_k'))_{k\in[0;\infty[}$ that satisfy $v = v_0$ and for all $k \in [0; \infty[$ with $v_k \in V_i$ we have $v_k' = \sigma_i(v_k)$.

As it turns out, there exist *optimal positional strategies* σ_i^* for each player i and a function $\nu : V \to \mathbb{Q}$ so that player 1 is able to secure a payoff of $\nu(v)$ against any other strategy of player 2 and vice versa, i.e., for all sequences $\check{e} \in \mathcal{P}_1(v, \sigma_1^*)$ and $\hat{e} \in \mathcal{P}_2(v, \sigma_2^*)$ we have

$$\nu_{\min}(\check{e}) \leq \nu(v) \leq \nu_{\max}(\hat{e}). \tag{17}$$

We call ν the *value function* of the MPG (V, E, w), see e.g. [6] for details. Note that σ_1^* is optimal in the sense that any deviation of player 1 from σ_1^* can only lead to a larger or equal payoff than $\nu(v)$ considering the worst case with respect to possible strategies of player 2. Similarly, a deviation of player 2 from σ_2^* may only lead to suboptimal payoff.

6.2 Feedback Entropy Characterization

Given a finite system $\Sigma = (X, U, F)$ and a nonempty set $Q \subseteq X$, we construct a MPG (V, E, w) so that the invariance entropy of Σ and Q can be characterized in terms of the value function of (V, E, w).

Let $V_1 := \{(A, u) \in \wp(Q) \times U \mid F(A, u) \subseteq Q\}$ where $\wp(Q)$ denotes the power set of Q, and consider for each $(A, u) \in V_1$ the set of sets

$$\mathcal{V}(A, u) := \{V \subseteq V_1 \mid F(A, u) \subseteq \cup_{(A', u') \in V} A'\}$$

with which we define $V_2 := \cup_{(A,u) \in V_1} \mathcal{V}(A, u)$ and the positions of the MPG follow by $V = V_1 \cup V_2$. We introduce the edges $E := E_1 \cup E_2$ of the MPG by

$$E_1 := \{(v_1, v_2) \in V_1 \times V_2 \mid v_2 \in \mathcal{V}(v_1)\}$$
$$E_2 := \{(v_2, v_1) \in V_2 \times V_1 \mid v_1 \in v_2\}.$$

The weights for $(v_1, v_2) \in E_1$ and $(v_2, v_1) \in E_2$ are given by $w(v_1, v_2) := \log_2 \#v_2$ and $w(v_2, v_1) := \log_2 \#v_2$. We refer to (V, E, w) as the MPG *associated* with Σ and Q.

THEOREM 5. *Consider a finite system $\Sigma = (X, U, F)$ and a nonempty, controlled invariant set Q. Let ν be the value function of the MPG (V, E, w) associated with Σ and Q. Then the invariance feedback entropy of Σ and Q satisfies*

$$h_{\text{inv}} = \max_{x \in Q} \min_{v \in \{(A,u) \in V_1 \mid x \in A\}} \nu(v) =: h_{\text{mpg}}. \tag{18}$$

PROOF. Before we show (18) let us point out that the controlled invariance of Q ensures that (V, E, w) is a MPG, i.e., for every $v \in V$ there exists $v' \in V$ so that $(v, v') \in E$.

We begin with the inequality $h_{\text{inv}} \geq h_{\text{mpg}}$. It follows from Theorem 1 that $h_{\text{inv}} < \infty$. Since Σ is finite the set of invariant covers of Σ and Q is finite and it follows that there exist an invariant cover $(\mathcal{A}, G)$ so that $h(\mathcal{A}, G) = h_{\text{inv}}$. For the sake of contradiction, suppose that $h(\mathcal{A}, G) < h_{\text{mpg}}$. Then there exists $\tau \in \mathbb{N}$ and a (τ, Q)-spanning set $\mathcal{S}$ so that $\frac{1}{\tau} \log_2 N(\mathcal{S}) < h_{\text{mpg}}$. For $t \in [0; \tau[$ we define the set $\mathcal{S}_t := \{\alpha|_{[0;t]} \mid \alpha \in \mathcal{S}\}$. Let σ_2^* be an optimal positional strategy for player 2. We construct a sequence $(v_k)_{k \in [0;\infty[}$ in V. We pick $A \in \mathcal{S}_0$ and set $v_0 := (A, G(A))$ and $v_1 := \{(A', u') \mid A' \in P(A) \wedge u' = G(A')\}$. For $t \in [1; \infty[$ we define by $v_{2t} := \sigma_2^*(v_{2t-1})$ and by $v_{2t+1} := \{(A, u) \mid A \in P(\alpha) \wedge u = G(\alpha(t))\}$ where $\alpha : [0; t] \to \mathcal{A}$ is implicitly given by the sequence that satisfies $(\alpha(t'), G(\alpha(t'))) = v_{2t'}$ for all $t' \in [0; t]$. We claim that the sequence $e := ((v_k, v'_k))_{k \in [0;\infty[}$ with $v'_k := v_{k+1}$ is an element of $\mathcal{P}_2(v_0, \sigma_2^*)$. Let $t \in [0; \infty[$ then we have $v_{2t} = (A, u)$ for some $A \in \mathcal{A}$ and $u = G(A)$, hence $F(A, u) \subseteq Q$ and we see that $v_{2t} \in V_1$. While it follows from (3) that $v_{2t+1} \in \mathcal{V}(v_{2t})$, hence $v_{2t+1} \in V_2$ and $(v_{2t}, v_{2t+1}) \in E_1$. From $v_{2t+2} = \sigma_2^*(v_{2t+1})$ follows that $(v_{2t+1}, v_{2t+2}) \in E_2$ and we have $(v_k, v_{k+1}) \in E$ for all $k \in [0; \infty[$ which shows that $((v_k, v'_k))_{k \in [0;\infty[}$ is a play. Moreover, $v_k \in V_2$ implies that $k = 2t + 1$ for some $t \in [0; \infty[$ and we have $v'_k = v_{2t+2} = \sigma_2^*(v_{2t+1})$ for all $t \in [0; \infty[$ so that $e = ((v_k, v'_k))_{k \in [0;\infty[}$ is an element of $\mathcal{P}_2(v_0, \sigma_2^*)$. Let $\alpha : [0; \infty[\to \mathcal{A}$ be implicitly given by the sequence that satisfies $(\alpha(t), G(\alpha(t))) = v_{2t}$ for all $t \in [0; \infty[$. Let $r = 2j\tau$ for some $j \in \mathbb{Z}_{\geq 0}$, and define $\alpha_j := \alpha|_{[j\tau;(j+1)\tau[}$. It follows from the fact that $v_{2t+2} \in v_{2t+1}$ and the definition of v_{2t+1} that $\alpha_j \in \mathcal{S}$. Therefore, we obtain

$$\sum_{k=r}^{r+2\tau-1} w((v_k, v'_k)) = 2 \sum_{t=0}^{\tau-1} \#v_{r+2t+1} = 2 \sum_{t=0}^{\tau-1} \log_2 \#P(\alpha_j|_{[0;t]})$$

which is bounded by $2 \log_2 N(\mathcal{S})$ and we deduce from (17) that $\frac{1}{\tau} \log_2 N(\mathcal{S}) \geq \nu_{\max}(e) \geq \nu(v_0)$. Since this inequality holds for every $v_0 = (A, G(A))$ with $A \in \mathcal{S}_0$ and $\mathcal{S}_0$ covers Q, we obtain a contradiction to $\frac{1}{\tau} \log_2 N(\mathcal{S}) < h_{\text{mpg}}$ and we see that $h_{\text{inv}} \geq h_{\text{mpg}}$ must hold.

We continue with the inequality $h_{\text{mpg}} \geq h_{\text{inv}}$. We define $(\mathcal{A}, G)$ implicitly by $A \in \mathcal{A}$ and $u = G(A)$ if and only if $(A, u) \in V_1$. It is easy to see by definition of V_1 that $(\mathcal{A}, G)$ is an invariant cover of Σ and Q. Let $V_0 \subseteq V_1$ be such that $\cup_{(A,u) \in V_0} A$ covers Q and $\max_{v \in V_0} \nu(v) = h_{\text{mpg}}$. Let σ_1^* be an optimal positional strategy for player 1. Let $\tau \in \mathbb{N}$ and consider the set $\mathcal{S} \subseteq \mathcal{A}^{[0;\tau[}$ implicitly defined by $\alpha \in \mathcal{S}$ if and only if there exists $((A_k, u_k), \bar{v}_k)_{k \in [0;\infty[} \in \mathcal{P}_1(v_0, \sigma_1^*)$ with $v_0 \in V_0$ so that $\alpha(t) = A_{2t}$ holds for for all $t \in [0; \tau[$. Let us show that $\mathcal{S}$ is a (τ, Q)-spanning set. Clearly $\{\alpha(0) \mid \alpha \in \mathcal{S}\}$ covers Q since $\cup_{(A,u) \in V_0} A$ covers Q and it remains to show (3). We fix $t \in [0; \tau - 1[$ and $\alpha_0 \in \mathcal{S}$ and pick $\alpha_j \in \mathcal{S}$ with $j \in [1; m]$, $m = \#P(\alpha_0|_{[0;t]})$ so that $P(\alpha_0|_{[0;t]}) = \{\alpha_j(t+1) \mid j \in [1; m]\}$ and $\alpha_0|_{[0;t]} = \alpha_j|_{[0;t]}$ holds for all $j \in [1; m]$. For every $j \in [0; m]$ there exists an associated play $(v_k^j = (A_k^j, u_k^j), \bar{v}_k^j)_{k \in [0;\infty[} \in \mathcal{P}_1(v_0, \sigma_1^*)$ that satisfies $\alpha_j(t') = A_{2t'}^j$ for all $t' \in [0; \tau[$. As σ_1^* is deterministic, we have $v_{2t+1}^0 = v_{2t+1}^j$ for all $j \in [1; m]$, which implies $P(\alpha_0|_{[0;t]}) = \{A \in \mathcal{A} \mid \exists_{u \in U} (A, u) \in v_{2t+1}^0\}$ so that $\#P(\alpha_0|_{[0;t]}) = \#v_{2t+1}^0$. As this holds for all $t \in [0; \tau - 1[$, we get $\frac{1}{2} \sum_{k=0}^{2\tau-1} w((v_k^0, \bar{v}_k^0)) + \log_2 \#V_0 \geq \sum_{t=0}^{\tau-1} \log_2 \#P(\alpha_0|_{[0;t]})$. This implies that for every $\tau \in \mathbb{N}$ there exists $v_0 \in V_0$ and a play $(v_k, \bar{v}_k)_{k \in [0;\infty[} \in \mathcal{P}_1(v_0, \sigma_1^*)$ so that

$$\frac{1}{2\tau} \sum_{k=0}^{2\tau-1} w((v_k, \bar{v}_k)) + \log_2 \frac{\#V_0}{\tau} \geq \frac{1}{\tau} \log_2 N(\mathcal{S})$$

holds. Since $\nu(v_0) \geq \nu_{\min}((v_k, \bar{v}_k)_{k \in [0;\infty[})$ holds for every play $(v_k, \bar{v}_k)_{k \in [0;\infty[}$ in $\mathcal{P}_1(v_0, \sigma_1^*)$ we get the desired inequality $h_{\text{mpg}} = \max_{v_0 \in V_0} \nu(v_0) \geq h_{\text{inv}}$. □

REMARK 1. *Let $n := \#X$ and $m := \#U$, then we obtain a bound on the number of vertices in V_1 by $m \cdot 2^n$. While the number of elements in $\mathcal{V}(v)$ for each $v \in V_1$ is bounded by $m \cdot 2^{2^n - 1}$ so that the number of elements in V is of the order of $m^2 \cdot 2^{2^n}$. The value function of a MPG can be computed in $O(\#V \cdot \#E \cdot \log_2 \#X)$ time [7], so that in its current form, the computation of h_{inv} based on Theorem 5 is far from practical and further investigations are needed.*

7. SUMMARY AND OUTLOOK

We have introduced a notion of invariance feedback entropy for discrete-time, nondeterministic systems in terms of invariant covers. We provided conditions for finiteness and established the equivalence with known notions of entropy in the deterministic case. We showed the data rate theorem and discussed potential alternatives of the data rate of a coder-controller. We used mean-payoff games to provide an algorithmic approach to determine the invariance feedback entropy of finite systems.

This work represents an initial attempt to develop a theory that explains data rate constraints of feedback control of nondeterministic control systems. Several important questions are open and further investigations are needed: What is the entropy of linear systems with bounded disturbances? Can we establish upper and lower bounds of the data-rate of sampled-data control systems as illustrated in Figure 2? Are there efficient means to construct the mean-payoff game?

8. ACKNOWLEDGMENTS

The work is supported by the TUM International Graduate School of Science and Engineering.

9. REFERENCES

[1] J. P. Hespanha, P. Naghshtabrizi, and Y. Xu. "A survey of recent results in networked control systems". In: *Proc. of the IEEE* 95.1 (2007), pp. 138–162.

[2] G. Nair et al. "Feedback control under data rate constraints: An overview". In: *Proc. of the IEEE* 95.1 (2007), pp. 108–137.

[3] G. N. Nair et al. "Topological feedback entropy and nonlinear stabilization". In: *IEEE Trans. Autom. Control* 49.9 (2004), pp. 1585–1597.

[4] F. Colonius and C. Kawan. "Invariance entropy for control systems". In: *SIAM J. Control Optim.* 48.3 (2009), pp. 1701–1721.

[5] F. Colonius, C. Kawan, and G. N. Nair. "A note on topological feedback entropy and invariance entropy". In: *Sys. Control Lett.* 62.5 (2013), pp. 377–381.

[6] A. Ehrenfeucht and J. Mycielski. "Positional strategies for mean payoff games". In: *Int. Journal of Game Theory* 8.2 (1979), pp. 109–113.

[7] U. Zwick and M. Paterson. "The complexity of mean payoff games on graphs". In: *Theoretical Computer Science* 158.1 (1996), pp. 343–359.

[8] R. T. Rockafellar and R. J-B Wets. *Variational analysis.* Vol. 317. Springer, 2009.

[9] C. G. Cassandras and S. Lafortune. *Introduction to discrete event systems.* Springer, 2009.

[10] C. Baier and J.-P. Katoen. *Principles of model checking.* MIT Press Cambridge, 2008.

[11] F. Colonius. "Entropy properties of deterministic control systems". In: *Proc. of the 54th IEEE Conf. on Decision and Control.* 2015, pp. 57–65.

[12] R. Freeman and P. V. Kokotovic. *Robust nonlinear control design: state-space and Lyapunov techniques.* Birkhäuser, 1996.

[13] F. Blanchini and S. Miani. *Set-Theoretic Methods in Control.* Birkhäuser, 2008.

[14] D. S. Laila, D. Nešić, and A. Astolfi. "Sampled-data Control of Nonlinear Systems". In: *Advanced Topics in Control Systems Theory.* Springer, 2006, pp. 91–137.

[15] J.-P. Aubin and H. Frankowska. *Set-valued analysis.* Birkhäuser, 1990.

[16] T. W. Gamelin and R. E. Greene. *Introduction to Topology.* 2nd Edition. Dover Publications, 1999.

[17] E. I. Silva, M. S. Derpich, and J. Østergaard. "A framework for control system design subject to average data-rate constraints". In: *IEEE Trans. Autom. Control* 56.8 (2011), pp. 1886–1899.

[18] G. N. Nair. "A nonstochastic information theory for feedback". In: *Proc. of the 51st IEEE Conf. on Decision and Control.* 2012, pp. 1343–1348.

[19] G. N. Nair. "A nonstochastic information theory for communication and state estimation". In: *IEEE Trans. Autom. Control* 58.6 (2013), pp. 1497–1510.

APPENDIX

PROOF OF LEMMA 1. We fix $\tau_1, \tau_2 \in \mathbb{N}$ and choose two minimal (τ_i, Q)-spanning sets $\mathcal{S}_i$, $i \in \{1,2\}$ in $(\mathcal{A}, G)$ so that $r_{\text{inv}}(\tau_i, Q) = N(\mathcal{S}_i)$. Let $\mathcal{S}$ be the set of sequences $\alpha : [0; \tau_1 + \tau_2[\to \mathcal{A}$ given by $\alpha(t) := \alpha_1(t)$ for $t \in [0; \tau_1[$ and $\alpha(t) := \alpha_2(t - \tau_1)$ for $t \in [\tau_1; \tau_1 + \tau_2[$, where $\alpha_i \in \mathcal{S}_i$ for $i \in \{1,2\}$. We claim that $\mathcal{S}$ is $(\tau_1 + \tau_2, Q)$-spanning in $(\mathcal{A}, G)$. It is easy to see that $\{A \in \mathcal{A} \mid \exists_{\alpha \in \mathcal{S}} A = \alpha(0)\}$ covers Q, since $\{A \in \mathcal{A} \mid \exists_{\alpha \in \mathcal{S}_1} A = \alpha(0)\}$ covers Q. Let $t \in [0; \tau_1 + \tau_2[$ and $\alpha \in \mathcal{S}$. If $t \in [0; \tau_1 - 1[$, we immediately see that $F(\alpha(t), G(\alpha(t))) \subseteq \cup_{A' \in P(\alpha|_{[0;t]})} A'$ since $\alpha_1 := \alpha|_{[0;\tau_1[} \in \mathcal{S}_1$ and $\mathcal{S}_1$ satisfies (3). Similarly, if $t \in [\tau_1; \tau_1 + \tau_2 - 1[$ we have $F(\alpha(t), G(\alpha(t))) \subseteq \cup_{A' \in P(\alpha|_{[0;t]})} A'$ since $\alpha_2 := \alpha|_{[\tau_1;\tau_1+\tau_2[} \in \mathcal{S}_2$ and $\mathcal{S}_2$ satisfies (3). For $t = \tau_1 - 1$, we know that $P(\alpha|_{[0;\tau_1[})$ equals $\{A \mid \exists_{\alpha_2 \in \mathcal{S}_2} \alpha_2(0) = A\}$ which covers Q and the inclusion $F(\alpha(t), G(\alpha(t))) \subseteq \cup_{A' \in P(\alpha|_{[0;t]})} A'$ follows. Hence $\mathcal{S}$ satisfies (3) and we see that $\mathcal{S}$ is (τ, Q)-spanning. Subsequently, for $i \in \{1,2\}$ and $\alpha \in \mathcal{S}_i$, $t \in [0; \tau_i - 1[$, let us use $P_i(\alpha|_{[0;t]}) := \{A \in \mathcal{A} \mid \exists_{\hat{\alpha} \in \mathcal{S}_i} \hat{\alpha}|_{[0;t]} = \alpha|_{[0;t]} \wedge A = \hat{\alpha}(t+1)\}$. Then we have $P(\alpha|_{[0;t]}) = P_1(\alpha_1|_{[0;t]})$ with $\alpha_1 := \alpha|_{[0;\tau_1[}$ if $t \in [0; \tau_1 - 1[$ and $P(\alpha|_{[0;t]}) = P_2(\alpha_2|_{[0;t-\tau_1]})$ with $\alpha_2 := \alpha|_{[\tau_1;\tau_1+\tau_2[}$ if $t \in [\tau_1; \tau_1 + \tau_2 - 1[$, while for $t = \tau_1 - 1$ we have $P(\alpha|_{[0;t]}) = P_2(\alpha_2)$ with $\alpha_2 := \alpha|_{[\tau_1;\tau_1+\tau_2[}$ and $P(\alpha) := P_1(\alpha_1)$ with $\alpha_1 := \alpha|_{[0;\tau_1[}$. Therefore, $N(\mathcal{S})$ is bounded by $N(\mathcal{S}_1) \cdot N(\mathcal{S}_2)$ and we have $r_{\text{inv}}(\tau_1 + \tau_2, Q) \leq r_{\text{inv}}(\tau_1, Q) \cdot r_{\text{inv}}(\tau_2, Q)$. Hence, $\tau \mapsto \log_2 r_{\text{inv}}(\tau, Q)$, $\mathbb{N} \to \mathbb{R}_{\geq 0}$ is a subadditive sequence of real numbers and (6) follows by [5, Lem. 2.1]. □

PROOF OF LEMMA 2. For every $t \in [0; \tau[$, we define the set $\mathcal{S}_t := \{\alpha \in \mathcal{A}^{[0;t]} \mid \exists_{\alpha' \in \mathcal{S}} \alpha'|_{[0;t]} = \alpha\}$. By definition of P we have for all $\alpha \in \mathcal{S}$ the equality $P(\alpha) = \mathcal{S}_0$, which shows the assertion for $\tau = 1$ since in this case we have $\mathcal{S}_0 = \mathcal{S}$. Subsequently, we assume $\tau > 1$. For $t \in [0; \tau[$ and $a_0 \dots a_t \in \mathcal{S}_t$ we use $Y(a_0 \dots a_t) := \{\alpha \in \mathcal{S} \mid a_0 \dots a_t = \alpha|_{[0;t]}\}$ to denote the sequences in $\mathcal{S}$ whose initial part is restricted to $a_0 \dots a_t$. For $t \in [0; \tau - 1[$ and $a_0 \dots a_t \in \mathcal{S}_t$ we have the inequality

$$\#Y(a_0 \dots a_t) \leq \#P(a_0 \dots a_t) \max_{a_{t+1} \in P(a_0 \dots a_t)} \#Y(a_0 \dots a_{t+1}).$$

For every $a_0 \dots a_{\tau-2} \in \mathcal{S}_{\tau-2}$ we have $\#Y(a_0 \dots a_{\tau-2}) = \#P(a_0 \dots a_{\tau-2})$ and we obtain a bound for $\#Y(a_0)$ by

$$\#P(a_0) \max_{a_1 \in P(a_0)} \#P(a_0 a_1) \cdots \max_{a_{\tau-2} \in P(a_0 \dots a_{\tau-3})} \#P(a_0 \dots a_{\tau-2})$$

so that $\#Y(a_0) \leq \max_{\alpha \in \mathcal{S}} \prod_{t=0}^{\tau-2} \#P(\alpha|_{[0;t]})$ holds for any $a_0 \in \mathcal{S}_0$. We use $\cup_{a_0 \in \mathcal{S}_0} Y(a_0) = \mathcal{S}$ and the fact that for every $\alpha \in \mathcal{S}$ we have $P(\alpha) = \mathcal{S}_0$ to arrive at desired inequality, $\#\mathcal{S} \leq \max_{\alpha \in \mathcal{S}} \prod_{t=0}^{\tau-1} \#P(\alpha|_{[0;t]})$. □

Robust Abstractions for Control Synthesis: Completeness via Robustness for Linear-Time Properties

Jun Liu
Department of Applied Mathematics
University of Waterloo
j.liu@uwaterloo.ca

ABSTRACT

We define robust abstractions for synthesizing provably correct and robust controllers for (possibly infinite) uncertain transition systems. It is shown that robust abstractions are sound in the sense that they preserve robust satisfaction of linear-time properties. We then focus on discrete-time control systems modelled by nonlinear difference equations with inputs and define concrete robust abstractions for them. While most abstraction techniques in the literature for nonlinear systems focus on constructing sound abstractions, we present computational procedures for constructing both sound and approximately complete robust abstractions for general nonlinear control systems without stability assumptions. Such procedures are approximately complete in the sense that, given a concrete discrete-time control system and an arbitrarily small perturbation of this system, there exists a finite transition system that robustly abstracts the concrete system and is abstracted by the slightly perturbed system simultaneously. A direct consequence of this result is that robust control synthesis for discrete-time nonlinear systems and linear-time specifications is robustly decidable. More specifically, if there exists a robust control strategy that realizes a given linear-time specification, we can algorithmically construct a (potentially less) robust control strategy that realizes the same specification. The theoretical results are illustrated with a simple motion planning example.

Keywords

Nonlinear systems; control synthesis; abstraction; robustness; linear-time property; linear temporal logic; decidability

1. INTRODUCTION

Abstraction serves as a bridge for connecting control theory and formal methods in the sense that hybrid control design for dynamical systems and high-level specifications

can be done using finite abstractions of these systems [,]. There has been a rich literature on computing abstractions for linear and nonlinear dynamical systems in the past decade (see, e.g., [, − , , , ,]). Early work on abstraction focuses on constructing symbolic models that are bisimilar (equivalent) to the original system. The seminal work in [ ] shows that bisimilar symbolic models exist for controllable linear systems. As a result, existence of controllers for such systems to meet linear-time properties (such as those specified by linear temporal logic [ ]) is decidable. For nonlinear systems that are incrementally stable [ ], it is shown in [ ] that approximately bisimilar models can be constructed (see also [ ], for construction of approximately bisimilar models for switched systems, and [ ] for its use in control synthesis). The work in [ ] considered symbolic models for nonlinear systems without stability assumptions, in which it is shown that symbolic models that approximately alternatingly simulate the sample-data representation of a general nonlinear control system can be constructed. The work in [ ] and [ ] both proposes computational procedures for constructing finite abstractions of discrete-time nonlinear systems. The abstraction techniques in [, ,] are conservative and sound in the sense that they are useful in the design of provably correct controllers, but do not necessarily yield a feasible design because the computational procedures for constructing abstractions for potentially unstable nonlinear systems are not complete.

Robustness is a central property to consider in control design, because all practical control systems need to be robust to imperfections in all aspects of control design and implementation, such as modelling, sensing, computation, communication, and actuation. For abstraction-based control design, how to preserve robustness poses a particular challenge because the hierarchical control design approach based on abstraction often use quantized state measurements (modelled as symbolic states in the abstraction) to compute appropriate control signals. Because of the state quantizers by definition are discontinuous, special attention is required to ensure that the resulting design is actually robust to measurement errors and disturbances. The work in [ ] (see also [ ]) proposes a novel notion of abstractions that are equipped with additional robustness margins to cope with different types of uncertainties in modelling, such as measurement errors, delays, and disturbances. The work in [ ] (see also [ ]) defines a new notation of system relations for abstraction-based control design. By explicitly considering the interconnection of state quantizers and feedback controllers, it is shown that the new system relation can

HSCC'17, April 18 - 20, 2017, Pittsburgh, PA, USA

© 2017 Copyright held by the owner/author(s). Publication rights licensed to ACM.
ISBN 978-1-4503-4590-3/17/04...$15.00

DOI: http://dx.doi.org/10.1145/3049797.3054970

also be used to design robust controllers against uncertainties and disturbances. The type of abstractions considered in [14, 15, 20, 21] resemble the approximate alternating simulations considered in [27] for nonlinear systems. These abstractions, nonetheless, are all conservative and sound. To the best knowledge of the authors, how to compute complete abstractions (or approximately complete) abstractions for general nonlinear systems without stability assumptions remains an open problem.

As an attempt to bridge this gap, in this paper, we define robust abstractions as a system relation from a (possibly infinite) transition system subject to uncertainty to anther transition system. We show that, while this abstraction relation is to some extent similar to the type of system relations considered in [15, 21, 27], it also has some subtle differences that are important for proving the approximate completeness results later in the paper. We show that robust abstractions are sound in the sense that they preserve robust satisfaction of linear-time properties. The main contributions of the paper include computational procedures for constructing both sound and approximately complete robust abstractions for general discrete-time nonlinear control systems without stability assumptions. We show that such procedures are complete in the sense that, given a concrete discrete-time control system and an arbitrarily small perturbation of this system, there exists a finite transition system that robustly abstracts the concrete system, whereas the perturbed system abstracts this finite transition system. An important consequence of this main result asserts that existence of robust controllers for discrete-time nonlinear systems and linear-time specifications is decidable. Finally, we would like to make clear upfront that the main point of this paper is not on providing more efficient algorithms for computing abstractions. Therefore, complexity issues, though important, are not a concern for the current paper and will be investigated in future work.

The organization of the paper is very straightforward. Section 2 presents some background material on transition systems and define robust abstractions. We highlight some similarities and subtle differences of the new abstraction relation with several variants of simulation relations in the literature. Section 3 presents the main results of the paper on construction of sound and approximately complete robust abstractions for discrete-time nonlinear control systems. A numerical example is used to illustrate the effectiveness of robust abstractions in Section 4. The paper is concluded in Section 5.

Notation: Let f be a (binary) relation from A to B, i.e., f is a subset of the Cartesian product $A \times B$. For each $a \in A$, $f(a)$ denotes the set $\{b : b \in B \text{ such that } (a, b) \in f\}$; for each $b \in B$, $f^{-1}(b)$ denotes the set $\{a : a \in A, (a, b) \in f\}$; for $A' \subseteq A$, $f(A') = \cup_{a \in A'} f(a)$; and for $B' \subseteq B$, $f^{-1}(B) = \cup_{b \in B'} f^{-1}(B)$. Let g be a relation from A to B and f be a relation from B to C. The composition of f and g, denoted by $f \circ g$, is a relation from A to C defined by

$$f \circ g = \{(a, c) : \exists b \in B \text{ s.t. } (a, b) \in g \text{ and } (b, c) \in f\}.$$

For two sets $A, B \subseteq \mathbb{R}^n$,

$$A + B = \{c : \exists a \in A, \exists b \in B \text{ s.t. } a + b = c\}$$

and $A \backslash B = \{a : a \in A, a \notin B\}$. For $a \in \mathbb{R}^n$ and $B \subseteq \mathbb{R}^n$, $a + B = \{a\} + B$. Let $|\cdot|$ denote the infinity norm in $\mathbb{R}^n$ and $\mathbb{B}$ denote the unit closed ball in infinity norm centred at the origin, i.e. $\mathbb{B} = \{x \in \mathbb{R}^n : |x| \leq 1\}$. The dimension of $\mathbb{B}$ will be clear from the context.

2. TRANSITION SYSTEMS AND ROBUST ABSTRACTIONS

2.1 Transition systems

DEFINITION 1. A *transition system* is a tuple

$$\mathcal{T} = (Q, A, R, \Pi, L),$$

where

- Q is the set of states;
- A is the set of actions;
- $R \subseteq Q \times A \times Q$ is the transition relation;
- Π is the set of atomic propositions;
- $L : Q \to 2^{\Pi}$ is the labelling function.

Consider the transition system $\mathcal{T}$ above. For each action $a \in A$ and $q \in Q$, the a-successor of q, denoted by $\mathrm{Post}_{\mathcal{T}}(q, a)$, is defined by

$$\mathrm{Post}_{\mathcal{T}}(q, a) = \{q' : q' \in Q \text{ s.t. } (q, a, q') \in R\}.$$

For each $q \in Q$, the set of admissible actions for q, denoted by $A_{\mathcal{T}}(q)$, is defined by

$$A_{\mathcal{T}}(q) = \{a : \mathrm{Post}_{\mathcal{T}}(q, a) \neq \emptyset\}.$$

In this paper, we assume that all transition systems have no terminal states in the sense that $A_{\mathcal{T}}(q) \neq \emptyset$ for all $q \in Q$.

An *execution* of $\mathcal{T}$ is an infinite alternating sequence of states and actions

$$\rho = q_0 a_0 q_1 a_1 q_2 a_2 \cdots,$$

where q_0 is some initial state and $(q_i, a_i, q_{i+1}) \in R$ for all $i \geq 0$. The *path* resulting from the execution ρ above is

$$\mathrm{Path}(\rho) = q_0 q_1 q_2 \cdots.$$

The *trace* of the execution ρ is defined by

$$\mathrm{Trace}(\rho) = L(q_0) L(q_1) L(q_2) \cdots.$$

A *control strategy* for a transition system $\mathcal{T}$ is a partial function $s : (q_0, q_1, \cdots, q_i) \mapsto a_i$ that maps the state history to the next action. An *s-controlled execution* of a transition system $\mathcal{T}$ is an execution of $\mathcal{T}$, where for each $i \geq 0$, the action a_i is chosen according to the control strategy s; s-controlled paths and traces are defined in a similar fashion.

2.2 Uncertainty transition systems

DEFINITION 2. A transition relation $\Delta \subseteq Q \times A \times Q$ is called an *uncertain transition relation* for $\mathcal{T} = (Q, A, R, \Pi, L)$, if the following two conditions hold:

(i) $R \cap \Delta = \emptyset$;
(ii) for each $(q, a, q') \in \Delta$, there exists some $(q, a, q'') \in R$.

DEFINITION 3. An *uncertain transition system* consisting of $\mathcal{T} = (Q, A, R, \Pi, L)$ as a nominal transition system and Δ as an uncertain transition relation for $\mathcal{T}$, denoted by $\mathcal{T} \oplus \Delta$, is defined by

$$\mathcal{T} \oplus \Delta = (Q, A, R \cup \Delta, \Pi, L).$$

It is clear from the above definition that, while Δ introduces additional transitions for the transition system $\mathcal{T}$, it does not add more admissible actions for any state. In other words, for all $q \in Q$, $A_{\mathcal{T}}(q) = A_{\mathcal{T}\oplus\Delta}(q)$.

Since an uncertain transition system is simply a transition system with additional transitions introduced by some uncertain transition relation, the execution (path, trace), control strategy, and controlled execution (path, trace) for an uncertain transition system are defined in the same way as for a nominal transition system.

2.3 Robust abstractions

We first define a notion of abstraction between transition systems for control synthesis.

Definition 4. For two transition systems

$$\mathcal{T}_1 = (Q_1, A_1, R_1, \Pi, L_1)$$

and

$$\mathcal{T}_2 = (Q_2, A_2, R_2, \Pi, L_2),$$

a relation $\alpha \subseteq Q_1 \times Q_2$ is said to be an *abstraction* from $\mathcal{T}_1$ to $\mathcal{T}_2$, if the following conditions are satisfied:

(i) for all $q_1 \in Q_1$, there exists $q_2 \in Q_2$ such that $(q_1, q_2) \in \alpha$ (i.e., $\alpha(q_1) \neq \emptyset$);

(ii) for all $(q_1, q_2) \in \alpha$ and $a_2 \in A_{\mathcal{T}_2}(q_2)$, there exists $a_1 \in A_{\mathcal{T}_1}(q_1)$ such that

$$\alpha(\mathrm{Post}_{\mathcal{T}_1}(q, a_1)) \subseteq \mathrm{Post}_{\mathcal{T}_2}(q_2, a_2); \tag{1}$$

for all $q \in \alpha^{-1}(q_2)$;

(iii) for all $(q_1, q_2) \in \alpha$, $L_2(q_2) \subseteq L_1(q_1)$.

If such a relation α exists, we say that $\mathcal{T}_2$ *abstracts* $\mathcal{T}_1$ and write $\mathcal{T}_1 \preceq_\alpha \mathcal{T}_2$ or simply $\mathcal{T}_1 \preceq \mathcal{T}_2$.

We then define robust abstractions as abstractions of uncertain transition systems.

Definition 5. Let Δ be an uncertain transition relation for $\mathcal{T}_1$. If there exists an abstraction α from $\mathcal{T}_1 \oplus \Delta$ to $\mathcal{T}_2$, i.e., $\mathcal{T}_1 \oplus \Delta \preceq_\alpha \mathcal{T}_2$, we say that α is a Δ-robust abstraction from $\mathcal{T}_1$ to $\mathcal{T}_2$ and $\mathcal{T}_2$ *Δ-robustly abstracts* $\mathcal{T}_1$. With a slight abuse of terminology, we sometimes also say that $\mathcal{T}_2$ is a Δ-robust abstraction of $\mathcal{T}_1$.

Remark 1. We highlight several differences between the notation of abstraction proposed in Definition 4 and other similar system relations in the literature. Apart from the obvious distinction that, in Definition 4, an explicit model of the uncertainty is considered (following [ ]), the abstraction defined by Definition 4 differs from several variants of simulation relations in the literature as elaborated below:

Finite abstractions with robustness margins: This notion of abstractions introduced in [,] is defined by introducing two positive parameters (γ_1, γ_2), which define the extra transitions to be added to the abstractions to ensure robustness. Suppose there is a metric d defined on Q_1. Then finite abstractions with robustness margins (γ_1, γ_2) amount to defining

$$\Delta = \{(q, a, q') : \exists (q_1, a, q_1') \in R_1 \text{ s.t.} \\ d(q_1, q) \le \gamma_1,\ d(q_1', q') \le \gamma_2\} \backslash R_1.$$

To establish $\mathcal{T}_1 \oplus \Delta \preceq_\alpha \mathcal{T}_2$, condition (1), which can be equivalently written as

$$\bigcup_{q\in\alpha^{-1}(q_2)} \alpha(\mathrm{Post}_{\mathcal{T}_1\oplus\Delta}(q, a_1)) = \alpha(\bigcup_{q\in\alpha^{-1}(q_2)} \mathrm{Post}_{\mathcal{T}_1\oplus\Delta}(q, a_1)) \\ \subseteq \mathrm{Post}_{\mathcal{T}_2}(q_2, a_2)$$

is essentially the over-approximation (of transitions) condition in [,]. The main difference lies in that Definition 4 does not assume that a metric is defined on Q_1 and the uncertainty model is not restricted to that defined by level sets of the distance function. Furthermore, here we define the abstraction relation on a general Kripke structure, whereas the work in [,] defines concrete abstractions from ordinary differential/difference equations with inputs to finite transition systems.

Feedback refinement relations [,]: Similar to [,], the abstraction relation considered in [,] also requires that, for each $(q_1, q_2) \in \alpha$, the admissible actions for each q_2 is a subset of the admissible actions for q_1. In Definition 4, for each $(q_1, q_2) \in \alpha$, it is not required that $A_{\mathcal{T}_2}(q_2) \subseteq A_{\mathcal{T}_1}(q_1)$, i.e., the admissible actions for q_1 do not have to be a subset of the admissible actions for q_2. This difference enables us to formulate and prove the approximate completeness results later in this paper (Section 3.3). Note that, when $A_{\mathcal{T}_2}(q_2) \subseteq A_{\mathcal{T}_1}(q_1)$, condition (1) can be simplified to: for each $(q_1, q_2) \in \alpha$ and every $a \in A_{\mathcal{T}_2}(q_2)$,

$$\alpha(\mathrm{Post}_{\mathcal{T}_1}(q_1, a)) \subseteq \mathrm{Post}_{\mathcal{T}_2}(q_2, a). \tag{2}$$

In other words, the same action a used by q_2 is assumed to be available (and used) for all $q_1 \in \alpha^{-1}(q_2)$, because $A_{\mathcal{T}_2}(q_2) \subseteq A_{\mathcal{T}_1}(q_1)$.

Alternating simulations [,]: The notion of alternating simulations [,] stipulates that, for each $(q_1, q_2) \in \alpha$ and every $a_2 \in A_{\mathcal{T}_2}(q_2)$, there exists $a_1 \in A_{\mathcal{T}_2}(q_1)$ such that, for every $q_1' \in \mathrm{Post}_{\mathcal{T}_1}(q_1, a_1)$, there exists some state $q_2' \in \mathrm{Post}_{\mathcal{T}_2}(q_2, a_2)$ such that $(q_1', q_2') \in \alpha$. In other words, for each $(q_1, q_2) \in \alpha$ and every $a_2 \in A_{\mathcal{T}_2}(q_2)$, there exists $a_1 \in A_{\mathcal{T}_1}(q_1)$ such that

$$\alpha(q_1') \cap \mathrm{Post}_{\mathcal{T}_2}(q_2, a_2) \neq \emptyset, \tag{3}$$

for all $q_1' \in \mathrm{Post}_{\mathcal{T}_1}(q_1, a_1)$, as articulated in [,]. Clearly, (3) is a weaker condition than (1) or (2), unless α is single-valued. Furthermore, and more importantly, (3) does not stipulate the use of the same action a_1 for all $q \in \alpha^{-1}(q_2)$, i.e., a_1 may depend on q (concrete states corresponding to q_2). A consequence of the latter is that, to implement the controller, one needs knowledge of the concrete state rather than the abstract (symbolic) state alone.

We use a simple example to illustrate the differences discussed above.

Example 1. Consider three transition systems

$$\mathcal{T}_i = (Q_i, A_i, R_i, \Pi, L_i), \quad i = 1, 2, 3,$$

where $Q_1 = \{x_0, x_1, x_2\}$, $Q_2 = Q_3 = \{q_0, q_1\}$, $A_1 = \{a, b\}$, $A_2 = A_3 = \{1, 2, 3\}$, $\Pi = \{\text{Initial}, \text{Goal}\}$, $L_1(x_0) = L_1(x_1) = L_2(q_0) = L_3(q_0) = \{\text{Initial}\}$, and $L_1(x_2) = L_2(q_1) = L_3(q_1) = \{\text{Goal}\}$. The transition relations are shown in Figure 1.

Define an abstraction relation from $\mathcal{T}_1$ to $\mathcal{T}_2$ by

$$\alpha = \{(x_0, q_0), (x_1, q_0), (x_2, q_1)\}.$$

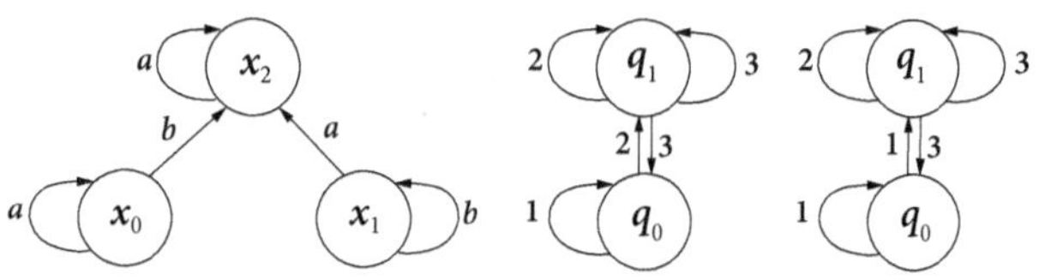

Figure 1: Transition systems $\mathcal{T}_1$ (left), $\mathcal{T}_2$ (middle), and $\mathcal{T}_3$ (right).

Then it can be easily verified that (3) is satisfied and α is an alternating simulation from $\mathcal{T}_1$ to $\mathcal{T}_2$. In fact, we can check that, for $(x_0, q_0) \in \alpha$, and action $1 \in A_2$, there exists $a \in A_1$ such that

$$\alpha(\mathrm{Post}_{\mathcal{T}_1}(x_0, a)) = \alpha(\{x_0\}) = \{q_0\} = \mathrm{Post}_{\mathcal{T}_2}(q_0, 1),$$

which implies (3). Similarly, for $(x_0, q_0) \in \alpha$, and action $2 \in A_2$, there exists $b \in A_1$ such that

$$\alpha(\mathrm{Post}_{\mathcal{T}_1}(x_0, b)) = \alpha(\{x_2\}) = \{q_1\} = \mathrm{Post}_{\mathcal{T}_2}(q_0, 2),$$

which also implies (3). For $(x_2, q_1) \in \alpha$, and action $3 \in A_2$, there exists $a \in A_1$ such that

$$\alpha(\mathrm{Post}_{\mathcal{T}_1}(x_2, a)) = \alpha(\{x_2\}) = \{q_1\} \subseteq \{q_0, q_1\} = \mathrm{Post}_{\mathcal{T}_2}(q_1, 3),$$

which implies (3). The rest can be checked in a similar fashion.

Suppose that one needs to design a control strategy for $\mathcal{T}_1$ such that all controlled executions of $\mathcal{T}_1$ starting from the 'Initial' set will eventually reach the 'Goal' set. Then, while one can find such a control strategy for $\mathcal{T}_2$, to implement this strategy on $\mathcal{T}_1$, however, $\mathcal{T}_1$ needs to be able to discriminate x_0 and x_1 and choose the appropriate actions (b for x_0 and a for x_1). This is not the case if only symbolic state information from the abstraction is available.

Note that, according to Definition 4, we do not have $\mathcal{T}_1 \preceq_\alpha \mathcal{T}_2$ because, for $(x_0, q_0) \in \alpha$ and action $1 \in A_2$, we have

$$\bigcup_{x \in \alpha^{-1}(q_0)} \alpha(\mathrm{Post}_{\mathcal{T}_1}(x, a)) = \alpha(\{x_0\}, \{x_2\})$$
$$= \{q_0, q_1\} \not\subseteq \{q_0\} = \mathrm{Post}_{\mathcal{T}_2}(q_0, 1),$$

$$\bigcup_{x \in \alpha^{-1}(q_0)} \alpha(\mathrm{Post}_{\mathcal{T}_1}(x, b)) = \alpha(\{x_1\}, \{x_2\})$$
$$= \{q_0, q_1\} \not\subseteq \{q_0\} = \mathrm{Post}_{\mathcal{T}_2}(q_0, 1),$$

Thus, (1) does not hold for either action a or b.

We can check that $\mathcal{T}_1 \preceq_\alpha \mathcal{T}_3$. Because the set of actions in $\mathcal{T}_2$ (and $\mathcal{T}_3$) is not a subset of the actions of $\mathcal{T}_1$ (in fact there are more actions in $\mathcal{T}_2$ and $\mathcal{T}_3$ than $\mathcal{T}_1$), α does not provide an abstraction relation from $\mathcal{T}_1$ to $\mathcal{T}_2$ or from $\mathcal{T}_1$ to $\mathcal{T}_3$ in the strict sense of the notions of simulation relations considered in [14, 15, 20, 21].

To consider a robust abstraction for $\mathcal{T}_1$, let $\Delta = \{(x_2, a, x_1)\}$. Then it can be verified that the transition system $\mathcal{T}_3$ is also a Δ-robust abstraction of $\mathcal{T}_1$.

We will state some immediate results that follow from Definition 4.

Proposition 1. *Let $\mathcal{T}$ be a transition system and Δ be an uncertain transition relation for $\mathcal{T}$. Then $\mathcal{T} \preceq \mathcal{T} \oplus \Delta$.*

Proof. Let $\mathcal{T} = (Q, A, R, \Pi, L)$. It is straightforward to check by Definitions 2 and 4 that the identity relation from Q to Q defines a Δ-robust abstraction from $\mathcal{T}$ to $\mathcal{T} \oplus \Delta$. □

Setting $\Delta = \emptyset$, a special case of Proposition 1 asserts that $\mathcal{T} \preceq \mathcal{T}$ for any transition system. It is also straightforward to verify that abstraction relations are transitive in the following sense.

Proposition 2. *Let $\mathcal{T}_i$ $(i = 1, 2, 3)$ be transition systems and Δ be an uncertain transition relation for $\mathcal{T}_1$. If $\mathcal{T}_1 \preceq_{\alpha_1} \mathcal{T}_2$ and $\mathcal{T}_2 \preceq_{\alpha_2} \mathcal{T}_3$, then $\mathcal{T}_1 \preceq_{\alpha_2 \circ \alpha_1} \mathcal{T}_3$.*

Proof. Let $\alpha_3 = \alpha_2 \circ \alpha_1$. We verify that conditions (i)–(iii) of Definition 4 are satisfied:

(i) For all $q_1 \in Q$, $\alpha_3(q_1)$ is non-empty, because $\alpha_1(q_1)$ is non-empty and $\alpha_2(q_2)$ is non-empty for any $q_2 \in Q_2$.

(ii) For any $(q_1, q_3) \in \alpha_3$, there exists $q_2 \in Q_2$ such that $(q_1, q_2) \in \alpha_1$ and $(q_2, q_3) \in \alpha_2$. For any $q_3 \in A_{\mathcal{T}_3}(q_3)$, there exists $a_2 \in A_{\mathcal{T}_2}(q_2)$ such that

$$\alpha_2(\mathrm{Post}_{\mathcal{T}_2}(q, a_2)) \subseteq \mathrm{Post}_{\mathcal{T}_3}(q_3, a_3),$$

for all $q \in \alpha_2^{-1}(q_3)$. For $a_2 \in A_{\mathcal{T}_2}(q_2)$, there exists $a_1 \in A_{\mathcal{T}_1}(q_1)$ such that

$$\alpha_1(\mathrm{Post}_{\mathcal{T}_1}(q, a_1)) \subseteq \mathrm{Post}_{\mathcal{T}_2}(q_2, a_2),$$

for all $q \in \alpha_1^{-1}(q_2)$. It follows that

$$\bigcup_{q \in \alpha_3^{-1}(q_3)} \alpha_3(\mathrm{Post}_{\mathcal{T}_1}(q, a_1))$$
$$= \bigcup_{q \in \alpha_3^{-1}(q_3)} \alpha_2 \circ \alpha_1(\mathrm{Post}_{\mathcal{T}_1}(q, a_1))$$
$$\subseteq \bigcup_{q \in \alpha_2^{-1}(q_2)} \alpha_2(\mathrm{Post}_{\mathcal{T}_2}(q, a_2))$$
$$\subseteq \mathrm{Post}_{\mathcal{T}_3}(q_3, a_3).$$

(iii) For any $(q_1, q_3) \in \alpha_3$, there exists $q_2 \in Q_2$ such that $(q_1, q_2) \in \alpha_1$ and $(q_2, q_3) \in \alpha_2$. Hence

$$L_3(q_3) \subseteq L_2(q_2) \subseteq L_1(q_1).$$

□

2.4 Soundness of abstractions

In this section, we prove that abstractions given by Definition 4 are sound in the sense of preserving realizability of linear-time properties.

A *linear-time (LT) property* [6] over a set of atomic propositions Π is a subset of $(2^\Pi)^\omega$, which is the set of all infinite words over the alphabet 2^Π, defined by

$$(2^\Pi)^\omega = \left\{ A_0 A_1 A_2 \cdots : A_i \in 2^\Pi, \quad i \geq 0 \right\}.$$

A particular class of LT properties can be conveniently specified by *linear temporal logic* (LTL [17]). This logic consists of propositional logic operators (e.g., **true**, **false**, *negation* ($\neg$), *disjunction* ($\vee$), *conjunction* ($\wedge$) and *implication* ($\rightarrow$)), and temporal operators (e.g., *next* ($\bigcirc$), *always* ($\Box$), *eventually* ($\Diamond$), *until* ($\mathcal{U}$) and *weak until* ($\mathcal{W}$)).

The syntax of LTL over a set of atomic propositions Π is defined inductively follows:

- **true** and **false** are LTL formulae;

- an atomic proposition $\pi \in \Pi$ is an LTL formula;
- if φ and ψ are LTL formulas, then $\neg\varphi$, $\varphi \vee \varphi$, $\bigcirc\varphi$, and $\varphi\mathcal{U}\varphi$ are LTL formulas.

The semantics of LTL is defined on infinite words over the alphabet 2^{Π}. Given a sequence $\sigma = A_0A_1A_2\cdots$ in 2^{Π}, we define $\sigma, i \vDash \varphi$, meaning that σ satisfies an LTL formula φ at position i, inductively as follows:

- $\sigma, i \vDash \textbf{true}$;
- $\sigma, i \vDash \pi$ if and only if $\pi \in A_i$;
- $\sigma, i \vDash \neg\varphi$ if and only if $\sigma, i \nvDash \varphi$;
- $\sigma, i \vDash \varphi_1 \vee \varphi_2$ if and only if $\sigma, i \vDash \varphi_1$ or $\sigma, i \vDash \varphi_2$;
- $\sigma, i \vDash \bigcirc\varphi$ if and only if $\sigma, i+1 \vDash \varphi$;
- $\sigma, i \vDash \varphi_1\mathcal{U}\varphi_2$ if and only if there exists $j \geq i$ such that $\sigma, j \vDash \varphi_2$ and $\sigma, k \vDash \varphi_1$ for all $i \leq k < j$;

We write $\sigma \vDash \varphi$, and say σ satisfies φ, if $\sigma, 0 \vDash \varphi$. An execution ρ of a transition system $\mathcal{T}$ is said to satisfy an LTL formula φ, written as $\rho \vDash \varphi$, if and only if its trace $\text{Trace}(\rho) \vDash \varphi$. Given a control strategy s for $\mathcal{T}$, if all s-controlled executions of $\mathcal{T}$ satisfy φ, we write $(\mathcal{T}, s) \vDash \varphi$. If such a control strategy s exists, we also say that φ is *realizable* for $\mathcal{T}$.

REMARK 1. For technical reasons, we assume that all LTL formulas have been transformed into positive normal form [, Chapter 5], where all negations appear only in front of the atomic propositions and only the following operators are allowed $\wedge$, $\vee$, $\bigcirc$, $\mathcal{U}$, and $\mathcal{W}$ (defined by $\varphi\mathcal{W}\psi = (\varphi\mathcal{U}\psi) \vee \Box\varphi$. We further assume that all negations of atomic propositions are replaced by new atomic propositions.

DEFINITION 6. Given an abstraction relation α from $\mathcal{T}_1$ to $\mathcal{T}_2$ and a control strategy μ_i for $\mathcal{T}_i$ $(i = 1, 2)$, μ_1 is called *α-implementation* of μ_2, if, for each $n \geq 0$,

$$u_n = \mu_1(x_0, x_1, x_2, \cdots, x_n)$$

is chosen according to

$$a_n = \mu_2(q_0, q_1, q_2, \cdots, q_n)$$

in such a way (as guaranteed by Definition 4 for $\mathcal{T}_1 \preceq_\alpha \mathcal{T}_2$) that

$$\alpha(\text{Post}_{\mathcal{T}_1}(x, u_n)) \subseteq \text{Post}_{\mathcal{T}_2}(q_n, a_n)$$

for all $x \in \alpha^{-1}(q_n)$, where $q_n \in \alpha(x_n)$.

We end this section by stating a soundness result for abstractions.

THEOREM 1. *Suppose that α is an abstraction from $\mathcal{T}_1$ to $\mathcal{T}_2$, i.e., $\mathcal{T}_1 \preceq_\alpha \mathcal{T}_2$ and and let φ be an LTL formula. If there exists a control strategy μ_2 for $\mathcal{T}_2$ such that $(\mathcal{T}_2, \mu_2) \vDash \varphi$, then there exists a control strategy μ_1, which is an α-implementation of μ_2, for $\mathcal{T}_1$ such that $(\mathcal{T}_1, \mu_1) \vDash \varphi$.*

PROOF. Let

$$\mathcal{T}_1 = (Q_1, A_1, R_1, \Pi, L_1)$$

and

$$\mathcal{T}_2 = (Q_2, A_2, R_2, \Pi, L_2).$$

We show that, by Definitions 4 and 6, a μ_1-controlled path of $\mathcal{T}_1$ always leads to a μ_2-controlled path of $\mathcal{T}_2$. Suppose we start with $x_k \in Q_1$ and let q_k be arbitrarily chosen from $\alpha(x_k)$, where $k \geq 0$. Suppose $a_k = \mu_2(q_0, q_1, q_2, \cdots, q_k)$ and $u_k = \mu_1(x_0, x_1, x_2, \cdots, x_k)$. Since $\alpha(\text{Post}_{\mathcal{T}_1}(x_k, u_k)) \subseteq \text{Post}_{\mathcal{T}_2}(q_k, a_k)$, we know that for any $q_{k+1} \in \alpha(x_{k+1})$ and $x_{k+1} \in \text{Post}_{\mathcal{T}_1}(x_k, u_k)$, we have $q_{k+1} \in \text{Post}_{\mathcal{T}_2}(q_k, a_k)$. This implies that (q_k, a_k, q_{k+1}) is a valid transition in $\mathcal{T}_2$ and therefore, by induction, $q_0q_1q_2\cdots$ is a μ_2-controlled path of $\mathcal{T}_2$, if $x_0x_1x_2\cdots$ is a μ_1-controlled path of $\mathcal{T}_1$. Furthermore, by Definitions 4, we have $L_2(q_k) \subseteq L_1(x_k)$ for all $k \geq 0$. Since the trace of $q_0q_1q_2\cdots$ satisfies φ, we know that the trace of $x_0, x_1, x_2\cdots$ also satisfies φ. $\Box$

Based on the proof, it is clear that an abstraction relation preserves not only temporal logic specifications but also linear-time properties in general, because we essentially proved that the controlled traces of $\mathcal{T}_1$ are included in the controlled traces of $\mathcal{T}_2$ (in fact, trace inclusion is equivalent to preservation of LT properties [, Theorem 3.15]).

3. ROBUST DECIDABILITY OF DISCRETE-TIME CONTROL SYNTHESIS

In this section, we investigate robust abstractions of discrete-time nonlinear systems modelled by nonlinear difference equations with inputs. We establish computational procedures for constructing sound and approximately complete robust abstractions for this class of control systems under very mild conditions.

3.1 Perturbed discrete-time control systems as uncertain transition systems

A *discrete-time control system* is modelled by a difference equation of the form

$$x(t+1) = f(x(t), u(t)), \tag{4}$$

where $x(t) \in X \subseteq \mathbb{R}^n$, $u(t) \in U \subseteq \mathbb{R}^m$, and $f : \mathbb{R}^n \times \mathbb{R}^m \to \mathbb{R}^n$.

A *solution* to (4) is an alternating sequence of states and control inputs of the form

$$x(0)u(0)x(1)u(1)x(2)u(2)\cdots,$$

such that (4) is satisfied.

A *control strategy* for (4) is a partial function

$$\sigma : (x(0), \cdots, x(t)) \mapsto u(t)$$

for all $t = 0, 1, 2, \cdots$, which maps the state history up to time t to the control input $u(t)$ at time t.

DEFINITION 7. The discrete-time control system (4) can be written as a transition system of the form

$$\mathcal{S} = (Q_\mathcal{S}, A_\mathcal{S}, R_\mathcal{S}, \Pi, L_\mathcal{S}) \tag{5}$$

by defining

- $Q_\mathcal{S} = X \cup \{X^c\}$;
- $A_\mathcal{S} = U$;
- $(x, u, x') \in R_\mathcal{S}$ if and only if one of the following holds: (i) $x' = f(x, u)$ and $x, x' \in X$; (ii) $x' = X^c$ and $f(x, u) \notin X$; (iii) $x' = x = X^c$;
- Π is a set of atomic propositions on $Q_\mathcal{S}$ and $\textbf{in} \in \Pi$;
- $L_\mathcal{S} : Q_\mathcal{S} \to 2^{\Pi}$ is a labelling function satisfying $\textbf{in} \in L_\mathcal{S}(q)$ for $q \neq X^c$ and $\textbf{in} \notin L_\mathcal{S}(X^c)$.

The state X^c and label **in** are introduced to precisely encode if an out-of-domain transition takes place.

We now introduce an uncertainty model for system (4).

DEFINITION 8. Consider system (4) subject to uncertainties of the form

$$x(t+1) = f(x(t), u(t)) + w(t), \tag{6}$$

where $w(t) \in \delta\mathbb{B}$ for some $\delta \geq 0$. Define Δ_δ to consist of transitions $(x, u, x') \notin R_\mathcal{S}$ such that one of the following holds: (i) $x' \in f(x,u) + \delta\mathbb{B}$ and $x, x' \in X$; (ii) $x' = X^c$ and $f(x,u) + w \notin X$ for some $w \in \delta\mathbb{B}$.

Clearly, $\mathcal{S} \oplus \Delta_\delta$ defined together by Definitions 7 and 8 exactly models (6) as summarized in the following proposition.

PROPOSITION 3. *Each solution of (6) that stays in X is an execution of $\mathcal{S}\oplus\Delta_\delta$. Conversely, each execution of $\mathcal{S}\oplus\Delta_\delta$ that stays in X is also a solution of (6).*

PROOF. This is straightforward to verify. Denote

$$\rho = x(0)u(0)x(1)u(1)x(2)u(2)\cdots.$$

If ρ is a solution of (6) such that $x(t) \in X$ for all $t \geq 0$. Then there exists $w(0)w(1)\cdots$ such that $x(t+1) = f(x(t), u(t)) + w(t)$, where $w(t) \in \delta\mathbb{B}$ for all $t \geq 0$, which implies that $(x(t), u(t), x(t+1)) \in R_\mathcal{S} \cup \Delta_\delta$. Thus ρ is also an execution of $\mathcal{S}\oplus\Delta_\delta$. Now suppose that ρ is an execution of $\mathcal{S}\oplus\Delta_\delta$ such that $x(t) \in X$ for all $t \geq 0$. Then $x(t+1) = f(x(t), u(t)) + w(t)$, where $w(t) \in \delta\mathbb{B}$ for all $t \geq 0$. This shows that ρ is a solution of (6). □

Because of this proposition, in the sequel, when proving soundness results, we always assume that out-of-domain solutions and paths are taken care of by enforcing the solutions and paths to stay in the domain through a safety specification, i.e., by including $\square(\mathbf{in})$ in the specification.

3.2 Soundness of robust abstractions for discrete-time control systems

COROLLARY 1. *Suppose there exists a transition system $\mathcal{T}$ such that $\mathcal{S} \oplus \Delta_\delta \preceq_\alpha \mathcal{T}$, where $\mathcal{S}$ and Δ_δ are defined by Definitions 7 and 8. Let φ be an LTL formula over Π. If there exists a control strategy μ for $\mathcal{T}$ such that $(\mathcal{T}, \mu) \vDash \varphi$, then there exists a control strategy κ, which is an α-implementation of μ, for $\mathcal{S} \oplus \Delta_\delta$ such that $(\mathcal{S} \oplus \Delta_\delta, \kappa) \vDash \varphi$.*

PROOF. It follows directly from Theorem 1. □

It is interesting to note that $(\mathcal{S} \oplus \Delta_\delta, \kappa) \vDash \varphi$ implies that solutions of (4) robustly satisfy φ in terms of not only additive disturbances modelled by (6), but also other types of uncertainties such as measurement errors. To illustrate this, consider a scenario where the controller κ is implemented on a system with measurement errors. We assume that this error is bounded, i.e., for each $x(t) \in \mathbb{R}^n$, its measurement is given by

$$\hat{x}(t) = x(t) + e(t), \tag{7}$$

where $e(t) \in \varepsilon\mathbb{B}$ for some $\varepsilon > 0$. To make the control strategy κ for (4) robust to measurement errors like (7), we can simply strengthen the labeling function L of $\mathcal{S}$ as follows. A labelling function $\hat{L} : \mathbb{R}^n \to 2^\Pi$ is said to be the *ε-strengthening* of another labelling function $L : \mathbb{R}^n \to 2^\Pi$, if $\pi \in \hat{L}(x)$ if and only if $\pi \in L(y)$ for all $y \in x + \varepsilon\mathbb{B}$.

The remaining technical results of the paper rely on the following assumption.

ASSUMPTION 1. *The function $f : \mathbb{R}^n \times \mathbb{R}^m$ is locally Lipschitz continuous in both arguments. The sets X and U are compact.*

The above assumption on f is very mild and is satisfied as long as the function $f : \mathbb{R}^n \times \mathbb{R}^m$ is differentiable with respect to both variables.

PROPOSITION 4. *Let $\hat{\mathcal{S}} = (Q, A, R, \Pi, \hat{L})$, which is obtained from $\mathcal{S}$ in Definition 7 by replacing L with its ε-strengthening $\hat{L}$. Suppose that the assumptions of Corollary 1 hold with $\hat{\mathcal{S}}$ in place of $\mathcal{S}$. Then $(\mathcal{S}, \kappa) \vDash \varphi$, subject to measurement errors described in (7), provided that $(L+1)\varepsilon \leq \delta$, where L is the uniform Lipschitz constant for both variables of f on the compact set $(X + \varepsilon\mathbb{B}) \times U$.*

PROOF. We have $\hat{\mathcal{S}} \oplus \Delta_\delta \preceq_\alpha \mathcal{T}$. The goal is to show that, despite the measurement errors, κ-controlled traces of $\mathcal{S}$ are a subset of the κ-controlled traces of $(\hat{\mathcal{S}}, \Delta)$ and therefore satisfies φ. Starting from $x(0)$, let $\hat{x}(0)$ be the measurement taken for $x(0)$. Suppose that an action $u(0) = \kappa(\hat{x}(0)) = \mu(q_0)$ is chosen by κ, where $q_0 \in \alpha(\hat{x}(0))$. Let L_1 be the labelling function for $\mathcal{T}$. Then $L_1(q_0) \subseteq \hat{L}(\hat{x}(0))$ by the definition of the robust abstraction. Since $\hat{L}$ is the ε-strengthening of L and $x(0) \in \hat{x(0)} + \varepsilon\mathbb{B}$, it follows that $L_1(q_0) \subseteq \hat{L}(\hat{x}(0)) \subseteq L(x(0))$.

We suppose by induction that $L_1(q_k) \subseteq L(x(k))$ holds for some $k \geq 0$, where $q_k \in \alpha(\hat{x}(k))$ and $\hat{x}(k) \in x(k) + \varepsilon\mathbb{B}$. The action at time k is given by $u(k) = \kappa(\hat{x}(0), \cdots, \hat{x}(k))$, which implements $a_k = \mu(q_0, \cdots, q_k)$ in the sense of Definition 6. The next state under $u(k)$ is given by $x(k+1) = f(x(k), u(k))$, whose measurement is $\hat{x}(k+1) = x(k+1) + e(k+1) \in x(k+1) + \varepsilon\mathbb{B}$. Hence $L_1(q_{k+1}) \subseteq \hat{L}(\hat{x}(k+1))$ implies $L_1(q_{k+1}) \subseteq \hat{L}(\hat{x}(k+1))L(x(k+1))$. Thus, $L(q_k) \subseteq L(x(k))$ for all $k \geq 0$.

We show that (q_k, a_k, q_{k+1}) is a valid transition in $\mathcal{T}$. Note that

$$\begin{aligned}
&\hat{x}(k+1) \\
&= x(k+1) + e(k+1) \\
&= f(x(k), u(k)) + e(k+1) \\
&= f(\hat{x}(k), u(k)) + (f(x(k), u(k)) - f(\hat{x}(k), u(k))) + e(k+1).
\end{aligned}$$

Since f is L-Lipschitz continuous in both arguments on the compact set $(X + \varepsilon\mathbb{B}) \times U$, the above equation shows that

$$\hat{x}(k+1) \in f(\hat{x}(k), u(k)) + (L+1)\varepsilon\mathbb{B} \subseteq f(\hat{x}(k), u(k)) + \delta\mathbb{B},$$

because $(L+1)\varepsilon \leq \delta$. Hence, by the choice of $u(k)$ by κ (which is an α-implementation of μ), we have

$$\begin{aligned}
q_{k+1} &\in \alpha(\hat{x}(k+1)) \\
&\subseteq \alpha(f(\hat{x}(k), u(k)) + \delta\mathbb{B}) \\
&\subseteq \alpha(\mathrm{Post}_{\hat{\mathcal{S}}\oplus\Delta}(\hat{x}(k), u(k))) \\
&\subseteq \mathrm{Post}_\mathcal{T}(q_k, a_k),
\end{aligned}$$

where $\hat{x}(k) \in \alpha^{-1}(q_k)$, which shows that (q_k, a_k, q_{k+1}) is a valid transition in $\mathcal{T}$ and therefore $q_0q_1q_2\cdots$ is a valid path for $\mathcal{T}$. Since the trace of this path satisfies φ and $L_1(q_k) \subseteq L(x(k))$ for all $k \geq 0$, it follows that the trace of $x(0)x(1)x(2)\cdots$ also satisfies φ. □

REMARK 2. The soundness result above states that to cope with measurement errors, we only need to choose δ

sufficiently large such that $(L+1)\varepsilon \leq \delta$ and strengthen the labelling function by a factor of ε. This condition simplifies the two robustness margins (γ_1, γ_2) considered in the work [,] and also does not require that the abstraction relation to be non-deterministic in order to be robust with respect to measurement errors as stated in [, Section VI.6].

3.3 Approximate completeness of robust abstractions for discrete-time control systems

In this section, we show that, under Assumption 1, computing robust abstractions for the discrete-time control system (4) is approximately complete, in the sense that, for arbitrary numbers $0 \leq \delta_1 < \delta_2$, we can find a finite transition system $\mathcal{T}$ such that $\mathcal{S} \oplus \Delta_{\delta_1} \preceq \mathcal{T} \preceq \mathcal{S} \oplus \Delta_{\delta_2}$, where $\mathcal{S}$ and Δ_{δ_i} $(i = 1, 2)$ are defined in Definitions 7 and 8. This result is made precise by the following theorem, which we present as the main result of the paper.

THEOREM 2. *For any numbers $0 \leq \delta_1 < \delta_2$, let Δ_{δ_i} $(i = 1, 2)$ be given by Definition 8 with $\delta = \delta_i$. For any numbers $0 \leq \varepsilon_1 < \varepsilon_2$, let $L_{\mathcal{S}_i}$ $(i = 1, 2)$ be the ε_i-strengthening of $L_{\mathcal{S}}$. Let*

$$\mathcal{S}_i = (Q_{\mathcal{S}}, A_{\mathcal{S}}, R_{\mathcal{S}} \cup \Delta_{\delta_i}, \Pi, L_{\mathcal{S}_i}), \quad i = 1, 2.$$

Then there exists a finite transition system $\mathcal{T}$ such that

$$\mathcal{S}_1 \preceq \mathcal{T} \preceq \mathcal{S}_2. \tag{8}$$

To prove Theorem 2, we need the following lemma on over-approximation of the reachable set of a box in $\mathbb{R}^n$ under a nonlinear map.

LEMMA 1. *Fix any $\delta > 0$, any box (also called an interval or a hyperrectangle) $[x] \subseteq \mathbb{R}^n$, and any $u \in U$. For all $\varepsilon > 0$, there exists a finitely terminated algorithm to compute an over-approximation of the reachable set of $[x]$ under (6), i.e., the set*

$$Reach_{(6)}([x], u) = f([x], u) + \delta\mathbb{B},$$

such that

$$Reach_{(6)}([x], u) \subseteq \widehat{Reach}_{(6)}([x], u) \subseteq Reach_{(6)}([x], u) + \varepsilon\mathbb{B},$$

where $\widehat{Reach}_{(6)}([x], u)$ is the computed over-approximation given as a union of boxes.

PROOF. This is a well-known result in interval analysis, known as outer approximation of the image set of a function. It can be proved, for example, using the results in [, Chapter 3]. Here we include a proof for completeness. Let $\mathbb{IR}^n$ denote the set of all boxes in $\mathbb{R}^n$. Let $[f_u] : \mathbb{IR}^n \to \mathbb{IR}^m$ be a *convergent inclusion function* [ ] of $f(\cdot, u)$, which satisfies the following two conditions:

- $f([y], u) \subseteq [f_u]([y])$ for all $[y] \in \mathbb{IR}^n$;
- $\lim_{w([y]) \to 0} w([f_u]([y])) = 0$,

where $w([y])$ is the width of $[y]$, given by $\max_{1 \leq i \leq n}\{\overline{y_i} - \underline{y_i}\}$ if we write $[y] = [y_1] \times \cdots \times [y_n] \subseteq \mathbb{R}^n$ and $[y_i] = [\underline{y}_i, \overline{y}_i] \subseteq \mathbb{R}$ for $i = 1, \cdots, n$. Without loss of generality, assume that $\varepsilon < 1$. Because f is L-Lipschitz continuous on $[x]$ for some $L > 0$, we can find an inclusion function such that $w([f_u]([y])) \leq Lw([y])$ for any subintervals of $[x]$. We mince the interval $[x]$ into subintervals such that the largest width of among these subintervals is smaller than $\frac{\varepsilon}{2L}$. For each such interval $[y]$, we evaluate $[f_u]([y])$ and obtain the interval $[z] = [f_u]([y]) + \delta\mathbb{B}$. Let $\mathcal{Y}$ denote the collection of all such intervals[1] and let Y be its union. We claim that

$$Y = \widehat{\text{Reach}}_{(6)}([x], u)$$

satisfies the requirement of this lemma. This is clearly true because, for each interval $[z] = [f_u]([y]) + \delta\mathbb{B}$, we have $f([y]) + \delta\mathbb{B} \subseteq [z]$ and the distance from $[z]$ to the true reachable set $\text{Reach}_{(6)}([x], u)$ is bounded by $w([f_u]([y])) \leq L \cdot w([y]) \leq \frac{\varepsilon}{2}$. The proof for Lemma 1 is also summarized in pseudo code format in Algorithm 1. □

Algorithm 1 Computation of an over-approximation of $\text{Reach}_{(6)}([x], u)$ (Lemma 1)

Input: $[x]$, δ, $\varepsilon > 0$, the Lipschitz constant L for $f(\cdot, u)$, and a centred convergent inclusion function $[f_u]$ for $f(\cdot, u)$

```
List ← [x]
𝒴 ← ∅
while List ≠ ∅ do
    [y] ← First(List)
    List ← List \ {[x]}
    if w([y]) ≤ ε/(2L) then
        [z] ← [f_u]([y]) + δ𝔹
        𝒴 ← 𝒴 ∪ {[z]}
    else
        {Left[y], Right[y]} = Bisect([y])
        List ← List ∪ {Left[y], Right[y]}
Y ← ∪_{[z]∈𝒴} [z]
return Y = Reach^_(6)([x], u)
```

PROOF OF THEOREM 2. The proof is constructive and we construct a finite transition system

$$\mathcal{T} = (Q_{\mathcal{T}}, A_{\mathcal{T}}, R_{\mathcal{T}}, \Pi, L_{\mathcal{T}})$$

as follows.

For a positive integer k, let $\mathbb{Z}^k$ denote the k-dimensional integer lattice, i.e., the set of all k-tuples of integers. For parameters $\eta > 0$ and $\mu > 0$ (to be chosen later), define

$$[\mathbb{R}^n]_\eta = \eta\mathbb{Z}^n, \quad [\mathbb{R}^m]_\mu = \mu\mathbb{Z}^m,$$

where $\mu\mathbb{Z}^k = \{\mu z : z \in \mathbb{Z}^k\}$ (for $k = n, m$). Define a relation α from $Q_{\mathcal{S}}$ to $[\mathbb{R}^n]_\eta \cup \{X^c\}$ by

$$\left\{(x, q) : q = \eta\lfloor\frac{x}{\eta}\rfloor, x \in X\right\} \cup \{(X^c, X^c)\},$$

where $\lfloor\cdot\rfloor$ is the floor function (i.e., $\lfloor x\rfloor = (\lfloor x_1\rfloor, \cdots, \lfloor x_n\rfloor)$ and $\lfloor x_i\rfloor$ gives the largest integer less than or equal to x_i). Let $Q_{\mathcal{T}}$ be $\alpha(Q_{\mathcal{S}})$ and $A_{\mathcal{T}} = \left\{a : \exists u \in A_{\mathcal{S}} \text{ s.t. } a = \mu\lfloor\frac{u}{\mu}\rfloor\right\}$ (which are both non-empty by definition and are finite because X and U are compact). Note that this gives a deterministic relation in the sense that $\alpha(x)$ is single-valued for all x. It is straightforward to verify that

$$\alpha^{-1}(\alpha(B)) \subseteq B + \eta\mathbb{B}, \tag{9}$$

for any set $B \subseteq \mathbb{R}^n \cup X^c$, with the slight abuse of notation that $X^c + x = X^c$ for any $x \in \mathbb{R}^n$.

[1]Such a collection $\mathcal{Y}$ is called a non-regular paving of $\mathbb{R}^n$, which can be regularized [, Chapter 3] to reduce the number of boxes and hence reduce complexity, but this is not necessary for our purpose.

We next construct $R_{\mathcal{T}}$. For each $q \in Q_{\mathcal{T}}$ and $a \in A_{\mathcal{T}}$, denote by

$$\text{Reach}_{\mathcal{S}_1}(\alpha^{-1}(q), a) = \bigcup_{x \in \alpha^{-1}(q)} \text{Post}_{\mathcal{S}_2}(x, a).$$

We let (q, a, q') be included in $R_{\mathcal{T}}$ if and only if

$$q' \in \alpha(\widehat{\text{Reach}_{\mathcal{S}_1}}(\overline{\alpha^{-1}(q)}, a)),$$

i.e.,

$$\text{Post}_{\mathcal{T}}(q, a) = \alpha(\widehat{\text{Reach}_{\mathcal{S}_1}}(\overline{\alpha^{-1}(q)}, a)), \tag{10}$$

where $\widehat{\text{Reach}_{\mathcal{S}_1}}(\overline{\alpha^{-1}(q)}, a)$ is computed from Lemma 1 by setting $[x] = \overline{\alpha^{-1}(q)}$, $u = a$, and $\delta = \delta_1$. In particular, we set $\widehat{\text{Reach}_{\mathcal{S}_1}}(\overline{\alpha^{-1}(q)}, a) = \widehat{\text{Reach}}_{(6)}([x], u)$, if $\widehat{\text{Reach}}_{(6)}([x], u) \subseteq X$, and

$$\widehat{\text{Reach}_{\mathcal{S}_1}}(\overline{\alpha^{-1}(q)}, a) = \widehat{\text{Reach}}_{(6)}([x], u) \cup \{X^c\},$$

if $\widehat{\text{Reach}}_{(6)}([x], u) \not\subseteq X$.

Then it follows from Lemma 1 that

$$\begin{aligned}\alpha(\bigcup_{x \in \alpha^{-1}(q)} \text{Post}_{\mathcal{S}_1}(x, a)) &\subseteq \alpha(\text{Reach}_{\mathcal{S}_1}(\overline{\alpha^{-1}(q)}, a)) \\ &\subseteq \alpha(\widehat{\text{Reach}_{\mathcal{S}_1}}(\overline{\alpha^{-1}(q)}, a)) \\ &= \text{Post}_{\mathcal{T}}(q, a),\end{aligned}$$

which verifies condition (ii) of Definition 4 for $\mathcal{S}_1 \preceq_\alpha \mathcal{T}$.

Consider α^{-1} as a relation from $Q_{\mathcal{T}}$ to $Q_{\mathcal{S}}$. Then for each $x \in Q_{\mathcal{S}}$ and $u \in A_{\mathcal{S}}$, we can choose $a = \mu \lfloor \frac{u}{\mu} \rfloor \in A_{\mathcal{T}}$ such that

$$\begin{aligned}\alpha^{-1}(\bigcup_{q \in \alpha(x)} \text{Post}_{\mathcal{T}}(q, a)) &= \alpha^{-1}(\text{Post}_{\mathcal{T}}(q, a)) \\ &\subseteq \alpha^{-1}(\alpha(\widehat{\text{Reach}_{\mathcal{S}_1}}(\overline{\alpha^{-1}(q)}, a))) \\ &\subseteq \widehat{\text{Reach}_{\mathcal{S}_1}}(\overline{\alpha^{-1}(q)}, a) + \eta\mathbb{B} \\ &\subseteq \text{Reach}_{\mathcal{S}_1}(\overline{\alpha^{-1}(q)}, a) + (\eta + \varepsilon)\mathbb{B}.\end{aligned}$$

where we used (10), (9), and Lemma 1. We claim that, if we can choose η, μ, and ε sufficiently small such that

$$\delta_1 + L(\eta + \mu) + \eta + \varepsilon \le \delta_2, \tag{11}$$

then

$$\text{Reach}_{\mathcal{S}_1}(\overline{\alpha^{-1}(q)}, a) + (\eta + \varepsilon)\mathbb{B} \subseteq \text{Post}_{\mathcal{S}_2}(x, u). \tag{12}$$

Note that $\overline{\alpha^{-1}(q)} \subseteq x + \eta\mathbb{B}$ and $a \in u + \mu\mathbb{B}$. We first assume that $X^c \notin \text{Reach}_{\mathcal{S}_1}(\overline{\alpha^{-1}(q)}, a)$. Without loss of generality, we can assume that $\eta \le 1$ and $\mu \le 1$. Because f is Lipschitz continuous in both arguments on the compact set $(X + \mathbb{B}) \times (U + \mathbb{B})$ (we use L to indicate the uniform Lipschitz constant for both variables on this set), it follows that

$$\text{Reach}_{\mathcal{S}_1}(\overline{\alpha^{-1}(q)}, a) \subseteq f(x, u) + [\delta_1 + L(\eta + \mu)]\mathbb{B}.$$

Combining the displayed equations above, we obtain

$$\begin{aligned}\alpha^{-1}(\bigcup_{q \in \alpha(x)} \text{Post}_{\mathcal{T}}(q, a)) &\subseteq f(x, u) + \delta_2\mathbb{B} \\ &= \text{Post}_{\mathcal{S}_2}(x, u),\end{aligned}$$

which verifies condition (ii) of Definition 4 for $\mathcal{T} \preceq_\alpha \mathcal{S}_2$, because $X^c \in \alpha^{-1}(\bigcup_{q \in \alpha(x)} \text{Post}_{\mathcal{T}}(q, a))$ would also imply $X^c \in \text{Post}_{\mathcal{S}_2}(x, u)$.

Now we define $L_{\mathcal{T}}$. For each $q \in Q_{\mathcal{T}}$, define

$$\pi \in L_{\mathcal{T}}(q)$$

if and only if $\pi \in L_{\mathcal{S}}(x)$ for all $x \in q + \frac{\varepsilon_1 + \varepsilon_2}{2}\mathbb{B}$. Choose η sufficiently small such that $\eta + \frac{\varepsilon_1 + \varepsilon_2}{2} < \varepsilon_2$. This is possible because $\varepsilon_2 > \varepsilon_1$. To verify condition (iii) of Definition 4 for $\mathcal{S}_1 \preceq_\alpha \mathcal{T}$ and $\mathcal{T} \preceq_{\alpha^{-1}} \mathcal{S}_2$, we need to check that

$$L_{\mathcal{S}_2}(x) \subseteq L_{\mathcal{T}}(q) \tag{13}$$

and

$$L_{\mathcal{T}}(q) \subseteq L_{\mathcal{S}_1}(x) \tag{14}$$

for all $(x, q) \in \alpha$. Fix any $(x, q) \in \alpha$. If $\pi \in L_{\mathcal{S}_2}(x)$, then $\pi \in L_{\mathcal{S}}(y)$ for all $y \in x + \varepsilon_2\mathbb{B}$. Since $q + \frac{\varepsilon_1 + \varepsilon_2}{2}\mathbb{B} \subseteq x + [\eta + \frac{\varepsilon_1 + \varepsilon_2}{2}]\mathbb{B} \subseteq x + \varepsilon_2\mathbb{B}$, we have $\pi \in L_{\mathcal{S}}(y)$ for all $y \in q + \frac{\varepsilon_1 + \varepsilon_2}{2}\mathbb{B}$ and $\pi \in L_{\mathcal{T}}(q)$. Hence, (13) holds. If $\pi \in L_{\mathcal{T}}(q)$, then $\pi \in L_{\mathcal{S}}(y)$ for all $y \in q + \frac{\varepsilon_1 + \varepsilon_2}{2}\mathbb{B}$ by the definition of $L_{\mathcal{T}}$. Since $x + \varepsilon_1\mathbb{B} \subseteq q + (\eta + \varepsilon_1)\mathbb{B} \subseteq q + \frac{\varepsilon_1 + \varepsilon_2}{2}\mathbb{B}$, we have $\pi \in L_{\mathcal{S}}(y)$ for all $y \in x + \varepsilon_1\mathbb{B}$ and $\pi \in L_{\mathcal{S}_1}(x)$. Hence, (14) holds.

We have verified $\mathcal{S}_1 \preceq \mathcal{T} \preceq \mathcal{S}_2$ by checking all the conditions of Definition 4. The main steps of the proof are also summarized in pseudo code format in Algorithm 2. □

Algorithm 2 Computation of an approximately complete robust abstraction $\mathcal{T}$ for $\mathcal{S}$ (Theorem 2)

Input: $\mathcal{S} = (Q_{\mathcal{S}}, A_{\mathcal{S}}, R_{\mathcal{S}}, \Pi, L_{\mathcal{S}})$, numbers $0 \le \delta_1 < \delta_2$ and $0 \le \varepsilon_1 < \varepsilon_2$

Set $L_{\mathcal{S}_i}$ be the ε_i-strengthening of $L_{\mathcal{S}}$ $(i = 1, 2)$
Set Δ_{δ_i} according to Definition 8 $(i = 1, 2)$
Set $\mathcal{S}_i = (Q_{\mathcal{S}}, A_{\mathcal{S}}, R_{\mathcal{S}} \cup \Delta_{\delta_i}, \Pi, L_{\mathcal{S}_i})$ $(i = 1, 2)$
Choose rational numbers $\eta \in (0, 1)$ and $\varepsilon \in (0, 1)$ such that $\delta_1 + L(\eta + \mu) + \eta + \varepsilon \le \delta_2$ and $\eta + \frac{\varepsilon_1 + \varepsilon_2}{2} < \varepsilon_2$, where L is the uniform Lipschitz constant of f on the compact set $(X + \mathbb{B}) \times (U + \mathbb{B})$
Set $Q_{\mathcal{T}} = \left\{x \in [\mathbb{R}^n]_\eta : \exists x \in Q_{\mathcal{S}} \text{ s.t. } x = \eta \lfloor \frac{u}{\eta} \rfloor \right\} \cup \{X^c\}$
Set $A_{\mathcal{T}} = \left\{a \in [\mathbb{R}^m]_\mu : \exists u \in A_{\mathcal{S}} \text{ s.t. } a = \mu \lfloor \frac{u}{\mu} \rfloor \right\}$
for all $q \in Q_{\mathcal{T}}$ **do**
  $L_{\mathcal{T}}(q) \leftarrow \emptyset$
  for all $\pi \in \Pi$ **do**
    if $\pi \in L_{\mathcal{S}}(x)$ for all $x \in q + \frac{\varepsilon_1 + \varepsilon_2}{2}\mathbb{B}$ **then**
      $L_{\mathcal{T}}(q) \leftarrow L_{\mathcal{T}}(q) \cup \{\pi\}$
$R_{\mathcal{T}} \leftarrow \emptyset$
for all $q \in Q_{\mathcal{T}}$ **do**
  for all $a \in A_{\mathcal{T}}$ **do**
    if $q' \in \alpha(\widehat{\text{Reach}}_{(6)}(\overline{\alpha^{-1}(q)}, a))$ **then**
      $R_{\mathcal{T}} \leftarrow R_{\mathcal{T}} \cup \{(q, a, q')\}$
return $\mathcal{T} = (Q_{\mathcal{T}}, A_{\mathcal{T}}, R_{\mathcal{T}}, \Pi, L_{\mathcal{T}})$

Remark 3. While the disturbance sets are so chosen for simplicity of presentation, they do not have to be of the form $\delta\mathbb{B}$. In fact, if we choose two arbitrary sets W_1 and W_2 in place of $\delta_1\mathbb{B}$ and $\delta_2\mathbb{B}$ in Definition 8 such that there exists $\varepsilon > 0$ such that $W_1 + \varepsilon\mathbb{B} \subseteq W_2$, then a completeness result similar to Theorem 2 can be stated. Furthermore, δ can be a vector in $\mathbb{R}^n$ instead of a scalar, in which case $\delta_i\mathbb{B}$ becomes a hyperrectangle and the condition $0 \le \delta_1 < \delta_2$ is a componentwise inequality.

REMARK 4. In the proof of Theorem 2, we in fact construct a single-valued abstraction relation α. While the main results of the paper are presented for the case where α can be multi-valued, it appears, in view of the proof of Theorem 2, that for practice purposes, α may always be chosen to be deterministic, while still preserving robustness (see also Remark 2).

Finally, we would like to point out that Theorem 2 shows that there exists an *approximately complete* abstraction procedure for discrete-time nonlinear control systems of the form (4) in the sense that, if a specification φ is realizable for $\mathcal{S}_2$ (namely, a δ_2-perturbation of $\mathcal{S}$), then there is a robust abstraction $\mathcal{T}$ of $\mathcal{S}_1$, which is a δ_1-perturbation of $\mathcal{S}$, such that φ is realizable for $\mathcal{T}$ and hence it is also realizable for $\mathcal{S}_1$. Note that $\mathcal{S}_1$ and $\mathcal{S}_2$ can be made arbitrarily close by choosing δ_2 close to δ_1 and ε_2 close to ε_1. Since the proof of above theorem is constructive, we can algorithmically synthesize a control strategy for $\mathcal{S}_1$ by computing $\mathcal{T}$ first and then solving a discrete synthesis problem for $\mathcal{T}$ with the specification φ. We summarize this in the following corollary.

COROLLARY 2. *Let $\mathcal{S}_1$, $\mathcal{S}_2$, and φ be as defined in Theorem 2. There is a decision procedure to answer one of the following two questions:*

(i) there exists a control strategy κ (and one can algorithmically construct it) such that $(\mathcal{S}_1, \kappa) \models \varphi$;

(ii) φ is not realizable for $\mathcal{S}_2$.

4. AN EXAMPLE

We use a simple motion planning example to illustrate our results. Consider a vehicle steering problem, where the dynamics of the vehicle are given by the so-called bicycle model [ ]. The same example is used for illustration of abstraction-based control design in [, ,]. The model is given by

$$\begin{bmatrix} \dot{x}_1 \\ \dot{x}_2 \\ \dot{x}_3 \end{bmatrix} = \begin{bmatrix} u_1 \cos(\alpha + x_3)/\cos(\alpha) \\ u_1 \sin(\alpha + x_3)/\cos(\alpha) \\ u_1 \tan(u_2) \end{bmatrix},$$

where $(x_1, x_2, x_3) = (x, y, \theta)$, $(u_1, u_2) = (v, \varphi)$, and $\alpha = \arctan(a \tan(u_2)/b)$. The constant $b = 1$ is the wheel base and $a = 0.5$ is the distance between centre of mass and rear wheels. The states consist of the coordinates of the centre of the mass (x, y) and the heading angle θ. The controls consist of the wheel speed v and the steering angle φ. The variable α is the angle of velocity depending on φ.

Let $X = [7, 10] \times [0, 4.5] \times [-\pi, \pi]$ and $U = [-1, 1] \times [-1, 1]$. Consider a workspace and a specification given by $\varphi = A_I \wedge \Box(\neg A_O) \wedge \Diamond A_G$, where $A_I = [7.6, 0.4, \pi/2]^T$, $A_G = [9, 9.6] \times [0, 0.6] \times [-\pi, \pi]$, $A_O = A_{O1} \cup A_{O2} \cup A_{O3}$, $A_{O1} = [8.2, 8.4] \times [0, 3.6] \times [-\pi, \pi]$, $A_{O2} = [8.4, 9.4] \times [3.4, 3.6] \times [-\pi, \pi]$, $A_{O3} = [9.4, 10] \times [2.4, 2.6] \times [-\pi, \pi]$.

To design a control strategy to realize this specification, we discretize the model using a sampling time step $\tau = 0.3$. We first consider the case with no disturbance, i.e., $\delta = 0$. Using the discretization parameters $\eta = 0.2$ and $\mu = 0.3$, the resulting nominal abstraction consists of 12,880 states and 3,023,040 transitions. The computation time was 7.3s for computing the abstraction and 8.6s for solving the synthesis problem on a 2.2GHz Intel Core i7 processor. To design a robust control strategy, we consider an additive disturbance of size $\delta = 0.05$ on the right-hand side of the discretized system. We compute a robust abstraction by setting $\delta = 0.05$ and $\eta = 0.05$. The resulting robust abstraction consists of $782,691$ states and $1,727,548,752$ transitions. The computation time was $2,327$s for abstraction and $2,289$s for synthesis on the same processor. We used a modified version of the toolbox SCOTS [ ] with an interval arithmetic extension to solve this example.

A feasible trajectory resulting from the nominal controller is shown in Figure 2, where no disturbance was added. A feasible trajectory resulting from a robust controller is shown in Figure 3 (left), where an additive disturbance of size $\delta = 0.05$ was added. Using the same controller, a simulated trajectory shown in Figure 3 (right) with an additive disturbance of size $\delta = 0.15$ fails to satisfy the specification. Furthermore, Theorem 2 implies that, for any $0.05 \leq \delta_1 < \delta_2$, by further refining the abstraction, we should be able to assert that either the specification is robustly realizable with a disturbance of size δ_1 or the specification is not realizable with a disturbance of size δ_2.

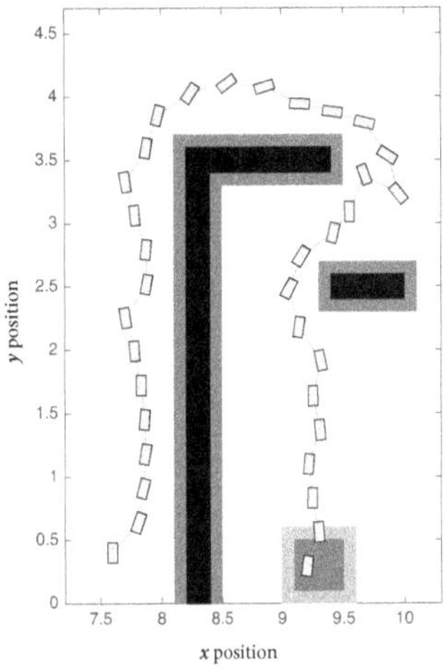

Figure 2: A simulated trajectory from a nominal abstraction that satisfies the specification.

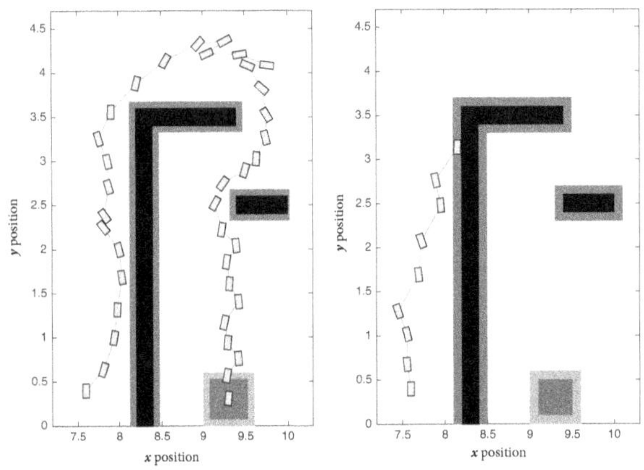

Figure 3: A valid trajectory (left) obtained from a robust abstraction with $\delta = 0.05$ and a failed trajectory (right) with disturbance size $\delta = 0.15$.

5. CONCLUSIONS AND DISCUSSIONS

We proposed a computational framework for designing robust abstractions for control synthesis. It is shown that robust abstractions are not only sound in the sense that they preserve robust satisfaction of linear-time properties, but also approximately complete in the sense that, given a concrete discrete-time control system and an arbitrarily small perturbation of this system, there exists a finite transition system that robustly abstracts the concrete system and is abstracted by the perturbed system at the same time. Consequently, the existence of controllers for a general discrete-time nonlinear control system and linear-time specifications is robustly decidable: if a specification is robustly realizable, there is a decision procedure to find a (potentially less) robust control strategy.

It is interesting to note that the connection between robustness and decidability appeared in different contexts. Recently, the notion of δ-decidability for satisfiability over the reals [ ] and δ-reachability analysis [ ] have been proposed to turn otherwise undecidable problems into decidable ones. A notion of "robustness implies decidability" was proposed in early work in [ ] for verifying bounded properties for polynomial hybrid automaton and in [ ] for reachability analysis of several simple models of hybrid systems. Finally, the early work in [ ] showed that *robust* stability is decidable for linear systems in the context of output feedback stabilization. In this sense, the current work can serve as an example of "robustness implies decidability" in the context of linear-time logic control synthesis for nonlinear systems.

6. ACKNOWLEDGMENTS

This research was supported in part by NSERC Canada and the University of Waterloo. The author would like to thank Necmiye Ozay and Yinan Li for stimulating discussions on related topics and the anonymous reviewers for helpful comments and suggestions.

7. REFERENCES

[1] R. Alur, T. A. Henzinger, G. Lafferriere, and G. J. Pappas. Discrete abstractions of hybrid systems. *Proceedings of the IEEE*, 88(7):971–984, 2000.

[2] B. Anderson, N. Bose, and E. Jury. Output feedback stabilization and related problems-solution via decision methods. *IEEE Transactions on Automatic control*, 20(1):53–66, 1975.

[3] D. Angeli et al. A lyapunov approach to incremental stability properties. *IEEE Transactions on Automatic Control*, 47(3):410–421, 2002.

[4] E. Asarin and A. Bouajjani. Perturbed turing machines and hybrid systems. In *Proc. of LICS*, pages 269–278. IEEE, 2001.

[5] K. J. Aström and R. M. Murray. *Feedback Systems: An Introduction for Scientists and Engineers*. Princeton University Press, 2010.

[6] C. Baier and J.-P. Katoen. *Principles of Model Checking*. MIT Press, 2008.

[7] M. Fränzle. What will be eventually true of polynomial hybrid automata? In *Proc. of TACS*, pages 340–359. Springer, 2001.

[8] S. Gao, J. Avigad, and E. M. Clarke. δ-complete decision procedures for satisfiability over the reals. In *Proc. of IJCAR*, pages 286–300. Springer, 2012.

[9] A. Girard. Controller synthesis for safety and reachability via approximate bisimulation. *Automatica*, 48(5):947–953, 2012.

[10] A. Girard, G. Pola, and P. Tabuada. Approximately bisimilar symbolic models for incrementally stable switched systems. *IEEE Trans. on Automatic Control*, 55:116–126, 2010.

[11] L. Jaulin. *Applied Interval Analysis*. Springer Science & Business Media, 2001.

[12] S. Kong, S. Gao, W. Chen, and E. Clarke. dreach: δ-reachability analysis for hybrid systems. In *Proc. of TACAS*, pages 200–205. Springer, 2015.

[13] Y. Li, J. Liu, and N. Ozay. Computing finite abstractions with robustness margins via local reachable set over-approximation. In *Proc. ADHS*, 2015.

[14] J. Liu and N. Ozay. Abstraction, discretization, and robustness in temporal logic control of dynamical systems. In *Proc. of HSCC*, pages 293–302, 2014.

[15] J. Liu and N. Ozay. Finite abstractions with robustness margins for temporal logic-based control synthesis. *Nonlinear Analysis: Hybrid Systems*, 22:1–15, 2016.

[16] N. Ozay, J. Liu, P. Prabhakar, and R. M. Murray. Computing augmented finite transition systems to synthesize switching protocols for polynomial switched systems. In *Proc. of ACC*, pages 6237–6244, 2013.

[17] A. Pnueli. The temporal logic of programs. In *Proc. of FOCS*, pages 46–57. IEEE, 1977.

[18] G. Pola, A. Girard, and P. Tabuada. Approximately bisimilar symbolic models for nonlinear control systems. *Automatica*, 44(10):2508–2516, 2008.

[19] G. Reissig. Computing abstractions of nonlinear systems. *IEEE Trans. Automatic Control*, 56:2583–2598, 2011.

[20] G. Reissig and M. Rungger. Feedback refinement relations for symbolic controller synthesis. In *Proc. of CDC*, pages 88–94. IEEE, 2014.

[21] G. Reissig, A. Weber, and M. Rungger. Feedback Refinement Relations for the Synthesis of Symbolic Controllers. *IEEE Transactions on Automatic Control, to appear*, 2016.

[22] M. Rungger and M. Zamani. Scots: A tool for the synthesis of symbolic controllers. In *Proc. of HSCC*, pages 99–104. ACM, 2016.

[23] P. Tabuada. *Verification and Control of Hybrid Systems: A Symbolic Approach*. Springer, 2009.

[24] P. Tabuada and G. J. Pappas. Linear time logic control of discrete-time linear systems. *IEEE Trans. on Automatic Control*, 51(12):1862–1877, 2006.

[25] Y. Tazaki and J. Imura. Discrete abstractions of nonlinear systems based on error propagation analysis. *IEEE Trans. Automatic Control*, 57:550–564, 2012.

[26] U. Topcu, N. Ozay, J. Liu, and R. M. Murray. On synthesizing robust discrete controllers under modeling uncertainty. In *Proc. of HSCC*, pages 85–94. ACM, 2012.

[27] M. Zamani, G. Pola, M. Mazo, and P. Tabuada. Symbolic models for nonlinear control systems without stability assumptions. *IEEE Transactions on Automatic Control*, 57(7):1804–1809, 2012.

Formal Synthesis of Stabilizing Controllers for Switched Systems

Pavithra Prabhakar*
Kansas State University, Manhattan, KS
pprabhakar@ksu.edu

Miriam García Soto†
IMDEA Software Institute &
Universidad Politécnica de Madrid, Spain
miriam.garcia@imdea.org

ABSTRACT

In this paper, we describe an abstraction-based method for synthesizing a state-based switching control for stabilizing a family of dynamical systems. Given a set of dynamical systems and a set of polyhedral switching surfaces, the algorithm synthesizes a strategy that assigns to every surface the linear dynamics to switch to at the surface. Our algorithm constructs a finite game graph that consists of the switching surfaces as the existential nodes and the choices of the dynamics as the universal nodes. In addition, the edges capture quantitative information about the evolution of the distance of the state from the equilibrium point along the executions. A switching strategy for the family of dynamical systems is extracted by finding a strategy on the game graph which results in plays having a bounded weight. Such a strategy is obtained by reducing the problem to the strategy synthesis for an energy game, which is a well-studied problem in the literature. We have implemented our algorithm for polyhedral inclusion dynamics and linear dynamics. We illustrate our algorithm on examples from these two classes of systems.

CCS Concepts

•**Theory of computation** → **Abstraction;** *Logic and verification; Algorithmic game theory;* •**Computer systems organization** → **Embedded and cyber-physical systems;**

Keywords

Hybrid systems; stability; control synthesis; game theory; switched systems

*Pavithra Prabhakar is partially supported by NSF CAREER award no. 1552668.
†Miriam García Soto is partially supported by BES-2013-065076 grant from the Spanish Ministry of Economy and Competitiveness.

HSCC '17, April 18–20, 2017, Pittsburgh, PA, USA.
© 2017 ACM. ISBN 978-1-4503-4590-3/17/04...$15.00.
DOI: http://dx.doi.org/10.1145/3049797.3049822

1. INTRODUCTION

One of the fundamental requirements in control design for cyber-physical systems is stability. Stability is a robustness property that captures the notion that small perturbations in the initial state of the system result in only small deviations in the behaviors of the system. This robustness property accounts for certain deviations in the implementation as compared to the design. In this paper, we consider the problem of computing a supervisory controller that switches between a set of given dynamical systems to obtain a switched system that is stable. Switching strategies are broadly of two kinds, one that specifies the switching times and the other that specifies the switching surfaces [15]. Here, we focus on strategies of the latter kind.

Stability analysis is a classical problem studied in control theory. For a linear dynamical system $\dot{x} = Ax$, stability can be characterized in terms of the eigenvalues of the matrix A, which can be efficiently determined when the elements of A are rational. However, complete characterization of stability is not known even for switched linear systems. For instance, eigenvalue based analysis does not carry over to switched linear systems; one can construct two systems — one stable and the other unstable — by switching between the same two linear dynamical systems [4]. Hence, restrictions on the dynamics and switching law that enforce stability have been investigated. For instance, a system that switches arbitrarily among a set of linear dynamics is stable, if the corresponding matrices are pairwise commutative or symmetric [20, 33].

More generally, Lyapunov functions are used to establish stability. A Lyapunov function is a function from the state space to non-negative reals such that the value of function along any execution decreases. Again, for linear systems, it is well known that there exist quadratic Lyapunov functions that can be computed by solving certain Linear Matrix Inequalities (LMIs). For switched systems, this framework has been extended to common and multiple Lyapunov functions. A common Lyapunov function consists of a single function which serves as a Lyapunov function for all the dynamical systems in the switched system. A multiple Lyapunov function consists of multiple functions, each of which serves as a Lyapunov function for certain dynamical system in the switched system, and in addition, consists of certain constraints that need to be satisfied by these functions at the switching surfaces. In [26, 27], necessary and sufficient conditions for the existence of common quadratic Lyapunov functions for arbitrary switched linear systems have been explored. Necessary and sufficient condition for robust asymptotic stability has been investigated in [3], which provides a semi decidable algorithm for stability analysis. Constraints on the switching, such as, slow switching characterized by average dwell time, that ensure stability have been investigated in [19]. For constrained switching, multiple Lyapunov functions have been studied in [9] including piecewise quadratic Lyapunov functions [13].

This paper focuses on the stabilization problem, namely, the synthesis of a switching logic that renders the system stable. Control Lyapunov functions are the analogue of Lyapunov functions for stabilizability. Quadratic and piecewise quadratic switching stabilization of linear systems has been explored in [32, 28, 22] and necessary and sufficient conditions for stabilization that lead to semi decidable algorithms have been explored in [16]. Both stability analysis and stabilization problem are undecidable for very simple dynamics, and hence, there are no complete algorithmic methods for stabilizable control synthesis. See [17] for a recent survey on stability and stabilization of switched linear systems.

In this paper, we explore an alternate method based on abstractions. Abstractions [12] construct simpler systems for the purpose of design and analysis. More precisely, to analyse the correctness of a system $\mathcal{S}$, a simpler system $\hat{\mathcal{S}}$ is constructed, such that, the correctness of $\hat{\mathcal{S}}$ implies the correctness of $\mathcal{S}$. Hence, the simpler system $\hat{\mathcal{S}}$ is analysed to infer the correctness of $\mathcal{S}$. In general, the abstraction is conservative and hence, the violation of the property by $\hat{\mathcal{S}}$ does not imply the violation of the property by $\mathcal{S}$. Abstractions for safety analysis have been explored in [1, 6, 2, 30]; more recently, abstractions have been explored for stability analysis [24]. Abstractions for controller synthesis follow the same general paradigm. Here, a simpler finite state abstract game is constructed from the continuous/switched system and a strategy for this abstract game is used to extract a controller for the original system [18, 11, 21, 31, 29]. These works consider safety and linear temporal logic objectives.

In this paper, we explore abstraction based controller synthesis for the stabilization problem. Given a set of dynamical systems and polyhedral switching surfaces, we construct a finite weighted (game) graph, that abstracts the switching synthesis problem into a strategy synthesis problem on the game graph. More precisely, if there exists a strategy on the game graph such that all the paths in the graph that conform with the strategy have bounded weights, then a switching control for the family of dynamical systems can be extracted from the strategy. We solve the strategy synthesis problem by reducing it into an energy game problem for which several algorithms have been proposed in the literature [5]. We apply our algorithm to the stabilization problem of a family of polyhedral inclusion dynamics and a family of linear dynamical systems. Here, we do not explore the choice of the polyhedral switching surfaces, and discuss briefly the computational aspects in the graph construction. These will be explored in detail in a future work.

2. PRELIMINARIES

In this section, we present some basic definitions and concepts required in the rest of the paper.

Numbers, functions and sequences..

Let $\mathbb{R}$, $\mathbb{Q}$ and $\mathbb{N}$ denote the set of real, rational and natural numbers, respectively. $\mathbb{R}_{\geqslant 0}$ denotes the set of non-negative real numbers and $\mathbb{R}_{\geqslant 0}^{\infty}$ denotes the set $\mathbb{R}_{\geqslant 0} \cup \{+\infty\}$.

Given a function $f : A \to B$, the domain of f, namely, A, is denoted $dom(f)$. The restriction of f to a subset $C \subseteq A$ is denoted as $f\lceil_C$.

Given a set A, the set of finite sequences over A with zero or more elements is denoted as A^* and the set of finite sequences over A with one or more elements is denoted as A^+. The set A^*B denotes the set of finite sequences conformed by a concatenation of a sequence in A^* and an element in B. The last term in a sequence η is denoted as $last(\eta)$. We refer to the cardinality of a sequence η as $|\eta|$.

The space $\mathbb{R}^n$*..*

The interior of a set $A \subseteq \mathbb{R}^n$ is denoted as $\mathring{A}$, and the closure as $\overline{A}$.

A *polyhedral partition* of an n-dimensional real space $X \subseteq \mathbb{R}^n$ is a finite set of closed convex polyhedra $R = \{\Omega_1, \dots, \Omega_k\}$ such that $X = \cup_{\Omega \in R} \Omega$, $\mathring{\Omega}_i \neq \emptyset$ for every i and $\mathring{\Omega}_i \cap \mathring{\Omega}_j = \emptyset$ for every $i \neq j$. A *valid* set of *facets* $\mathcal{F}$ of X is a set of maximal closed convex subsets of the boundary of the polyhedral sets contained in a polyhedral partition R of X, that is, $\mathcal{F} = \{f \mid f = \Omega \cap \Omega', \Omega, \Omega' \in R, \Omega \neq \Omega', dim(f) = n-1\}$ for some polyhedral partition R.

3. SWITCHING STABILIZATION PROBLEM

In this section, we formalize the switching stabilization problem for a family of differential inclusions. Given a set of differential inclusions, our goal is to synthesize a state based switching logic that results in a stable switched system.

Consider a family of n-dimensional dynamical systems determined by differential inclusions of the form:

$$\dot{x}(t) \in g_p(x(t)),\ p \in \mathcal{P}, \tag{1}$$

where $x(t) \in \mathbb{R}^n$ is the state at time t, $\mathcal{P}$ is a finite set of operational modes, and for every $p \in \mathcal{P}$, the multivalued map $g_p : \mathbb{R}^n \to 2^{\mathbb{R}^n}$ specifies the dynamics in the mode. We will refer to the above as the system $\mathcal{S} = (\mathcal{P}, \{g_p\}_{p \in \mathcal{P}})$.

A switched system is then obtained by switching between the dynamical systems at certain switching facets. Our definition is slightly different from a standard state dependent strategy, where every state is assigned a dynamics from the family. Our system will follow its current dynamics until it reaches a switching facet upon which it changes its dynamics as dictated by a switching policy.

Definition 1. *Given a system $\mathcal{S} = (\mathcal{P}, \{g_p\}_{p \in \mathcal{P}})$ and a finite set of valid facets $\mathcal{F}$ in $\mathbb{R}^n$, a* switching strategy *is a function $\alpha : \mathcal{F}^+ \to \mathcal{P}$.*

We seek a strategy that could potentially have memory, that is, the mode being chosen could depend not only on the current facet but also the sequence of facets seen until then. However, our algorithm will find memoryless strategies where the choice depends only on the current facet.

Definition 2. *Given a system $\mathcal{S} = (\mathcal{P}, \{g_p\}_{p \in \mathcal{P}})$ and a switching strategy α, the tuple $(\mathcal{P}, \{g_p\}_{p \in \mathcal{P}}, \alpha)$ is a* switched system *and it is denoted by $\mathcal{S}_\alpha$.*

Next, we define partial executions which capture the solution of the switched system starting from a switching facet before it reaches the next switching facet.

Definition 3. *Given a system $\mathcal{S} = (\mathcal{P}, \{g_p\}_{p \in \mathcal{P}})$, a valid set of facets $\mathcal{F}$ and a $p \in \mathcal{P}$, a* p-partial execution *is a* *function* $x : [T_1, T_2) \to \mathbb{R}^n$, *where* $T_1 \in \mathbb{R}_{\geqslant 0}$ *and* $T_2 \in \mathbb{R}^{\infty}_{\geqslant 0}$, *such that there exists a non-negative real* $T \in [T_1, T_2)$ *and a facet* $f \in \mathcal{F}$, *satisfying*

- *for all* $t \in [T_1, T]$, $x(t) \in f$,
- *for all* $t \in (T, T_2)$, $x(t) \notin f'$, *for any* $f' \in \mathcal{F}$, *and*
- *for all* $t \in [T_1, T_2)$, $\dot{x}(t) \in g_p(x(t))$.

A partial execution is a p-partial execution for some p. Note that it starts in some facet and then possibly goes out of the facet, but does not re-enter any other facet. We then define an execution of the system as a sequence of partial executions which can be joined together.

Definition 4. *An* execution *of a switched system* $\mathcal{S}_\alpha$ *is a continuous function* $x : [0, T) \to \mathbb{R}^n$ *with* $T \in \mathbb{R}^{\infty}_{\geqslant 0}$, *such that there exist finite or infinite sequences of valid facets* $f_1, f_2, \ldots$ *in* $\mathcal{F}$, *of modes* $p_1, p_2, \ldots$ *in* $\mathcal{P}$ *and of partial executions* $x_1, x_2, \ldots$ *of* $\mathcal{S}$ *and* $\mathcal{F}$, *where* $dom(x_i) = [T_{i-1}, T_i)$ *and* x_i *is a* p_i*-partial execution for every* i; *satisfying:*

- $[0, T) = \bigcup_i [T_{i-1}, T_i)$,
- $x \restriction_{[T_{i-1}, T_i)} = x_i$ *for every* i,
- $x_i(T_{i-1}) \in f_i$ *for every* i *and*
- $\alpha(f_1, \ldots, f_i) = p_i$ *for every* i.

Let $Exec(\mathcal{S}_\alpha)$ denote the set of all executions of $\mathcal{S}_\alpha$.

Next, we introduce the notion of stability for a switched system. Stability is a property of a system which ensures that small perturbations in the initial state of the system lead to small variations in its behavior. We focus on a classical notion of stability, namely, Lyapunov stability. We will fix origin $\bar{0}$ to be the equilibrium point in this paper.

Definition 5. *A switched system* $\mathcal{S}_\alpha$ *is* Lyapunov stable *with respect to the origin* $\bar{0}$, *if for every* $\varepsilon > 0$ *there exists a* $\delta > 0$ *such that every execution* $x \in Exec(\mathcal{S}_\alpha)$ *with* $||x(0)|| < \delta$ *satisfies* $||x(t)|| < \varepsilon$ *for all* $t > 0$.

Note that in the sequel every time we refer to stability it is Lyapunov stability with respect to the origin. Given a family of dynamical systems, our goal is to construct a stable switched system. The switching strategy is determined by considering a set of switching facets and assigning a dynamical system to each of them. The dynamical system associated to a facet describes the evolution of the switched system after reaching the facet.

Problem 1 (Stabilization problem). *Given a system* $\mathcal{S} = (\mathcal{P}, \{g_p\}_{p \in \mathcal{P}})$ *and a set of valid facets* $\mathcal{F}$, *find a switching strategy* $\alpha : \mathcal{F}^+ \to \mathcal{P}$ *such that the switched system* $\mathcal{S}_\alpha$ *is stable.*

Note that we restrict ourselves to certain switching sets. Nevertheless, we can choose any polyhedral partition in order to determine the facets for switching.

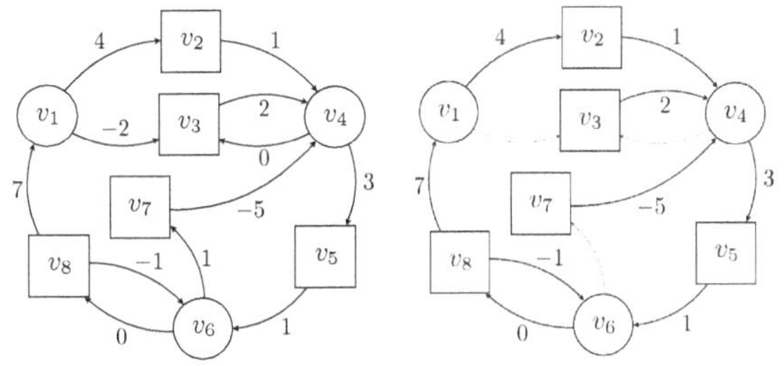

(a) Game graph G (b) Strategy over G

Figure 1: Game graph and strategy

4. GAMES

The synthesis problem is going to be solved by reducing to certain problems on games. More precisely, we transform the stabilization problem into finding a strategy in a finite weighted game graph. Here we present the concept of game and associated notions.

A game is played between a player and an adversary, where the goal of the player is to achieve a certain objective, whereas, that of the adversary is to thwart the efforts of the player. We want to find a strategy for the player which will allow her to achieve the objective for any strategy of the environment. The game is specified using a game graph that consists of a set of nodes partitioned between the player and the adversary. At each point, depending on the node, the player or the adversary get to choose an edge and make a transition to a node, and then the game continues from the new node. The objective corresponds to ensuring that the sequence of nodes in a play satisfy certain conditions. A winning strategy corresponds to a strategy of the player which ensures that the condition holds for every play resulting from the strategy.

Definition 6. *A* game graph *is a weighted graph* $G = (V, E, W)$ *where* $V = V_0 \cup V_1$, $V_0 \cap V_1 = \emptyset$, E *is a subset of* $V_0 \times V_1 \cup V_1 \times V_0$ *and* W *is a weight function mapping edges to rational numbers,* $W : E \to \mathbb{Q}$.

The partition of the nodes indicates that the nodes in V_0 are those where the player makes a choice, while nodes in V_1 are those where the adversary makes a choice.

Figure 1(a) shows a game graph. The nodes represented by circles are those where the player makes a decision and the nodes represented by squares are those where the adversary makes a decision.

Definition 7. *A* play *in* G *is an infinite sequence of nodes* $\tau = v_1 v_2 \ldots v_k \ldots$ *such that* $(v_i, v_{i+1}) \in E$ *for every* $i \geqslant 1$. *The set of all plays in* G *is denoted as* $Plays(G)$. *The set of edges in a play* τ *is denoted as* $E(\tau)$.

We say that the weight of a play $\tau = v_1 v_2 \ldots$ is bounded by b, denoted $W(\tau) \leqslant b$, if $\sum_{i=1}^{j} W(v_i, v_{i+1}) \leqslant b$ for every j.

Definition 8. *A* strategy *in* G *is a function* $\sigma : V^* V_0 \to V_1$ *such that for every* $\tau \in V^* V_0$, $(last(\tau), \sigma(\tau)) \in E$. *A strategy* σ *is said to be* memoryless *if for every* $\tau_1, \tau_2 \in V^* V_0$ *with* $last(\tau_1) = last(\tau_2)$, $\sigma(\tau_1) = \sigma(\tau_2)$.

Algorithm 1 Stabilizing switching strategy synthesis

Require: $\mathcal{S}, \mathcal{F}$
Ensure: α
1: $G := \textit{Game-graph}(\mathcal{S}, \mathcal{F})$
2: $\sigma := \textit{Winning-bounded-strategy}(G)$
3: $\alpha := \textit{Extract}(\sigma)$
4: **return** α

Notation.- For simplicity, we denote a memoryless strategy as a function $\sigma : V_0 \to V_1$.

Definition 9. *A finite or infinite sequence of nodes* $\tau = v_0v_1\ldots$ *is* consistent with a strategy σ *if for all* $\tau' = v_0v_1\ldots v_k$ *subsequence of* τ *with* $\tau' \in V^*V_0$, $\sigma(\tau') = v_{k+1}$.

In Figure 1(b), the solid outgoing arrows from the circles show a memoryless strategy for the player in the game graph, which specifies the choices of the player when in those nodes. The strategy induces a subgraph, defined by all the solid arrows.

We consider two types of objectives for the game; one requires to ensure that the weight of the plays remains bounded, and the other requires that the energy associated with the prefixes of the play remains positive when started with some given positive energy. Next, we define the winning strategies with respect to these objectives. A winning bounded strategy states that the weight of the plays consistent with the strategy is bounded from above.

Definition 10. *A strategy* σ *is a* winning bounded strategy *for a game graph G if there exists a value* $M \in \mathbb{Z}$ *such that for every* $\tau \in \textit{Plays}(G)$ *consistent with* σ, $W(\tau) \leqslant M$.

A winning energy strategy states that the player sustains a positive energy value whatever the choices of the adversary are.

Definition 11. *A strategy* σ *is a* winning energy strategy *for a game graph G if there exists a value* $w_0 \in \mathbb{N}$ *such that for every play in G consistent with* σ *of the form* $\tau = v_1v_2\ldots$, $w_0 + \sum_{i=1}^{j} W(v_i, v_{i+1}) \geqslant 0$ *for all* $j > 0$.

5. SWITCHING STRATEGY SYNTHESIS FOR STABILIZATION

In this section, we present a comprehensive abstraction-based approach for synthesizing a switching strategy that stabilizes the system. We will address some of the computational issues in the next section.

Let us fix a system $\mathcal{S} = (\mathcal{P}, \{g_p\}_{p\in\mathcal{P}})$ and a valid set of switching facets $\mathcal{F}$. The synthesis algorithm is shown in Algorithm 1. It proceeds in three steps:

Step 1 It constructs a game graph, $G(\mathcal{S}, \mathcal{F})$ which *abstracts* the system $\mathcal{S}$ by using the facets $\mathcal{F}$.

Step 2 It searches for a *winning bounded strategy* σ for the game graph $G(\mathcal{S}, \mathcal{F})$.

Step 3 A *stabilizing switching strategy* α for $\mathcal{S}$ and $\mathcal{F}$ is extracted from the winning bounded strategy σ.

Consider, for instance, the linear dynamical systems shown in Figure 2. They are specified by $\dot{x} = A_1x$ and $\dot{x} = A_2x$ and the family of dynamical systems is denoted as $\mathcal{S}_1 = (\{1,2\}, \{A_1, A_2\})$, where

Algorithm 2 Winning bounded strategy

Require: G
Ensure: σ
1: $G^e := \textit{Energy-game-graph}(G)$
2: $\sigma := \textit{Winning-energy-strategy}(G^e)$
3: **return** σ

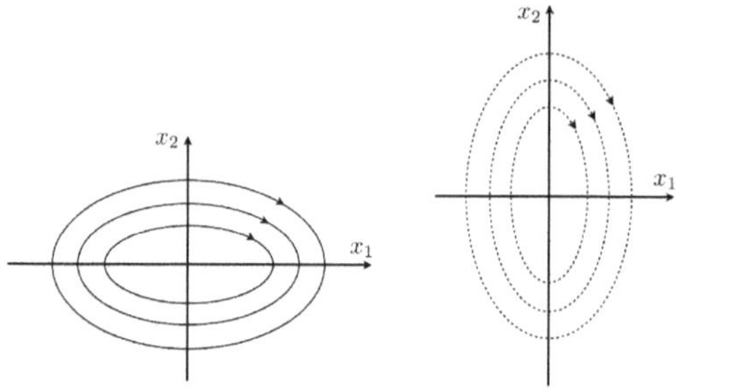

(a) $\dot{x} = A_1x$ (b) $\dot{x} = A_2x$

Figure 2: Sample trajectories

$$A_1 = \begin{pmatrix} 0 & 1 \\ -0.1 & 0 \end{pmatrix} \quad \text{and} \quad A_2 = \begin{pmatrix} 0 & 1 \\ -4 & 0 \end{pmatrix}$$

We consider the state space $\mathbb{R}^2$ partitioned into four operating regions, $\{\Omega_1, \Omega_2, \Omega_3, \Omega_4\}$, which correspond to the four quadrants and are separated by the following facets, $\mathcal{F} = \{f_1, f_2, f_3, f_4\}$, where $f_1 = \{(x_1, x_2) \in \mathbb{R}^2 : x_1 = 0, x_2 \geqslant 0\}$, $f_2 = \{(x_1, x_2) \in \mathbb{R}^2 : x_1 \geqslant 0, x_2 = 0\}$, $f_3 = \{(x_1, x_2) \in \mathbb{R}^2 : x_1 = 0, x_2 \leqslant 0\}$ and $f_4 = \{(x_1, x_2) \in \mathbb{R}^2 : x_1 \leqslant 0, x_2 = 0\}$. We want to find a switching strategy $\alpha : \mathcal{F}^+ \to \mathcal{P}$ which stabilizes the system $\mathcal{S}_1$. The switching strategy will associate with each sequence of facets a dynamical system in the family, which describes the evolution of the system when starting from the last facet. Next, we explain in detail, the enumerated steps for this switching strategy construction.

5.1 Game graph construction

First, we explain the construction of the game graph which abstracts the system $\mathcal{S}$. This extends the quantitative predicate abstraction method in [24] developed for stability verification. Predicate abstraction [12] is an abstraction technique that constructs a finite graph which over approximates the behaviors of a given system by using a finite set of predicates that partition the state space. Hence, properties such as safety can be inferred by analysing the finite abstract system. Predicate abstraction of discrete and hybrid systems has been applied for safety verification [1, 2, 30]. However, qualitative abstract graphs do not suffice for stability analysis, and hence, a quantitative predicate abstraction was proposed in [24]. Here we borrow the ideas to construct a game graph for solving the stabilization problem.

Let us consider the system $\mathcal{S} = (\mathcal{P}, \{g_p\}_{p\in\mathcal{P}})$ and a valid set of facets $\mathcal{F}$ along with the polyhedral partition R that defines the facets. The player nodes of the game graph correspond to the facets, and the adversary nodes correspond to the pairs of modes and facets, $(p, f) \in \mathcal{P} \times \mathcal{F}$. From every node f, there are edges to the nodes (p, f) for every $p \in \mathcal{P}$. The edge corresponds to the fact that in the facet f, the system chooses to execute the dynamics p. From a node (p, f), there is an edge to every node f' such that the facet

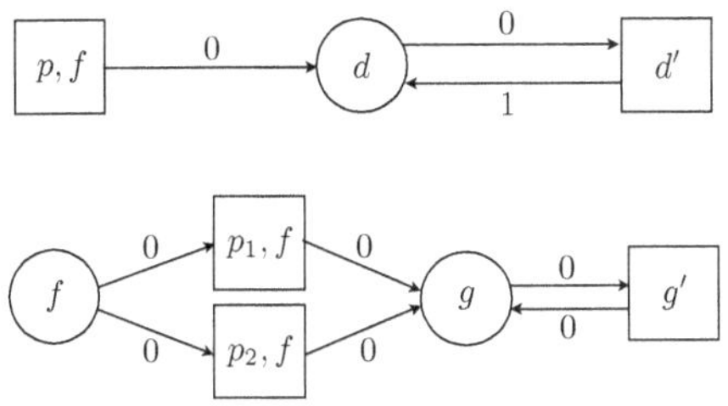

Figure 3: (a) Unbounded executions (b) Non-existence of p-partial executions which reach another facet

f' can be reached by executing the dynamics p from f (without touching any other facets). More precisely, the edge is added if some point in f can reach some point in f' by a p-partial execution. Further, the weight on an edge $((p, f), f')$ will provide an upper bound on the logarithm of the scalings associated with p-executions from f to f'; scaling of an execution captures the ratio of the distance of the execution from the origin when in f' as compared to its distance when it starts at f. It captures the factor by which the state is farther from the origin at the end as compared to where it started. A winning bounded strategy for this game graph indicates a strategy for the system $\mathcal{S}$ for which the scalings associated with the resulting executions are bounded, which in turn implies Lyapunov stability. Next, we present the concepts required to formalize the game graph construction.

Definition 12. *Given a region $\Omega \in R$, states x_1, x_2 and $p \in \mathcal{P}$, we denote by $x_1 \xrightarrow{p,\Omega} x_2$ the fact that there exists a p-partial solution $x : [T_1, T_2) \to \mathbb{R}^n$ such that $x(T_1) = x_1$, $x(t) \in \Omega$ for all $T_1 < t < T_2$, and $\lim_{t \to T_2} x(t) = x_2$.*

$x_1 \xrightarrow{p,\Omega} x_2$ denotes the fact that there exists a p-partial execution x starting at x_1 which converges to x_2 and remains within the region Ω at the intermediate times. We use converges instead of reaches only because the domain of our partial executions is right open.

Definition 13. *Given $f \in \mathcal{F}$, a region $\Omega \in R$, a set $P \subseteq \mathbb{R}^n$ and $p \in \mathcal{P}$, the scaling is given by*

$$SC(\Omega, (p, f), P) = \sup\{\frac{||x_2||}{||x_1||} \,|\, x_1 \in f, x_2 \in P, x_1 \xrightarrow{p,\Omega} x_2\}.$$

Our objective is to capture executions of the switched system by paths in the game graph such that its p-partial sub-executions correspond to the edges in the game graph. The game graph construction, informally described earlier, captures all p-partial executions that traverse between two facets. However, it does not account for those which start at a facet and remain within an adjacent region, never reaching another facet. Hence, we add additional elements to the game graph to capture these executions. We check if the scaling of the executions in the region are unbounded, by checking if $SC(\Omega, (p, f), \Omega) = \infty$, that is, the scaling associated with the executions starting from p while in a region Ω do not have a bound. If the scalings evaluate to infinity for some Ω, then we add the substructure shown in Figure 3. This is also illustrated in the experiments in Section 7.1 (see Figure 9 and Figure 6). We add two nodes, d and d', and three edges, $((p, f), d)$, (d, d') and (d', d), with weights 0, 0 and 1 respectively. If the scalings of the executions associated with a region are bounded, then they do not have any effect on the stability (they are trivially stable) and hence, we can ignore these executions. However, in some cases, all the executions out of (p, f) may not reach any other facets; hence, to ensure that all plays of the game graph are infinite we add some dummy nodes and edges as shown in Figure 3. It consists of a cycle with two new nodes, g and g' and edges (g, g') and (g', g). The node (p, f) has an edge $((p, f), g)$. All these new edges are annotated with weight equal to 0.

Remark. Note that the weights on the edges only capture the scalings when the executions touch the facets. It may appear that we ignore the scalings of the executions between the facets, however, the check $SC(\Omega, (p, f), \Omega) \neq \infty$, also ensure that there is a bound on the scaling of the executions between facets. However, the exact values of these bounds are not necessary for stability analysis as will be obvious from the proof.

Next, we introduce the formal definition for the abstract game graph.

Definition 14. *A game graph induced by a system $\mathcal{S}$ and a set of facets $\mathcal{F}$, denoted $G(\mathcal{S}, \mathcal{F}) = (V, E, W)$, satisfies:*

- $V = V_0 \cup V_1$ *where*
  - $V_0 = \mathcal{F} \cup \{d, g\}$,
  - $V_1 = (\mathcal{P} \times \mathcal{F}) \cup \{d', g'\}$;
- $E = E_0 \cup E_1 \cup E_1^d \cup E_1^g \cup E_0^* \cup E_1^*$ *where*
  - $E_0 = \{(f, (p, f)) \,|\, f \in \mathcal{F}, p \in \mathcal{P}\}$,
  - $E_1 \supseteq \{((p, f_1), f_2) \,|\, \exists \Omega \in R, x_1 \in f_1$ *and* $x_2 \in f_2$ *such that* $x_1 \xrightarrow{p,\Omega} x_2\} = E_1^{exact}$,
  - $E_1^d = \{((p, f), d) \,|\, \exists \Omega \in R : SC(\Omega, (p, f), \Omega) = \infty\}$,
  - $E_1^g = \{((p, f), g) \,|\, \nexists f' : ((p, f), f') \in E_1 \cup E_1^d\}$,
  - $E_0^* = \{(d, d'), (g, g')\}$,
  - $E_1^* = \{(d', d), (g', g)\}$;
- $W(e) : E \to \mathbb{Q}$ *where*
  - $W(e) = 0$ *if* $e \in E \setminus (E_1 \cup \{(d', d)\})$,
  - $W(((p, f_1), f_2)) \geqslant ln(SC(\Omega, (p, f_1), f_2))$ *for all* $\Omega \in R$,
  - $W((d', d)) = 1$.

Here ln denotes the natural logarithm.

Remark. The game graph is an over approximation of the executions of the system $\mathcal{S}$. Firstly, the edges are added if there is at least one execution between two facets. Note that if there is an execution from facet f_1 to f_2 and one from f_2 to f_3, it does not necessarily imply that there is an execution from f_1 to f_3 which goes through f_2. Hence, the game graph may have a path which does not correspond to any executions. However, every execution is captured by a path in the graph.

Secondly, we require E_1 to contain E_1^{exact} and not be equal to it. This is because in general we will not be able to

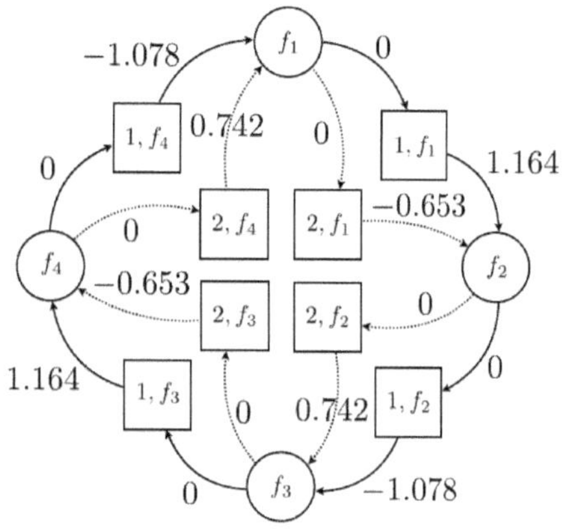

Figure 4: Game graph

compute E_1^{exact}. More discussion on computation of the graph will appear in Section 6. However, our results hold even for this relaxed set, that is, if we find a strategy for the game graph, we can extract one for the original system. This is because a relaxed E_1 just implies that we are considering a more general adversary than what is required. However, from the point of view of succeeding in finding a strategy for the game graph, it is desirable to have E_1 to be close to E_1^{exact}.

The game graph induced by the system $\mathcal{S}_1 = (\{1,2\}, \{A_1, A_2\})$ described in the previous section and depicted in Figure 2, is shown in Figure 4. The circles correspond to the facets f_1, f_2, f_3 and f_4 corresponding to the four axes as explained in Section 5. In this state, the player makes the choice regarding the dynamics (potentially depending on her previous choices). From each of the nodes f_i, there is an edge to (p, f_i) with weight 0 to capture the possible choices. The nodes (p, f_i) correspond to the adversary and has an edge to facets f_j to which the system can evolve from f_i using the dynamics p. Here, the strategy (choices of the player) need to be such that the resulting play is winning for any of the edges taken from (p, f_i). These facets have a weight that is an upper bound on the logarithm of the scaling of the executions between the facets. For instance, the edge $((2, f_1), f_2)$ states that there is potentially a 2-partial execution starting from f_1 that will evolve through some quadrant (the first) following the linear dynamics related to A_2 and reach f_2. Its weight 0.742 signifies that any 2-execution starting from f_1 and reaching f_2 will be at most $e^{0.742}$ times the distance to the origin as compared to the distance when it started. A positive value indicates that the execution is moving farther, and a negative value indicates the execution is getting closer to the origin. Note that the scaling of an execution consisting of a p_1-execution x_1 followed by a p_2-execution x_2 is the product of the two scalings. The logarithm of the scaling would be the sum of the logarithms of the scaling.

Our next objective is to establish the main result of the paper. We will show that a strategy for the game graph will yield a stabilizing switching strategy for the system. First, we need the definition of a strategy for the system that can be extracted from a strategy for the game graph.

Definition 15. *Given a system $\mathcal{S}$, a valid set of facets $\mathcal{F}$, the induced game graph $G(\mathcal{S}, \mathcal{F})$ and a strategy $\sigma : V^* V_0 \rightarrow V_1$ for $G(\mathcal{S}, \mathcal{F})$, we say that $\alpha_\sigma : \mathcal{F}^+ \rightarrow \mathcal{P}$ is a* switching strategy *induced by σ if for a sequence $\tau = f_1, (p_1, f_1), f_2, (p_2, f_2), \dots, f_k$ consistent with σ, $\alpha_\sigma(f_1, f_2, \dots, f_k) = \sigma(\tau)_\mathcal{P}$.*

Theorem 1. *Given a system $\mathcal{S}$ and a valid set of facets $\mathcal{F}$, if there exists a winning bounded strategy σ for the induced game graph $G(\mathcal{S}, \mathcal{F})$, then any induced strategy α_σ solves the stabilization problem for $\mathcal{S}$ and $\mathcal{F}$.*

PROOF. We need to show that the switched system $(\mathcal{P}, \{g_p\}_{p \in \mathcal{P}}, \alpha_\sigma)$ is stable. Let M be the bound on the weight of all consistent plays of σ. Consider an execution $x : [0, T) \rightarrow \mathbb{R}^n$ of the system $(\mathcal{P}, \{g_p\}_{p \in \mathcal{P}}, \alpha_\sigma)$, that is represented as a sequence of partial executions, $x = x_1 x_2 \dots$, as in Definition 3, that is, each x_i is a p_i-partial execution and $x_i(T_{i-1}) \in f_i \in \mathcal{F}$. Since, $\alpha_\sigma(f_1, \dots, f_k) = p_k$, the play $\tau = f_1(p_1, f_1) f_2(p_2, f_2) f_3 \dots$ in $G(\mathcal{S}, \mathcal{F})$ is consistent with σ. The weight of the path $f_i(p_i, f_i) f_{i+1}$ is a bound on the logarithm of the scaling $||x_{i+1}(T_i)|| / ||x_i(T_{i-1})||$, which is given by $W((f_i, (p_i, f_i))) + W(((p_i, f_i), f_{i+1}))$. Hence, the logarithm of any scaling associated with any prefix of the execution x of the form $x_1 \dots x_k$ is bounded by the value $\sum_{i=1}^{k-1} [W((f_i, (p_i, f_i))) + W(((p_i, f_i), f_{i+1}))]$, which in turn is bounded by M. We know that the scaling of $x_1 \dots x_k$ is bounded for every k. We want to show that the scaling $||x(t)|| / ||x(0)||$ is bounded for times t which correspond to interior of the domain of some x_i. More precisely, we want to show that the scalings associated with $x_i : [T_i, T_{i+1}) \rightarrow \mathbb{R}^n$ is bounded at time $t \in [T_i, T_{i+1})$. Note that since σ is a bounded winning strategy, we know that any finite sequence $\tau' = f_1'(p_1', f_1) f_2' \dots f_n'$ consistent with it will not choose a p such that (p, f_n') has an edge to d, otherwise, this play can be extended to a play with unbounded weight that is consistent with σ (since from d, σ is forced to choose d' and d' has an edge back to d). Therefore, we can conclude that every mode p that is chosen from a node f in a consistent play is such that p-executions from f are bounded. For every facet f and mode p that appears in any consistent play of the game graph, let N_p be a bound on the logarithms of the scalings associated with p executions from f. Let N be the maximum of all the N_ps. Now, we can conclude that the logarithm of the scaling associated with any x is bounded from above by $M + N$. Given any $\epsilon > 0$, we choose $\delta < \epsilon / (e^{M+N})$. We know that any execution of the switched system starting within the δ ball will not leave the δe^{M+N} ball, that is, the ϵ ball. Hence, the system is Lyapunov stable. □

5.2 Winning bounded strategy computation

Next we solve the problem of synthesizing a winning bounded strategy for a game graph G. Our broad approach is to reduce the problem of winning bounded strategy synthesis to that of winning energy strategy synthesis. The latter can be solved using the algorithm in [5] which outputs a memoryless winning energy strategy. First, we state the results that have been established in [5] on winning energy strategies.

Theorem 2. *[5] Given a game graph (V, E, W) where $W : E \rightarrow \mathbb{Z}$, if there exists a winning energy strategy, then there exists a memoryless winning energy strategy. Further, there is an algorithm which returns a memoryless winning energy strategy if it exists.*

We reduce the problem of finding a winning bounded strategy for the game graph G to finding a winning energy strategy for a game graph G^e. The transformation from G to G^e is achieved in two steps. Note that in Theorem 2 the weights are required to be integers. To ensure this, we multiply all the weights in G by a value which is the least common multiple of all the denominators of the rational weights. More precisely, let the weight of an edge e in E be the rational expressed as $\frac{a_e}{b_e}$. We denote by $\text{LCM}_G \in \mathbb{Z}$ the least common multiple of $\{b_e : e \in E\}$. It is clear that by multiplying each of the weights by LCM_G, we obtain integer values. Next, note that the condition for a winning energy strategy requires that the weights along a play are lower bounded by a value, whereas that for bounded strategy requires that the weights are upper bounded by a value. To accommodate this, we negate the values of the weights.

The formal definition of the energy game is given below, followed by the theorem which states that the transformation preserves existence of corresponding kind of strategies.

Definition 16. *Let $G = (V, E, W)$ be a game graph. The* induced energy game graph *is $G^e = (V, E, W^e)$ where $W^e \equiv -\text{LCM}_G \cdot W$.*

Theorem 3. *Let G be a game graph and G^e the induced energy game graph. Then, there exists a winning bounded strategy for G if and only if there exists a winning energy strategy for G^e. Moreover, σ is a winning bounded strategy for G if and only if σ is a winning energy strategy for G^e.*

PROOF. Note that if σ is a winning bounded strategy for G, then for every play $\tau = v_1, v_2, \ldots$ consistent with σ satisfies $W(\tau) \leqslant M$, that is, $\sum_{i=1}^{j} W(v_i, v_{i+1}) \leqslant M$. Then

$$\text{LCM}_G \cdot M + \sum_{i=1}^{j}(-\text{LCM}_G \cdot W(v_i, v_{i+1})) \geqslant 0,$$

that is, $\max(0, \text{LCM}_G \cdot M) + \sum_{i=1}^{j} W^e(v_i, v_{i+1}) \geqslant 0$. Hence, σ is a winning energy strategy for G^e with the initial energy $\max(0, \text{LCM}_G \cdot M) \in \mathbb{N}$. The argument in the other direction is similar. □

We solve the problem of finding winning bounded strategy for G by finding the winning energy strategy for G^e and solving the latter. Since memoryless winning energy strategies are sufficient for G^e, from Theorem 3, memoryless winning bounded strategies suffice for G. We find memoryless winning energy strategy for G^e using the algorithm in [5]. The algorithm computes a "small energy progress measure" that provides an initial energy on each of the nodes such that on every edge the weight on the target is a lower bound on the sum of the weight of the source together with the weight of the edge. This condition holds for some edge from a player node and every edge from an adversary node. A memoryless strategy can then be extracted from it by choosing the edge from the player node that satisfies this property. The initial energy progress measure for every node is set to zero. After i iterations, the progress measure ensures that the condition on winning energy strategy is satisfied by all plays up to length i. The iteration is similar to a standard value iteration, and converges in a finite number of steps. A winning strategy can be constructed either during the computation of the small energy measure or can be extracted from the small energy measure.

For the game graph shown in Figure 4, after multiplying their weights by the corresponding $-\text{LCM}_G$, a memoryless winning bounded strategy σ is obtained. It is defined as $\sigma(f_1) = 1$, $\sigma(f_2) = 2$, $\sigma(f_3) = 1$ and $\sigma(f_4) = 2$. From this strategy, the stabilizing switching strategy for the system $\mathcal{S} = (\{1,2\}, \{A_1, A_2\})$ is as follows:

$$\alpha_\sigma(\tau) = \begin{cases} 1 & \text{if } \mathit{last}(\tau) \in \{f_1, f_3\} \\ 2 & \text{if } \mathit{last}(\tau) \in \{f_2, f_4\} \end{cases}$$

6. GAME GRAPH COMPUTATION

In this section, we discuss the computational issues related to the game graph construction. The crux of the edge and the weight computation lie in computing a reachability relation $R(P_1, P_2, P_3, dyn)$, namely, given three polyhedral sets $P_1, P_2, P_3 \subseteq \mathbb{R}^n$ and a dynamical system dyn, it consists of all the pair of points (x_1, x_2) such that from the point $x_1 \in P_1$, by following the dynamics dyn, $x_2 \in P_2$ is reached, while always remaining within P_3 at the interior points. Then the weight correspond to

$$w = \sup\{\frac{||x_2||}{||x_1||} \mid (x_1, x_2) \in R(P_1, P_2, P_3, dyn)\} \qquad (2)$$

Our objective is to compute the set $R(P_1, P_2, P_3, dyn)$ and the weight given in Equation 2. In this section, we discuss the computation of these entities when dyn is a polyhedral inclusion dynamics or a linear dynamics. First, it was observed in [23, 25] that Lyapunov stability is a local property whose satisfaction depends only on a small neighborhood of the origin, and hence, the only switching surface that play a role in determining stability are those that contain the origin. Further, both polyhedral inclusion dynamics $\dot{x} \in P$, where P is a polyhedron, and linear dynamics $\dot{x} = Ax$, where A is a matrix, are scaling closed, namely, if there is an execution from x to y, then there is an execution from αx to αy. This is evident from the solutions of these systems, namely, $x(t) = x(0) + ct$ for some $c \in P$, and $x(t) = e^{At}x(0)$, respectively. Hence, as argued in [23, 25], it suffices to restrict our attention to facets that are upward scaling closed, that is, facets f such that if $x \in f$, then $\beta x \in f$ for all $\beta > 0$.

First let us consider the polyhedral inclusion dynamics $\dot{x} \in P$. Note that $R(P_1, P_2, P_3, dyn)$ is the pairs (x_1, x_2) which satisfy $x_1 \in P_1$, $x_2 \in P_2$, $x_2 = x_1 + ct$, $c \in P$, $x_1 + ct' \in P_3$ for all $0 < t' < t$. These constraints can be transformed into a set of linear constraints. For instance, checking $x_1 + ct' \in P_3$ for all $0 < t' < t$ is equivalent to just checking that $x_1 \in P_3$ and $x_1 + ct \in P_3$. The non-linear term ct can be eliminated as well, see [24] for details. Hence, the edge computation is reduced to a feasibility checking of linear constraints. To compute the scaling, we need to optimize the value of $||x_2||/||x_1||$. It was shown in [24] that we can restrict the optimization to x_1 such that $||x_1||$ is 1 and the optimization can be reduced to polynomially many linear programming problems in the dimension of the system. We use these ideas for scaling computation in our tool and experiments.

The reachability relation $R(P_1, P_2, P_3, dyn)$ cannot be computed exactly when dyn is a linear dynamical system $\dot{x} = Ax$, since the solutions for these systems involve an exponential function, and hence, needs to be approximated. There are several techniques for over approximating the reachability relation that use sample values to construct over approximations represented by polyhedra (zonotopes, boxes) or polynomials (ellipsoids) [7, 14, 10]. However, these approximations can be computed only for a bounded time, and

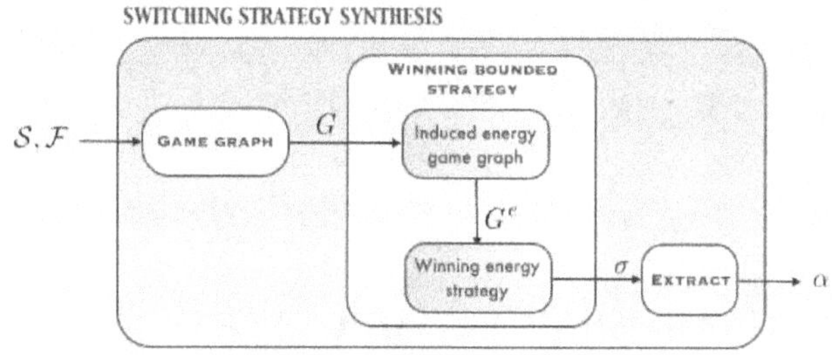

Figure 5: Tool Architecture

hence work well if an upper bound on the time to reach the target polyhedron P_2 from the polyhedron P_1 is known a priori. To overcome the drawback of the time bound computation, we use an alternate technique to compute the over approximations, namely, hybridization [8, 25]. Here, we divide the state space (here P_3) into a finite number of regions and approximate the linear dynamics in each of the regions by a polyhedral dynamics (see [25] for more details). We then compute the reachable set of these polyhedral dynamics (a switched system) which provides an upper bound on the reachable set $R(P_1, P_2, P_3, dyn)$. Further the computed set is a finite set of polyhedra, hence, the weight can be computed again by solving some linear programming problems.

Synthesis Algorithm Summary.

Here we recap the steps for synthesizing a switching strategy that stabilizes a given system $\mathcal{S} = (\mathcal{P}, \{g_p\}_{p\in\mathcal{P}})$ by considering a valid set of switching facets $\mathcal{F}$. They are summarized at the beginning of Section 5. The construction of the game graph $G(\mathcal{S}, \mathcal{F})$, which corresponds to Step 1, is explained in Definition 14; and details on its construction are discussed at Section 6. The search for a winning bounded strategy σ for the constructed game graph $G(\mathcal{S}, \mathcal{F})$, corresponds to Algorithm 1 in [5], which is justified at the beginning of Subsection 5.2. Finally, Step 3, which corresponds to the extraction of a stabilizing switching strategy α from σ, is explained at the end of Subsection 5.2.

7. IMPLEMENTATION

In this section, we explain some details of the implementation of the algorithm for solving the stabilization problem. We have implemented the full procedure for a family of systems with polyhedral inclusion dynamics and linear dynamics. A general flowchart of the prototype tool is shown in Figure 5. The input to the procedure is a family of polyhedral or linear systems $\mathcal{S}$ and a set of valid facets $\mathcal{F}$ that are obtained from some polyhedral partition of the state space; and the output is a stabilizing switching strategy. The first module "game graph" constructs the abstract game graph $G(\mathcal{S}, \mathcal{F})$ as defined in Definition 14. This game graph is the input to the "winning bounded strategy" module, that transforms the game graph and reduces the winning bounded strategy synthesis to winning energy strategy synthesis as in Definition 16 by modifying the weights. The winning energy strategy synthesized is also a winning bounded strategy, and it is output by the module. The module "Extract" outputs a switching strategy corresponding to a winning bounded strategy as described in Definition 15. If a strategy does not exist at any stage of the procedure, an empty strategy is returned.

The prototype has been implemented in Python. The edge and weight computation involve the computation of a reachability relation and optimization. We use the Parma Polyhedra Library (PPL) to perform all the polyhedral operations involved in the reachability relation computation and the optimizations required during scaling computation are performed using the GLPK package for solving linear programming problems. Our procedure requires several preprocessing steps on the game graph as well as the implementation of the strategy synthesis algorithm for which we use the NetworkX package. The graph construction algorithm takes time polynomial in the number of facets, the dynamics and the dimension; and the size of the graph is also polynomial in these parameters. The synthesis algorithm on the abstract game graph is polynomial in the size of the graph and the maximum constant appearing on the edges.

This implementation allows us to synthesize automatically a stabilizing switching strategy for a family of polyhedral inclusion dynamics or linear dynamics. Next, we illustrate the process for each of these cases.

7.1 Experiments

Here, we enumerate the computational details for two different experiments. One considers a family of polyhedral dynamical systems and the other considers a family of linear dynamical systems.

Polyhedral dynamics.

We consider a family of four polyhedral dynamical systems in $\mathbb{R}^2$. They are specified by $\dot{x} \in P_i$, where P_i corresponds to a single vector for each system: $P_1 = (1, 1)$, $P_2 = (-1, -1)$, $P_3 = (-1, 1)$ and $P_4 = (1, -1)$. The family of systems is denoted as $\mathcal{S} = (\{1, 2, 3, 4\}, \{P_1, P_2, P_3, P_4\})$. The set of valid facets are the semi axes of the plane, that is $\mathcal{F} = \{f_1, f_2, f_3, f_4\}$ where $f_1 = \{(x_1, x_2) \in \mathbb{R}^2 : x_1 = 0, x_2 \geqslant 0\}$, $f_2 = \{(x_1, x_2) \in \mathbb{R}^2 : x_1 \geqslant 0, x_2 = 0\}$, $f_3 = \{(x_1, x_2) \in \mathbb{R}^2 : x_1 = 0, x_2 \leqslant 0\}$ and $f_4 = \{(x_1, x_2) \in \mathbb{R}^2 : x_1 \leqslant 0, x_2 = 0\}$. These facets divide the state space into four operating regions, $\{\Omega_1, \Omega_2, \Omega_3, \Omega_4\}$, which correspond to the first, second, third and fourth planar quadrants, respectively. We illustrate partially the computation of the game graph $G(\mathcal{S}, \mathcal{F}) = (V_0 \cup V_1, E, W)$. We restrict this computation to the first quadrant, which contains the pair of facets f_1 and f_2, and their common region Ω_1. These two facets will be nodes in V_0. For V_1, we include the nodes $(1, f_1)$, $(2, f_1)$, $(3, f_1)$, $(4, f_1)$, $(1, f_2)$, $(2, f_2)$, $(3, f_2)$ and $(4, f_2)$. We construct edges in E_0 from f_1 to all the nodes of the form (p, f_1), and analogously, we construct edges from f_2 to (p, f_2), where $p \in \{1, 2, 3, 4\}$. The weight for all these edges is 0. In E_1, we obtain the edges $((4, f_1), f_2)$ and $((3, f_2), f_1)$, with $SC(\Omega_1, (4, f_1), f_2) = 1$ and $SC(\Omega_1, (3, f_2), f_1) = 1$. The set E_1^d contains $((1, f_1), d)$ and $((1, f_2), d)$. with weight value 0. The edges in E_1^g, are $((2, f_1), g)$, $((2, f_2), g)$, $((3, f_1), g)$ and $((4, f_2), g)$, all of them with weight equal to 0. The graph obtained for the first quadrant is shown in Figure 6. The computation for the rest of the quadrants is similar to that presented above.

The scalings associated with the edges E_1 of the game graph $G(\mathcal{S}, \mathcal{F})$ are 1s. Hence, in the induced energy game graph, all weights are equal to 0 except for the edge (d', d), which has weight equal to -1. (Recall that all the weights

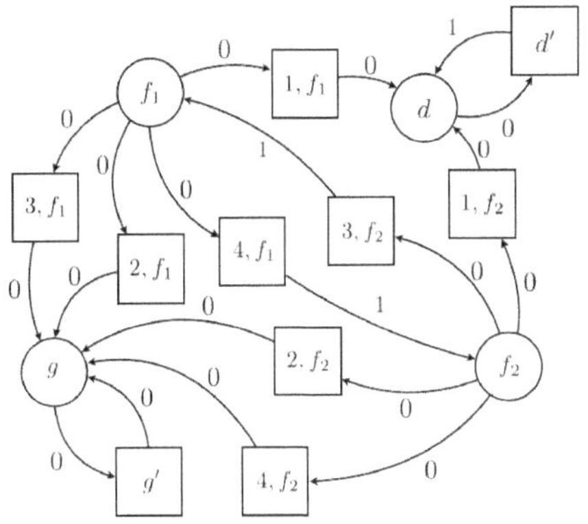

Figure 6: Partial game graph

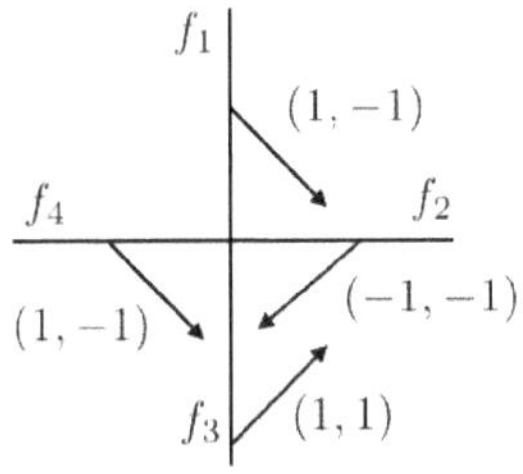

Figure 7: Stabilizing switching strategy

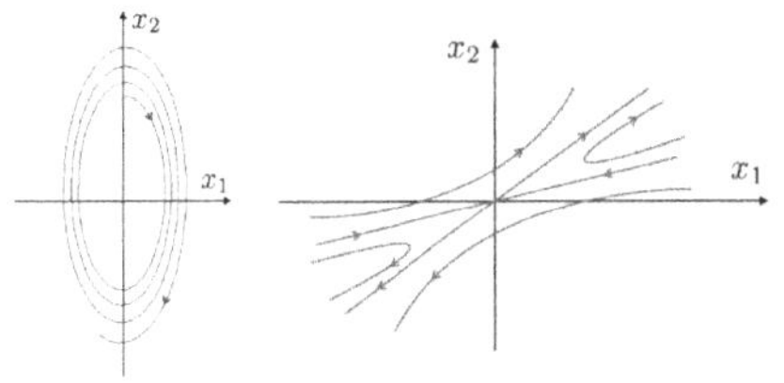

(a) $\dot{x} = A_1 x$ (b) $\dot{x} = A_2 x$

Figure 8: Phase portraits

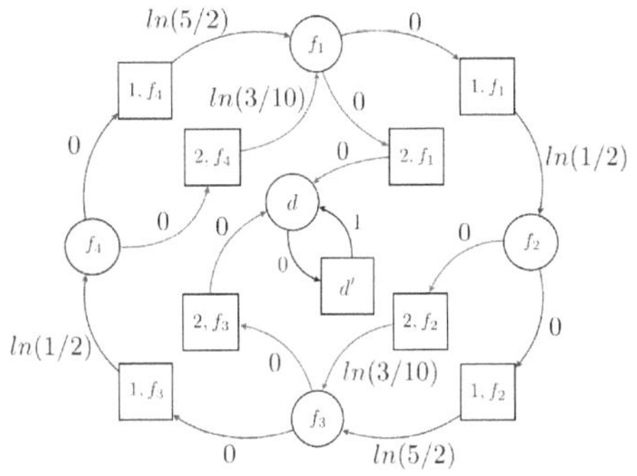

Figure 9: Game graph

in the induced graph are negated). The tool returns the following winning energy strategy; $\sigma : V_0 \to V_1$ where $\sigma(f_1) = (4, f_1)$, $\sigma(f_2) = (2, f_2)$, $\sigma(f_3) = (1, f_3)$ and $\sigma(f_4) = (4, f_4)$. From σ, the following switching strategy is computed; $\alpha_\sigma : \mathcal{F}^+ \to \mathcal{P}$ where

$$\alpha_\sigma(\tau) = \begin{cases} 4 & \text{if } last(\tau) \in \{f_1, f_4\} \\ 2 & \text{if } last(\tau) = f_2 \\ 1 & \text{if } last(\tau) = f_3 \end{cases}$$

This switching strategy is depicted in Figure 7, where the semi axes correspond to the facets. For every point in a facet, an execution of the synthesized switched system starting from it, evolves by following the vector outgoing from the facet.

Linear dynamics.

We consider a family of linear systems in the two dimensional real state space. denoted as $\mathcal{S} = (\{1, 2\}, \{A_1, A_2\})$, where $A_1 = \begin{pmatrix} 0 & 1 \\ -5 & 0.1 \end{pmatrix}$ and $A_2 = \begin{pmatrix} -1 & 4 \\ -0.2 & 1 \end{pmatrix}$.

Sample trajectories of these systems are shown in Figures 8(a) and 8(b). The polyhedral partition is obtained by dividing the state space, as in the previous experiment, with the two coordinate axes $\{x_1 = 0, x_2 = 0\}$. They partition the state space into four operating regions, $\{\Omega_1, \Omega_2, \Omega_3, \Omega_4\}$, which coincide with the four quadrants and are separated by the same facets as in the previous experiment, $\mathcal{F} = \{f_1, f_2, f_3, f_4\}$. Then, we compute the game graph $G(\mathcal{S}, \mathcal{F}) = (V, E, W)$, where $V_0 = \mathcal{F}$, $V_1 = \{(1, f_1), (2, f_1), (1, f_2), (2, f_2), (1, f_3), (2, f_3), (1, f_4), (2, f_4)\}$, $E_0 = \{(f_1, (1, f_1)), (f_1, (2, f_1)), (f_2, (1, f_2)), (f_2, (2, f_2)), (f_3, (1, f_3)), (f_3, (2, f_3)), (f_4, (1, f_4)), (f_4, (2, f_4))\}$, $E_1 = \{((1, f_1), f_2), ((1, f_2), f_3), ((2, f_2), f_3), ((1, f_3), f_4), ((1, f_4), f_1), ((2, f_4), f_1)\}$, $E_1^* = \{((2, f_1), d), ((2, f_3), d)\}$ and $E_0^* = \{(d', d)\}$. The weights for every $e \in E_0 \cup E_1^*$ are equal to 0, for (d', d) equal to 1 and for $e \in E_1$ we obtain the following scaling values: $SC(\Omega_1, ((1, f_1), f_2) = 1/2$, $SC(\Omega_2, ((1, f_2), f_3) = 5/2$, $SC(\Omega_2, ((2, f_2), f_3) = 3/10$, $SC(\Omega_3, ((1, f_3), f_4) = 1/2$, $SC(\Omega_4, ((1, f_4), f_1) = 5/2$ and $SC(\Omega_4, ((2, f_4), f_1) = 3/10$.

We compute the natural logarithm of the different scaling values: $ln(1/2) = -\frac{6243314768165359}{9007199254740992}$, $ln(5/2) = \frac{1031651649657871}{1125899906842624}$ and $ln(3/10) = -\frac{5422211472926497}{4503599627370496}$.

The game graph $G(\mathcal{S}, \mathcal{F})$ is shown in Figure 9. The winning energy strategy $\sigma : V_0 \to V_1$ computed is defined as follows: $\sigma(f_1) = (1, f_1)$, $\sigma(f_2) = (2, f_2)$, $\sigma(f_3) = (1, f_3)$ and $\sigma(f_4) = (2, f_4)$. From the winning energy strategy, we extract a stabilizing switching strategy $\alpha_\sigma : V \to \mathcal{P}$, that is

$$\alpha_\sigma(\tau) = \begin{cases} 1 & \text{if } last(\tau) \in \{f_1, f_3\} \\ 2 & \text{if } last(\tau) \in \{f_2, f_4\} \end{cases}$$

8. CONCLUSION

In this paper, we proposed an abstraction technique and a game based approach for synthesizing a switching logic for stabilization. While abstraction based approaches have been proposed for correct by construction of systems that satisfy certain temporal logic formulas, to the best of our knowledge, the same has not been explored for stabilization. Stability is a robustness property that is required of all control systems. Our approach can be combined with those for temporal logic properties to obtain stable controllers that satisfy temporal logic formulas. We intend to explore this in the future.

9. REFERENCES

[1] R. Alur, T. Dang, and F. Ivancic. Counter-Example Guided Predicate Abstraction of Hybrid Systems. In *TACAS*, pages 208–223, 2003.

[2] R. Alur, T. Dang, and F. Ivancic. Predicate abstraction for reachability analysis of hybrid systems. *ACM Transactions on Embedded Computing Systems*, 5(1):152–199, 2006.

[3] P. Bauer, K. Premaratne, and J. Duran. A necessary and sufficient condition for robust asymptotic stability of time-variant discrete systems. *Automatic Control, IEEE Transactions on*, 38(9):1427–1430, Sep 1993.

[4] M. Branicky. Stability of hybrid systems. In H. Unbehauen, editor, *Encylopedia of Life Support Systems*, volume Theme 6.43:Control Sytems, Robotics and Automation, chapter Article 6.43.28.3. UNESCO Publishing, 2004.

[5] L. Brim, J. Chaloupka, L. Doyen, R. Gentilini, and J. Raskin. Faster algorithms for mean-payoff games. *Formal Methods in System Design*, 38(2):97–118, 2011.

[6] E. Clarke, A. Fehnker, Z. Han, B. Krogh, J. Ouaknine, O. Stursberg, and M. Theobald. Abstraction and Counterexample-Guided Refinement in Model Checking of Hybrid Systems. *International Journal on Foundations of Computer Science*, 14(4):583–604, 2003.

[7] T. Dang and O. Maler. Reachability analysis via face lifting. In *HSCC*, pages 96–109, 1998.

[8] T. Dang, O. Maler, and R. Testylier. Accurate hybridization of nonlinear systems. In *Proceedings of the International Conference on Hybrid Systems: Computation and Control*, pages 11–20, 2010.

[9] R. DeCarlo, M. Branicky, S. Pettersson, and B. Lennartson. Perspectives and results on the stability and stabilizability of hybrid systems. *Proceedings of the IEEE*, 88(7):1069–1082, July 2000.

[10] G. Frehse, C. Le Guernic, A. Donzé, S. Cotton, R. Ray, O. Lebeltel, R. Ripado, A. Girard, T. Dang, and O. Maler. Spaceex: Scalable verification of hybrid systems. In *CAV*, pages 379–395, 2011.

[11] A. Girard. Controller synthesis for safety and reachability via approximate bisimulation. *Automatica*, 48(5):947–953, 2012.

[12] S. Graf and H. Saidi. Construction of abstact state graphs with PVS. In *CAV*, pages 72–83, 1997.

[13] M. Johansson. *Piecewise Linear Control Systems.* Springer, 2003.

[14] A. Kurzhanski and P. Varaiya. Ellipsoidal techniques for reachability analysis. In *HSCC*, pages 202–214, 2000.

[15] D. Liberzon, J. P. Hespanha, and A. S. Morse. Stability of switched systems: a lie-algebraic condition. *Systems Control Lett*, 37:117–122, 1999.

[16] H. Lin and P. J. Antsaklis. Switching stabilizability for continuous-time uncertain switched linear systems, 2007.

[17] H. Lin and P. J. Antsaklis. Stability and stabilizability of switched linear systems: A survey of recent results. *IEEE Trans. Automat. Contr.*, 54(2):308–322, 2009.

[18] T. Moor, J. Raisch, and S. O'Young. Discrete supervisory control of hybrid systems based on l-complete approximations. *Discrete Event Dynamic Systems*, 12(1):83–107, 2002.

[19] A. S. Morse. Supervisory control of families of linear set-point controllers - part 1: Exact matching. *IEEE Trans. Automat. Contr*, 41:1413–1431, 1998.

[20] K. Narendra and J. Balakrishnan. A common lyapunov function for stable lti systems with commuting a-matrices. *Automatic Control, IEEE Transactions on*, 39(12):2469–2471, Dec 1994.

[21] N. Ozay, J. Liu, P. Prabhakar, and R. M. Murray. Computing augmented finite transition systems to synthesize switching protocols for polynomial switched systems. In *ACC*, pages 6237–6244, 2013.

[22] S. Pettersson. Synthesis of switched linear systems. In *CDC*, volume 5, pages 5283–5288 Vol.5, 2003.

[23] P. Prabhakar and M. G. Soto. Abstraction based model-checking of stability of hybrid systems. In *CAV*, pages 280–295, 2013.

[24] P. Prabhakar and M. G. Soto. An algorithmic approach to stability verification of polyhedral switched systems. In *ACC*, pages 2318–2323, 2014.

[25] P. Prabhakar and M. G. Soto. Hybridization for stability analysis of switched linear systems. In *Proceedings of the International Conference on Hybrid Systems: Computation and Control*, 2016.

[26] R. Shorten and K. Narendra. Necessary and sufficient conditions for the existence of a common quadratic lyapunov function for two stable second order linear time-invariant systems. In *ACC*, volume 2, pages 1410–1414, Jun 1999.

[27] R. Shorten, K. Narendra, and O. Mason. A result on common quadratic lyapunov functions. *Automatic Control, IEEE Transactions on*, 48(1):110–113, Jan 2003.

[28] E. Skafidas, R. J. Evans, A. V. Savkin, and I. R. Petersen. Stability results for switched controller systems. In *Automatica*, volume 35, pages 553–564, 1999.

[29] P. Tabuada. *Verification and Control of Hybrid Systems: A Symbolic Approach.* Springer Publishing Company, Incorporated, 1st edition, 2009.

[30] A. Tiwari. Abstractions for hybrid systems. *Formal Methods in System Design*, 32(1):57–83, 2008.

[31] A. Ulusoy and C. Belta. Receding horizon temporal logic control in dynamic environments. *I. J. Robotic Res.*, 33(12):1593–1607, 2014.

[32] G. Zhai. Quadratic stabilizability of discrete-time switched systems via state and output feedback. In *CDC*, volume 3, pages 2165–2166, 2001.

[33] G. Zhai, H. Lin, and P. Antsaklis. Controller failure time analysis for symmetric h infin; control systems. In *CDC*, volume 3, pages 2459–2464, Dec 2003.

Convex Interpolation Control with Formal Guarantees for Disturbed and Constrained Nonlinear Systems

Bastian Schürmann
Technische Universität München
bastian.schuermann@tum.de

Matthias Althoff
Technische Universität München
althoff@tum.de

ABSTRACT

A new control method for nonlinear systems is presented which solves reach-avoid problems by interpolating optimal solutions using convex combinations. It also provides formal guarantees for constraint satisfaction and safety. Reach-avoid problems are important control tasks, which arise in many modern cyber-physical systems, including autonomous driving and robotic path planning. We obtain our control policy by computing the optimal input trajectories for finitely many extreme states only and combining them using convex combinations for all states in a continuous set. Our approach has very low online computation complexity, making it applicable for fast dynamical systems. Iterating through our approach leads to a new form of feedback control with formal guarantees in the presence of disturbances. We demonstrate the new control method for a control problem in automated driving and show the advantages compared to a classical control method.

Keywords

Interpolation Control, Reach-Avoid Problems, Nonlinear Control, Robust Control, Formal Verification, Convex Combinations

1. INTRODUCTION

Reach-avoid problems are important problems in cyber-physical systems and arise in many different application fields. For instance, autonomous cars should reach a desired position while avoiding other traffic participants and staying on the road. Another example is robot manipulators whose end-effector must reach a desired position without colliding with surrounding persons or objects. The goal is to always find a controller which steers all states from a given initial set into a set around a target state. Until reaching the final set, the system trajectories must avoid unsafe sets, such as obstacles, and satisfy constraints, for example input limitations. The task becomes even harder if the final set

HSCC'17, April 18 - 20, 2017, Pittsburgh, PA, USA

© 2017 Copyright held by the owner/author(s). Publication rights licensed to ACM.
ISBN 978-1-4503-4590-3/17/04... $15.00

DOI: http://dx.doi.org/10.1145/3049797.3049800

must be reached at a given point in time. For a single initial state, this can be achieved by solving a constraint optimization problem. The difficulty arises if one wants to control all states of a given initial set, which is required when the exact initial state is not known before runtime. The traditional approach would lead to infinitely many optimization problems and would therefore be infeasible.

Our goal is to provide a solution to this problem by extending the control inputs for finitely many states to a whole set of infinitely many states, while still ensuring that the final set is reached and that the constraints are satisfied. To do so, we present a novel control approach which utilizes optimal input trajectories for the extreme states of the initial set and uses convex combinations of these inputs to control the current state. By iterating this process over several steps, we obtain a feedback policy which ensures stability and robustness against disturbances, thereby combining the advantages of optimal (open-loop) control and feedback control. This idea provides a new way of viewing control theory: instead of looking for a feedback control law, which offers a stable closed-loop behavior, we directly use finitely many optimal open-loop inputs to control the system. Because of the way we compute the inputs for arbitrary states from finitely many optimal input trajectories, we achieve formal guarantees for the whole set of controlled states. Since the online complexity is low, fast sampling times can be achieved. At the same time, the basic idea of our approach is rather simple, both to understand as well as to implement, which facilitates its applicability in industry.

We apply our technique to maneuver automata, resulting in hybrid dynamics. Maneuver automata [13, 22] are used for online path planning tasks, where it is not possible to solve reach-avoid problems for fast and complex dynamical systems online. Instead, the overall path planning task is split into smaller reach-avoid problems, which can be solved offline (Fig. 1, ①). The solutions, so-called motion primitives [13], are stored as states in a maneuver automaton. Therein, two maneuvers can be safely connected if the reachable set of the previous motion primitive is completely contained in the initial set of the succeeding one (Fig. 1, ②). The maneuver automaton can then be used for online path-planning by simply connecting the pre-computed motion primitives along the transitions of the maneuver automaton and checking whether the possible plans do not enter unsafe regions (Fig. 1, ③-⑥). [22, 14] improve the applicability of maneuver automata for real systems by making them safe in uncertain environments through tools from formal verification (see e.g., [4, 1] and references therein). While this is a big advantage, the authors in [14] faced the challenge of ensuring that the reachable set of a motion primitive ends in the initial set of the next one in order to increase the number of transitions in the automaton. Our new control approach offers a solution to this problem.

Besides the hybrid dynamics of the maneuver automaton, the dynamics of the system without a controller could be hybrid as well. Our new method is based on combining optimal control with reachability analysis. Since approaches which deal with hybrid dynamics exist for both methods (e.g. [20, 4, 1]), we can also extend our approach to the case that the uncontrolled system is hybrid. Due to space limitations, however, we focus in this paper only on continuous dynamics of the uncontrolled system so that we are able to describe this new approach in detail.

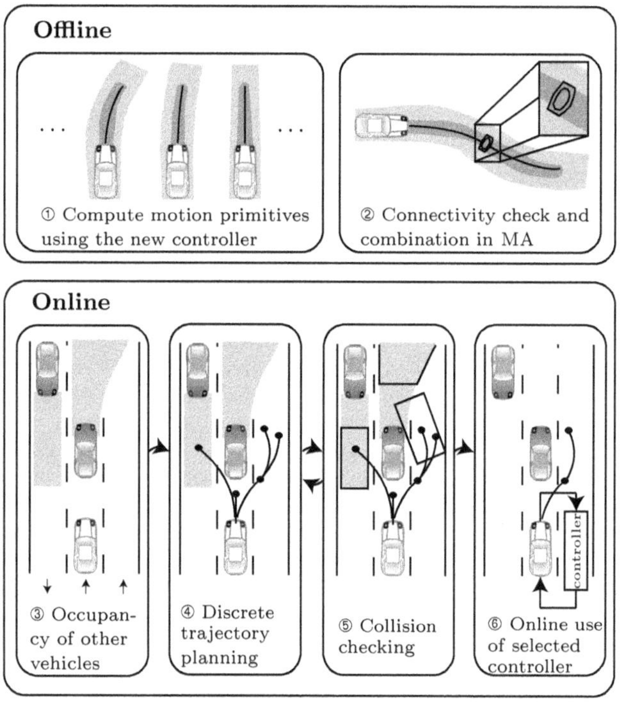

Figure 1: Overview of robust maneuver automata (MA) design for an example in automated driving using our convex control approach.

Related Literature. The idea of interpolating between finitely many offline computed solutions in order to obtain fast, near-optimal online control has been discussed in [31], although without providing guarantees or considering disturbances. Controlling all states around a single trajectory is achieved by exploiting the so-called trajectory robustness in [16]. This method is restricted to feedback-linearizable and differentially flat systems, and it also does not take disturbances into account. One way to obtain optimal control inputs which satisfy input and state constraints is to solve the Hamilton-Jacobi-Bellman (HJB) equation or use dynamic programming [5, 7, 21, 18]. However, an analytic solution of the HJB equation is only possible for relatively simple and small dimensional systems, and it becomes difficult to use for more complex and disturbed systems. For linear systems in particular, there exist several methods [8, 9] for systematically computing the optimal feedback control law for different regions in the state space depending on the goal region and the convex state and input constraints. These techniques are often used for explicit model predictive control (MPC) [8, 9]. However, since they have to divide the state space into different regions, this can become easily computationally intractable if the number of dimensions and constraints grows, especially if disturbance effects have to be taken into account. This curse of dimensionality is a common problem for techniques which rely on discretizing the state and input spaces, such as most abstraction-based control approaches [19, 17, 34], which are able to take complex specifications into account. Some recent approaches [33, 12] avoid computing complete abstractions of the state space, while still being able to consider complex specifications, by solving reachability problems in a similar way as for maneuver automata. A different approach is used in [30, 22], where the authors use sums-of-squares techniques to find special LQR tracking controllers. These controllers are then used to compute so-called LQR trees. However, these methods also suffer from the curse of dimensionality, as the complexity of sum-of-squares techniques grows very fast with the dimension. Less affected by the curse of dimensionality is implicit MPC, where tube-based approaches [23, 26] use an additional feedback controller to keep the system along an optimized trajectory despite disturbances. However, tube-based MPC loses optimality by using a fixed feedback controller, which is not optimized further, even though some approaches allow adapting the tube size during optimization [27]. Also, most efficient tube-based MPC approaches are restricted to linear systems, as they depend on the superposition principle.

Organization. The remainder of the paper is organized as follows: We begin with a formal problem statement in Sec. 2. In Sec. 3, we describe the convex control approach. For faster online computation, we discuss closed-form expressions of convex combinations in Sec. 4. Sec. 5 shows a linear approximation of the convex control approach for computational reasons. We demonstrate the applicability of our approach in a numerical example in Sec. 6. In Sec. 7 we discuss the complexity and optimality of our approach, before we conclude with a summary and an outlook in Sec. 8.

2. PROBLEM FORMULATION

In this paper, we consider a disturbed, nonlinear, time-continuous system of the form

$$\dot{x}(t) = f(x(t), u(t), w(t)), \tag{1}$$

with states $x(t) \in \mathbb{R}^n$, inputs $u(t) \in \mathbb{R}^m$, and disturbances $w(t) \in \mathcal{W} \subset \mathbb{R}^d$ ($\mathcal{W}$ is compact, i.e., closed and bounded). We do not require any stochastic properties for $w(\cdot)$; we only assume that any possible disturbance trajectory is bounded at any point in time in the compact set $\mathcal{W}$. We denote this by $w(\cdot) \in \mathcal{W}$, which is a shorthand for $w(t) \in \mathcal{W}, \forall t \in [0, t_f]$, where $t_f \in \mathbb{R}_0^+$ is the final time. The same shorthand is also used for states and inputs throughout the paper. We denote the solution of (1) with initial state $x(0)$, input $u(\cdot)$, and disturbance $w(\cdot)$ at time t as $\xi(x(0), u(\cdot), w(\cdot), t)$. The solution satisfies the following two properties:

1. $\xi(x(0), u(\cdot), w(\cdot), 0) = x(0)$

2. $\dot{\xi}(x(0), u(\cdot), w(\cdot), t) = f(\xi(x(0), u(\cdot), w(\cdot), t), u(t), w(t))$, $\forall t \in \mathbb{R}_0^+$.

Sometimes, when we consider the undisturbed nominal system, we use $\xi(x(0), u(\cdot), 0, \cdot)$ to denote the solution without disturbances, i.e., $\mathcal{W} = 0$.

The task is to find a control algorithm $u_{control}(x, t)$ for system (1) which guarantees that all states in an initial set $\mathcal{S}_{init} \subset \mathbb{R}^n$ are steered into a final set $\mathcal{S}_f \subset \mathbb{R}^n$ around an end state $x^{(f)}$ after time t_f, despite the disturbance set $\mathcal{W}$. We minimize the size of the final set by solving

$$\min_{u_{control}} \rho(\mathcal{S}_f, x^{(f)}), \tag{2}$$

where $\rho(\mathcal{S}_f, x_f) \to \mathbb{R}_0^+$ is a cost function measuring the distance of the states in $\mathcal{S}_f$ to $x^{(f)}$. Furthermore, we consider convex constraints on the states and inputs, i.e.,

$$\xi(x(0), u(\cdot), w(\cdot), \cdot) \in \mathcal{X}, \tag{3}$$

$$u(\cdot) \in \mathcal{U}, \tag{4}$$

where $\mathcal{X}$ and $\mathcal{U}$ are both convex sets in $\mathbb{R}^n$ and $\mathbb{R}^m$, respectively. The distance function $\rho(\mathcal{S}_f, x^{(f)})$ can have different possible forms. One example would be

$$\rho(\mathcal{S}_f, x^{(f)}) = max\{\|x - x^{(f)}\|_2 | x \in \mathcal{S}_f\}.$$

Note that during offline computation, the locations of most non-convex constraints, such as other traffic participants in automated driving or human workers surrounding robots, are not known. Therefore, we use this approach to compute the motion primitives offline in advance, while taking convex input constraints, e.g., maximum acceleration or steering, and convex state constraints, e.g., maximum velocity, into account. The non-convex dynamical constraints are handled during the online planning using the maneuver automaton as described in the introduction, see Fig. 1.

For the majority of this paper, we want to find a final set $\mathcal{S}_f$ which is as small as possible. If the task is instead to steer all states into a given final set, then we would have to adapt the algorithms by adding this as an additional constraint. In this case, however, it might be possible that no solution can be found, depending on the choice of constraints, final time, and final set.

3. CONVEX CONTROL

In order to solve the previously-stated problem, we propose a convex control approach: The basic idea is to use a convex combination of control inputs computed for the extreme states of an initial set $\mathcal{S}_{init}$ in order to ensure that all trajectories starting in this initial set will end in a desired set $\mathcal{S}_f$. A very similar idea has been used in parametrized tube MPC [26], where control inputs are also computed as convex combinations of extreme input values. This approach, however, is only used for linear systems and not for disturbed, nonlinear systems, as considered in this paper. Computing convex combinations of extreme inputs has also been used for reachability analysis of linear systems, see e.g. [11]. The focus in this case is on the reachable sets rather than optimal control inputs, however.

For our convex control approach, we consider the initial set $\mathcal{S}_{init}$ to be given by a polytope P, defined by its p extreme states $\hat{x}^{(i)}, i = 1, \ldots, p$. We assume to know for each of the extreme states $\hat{x}^{(i)}$ a piecewise-continuous control input $\hat{u}^{(i)}(\cdot), i = 1, \ldots, p$, which steers this state into the desired set $\mathcal{S}_f$. To obtain the control input which steers an arbitrary state $x(0) \in P$ into the desired set $\mathcal{S}_f$, we express $x(0)$ as a convex combination of the extreme states $\hat{x}^{(i)}$ by choosing $\lambda_i(x(0))$ such that

$$x(0) = \sum_{i=1}^{p} \lambda_i(x(0))\hat{x}^{(i)}, \tag{5}$$

with $\lambda_i(x(0)) \geq 0, \sum_{i=1}^{p} \lambda_i(x(0)) = 1$. We then use the same parameters $\lambda_i(x(0))$ to compute the corresponding control input $u_{conv}(x(0), \cdot)$ for the state $x(0)$ as a convex combination of the control inputs $\hat{u}^{(i)}(\cdot)$ of the extreme states $\hat{x}^{(i)}$, i.e.,

$$u_{conv}(x(0), \cdot) = \sum_{i=1}^{p} \lambda_i(x(0))\hat{u}^{(i)}(\cdot). \tag{6}$$

This is illustrated in Fig. 2. Note that the controller $u_{conv}(x(0), \cdot)$ provides an open loop control input. Feedback is realized by iteratively applying (6). As we see in Sec. 4, it is even possible to obtain closed-form expressions of the convex combinations, such that the system of inequalities in (5) does not to have to be solved online.

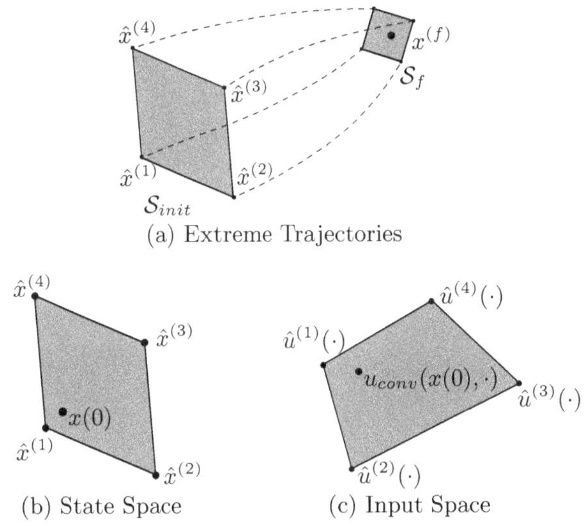

Figure 2: Basic idea of the convex control approach: Compute input trajectories which control the extreme states $\hat{x}^{(i)}$ of the initial set $\mathcal{S}_{init}$ close to the desired final state $x^{(f)}$ (a). Express state $x(0) \in \mathcal{S}_{init}$ as a convex combination of extreme states $\hat{x}^{(i)}$ (b). Use the same convex combination to compute the corresponding control input $u_{conv}(x(0), \cdot)$ using the control inputs $\hat{u}^{(i)}(\cdot)$ of the extreme states (c).

3.1 Convex Control for Linear Systems

Before we consider disturbed, nonlinear systems, we illustrate first how our approach works for undisturbed, linear systems of the form

$$\dot{x}(t) = Ax(t) + Bu(t), \tag{7}$$

with $x(t) \in \mathbb{R}^n, u(t) \in \mathbb{R}^m, A \in \mathbb{R}^{n\times n}$, and $B \in \mathbb{R}^{n\times m}$. In order to solve the control problem, we perform the following two steps:

Step 1: For each of the extreme states $\hat{x}^{(i)}, i = 1, \ldots, p$, of the initial set, we solve a constrained optimization problem of the form

$$\forall \hat{x}^{(i)} : \min_{\hat{u}^{(i)}(\cdot)} J_{linear}(\|\xi(\hat{x}^{(i)}, \hat{u}^{(i)}(\cdot), 0, t_f) - x^{(f)}\|),$$
$$\text{w.r.t. } (3), (4),$$

to find an input sequence which returns a solution that ends as close as possible to $x^{(f)}$ while satisfying the state and input constraints (3)-(4). The norm and the exact form of the cost function can be freely chosen depending on the specific problem.

Step 2: For a given state in the initial set: express it as a convex combination of the extreme states by solving (5) (or using a closed-form expression from Sec. 4) and use the same convex combination of the corresponding input sequences (6) to control it to the final set.

By applying these two steps, we obtain for each extreme state $\hat{x}^{(i)}$ an input sequence $\hat{u}^{(i)}$, such that the corresponding state trajectory ends close (see (2)) to the desired final state $x^{(f)}$ after a fixed time t_f. If all input sequences $\hat{u}^{(i)}(\cdot)$ and corresponding state trajectories $\xi(\hat{x}^{(i)}, \hat{u}^{(i)}(\cdot), 0, \cdot)$ satisfy the input and state constraints, respectively, then, all trajectories starting in the initial set $\mathcal{S}_{init}$ under the convex control law (6) end in the a priori known compact set

$$\mathcal{S}_f = \mathbf{conv}(\xi(\hat{x}^{(1)}, \hat{u}^{(1)}(\cdot), 0, t_f), \ldots, \xi(\hat{x}^{(p)}, \hat{u}^{(p)}(\cdot), 0, t_f)),$$

where $\mathbf{conv}(\cdot)$ denotes the convex hull. Moreover, all trajectories satisfy the state constraints (3) and input constraints (4) at all times.

This directly results from the way we compute the control law and from the convexity of linear systems. Using (5) and (6) it follows from the superposition principle that $\forall t \in [0, t_f]$:

$$\begin{aligned}
&\xi(x(0), u_{conv}(x(0), \cdot), 0, t) \\
&= \xi\left(\sum_{i=1}^{p} \lambda_i(x(0))\hat{x}^{(i)}, \sum_{i=1}^{p} \lambda_i(x(0))\hat{u}^{(i)}(\cdot), 0, t\right) \\
&= \sum_{i=1}^{p} \lambda_i(x(0))\xi(\hat{x}^{(i)}, \hat{u}^{(i)}(\cdot), 0, t),
\end{aligned}$$

i.e., any trajectory starting in the initial set lies inside the convex set of the extreme trajectories. Since the extreme trajectories satisfy the convex state constraints, any inner trajectory satisfies the state constraints as well. The control inputs are convex combinations of the extreme inputs, which are contained in the convex input constraint $\mathcal{U}$. Therefore, it follows from convexity that the control inputs are in the set $\mathcal{U}$ as well.

3.2 Convex Control for Nonlinear Systems with Disturbances

Before we extend this idea to nonlinear systems with disturbances (1), let us first define reachable sets and zonotopes, as they are important for the rest of the paper.

Definition 1 (Reachable Set). *For a system (1), the reachable set $\mathcal{R}_{t,u,\mathcal{W}}(\mathcal{S}) \subset \mathbb{R}^n$ for a time t, an input function $u : \mathbb{R}_0^+ \to \mathbb{R}^m$, disturbances $w(\cdot) \in \mathcal{W}$, and an initial set $\mathcal{S} \subset \mathbb{R}^n$ is the set of end states of trajectories starting in $\mathcal{S}$ after time t, i.e.,*

$$\mathcal{R}_{t,u,\mathcal{W}}(\mathcal{S}) = \{x(t) \in \mathbb{R}^n | \exists x(0) \in \mathcal{S}, \exists w(\cdot) \in \mathcal{W} : \xi(x(0), u(\cdot), w(\cdot), t) = x(t)\}.$$

The reachable set over a time interval $[t_1, t_2]$ is the union of all reachable sets for these time points, i.e.,

$$\mathcal{R}_{[t_1,t_2],u,\mathcal{W}}(\mathcal{S}) = \bigcup_{t \in [t_1,t_2]} \mathcal{R}_{t,u,\mathcal{W}}(\mathcal{S}).$$

If we consider the reachable set for a system with feedback $u_{fb}(x(t))$, then we denote by $\mathcal{R}_{t,u_{fb},\mathcal{W}}(\mathcal{S})$ the reachable set obtained if we consider the closed-loop dynamics $\dot{x}(t) = f(x(t), u_{fb}(x(t)), w(t))$ and no open-loop inputs.

All methods used in the reachablility analysis are over-approximative, i.e., the real reachable set is guaranteed to lie inside the computed reachable set. We have to compute over-approximations, as it is impossible to compute exact reachable sets for most systems [24]. Since we guarantee the constraint satisfaction for the over-approximated reachable set, the real reachable set satisfies the constraints as well, i.e., our algorithm is sound. Because we cannot compute the exact reachable set, we are also unable to provide error bounds for the approximations. Simulations indicate however, that over-approximations can be tightly computed [1]. In this work, we apply the reachability algorithms from [1], which use zonotopes as a set representation:

Definition 2 (Zonotope). *A set is called a zonotope if it can be written as*

$$\mathcal{Z} = \{x \in \mathbb{R}^n | x = c_{\mathcal{Z}} + G_{\mathcal{Z}}\alpha, \alpha_i \in [-1, 1]\},$$

with $\alpha \in \mathbb{R}^q$ and α_i denoting the $i-th$ entry of the vector α. Therein $c_{\mathcal{Z}} \in \mathbb{R}^n$ defines the center of the zonotope, and the matrix $G_{\mathcal{Z}} \in \mathbb{R}^{n \times q}$ contains the $q = on$ generators as its columns, with o denoting the order of the zonotope. A zonotope with n linearly independent generators is called a parallelotope.

Since nonlinear dynamics in general do not preserve convexity [32], convex control cannot be applied in the same way as in the linear case. Instead, we divide the control problem into intermediate steps and iteratively apply the convex control law to steer the system along a reference trajectory. For each time step, we compute the reachable set using techniques from formal verification [1], thereby ensuring that the constraints are always satisfied despite disturbances and nonlinear dynamics. By recomputing the convex control inputs in each time step, we realize feedback and counteract the effects from disturbances. Through the use of reachability analysis, we have a separation of concerns: the optimization provides performance, while the reachability analysis provides guarantees for the satisfaction of all constraints. Therefore, the guarantees still hold if we cannot find optimal solutions for the optimal control problems as long as we find solutions which satisfy the constraints. The new control approach is presented in Alg. 1 and is illustrated in Fig. 3. It consists of three major steps:

Step 1: We first solve a constrained, nonlinear optimization problem in *center_optimal_control* (Alg. 1, line 1) for the nominal system in order to find a trajectory $x^{(c)}(\cdot)$ which starts in $x^{(c)}(0)$, the center of $\mathcal{S}_{init}$, and ends as close as possible to $x^{(f)}$. To solve this control problem efficiently, piecewise-continuous control inputs are computed

Algorithm 1 Offline Part of the Convex Control Algorithm for Nonlinear Systems with Disturbances

1: $(x^{(c)}(\cdot), u^{(c)}(\cdot)) \leftarrow$ *center_optimal_control*$(x^{(c)}(0), x^{(f)}, t_f, N, \bar{\mathcal{X}}, \mathcal{U})$
2: Initialize: $\mathcal{S}_{reach,1} \leftarrow \mathcal{S}_{init}$
3: **for** $k = 1, \ldots, N$ **do**
4: $\quad \bar{\mathcal{P}}_k \leftarrow$ *compute_parallelotope_approx*$(\mathcal{S}_{reach,k})$
5: $\quad (\hat{x}^{(1,k)}, \ldots, \hat{x}^{(2^n,k)}) \leftarrow$ *comp_extreme_pts*$(\bar{\mathcal{P}}_k)$
6: $\quad$ **for** $i = 1, \ldots, 2^n$ **do**
7: $\quad\quad \hat{u}^{(i,k)}(\cdot) \leftarrow$ *optimal_corner_control*$(\hat{x}^{(i,k)}, x^{(c)}(t_{k+1}), \bar{\mathcal{X}}, \mathcal{U})$
8: $\quad$ **end for**
9: $\quad \mathcal{S}_{reach,k+1} \leftarrow$ *comp_reach_set*$(\mathcal{S}_{reach,k}, \hat{u}^{(1,k)}(\cdot), \ldots, \hat{u}^{(2^n,k)}(\cdot), \mathcal{W})$
10: **end for**

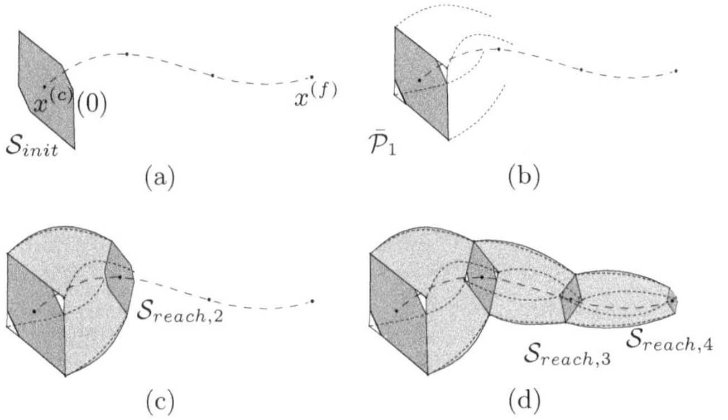

Figure 3: Convex control for nonlinear systems: Compute a reference trajectory $x^{(c)}(\cdot)$ from the center $x^{(c)}(0)$ of the initial set $\mathcal{S}_{init}$ to the final state $x^{(f)}$ (a). Over-approximate the initial set by a parallelotope $\bar{\mathcal{P}}_1$, and compute optimal trajectories for the extreme states (b). Compute the reachable set $\mathcal{S}_{reach,2}$ for one time step under the convex control law while taking all possible disturbance effects into account (c). Repeat the procedure (d).

for N time steps of length $\Delta t = \frac{t_f}{N}$. For an easier notation, we introduce $t_i = i\Delta t$.

Since we solve the optimization problem for the undisturbed system, we have to tighten the nominal state constraints such that the disturbed system still satisfies the original state constraints. We therefore define tightened state constraints as

$$\xi(x(0), u(\cdot), 0, \cdot) \in \bar{\mathcal{X}} \subseteq \mathcal{X}. \tag{8}$$

We discuss how to compute them at the end of this section.

The cost function of the optimization problem is chosen as

$$\min_{u^{(c)}(\cdot)} J_{center}(\|\xi(x^{(c)}(0), u^{(c)}(\cdot), 0, t_f) - x^{(f)}\|, \|u^{(c)}(\cdot)\|),$$
$$\text{w.r.t. } (8), (4).$$

Therein, $\|u^{(c)}(\cdot)\|$ denotes some norm on the input trajectory. We aim for a center trajectory which ends close to the desired end state and whose control inputs are not too large, such that we have some input capacities left for the inputs of the extreme states, which are explained in the next step. The resulting center trajectory is denoted by

$$x^{(c)}(\cdot) = \xi(x^{(c)}(0), u^{(c)}(\cdot), 0, \cdot).$$

Step 2: While step 1 is performed only once, we perform steps 2 and 3 for each time step k, $k = 1, \ldots, N$ (see Alg. 1). At time step k, we over-approximate the reachable set $\mathcal{S}_{reach,k}$ of the previous time step by a parallelotope $\bar{\mathcal{P}}_k$ in *compute_parallelotope_approx* (Alg. 1, line 4), i.e., $\mathcal{S}_{reach,k} \subseteq \bar{\mathcal{P}}_k$. At the first time step $k = 1$, we over-approximate the initial set $\mathcal{S}_{init}$ (line 2). There exist efficient algorithms to formally compute parallelotope over-approximations for zonotopes, see e.g., [1] and the references therein. We use parallelotopes, since they offer a good combination of a small number of extreme states and enclosed volume, and since analytical, closed-form expressions for convex combinations in parallelotopes exist (see Sec. 4).

For the parallelotope $\bar{\mathcal{P}}_k$, we compute the 2^n extreme states $\hat{x}^{(1,k)}, \ldots, \hat{x}^{(2^n,k)}$ in *comp_extreme_pts* (line 5). Computing the extreme states of a parallelotope $\mathcal{P}$ with center $c_{\mathcal{P}}$ and generator matrix $G_{\mathcal{P}}$ can be done in a numerically stable way by adding all 2^n combinations of the generators, i.e.,

$$\{\hat{x}^{(1)}, \ldots, \hat{x}^{(2^n)}\} = c_{\mathcal{P}} \pm g_{\mathcal{P}}^{(1)} \pm \cdots \pm g_{\mathcal{P}}^{(n)}, \tag{9}$$

where $g_{\mathcal{P}}^{(i)}$ denotes the i−th column of $G_{\mathcal{P}}$. This is an advantage over general polytopes in half-space representation, for which it is much harder and numerically less reliable to compute the extreme states. We use the extreme states for the convex control strategy by solving a nonlinear optimal control problem with the nominal system dynamics for one time step. This is done in *optimal_corner_control* (lines 6-8) by solving for each extreme state $\hat{x}^{(i,k)}$:

$$\min_{\hat{u}^{(i,k)}(\cdot)} J_{corner}(\|\xi(\hat{x}^{(i,k)}, \hat{u}^{(i,k)}(\cdot), 0, \Delta t) - x^{(c)}(t_{k+1})\|),$$
$$\text{w.r.t. } (8), (4). \tag{10}$$

This steers all extreme states as close as possible to the optimal center trajectory.

Step 3: In the third step, we use the control inputs of the extreme states of the parallelotope $\bar{\mathcal{P}}_k$ to obtain the convex control law in (6) for each state inside the reachable set of the last step $\mathcal{S}_{reach,k}$. After computing the convex control law $u_{conv}(x, \cdot)$, we use formal reachability analysis tools [1] in *comp_reach_set* (line 9) to obtain an over-approximation of the reachable sets $\bar{\mathcal{R}}_{\Delta t, u_{conv}, \mathcal{W}}(\mathcal{S}_{reach,k}) \supseteq \mathcal{R}_{\Delta t, u_{conv}, \mathcal{W}}(\mathcal{S}_{reach,k})$ and $\bar{\mathcal{R}}_{[0,\Delta t], u_{conv}, \mathcal{W}}(\mathcal{S}_{reach,k}) \supseteq \mathcal{R}_{[0,\Delta t], u_{conv}, \mathcal{W}}(\mathcal{S}_{reach,k})$. We require the reachable sets for time intervals to ensure the satisfaction of state constraints for all points in time. In addition, we use the reachable sets at times t_k to compute the parallelotope over-approximations and to initialize the reachability analysis for the next time step. Therefore, we compute reachable sets for time intervals and time points.

The over-approximation of the reachable set is the initial set for the next time step $k + 1$, i.e.,

$$\mathcal{S}_{reach,k+1} = \bar{\mathcal{R}}_{\Delta t, u_{conv}, \mathcal{W}}(\mathcal{S}_{reach,k}),$$

and we use this to continue with Step 2. By iterating Steps 2 and 3 for all N time steps, we obtain with $\mathcal{S}_f = \mathcal{S}_{reach,N+1}$

the over-approximation of the final reachable set of all states starting in the initial set $\mathcal{S}_{init}$ despite disturbances.

After the controller is computed offline using Alg. 1, we save the computed extreme states $\hat{x}^{(i,k)}$ together with the corresponding input trajectories $\hat{u}^{(i,k)}(\cdot)$ in a look-up table. In each time step during the online application of the convex controller, the current state $x(t_k)$ is expressed as a convex combination of the corresponding extreme states $\hat{x}^{(i,k)}$. The control input $u_{conv}(x(t_k),\cdot)$ is obtained from the convex combination of the extreme inputs $\hat{u}^{(i,k)}(\cdot)$ using the same parameters $\lambda_{i,k}(x(t_k))$ as described at the beginning of this section in (5) and (6).

The results of the convex control approach for nonlinear systems are summarized in the following theorem, which is the main result of this paper:

THEOREM 1. *We consider a nonlinear system with disturbances* (1) *and with state and input constraints* (3)-(4). *We assume that we have found a convex controller for this system using Algorithm 1. If*

$$\bar{\mathcal{R}}_{[0,t_f],u_{conv},\mathcal{W}}(\mathcal{S}_{init}) \subseteq \mathcal{X}, \tag{11}$$

then any trajectory $\xi(x(0), u_{conv}(x(0),\cdot), w(\cdot), \cdot)$ *which starts in the initial set will end after time* t_f *in* $\mathcal{S}_f = \mathcal{S}_{reach,N+1}$, *i.e.,* $\xi(x(0), u_{conv}(x(0),\cdot), w(\cdot), t_f) \in \mathcal{S}_f, \forall x(0) \in \mathcal{S}_{init}, \forall w(\cdot) \in \mathcal{W}$. *Moreover, every trajectory satisfies the state constraints and the applied inputs satisfy the input constraints despite the presence of disturbances, i.e.,* $\forall x(0) \in \mathcal{S}_{init}, \forall w(\cdot) \in \mathcal{W}, \forall t \in [0,t_f]$:

$$\xi(x(0), u_{conv}(x(0),\cdot), w(\cdot), t) \in \mathcal{X} \wedge u_{conv}(x(0),t) \in \mathcal{U}.$$

PROOF. From the definition of the reachable set and the way we compute $\mathcal{S}_f$ as the over-approximation of the final reachable set, it follows that $\forall x(0) \in \mathcal{S}_{init}, \forall w(\cdot) \in \mathcal{W}$:

$$\xi(x(0), u_{conv}(x(0),\cdot), w(\cdot), t_f) \in \mathcal{R}_{t_f,u_{conv},\mathcal{W}}(\mathcal{S}_{init}) \subseteq \bar{\mathcal{R}}_{t_f,u_{conv},\mathcal{W}}(\mathcal{S}_{init}) = \mathcal{S}_f.$$

In the same way, it follows from assumption (11) that

$$\mathcal{R}_{[0,t_f],u_{conv},\mathcal{W}}(\mathcal{S}_{init}) \subseteq \bar{\mathcal{R}}_{[0,t_f],u_{conv},\mathcal{W}}(\mathcal{S}_{init}) \subseteq \mathcal{X},$$

and therefore, the state constraint is satisfied for any trajectory starting in the initial set.

When computing the control inputs $\hat{u}^{(i,k)}(\cdot)$ of the extreme states $\hat{x}^{(i,k)}$ in (10), we restrict them to lie in the input set $\mathcal{U}$ at all times. Since the input set is convex, and since any convex combination of points in a convex set lies again in the convex set [10], it follows that any convex combination of these inputs, and therefore any control input from our convex controller, satisfies the input constraints. □

Tightened State Constraints. In general it is hard to know in advance how much tighter the new state constraints have to be, and there exists no general solution for this problem in literature for disturbed, nonlinear systems. Since we combine controller synthesis with reachable set computation, we can check offline if the controller satisfies all constraints, and if not, adapt the tightened state constraints. Since we know which state constraints have been violated, we can adapt exactly these constraints. By iteratively tightening the nominal state constraints offline in advance until all constraints are satisfied by the real system, we obtain a formally correct controller for the online application. The reachability analysis in [1] relies on linearizing the dynamics and over-approximating the linearization errors and disturbance. Therefore, we are able to use these over-approximations to obtain good initial estimates of how much we have to tighten the state constraints.

4. CLOSED-FORM EXPRESSION OF CONVEX COMBINATIONS

When applying the proposed convex control law (6), at each new time step, we have to find the parameters $\lambda_i(x)$ to express a state x as a convex combination of the extreme states $\hat{x}^{(i)}$. Utilizing solvers for this problem is computationally expensive, especially for higher dimensional systems, and they would only provide an implicit solution. The computation time would restrict the sampling times of our controller, and the implicit solutions would prohibit the application of reachability analysis, which relies on an explicit, closed-form expression of the closed-loop dynamics.

To overcome these problems, closed-form expressions of convex combinations of simplices, parallelotopes, and general polytopes are presented in [28]. As mentioned before, parallelotopes offer a good combination of enclosed volume and a small number of extreme states. While simplices for example have the advantage that they have only $n+1$ extreme states, the enclosed volume is smaller and has an "impractical" shape for our application purposes. On the other hand, objects like higher-order zonotopes or general polytopes may better describe certain shapes, but when applied, the number of vertices increases significantly. Therefore we use parallelotopes to over-approximate the reachable set for the convex control computation in Step 2 in Sec. 3.2. We use these parallelotope over-approximations only to obtain the input combination and use the actual high-order zonotope for reachability analysis. In doing so, we avoid the error due to this over-approximation such that it has no significant impact on the reachability analysis.

The following theorem shows how to obtain closed-form expressions of convex combinations for parallelotopes:

THEOREM 2 ([28]). *We consider a parallelotope* $\mathcal{P} \subset \mathbb{R}^n$ *given by*

$$\mathcal{P} = \{x \in \mathbb{R}^n | x = c_{\mathcal{P}} + G_{\mathcal{P}}\alpha(x), \alpha_i(x) \in [-1,1]\},$$

with 2^n *extreme states* $\hat{x}^{(1)}, \ldots, \hat{x}^{(2^n)}$, *see* (9). *Given a state* $x \in \mathcal{P}$, *this state can be expressed as a convex combination of the extreme states as* $x = \sum_{i=1}^{2^n} \lambda_i(x)\hat{x}^{(i)}$, *where the parameters* $\lambda_i(x)$ *are given by the following closed-form expression*

$$\lambda_i(x) = \prod_{j=1}^{n} \mu_{i,j}, \tag{12}$$

where

$$\mu_{i,j} = \begin{cases} x'_j & \text{if } \alpha_j(\hat{x}^{(i)}) = 1 \\ 1 - x'_j & \text{if } \alpha_j(\hat{x}^{(i)}) = -1. \end{cases} \tag{13}$$

Thereby, x' *is the transformed state of* x *under the affine transformation*

$$x' = \frac{1}{2}G_{\mathcal{P}}^{-1}(x - c_{\mathcal{P}}) + \frac{1}{2}\mathbf{1} \tag{14}$$

and x'_j *denotes its* $j-th$ *entry.*

The proof as well as results for sets other than parallelotopes can be found in [28]. Note that for a point $\hat{x}^{(i)} \in \mathcal{P}$ to be an extreme point, the entries in the corresponding parameter vector $\alpha(\hat{x}^{(i)})$ must all be ± 1; therefore, one of the cases in (13) is always satisfied. Also, $G_{\mathcal{P}}^{-1}$ always exists since $G_{\mathcal{P}}$ has full rank.

With this theorem, we are able to pre-compute the convex combinations for the parallelotopes at different points in time. Since we know the parallelotopes in advance, we can compute all matrices and matrix inverses of Thm. 2 offline. During the online computation, we simply plug in the current state in (14) and use the result to compute the $\lambda_i(x)$. The computation of all $\lambda_i(x)$ for a ten-dimensional parallelotope can be performed in around 0.1ms which is over 200 times faster than using linear programming solvers [28].

5. LINEAR APPROXIMATION OF THE CONVEX CONTROL APPROACH

The convex controller described in Sec. 3 is a nonlinear controller as can be seen by looking at the closed-form expressions of $\lambda_i(x)$ in (12), where the different entries x'_j are multiplied with each other. Although a convex combination is a linear combination of the extreme states, the parameters $\lambda_i(x)$ have a nonlinear dependency on the initial state for systems with dimensions greater than one. This increases the nonlinearity of the whole closed-loop system, which leads to larger computation errors during the reachability computation, as well as to a higher computational complexity of the reachability computation itself [1].

In order to overcome these problems, we present an alternative approach where we use a linear approximation of the convex control approach. To do so, we take advantage of the fact that efficient techniques for reachability analysis use zonotopes as set representation [3, 1]. We use the zonotope representation of the state set to compute a corresponding zonotope representation for the inputs. We modify only the third step in Sec. 3.2 by adding the input approximation, as shown in Alg. 2. For simpler computations, we restrict our considerations to piecewise-constant inputs, and we use the constant value u to also denote the constant input trajectory $u(\cdot)$, with $u(t) = u, \forall t$.

Algorithm 2 Convex Control Algorithm for Nonlinear Systems with Disturbances Using Linear Input Combinations

1: ... (Lines 1 to 8 as in Alg. 1)
2: $\mathcal{Z}_{U,k} \leftarrow$ *opt_input_zonotope*($\bar{\mathcal{P}}_k$, $\hat{u}^{(1,k)}, \dots, \hat{u}^{(2^n,k)}$)
3: $\mathcal{S}_{reach,k+1} \leftarrow$ *compute_reachable_set*($\mathcal{S}_{reach,k}$, $\mathcal{Z}_{U,k}$, $\mathcal{W}$)
4: **end for** (from last line of Alg. 1)

Any state x in a parallelotope $\mathcal{P}$ is uniquely defined by the parameters $\alpha(x)$, i.e., $x = c_{\mathcal{P}} + G_{\mathcal{P}}\alpha(x)$, and therefore $\alpha(x)$ can be obtained by

$$\alpha(x) = G_{\mathcal{P}}^{-1}(x - c_{\mathcal{P}}), \tag{15}$$

where $G_{\mathcal{P}}^{-1}$ exists since $\mathcal{P}$ is a parallelotope.

In every time step $k = 1, \dots, N$, we want to find an input zonotope $\mathcal{Z}_{U,k}$ with center $c_{\mathcal{Z}_{U,k}}$ and generator matrix $G_{\mathcal{Z}_{U,k}}$ such that we obtain the corresponding control input for any state $x(t_k) \in \bar{\mathcal{P}}_k$ by just using $\alpha(x(t_k))$ in

$$u_{zono}(x(t_k)) = c_{\mathcal{Z}_{U,k}} + G_{\mathcal{Z}_{U,k}}\alpha(x(t_k)). \tag{16}$$

By plugging (15) into (16), we obtain

$$u_{zono}(x(t_k)) = c_{\mathcal{Z}_{U,k}} + G_{\mathcal{Z}_{U,k}} G_{\bar{\mathcal{P}}_k}^{-1}(x(t_k) - c_{\bar{\mathcal{P}}_k}), \tag{17}$$

which is linear in $x(t_k)$ as desired.

We now have to choose the center $c_{\mathcal{Z}_{U,k}}$ and generator matrix $G_{\mathcal{Z}_{U,k}}$ of $\mathcal{Z}_{U,k}$, which best match the desired inputs. Clearly, as this is a linear approximation of the nonlinear convex input combinations, we cannot match the input for every state in $\bar{\mathcal{P}}_k$ exactly. We choose $c_{\mathcal{Z}_{U,k}}$ and $G_{\mathcal{Z}_{U,k}}$ in *opt_input_zonotope* (Alg. 2, line 2) by solving an optimization problem such that the difference between the optimal inputs for the extreme states $\hat{u}^{(i,k)}$ and the inputs from the input zonotope $\mathcal{Z}_{U,k}$ for the corresponding $\alpha(\hat{x}^{(i)})$ is minimized:

$$\min_{c_{\mathcal{Z}_{U,k}}, G_{\mathcal{Z}_{U,k}}} \sum_{i=1}^{2^n} \left\| \hat{u}^{(i,k)} - (c_{\mathcal{Z}_{U,k}} + G_{\mathcal{Z}_{U,k}}\alpha(\hat{x}^{(i,k)})) \right\|$$
$$\text{w.r.t. } c_{\mathcal{Z}_{U,k}} + G_{\mathcal{Z}_{U,k}}\alpha(\hat{x}^{(i,k)}) \in \mathcal{U}, \forall i \in \{1, \dots, 2^n\}. \tag{18}$$

Now, we have the desired linear control law $u_{zono}(\cdot)$ for any state in $\bar{\mathcal{P}}_k$ with (17). Using Alg. 2 and therefore replacing u_{conv} by u_{zono} in Thm. 1 ensures that the results of Thm. 1 also hold in the case of the new control law. We do not change anything about the reachability computation, with the exception of considering the new control law u_{zono}, in *compute_reachable_set* (line 3). Therefore, our algorithm is still sound and we have guarantees for satisfaction of the state constraints. Because of (18) and since $\mathcal{U}$ is convex it holds that $\forall k$

$$\mathcal{Z}_{U,k} = \mathbf{conv}\left(u_{zono}(\hat{x}^{(1,k)}), \dots, u_{zono}(\hat{x}^{(2^n,k)})\right) \subseteq \mathcal{U},$$

and therefore the input constraints are satisfied as well.

6. NUMERICAL EXAMPLE

In this section, we provide a numerical example to show the applicability of the proposed control approach for a constrained, nonlinear system. We choose a kinematic model of a vehicle, which is broadly used to model the most important dynamics of a car [25]:

$$\dot{v} = a + w_1,\ \dot{\Psi} = b + w_2,\ \dot{x} = v\,cos(\Psi),\ \dot{y} = v\,sin(\Psi), \tag{19}$$

where the states v, Ψ, x, and y are the velocity, the orientation, and the positions in x and in y directions, respectively. The acceleration a and the normalized steering angle b are the inputs, and w_1 and w_2 are additive disturbances. They are constrained to lie in the intervals $a \in [-9.81, 9.81]\frac{m}{s^2}$, $b \in [-0.4, 0.4]\frac{rad}{s}$, $w_1 \in [-0.5, 0.5]\frac{m}{s^2}$, and $w_2 \in [-0.02, 0.02]\frac{rad}{s}$.

We use our convex control approach to compute a maneuver automaton for this model. Due to space limitations, we present the maneuver automaton only for the three discrete states "drive straight", "turn left", and "turn right", at velocities around $20\frac{m}{s}$. However, we can add additional maneuvers simply by repeating the procedure for other final states. Following the techniques introduced in [14], we can only connect two motion primitives if the reachable set of the first one lies completely in the initial set of the second one, see Fig. 1, ②. Since the car dynamics are independent of the absolute position and orientation, it suffices if we end in a set with the same size as the initial set, but which can be shifted in position and orientation. However, in the velocity dimension, we have to end in the initial set again. Therefore, it must hold that $\mathcal{S}_{reach,N+1} - \left[0, \Psi^{(f)}, x^{(f)}, y^{(f)}\right]^T \subseteq \mathcal{S}_{init}$. We choose for all maneuvers the initial set as the box $[19.8, 20.2]\frac{m}{s} \times [-0.02, 0.02]rad \times [-0.2, 0.2]m \times [-0.2, 0.2]m$. We apply our convex control approach three times for different final states, corresponding to the three maneuvers. The final states are given for the "drive straight" maneuver by $\left[20\,\frac{m}{s}, 0\,rad, 20\,m, 0\,m\right]^T$ and for the "turn left" and "turn right" maneuvers by $\left[20\,\frac{m}{s}, \pm 0.2\,rad, 19.87\,m, \pm 1.99\,m\right]^T$. Each final state must be reached in one second. We divide the main trajectory into 10 sections and apply four different piece-wise constant control values for each section of the reference trajectory. For the local controllers, we choose the cost function as

$$J_{corner} = (\hat{x}^{(i,k+1)} - x^{(c)}(t_{k+1}))^T Q (\hat{x}^{(i,k+1)} - x^{(c)}(t_{k+1})),$$

with $\hat{x}^{(i,k+1)} = \xi(\hat{x}^{(i,k)}, \hat{u}^{(i,k)}(\cdot), 0, \Delta t)$ and Q being a diagonal matrix with $[2, 5, 1, 1]$ on the diagonal.

6.1 Computational Results

We implement our approach in MATLAB and use the ACADO toolbox [15] to solve the optimal control problems with a multiple shooting algorithm. For the reachability computation, we use the CORA toolbox [2], where the disturbances are handled as an uncontrollable input. Since the CORA toolbox works with zonotopes, we use the techniques presented in Sec. 5 to obtain a parallelotope approximating the inputs.

The computation of each maneuver takes around 10 seconds, which can be performed offline. The computations are performed on a computer with a 3.1 GHz dual-core i7 processor and 16 GB memory and without using parallel computing. The online computation of the input values can be performed in around 0.01ms, making it applicable to fast systems.

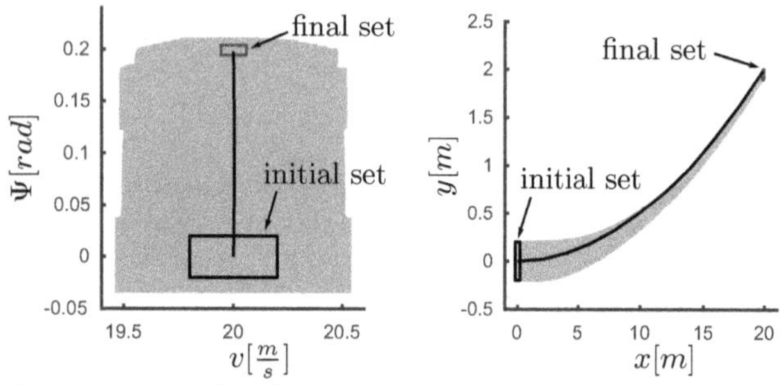

(a) Turn Left, (v, Ψ) plane (b) Turn Left, (x, y) plane

Figure 4: Reachable sets for the "turn left" maneuver with the convex controller. The initial set is plotted in black, the final set in blue, and the reachable set for all times between in gray. The black line shows the center trajectory $x^{(c)}(\cdot)$.

The whole reachable set is shown for the "turn left" maneuver in Fig. 4. In Fig. 5, the initial sets (black) and (shifted) final sets for all motion primitives are plotted. For the convex controller, all final sets (blue) lie around the final states and are completely contained in the desired set, i.e., the shifted initial set. Therefore, we are able to connect all maneuvers with each other and obtain a fully connected

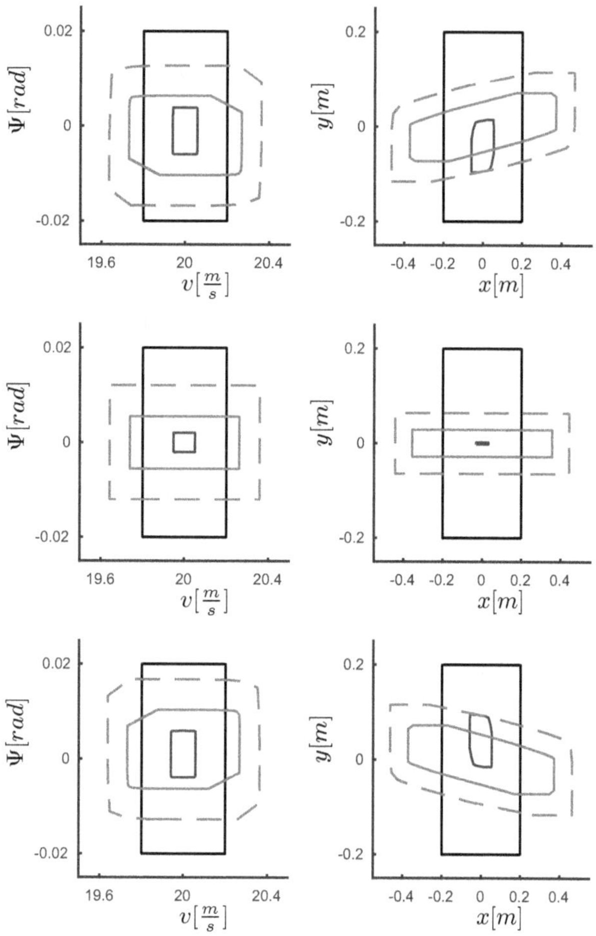

Figure 5: Initial (black) and shifted final sets (blue) for the convex controller, projected to the (v, Ψ) and the (x, y) planes, for the "turn left" (top), "drive straight" (center), and "turn right" (bottom) maneuvers. For comparison the final sets of two LQR controllers (red).

maneuver automaton. The controller satisfies the input constraints at all times due to the way we computed it.

6.2 Comparison with LQR Controller

For comparison, we have also implemented an LQR-tracking controller (red, solid in Fig. 5). It uses the same center-trajectory as a reference trajectory. In each step, we linearize the system around the corresponding state on the center trajectory and compute an LQR controller. We use the same Q matrix as for the corner trajectories. To weight the inputs we choose the R matrix for the Ricatti equation to be the identity matrix. As we see in Fig. 5, the shifted reachable sets exceed the initial sets, making it impossible to combine the maneuver with other maneuvers. Moreover, since the LQR controller does not take input constraints into account, it uses inputs for b in (19) up to $0.54\frac{rad}{s}$, which is more than the maximally allowed value. By decreasing the weights of the inputs, we can move the final sets inside the initial sets; however, the input constraints violation increases even more in this case. If we increase the weights on the inputs to $R = 4I$, we obtain a maximal $b = 0.40\frac{rad}{s}$, which barely satisfies the constraint. However, the reachable sets (red, dashed in Fig. 5) are very large and not suitable for a maneuver automaton at all. Therefore, we cannot achieve both a good final set and input satisfaction with LQR controllers. This shows the advantage of the convex control approach, which optimizes the reachable set while ensuring the satisfaction of the constraints.

7. DISCUSSION OF THE ALGORITHM

Let us now discuss the complexity and optimality of the proposed algorithms.

7.1 Optimality

Finding optimal solutions for a nonlinear, disturbed system is a hard task, and in most cases it is not possible to obtain globally optimal solutions. This is also true for the nonlinear programming algorithms which we use to obtain the solutions for the reference trajectory and the corner trajectories.

While we have no guarantees that our overall dynamics results in a globally optimal solution, numerical solvers for optimizing open-loop trajectories work very efficiently and converge for many initial states to (locally) optimal solutions. Direct optimization methods in particular have shown very good performance in recent years [6]. With our method we are able to transfer the good results from optimizing single, open-loop trajectories to a whole set of trajectories. Through the iterative application, we obtain therefore a robust, closed-loop algorithm. It is a general problem to efficiently obtain globally optimal solutions for nonlinear disturbed systems [29, 5].

While this general problem is still unsolved and even though we have no guarantees for optimality (which no efficient approach can provide for disturbed, nonlinear systems), we have guarantees that the computed final set is reached and all constraints are satisfied despite disturbances. As we see in Sec. 6, the optimized solution performs much better than other methods using standard LQR tracking controllers. Since the computation is done offline, one can make changes in the parameters (e.g., weighting matrices in the cost functions or number of time steps) or the desired final state if the results are not satisfying. This is of course also the case if the shifted final set is not in the initial set, as desired for maneuver automata. In this case we have to change parameters or know that these maneuvers cannot be combined.

7.2 Complexity

In order to discuss the complexity for our algorithm, we have to distinguish between offline and online complexity, where online complexity is more important, as it restricts sampling times and therefore control performance. For offline complexity, we are not able to provide an exact bound, since nonlinear programming algorithms have no convergence guarantees. As mentioned before, even though they have no guarantees, they are often quite fast, especially for short time horizons, as needed for the corner trajectories. We can argue that if the optimal control problem is hardly solvable for undisturbed open-loop trajectories, then we cannot expect it to be solved more easily for a set of initial states and disturbances. If we can solve the optimal control problems for the extreme states, then the complexity of our algorithm grows with 2^n, with n denoting the dimension of the state space, since a parallelotope has 2^n extreme states for which we have to compute the optimal input trajectories. While this is exponential, it is much better than other comparable algorithms, which rely on discretizing the state space (like explicit MPC or abstraction-based control) and have exponential complexity with a larger base: k^n, where k denotes the number of discretized states in each dimension. Therein, k can easily be 30 or 100. The reachability analysis which we use has a complexity of $\mathcal{O}(n^3)$, which is therefore negligible for the overall complexity.

The online complexity of our approach is very low, as it consists only of matrix vector multiplications and in the case of closed-form expression of the convex combinations, plugging the current state into a closed-form formula. Clearly, since we have 2^n extreme points, we have to compute 2^n weights, but each computation can be done very fast (around 0.1ms for all weights of a ten-dimensional system [28]). If we use the linear approximation of the inputs as presented in Sec. 5, the computation simplifies to a matrix vector multiplication only and has complexity $\mathcal{O}(n^2)$. Therefore, we can have high sampling times, as high as we could achieve with piecewise-constant feedback matrices. The efficiency of our approach can also be seen in the fast computation times of around 10 seconds for the offline part and around 0.01 milliseconds for the online part, see Sec. 6.

8. CONCLUSION

In this paper, we present a novel control approach which solves reach-avoid problems and can be used to generate robust maneuver automata. The approach allows us to steer all states from an initial set to a final set by only computing optimal input trajectories for the extreme states. By interpolating between these extreme state inputs using convex combinations, we obtain fast online controllers with very low computational complexity, as most computation tasks can be performed offline in advance. The use of tools from formal verification allows us to achieve provable safety and formal guarantees. The approach works for linear and nonlinear systems even in the presence of disturbances.

The presented control approach is a novel way of viewing closed-loop control by combining the optimized solutions from open-loop control with the stability and robustness of feedback control. By using closed-form expressions for the convex combinations and linear approximations for the control inputs, we provide two ways to make the convex controllers even more efficient and faster, so that the online complexity is only $\mathcal{O}(n^2)$. The applicability is shown in the numerical example, where we are able to obtain a completely connected maneuver automaton for an autonomous vehicle.

We believe that the convex control approach is a very useful tool in control theory which can be used for many applications. Therefore, there are many future extensions possible. The next steps include computing of larger maneuver automata and testing them on real autonomous cars, as well as applying our approach to other application areas.

Acknowledgments

The author gratefully acknowledges financial support from the European Commission project UnCoVerCPS under grant number 643921 and the German Research Foundation (DFG) under grant number AL 1185/3-1.

9. REFERENCES

[1] M. Althoff. *Reachability Analysis and its Application to the Safety Assessment of Autonomous Cars.* PhD thesis, Technische Universität München, 2010.

[2] M. Althoff. An introduction to CORA 2015. In *Proc. of the Workshop on Applied Verification for Continuous and Hybrid Systems*, pages 120–151, 2015.

[3] M. Althoff and G. Frehse. Combining zonotopes and support functions for efficient reachability analysis of linear systems. In *Proc. of the 55th IEEE Conference on Decision and Control*, pages 7439–7446, 2016.

[4] E. Asarin, T. Dang, G. Frehse, A. Girard, C. Le Guernic, and O. Maler. Recent progress in continuous and hybrid reachability analysis. In *Proc. of the IEEE Conference on Computer Aided Control Systems Design*, pages 1582–1587, 2006.

[5] D. P. Bertsekas. *Dynamic Programming and Optimal Control.* Athena Scientific Belmont, MA, 3rd edition, 2005.

[6] J. T. Betts. *Practical Methods for Optimal Control and Estimation Using Nonlinear Programming.* Society for Industrial and Applied Mathematics, 2010.

[7] F. Blanchini and S. Miani. *Set-Theoretic Methods in Control.* Springer, 2008.

[8] F. Borrelli. *Constrained Optimal Control of Linear and Hybrid Systems.* Springer, 2003.

[9] F. Borrelli, A. Bemporad, and M. Morari. *Predictive Control for linear and hybrid systems.* Cambridge University Press, 2011/2015.

[10] S. Boyd and L. Vandenberghe. *Convex Optimization.* Cambridge University Press, 2004.

[11] T. X. T. Dang. *Vérification Et Synthèse Des Systèmes Hybrides.* PhD thesis, Institut National Polytechnique de Grenoble, 2000.

[12] J. A. DeCastro and H. Kress-Gazit. Nonlinear controller synthesis and automatic workspace partitioning for reactive high-level behaviors. In *Proc. Hybrid Systems: Computation and Control*, 2016.

[13] E. Frazzoli, M. Dahleh, and E. Feron. Maneuver-based motion planning for nonlinear systems with symmetries. *IEEE Transactions on Robotics*, 21(6):1077–1091, 2005.

[14] D. Heß, M. Althoff, and T. Sattel. Formal verification of maneuver automata for parameterized motion primitives. In *Proc. of the International Conference on Intelligent Robots and Systems*, pages 1474–1481, 2014.

[15] B. Houska, H. Ferreau, and M. Diehl. ACADO Toolkit – An Open Source Framework for Automatic Control and Dynamic Optimization. *Optimal Control Applications and Methods*, 32(3):298–312, 2011.

[16] A. A. Julius and A. K. Winn. Safety controller synthesis using human generated trajectories: Nonlinear dynamics with feedback linearization and differential flatness. In *Proc. of the American Control Conference*, pages 709–714, 2012.

[17] M. Kloetzer and C. Belta. A fully automated framework for control of linear systems from temporal logic specifications. *IEEE Transactions on Automatic Control*, 53(1):287–297, 2008.

[18] A. B. Kurzhanski, I. M. Mitchell, and P. Varaiya. Optimization techniques for state-constrained control and obstacle problems. *Journal of Optimization Theory and Applications*, 128(3):499–521, 2006.

[19] J. Liu, U. Topcu, N. Ozay, and R. M. Murray. Reactive controllers for differentially flat systems with temporal logic constraints. In *Proc. of the Conference on Decision and Control*, pages 7664–7670, 2012.

[20] J. Lunze and F. Lamnabhi-Lagarrigue. *Handbook of hybrid systems control: theory, tools, applications.* Cambridge University Press, 2009.

[21] J. Lygeros, C. Tomlin, and S. Sastry. Controllers for reachability specifications for hybrid systems. *Automatica*, 35(3):349–370, 1999.

[22] A. Majumdar and R. Tedrake. Robust online motion planning with regions of finite time invariance. In *Algorithmic Foundations of Robotics X*, pages 543–558. Springer, 2013.

[23] D. Q. Mayne, M. M. Seron, and S. V. Raković. Robust model predictive control of constrained linear systems with bounded disturbances. *Automatica*, 41(2):219 – 224, 2005.

[24] A. Platzer and E. M. Clarke. The image computation problem in hybrid systems model checking. In *International Workshop on Hybrid Systems: Computation and Control*, pages 473–486, 2007.

[25] R. Rajamani. *Vehicle Dynamics and Control.* Springer, 2012.

[26] S. V. Raković, B. Kouvaritakis, M. Cannon, C. Panos, and R. Findeisen. Parameterized tube model predictive control. *IEEE Transactions on Automatic Control*, 57(11):2746–2761, 2012.

[27] S. V. Raković, B. Kouvaritakis, R. Findeisen, and M. Cannon. Homothetic tube model predictive control. *Automatica*, 48(8):1631–1638, 2012.

[28] B. Schürmann, A. El-Guindy, and M. Althoff. Closed-form expressions of convex combinations. In *Proc. of the American Control Conference*, pages 2795–2801, 2016.

[29] O. Schütze. *Set Oriented Methods for Global Optimization.* PhD thesis, Univ. Paderborn, 2004.

[30] R. Tedrake, I. R. Manchester, M. Tobenkin, and J. W. Roberts. LQR-trees: Feedback motion planning via sums-of-squares verification. *The International Journal of Robotics Research*, 29(8):1038–1052, 2010.

[31] P. Tsiotras and R. S. Diaz. Real-time near-optimal feedback control of aggressive vehicle maneuvers. In *Optimization and Optimal Control in Automotive Systems*, pages 109–129. Springer, 2014.

[32] A. Weber and G. Reissig. Classical and strong convexity of sublevel sets and application to attainable sets of nonlinear systems. *SIAM Journal on Control and Optimization*, 52(5):2857–2876, 2014.

[33] E. M. Wolff, U. Topcu, and R. M. Murray. Automaton-guided controller synthesis for nonlinear systems with temporal logic. In *Proc. of the International Conference on Intelligent Robots and Systems*, pages 4332–4339, 2013.

[34] M. Zamani, G. Pola, M. Mazo Jr., and P. Tabuada. Symbolic models for nonlinear control systems without stability assumptions. *IEEE Transactions on Automatic Control*, 57(7):1804–1809, 2012.

Scheduling of Embedded Controllers Under Timing Contracts *

Mohammad Al Khatib
L2S, CNRS
CentraleSupélec
Université Paris-Sud
Université Paris-Saclay
F-91192 Gif-sur-Yvette
mohammad.alkhatib
@l2s.centralesupelec.fr

Antoine Girard
L2S, CNRS
CentraleSupélec
Université Paris-Sud
Université Paris-Saclay
F-91192 Gif-sur-Yvette
antoine.girard
@l2s.centralesupelec.fr

Thao Dang
Verimag, CNRS
Université Grenoble Alpes
F-38000 Grenoble
thao.dang@imag.fr

ABSTRACT

Timing contracts for embedded controller implementation specify the constraints on the time instants at which certain operations are performed such as sampling, actuation, computation, etc. Several previous works have focused on stability analysis of embedded control systems under such timing contracts. In this paper, we consider the scheduling of embedded controllers on a shared computational platform. Given a set of controllers, each of which is subject to a timing contract, we synthesize a dynamic scheduling policy, which guarantees that each timing contract is satisfied and that the shared computational resource is allocated to at most one embedded controller at any time. The approach is based on a timed game formulation whose solution provides a suitable scheduling policy. In the second part of the paper, we consider the problem of synthesizing a set of timing contracts that guarantee at the same time the schedulability and the stability of the embedded controllers.

Keywords

Embedded control; Sampled-data systems; Scheduling; Timed automata; Stability

1. INTRODUCTION

Cyber-physical systems (CPS) consisting of integration of computing devices with physical processes are to become ubiquitous in modern societies (autonomous vehicles, smart buildings, robots, etc.) and will practically impact the life of citizens in all their aspects (housing, transportation, health, industry, assistance to the elderly, etc.). Therefore, high-confidence tools for the analysis and design of CPS, being able to cope with the tight interactions between cyber and physical components are urgently needed.

Design of complex CPS can be tackled by decomposing the global design problem into smaller sub-problems. This approach can be formally implemented using *contract based design* [36, 10, 9]. For instance, for embedded controller implementation, [19] proposed the use of timing contracts, which specify the constraints on the time instants at which certain operations are performed such as sampling, actuation or computation. Under such contracts, the control engineers are responsible for designing a control law that is robust to all possible timing variation specified in the contract while the software engineers can focus on implementing the proposed control law so as to satisfy the timing contract. Several previous works have taken the point of view of control engineers, by developing techniques for robust stability analysis of embedded control systems under such timing contracts (see e.g. [15, 20, 7, 2]).

In the first part of this paper, we adopt the point of view of the software engineer who has to implement several controllers, each subject to a timing contract, on a shared computational platform. Given best and worst case execution times for each control task, we synthesize a dynamic scheduling policy, which guarantees that each timing contract is satisfied and that the shared computational resource is allocated to at most one controller at any time. Our approach is based on the use of timed game automata [33, 13] and we show that the scheduling problem can be formulated as a timed safety game, which can be solved by the tool UPPAAL-TIGA [8], and whose solution provides a suitable scheduling policy.

In the second part of the paper, we address the requirement engineering problem, which consists in synthesizing a set of timing contracts that guarantee at the same time the schedulability and the stability of the embedded controllers. We use a re-parametrization of contracts, which provides some monotonicity property to the problem and allows us to develop an effective synthesis method based on guided sampling of the timing contract parameter space.

The paper is organized as follows. The problem setting is given in Section 2, where we introduce the considered classes of systems and timing contracts and where we formulate the

*This work was supported by the Agence Nationale de la Recherche (COMPACS project ANR-13-BS03-0004) and by the Labex DigiCosme, Université Paris-Saclay (CODECSYS project).

HSCC'17, April 18-20, 2017, Pittsburgh, PA, USA
© 2017 ACM. ISBN 978-1-4503-4590-3/17/04...$15.00
DOI: http://dx.doi.org/10.1145/3049797.3049816

stability verification, schedulability verification and timing contract synthesis problems. Section 3 provides a solution to the schedulability verification problem based on timed games. Then, the timing contract synthesis problem is addressed in Section 4. Section 5 shows an application of our approach using an illustrative example.

Notations. Let $\mathbb{R}$, $\mathbb{R}_0^+$, $\mathbb{R}^+$, $\mathbb{R}_0^-$, $\mathbb{R}^-$, $\mathbb{N}$, $\mathbb{N}^+$ denote the sets of reals, non-negative reals, positive reals, non-positive reals, negative reals, non-negative integers and positive integers, respectively. For $I \subseteq \mathbb{R}_0^+$, let $\mathbb{N}_I = \mathbb{N} \cap I$. Given a vector $p \in \mathbb{R}^n$, its i-th element is denoted by p_i. Given two vectors $p, p' \in \mathbb{R}^n$, the inequality $p \leq p'$ is interpreted componentwise. For a set S, we denote the set of all subsets of S by 2^S.

2. PROBLEM FORMULATION

2.1 Sampled-data systems

In this work, we consider sampled-data systems that take into account the sequences of sampling and actuation instants $(t_k^s)_{k\in\mathbb{N}}$ and $(t_k^a)_{k\in\mathbb{N}}$:

$$\dot{x}(t) = Ax(t) + Bu(t), \quad \forall t \in \mathbb{R}_0^+ \tag{1}$$

$$u(t) = Kx(t_k^s), \quad t_k^a < t \leq t_{k+1}^a \tag{2}$$

where $x(t) \in \mathbb{R}^n$ is the state of the system, $u(t) \in \mathbb{R}^m$ is the control input, the matrices $A \in \mathbb{R}^{n\times n}$, $B \in \mathbb{R}^{n\times m}$, $K \in \mathbb{R}^{m\times n}$ and $k \in \mathbb{N}$. In addition, it is assumed that for all $t \in [0, t_0^a]$, $u(t) = 0$.

We assume that the sequence of sampling and actuation instants (t_k^s) and (t_k^a) satisfy a *timing contract* $\theta(\underline{\tau}, \overline{\tau}, \underline{h}, \overline{h})$ given by

$$\begin{array}{ll} 0 \leq t_0^s, & \\ t_k^s \leq t_k^a \leq t_{k+1}^s, & \forall k \in \mathbb{N} \\ \tau_k = t_k^a - t_k^s \in [\underline{\tau}, \overline{\tau}], & \forall k \in \mathbb{N} \\ h_k = t_{k+1}^s - t_k^s \in [\underline{h}, \overline{h}], & \forall k \in \mathbb{N} \end{array} \tag{3}$$

where $\underline{\tau} \in \mathbb{R}_0^+$, $\overline{\tau} \in \mathbb{R}_0^+$, $\underline{h} \in \mathbb{R}^+$ and $\overline{h} \in \mathbb{R}^+$ provide bounds on the sampling-to-actuation delays (which includes time for computation of the control law) and sampling periods provided that $t_k^s \leq t_k^a \leq t_{k+1}^s$ for all $k \in \mathbb{N}$. Note that we impose $\underline{h} \neq 0$ to prevent Zeno behavior. Moreover, these parameters must belong to the following set so that the time intervals given in (3) are always non-empty and it is always possible to choose $t_{k+1}^s \geq t_k^a$:

$$\mathcal{C} = \left\{(\underline{\tau}, \overline{\tau}, \underline{h}, \overline{h}) \in \mathbb{R}_0^+ \times \mathbb{R}_0^+ \times \mathbb{R}^+ \times \mathbb{R}^+ : \underline{\tau} \leq \overline{\tau} \leq \overline{h}, \underline{h} \leq \overline{h}\right\}.$$

2.2 Stability verification

We consider the notion of stability in the following sense:

Definition 1. The system $\mathcal{S} = (A, B, K)$ is *globally uniformly exponentially stable* (GUES) under timing contract $\theta(\underline{\tau}, \overline{\tau}, \underline{h}, \overline{h})$ if there exist $\lambda \in \mathbb{R}^+$ and $C \in \mathbb{R}^+$ such that, for all sequences $(t_k^s)_{k\in\mathbb{N}}$ and $(t_k^a)_{k\in\mathbb{N}}$ verifying (3), the solutions of (1-2) verify

$$\|x(t)\| \leq Ce^{-\lambda(t-t_0^s)} \|x(t_0^s)\|, \ \forall t \geq t_0^s.$$

We then define the stability verification problem as follows:

PROBLEM 1 (STABILITY VERIFICATION). *Given a system $\mathcal{S} = (A, B, K)$ and a timing contract $\theta(\underline{\tau}, \overline{\tau}, \underline{h}, \overline{h})$ verify that $\mathcal{S}$ is GUES under timing contract $\theta(\underline{\tau}, \overline{\tau}, \underline{h}, \overline{h})$.*

Several approaches are presented in the literature to solve instances of Problem 1. A non-exhaustive list is given in Table 1. From the modeling perspective, the problem can be tackled using difference inclusions, time-delay systems or hybrid systems. On the computational side, the approaches are based on semi-definite programming (Linear Matrix Inequalities (LMI) or Sum Of Squares (SOS) formulations), invariant sets or reachability analysis. Let us remark that approaches [15, 20, 7, 2] appear to be able to address all instances of Problem 1.

2.3 Scheduling

We consider a collection of $N \in \mathbb{N}^+$ sampled-data systems $\{\mathcal{S}_1, \dots, \mathcal{S}_N\}$ of the form (1-2) where each system $\mathcal{S}_i = (A_i, B_i, K_i)$, is subject to a timing contract $\theta(\underline{\tau}^i, \overline{\tau}^i, \underline{h}^i, \overline{h}^i)$ of the form (3), with parameters $(\underline{\tau}^i, \overline{\tau}^i, \underline{h}^i, \overline{h}^i) \in \mathcal{C}$, $i \in \mathbb{N}_{[1,N]}$.

In addition, we assume that these systems share a single processor to compute the value of their control inputs given by (2). The time required to compute these inputs is assumed to belong to some known interval $[\underline{c}^i, \overline{c}^i]$, with $0 \leq \underline{c}^i \leq \overline{c}^i$, where $\underline{c}^i$ and $\overline{c}^i$ denote the best and worst case execution time to compute the input of systems $\mathcal{S}_i$, $i \in \mathbb{N}_{[1,N]}$.

The timing of events in the k-th control cycle of system $\mathcal{S}_i$ starts at instant $t_k^{s_i}$ when sampling occurs. Then, system $\mathcal{S}_i$ gains access to the computational resource at instant $t_k^{b_i}$, at which computation of the control input value begins. The computational resource is released at instant $t_k^{e_i}$, at which computation of the control input value ends. After that, actuation occurs at instant $t_k^{a_i}$. Formally, the sequences $(t_k^{s_i})_{k\in\mathbb{N}}$, $(t_k^{b_i})_{k\in\mathbb{N}}$, $(t_k^{e_i})_{k\in\mathbb{N}}$, and $(t_k^{a_i})_{k\in\mathbb{N}}$ satisfy the following constraints for all $i \in \mathbb{N}_{[1,N]}$:

$$\begin{array}{ll} 0 \leq t_0^{s_i} & \\ t_k^{s_i} \leq t_k^{b_i} \leq t_k^{e_i} \leq t_k^{a_i} \leq t_{k+1}^{s_i}, & \forall k \in \mathbb{N} \\ c_k^i = t_k^{e_i} - t_k^{b_i} \in [\underline{c}^i, \overline{c}^i], & \forall k \in \mathbb{N} \\ \tau_k^i = t_k^{a_i} - t_k^{s_i} \in [\underline{\tau}^i, \overline{\tau}^i], & \forall k \in \mathbb{N} \\ h_k^i = t_{k+1}^{s_i} - t_k^{s_i} \in [\underline{h}^i, \overline{h}^i], & \forall k \in \mathbb{N} \end{array} \tag{4}$$

In addition, a conflict arises if several systems request access to the computational resource at the same time. Let us define the following property, for $i \in \mathbb{N}_{[1,N]}$:

$$\mathsf{Com}(\mathcal{S}_i, t) \equiv \bigvee_{k\in\mathbb{N}} \left(t \in [t_k^{b_i}, t_k^{e_i})\right).$$

$\mathsf{Com}(\mathcal{S}_i, t)$ is true if and only if the computational resource is used by system $\mathcal{S}_i$ at time t. Then, in order to prevent conflicting accesses to the computational resource the following property must hold:

$$\begin{array}{c} \forall t \in \mathbb{R}_0^+, \forall (i,j) \in \mathbb{N}_{[1,N]}^2 \text{ with } i \neq j, \\ \mathsf{Com}(\mathcal{S}_i, t) \wedge \mathsf{Com}(\mathcal{S}_j, t) \equiv \mathsf{False}. \end{array} \tag{5}$$

REMARK 1. *It is straightforward to verify that for any sequences $(t_k^{s_i})_{k\in\mathbb{N}}$, $(t_k^{b_i})_{k\in\mathbb{N}}$, $(t_k^{e_i})_{k\in\mathbb{N}}$, and $(t_k^{a_i})_{k\in\mathbb{N}}$ satisfying (4-5), the sequences $(t_k^{s_i})_{k\in\mathbb{N}}$ and $(t_k^{a_i})_{k\in\mathbb{N}}$ satisfy the timing contract $\theta(\underline{\tau}^i, \overline{\tau}^i, \underline{h}^i, \overline{h}^i)$.*

We aim at synthesizing a dynamic scheduling policy, generating sequences of timing events satisfying (4-5). The

Table 1: **Methods that can solve instances of Problem 1 with description of the modeling, computational approaches, and list of restrictions.**

	Models	Algorithm	Restrictions
[15]	difference inclusion	LMI	–
[20]		LMI	–
[26]		LMI	$\underline{\tau} = \overline{\tau} = 0$
[27]		LMI	$\underline{\tau} = \overline{\tau} = 0$
[37]		SOS	$\underline{\tau} = \overline{\tau} = 0$
[22]		Invariant sets	$\underline{\tau} = \overline{\tau} = 0$
[1]		Reachability analysis	$\underline{\tau} = \overline{\tau} = 0$
[2]		Reachability analysis	–
[30]	time-delay systems	LMI	$\underline{h} = 0$
[24]		LMI	$\underline{h} = \overline{h}$, $\underline{\tau} = 0$
[31]		LMI	$\underline{\tau} = \overline{\tau} = 0$
[23]		LMI	$\underline{h} = \underline{\tau} = \overline{\tau} = 0$
[7]	hybrid systems	SOS	–
[25]		LMI	$\underline{\tau} = 0$, $\underline{h} = 0$

scheduler has control over the sampling and actuation instants $(t_k^{s_i})_{k\in\mathbb{N}}$, $(t_k^{a_i})_{k\in\mathbb{N}}$ and over the instants $(t_k^{b_i})_{k\in\mathbb{N}}$ when computation begins. However, the execution time $(c_k^i)_{k\in\mathbb{N}}$ and thus the instants when computation ends $(t_k^{e_i})_{k\in\mathbb{N}}$ is determined by the environment and are thus uncontrollable from the point of view of the scheduler. Then, we consider the following schedulability property:

Definition 2. The set of control tasks $\mathcal{T} = \{(\underline{c}^1, \overline{c}^1), \ldots, (\underline{c}^N, \overline{c}^N)\}$ is *schedulable* under timing contracts $\Theta = \{\theta(\underline{\tau}^1, \overline{\tau}^1, \underline{h}^1, \overline{h}^1), \ldots, \theta(\underline{\tau}^N, \overline{\tau}^N, \underline{h}^N, \overline{h}^N)\}$, if for all sequences $(c_k^i)_{k\in\mathbb{N}}$ with $c_k^i \in [\underline{c}^i, \overline{c}^i]$, for all $k \in \mathbb{N}$ and $i \in \mathbb{N}_{[1,N]}$, there exist sequences $(t_k^{s_i})_{k\in\mathbb{N}}$, $(t_k^{b_i})_{k\in\mathbb{N}}$, $(t_k^{e_i})_{k\in\mathbb{N}}$, and $(t_k^{a_i})_{k\in\mathbb{N}}$ satisfying (4-5), for all $i \in \mathbb{N}_{[1,N]}$.

Then, we define the scheduling problem as follows:

Problem 2 (Schedulability verification). *Given a set of control tasks $\mathcal{T} = \{(\underline{c}^1, \overline{c}^1), \ldots, (\underline{c}^N, \overline{c}^N)\}$ and timing contracts $\Theta = \{\theta(\underline{\tau}^1, \overline{\tau}^1, \underline{h}^1, \overline{h}^1), \ldots, \theta(\underline{\tau}^N, \overline{\tau}^N, \underline{h}^N, \overline{h}^N)\}$, verify that $\mathcal{T}$ is schedulable under timing contracts Θ.*

In Section 3, we will provide a solution to the schedulability verification problem. In addition, our approach will allow us to synthesize a dynamic scheduling policy for generating the sequences $(t_k^{s_i})_{k\in\mathbb{N}}$, $(t_k^{b_i})_{k\in\mathbb{N}}$, $(t_k^{e_i})_{k\in\mathbb{N}}$, and $(t_k^{a_i})_{k\in\mathbb{N}}$ satisfying (4-5), for all $i \in \mathbb{N}_{[1,N]}$.

Related work. In real-time scheduling of multiple tasks on a single processor, the objective is to obtain a calculation model related to concurrent execution of a given number of tasks [14, 16, 12]. In case some of the tasks are control tasks, scheduling and controller co-design problems are studied for periodic [6, 34], event-triggered [38], and self-triggered [17, 28] real-time implementations of the controller. In the same context, [32, 5, 4, 35] synthesize schedules based on the worst case execution time of the computational resource. In such a case, stability is guaranteed for each control loop but the schedule is conservative as long as the worst case computational time is assumed at every period for each task. Unlike these approaches, we decouple the controller stability problem and the scheduling design, using timing contracts, in order to synthesize conflict-free schedules using timed game automata. In fact, scheduling with timed automata are examined in literature [18, 21, 28] where in [21] an application on a steel plant is studied.

The closest approach to our work is that depicted in [28] were the scheduling problem is reformulated in terms of timed game automata [13]. Although, therein the approach has the advantage of employing event-triggered controllers and eventually improves the resource utilization over the network, however it can only solve instances of our problem where $t_k^{s_i} = t_k^{b_i}$, $t_k^{e_i} = t_k^{a_i}$ and $\underline{\tau} = \overline{\tau} = \overline{c}^i = \underline{c}^i = c \in \mathbb{R}^+$ for all $k \in \mathbb{N}$ and $i \in \mathbb{N}_{[1,N]}$.

2.4 Timing contract synthesis

In Section 4, we will consider the problem of synthesizing a set of timing contracts that guarantee at the same time the stability of the systems and the schedulability of control tasks.

Given the bounds on the parameters $0 \le \tau_{min}^i \le \tau_{max}^i$, $0 < h_{min}^i \le h_{max}^i$, with $\tau_{min}^i \le h_{min}^i$, $\tau_{max}^i \le h_{max}^i$, let

$$\mathcal{D}_i = [\tau_{min}^i, \tau_{max}^i]^2 \times [h_{min}^i, h_{max}^i]^2, \quad i \in \mathbb{N}_{[1,N]}, \qquad (6)$$

with $N \in \mathbb{N}^+$, the timing contract synthesis problem is formalized as follows:

Problem 3 (Timing contract synthesis). *Given a collection of systems $\{\mathcal{S}_1, \ldots, \mathcal{S}_N\}$, where $\mathcal{S}_i = (A_i, B_i, K_i)$ with $A_i \in \mathbb{R}^{n_i \times n_i}$, $B_i \in \mathbb{R}^{n_i \times m_i}$, and $K_i \in \mathbb{R}^{m_i \times n_i}$, $i \in \mathbb{N}_{[1,N]}$, a set of control tasks $\mathcal{T} = \{(\underline{c}^1, \overline{c}^1), \ldots, (\underline{c}^N, \overline{c}^N)\}$ with $0 \le \underline{c}^i \le \overline{c}^i$, $i \in \mathbb{N}_{[1,N]}$, and parameter sets $\mathcal{D}_i$, $i \in \mathbb{N}_{[1,N]}$, synthesize a set $\mathcal{P}^* \subseteq (\mathcal{C}^N) \cap (\mathcal{D}_1 \times \cdots \times \mathcal{D}_N)$ such that for all $(\underline{\tau}^1, \overline{\tau}^1, \underline{h}^1, \overline{h}^1, \ldots, \underline{\tau}^N, \overline{\tau}^N, \underline{h}^N, \overline{h}^N) \in \mathcal{P}^*$:*

1. *System $\mathcal{S}_i = (A_i, B_i, K_i)$ is GUES under timing contract $\theta(\underline{\tau}_i, \overline{\tau}_i, \underline{h}_i, \overline{h}_i)$, for all $i \in \mathbb{N}_{[1,N]}$.*
2. *The set of control tasks $\mathcal{T} = \{(\underline{c}^1, \overline{c}^1), \ldots, (\underline{c}^N, \overline{c}^N)\}$ is schedulable under timing contracts $\Theta = \{\theta(\underline{\tau}^1, \overline{\tau}^1, \underline{h}^1, \overline{h}^1), \ldots, \theta(\underline{\tau}^N, \overline{\tau}^N, \underline{h}^N, \overline{h}^N)\}$.*

3. SCHEDULING

In this section, we provide a solution to Problem 2. Our approach is based on timed automata [3] and timed game automata [33], which we briefly introduce in the following.

3.1 Timed and timed game automata

Let C be a finite set of real-valued variables called clocks. We denote by $\mathcal{B}(C)$ the set of conjunctions of clock constraints of the form $c \sim \alpha$ where $\alpha \in \mathbb{R}_0^+$, $c \in C$ and $\sim \in \{<, \leq, =, >, \geq\}$. We define a timed automaton (TA) and a timed game automaton (TGA) as in [13]:

Definition 3. A *timed automaton* is a sextuple (L, l_0, Act, C, E, I) where

- L is a finite set of locations;
- $l_0 \in L$ is the initial location;
- Act is a set of actions;
- C is a finite set of real-valued clocks;
- $E \subseteq L \times \mathcal{B}(C) \times Act \times 2^C \times L$ is the set of edges;
- $Inv : L \to \mathcal{B}(C)$ is a function that assigns invariants to locations.

Definition 4. A *timed game automaton* is a septuple $(L, l_0, Act_c, Act_u, C, E, I)$ such that $(L, l_0, Act_c \cup Act_u, C, E, I)$ is a timed automaton and $Act_c \cap Act_u = \emptyset$, where Act_c defines a set of controllable actions and Act_u defines a set of uncontrollable actions.

Formal semantics of TA and TGA are given in [13]. Informally, semantics of a TA is described by a transition system whose state consists of the current location and value of the clocks. Then, the execution of a TA can be described by two types of transitions defined as follows:

- time progress: the current location $l \in L$ is maintained and the value of the clocks grow at unitary rate; these transitions are enabled as long as the value of the clocks satisfies $Inv(l)$.
- discrete transition: an instantaneous transition from the current location $l \in L$ to a new location $l' \in L$ labelled by an action $a \in Act$ is triggered; these transitions are enabled if there is an edge $(l, G, a, C', l') \in E$, such that the value of the clocks satisfies G; in that case, the value of the clocks belonging to C' resets to zero.

The semantics of TGA is similar to that of TA with the specificity that discrete transitions labelled by a controllable action (i.e. $a \in Act_c$) are triggered by a controller, while discrete transitions labelled by an uncontrollable action (i.e. $a \in Act_u$) are triggered by the environment/opponent.

In the following, we consider *safety games* (see e.g. [13]) defined by a set of unsafe locations $L_u \subseteq L$. A solution to the safety game is given by a winning strategy for the controller such that under any behavior of the environment/opponent, the set of unsafe locations is avoided by all executions of the TGA.

3.2 Scheduling using TGA

In this section, we propose a solution to Problem 2 based on a reformulation using timed game automata.

Definition 5. Let $i \in \mathbb{N}_{[1,N]}$, the timed game automaton generated by control task $(\underline{c}^i, \overline{c}^i)$ and timing contract $\theta(\underline{\tau}^i, \overline{\tau}^i, \underline{h}^i, \overline{h}^i)$ is displayed in Figure 1 and is formally defined by $\mathsf{TGA}_i = (L^i, l_0^i, Act_c^i, Act_u^i, C^i, E^i, Inv^i)$ where

- $L^i = \{Init^i, Presam^i, Precomp^i, Comp^i, Preac^i\}$;
- $l_0^i = Init^i$;
- $Act_c^i = \{sample^i, begin^i, actuate^i\}$;
- $Act_u^i = \{end^i, in^i\}$;
- $C^i = \{c^i, k^i\}$;
- $E^i = \{(Init^i, c^i \geq 0, in^i, \{c^i\}, Presam^i),$ $(Presam^i, c^i \geq \underline{h}^i, sample^i, \{c^i\}, Precomp^i),$ $(Precomp^i, c^i \geq 0, begin^i, \{k^i\}, Comp^i),$ $(Comp^i, k^i \geq \underline{c}^i, end^i, \emptyset, Preac^i),$ $(Preac^i, c^i \geq \underline{\tau}^i, actuate^i, \emptyset, Presam^i)\}$;
- $Inv^i(Init^i) = \{c^i \geq 0\}$, $Inv^i(Presam^i) = \{c^i \leq \overline{h}^i\}$, $Inv^i(Precomp^i) = \{c^i \leq \overline{\tau}^i - \overline{c}^i\}$, $Inv^i(Comp^i) = \{k^i \leq \overline{c}^i\}$, $Inv^i(Preac^i) = \{c^i \leq \overline{\tau}^i\}$.

Let the sequences $(t_k^{s_i})$, $(t_k^{a_i})$, $(t_k^{b_i})$ and $(t_k^{e_i})$ be given by the instants of the discrete transitions labelled by actions $sample^i$, $actuate^i$, $begin^i$ and end^i, respectively. It is easy to see that these sequences satisfy the constraints given by (4). Conversely, one can check that all sequences satisfying (4) can be generated by executions of TGA_i.

Moreover, let us remark that the controllable actions are $sample^i$, $actuate^i$, $begin^i$ which means that the controller determines the instants when sampling and actuation occur and when computation begins. However, end^i is uncontrollable, which means that the execution time, and thus the instant at which computation ends is determined by the environment. This is consistent with the problem formulation in Section 2.

Finally, the computational resource is used by system $\mathcal{S}_i$ if the current location of TGA_i is $Comp^i$. To take into account the constraint given by (5), stating that two systems cannot access the computational resource at the same time, we need to define the composition of the timed game automata defined above:

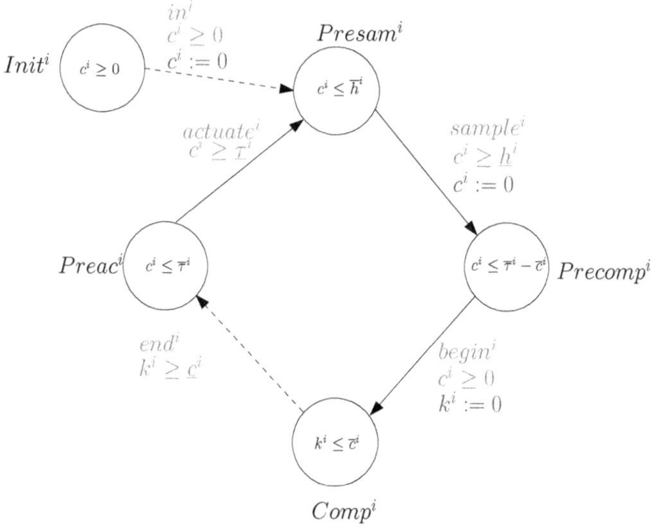

Figure 1: TGA^i where plain edges correspond to controllable actions while dashed edges correspond to uncontrollable actions.

Definition 6. The timed game automaton generated by the set of control tasks $\mathcal{T} = \{(\underline{c}^1, \overline{c}^1), \ldots, (\underline{c}^N, \overline{c}^N)\}$ and timing contracts $\Theta = \{\theta(\underline{\tau}^1, \overline{\tau}^1, \underline{h}^1, \overline{h}^1), \ldots, \theta(\underline{\tau}^N, \overline{\tau}^N, \underline{h}^N, \overline{h}^N)\}$ is given by $\mathsf{TGA} = (\overline{L}, \overline{l}_0, \overline{Act}_c, \overline{Act}_u, \overline{C}, \overline{E}, \overline{Inv})$ where

- $\overline{L} = L^1 \times \cdots \times L^N$, thus $l = (l^1, \ldots, l^N) \in L$ denotes the location of TGA;
- $\overline{l}_0 = (Init^1, \ldots, Init^N)$;
- $\overline{Act}_c = \bigcup_{i=1}^N Act_c^i$;
- $\overline{Act}_u = \bigcup_{i=1}^N Act_u^i$;
- $\overline{C} = \bigcup_{i=1}^N C^i$;
- $\overline{E} = \{(l_m, \lambda, act, C', l_n) \in \overline{L} \times \mathcal{B}(\overline{C}) \times (\overline{Act}_c \cup \overline{Act}_u) \times \overline{L} : \exists i \in \mathbb{N}_{[1,N]}, l_m^j = l_n^j \ \ \forall j \neq i \text{ and } (l_m^i, \lambda, act, C', l_n^i) \in E^i\}$;
- $Inv(l) = \bigwedge_{i=1}^N Inv^i(l^i)$, $i \in \mathbb{N}_{[1,N]}$.

TGA describes the parallel evolution of the $\mathsf{TGA}_1, \ldots, \mathsf{TGA}_N$. Then, the set of locations corresponding to conflicting accesses to the computational resources is $\overline{L}_u \subseteq \overline{L}$ defined by:

$$\overline{L}_u = \{l \in \overline{L} : \exists (i,j) \in \mathbb{N}_{[1,N]}^2, i \neq j, \quad (l^i = Comp^i) \wedge (l^j = Comp^j)\}. \tag{7}$$

From the previous discussions, it follows that $\mathcal{T}$ is *schedulable* under timing contracts Θ if there is a winning strategy to the safety game defined by the timed game automaton TGA and the set of unsafe locations $\overline{L}_u$. From the practical point of view, the safety game can be solved using the tool UPPAAL-TIGA [8]. The tool synthesizes a winning strategy when it exists, which provides us with a dynamic scheduling policy for generating the sequences $(t_k^{s_i})_{k \in \mathbb{N}}$, $(t_k^{b_i})_{k \in \mathbb{N}}$, $(t_k^{e_i})_{k \in \mathbb{N}}$, and $(t_k^{a_i})_{k \in \mathbb{N}}$ satisfying (4-5), for all $i \in \mathbb{N}_{[1,N]}$.

4. TIMING CONTRACT SYNTHESIS

In this section, we propose a solution to Problem 3. Given a collection of systems $\{\mathcal{S}_1, \ldots, \mathcal{S}_N\}$, a set of control tasks $\mathcal{T} = \{(\underline{c}^1, \overline{c}^1), \ldots, (\underline{c}^N, \overline{c}^N)\}$ with $0 \leq \underline{c}^i \leq \overline{c}^i$, $i \in \mathbb{N}_{[1,N]}$, and parameter sets $\mathcal{D}_1, \ldots, \mathcal{D}_N$, we use a previous result [2] and a monotonicity property to design an algorithm that synthesizes a set of timing contracts ensuring stability of each system $\mathcal{S}_i$ and schedulability of $\mathcal{T}$. The workflow of the proposed approach is depicted in Figure 2. The problem is divided into two parts. First, we synthesize timing contract giving a guarantee on stability for every system $\mathcal{S}_i$, $i \in \mathbb{N}_{[1,N]}$, where a set $\mathcal{P}_{st}$ is synthesized as explained in Section 4.1. Also in this part, when it is necessary we could use any method from Section 2.2 for checking stability. In the second part, we follow the steps illustrated in Section 4.2 to synthesize a set $\underline{\mathcal{P}}'$ giving a guarantee on schedulability. Notice that the method proposed in Section 3 is used for checking schedulability of control tasks. As a consequence, a solution to Problem 3 is given by $\mathcal{P}^*$.

4.1 Guarantee on stability

For $i \in \mathbb{N}_{[1,N]}$, we consider each of the systems $\mathcal{S}_i = (A_i, B_i, K_i)$ and the set $\mathcal{D}_i$ given by (9), $i \in \mathbb{N}_{[1,N]}$. We use Algorithm 2 in [2] to synthesize a set $\mathcal{C}_i^* \subseteq \mathcal{C} \cap \mathcal{D}_i$ such

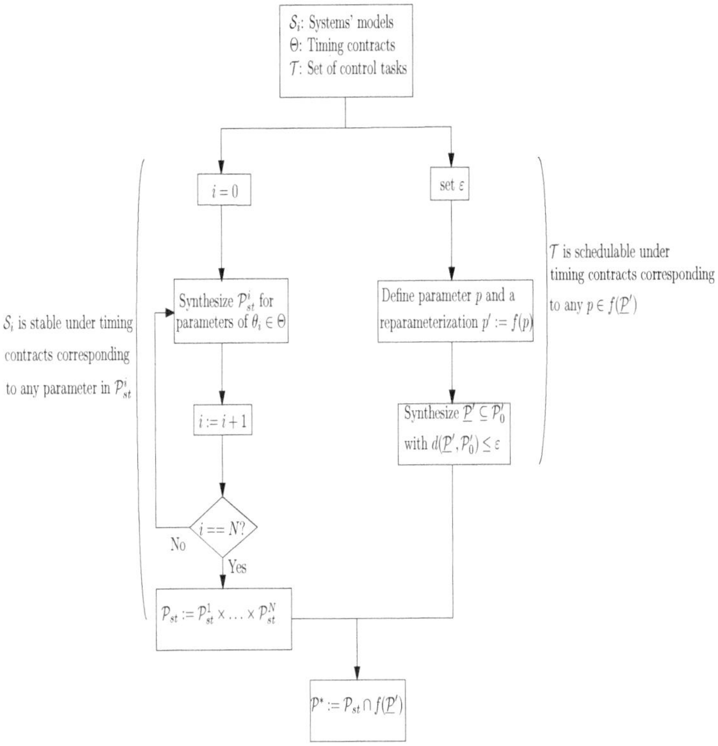

Figure 2: Workflow of the proposed approach.

that for all $(\underline{\tau}^i, \overline{\tau}^i, \underline{h}^i, \overline{h}^i) \in \mathcal{C}_i^*$, $\mathcal{S}_i$ is GUES under timing contract $\theta(\underline{\tau}_i, \overline{\tau}_i, \underline{h}_i, \overline{h}_i)$.

Then, defining the set $\mathcal{P}_{st} = \mathcal{C}_1^* \times \cdots \times \mathcal{C}_N^*$, it follows that for all $(\underline{\tau}^1, \overline{\tau}^1, \underline{h}^1, \overline{h}^1, \ldots, \underline{\tau}^N, \overline{\tau}^N, \underline{h}^N, \overline{h}^N) \in \mathcal{P}_{st}$, system $\mathcal{S}_i = (A_i, B_i, K_i)$ is GUES under timing contract $\theta(\underline{\tau}_i, \overline{\tau}_i, \underline{h}_i, \overline{h}_i)$, for all $i \in \mathbb{N}_{[1,N]}$.

4.2 Guarantee on schedulability

In this section, given the set $\mathcal{P}_{st}$, defined in the previous section, we solve Problem 3 by synthesizing a set $\mathcal{P}^* \subseteq \mathcal{P}_{st}$ such that for all $(\underline{\tau}^1, \overline{\tau}^1, \underline{h}^1, \overline{h}^1, \ldots, \underline{\tau}^N, \overline{\tau}^N, \underline{h}^N, \overline{h}^N) \in \mathcal{P}^*$, the set of control tasks $\mathcal{T}$ is schedulable under timing contracts $\Theta = \{\theta(\underline{\tau}^1, \overline{\tau}^1, \underline{h}^1, \overline{h}^1), \ldots, \theta(\underline{\tau}^N, \overline{\tau}^N, \underline{h}^N, \overline{h}^N)\}$.

The timing contract parameters are given by the vector $p = (\underline{\tau}^1, \overline{\tau}^1, \underline{h}^1, \overline{h}^1, \ldots, \underline{\tau}^N, \overline{\tau}^N, \underline{h}^N, \overline{h}^N)$. We then define the following Boolean function for $p \in \mathcal{C}^N \cap (\mathcal{D}_1 \times \cdots \times \mathcal{D}_N)$:

$$\mathsf{Sched}(p) \equiv \mathcal{T} \text{ is } \textit{schedulable} \text{ under timing contracts } \Theta.$$

In order to solve Problem 3 we need to compute (a subset of) the set $\mathcal{P}_0$ defined by

$$\mathcal{P}_0 = \{p \in \mathcal{C}^N \cap (\mathcal{D}_1 \times \cdots \times \mathcal{D}_N) : \mathsf{Sched}(p)\}.$$

Re-parametrization

We define a new parameter $p' \in \mathcal{D}_1' \times \cdots \times \mathcal{D}_N'$ with

$$\mathcal{D}_i' = [\tau_{min}^i, \tau_{max}^i] \times [-\tau_{max}^i, -\tau_{min}^i] \times [h_{min}^i, h_{max}^i] \times [-h_{max}^i, -h_{min}^i], \ \ i \in \mathbb{N}_{[1,N]}, \tag{8}$$

such that $p' = (\beta_1^1, \beta_2^1, \beta_3^1, \beta_4^1, \ldots, \beta_1^N, \beta_2^N, \beta_3^N, \beta_4^N)$. We further define the map $f : (\mathcal{D}_1' \times \cdots \times \mathcal{D}_N') \to (\mathcal{D}_1 \times \cdots \times \mathcal{D}_N)$

such that $f(p') = p = (\underline{\tau}^1, \overline{\tau}^1, \underline{h}^1, \overline{h}^1, \dots, \underline{\tau}^N, \overline{\tau}^N, \underline{h}^N, \overline{h}^N)$, where for all $i \in \mathbb{N}_{[1,N]}$

$$\underline{\tau}^i = \beta_1^i,\ \overline{\tau}^i = \min(-\beta_2^i, -\beta_4^i),\ \underline{h}^i = \beta_3^i,\ \overline{h}^i = -\beta_4^i.$$

We associate to the parameter p' a constraint set $(\mathcal{C}')^N$ where

$$\mathcal{C}' = \left\{ \beta \in \mathbb{R}_0^+ \times \mathbb{R}_0^- \times \mathbb{R}^+ \times \mathbb{R}^- : \begin{array}{c} \beta_1 \leq \min(-\beta_2, -\beta_4) \\ \beta_3 \leq -\beta_4 \end{array} \right\}.$$

Last we define the set $\mathcal{P}'_o$ by :

$$\mathcal{P}'_o = \left\{ p' \in \mathcal{D}'_1 \times \dots \times \mathcal{D}'_N : ((p' \in (\mathcal{C}')^N) \wedge \mathsf{Sched}(f(p'))) \right\}.$$

One can check that the following relation holds:

$$\mathcal{P}_o = f(\mathcal{P}'_o). \tag{9}$$

We can then show that $\mathcal{P}'_o$ satisfies the following monotonicity property:

Proposition 1. *For all $p'_1, p'_2 \in \mathcal{D}'_1 \times \dots \times \mathcal{D}'_N$, the following implications hold:*

$$((p'_2 \leq p'_1) \wedge (p'_1 \in \mathcal{P}'_o)) \implies p'_2 \in \mathcal{P}'_o.$$

$$((p'_2 \leq p'_1) \wedge (p'_2 \notin \mathcal{P}'_o)) \implies p'_1 \notin \mathcal{P}'_o.$$

Proof. Let $p'_1 = (\beta_1^1, \beta_2^1, \beta_3^1, \beta_4^1, \dots, \beta_1^N, \beta_2^N, \beta_3^N, \beta_4^N)$ and $p'_2 = (\alpha_1^1, \alpha_2^1, \alpha_3^1, \alpha_4^1, \dots, \alpha_1^N, \alpha_2^N, \alpha_3^N, \alpha_4^N)$. We assume $p'_2 \leq p'_1$ and $p'_1 \in \mathcal{P}'_o$. Then $p'_1 \in (\mathcal{C}')^N$ which implies $\alpha_1^i \leq \beta_1^i \leq -\beta_2^i \leq \alpha_2^i$, $\alpha_1^i \leq \beta_1^i \leq -\beta_4^i \leq -\alpha_4^i$, and $\alpha_3^i \leq \beta_3^i \leq -\beta_4^i \leq -\alpha_4^i$ for all $i \in \mathbb{N}_{[1,N]}$. Thus $p'_2 \in (\mathcal{C}')^N$. We also have $\mathsf{Sched}(f(p'_1))$. In this case, $p_1 = f(p'_1) = (\underline{\tau}_1^1, \overline{\tau}_1^1, \underline{h}_1^1, \overline{h}_1^1, \dots, \underline{\tau}_1^N, \overline{\tau}_1^N, \underline{h}_1^N, \overline{h}_1^N)$ and $p_2 = f(p'_2) = (\underline{\tau}_2^1, \overline{\tau}_2^1, \underline{h}_2^1, \overline{h}_2^1, \dots, \underline{\tau}_2^N, \overline{\tau}_2^N, \underline{h}_2^N, \overline{h}_2^N)$ satisfy $p_1 \in \mathcal{C}^N$, $p_2 \in \mathcal{C}^N$ and for all $i \in \mathbb{N}_{[1,N]}$

$$\underline{\tau}_2^i \leq \underline{\tau}_1^i,\ \overline{\tau}_2^i \geq \overline{\tau}_1^i,\ \underline{h}_2^i \leq \underline{h}_1^i,\ \overline{h}_2^i \geq \overline{h}_1^i. \tag{10}$$

It is easy to check that if $\mathcal{T}$ is schedulable under timing contracts $\Theta_1 = \{\theta(\underline{\tau}_1^1, \overline{\tau}_1^1, \underline{h}_1^1, \overline{h}_1^1), \dots, \theta(\underline{\tau}_1^N, \overline{\tau}_1^N, \underline{h}_1^N, \overline{h}_1^N)\}$ then $\mathcal{T}$ is schedulable under timing contracts $\Theta_2 = \{\theta(\underline{\tau}_2^1, \overline{\tau}_2^1, \underline{h}_2^1, \overline{h}_2^1), \dots, \theta(\underline{\tau}_2^N, \overline{\tau}_2^N, \underline{h}_2^N, \overline{h}_2^N)\}$ for all $p_2 \in \mathcal{C}$ satisfying (10). Thus, $\mathsf{Sched}(f(p'_2))$ holds and $p'_2 \in \mathcal{P}'_o$.

This proves the first implication. For the second implication, it is sufficient to check that

$$\begin{aligned} & ((p'_2 \leq p'_1) \wedge (p'_1 \in \mathcal{P}'_o)) \implies p'_2 \in \mathcal{P}'_o \\ \equiv\ & \neg(p'_2 \leq p'_1) \vee (p'_1 \notin \mathcal{P}'_o) \vee (p'_2 \in \mathcal{P}'_o) \\ \equiv\ & ((p'_2 \leq p'_1) \wedge (p'_2 \notin \mathcal{P}'_o)) \implies p'_1 \notin \mathcal{P}'_o. \end{aligned}$$

□

Now using Proposition 1 and the set $\mathcal{P}_{st}$ obtained in Section 4.1 we can sample the parameter space to solve Problem 3.

Theorem 1. *Let $\underline{p}^1, \dots, \underline{p}^{M_1} \in \mathcal{P}'_o$, and $\overline{p}^1, \dots, \overline{p}^{M_2} \in \mathcal{D}'_1 \times \dots \times \mathcal{D}'_N \setminus \mathcal{P}'_o$ and let*

$$\underline{\mathcal{P}}' = \bigcup_{j=1}^{M_1} \{p' \in \mathcal{D}'_1 \times \dots \times \mathcal{D}'_N : \underline{p}^j \geq p'\},$$

$$\overline{\mathcal{P}}' = (\mathcal{D}'_1 \times \dots \times \mathcal{D}'_N) \setminus \bigcup_{j=1}^{M_2} \{p' \in \mathcal{D}'_1 \times \dots \times \mathcal{D}'_N : p' \geq \overline{p}^j\}.$$

Then, $\underline{\mathcal{P}}' \subseteq \mathcal{P}'_o \subseteq \overline{\mathcal{P}}'$. Moreover, $\mathcal{P}^* = f(\underline{\mathcal{P}}') \cap \mathcal{P}_{st}$ is a solution to Problem 3

Proof. $\underline{\mathcal{P}}' \subseteq \mathcal{P}'_o \subseteq \overline{\mathcal{P}}'$ is a direct consequence of Proposition 1. Then, it follows that $\mathcal{P}^*$ is a solution to Problem 3. □

4.3 Algorithm for timing contract synthesis

Theorem 1 shows that it is possible to compute under and over-approximations of the set $\mathcal{P}'_o$ by sampling the parameter space $\mathcal{D}'_1 \times \dots \times \mathcal{D}'_N$. In this section, given the set $\mathcal{P}_{st}$ from Section 4.1, we use this property to design a synthesis algorithm. Similar algorithms have been used in [29, 39] for computing an approximation of the Pareto front of a monotone multi-criteria optimization problem. Indeed, this latter problem can be tackled by computing an under and over-approximation of a set satisfying a monotonicity property similar to that of Proposition 1.

Algorithm 1. *Timing contract synthesis*

function *TC_Synth*($\mathcal{T}$,$\{\mathcal{D}_1, \dots, \mathcal{D}_N\}$,$\mathcal{P}_{st}$)
input: $\mathcal{T}$, $\mathcal{D}_i = [\tau_{min}^i, \tau_{max}^i]^2 \times [h_{min}^i, h_{max}^i]^2, i \in \mathbb{N}_{[1,N]}$, $\mathcal{P}_{st} \subseteq \mathcal{C}^N \cap (\mathcal{D}_1 \times \dots \times \mathcal{D}_N)$,
output: $\mathcal{P}^* \subseteq \mathcal{C}^N \cap (\mathcal{D}_1 \times \dots \times \mathcal{D}_N)$
parameter: $\varepsilon \in \mathbb{R}^+$
1: ***if*** $p'_{max} \in \mathcal{P}'_o$ ***then***
2:     *return* $(\mathcal{D}_1 \times \dots \times \mathcal{D}_N) \cap \mathcal{P}_{st}$;
3: ***else*** $\overline{\mathcal{P}}' := (\mathcal{D}'_1 \times \dots \times \mathcal{D}'_N) \setminus \{p'_{max}\}$;
4: ***end if***
5: ***if*** $p'_{min} \notin \mathcal{P}'_o$ ***then***
6:     *return* $\emptyset$;
7: ***else*** $\underline{\mathcal{P}}' := \{p'_{min}\}$;
8: ***end if***
9: ***while*** $d(\underline{\mathcal{P}}', \overline{\mathcal{P}}') > \varepsilon$ ***do***   ▷ *main loop*
10:     *Pick* $p' \in \overline{\mathcal{P}}' \setminus \underline{\mathcal{P}}'$;   ▷ *select next sample*
11:     ***if*** $p' \in \mathcal{P}'_o$ ***then***
12:         $\underline{\mathcal{P}}' := \underline{\mathcal{P}}' \cup \{p'_* \in (\mathcal{D}'_1 \times \dots \times \mathcal{D}'_N) : p'_* \leq p'\}$;
13:     ***else*** $\overline{\mathcal{P}}' := \overline{\mathcal{P}}' \setminus \{p'_* \in (\mathcal{D}'_1 \times \dots \times \mathcal{D}'_N) : p' \leq p'_*\}$;
14:     ***end if***
15: ***end while***
16: *return* $f(\underline{\mathcal{P}}') \cap \mathcal{P}_{st}$;

Algorithm 1 computes an under-approximation $\underline{\mathcal{P}}'$ and an over-approximation $\overline{\mathcal{P}}'$ of the set $\mathcal{P}'_o$ by sampling iteratively the parameter space $\mathcal{D}'_1 \times \dots \times \mathcal{D}'_N$.

Lines 1 to 8 initialize these approximations by testing both the lower bound $p'_{min} = (\tau_{min}^1, -\tau_{max}^1, h_{min}^1, -h_{max}^1, \dots, \tau_{min}^N, -\tau_{max}^N, h_{min}^N, -h_{max}^N)$ and the upper bound $p'_{max} = (\tau_{max}^1, -\tau_{min}^1, h_{max}^1, -h_{min}^1, \dots, \tau_{max}^N, -\tau_{min}^N, h_{max}^N, -h_{min}^N)$ of the set $\mathcal{D}'_1 \times \dots \times \mathcal{D}'_N$. If $p'_{max} \in \mathcal{P}'_o$, then by Theorem 1, $f(\mathcal{D}'_1 \times \dots \times \mathcal{D}'_N) \cap \mathcal{P}_{st} = (\mathcal{D}_1 \times \dots \times \mathcal{D}_N) \cap \mathcal{P}_{st}$ is a solution to Problem 3. Note that in that case, all timing-contract parameters, $(\underline{\tau}_1^1, \overline{\tau}_1^1, \underline{h}_1^1, \overline{h}_1^1, \dots, \underline{\tau}_1^N, \overline{\tau}_1^N, \underline{h}_1^N, \overline{h}_1^N) \in \mathcal{D}_1 \times \dots \times \mathcal{D}_N$ guarantee the schedulability of $\mathcal{T}$ under timing contracts $\Theta = \{\theta(\underline{\tau}^1, \overline{\tau}^1, \underline{h}^1, \overline{h}^1), \dots, \theta(\underline{\tau}^N, \overline{\tau}^N, \underline{h}^N, \overline{h}^N)\}$. If $p_{max} \notin \mathcal{P}'_o$, then $(\mathcal{D}'_1 \times \dots \times \mathcal{D}'_N) \setminus \{p'_{max}\}$ is an over-approximation of $\mathcal{P}'_o$. Similarly, if $p'_{min} \notin \mathcal{P}'_o$, then by Theorem 1, $\mathcal{P}'_o = \emptyset$. Note that in that case, no timing-contracts can guarantee the schedulability of $\mathcal{T}$. If $p'_{min} \in \mathcal{P}'_o$, then $\{p'_{min}\}$ is an under-approximation of $\mathcal{P}'_o$.

Lines 9 to 14 describe the main loop of the timing contract synthesis algorithm. At any time of the execution, $\underline{\mathcal{P}}' \subseteq \mathcal{P}'_o \subseteq \overline{\mathcal{P}}'$ holds. We pick a sample $p' \in \overline{\mathcal{P}}' \setminus \underline{\mathcal{P}}'$

which is the unexplored parameter region lying in the over-approximation of $\mathcal{P}'_o$ but not in its under-approximation. If $p' \in \mathcal{P}'_o$ (or if $p' \notin \mathcal{P}'_o$), then we update the under-approximation $\underline{\mathcal{P}}'$ (or the over-approximation $\overline{\mathcal{P}}'$) according to Theorem 1. The algorithm stops when the Hausdorff distance between the $\underline{\mathcal{P}}'$ and $\overline{\mathcal{P}}'$ becomes smaller than ε. One rising issue is that the choice of the sample $p' \in \overline{\mathcal{P}}' \setminus \underline{\mathcal{P}}'$, at line 10, is crucial for the efficiency of the algorithm. In our implementation, we use the selection criteria proposed in [29] which consists in choosing the sample that will produce the fastest decrease of the Hausdorff distance $d(\underline{\mathcal{P}}', \overline{\mathcal{P}}')$. In [39] an alternative selection criteria based on multiscale grid exploration is proposed.

Finally, it is important to note that Algorithm 1 needs testing if the samples $p' \in \mathcal{P}'_o$, which requires checking the condition $\mathsf{Sched}(f(p'))$. In our implementation, this is done using the method proposed in Section 3, which assures us that the set $f(\underline{\mathcal{P}}')$ tends to $\mathcal{P}_0$ as $\varepsilon \to 0$, where $\mathcal{P}_0$ is the set of all solutions $(\underline{\tau}^1, \overline{\tau}^1, \underline{h}^1, \overline{h}^1, \dots, \underline{\tau}^N, \overline{\tau}^N, \underline{h}^N, \overline{h}^N)$ such that $\mathcal{T}$ is schedulable under timing contracts $\Theta = \{\theta(\underline{\tau}^1, \overline{\tau}^1, \underline{h}^1, \overline{h}^1), \dots, \theta(\underline{\tau}^N, \overline{\tau}^N, \underline{h}^N, \overline{h}^N)\}$.

5. ILLUSTRATIVE EXAMPLE

In this section, we verify the stability and the schedulability of two systems sharing a common computational resource under given timing contracts. Then, we show an application of the timing contract synthesis algorithm.

We implemented the scheduling approach presented in Section 3 in UPPAAL-TIGA [8] and Algorithm 1 in Matlab. All reported experiments are realized on a desktop with i7 4790 processor of frequency 3.6 GHz and a 8 GB RAM.

We consider two systems $\mathcal{S}_1 = (A_1, B_1, K_1)$ and $\mathcal{S}_2 = (A_2, B_2, K_2)$, taken from [11], given by the following matrices:

$$A_1 = \begin{pmatrix} 0 & 1 \\ 0 & -0.1 \end{pmatrix},\ B_1 = \begin{pmatrix} 0 \\ 0.1 \end{pmatrix},\ K_1 = \begin{pmatrix} -3.75 & -11.5 \end{pmatrix}. \tag{11}$$

$$A_2 = \begin{pmatrix} 0 & 1 \\ -2 & 0.1 \end{pmatrix},\ B_2 = \begin{pmatrix} 0 \\ 1 \end{pmatrix},\ K_2 = \begin{pmatrix} 1 & 0 \end{pmatrix}. \tag{12}$$

Furthermore, we set the best and worst case execution times for each task as $\underline{c}^1 = 0.12$, $\overline{c}^1 = 0.35$, $\underline{c}^2 = 0.04$, and $\overline{c}^2 = 0.12$.

5.1 Stability verification

Using Algorithm 1 in [2] we could verify that systems $\mathcal{S}_1$ and $\mathcal{S}_2$ are GUES under timing contracts $\theta(0.1, 0.35, 0.3, 0.85)$ and $\theta(0.2, 0.6, 0.8, 1.15)$ respectively. The computation times required for stability verification are 1.96 seconds and 1.5 seconds, respectively.

5.2 Scheduling

Now, we consider the set of control tasks $\mathcal{T} = \{(\underline{c}^1, \overline{c}^1), (\underline{c}^2, \overline{c}^2)\}$ and the same timing contracts $\Theta = \{\theta(0.1, 0.35, 0.3, 0.85), \theta(0.2, 0.6, 0.8, 1.15)\}$ as in the previous section.

In order to solve the scheduling problem, we associate to $\mathcal{T}$ the timed game automaton TGA as given in Definition 6. Following the approach in Section 3, we solve the safety game on TGA to find a strategy (if it exists) for the triggering of controllable actions that occur at $(t_k^{s_i})_{k\in\mathbb{N}}$, $(t_k^{b_i})_{k\in\mathbb{N}}$, and $(t_k^{a_i})_{k\in\mathbb{N}}$, with $i \in \mathbb{N}_{[1,2]}$, guaranteeing that the set of bad states L_u of the system, given by (13), is never reached regardless of when uncontrollable actions occurring at $(t_k^{e_i})_{k\in\mathbb{N}}$, $i \in \mathbb{N}_{[1,2]}$, are exactly taken.

Using UPPAAL-TIGA, we successfully prove that $\mathcal{T}$ is schedulable under timing contracts Θ, and thus a scheduling policy was found. The computation time required to solve the game was 1.37 seconds.

Figure 3 shows the timing of events resulting from this scheduling policy. The first and second plots show that the timing contracts $\theta(0.1, 0.35, 0.3, 0.85)$ and $\theta(0.2, 0.6, 0.8, 1.15)$ are respected for both systems $\mathcal{S}_1$ and $\mathcal{S}_2$ respectively. The third plot shows that only one of the two systems gains access to the shared processor at a time since it appears clearly that

$$\text{for all } t \in \mathbb{R}_0^+, \mathsf{Com}(\mathcal{S}_1, t) \wedge \mathsf{Com}(\mathcal{S}_2, t) \equiv \mathsf{False}.$$

One can notice that in the first three control cycles of $\mathcal{S}_2$, the beginning of the computation has to be delayed until the computational resource is released by $\mathcal{S}_1$.

Using this scheduling policy, Figure 4 shows results of simulating $\mathcal{S}_1$ and $\mathcal{S}_2$, when they share a single processor to compute the value of their control inputs, for the initial states $x_0^1 = \binom{2}{3}$ and $x_0^2 = \binom{2}{3}$ with $t_0^{s1} = 0.4$ and $t_0^{s2} = 0.9$. As shown, trajectories of both systems converge to zero and therefore the scheduling policy in this case guarantees the exponential stability of each system.

5.3 Timing contract synthesis

We now consider the timing contract synthesis problem for systems $\mathcal{S}_1$ and $\mathcal{S}_2$ and the set of control tasks $\mathcal{T} = \{(\underline{c}^1, \overline{c}^1), (\underline{c}^2, \overline{c}^2)\}$. We fix $\underline{\tau}^1 = 0.1$, $\underline{h}^1 = 0.3$, $\underline{\tau}^2 = 0.2$, and $\underline{h}^2 = 0.8$ and consider the following bounds on parameters $\mathcal{D}_1 = [0.1, 0.1] \times [0.1, 0.76] \times [0.3, 0.3] \times [0.3, 1.72]$ and $\mathcal{D}_2 = [0.2, 0.2] \times [0.2, 1.16] \times [0.8, 0.8] \times [0.8, 2.02]$.

Using Algorithm 2 in [2], we synthesize the set $\mathcal{P}_{st} = \mathcal{C}_1^* \times \mathcal{C}_2^* \subseteq \mathcal{C}^2 \cap (\mathcal{D}_1 \times \mathcal{D}_2)$ such that for all $(\underline{\tau}^1, \overline{\tau}^1, \underline{h}^1, \overline{h}^1, \underline{\tau}^2, \overline{\tau}^2, \underline{h}^2, \overline{h}^2) \in \mathcal{P}_{st}$, system $\mathcal{S}_i = (A_i, B_i, K_i)$ is GUES under timing contract $\theta(\underline{\tau}_i, \overline{\tau}_i, \underline{h}_i, \overline{h}_i)$, for all $i \in \mathbb{N}_{[1,2]}$. The sets $\mathcal{C}_1^*$ and $\mathcal{C}_2^*$, in the $(\overline{\tau}^1, \overline{h}^1)$ plane and $(\overline{\tau}^2, \overline{h}^2)$ plane respectively, are shown by Figure 5.

Then, we search for a set $\mathcal{P}^* \subseteq \mathcal{P}_{st}$ such that for all $(\underline{\tau}^1, \overline{\tau}^1, \underline{h}^1, \overline{h}^1, \underline{\tau}^2, \overline{\tau}^2, \underline{h}^2, \overline{h}^2) \in \mathcal{P}^*$, the set of control tasks $\mathcal{T}$ is schedulable under timing contracts $\Theta = \{\theta(\underline{\tau}^1, \overline{\tau}^1, \underline{h}^1, \overline{h}^1), \theta(\underline{\tau}^2, \overline{\tau}^2, \underline{h}^2, \overline{h}^2)\}$. We set the parameter $\varepsilon = 0.04$, and apply Algorithm 1 to compute the set $\mathcal{P}^*$. The algorithm tested 944 parameter samples and the computation time was 43.4 minutes. A section of the sets $f(\underline{\mathcal{P}}')$ and $\mathcal{P}^*$ in the $(0.1, \overline{\tau}^1, 0.3, \overline{h}^1, 0.6, 0.6, 1.15, 1.15)$ domain is shown in Figure 6.

6. CONCLUSION

In this work, we proposed useful tools for contract-based design of embedded control systems under the form of a scheduling approach and an algorithm for timing contract synthesis. These tools can be used by control and software engineers to derive requirements that must be met by the real-time implementation of a control law. The validity of our approach has been shown on examples. As future work, it would be interesting to handle the problem of controller

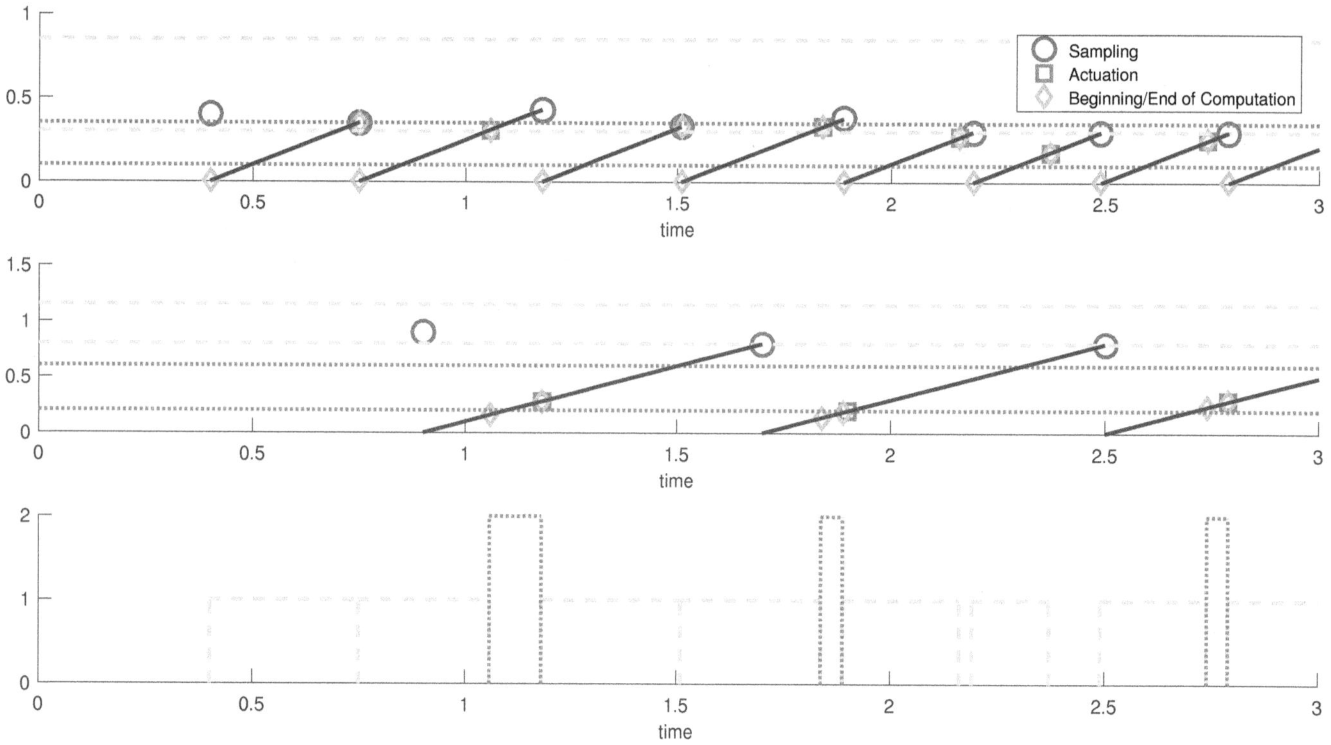

Figure 3: Timing of events (sampling, beginning/end of computation, and actuation) for systems $\mathcal{S}_1$ (first plot) and $\mathcal{S}_2$ (second plot) during the first 3 seconds; dotted lines represent constraints on actuation instants, while dashed lines represent constraints on sampling instants. In the third plot, the dotted line represents $\mathsf{Com}(\mathcal{S}_2, t)$ (less frequent) and the dashed line represents $\mathsf{Com}(\mathcal{S}_1, t)$ (more frequent).

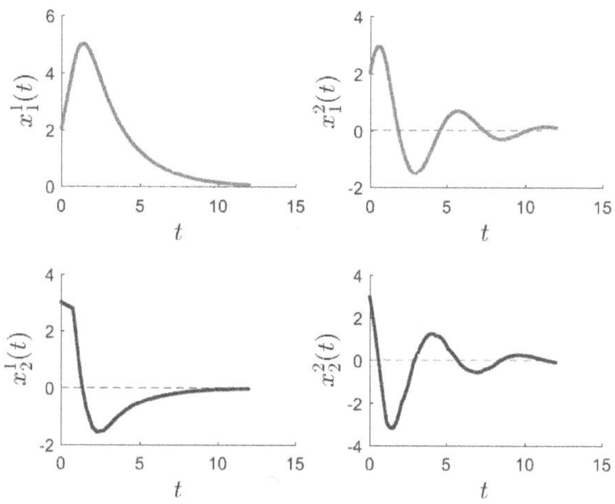

Figure 4: Trajectories for systems $\mathcal{S}_1$ (left) and $\mathcal{S}_2$ (right) using the synthesized scheduling policy.

synthesis given a timing contract, and to co-synthesize the controller and the timing contracts guaranteeing the schedulability of the latter and the stability of each of the systems.

References

[1] M. Al Khatib, A. Girard, and T. Dang. Stability verification and timing contract synthesis for linear impulsive systems using reachability analysis. *Nonlinear Analysis: Hybrid Systems*, 2016. http://dx.doi.org/10.1016/j.nahs.2016.08.007.

[2] M. Al Khatib, A. Girard, and T. Dang. Verification and synthesis of timing contracts for embedded controllers. In *Proceedings of the 19th International Conference on Hybrid Systems: Computation and Control*, pages 115–124. ACM, 2016.

[3] R. Alur and D. L. Dill. A theory of timed automata. *Theoretical Computer Science*, 126(2):183–235, 1994.

[4] A. Aminifar, P. Eles, and Z. Peng. Jfair: a scheduling algorithm to stabilize control applications. In *Real-Time and Embedded Technology and Applications Symposium (RTAS)*, pages 63–72. IEEE, 2015.

[5] A. Aminifar, S. Samii, P. Eles, Z. Peng, and A. Cervin. Designing high-quality embedded control systems with guaranteed stability. In *Real-Time Systems Symposium (RTSS)*, pages 283–292. IEEE, 2012.

[6] A. Aminifar, P. Tabuada, P. Eles, and Z. Peng. Self-triggered controllers and hard real-time guarantees. In *Design, Automation & Test in Europe*

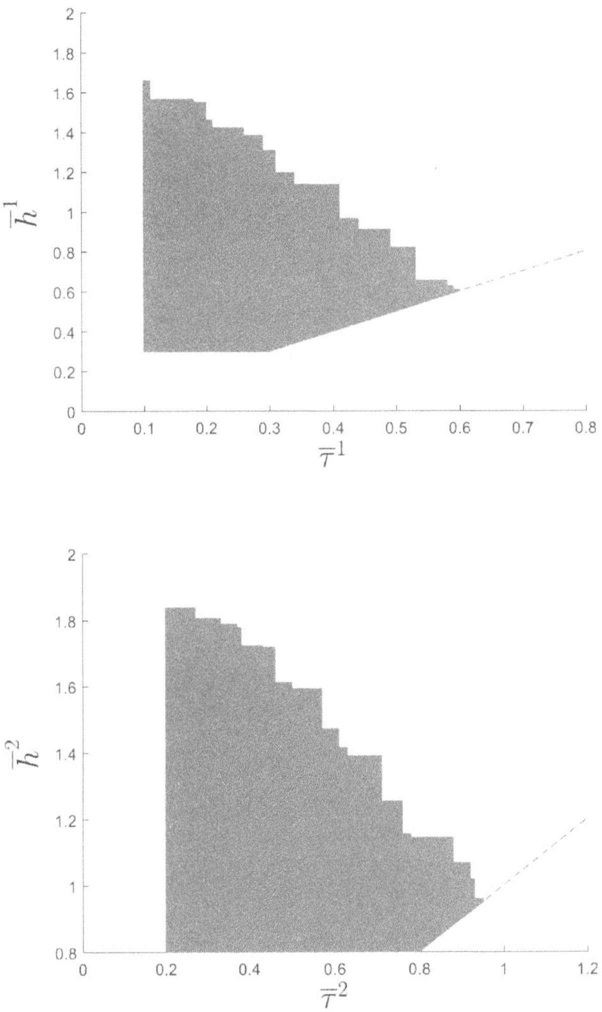

Figure 5: Timing contract parameters that guarantee stability for each system $\mathcal{S}_1$ and $\mathcal{S}_2$: $\mathcal{C}_1^*$ (top) and $\mathcal{C}_2^*$ (bottom).

Conference & Exhibition (DATE), pages 636–641. IEEE, 2016.

[7] N. W. Bauer, P. J. H. Maas, and W. P. M. H. Heemels. Stability analysis of networked control systems: A sum of squares approach. *Automatica*, 48(8):1514–1524, 2012.

[8] G. Behrmann, A. Cougnard, A. David, E. Fleury, K. G. Larsen, and D. Lime. UPPAAL-TIGA: Time for playing games! In *International Conference on Computer Aided Verification*, pages 121–125. Springer, 2007.

[9] A. Benveniste, B. Caillaud, D. Nickovic, R. Passerone, J.-B. Raclet, P. Reinkemeier, A. Sangiovanni-Vincentelli, W. Damm, T. Henzinger, and K. Larsen. Contracts for systems design: methodology and application cases. Research Report RR-8760, Inria Rennes Bretagne Atlantique ; INRIA, July 2015.

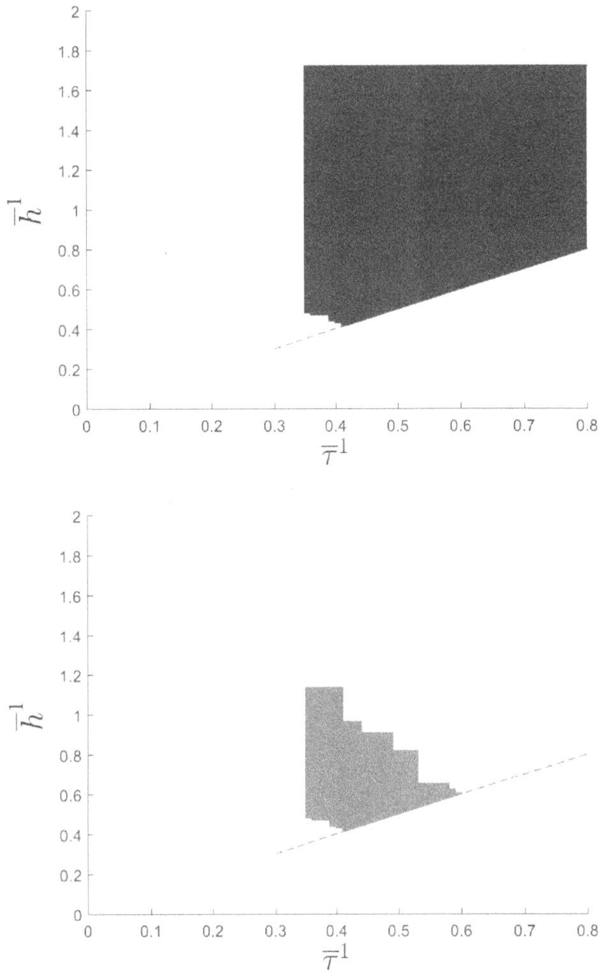

Figure 6: A 2D section of $f(\underline{\mathcal{P}}')$ (top) and $\mathcal{P}^*$ (bottom) in the $(0.1, \overline{\tau}^1, 0.3, \overline{h}^1, 0.6, 0.6, 1.15, 1.15)$ domain.

[10] A. Benveniste, B. Caillaud, D. Nickovic, R. Passerone, J.-B. Raclet, P. Reinkemeier, A. Sangiovanni-Vincentelli, W. Damm, T. Henzinger, and K. Larsen. Contracts for systems design: theory. Research Report RR-8759, Inria Rennes Bretagne Atlantique ; INRIA, July 2015.

[11] C. Briat. Convex conditions for robust stability analysis and stabilization of linear aperiodic impulsive and sampled-data systems under dwell-time constraints. *Automatica*, 49(11):3449–3457, 2013.

[12] G. Buttazzo. *Hard real-time computing systems: predictable scheduling algorithms and applications*, volume 24. Springer Science & Business Media, 2011.

[13] F. Cassez, A. David, E. Fleury, K. G. Larsen, and D. Lime. Efficient on-the-fly algorithms for the analysis of timed games. In *CONCUR 2005-Concurrency Theory*, pages 66–80. Springer-Verlag, 2005.

[14] A. Çela, M. B. Gaid, X.-G. Li, and S.-I. Niculescu. *Optimal design of distributed control and embedded systems.* Springer Science & Business Media, 2013.

[15] M. B. G. Cloosterman, L. Hetel, N. Van De Wouw, W. P. M. H. Heemels, J. Daafouz, and H. Nijmeijer. Controller synthesis for networked control systems. *Automatica*, 46(10):1584–1594, 2010.

[16] F. Cottet, J. Delacroix, C. Kaiser, and Z. Mammeri. Scheduling in real-time systems. *Scheduling in Real-Time Systems*, page 282, 2002.

[17] S.-L. Dai, H. Lin, and S. S. Ge. Scheduling-and-control codesign for a collection of networked control systems with uncertain delays. *IEEE Transactions on Control Systems Technology*, 18(1):66–78, 2010.

[18] A. David, J. Illum, K. G. Larsen, and A. Skou. Model-based framework for schedulability analysis using uppaal 4.1. *Model-based design for embedded systems*, 1(1):93–119, 2009.

[19] P. Derler, E. A. Lee, S. Tripakis, and M. Törngren. Cyber-physical system design contracts. In *ACM/IEEE International Conference on Cyber-Physical Systems*, pages 109–118, 2013.

[20] M. C. F. Donkers, W. P. M. H. Heemels, N. Van De Wouw, and L. Hetel. Stability analysis of networked control systems using a switched linear systems approach. *IEEE Transactions on Automatic Control*, 56(9):2101–2115, 2011.

[21] A. Fehnker. *Scheduling a steel plant with timed automata.* Computing Science Institute Nijmegen, Faculty of Mathematics and Informatics, Catholic University of Nijmegen, 1999.

[22] M. Fiacchini and I.-C. Morarescu. Set theory conditions for stability of linear impulsive systems. In *IEEE Conference on Decision and Control*, pages 1527–1532, 2014.

[23] H. Fujioka. Stability analysis of systems with aperiodic sample-and-hold devices. *Automatica*, 45(3):771–775, 2009.

[24] H. Gao, X. Meng, T. Chen, and J. Lam. Stabilization of networked control systems via dynamic output-feedback controllers. *SIAM Journal on Control and Optimization*, 48(5):3643–3658, 2010.

[25] W. P. M. H. Heemels, A. R. Teel, N. Van de Wouw, and D. Nešić. Networked control systems with communication constraints: Tradeoffs between transmission intervals, delays and performance. *IEEE Transactions on Automatic Control*, 55(8):1781–1796, 2010.

[26] L. Hetel, J. Daafouz, S. Tarbouriech, and C. Prieur. Stabilization of linear impulsive systems through a nearly-periodic reset. *Nonlinear Analysis: Hybrid Systems*, 7(1):4–15, 2013.

[27] L. Hetel, A. Kruszewski, W. Perruquetti, and J.-P. Richard. Discrete and intersample analysis of systems with aperiodic sampling. *IEEE Transactions on Automatic Control*, 56(7):1696–1701, 2011.

[28] A. S. Kolarijani, D. Adzkiya, and M. Mazo. Symbolic abstractions for the scheduling of event-triggered control systems. In *54th IEEE Conference on Decision and Control (CDC)*, pages 6153–6158. IEEE, 2015.

[29] J. Legriel, C. Le Guernic, S. Cotton, and O. Maler. Approximating the pareto front of multi-criteria optimization problems. In *Tools and Algorithms for the Construction and Analysis of Systems*, pages 69–83. Springer, 2010.

[30] K. Liu, E. Fridman, and L. Hetel. Networked control systems in the presence of scheduling protocols and communication delays. *SIAM Journal on Control and Optimization*, 53(4):1768–1788, 2015.

[31] K. Liu, V. Suplin, and E. Fridman. Stability of linear systems with general sawtooth delay. *IMA Journal of Mathematical Control and Information*, 27(4):419–436, 2010.

[32] R. Majumdar, I. Saha, and M. Zamani. Performance-aware scheduler synthesis for control systems. In *International Conference on Embedded Software*, pages 299–308. ACM, 2011.

[33] O. Maler, A. Pnueli, and J. Sifakis. On the synthesis of discrete controllers for timed systems. In *Annual Symposium on Theoretical Aspects of Computer Science*, pages 229–242. Springer, 1995.

[34] P. Naghshtabrizi and J. P. Hespanha. Analysis of distributed control systems with shared communication and computation resources. In *American Control Conference*, pages 3384–3389. IEEE, 2009.

[35] I. Saha, S. Baruah, and R. Majumdar. Dynamic scheduling for networked control systems. In *Proceedings of the 18th International Conference on Hybrid Systems: Computation and Control*, pages 98–107. ACM, 2015.

[36] A. Sangiovanni-Vincentelli, W. Damm, and R. Passerone. Taming dr. frankenstein: Contract-based design for cyber-physical systems. *European Journal of Control*, 18(3):217–238, 2012.

[37] A. Seuret and M. Peet. Stability analysis of sampled-data systems using sum of squares. *IEEE Transactions on Automatic Control*, 58(6):1620–1625, 2013.

[38] P. Tabuada. Event-triggered real-time scheduling of stabilizing control tasks. *IEEE Transactions on Automatic Control*, 52(9):1680–1685, 2007.

[39] P. Tendulkar. *Mapping and Scheduling on Multi-core Processors using SMT Solvers.* PhD thesis, Universite de Grenoble I-Joseph Fourier, 2014.

Convex and Combinatorial Optimization for Dynamic Robots in the Real World

Russ Tedrake
MIT Computer Science and Artificial Intelligence Laboratory
& Toyota Research Institute
Cambridge, MA, USA 02139
russt@mit.edu

ABSTRACT

Humanoid robots walking across intermittent terrain, robotic arms grasping multifaceted objects, UAVs darting left or right around a tree, or autonomous vehicles making discrete navigation decisions in traffic... many of the dynamics and control problems we face today have both rich nonlinear dynamics and an inherently combinatorial structure. In this talk, I'll review some recent work on optimization-based planning and control methods which address these two challenges simultaneously. All of these can be modeled as hybrid systems, but in some cases more efficient optimizations are possible by using alternative formulations, such as (measure-) differential inclusions. I'll present our explorations with mixed-integer convex-, semidefinite-programming-relaxations, and satisfiability-modulo- theory(SMT)-based methods applied to hard problems in legged locomotion over rough terrain, grasp optimization, and UAVs flying through highly cluttered environments.

CCS Concepts/ACM Classifiers

• **Theory of computation~Mathematical optimization**
• **Theory of computation~Mixed discrete-continuous optimization** • **Computer systems organization~Robotic control** • *Computing methodologies~Robotic planning*

Author Keywords

Optimization; Motion Planning; Feedback Control; Humanoid Robots; Unmanned Aerial Vehicles

BIOGRAPHY

Russ is a Professor of Electrical Engineering and Computer Science, Aeronautics and Astronautics, and Mechanical Engineering at MIT, the Director of the Center for Robotics at the Computer Science and Artificial Intelligence Lab, and was the leader of Team MIT's entry in the DARPA Robotics Challenge. Russ is also the Vice President of Simulation and Control at the new Toyota Research Institute. He is a recipient of the NSF CAREER Award, the MIT Jerome Saltzer Award for undergraduate teaching, the DARPA Young Faculty Award in Mathematics, the 2012 Ruth and Joel Spira Teaching Award, and was named a Microsoft Research New Faculty Fellow.

HSCC'17, April 18–20, 2017, Pittsburgh, PA, USA.
ACM ISBN 978-1-4503-4590-3/17/04.
http://dx.doi.org/10.1145/3049797.3049803

Coupling Policy Iterations with Piecewise Quadratic Lyapunov Functions

Assalé Adjé
Université of Perpignan Via Domitia
LAMPS
France
assale.adje@univ-perp.fr

ABSTRACT

We recently constructed piecewise quadratic Lyapunov functions to compute overapproximations over the reachable values set of piecewise affine discrete-time systems. The overapproximations can be viewed as the solutions of an inverse problem. However these overapproximations can be loose. In this paper, we refine the latter overapproximations extending previous works combining policy iterations with quadratic Lyapunov functions.

1. INTRODUCTION

Several catastrophic events showed the importance of the formal verification of programs. Some of these failures are caused by overflows. A method to prove the absence of overflows in numerical programs consists in providing precise safe bounds over the values taken by the variable of the analyzed program.

In this paper, we are interesting in a particular class of numerical programs: single while loop programs with a switch-case structure inside the loop body. Moreover, we suppose that test and assignment functions are affine. Such a program can be represented as a piecewise affine discrete-time system. To compute bouns over the values taken by the variable of the analyzed program is thus reduced to overapproximate the reachable values set of a piecewise affine discrete-time system. Hence, we propose to compute *automatically* precise bounds over piecewise affine discrete-time systems using policy iterations and piecewise quadratic Lyapunov functions.

Initially the policy iterations algorithm solves stochastic control problems [16] which are equivalent to solve fixed point problems involving maxima of affine functions. The policy iteration algorithm was then extended to zero-sum two-player stochastic games [15], this extension allows the computation of the unique fixed point of a contractive piecewise affine function. The very first extension of the policy iterations algorithm in program analysis was in 2005 by Costan et al [9]. Since then, the use of policy iterations in various verification problems greatly increases: in [3, 14], the authors describe a policy iteration algorithm to overapproximate the reachable values set of numerical programs with affine assignments; in [19], the author proves termination using policy iterations; in [26, 28] the authors propose to embed policy iterations for programs dealing with both numerical and boolean variables.

The method developed in [2] allows to compute bounds over the state-variable of a piecewise affine system. The method relies on the synthesis of a piecewise quadratic Lyapunov function for the considered system. The optimal value of the formulated maximization problem furnishes an upper bound on the maximal value of the Euclidian norm of the state variable. This upper bound can be very loose since it combines all the coordinates together. To obtain tigher results, we propose to use a templates based method. A templates method consists in representing sets as sublevel sets of *given* functions called *templates*. Then an overapproximation in this context is computed from a vector of bounds over the templates. The most precise overapproximation with respect to these templates is provided by the vector of bounds satisfying a smallest fixed point equation. In our context, the generated piecewise quadratic Lyapunov function is used as a template. We complete the templates basis by the square of variables. Finally we use policy iterations to solve the (smallest) fixed point equation. Thus, the developed policy iterations algorithm leads to tighter bounds over the reachable values set.

Related Works. The use of a quadratic Lyapunov function as a quadratic template was explicitly done in [25] but one quadratic Lyapunov function is not sufficient to prove the boundedness of reachable values set of a piecewise affine system unless it exists a common quadratic Lyapunov function. Then, we deal with piecewise quadratic Lyapunov functions. Hence the works on the computation of piecewise quadratic Lyapunov functions [11, 12, 17, 21] are also related to this paper. Their authors are interested in proving stability of piecewise affine systems. However, as classical quadratic Lyapunov functions, piecewise quadratic Lyapunov functions provide sublevel invariant sets for the considered system. We use this latter interpretation for a verification purpose to compute an overapproximation of the reachable values set.

In this paper, we aboard the reachability problem as we are interested in reachable values sets. In [6], the authors consider the complexity of some reachability problem such as: Is a certain value can be attained? When this value is at-

HSCC'17, April 18-20, 2017, Pittsburgh, PA, USA
© 2017 ACM. ISBN 978-1-4503-4590-3/17/04...$15.00
DOI: http://dx.doi.org/10.1145/3049797.3049825

tained?...In our work, we do not consider complexity issues but we want to represent a reachable value set in a computable way. So we avoid complexity issues by using computable representations which present some conservatism. We can cite the work of Rakovic et al [23]. The authors propose to deal with set invariance and present some results about sets that are invariant according to certain piecewise affine dynamics and some control. In our work, we are interesting in computing invariants set that contain initial conditions and thus the whole reachable value sets.

Another interesting tool could be the tropical polyhedra domain [4]. It generates disjunctions of zones as invariants. Nevertheless, the latter invariants did not encode quadratic relations between variables.

The works about verifying hybrid systems (see [27] and references therein) could give us some inspirations. First, the studies concern continuous dynamics whereas we are interested in discrete-time systems. Up to some adaptation, this first inconvenient could be overcomed. Second, tools to study safety problems are mainly limited to a bounded time analysis and perform a huge number of steps to obtain a sufficient precision. We propose to compute a safe guaranteed overapproximation which is valid whatever the time in a small number of iterations.

Policy iteration algorithms in templates domain proposed in [3] used quadratic templates and did not handle piecewise quadratic templates. In this paper, we adapt policy iteration based on Lagrange duality [1] to piecewise quadratic functions.

Contributions. The first contribution of the paper is the formalisation of piecewise quadratic Lyapunov functions to compute an overapproximation of the reachable values set of a piecewise affine discrete-time dynamical system. This formalisation uses the theory of cone-copositive matrices which is also an original contribution in this context.

The main contribution of the article is the extension of the policy iterations algorithm to the piecewise quadratic templates. Indeed, a policy iterations algorithm has just been constructed in the case of quadratic functions.

Notations. Numbers. $\mathbb{N}$ denotes the set of nonnegative integers, then for $d \in \mathbb{N}$, $[d] = \{1, \ldots, d\}$. $\mathbb{R}$ is the set of reals, $\mathbb{R}_+$ the set of nonnegative reals and $\mathbb{R}^d$ denotes the set of vectors of d reals. We denote by $\wp(\mathbb{R}^d)$ the set of subsets of $\mathbb{R}^d$.

Inequalities. For $y, z \in \mathbb{R}^d$, $y < z$ (resp. $y \leq z$) means $\forall l \in [d]$, $y_l < z_l$, (resp. $\forall l \in [d]$, $y_l \leq z_l$) and $y \leq_{w,s} z$ is a mix of weak and strict inequalities.

Matrices. $\mathbb{M}_{n \times m}$ is the set of matrices with n rows and m columns. $0_{n,m}$ and 0_n are respectively the null matrices of $\mathbb{M}_{n\times m}$ and $\mathbb{M}_{n\times n}$. Id_n is the identity matrix of $\mathbb{M}_{n\times n}$. $M^\intercal$ is the transpose of $M \in \mathbb{M}_{n\times m}$. $\mathbb{S}_n$ is the set of symmetric matrices of size $n \times n$. $A \succeq 0$ means that A is semi-definite positive i.e. $A \in \mathbb{S}_d$ and $\forall x \in \mathbb{R}^d$, $x^\intercal A x \geq 0$. $\mathbb{S}_d^+$ is the convex cone of semidefinite positive matrices.

2. PIECEWISE AFFINE DISCRETE-TIME SYSTEMS

Our very first motivation is the verification of programs. Indeed, we want to prove that the values taken by the variable of the program are bounded. To prove it, it suffices to compute bounds over the values taken by each variable. The considered programs consist of a single loop with possibly a complicated switch-case type loop body supposed to be written as a nested sequence of *if then else* (*ite* for short) statements, or a *switch* $c1 \to inst1; c2 \to instr2; c3 \to instr3$. Moreover, we assume that the analyzed programs are written in affine arithmetic: the assignments of the programs are of the form $v_j = \sum_{i=1}^d a_i v_i + c$ where a_i and c are scalars and v_j denotes a variable of the program. So, the programs analyzed here can be viewed as piecewise affine discrete-time systems as we can see at Example 1. In the rest of the paper, we only consider piecewise affine discrete-time systems. Finally, the verification problem boils down to compute an overapproximation of the reachable states of a piecewise affine discrete-time system.

Piecewise affine systems (PWA for short) are defined as systems the dynamic of which is piecewise affine. Thus the dynamic is characterized by a polyhedral partition and a family of affine maps relative to this partition. Here, a polyhedral partition is a family of convex polyhedra such that:

$$\bigcup_{i\in\mathcal{I}} X^i = \mathbb{R}^d \text{ and } \forall i, j \in \mathcal{I},\ i \neq j\ X^i \cap X^j = \emptyset\ . \quad (1)$$

The convex polyhedron X^i can contain both strict and weak inequalities and is represented by $T^i \in \mathbb{M}_{n_i \times m}$ and $c^i \in \mathbb{R}^{n_i}$. We denote by T_s^i (resp. T_w^i) and c_s^i (resp. c_w^i) the parts of T^i and c^i corresponding to strict (resp. weak) inequalities:

$$\begin{aligned} X^i &= \left\{x \in \mathbb{R}^d \,\middle|\, T^i x \leq_{w,s} c^i\right\} \\ &= \left\{x \in \mathbb{R}^d \,\middle|\, T_s^i x < c_s^i,\ T_w^i x \leq c_w^i\right\} \end{aligned} \quad (2)$$

Definition 1 (Piecewise Affine System). *A PWA is characterized by the triple $(X^0, \mathcal{X}, \mathcal{A})$ where:*

- *X^0 is the polytope of the initial conditions of the form (2);*
- *$\mathcal{X} := \{X^i, i \in \mathcal{I}\}$ is a polyhedral partition i.e. satisfying (1);*
- *$\mathcal{A} := \{x \mapsto f^i(x) = A^i x + b^i, i \in \mathcal{I}\}$ where $A^i \in \mathbb{M}_{d\times d}$ and $b^i \in \mathbb{R}^d$;*

And satisfies the following relation for all $k \in \mathbb{N}$:

$$x_0 \in X^0,\ \text{if } x_k \in X^i,\ x_{k+1} = f^i(x_k)\ . \quad (3)$$

Let $P = (X^0, \mathcal{X}, \mathcal{A})$ be a PWA. We need some notations for the rest of the paper. First we define the reachable values set $\mathcal{R}$ of P:

$$\mathcal{R} := \bigcup_{k\in\mathbb{N}} \mathbb{A}^k(X^0), \text{ where } \mathbb{A}(x) = f^i(x) \text{ if } x \in X^i \quad (4)$$

We define the set of possible switches:

$$\begin{aligned} \mathrm{Sw} &:= \{(i,j) \in \mathcal{I}^2 \mid \mathcal{R} \cap X^{ij} \neq \emptyset\} \\ &\text{where } X^{ij} = X^i \cap {f^i}^{-1}(X^j)\ . \end{aligned} \quad (5)$$

Finally, we define the set of indices of polyhedra of $\mathcal{X}$ which meet the polyhedron of possible initial conditions:

$$\mathrm{In} := \{i \in \mathcal{I} \mid X^{i0} \neq \emptyset\} \text{ where } X^{i0} = X^i \cap X^0\ . \quad (6)$$

We introduce for $i \in \mathcal{I}$, the following matrix of $\mathbb{M}_{(d+1)\times(d+1)}$:

$$F^i = \begin{pmatrix} 1 & 0_{1\times d} \\ b^i & A^i \end{pmatrix}\ . \quad (7)$$

Eq. (3) can be rewritten as $(1, x_{k+1})^\intercal = F^i(1, x_k)$.

Example 1. *Let us consider the following program : a single while loop with a ite instruction in the loop body.*

```
(x,y)∈ [0,3] × [0,2];
while(true){
    ox=x;
    oy=y;
    if (3*ox+8*oy < -3 ){
        x=0.4197*ox-0.2859*oy+2;
        y=-0.5029*ox+0.1679*oy+5;
    }
    else{ \\3*ox+8*oy>=-3
        x=-0.0575*ox-0.4275*oy-4;
        y=-0.3334*ox-2682*oy+4;
    }
}
```

The initial condition X^0 of the piecewise affine systems is $(x,y) \in [0,3]\times[0,2]$. We can rewrite this program as a piecewise affine discrete-time dynamical systems using our notations. To do so, we have to exhibit the matrices T_s^i and T_w^i and vectors c_s^i and c_w^i (see Eq. (2)) and the matrices F^i (see Eq. (7)):

$$F^1 = \begin{pmatrix} 1 & 0 & 0 \\ 2 & 0.4197 & 0.2859 \\ 5 & 0.5029 & 0.1679 \end{pmatrix}, \left\{ \begin{array}{l} T_s^1 = (3 \quad 8) \\ c_s^1 = -3 \end{array} \right.$$

$$F^2 = \begin{pmatrix} 1 & 0 & 0 \\ -4 & -0.0575 & 0.4275 \\ 4 & -0.3334 & -0.2682 \end{pmatrix}, \left\{ \begin{array}{l} T_w^2 = (-3 \quad -8) \\ c_w^2 = 3 \end{array} \right.$$

We are interested in computing *automatically* precise over-approximation of $\mathcal{R}$. First, we propose to compute an over-approximation of $\mathcal{R}$ as a set $S \subseteq \mathbb{R}^d$ such that $X^0 \subseteq S$ and $\forall i \in \mathcal{I},\ x \in S \cap X^i \implies A^i x + b^i \in S$. From the latter invariance condition, a sublevel of a Lyapunov function containing the initial states can be such a set S.

From now on, we consider a fixed $P = (X^0, \mathcal{X}, \mathcal{A})$ following Def. 1.

3. WEAK PIECEWISE QUADRATIC LYAPUNOV FUNCTIONS

In this paper, we use weak piecewise quadratic Lyapunov functions to compute directly an overapproximation of reachable values set.

Let q be a quadratic form i.e. a function such that for all $y \in \mathbb{R}^d$, $q(y) = y^\intercal A_q y + b_q^\intercal y + c_q$ where $A_q \in \mathbb{S}_d$, $b_q \in \mathbb{R}^d$ and $c_q \in \mathbb{R}$. We define the lift-matrix of q, the matrix of $\mathbb{S}_{d+1}$ defined as follows:

$$\mathbf{M}(A_q, b_q, c_q) = \mathbf{M}(q) = \begin{pmatrix} c_q & (b_q/2)^\intercal \\ (b_q/2) & A_q \end{pmatrix} \tag{8}$$

It is obvious that the $q \mapsto \mathbf{M}(q)$ is linear. Let $A \in \mathbb{M}_{d\times d}$, $b \in \mathbb{R}^d$, and q be a quadratic form, we have, for all $x \in \mathbb{R}^d$:

$$q(Ax+b) = \begin{pmatrix} 1 \\ x \end{pmatrix}^\intercal \begin{pmatrix} 1 & 0_{1\times d} \\ b & A \end{pmatrix}^\intercal \mathbf{M}(q) \begin{pmatrix} 1 & 0_{1\times d} \\ b & A \end{pmatrix} \begin{pmatrix} 1 \\ x \end{pmatrix}. \tag{9}$$

Lemma 1. *Let $A \in \mathbb{S}_d$, $b \in \mathbb{R}^d$ and $c \in \mathbb{R}$. Then: $(\forall y \in \mathbb{R}^d,\ y^\intercal A y + b^\intercal y + c \geq 0) \iff \mathbf{M}(A,b,c) \in \mathbb{S}_{d+1}^+$*

Proof. It suffices to remark that for all $t \neq 0$, for all $y \in \mathbb{R}^d$, $t^2 q(t^{-1}y) = \begin{pmatrix} 1 \\ y \end{pmatrix}^\intercal \mathbf{M}(q) \begin{pmatrix} 1 \\ y \end{pmatrix}$. □

Definition 2 ((Cone)-copositive matrices). *Let $M \in \mathbb{M}_{m\times d}$. A matrix $Q \in \mathbb{S}_d$ is said to be M-copositive iff:*

$$My \geq 0 \implies y^\intercal Q y \geq 0$$

An Id_d-copositive matrix is called a copositive matrix. *We denote by $\mathbf{C}_d(M)$ the set of M-copositive matrices and $\mathbf{C}_d$ the set of copositive matrices.*

The notion of cone-copositive matrix involves conic polyhedra but can be easily extended to non-conic polyhedra by using $Mx \leq p \iff \begin{pmatrix} 1 & 0_{1\times d} \\ p & -M \end{pmatrix}\begin{pmatrix} 1 \\ x \end{pmatrix} \geq 0$.

Lemma 2. *Let $q : \mathbb{R}^d \to \mathbb{R}^d$ be a quadratic function. Let $M \in \mathbb{M}_{m\times d}$, $p \in \mathbb{R}^m$ and consider $C = \{x \mid Mx \leq p\}$. Then $\mathbf{M}(q) \in \mathbf{C}_{d+1}\left(\begin{pmatrix} 1 & 0_{1\times d} \\ p & -M \end{pmatrix}\right) \implies (q(x) \geq 0,\ \forall x \in C)$.*

We introduce the following matrices:

$$\forall i \in \mathcal{I},\ E^i = \begin{pmatrix} 1 & 0_{1\times d} \\ c^i & -T^i \end{pmatrix}, \tag{10a}$$

$$\forall (i,j) \in \mathcal{I}^2,\ E^{ij} = \begin{pmatrix} 1 & 0_{1\times d} \\ c^i & -T^i \\ c^j - T^j b^i & -T^j A^i \end{pmatrix}, \tag{10b}$$

$$\forall i \in \mathrm{In},\ E^{i0} = \begin{pmatrix} 1 & 0_{1\times d} \\ c^i & -T^i \\ c^0 & -T^0 \end{pmatrix}. \tag{10c}$$

We will denote by n_i the number of rows of E^i, n_{ij} the number of rows of E^{ij} and n_{i0} the number of rows of E^{i0}.

Lemma 3. *For all $i \in \mathcal{I}$, $X^i \subseteq \{x \mid E^i(1\ x^\intercal)^\intercal \geq 0\}$, for all $(i,j) \in \mathrm{Sw}$, $X^{ij} \subseteq \{x \mid E^{ij}(1\ x^\intercal)^\intercal \geq 0\}$ and for all $i \in \mathrm{In}$, $X^{i0} \subseteq \{x \mid E^{i0}(1\ x^\intercal)^\intercal \geq 0\}$.*

Definition 3 (wPQL functions). *A function L is a weak piecewise quadratic Lyapunov function (wPQL for short) for P if and only if there exist a family $\{(P^i, q^i), P^i \in \mathbb{S}_d, q^i \in \mathbb{R}^d,\ i \in \mathcal{I}\}$ and two reals α and β such that:*

1. *$\forall i \in \mathcal{I}$, $\forall x \in X^i$, $L(x) = L^i(x) = x^\intercal P^i x + 2x^\intercal q^i$;*
2. *$\forall i \in \mathcal{I}$:*

$$\mathbf{M}(P^i, 2q^i, -\alpha) - \mathbf{M}(\mathrm{Id}, 0, -\beta) \in \mathbf{C}_{d+1}\left(E^i\right)\ ; \tag{11}$$

3. *$\forall (i,j) \in \mathrm{Sw}$:*

$$\mathbf{M}(P^i, 2q^i, 0) - F^{i\intercal}\mathbf{M}(P^j, 2q^j, 0)F^i \in \mathbf{C}_{d+1}\left(E^{ij}\right)\ ; \tag{12}$$

4. *$\forall i \in \mathrm{In}$:*

$$-\mathbf{M}(P^i, 2q^i, -\alpha) \in \mathbf{C}_{d+1}\left(E^{i0}\right). \tag{13}$$

Proposition 1 (Bounded trajectories). *Suppose that P admits a wPQL function represented by $\{(P^i, q^i), P^i \in \mathbb{S}_d, q^i \in \mathbb{R}^d,\ i \in \mathcal{I}\}$ and reals α and β. Let $i \in \mathcal{I}$, $S_\alpha^i = \{x \in X^i \mid L^i(x) \leq \alpha\} = \{x \in X^i \mid x^\intercal P^i x + 2x^\intercal q^i \leq \alpha\}$ and $S = \cup_{i\in\mathcal{I}} S_\alpha^i$. Then, $\mathcal{R} \subseteq S \subseteq \{x \in \mathbb{R}^d \mid \|x\|_2^2 \leq \beta\}$.*

Proof. First, we prove that $S \subseteq \{x \in \mathbb{R}^d \mid \|x\|_2^2 \leq \beta\}$. Let $i \in \mathcal{I}$ and $x \in X^i$. From Eq. (11), Lemma 2 and Lemma 3, $x^\intercal P^i x + 2x^\intercal q^i - \alpha - \|x\|_2^2 + \beta \geq 0$ which implies that $S \subseteq \{x \in \mathbb{R}^d \mid \|x\|_2^2 \leq \beta\}$.

From Eq. (4), to prove the first inclusion, we have to show that for all $k \in \mathbb{N}$, $\mathbb{A}^k(X^0) \subseteq S$. We prove it by induction on k. Let $x \in X^0$. Since $\mathcal{X}$ satisfies (1), there exists a unique $i \in \mathrm{In}$ such that $x \in X^{i0}$. From Eq. (13), Lemma 2 and Lemma 3, $L^i(x) \le \alpha$. Now suppose $\mathbb{A}^k(X^0) \subseteq S$ for some $k \in \mathbb{N}$. Let $y \in \mathbb{A}^{k+1}(X^0)$. Then $y = \mathbb{A}(x)$ for some $x \in \mathbb{A}^k(X^0)$. Since $\mathcal{X}$ satisfies (1), there exists an unique $(i,j) \in \mathrm{Sw}$ such that $x \in X^{ij}$ (hence $y \in X^j$). As $x \in X^i$ and $x \in S$, then $x \in S^i_\alpha$. From Eq. (12), Lemma 2 and Lemma 3, $0 \le L^i(x) - L^j(y) = L^i(x) - \alpha - (L^j(y) - \alpha)$. Finally $y \in S^j_\alpha \subseteq S$ as $x \in S^i_\alpha$. □

3.1 Computational issues

To construct wPQL functions, we are faced with two issues. First, we must know the sets of indices Sw and In. Second we have to manipulate cone-copositive constraints.

3.1.1 The computation of sets Sw *and* In

To set Sw relies on $\mathcal{R}$, the set we want approximate. To overcome this issue, we just remove the intersection with $\mathcal{R}$:

$$\overline{\mathrm{Sw}} := \{(i,j) \in \mathcal{I}^2 \mid X^{ij} \neq \emptyset\} \ . \tag{14}$$

The polyhedra X^i and X^j can contain strict inequalities. Hence to compute $\overline{\mathrm{Sw}}$ we need Motzkin's theorem [22]. This alternative theorem permits to compute exactly the set In. The direct application of Motzkin's transposition theorem [22] yields to the next proposition.

PROPOSITION 2. *The couple* $(i,j) \in \overline{\mathrm{Sw}}$ *if and only if:*

$$\left\{\begin{array}{l} \begin{pmatrix} 1 & 0_{1\times d} \\ c_s^i & -T_s^i \\ c_s^j - T_s^j b^i & -T_s^j A^i \end{pmatrix}^{\intercal} p^s + \begin{pmatrix} c_w^i & -T_w^i \\ c_w^j - T_w^j b^i & -T_w^j \end{pmatrix}^{\intercal} p = 0 \\ \sum_k p_k^s = 1,\ p^s \ge 0,\ p \ge 0 \end{array}\right.$$

has no solution.

The index $i \in \mathrm{In}$ *if and only if:*

$$\left\{\begin{array}{l} \begin{pmatrix} 1 & 0_{1\times d} \\ c_s^i & -T_s^i \\ c_s^0 & -T_s^0 \end{pmatrix}^{\intercal} p^s + \begin{pmatrix} c_w^i & -T_w^i \\ c_w^0 & -T_w^0 \end{pmatrix}^{\intercal} p = 0 \\ \sum_k p_k^s = 1,\ p^s \ge 0,\ p \ge 0 \end{array}\right.$$

has no solution.

3.1.2 Cone-copositive constraints

The interested reader can refer to [7] a list of exciting papers about the representation of cone-copositive matrices.

PROPOSITION 3 (TH. 2.1 OF [18]). *For all* $M \in \mathbb{M}_{m\times d}$, *we have:*

$$\{M^{\intercal} C M + S \mid C \in \mathbf{C}_d \text{ and } S \in \mathbb{S}_d^+\} \subseteq \mathbf{C}_d(M) \qquad (\Delta)$$

If the rank of M *is equal to* m, *then* (Δ) *is an equality.*

The next proposition discusses a simple characterization of copositive matrices.

PROPOSITION 4 ([10, 20]). *We have:* $\forall d \in \mathbb{N}$: $\mathbb{S}_d^{\ge 0} + \mathbb{S}_d^+ \subseteq \mathbf{C}_d$. *If* $d \le 4$ *then* $\mathbf{C}_d = \mathbb{S}_d^{\ge 0} + \mathbb{S}_d^+$.

COROLLARY 1. *Let* $M \in \mathbb{M}_{m\times d}$. *Then:*

$$\mathbf{C}_d(M) \supseteq \left\{ Q \in \mathbb{S}_d \;\middle|\; \begin{array}{l} \exists W_p \in \mathbb{S}_m^{\ge 0},\ W_+ \in \mathbb{S}_m^+, \text{ s.t.} \\ Q - M^{\intercal}(W_p + W_+)M \succeq 0 \end{array} \right\} \qquad (\star)$$

If M *has full row rank and* $d \le 4$, *then* $(\star)$ *is actually an equality.*

The computation of copositive constraints is a quite recent field of research. Algorithms exist (e.g. [8]) but for the knowledge of the author no tools are available. In this paper, in practice, we use Corollary 1 and we replace $\mathbf{C}_d(M)$ by the right-hand side of Eq. $(\star)$.

3.1.3 Computation of weak piecewise quadratic Lyapunov functions using SDP solvers

Finally, we construct wPQL functions using semidefinite programming. We define the notion of computable wPQL functions.

DEFINITION 4 (COMPUTABLE WPQL FUNCTIONS). *A function* L *is a computable wPQL for* P *if and only if there exist two reals* α *and* β *and four families:*

- $\mathcal{P} := \{(P^i, q^i), P^i \in \mathbb{S}_d, q^i \in \mathbb{R}^d,\ i \in \mathcal{I}\}$
- $\mathcal{W} := \{(W_p^i, W_+^i) \in \mathbb{S}_{n_i+1}^{\ge 0} \times \mathbb{S}_{n_i+1}^+, i \in \mathcal{I}\}$,
- $\mathcal{U} := \{(U_p^{ij}, U_+^{ij}) \in \mathbb{S}_{n_{ij}}^{\ge 0} \times \mathbb{S}_{n_{ij}}^+, (i,j) \in \overline{\mathrm{Sw}}\}$
- $\mathcal{Z} := \{(Z_p^{i0}, Z_+^{i0}) \in \mathbb{S}_{n_{i0}}^{\ge 0} \times \mathbb{S}_{n_{i0}}^+, i \in \mathrm{In}\}$

such that:

1. $\forall i \in \mathcal{I}, \forall x \in X^i$, $L(x) = L^i(x) = x^{\intercal} P^i x + 2x^{\intercal} q^i$;
2. $\forall i \in \mathcal{I}$:
$$\begin{array}{r} \mathbf{M}(P^i, 2q^i, -\alpha) - \mathbf{M}(\mathrm{Id}, 0, -\beta) \\ - E^{i\intercal}(W_p^i + W_+^i)E^i \end{array} \succeq 0\ ; \tag{15}$$
3. $\forall (i,j) \in \overline{\mathrm{Sw}}$:
$$\begin{array}{r} \mathbf{M}(P^i, 2q^i, 0) - F^{i\intercal}\mathbf{M}(P^j, 2q^j, 0)F^i \\ - E^{ij\intercal}(U_p^{ij} + U_+^{ij})E^{ij} \end{array} \succeq 0\ ; \tag{16}$$
4. $\forall i \in \mathrm{In}$:
$$-\mathbf{M}(P^i, 2q^i, -\alpha) - E^{i0\intercal}\left(Z_p^{0i} + Z_+^{0i}\right)E^{i0} \succeq 0; \tag{17}$$

Let us consider the problem:

$$\begin{array}{ll} \inf\limits_{\substack{\mathcal{P},\mathcal{W},\mathcal{U},\mathcal{Z},\\ \alpha,\beta}} & \alpha + \beta \\ \text{s.t.} & \left\{\begin{array}{l} (\mathcal{P},\mathcal{W},\mathcal{U},\mathcal{Z},\alpha,\beta) \text{ satisfies (15), (16) and (17)} \\ \alpha \ge 0,\ \beta \ge 0 \end{array}\right. \end{array} \tag{PSD}$$

Problem (PSD) is thus a semi-definite program. The use of the sum $\alpha + \beta$ as objective function enforces the functions L^is to provide a minimal bound β and a minimal ellipsoid containing the initial conditions. The constraint $\beta \ge 0$ is obvious since β represents a norm. However, $\alpha \ge 0$ is less natural but ensures that the objective function is bounded from below. The presence of the constraint $\alpha \ge 0$ does not affect the feasibility. Note that to reduce the size of the problem, we can take $q^i = 0$ and get an homogeneous wPQL function.

We remark the presence of $(1, 0_{1\times d})$ in the contruction of matrices E^i, E^{ij} and E^{i0} (see Eqs (10)). It would be more natural to express them without this vector. However, when we replace the cone-copositivity constraints by right-hand-side of Eq. ($\star$), we allow symmetry as it is shown in Example 2. The vector $(1, 0_{1\times d})$ aims to break it.

EXAMPLE 2 (WHY $(1, 0_{1\times d})$ IN EQS (10)?). *Let us consider* $X = \{x \in \mathbb{R} \mid x \leq 1\}$. *Let* $u(x) = (1, x)$, *and* $M = (1\ -1)$. *Then* $X = \{x \mid Mu(x)^\intercal \geq 0\}$.

Now let $W \geq 0$ *and define* $X' = \{x \mid u(x)M^\intercal W M u(x)^\intercal \geq 0\}$. *Since* $u(x)M^\intercal W M u(x)^\intercal = W u(x) M^\intercal M u(x)^\intercal = 2W(1-x)^2$, $X' = \mathbb{R}$ *for all* $W \geq 0$.

Now let us take $E = \left(\begin{smallmatrix} 1 & 0 \\ 1 & -1 \end{smallmatrix}\right)$ *and let* $W = \left(\begin{smallmatrix} w_1 & w_3 \\ w_3 & w_2 \end{smallmatrix}\right)$ *with* $w_1, w_2, w_3 \geq 0$ *and define* $\overline{X} = \{x \mid u(x)E^\intercal W E u(x)^\intercal \geq 0\}$. *Hence,* $u(x)E^\intercal \left(\begin{smallmatrix} w_1 & w_3 \\ w_3 & w_2 \end{smallmatrix}\right) E u(x)^\intercal = w_1 + 2w_3(1-x) + w_2(1-x)^2$. *Taking for example* $w_2 = w_1 = 0$ *and* $w_3 > 0$ *implies that* $\overline{X} = X$.

PROPOSITION 5. *Assume that Problem* (PSD) *has a feasible solution* $(\mathcal{P}, \mathcal{W}, \mathcal{U}, \mathcal{Z}, \alpha, \beta)$. *Then:*

1. The family $\mathcal{P}$ *defines a wPQL function* L;

2. There exists $(\mathcal{P}, \mathcal{W}, \mathcal{U}, \mathcal{Z}, \alpha, \beta)$ *satisfiying* (15), (16) *and* (17) *if and only if Problem* (PSD) *is feasible;*

3. Let $(i, j) \in \overline{\text{Sw}}$. *Let us define the permutation* σ *as follows:* $\sigma(k) = n_i$ *if* $k = 1$, $k-1$ *if* $2 \leq k \leq n_i$ *and* k *otherwise. and* P_σ *the associated permutation matrix*[1]. *Then, we have:*

$$\begin{aligned} & F^{i\intercal}\mathbf{M}(\text{Id}, 0, 0)F^i \\ \preceq\ & \mathbf{M}(P^i, 2q^i, -\alpha) + \mathbf{M}(0, 0, \beta) \\ & -E^{ij\intercal}\left(P_\sigma^\intercal \begin{pmatrix} 0_{n_i-1} & 0_{n_i-1,n_j} \\ 0_{n_j,n_i-1} & W_p^j + W_+^j \end{pmatrix} P_\sigma + U_p^{ij} + U_+^{ij}\right) E^{ij}\ ; \end{aligned}$$

4. We have $\sup_{x \in X^0} \|x\|_2^2 \leq \beta$;

5. Assume that $(\mathcal{P}, \mathcal{W}, \mathcal{U}, \mathcal{Z}, \alpha, \beta)$ *is optimal with* $\alpha > 0$. *Then,* $\sup_{x \in X^0} L(x) = \alpha$.

PROOF. *1.* This follows readily from Corollary 1.

2. The "if" part is obvious. Let us focus on the "only if" part and let $S^1 := (\mathcal{P}, \mathcal{W}, \mathcal{U}, \mathcal{Z}, \alpha, \beta)$ satisfiying (15), (16) and (17). From Th. 1, $\beta \geq 0$. Let us suppose that $\alpha < 0$ otherwise the proof is finished. Let us prove that $S^2 := (\mathcal{P}, \mathcal{W}, \mathcal{U}, \mathcal{Z}, 0, \beta - \alpha)$ is feasible for Problem (PSD). First $\beta - \alpha \geq 0$ since $\beta \geq 0$ and $\alpha < 0$. Second, $\mathbf{M}(P^i, 2q^i, 0) - \mathbf{M}(\text{Id}, 0, -(\beta-\alpha)) - E^{i\intercal}\left(W_p^i + W_+^i\right)E^i = \mathbf{M}(P^i, 2q^i, -\alpha) - \mathbf{M}(\text{Id}, 0, -\beta) - E^{i\intercal}\left(W_p^i + W_+^i\right)E^i$ thus S^2 satisfies (15) as S^1 does. Since α and β do not appear in (16), S^2 satisfies (16). Finally, $-\mathbf{M}(P^i, 2q^i, 0) - E^{i0\intercal}\left(Z_p^{0i} + Z_+^{0i}\right)E^{i0} = -\mathbf{M}(P^i, 2q^i, \alpha - \alpha) - E^{i0\intercal}\left(Z_p^{0i} + Z_+^{0i}\right)E^{i0} = \mathbf{M}(0, 0, -\alpha) - \mathbf{M}(P^i, 2q^i, -\alpha) - E^{i0\intercal}\left(Z_p^{0i} + Z_+^{0i}\right)E^{i0}$. We conclude that S^2 satisfies (17) as S^1 does.

3. Let $(i, j) \in \overline{\text{Sw}}$. We have, $\mathbf{M}(P^j, 2q^j, -\alpha) - \mathbf{M}(\text{Id}, 0, -\beta) - E^{j\intercal}\left(W_p^j + W_+^j\right)E^j \succeq 0$. Hence, $F^{i\intercal}\big(\mathbf{M}(P^j, 2q^j, -\alpha) - \mathbf{M}(\text{Id}, 0, -\beta) - E^{j\intercal}\left(W_p^j + W_+^j\right)E^j\big)F^i \succeq 0$. Thus, $F^{i\intercal}\mathbf{M}(P^j, 2q^j, -\alpha)F^i - F^{i\intercal}E^{j\intercal}\left(W_p^j + W_+^j\right)E^jF^i \succeq F^{i\intercal}\mathbf{M}(\text{Id}, 0, -\beta)F^i$. Hence, $-F^{i\intercal}E^{j\intercal}\left(W_p^j + W_+^j\right)E^jF^i + \mathbf{M}(P^i, 2q^i, 0) - E^{ij\intercal}\left(U_p^{ij} + U_+^{ij}\right)E^{ij} \succeq F^{i\intercal}\mathbf{M}(\text{Id}, 0, -\beta)F^i$. By using $F^{i\intercal}\mathbf{M}(0, 0, -\beta)F^i = \mathbf{M}(0, 0, -\beta)$, we get that $F^{i\intercal}\mathbf{M}(\text{Id}, 0, 0)F^i \preceq -F^{i\intercal}E^{j\intercal}\left(W_p^j + W_+^j\right)E^jF^i + \mathbf{M}(P^i, 2q^i, 0) - E^{ij\intercal}\left(U_p^{ij} + U_+^{ij}\right)E^{ij} + \mathbf{M}(0, 0, \beta)$. To end with the proof, it suffices to remark that $E^{ij} = P_\sigma^\intercal \begin{pmatrix} c^i & -T^i \\ & E^jF^i \end{pmatrix}$.

4. Since $\mathcal{P}$ is wPQL, then from Th. 1 $\mathcal{R} \subseteq \{x \in \mathbb{R}^d \mid \|x\|_2^2 \leq \beta\}$ and since $X^0 \subseteq \mathcal{R}$, $\sup_{x \in X^0} \|x\|_2^2 \leq \beta$.

5. Assume that $(\mathcal{P}, \mathcal{W}, \mathcal{U}, \mathcal{Z}, \alpha, \beta)$ is an optimal solution with $\alpha > 0$ and suppose that $\sup_{x \in X^0} L(x) \neq \alpha$. From Constraint (17), we have for all $i \in \text{In}$, $X^i \cap X^0 \subseteq \{x \mid L^i(x) \leq \alpha\}$ and thus for all $i \in \text{In}$, $\sup_{x \in X^i \cap X^0} L^i(x) \leq \alpha$. Since $\sup_{x \in X^0} L(x) = \sup_{i \in \text{In}} \sup_{x \in X^i \cap X^0} L^i(x)$, we get $\sup_{x \in X^0} L(x) \leq \alpha$. Now let $\epsilon > 0$ such that $\gamma = \alpha - \epsilon \geq 0$ and $\sup_{x \in X^0} L(x) \leq \gamma$. Let us define the matrix N by $N_{l,m} = 1$ if $l = m = 1$ and 0 otherwise. We have $-\mathbf{M}(P^i, 2q^i, -\gamma) - E^{i0\intercal}\left(Z_p^{0i} + Z_+^{0i}\right)E^{i0} = -\mathbf{M}(L^i) + \gamma N - E^{i0\intercal}\left(Z_p^{0i} + Z_+^{0i}\right)E^{i0}$. From $E_{1,1}^{i0} = 1$, we get $E^{i0\intercal}NE^{i0} = N$. So, $-\mathbf{M}(P^i, 2q^i, -\gamma) - E^{i0\intercal}\left(Z_p^{0i} + Z_+^{0i}\right)E^{i0} = -\mathbf{M}(L^i) + \alpha N - E^{i0\intercal}\left(Z_p^{0i} + \epsilon N + Z_+^{0i}\right)E^{i0}$. Now, $\mathbf{M}(P^i, 2q^i, -\gamma) - \mathbf{M}(\text{Id}, 0, -\beta) - E^{i\intercal}\left(W_p^i + W_+^i\right)E^i = \mathbf{M}(P^i, 2q^i, -\alpha) - \mathbf{M}(\text{Id}, 0, -\beta) - E^{i\intercal}\left(W_p^i + W_+^i\right)E^i + \epsilon N$. From Constraint (15), $\mathbf{M}(P^i, 2q^i, -\gamma) - \mathbf{M}(\text{Id}, 0, -\beta) - E^{i\intercal}\left(W_p^i + W_+^i\right)E^i$ is positive semidefinite. We conclude that $(\mathcal{P}, \mathcal{W}, \mathcal{U}, \mathcal{Z}', \gamma, \beta)$ with $\mathcal{Z}' = \{(Z_p^{i0} + \epsilon N, Z_+^{i0}) \in \mathbb{S}_{n_{i0}}^{\geq 0} \times \mathbb{S}_{n_{i0}}^+, i \in \text{In}\}$ is feasible and $\gamma + \beta = \alpha + \beta - \epsilon$ thus $(\mathcal{P}, \mathcal{W}, \mathcal{U}, \mathcal{Z}, \alpha, \beta)$ cannot be optimal. $\square$

4. POLICY ITERATION ALGORITHM

In this section, we give details about the policy iteration algorithm which aims to make more accurate the overapproximation found directly from the computation of a wPQL function.

4.1 Sublevel Modelisation

In Def. 4, β is an upper bound on the Euclidian norm of the state variable. We do not have a precise upper bound on each coordinate considered separetely neither a precise upper bound on the state variable considering a specific cell. To obtain tigher bounds, we intersect S_α with other sublevel sets. In [25], the authors propose to combine quadratic Lyapunov functions with the square of coordinate. In this paper, we apply this technique replacing quadratic Lyapunov functions by wPQL functions. Thus we are interested in a set V of the form $S_\alpha \cap \cup_{i \in \mathcal{I}}\{y \in X^i \mid y_l^2 \leq \beta_l^i, l = 1, \ldots, d\}$. The computation of V is thus reduced to compute β_l^i. In verification of programs, the method is called a *templates domain abstraction* (for more background [3]).

We can deduce from Eq. (4) that $\mathcal{R} = \mathbb{A}(\mathcal{R}) \cup X^0$. We introduce the map $F : \wp(\mathbb{R}^d) \mapsto \wp(\mathbb{R}^d)$ defined by

$$C \mapsto F(C) := \mathbb{A}(C) \cup X^0\ .$$

Hence, $\mathcal{R}$ is the smallest fixed point of F in the sense of if $C = F(C)$ then $\mathcal{R} \subseteq C$. From Tarski's theorem [29], since F is monotone on $\wp(\mathbb{R}^d)$, then:

$$\mathcal{R} = \inf\{C \in \wp(\mathbb{R}^d) \mid F(C) \subseteq C\}; \qquad (18)$$

Any set C such that $F(C) \subseteq C$ satisfies $\mathcal{R} \subseteq C$. We propose to consider a restricted family of such sets C parameterized by $\omega \in \mathbb{R}^{d+1}$:

$$C(\omega) := \{x \in \mathbb{R}^d \mid \forall k \in [d],\ x_k^2 \leq \omega_k, L(x) \leq \omega_{d+1}\}$$

where L is a wPQL function for the PWA P. A set $C(\omega)$ is just the intersection of a sublevel of a wPQL function with a cartesian product of intervals. We define:

$$\forall k \in [d],\ X_k^0 = \sup_{y \in X^0} y_k^2 \text{ and } X_{d+1}^0 = \sup_{y \in X^0} L(y)$$

[1] $[P_\sigma]_{lk} = 1$ if $l = \sigma(k)$; 0 otherwise and $P_\sigma^{-1} = P_\sigma^\intercal$.

The numbers X_k^0 allows to construct interval bounds for the k-th coordinate of an initial value whereas X_{d+1}^0 refers to the maximum value of the wPQL function L over X^0.

We also define for all $(i,j) \in \overline{\mathrm{Sw}}$ and for all $\omega \in \mathbb{R}^{d+1}$:

$$\forall\, k \in [d], \quad F_{ij,k}^\sharp(\omega) = \sup_{\substack{\forall\, k\in[d],\ x_k^2 \le \omega_k,\\ L^i(x)\le\omega_{d+1},\ x\in X^{ij}}} (A_{k\cdot}^i x + b_k^i)^2$$

and

$$F_{ij,d+1}^\sharp(\omega) = \sup_{\substack{\forall\, k\in[d],\ x_k^2 \le \omega_k,\\ L^i(x)\le\omega_{d+1},\ x\in X^{ij}}} L^j(A^i x + b^i)$$

and finally, we define for all $\omega \in \mathbb{R}^{d+1}$:

$$\forall\, l \in [d+1],\ F_l^\sharp(\omega) = \sup\{\sup_{(i,j)\in\overline{\mathrm{Sw}}} F_{ij,l}^\sharp(\omega), X_l^0\}$$

and $F^\sharp(\omega) = (F_1^\sharp(\omega), \ldots, F_{d+1}^\sharp(\omega))$. The map F acts on sets whereas $F^\sharp$ acts on vectors of $\mathbb{R}^{d+1}$. Prop. 6 highlights the link between the two maps.

PROPOSITION 6. *The following statements hold:*

1. $F(C(\omega)) \subseteq C(\omega) \iff F^\sharp(\omega) \le \omega$*;*

2. $\mathcal{R} \subseteq \inf\{C(\omega) \mid \omega \in \mathbb{R}^{d+1}$ *s.t.* $F^\sharp(\omega) \le \omega\}$*;*

3. For all $\omega \in \mathbb{R}^{d+1}$ *and all* $l \in [d+1]$, $F_{ij,l}^\sharp(\omega)$ *is the optimal value of quadratic program;*

4. For all $k \in [d]$, $X_k^0 = \max\{(\inf_{x\in X^0} x_k)^2, (\sup_{x\in X^0} x_k)^2\}$ *and if L is a computable wPQL function constructed from an optimal solution* $(\mathcal{P}, \mathcal{W}, \mathcal{U}, \mathcal{Z}, \alpha, \beta)$ *of* (PSD) *with* $\alpha > 0$, *then* $X_{d+1}^0 = \alpha$.

PROOF. *1.* We remark that $F(C(\omega)) \subseteq C(\omega)$ iff for all $k \in [d]$, $\sup_{y\in F(C(\omega))} y_k^2 \le \omega_k$ and $\sup_{y\in F(C(\omega))} L(y) \le \omega_{d+1}$. We only give details for the first inequality, the proof of the second follows the same idea. For all $k \in [d]$:

$$\begin{aligned}\sup_{y\in F(C(\omega))} y_k^2 &= \sup\{\sup_{y\in \mathbb{A}(C(\omega))} y_k^2, \sup_{y\in X^0} y_k^2\}\\ &= \sup\{\sup_{(i,j)\in\overline{\mathrm{Sw}}}\ \sup_{\substack{y=A^i x+b^i,\\ x\in C(\omega),\\ x\in X^{ij}}} y_k^2, \sup_{y\in X^0} y_k^2\} = F_k^\sharp(\omega)\end{aligned}$$

2. From Eq. (18), $\mathcal{R} \subseteq \inf\{C(\omega) \mid \omega \in \mathbb{R}^{d+1},\ F^\sharp(C(\omega)) \subseteq C(\omega)\}$. We conclude using the first point.

3. Direct from the definition of $F_{ij,l}^\sharp(\omega)$.

4. Let $k \in [d]$. Since X^0 is compact and $x \mapsto x_k$ is continuous, there exist $u, z \in X^0$ such that $u_k = \inf_{x\in X^0} x_k$ and $z_k = \sup_{x\in X^0} x_k$. Hence for all $x \in X^0$, $x_k^2 \le \max(z_k^2, u_k^2)$. Since z and u belong to X^0, then $X_k^0 = \max(z_k^2, u_k^2)$. Since $(\mathcal{P}, \mathcal{W}, \mathcal{U}, \mathcal{Z}, \alpha, \beta)$ is an optimal solution of Problem (PSD) and $\alpha > 0$ then $X_{d+1}^0 = \alpha$ from Prop. 5. □

Now, we assume that Problem (PSD) has an optimal solution $(\mathcal{P}, \mathcal{W}, \mathcal{U}, \mathcal{Z}, \alpha, \beta)$ with $\alpha > 0$ and we denote by L the associated wPQL function.

From Prop. 6, to compute $F_{ij,l}^\sharp(\omega)$ is reduced to solve a quadratic maximization known to be NP-Hard [30]. So we propose to compute instead a safe overapproximation using Lagrange duality and semi-definite programming.

4.2 Relaxed functional

In this subsection, we define the function on which we compute a fixed point.

For this subsection, we fix $(i,j) \in \overline{\mathrm{Sw}}$ and $\omega \in \mathbb{R}^{d+1}$. For all $k \in [d]$, we write $\mathbf{M}_k$ for $\mathbf{M}(x \mapsto x_k^2)$ and for all $i \in \mathcal{I}$, $\mathbf{M}_L^i$ for $\mathbf{M}(L^i)$. The matrix $\mathbf{N} \in \mathbb{M}_{(d+1)\times(d+1)}$ is defined by $\mathbf{N}_{l,m} = 1$ if $l = m = 1$ and 0 otherwise.

Let $\lambda \in \mathbb{R}_+^{d+1}$, $Y \in \mathbb{S}_{n_{ij}}^{\ge 0}$ and $Z \in \mathbb{S}_{n_{ij}}^+$. We construct the auxiliary matrices:

$$\begin{aligned}&\Phi_{ij,k}(\lambda, Y, Z) =\\ &F^{i\intercal}\mathbf{M}_k F^i - \sum_{l=1}^d \lambda_l \mathbf{M}_l - \lambda_{l+1}\mathbf{M}_L^i + E^{ij\intercal}(Y+Z)E^{ij}\\ &\Phi_{ij,d+1}(\lambda, Y, Z) =\\ &F^{i\intercal}\mathbf{M}_L^j F^i - \sum_{l=1}^d \lambda_l \mathbf{M}_l - \lambda_{l+1}\mathbf{M}_L^i + E^{ij\intercal}(Y+Z)E^{ij}\end{aligned} \tag{19}$$

For all $l \in [d+1]$, for all $\omega \in \mathbb{R}_+^{d+1}$:

$$\begin{aligned}&F_{ij,l}^{\mathcal{R}}(\omega) =\\ &\inf_{\lambda,\eta,Y,Z} \quad \eta\\ &\text{s.t.} \quad \begin{cases}(\eta - \sum_{k=1}^{d+1}\lambda_k\omega_k)\mathbf{N} - \Phi_{ij,l}(\lambda, Y, Z) \succeq 0,\\ \lambda \in \mathbb{R}_+^{d+1},\ \eta \in \mathbb{R},\ Y \ge 0,\ Z \succeq 0\end{cases}\end{aligned} \tag{20}$$

$$F_l^{\mathcal{R}}(\omega) = \sup\{\sup_{(i,j)\in\overline{\mathrm{Sw}}} F_{ij,l}^{\mathcal{R}}(\omega), X_l^0\}$$

and $F^{\mathcal{R}}(\omega) = (F_1^{\mathcal{R}}(\omega), \ldots, F_{d+1}^{\mathcal{R}}(\omega))$. The map $F^{\mathcal{R}}$ is computable overapproximation of $F^\sharp$. Indeed, $F^{\mathcal{R}}(\omega)$ is the optimal value of a semidefinite program which can be solved in polynomial time[2] and thus relies on SDP solvers.

PROPOSITION 7 (SAFE OVERAPPROXIMATION). *The following assertions are true:*

1. For all $l \in [d+1]$, $F_l^{\mathcal{R}}$ *is the optimal value of a SDP program;*

2. $F^\sharp \le F^{\mathcal{R}}$.

PROOF. *1.* The first statement is straightforward.

2. We have to prove that for all $k \in [d+1]$, for all $\omega \in \mathbb{R}^{d+1}$, $F_{ij,k}^\sharp(\omega) \le F_{ij,k}^{\mathcal{R}}(\omega)$. We do the proof for the case $k = d+1$. The other cases follows the same proof constructions.

Applying the Weak Duality Theorem (see e.g. [5, Sect. 5.3]), we obtain:

$$\begin{aligned}F_{ij,d+1}^\sharp(\omega) \le \inf_{\lambda\in\mathbb{R}_+^{d+1}} \sup_{x\in X^{ij}} L^j(f^i(x)) + \sum_{k=1}^d \lambda_k(\omega_k - x_k^2)\\ + \lambda_{d+1}(\omega_{d+1} - L^i(x))\end{aligned}$$

Let us write $q_{\eta,\lambda} := \eta - L^j(f^i(x)) - \sum_{k=1}^d \lambda_k(\omega_k - x_k^2) - \lambda_{d+1}(\omega_{d+1} - L^i(x))$. Then $\sup_{x\in X^{ij}} L^j(f^i(x)) + \sum_{k=1}^d \lambda_k(\omega_k - x_k^2) + \lambda_{d+1}(\omega_{d+1} - L^i(x)) = \inf\{\eta \mid q_{\eta,\lambda}(x) \ge 0,\ \forall x \in X^{ij}\}$.

From Lemma 2, $\mathbf{M}(q_{\eta,\lambda}) \in \mathbf{C}_{d+1}(E^{ij}) \implies (q_{\eta,\lambda}(x) \ge 0,\ \forall x \in X^{ij})$. From Corollary 1, $(\mathbf{M}(q_{\eta,\lambda}) - E^{ij\intercal}(Y+Z)E^{ij} \succeq 0$ for some $Y \ge 0$ and $Z \succeq 0) \implies \mathbf{M}(q_{\eta,\lambda}) \in \mathbf{C}_{d+1}(E^{ij})$. Now from Eq. (9) and since $A \to \mathbf{M}(A)$ is linear, we have $\mathbf{M}(q_{\eta,\lambda}) = (\eta - \sum_{k=1}^{d+1}\lambda_k\omega_k)N - \Phi_{ij,d+1}(\lambda, Y, Z) + E^{ij\intercal}(Y+Z)E^{ij}$. Since $F_{ij,l}^{\mathcal{R}}$ is the infimum of η over the constraint $(\eta - \sum_{k=1}^{d+1}\lambda_k\omega_k)N - \Phi_{ij,d+1}(\lambda, Y, Z) \succeq 0$, $\lambda \in \mathbb{R}_+^{d+1}$, $\eta \in \mathbb{R}$, $Y \ge 0$ and $Z \succeq 0$, this achieves the proof. □

[2]The term "polynomial time" here must be taken very carefully. Some precisions over the complexity analysis of SDP problems can be found in [24].

LEMMA 4. *Let $(i,j) \in \overline{\text{Sw}}$, $l \in [d+1]$ and $\omega \in \mathbb{R}^{d+1}$. Then:*

$$F^{\mathcal{R}}_{ij,l}(\omega) = \inf_{\lambda \in \mathbb{R}^{d+1}_+} F^{\lambda}_{ij,l}(\omega)$$

where

$$F^{\lambda}_{ij,l}(\omega) = \sum_{m=1}^{d+1} \lambda_m \omega_m + \inf_{\substack{Y \succeq 0\\ Z \succeq 0}} \sup_{x \in \mathbb{R}^d} \begin{pmatrix}1\\x\end{pmatrix}^{\intercal} \Phi_{ij,l}(\lambda, Y, Z) \begin{pmatrix}1\\x\end{pmatrix} \tag{21}$$

PROPOSITION 8. *Let $(i,j) \in \overline{\text{Sw}}$, $l \in [d+1]$, $\lambda \in \mathbb{R}^{d+1}_+$. The following statements are true:*

1. *$F^{\lambda}_{ij,l}$ is affine;*
2. *$F^{\lambda}_{ij,l}$, $F^{\mathcal{R}}_{ij,l}$ and $F^{\mathcal{R}}_l$ are monotone;*
3. *$F^{\mathcal{R}}_{ij,l}$ and $F^{\mathcal{R}}_l$ are upper semi-continuous.*

PROOF. The first assertion follows readily from Eq. (21). The function $w \mapsto F^{\lambda}_{ij,l}(w)$ is monotone from the positivity of λ and the two last functions are monotone as the supremum of monotone functions. The function $w \mapsto F^{\mathcal{R}}_{ij,l}(w)$ is upper semi-continuous as the infimum of continuous functions and $w \mapsto F^{\mathcal{R}}_l(w)$ is upper semi-continuous as the finite supremum of upper semi-continuous functions. □

To be able to perform a new step in policy iteration, we need a selection property. In our case, the selection property relies on the existence of an optimal dual solution.

DEFINITION 5 (SELECTION PROPERTY). *Let $(i,j) \in \overline{\text{Sw}}$ and $l \in [d+1]$. We say that $\omega \in \mathbb{R}^{d+1}$ satisfies the selection property if there exists $\lambda \in \mathbb{R}^{d+1}_+$ such that:*

$$F^{\mathcal{R}}_{ij,l}(\omega) = F^{\lambda}_{ij,l}(\omega) \tag{22}$$

We define:

$$\text{Sol}_{\lambda}((i,j), l, \omega) := \{\lambda \in \mathbb{R}^{d+1}_+ \mid F^{\mathcal{R}}_{ij,l}(\omega) = F^{\lambda}_{ij,l}(\omega)\}$$

and

$$\mathcal{S} := \{\omega \in \mathbb{R}^{d+1} \mid \forall (i,j) \in \overline{\text{Sw}}, \forall l \in [d+1], \text{Sol}_{\lambda}((i,j), l, \omega) \neq \emptyset\} .$$

COROLLARY 2. *Let $(i,j) \in \overline{\text{Sw}}$, $l \in [d+1]$ and $\omega \in \mathcal{S}$. Now let $\overline{\lambda} \in \text{Sol}_{\lambda}((i,j), \omega, p)$, then:*

$$\inf_{\substack{Y \succeq 0\\ Z \succeq 0}} \sup_{x \in \mathbb{R}^d} \begin{pmatrix}1\\x\end{pmatrix}^{\intercal} \Phi_{ij,l}(\lambda, Y, Z) \begin{pmatrix}1\\x\end{pmatrix} = F^{\mathcal{R}}_{ij,l}(\omega) - \sum_{m=1}^{d+1} \overline{\lambda}_m \omega_m .$$

Let $(i,j) \in \overline{\text{Sw}}$, $l \in [d+1]$ and $\omega \in \mathcal{S}$. From Corollary 2, for all $\lambda \in \text{Sol}_{\lambda}((i,j), l, \omega)$, for all $v \in \mathbb{R}^{d+1}$, we have:

$$F^{\lambda}_{ij,l}(v) = \sum_{m=1}^{d+1} \lambda_m v_m + F^{\mathcal{R}}_{ij,l}(\omega) - \sum_{m=1}^{d+1} \overline{\lambda}_m \omega_m \tag{23}$$

We remark that $F^{\lambda}_{ij,l}(\omega) = F^{\mathcal{R}}_{ij,l}(\omega)$.

From the first statement of Prop. 6 and the second assertion of Prop. 7, the most precise overapproximation of $\mathcal{R}$ (with this templates basis) is given by $\overline{\omega} = \inf\{\omega \in \mathbb{R}^{d+1} \mid F^{\mathcal{R}}(\omega) \leq \omega\}$. From Tarski's theorem, $\overline{\omega}$ is the smallest fixed point of $F^{\mathcal{R}}$. However, the smallest is difficult to get and since any vector ω such that $F^{\mathcal{R}}(\omega) \leq \omega$ furnishes a valid but less precise overapproximation of $\mathcal{R}$, we perform policy iterations until a fixed point is reached.

4.3 Policies definition

A policy iteration algorithm can be used to solve a fixed point equation for a monotone function written as an infimum of a family of simpler monotone functions, obtained by selecting *policies*, see [9, 13] for more background. The idea is to solve a sequence of fixed point problems involving the simple functions. In the present setting, we look for a representation of the relaxed function:

$$\forall (i,j) \in \overline{\text{Sw}}, \forall l \in [d+1], \; F^{\mathcal{R}}_{ij,l} = \inf_{\pi \in \Pi} F^{\pi}_{ij,l} \tag{24}$$

where the infimum is taken over a set Π whose elements π are called *policies*, and where each function F^{π} is required to be monotone. The correctness of the algorithm relies on a selection property, meaning in the present setting that for each argument $((i,j), l, \omega)$ there must exist a policy π such that $F^{\mathcal{R}}_{ij,l}(\omega) = F^{\pi}_{ij,l}(\omega)$. The idea of the algorithm is to start from a policy π^0, compute the smallest fixed point ω of F^{π^0}, evaluate $F^{\mathcal{R}}$ at point ω, and, if $\omega \neq F^{\mathcal{R}}(\omega)$, determine the new policy using the selection property at point ω.

Let us now identify the policies. Lemma 4 shows that for all $l \in [d+1]$, $F^{\mathcal{R}}_{ij}$ can be written as the infimum of the family of affine functions F^{λ}_{ij}, the infimum being taken over the set of $\lambda \in \mathbb{R}^{d+1}_+$. When $\omega \in \mathcal{S}$ is given, choosing a policy π consists in selecting, for each $(i,j) \in \overline{\text{Sw}}$ and for all $l \in [d+1]$, a vector $\lambda \in \text{Sol}_{\lambda}((i,j), l, \omega)$. We denote by $\pi_{ij,l}(\omega)$ the value of λ chosen by the policy π. Then, the map $F^{\pi_{ij,l}}_{ij,l}$ in Eq. (24) is obtained by replacing $F^{\mathcal{R}}_{ij,l}$ by $F^{\lambda}_{ij,l}$ appearing in Eq. (23). Finally, we define, for all $l \in [d+1]$:

$$F^{\pi}_l(\omega) = \sup\{\sup_{(i,j) \in \overline{\text{Sw}}} F^{\pi_{ij,l}}_{ij,l}(\omega), X^0_l\}$$

and $F^{\pi} = (F^{\pi}_1, \ldots, F^{\pi}_{d+1})$.

Now, we can define concretely the policy iteration algorithm at Algorithm 1.

Algorithm 1 Policy Iteration with wPQL functions

1. Choose $\pi^0 \in \Pi$, $k = 0$.
2. Define F^{π^k} by choosing λ according to policy π^k using Eq. (23).
3. Compute the smallest fixed point ω^k in $\mathbb{R}^{d+1}$ of F^{π^k}.
4. If $\omega^k \in \mathcal{S}$ continue otherwise return ω^k.
5. Evaluate $F^{\mathcal{R}}(\omega^k)$, if $F^{\mathcal{R}}(\omega^k) = \omega^k$ return ω^k otherwise take π^{k+1} s.t. $F^{\mathcal{R}}(\omega^k) = F^{\pi^{k+1}}(\omega^k)$. Increment k and go to 2.

4.4 Some details about Policy Iteration algorithm

Initialization. Policy iteration algorithm needs an initial policy. Recall that L was computed from an optimal solution $(\mathcal{P}, \mathcal{W}, \mathcal{U}, \mathcal{Z}, \alpha, \beta)$ of Problem (PSD) with $\alpha > 0$. The first policy is given by an element in $\text{Sol}_{\lambda}((i,j), l, w^0)$ where w^0 is defined by:

$$\forall k \in [d], \; \omega^0_k = \beta, \; w^0_{d+1} = \alpha \tag{25}$$

PROPOSITION 9. *The vector ω^0 satisfies $F^{\mathcal{R}}(\omega^0) \leq \omega^0$.*

PROOF. From Prop. 5, we have for all $k \in [d]$, $X_k^0 \leq \beta = \omega_k^0$ and $X_{d+1}^0 = \alpha = \omega_{d+1}^0$. Let $(i,j) \in \overline{Sw}$ and $l \in [d+1]$. We have to prove that $F_{ij,l}^{\mathcal{R}}(\omega^0) \leq \omega^0$. It suffices to prove there exist $\lambda \geq 0$, $Y \geq 0$ and $Z \succeq 0$ such that:

$$(\omega_l^0 - \sum_{k=1}^{d+1} \lambda_k \omega_k)N - \Phi_{ij,l}(\lambda, Y, Z) \succeq 0 \tag{26}$$

Indeed, if Eq. (26) holds then $(\omega_l^0(p), \lambda, Y, Z)$ is feasible for the SDP problem (20) and thus $F_{ij,l}^{\mathcal{R}}(\omega^0) \leq \omega_l^0$.

Let us define $\bar{\lambda}$ by $\bar{\lambda}_{d+1} = 1$ and $\bar{\lambda}_k = 0$ for all $k \in [d]$. Let us simply write $S := (\mathcal{P}, \mathcal{W}, \mathcal{U}, \mathcal{Z}, \alpha, \beta)$.

Let $l = d+1$ and extract U_p^{ij} and U_+^{ij} from $\mathcal{U}$. Then, $(\omega_{d+1}^0 - \sum_{k=1}^{d+1} \bar{\lambda}_k \omega_k)N - \Phi_{ij,l}(\bar{\lambda}, U_p^{ij}, U_+^{ij}) = -F^{i\intercal}\mathbf{M}_L^j F^i + \mathbf{M}_L^i - E^{ij\intercal}(U_p^{ij} + U_+^{ij})E^{ij}$. Since S satisfies Eq. (16) as an optimal solution of Problem (PSD), Eq (26) holds with $\lambda = \bar{\lambda}$, $Y = U_p^{ij}$ and $Z = U_+^{ij}$.

Let $l \in [d]$, $\bar{Y} = P_\sigma^\intercal \begin{pmatrix} 0_{n_i-1} & 0_{n_i-1,n_j} \\ 0_{n_j,n_i-1} & W_p^j \end{pmatrix} P_\sigma + U_p^{ij}$ and $\bar{Z} = P_\sigma^\intercal \begin{pmatrix} 0_{n_i-1} & 0_{n_i-1,n_j} \\ 0_{n_j,n_i-1} & W_+^j \end{pmatrix} P_\sigma + U_+^{ij}$ where P_σ is the permutation matrix defined at Prop 5, W_p^j and W_+^j are extracted from $\mathcal{W}$ and U_p^{ij} and U_+^{ij} are extracted from $\mathcal{U}$. We have $(\omega_l^0 - \sum_{k=1}^{d+1} \bar{\lambda}_k \omega_k)N - \Phi_{ij,l}(\bar{\lambda}, \bar{Y}, \bar{Z}) = \mathbf{M}(0, 0, \beta - \alpha) - F^{i\intercal}\mathbf{M}_l F^i + \mathbf{M}_L^i - E^{ij\intercal}(\bar{Y} + \bar{Z})E^{ij}$. Now, remark that $\mathbf{M}_l \preceq \mathbf{M}(\mathrm{Id}, 0, 0)$ and thus $-F^{i\intercal}\mathbf{M}_l F^i + \mathbf{M}(P^i, 2q^i, -\alpha) - E^{ij\intercal}(\bar{Y} + \bar{Z})E^{ij} + \mathbf{M}(0,0,\beta) \preceq -F^{i\intercal}\mathbf{M}(\mathrm{Id}, 0, 0)F^i + \mathbf{M}(P^i, 2q^i, -\alpha) - E^{ij\intercal}(\bar{Y}+\bar{Z})E^{ij} + \mathbf{M}(0,0,\beta)$. We conclude that Eq (26) holds with $\lambda = \bar{\lambda}$, $Y = \bar{Y}$ and $Z = \bar{Z}$ from the second assertion of Prop. 5. □

Smallest fixed point computation associated to a policy. For the third step of Algorithm 1, using Lemma 4, F^π is monotone and affine, we compute the smallest fixed point of F^π by solving the following LP see [13, Section 4]:

$$\min \left\{ \sum_{k=1}^{d+1} w_k \text{ s.t. } F^\pi(w) \leq w \right\} \tag{27}$$

Convergence. In [1], it is proved that the policy iterations algorithm in the quadratic setting converges towards a fixed point of $F^{\mathcal{R}}$. Here, we establish a similar result (Th. 1). Combined with Prop. 7, this fixed point provides a safe over-approximation of $\mathcal{R}$.

Let $(w^l)_{l\in\mathbb{N}}$ be the sequence generated by Algorithm 1. If $w^l \notin \mathcal{S}$ and $w^{l-1} \in \mathcal{S}$, then we set $w^k = w^l$ for all $k \geq l$.

THEOREM 1. *The following assertions hold:*
1. For all $l \in \mathbb{N}$, $F^{\mathcal{R}}(w^l) \leq w^l$;
2. The sequence $(w^l)_{l\geq 0}$ is decreasing. Moreover for all $l \in \mathbb{N}$ such that $w^{l-1} \in \mathcal{S}$ either $w^l = w^{l-1}$ and $F^{\mathcal{R}}(w^l) = w^l$ or $w^l < w^{l-1}$;
3. For all $l \in \mathbb{N}$, for all $k \in [d+1]$, $X_k^0 \leq w_k^l \leq w_k^0$;
4. The limit w^∞ of $(w^l)_{l\geq 0}$ satisfies: $F^{\mathcal{R}}(w^\infty) \leq w^\infty$. Moreover if $\forall k \in \mathbb{N}$, $w^k \in \mathcal{S}$ then $F^{\mathcal{R}}(w^\infty) = w^\infty$.

PROOF. *1.* From Prop. 9, $F^{\mathcal{R}}(w^0) \leq w^0$. Now, let $l > 0$ and assume $w^{l-1} \in \mathcal{S}$, there exists π^l such that, $F^{\pi^l}(w^l) = w^l$ and since $F^{\mathcal{R}} = \inf_\pi F^\pi$, we get $F^{\mathcal{R}}(w^l) \leq F^{\pi^l}(w^l) = w^l$. If $w^{l-1} \notin \mathcal{S}$, then there exists $k \in \mathbb{N}$, $k \leq l-1$ such that $w^{k-1} \in \mathcal{S}$ and $w^l = w^k$, and thus $F^{\mathcal{R}}(w^k) \leq w^k$.

2. Let $l \in \mathbb{N}$, if $w^{l-1} \notin \mathcal{S}$, $w^l = w^{l-1}$. Now suppose $w^{l-1} \in \mathcal{S}$. There exists $\pi^l \in \Pi$ such that $F^{\mathcal{R}}(w^{l-1}) = F^{\pi^l}(w^{l-1}) \leq w^{l-1}$ and since $w^l = \inf\{v \in \mathbb{R}^{d+1} \mid F^{\pi^l}(v) \leq v\}$ then $w^l \leq w^{l-1}$. Now if $w^l = w^{l-1}$, $F^{\mathcal{R}}(w^{l-1}) = F^{\mathcal{R}}(w^l) = F^{\pi^l}(w^{l-1}) = F^{\pi^l}(w^l) = w^l = w^{l-1}$.

3. From Prop. 6, Prop. 7 and the first assertion, $X_k^0 \leq F_k^\sharp(w^l) \leq F_k^{\mathcal{R}}(w^l) \leq w_k^l$.

4. First, w^∞ exists since $(w_l)_{l\in\mathbb{N}}$ is decreasing and bounded from below (third assertion). Then, for all $l \in \mathbb{N}$, $w^\infty \leq w^l$ and since $F^{\mathcal{R}}$ is monotone (Prop. 8) $F^{\mathcal{R}}(w^\infty) \leq F^{\mathcal{R}}(w^l) \leq w^l$. Taking the infimum over l, we get $F^{\mathcal{R}}(w^\infty) \leq w^\infty$. Now we prove that $w^\infty \leq F^{\mathcal{R}}(w^\infty)$. Let $l \in \mathbb{N}$. Since $w^l \in \mathcal{S}$, there exists $\pi^{l+1} \in \Pi$ such that $F^{\pi^{l+1}}(w^l) = F^{\mathcal{R}}(w^l)$. Moreover, $w^{l+1} \leq w^l$ and since $F^{\pi^{l+1}}$ is monotone: $w^{l+1} = F^{\pi^{l+1}}(w^{l+1}) \leq F^{\pi^{l+1}}(w^l) = F^{\mathcal{R}}(w^l)$. Now by taking the infimum on l, we get $w^\infty = \inf_l w^{l+1} = \inf_l w^l \leq \inf_l F^{\mathcal{R}}(w^l)$. Finally, since $F^{\mathcal{R}}$ is upper semicontinuous (Prop. 8), then $\inf_k F^{\mathcal{R}}(w^k) = \limsup_k F^{\mathcal{R}}(w^k) \leq F^{\mathcal{R}}(\lim_k w^k) = F^{\mathcal{R}}(w^\infty)$. Hence, $w^\infty \leq F^{\mathcal{R}}(w^\infty)$. □

5. EXAMPLES

The following examples are performed using YALMIP interfaced with the SDP solver MOSEK.

5.1 Example from [21] slighty modified

Consider the followinf PWA: $X^0 = [-1,1] \times [-1,1]$, and, for all $k \in \mathbb{N}$:

$$x_{k+1} = \begin{cases} A^1 x_k & \text{if } x_{k,1} \geq 0 \text{ and } x_{k,2} \geq 0 \\ A^2 x_k & \text{if } x_{k,1} \geq 0 \text{ and } x_{k,2} < 0 \\ A^3 x_k & \text{if } x_{k,1} < 0 \text{ and } x_{k,2} < 0 \\ A^4 x_k & \text{if } x_{k,1} < 0 \text{ and } x_{k,2} \geq 0 \end{cases}$$

with

$$A^1 = \begin{pmatrix} -0.04 & -0.461 \\ -0.139 & 0.341 \end{pmatrix}, \ A^2 = \begin{pmatrix} 0.936 & 0.323 \\ 0.788 & -0.049 \end{pmatrix}$$
$$A^3 = \begin{pmatrix} -0.857 & 0.815 \\ 0.491 & 0.62 \end{pmatrix}, \ A^4 = \begin{pmatrix} -0.022 & 0.644 \\ 0.758 & 0.271 \end{pmatrix}$$

Then, we have $X^1 = \mathbb{R}_+ \times \mathbb{R}_+$, $X^2 = \mathbb{R}_+ \times \mathbb{R}_-^*$, $X^3 = \mathbb{R}_-^* \times \mathbb{R}_-^*$ and $X^4 = \mathbb{R}_-^* \times \mathbb{R}_+$.

From Prop. 2, In $= \{1,2,3,4\}$ and $\overline{\mathrm{Sw}} = \{(i,j) \mid S(i,j) = 1\}$ with $S = \begin{pmatrix} 1&0&1&1 \\ 1&0&0&1 \\ 0&1&1&0 \\ 1&1&0&0 \end{pmatrix}$.

By solving Problem PSD, we get a (optimal) wPQL function L characterized by the following matrices:

$$P^1 = \begin{pmatrix} 1.1178 & -0.1178 \\ -0.1178 & 1.1178 \end{pmatrix}, \ P^2 = \begin{pmatrix} 1.5907 & 0.5907 \\ 0.5907 & 1.5907 \end{pmatrix},$$
$$P^3 = \begin{pmatrix} 1.3309 & -0.3309 \\ -0.3309 & 1.3309 \end{pmatrix}, \ P^4 = \begin{pmatrix} 1.2558 & 0.2558 \\ 0.2558 & 1.2558 \end{pmatrix}$$

Since $\alpha = \beta = 2$, then $\mathcal{R} \subseteq \{x \in \mathbb{R}^2 \mid L(x) \leq 2\} \subseteq \{x \in \mathbb{R}^2 \mid \|x\|_2^2 \leq 2\}$. The sets $\mathcal{R}$ (discretized version) and $\{x \in \mathbb{R}^2 \mid L(x) \leq 2\}$ are depicted at Figure 1a. Then we enter into policy iteration algorithm. Fròm Eq. (25), we define w^0 by $w_1^0 = 2.0000$, $w_2^0 = 2.0000$, $w_3^0 = 2.0000$. Then we compute the image of w^0 by the relaxed semantics $F^{\mathcal{R}}(w^0)$ using semidefinite programming (see Eq. (20)). We check that w^0 is not a fixed point of $F^{\mathcal{R}}$ and then the initial policy

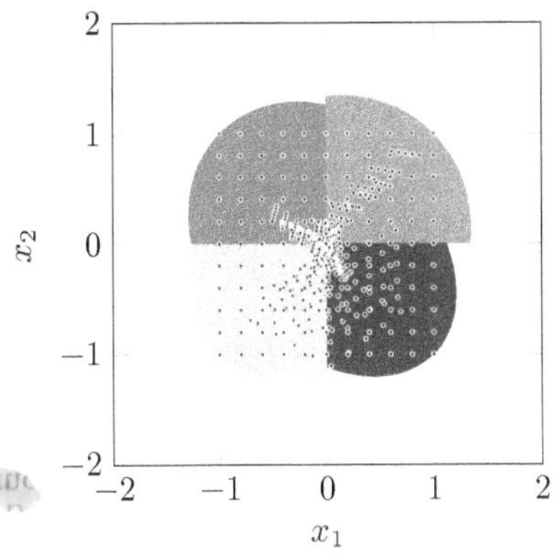

(a) First overapproximation found by (PSD)

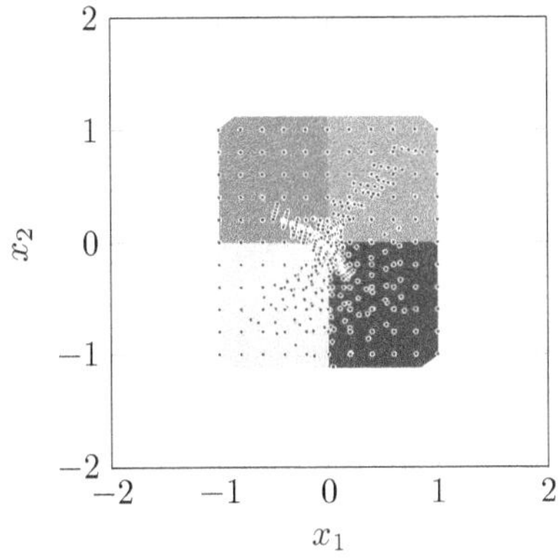

(b) Final overapproximation found by policy iterations

Figure 1: (Discretized) $\mathcal{R}$ in yellow and initial (Fig. 1a) and last overapproximations (Fig. 1b) of $\mathcal{R}$.

$\pi^0((i,j),l,w^0)$ is the vector λ extracted from the optimal solutions (λ, Y, Z) of the semidefinite programs involved in the computation of $F^{\mathcal{R}}(w^0)$. For example, for $(1,3) \in \overline{\text{Sw}}$ and $l = 1$, $\pi^0((1,3),1,w^0) = (0.0000, 0.0000, 0.0430)^\intercal$, where the first two zeros are the Lagrange multipliers associated to $\mathbf{M}_1$ and $\mathbf{M}_2$ and 0.0430 is the Lagrange multiplier associated to $\mathbf{M}(L^1)$. We compute the smallest fixed point associated to π^0 using the LP (27):

$$w_1^1 = 1.1036,\ w_2^1 = 1.2443,\ w_3^1 = 2.0000$$

Moreover, at each step k, policy iterations provides auxiliary values which represent the overapproximations of the polyhedra $\mathcal{R} \cap X^i \cap A^{i^{-1}}(X^j)$ by ellipsoids of the form $\{x \in \mathbb{R}^2 \mid x_1^2 \leq w_{ij,1}^k,\ x_2^2 \leq w_{ij,2}^k,\ L(x_1,x_2) \leq w_{ij,3}^k\}$. For example, for $k = 0$:

$$\begin{array}{l} w_{11,1} = 0.0000,\ w_{11,2} = 0.0000,\ w_{11,3} = 0.0000 \\ w_{13,1} = 0.0573,\ w_{13,2} = 0.0213,\ w_{13,3} = 0.0213 \\ w_{14,1} = 0.3012,\ w_{14,2} = 0.1447,\ w_{14,3} = 0.1447 \end{array}$$

Note that we found that for $(i,j) = (1,1)$, $w_{ij,1}^1 = w_{ij,2}^1 = w_{ij,3}^1 = 0$ which means that $\mathcal{R} \cap X^1 \cap A^{1^{-1}}(X^1)$ is reduced to the singleton $(0,0)$. The invariant found is depicted at Figure 1b. Finally, we find after two iterations that for all $k \in \mathbb{N}$, $x_{1,k}^2 \leq 1$, $x_{2,k}^2 \leq 1.2443$ and $L(x_{1,k}, x_{2,k}) \leq 2$.

5.2 A (piecewise) affine example

We now consider the following PWA: $X^0 = [0,3] \times [0,2]$ and for all $k \in \mathbb{N}$:

$$x_{k+1} = \begin{cases} A^1 x_k + b^1 & \text{if } T(x_k) < c \\ A^2 x_k + b^2 & \text{if } T(x_k) \geq c \end{cases}$$

with

$$A^1 = \begin{pmatrix} 0.4197 & -0.2859 \\ 0.5029 & 0.1679 \end{pmatrix},\quad b^1 = \begin{pmatrix} 2.0000 \\ 5.0000 \end{pmatrix},$$
$$A^2 = \begin{pmatrix} -0.0575 & -0.4275 \\ -0.3334 & -0.2682 \end{pmatrix},\quad b^2 = \begin{pmatrix} -4.0000 \\ 4.0000 \end{pmatrix}$$

$$T = \begin{pmatrix} 3.0000 & 8.0000 \end{pmatrix} \text{ and } c = -3.0000$$

By Prop. 2, $\overline{\text{Sw}} = \mathcal{I}^2 = \{(1,1),(1,2),(2,1),(2,2)\}$ and $\text{In} = \{2\}$. Using Problem (PSD), we compute the wPQL function L characterized by:

$$P^1 = \begin{pmatrix} 2.9888 & -1.7890 \\ -1.7890 & 8.0295 \end{pmatrix},\quad q^1 = \begin{pmatrix} -14.7283 \\ -94.1347 \end{pmatrix}$$
and
$$P^2 = \begin{pmatrix} 2.7192 & 2.0930 \\ 2.0930 & 6.1110 \end{pmatrix},\quad q^2 = \begin{pmatrix} 5.5737 \\ -16.4198 \end{pmatrix}$$

and the invariant found is $\{x \in \mathbb{R}^2 \mid L(x) \leq 58.1165\}$ and an upper bound over the square Euclidian norm of the state variable is 286.4932. We run the policy iteration to get finally after 4 iterations the following bound vector:

$$w_1 = 41.8956,\ w_2 = 31.4449,\ w_3 = 58.1165$$

corresponding to the invariant set $\{x \in \mathbb{R}^2 \mid x_i^2 \leq w_i,\ L(x) \leq w_3\}$.

We obtain interesting information during policy iterations. At step $k = 0$, when we select the initial policy, the SDP solver returns for all $l = 1,2,3$, $F_{11,l}^{\mathcal{R}}(w^0) = -\infty$ and from Prop. 7 this implies that $\sup_{x \in \mathcal{R} \cap X^1 \cap f^{1^{-1}}(X^1)} p(A^1 x + b^1)$ is not feasible hence $(1,1) \notin \text{Sw}$. At the iteration step $k = 1$, the SDP solver provides for all $l = 1,2,3$, $F_{21,l}^{\mathcal{R}}(w^1) = -\infty$ and from Prop. 7 this implies that $(2,1) \notin \text{Sw}$. Finally, $\text{Sw} \subseteq \{(1,2),(2,2)\}$. Recalling that $1 \notin \text{In}$, we conclude that the system state variable only stays in X^2 and thus the system is actually equivalent to a *constrained affine system*. This information is computed *automatically*.

6. CONCLUSION AND FUTURE WORKS

We have developed a method to compute *automatically* by semi-definite programming precise bounds over the reachable values set of a piecewise affine system. The method combines weak piecewise quadratic Lyapunov functions to generate a first overapproximation and policy iterations used to reduce the initial overapproximation.

Future works could be to design a repartitioning method in order to improve the feasibility of Problem (PSD). In the same direction, we could use SOS programming to rewrite copositive constraints. Also, future works should contain the study of the optimality of the presented policy iterations algorithm (providing the most precise overapproximation considering bounding the square of coordinates variables or not).

7. REFERENCES

[1] A. Adjé. Policy iteration in finite templates domain. In *Numerical Software Verification (NSV 2014)*, 2014.

[2] A. Adjé and P.-L. Garoche. Automatic Synthesis of Piecewise Linear Quadratic Invariants for Programs. In *Verification, Model Checking, and Abstract Interpretation - 16th International Conference, VMCAI 2015, Mumbai, India, January 12-14, 2015. Proceedings*, pages 99–116, 2015.

[3] A. Adjé, S. Gaubert, and E. Goubault. Coupling Policy Iteration with Semi-Definite Relaxation to Compute Accurate Numerical Invariants in Static Analysis. *Logical Methods in Computer Science*, 8(1), 2012.

[4] X. Allamigeon. *Static Analysis of Memory Manipulations by Abstract Interpretation — Algorithmics of Tropical Polyhedra, and Application to Abstract Interpretation*. PhD thesis, École Polytechnique, Palaiseau, France, November 2009.

[5] A. Auslender and M. Teboulle. *Asymptotic Cones and Functions in Optimization and Variational Inequalities*. Springer Science & Business Media, 2006.

[6] H. Bazille, O. Bournez, W. Gomaa, and A. Pouly. On The Complexity of Bounded Time Reachability for Piecewise Affine Systems. In *Reachability Problems: 8th International Workshop, RP 2014, Oxford, UK, September 22-24, 2014. Proceedings*, pages 20–31, Cham, 2014. Springer International Publishing.

[7] I. M. Bomze, W. Schachinger, and G. Uchida. Think Co(mpletely)positive ! Matrix Properties, Examples and a Clustered Bibliography on Copositive Optimization. *Journal of Global Optimization*, 52(3):423–445, 2012.

[8] S. Bundfuss and M. Dür. An Adaptive Linear Approximation Algorithm for Copositive Programs. *SIAM J. on Optimization*, 20(1):30–53, March 2009.

[9] A. Costan, S. Gaubert, E. Goubault, M. Martel, and S. Putot. A Policy Iteration Algorithm for Computing Fixed Points in Static Analysis of Programs. In *Computer aided verification*, pages 462–475. Springer, 2005.

[10] P. H. Diananda. On Non-negative Forms in Real Variables Some or All of Which are Non-negative. *Mathematical Proceedings of the Cambridge Philosophical Society*, 58:17–25, 1 1962.

[11] Gang Feng. Stability Analysis of Piecewise Discrete-time Linear Systems. *IEEE Transactions on Automatic Control*, 47(7):1109, 2002.

[12] Giancarlo Ferrari-Trecate, Francesco Alessandro Cuzzola, Domenico Mignone, and Manfred Morari. Analysis of Discrete-time Piecewise Affine and Hybrid Systems. *Automatica*, 38(12):2139–2146, 2002.

[13] S. Gaubert, E. Goubault, A. Taly, and S. Zennou. Static Analysis by Policy Iteration on Relational Domains. In *Programming Languages and Systems*, pages 237–252. Springer, 2007.

[14] T. Gawlitza, H. Seidl, A. Adjé, S. Gaubert, and E. Goubault. Abstract Interpretation Meets Convex Optimization. *J. Symb. Comput.*, 47(12):1416–1446, 2012.

[15] A. J. Hoffman and R. M. Karp. On Nonterminating Stochastic Games. *Management Science*, 12(5):359–370, 1966.

[16] R. A. Howard. *Dynamic Programming and Markov Processes*. MIT Press, Cambridge, MA, 1960.

[17] M. Johansson. On Modeling, Analysis and Design of Piecewise Linear Control Systems. In *Circuits and Systems, 2003. ISCAS '03. Proceedings of the 2003 International Symposium on*, volume 3, pages III–646–III–649 vol.3, May 2003.

[18] D.H. Martin and D.H. Jacobson. Copositive Matrices and Definiteness of Quadratic Forms Subject to Homogeneous Linear Inequality Constraints. *Linear Algebra and its Applications*, 35(0):227 – 258, 1981.

[19] D. Massé. Proving Termination by Policy Iteration. *Electronic Notes in Theoretical Computer Science*, 287(0):77 – 88, 2012. Proceedings of the Fourth International Workshop on Numerical and Symbolic Abstract Domains, NSAD 2012.

[20] J. E. Maxfield and H. Minc. On the Matrix Equation $X'X = A$. *Proceedings of the Edinburgh Mathematical Society (Series 2)*, 13:125–129, 12 1962.

[21] D. Mignone, G. Ferrari-Trecate, and M. Morari. Stability and Stabilization of Piecewise Affine and Hybrid systems: an LMI approach. In *Decision and Control, 2000. Proceedings of the 39th IEEE Conference on*, volume 1, pages 504–509 vol.1, 2000.

[22] T. S. Motzkin. Two Consequences of the Transposition Theorem on Linear Inequalities. *Econometrica*, 19(2):184–185, 1951.

[23] SV Rakovic, P Grieder, M Kvasnica, DQ Mayne, and M Morari. Computation of Invariant Sets for Piecewise Affine Discrete Time Systems Subject to Bounded Disturbances. In *Decision and Control, 2004. CDC. 43rd IEEE Conference on*, volume 2, pages 1418–1423. IEEE, 2004.

[24] M. V. Ramana and P. M. Pardalos. Semidefinite Programming. *Interior point methods of mathematical programming*, 5:369–398, 1997.

[25] P. Roux, R. Jobredeaux, P.-L. Garoche, and E. Feron. A Generic Ellipsoid Abstract Domain for Linear Time Invariant Systems. In *Hybrid Systems: Computation and Control (part of CPS Week 2012), HSCC'12, Beijing, China, April 17-19, 2012*, pages 105–114, 2012.

[26] P. Schrammel and P. Subotic. Logico-Numerical Max-Strategy Iteration. In Roberto Giacobazzi, Josh Berdine, and Isabella Mastroeni, editors, *Verification, Model Checking, and Abstract Interpretation*, volume 7737 of *Lecture Notes in Computer Science*, pages 414–433. Springer Berlin Heidelberg, 2013.

[27] S. Schupp, E. Ábrahám, X. Chen, I. Ben Makhlouf, G. Frehse, S. Sankaranarayanan, and S. Kowalewski. Current Challenges in the Verification of Hybrid Systems. In *Cyber Physical Systems. Design, Modeling, and Evaluation - 5th International Workshop, CyPhy 2015, Amsterdam, The Netherlands, October 8, 2015, Proceedings*, pages 8–24, 2015.

[28] P. Sotin, B. Jeannet, F. Védrine, and E. Goubault. Policy iteration within logico-numerical abstract domains. In *Automated Technology for Verification and Analysis*, pages 290–305. Springer, 2011.

[29] A. Tarski. A lattice-theoretical fixpoint theorem and its applications. *Pacific J. Math.*, 5(2):285–309, 1955.

[30] S. A. Vavasis. Quadratic programming is in NP. *Information Processing Letters*, 36(2):73 – 77, 1990.

Robust Model Checking of Timed Automata under Clock Drifts

Nima Roohi
Department of Computer Science, University of Illinois at Urbana-Champaign, Illinois, USA
roohi2@illinois.edu

Pavithra Prabhakar
Department of Computer Science, Kansas State University, KS, USA
pprabhakar@ksu.edu

Mahesh Viswanathan
Department of Computer Science, University of Illinois at Urbana-Champaign, Illinois, USA
vmahesh@illinois.edu

ABSTRACT

Timed automata have an idealized semantics where clocks are assumed to be perfectly continuous and synchronized, and guards have infinite precision. These assumptions cannot be realized physically. In order to ensure that correct timed automata designs can be implemented on real-time platforms, several authors have suggested that timed automata be studied under robust semantics. A timed automaton $\mathcal{H}$ is said to robustly satisfy a property if there is a positive ϵ and/or a positive δ such that the automaton satisfies the property even when the clocks are allowed to drift by ϵ and/or guards are enlarged by δ. In this paper we show that, 1. checking ω-regular properties when only clocks are perturbed or when both clocks and guards are perturbed, is PSPACE-complete; and 2. one can compute the exact reachable set of a bounded timed automaton when clocks are drifted by infinitesimally small amount, using polynomial space. In particular, we remove the restrictive assumption on the timed automaton that its region graph only contains progress cycles, under which the second result above has been previously established.

1. INTRODUCTION

Timed automata [2] are the standard formal model for real-time systems because they are an elegant and expressive formalism, and, yet are amenable to algorithmic analysis [14, 18]. However, timed automata have an idealistic semantics that makes assumptions that are physically unrealizable. In timed automata, time is measured by perfectly continuous and synchronous clocks that have infinite precision as opposed to finite precision, almost synchronized, digital clocks that are accessed by implementations. Timed automata can also respond instantaneously to events whereas physical realizations of the real-time systems react with some non-zero delay. Finally, timed automata allow modelling control algorithms that exhibit Zeno behaviors, have unrealistic convergence properties [10], or isolated behaviors [12]. These deficiencies have been observed by a number of researchers [1, 3, 10, 12, 16, 17]. In order to ensure that correct timed automata yield correct, implementable designs, the remedy suggested by these papers is to consider a *robust* semantics for timed automata.

HSCC'17, April 18 - 20, 2017, Pittsburgh, PA, USA

ACM ISBN 978-1-4503-4590-3/17/04...$15.00

DOI: http://dx.doi.org/10.1145/3049797.3049821

Starting from the seminal work of [12] where a topological notion of robustness was proposed, different notions of robustness have been considered [3, 15, 16]. One notion of robustness that has been studied extensively, is the following. For a timed automaton $\mathcal{H}$, using $\mathcal{H}^{\epsilon}_{\delta}$ to denote the automaton similar to $\mathcal{H}$ with guards enlarged by δ and clocks allowed to drift by ϵ, robust satisfaction of φ asks if there is some $\epsilon \in \mathbb{R}_+$ and $\delta \in \mathbb{R}_+$ such that $\mathcal{H}^{\epsilon}_{\delta}$ satisfies φ. This notion of robustness has been shown to imply implementability in real-time platforms [11, 16].

The algorithmic complexity of checking the robustness of timed automata designs has received much attention. For a timed automaton $\mathcal{H}$, let us denote by $\mathcal{H}^{\epsilon}$ the semantics where clocks can drift by ϵ (but guards remain unperturbed), and by $\mathcal{H}_{\delta}$ the one where guards are enlarged by δ (but clocks do not drift). Robust satisfaction under only clock drifts asks if for some $\epsilon \in \mathbb{R}_+$, $\mathcal{H}^{\epsilon}$ satisfies the property, while robust satisfaction under only enlarged guards asks if for some $\delta \in \mathbb{R}_+$, $\mathcal{H}_{\delta}$ satisfies the property. For safety properties, and bounded timed automata [1] the problem was first considered in [15]. It is shown that robustness with only clocks drifts with respect to safety properties can be decided in PSPACE. These results were generalized in [11] where safety verification under both clock drifts and enlarged guards is solved in PSPACE. The approach in both [15] and [11] is based on computing the reachable states under infinitesimal guard and clock perturbations (or only guard or only clock perturbations), referred to as $\mathsf{limreach}^{\epsilon}_{\delta}(\mathcal{H})$ (or $\mathsf{limreach}_{\delta}(\mathcal{H})$ or $\mathsf{limreach}^{\epsilon}(\mathcal{H})$). It is shown that $\mathcal{H}$ is robustly safe (under just clock drifts, or guard perturbations, or both) iff the corresponding limreach set is disjoint from the unsafe states. Moreover, it is observed in [11] that the three limreach sets coincide, that is,

$$\mathsf{limreach}^{\epsilon}_{\delta}(\mathcal{H}) = \mathsf{limreach}^{\epsilon}(\mathcal{H}) = \mathsf{limreach}_{\delta}(\mathcal{H}) \tag{1}$$

Except the results about disjointness of unsafe and limreach sets, all the above results on safety verification (including the fact that limreach sets coincide) in [11, 15] are established for timed automata that satisfy the *progress cycle assumption (PCA)* which requires that every cycle in the region graph of $\mathcal{H}$ resets every clock of timed automaton at least once.

[1]A timed automaton is *bounded* if the invariant of every location is bounded.

The progress cycle assumption can be restrictive when modeling real-time systems because it does not allow the design to measure time spent in cycles. Therefore, the decidability of robust verification without the progress cycle assumption was investigated in [8]. The results from [11, 15] were generalized in a couple of directions. First the progress cycle assumption was removed. Second, general ω-regular properties were considered as opposed to just safety. In addition, the restriction to bounded timed automata was also removed; this restriction to bounded automata is, however, not limiting because every timed automaton is weakly bisimilar to a bounded timed automaton [5, 7]. However, in some respects, the results in [8] are also less general than those in [11]; the paper [8] only considers robustness with respect to perturbation of guards alone.

In this paper, we continue this line of investigation. In the absence of the progress cycle assumption, we ask what is the complexity of robustly verifying a property when clocks are allowed to drift, as well. Our first observation is that an automaton $\mathcal{H}$ robustly satisfies a property $\Box\Diamond B$ when both clocks and guards are perturbed iff $\mathcal{H}$ robustly satisfies the same property when only guards are enlarged. In addition, $\mathsf{limreach}^{\epsilon}_{\delta}(\mathcal{H}) = \mathsf{limreach}_{\delta}(\mathcal{H})$. Thus, using the algorithm in [8], one can verify designs under both clock drifts and guard perturbation. On the other hand, we show that robustness when only clocks are drifted is not equivalent with the *stronger* notion of robustness when both guards and clocks are perturbed. More precisely, we show that there are timed automata that are robust when only clocks are drifted, but not when both guards and clocks are perturbed (see Example 12). This is in contrast to Equation (1) that holds under the progress cycle assumption. We then present an algorithm to check ω-regular properties when only clocks are drifted. We show that a timed automaton $\mathcal{H}$ robustly satisfies a property $\Box\Diamond B$ when only clocks are drifted iff there is a constant δ_1 (depending only on the size of $\mathcal{H}$) such that the automaton in which only the guard constraints involving *positive* constants are perturbed by δ_1, satisfies $\Box\Diamond B$. This observation can be exploited to give a PSPACE algorithm. We also show that this problem is PSPACE-hard, thus establishing the optimality of our algorithm.

Next, we consider the problem of computing $\mathsf{limreach}^{\epsilon}$ for bounded timed automata in the absence of the progress cycle assumption. While the algorithm to verify ω-regular properties discussed in the previous paragraph also applies to robust safety verification, computing $\mathsf{limreach}^{\epsilon}$ is of independent interest just like computing reachable sets is an important task independent of safety verification. Puri's algorithm [15] (generalized in [11]) works by iteratively adding the (topological) closure of regions on progress cycles that have a non-empty intersection with the current limreach set. We show that the (almost) same algorithm correctly computes $\mathsf{limreach}^{\epsilon}$ even when the progress cycle assumption does not hold. This algorithm can be shown to use polynomial space. Our contributions, in the context of previous results, is summarized in Table 1. As can be seen from the table, the results in this paper cannot be used to compute $\mathsf{limreach}^{\epsilon}_{\delta}$ nor $\mathsf{limreach}_{\delta}$, in the absence of the progress cycle assumption.

Problem / Assumption	With PCA	Without PCA
$\mathsf{limreach}^{\epsilon}_{\delta}$ computation	✓ [11]	
$\mathsf{limreach}_{\delta}$ computation	✓ [11]	
$\mathsf{limreach}^{\epsilon}$ computation	✓ [11, 15]	(✓)
Robust ω-regular	(✓)	(✓)
Robust ω-regular with only Enlarged Guards	✓ [6]	✓ [8]
Robust ω-regular with only Drifted Clocks	(✓)	(✓)

Table 1: Summary of Robust Model Checking Problem Results: Check marks indicate that the corresponding problem is solvable in polynomial space; check marks within parenthesis are established in this paper and those without the parenthesis were established in the reference cited alongside. Recall that PCA refers to the Progress Cycle Assumption.

2. PRELIMINARIES

The sets of *natural*, *positive natural*, *positive rational*, *real*, *positive real*, and *non-negative real*, numbers are represented by $\mathbb{N}$, $\mathbb{N}_{+}$, $\mathbb{Q}_{+}$, $\mathbb{R}$, $\mathbb{R}_{+}$, and $\mathbb{R}_{\geq 0}$, respectively. For $r \in \mathbb{R}_{\geq 0}$, we define $\lfloor r \rfloor$ to be integer part of r, and $\langle r \rangle$ to be $r - \lfloor r \rfloor$. Similarly, $\lceil r \rceil$ is the smallest integer not smaller than r. For $a, b \in \mathbb{R} \cup \{-\infty, \infty\}$, $[a, b] := \{x \in \mathbb{R} \mid a \leq x \leq b\}$ is the *interval* of real numbers between a and b. The set of *intervals* will be denoted by $\mathcal{I}$. Note that $\mathcal{I}$ is closed under finite intersection. An interval $I = [a, b]$ is said to be *bounded* if neither a nor b are in $\{-\infty, \infty\}$.

Let A and B be two arbitrary sets. Size of A is denoted by $|A|$. The power set of A is represented by 2^A. The Cartesian product of A and B is represented by $A \times B$. For a tuple $p := (a, b)$, elements a and b are represented by $\mathsf{fst}(p)$ and $\mathsf{snd}(p)$, respectively. If $A, B \subseteq \mathbb{R}$ then $A + B := \{a + b \mid a \in A \wedge b \in B\}$. The set of functions from A to B is represented by B^A or $A \to B$. For a function $f \in A \to B$, $\mathsf{dom}(f)$ denotes the domain of f. For any two functions $f, g \in A \to \mathbb{R}$, the function $f - g \in A \to \mathbb{R}$ maps x to $f(x) - g(x)$. For any $C \subseteq A$, $f[C \leftarrow 0] \in A \to \mathbb{R}$ maps x to 0 if $x \in C$ and maps x to $f(x)$ if $x \notin C$. Consider $D \subseteq 2^B$. If D is closed under intersection, and $f, g \in D^A$, $f \dot{\cap} g \in A \to D$ is the function $(f \dot{\cap} g)(x) := f(x) \cap g(x)$. For functions $f \in A \to D$ and $g \in A \to B$, we say $g \dot{\in} f$ iff $\forall x \in A \bullet g(x) \in f(x)$.

For a set A, ε denotes the empty sequence, A^n (for $n \in \mathbb{N}$) the set of sequences of length n, A^* the set of finite sequences, A^ω the set of infinite sequences, and $A^\infty = A^* \cup A^\omega$ the set of finite and infinite sequences. We will often abuse notation and refer to both A and A^1 (sequences of length 1) as A. For two sets of sequences X and Y, XY denotes the set of sequences formed by concatenating a sequence from X with a sequence from Y. For a sequence σ, σ_i will denote the ith element in the sequence σ; the first element of the sequence is assumed to have index 0.

For any two points $p, p' \in \mathbb{R}^A$ and two subsets $P, P' \subseteq \mathbb{R}^A$ we define $\mathsf{d}_\infty(p, p') := \max\{|p(a) - p'(a)| \mid a \in A\}$, $\mathsf{d}_\infty(p, P') := \inf\{\mathsf{d}_\infty(p, p') \mid p' \in P'\}$, and $\mathsf{d}_\infty(P, P') := \max\{\sup_{p \in P} \mathsf{d}_\infty(p, P'), \sup_{p' \in P'} \mathsf{d}_\infty(p', P)\}$.

2.1 Timed Automata

In this section we define timed automata and its semantics under different kinds of perturbation. For an introduction to the theory of timed automata see [2].

Definition 1. *A timed automaton $\mathcal{H}$ is a tuple* $(\mathtt{Q}, \mathtt{X}, \mathtt{Q}^{\mathsf{init}}, \mathtt{I}, \mathtt{E})$, *where*

- $\mathtt{Q}$ *is a finite non-empty set of (discrete)* locations.
- $\mathtt{X}$ *is a finite non-empty set of* clocks.

- $\mathtt{Q}^{\mathsf{init}} \subseteq \mathtt{Q}$ *is a set of* initial locations.
- $\mathtt{I} \in \mathtt{Q} \to \mathcal{I}^{\mathtt{X}}$ *maps each location* q *to a rectangular set as the* invariant *of clocks in* q.
- $\mathtt{E}$ *is a finite set of* edges. *Each edge* $e \in \mathtt{E}$ *itself is a tuple* (s, d, l, g, r) *in which*
  - $s, d \in \mathtt{Q}$ *are* source *and* destination *locations, respectively.*
  - $l \subseteq \mathtt{E}$ *is the* label *of* e,
  - $g \in \mathcal{I}^{\mathtt{X}}$ *is a rectangular set, the* guard *of* e.
  - $r \subseteq \mathtt{X}$ *is the set of clocks that are* reset to 0 *after taking* e.

  We write $\mathtt{S}e$, $\mathtt{D}e$, $\mathtt{L}e$, $\mathtt{G}e$, *and* $\mathtt{R}e$ *to denote the source, destination, label, guard and reset associated with the edge* e, *respectively.*

A valuation function $\nu \in \mathbb{R}_{\geq 0}^{\mathtt{X}}$ *assigns a non-negative value to each clock of* $\mathcal{H}$. *We denote the set of all valuations by* $\mathtt{V}_{\mathcal{H}}$. *Furthermore, let* $\mathsf{M} \in \mathbb{R}_{\geq 0}$ *be the maximum constant appearing in the specification of guards of edges and invariants of locations in* $\mathcal{H}$. *We refer to the different elements of* $\mathcal{H}$, *by adding* $\mathcal{H}$ *as a subscript. For example,* $\mathtt{X}_{\mathcal{H}}$ *is the set of clocks of* $\mathcal{H}$. *But we may omit the subscript whenever it is clear from the context. Also, we denote* $\mathtt{I}(q)(x)$ *and* $(\mathtt{G}e)(x)$ *respectively by* $\mathtt{I}(q, x)$ *and* $\mathtt{G}(e, x)$. *Finally, a timed automaton is said to be* bounded *iff all intervals specifying the invariants are bounded.*

For a timed automaton $\mathcal{H}$, we consider two types of perturbations. By $\mathcal{H}_{\delta}^{\epsilon}$, we refer to the semantics where guards are enlarged by δ and clocks are allowed to drift by ϵ. On the other hand, $\mathcal{H}_{+\delta}^{\epsilon}$ refers to the semantics where clocks are allowed to drift by ϵ but *only positive* guards are perturbed by δ. Before defining these semantics, we introduce some notation. For an interval $I = [a, b]$ and $\delta \in \mathbb{R}_{\geq 0}$, $I_{\delta} := [a-\delta, b+\delta]$. On the other hand, $I_{+\delta} := [c, d]$, where

$$c = \begin{cases} a - \delta & \text{if } a > 0 \\ a & \text{otherwise} \end{cases} \qquad d = \begin{cases} b + \delta & \text{if } b > 0 \\ b & \text{otherwise} \end{cases}$$

Definition 2. *For any timed automaton* $\mathcal{H}$ *and* $\epsilon, \delta \in \mathbb{R}_{\geq 0}$, *the semantics of* $\mathcal{H}_{\eta}^{\epsilon}$, *where* $\eta \in \{\delta, +\delta\}$, *is defined to be the transition system* $(\mathtt{S}, \Sigma, \to, \mathtt{S}^{\mathsf{init}})$ *where*

- $\mathtt{S} := \mathtt{Q} \times \mathtt{V}$,
- $\Sigma := \mathtt{E} \cup \mathbb{R}_{\geq 0}$,
- $\mathtt{S}^{\mathsf{init}} := \{(q, 0^{\mathtt{X}}) \mid q \in \mathtt{Q}^{\mathsf{init}} \wedge 0^{\mathtt{X}} \dot{\in} \mathtt{I}_{\eta}(q)\}$, *and*
- $\to := \to_1 \cup \to_2$ *where*
  - $\to_1$ *is the set of* continuous *transitions and for all* $t \in \mathbb{R}_{\geq 0}$ *we have* $(q, \nu) \xrightarrow{t}_1 (q', \nu')$ *iff 1.* $q = q'$, *2.* $\nu, \nu' \dot{\in} \mathtt{I}_{\eta}(q)$, *and 3.* $(\nu' - \nu) \dot{\in} [t(1-\epsilon), t(1+\epsilon)]^{\mathtt{X}}$
  - $\to_2$ *is the set of* discrete *transitions and for any* $e \in \mathtt{E}$ *we have* $(q, \nu) \xrightarrow{e}_2 (q', \nu')$ *iff 1.* $q = \mathtt{S}e$, *2.* $q' = \mathtt{D}e$, *3.* $\nu \dot{\in} \mathtt{I}_{\eta}(q) \dot{\cap} \mathtt{G}_{\eta}(e)$, *4.* $\nu' = \nu[\mathtt{R}e \leftarrow 0]$, *and 5.* $\nu' \dot{\in} \mathtt{I}_{\eta}(q')$.

When either ϵ or δ is 0, we will drop it from the superscript/subscript. In particular, for $\epsilon, \delta \in \mathbb{R}_{+}$, $\mathcal{H}^{\epsilon}$ refers to $\mathcal{H}_{0}^{\epsilon}$, $\mathcal{H}_{\delta}$ refers to $\mathcal{H}_{\delta}^{0}$, and $\mathcal{H}_{+\delta}$ is $\mathcal{H}_{+\delta}^{0}$. Finally, we will abuse notation and use $\mathcal{H}$ to refer to both the timed automaton and its *standard semantics* $\mathcal{H}_{0}^{0}$.

Consider a timed automaton $\mathcal{H}$, $\epsilon, \delta \in \mathbb{R}_{\geq 0}$, and $\eta \in \{\delta, +\delta\}$. Let $\mathcal{T}$ be $\mathcal{H}_{\eta}^{\epsilon}$. A *trajectory* of $\mathcal{T}$ is a non-empty sequence of the form $s_0, (t_1, e_1), s_1, (t_2, e_2), s_2, \ldots$, where s_i is the state of $\mathcal{T}$ immediately after the ith discrete transition, t_i is the time (after transition $i-1$) the ith discrete transition is taken, and e_i is the edge of the discrete i^{th} transition. Formally, a trajectory τ of $\mathcal{T}$ starting from state s is a sequence in $\mathtt{S}((\mathbb{R}_{\geq 0} \times \mathtt{E})\mathtt{S})^{\infty}$ such that $\tau_0 = s$, and for every i (with $2i + 2 \leq$ length of τ), there is a state s_i such that

$$\tau_{2i} \xrightarrow{\mathsf{fst}(\tau_{2i+1})}_{\mathcal{T}} s_i \xrightarrow{\mathsf{snd}(\tau_{2i+1})}_{\mathcal{T}} \tau_{2i+2}.$$

The set of *trajectories*, *finite trajectories*, and *infinite trajectories* of $\mathcal{T}$ is denoted by $[\![\mathcal{T}]\!]_{\infty}$, $[\![\mathcal{T}]\!]_{*}$, and $[\![\mathcal{T}]\!]_{\omega}$, respectively. We will use $\mathsf{first}(\tau)$ to refer to the starting state of trajectory τ (namely, state τ_0), and, if τ is finite, $\mathsf{last}(\tau)$ to the last state in the sequence. Let $\tau \in [\![\mathcal{T}]\!]_{\infty}$ be a sequence with k elements. Observe that k is either infinite or it is an odd number. The *length* of a trajectory τ is defined to be the *number of discrete steps*; it is denoted as $|\tau| = \lfloor k/2 \rfloor$. We define $\mathsf{duration}(\tau) := \sum_{i<|\tau|} \mathsf{fst}(\tau_{2i+1})$, to be the sum of the time taken at each step of the trajectory. A trajectory τ is said to be an *execution* if $\mathsf{first}(\tau) \in \mathtt{S}^{\mathsf{init}}$, i.e., it starts from an initial state. We denote the set of *executions*, *finite executions*, and *infinite executions* of $\mathcal{T}$ by $[\![\mathcal{T}]\!]_{\infty}^{0}$, $[\![\mathcal{T}]\!]_{*}^{0}$, and $[\![\mathcal{T}]\!]_{\omega}^{0}$, respectively. For any $T \in \mathbb{R}$ and trajectory $\tau \in [\![\mathcal{T}]\!]_{\infty}$, we say that a trajectory τ is T*-time-bounded* iff $\mathsf{duration}(\tau) \leq T$. Also, $\mathsf{locs}(\tau)$ is the set of locations visited by τ, $\mathtt{inf}(\tau)$ is the set of edges visited infinitely often by τ, and $\mathtt{trace}(\tau)$ is the sequence of edges visited by τ. For a finite trajectory $\tau \in [\![\mathcal{T}]\!]_{*}$ and a trajectory $\tau' = s\sigma \in [\![\mathcal{T}]\!]_{\infty}$ starting from state $s = \mathsf{last}(\tau)$, concatenation of τ and τ', denoted as $\tau \frown \tau'$, is the trajectory/sequence $\tau\sigma$. Finally, we define $\mathsf{reach}(\mathcal{H}_{\delta}^{\epsilon}) := \{\nu \mid \exists \tau \in [\![\mathcal{H}_{\delta}^{\epsilon}]\!]_{*}^{0} \bullet \nu = \mathsf{last}(\tau)\}$, $\mathsf{limreach}^{\epsilon}(\mathcal{H}) := \bigcap_{\epsilon \in \mathbb{R}_{+}} \mathsf{reach}(\mathcal{H}^{\epsilon})$, $\mathsf{limreach}_{\delta}(\mathcal{H}) := \bigcap_{\delta \in \mathbb{R}_{+}} \mathsf{reach}(\mathcal{H}_{\delta})$, $\mathsf{limreach}_{\delta}^{\epsilon}(\mathcal{H}) := \bigcap_{\epsilon \in \mathbb{R}_{+}} \bigcap_{\delta \in \mathbb{R}_{+}} \mathsf{reach}(\mathcal{H}_{\delta}^{\epsilon})$.

An equivalence relation, called *region equivalence* plays a critical role in the reachability analysis of timed automata [2]. It is an equivalence on states, and equivalence classes of this relation are called *regions*. Region equivalence is defined as follows. Consider a timed automaton $\mathcal{H}$ with clocks $\mathtt{X}$, locations $\mathtt{Q}$, and maximum constant M. Let $\mathcal{T}$ be the transition system of $\mathcal{H}$ with states $\mathtt{S}$. Two states $(q_1, \nu_1), (q_2, \nu_2) \in \mathtt{S}$ are region equivalent, $(q_1, \nu_1) \sim (q_2, \nu_2)$, iff

1. Locations q_1 and q_2 are the same, i.e., $q_1 = q_2$,
2. For every $x \in \mathtt{X}$, either $\lfloor \nu_1(x) \rfloor = \lfloor \nu_2(x) \rfloor$ or both $\nu_1(x) > \mathsf{M}$ and $\nu_2(x) > \mathsf{M}$,
3. For every $x \in \mathtt{X}$, if $\nu_1(x) \leq \mathsf{M}$ then $\langle \nu_1(x) \rangle = 0$ iff $\langle \nu_2(x) \rangle = 0$, and
4. For every $x, y \in \mathtt{X}$, if $\nu_1(x) \leq \mathsf{M}$ and $\nu_2(y) \leq \mathsf{M}$ then $\langle \nu_1(x) \rangle \leq \langle \nu_1(y) \rangle$ iff $\langle \nu_2(x) \rangle \leq \langle \nu_2(y) \rangle$.

The number of equivalence classes of $\sim$, or regions, is bounded by $|\mathtt{Q}| \cdot |\mathtt{X}|! \cdot 2^{|\mathtt{X}|} \cdot (2\mathsf{M}+2)^{|\mathtt{X}|}$; thus, the number of regions is linear in $|\mathtt{Q}|$ and M and is singly exponential in $|\mathtt{X}|$. For a region r, $[r]$ will be the smallest (topologically) closed set containing r, and for a state s, $[s]$ will be the topological closure of the region containing s; thus, if $s \in r$ then $[s] = [r]$. Finally, for any two states $s_1 := (q_1, \nu_1)$ and $s_2 := (q_2, \nu_2)$ we define $\mathsf{d}_{\infty}(s_1, s_2)$ to be ∞ if $q_1 \neq q_2$ and $\mathsf{d}_{\infty}(\nu_1, \nu_2)$ otherwise. The importance of regions is captured in the following proposition that says that region equivalence is a bisimulation.

Proposition 3. *If* τ *is a finite trajectory starting at state* s *and* $s' \sim s$ *then there is a finite trajectory* τ' *starting from* s' *such that* $\mathtt{trace}(\tau) = \mathtt{trace}(\tau')$ *and* $\mathsf{last}(\tau) \sim \mathsf{last}(\tau')$.

Proposition 3 says the quotient of $\mathcal{T}$ with respect to $\sim$ is well defined. This quotient is called the *region graph* defined as $\mathcal{G} := (V, E)$, where V is the set of regions, and for $\sigma \in \mathtt{E} \cup \{\mathsf{time}\}$, $(r_1, \sigma, r_2) \in E$ iff $\exists s_1 \in r_1, s_2 \in r_2 \bullet$ if $\sigma \in \mathtt{E}$, $s_1 \xrightarrow{\sigma} s_2$ and if $\sigma = \mathsf{time}$, then $r_1 \neq r_2$ and there is

$t \in \mathbb{R}_{\geq 0}$ such that $s_1 \xrightarrow{t} s_2$. For any set of regions A, we define $\mathsf{reach}(\mathcal{G}, A)$ to be the set of nodes in $\mathcal{G}$ reachable from A. A path π in the region graph is called *progress cycle* iff the first and last nodes in π are the same and every clock in $\mathtt{X}$ is reset at least once along the edges of π. Finally, a timed automaton $\mathcal{H}$ is said to satisfy the *progress cycle assumption (PCA)* if every cycle in its region graph $\mathcal{G}$ is a progress cycle.

We conclude this section by defining the main verification problems that we consider in this paper. Recall that the classical safety and ω-regular model checking problems can be defined as follows:

Problem 4. *Let $\mathcal{H}$ be a timed automaton with only integer constants, $Q \subseteq \mathtt{Q}_{\mathcal{H}}$ be an arbitrary set of locations, and $B \subseteq \mathtt{E}_{\mathcal{H}}$ be an arbitrary subset of edges. $\mathcal{H}$ is said satisfy the safety property $\Box Q$ (denoted $\mathcal{H} \models \Box Q$) if no control location* outside *Q is reachable, that is, it is not the case that there is $q \notin Q$ and $\nu \in \mathtt{V}_{\mathcal{H}}$ such that $(q, \nu) \in \mathsf{reach}(\mathcal{H})$. Also, $\mathcal{H}$ is said to satisfy* ω-regular property *$\Box\Diamond B$ (denoted by $\mathcal{H} \models \Box\Diamond B$), iff $\forall \tau \in [\![\mathcal{H}]\!]^0_\omega \bullet \mathtt{inf}(\tau) \cap B \neq \emptyset$.*

The safety and ω-regular model checking problems are that given timed automaton $\mathcal{H}$, sets $Q \subseteq \mathtt{Q}_{\mathcal{H}}$ and $B \subseteq \mathtt{E}_{\mathcal{H}}$, determine if $\mathcal{H} \models \Box Q$ and $\mathcal{H} \models \Box\Diamond B$, respectively.

Note that the safety and ω-regular model checking problems as stated are a special case of general safety and ω-regular verification. However, the general regular safety and ω-regular property verification problems can be reduced to these special cases by taking a cross product of $\mathcal{H}$ and an appropriate property automaton [4]. In this paper we consider robust versions of these classical problems.

Problem 5. *Let $\mathcal{H}$ be a timed automaton with only integer constants, and $B \subseteq \mathtt{E}_{\mathcal{H}}$ be an arbitrary subset of edges. The* robust ω-regular model checking *problem asks if there are $\epsilon, \delta \in \mathbb{R}_+$ such that $\mathcal{H}^\epsilon_\delta \models \Box\Diamond B$.*

Two variants of the above problem that we will also consider are as follows. The robust ω-regular model checking problem when only guards are enlarged *asks if there is $\delta \in \mathbb{R}_+$ such that $\mathcal{H}_\delta \models \Box\Diamond B$. The* robust ω-regular model checking problem when only clocks drift *asks if there is $\epsilon \in \mathbb{R}_+$ such that $\mathcal{H}^\epsilon \models \Box\Diamond B$.*

Robust versions of the safety verification problem are defined similarly; the formal definition is skipped in the interest of space.

3. ROBUST ω-REGULAR MODEL CHECKING

In this section, we present our results for the robust ω-regular model checking problem when both clocks and guards are perturbed and the robust ω-regular model checking problem when only clocks are perturbed. Recall that the robust ω-regular model checking problem when only guards are enlarged was solved in [8].

3.1 Robust ω-regular model checking when both guards and clocks are perturbed

Our main result in this section is that robust ω-regular model checking problem when both guards and clocks are perturbed is equivalent to the robust ω-regular model checking problem when only guards are perturbed. This is formalized in the following theorem.

Theorem 6. *For any timed automaton $\mathcal{H}$ and B a subset of $\mathtt{E}_{\mathcal{H}}$,*

$$\left(\exists \epsilon, \delta \in \mathbb{R}_+ \bullet \mathcal{H}^\epsilon_\delta \models \Box\Diamond B\right) \Leftrightarrow \left(\exists \delta' \in \mathbb{R}_+ \bullet \mathcal{H}_{\delta'} \models \Box\Diamond B\right)$$

Note that the implication from left to right is trivial, since if $\mathcal{H}^\epsilon_\delta \models \Box\Diamond B$ then by assigning δ to δ', we obtain $\mathcal{H}_{\delta'} \models \Box\Diamond B$ as well. The non-trivial part of the proof lies in showing the other direction. It requires the robustness under perturbed guards to be transferred to that under clock drifts and perturbed guards, which is facilitated by the following lemma.

Lemma 7. *For any timed automaton $\mathcal{H}$, $\epsilon \in (0, \frac{1}{4})$, $\gamma \in (0, \frac{\mathsf{M}}{2})$, and $\tau \in [\![\mathcal{H}^\epsilon_\gamma]\!]^0_\infty$, there is $\tau' \in [\![\mathcal{H}_{2\mathsf{M}\epsilon+\gamma}]\!]^0_\infty$, such that τ and τ' have the exact same sequence of discrete and continuous transitions. Here, M is the largest constant appearing in the constraints of $\mathcal{H}$.*

Proof. Fix $\epsilon \in (0, \frac{1}{4})$, $\gamma \in (0, \frac{\mathsf{M}}{2})$, and $\tau \in [\![\mathcal{H}^\epsilon_\gamma]\!]^0_\infty$. Let $\delta := 2\epsilon\mathsf{M} + \gamma$. Obviously, the set of edges that are enabled initially in $\mathcal{H}^\epsilon_\gamma$ corresponds to a subset of the edges that are initially enabled in $\mathcal{H}_\delta$. We show the same is true at any step in τ. For any variable $x \in \mathtt{X}$ if valuation ν_x satisfies guard g at the time of taking edge e in $\mathcal{H}^\epsilon_\gamma$, there are two cases:

1. $g := x \rhd c$ for some integer $c \in \{0, \ldots, \mathsf{M}\}$ and $\rhd \in \{>, \geq\}$. Time taken by x to reach its current value since its last reset (or since the beginning of time if x has never been reset) is at least $\frac{c-\gamma}{1+\epsilon}$. We show that this time is big enough for the enlarged guard $x \rhd c - \delta$ to be satisfied when x evolves without clock drifts.

$$\begin{array}{ll} (\mathsf{M} \rhd c) & \Rightarrow \\ (2\mathsf{M} + \gamma + 2\epsilon\mathsf{M} \rhd c) & \Rightarrow \\ \left(0 \rhd -2\epsilon\mathsf{M} + c\epsilon - \gamma\epsilon - 2\epsilon^2\mathsf{M}\right) & \Rightarrow \\ \left(c - \gamma \rhd c - \gamma - 2\epsilon\mathsf{M} + c\epsilon - \gamma\epsilon - 2\epsilon^2\mathsf{M}\right) & \Rightarrow \\ \left(c - \gamma \rhd (1+\epsilon)(c - \gamma - 2\epsilon\mathsf{M})\right) & \Rightarrow \\ \left(\dfrac{c-\gamma}{1+\epsilon} \rhd c - \gamma - 2\epsilon\mathsf{M} = c - \delta\right) & \end{array}$$

2. $g := x \lhd c$ for some integer $c \in \{0, \ldots, \mathsf{M}\}$ and $\lhd \in \{<, \leq\}$. Time taken by x to reach its current value, since its last reset (or since the beginning of time if x has never been reset) is at most $\frac{c+\gamma}{1-\epsilon}$. We show that this time is small enough for the enlarged guard $x \lhd c + \delta$ to be satisfied when there are no clock drifts. Again,

$$\begin{array}{ll} (c \leq \mathsf{M}) & \Rightarrow \\ \left(c + \dfrac{\mathsf{M}}{2} + \dfrac{\mathsf{M}}{2} \leq 2\mathsf{M}\right) & \Rightarrow \\ (c + 2\epsilon\mathsf{M} + \gamma \lhd 2\mathsf{M}) & \Rightarrow \\ \left(0 \lhd 2\epsilon\mathsf{M} - c\epsilon - 2\epsilon^2\mathsf{M} - \epsilon\gamma\right) & \Rightarrow \\ \left(c + \gamma \lhd c + \gamma + 2\epsilon\mathsf{M} - c\epsilon - 2\epsilon^2\mathsf{M} - \epsilon\gamma\right) & \Rightarrow \\ \left(c + \gamma \lhd (1-\epsilon)(c + 2\epsilon\mathsf{M} + \gamma)\right) & \Rightarrow \\ \left(\dfrac{c+\gamma}{1-\epsilon} \lhd c + 2\epsilon\mathsf{M} + \gamma = c + \delta\right) & \end{array}$$

Note that variables are reset at the exact same times in $\tau \in [\![\mathcal{H}^\epsilon_\gamma]\!]^0_\infty$ and $\tau \in [\![\mathcal{H}_\delta]\!]^0_\infty$. So whenever a variable is reset in $\tau \in [\![\mathcal{H}^\epsilon_\gamma]\!]^0_\infty$ at time t, the same variable is reset in $\tau \in [\![\mathcal{H}_\delta]\!]^0_\infty$ at time t. This makes the values of x in two executions 0 at time t. ☐

The right to left implication of Theorem 6 follows directly from Lemma 7. If $\mathcal{H}_{\delta'} \models \Box\Diamond B$, then by choosing any $\epsilon \in (0, \frac{1}{4})$ and $\delta \in (0, \frac{\mathsf{M}}{2})$ such that $2\mathsf{M}\epsilon + \delta < \delta'$, we know any execution in $[\![\mathcal{H}^{\epsilon}_{\delta}]\!]^{0}_{\omega}$ has a corresponding execution in $[\![\mathcal{H}_{\delta'}]\!]^{0}_{\omega}$ with the same sequence of discrete transitions. Lemma 7 also implies $\mathsf{limreach}^{\epsilon}_{\delta}(\mathcal{H})$ is subset of $\mathsf{limreach}_{\delta}(\mathcal{H})$ and therefore they are equal even when the progress cycle assumption does not hold. This is formalized in the Corollary 8.

Corollary 8. *For any bounded timed automaton $\mathcal{H}$, we have* $\mathsf{limreach}^{\epsilon}_{\delta}(\mathcal{H}) \subseteq \mathsf{limreach}_{\delta}(\mathcal{H})$.

Proof. $\mathsf{limreach}_{\delta}(\mathcal{H})$ is taken to be the intersection of the reach set of $\mathcal{H}_{\delta}$ for all δ. Since the guards are perturbed in $\mathcal{H}_{\delta}$, we can (without loss of generality) assume that the intervals are closed in $\mathcal{H}_{\delta}$ when defining $\mathsf{limreach}_{\delta}(\mathcal{H})$ [11]. Thus, $\mathsf{reach}(\mathcal{H}_{\delta})$ is a closed set, for any $\delta \in \mathbb{R}_{+}$. Let $s \in \mathsf{limreach}^{\epsilon}_{\delta}(\mathcal{H})$ be an arbitrary state. For any $\delta \in \mathbb{R}_{+}$, we will show $s \in \mathsf{reach}(\mathcal{H}_{\delta})$, thus establishing the claim. Since $\mathsf{reach}(\mathcal{H}_{\delta})$ is closed, we can establish this by showing that $\mathsf{d}_{\infty}(s, \mathsf{reach}(\mathcal{H}_{\delta}))$ is arbitrarily small, or more precisely, for any $\kappa \in \mathbb{R}_{+}$, $\mathsf{d}_{\infty}(s, \mathsf{reach}(\mathcal{H}_{\delta})) < \kappa$.

Let us fix $\kappa \in \mathbb{R}_{+}$. Pick $\epsilon \in (0, \frac{1}{4})$ and $\gamma \in (0, \frac{\mathsf{M}}{2})$ such that $2\mathsf{M}\epsilon + \gamma < \delta$ and $2\mathsf{M}\epsilon < \kappa$. Since $s \in \mathsf{reach}(\mathcal{H}^{\epsilon}_{\gamma})$ we know there is an execution $\tau \in [\![\mathcal{H}^{\epsilon}_{\gamma}]\!]^{0}_{*}$ such that $\mathsf{last}(\tau) = s$. By Lemma 7 we know there is an execution $\tau' \in [\![\mathcal{H}_{2\mathsf{M}\epsilon+\gamma}]\!]^{0}_{*} \subseteq [\![\mathcal{H}_{\delta}]\!]^{0}_{*}$ with the same sequence of discrete and continuous transitions as τ. Since $\mathcal{H}$ is bounded and $\epsilon < \frac{1}{2}$, every variable is reset at least once every $2\mathsf{M}$ units of time. Since the clocks are drifted by at most ϵ in $\mathcal{H}^{\epsilon}_{\gamma}$ and variables are reset at the exact same times in τ and τ', $\mathsf{d}_{\infty}(s, \mathsf{last}(\tau')) \leq 2\mathsf{M}\epsilon < \kappa$. Therefore, $\mathsf{d}_{\infty}(s, \mathsf{reach}(\mathcal{H}_{\delta})) < \kappa$. ☐

To obtain an algorithm for robust ω-regular model checking problem when both guards and clocks are perturbed, we resort to the results in [8] for robust ω-regular model checking problem when only guards are perturbed. The algorithm in [8] provides a computable value δ_0, such that the $\mathcal{H}_{\delta_0} \models \Box\Diamond B$ iff there is $\delta \in \mathbb{R}_{+}$ such that $\mathcal{H}_{\delta} \models \Box\Diamond B$. We recall this result from [8].

Theorem 9 (Based on Lemma 11 and Theorem 3 in [8]). *Let $\mathcal{H}$ be a timed automaton, W be its number of regions, and B be a subset of $\mathtt{E}_{\mathcal{H}}$. Then*

1. $\forall \delta \in \mathbb{R}_{+}, \tau \in [\![\mathcal{H}_{\delta_0}]\!]^{0}_{\omega} \bullet \exists \tau' \in [\![\mathcal{H}_{\delta}]\!]^{0}_{\omega} \bullet \mathtt{inf}(\tau) = \mathtt{inf}(\tau')$
2. $\exists \delta \in \mathbb{R}_{+} \bullet \mathcal{H}_{\delta} \models \Box\Diamond B \Leftrightarrow \mathcal{H}_{\delta_0} \models \Box\Diamond B$

where $\delta_0 := \frac{1}{2}\left(8|\mathtt{X}|^2(W+1)\right)^{-1}$ *if $\mathcal{H}$ satisfies the progress cycle assumption, otherwise*
$\delta_0 := \frac{1}{2}(5(W+1)|\mathtt{X}|^3(2|\mathtt{Q}|(|\mathtt{X}|!)4^{|\mathtt{X}|}+4)^2)^{-1}$.

Proof. The second result follows immediately from the first one. As far as the first result is concerned, the only difference when compared to the observations in [8], is that here $\mathtt{inf}(\cdot)$ returns the set of edges, as opposed to the set of locations, that are visited infinitely often. This is not a problem since the proof in [8] essentially obtains τ' from τ by 1. repeating some subexecutions of τ a finite number of times (duration of continuous transitions may change during this step), and 2. repeating the previous step for a finite number of times. ☐

In order to solve robust ω-regular model checking when both guards and clocks are perturbed, our algorithm first checks $\mathcal{H}_{\delta_0} \models \Box\Diamond B$ where δ_0 is introduced by Theorem 9. If $\mathcal{H}_{\delta_0} \not\models \Box\Diamond B$ then clearly $\mathcal{H}$ does *not* robustly satisfy $\Box\Diamond B$ when both guards and clocks are perturbed. On the other hand, if $\mathcal{H}_{\delta_0} \models \Box\Diamond B$ then using Lemma 7 we know $\mathcal{H}^{\epsilon_1}_{\delta_1} \models \Box\Diamond B$ for any $\delta_1, \epsilon_1 \in \mathbb{R}_{+}$ that satisfy $2\mathsf{M}\epsilon_1 + \delta_1 < \delta_0$.

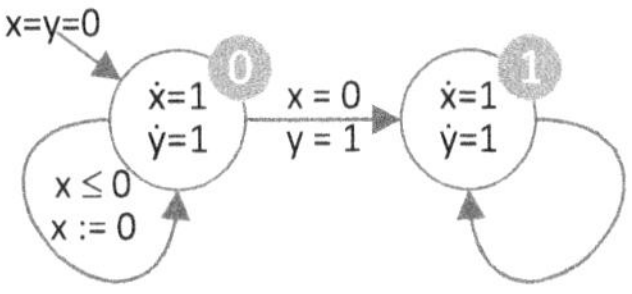

Figure 1: $\exists \epsilon \in \mathbb{R}_{+} \bullet \mathcal{H}^{\epsilon} \models \Box\Diamond B$ does not always imply $\exists \delta \in \mathbb{R}_{+} \bullet \mathcal{H}_{\delta} \models \Box\Diamond B$

Theorem 10. *Let $\mathcal{H}$ be a timed automaton and B be a subset of $\mathtt{E}_{\mathcal{H}}$. Let δ_0 be as defined in Theorem 9. Then, for any, ϵ_1, δ_1 such that $2\mathsf{M}\epsilon_1 + \delta_1 \leq \delta_0$, the following holds:*

$$\left(\exists \epsilon, \delta \in \mathbb{R}_{+} \bullet \mathcal{H}^{\epsilon}_{\delta} \models \Box\Diamond B\right) \Leftrightarrow (\mathcal{H}_{\delta_0} \models \Box\Diamond B) \Leftrightarrow (\mathcal{H}^{\epsilon_1}_{\delta_1} \models \Box\Diamond B)$$

Since the robust ω-regular model checking problem when only guards are perturbed is PSPACE-complete, from Theorem 10, we obtain the following:

Corollary 11. *The robust ω-regular model checking problem when both guards and clocks are perturbed is PSPACE-complete.*

While robust ω-regular model checking problem when both guards and clocks are perturbed and when only guards are perturbed are equivalent (Theorem 6), the same is surprisingly not true for the case when only clocks are drifted. This is demonstrated by our next example.

Example 12. *In this example, we show that*

$$\left(\exists \epsilon \in \mathbb{R}_{+} \bullet \mathcal{H}^{\epsilon} \models \Box\Diamond B\right) \not\Rightarrow \left(\exists \delta \in \mathbb{R}_{+} \bullet \mathcal{H}_{\delta} \models \Box\Diamond B\right)$$

Consider the timed automaton $\mathcal{H}$ in Figure 1. It starts at location 0 with $x = y = 0$ and both the variables evolve at rate 1. Note that e_1, the self loop on location 0, can only be taken when $x = 0$, that is, it is feasible only at time 0. Hence, the edge e_2 from location 0 to location 1 can never be taken, since once time passes both x and y will have non-zero values and the value of x can never be reset.

Taking $B := \{e_1\}$, consider the ω-regular property $\Box\Diamond B$. Note that the only infinite execution τ of the timed automaton is the one which traverses e_1 repeatedly without time elapsing. This satisfies the condition $\Box\Diamond B$. Moreover, even if we allow clock drifts, we will still have only one infinite execution, namely, τ. Hence, $\mathcal{H}^{\epsilon} \models \Box\Diamond B$ (for any $\epsilon \in [0, 1)$).

However, we argue that for any δ, $\mathcal{H}_{\delta} \not\models \Box\Diamond B$, since, there will be infinite trajectories that visit location 1 and execute e_3, the self loop on location 1, repeatedly. To see this, note that a δ enlargement of the guard $x \leq 0$ will lead to $x \leq \delta$. Hence, by repeatedly taking e_1 every δ units of time, the value $x = 0$ and $y \in [1-\delta, 1+\delta]$ can be reached. Hence, the edge to location 1 can be taken.

Observe that the same example works if we bound guards and invariants. Furthermore, this example also shows that $\mathsf{limreach}^{\epsilon}(\mathcal{H}) \neq \mathsf{limreach}_{\delta}(\mathcal{H})$, a fact we mentioned in the introduction.

3.2 Robust ω-regular model checking when only clocks are perturbed

In Example 12, we showed that even if there exists an $\epsilon \in \mathbb{R}_{+}$ such that $\mathcal{H}^{\epsilon} \models \Box\Diamond B$, there may not exist a $\delta \in \mathbb{R}_{+}$ such that $\mathcal{H}_{\delta} \models \Box\Diamond B$. However, we show that the implication holds when we consider a weaker notion of guard perturbations.

Theorem 13. *For any timed automaton $\mathcal{H}$ and B a subset of* E,

$$\left(\exists\epsilon \in \mathbb{R}_+ \bullet \mathcal{H}^\epsilon \models \Box\Diamond B\right) \Leftrightarrow \left(\exists\delta \in \mathbb{R}_+ \bullet \mathcal{H}_{+\delta} \models \Box\Diamond B\right)$$

The crux of the proof of Theorem 13 lies in the following lemma which establishes the connection between the trace language of automata under clock drifts and the trace language of automata when positive guard constants are perturbed.

Lemma 14. *For a timed automaton $\mathcal{H}$ with maximum constant* M *and $\epsilon \in (0, \frac{1}{2})$ the following holds:*

$$\mathtt{trace}\left(\llbracket\mathcal{H}_{+\frac{\epsilon}{2}}\rrbracket^0_\infty\right) \subseteq \mathtt{trace}(\llbracket\mathcal{H}^\epsilon\rrbracket^0_\infty) \subseteq \mathtt{trace}(\llbracket\mathcal{H}_{+2\mathsf{M}\epsilon}\rrbracket^0_\infty)$$

Proof. $\mathcal{H}^\epsilon$ is an initialized rectangular automaton. In [13], Henzinger *et al.* describe a transformation from 1. an initialized rectangular automaton $\mathcal{H}^\epsilon$ into an initialized multirate hybrid automaton $\mathcal{H}'$ that is trace equivalent with $\mathcal{H}^\epsilon$, and 2. $\mathcal{H}'$ to a timed automaton $\mathcal{H}''$ which is bisimilar to $\mathcal{H}'$.

Initialized multirate hybrid automaton $\mathcal{H}'$ is obtained from $\mathcal{H}$ by replacing every variable $x \in \mathtt{X}_\mathcal{H}$ by two variables x_l and x_u. Initially all variables in $\mathcal{H}'$ are zero. $\mathcal{H}$ and $\mathcal{H}'$ have the same set of (initial) locations and none of them has invariant in $\mathcal{H}'$. For any location $q \in \mathtt{Q}_\mathcal{H}$ and variable $x \in \mathtt{X}_\mathcal{H}$, $\mathtt{Flow}_{\mathcal{H}'}(q, x_l) = 1 - \epsilon$ and $\mathtt{Flow}_{\mathcal{H}'}(q, x_u) = 1 + \epsilon$ (recall that $\mathtt{Flow}(q, x)$ is rate at which variable x changes in location q). There is a bijection between edges of $\mathcal{H}$ and $\mathcal{H}'$. For any edge $e \in \mathtt{E}_\mathcal{H}$ there is an edge $e' \in \mathtt{E}_{\mathcal{H}'}$ such that 1. e' has the same source and destination as e, 2. For any $x \in \mathtt{X}_\mathcal{H}$ we have $x \in \mathtt{R}_\mathcal{H}e \Leftrightarrow x_l, x_u \in \mathtt{R}_{\mathcal{H}'}e'$, 3. For any $x \in \mathtt{X}_\mathcal{H}$ and constant $c \in \mathbb{R}$ we have $(x \le c) \in \mathtt{G}_\mathcal{H}e \Leftrightarrow (x_l \le c) \in \mathtt{G}_{\mathcal{H}'}e'$ and $(x \ge c) \in \mathtt{G}_\mathcal{H}e \Leftrightarrow (x_u \ge c) \in \mathtt{G}_{\mathcal{H}'}e'$.

Timed automaton $\mathcal{H}''$ is obtained from $\mathcal{H}'$ by 1. setting $\mathtt{Flow}_{\mathcal{H}''}(q, x_l) = \mathtt{Flow}_{\mathcal{H}''}(q, x_u) = 1$ for all $q \in \mathtt{Q}_\mathcal{H}$ and $x \in \mathtt{X}_\mathcal{H}$. 2. every guard $x_l \le c$ is replaced by $x_l \le \frac{c}{1-\epsilon}$, and 3. every guard $x_u \ge c$ is replaced by $x_u \ge \frac{c}{1+\epsilon}$. Note that x_l and x_u are both reset at the exact same times to zero, they have the same initial value and reset to the same value. Therefore, one can merge these two variables into one and combine their guards together. This is possible since $\mathcal{H}$ is a timed automaton.

If $c = 0$ then $\frac{c}{1-\epsilon} = \frac{c}{1+\epsilon} = 0$. This corresponds to not changing zero guards. Next we show for $c \ge 1$ the following are true: 1. $c+\epsilon \le \frac{c}{1-\epsilon} \le c+2\mathsf{M}\epsilon$, and 2. $c-\mathsf{M}\epsilon \le \frac{c}{1+\epsilon} \le c-\frac{\epsilon}{2}$.

$$\left(\tfrac{c}{1-\epsilon} \le c + 2\mathsf{M}\epsilon\right) \Leftrightarrow (c \le c - c\epsilon + 2\mathsf{M}\epsilon - 2\mathsf{M}\epsilon^2) \Leftrightarrow (c + 2\mathsf{M}\epsilon \le 2\mathsf{M})$$

$$\left(c + \epsilon \le \tfrac{c}{1-\epsilon}\right) \Leftrightarrow (c - c\epsilon + \epsilon - \epsilon^2 \le c) \Leftrightarrow (1 - \epsilon \le c)$$

$$\left(\tfrac{c}{1+\epsilon} \le c - \tfrac{\epsilon}{2}\right) \Leftrightarrow \left(c \le c + c\epsilon - \tfrac{\epsilon}{2} - \tfrac{\epsilon^2}{2}\right) \Leftrightarrow \left(\tfrac{1}{2} + \tfrac{\epsilon}{2} \le c\right)$$

$$\left(c - \mathsf{M}\epsilon \le \tfrac{c}{1+\epsilon}\right) \Leftrightarrow (c + c\epsilon - \mathsf{M}\epsilon - \mathsf{M}\epsilon^2 \le c) \Leftrightarrow (c - \mathsf{M}\epsilon \le \mathsf{M})$$

This means that if we enlarge guards with $2\mathsf{M}\epsilon$, any time a guard is enabled in $\mathcal{H}''$ the same guard is enabled in $\mathcal{H}_{+2\mathsf{M}\epsilon}$. Similarly, if we enlarge guards with $\frac{\epsilon}{2}$, any time a guard is enabled in $\mathcal{H}_{+\frac{\epsilon}{2}}$ the same guard is enabled in $\mathcal{H}''$. The proof is complete once we remember that $\mathcal{H}^\epsilon$ and $\mathcal{H}''$ are trace equivalent. □

Next, we present an algorithm for robust ω-regular model checking problem when only positive guards are perturbed. The main technical observation is that there exists a computable δ_1 such that for all positive guard perturbations $\delta \in (0, \delta_1)$, the set of edges that are visited infinitely often along the executions of $\mathcal{H}_{+\delta_1}$ are contained in that of $\mathcal{H}_{+\delta}$. Therefore, if $\mathcal{H}_{+\delta} \models \Box\Diamond B$ for some δ, then $\mathcal{H}_{+\delta_1} \models \Box\Diamond B$ (the other implication is trivial). These observations are captured in Lemma 15 and Theorem 16. We first need a few definitions.

For any timed automaton $\mathcal{H}$ and any two edges $e_1, e_2 \in \mathtt{E}$, let $\mathtt{succ}(e_1, e_2)$ be a predicate that returns true iff 1. $\mathtt{D}e_1 = \mathtt{S}e_2$, and 2. $\forall x \in \mathtt{R}e_1 \bullet (x = 0) \wedge \mathtt{G}e_2 \not\Rightarrow \bot$. The second condition means if x is reset by e_1 then predicate $x = 0$ is consistent with the guard of e_2. Intuitively, $\mathtt{succ}(e_1, e_2)$ is true iff e_1 and e_2 can be merged. When this is the case, we define $e := \mathtt{merge}(e_1, e_2)$ to be the edge $(\mathtt{S}e_1, \mathtt{D}e_2, \mathtt{G}e_1 \wedge g, \mathtt{R}e_1 \cup \mathtt{R}e_2, \mathtt{L}e_1 \cup \mathtt{L}e_2 \cup \{e_1, e_2\})$ where for any guard $(x \bowtie c) \in \mathtt{G}e_2$ if $x \notin \mathtt{R}e_1$ then $(x \bowtie c) \in g$, otherwise, g does not constrain x. It is easy to see that if $s_1 \xrightarrow{e_1} s_2 \xrightarrow{0} s_3 \xrightarrow{e_2} s_4$, for some $s_1, s_2, s_3, s_4 \in \mathtt{S}_\mathcal{H}$ then $s_1 \xrightarrow{e} s_4$. Let $\mathtt{E}^s$ be the smallest set that contains $\mathtt{E}$ and for any two edges $e_1, e_2 \in \mathtt{E}^s$ if $\mathtt{succ}(e_1, e_2)$ then $\mathtt{merge}(e_1, e_2) \in \mathtt{E}^s$. Let $\mathcal{H}^s$ be same as $\mathcal{H}$ except its set of edges is replaced by $\mathtt{E}^s$ and q is an initial location in $\mathcal{H}^s$ iff $q \in \mathtt{Q}^{\mathsf{init}}_\mathcal{H}$ or $(q', 0^{\mathtt{X}}) \xrightarrow{e} (q, 0^{\mathtt{X}})$ for some $q' \in \mathtt{Q}^{\mathsf{init}}_\mathcal{H}$ and $e \in \mathtt{E}^s$. Intuitively, q is an initial location in $\mathcal{H}^s$ iff q is an initial location of $\mathcal{H}$ or it can be reached using an execution of 0 duration. Note that $|\mathtt{E}^s| < \infty$ therefore $\mathcal{H}^s$ is a well defined timed automaton. Finally, by construction, for any two states $s, s' \in \mathtt{S}_\mathcal{H} = \mathtt{S}_{\mathcal{H}^s}$ and $e \in \mathtt{E}^s$ if $s \xrightarrow{e} s'$ and e is a merge of $e_1, \ldots, e_n \in \mathtt{E}_\mathcal{H}$ in the given order (we don't need $\mathtt{merge}$ to be associative) then $s_0 \xrightarrow{e_1} s'_1 \xrightarrow{0} s_1 \xrightarrow{e_2} \cdots \xrightarrow{0} s'_n \xrightarrow{e_n} s_n$ for some $s_0, \ldots, s_n, s'_1, \ldots, s'_n \in \mathtt{S}_\mathcal{H}$ such that $s_0 = s$ and $s_n = s'$. Furthermore, $\mathtt{L}e = \{e_1, \ldots, e_n\}$.

Lemma 15. *Let $\mathcal{H}$ be a timed automaton and $\delta_1 := \frac{\delta_0}{24}$, where δ_0 is defined as in Theorem 9. For any $\delta \in (0, \delta_1)$ and execution $\tau \in \llbracket\mathcal{H}_{+\delta_1}\rrbracket^0_\omega$ there is execution $\tau' \in \llbracket\mathcal{H}_{+\delta}\rrbracket^0_\omega$ such that $\mathtt{inf}(\tau) = \mathtt{inf}(\tau')$.*

Proof. If $\mathsf{duration}(\tau) = 0$ the theorem is trivially true. Therefore, for the rest of the proof assume $\mathsf{duration}(\tau) > 0$.

1. Suppose τ has infinitely many non-zero time transitions. We prove this part for $\delta_1 := \delta_0$ (which is stronger than $\delta_1 := \frac{\delta_0}{24}$). After any non-zero time transition, value of no variable is zero. Therefore, none of the guards of the form $x \le 0$ are satisfied. Construct an execution $u \in \llbracket\mathcal{H}^s_{+\delta_1}\rrbracket^0_\omega$ from τ by removing all zero time transitions and merging edges that their in-between-time-transitions have been removed. Also, if u does not start with non-zero time transition, remove e_0 the first discrete transition of it. After this we know u starts with a non-zero time transition and $x \le 0$ is never used in its guards. Theorem 9 only uses edges of u and guards of u are the same in $\mathcal{H}^s_{+\delta_1}$ and $\mathcal{H}^s_{\delta_1}$. Therefore, by Theorem 9 there is an execution $u' \in \llbracket\mathcal{H}^s_{+\delta}\rrbracket^0_\omega$ such that $\mathtt{inf}(u') = \mathtt{inf}(u)$. If we replace any edge e in u that belongs to $\mathtt{E}^s \setminus \mathtt{E}$ with some sequence of edges from $\mathtt{L}e$ and do the same for e_0 (if it was initially removed), we get an execution $\tau'' \in \llbracket\mathcal{H}_{+\delta_1}\rrbracket^0_\omega$. If we do the same to u', we get an execution $\tau' \in \llbracket\mathcal{H}_{+\delta}\rrbracket^0_\omega$. Furthermore, we know $\mathtt{inf}(\tau') = \mathtt{inf}(\tau'')$. This part is complete once we notice $\mathtt{inf}(\tau) = \mathtt{inf}(\tau'')$ since edges in $\mathtt{E}^s$ keep track of set of edges that they visit internally.

2. Next suppose $\tau := \tau^1 \frown \tau^2$ for some $\tau^1 \in [\![\mathcal{H}_{+\delta_1}]\!]^0_*$ and $\tau^2 \in [\![\mathcal{H}_{+\delta_1}]\!]_\omega$ such that $\mathsf{duration}(\tau^2) = 0$. Let $Y \subseteq \mathtt{X}$ be the possibly empty set of variables such that for any $x \in Y$ the guard $x \leq 0$ occurs infinitely often in τ. Let $\tau := \tau^3 \frown \tau^4$ for some $\tau^3 \in [\![\mathcal{H}_{+\delta_1}]\!]^0_*$ and $\tau^4 \in [\![\mathcal{H}_{+\delta_1}]\!]_\omega$ such that $\mathsf{duration}(\tau^4) = 0$, all variables in Y are always zero in τ^4, and $x \leq 0$ appears in guards of τ^4 only for $x \in Y$. For any variable $x \in \mathtt{X}$, let $\tau^4_x \in [\![\mathcal{H}_{+\delta_1}]\!]_\infty$ be the longest prefix of τ^4 that either never resets x or resets x only on its last step. Also, let g_x be the conjunction of all guards on x in τ^4_x that are not $x \leq 0$. Furthermore, let $g := \bigwedge_{x \in \mathtt{X}} g_x$, and let g_δ be g enlarged by δ. Note that g_{δ_1} is satisfied by $\mathsf{last}(\tau^3)$. Let q be the last location visited in τ^3. Add a new location q' to $\mathtt{Q}_\mathcal{H}$ and two new edges e and e' to $\mathtt{E}_\mathcal{H}$. e is from q to q' with guard $g \wedge \bigwedge_{x \in Y} x \leq 0$ that resets no variable, and e' is a self-loop on q' with guard g that also resets no variable. Call the new timed automaton $\mathcal{H}'$.
Let $u := u^1 \frown u^2$ for some $u^1 \in [\![\mathcal{H}'_{+2\delta_1}]\!]^0_*$ and $u^2 \in [\![\mathcal{H}'_{+2\delta_1}]\!]_\omega$ such that $u^1 := \mathsf{first}(\tau^3) \xrightarrow{\tau^3} \mathsf{last}(\tau^3) \xrightarrow{e} s$ and $u^2 := s_n \xrightarrow{t_n} s'_n \xrightarrow{e'} s_{n+1}$ for some $s, s_0, s'_0, s_1, s'_1, s_2, s'_2, \ldots \in \mathtt{S}_{\mathcal{H}'}$ where $s_0 = s$ and $t_n := \frac{\delta_1}{2^{n+1}}$ for all $n \in \mathbb{N}$. Since $\mathsf{duration}(u^2) = \delta_1$ we know $g_{2\delta_1}$ is always satisfied in u^2 and therefore u is a valid execution.
Let δ'_0 be the maximum enlargement Theorem 9 allows for $\mathcal{H}'$. Since $\mathcal{H}'$ has only one location more than $\mathcal{H}$ and number of edges does not matter in Theorem 9, we know $2\delta_1 \leq \delta'_0$. So we can use the previous case and find $u' \in [\![\mathcal{H}'_{+\delta}]\!]^0_\omega$ such that $\mathtt{inf}(u) = \inf(u') = \{e'\}$. By construction of $\mathcal{H}'$, we know u' can be written as $u'^1 \frown u'^2$ for some $u'^1 \in [\![\mathcal{H}'_{+\delta}]\!]^0_*$ and $u'^2 \in [\![\mathcal{H}'_{+\delta}]\!]_\omega$ such that the last edge in u'^1 is e, e is used only once in u'^1, and the only edge in u'^2 is e'.
Inside u', right before and after taking e, g_δ is satisfied and all variables in Y are zero. Let $\tau' := \tau'^1 \frown \tau'^2$, where τ'^1 is obtained from u'^1 by removing e and the time transition after that, and τ'^2 is obtained from τ^4 by using the same trace and setting all time transitions equal to zero. We show that $\tau' \in [\![\mathcal{H}_{+\delta}]\!]^0_\omega$.
We know at the end of τ'^1 and everywhere in τ'_2 all variables in Y are zero which is the same in τ^4. For any variable $x \notin Y$ we know value of x satisfies g_δ at the end of τ'^1 and this value does not change in τ'^2 until x gets reset to 0. During this time it always satisfies g_δ and after it gets reset to 0 it remains 0 both in τ'^2 and τ^4.

□

Theorem 16. *For any timed automaton $\mathcal{H}$ and B a subset of* $\mathtt{E}$*,*

$$\left(\exists \delta \in \mathbb{R}_+ \bullet \mathcal{H}_{+\delta} \models \Box\Diamond B\right) \Leftrightarrow (\mathcal{H}_{+\delta_1} \models \Box\Diamond B)$$

where δ_1 is as defined in Lemma 15.

The above observations together give us the following result.

Theorem 17. *Let $\mathcal{H}$ be a timed automaton with maximum constant* M *and let B be a subset of* $\mathtt{E}$*. Let δ_1 be as defined in Lemma 15, and let $\epsilon_1 := \frac{\delta_1}{2\mathsf{M}}$. Then:*

$$\left(\exists \epsilon \in \mathbb{R}_+ \bullet \mathcal{H}^\epsilon \models \Box\Diamond B\right) \Leftrightarrow (\mathcal{H}_{+\delta_1} \models \Box\Diamond B) \Leftrightarrow (\mathcal{H}^{\epsilon_1} \models \Box\Diamond B)$$

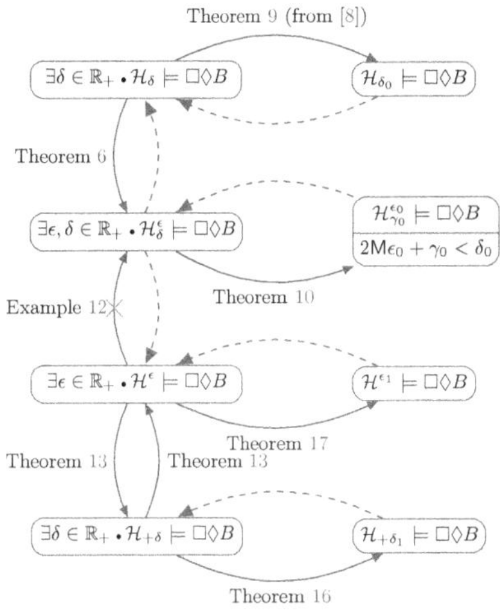

Figure 2: Overview of the results in Section 3. δ_0 is defined in Theorem 9, $\delta_1 := \frac{\delta_0}{24}$, $\epsilon_1 := \frac{\delta_1}{2\mathsf{M}}$, and M is the maximum constant appeared in $\mathcal{H}$. Arrows are implications. Implications of dashed arrows are obvious. All problems are in PSPACE-complete.

Proof. Using Theorem 13 and Lemma 15 we only need to show $\exists \epsilon \in \mathbb{R}_+ \bullet \mathcal{H}^\epsilon \models \Box\Diamond B$ implies $\mathcal{H}^{\epsilon_1} \models \Box\Diamond B$. If $\epsilon \geq \epsilon_1$ then we are done. Otherwise, *wlog.* we can assume $\epsilon < \frac{1}{2}$ and using Lemma 14 we know for any $\tau \in [\![\mathcal{H}^{\epsilon_1}]\!]^0_\omega$ if τ visits any element of B infinitely often then there is $\tau' \in [\![\mathcal{H}_{+2\mathsf{M}\epsilon_1}]\!]^0_\omega$ that visits the same set infinitely often. Next, using $2\mathsf{M}\epsilon_1 \leq \delta_1$ and Theorem 13, there is $\tau'' \in [\![\mathcal{H}_{+\frac{\epsilon}{2}}]\!]^0_\omega$ that visits the same set of edges infinitely often. Finally, using Lemma 14 we know there is $\tau''' \in [\![\mathcal{H}^\epsilon]\!]^0_\omega$ that visits the same element in B infinitely often. □

Theorem 17 gives a simple algorithm to solve robust ω-regular model checking problem when only clocks are drifted (compute δ_1 and check that $\mathcal{H}_{+\delta_1} \models \Box\Diamond B$). Since $\mathcal{H}_{+\delta_1}$ is a timed automaton, δ_1 is only exponentially small, and ω-regular model checking problem for timed automaton can be solved in PSPACE, we have a simple upper bound on the complexity. We show that in fact this complexity bound is tight.

Corollary 18. *The robust ω-regular model checking problem when only clocks are drifted is PSPACE-complete.*

Proof. PSPACE-completeness when guards are enlarged by δ_0 has been established in [8]. Bouyer *et al.* proved for any poly-space bounded Turing machine $\mathcal{A}$ there is a timed automaton $\mathcal{H}$ and property $\Box\Diamond B$ such that $\mathcal{A}$ accepts the zero input iff $\mathcal{H}_{\delta_0} \models \Box\Diamond B$ and iff $\mathcal{H} \models \Box\Diamond B$. With the help of Lemma 7 and using $\epsilon_0 := \frac{\delta_0}{2\mathsf{M}}$ we have $(\mathcal{H} \models \Box\Diamond B) \Rightarrow (\mathcal{H}_{\delta_0} \models \Box\Diamond B) \Rightarrow (\mathcal{H}^{\epsilon_0} \models \Box\Diamond B) \Rightarrow (\mathcal{H} \models \Box\Diamond B)$. Therefore, $\mathcal{A}$ accepts the zero input iff $\mathcal{H}^{\epsilon_0} \models \Box\Diamond B$. □

4. COMPUTING LIMIT REACHABLE SETS UNDER CLOCK DRIFTS

In this section, we will prove that $\mathsf{limreach}^\epsilon(\mathcal{H})$ is computable in polynomial space for a *bounded* timed automaton $\mathcal{H}$. Recall that, a timed automaton $\mathcal{H}$ is bounded if the invariants of $\mathcal{H}$ are bounded by M, the maximum constant appearing in the constraints of $\mathcal{H}$. Restricting our attention to bounded timed automata is not limiting. It is well known [5, 7], that for any timed automaton $\mathcal{H}$, one can construct a bounded timed automaton $\mathsf{bnd}(\mathcal{H})$ that is weakly bisimilar to $\mathcal{H}$. In fact, the construction also works when $\mathcal{H}$ is perturbed. Thus, given that we show how to compute $\mathsf{limreach}^{\epsilon}(\mathcal{H})$ for a bounded automaton $\mathcal{H}$, we can compute the set of regions containing states that belong to $\mathsf{limreach}^{\epsilon}(\mathcal{H}')$ for any (not necessarily bounded) timed automaton $\mathcal{H}'$.

The algorithm to compute $\mathsf{limreach}^{\epsilon}(\mathcal{H})$ is very similar to the one for timed automata under the progress cycle assumption, and is shown as Algorithm 1. Lines 1 to 3 compute the set $\mathcal{C}$ of all progress cycles whose length are bounded by $W + 2W|\mathtt{X}|$, where W is the number of regions of $\mathcal{H}$. The rest of the algorithm is similar to the approach in [11, 15]; the algorithm first computes the reachable regions assuming there is no perturbation (Line 4). It then iteratively adds closure of initial regions of progress cycles that are not in the current set of reachable regions but have non-empty intersection with it, and recomputes the reachable regions, until a fixpoint is reached. At that point the set J^* is the set of limit reachable states of $\mathcal{H}$ (Line 9).

Algorithm 1: Computing the limit reachable set of a bounded timed automaton

Input : Bounded timed automaton $\mathcal{H}$
Output : $\mathsf{limreach}^{\epsilon}(\mathcal{H})$

1 $\mathcal{G} \leftarrow$ the region graph of $\mathcal{H}$
2 $W \leftarrow$ number of nodes in $\mathcal{G}$
3 $\mathcal{C} \leftarrow$ the set of progress cycles in $\mathcal{G}$ of length $\leq W + 2W|\mathtt{X}|$
4 $J^* \leftarrow \bigcup_{s \in \mathsf{s}_{\mathsf{init}}} \mathsf{reach}(\mathcal{G}, [s])$
5 **while** $\exists p \in \mathcal{C} \bullet [p_0] \not\subseteq J^* \wedge J^* \cap [p_0] \neq \emptyset$ **do**
6 $\quad J^* \leftarrow J^* \cup [p_0]$
7 $\quad J^* \leftarrow \mathsf{reach}(\mathcal{G}, J^*)$
8 **end**
9 **return** J^*

The main observation in this section is that J^* is indeed $\mathsf{limreach}^{\epsilon}(\mathcal{H})$, which is stated next. Later in the section we argue that Algorithm 1 can in fact, be implemented in such a way that it uses only polynomial space.

Theorem 19. *For a timed automaton $\mathcal{H}$, let J^* be the set returned on Line 9 in Algorithm 1. We have:*

$$\mathsf{limreach}^{\epsilon}(\mathcal{H}) = J^*$$

The proof of $J^* \subseteq \mathsf{limreach}^{\epsilon}(\mathcal{H})$ follows from the observations in [11][2]. To show that $\mathsf{limreach}^{\epsilon}(\mathcal{H}) \subseteq J^*$, from Algorithm 1, we observe that J^* is a (topologically) closed set. If we show that $\mathsf{d}_{\infty}(\mathsf{limreach}^{\epsilon}(\mathcal{H}), J^*) = 0$, then the result follows immediately. This is the crux of the proof. We state this observation in a slightly stronger form below as Lemma 23. Before presenting this lemma and its proof, we recall 3 observations from [9, 11] that we will use. The first observation (from [11]) is that if the distance between the closure of two regions is small, then they have a non-empty intersection.

Lemma 20 (Lemma 16 in [11])**.** *For any timed automaton $\mathcal{H}$ and for any two regions r_1 and r_2, if $\mathsf{d}_{\infty}([r_1], [r_2]) < \frac{1}{|\mathtt{X}|}$ then $[r_1] \cap [r_2] \neq \emptyset$.*

Next, we recall a result from [11] that shows that for any distance bound α and number of steps k, all trajectories of certain perturbed timed automata $\mathcal{H}^{\epsilon}_{\delta}$ are close to some trajectory of $\mathcal{H}$.

Theorem 21 (Theorem 44 in [11])**.** *Let $\mathcal{H}$ be a bounded timed automaton. For any distance $\alpha \in (0, 1)$ and number of steps $k \in \mathbb{N}$, there are two numbers $D(\alpha, k), E(\alpha, k) \in \mathbb{R}_+$ such that for any $\epsilon \in [0, E(\alpha, k)]$, $\delta \in [0, D(\alpha, k)]$, and a trajectory $\tau' \in [\![\mathcal{H}^{\epsilon}_{\delta}]\!]_*$ such that $|\tau'| \leq k$ there is a trajectory $\tau \in [\![\mathcal{H}]\!]_*$ with the following properties:*

1. *$\mathsf{first}(\tau) \in [\mathsf{first}(\tau')]$*
2. *$\mathtt{trace}(\tau) = \mathtt{trace}(\tau')$,*
3. *τ is close to τ' in the following sense: $\forall i \in \{0, \ldots, |\tau|\} \bullet \mathsf{d}_{\infty}(\tau_{2i}, \tau'_{2i}) < \alpha$.*

Finally, we recall a result about monotonic rectangular hybrid automata from [9] that we apply to clock drifted timed automata. The result states that corresponding to any trajectory of duration T between two states in $\mathsf{S}_{\mathcal{H}^{\epsilon}}$, there is a trajectory of the same duration between the same states such that number of steps is bounded by a function of T and $\mathcal{H}$. We state this observation for $\mathcal{H}^{\epsilon}$ in a slightly different form than is proved in [9].

Theorem 22 (Based on Theorem 2 in [9])**.** *Let $\mathcal{H}$ be a timed automaton with M as the maximum constant appearing in its constraints, $\epsilon \in [0, 1]$ be a perturbation, and $T \in \mathbb{R}_{\geq 0}$ be a time bound. Then for any $\tau \in [\![\mathcal{H}^{\epsilon}]\!]_*$ there is $\tau' \in [\![\mathcal{H}^{\epsilon}]\!]_*$ with the following properties:*

1. *$\mathsf{first}(\tau') = \mathsf{first}(\tau)$,*
2. *$\mathsf{last}(\tau') = \mathsf{last}(\tau)$,*
3. *$\mathsf{locs}(\tau') = \mathsf{locs}(\tau)$,*
4. *$\mathsf{duration}(\tau') = \mathsf{duration}(\tau)$, and*
5. *$|\tau'| \leq F(\mathcal{H}, T) = 24(2\lceil T \rceil + 1) \times |\mathtt{X}|^2 \times |\mathtt{Q}|^2 \times (2\mathsf{cmax} + 3)^{2|\mathtt{X}|}$, where $\mathsf{cmax} := \max\{2, \mathsf{M}\}$.*

Proof. The result follows from the observation in [9] about monotonic rectangular hybrid automata; $\mathcal{H}^{\epsilon}$ is such an automaton, where the maximum rate of any clock (called rmax in [9]) is bounded by 2. Note that items 3 and 4 are not explicitly mentioned in Theorem 2 in [9], but they follow from the proof in [9]. □

We have now all the results from previous papers that we need to establish the proof of Lemma 23. It is useful to contrast the statements of Lemma 23 and Theorem 21. First, Lemma 23 applies to all trajectories and not just those with a bounded number of steps. Second, in Lemma 23 closeness is measured with respect to J^* (as opposed to trajectories of $\mathcal{H}$).

Lemma 23. *Let $\mathcal{H}$ be a bounded timed automaton with clocks $\mathtt{X}$. For any distance $\alpha \in \left(0, \frac{1}{2|\mathtt{X}|}\right)$ there is $E \in \mathbb{R}_+$ such that for any $\epsilon \in [0, E]$ and for any $\tau' \in [\![\mathcal{H}^{\epsilon}]\!]_*$ such that $\mathsf{first}(\tau') \in J^*$ we have $\mathsf{d}_{\infty}(\mathsf{last}(\tau'), J^*) < \alpha$; here J^* refers to the set returned on Line 9 in Algorithm 1.*

[2] The algorithm in [11] only considers simple cycles, i.e., cycles whose length is bounded by W. However, the proof of $J^* \subseteq \mathsf{limreach}^{\epsilon}(\mathcal{H})$ in [11] does not rely on the assumption, and so eventhough our algorithm may consider non-simple cycles in its analysis, this is does not result in any additional reachable states.

Proof. The proof of this theorem is similar to the proof of Theorem 45 in [11] with significant departures. Let M be the maximum constant appearing on constraints of $\mathcal{H}$. We know M is a bound on clock values in $\mathcal{H}$. Let W be the number of regions in the region graph of $\mathcal{H}$ (as in line 2). Take $k = F(\mathcal{H}, 6\mathsf{M}W + 2\mathsf{M})$, where is F is the function from Theorem 22. We will prove that the desired $E = \min\{\frac{1}{3}, E(\alpha, k)\}$, where $E(\alpha, k)$ is from Theorem 21. Fix E to be this value. Notice that for this choice of E, the rate of every variable in $\mathcal{H}^\epsilon$ is $\geq 1 - \epsilon > \frac{1}{2}$. This is the reason we choose E to be at most $\frac{1}{3}$.

The proof is by induction on $|\tau'|$. For the base case, consider τ' such that $|\tau'| \leq k$. From Theorem 21 and the definition of E, there is a trajectory $\tau \in [\![\mathcal{H}]\!]_*$ that is α-close to τ'. Since J^* is a closed set, $\mathsf{first}(\tau) \in [\mathsf{first}(\tau')] \subseteq J^*$. Finally, observe that $\mathsf{reach}(\mathcal{G}, J^*) \subseteq J^*$ ($\mathcal{G}$ is the region graph of $\mathcal{H}$) and so $\mathsf{last}(\tau) \in J^*$. From Theorem 21, we have $\mathsf{d}_\infty(\mathsf{last}(\tau), \mathsf{last}(\tau')) < \alpha$ and so $\mathsf{d}_\infty(\mathsf{last}(\tau'), J^*) < \alpha$.

For the inductive step, if $|\tau'| > F(\mathcal{H}, \mathsf{duration}(\tau'))$ then Theorem 22 ensures that there is a trajectory $\tau'' \in [\![\mathcal{H}^\epsilon]\!]_*$ that starts and ends in the same state and has fewer steps. The lemma then follows by the induction hypothesis applied to τ''.

Let us, therefore, assume that $|\tau'| \leq F(\mathcal{H}, \mathsf{duration}(\tau'))$ and $\mathsf{duration}(\tau') > 6\mathsf{M}W + 2\mathsf{M}$. Observe that all clocks in $\mathcal{H}^\epsilon$ are bounded by M, and the rate of every clock is $\geq 1 - \epsilon > \frac{1}{2}$. So no time transition has duration $2\mathsf{M}$ or longer. Thus, without loss of generality, we can write τ' as $\tau' = \tau_{\mathsf{first}} \frown \tau_{\mathsf{last}}$, where $\mathsf{duration}(\tau_{\mathsf{last}})$ is between $6\mathsf{M}W$ and $6\mathsf{M}W + 2\mathsf{M}$. From Theorem 22, there is $\tau'' \in [\![\mathcal{H}^\epsilon]\!]_*$ such that 1. $|\tau''| \leq k = F(\mathcal{H}', 6\mathsf{M}W + 2\mathsf{M})$, 2. $\mathsf{duration}(\tau'') = \mathsf{duration}(\tau_{\mathsf{last}})$, 3. $\mathsf{first}(\tau'') = \mathsf{first}(\tau_{\mathsf{last}})$, and 4. $\mathsf{last}(\tau'') = \mathsf{last}(\tau_{\mathsf{last}}) = \mathsf{last}(\tau')$. By Theorem 21 we know there is $\tau \in [\![\mathcal{H}]\!]_*$ that stays α-close to τ'' every step of the way. Let ν_i and ν_i'' be respectively states of τ and τ'' at step i. Applying the induction hypothesis to τ'', for any $i < |\tau''|$, we have $\mathsf{d}_\infty(\nu_i'', J^*) \leq \alpha$. Thus, by triangle inequality, for any $i < |\tau''|$,

$$\mathsf{d}_\infty(\nu_i, J^*) \leq \mathsf{d}_\infty(\nu_i, \nu_i'') + \mathsf{d}_\infty(\nu_i'', J^*) \leq 2\alpha < \frac{1}{|\mathtt{X}|}$$

Thus, using Lemma 20, we have $[\nu_i] \cap J^* \neq \emptyset$ for any $i < |\tau''|$.

The previous paragraph establishes the closeness of every state ν_i'', except possible the last; we need to show that $\mathsf{last}(\tau_{\mathsf{last}}) = \mathsf{last}(\tau'')$ is close. By construction, we know that $\mathsf{d}_\infty(\mathsf{last}(\tau''), \mathsf{last}(\tau)) \leq \alpha$. Thus, proving $\mathsf{last}(\tau) \in J^*$ will complete the induction step.

Next, because $\mathcal{H}^\epsilon$ is bounded and the rate of every variable is $> \frac{1}{2}$, every variable is reset within $2\mathsf{M}$ time since its last reset. Thus, in any trajectory of duration $\geq 2\mathsf{M}$, every variable is reset. Based on these observations, we can partition τ'' as $\tau'' = \tau_1'' \frown \tau_2'' \frown \cdots \frown \tau_m''$, where for every i, 1. $\mathsf{duration}(\tau_i'') \leq 2\mathsf{M}$, 2. every variable is reset in subtrajectory τ_i'', and 3. $m \geq 6\mathsf{M}W/2\mathsf{M} = 3W \geq W + 2$. Since $\mathtt{trace}(\tau) = \mathtt{trace}(\tau'')$, we can partition τ similarly into $\tau = \tau_1 \frown \cdots \frown \tau_m$, where every variable is reset in each subtrajectory τ_i. The proof can now be completed using two technical lemmas that are proved next. We will show

- There is a $j < |\tau|$ such that there is a subtrajectory of τ starting from ν_j that is a progress cycle (Lemma 24).
- $[\nu_j]$ is, in fact, part of a progress cycle of length $\leq W + 2W|\mathtt{X}|$ (Lemma 25).

Assuming the above hold, we can conclude that $\nu_j \in J^*$ because of line 6 of Algorithm 1. Also, since τ is a trajectory of $\mathcal{H}$, we can conclude that $\nu_i \in J^*$ for all $i \geq j$ (Line 7 of Algorithm 1), completing the proof of the induction step. □

Lemma 24. *Let $\mathcal{H}$ be a timed automaton with W regions in its region graph. Let τ be any trajectory of $\mathcal{H}$ such that*

$$\tau = \tau_1 \frown \tau_2 \frown \cdots \frown \tau_m$$

where $m \geq W + 2$ and every variable of $\mathcal{H}$ is reset in each τ_i (for every i). Then there is a subtrajectory of τ that is a progress cycle.

Proof. As $m \geq W + 2$ and the number of regions is bounded by W, by pigeon-hole principle, there must be s, t and region r such that 1. $t \geq s + 2$, and 2. r is visited in both τ_s and τ_t. These observations ensure that there is a subtrajectory of $\tau_s \frown \cdots \frown \tau_t$ that forms a cycle, and since there is an index u between s and t, it is also a progress cycle since all the variables will be reset in τ_u. □

Lemma 25. *Let $\mathcal{H}$ be any timed automaton with $\mathcal{G}$ as its region graph and W as the number of nodes in $\mathcal{G}$. For any cycle π in $\mathcal{G}$ there is a cycle π' in $\mathcal{G}$ such that*

1. *$|\pi'| \leq W + 2W|\mathtt{X}|$,*
2. *$\pi_0 = \pi_0'$ (they start from the same node), and*
3. *π and π' reset the same set of clocks.*

We conclude this section by observing that $\mathsf{limreach}^\epsilon(\mathcal{H})$ can be computed in polynomial space.

Theorem 26. *For any bounded timed automaton $\mathcal{H}$, $\mathsf{limreach}^\epsilon(\mathcal{H})$ can be computed by an algorithm that uses space that is bounded by a polynomial function of $|\mathcal{H}|$.*

Proof. From Theorem 19, we know that $J^* = \mathsf{limreach}^\epsilon(\mathcal{H})$. If we show that Algorithm 1 uses only polynomial space, then we are done. Unfortunately, as presented, Algorithm 1 uses exponential space and runs in exponential time. But small changes to the presentation of Algorithm 1 establish the complexity bounds stated in the theorem.

First observe that J^* is a union of regions of $\mathcal{H}$. Therefore, if we show that, given a region r of $\mathcal{H}$, the problem of determining if $r \in J^*$ can be solved in polynomial space then we will establish the complexity bounds. Based on lines 3 through 7, we conclude that $r \in J^*$ iff there is a path $\pi := \pi_0\pi_1\pi_2 \ldots \pi_{2m}$, for some $m \leq W$ such that

1. π_0 is an initial region of $\mathcal{H}'$,
2. π_{2i+1} is reachable from π_{2i}, for $0 \leq i \leq m$,
3. $[\pi_{2i}] \cap \pi_{2i-1} \neq \emptyset$, for $1 \leq i \leq m$, and
4. for $1 \leq i \leq m$, π_{2i} is on a progress cycle.

By progressively guessing regions on a path/cycle, each of the above conditions can be checked in (nondeterministic) polynomial space, giving us the necessary bounds. □

5. EXPERIMENTAL RESULTS

We applied the above algorithmic ideas to verify the robustness of two protocols. Models of both protocols are available in UPPAAL. The first one we considered is Fischer's mutual exclusion protocol for n processes. Any mutual exclusion protocol must satisfy at least three properties: 1. no two processes enter a critical section at the same time, 2. there are no deadlocks in the system, and 3. any request to access a critical section will eventually be granted. The first property is a safety property and the next two are liveness properties. Each of these properties can be verified to hold for the unperturbed protocol using UPPAAL for $n \leq 6$ in less 2 seconds. Using UPPAAL, we could also show that the system satisfies each of these properties when there are 6 processes and guards are enlarged by $\delta := 0.01$ [3]; the verification time for this was also less than 2 seconds. Therefore, using Lemma 7 and knowing the maximum constant in this model is 3, the model is also robust with $\epsilon := \frac{0.01}{12}$ and $\delta := \frac{0.01}{2}$.

The next example we verified, is 2Doors. It involves two doors and two users that interact using the following rules: 1. a room has two doors which cannot be opened at the same time, 2. a door starts to open if its button is pushed, 3. it takes six seconds for a door to open, and thereafter it says open for at least four seconds, but no more than eight seconds, 4. it takes six seconds for a door to close and it stays closed for at least five seconds. We checked the following properties: 1. Mutex: The two doors are never open at the same time. 2. Either of doors can be opened. 3. Liveness: Whenever a button is pushed, the corresponding door will eventually open. 4. The system is deadlock-free. Using UPPAAL, in less than 2 seconds we could show that the system satisfies each of these properties when guards are enlarged by $\delta := 0.0001$. Therefore, using Lemma 7 and knowing the maximum constant in this model is 8, the model is also robust with $\epsilon := \frac{0.0001}{32}$ and $\delta := \frac{0.0001}{2}$.

Note that properties we checked in these two examples are not necessarily expressible using the special type of (robust) ω-regular model checking problems we have considered in this paper. However, Lemma 7 establishes language inclusion between executions of $\mathcal{H}$ under different types of perturbation, regardless of the property one might want to check.

6. CONCLUSION

In this paper we have investigated the robust model checking problem for timed automata without the progress cycle assumption, when only clocks are allowed to drift and when both guards and clocks are perturbed. We first showed that robust model checking of ω-regular properties with only enlarged guards is equivalent to the case when guards and clock rates are perturbed, and obtained a PSPACE-complete algorithm for the later case. We then gave another PSPACE-complete algorithm for model checking ω-regular properties when only clocks are allowed to drift. Finally, we gave a polynomial space algorithm to compute $\mathsf{limreach}^{\epsilon}(\mathcal{H})$. However, our results do not yield an algorithm to compute $\mathsf{limreach}^{\epsilon}_{\delta}(\mathcal{H})$ ($= \mathsf{limreach}_{\delta}(\mathcal{H})$). This is a possible direction for future exploration.

7. ACKNOWLEDGEMENT

We gratefully ackowledge the support of the following grants — Nima Roohi was partially supported by NSF CNS 1329991 and AFOSR FA9950-15-1-0059; Pavithra Prabhakar was partially supported by NSF CAREER Award 1552668; and Mahesh Viswanathan was partially supported by NSF CCF 1422798, NSF CNS 1329991 and AFOSR FA9950-15-1-0059.

[3] The model has a strict inequality $x > k$. We first replace that with $x \geq k+1$ and positively verified that all properties are still satisfied.

8. REFERENCES

[1] K. Altisen and S. Tripakis. Implementation of timed automata: An issue of semantics or modeling? In *Proceedings of FORMATS*, pages 273–288, 2005.

[2] R. Alur and D. L. Dill. A theory of timed automata. *TCS*, 126:183–235, 1994.

[3] R. Alur, S. L. Torre, and P. Madhusudan. Perturbed timed automata. In *Proceedings of HSCC*, pages 70–85, 2005.

[4] C. Baier and J.-P. Katoen. *Principles of Model Checking (Representation and Mind Series)*. 2008.

[5] G. Behrmann, A. Fehnker, T. Hune, K. Larsen, P. Pettersson, J. Romijn, and F. Vaandrager. Minimum-cost reachability for priced timed automata. In *Proceedings of HSCC*, pages 147–161, 2001.

[6] P. Bouyer, N. Markey, and P.-A. Reynier. Robust model-checking of linear-time properties in timed automata. In *Proceedings of LATIN*, pages 238–249, 2006.

[7] P. Bouyer and F. Chevalier. On conciseness of extensions of timed automata. *J. Autom. Lang. Comb.*, 10(4):393–405, April 2005.

[8] P. Bouyer, N. Markey, and O. Sankur. Robust model-checking of timed automata via pumping in channel machines. In *Proceedings of FORMATS*, pages 97–112, 2011.

[9] T. Brihaye, L. Doyen, G. Geeraerts, J. Ouaknine, J. F. Raskin, and J. Worrell. Time-bounded reachability for monotonic hybrid automata: Complexity and fixed points. In *Proceedings of ATVA*, volume 8172 of *LNCS*, pages 55–70, 2013.

[10] F. Cassez, T. Henzinger, and J.-F. Raskin. A comparison of control problems for timed and hybrid systems. In *Proceedings of HSCC*, pages 134–148, 2002.

[11] M. de Wulf, L. Doyen, N. Markey, and J.-F. Raskin. Robust safety of timed automata. *Formal Methods in System Design*, 33(1):45–84, 2008.

[12] V. Gupta, T. Henzinger, and R. Jagadeesan. Robust timed automata. In *Proceedings of the International Workshop on Hybrid and real-time Systems*, pages 331–345, 1997.

[13] T. A. Henzinger, P. W. Kopke, A. Puri, and P. Varaiya. What's decidable about hybrid automata? In *Journal of Computer and System Sciences*, pages 373–382, 1995.

[14] K. Larsen, P. Pettersson, and W. Yi. UPPAAL in a nutshell. *International Journal on Software Tools for Technology Transfer*, 1:134–152, 1997.

[15] A. Puri. Dynamical properties of timed automata. *Discrete Event Dynamic Systems*, 10(1-2):87–113, 2000.

[16] M. D. Wulf, L. Doyen, and J.-F.Raskin. Almost ASAP semantics: From timed models to timed implementations. *Formal Aspects of Computing*, 17(3):319–341, 2005.

[17] M. D. Wulf, L. Doyen, N. Markey, and J.-F. Raskin. Robustness and implementability of timed automata. In *Proceedings of FORMATS*, pages 118–133, 2004.

[18] S. Yovine. KRONOS: A verification tool for real-time systems. *International Journal on Software Tools for Technology Transfer*, 1:123–133, 1997.

Safety Verification of Nonlinear Hybrid Systems Based on Invariant Clusters

Hui Kong
IST Austria
Klosterneuburg, Austria
hui.kong@ist.ac.at

Sergiy Bogomolov
Australian National University
Canberra, Australia
sergiy.bogomolov@anu.edu.au

Christian Schilling
University of Freiburg
Freiburg, Germany
schillic@informatik.uni-freiburg.de

Yu Jiang
Tsinghua University, Beijing
Henan University, Kaifeng
China
jy1989@mail.tsinghua.edu.cn

Thomas A. Henzinger
IST Austria
Klosterneuburg, Austria
tah@ist.ac.at

ABSTRACT

In this paper, we propose an approach to automatically compute invariant clusters for nonlinear semialgebraic hybrid systems. An invariant cluster for an ordinary differential equation (ODE) is a multivariate polynomial invariant $g(\vec{u}, \vec{x}) = 0$, parametric in $\vec{u}$, which can yield an infinite number of concrete invariants by assigning different values to $\vec{u}$ so that every trajectory of the system can be overapproximated precisely by the intersection of a group of concrete invariants. For semialgebraic systems, which involve ODEs with multivariate polynomial right-hand sides, given a template multivariate polynomial $g(\vec{u}, \vec{x})$, an invariant cluster can be obtained by first computing the remainder of the Lie derivative of $g(\vec{u}, \vec{x})$ divided by $g(\vec{u}, \vec{x})$ and then solving the system of polynomial equations obtained from the coefficients of the remainder. Based on invariant clusters and sum-of-squares (SOS) programming, we present a new method for the safety verification of hybrid systems. Experiments on nonlinear benchmark systems from biology and control theory show that our approach is efficient.

CCS Concepts

•General and reference → Verification; •Theory of computation → Timed and hybrid models; •Software and its engineering → Formal methods; Model checking;

Keywords

hybrid system; nonlinear system; semialgebraic system; invariant; safety verification; SOS programming

HSCC'17, April 18 - 20, 2017, Pittsburgh, PA, USA

ISBN 978-1-4503-4590-3/17/04...$15.00

DOI: http://dx.doi.org/10.1145/3049797.3054966

1. INTRODUCTION

A hybrid system [17] is a dynamical system that exhibits both discrete and continuous behaviors. In this paper, we consider the safety verification problem for hybrid systems. In other words, we want to automatically check whether a set of bad states can be reached from a set of initial states. For systems described by nonlinear differential equations this task is particularly complicated as computing the exact reachable set is usually infeasible. Existing approaches are mainly based on approximate reachable set computation [2, 9, 4, 6] and abstraction [33, 1, 11, 13, 5, 8, 7].

An invariant is a special kind of overapproximation for the reachable set of a system. Since invariants do not involve direct computation of the reachable set, they are especially suitable for dealing with nonlinear hybrid systems. However, automatically and efficiently generating sufficiently strong invariants is challenging [26, 12, 28, 24, 20, 27, 16, 29, 18].

In this work, we propose an approach to automatically compute *invariant clusters* for a class of nonlinear semialgebraic systems whose trajectories are algebraic, i.e., every trajectory of the system is essentially a subset of the intersection of zero level sets of a group of multivariate polynomials. An invariant cluster for a semialgebraic system is a parameterized multivariate polynomial invariant $g(\vec{u}, \vec{x}) = 0$, with parameter $\vec{u}$, which can yield an infinite number of concrete invariants by assigning different values to $\vec{u}$ so that every trajectory of the system can be overapproximated precisely by the intersection of a group of concrete invariants.

We roughly describe the idea of computing invariant clusters. A sufficient condition for a trajectory of a semialgebraic system to start from and to always stay in the zero level set of a multivariate polynomial $g(\vec{x})$ (i.e., $\{\vec{x} \in \mathbb{R}^n \mid g(\vec{x}) = 0\}$) is that the Lie derivative $\mathcal{L}_{\vec{f}} g$ of $g(\vec{x})$ on the vector flow $\vec{f}$ can be divided exactly by $g(\vec{x})$ (i.e., the remainder of $\mathcal{L}_{\vec{f}} g$ w.r.t. $g(\vec{x})$ must be identical to 0). Therefore, if some $g(\vec{x})$ satisfies this condition, $g(\vec{x}) = 0$ is an invariant of the system. Given a template polynomial $g(\vec{u}, \vec{x})$ with $\vec{u}$ as its coefficients, we can compute the remainder $r(\vec{u}, \vec{x})$ of $\mathcal{L}_{\vec{f}} g$ w.r.t. $g(\vec{u}, \vec{x})$ symbolically. Moreover, $r(\vec{u}, \vec{x}) \equiv 0$ implies that all the coefficients $a_i(\vec{u})$ of the monomials in $\vec{x}$ in $r(\vec{u}, \vec{x})$ are equal to 0; thus we can set up a system P of polynomial equations in $\vec{u}$ from the coefficients $a_i(\vec{u})$. By solving P we get a set $\mathcal{C}$ of constraints on $\vec{u}$. For those elements in $\mathcal{C}$ that are linear in $\vec{u}$, the corresponding parameterized polynomial equations $g(\vec{u},\vec{x}) = 0$ form an infinite set of invariants, which we call invariant clusters. Based on invariant clusters and sum-of-squares (*SOS*) programming, we propose a new method for the safety verification of hybrid systems.

The main contributions of this paper are as follows: 1) We propose to generate invariant clusters for nonlinear semialgebraic systems based on computing the remainder of the Lie derivative of a template polynomial $g(\vec{u},\vec{x})$ w.r.t. $g(\vec{u},\vec{x})$ and solving the system of polynomial equations obtained from the coefficients of the remainder. 2) We present a method to overapproximate trajectories precisely by using invariant clusters. 3) We apply invariant clusters to the safety verification of semialgebraic hybrid systems based on *SOS* programming. 4) We implemented a prototype tool to perform the aforementioned steps automatically. Experiments show that our approach is effective and efficient.

The paper is organized as follows. Section 2 is devoted to the preliminaries. In Section 3, we introduce the approach to computing invariant clusters and using them to characterize trajectories. In Section 4, we present a method to verify safety properties for semialgebraic continuous and hybrid systems based on invariant clusters. In Section 5, we present our experimental results. In Section 6, we introduce some related works. Finally, we conclude our paper in Section 7.

2. PRELIMINARIES

In this section, we recall some concepts used throughout the paper. We first clarify some notation conventions. If not specified otherwise, we decorate vectors $\vec{\cdot}$, we use the symbol $\mathbb{K}$ for a field, $\mathbb{R}$ for the real number field and $\mathbb{N}$ for the set of natural numbers, and we consider multivariate polynomials, e.g., elements of the ring $\mathbb{K}[\vec{x}]$, where the components of $\vec{x}$ act as indeterminates. In addition, for all the polynomials $g(\vec{u},\vec{x})$, we denote by $\vec{u}$ the vector composed of all the u_i and denote by $\vec{x}$ the vector composed of all the remaining variables that occur in the polynomial.

DEFINITION 1 (IDEAL). *[10] A subset I of $\mathbb{K}[\vec{x}]$, is called an **ideal** if 1) $0 \in I$; 2) if $p, q \in I$, then $p + q \in I$; and 3) if $p \in I$ and $q \in \mathbb{K}[\vec{x}]$, then $pq \in I$.*

DEFINITION 2 (GENERATED IDEAL). *[10] Let $g_1, \ldots, g_s$ be polynomials in $\mathbb{K}[\vec{x}]$. The **ideal generated by** $\{g_1, \ldots, g_s\}$ is*

$$\langle g_1, \ldots, g_s\rangle \overset{def}{=} \Big\{ \sum_{i=1}^{s} h_i g_i \mid h_1, \ldots, h_s \in \mathbb{K}[\vec{x}] \Big\}.$$

DEFINITION 3 (ALGEBRAIC VARIETY). *Let $\mathbb{K}$ be an algebraically closed field and $I \subset \mathbb{K}[\vec{x}]$ be an ideal. We define the **algebraic variety** of I as*

$$\mathbb{V}(I) \overset{def}{=} \{\vec{x} \in \mathbb{K}^n \mid f(\vec{x}) = 0 \text{ for } f \in I\}.$$

Next, we present the notation of the Lie derivative, which is widely used in the discipline of differential geometry. Let $\vec{f} : \mathbb{R}^n \to \mathbb{R}^n$ be a continuous vector field such that $\dot{x}_i = f_i(\vec{x})$ where $\dot{x}_i$ is the time derivative of $x_i(t)$.

DEFINITION 4 (LIE DERIVATIVE). *For a given polynomial $p \in \mathbb{K}[\vec{x}]$ over $\vec{x} = (x_1, \ldots, x_n)$ and a continuous system $\dot{\vec{x}} = \vec{f}$, where $\vec{f} = (f_1, \ldots, f_n)$, the **Lie derivative** of $p \in \mathbb{K}[\vec{x}]$ along f of order k is defined as follows.*

$$\mathcal{L}^k_{\vec{f}} p \overset{def}{=} \begin{cases} p, & k = 0 \\ \sum_{i=1}^{n} \frac{\partial \mathcal{L}^{k-1}_{\vec{f}} p}{\partial x_i} \cdot f_i, & k \geq 1 \end{cases}$$

Essentially, the k-th order Lie derivative of p is the k-th derivative of p w.r.t. time, i.e., reflects the change of p over time. We write $\mathcal{L}_{\vec{f}} p$ for $\mathcal{L}^1_{\vec{f}} p$.

We also use the following theorem for deciding the existence of a real solution of a system of polynomial constraints.

THEOREM 1 (REAL NULLSTELLENSATZ). *[32] The system of multivariate polynomial equations and inequalities $p_1(\vec{x}) = 0, \ldots, p_{m_1}(\vec{x}) = 0, \quad q_1(\vec{x}) \geq 0, \ldots, q_{m_2}(\vec{x}) \geq 0$, $r_1(\vec{x}) > 0, \ldots, r_{m_3}(\vec{x}) > 0$ either has a solution in $\mathbb{R}^n$, or there exists the following polynomial identity*

$$\sum_{i=1}^{m_1} \beta_i p_i + \sum_{v \in \{0,1\}^{m_2}} \delta_v \prod_{j=1}^{m_2} q_j^{v_j} + \prod_{k=1}^{m_3} r_k^{d_k} + \sum_{v \in \{0,1\}^{m_3}} \eta_v \prod_{k=1}^{m_3} r_k^{v_k} + s = 0 \tag{1}$$

where $d_k \in \mathbb{N}$ and p_i, q_j, r_k, β_i are polynomials and δ_v, η_v, s are SOS (sum-of-squares) polynomials in $\mathbb{R}[\vec{x}]$.

REMARK 1. *Theorem 1 enables efficient decision if a system of polynomial constraints has a real solution. By moving the term s in equation (1) to the right-hand side and denoting the remaining terms by $R(\vec{x},\vec{y})$, we have $-R(\vec{x},\vec{y}) = s$, which means that $-R(\vec{x},\vec{y})$ is SOS. Hence finding a set of polynomials $\beta_j, r_k, \delta_v, \eta_v, s$ and some d_k's that make $-R(\vec{x},\vec{y})$ SOS is sufficient to prove that the system has no real solution, which can be done efficiently by SOS programming [25].*

In this paper, we focus on semialgebraic continuous and hybrid systems; we define them in the following.

DEFINITION 5 (SEMIALGEBRAIC SYSTEM). *A **semialgebraic system** is a triple $M \overset{def}{=} \langle X, \vec{f}, X_0\rangle$, where*

1. *$X \subseteq \mathbb{R}^n$ is the state space of the system M,*
2. *$\vec{f} \in \mathbb{R}[\vec{x}]^n$ is a locally Lipschitz continuous polynomial vector field function, and*
3. *$X_0 \subseteq X$ is the initial set, which is semialgebraic [32].*

The local Lipschitz continuity guarantees the existence and uniqueness of the differential equation $\dot{\vec{x}} = \vec{f}$ locally. A trajectory of a semialgebraic system is defined as follows.

DEFINITION 6 (TRAJECTORY). *Given a semialgebraic system M, a **trajectory** originating from a point $\vec{x}_0 \in X_0$ to time $T > 0$ is a continuous and differentiable function $\vec{x}(t)$: $[0,T) \to \mathbb{R}^n$ such that 1) $\vec{x}(0) = \vec{x}_0$, and 2) $\forall \tau \in [0,T)$: $\frac{d\vec{x}}{dt}\big|_{t=\tau} = \vec{f}(\vec{x}(\tau))$. T is assumed to be within the maximal interval of existence of the solution from $\vec{x}_0$.*

DEFINITION 7 (SAFETY). *Given an unsafe set $X_U \subseteq X$, a semialgebraic system $M = \langle X, \vec{f}, X_0\rangle$ is said to be **safe** if no trajectory $\vec{x}(t)$ of M satisfies both $\vec{x}(0) \in X_0$ and $\exists \tau \in \mathbb{R}_{\geq 0} : \vec{x}(\tau) \in X_U$.*

DEFINITION 8 (HYBRID SYSTEM). *A **hybrid system** is described by a tuple $\mathcal{H} \overset{def}{=} \langle L, X, E, G, R, I, F\rangle$, where*

- *L is a finite set of locations (or modes),*
- *$X \subseteq \mathbb{R}^n$ is the continuous state space. The hybrid state space of the system is denoted by $\mathcal{X} = L \times X$ and a state is denoted by $(l, \vec{x}) \in \mathcal{X}$,*

- $E \subseteq L \times L$ *is a set of discrete transitions, together with a guard mapping* $G : E \rightarrow 2^X$ *and a reset mapping* $R : E \times X \rightarrow 2^X$,
- $I : L \rightarrow 2^X$ *is an invariant mapping, and*
- $F : L \times X \rightarrow \mathbb{R}^n$ *is a vector field mapping that assigns to each location* l *a vector field* $\vec{f}$.

The transition and dynamic structure of the hybrid system defines a set of trajectories. A trajectory is a sequence originating from a state $(l_0, \vec{x}_0) \in \mathcal{X}_0$, where $\mathcal{X}_0 \subseteq \mathcal{X}$ is an initial set, and consisting of a series of interleaved continuous flows and discrete transitions. During the continuous flows, the system evolves following the vector field $F(l)$ at some location $l \in L$ as long as the invariant condition $I(l)$ is not violated. At some state $(l, \vec{x})$, if there is a discrete transition $(l, l') \in E$ such that $(l, \vec{x}) \in G(l, l')$ (we write $G(l, l')$ for $G((l, l'))$), the discrete transition can be taken and the system state can be reset to $R((l, l'), \vec{x})$. The problem of safety verification of a hybrid system is to prove that an unsafe set X_U cannot be reached from an initial set X_0.

3. COMPUTING INVARIANT CLUSTERS

In this section, we introduce the *invariant cluster* and show how to compute a set of invariant clusters and use it to overapproximate all trajectories of a semialgebraic system.

3.1 Invariants and invariant clusters

Given a semialgebraic system M, if we can find a multivariate polynomial $g(\vec{x}) \in \mathbb{R}[\vec{x}]$ such that for any trajectory $\vec{x}(t)$ of M, $g(\vec{x}(0)) \sim 0$ implies $g(\vec{x}(t)) \sim 0$ for all $t > 0$, where $\sim \in \{<, \leq, =, \geq, >\}$, then $g(\vec{x}) \sim 0$ is an *invariant* of the system. We call $g(\vec{x})$ an *invariant polynomial* of M. A trajectory $\vec{x}(t)$ is said to be *algebraic* if there exists a nonzero polynomial invariant $g(\vec{x}) = 0$ for $\vec{x}(t)$. Next we present a sufficient condition for $g(\vec{x})$ to be an invariant polynomial.

PROPOSITION 1. *Let* $M = \langle X, \vec{f}, X_0 \rangle$ *be a semialgebraic system and* $g(\vec{x}) \in \mathbb{R}[\vec{x}]$. *Then* $g \sim 0$ *is an invariant of* M *for every* $\sim \in \{<, \leq, =, \geq, >\}$ *if* $g(\vec{x})$ *satisfies*

$$\mathcal{L}_{\vec{f}} g \in \langle g \rangle \tag{2}$$

Proposition 1 states that all the polynomial equations and inequalities $g \sim 0$ are invariants of M if the Lie derivative of g belongs to the ideal $\langle g \rangle$. Note that every invariant satisfying condition (2) defines an enclosed region for trajectories, that is, no trajectory can enter or leave the region.

For a semialgebraic system whose trajectories are algebraic, the trajectories can usually be divided into several groups, and in each group all trajectories show similar curves. Essentially, these similar curves can be described identically by a unique parameterized polynomial equation that we characterize as an invariant cluster. The computation method of invariant clusters is presented in Subsection 3.2.

DEFINITION 9 (INVARIANT CLUSTER). *An* ***invariant cluster*** C *of a semialgebraic system is a set of invariants that can be uniformly described as* $C = \{g(\vec{u}, \vec{x}) = 0 \mid \vec{u} \in \mathbb{R}^K \setminus \{\vec{0}\}\}$, *where* $g(\vec{u}, \vec{x}) = \sum_{i=1}^{M} c_i(\vec{u}) X^i$ *satisfies* $\mathcal{L}_{\vec{f}} g \in \langle g \rangle$ *and* $c_i(\vec{u}) \in \mathbb{R}[\vec{u}]$ *are fixed linear polynomials in* $\vec{u} = (u_1, \cdots, u_K)$, X^i *are monomials in* $\vec{x} = (x_1, \cdots, x_n)$, *and* $M, K \in \mathbb{N}$.

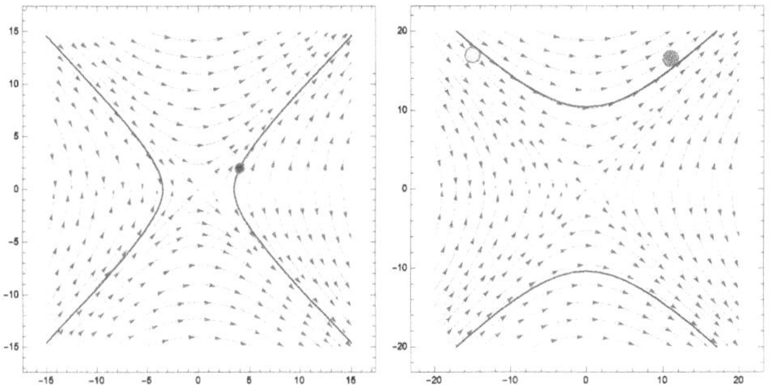

(a) (b)

Figure 1: (a) Example 2. Curve defined by invariant cluster of Class$(C^*, \vec{x}_0)$ for $\vec{x}_0 = (4, 2)$. (b) Example 6. X_0: $(x+15)^2+(y-17)^2 \leq 1$, X_U: $(x_1-11)^2+(y_1-16.5)^2 \leq 1$.

Note that by requiring $\vec{u} \neq \vec{0}$ in Definition 9 as well as other related definitions, we exclude the trivial invariant $0 = 0$. Given an invariant cluster, by varying the parameter $\vec{u}$ we may obtain an infinite set of concrete invariants for the system. To be intuitive, we present a running example to demonstrate the related concepts throughout the paper.

EXAMPLE 1 (RUNNING EXAMPLE). *Consider the semialgebraic system* M_1 *described by* $[\dot{x}, \dot{y}] = [y^2, xy]$. *The set* $C^* = \{u_1 - u_3(x^2 - y^2) = 0 \mid (u_1, u_3) \in \mathbb{R}^2 \setminus \{\vec{0}\}\}$ *is an invariant cluster. It is easy to verify that the polynomial* $u_1 - u_3(x^2 - y^2)$ *satisfies condition (2) for all* $(u_1, u_3) \in \mathbb{R}^2$.

DEFINITION 10 (INVARIANT CLASS). *Given a semialgebraic system* M *with an initial point* $\vec{x}_0$ *and an invariant cluster* $C = \{g(\vec{u}, \vec{x}) = 0 \mid \vec{u} \in \mathbb{R}^K \setminus \{\vec{0}\}\}$ *of* M, *where* $K \in \mathbb{N}$, *an* ***invariant class*** *of* C *at* $\vec{x}_0$, *denoted by* **Class**$(C, \vec{x}_0)$, *is the set* $\{g(\vec{u}, \vec{x}) = 0 \mid g(\vec{u}, \vec{x}_0) = 0,\ \vec{u} \in \mathbb{R}^K \setminus \{\vec{0}\}\}$.

Given an invariant cluster C, by substituting a specific point $\vec{x}_0$ for $\vec{x}$ in $g(\vec{u}, \vec{x}) = 0$ we get a constraint $g(\vec{u}, \vec{x}_0) = 0$ on $\vec{u}$, which yields a subset **Class**$(C, \vec{x}_0)$ of C. Apparently, every member of **Class**$(C, \vec{x}_0)$ is an invariant for the trajectory originating from $\vec{x}_0$.

EXAMPLE 2 (RUNNING EXAMPLE). *For the given invariant cluster* C^* *in Example 1 and a given initial point* $\vec{x}_0 = (4, 2)$, *we get the invariant class* **Class**$(C^*, \vec{x}_0) = \{u_1 - u_3(x^2 - y^2) = 0 \mid u_1 - 12u_3 = 0, (u_1, u_3) \in \mathbb{R}^2 \setminus \{\vec{0}\}\}$. *Every member of* **Class**$(C^*, \vec{x}_0)$ *is an invariant for the trajectory of* M_1 *originating from* $\vec{x}_0$. *The algebraic variety defined by* **Class**$(C^*, \vec{x}_0)$ *is shown in Figure 1(a).*

An invariant class has the following important properties.

THEOREM 2. *Given an* n*-dimensional semialgebraic system* M *and an invariant class* $D = \{g(\vec{u}, \vec{x}) = 0 \mid g(\vec{u}, \vec{x}_0) = 0,\ \vec{u} \in \mathbb{R}^K \setminus \{\vec{0}\}\}$ *of* M *at a specified point* $\vec{x}_0$, *let* D_g *be the set of all invariant polynomials occurring in* D *and* $\pi_{\vec{x}_0}$ *be the trajectory of* M *originating from* $\vec{x}_0$. *Then,*

1. $\pi_{\vec{x}_0} \subseteq \mathbb{V}(D_g)$;
2. *there exists a subset* B *of* D_g *consisting of* m *members such that* $\langle D_g \rangle = \langle B \rangle$, *where* m *is the dimension of the hyperplane* $g(\vec{u}, \vec{x}_0) = 0$ *in terms of* $\vec{u}$ *in* $\mathbb{R}^K$ *and* $\langle D_g \rangle$ *and* $\langle B \rangle$ *denote the ideal generated by the members of* D_g *and* B, *respectively.*

Algorithm 1: Computation of invariant clusters

input : f: n-dimensional polynomial vector field;
N: upper bound for invariant polynomial degree
output: CFamily: a set of invariant clusters

1 CFamily $\leftarrow \emptyset$;
2 **for** $i \leftarrow 1$ **to** N **do**
3 $g_{\vec{u},\vec{x}} \leftarrow$ generate parameterized polynomial over $\vec{x}$ of degree i;
4 $L_f g \leftarrow$ compute the Lie derivative of $g_{\vec{u},\vec{x}}$;
5 **foreach** *monomial order* $\mathcal{O}$ *of* $\vec{x}$ **do**
6 $R_{\vec{u},\vec{x}} \leftarrow$ compute remainder of $L_f g$ w.r.t. g by $\mathcal{O}$;
7 Coeffs $\leftarrow$ collect coefficients of $\vec{x}$ in $R_{\vec{u},\vec{x}}$;
8 Solution $\leftarrow$ solve system Coeffs on $\vec{u}$;
9 CFamily $\leftarrow$ CFamily $\cup$ Solution;

REMARK 2. *The first property in Theorem 2 reveals that a trajectory $\pi_{\vec{x}_0}$ is always contained in the intersection of all the invariants in the invariant class D of $\vec{x}_0$. The second property asserts that the invariant class can be generated by a finite subset B of D if it consists of an infinite number of invariants. The algebraic variety $\mathbb{V}(B)$ (which is equivalent to $\mathbb{V}(D_g)$) forms an overapproximation for $\pi_{\vec{x}_0}$ and the quality of the overapproximation depends largely on the dimension m of $\mathbb{V}(B)$ (the lower the better). In the ideal case $m = 1$, $\mathbb{V}(B)$ shrinks to an algebraic curve and hence some part matches the trajectory precisely. In the case of $m > 1$, $\mathbb{V}(B)$ is usually a hypersurface. To make the overapproximation less conservative, we may take the union of multiple invariant classes from different invariant clusters (if they exist) to reduce the dimension of the algebraic variety.*

3.2 Invariant cluster computation

According to Proposition 1, if we can find a polynomial $g(\vec{x})$ such that $\mathcal{L}_{\vec{f}} g \in \langle g \rangle$, which is equivalent to that the remainder of $\mathcal{L}_{\vec{f}} g$ w.r.t. $g(\vec{x})$ is identical to 0, then $g(\vec{x}) = 0$ is an invariant of M. The idea is as follows. We first establish a template $g(\vec{u}, \vec{x})$ for $g(\vec{x})$ with parameter $\vec{u}$ and then compute the remainder $r(\vec{u}, \vec{x})$ of $\mathcal{L}_{\vec{f}} g$ w.r.t. $g(\vec{u}, \vec{x})$. According to the procedure of polynomial division [10], $r(\vec{u}, \vec{x})$ must be of the form $\sum_{i=1}^{K} \frac{b_i(\vec{u})}{u_j^d} X^i$, where $d \in \mathbb{N}$, $b_i(\vec{u})$ are homogeneous polynomials of degree $d+1$ over $\vec{u}$, u_j is the coefficient of the leading term of $g(\vec{u}, \vec{x})$ by some specified monomial order of $\vec{x}$, and X^i are monomials in $\vec{x}$. Since $r(\vec{u}, \vec{x}) \equiv 0$ implies $u_j \neq 0$ and $b_i(\vec{u}) = 0$ for all $i = 1, \dots, K$, we obtain a system $\mathcal{C}$ of homogeneous polynomial equations in $\vec{u}$ plus $u_j \neq 0$ from the coefficients of $r(\vec{u}, \vec{x})$. Solving $\mathcal{C}$ may yield a set of invariant clusters of M if it exists. Note that all the aforementioned steps can be performed automatically in mathematical software such as *Maple*. Pseudocode for computing invariant clusters is shown in Algorithm 1. The motivation for the loop in line 5 is that the remainder may vary from the monomial order of $\vec{x}$ and produce different solutions. Using multiple orders helps to get more solutions.

REMARK 3. *In Algorithm 1, the key steps are computing the remainder in line 4 and solving the system of equations on $\vec{u}$ in line 8. The former takes only linear time and hence is very efficient. The latter involves solving a system of homogeneous polynomial equations, which is NP-complete [3]. In our implementation in* Maple, *we use the command* `solve`, *a sophisticated solver that combines a number of algorithms, including Gröbner basis and the elimination method based on resultants, and selects the best algorithm on the fly. In our experiments on nonlinear (parametric) systems of dimensions ranging from 2 to 8 the solver quickly determines whether a solution exists in most cases.*

Like most invariant generation approaches our approach is limited. Essentially, an invariant cluster could be an infinite set of Darboux polynomials and first integrals, which means that our approach applies only to integrable systems [14].

EXAMPLE 3 (RUNNING EXAMPLE). *According to Algorithm 1, the steps for computing the invariant clusters of degree 2 are as follows:*

1. *Generate the template polynomial of degree 2:*
$$g_2(\vec{u}, \vec{x}) = u_6 x^2 + u_5 xy + u_4 x + u_3 y^2 + u_2 y + u_1$$
2. *Compute the Lie derivative $\mathcal{L}_{\vec{f}} g_2$ using Definition 4:*
$$\mathcal{L}_{\vec{f}} g_2 = \frac{\partial g_2}{\partial x}\dot{x} + \frac{\partial g_2}{\partial y}\dot{y} = u_5 x^2 y + (2\,u_3 + 2\,u_6)\,xy^2 + u_2 xy + y^3 u_5 + u_4 y^2$$
3. *Compute the remainder of $\mathcal{L}_{\vec{f}} g_2$ w.r.t. g_2 by graded reverse lexicographic (*grevlex*) order of (x, y). Using this order, the leading term of $\mathcal{L}_{\vec{f}} g_2$ and g_2 is $u_5 x^2 y$ and $u_6 x^2$, respectively. Then:*
$$r(\vec{u}, \vec{x}) = \mathcal{L}_{\vec{f}} g_2 - \frac{u_5 y}{u_6} g_2 = \Big(\left(2\,u_3 u_6 - u_5^2 + 2\,u_6^2\right) xy^2 + \left(u_2 u_6 - u_4 u_5\right) xy + \left(-u_3 u_5 + u_5 u_6\right) y^3 + \left(-u_2 u_5 + u_4 u_6\right) y^2 - u_1 u_5 y \Big) \frac{1}{u_6}$$
4. *Collect the coefficients of $r(\vec{u}, \vec{x})$:*
$$S := \left\{ \frac{u_2 u_6 - u_4 u_5}{u_6}, \frac{-u_3 u_5 + u_5 u_6}{u_6}, \frac{-u_2 u_5 + u_4 u_6}{u_6}, \frac{2\,u_3 u_6 - u_5^2 + 2\,u_6^2}{u_6}, -\frac{u_1 u_5}{u_6} \right\}$$
5. *Solve the system formed by S. To save space, we just present one of the six solutions we obtained:*
$$C_6 = \{u_6 = -u_3, u_2 = u_4 = u_5 = 0, u_3 = u_3, u_1 = u_1\}$$
6. *Substitute the above solution C_6 for $\vec{u}$ in $g_2(\vec{u}, \vec{x})$. We get the following parameterized invariant polynomial:*
$$g_2(\vec{u}, \vec{x}) = -u_3 x^2 + u_3 y^2 + u_1$$

The other five solutions obtained in step 5. are in fact the products of the invariant polynomials $\{u_2 y, u_1(x+y), u_1(x-y)\}$ that were obtained when initially computing the invariants of degree 1. Hence they cannot increase the expressive power of the set of invariant clusters and should be dropped. The above solution is the one we have given in Example 1.

3.3 Overapproximating trajectories by invariant classes

In this section, we address how to overapproximate trajectories precisely by using invariant classes.

Algorithm 2: Computation of invariant classes

input : CFamily: set of invariant clusters;
$\vec{x}_0$: an initial point

output: ICls: list of invariant classes

ICls $\leftarrow \emptyset$;
foreach $C \in$ CFamily **do**
  D $\leftarrow$ **Class**$(C, \vec{x}_0)$;
  if D $\neq \emptyset$ **then**
    $m \leftarrow$ dimension of the hyperplane $g(\vec{u}, \vec{x}_0) = 0$ defining D;
    if $m \geq 1$ **then**
      Basis $\leftarrow$ basis $\{u_1, \ldots, u_m\}$ of $g(\vec{u}, \vec{x}_0) = 0$;
      D $\leftarrow \{g(\vec{u}_1, \vec{x}), \ldots, g(\vec{u}_m, \vec{x})\}, u_i \in$ Basis;
    ICls $\leftarrow$ ICls $\cup$ D;

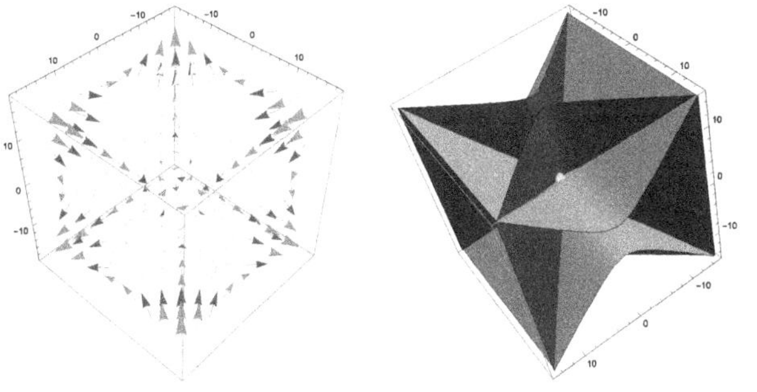

(a) (b)

Figure 2: (a) 3D vector field of Example 4. (b) The intersection of the invariants $y^2 - x^2 - 3 = 0$ (blue) and $z^2 - x^2 - 8 = 0$ (orange) overapproximates the trajectory originating from $\vec{x}_0 = (1, 2, 3)$ (green ball).

Invariant clusters can be divided into two categories according to the number of invariant classes that they can yield by varying the parameter $\vec{u}$. 1) **finite invariant cluster**: This kind of invariant cluster can yield only one invariant class no matter how $\vec{u}$ changes. For example, $\{u_1(x-y) = 0 \mid u_1 \in \mathbb{R} \setminus \{0\}\}$ is such an invariant cluster for the running example. The trajectories covered by this invariant class are very limited. Moreover, the overapproximation is conservative due to the high dimension of the algebraic variety defined by the invariant class. 2) **infinite invariant cluster**: One such invariant cluster C can yield an infinite number of invariant classes **Class**$(C, \vec{x}_0)$ as the initial point $\vec{x}_0$ varies, e.g., the invariant cluster C^* in Example 1. For the trajectory $\pi_{\vec{x}_0}$, the overapproximating precision of **Class**$(C, \vec{x}_0)$ depends largely on the dimension m of the algebraic variety defined by **Class**$(C, \vec{x}_0)$. In the best case $m = 1$ we have a curve-to-curve match in part for the trajectory.

Next we introduce how to identify the invariant classes for a given point $\vec{x}_0$ from a set of invariant clusters and how to get a finite representation. To be intuitive, we first present a 3-dimensional system and a set of invariant clusters for it.

EXAMPLE 4. *Consider the following semialgebraic system M_2: $[\dot{x}, \dot{y}, \dot{z}] = [yz, xz, xy]$. We obtain a set of invariant clusters consisting of 7 elements. Here we only present the infinite invariant cluster due to the page limit.*

$$C_7 = \{g_7(\vec{u}, \vec{x}) = (-u_5 - u_6)x^2 + u_5 y^2 + u_6 z^2 + u_0 = 0 \mid \vec{u} \in \mathbb{R}^3 \setminus \{\vec{0}\}\}$$

The invariant clusters are capable of overapproximating all the trajectories of the system M_2. For any given initial state, how can we identify the invariant classes from the set of invariant clusters? Suppose we want to find the invariant classes that can overapproximate the trajectory from the state $\vec{x}_0 = (1, 2, 3)$. According to Theorem 2, we have Algorithm 2 for this purpose.

REMARK 4. *In Algorithm 2, we enumerate the invariant clusters to find out which one can provide a non-empty invariant class* **Class**$(C, \vec{x}_0)$ *for $\vec{x}_0$. For a* **Class**$(C, \vec{x}_0)$ *to be nonempty, the corresponding hyperplane $g(\vec{u}, \vec{x}_0) = 0$ must have at least one solution to $\vec{u} \in \mathbb{R}^K \setminus \{\vec{0}\}$, which is equivalent to that its dimension must be at least 1. For a hyperplane in $\mathbb{R}^K$, its dimension is equal to $K - 1$. Therefore,* **Class**$(C, \vec{x}_0)$ *must be nonempty if $K > 1$ and the basis of the hyperplane can be obtained through a basic linear algebraic computation (which will be illustrated in what follows). However, in case $g(\vec{u}, \vec{x}_0)$ evaluates to 0, the hyperplane degenerates to the space $\mathbb{R}^K \setminus \{\vec{0}\}$ and the dimension will be K. Therefore, an invariant class with $K = 1$ is nonempty iff $g(\vec{u}, \vec{x}_0)$ evaluates to 0. For example, given an invariant cluster $C^0 = \{u_1(x - y) = 0 \mid u_1 \in \mathbb{R} \setminus \{0\}\}$ and a point $\vec{x}_0 = (x_0, y_0)$,* **Class**$(C^0, \vec{x}_0)$ *is equal to C^0 if $x_0 = y_0$, and otherwise* **Class**$(C^0, \vec{x}_0)$ *is empty.*

EXAMPLE 5. *We continue from Example 4. For the given point $\vec{x}_0 = (1, 2, 3)$, according to Algorithm 2, we find that only* **Class**$(C_7, \vec{x}_0) = \{g_7(\vec{u}, x, y, z) = 0 \mid 3u_5 + 8u_6 + u_0 = 0, \vec{u} \in \mathbb{R}^3 \setminus \{\vec{0}\}\}$ *is nonempty. The dimension of the hyperplane $H: 3u_5 + 8u_6 + u_0 = 0$ is 2. Since $u_0 = -3u_5 - 8u_6$, to get the basis of H, we can write $(u_0, u_5, u_6) = (-3u_5 - 8u_6, u_5, u_6) = u_5(-3, 1, 0) + u_6(-8, 0, 1)$. Hence we have the basis $\{(-3, 1, 0), (-8, 0, 1)\}$ for H. As a result, we get a finite representation $B = \{y^2 - x^2 - 3 = 0,\ z^2 - x^2 - 8 = 0\}$ for* **Class**$(C_7, \vec{x}_0)$. *It is easy to check by the* Maple *function* `HilbertDimension` *that $dim(B) = 1$. Thus we obtain an algebraic variety $\mathbb{V}(B)$ that provides in part a curve-to-curve match to the trajectory $\pi_{\vec{x}_0}$. The 3-D vector field and the algebraic curve $\mathbb{V}(B)$ are shown in Figure 2.*

4. SAFETY VERIFICATION

4.1 Safety Verification of Continuous Systems

In this subsection, we show how to verify a safety property for a nonlinear system based on invariant clusters.

In Section 3, we have seen that a trajectory can be overapproximated by an invariant class. Since an invariant class is determined uniquely by a single hyperplane $g(\vec{u}, \vec{x}_0) = 0$ in $\mathbb{R}^K$ for an initial point $\vec{x}_0$, and a hyperplane without constant term (which holds for $g(\vec{u}, \vec{x}_0) = 0$) is uniquely determined by its normal vector, we can verify that two states do not lie on the same trajectory using the following theorem.

THEOREM 3. *Given a semialgebraic system $M = \langle X, \vec{f}, X_0 \rangle$ and an invariant cluster $C = \{g(\vec{u}, \vec{x}) = 0 \mid \vec{u} = (u_1, \cdots, u_K) \in \mathbb{R}^K \setminus \{\vec{0}\}\}$ of M with $K > 1$, where $g(\vec{u}, \vec{x}) = \sum_{i=1}^{K} \psi_i(\vec{x}) u_i$ and $\psi_i(\vec{x}) \in \mathbb{R}[\vec{x}]$, an initial set X_0, and an unsafe set X_U,* *if there exists a pair of states $(\vec{x}_1, \vec{x}_2) \in X_0 \times X_U$ such that $\vec{x}_1$ and $\vec{x}_2$ lie on the same trajectory, one of the following two formulae must hold:*

$$(i) \quad \exists k \in \mathbb{R}\backslash\{0\} : \; k\psi_i(\vec{x}_1) = \psi_i(\vec{x}_2), i = 1, \ldots, K \qquad (3)$$

$$(ii) \quad \psi_i(\vec{x}_1) = \psi_i(\vec{x}_2) = 0, i = 1, \ldots, K \qquad (4)$$

Moreover, if some $\psi_i(\vec{x}) \equiv 1$, i.e., $g(\vec{u}, \vec{x})$ contains a constant term u_i, then formula (3) simplifies to

$$\psi_i(\vec{x}_1) = \psi_i(\vec{x}_2), i = 1, \ldots, K \qquad (5)$$

REMARK 5. *Instead of computing the invariants explicitly, Theorem 3 provides an alternative way to verify that two states $\vec{x}_1, \vec{x}_2$ do not lie on the same trajectory by checking the difference between the normal vectors of $g(\vec{u}, \vec{x}_1) = 0$ and $g(\vec{u}, \vec{x}_2) = 0$. Let us take Example 4 for illustration. We think of C_7 as a hyperplane over $\vec{u} \in \mathbb{R}^3$: $u_0 + (y^2 - x^2)u_5 + (z^2 - x^2)u_6 = 0$, hence the corresponding normal vector is $\vec{\mathcal{N}}(\vec{x}) = (1, y^2 - x^2, z^2 - x^2)$. Given two random points $\vec{x}_1 = (1, 2, 3)$ and $\vec{x}_2 = (5, \sqrt{27}, \sqrt{34})$, it is easy to verify that $\vec{\mathcal{N}}(\vec{x}_1) \neq \vec{\mathcal{N}}(\vec{x}_2)$, which means that $\vec{x}_1$ and $\vec{x}_2$ are not on the same trajectory. Alternatively, we can argue that the invariant class of $\vec{x}_1$ is $\{y^2 - x^2 - 3 = 0, z^2 - x^2 - 8 = 0\}$ and $\vec{x}_2$ does not belong to its solution set.*

Now we demonstrate how to verify a safety property of semialgebraic systems. Assume X_0 and X_U can be written as semialgebraic sets, i.e., $X_0 = \{\vec{x}_1 \in \mathbb{R}^n \mid p_{i_1}(\vec{x}_1) = 0, q_{j_1}(\vec{x}_1) \geq 0, r_{k_1}(\vec{x}_1) > 0, i_1 = 1, \ldots, l_1, j_1 = 1 \ldots m_1, k_1 = 1, \ldots, n_1\}$ and $X_U = \{\vec{x}_2 \in \mathbb{R}^n \mid p_{i_2}(\vec{x}_2) = 0, q_{j_2}(\vec{x}_2) \geq 0, r_{k_2}(\vec{x}_2) > 0, i_2 = l_1+1, \ldots, l_1+l_2, j_2 = m_1+1, \ldots, m_1+m_2, k_2 = n_1 + 1, \ldots, n_1 + n_2\}$. Then we have the following theorem for deciding the safety of a semialgebraic system.

THEOREM 4. *Given a semialgebraic system $M = \langle X, \vec{f}, X_0 \rangle$ and invariant cluster $C = \{g(\vec{u}, \vec{x}) = 0 \mid \vec{u} \in \mathbb{R}^K \setminus \{\vec{0}\}\}$ of M with $K \geq 2$, suppose the normal vector of the hyperplane $g(\vec{u}, \vec{x}) = 0$ over $\vec{u}$ is $(1, \psi_1(\vec{x}), \ldots, \psi_K(\vec{x}))$. Then the system M is safe if there exists the following polynomial identity*

$$\sum_{k=1}^{K} \gamma_k(\psi_k(\vec{x}_1) - \psi_k(\vec{x}_2)) + \sum_{i=1}^{l_1+l_2} \beta_i p_i + \sum_{v \in \{0,1\}^{m_1+m_2}} \delta_v \prod_{j=1}^{m_1+m_2} q_j^{v_j}$$
$$+ \sum_{v \in \{0,1\}^{n_1+n_2}} \eta_v \prod_{k=1}^{n_1+n_2} r_k^{v_k} + \prod_{k=1}^{n_1+n_2} r_k^{d_k} + s = 0 \qquad (6)$$

where $d_k \in \mathbb{N}$ and β_i, γ_k are polynomials and δ_v, η_v, s are SOS polynomials in $\mathbb{R}[\vec{x}_1, \vec{x}_2]$.

REMARK 6. *Theorem 4 transforms the safety verification problem into a decision problem about the existence of a real solution of a system of polynomial equations and inequalities. As noted in Remark 1, this decision problem can be solved by SOS programming. Our implementation uses the efficient tool* SOSTOOLS *[25].*

In Theorem 4, we deal with a general semialgebraic system where the initial set and the unsafe set are represented by a set of polynomial equations and inequalities. However, if the system is described by much simpler set representations such as a single polynomial equation or inequality, the programming problem can be simplified correspondingly. If, e.g., both sets can be represented or overapproximated by a single polynomial equation $I(\vec{x}_1) = 0$ and $U(\vec{x}_2) = 0$, respectively, then the programming problem simplifies to (see [32])

$$\sum_{j=1}^{K} \alpha_j(\psi_j(\vec{x}_1) - \psi_j(\vec{x}_2)) + \beta I + \theta U - 1 \quad \text{is an } SOS \qquad (7)$$

where $(\psi_1(\vec{x}), \ldots, \psi_K(\vec{x}))$ is the same as in Theorem 4 and $\alpha_j, \beta, \theta \in \mathbb{R}[\vec{x}_1, \vec{x}_2]$. Algorithm 3 summarizes safety verification based on the condition (7).

Algorithm 3: Safety verification

---

input : $\vec{\psi}$: the K-dimensional normal vector of an invariant cluster;
I($\vec{x}_1$): the initial set; U($\vec{x}_2$): the unsafe set;
N: the maximum degree of programming polynomials $\vec{\alpha}, \beta, \theta$

output : IsSafe: whether the system is safe

IsSafe ← False;
for $i \leftarrow 1$ **to** N **do**
  $\vec{\alpha} \leftarrow$ generate a vector of polynomials of degree i;
  $\beta \leftarrow$ generate a polynomial of degree i for I($\vec{x}_1$);
  $\theta \leftarrow$ generate a polynomial of degree i for U($\vec{x}_2$);
  $P \leftarrow \sum_{j=1}^{K} \alpha_j(\vec{\psi}_j(\vec{x}_1) - \vec{\psi}_j(\vec{x}_2)) + \beta\text{I} + \theta\text{U} - 1$;
  Solution ← perform *SOS* programming on P;
  if Solution *is found* **then**
    IsSafe ← True;
    break;

EXAMPLE 6 (RUNNING EXAMPLE 2). *Given the semialgebraic system M_3 by $[\dot{x}, \dot{y}] = [y^2, xy]$ and the initial set $X_0 = \{(x, y) \in \mathbb{R}^2 \mid I(x, y) = (x+15)^2 + (y-17)^2 - 1 \leq 0\}$, verify that the unsafe set $X_U = \{(x, y) \in \mathbb{R}^2 \mid U(x, y) = (x - 11)^2 + (y - 16.5)^2 - 1 \leq 0\}$ cannot be reached. The parameter space of $C^* = \{g(\vec{u}, \vec{x}) = u_1 - u_3(x^2 - y^2) = 0 \mid (u_1, u_3) \in \mathbb{R}^2 \setminus \{\vec{0}\}\}$ has dimension 1 and hence can provide an invariant class for every state in X_0 and X_U. The normal vector of the hyperplane $g(\vec{u}, \vec{x}) = 0$ is $(1, \psi_1(x, y)) = (1, y^2 - x^2)$. Let $\varphi(x_1, y_1, x_2, y_2) = \psi_1(x_1, y_1) - \psi_1(x_2, y_2)$. By Theorem 4 we only need to verify whether the following system of equations has no real solution.*

$$I(x_1, y_1) = (x_1 + 15)^2 + (y_1 - 17)^2 - 1 = 0$$
$$U(x_2, y_2) = (x_2 - 11)^2 + (y_2 - 16.5)^2 - 1 = 0$$
$$\varphi(x_1, y_1, x_2, y_2) = y_1^2 - x_1^2 - (y_2^2 - x_2^2) = 0$$

Note that we substitute (x_1, y_1), (x_2, y_2) for (x, y) in $I(x, y)$ and $U(x, y)$, respectively, to denote the different points in X_0 and X_U. To prove that the system is safe, we need to find $\alpha_i \in \mathbb{R}[x_1, y_1, x_2, y_2], i = 1, 2, 3$ such that $Prog = \alpha_1 I + \alpha_2 U + \alpha_3\varphi - 1$ is SOS. We find three polynomials of degree 2 for α_i, respectively, hence the system is safe. Observe that the relative position of X_U is very close to the reachable set from X_0 (see Figure 1(b)). We failed to find a barrier certificate for this system using the methods in [20, 24].

In Theorem 4, we presented a sufficient condition for deciding if a semialgebraic system is safe. The theory originated from the fact that the system is safe if there is no invariant class intersecting both the initial and the unsafe set, which is equivalent to that the formula (6) holds. To verify the latter, we need to find a set of witness polynomials by *SOS* programming. However, as the dimension of the system increases, the number of parametric polynomials involved increases correspondingly, which also leads to an increase in computational complexity. In what follows, we present a new method for safety verification that avoids this problem. The new method is based on Proposition 1, i.e., for any polynomial $g(\vec{x})$ satisfying $\mathcal{L}_{\vec{f}}g \in \langle g \rangle$, $g(x) \sim 0$ is an invariant for any $\sim \in \{<, \leq, =, \geq, >\}$.

PROPOSITION 2. *Given a semialgebraic system* $M = \langle X, \vec{f}, X_0 \rangle$ *and an invariant cluster* $C = \{g(\vec{u}, \vec{x}) = 0 \mid \vec{u} \in \mathbb{R}^K \setminus \{\vec{0}\}\}$ *of* M, *let* X_0 *and* X_U *be the initial set and the unsafe set, respectively. Then, the system is safe if there exists a* $\vec{u}^* \in \mathbb{R}^K \setminus \{\vec{0}\}$ *such that*

$$\forall \vec{x} \in X_0 : g(\vec{u}^*, \vec{x}) \geq 0 \quad (8)$$

$$\forall \vec{x} \in X_U : g(\vec{u}^*, \vec{x}) < 0 \quad (9)$$

According to Proposition 2, to verify the safety property, it suffices to find a $\vec{u}^* \in \mathbb{R}^K \setminus \{\vec{0}\}$ which satisfies the constraints (8) and (9). There are some constraint solving methods available, e.g, *SMT* solvers. However, the high complexity of *SMT* theories limits the applicability. In the following, we transform the above constraint-solving problem into an *SOS* programming problem, which can be solved efficiently. We write $\vec{P}(\vec{x}) \succeq \vec{0}$ to denote $p_i(\vec{x}) \geq 0, i = 1, \ldots, m$ for a polynomial vector $\vec{P}(\vec{x}) = (p_1(\vec{x}), \ldots, p_m(\vec{x}))$.

PROPOSITION 3. *Given a semialgebraic system* $M = \langle X, \vec{f}, X_0 \rangle$ *and an invariant cluster* $C = \{g(\vec{u}, \vec{x}) = 0 \mid \vec{u} \in \mathbb{R}^K \setminus \{\vec{0}\}\}$ *of* M *and a constant* $\epsilon \in \mathbb{R}_{>0}$, *let* $X_0 = \{\vec{x} \in \mathbb{R}^n \mid \vec{I} \succeq \vec{0}, \vec{I} \in \mathbb{R}[\vec{x}]^{m_1}\}$ *and* $X_U = \{\vec{x} \in \mathbb{R}^n \mid \vec{U} \succeq \vec{0}, \vec{U} \in \mathbb{R}[\vec{x}]^{m_2}\}$. *Then, the system is safe if there exist a* $\vec{u}^* \in \mathbb{R}^K \setminus \{\vec{0}\}$ *and two SOS polynomial vectors* $\vec{\mu}_1 \in \mathbb{R}[\vec{x}]^{m_1}$, $\vec{\mu}_2 \in \mathbb{R}[\vec{x}]^{m_2}$ *such that the following are SOS polynomials.*

$$g(\vec{u}^*, \vec{x}) - \vec{\mu}_1 \cdot \vec{I} \quad (10)$$

$$- g(\vec{u}^*, \vec{x}) - \vec{\mu}_2 \cdot \vec{U} - \epsilon \quad (11)$$

Similar to Theorem 4, Proposition 3 also reduces to an *SOS* programming problem. However, the ideas behind the theories are different. By Theorem 4 we attempt to prove no invariant class overapproximating the trajectory can intersect both X_0 and X_U, while by Proposition 3 we mean to find a hypersurface that can separate the reachable set from X_U. Apparently, there must exist no invariant class intersecting both X_0 and X_U if there exists such a hypersurface, but not vice versa. Hence the latter is more conservative than the former, but it is also more efficient in theory because it usually involves less unknown polynomials. For example, for an n-dimensional system with X_0 and X_U defined by a single polynomial inequality, respectively, we usually need $n+1$ unknown polynomials for the former method, however, we need only 2 for the latter. We omit the algorithm based on Proposition 3, which is similar to Algorithm 3.

4.2 Safety Verification of Hybrid Systems

A hybrid system consists of a set of locations and a set of discrete transitions between locations. In general, different locations have different continuous dynamics and hence correspond to different invariant clusters. An invariant for the hybrid system can be synthesized from the set of invariant clusters of all locations. The idea is to pick a polynomial $g_l(\vec{u}_l^*, \vec{x})$ from the respective invariant cluster C_l for each location l such that $g_l(\vec{u}_l^*, \vec{x}) \geq 0$ is an invariant for the location l and all the invariants coupled together through the constraints at the discrete transitions form a hybrid invariant for the hybrid system.

PROPOSITION 4. *Given an* n*-dimensional hybrid system* $\mathcal{H} = \langle L, X, E, G, R, I, F \rangle$ *and a set of invariant clusters* $\{C_l, l = 1, \ldots, n\}$, *where* $C_l = \{g_l(\vec{u}_l, \vec{x}) = 0 \mid \vec{u}_l \in \mathbb{R}^{K_l} \setminus \{\vec{0}\}\}$ *with* $K_l > 1$ *is an invariant cluster for location* l, *the system is safe if there exists a set* $S_{\vec{u}} = \{\vec{u}_l^* \in \mathbb{R}^{K_l} \setminus \{\vec{0}\}, l = 1, \ldots, n\}$ *such that, for all* $l \in L$ *and* $(l, l') \in E$, *the following formulae hold:*

$$\forall \vec{x} \in \mathrm{Init}(l) : g_l(\vec{u}_l^*, x) \geq 0 \quad (12)$$

$$\forall \vec{x} \in G(l, l'), \forall \vec{x}' \in R((l, l'), \vec{x}) : g_l(\vec{u}_l^*, \vec{x}) \geq 0 \implies g_{l'}(\vec{u}_{l'}^*, \vec{x}') \geq 0 \quad (13)$$

$$\forall \vec{x} \in I(l) \cap \mathrm{Uns}(l) : g_l(\vec{u}_l^*, \vec{x}) < 0 \quad (14)$$

where Init(l) *and* Uns(l) *denote respectively the initial set and the unsafe set at location* l.

Similar to Proposition 2, we further transform the problem into an *SOS* programming problem. Consider a semialgebraic hybrid system $\mathcal{H} = \langle L, X, E, G, R, I, F \rangle$, where the mappings G, R, and I are defined in terms of polynomial inequalities as follows:

$$G : (l, l') \mapsto \{\vec{x} \in \mathbb{R}^n \mid \vec{G}_{ll'} \succeq 0, \vec{G}_{ll'} \in \mathbb{R}[\vec{x}]^{m_{ll'}}\}$$

$$R : ((l, l'), \vec{x}) \mapsto \{\vec{x} \in \mathbb{R}^n \mid \vec{R}_{ll'\vec{x}} \succeq 0, \vec{R}_{ll'\vec{x}} \in \mathbb{R}[\vec{x}]^{n_{ll'}}\}$$

$$I : l \mapsto \{\vec{x} \in \mathbb{R}^n \mid \vec{I}_l \succeq 0, \vec{I}_l \in \mathbb{R}[\vec{x}]^{p_l}\}$$

and the mappings of the initial and the unsafe set are defined as follows:

$$\mathrm{Init} : l \mapsto \{\vec{x} \in \mathbb{R}^n \mid \vec{\mathrm{Init}}_l \succeq 0, \vec{\mathrm{Init}}_l \in \mathbb{R}[\vec{x}]^{r_l}\}$$

$$\mathrm{Uns} : l \mapsto \{\vec{x} \in \mathbb{R}^n \mid \vec{\mathrm{Uns}}_l \succeq 0, \vec{\mathrm{Uns}}_l \in \mathbb{R}[\vec{x}]^{s_l}\}$$

where $m_{ll'}$, $n_{ll'}$, r_l, p_l and s_l are the dimensions of the polynomial vector spaces. Then we have the following proposition for safety verification of $\mathcal{H}$.

PROPOSITION 5. *Let the hybrid system* $\mathcal{H}$, *the initial set mapping* Init, *and the unsafe set mapping* Uns *be defined as above. Given a set of invariant clusters* $\{C_l, l = 1, \ldots, n\}$ *of* $\mathcal{H}$ *where* $C_l = \{g_l(\vec{u}_l, \vec{x}) = 0 \mid \vec{u}_l \in \mathbb{R}^{K_l} \setminus \{\vec{0}\}\}$ *with* $K_l > 1$ *is an invariant cluster for location* l, *a set* $S_\gamma = \{\gamma_{ll'} \in \mathbb{R}_{\geq 0}, (l, l') \in E\}$ *of constants, and a constant vector* $\vec{\epsilon} \in \mathbb{R}^n_{>0}$, *the system is safe if there exists a set* $S_u = \{\vec{u}_l^* \in \mathbb{R}^{K_l} \setminus \{\vec{0}\}, l = 1, \ldots, n\}$ *and five sets of SOS polynomial vectors* $\{\vec{\theta}_l \in \mathbb{R}[\vec{x}]^{s_l}, l \in L\}$, $\{\vec{\kappa}_{ll'} \in \mathbb{R}[\vec{x}]^{p_{ll'}}, (l, l') \in E\}$, $\{\vec{\sigma}_{ll'} \in \mathbb{R}[\vec{x}]^{q_{ll'}}, (l, l') \in E\}$, $\{\vec{\eta}_l \in \mathbb{R}[\vec{x}]^{t_l}, l \in L\}$, *and* $\{\vec{\nu}_l \in \mathbb{R}[\vec{x}]^{w_l}, l \in L\}$ *such that the following polynomials are SOS for all* $l \in L$ *and* $(l, l') \in E$:

$$g_l(\vec{u}_l^*, \vec{x}) - \vec{\theta}_l \cdot \vec{\mathrm{Init}}_l \quad (15)$$

$$g_{l'}(\vec{u}_{l'}^*, \vec{x}') - \gamma_{ll'} g_l(\vec{u}_l^*, \vec{x}) - \vec{\kappa}_{ll'} \cdot G_{ll'} - \vec{\sigma}_{ll'} \cdot R_{ll'\vec{x}} \quad (16)$$

$$- \vec{\nu}_l \cdot I_l - \vec{\eta}_l \cdot \vec{\mathrm{Uns}}_l - g_l(\vec{u}_l^*, \vec{x}) - \epsilon_l \quad (17)$$

The algorithm for computing invariants for semialgebraic hybrid systems based on Proposition 5 is very similar to Algorithm 3 for semialgebraic continuous systems except that it involves more *SOS* constraints on discrete transitions.

5. IMPLEMENTATION & EXPERIMENTS

Based on the approach presented in this paper, we implemented a prototype tool in *Maple* and *Matlab*, respectively. In *Maple*, we implemented the tool for computing invariant clusters and identifying invariant classes based on remainder computation. In *Matlab*, we implemented the tool for safety verification based on the *SOS* programming tool package *SOSTOOLS*. Currently, we manually transfer the invariant clusters computed in *Maple* to *Matlab* for safety verification.

Now we present the experimental results on nonlinear benchmark systems, run on a laptop with a 3.1GHz *Intel Core i7* CPU and 8 GB memory.

5.1 Longitudinal Motion of an Airplane

In this experiment, we study the 6th order longitudinal equations of motion that capture the vertical motion (climbing, descending) of an airplane [31, Chapter 5]. Let g denote the gravity acceleration, m the total mass of an airplane, M the aerodynamic and thrust moment w.r.t. the y axis, (X, Z) the aerodynamics and thrust forces w.r.t. axis x and z, and I_{yy} the second diagonal element of its inertia matrix. Then the motion of the airplane is described as follows.

$$\begin{aligned} \dot{v} &= \frac{X}{m} - g\sin(\theta) - qw, & \dot{w} &= \frac{Z}{m} + g\cos(\theta) + qv, \\ \dot{x} &= w\sin(\theta) + v\cos(\theta), & \dot{z} &= -v\sin(\theta) + w\cos(\theta), \\ \dot{\theta} &= q, & \dot{q} &= \frac{M}{I_{yy}}, \end{aligned}$$

where the meanings of the variables are as follows: v: axial velocity, w: vertical velocity, x: range, z: altitude, q: pitch rate, θ: pitch angle.

To transform the above system into a semialgebraic system, we first introduce two additional variables d_1, d_2 such that $d_1 = \sin(\theta)$, $d_2 = \cos(\theta)$ and then substitute d_1 and d_2 respectively for $\sin(\theta)$ and $\cos(\theta)$ in the model. In addition, we get two more constraints $\dot{d_1} = qd_2$ and $\dot{d_2} = -qd_1$. As a result, the dimension of the system rises to 8. For this system, using the method in [12], Ghorbal et al. spent **1** hour finding three invariant polynomials of degree 3 on a laptop with a 1.7GHz *Intel Core i5* CPU and 4 GB memory. Using our method, we spent only **0.484** seconds obtaining an invariant cluster $g_9(\vec{u}, \vec{x}) = 0$ of degree 3. By applying the constraint $d_1^2 + d_2^2 = 1$, we reduce the normal vector of the hyperplane $g_9(\vec{u}, \vec{x}) = 0$ in $\vec{u}$ to $(1, \psi_1, \psi_2, \psi_3)$, where ψ_1, ψ_2, ψ_3 are defined as follows.

$$\begin{aligned} \psi_1 &= \frac{Mmz}{I_{yy}Z} + \frac{gm\theta}{Z} + \left(\frac{mqv}{Z} + 1\right)\sin(\theta) \\ &\quad + \left(\frac{X}{Z} - \frac{mqw}{Z}\right)\cos(\theta) \\ \psi_2 &= -\frac{Xz}{Z} + x - \frac{gI_{yy}X\theta}{ZM} - I_{yy}\left(\frac{Xqv}{ZM} + \frac{qw}{M}\right)\sin(\theta) \\ &\quad + I_{yy}\left(\frac{Xqw}{ZM} - \frac{qv}{M} - \frac{X^2 + Z^2}{ZMm}\right)\cos(\theta) \\ \psi_3 &= q^2 - 2\frac{M\theta}{I_{yy}} \end{aligned}$$

Given a symbolic initial point $\vec{x}_0 = (v_0, w_0, x_0, z_0, \theta_0, q_0, d_1^0, d_2^0)$, we have verified that our invariant cluster defines the same algebraic variety as defined by the invariants in [12] by comparing their Gröbner bases. However, our method is much more efficient. Moreover, we also obtained the invariant clusters of higher degrees $(4 - 6)$ quickly. The experimental result is shown in Table 1. The first column is the degree of the invariants, the second column is the variables to be decided, the third column is the computing time in seconds, and the last column is the number of invariant clusters generated. As can be seen, in the most complicated case, where the number of the indeterminates reaches up to 3003, we spent only 200.9 seconds to discover an invariant cluster of degree 6. However, we found that these higher order invariant clusters have the same expressive power as the invariant cluster of degree 3 in terms of algebraic variety.

5.2 Looping particle

Consider a heavy particle on a circular path of radius r whose motion is described by the following differential equation

$$\begin{bmatrix} \dot{x} \\ \dot{y} \\ \dot{\omega} \end{bmatrix} = \begin{bmatrix} r\dot{\cos(\theta)} \\ r\dot{\sin(\theta)} \\ -\frac{g\cos(\theta)}{r} \end{bmatrix} = \begin{bmatrix} -r\sin(\theta)\dot{\theta} \\ r\cos(\theta)\dot{\theta} \\ -\frac{g(r\cos(\theta))}{r^2} \end{bmatrix} = \begin{bmatrix} -y\omega \\ x\omega \\ -\frac{gx}{r^2} \end{bmatrix}$$

Note that the above is a parameterized system with gravity acceleration g and radius r as parameters. Our tool finds the following invariant cluster consisting of a parametric polynomial of degree 2: $\{g(\vec{u}, \vec{x}) = 0 \mid g(\vec{u}, \vec{x}) = u_5x^2 + u_5y^2 + u_2\omega^2 + \frac{2u_2g}{r^2}y + u_0, \vec{u} \in \mathbb{R}^3 \setminus \{\vec{0}\}\}$. Given an arbitrary point $(x_0, y_0, \omega_0) = (2, 0, \omega_0)$, we get the invariant class $\{g(\vec{u}, \vec{x}) = 0 \mid (x_0^2 + y_0^2)u_5 + (\omega_0^2 + \frac{2g}{r^2}y_0)u_2 + u_0 = 0, \vec{u} \in \mathbb{R}^3 \setminus \{\vec{0}\}\}$. According to Algorithm 2, the algebraic variety representing the trajectory originating from (x_0, y_0, ω_0) is $\{(x, y, \omega) \in \mathbb{R}^3 \mid x^2 + y^2 - x_0^2 - y_0^2 = 0, \omega^2 + \frac{2g}{r^2}y - \omega_0^2 - \frac{2g}{r^2}y_0 = 0\}$. The results in [26] and [29] are special cases of our result when setting $(r, g) = (2, 10)$ and $(r, g, x_0, y_0) = (2, 10, 2, 0)$, respectively. Therefore, our method is more powerful in finding parameterized invariants for parameterized systems. See Table 1 for detailed experimental results.

5.3 Coupled spring-mass system

Consider a system with two springs of weights w_1, w_2.

$$\begin{bmatrix} \dot{x_1} \\ \dot{v_1} \\ \dot{x_2} \\ \dot{v_2} \end{bmatrix} = \begin{bmatrix} v_1 \\ -\frac{k_1}{m_1}x_1 - \frac{k_2}{m_1}(x_1 - x_2) \\ v_2 \\ -\frac{k_2}{m_2}(x_2 - x_1) \end{bmatrix}$$

One spring, having spring constant k_1, is attached to the ceiling, and the weight w_1 of mass m_1 is attached to the lower end of this spring. Attached to weight w_1 is a second spring with spring constant k_2, and the weight w_2 of mass m_2 is attached to the lower end of this spring. x_1 and x_2 denote the displacements of the center of masses of the weights w_1 and w_2 from equilibrium, respectively.

In this experiment, we first consider an instantiated version of the system by using the same parameters as in [28]: $\frac{k_1}{m_1} = \frac{k_2}{m_2} = k$ and $m_1 = 5m_2$. The experimental result is presented in Table 1. We found that the expressive power of the invariant clusters does not increases any more as the degree of the invariant clusters is greater than 3 and it took only 0.25 seconds to compute the invariant cluster of degree 3. Finally, we perform the computation directly on the fully parameterized system and we get the following parameterized invariant cluster that enables us to analyze the

Table 1: Benchmark results for the Longitudinal Motion of an Airplane (B1), the Looping Particle system (B2), and the Coupled Spring-Mass system (B3).

Degree of invariants	No. of variables B1	B2	B3	Running time (sec) B1	B2	B3	No. of invariant clusters B1	B2	B3
1	9	4	6	0.016	0.015	0.047	0	0	0
2	45	10	21	0.031	0.047	0.078	1	1	0
3	165	20	56	0.484	0.049	0.250	1	0	1
4	495	35	126	3.844	0.156	1.109	1	1	1
5	1287	56	252	25.172	0.703	6.641	1	0	1
6	3003	84	462	200.903	3.000	32.109	1	1	1

system properties under different parameter settings.

$$\begin{aligned} g(\vec{u},\vec{x}) &= u_8 v_1 v_2 + \frac{k_2 x_1 x_2 (m_1 u_8 - 2m_2 u_{10})}{m_1 m_2} + u_{10} v_1^2 + u_1 \\ &+ \frac{1}{2}\frac{v_2^2 (k_1 m_2 u_8 - k_2 m_1 u_8 + k_2 m_2 u_8 + 2k_2 m_2 u_{10})}{k_2 m_1} \\ &+ \frac{1}{2}\frac{(2k_1 m_2 u_{10} - k_2 m_1 u_8 + 2k_2 m_2 u_{10}) x_1^2}{m_1 m_2} \\ &+ \frac{1}{2}\frac{(k_1 m_2 u_8 - k_2 m_1 u_8 + 2k_2 m_2 u_{10}) x_2^2}{m_1 m_2} \end{aligned}$$

5.4 Hybrid controller

Consider a hybrid controller consisting of two control modes. The discrete transition diagram of the system is shown in Figure 3(a) and the vector fields describing the continuous behaviors are given as follows:

$$f_1(\vec{x}) = \begin{bmatrix} y^2 + 10y + 25 \\ 2xy + 10x - 40y - 200 \end{bmatrix},$$

$$f_2(\vec{x}) = \begin{bmatrix} -y^2 - 10y - 25 \\ 8xy + 40x - 160y - 800 \end{bmatrix}$$

The system starts from some point in $X_0 = \{(x, y) \in \mathbb{R}^2 \mid (x-9)^2+(y-20)^2 \leq 4\}$ and then evolves following the vector field $f_1(\vec{x})$ at location l_1 (Switch-On). The value of x keeps increasing until it reaches 35. Then the system switches to location l_2 (Switch-Off) without performing any reset operation. At location l_2, the system operates following the vector field $f_2(\vec{x})$ and the value of x keeps decreasing. As the value of x drops to 5, the system switches immediately back to location l_1 again. Our objective is to verify that the value of y will never exceed 48 in both locations.

For the convenience of *SOS* programming, we define the unsafe set as $\text{Uns}(l_1) = \text{Uns}(l_2) = \{(x, y) \in \mathbb{R}^2 \mid 48 < y < 60\}$, which is sufficient to prove $y \leq 48$ in locations l_1 and l_2. According to the theory proposed in Section 4.2, we first find an invariant cluster for each location, which consists of a parameterized polynomial, respectively: $g_1(\vec{u}_1, \vec{x}) = -\frac{1}{5}u_{12}x^2 + \frac{1}{10}u_{12}y^2 + 8u_{12}x + u_{12}y + u_{11}$ and $g_2(\vec{u}_2, \vec{x}) = \frac{4}{5}u_{22}x^2 + \frac{1}{10}u_{22}y^2 - 32u_{22}x + u_{22}y + u_{21}$. In the second phase, we make use of the constraint condition in Proposition 5 to compute a pair of vectors $\vec{u}_1^*$ and $\vec{u}_2^*$. By setting $\gamma_{12} = \gamma_{21} = 1$, our tool found a pair of $\vec{u}_1^* = (u_{11}, u_{12}) = (2.9747, 382.14)$ and $\vec{u}_2^* = (u_{21}, u_{22}) = (2.9747, 138.44)$. As shown in Figure 3(b), the curves of $g_1(\vec{u}_1^*, \vec{x}) = 0$ and $g_2(\vec{u}_2^*, \vec{x}) = 0$ form an upper bound for the reachable set in location l_1 and l_2, respectively, which lie below the unsafe region $y \geq 48$. Therefore, the system is safe.

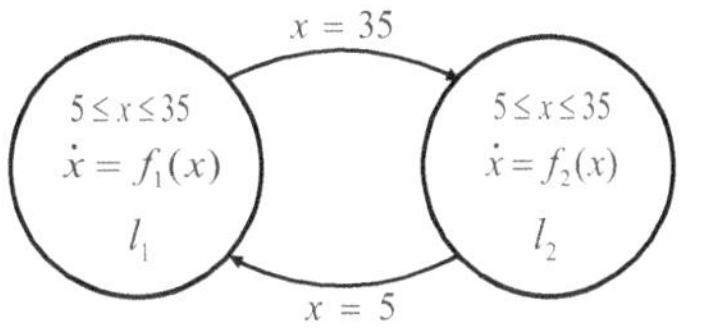

(a)

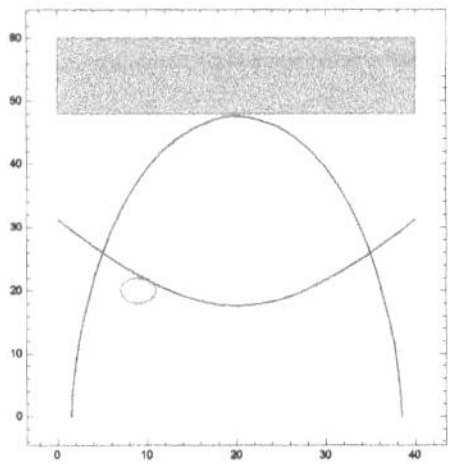

(b)

Figure 3: Hybrid controller from Subsection 5.4. (a) Hybrid automaton. (b) Hybrid invariant. Solid patch in green: initial set. Curve in blue: invariant for l_1. Curve in purple: invariant for l_2. Red shadow region on the top: unsafe region.

6. RELATED WORK

Many recent efforts have been made toward generating invariants for hybrid systems. Matringe et al. reduce the invariant generation problem to the computation of the associated eigenspaces by encoding the invariant constraints as symbolic matrices [26]. Ghorbal et al. use the invariant algebraic set formed by a polynomial and a finite set of its successive Lie derivatives to overapproximate vector flows [12]. Both of the aforementioned methods involve minimizing the rank of a symbolic matrix. Although in theory the problem of minimizing the rank of a symbolic matrix lies in the same complexity class as that of our problem, experiments show that our approach is more powerful in practice. Sankaranarayanan discovers invariants based on invariant ideal and pseudo ideal iteration [28], but this method is limited to algebraic systems. Moreover, none of the aforementioned methods involve verifying safety properties based on the invariants obtained. Tiwari et al. compute invariants for some special types of linear and nonlinear systems based on *Syzygy* computation and Gröbner basis theory as well as linear constraint solving [34]. Platzer et al. use quantifier elimination to find differential invariants [23]. Another approach considers barrier certificates based on different inductive conditions [24, 20, 21] which can be solved by *SOS* programming efficiently but is limited by the conservative inductive condition. Carbonell et al. generate invariants for linear systems [27]. Some other approaches focusing on different features of systems have also been proposed for constructing inductive invariants [19, 16, 29, 30, 22, 15].

7. CONCLUSION

In this paper, we proposed an approach to automatically generate invariant clusters for semialgebraic hybrid systems. Invariant clusters can overapproximate trajectories of the system precisely. They can be obtained efficiently by computing the remainder of the Lie derivative of a template polynomial $g(\vec{u},\vec{x})$ w.r.t. $g(\vec{u},\vec{x})$ and then solving a system of homogeneous polynomial equations obtained from the remainder. Based on invariant clusters and *SOS* programming, we proposed a new method for safety verification of hybrid systems. Experiments show that our approach is efficient for a large class of biological and control systems.

Acknowledgment

This research was supported in part by the Austrian Science Fund (FWF) under grants S11402-N23 (RiSE/SHiNE) and Z211-N23 (Wittgenstein Award), and by the ARC project DP140104219 (Robust AI Planning for Hybrid Systems).

8. REFERENCES

[1] R. Alur, T. Dang, and F. Ivančić. Progress on reachability analysis of hybrid systems using predicate abstraction. In *HSCC*. 2003.

[2] E. Asarin, T. Dang, and A. Girard. Reachability analysis of nonlinear systems using conservative approximation. In *HSCC*. 2003.

[3] A. Ayad. A survey on the complexity of solving algebraic systems. In *International Mathematical Forum*, volume 5, 2010.

[4] S. Bogomolov, A. Donzé, G. Frehse, R. Grosu, T. T. Johnson, H. Ladan, A. Podelski, and M. Wehrle. Guided search for hybrid systems based on coarse-grained space abstractions. *STTT*, 2015.

[5] S. Bogomolov, G. Frehse, M. Greitschus, R. Grosu, C. S. Pasareanu, A. Podelski, and T. Strump. Assume-guarantee abstraction refinement meets hybrid systems. In *HVC*, 2014.

[6] S. Bogomolov, G. Frehse, R. Grosu, H. Ladan, A. Podelski, and M. Wehrle. A box-based distance between regions for guiding the reachability analysis of SpaceEx. In *CAV*, 2012.

[7] S. Bogomolov, C. Herrera, M. Muñiz, B. Westphal, and A. Podelski. Quasi-dependent variables in hybrid automata. In *HSCC*, 2014.

[8] S. Bogomolov, C. Schilling, E. Bartocci, G. Batt, H. Kong, and R. Grosu. Abstraction-based parameter synthesis for multiaffine systems. In *HVC*, 2015.

[9] X. Chen, E. Ábrahám, and S. Sankaranarayanan. Taylor model flowpipe construction for non-linear hybrid systems. In *RTSS*, 2012.

[10] D. A. Cox, J. Little, and D. O'Shea. *Ideals, Varieties, and Algorithms: An Introduction to Computational Algebraic Geometry and Commutative Algebra.* Springer, 2007.

[11] T. Dang, O. Maler, and R. Testylier. Accurate hybridization of nonlinear systems. In *HSCC*, 2010.

[12] K. Ghorbal and A. Platzer. Characterizing algebraic invariants by differential radical invariants. In *TACAS*. 2014.

[13] A. Girard and S. Martin. Synthesis for constrained nonlinear systems using hybridization and robust controllers on simplices. *IEEE Trans. Automat. Contr.*, 57(4), 2012.

[14] A. Goriely. *Integrability and nonintegrability of dynamical systems*, volume 19. World Scientific, 2001.

[15] E. Goubault, J. Jourdan, S. Putot, and S. Sankaranarayanan. Finding non-polynomial positive invariants and Lyapunov functions for polynomial systems through Darboux polynomials. In *ACC*, 2014.

[16] S. Gulwani and A. Tiwari. Constraint-based approach for analysis of hybrid systems. In *CAV*, 2008.

[17] T. A. Henzinger. The theory of hybrid automata. In *LICS*, 1996.

[18] Y. Jiang, H. Liu, H. Kong, R. Wang, M. Hosseini, J. Sun, and L. Sha. Use runtime verification to improve the quality of medical care practice. In *ICSE*, 2016.

[19] T. T. Johnson and S. Mitra. Invariant synthesis for verification of parameterized cyber-physical systems with applications to aerospace systems. In *AIAA Infotech at Aerospace Conference*, 2013.

[20] H. Kong, F. He, X. Song, W. N. Hung, and M. Gu. Exponential-condition-based barrier certificate generation for safety verification of hybrid systems. In *CAV*, 2013.

[21] H. Kong, X. Song, D. Han, M. Gu, and J. Sun. A new barrier certificate for safety verification of hybrid systems. *The Computer Journal*, 57(7):1033–1045, 2014.

[22] J. Liu, N. Zhan, and H. Zhao. Computing semi-algebraic invariants for polynomial dynamical systems. In *EMSOFT*, 2011.

[23] A. Platzer and E. Clarke. Computing differential invariants of hybrid systems as fixedpoints. In *CAV*, 2008.

[24] S. Prajna and A. Jadbabaie. Safety verification of hybrid systems using barrier certificates. *HSCC*, 2004.

[25] S. Prajna, A. Papachristodoulou, P. Seiler, and P. A. Parrilo. *SOSTOOLS and its control applications.* 2005.

[26] R. Rebiha, A. V. Moura, and N. Matringe. Generating invariants for non-linear hybrid systems. *TCS*, 594, 2015.

[27] E. Rodríguez-Carbonell and A. Tiwari. Generating polynomial invariants for hybrid systems. *HSCC*, 2005.

[28] S. Sankaranarayanan. Automatic invariant generation for hybrid systems using ideal fixed points. In *HSCC*, 2010.

[29] S. Sankaranarayanan, H. Sipma, and Z. Manna. Constructing invariants for hybrid systems. *HSCC*, 2004.

[30] B. Sassi, M. Amin, A. Girard, and S. Sankaranarayanan. Iterative computation of polyhedral invariants sets for polynomial dynamical systems. In *CDC*, 2014.

[31] R. F. Stengel. Flight dynamics. *Fluid Dynamics*, 1, 2004.

[32] G. Stengle. A Nullstellensatz and a Positivstellensatz in semialgebraic geometry. *Mathematische Annalen*, 207(2), 1974.

[33] A. Tiwari. Abstractions for hybrid systems. *Formal Methods in System Design*, 32(1), 2008.

[34] A. Tiwari and G. Khanna. Nonlinear systems: Approximating reach sets. *HSCC*, 2004.

HyLAA: A Tool for Computing Simulation-Equivalent Reachability for Linear Systems

Stanley Bak
Air Force Research Laboratory
Aerospace Systems Directorate
stanleybak@gmail.com

Parasara Sridhar Duggirala
Department of Computer Science and Engineering
University of Connecticut
psd@uconn.edu

ABSTRACT

Simulations are a practical method of increasing the confidence that a system design is correct. This paper presents techniques which aim to determine all the states that can be reached using a particular hybrid automaton simulation algorithm, a property we call *simulation-equivalent* reachability. Although this is a slightly weaker property than traditional reachability, its computation can be efficient and accurate.

We present HyLAA, the first tool for simulation-equivalent reachability for hybrid automata with affine dynamics. HyLAA's analysis is exact; upon completion, the tool provides a concrete simulation trace to an unsafe state if and only if the hybrid automaton simulation engine could produce such a trace. In the backend, the tool implements an efficient algorithm for continuous post that exploits the superposition principle of linear systems, requiring only $n + 1$ simulations per mode for an n-dimensional linear system. This technique is capable of analyzing a replicated helicopter system with over 1000 state variables in less than 20 minutes. The tool also contains several novel performance enhancements, such as invariant constraint elimination, warm-start linear programming, and trace-guided set deaggregation.

1. INTRODUCTION

Cyber-physical systems (CPS) that involve interaction between software and the physical world can naturally be modeled using the hybrid automaton formalism. These models allow a mix of discrete and continuous behaviors. Often, the continuous evolution is defined with differential equations that are linear (or affine). Such differential equations represent commonly observed physical systems such as autonomous vehicles, hardware circuits, biological systems, etc. As these CPS are deployed in safety-critical scenarios, it is important to ensure that these systems satisfy the *safety* specification. Further, if a given system design does not satisfy the safety specification, it is useful for debugging to provide the system designer with a concrete counterexample which violates the specification.

Due to increased complexity of CPS, a model-based design framework is increasingly being adopted by industries to do design and development. In this approach, the CPS is modeled in a framework such as Simulink/Stateflow or Modelica and is tested under varying scenarios by using numerical simulations. These simulations, even when they have numerical errors, are regarded as very close approximations of the real behaviors and used for system design and debugging. For CPS, the space of uncertainties is often uncountable, and therefore, one cannot usually conclude that the system satisfies the safety specification from a finite number of sample simulations.

In this paper, we introduce a tool called **HyLAA** (**Hy**brid **L**inear **A**utomata **A**nalyzer) that performs simulation-based verification for hybrid automata with linear ODEs. HyLAA implements an algorithm that computes the reachable set of states of an n-dimensional linear system using only $n+1$ simulations [10]. HyLAA's goal is to perform *simulation-equivalent* reachability for bounded time. That is, it computes the set of states that would be encountered by a hybrid automaton simulation algorithm for all possible nondeterministic choices in the initial state and the discrete transitions. HyLAA declares a system to be safe if and only if all the simulations are safe; it declares a system to be unsafe if and only if there exists a counterexample simulation trace that violates the safety property, and it produces such a trace.

For efficiency, the tool makes two assumptions. First, numerical computations are considered exact and errors due to floating point computations are ignored. Second, the tool assumes that the underlying ODE simulation engine provides exact simulations for the dynamics. We believe that these assumptions are reasonable, given the crucial role floating-point simulations already play in system analysis and design. In practice, floating point errors are usually small, and to reduce/eliminate these errors further, one can use simulation engines with arbitrary precision [1, 12, 5]. Analysis of HyLAA is different from other simulation based verification tools such as C2E2 [9], Breach [8], or Strong [7] in two aspects. First, these tools aim to prove safety irrespective of the semantics of the simulation engine used. Second, in worst case, the number of simulations would be exponential in the number of dimensions.

To clarify, we emphasize the differences between a *hybrid automaton simulation algorithm* and an *ODE simulation engine*. A simulation of hybrid automaton records an execution of

DISTRIBUTION A. Approved for public release; Distribution unlimited. (Approval AFRL PA #88ABW-2016-2897, 30 SEPT 2016)

HSCC'17, April 18 - 20, 2017, Pittsburgh, PA, USA

ACM ISBN 978-1-4503-4590-3/17/04...$15.00

DOI: http://dx.doi.org/10.1145/3049797.3054973

the hybrid automaton starting from an initial state while taking into account the different modes, invariants and discrete transitions(the specific algorithm is presented later). To do this, HyLAA makes use of an ODE simulation engine, which can only simulate the behavior of the system according to a given differential equation. In the context of MATLAB, a hybrid automaton simulation algorithm would be similar to simulation engine underlying Simulink / Stateflow (although our semantics are slightly different, see the next section), whereas an ODE simulation engine refers to a standard ODE solver such as `ode45`.

2. PRELIMINARIES

We consider affine hybrid automata defined as follows.

DEFINITION 1. *An affine hybrid automaton is defined as a tuple* $\langle Loc, X, Flow, Inv, Trans, Guard\rangle$ *where*

Loc is a finite set of locations (also called modes).

$X \subseteq \mathbb{R}^n$ *is the state space of the behaviors.*

$Flow : Loc \rightarrow AffineDeq(X)$ *assigns an affine differential equation* $\dot{x} = A_l x + B_l$ *for location* l *of the hybrid automaton.*

$Inv : Loc \rightarrow 2^{\mathbb{R}^n}$ *assigns an invariant set for each location.*

$Trans \subseteq Loc \times Loc$ *is the set of discrete transitions.*

$Guard : Trans \rightarrow 2^{\mathbb{R}^n}$ *defines the set of states where a discrete transition is enabled.*

For the hybrid automata we consider, the invariants and guards are given as conjunction of linear constraints.

A reachability problem combines an affine hybrid automaton with an *initial set of states Q*, which is a finite set of elements in $Loc \times 2^{\mathbb{R}^n}$, where second element in the pair is given as conjunction of linear constraints. An *initial state* q_0 is a pair (Loc_0, x_0), where an element exists in the initial set of states with the given location Loc_0, and the point x_0 satisfies both the corresponding linear constraints and the invariant of Loc_0. Unsafe states are indicated by having an explicit set of error modes, $U \subseteq Loc$.

Given an initial state $q_0 = (Loc_0, x_0)$, an execution of the hybrid automaton $\sigma(x_0) = \tau_0 a_1 \tau_1 a_2 \ldots$ is a sequence of trajectories and actions such that each τ_i is the solution of the affine differential equation for the location Loc_i and respects its invariant, (τ_0 starts from Loc_0), the state before a discrete transition a_i should satisfy the $Guard(a_i)$ and the state after the discrete transition satisfies the invariant of the successor mode Loc_{i+1}. We abuse notation and denote the state of the system following a trajectory after time t as $\tau_i(q_0, t)$ where q_0 is the initial state of the trajectory.

The closed form expression for the trajectories is given using the state transformation matrix $\Phi_i : \mathbb{R}_{\geq 0} \times \mathbb{R}_{\geq 0} \rightarrow \mathbb{R}^{n \times n}$ where $\tau_i(x_0, t) = \Phi_i(t, 0)x_0 + \int_0^t \Phi(t, s)B_i(s)ds$. For linear time invariant systems (LTIs), the state transformation matrix $\Phi_i(t_2, t_1) = e^{A_i(t_2 - t_1)}$. For efficiently analyzing these models, numerical simulations from an ODE simulation engine are routinely used. We now define a trace produced by a hybrid automaton simulation algorithm.

DEFINITION 2. *Given a hybrid automaton H and an initial set of states Q, a sequence* $\rho_H(q_0, h) = q_0, q_1, q_2, \ldots$*, where each* $q_i = (Loc_i, x_i)$*, is called a* (q_0, h)*-simulation of H if and only if* $q_0 \in Q$ *and each pair* (q_i, q_{i+1}) *corresponds to either (i) a continuous trajectory in location* $Loc_i = Loc_{i+1}$ *such that a trajectory starting from* x_i *would reach* x_{i+1} *after h time units with* $x_i \in Inv(Loc_i)$*, or (ii) a discrete transition from* Loc_i *to* Loc_{i+1} *where* $a = (Loc_i, Loc_{i+1})$ *and* $a \in Trans$ *such that* $x_i = x_{i+1}$*,* $x_i \in Guard(a)$ *and* $x_{i+1} \in Inv(Loc_{i+1})$*. We drop the subscript when it is clear from context. Bounded-time variants of these simulations are called* (q_0, h, T)*-simulations.*

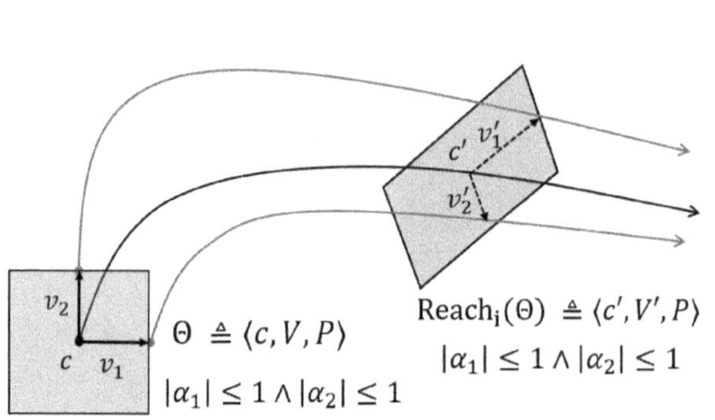

Figure 1: Due to superposition, $\tau(c + v_1 + v_2, t) = c' + v_1' + v_2'$, where $c' = \tau(c, t)$, $v_1' = \tau(c + v_1, t) - \tau(c, t)$ and $v_2' = \tau(c + v_2, t) - \tau(c, t)$. In the star representation, only the center and the basis vectors change as time elapses. The star's predicate, $|\alpha_1| \leq 1 \wedge |\alpha_2| \leq 1$ remains the same.

For these simulations, h is called the *step size* and T is called *time bound*. Pairs of states corresponding to (i) are said to arise from a *continuous-post step*, and pairs from condition (ii) come from a *discrete-post step*.

Notice that hybrid automaton simulation traces which conform to Definition 2 do not check if the invariant is violated for the entire time interval, but only at multiples of the step size h. Also, the discrete transitions are only enabled at time instances that are multiples of h and nondeterminism is allowed in discrete transitions if more than one guard is satisfied, or the invariant remains true. One subtlety is that discrete-post pairs only have the invariant checked in the first state. This has the effect of allowing discrete transitions from states where the invariant is false (i.e., guards are checked before invariants). This is necessary to handle the common case of systems where a guard is the negation of a location's invariant, and a step of the simulation may jump over the boundary. If such behaviors are not desired, the guards can be explicitly strengthened to include the negation of the invariant.

For readers familiar with the simulation engines in standard tools like Simulink / Stateflow or Modelica, the described trajectories do not perform any special *zero-crossing detection* and the transitions are not necessarily *urgent*. In this paper, we attempt to determine if an affine hybrid automaton is safe with respect all bounded-time simulations that conform to the conditions in Definition 2.

DEFINITION 3. *A given simulation* $\rho_H(q_0, h)$ *is said to be safe with respect to an unsafe set of modes U if and only if* $\forall (Loc_i, x_i) \in \rho_H(q_0, h)$*,* $Loc_i \notin U$*. Safety for time-bounded simulations are defined similarly.*

DEFINITION 4. *A hybrid automaton H with an initial set of states Q, time bound T, and unsafe set of modes U is said to be safe if all simulations starting from Q for bounded time T are safe.*

Solutions to linear ODEs (in our case trajectories τ_i in each mode) satisfy a superposition property, illustrated in Figure 1. Given any initial state x_0, vectors $v_1, \ldots, v_m$ where $v_i \in \mathbb{R}^n$, and scalars $\alpha_1, \ldots, \alpha_m$,

$$\tau_i(x_0 + \Sigma_{i=1}^m \alpha_i v_i, t) = \tau_i(x_0, t) + \Sigma_{i=1}^m \alpha_i(\tau_i(x_0 + v_i, t) - \tau_i(x_0, t)).$$

Before describing the algorithm for computing the reachable set, we finally introduce a data structure called a *generalized star*, which is used to represent the reachable set of states in HyLAA.

DEFINITION 5. *A* generalized star Θ *is a tuple* $\langle c, V, P\rangle$ *where* $c \in \mathbb{R}^n$ *is called the* center, $V = \{v_1, v_2, \ldots, v_m\}$ *is a set of* m $(\leq n)$ *vectors in* $\mathbb{R}^n$ *called the* basis vectors, *and* $P : \mathbb{R}^n \rightarrow \{\top, \bot\}$ *is a predicate. A generalized star* Θ *defines a subset of* $\mathbb{R}^n$ *as follows.*

$$[\![\Theta]\!] = \{x \mid \exists \bar{\alpha} = [\alpha_1, \ldots, \alpha_m]^T \text{ such that } x = c + \Sigma_{i=1}^{n} \alpha_i v_i \text{and } P(\bar{\alpha}) = \top\}$$

Sometimes we will refer to both Θ *and* $[\![\Theta]\!]$ *as* Θ*. In this paper, we consider predicates* P *that are conjunctions of linear constraints.*

3. REACHABILITY ALGORITHM

In this section, we present an algorithm for computing the simulation-equivalent reachable set of states for linear hybrid systems. The description is divided into two parts: (1) computing the set of states for the linear dynamics without considering the invariants and discrete transitions, and (2) accommodating the invariants in each location and accounting for discrete transitions between locations.

3.1 Continuous Dynamics

States reachable under continuous evolution are computed by exploiting the superposition principle and using the *generalized star* representation. For an n-dimensional linear system, this technique requires at most $n+1$ simulations. Let the initial set of states Q be given as a generalized star $\langle c, V, P\rangle$ where $V = \{v_1, v_2, \ldots, v_m\}$. The ODE simulation engine for continuous dynamics, with initial state x_0, step size h, and number of steps k, denoted $\rho(x_0, h, k)$, returns a sequence $x_0, x_1, \ldots, x_k$ such that $x_i = \tau(x_0, i \cdot h)$. We denote x_i as $\rho(x_0, h, k)[i]$. The reachable set at time instances $i \cdot h$ is computed by Algorithm 1 as a generalized star.

Algorithm 1: Algorithm that computes the simulation-equivalent reachable set at time instances $i \cdot h$ from $n+1$ simulations.

---

input : Initial Set: $\Theta \triangleq \langle c, V, P\rangle$, time step: h, steps: k
output: $Reach(\Theta) = Reach_0(\Theta), \ldots, Reach_k(\Theta)$
1 **for** *each i from* 0 *to* k **do**
2 $\quad c' \leftarrow \rho(c, h, k)[i]$;
3 $\quad$ **for** *each* $v_j \in V$ **do**
4 $\quad\quad x'_j \leftarrow \rho(c + v_j, h, k)[i]$;
5 $\quad\quad v'_j \leftarrow x'_j - c'$;
6 $\quad V' \leftarrow \{v'_1, \ldots, v'_m\}$;
7 $\quad Reach_i(\Theta) \leftarrow \langle c', V', P\rangle$;
8 $\quad$ Append $Reach_i(\Theta)$ to $Reach(\Theta)$;
9 **return** $Reach(\Theta)$;

The algorithm in line 2 computes the state of trajectory starting from the initial state c at time $i \cdot h$ as c'. The loop in lines 3 to 5 computes x'_j, the state of the trajectory starting from $c+v_j$ at time $i \cdot h$. The reachable set at time $i \cdot h$ is given as as generalized star $\langle c', V', P\rangle$, where $V' = \{v'_1, \ldots, v'_n\}$ with $v'_j = x'_j - c'$. The correctness of Algorithm 1 follows from the superposition principle and has been previously established [10]. An illustration of the reachable set computation as described in the algorithm is presented in Figure 1.

With this algorithm, extracting concrete trajectories which reach a given star is straightforward. This process involves expressing the desired point as a vector sum of star's center and scalar multiples along each of the basis vectors. The scalar multiples, for an ordered basis set, is called a *basis point*. The desired trajectory is the sequence of points where the state at discrete time step is obtained by the vector sum of the corresponding center and the multiplication of basis point with the corresponding basis vector matrix.

3.2 Hybrid Dynamics

In this section, we use the described continuous-post algorithm while accounting for invariants and discrete transitions to perform simulation-equivalent reachability. The pseudo-code is given in Algorithm 2.

Algorithm 2: Algorithm that computes the simulation-equivalent reachable set for hybrid automata.

---

input : Initial set of states: Q, Time step: h
output: Simulation-equivalent reachable set
1 $ReachSet \leftarrow \emptyset$; cur_state $\leftarrow \emptyset$; waiting $\leftarrow \emptyset$;
2 **for** $q \in Q$ **do**
3 $\quad push$(waiting, q);
4 **while** $\neg empty$(waiting) $\vee$ cur_state $\neq \emptyset$ **do**
5 $\quad$ **if** cur_state $= \emptyset$ **then**
6 $\quad\quad$ /* discrete-post step */
7 $\quad\quad \langle\Theta, l\rangle \leftarrow pop$(waiting);
8 $\quad\quad \Theta \leftarrow \Theta \cap Inv(l)$;
9 $\quad\quad$ **if** $\Theta \neq \emptyset$ **then**
10 $\quad\quad\quad$ **for** $q \in$ discreteTransitions(Θ, l) **do**
11 $\quad\quad\quad\quad push$(waiting, q);
12 $\quad\quad\quad$ cur_state $\leftarrow \langle\Theta, l\rangle$;
13 $\quad\quad\quad ReachSet \leftarrow$ cur_state $\cup\ ReachSet$;
14 $\quad$ **else**
15 $\quad\quad$ /* continuous-post step */
16 $\quad\quad \langle\Theta, l\rangle \leftarrow$ cur_state;
17 $\quad\quad \Theta \leftarrow Alg1(\Theta, h, 1)$;
18 $\quad\quad$ **for** $q \in$ discreteTransitions(Θ, l) **do**
19 $\quad\quad\quad push$(waiting, q);
20 $\quad\quad \Theta \leftarrow \Theta \cap Inv(l)$;
21 $\quad\quad$ **if** $\Theta \neq \emptyset$ **then**
22 $\quad\quad\quad$ cur_state $\leftarrow \langle\Theta, l\rangle$;
23 $\quad\quad\quad ReachSet \leftarrow$ cur_state $\cup\ ReachSet$;
24 $\quad\quad$ **else**
25 $\quad\quad\quad$ cur_state $\leftarrow \emptyset$;
26 **return** $ReachSet$;

For each given iteration of the outermost loop, the algorithm performs one discrete transition or computes the reachable set according to continuous evolution by one step. First, each of the elements of the initial set of states Q, which are pairs of stars and locations, are pushed onto the waiting list in line 3.

Initially, the reachable set for discrete transitions is calculated in lines 7 to 13 (called discrete post). In a discrete-post step, the set of states that violate the invariant are pruned in line 8, followed by checking for guard successors in line 10. Pruning the set of states that violate the invariant first ensures two conditions as required in Definition 2: (i) all initial states satisfy the invariant of initial location, and (ii) after each discrete-post step, the invariant of the destination mode is satisfied. If the set of states that satisfy the invariant is nonempty, in line 12 the star is assigned to cur_state and then it gets added to the final reachable set.

After cur_state is assigned, the algorithm will compute the reachable set with the continuous dynamics (called continuous post). In line 17, the earlier continuous algorithm is called for a single step h. In the continuous-post operation, guard checking (line 18) is performed *before* invariant trimming (line 20). This is needed to maintain the condition of valid simulations in Definition 2 that discrete-post steps are possible even if the destination state does not satisfy the invariant of the current mode (this was to be able simulate the common case of guards being the complements of a state's invariant). Finally, if the reachable set for one step satisfies the invariant, line 22 updates cur_state and adds it to the final reachable set. Otherwise, cur_state is discarded, and the next state can be removed from the waiting list.

As a side effect, this algorithm always keeps track of the reachable set that satisfies the invariant (line 20). That is, if the invariant is violated by a given state in the current reachable set, its future continuous trajectory is not part of the reachable set. Without this operation, some of the states which have previously violated the invariant could re-enter the invariant region, and then appear to be reachable. A simulation trajectory as defined in Definition 2, however, could not contain such states. Some reachable set computation tools postpone the pruning of the reachable set until all continuous-post steps complete (the invariant becomes completely false or the time bound is reached), which can lead to this type of error. A demonstration of this is provided in Section 4.2.

The HyLAA implementation has several enhancements to the described algorithm. In HyLAA, time is tracked by maintaining the cumulative number of continuous-post operations performed on each star, and another condition for stopping a continuous-post step is if the number of steps performed exceeds the desired time bound. Additionally, the guard check in the discrete-post logic is optional, depending on if the user wants to support urgent transitions, where no time elapses. It may be desirable to disable these since they can lead to infinite loops where time does not pass (Zeno behavior). Further, star aggregation may need to be performed in order to prevent large numbers of states from being added to the waiting list. However, aggregated stars may be overapproximative and not correspond to real simulations, so deaggregation may be necessary to find concrete counter-example traces. This approach will be discussed more in Section 4.4.

In terms of efficiency and data structures, the predicates in stars are conjunctions of linear constraints. Checking for intersections with guards and invariants (which are linear constraints), can be done by performing a linear optimization in the normal direction of the linear constraint's hyperplane, subject to the constraints that the predicate of the star is true. If an intersection exists, pruning states that violate invariant would require adding an extra constraint to the star. Checking if a star is empty can also be done by checking if any point satisfies the star's linear constraints (the objective can be 0). Thus all the main operations needed for Algorithm 2 can be exactly and efficiently performed.

4. HYLAA TOOL IMPLEMENTATION

The HyLAA tool implements the theory presented in Section 3. The tool is developed in Python, although many of the core computation components are libraries written in other languages. Simulations are performed using `scipy`, which uses the FORTRAN library `odepack`'s `lsoda` solver. This solver supports a wide variety of differential equations and allows the user to set the simulation accuracy. Linear programming is performed using the `glpk` library, and matrix operations are done using `numpy`. Visualization for the reachable set is provided using the libraries in `matplotlib`. HyLAA supports a live animation mode which shows the generalized stars during the course of the computation, a step-by-step mode when the user presses a button before each continuous or discrete-post operation, and a video export mode that uses `ffmpeg` to output the visualization to a file format such as `.mp4`. The model input file is Python code instantiating HyLAA-specific objects. To ease model development, we have created a printer using the HyST model conversion tool [2]. This allows input models to be created in the SpaceEx [11] format using the SpaceEx model editor, and then exported and used by HyLAA.

In this section, we describe three novel features of HyLAA namely, invariant constraint propagation, warm-start optimization, and trace based aggregation and present some experimental evaluation in comparison to other tools. Owing to space limitations, all the three features have not been fully described and proofs of correctness are not presented. The experimental evaluations have been limited to instances that highlight the new features in HyLAA and are not extensive. The algorithms behind each of the features and the corresponding correctness proofs are presented in other work [4].

4.1 Continuous-Post Scalability

We first evaluate the scalability of HyLAA, which uses the $n+1$ simulations approach described in Section 3.1. In order to do this, we use the helicopter/controller benchmark provided on the SpaceEx website[1]. We use the same parameters as the `x8_over_time_large` variant of the benchmark, which consists of a 28-dimensional helicopter plus a time dimension, a nondeterministic set of initial states with a 30 second target time and a 0.1 second step size. As this system contains no discrete switches, it serves as an evaluation of the efficiency of the continuous-post operation. We compared HyLAA with `supp` and `stc` scenarios in SpaceEx [11] using the default accuracy settings. In order to show scalability, we replicated the helicopter several times within the same model. This was repeated until the computation did not finish within the 20 minute timeout. We also attempted to use the linear reachability mode from Flow* [6] 2.0.0, but did not succeed in finding a suitable set of parameters with the 0.1 time step, although we did get Flow* to complete the single helicopter case with a smaller time step in about 10 minutes. The results are shown in Figure 2. HyLAA's approach generally performs better, and is able to complete a 365 dimensional system (13 helicopters) in under a minute, and a 1065 dimensional system (38 helicopters) in under 20 minutes. The execution of the reachability tools was scripted using the `hypy` library [3], along with a model transformation pass for replicating the helicopter system written in HyST [2]. The measurements were performed using a 2.30GHz Intel i5-

[1] http://spaceex.imag.fr/news/helicopter-example-posted-39

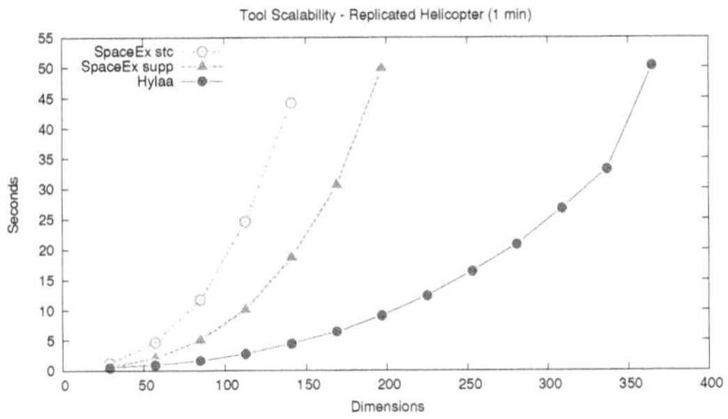

(a) 1 min limit

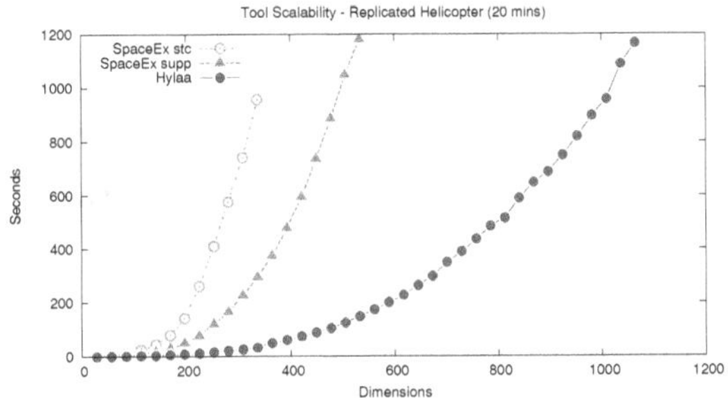

(b) 20 min limit

Figure 2: Scalability of reachability computation on the replicated helicopter system with a one minute and 20 minute time limit. The $n + 1$ simulation continuous-post operation in HyLAA is generally faster than the supp and stc methods implemented in SpaceEx.

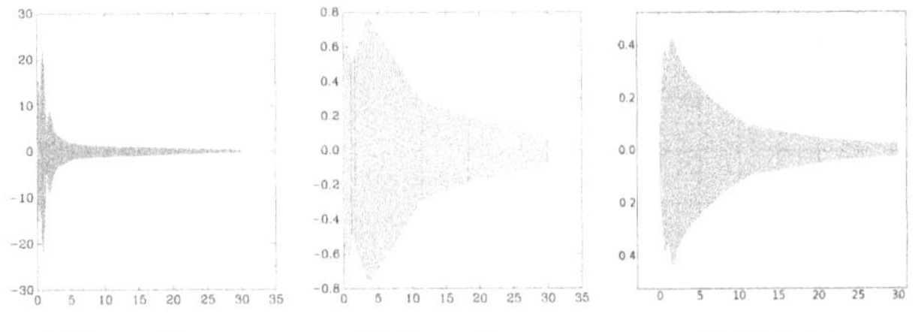

(a) SpaceEx supp (b) SpaceEx stc (c) HyLAA

Figure 3: Plots of x_8 over time for a two-helicopter system show that the default settings used for measuring SpaceEx produce less accurate reachability plots than HyLAA. Note the y-axis scale with the supp method is much larger.

5300U CPU with 16 GB ram running Ubuntu 14.04 x64.

Note that the guarantees provided by SpaceEx and HyLAA are different. SpaceEx computes reachable set that includes states encountered by trajectories at all time instances whereas HyLAA computes reachable set at discrete instances of time. However, HyLAA can produce concrete counterexample traces. We would also like to highlight that there is an inherent challenge in comparing reachability tools, since the choice of parameters often provides a trade off between accuracy and runtime. Under the measured default parameters, Figure 3 compares output plots for the 2-helicopter case for x_8 over time, which shows that HyLAA's result appears more accurate. While the supp scenario seems to reach states where $x_8 > 20$, HyLAA's output always remains bounded in $[-0.45, 0.45]$. Furthermore, HyLAA's accuracy does not change for higher dimensional variants. Of course, we could increase SpaceEx's accuracy through parameter selection, but this would serve only to increase the computation times measured in Figure 2, and it would be difficult to justify one choice of parameters over another.

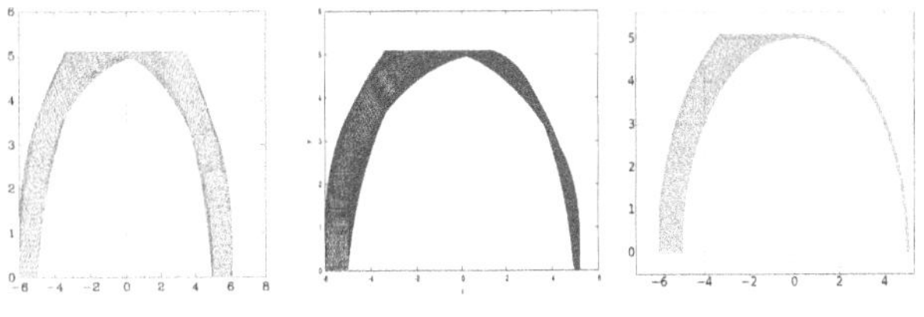

(a) SpaceEx stc (b) Flow* (c) HyLAA

Figure 4: Invariant trimming is performed when $y > 5.1$.

4.2 Invariant Constraint Elimination

During a continuous-post operation, it is possible that the generalized star being tracked has a partial intersection with the invariant. HyLAA eliminates states where the invariant is violated by adding an additional linear constraint into the predicate of the generalized star. This constraint is propagated forward in time and is added to predicates of all the following generalized stars. Therefore, successive time steps with a partial invariant intersection result in more constraints being added to the star. For this reason, HyLAA checks if each newly-added constraint is strictly stronger than the previous one, and drops the previous one if so. Without this optimization, the number of constraints added would be equal to the number of steps where a partial intersection takes place, which gets larger as the step size is decreased.

An example demonstrating this is the harmonic oscillator system, with $\dot{x} = y$ and $\dot{y} = -x$. Trajectories of this system rotate clockwise around the origin. The initial states are $x \in [-6, -5]$ and $y \in [0, 1]$, and the single mode's invariant is taken as $0 \leq y \leq 5.1$. In this system, trajectories from most of the initial states actually violate the invariant, and should be pruned from the reachable set.

Reachability plots for this system in SpaceEx stc, Flow* and HyLAA are shown in Figure 4. Notice that SpaceEx does not perform such pruning during the continuous-post operation (instead postponing it until afterwards), resulting in large error in the computed set of states. Flow*'s result appears correct, with the seeming overapproximation being an artifact of the octagon plotting mode. HyLAA's generalized star adds several constraints to account for the invariant and hence the final star in the reachable set has 79 constraints. With invariant constraint elimination, this number is reduced to 25.

4.3 Warm-Start Linear Programming

At each step during a continuous-post operation, the generalized star representation of reachable set must handle possible discrete transitions by checking if a guard condition can be satisfied. Moreover, additional constraints might be added to the star to prune the states that violate invariant. If plotting is enabled, the generalized star set has to be projected accurately on a 2-d plane for visualization. A simple box overapproximation can be rendered by finding maximum and minimum values of each axis variables. To obtain a more accurate plot, HyLAA chooses a number equidistant angles (for example, 64), maximizes the cost function along these directions, and renders the projection on 2d plane. Since these operations are performed by solving linear programing (LP) problems, the optimization of the LP engine is essential to HyLAA's performance.

HyLAA uses the GNU Linear Programming Kit (glpk) to solve LPs, which is an optimized ANSI C implementation that gets called from HyLAA's Python code. Internally, `glpk` uses a two-phase Simplex method to solve LPs. The first phase comes up with a feasible solution and the second phase applies the simplex heuristics to drive the feasible solution to the optimal solution. To improve the performance of solving multiple linear programs, HyLAA uses a warm-start LP optimization. Here, HyLAA stores the solution of the previous LP, and uses it as an initial guess for subsequent LPs. This allows `glpk` to skip the first phase of LP, and in many instances the second phase as well. For example, when plotting, a vertex of the star is the maximal point for many plotting directions. In these cases, the LP engine would be able to detect this and terminate immediately with zero additional Simplex iterations.

This warm-start optimization is helpful during guard (and invariant) intersections as well. For guard intersections, HyLAA finds the vertex of the star that is closest to the guard. After a single time step, the basis vectors in the star often only change slightly, and thus the same vertex of the star is often remains the closest one to the guard. The previous LP solution, in this case, would immediately lead to the new LP solution and improves the efficiency of HyLAA.

4.4 Trace-Guided Deaggregation

A well-known issue with flow-pipe construction reachability analysis is that, upon encountering a guard intersection, a single set of states might yield to multiple states in the successor location after a discrete transition. This can be observed in the invariant trimming example in Figure 4. If there was a guard with condition $y \geq 5.1$, then the guard would be enabled at multiple time steps, creating several successor stars in the next mode. As the time duration for which the guard is enabled remains constant, using a smaller step size might increase the number of successor stars. In the worst case, every star set has multiple successor stars during a discrete transition, leading to an exponential increase in the number of stars to be tracked after a few discrete transitions.

One common solution to this problem is to aggregate states in the same mode prior to each continuous-post operation. While this prevents the exponential problem described above, it might lead to a different set of potential problems. First, the aggregation is usually not exact. For generalized stars where the predicate is a set of linear constraints, for example, the exact union of two stars cannot generally be expressed using a conjunction of linear constraints. To see this, notice that a set of linear constraints defines a convex set, whereas the union of two stars can be non-convex, or even disjoint. Since the aggregation is not exact, it is no longer the case that if an aggregated star reaches an unsafe state then a concrete trace exists to the unsafe state. Second, in general, full aggregation based on convex representations (such as support functions in SpaceEx or parallelotopes in Flow*) cannot bound error. To see this, imagine the single mode whose reachable set was shown in Figure 4 contains a guard with a *true* condition. Since the guard is always enabled, all of the states in the plot would be aggregated. Therefore, perfect convex aggregation would include all of the states in the middle of the semi-circle, that are not part of the reachable set.

Thus, it is undesirable not to do aggregation due to exponential blowup in tracked states, but it is also undesirable to do aggregation due to unbounded error with convex overapproximations. HyLAA includes a compromise between these two, where aggregation is performed aggressively, but, upon reaching a guard, a concrete trace needs to be generated which reaches the guard. If such a trace cannot be generated, it means one of the stars along the path from the initial states to the current star includes an aggregated star which contributes to the overapproximation. This aggregated star is identified by backtracking, split into two smaller aggregated stars with less overapproximation, and the reachable set computation is resumed with the new aggregated stars. In this way, a guard is taken if and only if a concrete trace exists to the guard. Since the set of unsafe states is defined as subset of modes in the hybrid automaton, such a state will only be reached if there exists a concrete path. To the authors knowledge, this is the first approach to offer such aggregation and deaggregation strategies. A video demonstration of the deaggregation method is available on HyLAA website [2].

5. CONCLUSION

In this paper, we have presented a tool called HyLAA for performing simulation-equivalent reachability of affine hybrid automata. HyLAA can efficiently compute all the states reached by a specific hybrid automaton simulation algorithm. We have demonstrated the efficiency of the continuous-post operation on HyLAA by computing reachable set of a 1065 dimensional system in under 20 minutes, and described several improvements to handle the discrete transitions.

HyLAA is still in its early phases and many further enhancements are being considered. We plan to add support for resets on guards, as well as support for nondeterministic inputs within the differential equations. We wish to add support for hierarchical models and parallelize the simulation engine to improve scalability.

6. REFERENCES

[1] *Computer Assisted Proofs in Dynamic Groups (CAPD).* http://capd.ii.uj.edu.pl/index.php.

[2] S. Bak, S. Bogomolov, and T. T. Johnson. HyST: A source transformation and translation tool for hybrid automaton models. In *18th International Conference on Hybrid Systems: Computation and Control*, Seattle, Washington, Apr. 2015. ACM.

[3] S. Bak, S. Bogomolov, and C. Schilling. High-level hybrid systems analysis with hypy. In *ARCH 16: Proc. of the 3rd Workshop on Applied Verification for Continuous and Hybrid Systems*, 2016.

[4] S. Bak and P. S. Duggirala. Rigorous simulation-based analysis of linear hybrid systems. In *Tools and Algorithms for the Construction and Analysis of Systems*. Springer, 2017.

[5] O. Bouissou and M. Martel. GRKLib: a guaranteed runge kutta library. In *IMACS*, 2006.

[6] X. Chen, E. Abraham, and S. Sankaranarayanan. Taylor model flowpipe construction for non-linear hybrid systems. *2013 IEEE 34th Real-Time Systems Symposium*, 0:183–192, 2012.

[7] Y. Deng, A. Rajhans, and A. A. Julius. STRONG: a trajectory-based verification toolbox for hybrid systems. In *Quantitative Evaluation of Systems*, pages 165–168. Springer, 2013.

[8] A. Donzé. Breach, a toolbox for verification and parameter synthesis of hybrid systems. In *Computer Aided Verification*, pages 167–170. Springer, 2010.

[9] P. S. Duggirala, S. Mitra, M. Viswanathan, and M. Potok. C2E2: a verification tool for stateflow models. In *Tools and Algorithms for the Construction and Analysis of Systems*, pages 68–82. Springer, 2015.

[10] P. S. Duggirala and M. Viswanathan. Parsimonious, simulation based verification of linear systems. In *International Conference on Computer Aided Verification*, pages 477–494. Springer, 2016.

[11] G. Frehse, C. Le Guernic, A. Donzé, S. Cotton, R. Ray, O. Lebeltel, R. Ripado, A. Girard, T. Dang, and O. Maler. SpaceEx: Scalable verification of hybrid systems. In *Proc. 23rd International Conference on Computer Aided Verification (CAV)*, LNCS. Springer, 2011.

[12] N. Nedialkov. VNODE-LP: Validated solutions for initial value problem for ODEs. Technical report, McMaster University, 2006.

[2] http://stanleybak.com/hylaa/#hscc2017

Dynamic Periodic Event-Triggered Control for Linear Systems

Dominicus P. Borgers
d.p.borgers@tue.nl

Victor S. Dolk
v.s.dolk@tue.nl

W.P. Maurice H. Heemels
m.heemels@tue.nl

Control Systems Technology Group, Department of Mechanical Engineering
Eindhoven University of Technology, Eindhoven, The Netherlands

ABSTRACT

In event-triggered control systems, events are typically generated when a *static* function of the output (or state) of the system exceeds a given threshold. Recently, event-generators have been proposed that generate events based on an additional dynamic variable, with dynamics that depend on the output of the system. It is shown that these *dynamic* event-generators are able to guarantee the same performance as their static counterparts, while typically generating significantly fewer events. However, all dynamic event-generators available in literature require continuous measuring of the output of the plant, which is difficult to realize on digital platforms. In this paper, we propose new dynamic event-generators for linear systems, which require only periodic sampling of the output, and are therefore easy to implement on digital platforms. Based on hybrid modelling techniques combined with constructive designs of Lyapunov/storage functions for the resulting hybrid models, it is shown that these (dynamic periodic) event-generators lead to closed-loop systems which are globally exponentially stable (GES) with a guaranteed decay rate and $\mathcal{L}_2$-stable with a guaranteed $\mathcal{L}_2$-gain. The benefits of these new event-generators are also demonstrated via a numerical example.

Keywords

Event-triggered control; Hybrid systems; Impulsive systems; Riccati differential equations; $\mathcal{L}_2$ stability; Global exponential stability

1. INTRODUCTION

In most digital control systems, the measured output of the plant is periodically transmitted to the controller. Hence, the transmission times $\{t_k\}_{k\in\mathbb{N}}$ are determined in open-loop, as they are independent of the state of the system. This possibly leads to a waste of (e.g., computation, communication, and energy) resources, as many of the transmissions are actually not necessary to achieve the desired performance guarantees. In recent years, many *event-triggered control* (ETC) strategies have been proposed which generate the transmission times based on a triggering condition involving the current state or output measurement of the plant and the most recently transmitted measurement data, see, e.g., [4,15,18,23] and the references therein. This brings a *feedback* mechanism into the sampling and communication process, such that measurement data is only transmitted to the controller when needed in order to guarantee the required stability and performance properties of the system.

The ETC strategies in the works mentioned above can be categorized as *continuous* event-triggered control (CETC) strategies, as the triggering condition (and thus the state or output of the system) has to be monitored continuously. As this can be difficult to realize on digital platforms, many CETC controllers are implemented using a discretized version in practice. A better solution to this problem is to use *periodic* event-triggered control (PETC), in which the triggering condition is only checked periodically at fixed equidistant time instances. This enables (easier) implementation on digital platforms, such that the event-generator that is implemented in practice is identical to its original design, instead of a discrete approximation as in the CETC case. Note that PETC differs from standard periodic sampled-data control, as in PETC the event/transmission times are only a subset of the sampling times and can be aperiodic. Of course, event-triggered control schemes for discrete-time systems (e.g., [6,8,16,19,26]) can also be interpreted as PETC schemes, but these do not take into account the inter-sample behavior of the underlying continuous process.

In the past few years, various PETC strategies have been proposed for linear systems [5,12–15] and for nonlinear systems, see, e.g., [3,20,24]. In all these works, events are triggered whenever a certain *static* function of the state or output exceeds a given threshold. Hence, the event-generators do not have any dynamics of their own, and can be categorized as *static* periodic event-generators.

More recently, *continuous* event-generators have been proposed which generate events based on an additional dynamic variable (with dynamics that depend on the state or output of the system), leading to *dynamic* continuous event-generators. Dynamic continuous event-generators have been proposed for nonlinear systems in [7,10,21], and for linear systems in [2]. In these works, it is shown that dynamic event-generators are able to guarantee the same performance as their static counterparts, while typically generating significantly fewer events. However, the proposed

HSCC'17, April 18-20, 2017, Pittsburgh, PA, USA

DOI: http://dx.doi.org/10.1145/3049797.3049815

event-generators in [2,7,10,21] are all CETC solutions, and therefore difficult to implement in practice. To the best of the authors' knowledge, *dynamic* PETC solutions have not yet been proposed in literature.

As dynamic event-generators show great potential in CETC systems, we would like to exploit their benefits also in the context of PETC systems. Therefore, in this work, we propose two designs of dynamic periodic event-generators for linear systems. Our designs are based on ideas from [2] and [12], making use of hybrid modeling techniques and matrix Riccati differential equations. The first variant requires that the event-generator has access to the complete state of the plant, while the second is purely based on output measurements. Both dynamic event-generators we propose lead to closed-loop systems which are globally exponentially stable (GES) with a guaranteed decay rate and $\mathcal{L}_2$-stable with a guaranteed $\mathcal{L}_2$-gain. We show via a numerical example that both dynamic event-generators we propose outperform the static event-generator of [12], in the sense that identical decay rate and $\mathcal{L}_2$-gain guarantees are achieved with significantly fewer events.

1.1 Notation

For a vector $x \in \mathbb{R}^{n_x}$, we denote by $|x| := \sqrt{x^\top x}$ its Euclidean norm. For a symmetric matrix $A \in \mathbb{R}^{n \times n}$, we denote by $\lambda_{max}(A)$ and $\lambda_{min}(A)$ its maximum and minimum eigenvalue, respectively. For a matrix $P \in \mathbb{R}^{n\times n}$, we write $P \succ 0$ ($P \succeq 0$) if P is symmetric and positive (semi-)definite, and $P \prec 0$ ($P \preceq 0$) if P is symmetric and negative (semi-)definite. By I and O we denote the identity and zero matrix of appropriate dimensions, respectively. For a measurable signal $w : \mathbb{R}_{\geqslant 0} \to \mathbb{R}^{n_w}$, we write $w \in \mathcal{L}_2$ if $\|w\|_{\mathcal{L}_2} < \infty$, where $\|w\|_{\mathcal{L}_2} := \left(\int_0^\infty |w(t)|^2 \mathrm{d}t\right)^{1/2}$ denotes its $\mathcal{L}_2$-norm. By $\mathbb{N}$ we denote the set of natural numbers including zero, i.e., $\mathbb{N} := \{0, 1, 2, \dots\}$. A function $\gamma : \mathbb{R}_{\geqslant 0} \to \mathbb{R}_{\geqslant 0}$ is a $\mathcal{K}$-function if it is continuous, strictly increasing and $\gamma(0) = 0$, and a $\mathcal{K}_\infty$-function if it is a $\mathcal{K}$-function and, in addition, $\gamma(s) \to \infty$ as $s \to \infty$. A function $\beta : \mathbb{R}_{\geqslant 0} \times \mathbb{R}_{\geqslant 0} \to \mathbb{R}_{\geqslant 0}$ is a $\mathcal{KL}$-function if for each fixed $t \in \mathbb{R}_{\geqslant 0}$ the function $\beta(\cdot, t)$ is a $\mathcal{K}$-function and for each fixed $s \in \mathbb{R}_{\geqslant 0}$, $\beta(s,t)$ is decreasing in t and $\beta(s,t) \to 0$ as $t \to \infty$. For vectors $x_i \in \mathbb{R}^{n_i}$, $i \in \{1, 2, \dots, N\}$, we denote by $(x_1, x_2, \cdots, x_N)$ the vector $[x_1^\top x_2^\top \cdots x_N^\top]^\top \in \mathbb{R}^n$ with $n = \sum_{i=1}^N n_i$. For brevity, we sometimes write symmetric matrices of the form $\left[\begin{smallmatrix} A & B \\ B^\top & C \end{smallmatrix}\right]$ as $\left[\begin{smallmatrix} A & B \\ \star & C \end{smallmatrix}\right]$ or $\left[\begin{smallmatrix} A & \star \\ B^\top & C \end{smallmatrix}\right]$. For a left-continuous signal $f : \mathbb{R}_{\geqslant 0} \to \mathbb{R}^n$ and $t \in \mathbb{R}_{\geqslant 0}$, we use $f(t^+)$ to denote the limit $f(t^+) = \lim_{s \to t, s > t} f(s)$.

2. CONTROL SETUP

In this paper, we consider the event-triggered control setup as shown in Figure 1, in which the plant $\mathcal{P}$ is given by

$$\mathcal{P} : \begin{cases} \frac{\mathrm{d}}{\mathrm{d}t} x_p(t) = A_p x_p(t) + B_p u(t) + B_{pw} w(t) \\ y(t) = C_y x_p(t) + D_y u(t) \\ z(t) = C_z x_p(t) + D_z u(t) + D_{zw} w(t) \end{cases} \tag{1}$$

and the controller $\mathcal{C}$ is given by

$$\mathcal{C} : \begin{cases} \frac{\mathrm{d}}{\mathrm{d}t} x_c(t) = A_c x_c(t) + B_c \hat{y}(t) \\ u(t) = C_u x_c(t) + D_u \hat{y}(t). \end{cases} \tag{2}$$

Here, $x_p(t) \in \mathbb{R}^{n_{x_p}}$ denotes the state of the plant $\mathcal{P}$, $y(t) \in \mathbb{R}^{n_y}$ its measured output, $z(t) \in \mathbb{R}^{n_z}$ the performance output, and $w(t) \in \mathbb{R}^{n_w}$ a disturbance at time $t \in \mathbb{R}_{\geqslant 0}$. Furthermore, $x_c(t) \in \mathbb{R}^{n_{x_c}}$ denotes the state of the controller $\mathcal{C}$, $u(t) \in \mathbb{R}^{n_u}$ is the control input at time $t \in \mathbb{R}_{\geqslant 0}$, and $\hat{y}(t) \in \mathbb{R}^{n_y}$ denotes the output that is available at the controller, given by

$$\hat{y}(t) = y(t_k), \quad t \in (t_k, t_{k+1}], \tag{3}$$

where the sequence $\{t_k\}_{k \in \mathbb{N}}$ denotes the event (or transmission) times which are generated by the event-generator specified below.

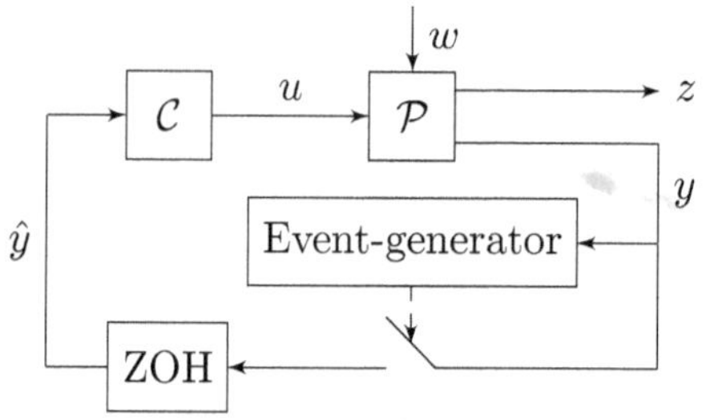

Figure 1: Event-triggered control setup.

In this work, the plant's output y is sampled periodically at fixed sample times $s_n = nh$, $n \in \mathbb{N}$, where $h \in \mathbb{R}_{>0}$ is the sample period. At each sample time s_n, $n \in \mathbb{N}$, the event-generator decides whether or not the measured output $y(s_n)$ should be transmitted to the controller. Hence, the sequence of event times $\{t_k\}_{k \in \mathbb{N}}$ is a subsequence of the sequence of sample times $\{s_n\}_{n \in \mathbb{N}}$.

Define the state $\xi := (x_p, x_c, \hat{y}) \in \mathbb{R}^{n_\xi}$, with $n_\xi = n_{x_p} + n_{x_c} + n_y$, and introduce a timer variable $\tau \in [0, h]$, which keeps track of the time that has elapsed since the latest sample time, and a dynamic variable $\eta \in \mathbb{R}$, which will be included in the event-generator. Lastly, define the matrix $Y \in \mathbb{R}^{2n_y \times n_\xi}$ as

$$Y := \begin{bmatrix} C_y & D_y C_u & D_y D_u \\ O & O & I \end{bmatrix} \tag{4}$$

such that $\zeta := (y, \hat{y}) = Y\xi$, and the signal $\hat{o} : \mathbb{R}_{\geqslant 0} \to \mathbb{R}^{2n_y} \times [0, h] \times \mathbb{R}$ as

$$\hat{o}(t) := (\zeta(s_n), \tau(t), \eta(t)), \quad t \in (s_n, s_{n+1}], \; n \in \mathbb{N}, \tag{5}$$

which is the information that is available to the event-generator at time $t \in \mathbb{R}_{\geqslant 0}$.

The dynamic variable η will evolve according to

$$\frac{\mathrm{d}}{\mathrm{d}t}\eta(t) = \Psi(\hat{o}(t)), \qquad t \in (s_n, s_{n+1}), \; n \in \mathbb{N}, \tag{6a}$$

$$\eta(t^+) = \eta_T(\hat{o}(t)), \qquad t \in \{t_k\}_{k \in \mathbb{N}}, \tag{6b}$$

$$\eta(t^+) = \eta_N(\hat{o}(t)), \qquad t \in \{s_n\}_{n \in \mathbb{N}} \setminus \{t_k\}_{k \in \mathbb{N}}, \tag{6c}$$

where the functions $\Psi : \mathbb{R}^{2n_y} \times [0, h] \times \mathbb{R} \to \mathbb{R}$, $\eta_T : \mathbb{R}^{2n_y} \times [0, h] \times \mathbb{R} \to \mathbb{R}$ and $\eta_N : \mathbb{R}^{2n_y} \times [0, h] \times \mathbb{R} \to \mathbb{R}$ are to be designed. Note that at transmission times t_k, $k \in \mathbb{N}$, the variable η is updated differently than at the other sample times $s_n \neq t_k$, $n, k \in \mathbb{N}$, at which no transmission occurs.

Now, we can write the hybrid closed-loop system as

$$\frac{\mathrm{d}}{\mathrm{d}t}\begin{bmatrix}\xi(t)\\ \tau(t)\\ \eta(t)\end{bmatrix}=\begin{bmatrix}A\xi(t)+Bw(t)\\ 1\\ \Psi(\hat{o}(t))\end{bmatrix},\quad \begin{matrix}t\in(s_n,s_{n+1}),\\ n\in\mathbb{N},\end{matrix} \tag{7a}$$

$$\begin{bmatrix}\xi(t^+)\\ \tau(t^+)\\ \eta(t^+)\end{bmatrix}=\begin{bmatrix}J\xi(t)\\ 0\\ \eta_T(\hat{o}(t))\end{bmatrix},\quad t\in\{t_k\}_{k\in\mathbb{N}} \tag{7b}$$

$$\begin{bmatrix}\xi(t^+)\\ \tau(t^+)\\ \eta(t^+)\end{bmatrix}=\begin{bmatrix}\xi(t)\\ 0\\ \eta_N(\hat{o}(t))\end{bmatrix},\quad \begin{matrix}t\in\\ \{s_n\}_{n\in\mathbb{N}}\setminus\{t_k\}_{k\in\mathbb{N}}\end{matrix} \tag{7c}$$

$$z(t)=C\xi(t)+Dw(t), \tag{7d}$$

where

$$A=\begin{bmatrix}A_p & B_pC_u & B_pD_u\\ O & A_c & B_c\\ O & O & O\end{bmatrix},\ B=\begin{bmatrix}B_{pw}\\ O\\ O\end{bmatrix},$$

$$C=\begin{bmatrix}C_z & D_zC_u & D_zD_u\end{bmatrix},\ D=D_{zw},\text{ and}$$

$$J=\begin{bmatrix}I & O & O\\ O & I & O\\ C_y & D_yC_u & D_yD_u\end{bmatrix}.$$

At sample times $s_n=nh$, $n\in\mathbb{N}$, the reset (7b) occurs when an event is triggered by the event-generator, otherwise the state (ξ,τ,η) jumps according to (7c). In between sample times, the system evolves according to the differential equation (7a), where $\big(\xi(s_n^+),\tau(s_n^+),\eta(s_n^+)\big)$ given by (7b) or (7c) denotes the starting point for the solution to (7a) in the interval $(s_n,s_{n+1}]$, $n\in\mathbb{N}$. Hence, the solutions we consider are left-continuous signals.

In this work, the sequence of event/transmission times $\{t_k\}_{k\in\mathbb{N}}$ is generated by *dynamic* periodic event-generators of the form

$$t_0=0,\ t_{k+1}=\min\{t>t_k\mid \eta_N(\hat{o}(t))\leqslant 0\wedge\zeta^\top(t)Q\zeta(t)\geqslant 0,\ t=nh,\ n\in\mathbb{N}\}, \tag{8}$$

where the scalar $h\in\mathbb{R}_{>0}$ and the matrix $Q\in\mathbb{R}^{2n_y\times 2n_y}$ are design parameters, in addition to the functions Ψ, η_T, and η_N. Note that the function η_N appears both in the update dynamics (6c), as well as in the triggering condition in (8).

With the model (6), (8), we can also capture *static* periodic event-generators by choosing $\eta(0)=0$ and

$$\Psi(\hat{o})=0 \tag{9a}$$
$$\eta_T(\hat{o})=0 \tag{9b}$$
$$\eta_N(\hat{o})=0 \tag{9c}$$

for all $\hat{o}\in\mathbb{R}^{2n_y}\times\mathbb{R}_{\geqslant 0}\times\mathbb{R}_{\geqslant 0}$, as then we have that $\eta(t)=0$ for all $t\in\mathbb{R}_{\geqslant 0}$, and the dynamic periodic event-generator (8) reduces to static periodic event-generators as in [12], given by

$$t_0=0,\ t_{k+1}=\min\{t>t_k\mid \zeta^\top(t)Q\zeta(t)\geqslant 0,\ t=nh,\ n\in\mathbb{N}\}, \tag{10}$$

which only has h and Q as design parameters. A possible choice for Q is given by

$$Q=\begin{bmatrix}(1-\sigma^2)I & -I\\ -I & I\end{bmatrix} \tag{11}$$

with $\sigma\in(0,1)$, such that (10) reduces to

$$t_0=0,\ t_{k+1}=\min\{t>t_k\mid |\hat{y}(t)-y(t)|^2\geqslant\sigma^2|y(t)|^2,\ t=nh,\ n\in\mathbb{N}\},$$

which can be seen as the digital version of static continuous event-generators [23] of the type

$$t_0=0,\ t_{k+1}=\inf\{t\geqslant t_k\mid |\hat{y}(t)-y(t)|^2\geqslant\sigma^2|y(t)|^2,\ t\in\mathbb{R}_{\geqslant 0}\}.$$

Other control setups and other choices of Q are also possible, see e.g., [12].

We will consider the following two notions of stability.

DEFINITION 2.1. *The PETC system (7)-(8) is said to be globally exponentially stable (GES), if there exist a function $\beta\in\mathcal{KL}$ and scalars $c>0$ and $\rho>0$ such that for any initial condition $\xi(0)=\xi_0\in\mathbb{R}^{n_\xi}$, $\tau(0)=0$, $\eta(0)=0$, all corresponding solutions to (7)-(8) with $w=0$ satisfy $|\xi(t)|\leqslant ce^{-\rho t}|\xi_0|$ and $|\eta(t)|\leqslant\beta(|\xi_0|,t)$ for all $t\in\mathbb{R}_{\geqslant 0}$. In this case, we call ρ a (lower bound on the) decay rate.*

Note that we only require exponential decay of the state variable ξ, as we are mainly interested in the control performance regarding the plant and controller states, which are captured in ξ. In addition, we require that η stays bounded by a $\mathcal{KL}$-function for practical implementability. We do not put any constraint on the variable τ as it is only used for modelling purposes.

DEFINITION 2.2. *The PETC system (7)-(8) is said to have an $\mathcal{L}_2$-gain from w to z smaller than or equal to θ, if there exists a function $\delta\in\mathcal{K}_\infty$ such that for any initial condition $\xi(0)=\xi_0\in\mathbb{R}^{n_\xi}$, $\tau(0)=0$, $\eta(0)=0$, all corresponding solutions to (7)-(8) with $w\in\mathcal{L}_2$ satisfy $\|z\|_{\mathcal{L}_2}\leqslant\delta(|\xi_0|)+\theta\|w\|_{\mathcal{L}_2}$.*

In the next section, we will present the stability analysis of the static PETC system (7) with (9) and (10), which leads to designs for h and Q. Building upon the design and stability analysis of the static PETC system, we then present our design for the functions Ψ, η_T, and η_N in the dynamic event-generator in Section 4.

3. STATIC PETC

To analyze the stability and $\mathcal{L}_2$-gain of the static PETC system (7) with (9) and (10), we will use the Lyapunov/storage function U given by

$$U(\xi,\tau,\eta)=V(\xi,\tau)+\eta, \tag{12}$$

with V given by

$$V(\xi,\tau)=\xi^\top P(\tau)\xi,\quad \tau\in[0,h], \tag{13}$$

where $P:[0,h]\to\mathbb{R}^{n_\xi\times n_\xi}$ is a continuously differentiable function with $P(\tau)\succ 0$ for $\tau\in[0,h]$. The function P will be chosen such that (12) becomes a storage function [22,25] for the PETC system (7), (10) with the supply rate $\theta^{-2}z^\top z-w^\top w$ and decay rate 2ρ.

In order to do so, we select the function $P : [0,h] \to \mathbb{R}^{n_\xi \times n_\xi}$ to satisfy the Riccati differential equation (where we omitted τ for compactness of notation)

$$\begin{aligned} \tfrac{\mathrm{d}}{\mathrm{d}\tau} P = & -A^\top P - PA - 2\rho P - \theta^{-2} C^\top C \\ & - (PB + \theta^{-2} C^\top D) M (B^\top P + \theta^{-2} D^\top C), \end{aligned} \quad (14)$$

provided the solution exists on $[0,h]$ for the desired values of $\rho > 0$ and θ. Here, $M := (I - \theta^{-2} D^\top D)^{-1}$ is assumed to exist and to be positive definite, which means that $\theta^2 > \lambda_{max}(D^\top D)$.

In order to find the explicit expression for P, we introduce the Hamiltonian matrix

$$H := \begin{bmatrix} A + \rho I + \theta^{-2} BMD^\top C & BMB^\top \\ -C^\top LC & -\left(A + \rho I + \theta^{-2} BMD^\top C\right)^\top \end{bmatrix}$$

in which $L := (\theta^2 I - DD^\top)^{-1}$, and we define the matrix exponential

$$F(\tau) := e^{-H\tau} = \begin{bmatrix} F_{11}(\tau) & F_{12}(\tau) \\ F_{21}(\tau) & F_{22}(\tau) \end{bmatrix}. \quad (15)$$

ASSUMPTION 3.1. *$F_{11}(\tau)$ is invertible for all $\tau \in [0,h]$.*

Assumption 3.1 can always be satisfied by choosing h sufficiently small, as $F_{11}(0) = I$ and F_{11} is a continuous function. The function $P : [0,h] \to \mathbb{R}^{n_\xi \times n_\xi}$ is now explicitly defined for $\tau \in [0,h]$ by

$$\begin{aligned} P(\tau) = & (F_{21}(h-\tau) + F_{22}(h-\tau)P(h)) \\ & (F_{11}(h-\tau) + F_{12}(h-\tau)P(h))^{-1}, \end{aligned} \quad (16)$$

see [1,12] for further details.

Before stating the next theorem (which is a slight variation of [12, Theorem III.2]), let us introduce the notation $P_0 := P(0)$, $P_h := P(h)$, $\bar{F}_{11} := F_{11}(h)$, $\bar{F}_{12} := F_{12}(h)$, $\bar{F}_{21} := F_{21}(h)$, and $\bar{F}_{22} := F_{22}(h)$, the matrix

$$\bar{G} := \bar{F}_{11}^{-\top} P_h \bar{F}_{11}^{-1} + \bar{F}_{21} \bar{F}_{11}^{-1}, \quad (17)$$

and a matrix $\bar{S}$ that satisfies $\bar{S}\bar{S}^\top := -\bar{F}_{11}^{-1}\bar{F}_{12}$. A matrix $\bar{S}$ exists under Assumption 3.1, because this assumption will guarantee that the matrix $-\bar{F}_{11}^{-1}\bar{F}_{12}$ is positive semi-definite.

THEOREM 3.2. *If there exist matrices $N_T, N_N \in \mathbb{R}^{2n_y \times 2n_y}$ with $N_T, N_N \succeq 0$ and $P_h \in \mathbb{R}^{n_\xi \times n_\xi}$ with $P_h \succ 0$, and scalars $\beta, \mu, \theta, \rho \in \mathbb{R}_{\geqslant 0}$, such that*

$$\begin{bmatrix} P_h - Y^\top (N_T + \mu Q) Y - J^\top \bar{G} J & J^\top \bar{F}_{11}^{-\top} P_h \bar{S} \\ \star & I - \bar{S}^\top P_h \bar{S} \end{bmatrix} \succ 0, \quad (18)$$

$$\begin{bmatrix} P_h - Y^\top (N_N - \beta Q) Y - \bar{G} & \bar{F}_{11}^{-\top} P_h \bar{S} \\ \star & I - \bar{S}^\top P_h \bar{S} \end{bmatrix} \succ 0, \quad (19)$$

and Assumption 3.1 hold, then the static PETC system (7) with (9) and (10) is GES with decay rate ρ, and has an $\mathcal{L}_2$-gain from w to z smaller than or equal to θ.

The proof of Theorem 3.2 is given in [12] for the system (7) with (9) and (10) with η absent. However, as here we have added the variable η to the closed loop, and our results in Section 4 build upon the proof of Theorem 3.2, we provide a sketch of the proof below.

PROOF. The proof is based on the storage function U given by (12) with V as defined in (13). However, we only need to consider the function V, as it holds that $\eta(t) = 0$ for all $t \in \mathbb{R}_{\geqslant 0}$ and thus in this case $U = V$.

The proof consists of showing that the function V is a proper function and satisfies for all $\xi \in \mathbb{R}^{n_\xi}$ and all $\tau \in [0,h]$,

$$c_1 |\xi|^2 \leqslant V(\xi,\tau) \leqslant c_2 |\xi|^2 \quad (20)$$

with $c_2 \geqslant c_1 > 0$, has a supply rate $\theta^{-2} z^\top z - w^\top w$ [22,25] and decay rate 2ρ during flow (7a), and is nonincreasing along jumps (7b) and (7c).

The first property follows from Assumption 3.1, as this assumption guarantees that $P(\tau) \succ 0$ for all $\tau \in [0,h]$, see [1, 12]. Hence, (20) holds with

$$c_1 = \min_{\tau \in [0,h]} \lambda_{min}(P(\tau)), \text{ and} \quad (21a)$$

$$c_2 = \max_{\tau \in [0,h]} \lambda_{max}(P(\tau)), \quad (21b)$$

where $c_2 \geqslant c_1 > 0$.

For brevity, we will use the notation $V(t) = V(\xi(t), \tau(t))$ in the remainder.

The second property follows directly from (14) and (7a) as these differential equations guarantee that

$$\tfrac{\mathrm{d}}{\mathrm{d}t} V(t) \leqslant -2\rho V(t) - \theta^{-2} z(t)^\top z(t) + w(t)^\top w(t) \quad (22)$$

during flow (7a) when $\tau \in [0,h]$, (see [12]).

Finally, we show that V does not increase along jumps. In [12], it is shown that

$$\begin{aligned} P_0 = & \bar{F}_{21}\bar{F}_{11}^{-1} + \\ & \bar{F}_{11}^{-\top} \left(P_h + P_h \bar{S} \left(I - \bar{S}^\top P_h \bar{S} \right)^{-1} \bar{S}^\top P_h \right) \bar{F}_{11}^{-1}. \end{aligned} \quad (23)$$

By applying a Schur complement it follows from (18) that along jumps (7b) (when $\tau = h$ and $\zeta^\top Q \zeta \geqslant 0$) we have

$$\begin{aligned} V(t^+) &= \xi(t)^\top J^\top P_0 J \xi(t) \\ &\leqslant \xi(t)^\top P_h \xi(t) - \zeta(t)^\top (N_T + \mu Q) \zeta(t) \quad (24a) \\ &\leqslant \xi(t)^\top P_h \xi(t) = V(t), \quad (24b) \end{aligned}$$

and it follows from (19) that along jumps (7c) (when $\tau = h$ and $\zeta^\top Q \zeta \leqslant 0$) we have

$$\begin{aligned} V(t^+) &= \xi(t)^\top P_0 \xi(t) \\ &\leqslant \xi(t)^\top P_h \xi(t) - \zeta(t)^\top (N_N - \beta Q) \zeta(t) \quad (25a) \\ &\leqslant \xi(t)^\top P_h \xi(t) = V(t). \quad (25b) \end{aligned}$$

Combining (20), (22), (25b), and (24b) indeed establishes the upper bound θ on the $\mathcal{L}_2$-gain of the PETC system (7) with (9) and (10) [12]. Furthermore, when $w = 0$, it follows that for all $t \in \mathbb{R}_{\geqslant 0}$

$$|\xi(t)| \leqslant c e^{-\rho t} |\xi(0)| \quad (26)$$

with $c = \sqrt{c_1/c_2}$, which proves that the system is GES with decay rate ρ. □

Note that the conditions of Theorem 3.2 depend nonlinearly on the design variables h and Q, and the control performance measures ρ and θ. However, by fixing the variables h, Q, ρ, and θ, inequalities (18) and (19) become LMIs, in which case the parameters P_h, P_0, N_T, N_N, μ, and β can be synthesized numerically via semi-definite programming (e.g., using Yalmip/SeDuMi[17] in MATLAB).

The $\mathcal{L}_2$-gain estimate θ can be optimized via bisection when h, Q, and ρ are fixed. Although the optimization is non-convex and we should expect to find local optima, good results can be found with proper initial estimates. The same holds for the decay rate ρ (when h, Q, and θ are fixed) and the sample period h (when Q, ρ and θ are fixed). Finally, when Q is given by (11), the design freedom in Q is reduced to the scalar σ, which can also be optimized via bisection when h, ρ, and θ are fixed.

In [13] it is shown that stability and contractivity (in the sense that the $\mathcal{L}_2$-gain is smaller than 1) of the hybrid system (7) with (9) and (10) is equivalent to stability and contractivity (in the sense that the l_2-gain is smaller than 1) of a specific discrete-time piecewise-linear system. Hence, the $\mathcal{L}_2$-gain of the hybrid system (7) with (9) and (10) can be determined by studying the l_2-gain of a discrete-time piecewise linear system, for which less conservative methods are available using piecewise quadratic Lyapunov/storage functions and S-procedure relaxations, see [13, Theorem V.1]. Moreover, in [13, Section IV] it is shown that the LMI conditions in Theorem 3.2 (or [12, Theorem III.2]) with $\rho = 0$ and $\theta = 1$ can be interpreted as l_2-gain conditions on the discrete-time piecewise linear system using a common quadratic Lyapunov/storage function. Here we take a different approach and do not reduce the conservatism in our $\mathcal{L}_2$-gain estimate as in, e.g., [13]. Instead, in the next section we will exploit this conservatism in our analysis in order to *extend* the transmission intervals, and, correspondingly, further reduce the amount of communication in the system, while preserving the same $\mathcal{L}_2$-gain guarantee. Details will be given in the next section on this new approach.

REMARK 3.3. *When Q is given by (11) with $\sigma = 0$, the static PETC system (7) with (9) and (10) reduces to a sampled-data system. Moreover, the related discrete-time piecewise linear system in this case reduces to a discrete-time LTI system, for which the l_2-gain conditions using a common quadratic Lyapunov/storage function are non-conservative (see [9, Lemma 5.1]). Hence, for sampled-data systems, Theorem 3.2, [12, Theorem III.2], and [13, Theorem V.1] are equivalent and can all be used to determine exact (i.e., non-conservative) $\mathcal{L}_2$-gains.*

4. DYNAMIC PETC

In this section we present our design for the dynamics (6) of the variable η, which is included in the dynamic event-generator (8). The idea is as follows. In Section 3, the function V (and, hence, also the Lyapunov/storage function U) is often strictly decreasing along jumps (7b) and (7c). However, to guarantee GES and $\mathcal{L}_2$-stability, it is sufficient if U is nonincreasing along jumps [11]. To get less conservative results, we will store this 'unnecessary' decrease of V as much as possible in the dynamic variable η, which acts as a buffer. When a transmission is necessary according to the static event-generator, we might choose not to transmit at this sample time. As the state then jumps according to (7c), we can no longer guarantee that V does not increase along this jump. However, an increase of V can be compensated by reducing η, and hence we can defer the transmission until the buffer η is no longer large enough. The transmission only needs to occur if the buffer η would become negative otherwise. As a result, the stability analysis becomes less conservative, and the same $\mathcal{L}_2$-gain and decay rate can be guaranteed with typically fewer transmissions. In this way, our design leads to a dynamic PETC system (7), (8) with the same $\mathcal{L}_2$-gain θ and decay rate ρ as the static PETC system (7), (10), but with a significant reduction in the number of transmissions, as we will see in Section 5.

First, we choose the flow dynamics (6a) of η as

$$\Psi(\hat{o}) = -2\rho\eta, \text{ for } \tau \in (0, h]. \tag{27}$$

REMARK 4.1. *As Ψ is given by (27), it follows that $\eta(s_{n+1}) = e^{-2\rho h}\eta(s_n^+)$. Thus, since the event-generator only needs to know the value of η at sample times s_n, $n \in \mathbb{N}$, the variable η does not need to continuously evolve according to (27) in the event-generator. Instead we can use the discrete-time dynamics just described.*

For the functions η_T and η_N, we provide the following two designs.

1) State-based dynamic PETC:

$$\eta_T(\hat{o}) = \eta + \xi^\top (P_h - J^\top P_0 J)\xi, \tag{28a}$$

$$\eta_N(\hat{o}) = \eta + \xi^\top (P_h - P_0)\xi. \tag{28b}$$

2) Output-based dynamic PETC:

$$\eta_T(\hat{o}) = \eta + \zeta^\top (N_T + \mu Q)\zeta, \tag{29a}$$

$$\eta_N(\hat{o}) = \eta + \zeta^\top (N_N - \beta Q)\zeta. \tag{29b}$$

Here, the scalars ρ, μ, and β, and the matrices N_T, N_N, P_0, and P_h follow from the stability analysis of the static PETC system in Theorem 3.2.

The first design requires that the full state $\xi(s_n)$ is known to the event-generator at sample time s_n, $n \in \mathbb{N}$. This is the case when $y = (x_p, x_c)$ (e.g., when $\mathcal{C}$ is a static state-feedback controller in which case $y = x_p$ and $n_{x_c} = 0$), as then $\zeta = \xi$. When $y = x_p$ and $n_{x_c} \neq 0$, a copy of the controller could be included in the event-generator in order to track the controller state x_c.

The second design is more conservative, but can also be used in case the event-generator does not have access to the complete vector (x_p, x_c), in which case $\zeta \neq \xi$. Hence, this choice can be used for output-based dynamic PETC.

THEOREM 4.2. *If the conditions of Theorem 3.2 hold, then the dynamic PETC system (7) with (8), (27), and (28) or (29) is GES with decay rate ρ, and has an $\mathcal{L}_2$-gain from w to z smaller than or equal to θ.*

PROOF. Consider again the Lyapunov/storage function U given by (12) with V as defined in (13).

First, we show that U is a proper storage function, by showing that $\eta(t) \geqslant 0$ for all $t \in \mathbb{R}_{\geqslant 0}$, and that U satisfies for all $\xi \in \mathbb{R}^{n_\xi}$, $\tau \in [0, h]$, and all $\eta \in \mathbb{R}_{\geqslant 0}$,

$$c_1|\xi|^2 + |\eta| \leqslant U(\xi, \tau, \eta) \leqslant c_2|\xi|^2 + |\eta|, \tag{30}$$

where c_1 and c_2 are given by (21). As $\eta(0) = 0$, it follows from (27) that $\eta(t) \geqslant 0$ for all $t \in [0, h]$, and hence, that $\eta(s_1) \geqslant 0$. Next, given event-generator (8), a transmission (7b) occurs in case $\zeta(s_1)^\top Q\zeta(s_1) \geqslant 0$ and $\eta_N(\hat{o}(s_1)) \leqslant 0$. In this case, $\eta_T(\hat{o}(s_1)) \geqslant 0$ follows from (24b) when η_T is given by (28a), or from $N_T \succeq 0$ and $\mu \geqslant 0$ when η_T is given by (29a). Otherwise, if $\zeta(s_1)^\top Q\zeta(s_1) \leqslant 0$ or $\eta_N(\hat{o}(s_1)) \geqslant 0$, no transmission occurs, and the state jumps according to (7c). Observe however that when $\zeta(s_1)^\top Q\zeta(s_1) \leqslant 0$ it holds that $\eta_N(\hat{o}(s_1)) \geqslant 0$, which follows from (25b) when η_N is given by (28b), or from $N_N \succeq 0$ and $\beta \geqslant 0$ when η_N is given by (29b). Hence, in all cases it holds that $\eta(s_1^+) \geqslant 0$. It follows by induction that $\eta(t) \geqslant 0$ for all $t \in \mathbb{R}_{\geqslant 0}$. Property (30) then follows by combining (20) and (12).

It remains to show that U has a supply rate $\theta^{-2}z^\top z - w^\top w$ and decay rate 2ρ during flow (7a), and is nonincreasing along jumps (7b) and (7c). For brevity, we will use the notation $V(t) = V(\xi(t), \tau(t))$ and $U(t) = U(\xi(t), \tau(t), \eta(t))$ in the remainder.

From (14) and (27) it follows (using (22)) that

$$\begin{aligned}\tfrac{\mathrm{d}}{\mathrm{d}t}U(t) &\leqslant -2\rho V(t) - 2\rho\eta(t) - \theta^{-2}z(t)^\top z(t) + w(t)^\top w(t) \\ &= -2\rho U(t) - \theta^{-2}z(t)^\top z(t) + w(t)^\top w(t) \qquad (31)\end{aligned}$$

during flow (7a).

Finally, we show that

$$U(t^+) \leqslant U(t) \qquad (32)$$

holds along jumps. When using (28), we find along transmissions (7b) that

$$\begin{aligned}U(t^+) &= \xi^\top J^\top P_0 J\xi + \eta + \xi^\top (P_h - J^\top P_0 J)\xi \\ &= \xi^\top P_h \xi + \eta = U(t)\end{aligned}$$

and along non-transmission jumps (7c) that

$$\begin{aligned}U(t^+) &= \xi^\top P_0 \xi + \eta + \xi^\top (P_h - P_0)\xi \\ &= \xi^\top P_h \xi + \eta = U(t).\end{aligned}$$

Hence, (32) holds with equality. Alternatively, when using (29), we find (using (24a)) that along transmissions (7b) it holds that

$$\begin{aligned}U(t^+) &= \xi^\top J^\top P_0 J\xi + \eta + \zeta^\top (N_T + \mu Q)\zeta \\ &\leqslant \xi^\top P_h \xi + \zeta^\top (N_T + \mu Q - N_T - \mu Q)\zeta + \eta \\ &= U(t)\end{aligned}$$

and along non-transmission jumps (7c) (using (25a)) that

$$\begin{aligned}U(t^+) &= \xi^\top P_0 \xi + \eta + \zeta^\top (N_N - \beta Q)\zeta \\ &\leqslant \xi^\top P_h \xi + \zeta^\top (N_N - \beta Q - N_N + \beta Q)\zeta + \eta \\ &= U(t).\end{aligned}$$

Equations (30), (31), and (32) together prove that the system has an $\mathcal{L}_2$-gain from w to z smaller than or equal to θ [22, 25]. Furthermore, in case $w = 0$, we obtain

$$U(t) \leqslant e^{-2\rho t} U(0) \qquad (33)$$

$$c_1 |\xi(t)|^2 + \eta(t) \leqslant e^{-2\rho t}(c_2 |\xi(0)|^2 + \eta(0)), \qquad (34)$$

and, since $\eta(0) = 0$ and $\eta(t) \geqslant 0$ for all $t \in \mathbb{R}_{\geqslant 0}$, we find

$$|\xi(t)| \leqslant c e^{-\rho t} |\xi(0)|, \text{ and} \qquad (35)$$

$$|\eta(t)| \leqslant c_2 e^{-2\rho t} |\xi(0)|^2 \qquad (36)$$

with $c = \sqrt{c_1/c_2}$, which proves that the system is GES with decay rate ρ. □

While the static periodic event-generator only has design parameters h and Q, the state-based dynamic event-generator has design parameters h, Q, ρ, P_0, and P_h, and the output-based dynamic event-generator has design parameters h, Q, ρ, N_T, N_N, μ, and β. However, as already mentioned in Section 3, for fixed h, Q, ρ, and θ, inequalities (18) and (19) are LMIs, in which case the parameters P_h, P_0, N_T, N_N, μ, and β can be synthesized (and optimized) numerically via semi-definite programming (e.g., using Yalmip/SeDuMi in MATLAB). Hence, the design of these extra parameters follows directly and naturally from the design and stability analysis of the static event-generator. Of course, manual tuning of one or more of these parameters is also possible, but can be difficult given the large design space.

5. NUMERICAL EXAMPLE

In this section, we consider the example from [23], with open-loop unstable plant $\mathcal{P}$ given by (1) with $n_{x_p} = n_y = 2$ and

$$A_p = \begin{bmatrix} 0 & 1 \\ -2 & 3 \end{bmatrix}, \quad B_p = \begin{bmatrix} 0 \\ 1 \end{bmatrix}, \quad B_{pw} = \begin{bmatrix} 1 \\ 0 \end{bmatrix},$$

$$C_y = C_z = I, \quad D_y = D_z = D_{zw} = O,$$

and controller $\mathcal{C}$ given by (2) with $n_{x_c} = 0$ and

$$D_u = \begin{bmatrix} 1 & -4 \end{bmatrix}.$$

Note that this is a static state-feedback controller, and thus both (28) and (29) can be used.

5.1 Results for Theorems 3.2 and 4.2

In Figure 2(a) we show the guaranteed $\mathcal{L}_2$-gain θ as a function of the timer threshold h based on Theorem 3.2, where we used $\rho = 0$ and Q as in (11) with $\sigma = 0.2$. This $\mathcal{L}_2$-gain holds for the static event-generator (10) with (9), as well as for the state-based dynamic event-generator (8) with (27) and (28), and the output-based dynamic event-generator (8) with (27) and (29). For each h, the $\mathcal{L}_2$-gain θ is minimized via a bisection algorithm, and the matrices N_T, N_N, P_h and P_0 and scalars μ and β are found numerically by solving the LMIs (18) and (19). Additionally, for the three different event-generators, Figure 2(a) shows the actual ratios $\|z\|_{\mathcal{L}_2}/\|w\|_{\mathcal{L}_2}$ for the disturbance w given by

$$w(t) = e^{-0.2t}\sin(t/4), \quad t \in \mathbb{R}_{\geqslant 0}, \qquad (37)$$

which have been obtained by simulating the PETC systems for 120 time units with $\xi(0) = (0, 0, 0, 0)$ and disturbance w given by (37). Figure 2(b) shows the average inter-event times τ_{avg} = (total number of events)/(simulation time) for the static and dynamic event-generators, which have been obtained by the same simulations.

Note that the conservatism in the $\mathcal{L}_2$-gain analysis of Theorem 3.2 is purely caused by the fact that the jump map given by (7b) and (7c) is piecewise linear, see also Remark 3.3. Hence, when h decreases, also the conservatism in the $\mathcal{L}_2$-gain analysis increases (as also the number of jumps increases). This explains why the guaranteed $\mathcal{L}_2$-gain θ increases when h becomes small.

The dynamic event-generators exploit (part of) the conservatism in the $\mathcal{L}_2$-gain analysis of Theorem 3.2 by storing as much as possible of the unnecessary decrease of V in the buffer η. Transmissions are then postponed (compared to when using the static event-generator) by generating events only when this buffer would become empty (or negative) otherwise. This leads to significantly larger τ_{avg}, see Figure 2(b), while the control performance guarantees

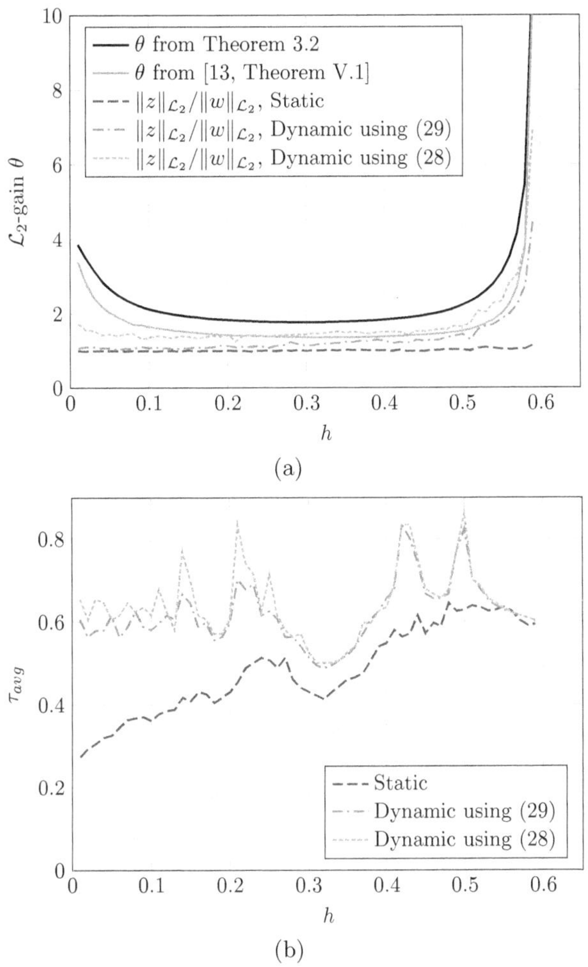

Figure 2: Guaranteed $\mathcal{L}_2$-gains θ (solid lines) and actual ratios $\|z\|_{\mathcal{L}_2}/\|w\|_{\mathcal{L}_2}$ (dashed lines) for varying h (a) and average inter-event times τ_{avg} for varying h (b).

are not affected (although the actual ratios $\|z\|_{\mathcal{L}_2}/\|w\|_{\mathcal{L}_2}$ do increase, see Figure 2(a)).

5.2 Comparison to [13]

As already mentioned, for the static PETC system (7) with (9) and (10), a tighter upper bound θ on the $\mathcal{L}_2$-gain can be calculated using [13, Theorem V.1]. Our new dynamic PETC systems cannot be captured in the framework of [13] because of the quadratic terms in (28a), (28b), (29a), and (29b). Hence, we can only compare our new results for dynamic PETC systems in Theorem 4.2 to [13, Theorem V.1] for static PETC systems. In order to do so, the $\mathcal{L}_2$-gain estimate using [13, Theorem V.1] is also shown in Figure 2(a) (where we partitioned the state-space into two regions using $X_1 = Y^\top QY$ and $X_2 = -Y^\top QY$, see [13] for more details).

In Figure 2(a) we can see that when an $\mathcal{L}_2$-gain $\theta = 2.2$ is acceptable, we can select $h = 0.56$ when using the static event-generator (based on [13, Theorem V.1]), or $h = 0.50$ when using either of the dynamic event-generators (based on Theorem 3.2 / 4.2). In Figure 2(b) we can then see that for the disturbance w given by (37), the average inter-event time τ_{avg} for both dynamic event-generators with $h = 0.50$ is much higher than τ_{avg} of the static event-generator with $h = 0.56$. Hence, for identical control performance guarantees, we can find a higher guaranteed minimum inter-event time h when using static PETC, but higher average inter-event times τ_{avg} might be obtained by using dynamic PETC (although no guarantees can be given as τ_{avg} depends on the disturbance w). As a result, there is no clear answer to whether static or dynamic PETC is better, and which PETC variant one should use depends on the constraints and requirements of the control problem at hand (e.g., whether a higher h or higher τ_{avg} is preferred).

6. CONCLUSIONS AND FUTURE WORK

We proposed two (state-based and output-based) dynamic periodic event-generators for linear systems. Our designs lead to closed-loop hybrid systems which are globally exponentially stable with a guaranteed decay rate and $\mathcal{L}_2$-stable with a guaranteed $\mathcal{L}_2$-gain. Moreover, for identical control performance guarantees, our new dynamic periodic event-generators typically generate fewer events than the corresponding static periodic event-generator. Finally, our new dynamic event-generators are the first in literature that only require periodic sampling of the state or output of the system, making our new designs much easier to implement on digital platforms than other dynamic event-generators that require continuous measuring of the system.

Future work includes the addition of (variable) communication delays and experimental validation.

7. ACKNOWLEDGEMENTS

This work is supported by the Innovational Research Incentives Scheme under the VICI grant "Wireless control systems: A new frontier in automation" (No. 11382) awarded by NWO (The Netherlands Organisation for Scientific Research) and STW (Dutch Technology Foundation), and the STW project "Integrated design approach for safety-critical real-time automotive systems" (No. 12698).

8. REFERENCES

[1] T. Başar and P. Bernhard. *H^∞-Optimal Control and Relaxed Minimax Design Problems: A Dynamic Game Approach.* Birkhäuser, Boston, MA, USA, 2nd edition, 1995.

[2] D. P. Borgers, V. S. Dolk, and W. P. M. H. Heemels. Dynamic event-triggered control with time-regularization for linear systems. In *55th IEEE Conf. Decision and Control*, pages 1352–1357, 2016.

[3] D. P. Borgers, R. Postoyan, A. Anta, P. Tabuada, D. Nešić, and W. P. M. H. Heemels. Periodic event-triggered control of nonlinear systems using overapproximation techniques. Submitted.

[4] C. G. Cassandras. The event-driven paradigm for control, communication and optimization. *J. Control and Decision*, 1(1):3–17, 2014.

[5] X. Chen and F. Hao. Periodic event-triggered state-feedback and output-feedback control for linear systems. *Int. J. Control, Automation and Systems*, 13(4):779–787, 2015.

[6] R. Cogill. Event-based control using quadratic approximate value functions. In *48th IEEE Conf.*

Decision and Control and Chinese Control Conf., pages 5883–5888, 2009.

[7] V. S. Dolk, D. P. Borgers, and W. P. M. H. Heemels. Output-based and decentralized dynamic event-triggered control with guaranteed $\mathcal{L}_p$-gain performance and Zeno-freeness. *IEEE Trans. Automat. Contr.*, 62(1):34–49, 2017.

[8] A. Eqtami, D. V. Dimarogonas, and K. J. Kyriakopoulos. Event-triggered control for discrete-time systems. In *Proc. Amer. Control Conf.*, pages 4719–4724, 2010.

[9] P. Gahinet and P. Apkarian. A linear matrix inequality approach to H_∞ control. *Int. J. Robust Nonlinear Control*, 4(4):421–448, 1994.

[10] A. Girard. Dynamic triggering mechanisms for event-triggered control. *IEEE Trans. Automat. Contr.*, 60(7):1992–1997, 2015.

[11] R. Goebel, R. G. Sanfelice, and A. R. Teel. *Hybrid Dynamical Systems: Modeling, Stability, and Robustness.* Princeton University Press, 2012.

[12] W. P. M. H. Heemels, M. C. F. Donkers, and A. R. Teel. Periodic event-triggered control for linear systems. *IEEE Trans. Automat. Contr.*, 58(4):847–861, 2013.

[13] W. P. M. H. Heemels, G. E. Dullerud, and A. R. Teel. $\mathcal{L}_2$-gain analysis for a class of hybrid systems with applications to reset and event-triggered control: A lifting approach. *IEEE Trans. Automat. Contr.*, 61(10):2766–2781, 2016.

[14] W. P. M. H. Heemels, J. H. Sandee, and P. P. J. van den Bosch. Analysis of event-driven controllers for linear systems. *Int. J. Control*, 81(4):571–590, 2008.

[15] T. Henningsson, E. Johannesson, and A. Cervin. Sporadic event-based control of first-order linear stochastic systems. *Automatica*, 44(11):2890–2895, 2008.

[16] L. Li and M. Lemmon. Weakly coupled event triggered output feedback system in wireless networked control systems. In *Allerton Conf. Commun., Control and Computing*, 2011.

[17] J. Löfberg. YALMIP: a toolbox for modeling and optimization in MATLAB. In *IEEE Int. Symp. Computer Aided Control Systems Design*, pages 284–289, 2004.

[18] M. Miskowicz. Send-on-delta concept: An event-based data reporting strategy. *Sensors*, 6(1):49–63, 2006.

[19] A. Molin and S. Hirche. On the optimality of certainty equivalence for event-triggered control systems. *IEEE Trans. Automat. Contr.*, 58(2):470–474, 2013.

[20] R. Postoyan, A. Anta, W. P. M. H. Heemels, P. Tabuada, and D. Nešić. Periodic event-triggered control for nonlinear systems. In *52nd IEEE Conf. Decision and Control*, pages 7397–7402, 2013.

[21] R. Postoyan, P. Tabuada, D. Nešić, and A. Anta. A framework for the event-triggered stabilization of nonlinear systems. *IEEE Trans. Automat. Contr.*, 60(4):982–996, 2015.

[22] A. Schaft, van der. *L_2-Gain and Passivity Techniques in Nonlinear Control*, volume 218 of *Lecture Notes in Control and Information Sciences.* Springer Verlag, Berlin, Germany, 1996.

[23] P. Tabuada. Event-triggered real-time scheduling of stabilizing control tasks. *IEEE Trans. Automat. Contr.*, 52(9):1680–1685, 2007.

[24] W. Wang, R. Postoyan, D. Nešić, and W. P. M. H. Heemels. Stabilization of nonlinear systems using state-feedback periodic event-triggered controllers. In *IEEE 55th Conf. Decision and Control*, pages 6808–6813, 2016.

[25] J. C. Willems. Dissipative dynamical systems part I: General theory. *Arch. Rational Mech. Anal.*, 45(5):321–351, 1972.

[26] J. K. Yook, D. M. Tilbury, and N. R. Soparkar. Trading computation for bandwidth: reducing communication in distributed control systems using state estimators. *IEEE Trans. Contr. Syst. Technol.*, 10(4):503–518, 2002.

On a Class of Maximal Invariance Inducing Control Strategies for Large Collections of Switched Systems

Petter Nilsson
Dept. of Electrical Engineering and Computer Science
University of Michigan
Ann Arbor, MI
pettni@umich.edu

Necmiye Ozay
Dept. of Electrical Engineering and Computer Science
University of Michigan
Ann Arbor, MI
necmiye@umich.edu

ABSTRACT

Modern control synthesis methods that are capable of delivering safety guarantees typically rely on finding invariant sets. Computing and/or representing such sets becomes intractable for high-dimensional systems and often constitutes the main bottleneck of computational procedures. In this paper we instead analytically study a particular high-dimensional system and propose a control strategy that we prove renders a set invariant whenever it is possible to do so. The control problem—the mode-counting problem with two modes in one dimension—is inspired by scheduling of thermostatically controlled loads (TCLs) and exhibits a trade-off between local safety constraints and a global counting constraint. We improve upon a control strategy from the literature to handle heterogeneity and derive sufficient conditions for the strategy to solve the problem at hand. In addition, we show that the conditions are also necessary for the problem to have a solution, which implies a type of optimality of the proposed control strategy. We outline more general problem instances where the same control strategy can be implemented and we give sufficient (but not necessary) conditions for the closed-loop system to satisfy its specification. We illustrate our results on a TCL scheduling example.

Keywords

Control of switched systems; Energy applications

1. INTRODUCTION

Formal safety verification of control systems and control synthesis techniques that automatically generate controllers with safety guarantees provide principled alternatives to testing and simulation before system deployment. Most of these techniques rely on computation of invariant sets or controlled invariant sets in order to show that the system trajectories do no leave the part of the state-space that is deemed safe [3]. Computing and/or representing invariant sets often becomes infeasible as the geometry of such sets can be fairly complex for high dimensional hybrid systems [16]. To partly alleviate this challenge, Hafner and Del Vecchio show that, for monotone systems, it is easier to devise an algorithm that checks whether a given state is inside, at the boundary, or outside of the maximal invariant set [6]. Instead of computing the invariant set explicitly, such an algorithm is then used within a supervisory controller in order to guarantee safety. A related recent result for cooperative systems [14] shows that if the goal is to find a (not necessarily maximal) controlled invariant set contained inside a rectangular set, there is almost no loss of generality in restricting attention to periodic input sequences, which again enables focusing on the controller instead of sets.

In this paper we seek another alternative: instead of computing the maximal invariant set, can we propose a controller and show that it enforces invariance of the maximal controlled invariant set, whenever that set is nonempty? This question is non-trivial to answer for arbitrary systems; therefore, we focus on a particular class of high dimensional switched systems, motivated by the thermostatically controlled load (TCL) coordination problem.

TCLs include air conditioners, water heaters, refrigerators, etc., that operate within a certain temperature range, called *dead band*, around a temperature set point. TCL owners are typically indifferent to small temperature perturbations around their desired set point. The idea behind TCL coordination is that an electric utility company can leverage this flexibility—which becomes meaningful for large collections of TCLs—to shape aggregate demand on the grid.

The efforts to model aggregate TCL systems can be traced back to 1985, when an aggregate model based on the Focker-Planck partial differential equation (PDE) was proposed [10]. The paper borrowed ideas from statistical physics: just as a large collection of particles can be described by a density, a large number of TCLs can be approximately represented by a "TCL density" function whose evolution is governed by a PDE. More recent work along the same lines have focused on models which are more amenable to control so that the flexibility in TCL operating conditions can be used to help improve power grid operations. In [5] a PDE-model with exposed parameters for the temperature dead band is derived, thus enabling analysis of control of these parameters. Another area of work has been focused on developing finite-state models. These are obtained by partitioning the TCL temperature range into "bins", and using discrete-time Markov chains to describe the evolution of a probability distribution over the resulting discrete state space [8, 15, 4]. In

HSCC '17, April 18–20, 2017, Pittsburgh, PA, USA.

DOI: http://dx.doi.org/10.1145/3049797.3049810

addition, estimation techniques for these models have been proposed to lower the amount of information required at a central control node [11].

As illustrated in [4, 5], if a universal set point temperature is imposed across a collection of TCLs, it can be treated as a control input that can be shaped in order to track reference demand. However, the tracking capability comes at the cost of modifying the set point temperature, which may result in a conflict with end user preferences. In [15, 7] a different approach is followed: the on/off-state of each individual TCL is treated as a potential control input. This additional control freedom can leverage more of the flexibility within a temperature range and can therefore potentially achieve reference tracking without violating end user constraints.

This approach is generalized in [13] into the so-called *mode-counting problem*. The fundamental challenge in such a problem is to satisfy local state constraints while simultaneously controlling the aggregate number of subsystems that are in a given mode. Such a constraint is important in TCL coordination: turning too many TCLs on or off at the same time may overload the electricity grid. The cited paper proposes a controller synthesis technique based on an approximately bisimilar abstraction and solves a discrete mode-counting problem on the abstraction via a linear program. In theory, the method can solve the mode-counting problem to an arbitrary precision, but it assumes knowledge of initial conditions.

In this paper we first focus on a special case of the mode-counting problem that is inspired by the TCL scheduling problem, where each individual subsystem has two modes and one-dimensional continuous dynamics. We show that a generalization of a control policy proposed in [7] is in a certain sense optimal for a heterogeneous family of TCLs, and derive analytic feasibility limits. The analysis shows that the control policy enforces invariance of the maximal controlled invariant set, without the need to explicitly deal with or express the controlled invariant set itself.

The problem at hand is related to schedulability theory. Previous work has identified the similar feasibility limits in the linear setting [12], but without showing that the control policy in [7] is in fact optimal. Another related work is [2] which considers schedulability of hybrid constant-rate systems, subsequently generalized to bounded-rate systems [1]. These papers present feasibility results in the form of linear programs that scale with the number of aggregate dynamical modes—in our case 2^N. By contrast, we provide closed-form formulas and an easy-to-implement control policy that achieves invariance whenever it is theoretically feasible.

This paper is structured as follows: the remainder of this section introduces relevant notation and formalizes the problem statement. In the following Section 2 we introduce time to exit—a key concept that is a novel addition to the policy in [7] and provides an abstraction that makes heterogeneity invisible to the central coordinator. Subsequently, in Section 3, we propose a control strategy to solve the problem and present our main results regarding its performance. Sufficient conditions for the strategy that apply in more general settings are presented in Section 4. The results are illustrated with simulations in Section 5 before the paper is concluded in Section 6. The proofs of the main results have been deferred to the appendix.

1.1 Preliminaries

We first introduce some notation. A set of integers from 1 to N is written as $[N] = \{1, 2, \ldots, N\}$. The indicator function of a set A is denoted $\mathbb{1}_A(x)$ and is equal to 1 if $x \in A$ and to 0 otherwise. We use the Nabla operator $\nabla_x f$ to denote the Jacobian of f with respect to x.

We will work with the usual definition of the flow $\phi_f(x,t)$ of a vector field $f : \mathbb{R}^n \to \mathbb{R}^n$. It is the solution at time t of the following differential equation:

$$\begin{cases} \frac{\mathrm{d}}{\mathrm{d}s} y(s) = f(y(s)), \\ y(0) = x. \end{cases}$$

Clearly, the flow operator satisfies the relation

$$\frac{\mathrm{d}}{\mathrm{d}t} \phi_f(x,t) = f\left(\phi_f(x,t)\right),$$

a fact that will be used extensively later in the paper.

1.2 Problem statement

In most of the literature on TCL modeling and control a one-dimensional linear switched ODE is used to model an individual TCL. A TCL has the two modes `on` and `off`, each inducing a globally stable equilibrium point. The temperature range between the two equilibria constitute the attainable temperatures. Typically, a subrange of this temperature range (the dead band) forms acceptable end user states, i.e., local safety constraints. Since the dead band is necessarily located between the equilibria, it follows that the flows corresponding to the two modes are sign-definite and have opposing signs. The following generalized problem formulation captures these characteristics.

PROBLEM 1. *Given N subsystems with states $\{x^i\}_{i\in[N]}$ s.t. $x^i \in \mathbb{R}$, obeying the dynamics*

$$\frac{\mathrm{d}}{\mathrm{d}t} x^i(t) = \begin{cases} f^i_{\mathtt{off}}\left(x^i(t)\right) & \text{if } \sigma^i(t) = \mathtt{off}, \\ f^i_{\mathtt{on}}\left(x^i(t)\right) & \text{if } \sigma^i(t) = \mathtt{on}, \end{cases} \tag{1}$$

local safe sets $S^i = [\underline{a}^i, \overline{a}^i]$, and global mode-counting bounds $[\underline{K}_{\mathtt{on}}, \overline{K}_{\mathtt{on}}]$, construct an aggregate switching policy $\{\sigma^i\}_{i\in[N]}$ such that for all trajectories $x^i : \mathbb{R}^+ \to \mathbb{R}$:

$$x^i(t) \in S^i, \quad \forall i \in [N], t \in \mathbb{R}^+, \tag{2}$$

$$\underline{K}_{\mathtt{on}} \leq \sum_{i=1}^{N} \mathbb{1}_{\{\mathtt{on}\}}\left(\sigma^i(t)\right) \leq \overline{K}_{\mathtt{on}}, \quad \forall t \in \mathbb{R}^+. \tag{3}$$

In accordance with the TCL setting, we assume that $f^i_{\mathtt{off}}$ is strictly positive on S and that $f^i_{\mathtt{on}}$ is strictly negative. With these assumptions, the `on` mode will always transport the state "downwards", while the `off` mode transports "upwards", as illustrated in Figure 1. In order for the problem to have a solution the initial conditions of all x^i's must evidently be inside their safe sets S^i.

Eq. (2) represents a local safety constraint while (3) is a global constraint that requires coordination between the different subsystems. Both constraints are trivial to satisfy by themselves, but when they have to be taken into account simultaneously a conflict arises. In this paper we propose a control strategy that resolves this conflict and prove that under certain assumptions—that apply for TCL dynamics—it is the best possible strategy.

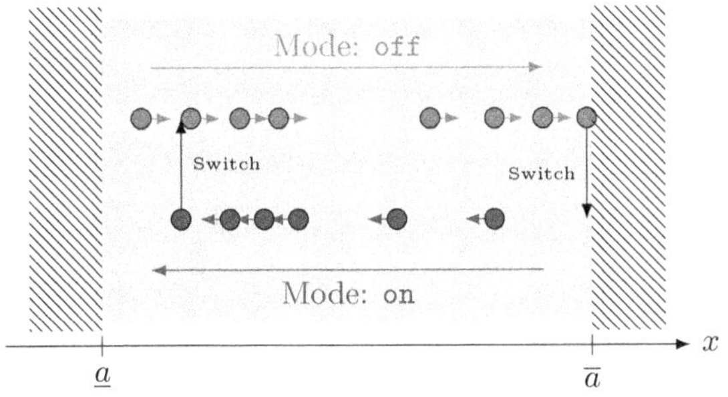

Figure 1: Illustration of the TCL scheduling problem with homogeneous local safety constraints; $\underline{a}^i = \underline{a}$ and $\overline{a}^i = \overline{a}$ for all $i \in [N]$. Each subsystem is illustrated with a colored circle; those that are in mode on are in blue and those that are in mode off are in red. The local safety constraints stipulate that each subsystem must remain in the interval $[\underline{a}, \overline{a}]$, while the global mode-counting constraint restricts the number of subsystems that can be in mode on at a given time. When a subsystem switches mode the direction of movement is reversed due to the assumption on signs of f_{on} and f_{off}.

The aggregate dynamics can be seen as an N-dimensional switched system with 2^N aggregate modes. For N's in the tens or hundreds of thousands, conventional computer-assisted analysis methods that do not exploit the symmetries of the problem become intractable.

2. TIME TO EXIT

In order to treat a heterogeneous family of subsystems in a cohesive manner we introduce *time to exit* as a way to assess the urgency to switch a given subsystem. As a one-dimensional quantity that abstracts away heterogeneity, the concept is well suited for general problems with constraints on mode counts. We therefore present formulas for arbitrary n-dimensional systems, although the main focus in this paper is the special setting with one-dimensional subsystems. The time to exit with respect to a set $S \subset \mathbb{R}^n$ is the minimal time it takes for the flow to reach the boundary of S.

DEFINITION 1. *Given a set $S \subset \mathbb{R}^n$, for $x \in S$ and a vector field $f : \mathbb{R}^n \to \mathbb{R}^n$, the* ***time to exit*** *$T_f(x)$ is the time it takes for the flow of f starting in x to reach ∂S:*

$$T_f(x) = \inf\{\tau \geq 0 : \phi_f(x,\tau) \in \partial S\}.$$

If the set S is not transient, $T_f(x)$ might be equal to $+\infty$. In the following we assume that the time to exit is finite, which is the case in Problem 1. We next define an operator that maps a given point x to the point on ∂S where the flow of f starting in x exits S.

DEFINITION 2. *For $f : \mathbb{R}^n \to \mathbb{R}^n$ and $x \in S$ with $T_f(x) < +\infty$, the* ***exit point*** *$U_f(x)$ is*

$$U_f(x) = \phi_f(x, T_f(x)).$$

We now analyze the dynamic evolution of the time to exit T_f. It is clear that T_f decreases with unit speed along a trajectory of f itself. Using the Lie derivative, this fact is expressed as $\mathcal{L}_f T_f(x) = -1$. However, we are also interested in how the time to exit with respect to f, T_f, varies along trajectories of a second vector field g. The infinitesimal change is given in terms of the Lie derivative $\mathcal{L}_g T_f$.

PROPOSITION 1. *Assume that ∂S is C^1 at $U_f(x)$. Then the Lie derivative of $T_f(x)$ with respect to g is expressed as follows:*

$$\mathcal{L}_g T_f(x) = -\frac{\left(\hat{n}^S_{U_f(x)}\right)^T (\nabla_x \phi_f)|_{(x,T_f(x))}\, g(x)}{\left(\hat{n}^S_{U_f(x)}\right)^T f(U_f(x))}, \tag{4}$$

where $\hat{n}^S_x$ is the outward-pointing unit normal of ∂S at x.

PROOF. By definition of the Lie derivative:

$$\begin{aligned}
\mathcal{L}_g T_f(x) &= \left.\frac{\mathrm{d}}{\mathrm{d}s}\right|_{s=0} T_f(\phi_g(x,s)) \\
&= \left.\frac{\mathrm{d}}{\mathrm{d}s}\right|_{s=0} \inf\left\{\tau : \phi_f\left(x + g(x)s + \mathcal{O}(s^2), \tau\right) \in \partial S\right\} \\
&= \left.\frac{\mathrm{d}}{\mathrm{d}s}\right|_{s=0} \inf\left\{\tau : \begin{array}{c}\phi_f(x,\tau) + (\nabla_x\phi_f)|_{(x,\tau)}\, g(x)s \\ +\, \mathcal{O}(s^2) \in \partial S\end{array}\right\} \\
&= \left.\frac{\mathrm{d}}{\mathrm{d}s}\right|_{s=0} T_f(x) + \inf\left\{\tau : \begin{array}{c}\phi_f(x, T_f(x)+\tau) \\ +\, (\nabla_x\phi_f)|_{(x,T_f(x)+\tau)}\, g(x)s \\ +\, \mathcal{O}(s^2) \in \partial S\end{array}\right\}.
\end{aligned}$$

For a small τ, $\phi_f(x, T_f(x)+\tau) = U_f(x) + f(U_f(x))\tau + \mathcal{O}(\tau^2)$. Since $U_f(x) \in \partial S$, it follows that the τ that achieves the infimum must counteract the effect of the s-term along the normal of ∂S, as displayed in Figure 2. Ignoring second-order terms, this is expressed by the relation

$$0 = \left\langle \hat{n}^S_{U_f(x)}, f(U_f(x))\tau + (\nabla_x\phi_f)|_{(x,T_f(x)+\tau)}\, g(x)s \right\rangle,$$

which, given that $\left\langle \hat{n}^S_{U_f(x)}, f(U_f(x))\right\rangle \neq 0$, by the implicit function theorem describes an implicit mapping $s \mapsto \tau$ defined around the origin, such that $0 \mapsto 0$. By writing

$$(\nabla_x\phi_f)|_{(x,T_f(x)+\tau)} = (\nabla_x\phi_f)|_{(x,T_f(x))} + \mathcal{O}(\tau);$$

differentiating the implicit relation with respect to s; and letting $s \to 0$; the result is obtained. □

The identity in Proposition 1 depends in an intricate way on the geometry of S and the vector field flow lines. We remark that the derivative of the flow operator with respect to the initial condition x can be written as the solution $\eta(t)$ of a matrix-valued ODE obtained by linearizing f along the flow [17, p. 154]:

$$\eta(0) = I, \quad \frac{\mathrm{d}}{\mathrm{d}s}\eta(s) = (\nabla_x f)|_{\phi_f(x,s)}\, \eta(s). \tag{5}$$

3. A SWITCHING STRATEGY FOR PROBLEM 1

We now apply the theory developed in the previous section to the study of Problem 1—the mode-counting problem for a collection of one-dimensional two-mode switched systems. In the interest of keeping notation simple, we omit the f's in subscripts and write ϕ^i_{on} instead of $\phi_{f^i_{\text{on}}}$, and similarly for T, U, and $\mathcal{L}$.

First we adapt Proposition 1 for the simplified geometry of Problem 1; one-dimensional sign-definite vector fields allow us to evaluate the exit point mapping without solving an ODE.

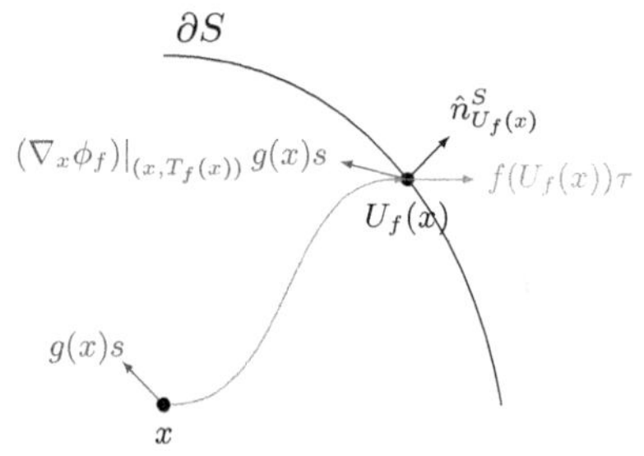

Figure 2: Illustration of the effect an infinitesimal movement along the vector field $g(x)$ has on the exit time $T_f(x)$ with respect to f. A movement $g(x)s$ at x is propagated along the flow line of f and results in the infinitesimal movement $\nabla_x\phi_f(x, T_f(x))g(x)s$ at $U_f(x)$. To compensate for this movement, τ must be chosen so that $f(U_f(x))\tau$ counteracts the effect in the normal direction.

PROPOSITION 2. *For the dynamics* (1) *and the safe set* $S^i = [\underline{a}^i, \overline{a}^i]$, *the expressions in Proposition 1 simplify to:*

$$\mathcal{L}^i_{off}T^i_{on}(x) = -\frac{f^i_{off}(x)}{f^i_{on}(x)}, \quad \mathcal{L}^i_{on}T^i_{off}(x) = -\frac{f^i_{on}(x)}{f^i_{off}(x)}. \tag{6}$$

PROOF. In the interest of brevity we do not solve (5) but opt for a simpler argument. For a one-dimensional vector field f we can for a small h write

$$\begin{aligned}\phi_f(x+h,t) &= \phi_f(x, t + h/f(x) + \mathcal{O}(h^2)) \\ &= \phi_f\left(\phi_f(x,t), h/f(x) + \mathcal{O}(h^2)\right) \\ &= \phi_f(x,t) + hf(\phi_f(x,t))/f(x) + \mathcal{O}(h^2).\end{aligned}$$

Thus we get,

$$\nabla_x\phi_f(x,t) = \lim_{h\to 0}\frac{h\frac{f(\phi_f(x,t))}{f(x)} + \mathcal{O}(h^2)}{h} = \frac{f(\phi_f(x,t))}{f(x)}.$$

Turning to (4), the simple geometry yields $U^i_{on}(x) = \underline{a}^i$ and $\hat{n}_{U_{on}(x)} = -1$. Thus,

$$f^i_{on}(\phi^i_{on}(x, T^i_{on}(x))) = f^i_{on}(U^i_{on}(x)) = f^i_{on}(\underline{a}^i),$$

which gives

$$\mathcal{L}^i_{off}T^i_{on}(x) = -\frac{f^i_{on}(\underline{a}^i)f^i_{off}(x)}{f^i_{on}(x)} / f^i_{on}(\underline{a}^i) = -\frac{f^i_{off}(x)}{f^i_{on}(x)}.$$

The expression for $\mathcal{L}^i_{on}T^i_{off}(x)$ is derived in an analogous fashion. □

Now, motivated by the control strategy proposed in [7], we propose a strategy for Problem 1 that only switches a subsystem if either the local state constraint or the global mode-counting bounds are about to be violated. In the referenced paper, the strategy was found to have good tracking performance[1] and robustness in a mildly heterogeneous setting, but no formal analysis was carried out. A key novelty in our work is that we use time to exit—rather than state value—to select which subsystem to switch to preserve mode-counting bounds. This modification allows us to work with truly heterogeneous collections of subsystems.

[1]Using the terminology of this paper, tracking translates to time-varying mode-counting bounds.

STRATEGY 1. *Switch subsystem i at a time instant t if one of the following conditions occur:*

1. *If $T^i_{off}(x^i(t)) = 0$, switch subsystem i to* **on**,
2. *If $T^i_{on}(x^i(t)) = 0$, switch subsystem i to* **off**,
3. *If $\sum_{j\in[N]} \mathbb{1}_{\{on\}}(\sigma^j(t^+)) < \underline{K}_{on}$ for $t^+ > t$, select the subsystem i in mode* **off** *with the largest time to* **on**-*exit, i.e.*
$$i = \underset{j\in[N]\,:\,\sigma^j(t)=off}{\arg\max}\; T^j_{on}(x^j(t)),$$
and switch it to **on**. *If the bound is still violated at t^+, repeat step 3.*
4. *If $\sum_{j\in[N]} \mathbb{1}_{\{on\}}(\sigma^j(t^+)) > \overline{K}_{on}$ for $t^+ > t$, select the subsystem i in mode* **on** *with the largest time to* **off**-*exit, i.e.*
$$i = \underset{j\in[N]\,:\,\sigma^j(t)=on}{\arg\max}\; T^j_{off}(x^j(t)),$$
and switch it to **off**. *If the bound is still violated at t^+, repeat step 4.*

REMARK 1. *In the event that more than $\overline{K}_{on}$ subsystems simultaneously satisfy the condition in 1., or analogously for $\underline{K}_{on}$ and condition 2., the strategy above is not well defined with respect to the dynamics. This is however a measure-zero event in the space of initial conditions. Let's call aggregate states where several subsystems have identical and non-zero times to exit* **degenerate**. *Since a mode perturbation (i.e., switching* **off** *some systems in the* **on** *mode while simultaneously switching* **on** *some systems in the* **off** *mode) can be applied whenever the system is in a degenerate state, we can without loss of generality disregard degenerate states provided that the initial condition itself is not degenerate.*

Alternatively, degenerate cases can be handled by adding a time margin $\tau > 0$ to the switching condition: if the times to exit of several subsystems cross into the margin region $[0, \tau]$ simultaneously, switch one subsystem i_1 when it crosses the margin ($T^{i_1}(x^{i_1}) = \tau$) and space out the remaining switches linearly such that the last switch for subsystem i_k occurs at the boundary when $T^{i_k}(x^{i_k}) = 0$.

Our results regarding the performance of this strategy rely on two assumptions. The first is a mild assumption that allows us to analyze the flow in a vicinity of the end points.

ASSUMPTION 1. *The functions f^i_{on} and f^i_{off} are continuous at $\underline{a}^i$ and at $\overline{a}^i$ for all $i \in [N]$.*

Secondly, we state an assumption that is crucial for proving "optimality" of Strategy 1.

ASSUMPTION 2. *The functions f^i_{on} and f^i_{off} are monotonically decreasing in S^i for all $i \in [N]$.*

Crucially, this assumption holds for typical TCL models, since the (absolute) flow velocity of a stable one-dimensional linear system is necessarily monotonically decreasing towards its equilibrium point. We are now in a position to state the main results of this paper.

THEOREM 1. *Assume that Assumption 1 holds and that the initial condition is not degenerate in the sense of Remark 1. Then, if*

$$\sum_{i\in[N]} \frac{\mathcal{L}^i_{off}T^i_{on}(\underline{a}^i)}{1+\mathcal{L}^i_{off}T^i_{on}(\underline{a}^i)} > \underline{K}_{on}, \text{ and,} \tag{7a}$$

$$\sum_{i\in[N]} \frac{\mathcal{L}^i_{on}T^i_{off}(\overline{a}^i)}{1+\mathcal{L}^i_{on}T^i_{off}(\overline{a}^i)} > N - \overline{K}_{on}, \tag{7b}$$

then Strategy 1 solves Problem 1.

Strategy 1 can also be used to satisfy time-varying mode-counting bounds.

COROLLARY 1. *Consider a generalization of Problem 1 with piecewise constant time-varying mode-counting bounds $\underline{K}_{on}(t)$ and $\overline{K}_{on}(t)$. If (7) holds for all $t \in \mathbb{R}^+$, then Strategy 1 enforces (2)-(3) for all $t \in \mathbb{R}^+$.*

The next result shows that under the additional monotonicity assumption the inequalities (7) are also (almost) necessary conditions for Problem 1 to have a solution.

THEOREM 2. *Assume that Assumption 1 and 2 hold. If the strict version of (7) is violated, i.e.,*

$$\sum_{i\in[N]} \frac{\mathcal{L}^i_{off}T^i_{on}(\underline{a}^i)}{1+\mathcal{L}^i_{off}T^i_{on}(\underline{a}^i)} < \underline{K}_{on}, \text{ or,} \tag{8a}$$

$$\sum_{i\in[N]} \frac{\mathcal{L}^i_{on}T^i_{off}(\overline{a}^i)}{1+\mathcal{L}^i_{on}T^i_{off}(\overline{a}^i)} < N - \overline{K}_{on}, \tag{8b}$$

then Problem 1 has no solution.

The proofs of these two results are presented in the appendix. Together, Theorem 1 and 2 allow us to make a conclusion about the maximal controlled invariant[2] set contained in the global safety set

$$\mathfrak{S} = \left\{ \prod_{i\in[N]} \{(x^i,\sigma^i)\} : \begin{array}{l} \underline{K}_{\text{on}} \le \sum_{i\in[N]} \mathbb{1}_{\{\text{on}\}}(\sigma^i) \le \overline{K}_{\text{on}}, \\ x^i \in S^i, \quad \forall i \in [N] \end{array} \right\}. \tag{9}$$

COROLLARY 2. *Assume that Assumptions 1 and 2 hold. Then, if (8) holds, the maximal controlled invariant set contained in $\mathfrak{S}$ is empty. Otherwise, the maximal controlled invariant set contained in $\mathfrak{S}$ is equal, up to closure, to $\mathfrak{S}$ itself.*

PROOF. Only the case when neither (7) nor (8) is true remains. In this case, due to monotonicity we can pick an $\epsilon > 0$ such that (7) is satisfied for the modified bounds $(\underline{a}^i)' = \underline{a}^i + \epsilon$, $(\overline{a}^i)' = \overline{a}^i - \epsilon$. Hence, the set

$$\mathfrak{S}' = \left\{ \prod_{i\in[N]} \{(x^i,\sigma^i)\} : \begin{array}{l} \underline{K}_{\text{on}} \le \sum_{i\in[N]} \mathbb{1}_{\{\text{on}\}}(\sigma^i) \le \overline{K}_{\text{on}} \\ \underline{a}^i + \epsilon \le x^i \le \overline{a}^i - \epsilon \quad \forall i \in [N] \end{array} \right\}.$$

is a controlled invariant set contained in $\mathfrak{S}$. Letting $\epsilon \to 0$ gives the result. □

[2]A set S is controlled invariant if for all initial states $x(0) \in S$, there is a switching policy such that $x(t) \in S$ for all $t \ge 0$.

REMARK 2. *If the monotonicity assumption Assumption 2 does not hold, a variation of Strategy 1 may still be optimal. Assume that two points $(\underline{a}^i)'$ and $(\overline{a}^i)'$ can be found such that $(\underline{a}^i)' < (\overline{a}^i)'$, and such that*

$$(\underline{a}^i)' \in \arg\max_{x\in S^i} \mathcal{L}^i_{off}T^i_{on}(x), \quad (\overline{a}^i)' \in \arg\max_{x\in S^i} \mathcal{L}^i_{on}T^i_{off}(x).$$

Then, if Strategy 1 is redefined to force switches at $(\underline{a}^i)'$ and $(\overline{a}^i)'$, the results from Theorem 1 and 2 still apply provided that initial conditions are within the range $\left[(\underline{a}^i)', (\overline{a}^i)'\right]$.

4. CONTROL STRATEGY GENERALIZATIONS

In the previous section we proposed Strategy 1 and proved that it enforces invariance whenever it is possible to do so in the setting with one-dimensional subsystems. Here we outline more general problem instances where the strategy can be applied, and give conditions analogous to (7) that guarantee that the strategy solves Problem 1. However, the additional generality comes at the cost of potential conservativeness: there are no results analogous to Theorem 2 in these cases. The proofs of these generalizations follow that of Theorem 1.

4.1 Uncertainty in vector fields

Suppose that there is some bounded parametric uncertainty $d^i \in D^i$ present in the dynamics, i.e.,

$$\frac{\mathrm{d}}{\mathrm{d}t}x^i(t) = f^i_{\sigma^i(t)}\left(x^i(t), d^i(t)\right), \quad d^i(t) \in D^i, \tag{10}$$

but that $f^i_{\text{on}}(x,d) < 0$ for all $(x,d) \in S^i \times D^i$ and that $f^i_{\text{off}}(x,d) > 0$ for all $(x,d) \in S^i \times D^i$.

Time to exit is no longer defined for such a system, but if the "undisturbed" time to exit corresponding to $d = 0$ is used, Strategy 1 can still be implemented. If the worst-case disturbance is taken into account at the boundaries of the S^i's, the following inequalities are obtained, that—if fulfilled—guarantee that the strategy solves Problem 1.

$$\sum_{i\in[N]} \min_{d^i\in D^i} \frac{f^i_{\text{off}}(\underline{a}^i,d^i)}{-f^i_{\text{on}}(\underline{a}^i,d^i) + f^i_{\text{off}}(\underline{a}^i,d^i)} > \underline{K}_{\text{on}}, \text{ and,} \tag{11a}$$

$$\sum_{i\in[N]} \min_{d^i\in D^i} \frac{f^i_{\text{on}}(\overline{a}^i,d^i)}{-f^i_{\text{on}}(\overline{a}^i,d^i) + f^i_{\text{off}}(\overline{a}^i,d^i)} > N - \overline{K}_{\text{on}}. \tag{11b}$$

4.2 Higher-dimensional systems

The concept of time to exit is defined for systems of arbitrary dimension, so Strategy 1 can be implemented also for arbitrary mode-counting problems provided that the time to exit can be computed. To arrive at sufficient conditions for correctness, we divide the boundary ∂S^i of the local safety set S^i into parts ∂S^i_{on} and $\partial S^i_{\text{off}}$ where the on and off modes may exit, respectively:

$$\partial S^i_{\text{off}} = \left\{x \in \partial S^i : \left\langle \hat{n}^{S^i}_x, f^i_{\text{off}}(x)\right\rangle \ge 0\right\}, \tag{12a}$$

$$\partial S^i_{\text{on}} = \left\{x \in \partial S^i : \left\langle \hat{n}^{S^i}_x, f^i_{\text{on}}(x)\right\rangle \ge 0\right\}. \tag{12b}$$

We will propose sufficient conditions to guarantee that the maximal invariant set contained in $\mathfrak{S}$ is equal to $\mathfrak{S}$ itself, which is sufficient for Strategy 1 to solve the generalized version of Problem 1. First, we require that the distance between the sets $\partial S^i_{\text{off}}$ and $\partial S^i_{\text{off}}$ is lower bounded by some

$\epsilon > 0$ for all $i \in [N]$. If, furthermore, the following generalizations of (7) hold:

$$\sum_{i\in[N]} \min_{\underline{a}^i \in \partial S^i_{\text{off}}} \frac{\mathcal{L}^i_{\text{off}} T^i_{\text{on}}\left(\underline{a}^i\right)}{1+\mathcal{L}^i_{\text{off}} T^i_{\text{on}}\left(\underline{a}^i\right)} > \underline{K}_{\text{on}}, \text{ and,} \tag{13a}$$

$$\sum_{i\in[N]} \min_{\overline{a}^i \in \partial S^i_{\text{on}}} \frac{\mathcal{L}^i_{\text{on}} T^i_{\text{off}}\left(\overline{a}^i\right)}{1+\mathcal{L}^i_{\text{on}} T^i_{\text{off}}\left(\overline{a}^i\right)} > N - \overline{K}_{\text{on}}, \tag{13b}$$

then $\mathfrak{S}$ is controlled invariant.

For higher-dimensional systems the maximal controlled invariant set contained in $\mathfrak{S}$ may exhibit a complicated geometry. In the one-dimensional case under the monotonicity assumption, it is, as stated in Corollary 2, either empty or equal (up to closure) to $\mathfrak{S}$ itself. In higher dimensions there is no corresponding result. Therefore, even if (13) does not hold, Strategy 1 may be able to enforce invariance of a smaller set.

5. EXAMPLE: TCL SCHEDULING

We illustrate the results with simulations of an aggregate TCL system. Following [7], the dynamics of an individual TCL can be modeled as follows:

$$\frac{\mathrm{d}}{\mathrm{d}t}\theta_i(t) = -a(\theta_i(t) - \theta_a) - bP_m \times \mathbb{1}_{\{\text{on}\}}(\sigma_i(t)). \tag{14}$$

We generated a heterogeneous collection of 1000 TCL's by sampling the parameter values a, θ_a, b and P_m around nominal values[3], and sampled individual temperature dead band parameters $\underline{a}^i$ and $\overline{a}^i$ uniformly from $[19, 20.9]$ and $[21, 23]$, respectively. In the sampling we made sure that fundamental problem assumptions were satisfied; in particular, that $f^i_{\text{on}} < 0$ and $f^i_{\text{off}} > 0$ on $[\underline{a}^i, \overline{a}^i]$. When this is true, both f^i_{on} and f^i_{off} are also monotonically decreasing on the safe set. Therefore Assumptions 1 and 2 hold and therefore condition (7) is tight.

Evaluating (7) showed that the largest possible $\underline{K}_{\text{on}}$ is 323, and the smallest possible $\overline{K}_{\text{on}}$ is 250 for the generated collection. In other words, any mode-counting bounds $[\underline{K}_{\text{on}}, \overline{K}_{\text{on}}]$ with $\underline{K}_{\text{on}} \leq 323$ and $\overline{K}_{\text{on}} \geq 250$ can be satisfied indefinitely while also respecting local safety constraints. Figure 3 displays the resulting mode-on-count during a simulation of Strategy 1 where the imposed mode-counting bounds are varying within the feasible values discussed above. Information about the times to exit is shown in Figure 4 and temperature traces of three individual TCL's are depicted in Figure 5.

Remark 3. *In the simulation a sample time* 0.01 *h was used to implement Strategy 1. Rather than switching a TCL at the instant it reaches the boundary of S^i, it is switched at the sample instant if it exited S^i during the last sample period. This implementation is practical due to its simplicity, but will lead to brief violations of local safety constraints. However, it follows from the monotonicity property and the reasoning in the appendix that no single state constraint will be permanently violated, and there is an upper bound on the magnitude of the violation that goes to 0 as the sample time decreases. The violations could also be corrected for by shrinking the local safety constraints by an appropriate margin.*

[3]The nominal values were chosen as $a = 0.25$, $b = 1.25$, $\theta_a = 28.6$, $P_m = 5.6$.

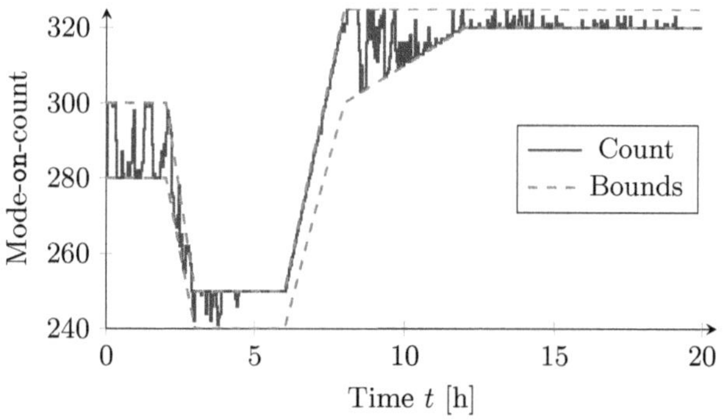

Figure 3: Actual mode-on-count (solid blue) and imposed mode on counting bounds (dashed green) in a Simulation of Strategy 1 for an example with 1000 heterogeneous TCL's. As can be seen, the imposed bounds are satisfied throughout the simulation.

If Strategy 1 is implemented in continuous time, it is shown in the appendix that it will not result in Zeno behavior as long as (7) *holds.*

6. CONCLUSIONS

In this paper we studied the mode-counting problem with two modes in one dimension, and proposed a control strategy that we proved to be optimal in a certain sense. Our analysis is grounded on careful consideration of the hybrid nature of the closed loop dynamics, where the control strategy imposes switching based on local end user constraints and global mode-counting constraints. The results imply tight bounds on the performance that can be achieved in steady state in TCL coordination applications, as demonstrated in Section 5.

Future work will be focused on two objectives. Firstly, we are interested in further investigating the short-horizon control properties of TCL scheduling. It can be shown that Strategy 1 is not the best possible strategy if (8) holds, in the sense that there is a different strategy that maintains $\mathfrak{S}$ invariant for a longer time (although no strategy can achieve invariance indefinitely). By finding strategies that maximize the time until local safety constraint violation we hope to put forward control schemes with short-term optimality conditions and simultaneously derive analytical bounds on tracking performance for larger classes of time-varying counting constraints. Similar control schemes will also be relevant to additional control objectives like minimizing the number of switches uniformly or on average while maintaining local safety and counting constraints.

Secondly, we hope to discover additional settings where the same approach can be applied: to propose a strategy and prove that it enforces invariance under some assumptions. When this is achievable, the control strategy becomes an implicit representation of a controlled invariant set. In this work the maximal controlled invariant set turned out to be either empty, or equal (up to closure) to the safe set itself. This is typically not the case; for more complex situations an implicit definition of a controlled invariant set through a control strategy may be the only practical option.

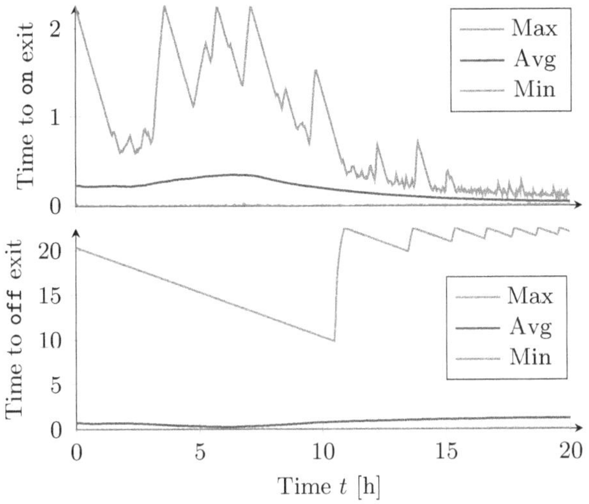

Figure 4: Time to exit for the simulation in Figure 3. The plots show maximal, average, and minimal times to exit for the two modes. As can be seen, the minimal times to exit remain above 0 which implies that local safety constraints are satisfied. In the latter part of the simulation, the lower mode-on-bound $\underline{K}_{\text{on}}$ is equal to 320 which is close to the largest feasible value 323. As a result, the subsystems congregate at the lower boundary which is illustrated by the fact that the times to on exit approach 0. This confirms the tightness of condition (7).

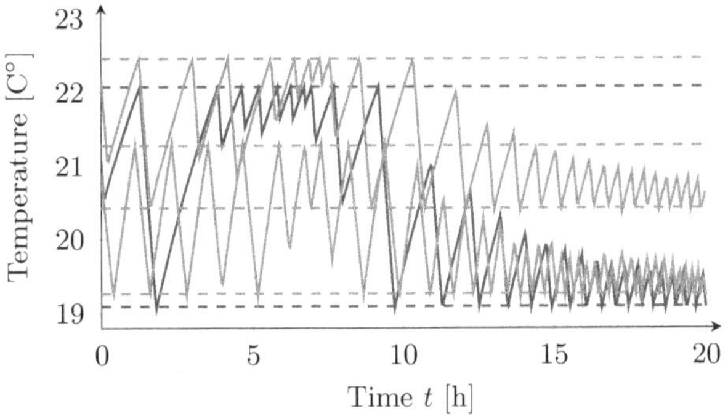

Figure 5: Illustration of temperature movement of three individual TCL's depicted in red, blue, and green. The dashed lines indicate heterogeneous local state constraints. As can be seen, Strategy 1 switches an individual TCL whenever those local safety constraints are about to be violated. Other switches are the result of necessity to enforce global mode-counting constraints. In the latter part of the simulation the imposed mode-on-count is high, as shown in Figure 4. As a consequence, the individual TCL's group in the lower parts of their temperature spectra, since the on fields f^i_{on} are relatively weaker there, thus enabling staying in mode on during a larger fraction of the time. The reverse holds around $t = 5$ h where the imposed mode-on-count is low.

APPENDIX

The proofs of Theorem 1 and 2 rely on a series of lemmas that are presented first. By without loss of generality excluding degenerate cases (c.f. Remark 1), subsystems can be assumed to arrive at boundaries $\underline{a}^i$ and $\overline{a}^i$ one by one. In this case, Strategy 1 enforces the constraints (2)-(3) for all times that the closed loop trajectory is defined. The challenge is to show that the trajectory is defined for all times which amounts to ruling out *Zeno behavior* [9]—accumulation of switching instances at a time t_Z beyond which the solution is undefined.

LEMMA 1. *Zeno behavior can only occur for Strategy 1 if a group $I \subset [N]$ of subsystems all congregate at either their lower or upper boundaries, but not both. That is, either $x^i(t) \to \underline{a}^i$ for all $i \in I$, or, $x^i(t) \to \overline{a}^i$ for all $i \in I$.*

PROOF. By the definition of Zeno behavior, an infinite number of switches must take place over a finite time interval $[0, t_Z)$. These switches must necessarily be undertaken by subsystems in some subset $I \subset [N]$, and we may assume that all subsystems in I switch an infinite amount of times by excluding those that do not. Consider a single subsystem $i \in I$ and some interval $[t_0, t_Z)$ so that the duration between switches of i is less than δ, where δ can be chosen arbitrarily small by adjusting t_0. By inspection of Strategy 1, it follows that either $T^i_{\texttt{on}}(x^i(t)) \leq \delta$ or $T^i_{\texttt{off}}(x^i(t)) \leq \delta$ for all $t \in [t_0, t_Z)$. Hence $x^i(t)$ approaches either $\underline{a}^i$ or $\overline{a}^i$.

We show that all systems in I must congregate at either the lower boundaries $\underline{a}^i$ or the upper boundaries $\overline{a}^i$, but not both. This trivially holds when I is a singleton. Now, assume for contradiction that I can be partitioned into nonempty sets $\underline{I}$ and $\overline{I}$ such that $x^i(t) \to \underline{a}^i$ for $i \in \underline{I}$ and $x^j(t) \to \overline{a}^j$ for $j \in \overline{I}$. By the same construction as above, we pick a $\delta > 0$ and an associated time interval $[t_0, t_Z)$ such that $T^i_{\texttt{on}}(x^i(t)) \leq \delta$ and $T^j_{\texttt{off}}(x^j(t)) \leq \delta$ for all $i \in \underline{I}$, all $j \in \overline{I}$, and all $t \in [t_0, t_Z)$. This is a contradiction of the behavior of Strategy 1. Indeed, for δ small enough $T^j_{\texttt{on}}(x^j) > T^i_{\texttt{on}}(x^i)$ for all $i \in \underline{I}, j \in \overline{I}$, in which case 1) x^i would never be switched from `off` to `on` unless all systems in $\overline{I}$ are already in `on`, and 2) x^j would never be switched from `on` to `off` unless all systems in $\overline{I}$ are already in `off`. But in such a situation no switches occur at all. Therefore either $\underline{I} = I$ or $\overline{I} = I$, which shows that either all subsystems congregate at $\underline{a}^i$, or all subsystems congregate at $\overline{a}^i$. □

LEMMA 2. *If Zeno behavior occurs by a group subsystems $I \subset [N]$ congregating at their lower boundaries $\underline{a}^i$, then*

$$\lim_{t \to t_Z} \sum_{i \in I} T^i_{on}(x^i(t)) = 0,$$

where t_Z is the Zeno time.

PROOF. It suffices to remark that the time between switches for a subsystem $i \in I$ goes to 0 as $t \to t_Z$, and that $\sup_{t' > t} T^i_{\texttt{on}}(x^i(t'))$ is upper bounded by the maximal time between switches on the interval $[t, t_Z)$. □

LEMMA 3. *Zeno behavior at the lower boundaries $\underline{a}^i$ for subsystems $I \subset [N]$ implies that exactly*

$$\max(0, \underline{K}_{on} - N + |I|)$$

*of the subsystems in I are in mode **on** for times close to the Zeno time.*

PROOF. We first show that all subsystems that are not in I must be in mode on. Assume that Zeno behavior occurs for a subset $I \subset [N]$ at the lower boundary, and assume for contradiction that there is a subsystem $j \in [N] \setminus I$ that is in mode off for all times $t \in [t_0, t_Z)$ for some t_0. By Lemma 2, $T^i_{\text{on}}(x^i(t)) \to 0$ for all $i \in I$ as $t \to t_Z$. It follows that $T^j_{\text{on}}(x^j(t)) > T^i_{\text{on}}(x^i(t))$ for t close enough to t_Z, so Strategy 1 switches subsystem j to on before switching subsystem i to on, for all $i \in I$. This is a contradiction.

Now, a subsystem in I can only be switched to mode on when condition 3. of Strategy 1 occurs. It follows that there are exactly $\underline{K}_{\text{on}}$ subsystems in mode on for all times $t \in [t_0, t_Z)$, and out of those,

$$\underline{K}_{\text{on}} - \min(\underline{K}_{\text{on}}, N - |I|) = \max(0, \underline{K}_{\text{on}} - N + |I|)$$

are members of I. □

LEMMA 4. *If (7) holds, then*

$$-\max(\underline{K}_{on} + |I| - N, 0) + \sum_{i \in I} \frac{\mathcal{L}^i_{off} T^i_{on}(\underline{a}^i)}{1 + \mathcal{L}^i_{off} T^i_{on}(\underline{a}^i)} > 0$$

for all sets $I \subset [N]$.

PROOF. If the max evaluates to 0, the inequality is evidently valid. If not, it suffices to note that

$$\mathcal{L}^i_{\text{off}} T^i_{\text{on}}(\underline{a}^i) / \left(1 + \mathcal{L}^i_{\text{off}} T^i_{\text{on}}(\underline{a}^i)\right) < 1 \text{ for all } i \in [N]$$

to obtain

$$\begin{aligned} -\underline{K}_{\text{on}} + (N - |I|) + \sum_{i \in I} \frac{\mathcal{L}^i_{\text{off}} T^i_{\text{on}}(\underline{a}^i)}{1 + \mathcal{L}^i_{\text{off}} T^i_{\text{on}}(\underline{a}^i)} \\ \geq -\underline{K}_{\text{on}} + \sum_{i \in [N]} \frac{\mathcal{L}^i_{\text{off}} T^i_{\text{on}}(\underline{a}^i)}{1 + \mathcal{L}^i_{\text{off}} T^i_{\text{on}}(\underline{a}^i)} > 0. \end{aligned}$$

□

LEMMA 5. *Under Assumption 2, $\mathcal{L}^i_{off} T^i_{on}(x)$ is monotonically decreasing in S^i.*

PROOF. By assumption, both $f^i_{\text{on}} < 0$ and $f^i_{\text{off}} > 0$ are monotonically decreasing in S^i. From Proposition 2:

$$\mathcal{L}^i_{\text{off}} T^i_{\text{on}}(x) = f^i_{\text{off}}(x) / (-f^i_{\text{on}}(x)).$$

As a quotient of a positive monotonically deceasing function and a positive monotonically increasing function, it is monotonically decreasing. □

The following proofs use the concept of a *cycle* in the state space which we introduce next.

DEFINITION 3. *A **cycle** for subsystem i is a continuous trajectory segment $x^i(t)$ on the bounded interval $[0, \tau_{on} + \tau_{off}]$ with exactly one switch such that $x^i(0) = x^i(\tau_{on} + \tau_{off})$.*

In the following we use a wider notion of a cycle as a collection of trajectory segments that—when patched together—satisfy Definition 3. The subsequent proofs rely on partitioning a trajectory into such generalized cycles, as illustrated in Figure 6. Any trajectory can be divided into cycles with the possible exception of bounded time intervals. We state this precisely in the next lemma.

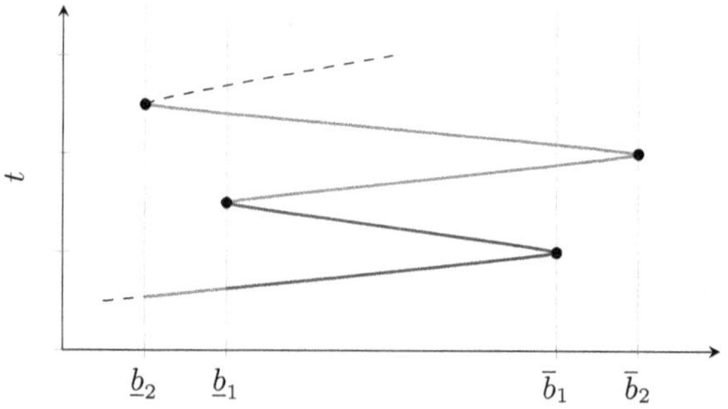

Figure 6: Illustration of cycle partitioning of a trajectory $x^i(t)$. The segment plotted in solid blue is a true cycle in the sense of Definition 3: it starts in mode off at $\underline{b}_1$, reaches $\overline{b}_1$, switches to mode on, and returns to $\underline{b}_1$. Therefore $\overline{b}_1 = \phi^i_{\text{off}}(\tau_{\text{off}}, \underline{b}_1)$ and $\underline{b}_1 = \phi^i_{\text{on}}(\tau_{\text{on}}, \overline{b}_1)$, where τ_{off} and τ_{on} are the times spent in mode off and on, respectively. The segments marked in red can be patched together to form a cycle.

LEMMA 6. *A trajectory $x^i(t)$ defined on an interval $[t_0, t_1]$ that satisfies the state constraints (2) can be divided into cycles in a way such that the duration of time not captured by cycles is at most*

$$\max_{t \in [t_0, t_1]} \left(T^i_{on}(x^i(t)), T^i_{off}(x^i(t))\right). \tag{15}$$

PROOF. Any segment $[t'_0, t'_1]$ such that $x^i(t'_0) = x^i(t'_1)$ can be recursively partitioned into cycles, as illustrated in Figure 6. The bound (15) captures the maximal possible time duration during which $x^i(t) \neq x^i(t')$ for all $t \neq t'$. □

From the definition of a cycle it follows that the time interval for a cycle starting in mode off can be divided into a mode-off interval $[0, \tau_{\text{off}}]$ and a mode-on interval $[\tau_{\text{off}}, \tau_{\text{off}} + \tau_{\text{on}}]$. The next lemma relates these times to the relative strengths of the vector fields, which is captured by $\mathcal{L}^i_{\text{off}} T^i_{\text{on}}$. This result also applies for cycles that are not connected in time, such as the red cycle in Figure 6.

LEMMA 7. *Consider a cycle for subsystem i with time τ_{on} in mode on and time τ_{off} in mode off. Let $\underline{b}$ and $\overline{b}$ be the extremal values of $x^i(t)$ during the cycle. Then,*

$$\frac{\int_{s=0}^{\tau_{off}} \mathcal{L}^i_{off} T^i_{on}\left(\phi^i_{off}(s, \underline{b})\right) \, \mathrm{d}s}{\tau_{on} + \tau_{off}} \leq \frac{\mathcal{L}^i_{off} T^i_{on}(\underline{b})}{1 + \mathcal{L}^i_{off} T^i_{on}(\underline{b})}. \tag{16}$$

Furthermore, if f^i_{off} and f^i_{on} are continuous at $\underline{b}$:

$$\lim_{\tau_{off} \to 0} \frac{\int_{s=0}^{\tau_{off}} \mathcal{L}^i_{off} T^i_{on}\left(\phi^i_{off}(s, \underline{b})\right) \, \mathrm{d}s}{\tau_{on} + \tau_{off}} = \frac{\mathcal{L}^i_{off} T^i_{on}(\underline{b})}{1 + \mathcal{L}^i_{off} T^i_{on}(\underline{b})}.$$

PROOF. Let $\overline{b} = \phi^i_{\text{off}}(\tau_{\text{off}}, \underline{b})$ be the maximal value of $x^i(t)$ during the cycle. By twice re-parameterizing an integral we can write τ_{on} as

$$\tau_{\text{on}} = \int_{s=0}^{\tau_{\text{on}}} \mathrm{d}s = \int_{x=\bar{b}}^{\underline{b}} \frac{\mathrm{d}x}{f^i_{\text{on}}(x)} \begin{pmatrix} \text{by ch. of vars:} \\ x = \phi^i_{\text{on}}(s,\bar{b}) \\ \mathrm{d}x = f^i_{\text{on}}(x)\,\mathrm{d}s \end{pmatrix} = \int_{x=\underline{b}}^{\bar{b}} -\frac{\mathrm{d}x}{f^i_{\text{on}}(x)}$$

$$= \int_{s=0}^{\tau_{\text{off}}} -\frac{f^i_{\text{off}}\left(\phi^i_{\text{off}}(s,\underline{b})\right)}{f^i_{\text{on}}\left(\phi^i_{\text{off}}(s,\underline{b})\right)}\,\mathrm{d}s \quad \begin{pmatrix} \text{by ch. of vars:} \\ x = \phi^i_{\text{off}}(s,\underline{b}) \\ \mathrm{d}x = f^i_{\text{off}}\left(\phi^i_{\text{off}}(s,\underline{b})\right)\mathrm{d}s \end{pmatrix}$$

$$= \int_{s=0}^{\tau_{\text{off}}} \mathcal{L}^i_{\text{off}} T^i_{\text{on}}\left(\phi^i_{\text{off}}(s,\underline{b})\right)\,\mathrm{d}s.$$

It follows that the left-hand side of (16) is actually an expression for $\tau_{\text{on}}/(\tau_{\text{on}}+\tau_{\text{off}})$—the fraction of time spent in mode on during the cycle. Furthermore, by denoting $\tau_{\text{on}}(\tau_{\text{off}}) = \int_{s=0}^{\tau_{\text{off}}} \mathcal{L}^i_{\text{off}} T^i_{\text{on}}\left(\phi^i_{\text{off}}(s,\underline{b})\right)\,\mathrm{d}s$,

$$\frac{\int_{s=0}^{\tau_{\text{off}}} \mathcal{L}^i_{\text{off}} T^i_{\text{on}}\left(\phi^i_{\text{off}}(s,\underline{b})\right)\,\mathrm{d}s}{\tau_{\text{on}}+\tau_{\text{off}}} = \frac{\frac{1}{\tau_{\text{off}}}\tau_{\text{on}}(\tau_{\text{off}})}{1+\frac{1}{\tau_{\text{off}}}\tau_{\text{on}}(\tau_{\text{off}})}. \tag{17}$$

The mapping $x \mapsto x/(1+x)$ is strictly increasing for $x \geq 0$, therefore (17) attains its maximal value for the largest possible $\frac{1}{\tau_{\text{off}}}\tau_{\text{on}}(\tau_{\text{off}})$. By Lemma 5;

$$\frac{1}{\tau_{\text{off}}}\tau_{\text{on}}(\tau_{\text{off}}) = \frac{1}{\tau_{\text{off}}}\int_{s=0}^{\tau_{\text{off}}} \mathcal{L}^i_{\text{off}} T^i_{\text{on}}\left(\phi^i_{\text{off}}(s,\underline{b})\right)\,\mathrm{d}s$$
$$\leq \frac{1}{\tau_{\text{off}}}\tau_{\text{off}} \sup_{u\in[0,\tau_{\text{off}}]} \mathcal{L}^i_{\text{off}} T^i_{\text{on}}\left(\phi^i_{\text{off}}(u,\underline{b})\right) = \mathcal{L}^i_{\text{off}} T^i_{\text{on}}(\underline{b}).$$

Plugging this into (17) proves the first claim. By taking the limit of the integral, it follows given the continuity assumption that the maximum is approached as $\tau_{\text{off}} \to 0$. □

Proof of Theorem 1. We need to prove that the strategy does not induce Zeno behavior. Assume for contradiction that Zeno behavior occurs at $t = t_Z$ but that (7) holds. Then by Lemma 1 we can select a subset of subsystems $I \subset [N]$ that congregate at the (w.l.o.g.) lower boundaries $\underline{a}^i$.

Consider a time $t < t_Z$ such that all switches that occur after t are switches of subsystems in I. We can pick a $\tau > 0$ such that the trajectory is defined on the whole time interval $[t, t+\tau]$. Define $\tau^*_{\text{on}} = \max_{i\in I}\sup_{s\geq t} T^i_{\text{on}}(x^i(s))$. By Lemma 2, $\tau^*_{\text{on}} \to 0$ as $t \to t_Z$. Consider the evolution of $\sum_{i\in I} T^i_{\text{on}}(x^i(t))$ on the interval $[t, t+\tau]$:

$$\sum_{i\in I} T^i_{\text{on}}(x^i(t+\tau)) = \sum_{i\in I} T^i_{\text{on}}(x^i(t)) + \int_{s=t}^{t+\tau} \frac{\mathrm{d}}{\mathrm{d}s}\sum_{i\in I} T^i_{\text{on}}(x^i(s))\,\mathrm{d}s. \tag{18}$$

By Lemma 3, out of the $|I|$ subsystems in I, $\max(\underline{K}_{\text{on}}+|I|-N,0)$ are in mode on. We recall that

$$\frac{\mathrm{d}}{\mathrm{d}s} T^i_{\text{on}}(x^i(s)) = \begin{cases} -1 & \text{if } \sigma^i(s) = \texttt{on}, \\ \mathcal{L}^i_{\text{off}} T^i_{\text{on}}(x^i(s)) & \text{if } \sigma^i(s) = \texttt{off}. \end{cases}$$

By splitting the integral we can therefore write

$$\int_{s=t}^{t+\tau} \sum_{i\in I} \frac{\mathrm{d}}{\mathrm{d}s} T^i_{\text{on}}(x^i(s))\,\mathrm{d}s = \sum_{i\in I}\int_{s=t}^{t+\tau} \frac{\mathrm{d}}{\mathrm{d}s} T^i_{\text{on}}(x^i(s))\,\mathrm{d}s \tag{19}$$
$$= \sum_{i\in I}\left(\int_{\substack{s\in[t,t+\tau] \\ \sigma^i(s)=\text{on}}} \frac{\mathrm{d}}{\mathrm{d}s} T^i_{\text{on}}(x^i(s))\,\mathrm{d}s + \int_{\substack{s\in[t,t+\tau] \\ \sigma^i(s)=\text{off}}} \frac{\mathrm{d}}{\mathrm{d}s} T^i_{\text{on}}(x^i(s))\,\mathrm{d}s \right)$$
$$= -\max(\underline{K}_{\text{on}}+|I|-N,0)\,\tau + \sum_{i\in I}\int_{\substack{s\in[t,t+\tau] \\ \sigma^i(s)=\text{off}}} \mathcal{L}^i_{\text{off}} T^i_{\text{on}}(x^i(s))\,\mathrm{d}s.$$

We consider the remaining integral. Each subsystem i in I will reach $\underline{a}^i$, switch to off, travel "upwards" until $T^i_{\text{on}}(x^i(t)) = \tau^{i,c}_{\text{on}}$ for some $\tau^{i,c}_{\text{on}} < \tau^*_{\text{on}}$, switch to on, and finally reach $\underline{a}^i$ again. We can thus partition the trajectory into a set of cycles Cyc_i in the sense of Definition 3. We split the integral above accordingly and obtain the following inequality due to possibly omitting times at the beginning and the end of $[t, t+\tau]$ that are not part of complete cycles (c.f. Lemma 6).

$$\int_{\substack{s\in[t,t+\tau] \\ \sigma^i(s)=\text{off}}} \mathcal{L}^i_{\text{off}} T^i_{\text{on}}(x^i(s))\,\mathrm{d}s \geq \sum_{c\in Cyc_i}\int_{s=0}^{\tau^{c,i}_{\text{off}}} \mathcal{L}^i_{\text{off}} T^i_{\text{on}}(\phi^i_{\text{off}}(\underline{a}^i,s))\,\mathrm{d}s,$$

where $\tau^{c,i}_{\text{off}}$ is the time spent in mode off by subsystem i during cycle c. By Lemma 7 we can bound this from below as

$$\sum_{c\in Cyc_i}\int_{s=0}^{\tau^{c,i}_{\text{off}}} \mathcal{L}^i_{\text{off}} T^i_{\text{on}}(\phi^i_{\text{off}}(\underline{a}^i,s))\,\mathrm{d}s$$
$$= \sum_{c\in Cyc_i}\left(\tau^{c,i}_{\text{off}}+\tau^{c,i}_{\text{on}}\right)\left(\frac{\mathcal{L}^i_{\text{off}} T^i_{\text{on}}(\underline{a}^i)}{1+\mathcal{L}^i_{\text{off}} T^i_{\text{on}}(\underline{a}^i)} - \delta(\tau^{c,i}_{\text{off}})\right)$$
$$\geq (\tau-\delta_\tau)\left(\frac{\mathcal{L}^i_{\text{off}} T^i_{\text{on}}(\underline{a}^i)}{1+\mathcal{L}^i_{\text{off}} T^i_{\text{on}}(\underline{a}^i)} - \delta\right),$$

where $\delta = \max_i \max_c \delta(\tau^{c,i}_{\text{off}}) \to 0$ as $\tau^*_{\text{on}} \to 0$ and $\delta_\tau < \tau$ has been subtracted to compensate for time before and after cycles. We thus obtain a lower bound for (19) as

$$\int_{s=t}^{t+\tau} \sum_{i\in I} \frac{\mathrm{d}}{\mathrm{d}s} T^i_{\text{on}}(x^i(s))\,\mathrm{d}s$$
$$\geq \left[\begin{array}{l} -\max(\underline{K}_{\text{on}}+|I|-N,0) \\ +\sum_{i\in I}\frac{\mathcal{L}^i_{\text{off}} T^i_{\text{on}}(\underline{a}^i)}{1+\mathcal{L}^i_{\text{off}} T^i_{\text{on}}(\underline{a}^i)} - \delta|I| \end{array}\right](\tau-\delta_\tau).$$

Now, by letting $\tau \to \tau_Z = t_Z - t$ in (18);

$$0 \geq \underbrace{\sum_{i\in I} T^i_{\text{on}}(x(t))}_{\geq 0} + \underbrace{\left[\begin{array}{l} -\max(\underline{K}_{\text{on}}+|I|-N,0) \\ +\sum_{i\in I}\frac{\mathcal{L}^i_{\text{off}} T^i_{\text{on}}(\underline{a}^i)}{1+\mathcal{L}^i_{\text{off}} T^i_{\text{on}}(\underline{a}^i)} - \delta|I| \end{array}\right]}_{A}\underbrace{(\tau_Z-\delta_{\tau_Z})}_{B}.$$

As $t \to t_Z$, $B \to 0$ from above, and

$$A \to -\max(\underline{K}_{\text{on}}+|I|-N,0) + \sum_{i\in I}\frac{\mathcal{L}^i_{\text{off}} T^i_{\text{on}}(\underline{a}^i)}{1+\mathcal{L}^i_{\text{off}} T^i_{\text{on}}(\underline{a}^i)},$$

which is strictly positive by Lemma 4. This is a contradiction of the last inequality, and thus of the Zeno behavior. □

PROOF OF THEOREM 2. We assume that the first inequality in (8) holds; the other case can be treated symmetrically. Assume for contradiction that a switching strategy $\{\sigma^i(t)\}_{i\in[N]}$ that generates infinite-time trajectories satisfying the constraints of Problem 1 exists. Then,

$$\frac{\mathrm{d}}{\mathrm{d}t}\sum_{i\in[N]} T^i_{\mathrm{on}}(x^i(t)) \leq -\underline{K}_{\mathrm{on}} + \sum_{\substack{i\in[N]\\ \sigma^i(t)=\mathtt{off}}} \mathcal{L}^i_{\mathtt{off}} T^i_{\mathrm{on}}(x^i(t)). \quad (20)$$

We integrate the right-hand sum over an interval $[0, t_f]$,

$$\int_{s=0}^{t_f} \sum_{\substack{i\in[N]\\ \sigma^i(t)=\mathtt{off}}} \mathcal{L}^i_{\mathtt{off}} T^i_{\mathrm{on}}(x^i(s))\,\mathrm{d}s = \sum_{i\in[N]} \int_{\substack{s\in[0,t_f]\\ \sigma^i(s)=\mathtt{off}}} \mathcal{L}^i_{\mathtt{off}} T^i_{\mathrm{on}}(x^i(s))\,\mathrm{d}s,$$

and seek to bound the integral for each $i \in [N]$. By Lemma 6 the trajectory can be partitioned into complete cycles $c \in Cyc_i$ with extremal points $\underline{b}_c$ and $\overline{b}_c$ so that the whole interval $[0, t_f]$ is covered except possibly for a total duration $\Delta^i_{t_f}$ at the beginning and the end of the interval $[0, t_f]$. We divide the integral into contributions from these cycles and use Lemma 7,

$$\begin{aligned}\int_{\substack{s\in[0,t_f]\\ \sigma^i(s)=\mathtt{off}}} \mathcal{L}^i_{\mathtt{off}} T^i_{\mathrm{on}}\left(x^i(s)\right)\mathrm{d}s &= \sum_{c\in Cyc_i} \int_{s=0}^{\tau^{c,i}_{\mathtt{off}}} \mathcal{L}^i_{\mathtt{off}} T^i_{\mathrm{on}}\left(\phi^i_{\mathtt{off}}(s, \underline{b}_c)\right)\mathrm{d}s \\ &\leq \sum_{c\in Cyc_i} \left(\tau^{c,i}_{\mathtt{off}} + \tau^{c,i}_{\mathrm{on}}\right) \frac{\mathcal{L}^i_{\mathtt{off}} T^i_{\mathrm{on}}(\underline{b}_c)}{1 + \mathcal{L}^i_{\mathtt{off}} T^i_{\mathrm{on}}(\underline{b}_c)} \\ &\leq \left(t_f - \Delta^i_{t_f}\right) \frac{\mathcal{L}^i_{\mathtt{off}} T^i_{\mathrm{on}}(\underline{a}^i)}{1 + \mathcal{L}^i_{\mathtt{off}} T^i_{\mathrm{on}}(\underline{a}^i)}.\end{aligned}$$

By Lemma 6 the non-cycle time $\Delta^i_{t_f}$ is bounded independently of t_f as $\Delta^i_{t_f} \leq \max\left(T^i_{\mathrm{on}}(\overline{a}), T^i_{\mathtt{off}}(\underline{a}^i)\right)$.

Using this upper bound and (8), integrating (20) yields

$$\begin{aligned}&\sum_{i\in[N]} T^i_{\mathrm{on}}(x^i(t_f)) - \sum_{i\in[N]} T^i_{\mathrm{on}}(x^i(0)) \\ &\leq -\underline{K}_{\mathrm{on}} t_f + \sum_{i\in[N]} \frac{\mathcal{L}^i_{\mathtt{off}} T^i_{\mathrm{on}}(\underline{a}^i)}{1 + \mathcal{L}^i_{\mathtt{off}} T^i_{\mathrm{on}}(\underline{a}^i)} (t_f - \bar{\Delta}^i_{t_f}) \\ &\leq \left(-\underline{K}_{\mathrm{on}} + \sum_{i\in[N]} \frac{\mathcal{L}^i_{\mathtt{off}} T^i_{\mathrm{on}}(\underline{a}^i)}{1 + \mathcal{L}^i_{\mathtt{off}} T^i_{\mathrm{on}}(\underline{a}^i)}\right) t_f - \bar{\Delta}_{t_f} \\ &\leq -\epsilon t_f - \bar{\Delta}_{t_f}\end{aligned}$$

for some $\epsilon > 0$ and where $\bar{\Delta}_{t_f}$ is bounded independently of t_f and i since each $\Delta^i_{t_f}$ is uniformly bounded. Letting $t_f \to \infty$ results in a violation of state constraints, which is a contradiction of the correctness of the switching strategy. □

Acknowledgments

The authors thank Johanna Mathieu for discussions motivating this work. Petter Nilsson is supported by NSF grant CNS-1239037. Necmiye Ozay is supported in part by NSF grants CNS-1446298 and ECCS-1553873, and DARPA grant N66001-14-1-4045.

A. REFERENCES

[1] R. Alur, V. Forejt, S. Moarref, and A. Trivedi. Safe schedulability of bounded-rate multi-mode systems. In *Proc. of HSCC*, pages 243–252, 2013.

[2] R. Alur, A. Trivedi, and D. Wojtczak. Optimal scheduling for constant-rate multi-mode systems. In *Proc. of HSCC*, pages 75–84, 2012.

[3] F. Blanchini. Survey paper: Set invariance in control. *Automatica*, 35(11):1747–1767, 1999.

[4] S. Esmaeil Zadeh Soudjani and A. Abate. Aggregation and control of populations of thermostatically controlled loads by formal abstractions. *IEEE Trans. on Control Systems Technology*, 23(3):975–990, 2015.

[5] A. Ghaffari, S. Moura, and M. Krstić. Modeling, control, and stability analysis of heterogeneous thermostatically controlled load populations using partial differential equations. *ASME Journal of Dynamic Systems, Measurement, and Control*, 137(10), 2015.

[6] M. R. Hafner and D. Del Vecchio. Computational tools for the safety control of a class of piecewise continuous systems with imperfect information on a partial order. *SIAM Journal on Control and Optimization*, 49(6):2463–2493, 2011.

[7] H. Hao, B. M. Sanandaji, K. Poolla, and T. L. Vincent. Aggregate Flexibility of Thermostatically Controlled Loads. *IEEE Trans. on Power Systems*, 30(1):189–198, 2015.

[8] S. Koch, J. L. Mathieu, and D. S. Callaway. Modeling and control of aggregated heterogeneous thermostatically controlled loads for ancillary services. In *Proc. of PSCC*, pages 1–7, 2011.

[9] D. Liberzon. *Switching in Systems and Control.* Springer, 2003.

[10] R. Malhame and C.-Y. Chong. Electric load model synthesis by diffusion approximation of a high-order hybrid-state stochastic system. *IEEE Trans. on Automatic Control*, 30(9):854–860, 1985.

[11] J. L. Mathieu, S. Koch, and D. S. Callaway. State estimation and control of electric loads to manage real-time energy imbalance. *IEEE Trans. on Power Systems*, 28(1):430–440, 2013.

[12] T. X. Nghiem, M. Behl, and R. Mangharam. Green scheduling of control systems for peak demand reduction. In *Proc. of IEEE CDC*, pages 5131–5136, 2011.

[13] P. Nilsson and N. Ozay. Control synthesis for large collections of systems with mode-counting constraints. In *Proc. of HSCC*, pages 205–214, 2016.

[14] S. Sadraddini and C. Belta. Safety control of monotone systems with bounded uncertainties. In *Proc. of IEEE CDC*, pages 4874–4879, 2016.

[15] B. M. Sanandaji, H. Hao, and K. Poolla. Fast regulation service provision via aggregation of thermostatically controlled loads. In *Proc. of HICSS*, pages 2388–2397, 2014.

[16] C. J. Tomlin, I. Mitchell, A. M. Bayen, and M. Oishi. Computational techniques for the verification of hybrid systems. *Proceedings of the IEEE*, 91(7):986–1001, 2003.

[17] W. Walter. *Ordinary Differential Equations.* Springer, 1998.

Sound and Automated Synthesis of Digital Stabilizing Controllers for Continuous Plants*

Alessandro Abate[1], Iury Bessa[2], Dario Cattaruzza[1], Lucas Cordeiro[1,2],
Cristina David[1], Pascal Kesseli[1] and Daniel Kroening[1]

[1]University of Oxford, Oxford, United Kingdom [2]Federal University of Amazonas, Manaus, Brazil

ABSTRACT

Modern control is implemented with digital microcontrollers, embedded within a dynamical plant that represents physical components. We present a new algorithm based on counter-example guided inductive synthesis that automates the design of digital controllers that are correct by construction. The synthesis result is sound with respect to the complete range of approximations, including time discretization, quantization effects, and finite-precision arithmetic and its rounding errors. We have implemented our new algorithm in a tool called DSSynth, and are able to automatically generate stable controllers for a set of intricate plant models taken from the literature within minutes.

Keywords

Digital control synthesis, CEGIS, finite-word-length representation, time sampling, quantization

1. INTRODUCTION

Modern implementations of embedded control systems have proliferated with the availability of low-cost devices that can perform highly non-trivial control tasks, with significant impact in numerous application areas such as environmental control and robotics [4, 17]. Correct control is non-trivial, however. The problem is exacerbated by artifacts specific to digital control, such as the effects of finite-precision arithmetic, time discretization and quantization noise introduced by A/D and D/A conversion. Thus, programming expertise is a key barrier to broad adoption of correct digital controllers, and requires considerable knowledge outside of the expertise of many control engineers.

Beyond classical a-posteriori validation in digital control, there has been plenty of previous work aiming at *verifying* a given designed controller, which however broadly lack automation. Recent work has studied the stability of digital controllers considering implementation aspects, i.e., fixed-point arithmetic and the word length [8]. They exploit advances in bit-accurate verification of C programs to obtain a verifier for software-implemented digital control.

By contrast, we leverage a very recent step-change in the automation and scalability of *program synthesis*. Program synthesis engines use a specification as the starting point, and subsequently generate a sequence of candidate programs from a given template. The candidate programs are iteratively refined to eventually satisfy the specification. Program synthesizers implementing Counter-Example Guided Inductive Synthesis (CEGIS) [34] are now able to generate programs for highly non-trivial specifications with a very high degree of automation. Modern synthesis engines combine automated testing, genetic algorithms, and SMT-based automated reasoning [1, 11].

By combining state-of-the-art synthesis engines we present a tool that automatically generates digital controllers for a given continuous plant model that are correct by construction. This approach delivers a high degree of automation, promises to reduce the cost and time of development of digital control dramatically, and requires considerably less expertise than a-posteriori verification. Specifically, we synthesize stable, software-implemented embedded controllers along with a model of a physical plant. Due to the complexity of such closed-loop systems, in this work we focus on linear models with known configurations, and perform parametric synthesis of stabilizing digital controllers (further closed-loop performance requirements are left to future work).

Our work addresses challenging aspects of the control synthesis problem. We perform digital control synthesis over a hybrid model, where the plant exhibits continuous behavior whereas the controller operates in discrete time and over a quantized domain. Inspired by a classical approach [4], we translate the problem into a single digital domain, i.e., we model a digital equivalent of the continuous plant by evaluating the effects of the quantizers (A/D and D/A converters) and of time discretization. We further account for uncertainties in the plant model. The resulting closed-loop system is a program with a loop that operates on bit-vectors encoded using fixed-point arithmetic with finite word length (FWL). The three effects of 1. uncertainties, 2. FWL representation and 3. quantization errors are incorporated into the model, and are taken into account during the CEGIS-based synthesis of the control software for the plant.

In summary, this paper makes the following original contributions.

- We automatically generate *correct-by-construction* digital controllers using an inductive synthesis approach.

*Supported by EPSRC grant EP/J012564/1, ERC project 280053 (CPROVER) and the H2020 FET OPEN SC[2].

HSCC '17, April 18–20, 2017, Pittsburgh, PA, USA.

ACM ISBN 978-1-4503-4590-3/17/04.
DOI: http://dx.doi.org/10.1145/3049797.3049802

Our application of program synthesis is non-trivial and addresses challenges specific to control systems, such as quantizers and FWL. In particular, we have found that a two-stage verification engine that continuously refines the precision of the fixed-point representation of the plant yields a speed-up of two orders of magnitude over a conventional one-stage verification engine.

- Experimental results show that DSSynth is able to efficiently synthesize stable controllers for a set of intricate benchmarks taken from the literature: the median runtime for our benchmark set considering the faster engine is 48 s, i.e., half of the controllers can be synthesized in less than one minute.

2. PRELIMINARIES

2.1 Discretization of the Plant

The digital controllers synthesized using the algorithm we present in this paper are typically used in closed loops with continuous (physical) plants. Thus, we consider continuous dynamics (the plant) and discrete parts (the digital controller). In order to obtain an overall model for the synthesis, we discretize the continuous plant and particularly look at the plant dynamics from the perspective of the digital controller.

As we only consider transfer function models and require a z-domain transfer function $G(z)$ that captures all aspects of the continuous plant, which is naturally described via a Laplace-domain transfer function $G(s)$. The continuous model of the plant must be discretized to obtain the corresponding coefficients of $G(z)$.

Among the discretization methods in the literature [17], we consider the sample-and-hold processes in complex systems [20]. On the other hand, the ZOH discretization models the exact effect of sampling and DAC interpolation over the plant.

ASSUMPTION 1. *The sample-and-hold effects of the ADC and the presence of the ZOH of the DAC are synchronized, namely there is no delay between sampling the plant output at the ADC and updating the DAC accordingly. The DAC interpolator is an ideal ZOH.*

LEMMA 1. *[4] Given a synchronized ZOH input and sample-and-hold output on the plant, with a sample time T satisfying the Nyquist criterion, the discrete pulse transfer function $G(z,T)$ is an exact z-domain representation of $G(s)$, and can be computed using the following formula:*

$$G(z,T) = (1 - z^{-1})\mathcal{Z}\left\{\mathcal{L}^{-1}\left\{\frac{G(s)}{s}\right\}_{t=kT}\right\}. \quad (1)$$

In this study, for the sake of brevity, we will use the notation $G(z)$ to represent the pulse transfer function $G(z,T)$. Lemma 1 ensures that the poles and zeros match under the $\mathcal{Z}\left\{\mathcal{L}^{-1}\left\{\cdot\right\}_{t=kT}\right\}$ operations, and it includes the ZOH dynamics in the $(1 - z^{-1})$ term. This is sufficient for stability studies over $G(s)$ [15], i.e., if there is any unstable pole (in the complex domain $\Re\{s\} > 0$), the pulse transfer function in (1) will also present the same number of unstable poles ($|z| > 1$) [17].

2.2 Model Imprecision, Finite Word Length Representation and Quantization Effects

Let $C(z)$ be a digital controller and $G(z)$ be a discrete-time representation of the plant, given as

$$C(z) = \frac{C_n(z)}{C_d(z)} = \frac{\beta_0 + \beta_1 z^{-1} + \ldots + \beta_{M_C} z^{-M_C}}{\alpha_0 + \alpha_1 z^{-1} + \ldots + \alpha_{N_C} z^{-N_C}}, \quad (2)$$

$$G(z) = \frac{G_n(z)}{G_d(z)} = \frac{b_0 + b_1 z^{-1} + \ldots + b_{M_G} z^{-M_G}}{a_0 + a_1 z^{-1} + \ldots + a_{N_G} z^{-N_G}}. \quad (3)$$

where $\vec{\beta}$ and $\vec{\alpha}$ are vectors containing the controller's coefficients; similarly, $\vec{b}$ and $\vec{a}$ denote the plant's coefficients; and finally $N_{(\cdot)}$ and $M_{(\cdot)}$ indicate the order of the polynomials, and we require in particular that $N_G \geq M_G$.

Uncertainties in $G(z)$ may appear owing to: 1. uncertainties in $G(s)$ (we denote the uncertain continuous plant by $\hat{G}(s) = \frac{G_n(s)+\Delta_p G_n(s)}{G_d(s)+\Delta_p G_d(s)}$ to explicitly encompass the effects of the uncertainty terms $\Delta_p G_{(\cdot)}(s)$) arising from tolerances/imprecision in the original model; 2. errors in the numerical calculations due to FWL effects (e.g., coefficient truncation and round-off, which will be denoted as $\Delta_b G_n(s), \Delta_b G_d(s)$); and 3. errors caused by quantization (which we model later as as external disturbances ν_1 and ν_2). These uncertainties are parametrically expressed by additive terms, eventually resulting in an uncertain model $\hat{G}(z)$, such that:

$$\hat{G}(z) = \frac{G_n(z) + \Delta G_n(z)}{G_d(z) + \Delta G_d(z)}, \quad (4)$$

which will be represented by the following transfer function:

$$\hat{G}(z) = \frac{\hat{b}_0 + \hat{b}_1 z^{-1} + \ldots + \hat{b}_{M_G} z^{-M_G}}{\hat{a}_0 + \hat{a}_1 z^{-1} + \ldots + \hat{a}_{N_G} z^{-N_G}}. \quad (5)$$

Notice that, due to the nature of the methods we use for the stability check, we require that the parametric errors in the plant have the same polynomial order as the plant itself (indeed, all other errors described in this paper fulfill this property). We also remark that, due to its native digital implementation, there are no parametric errors $(\Delta_p C_n(z), \Delta_p C_d(z))$ in the controller. Thus $\hat{C}(z) \equiv C(z)$.

We introduce next a notation based on the coefficients of the polynomial to simplify the presentation. Let $\mathcal{P}^N$ be the space of polynomials of order N. Let $P \in \mathcal{P}^{M,N}$ be a rational polynomial $\frac{P_n}{P_d}$, where $P_n \in \mathcal{P}^M$ and $P_d \in \mathcal{P}^N$. For a vector of coefficients

$$\vec{P} \in \mathbb{R}^{N+M+2} = [n_0 \; n_1 \; \ldots \; n_M \; d_0 \; d_1 \; \ldots \; d_N \;]^T \quad (6)$$

and an uncertainty vector

$$\Delta\vec{P} \in \mathbb{R}^{N+M+2} = [\Delta n_0 \; \ldots \; \Delta n_M \; \Delta d_0 \; \ldots \; \Delta d_N \;]^T \quad (7)$$

we write

$$\vec{\hat{G}} = \vec{G} + \Delta\vec{G}, \text{ where} \quad (8)$$

$$\vec{G} \in \mathbb{R}^{N_G+M_G+2} = [b_0 \; \ldots \; b_{M_G} \; a_0 \; \ldots \; a_{N_G} \;]^T,$$

$$\Delta\vec{G} \in \mathbb{R}^{N_G+M_G+2} = [\Delta b_0 \; \ldots \; \Delta b_{M_G} \; \Delta a_0 \; \ldots \; \Delta a_{N_G} \;]^T.$$

In the following we will either manipulate the transfer functions $G(z)$, $C(z)$ directly, or work over their respective coefficients $\vec{G}$, $\vec{C}$ in vector form.

A typical digital control system with a continuous plant and a discrete controller is illustrated in Figure 1. The DAC and ADC converters introduce quantization errors (notice

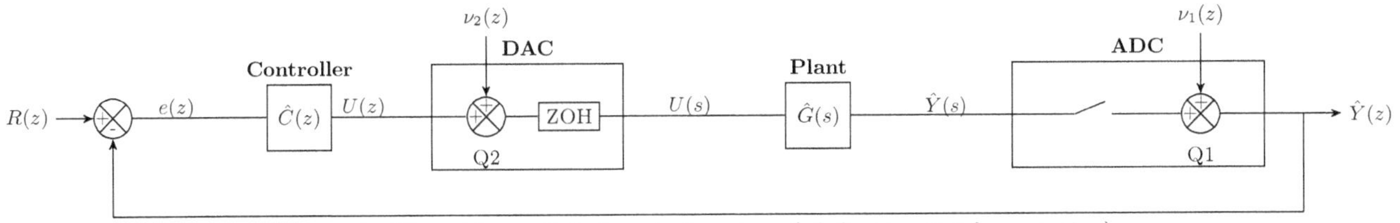

Figure 1: Closed-loop digital control system (cf. Section 2.2 for notation)

that each of them may have a different FWL representation than the controller), which are modeled as disturbances $\nu_1(z)$ and $\nu_2(z)$; $G(s)$ is the continuous-time plant model with parametric additive uncertainty $\Delta_p G_n(s)$ and $\Delta_p G_d(s)$ (as mentioned above); $R(z)$ is a given reference signal; $U(z)$ is the control signal; and $\hat{Y}(z)$ is the output signal affected by the disturbances and uncertainties in the closed-loop system The ADC and DAC may be abstracted by transforming the closed-loop system in Figure 1 into the digital system in Figure 2, where the effect of ν_1 and ν_2 in the output $Y(z)$ is additive noise.

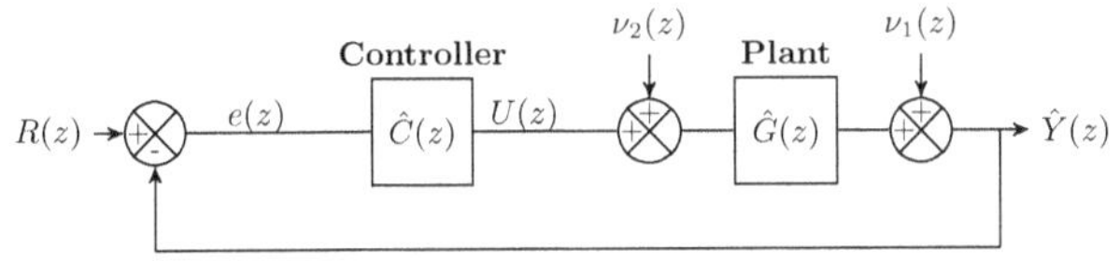

Figure 2: Fully digital equivalent to system in Figure 1

In Figure 2, two sources of uncertainty are illustrated: parametric uncertainties model the errors (which are represented by $\Delta_p \vec{G}$), and uncertainties for the quantizations in the ADC and DAC conversions (ν_1 and ν_2), which are assumed to be non-deterministic. Recall that we discussed how the quantization noise is an additive term, which means it does not enter parametrically in the transfer function. Instead, we later show that the system is stable given these non-deterministic disturbance.

The uncertain model may be rewritten as a vector of coefficients in the z-domain using equation (8) as $\vec{\hat{G}} = \vec{G} + \Delta_p \vec{G}$. The parametric uncertainties in the plant are assumed to have the same order as the plant model, since errors of higher order can move the closed-loop poles by large amounts, thus preventing any given controller from stabilizing such a setup. This is a reasonable assumption since most tolerances do not change the architecture of the plant.

Direct use of controllers in fixed-point representation.

Since the controller is implemented using finite representation, $C(z)$ also suffers disturbances from the FWL effects, with roundoffs in coefficients that may change closed-loop poles and zeros position, and consequently affect its stability, as argued in [8].

Let $\hat{C}(z)$ be the digital controller transfer function represented using this FWL with integer size I and fractional size F. The term I affects the range of the representation and is set to avoid overflows, while F affects the precision and the truncation after arithmetic operations. We shall denote the FWL domain of the coefficients by $\mathbb{R}\langle I, F\rangle$ and define a function

$$\mathcal{F}_n\langle I, F\rangle(P \in \mathcal{P}) : \mathcal{P}^n \to \mathcal{P}^n\langle I, F\rangle \tag{9}$$

$$\triangleq \tilde{P} \in \mathcal{P}^n\langle I, F\rangle : c_i \in \vec{P} \wedge \tilde{c}_i \in \vec{\tilde{P}} = \mathcal{F}_0\langle I, F\rangle(c_i),$$

where $\mathcal{P}^n$ is the space of polynomials of n-th order, $\mathcal{P}^n\langle I, F\rangle$ is the space of polynomials with coefficients in $\mathbb{R}\langle I, F\rangle$, and (as a special case) $\mathcal{F}_0\langle I, F\rangle(x)$ returns the element $\tilde{x} \in \mathbb{R}\langle I, F\rangle$ that is closest to the real parameter x.

Similarly, $\mathcal{F}_{n,m}\langle I, F\rangle(\cdot) : \mathcal{P}^{n,m} \to \mathcal{P}^{n,m}\langle I, F\rangle$ applies the same effect to a ratio of polynomials, where $\mathcal{P}^{n,m}$, $\mathcal{P}^{n,m}\langle I, F\rangle$ are rational polynomial domains.

Thus, the perturbed controller model $\tilde{C}(z)$ may be obtained from the original model $\hat{C}(z) = C(z) = \frac{C_n(z)}{C_d(z)}$ as follows:

$$\tilde{C}(z) = \mathcal{F}_{M_C,N_C}\langle I, F\rangle(C(z)) = \frac{\mathcal{F}_{M_C}\langle I, F\rangle(\hat{C}_n(z))}{\mathcal{F}_{N_C}\langle I, F\rangle(\hat{C}_d(z))}. \tag{10}$$

In the case of a digitally synthesized controller (as it is the case in this work), $\tilde{C}(z) \equiv \hat{C}(z) \equiv C(z)$ because the synthesis is performed directly using FWL representation. In other words, we synthesize a controller that is already in the domain $\mathbb{R}\langle I, F\rangle$ and has therefore no uncertainties entering because of FWL representations, that is, $\Delta_b C_n(z) = \Delta_b C_d(z) = 0$.

Fixed-point computation in program synthesis.

The program synthesis engine uses fixed-point arithmetic. Specifically, we use the domain $\mathbb{R}\langle I, F\rangle$ for the controller's coefficients and the domain $\mathbb{R}\langle I_p, F_p\rangle$ for the plant's coefficients, where I and F, as well as I_p and F_p, denote the number of bits for the integer and fractional parts, respectively, and where it is practically motivated to consider $\mathbb{R}\langle I_p, F_p\rangle \supseteq \mathbb{R}\langle I, F\rangle$.

Given the use of fixed-point arithmetic, we examine the discretization effect during these operations. Let $\tilde{C}(z)$ and $\tilde{G}(z)$ be transfer functions represented using fixed-point bit-vectors.

$$\tilde{C}(z) = \frac{\tilde{\beta}_0 + \tilde{\beta}_1 z^{-1} + ... + \tilde{\beta}_{M_C} z^{-M_C}}{\tilde{\alpha}_0 + \tilde{\alpha}_1 z^{-1} + ... + \tilde{\alpha}_{N_C} z^{-N_C}}, \tag{11}$$

$$\tilde{G}(z) = \frac{\tilde{b}_0 + \tilde{b}_1 z^{-1} + ... + \tilde{b}_{M_G} z^{-M_G}}{\tilde{a}_0 + \tilde{a}_1 z^{-1} + ... + \tilde{a}_{N_G} z^{-N_G}}. \tag{12}$$

Recall that since the controller is synthesized in the $\mathbb{R}\langle I, F\rangle$ domain, $\tilde{C}(z) \equiv \hat{C}(z) \equiv C(z)$. However, given a real plant $\hat{G}(z)$, we need to introduce $\tilde{G}(z) = \mathcal{F}_{M_G,N_G}\langle I_p, F_p\rangle(\hat{G}(z))$, where

$$\tilde{G}(z) = \frac{(\hat{b}_0 + \Delta_b \hat{b}_0) + ... + (\hat{b}_{M_G} + \Delta_b \hat{b}_{M_G}) z^{-M_G}}{(\hat{a}_0 + \Delta_b \hat{a}_0) + ... + (\hat{a}_{N_G} + \Delta_b \hat{a}_{N_G}) z^{-N_G}}$$

$$\vec{\tilde{G}} = \vec{\hat{G}} + \Delta_b \vec{G} = \vec{G} + \Delta_p \vec{G} + \Delta_b \vec{G}, \tag{13}$$

where $\Delta_b c_i = \tilde{c}_i - \hat{c}_i$ and $\Delta_b G$ represents the plant uncertainty caused by the rounding off effect. We capture the global uncertainty as $\Delta \vec{G} = \Delta_p \vec{G} + \Delta_b \vec{G}$.

2.3 Closed-Loop Stability Verification under Parametric Uncertainties, FWL Representation and Quantization Noise

Sound synthesis of the digital controller requires the consideration of the effect of FWL on the controller and of quantization disturbances in the closed-loop system. Let the quantizer $Q1$ (ADC) be the source of a white noise ν_1 and $Q2$ (DAC) be the source of a white noise ν_2. The following equation models the system in Figure 1, including the parametric uncertainties $\Delta\vec{G}$ and the FWL effects on the controller $\tilde{C}(z)$:

$$\hat{Y}(z) = \nu_1(z) + \hat{G}(z)\tilde{C}(z)R(z) + \hat{G}(z)\nu_2(z) - \hat{G}(z)\tilde{C}(z)\hat{Y}(z). \quad (14)$$

The above can be rewritten as follows:

$$\hat{Y}(z) = H_1(z)\nu_1(z) + H_2(z)\nu_2(z) + H_3(z)R(z), \quad (15)$$

where

$$H_1(z) = \frac{1}{1+\hat{G}(z)\tilde{C}(z)},$$

$$H_2(z) = \frac{\hat{G}(z)}{1+\hat{G}(z)\tilde{C}(z)},$$

$$H_3(z) = \frac{\hat{G}(z)\tilde{C}(z)}{1+\hat{G}(z)\tilde{C}(z)}.$$

ASSUMPTION 2. *The quantization noises ν_1 (from Q1) and ν_2 (from Q2) are uncorrelated white noises and their amplitudes are always bounded by the half of quantization step [4], i.e., $|\nu_1| \leq \frac{q_1}{2}$ and $|\nu_2| \leq \frac{q_2}{2}$, where q_1 and q_2 are the quantization steps of ADC and DAC, respectively.*

A discrete-time dynamical system is said to be Bounded-Input and Bounded-Output (BIBO) stable if bounded inputs necessarily result in bounded outputs. This condition holds true over an LTI model if and only if every pole of its transfer function lies inside the unit circle [5]. Analyzing Eq. (15), the following proposition provides conditions for the BIBO stability of the system in Figure 1, with regards to the exogenous signals $R(z)$, ν_1 and ν_2, which are all bounded (in particular, the bound on the quantization noise is given by Assumption 2).

PROPOSITION 1. *[8, 15] Consider a feedback closed-loop control system as given in Figure 1 with a FWL implementation of the digital controller $\tilde{C}(z) = \mathcal{F}_{M_C,N_C}\langle I,F\rangle(C(z))$ and uncertain discrete model of the plant from (6), (7)*

$$\hat{G}(z) = \frac{\hat{G}_n(z)}{\hat{G}_d(z)}, \quad \hat{\vec{G}} = \vec{G} + \Delta_p\vec{G}.$$

Then $\hat{G}(z)$ is BIBO-stable if and only if:

- *the roots of characteristic polynomial $S(z)$ are inside the open unit circle, where $S(z)$ is:*

$$S(z) = \tilde{C}_n(z)\hat{G}_n(z) + \tilde{C}_d(z)\hat{G}_d(z); \quad (16)$$

- *the direct loop product $\tilde{C}(z)\hat{G}(z)$ has no pole-zero cancellation on or outside the unit circle.*

Proposition 1 provides necessary (and sufficient) conditions for the controller to stabilize the closed-loop system, considering plant parametric uncertainties (i.e., $\Delta_p\vec{G}$), quantization noises (ν_1 and ν_2) and FWL effects in the control software. In particular, note that the model for quantization noise enters as a signal to be stabilized: in practice, if the quantization noise is bounded, the noise may be disregarded if the conditions on Proposition 1 are satisfied.

If the verification is performed using FWL arithmetic, the above equations must use $\tilde{G}(z)$ instead of $\hat{G}(z)$. The former will provide sufficient conditions for the latter to be stabilized.

3. AUTOMATED PROGRAM SYNTHESIS FOR DIGITAL CONTROL

3.1 Overview of the Synthesis Process

In order to synthesize closed-loop digital control systems, we use a program synthesis engine. Our program synthesizer implements Counter-Example Guided Inductive Synthesis (CEGIS) [34]. We start by presenting its general architecture followed by describing the parts specific to closed-loop control systems. A high-level view of the synthesis process is given in Figure 3. Steps 1 to 3 are performed by the user and Steps A to D are automatically performed by our tool for Digital Systems Synthesis, named DSSynth.

CEGIS-based control synthesis requires a formal verifier to check whether a candidate controller meets the requirements when combined with the plant. We use the Digital-System Verifier (DSVerifier) [19] in the verification module for DSSynth. It checks the stability of closed-loop control systems and considers finite-word length (FWL) effects in the digital controller and uncertainty parameters in the plant model (plant intervals) [8].

Given a plant model in ANSI-C syntax as input (Steps 1–3), DSSynth constructs a non-deterministic model to represent the plant family, i.e., it addresses plant variations as interval sets (Step A), and formulates a function (Step B) using implementation details provided in Steps 2 and 3 to calculate the controller parameters to be synthesized (Step C). Note that DSSynth synthesizes the controller for the desired numerical representation and realization form. Finally, DSSynth builds an intermediate ANSI-C code for the digital system implementation, which is used as input for the CEGIS engine (Step D).

This intermediate ANSI-C code model contains a specification ϕ for the property of interest (i.e., robust stability) and is passed to the Counterexample-Guided Inductive Synthesis (CEGIS) module of CBMC [9], where the controller is marked as the input variable to synthesize. CEGIS employs an iterative, counterexample-guided refinement process, which is explained in detail in Section 3.2. CEGIS reports a successful synthesis result if it generates a controller that is safe with respect to ϕ. In particular, the ANSI-C code model guarantees that a synthesized solution is complete and sound with respect to the stability property ϕ, since it does not depend on system inputs and outputs. In the case of stability, the specification ϕ consists of a number of assumptions on the polynomial coefficients, following Jury's Criteria, as well as the restrictions on the representation of these coefficients as discussed in detail in Section 3.3.

3.2 Architecture of the Program Synthesizer

The input specification provided to the program synthesizer is of the form $\exists\vec{P}.\forall\vec{x}.\sigma(\vec{x},\vec{P})$ where $\vec{P}$ ranges over functions,

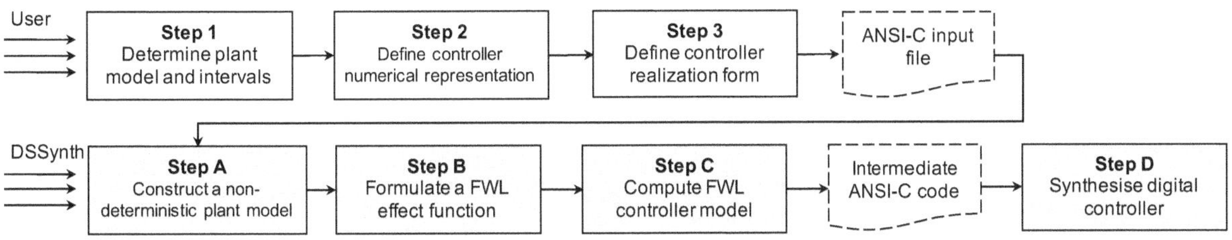

Figure 3: Overview of the synthesis process

$\vec{x}$ ranges over ground terms and σ is a quantifier-free formula. We interpret the ground terms over some finite domain $\mathcal{D}$.

The design of our synthesizer is given in Figure 4 and consists of two phases, SYNTHESIZE and VERIFY, which interact via a finite set of test vectors INPUTS that is updated incrementally. Given the aforementioned specification σ, the SYNTH procedure tries to find an existential witness $\vec{P}$ satisfying the specification $\sigma(\vec{x}, \vec{P})$ for all $\vec{x}$ in INPUTS (as opposed to all $\vec{x} \in \mathcal{D}$). If SYNTHESIZE succeeds in finding a witness $\vec{P}$, this witness is a candidate solution to the full synthesis formula. We pass this candidate solution to VERIFY, which checks whether it is a full solution (i.e., $\vec{P}$ satisfies the specification $\sigma(\vec{x}, \vec{P})$ for all $\vec{x} \in \mathcal{D}$). If this is the case, then the algorithm terminates. Otherwise, additional information is provided to the SYNTHESIZE phase in the form of a new counterexample that is added to the INPUTS set and the loop iterates again (the second feedback signal "Increase Precision" provided by the VERIFY phase in Figure 4 is specific to control synthesis and will be described in the next section).

Each iteration of the loop adds a new input to the finite set INPUTS that is used for synthesis. Given that the full set of inputs $\mathcal{D}$ is finite, this means that the refinement loop can only iterate a potentially very large but finite number of times.

3.3 Synthesis for Control

Formal specification of the stability property.

Next, we describe the specific property that we pass to the program synthesizer as the specification σ. There are a number of algorithms in our verification engine that can be used for stability analysis [7, 8]. Here we choose Jury's criterion [4] in view of its efficiency and ease of integration within DSSynth: we employ this method to check the stability in the z-domain for the characteristic polynomial $S(z)$ defined in (16). We consider the following form for $S(z)$:

$$S(z) = a_0 z^N + a_1 z^{N-1} + \cdots + a_{N-1} z + a_N = 0, a_0 \neq 0.$$

Next, the following matrix $M = [m_{ij}]_{(2N-2)\times N}$ is built from $S(z)$ coefficients:

$$M = \begin{pmatrix} V^{(0)} \\ V^{(1)} \\ \vdots \\ V^{(N-2)} \end{pmatrix},$$

where $V^{(k)} = [v_{ij}^{(k)}]_{2\times N}$ such that:

$$v_{ij}^{(0)} = \begin{cases} a_{j-1}, & \text{if } i = 1 \\ v^{0}_{(1)(N-j+1)}, & \text{if } i = 2 \end{cases}$$

$$v_{ij}^{(k)} = \begin{cases} 0, & \text{if } j > n-k \\ v_{1j}^{(k-1)} - v_{2j}^{(k-1)} \cdot \frac{v_{11}^{(k-1)}}{v_{21}^{(k-1)}}, & \text{if } j \leq n-k \text{ and } i = 1 \\ v^{k}_{(1)(N-j+1)}, & \text{if } j \leq n-k \text{ and } i = 2 \end{cases}$$

and where $k \in \mathbb{Z}$ is such that $0 < k < N-2$. We have that [4] $S(z)$ is the characteristic polynomial of a stable system if and only if the following four conditions hold: $R_1 : S(1) > 0$; $R_2 : (1)^N S(1) > 0$; $R_3 : |a_0| < a_N$; $R_4 : m_{11} > 0 \wedge m_{31} > 0 \wedge m_{51} > 0 \wedge \ldots \wedge m_{(2N-3)(1)} > 0$. The stability property is then encoded by a constraint of the form: $\phi_{stability} \equiv (R_1 \wedge R_2 \wedge R_3 \wedge R_4)$.

The synthesis problem.

The synthesis problem we are trying to solve is the following: find a digital controller $\tilde{C}(z)$ that makes the closed-loop system stable for all possible uncertainties $\tilde{G}(z)$ (13). When mapping back to the notation used for describing the general architecture of the program synthesizer, the controller $\tilde{C}(z)$ denotes P and $\tilde{G}(z)$ represents x.

As mentioned above, we compute the coefficients for $\tilde{C}(z)$ in the domain $\mathbb{R}\langle I, F\rangle$, and those for $\tilde{G}(z)$ in the domain $\mathbb{R}\langle I_p, F_p\rangle$. While the controller's precision $\langle I, F\rangle$ is given, we can vary $\langle I_p, F_p\rangle$ such that $\mathbb{R}\langle I_p, F_p\rangle \supseteq \mathbb{R}\langle I, F\rangle$. As the cost of SAT solving increases with in the size of the problem instance, our algorithm tries to solve the problem first for small I_p, F_p, iteratively increasing the precision if it is insufficient.

3.4 The SYNTHESIZE and VERIFY phases

The SYNTHESIZE phase uses BMC to compute a solution $\tilde{C}(z)$. There are two alternatives for the VERIFY phase. The first approach uses interval arithmetic [28] to represent the coefficients $[c_i - \Delta_p c_i - \Delta_b c_i,\ c_i + \Delta_p c_i - \Delta_b c_i + (2^{-F_p})]$ and rounds outwards. This0 allows us to simultaneously evaluate the full collection of plants $\hat{G}(s)$ (i.e., all concrete plants $G(s)$ in the range $G(s) \pm \Delta_p G(s)$) plus the effects of numeric calculations. Synthesized controllers are stable for all plants in the family. Preliminary experiments show that a synthesis approach using this verification engine has poor performance and we therefore designed a second approach. Our experimental results in Section 4 show that the speedup yielded by the second approach is in most cases of at least two orders of magnitude.

The second approach is illustrated in Figure 4 and uses a two-stage verification approach: the first stage performs potentially unsound fixed-point operations assuming a plant precision $\langle I_p, F_p\rangle$, and the second stage restores soundness by validating these operations using interval arithmetic on the synthesized controller. In more detail, in the first stage, denoted by UNCERTAINTY in Figure 4, assuming a precision $\langle I_p, F_p\rangle$ we check whether the system is unstable for the current candidate solution, i.e., if $\neg\phi_{stability}$ is satisfiable for $S(z)$. If this is the case, then we obtain a counterexample $\tilde{G}(z)$,

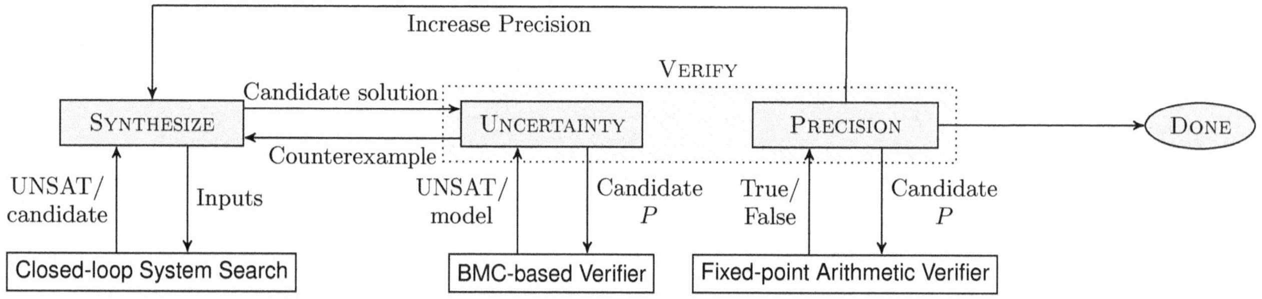

Figure 4: Counterexample-Guided Inductive Synthesis of Closed-loop Systems (Step D)

which makes the closed-loop system unstable. This uncertainty is added to the set INPUTS such that, in the subsequent SYNTHESIZE phase, we obtain a candidate solution consisting of a controller $C(z)$, which makes the closed-loop system stable for all the uncertainties accumulated in INPUTS.

If the UNCERTAINTY verification stage concludes that the system is stable for the current candidate solution, then we pass this solution to the second verification stage, PRECISION, which checks the propagation of the error in the fixed-point calculations using a Fixed-point Arithmetic Verifier based on interval arithmetic.

If the PRECISION verification returns *false*, then we increase the precision of $\langle I_p, F_p \rangle$ and re-start the SYNTHESIZE phase with an empty INPUTS set. Otherwise, we found a full sound solution for our synthesis problem and we are done.

In the rest of the paper, we will refer to the two approaches for the VERIFY phase as one-stage and two-stage, respectively.

3.5 Soundness

The SYNTHESISE phase generates potentially unsound candidate solutions. The soundness of the model is ensured by the VERIFY phase. If a candidate solution passes verification, it is necessarily sound.

The VERIFY phase has two stages. The first stage ensures that no counterexample plant with an unstable closed loop exists over finite-precision arithmetic. Since the actual plant uses reals, we need to ensure we do not miss a counterexample because of rounding errors. For this reason, the second verification stage uses an overapproximation with interval arithmetic with outward rounding. Thus, the first verification stage underapproximates and is used to generate counterexamples, and the second stage overapproximates and provides proof that no counterexample exists.

3.6 Illustrative Example

We illustrate our approach with a classical cruise control example from the literature [5]. It highlights the challenges that arise when using finite-precision arithmetic in digital control. We are given a discrete plant model (with a time step of 0.2 s), represented by the following z-expression:

$$G(z) = \frac{0.0264}{z - 0.9998}. \qquad (17)$$

Using an optimization tool, the authors of [36] have designed a high-performance controller for this plant, which is characterized by the following z-domain transfer function:

$$C(z) = \frac{2.72z^2 - 4.153z + 1.896}{z^2 - 1.844z + 0.8496}. \qquad (18)$$

The authors of [36] claim that the controller $C(z)$ in (18) stabilizes the closed-loop system for the discrete plant model $G(z)$ in (17). However, if the effects of finite-precision arithmetic are considered, then this closed-loop system becomes unstable. For instance, an implementation of $C(z)$ using $\mathbb{R}\langle 4, 16 \rangle$ fixed-point numbers (i.e., 4 bits for the integer part and 16 bits for the fractional part) can be modeled as:

$$\tilde{C}(z) := \frac{2.71998596191406 25z^2 - 4.1529998779296875z + 1.89599609375}{z^2 - 1.843994140625z + 0.8495941162109375}. \qquad (19)$$

The resulting system, where $\tilde{C}(z)$ and $G(z)$ are in the forward path, is unstable. Notice that this is disregarding further approximation effects on the plant caused by quantization in the verifier (i.e., $\tilde{G}(z)$). Figure 5a gives the Bode diagram for the digital controller represented in (18): as the phase margin is negative, the controller is unstable when considering the FWL effects.

3.7 Program Synthesis for the Example

We now demonstrate how our approach solves the synthesis problem for the example given in the previous section. Assuming a precision of $I_p = 16$, $F_p = 24$, we start with an a-priori candidate solution with all coefficients zero (the controller performs FWL arithmetic, hence we use $\tilde{C}(z)$):

$$\tilde{C}(z) = \frac{0z^2{+}0z{+}0}{0z^2{+}0z{+}0}.$$

In the first VERIFY stage, the UNCERTAINTY check finds the following counterexample:

$$\tilde{G}(z) = \frac{0.026506}{1.000610z + 1.002838}.$$

We add this counterexample to INPUTS and initiate the SYNTHESIZE phase, where we obtain the following candidate solution:

$$\tilde{C}(z) = \frac{12.402664z^2{-}11.439667z{+}0.596756}{4.003906z^2{-}0.287949z{+}0.015625}.$$

This time, the UNCERTAINTY check does not find any counterexample and we pass the current candidate solution to the PRECISION verification stage. We obtain the result *false*, meaning that the current precision is insufficient. Consequently, we increase our precision to $I_p = 20$, $F_p = 28$. Since the previous counterexamples were obtained at lower precision, we remove them from the set of counterexamples. Back in the SYNTHESIZE phase, we re-start the process with a candidate solution with all coefficients 0, as above. Next, the UNCERTAINTY verification stage provides the first counterexample at higher precision:

$$\tilde{G}(z) = \frac{0.026314}{0.999024z{-}1.004785}.$$

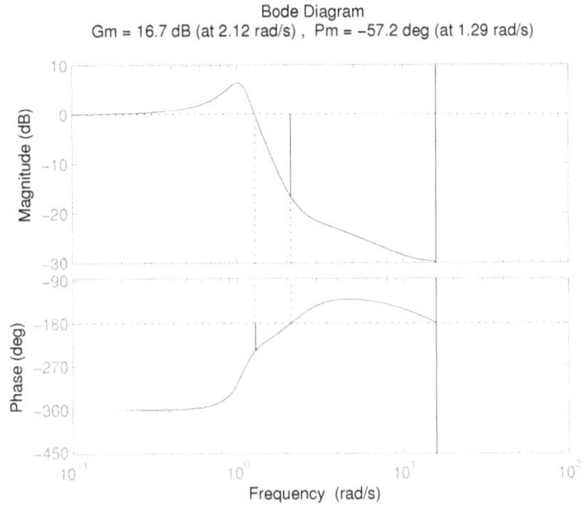

(a) Original controller [36]

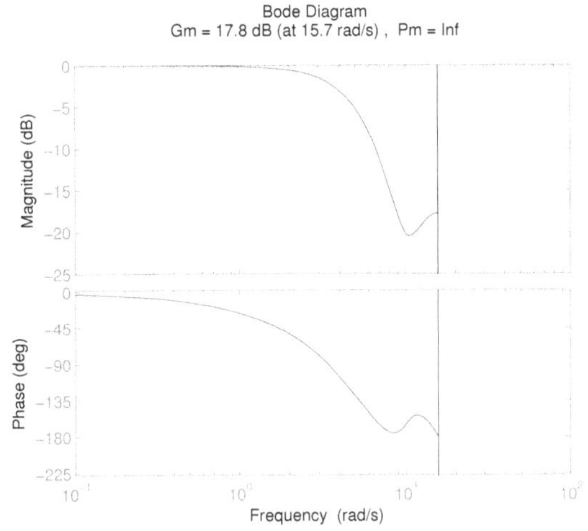

(b) Controller synthesized by DSSynth

Figure 5: Bode diagram for original controller in [36] and for newly synthesized closed-loop system

In the SYNTHESIZE phase, we get a new candidate solution that eliminates the new, higher precision counterexample:

$$\tilde{C}(z) = \frac{11.035202z^2+5.846100z+4.901855}{1.097901z^2+0.063110z+0.128357}.$$

This candidate solution is validated as the final solution by both stages UNCERTAINTY and PRECISION in the VERIFY phase. Figure 5 compares the Bode diagram using the digital controller represented by Eq. (18) from [36] (Figure 5a) and the final candidate solution from our synthesizer (Figure 5b). The DSSynth final solution is stable since it presents an infinite phase margin and a gain margin of 17.8 dB.

Figure 6 illustrates the step responses of the closed-loop system with the original controller represented by Eq. (18) (Figure 6a), the first (Figure 6b) and final (Figure 6c) candidate solutions provided by DSSynth. The step response in Figure 6a confirms the stability loss if we consider FWL effects. Figure 6b shows that the first candidate controller is able to stabilize the closed-loop system without uncertainties, but it is rejected during the PRECISION phase by DSSynth since this solution is not sound. Finally, Figure 6c shows a stable behavior for the final (sound) solution, which presents a lower settling time (hence the digitization effects).

4. EXPERIMENTAL EVALUATION

4.1 Description of the Benchmarks

The first set of benchmarks uses the discrete model G_1 of a cruise control system for a car, and accounts for rolling friction, aerodynamic drag, and the gravitational disturbance force [5]. The second set of benchmarks considers the discrete model G_2 of a simple spring-mass damper plant [36]. A third set of benchmarks uses the discrete model G_3 for satellite attitude dynamics [17], which require attitude control for orientation of antennas and sensors w.r.t. Earth. The fourth set of benchmarks presents an alternative discrete model G_4 of a cruise control system [36]. The fifth and sixth set of benchmarks describe the discrete model of a DC servo motor velocity dynamics [27, 35]. The seventh set of benchmarks contains a well-studied discrete non-minimal phase model G_7. Non-minimal phase models cause additional difficulties for the design of stable controllers [12]. The eighth set of benchmarks describes the discrete model G_8 for the *Helicopter Longitudinal Motion*, which provides the longitudinal motion dynamics of a helicopter [17]. The ninth set of benchmarks contains the discrete model G_9 for the known *Inverted Pendulum*, which describes a pendulum dynamics with its center of mass above its pivot point [17]. The tenth set of benchmarks contains the *Magnetic Suspension* discrete model G_{10}, which describes the dynamics of a mass that levitates with support only of a magnetic field [17]. The eleventh set of benchmarks contains the *Computer Tape Driver* discrete model G_{11}, which describes a system to read and write data on a storage device [17]. The last set of benchmarks considers a discrete model G_{12} that is typically used for evaluating stability margins and controller fragility [23, 24].

Additional benchmarks were created for the *Cruise Control System*, *Spring-mass damper* and *Satellite* considering parametric additive in the nominal plant model (represented by $\Delta_p\vec{G}$ in Eq. (13)). The uncertainties are deviations bounded to a maximum magnitude of 0.5 in each coefficient. These uncertain models are respectively represented by G_{1b}, G_{2b}, G_{3b} and G_{3d}.

All experiments have been conducted on a 12-core 2.40 GHz Intel Xeon E5-2440 with 96 GB of RAM and Linux OS. All times given are wall clock times in seconds, as measured by the UNIX date command. For the two-stage verification engine in Figure 4 we have applied a timeout of 8 hours per benchmark, whereas 24 hours have been set for the approach using a one-stage engine.

4.2 Objectives

Using the closed-loop control system benchmarks given in Section 4.1, our experimental evaluation aims to answer two research questions:

RQ1 **(performance)** does the CEGIS approach generate a FWL digital controller in a reasonable amount of time?

RQ2 **(sanity check)** are the synthesized controllers sound and can their stability be confirmed outside of our model?

4.3 Results

We give the run-times required to synthesize a stable controller for each benchmark in Table 1. Here, *Plant* is the discrete or continuous plant model, *Benchmark* is the name of the employed benchmark, *I* and *F* represent the

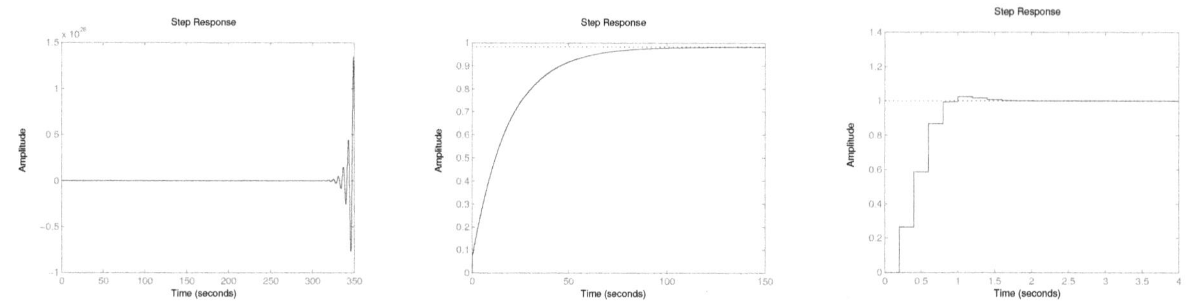

(a) Original controller (b) First solution by DSSynth (c) Final solution by DSSynth

Figure 6: Step responses for original [36] closed-loop system with FWL effects and for each SYNTHESIZE iteration of DSSynth

number of integer and fractional bits of the stable controller, respectively, while the two right columns display the total time (in seconds) required to synthesize a stable controller for the given plant.

For the majority of the benchmarks, the conjecture explained in Section 3.3 holds and the two-stage verification engine is able to find a stable solution in less than one minute for half of the benchmarks. This is possible if the inductive solutions need to be refined with few counterexamples and increments of the fixed-point precision. However, the benchmark *SatelliteB2* with uncertainty (G_{3b}) has required too many counterexamples to refine its solution. For this particular case, the one-stage engine is able to complement the two-stage approach and synthesizes a solution. It is important to reiterate that the one-stage verification engine does not take advantage of the inductive conjecture inherent to CEGIS, but instead fully explores the counterexample space in a single SAT instance. As expected, this approach is significantly slower on average and is only useful for benchmarks where the CEGIS approach requires too many refinement iterations such that exploring all counterexamples in a single SAT instance performs better. Our results suggest an average performance difference of at least two orders of magnitude, leading to the one-stage engine timing out on the majority of our benchmarks. Table 1 lists the results for both engines, where in 16 out of 23 benchmarks, the two-stage engine is faster.

The presence of uncertainty in some particular benchmarks (2, 4, 6 and 8) leads to harder verification conditions to be checked by the VERIFY phase, which impacts the overall synthesis time. However, considering the faster engine for each benchmark (marked in bold in Table 1), the median run-time is 48 s, implying that DSSynth can synthesize half of the controllers in less than one minute. Overall, the average fastest synthesis time considering both engines is approximately 42 minutes. We consider these times short enough to be of practical use to control engineers, and thus affirm RQ1. We further observe that the two-stage verification engine is able to synthesize stable controllers for 19 out of the 23 benchmarks, and can be complemented using the one-stage engine, which is faster for two benchmarks where the inductive conjectures fail. Both verification engines together enable controller synthesis for 20 out of 23 benchmarks. For the remaining benchmarks our approach failed to synthesize a stable controller within the time limits. This can be addressed by either increasing either the time limit or the fixed-point word widths considered, or by using floating-point arithmetic instead. The synthesized controllers have been

#	Plant	Benchmark	I	F	2-stage	1-stage
1	G_{1a}	CruiseControl02	4	16	**12 s**	67 s
2	G_{1b}	CruiseControl02†	4	16	14600 s	**52 s**
3	G_{2a}	SpgMsDamper	15	16	**52 s**	318 s
4	G_{2b}	SpgMsDamper†	15	16	✗	✗
5	G_{3a}	SatelliteB2	3	7	**36 s**	✗
6	G_{3b}	SatelliteB2†	3	7	✗	**4111 s**
7	G_{3c}	SatelliteC2	3	5	**3 s**	205 s
8	G_{3d}	SatelliteC2†	3	5	**50 s**	1315 s
9	G_4	Cruise	3	7	1 s	1 s
10	G_5	DCMotor	3	7	**1 s**	10 s
11	G_6	DCServomotor	4	11	**46 s**	✗
12	G_7	Doyleetal	4	11	**8769 s**	✗
13	G_8	Helicopter	3	7	**44 s**	✗
14	G_9	Pendulum	3	7	**1 s**	14826 s
15	G_{10}	Suspension	3	7	**1 s**	5 s
16	G_{11}	Tapedriver	3	7	1 s	1 s
17	G_{12a}	a_ST1_IMPL1	16	4	**11748 s**	✗
18	G_{12a}	a_ST1_IMPL2	16	8	**351 s**	✗
19	G_{12a}	a_ST1_IMPL3	16	12	**8772 s**	✗
20	G_{12b}	a_ST2_IMPL1	16	4	**1128 s**	✗
21	G_{12b}	a_ST2_IMPL2	16	8	✗	✗
22	G_{12b}	a_ST2_IMPL3	16	12	**15183 s**	✗
23	G_{12c}	a_ST3_IMPL1	16	4	✗	✗

Table 1: DSSynth results (✗ = time-out, † = uncertainty)

confirmed to be stable outside of our model representation using MATLAB, positively answering RQ2. A link to the full experimental environment, including scripts to reproduce the results, all benchmarks and the DSSynth tool, is provided in the footnote.[1]

4.4 Threats to Validity

We have reported a favorable assessment of DSSynth over a diverse set of real-world benchmarks. Nevertheless, this set of benchmarks is limited within the scope of this paper and DSSynth's performance needs to be assessed on a larger benchmark set in future work.

Furthermore, our approach to select suitable FWL word widths to model plant behavior employs a heuristic based on user-provided controller word-width specifications. Given the encouraging results of our benchmarks, this heuristic appears to be strong enough for the current benchmark set, but this may not generalize. Further experiments towards determining suitable plant FWL configurations may thus be necessary in future work.

Finally, the experimental results obtained using DSSynth for stability properties may not generalize to other properties.

[1] http://www.cprover.org/DSSynth/experiment.tar.gz CBMC (SHA-1 hash) version: 7a6cec1dd0eb8843559591105235f1f2c4678801

The inductive nature of the two-stage back-end of DSSynth increases performance significantly compared to the one-stage back-end, but this performance benefit introduced by CEGIS inductive generalizations may not be observed for other controller properties. Additional experiments are necessary to confirm that the performance of our inductive synthesis approach can be leveraged in those scenarios.

5. RELATED WORK

Robust Synthesis of Linear Systems.

The problem of parametric control synthesis based on stability measures for continuous Linear Time Invariant (LTI) Single Input-Single Output (SISO) systems has been researched for several decades. On a theoretical level it is a solved problem [37], for which researchers continuously seek better results for a number of aspects in addition to stability. A vast range of pole placement techniques such as Moore's algorithm for eigenstructure assignment [25] or the more recent Linear Quadratic Regulator (LQR) [6] have been used with increasing degrees of success. The latter approach highlights the importance of conserving energy during the control process, which results in lower running costs. Since real systems are subject to tolerance and noise as well as the need for economy, more recent studies focus on the problem of achieving robust stability with minimum gain [33, 26]. However, when applied with the aim of synthesizing a digital controller, many of these techniques lack the ability to produce sound or stable results because they disregard the effects of quantization and rounding. Recent papers on implementations/synthesis of LTI digital controllers [10, 18] focus on time discretization, failing to account for these error-inducing effects and can result in digital systems that are unstable even though they have been proven to be robustly stable in a continuous space.

Formal Verification of Linear Digital Controllers.

Various effects of discretizing dynamics, including delayed response [13] and Finite Word Length (FWL) semantics [3] have been studied, with the goal to either verify [7] or to optimize [29] given implementations.

There are two different problems that arise from FWL semantics. The first is the error in the dynamics caused by the inability to represent the exact state of the physical system while the second relates to rounding errors during computation. In [16], a stability measure based on the error of the digital dynamics ensures that the deviation introduced by FWL does not make the digital system unstable. A recent approach [38] uses the μ-calculus to directly model the digital controller so that the selected parameters are stable by design. Most work in verification focuses on finding a correct variant of a known controller, looking for optimal parameter representations using FWL, but ignore the effects of rounding errors due to issues of mathematical tractability. The analyses in [32, 36] rely on an invariant computation on the discrete system dynamics using Semi-Definite Programming (SDP). While the former uses BIBO properties to determine stability, the latter uses Lyapunov-based quadratic invariants. In both cases, the SDP solver uses floating-point arithmetic and soundness is checked by bounding the error. An alternative approach is taken by [30], where the verification of existing code is performed against a known model by extracting an LTI model of the code through symbolic execution. In order to account for rounding errors, an upper bound is introduced in the verification phase. If the error of the implementation is lower than this tolerance level, then the verification is successful.

Robust Synthesis of FWL Digital Controllers.

There is no technique in the existing literature for automatic synthesis of fixed-point digital controllers that considers FWL effects.

Other tools such as [14] are aimed at robust stability problems, but they fail to take the FWL effects into account. In order to provide a correct-by-design digital controller, [2] requires a user-defined finite-state abstraction to synthesize a digital controller based on high-level specifications. While this approach overcomes the challenges presented by the FWL problem, it still requires error-prone user intervention. A different solution that uses FWL as the starting point is an approach that synthesizes word lengths for known control problems [22]; however, this provides neither an optimal result nor a comprehensive solution for the problem.

The CEGIS Architecture.

Program synthesis is the problem of computing correct-by-design programs from high-level specifications. Algorithms for this problem have made substantial progress in recent years. One such approach [21] inductively synthesizes invariants to generate the desired programs.

Program synthesizers are an ideal fit for synthesis of parametric controllers since the semantics of programs capture effects such as FWL precisely. In [31], the authors use CEGIS for the synthesis of switching controllers for stabilizing continuous-time plants with polynomial dynamics. The work extends to its application on affine systems, finding its major challenge in the hardness of solving linear arithmetic with the state-of-the-art SMT solvers. Since this approach uses switching states instead of linear dynamics in the digital controller, it entirely circumvents the FWL problem. It is also not suitable for the kind of control we seek to synthesize. We require a combination of a synthesis engine with a control verification tool that addresses the challenges presented here in the form of FWL effects and stability measures for LTI SISO controllers. We take the former from [11] and the latter from [7] while enhancing the procedure by evaluating the quantization effects of the Hardware interfaces (ADC/DAC) to obtain an accurate discrete-time FWL representation of the continuous dynamics.

6. CONCLUSIONS

We have presented a method for synthesizing stable controllers, implemented in a tool called DSSynth. Our approach is it is fully automated and algorithmically and numerically sound. DSSynth marks the first use of the CEGIS that handles plants with uncertain models and FWL effects over the digital controller. We transform the traditional CEGIS refinement loop into a two-stage engine: here, the first stage performs fast, but potentially unsound fixed-point operations, whereas the second stage restores soundness by validating the operations performed by the first stage using interval arithmetic. Our experimental results show that DSSynth is able to synthesize stable controllers for most benchmarks within a reasonable amount of time fully automatically. Future work will be the extension of this CEGIS-based approach to further classes of systems, including those with state space.

7. REFERENCES

[1] R. Alur, D. Fisman, R. Singh, and A. Solar-Lezama. SyGuS-Comp 2016: Results and analysis. In *Workshop on Synthesis*, volume 229 of *EPTCS*, 2016.

[2] R. Alur, S. Moarref, and U. Topcu. Compositional synthesis with parametric reactive controllers. In *HSCC*. ACM, 2016.

[3] A. Anta, R. Majumdar, I. Saha, and P. Tabuada. Automatic verification of control system implementations. In *Embedded Software (EMSOFT)*, pages 9–18, 2010.

[4] K. Åström and B. Wittenmark. *Computer-controlled systems: theory and design.* 1997.

[5] K. J. Astrom and R. M. Murray. *Feedback Systems: An Introduction for Scientists and Engineers.* 2008.

[6] A. Bemporad, M. Morari, V. Dua, and E. N. Pistikopoulos. The explicit linear quadratic regulator for constrained systems. *Automatica*, 38(1), 2002.

[7] I. Bessa, H. Ismail, L. Cordeiro, and J. Filho. Verification of fixed-point digital controllers using direct and delta forms realizations. *Design Autom. for Emb. Sys.*, 20(2), 2016.

[8] I. Bessa, H. Ismail, R. Palhares, L. Cordeiro, and J. E. C. Filho. Formal non-fragile stability verification of digital control systems with uncertainty. *IEEE Transactions on Computers*, 66(3):545–552, 2017.

[9] E. M. Clarke, D. Kroening, and F. Lerda. A tool for checking ANSI-C programs. In *TACAS*, volume 2988, 2004.

[10] S. Das, I. Pan, K. Halder, S. Das, and A. Gupta. LQR based improved discrete PID controller design via optimum selection of weighting matrices using fractional order integral performance index. *Applied Mathematical Modelling*, 37(6), 2013.

[11] C. David, D. Kroening, and M. Lewis. Using program synthesis for program analysis. In *LPAR*, LNCS, 2015.

[12] J. C. Doyle, B. A. Francis, and A. R. Tannenbaum. *Feedback Control Theory.* 1991.

[13] P. S. Duggirala and M. Viswanathan. Analyzing real time linear control systems using software verification. In *IEEE Real-Time Systems Symposium*, Dec 2015.

[14] C. Economakos, G. Economakos, M. Skarpetis, and M. Tzamtzi. Automated synthesis of an FPGA-based controller for vehicle lateral control. In *MATEC Web of Conferences*, volume 41, 2016.

[15] S. Fadali and A. Visioli. *Digital Control Engineering: Analysis and Design*, volume 303 of *Electronics & Electrical.* 2009.

[16] I. J. Fialho and T. T. Georgiou. On stability and performance of sampled-data systems subject to wordlength constraint. *IEEE Trans. on Automatic Control*, 39(12), 1994.

[17] G. Franklin, D. Powell, and A. Emami-Naeini. *Feedback Control of Dynamic Systems.* 7th edition, 2015.

[18] S. Ghosh, R. K. Barai, S. Bhattarcharya, P. Bhattacharyya, S. Rudra, A. Dutta, and R. Pyne. An FPGA based implementation of a flexible digital PID controller for a motion control system. In *Computer Communication and Informatics (ICCCI)*. IEEE, 2013.

[19] H. Ismail, I. Bessa, L. C. Cordeiro, E. B. de Lima Filho, and J. E. C. Filho. DSVerifier: A bounded model checking tool for digital systems. In *SPIN*, volume 9232, 2015.

[20] R. Istepanian and J. F. Whidborne. *Digital controller implementation and fragility: A modern perspective.* 2012.

[21] S. Itzhaky, S. Gulwani, N. Immerman, and M. Sagiv. A simple inductive synthesis methodology and its applications. In *ACM Sigplan Notices*, volume 45. ACM, 2010.

[22] S. Jha and S. A. Seshia. Synthesis of optimal fixed-point implementations of numerical software routines. In *Numerical Software Verification (NSV)*, 2013.

[23] L. Keel and S. Bhattacharyya. Robust, fragile, or optimal? *IEEE Trans. on Automatic Control*, 42(8), 1997.

[24] L. Keel and S. Bhattacharyya. Stability margins and digital implementation of controllers. In *Proc. American Control Conference*, volume 5, 1998.

[25] G. Klein and B. Moore. Eigenvalue-generalized eigenvector assignment with state feedback. *IEEE Trans. on Automatic Control*, 22(1), 1977.

[26] U. Konigorski. Pole placement by parametric output feedback. *Systems & Control Letters*, 61(2), 2012.

[27] Y. Li, K. Ang, G. Chong, W. Feng, K. Tan, and H. Kashiwagi. CAutoCSD–evolutionary search and optimisation enabled computer automated control system design. *Int J Automat Comput*, 1(1), 2004.

[28] R. E. Moore. *Interval analysis*, volume 4. 1966.

[29] A. K. Oudjida, N. Chaillet, A. Liacha, M. L. Berrandjia, and M. Hamerlain. Design of high-speed and low-power finite-word-length PID controllers. *Control Theory and Technology*, 12(1), 2014.

[30] J. Park, M. Pajic, I. Lee, and O. Sokolsky. Scalable verification of linear controller software. In *TACAS*. Springer, 2016.

[31] H. Ravanbakhsh and S. Sankaranarayanan. Counter-example guided synthesis of control Lyapunov functions for switched systems. In *Conference on Decision and Control, CDC*, 2015.

[32] P. Roux, R. Jobredeaux, and P. Garoche. Closed loop analysis of control command software. In *HSCC*, 2015.

[33] R. Schmid, L. Ntogramatzidis, T. Nguyen, and A. Pandey. A unified method for optimal arbitrary pole placement. *Automatica*, 50(8), 2014.

[34] A. Solar-Lezama, L. Tancau, R. Bodík, S. A. Seshia, and V. A. Saraswat. Combinatorial sketching for finite programs. In *ASPLOS*, pages 404–415. ACM, 2006.

[35] K. Tan and Y. Li. Performance-based control system design automation via evolutionary computing. *Engineering Applications of Artificial Intelligence*, 14(4), 2001.

[36] T. E. Wang, P. Garoche, P. Roux, R. Jobredeaux, and E. Feron. Formal analysis of robustness at model and code level. In *HSCC*, 2016.

[37] W. Wonham. On pole assignment in multi-input controllable linear systems. *IEEE Trans. on Automatic Control*, 12(6), 1967.

[38] J. Wu, G. Li, S. Chen, and J. Chu. Robust finite word length controller design. *Automatica*, 45(12), 2009.

A Small Gain Theorem for Parametric Assume-Guarantee Contracts*

Eric S. Kim, Murat Arcak, Sanjit A. Seshia
{eskim, arcak, sseshia}@eecs.berkeley.edu
University of California at Berkeley, Berkeley, CA, USA
Department of Electrical Engineering and Computer Sciences

ABSTRACT

The problem of verifying properties of large, networked cyber-physical systems (CPS) is beyond the reach of most computational tools today. Two common "divide-and-conquer" techniques for CPS verification are assume-guarantee contracts from the formal methods literature and input-output properties from the control theory literature. Combining these two approaches, we first introduce the notion of a parametric assume-guarantee contract, which lets one reason about system behavior abstractly in a parameter domain. We next show how a finite gain property can be encoded in this form and provide a generalized small-gain theorem for parametric assume-guarantee contracts.

This theorem recovers the classical small gain theorem as a special case and its derivation highlights the connection between assume-guarantee reasoning and small-gain results. This new small-gain theorem applies to behaviors beyond bounded deviation from a nominal point to include a fragment of linear temporal logic with parametrized predicates that can encode safety, recurrence, and liveness properties. Our results are validated with an example which certifies that the interconnection of two freeway segments experiences intermittent congestion.

Keywords

Assume-Guarantee Contracts; Parametric Temporal Logic; Small Gain Theorem; Robustness

1. INTRODUCTION

Exploiting compositionality is a common procedure for the design and verification of systems consisting of a large number of interconnected components. Such techniques leverage higher level representations of component behavior to reason about the complete interconnected system's behavior. In the broader cyber-physical systems (CPS) literature, these higher level representations are commonly in the form of an input-output property or an assume-guarantee contract. The notion of assume-guarantee contract resembles the concepts of an input-output robustness property because both encode relationships between an environment and the behaviors exhibited by a system. Both theories are leveraged for compositional design and verification for an interconnection of systems.

We first introduce the notion of a parametric assume-guarantee contract. Contracts of this form permit us to write tighter guarantees on system behaviors as a response to the environment a system *actually* experiences once implemented and deployed; contracts without this form typically have coarse guarantees because assumptions need to account for all possible environments it *could* experience. Additionally, the parameterization of assumptions and guarantees permits us to reason about system behavior. A finite gain property can be encoded as a parametric assume-guarantee contract.

This paper's core technical contribution is to provide a small gain theorem for system behaviors satisfying a parametric assume-guarantee contract. The classical small-gain theorem, which establishes bounded input bounded output (BIBO) stability for a feedback interconnection is recovered as a special case. The new result opens a door to small gain-like results for a broader class of specifications beyond BIBO stability. This broader class of specifications requires a mild technical condition, which we show to also be satisfied by a fragment of linear temporal logic with parametrized predicates. This fragment may encode objectives such as safety, recurrence, and liveness properties.

We next discuss methods to verify that a system satisfies a parametric assume-guarantee contract. Our results are demonstrated with a freeway traffic flow example with hybrid dynamics. Two freeway segments are individually certified to have intermittent congestion. The concatenation is also certified to have intermittent congestion and a quantitative upper bound is established on its severity.

1.1 Related Work

The notions of input-output stability and robustness from the control theory literature have been extended to cyber-physical systems for both verification and controller synthesis. Definitions of robustness for systems with discrete input-output alphabets and associated verification algorithms were provided by Tarraf et al. [23] and Tabuada et al. [22]. Small-gain conditions are leveraged by Rungger et al. [21] for com-

*This work was supported in part by NSF grant CNS-1446145, the NSF Graduate Research Fellowship Program, NSF Expeditions grant CCF-1139138 and by STARnet, a Semiconductor Research Corporation program, sponsored by MARCO and DARPA.

HSCC'17, April 18 - 20, 2017, Pittsburgh, PA, USA

ISBN 978-1-4503-4590-3/17/04...$15.00

DOI: http://dx.doi.org/10.1145/3049797.3049805

positional construction of approximate discrete abstractions of continuous systems and Dallal et al. [6] to design customized compositional abstractions for a persistency specification. Majumdar et al. [16] argue that graceful degradation in performance in the presence of errors is a desirable property to enforce in systems. Bloem et al. [4] advocate for objectives with quantitative measures of "goodness" to distinguish between control strategies that both satisfy a Boolean specification. Indeed, robustness has been introduced into temporal logic to serve as a qualitative measure of satisfaction [10][9].

Compositionality in the formal methods literature has been approached through the notion of a contract which specifies a set of environments under which a component is guaranteed to exhibit a desired behavior [3]. Assume-guarantee contracts have been used for the verification of aircraft electrical systems [18], controller synthesis in traffic networks [13], and to certify stability for embedded systems in the presence of timing uncertainty [1].

To date, assume-guarantee contracts have been Boolean properties and do not incorporate notions of robustness as described above. To the authors' knowledge, there are no existing results that quantify how robust an interconnection of two systems is upon interconnection. The literature on assume-guarantee contracts with quantitative values primarly concerns verifying that a stochastic system satisfies a property with sufficiently high probability [14].

2. PRELIMINARIES

For a set $\mathcal{P}$, let $|\mathcal{P}|$, $2^{\mathcal{P}}$, $\mathcal{P} \times \mathcal{Q}$, $\mathcal{P}^*$, and $\mathcal{P}^\omega$ respectively represent $\mathcal{P}$'s cardinality, powerset (set of all subsets), Cartesian product with $\mathcal{Q}$, and sets of finite and infinite sequences of elements of $\mathcal{P}$. We let $\mapsto$ denote a functional map from a domain to codomain, and $\implies$ represent Boolean implication. Boolean true and false are denoted by $\top$ and $\bot$. For two functions f, g with appropriate domains and codomains, $(f \circ g)(x)$ denotes the function composition $f(g(x))$. The Boolean negation of a proposition a is $\neg a$ and we have logical operations $\wedge$ (and/conjunction) and $\vee$ (or/disjunction). The implication $A \implies B$ is equivalent to the logical statement $\neg A \vee B$; in other words, $A \implies B$ is violated only when A is true and B is false.

Given a space $\mathcal{X}$ equipped with a distance metric $d : \mathcal{X} \times \mathcal{X} \mapsto \mathbb{R}_{\geq 0}$, the closure of the set $\mathcal{L} \subseteq \mathcal{X}$ is denoted $\mathbf{cl}(\mathcal{L})$. The $\epsilon-$expansion of $A \subseteq \mathcal{X}$ for $\epsilon \geq 0$ is $\mathcal{B}_\epsilon(A) = \bigcup_{x \in A}\{y \in \mathcal{X} : d(x, y) \leq \epsilon\}$. A point x' is in the $\omega-$limit of a sequence $x[\cdot] = x[0]x[1]\ldots$ if and only if there exists a subsequence that converges to x'.

For a space $\mathcal{X}$ and an interval $I = [a, b]$ (where $a \leq b$, $a \in \mathbb{Z}_{\geq 0}, b \in \mathbb{Z}_{\geq 0} \cup \{\infty\}$) the space of signals $\mathcal{X}[\cdot]$ is given by a Cartesian product indexed by elements of I:

$$\mathcal{X}[\cdot] = \prod_{k \in I} \mathcal{X}. \tag{1}$$

For a signal $x[\cdot] \in \mathcal{X}[\cdot]$, let $x[k]$ represent its value at time k.

In this paper, a dynamical system Σ is viewed as a relation between inputs and output signals $\Sigma \subseteq \mathcal{U}[\cdot] \times \mathcal{Y}[\cdot]$. We assume that any input $u[\cdot]$ is paired with at least one $y[\cdot]$ via the relation Σ. Such a $y[\cdot]$ is unique if Σ is deterministic and we say $y[\cdot] = \Sigma(u[\cdot])$ holds. If Σ is non-deterministic then $y[\cdot]$ is not necessarily unique and we say that $y[\cdot] \in \Sigma(u[\cdot])$.

3. SPECIFICATIONS

An input-output specification $\phi \subseteq \mathcal{U}[\cdot] \times \mathcal{Y}[\cdot]$ for a dynamical system is a logical statement describing a set of desirable input-output behaviors. An input specification is a subset of $\mathcal{U}[\cdot]$ and an output specification is a subset of $\mathcal{Y}[\cdot]$. We signify that an input (resp. output) signal $z[\cdot]$ *satisfies* an input (resp. output) specification ϕ by $z[\cdot] \models \phi$. A system Σ satisfies ϕ if $\Sigma \subseteq \phi$. A specification ϕ over $\mathcal{Z}[\cdot]$ is *satisfiable* if there exists a $z[\cdot] \in \mathcal{Z}[\cdot]$ such that $z[\cdot] \models \phi$. A specification ϕ has an evaluation time $|\phi|$, which represents the minimum amount of time to determine if a signal satisfies or violates ϕ. If specification $\phi \subseteq \mathcal{U}[\cdot] \times \mathcal{Y}[\cdot]$ is associated with the time interval $I = [a, b]$ then generally $|\phi| = b - a$. Specification ϕ has *bounded evaluation time* if $|\phi| < \infty$.

One can project from a Boolean view of the specification ϕ to a set point of view with $\phi = \{z[\cdot] \in \mathcal{Z}[\cdot] : z[\cdot] \models \phi\}$. As expected $z[\cdot] \models \phi$ if and only if $z[\cdot] \in \phi$ (using the set theoretic definition of ϕ). It is typically easier to manipulate specifications as logical objects, but some notation overloading between the set/logic points of view may occur and is pointed out when appropriate.

A parametric input-output specification $\psi : \mathcal{P} \mapsto 2^{\mathcal{U}[\cdot] \times \mathcal{Y}[\cdot]}$ is a collection of specifications indexed by some parameter space $\mathcal{P}$. Parametric input specifications and parametric output specifications are defined analogously. For instance the input specification (in set form) $\psi(p) = \{u[\cdot] : \sqrt[p]{u[1]} > 4\}$ has parameter $p \in \mathbb{R}$. An example of a parametric output specification may be the set $\psi(p) = \{y[\cdot] : ||y[\cdot]||_2 < p\}$ of signals with Euclidean norm bounded by $p \in \mathbb{R}_{\geq 0}$.

We use the Hausdorff pseudo-metric to measure the difference between satisfiable specifications. Given a metric $d : \mathcal{X}[\cdot] \times \mathcal{X}[\cdot] \mapsto \mathbb{R}_{\geq 0} \cup \{\infty\}$ between signals, the Hausdorff between specifications ϕ_a and ϕ_b is:

$$\begin{aligned} d_H(\phi_a, \phi_b) &:= \inf\{\epsilon \geq 0 : \phi_a \subseteq \mathcal{B}_\epsilon(\phi_b) \text{ and } \phi_b \subseteq \mathcal{B}_\epsilon(\phi_a)\} \\ &:= \max\{\sup_{a \in \phi_a} \inf_{b \in \phi_b} d(a[\cdot], b[\cdot]), \sup_{b \in \phi_b} \inf_{a \in \phi_a} d(a[\cdot], b[\cdot])\} \end{aligned}$$

If $d_H(\phi_a, \phi_b) < \epsilon$, then for each signal that satisfies ϕ_a is at most ϵ for some signal that satisfies ϕ_b and vice versa. The Hausdorff distance can assume infinite values and is a pseudo-metric because $d_H(\phi_a, \phi_b) = 0$ implies $\mathbf{cl}(\phi_a) = \mathbf{cl}(\phi_b)$ rather than $\phi_a = \phi_b$. A parametric specification with a metric-equipped parameter space is Hausdorff continuous if it satisfies the standard $\epsilon - \delta$ definition. That is, any arbitrary small bound on the Hausdorff distance between specifications is satisfied for a sufficiently small parameter difference.

3.1 Assume-Guarantee Contracts

Assume-guarantee reasoning is a common way to abstract a system by encoding what behaviors can be expected under suitable assumptions [3][17]. The assumption is often viewed as an environment experienced by a system.

DEFINITION 1. *(Assume-Guarantee Contract) An assume guarantee contract $\mathcal{C}$ is a pair (ϕ_a, ϕ_g) consisting of an assumption ϕ_a and guarantee ϕ_g that encodes the requirement that the logical implication $\phi_a \implies \phi_g$ holds.*

A system $\Sigma \subseteq \mathcal{U}[\cdot] \times \mathcal{Y}[\cdot]$ satisfies $\mathcal{C} = (\phi_a, \phi_g)$ if $\Sigma \cap \phi_a \subseteq \phi_g$ (where ϕ_a, ϕ_g are viewed as sets) and satisfaction is depicted in Figure 1. Note that an assume-guarantee specification is automatically satisfied if the assumptions are not true; it

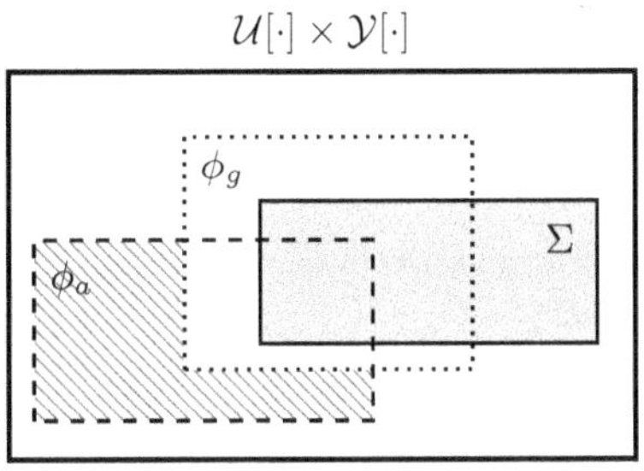

Figure 1: Illustration of system Σ (shaded box) satisfying an unsaturated contract $\mathcal{C} = (\phi_a, \phi_g)$. The space $\mathcal{U}[\cdot] \times \mathcal{Y}[\cdot]$ represets the set of all possible behaviors. The system's set of feasible behaviors does not always satisfy the guarantee (dotted box), but this is permitted because the assumption (dashed box) is not true when the violation occurs. A violation occurs only in the patterned region.

can only be violated when the assumption is true and the guarantee is false.

Any contract (ϕ_a, ϕ_g) can be transformed into its *saturated form* (ϕ'_a, ϕ'_g) where $\phi'_a := \phi_a$ and $\phi'_g := (\phi_a \implies \phi_g)$. Logically, a contract and its saturated form are equivalent. However, unlike the original guarantee ϕ_g which is permitted to be false when the assumption is false, the new guarantee ϕ'_g is false only when the system violates the contract. With respect to Figure 1, the new guarantee $\phi'_g := \neg\phi_a \vee \phi_g$ is the complement of the patterned region that signifies a contract violation.

The conjunction of saturated contracts is denoted by $\mathcal{C}^1 \wedge \mathcal{C}^2 = (\phi_a^1 \vee \phi_a^2, \phi_g^1 \wedge \phi_g^2)$ [3]. Thus a system that satisfies the conjunction of contracts can satisfy tighter guarantees under a wider range of environments/assumptions.

3.2 Parametric Assume Guarantee Contracts

Most assume-guarantee contracts make worst case assumptions about an environment's behavior at design time. A system's guarantee as a result is coarse in order to compensate for the uncertainty about which environment a system will experience once deployed.

In order to make guarantees more precise, we use parametric specifications to divide the assumption ϕ_a into smaller regions $\psi_a(p_a)$ where each p_a can be thought of as an "environmental scenario" parametrized over a set $\mathcal{P}_a$. Systems can provide a finer guarantee $\psi_g(p_g)$ on response to a smaller set of environment behaviors $\psi_a(p_a)$. The relationship between the assumption and guarantee is specified by the parameter map $\lambda : \mathcal{P}_a \mapsto \mathcal{P}_g$.

We define a set of contracts $\mathcal{C}(p_a)$ that correspond to each of these environment scenarios.

$$\mathcal{C}(p_a) := (\psi_a(p_a), \psi_a(p_a) \implies \psi_g(\lambda(p_a))). \tag{2}$$

DEFINITION 2. *(Parametric Assume-Guarantee Contract) Assume-guarantee contract $\mathcal{C} = (\phi_a, \phi_g)$ is in parametric form if there exists a parametric specification $\psi_a : \mathcal{P}_a \mapsto 2^{\mathcal{U}[\cdot]}$, parametric specification $\psi_g : \mathcal{P}_g \mapsto 2^{\mathcal{Y}[\cdot]}$, and parameter map $\lambda : \mathcal{P}_a \mapsto \mathcal{P}_g$ from assumption parameter space $\mathcal{P}_a$ to guarantee parameter space $\mathcal{P}_g$ such that:*

$$\phi_a = \bigvee_{p_a \in \mathcal{P}_a} \psi_a(p_a) \tag{3}$$

$$\phi_g = \bigwedge_{p_a \in \mathcal{P}_a} (\psi_a(p_a) \implies \psi_g(\lambda(p_a))). \tag{4}$$

The parametric contract can be viewed as a conjunction of smaller contracts $\mathcal{C} = \bigwedge_{p_a \in \mathcal{P}_a} \mathcal{C}(p_a)$.

For all the "assumption scenarios" that are satisfied by the environment, a corresponding guarantee is triggered. Likewise, unsatisfied assumptions do not trigger an obligation to satisfy a guarantee. Parametric assume-guarantee contracts calibrate the guarantees in response to only those environmental scenarios that are satisfied. They are robust in the sense that they are able to provide *some* guarantee despite uncertainties at design time about which environment assumptions will be satisfied after system deployment.

System Σ satisfies the parametric assume-guarantee contract if for all $p_a \in \mathcal{P}_a$:

$$\Sigma \cap \psi_a(p_a) \subseteq \psi_g(\lambda(p_a)).$$

We now show that a finite gain property can be encoded as a parametric assume-guarantee contract. Let $\mathcal{U}[\cdot]$ and $\mathcal{Y}[\cdot]$ be vector spaces equipped with a norm $||\cdot||$.

EXAMPLE 1 (BOUNDED GAIN). *The bounded gain condition $||y[\cdot]|| \leq \gamma||u[\cdot]|| + \beta$ can be encoded as a parametric assume-guarantee contract (ϕ_a, ϕ_b) where $\mathcal{P}_a = \mathcal{P}_g = \mathbb{R}_{\geq 0} \cup \{\infty\}$, $\psi_a(p_a) := ||u[\cdot]|| \leq p_a$, $\psi_g(p_g) := ||y[\cdot]|| \leq p_g$, and $\lambda(p_a) = \gamma p_a + \beta$.*

$$\phi_a := \bigvee_{p_a \in \mathcal{P}_a} (||u[\cdot]|| \leq p_a)$$

$$\phi_g := \bigwedge_{p_a \in \mathcal{P}_a} (||u[\cdot]|| \leq p_a \implies ||y[\cdot]|| \leq \gamma p_a + \beta)$$

When $||u[\cdot]|| = \infty$ then $||y[\cdot]||$ has a trivial upper bound ∞.

Example 1 highlights how the system's guarantee now adjusts to the environment it is in. If $u[\cdot]$ has a large norm, then $y[\cdot]$ will as well. The parametric assume-guarantee contract is also tight in the sense that a stricter norm bound on $u[\cdot]$ will also incur a stricter norm bound on $y[\cdot]$ automatically.

Note that when parameter spaces $\mathcal{P}_a, \mathcal{P}_g$ are singletons then the parametric contract is a regular assume-guarantee contract as detailed in the previous section. Although parametric assume-guarantee contracts permit us to adjust guarantees in response to assumptions, establishing that a system Σ satisfies such contracts may be difficult. Given a system Σ, calibrating the parameter map λ may require domain specific knowledge from the user. Parametric contracts also have more complex encodings which could incur a computational cost during verification. Some rules of thumb for picking the type of parametric specification and techniques to verify contract satisfaction are provided in latter sections.

4. A SMALL GAIN THEOREM FOR PARAMETRIC CONTRACTS

Consider the interconnection in Figure 2, which contains an exogenous environment and a feedback loop. Suppose for

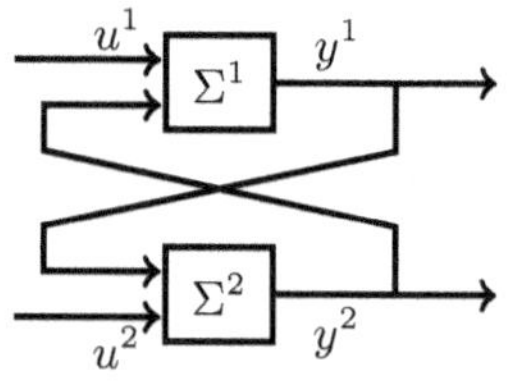

Figure 2: An interconnection with exogenous environment and feedback.

each system Σ^i where $i \in \{1,2\}$ the input space $\mathcal{U}^i = \mathcal{U}_e^i \times \mathcal{U}_f^i$ is partitioned into an exogenous environment $\mathcal{U}_e^i$ component and a feedback component $\mathcal{U}_f^i$. In order for the interconnection to be valid the spaces must match $\mathcal{U}_f^1 = \mathcal{Y}^2$ and $\mathcal{U}_f^2 = \mathcal{Y}^1$. The assume-guarantee contract framework [3][17] in its full generality ignores the roles of ports as inputs and outputs. With Figure 2 in mind, we place the following restriction on assumptions and guarantees.

ASSUMPTION 1. *Let $\psi_{af} : \mathcal{P}_{af} \mapsto 2^{\mathcal{U}_{af}[\cdot]}$ and $\psi_{ae} : \mathcal{P}_{ae} \mapsto 2^{\mathcal{U}_{ae}[\cdot]}$ be input parametric specifications over appropriate domains, and $\psi_g : \mathcal{P}_g \mapsto 2^{\mathcal{Y}[\cdot]}$ be an output parametric specification.*

The assumption parameter space is partitioned into two components $\mathcal{P}_a^i = \mathcal{P}_{ae}^i \times \mathcal{P}_{af}^i$ and the parametric input assumptions $\psi_a : \mathcal{P}_{ae}^i \times \mathcal{P}_{af}^i \mapsto 2^{\mathcal{U}^i[\cdot]}$ is the conjunction of two components

$$\psi_a^i(p_{ae}^i, p_{af}^i) := \psi_{ae}^i(p_{ae}^i) \wedge \psi_{af}^i(p_{af}^i). \tag{5}$$

The parameter map $\lambda^i : \mathcal{P}_{ae}^i \times \mathcal{P}_{af}^i \mapsto \mathcal{P}_g^i$ is adjusted to account for this decomposition of the input space.

4.1 Main Results

Due to the feedback loop in Figure 2, a few additional assumptions are required to derive a new assume-guarantee contract for the interconnected system. First, the exogenous environment and internal feedback assumptions for at least one system need to be satisfied. Second, the guarantees from one system need to imply that the assumptions for the other system hold.

THEOREM 1. *Consider the interconnection of two systems Σ^1, Σ^2 depicted in Figure 2. We assume the following.*

1. *Both systems satisfy their parametric assume guarantee contracts. That is for $i \in \{1,2\}$, $\Sigma_i \cap \phi_a^i \subseteq \phi_g^i$ where ϕ_a^i and ϕ_g^i are defined as*

$$\phi_a^i = \bigvee_{(p_{ae}^i, p_{af}^i) \in \mathcal{P}_a^i} \left(\psi_{ae}^i(p_{ae}^i) \wedge \psi_{af}^i(p_{af}^i)\right) \tag{6}$$

$$\phi_g^i = \bigwedge_{(p_{ae}^i, p_{af}^i) \in \mathcal{P}_a^i} (\psi_{ae}^i(p_{ae}^i) \wedge \psi_{af}^i(p_{af}^i) \tag{7}$$

$$\implies \psi_g^i(\lambda^i(p_{ae}^i, p_{af}^i))).$$

2. *The guarantee parameter spaces are subsets of the feedback components of the assumption parameter spaces, i.e., $\mathcal{P}_g^2 \subseteq \mathcal{P}_{af}^1$ and $\mathcal{P}_g^1 \subseteq \mathcal{P}_{af}^2$. Moreover, the guarantee $\psi_g^2(\cdot)$ from one system implies the feedback assumption $\psi_{af}^1(\cdot)$ and vice versa:*

$$\forall p \in \mathcal{P}_g^1 \quad \psi_g^2(p) \implies \psi_{af}^1(p) \tag{8}$$

$$\forall p \in \mathcal{P}_g^2 \quad \psi_g^1(p) \implies \psi_{af}^2(p). \tag{9}$$

This condition is trivially satisfied if $\psi_g^2(\cdot) = \psi_{af}^1(\cdot)$ and vice versa.

3. *There exist environment parameters $p_{ae}^1 \in \mathcal{P}_{ae}^1$ and $p_{ae}^2 \in \mathcal{P}_{ae}^2$ such that $\psi_{ae}^1(p_{ae}^1)$ and $\psi_{ae}^2(p_{ae}^2)$ are satisfied.*

4. *For either $i = 1,2$ there exists a feedback parameter $p_{af}^i[0] \in \mathcal{P}_{af}^i$ such that $\psi_{af}^i(p_{af}^i[0])$ is true.*

Without loss of generality let $i = 1$, define new feedback parameter maps $\hat{\lambda}^1(\cdot) = \lambda^1(p_{ae}^1, \cdot)$ and $\hat{\lambda}^2(\cdot) = \lambda^1(p_{ae}^2, \cdot)$ associated with exogenous environment assumptions p_{ae}^1, p_{ae}^2, and define guarantee parameter iterations

$$p_g^1[k+1] = (\hat{\lambda}^1 \circ \hat{\lambda}^2)(p_g^1[k]) \tag{10}$$

$$p_g^2[k+1] = (\hat{\lambda}^2 \circ \hat{\lambda}^1)(p_g^2[k]) \tag{11}$$

with initializations $p_g^1[0] = \hat{\lambda}^1(p_{af}^1[0])$, $p_g^2[0] = \hat{\lambda}^2(p_g^1[0])$. Then the guarantee simplifies to

$$\bigwedge_{k=0}^{\infty} \psi_g^1(p_g^1[k])) \wedge \bigwedge_{k=0}^{\infty} \psi_g^2(p_g^2[k]) . \tag{12}$$

For the case when $i = 2$ then a similar guarantee can be obtained by switching the indexes in (10), (11), and (12).

PROOF. Without loss of generality let $i = 1$. The existence of satisfying p_{ae}^1, p_{ae}^2 and $p_{af}^1[0]$ ensure that we can bootstrap an infinite sequence of implications from (7), (8) and (9). The parameters in this implication are generated from the sequences (10) and (11).

$$\begin{aligned}
&\psi_{ae}^1(p_{ae}^1) \wedge \psi_{ae}^2(p_{ae}^2) \wedge \psi_{af}^1(p_{af}^1[0]) \\
&\wedge (\psi_{ae}^1(p_{ae}^1) \wedge \psi_{af}^1(p_{af}^1[0]) \implies \psi_g^1(p_g^1[0])) \\
&\wedge (\psi_g^1(p_g^1[0]) \implies \psi_a^2(p_g^1[0])) \\
&\wedge (\psi_{ae}^2(p_{ae}^2) \wedge \psi_{af}^2(p_g^1[0]) \implies \psi_g^2(p_g^2[0])) \\
&\wedge (\psi_g^2(p_g^2[0]) \implies \psi_a^1(p_g^2[0])) \\
&\wedge (\psi_{ae}^1(p_{ae}^1) \wedge \psi_{af}^1(p_g^2[0]) \implies \psi_g^1(p_g^1[1])) \\
&\wedge \ldots
\end{aligned}$$

This infinite conjunction sequence contains within it (12) as a subsequence. □

The guarantee (12) can be simplified dramatically by investigating the contraction properties of the parameter iterations (10) and (11). To achieve this simplification we assume that the parameter sets $\mathcal{P}_g^i$ for $i = 1,2$ are equipped with distance metrics $d_{\mathcal{P}}^i : \mathcal{P}_g^i \times \mathcal{P}_g^i \mapsto \mathbb{R}_{\geq 0}$ and the input and output spaces $\mathcal{U}[\cdot] \times \mathcal{Y}[\cdot]$ are equipped with a distance metric.

THEOREM 2. *(Small Gain Theorem for Parametric Assume-Guarantee Contracts) Let $\mathcal{P}_g^1$ and $\mathcal{P}_g^2$ be metric spaces and $\psi_g^1(\cdot), \psi_g^2(\cdot)$ be specifications on a metric space. If in addition to the assumptions of Theorem 1 the following are also true:*

1. *Sequences generated by the iterations (10), (11) have nonempty $\omega-$limit sets W^1, W^2 respectively.*

2. *The specifications ψ_g^1, ψ_g^2 vary continuously with parameters everywhere in $\mathcal{P}_g^1, \mathcal{P}_g^2$, where the Hausdorff distance d_H is used as a metric between specifications. In other words for both $i = 1, 2$ for all $\epsilon^i > 0$ and $p \in \mathcal{P}_g^i$ there exists a $\delta^i > 0$ such that*

$$d_{\mathcal{P}}^i(p, \hat{p}^i) < \delta^i \implies d_H(\psi_g^i(p), \psi_g^i(\hat{p}^i)) < \epsilon^i$$

then the guarantee (12) is over-approximated by:

$$\bigwedge_{p^1 \in W^1} \mathbf{cl}(\psi_g^1(p^1)) \wedge \bigwedge_{p^2 \in W^2} \mathbf{cl}(\psi_g^2(p^2)) \qquad (13)$$

where $\mathbf{cl}(\psi)$ is the closure of the specification set ψ.

PROOF. Without loss of generality, we seek to prove that the ψ_g^1 component of formula (12) implies $\mathbf{cl}(\psi_g^1(p^1))$ for a p^1 in the ω-limit set W^1. Suppose $\epsilon > 0$. By Hausdorff continuity of ψ_g^1, there exists a δ such that $|p - p^1| < \delta$ implies $d_H(\psi_g^1(p), \psi_g^1(p^1)) < \epsilon$. Because $p^1 \in W^1$, there is a subsequence of (10) that converges to p^1 and for arbitrary δ. It follows that (12) consists of an infinite sequence of intersections that converge to $\psi_g^1(p^1)$ with arbitrary precision. Because of Hausdorff distance of zero implies that the closure of the two sets are equivalent, this infinite intersection then implies that $\mathbf{cl}(\psi_g^1(p^1))$ holds. Similar arguments can be made for any $p^1 \in W^1$ and for ψ_g^2. □

If the iterations (10) and (11) are contractions to a single point, then we can declare a new parametric assume-guarantee contract for the interconnected system in Figure 2 that is expressed between the exogenous inputs and the outputs.

COROLLARY 1. *If in addition to the assumptions of Theorem 2, the iterations (10) and (11) globally converge to fixed points for any initial parameters $p_{af}^1[0], p_{af}^2[0]$ then the interconnected system of Figure 2 satisfies the parametric assume-guarantee contract associated with*

$$\mathcal{U} := \mathcal{U}_e^1 \times \mathcal{U}_e^2$$
$$\mathcal{Y} := \mathcal{Y}^1 \times \mathcal{Y}^2$$
$$\mathcal{P}_a := \mathcal{P}_{ae}^1 \times \mathcal{P}_{ae}^2$$
$$\mathcal{P}_g := \mathcal{P}_g^1 \times \mathcal{P}_g^2$$
$$\psi_a(p_{ae}^1, p_{ae}^2) := \psi_{ae}^1(p_{ae}^1) \wedge \psi_{ae}^2(p_{ae}^2)$$
$$\psi_g(p_g^1, p_g^2) := \mathbf{cl}(\psi_g^1(\lambda^1(p_{ae}^1, p_{ae}^2))) \wedge \mathbf{cl}(\psi_g^2(\lambda^2(p_{ae}^1, p_{ae}^2))))$$

and $\lambda^1 : \mathcal{P}_{ae}^1 \times \mathcal{P}_{ae}^2 \mapsto \mathcal{P}_g^1$ and $\lambda^2 : \mathcal{P}_{ae}^1 \times \mathcal{P}_{ae}^2 \mapsto \mathcal{P}_g^1$ are the respective limit points of the iterations (10) and (11) as a function of exogenous environment assumptions p_{ae}^1 and p_{ae}^2.

4.2 Ensuring that Guarantees are Satisfiable

One technical issue with applying Theorem 2 to richer sets of behaviors is determining whether the guarantees (12) or (13) are nonempty sets and satisfiable. It is advantageous to design parametric specifications to ensure that satisfiability is maintained.

We link parameters to set containment through the notion of monotone specifications, which were previously advocated in the context of requirement mining [12]. Given a partially ordered parameter space $\mathcal{P}_g^1$ equipped with an ordering relation $\leq_{\mathcal{P}_g^1}$, the parametric output specification $\psi_g^1 : \mathcal{P}_g^1 \mapsto 2^{\mathcal{Y}[\cdot]}$ is monotone if $a \leq_{\mathcal{P}_g^1} b$ implies $\psi_g^1(a) \subseteq \psi_g^1(b)$.

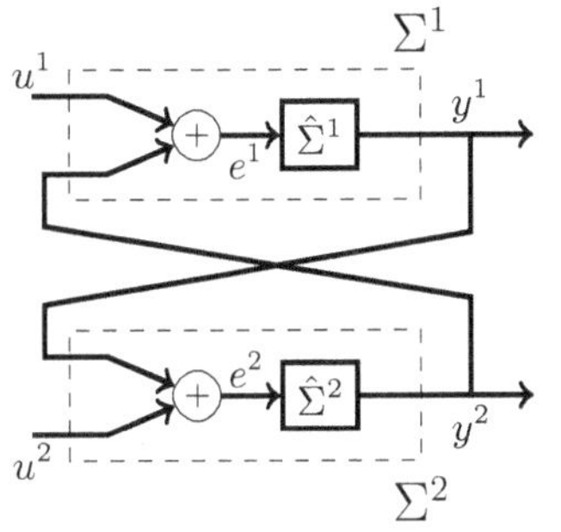

Figure 3: System interconnection for the classical small gain theorem. This interconnection is related to Figure 2 via composite systems Σ^1, Σ^2 which incorporate the addition blocks.

Proposition 1 uses these notions of monotonicity and set containment to give a sufficient condition for the guarantees to be nonempty.

PROPOSITION 1. *Suppose that*

1. *For both $i = 1, 2$ and all nonempty subsets $\mathcal{L}$ of parameter space $\mathcal{P}_g^i$, there exists a lower bound $p \in \mathcal{P}_g^i$ such that $p \leq_{\mathcal{P}_g^i} q$ for all $q \in \mathcal{L}$.*

2. *Parametric output guarantees $\psi_g^1(\cdot)$ and $\psi_g^2(\cdot)$ are monotone specifications and for all parameters $p^1 \in \mathcal{P}_g^1, p^2 \in \mathcal{P}_g^2$ the guarantees $\psi_g^1(p^1), \psi_g^2(p^2)$ are nonempty sets.*

Then the guarantees (12) and (13) are satisfiable/nonempty.

PROOF. Parameters that appear within the sequences (10) and (11) have a lower bound from the first condition and second conditions. Let these lower bounds be denoted as l^1 and l^2 respectively. The sets $\psi_g^1(l^1)$ and $\psi_g^2(l^2)$ are nonempty and $\psi_g^1(l^1) \subseteq \psi_g^1(p_g^1[k])$ and $\psi_g^2(l^2) \subseteq \psi_g^2(p_g^2[k])$ for all $k \in \mathbb{Z}_{\geq 0}$. Therefore, because $\psi_g^1(l^1) \subseteq \cap_{k \in \mathbb{Z}_{\geq 0}} \psi_g^1(p_g^1[k])$ and $\psi_g^2(l^2) \subseteq \cap_{k \in \mathbb{Z}_{\geq 0}} \psi_g^2(p_g^2[k])$, the guarantees (12) and (13) correspond to nonempty sets and are hence satisfiable. □

4.3 Classical Small Gain Theorem as a Special Case

Theorem 2 and Proposition 1 recover the small-gain theorem as stated in [7]. Given some norm, let $\mathcal{L}$ be the space of norm bounded signals. A signal $x[\cdot]$ has an associated T-truncated norm $|x[\cdot]|_T = |\mathbb{I}_T x[\cdot]|$. The signal $x[\cdot]$ is pointwise multiplied with $\mathbb{I}_T$ the indicator function on the time interval $[0, T]$ before the signal norm is taken. The $\mathcal{L}$-extended space $\mathcal{L}_e$ is defined as $\{x[\cdot] : \forall T > 0,\ |x[\cdot]|_T < \infty\}$ and it is clear that $\mathcal{L}$ is a strict subset of $\mathcal{L}_e$.

COROLLARY 2. *(Classical small gain theorem [7]) Let systems $\hat{\Sigma}^1, \hat{\Sigma}^2$ be input-output maps $\hat{\Sigma}^i : \mathcal{L}_e \mapsto \mathcal{L}_e$ and interconnected as in Figure 3. Let $e^1[\cdot], e^2[\cdot] \in \mathcal{L}_e$ and $u^1[\cdot], u^2[\cdot]$ be defined such that*

$$u^1[\cdot] = e^1[\cdot] - y^2[\cdot] \qquad (14)$$
$$u^2[\cdot] = e^2[\cdot] - y^1[\cdot]. \qquad (15)$$

Suppose there are four constants $\gamma^1, \gamma^2, \beta^1, \beta^2 \geq 0$ such that

$$|y^1[\cdot]|_T \leq \gamma^1 |e^1[\cdot]|_T + \beta^1 \qquad (16)$$
$$|y^2[\cdot]|_T \leq \gamma^2 |e^2[\cdot]|_T + \beta^2 \qquad (17)$$

for all T. If $\gamma^1\gamma^2 < 1$, then for all T:

$$|y^1[\cdot]|_T \leq \frac{1}{1-\gamma^1\gamma^2}\left(\gamma^1|u^1[\cdot]|_T + \gamma^1\gamma^2|u^2[\cdot]|_T + \gamma^1\beta^2 + \beta^1\right) \tag{18}$$

$$|y^2[\cdot]|_T \leq \frac{1}{1-\gamma^1\gamma^2}\left(\gamma^2|u^2[\cdot]|_T + \gamma^1\gamma^2|u^1[\cdot]|_T + \gamma^2\beta^1 + \beta^2\right). \tag{19}$$

PROOF. The interconnection defined by (14) and (15) is depicted in Figure 3 where the dashed boxes correspond to Σ^1, Σ^2 in Figure 2 used in Theorem 2. Via the triangle inequality, the bounds (16) and (17) are replaced with

$$|y^1[\cdot]|_T \leq \gamma^1|u^1[\cdot]|_T + \gamma^1|y^2[\cdot]|_T + \beta^1 \tag{20}$$
$$|y^2[\cdot]|_T \leq \gamma^2|u^2[\cdot]|_T + \gamma^2|y^1[\cdot]|_T + \beta^2. \tag{21}$$

The assumption parameters associated with the exogenous inputs u^1, u^2 are bounds on their truncated norms. The feedback assumptions pertain to norm bounds on y^1, y^2. The parameter spaces are $\mathcal{P}^1_{ae}, \mathcal{P}^1_{af}, \mathcal{P}^1_g = \mathbb{R}_{\geq 0} \cup \{\infty\}$. For system Σ^1, define the exogenous assumption, feedback assumption, and guarantee as

$$\psi^1_{ae}(p) = (|u^1[\cdot]|_T \leq p) \tag{22}$$
$$\psi^1_{af}(r) = (|y^2[\cdot]|_T \leq r) \tag{23}$$
$$\psi^1_g(r) = (|y^1[\cdot]|_T \leq r) \tag{24}$$

with the parameter iteration map $\lambda^1(p,r) = \gamma^1 p + \gamma^1 r + \beta^1$. With the above definitions, the bounds (20) can be replaced with a parametric assume-guarantee contract. Analogous definitions for Σ^2 lead to a similar reformulation of (21). The first condition of Theorem 1 is therefore satisfied. The second condition is satisfied because both the guarantees and feedback assumptions are of the same form. The third and fourth conditions of Theorem 1 are satisfied because the existence of $e^1[\cdot], e^2[\cdot] \in \mathcal{L}_e$ implies that their T-truncated norm is finite for some T. Via (16) and (17), $y^1[\cdot], y^2[\cdot]$ also have finite T-truncated norm for an identical T. Via the triangle inequality, $u^1[\cdot], u^2[\cdot]$ must have finite T-truncated norm and satisfy (22).

For fixed norm bounds on $u^1[\cdot], u^2[\cdot]$, the feedback iteration functions become $\hat{\lambda}^1(r) := \gamma^1|u^1[\cdot]|_T + \gamma^1 r + \beta^1$ and $\hat{\lambda}^2(r) := \gamma^2|u^2[\cdot]|_T + \gamma^2 r + \beta^2$. When $\gamma^1\gamma^2 < 1$ the parameter iterations converge to a pair of fixed points, which are given by the right hand sides of (18) and (19). Theorem 2 certifies that these bounds are in fact enforced. We know these guarantees are satisfiable via Proposition 1 because any subset of $\mathcal{P}^1_g, \mathcal{P}^2_g = \mathbb{R}_{\geq 0} \cup \{\infty\}$ has a lower bound within $\mathbb{R}_{\geq 0} \cup \{\infty\}$ and the guarantees ψ^1_g, ψ^2_g are non-empty for all parameters. □

5. HAUSDORFF CONTINUITY OF PARAMETRIC LINEAR TEMPORAL LOGIC

The results from the previous section place relatively mild conditions on guarantee specifications $\psi_g(\cdot)$ to provide a small gain result. These were satisfied when the parameteric specification corresponded to sublevel sets of a norm on signals. In this section, we consider a parametric temporal logic variant that can also be used by Theorem 2.

Temporal logic [19] is a powerful formalism to encode complex timing requirements and has been used as a specification language for controller synthesis and verification of cyber-physical systems. Linear temporal logic (LTL) is a specification language for discrete time systems. Predicates are encoded as statements that are true at a specific instant in time, and a set of temporal operators allow one to make statements that incorporate temporal constraints. In our problem formulation, LTL formulas $\phi \subseteq \mathcal{U}^\omega \times \mathcal{Y}^\omega$ can be thought of as sets of infinite length input-output sequences. We consider an LTL variant where input predicates are subsets of $\mathcal{U}$ of the form $f(x) \sim p$ where $\sim \in \{\leq, \geq\}$ and $f : \mathcal{U} \mapsto \mathbb{R}$ is a real-valued function. Output predicates are defined analogously. Definition 3 provides a syntax for constructing LTL formulas.

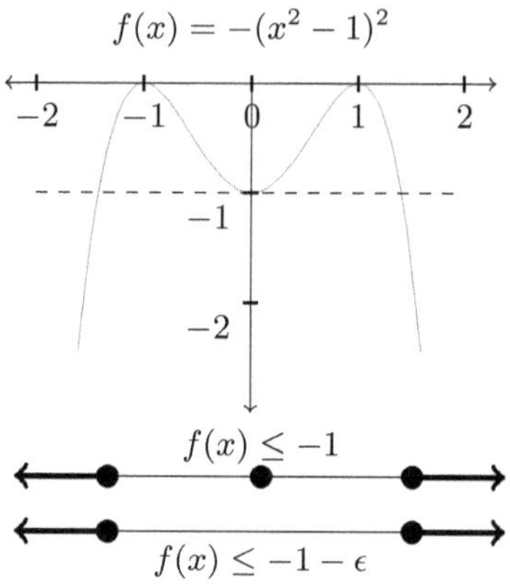

Figure 4: Parametric sublevel sets of non-convex continuous functions are not necessarily Hausdorff continuous.

DEFINITION 3. *Linear temporal logic formulas are constructed with the syntax below*

$$\phi = \top \mid f(\cdot) \sim p \mid \neg\phi \mid \phi_1 \vee \phi_2 \mid \phi_1 \wedge \phi_2 \mid \mathbf{X}\phi \mid \mathbf{F}\phi \mid \mathbf{G}\phi \mid \phi_1 \mathbf{U} \phi_2.$$

with parametric predicates $f(\cdot) \sim p$ where $p \in \mathbb{R}$ and $\sim \in \{\leq, \geq\}$. The semantics of the temporal operators $\mathbf{X}, \mathbf{F}, \mathbf{G}$, *and* $\mathbf{U}$ *are summarized below:*

- *Specification $\mathbf{X}\phi$ with the "next" operator $\mathbf{X}$ is true if and only if ϕ is true at the next time step.*
- *Specification $\mathbf{F}\phi$ with the "eventually" operator $\mathbf{F}$ is true if and only if ϕ is true at the current time step or there exists a future time step when ϕ is true.*
- *Specification $\mathbf{G}\phi$ with the "always" operator $\mathbf{G}$ is true if and only if ϕ is true at the present and all future time steps.*
- *Specification $\phi_1 \mathbf{U} \phi_2$ with the "until" operator $\mathbf{U}$ is true if and only if ϕ_2 is eventually true and ϕ_1 is true for all future time instances before ϕ_2 becomes true.*

The simplest parametric LTL formula is a parametric predicate, which takes the form of sublevel or superlevel set of a function. The parameter p corresponds to the level. Unfortunately, even for continuous functions $f(\cdot)$, the Hausdorff distance between sublevel sets does not vary continuously for all $p \in \mathbb{R}$. Consider the example given in Figure 4. Due to the presence of a spurious local minimum, perturbing p from $p = -1$ to $p = -1 - \epsilon$ for any $\epsilon > 0$ causes the point at zero to vanish from the sublevel set. The Hausdorff distance between the two sublevel sets is lower bounded in this example by $\sqrt{2}$ for all sufficiently small neighborhoods around $p = -1$.

To alleviate this issue of disconnected sublevel sets appearing with spurious local minima, we consider a fragment of LTL where the predicates are compact convex sets.

DEFINITION 4. *LTL formulas with convex parametric predicates are constructed with the following syntax.*

$$\phi = \top \mid f(\cdot) \leq p \mid g(\cdot) \geq q \mid \phi_1 \vee \phi_2 \mid \mathbf{X}\phi \mid \mathbf{F}\phi \mid \mathbf{G}\phi \mid \phi_1 \mathbf{U} \phi_2.$$

where for each predicate $f(\cdot) \leq p$ associated with a convex $f(\cdot)$ we restrict p to the domain $[\min_x f(x), \infty]$ and similarly $g(\cdot)$ is concave with $q \in [-\infty, \max_x g(x)]$.

We make the mild technical assumption that $f(\cdot)$ is uniformly continuous; that is, for all $\epsilon > 0$ there exists a δ where $d(x, y) < \delta$ implies $|f(x) - f(y)| < \epsilon$ for all appropriate x, y.

PROPOSITION 2. *The sublevel set of uniformly continuous convex predicates $f(\cdot) \leq p$ varies continuously with parameter $p \in [\min_x f(x), \infty]$ when the distance between predicates is given by the Hausdorff metric.*

PROOF. Consider two predicates $\psi(p) = f(x) \leq p$ and $\psi(p') = f(x) \leq p'$. Without loss of generality, we assume that $p < p'$. Suppose $\epsilon > 0$. Let $m^+ \geq 0$ be defined as

$$m^+ = \left(\sup_{x \in \mathcal{B}_\epsilon(\psi(p))} f(x) \right) - p.$$

m^+ is the least upper bound on how much $f(\cdot)$ may increase by bloating the set $\psi(p)$ by ϵ. Due to uniform continuity of $f(\cdot)$, m^+ is finite. Because $f(\cdot)$ is convex its sublevel sets cannot consist of many disjoint regions and $\{x : f(x) \leq p + am^+\} \subseteq \mathcal{B}_\epsilon(\psi(p))$ for all $0 < a < 1$. If $|p - p'| < am^+$ then $\psi(p') \subseteq \mathcal{B}_\epsilon(\psi(p))$. An identical argument can be made when $p' < p$. Thus, if the parameters $|p-p'| < am^+$ then the Hausdorff distance of the sublevel sets are bounded above by ϵ. $\square$

Note that the syntax in Definition 4 makes the curious choice of permitting disjunctions $\vee$ and not conjunctions $\wedge$. This choice was made due to the following property of the Hausdorff distance

$$d_H(A \cup B, C \cup D) \leq \max(d_H(A, C), d_H(B, D)) \qquad (25)$$

which upper bounds the distance between sets after a union. No analogous property exists for set intersections because they may be empty and the Hausdorff distance is ill defined. The potential loss of convexity under unions and disjunctions is not an issue because convexity of predicates in Definition 4 simply serves as a sufficient condition for predicates to be Hausdorff continuous and is not necessary.

THEOREM 3. *Let $\psi(\cdot)$ be a parametric specification constructed with the convex predicate LTL grammar from Definition 4. Define $N \in \mathbb{Z}_{\geq 0}$ to be the number of times a predicate appears in $\psi(\cdot)$ and parameter space $\mathcal{P} = [\min_x f_1(x), \infty] \times \ldots \times [\min_x f_N(x), \infty]$. Specifications constructed with the grammar $\psi(\cdot)$ are Hausdorff continuous where signals distances are measured with a supremum metric, $d(x[\cdot], y[\cdot]) = \sup_{k \in \mathbb{Z}_{\geq 0}} d(x[k], y[k])$*

PROOF. Suppose $\epsilon > 0$. Let m_i be defined as it appears at the end of the proof of Proposition 2 for predicate $f_i(p_i) \leq p_i$. Let $m = \min_{i \in \{1,\ldots,N\}} m_i$. Suppose that $x[\cdot] \models \psi(p)$ but $x[\cdot] \not\models \psi(p')$ and $\max_i(|p_i - p_i'|) < m$. Each predicate p_i in formula $\psi(p)$ has an associated infinite Boolean sequence where the k-th value is $\top$ if and only if $x[k] \models p_i$. For some time k, there must be at least one predicate that is different; for it to be otherwise would contradict the assertion that $x[\cdot] \not\models \psi(p')$. Given such a time step k, Proposition 2 and (25) guarantee that for any time step k when the difference arises, $x[k]$ must be less than a distance ϵ away from a point $y[k]$ that satisfies the same set of predicates for p'. Thus, $\psi(p) \subseteq \mathcal{B}_\epsilon(\psi(p'))$ where the $\epsilon-$expansion of $\psi(p')$ is with respect to the supremum metric. A similar argument can be made for the case when $x[\cdot] \models \psi(p')$ and $x[\cdot] \not\models \psi(p)$. $\square$

Theorem 3 augments Theorem 2 by providing a concrete instantiation of a class of Hausdorff continuous specifications with temporal logic operators.

6. CERTIFICATION OF PARAMETRIC CONTRACTS

To apply the results from previous sections we need to show that each system satisfies a parametric assume-guarantee contract. We pose a falsification problem that seeks to construct a violation of the contract. Consider a system Σ with a state space $\mathcal{X}$ and initial state set $\mathcal{X}_0$. The notation $y[\cdot] \in \Sigma(x[0], u[\cdot])$ signifies that output $y[\cdot]$ satisfies the dynamics Σ permitted by $x[0]$ and $u[\cdot]$. Let (ϕ_a, ϕ_g) be a parametric contract obtained from parametric specifications ψ_a, ψ_g and parameter map $\lambda : \mathcal{P}_a \mapsto \mathcal{P}_g$.

PROBLEM 1. *If there exist p, $x[0]$, and $u[\cdot]$ that satisfy constraints (27), (28) and (29) then Σ does not satisfy the parametric assume-guarantee contract (ϕ_a, ϕ_g).*

$$\begin{aligned} \textit{find} \quad & p \in \mathcal{P}_a, x[0] \in \mathcal{X}_0, u[\cdot] && (26)\\ \textit{subject to} \quad & u[\cdot] \models \psi_a(p) && (27)\\ & y[\cdot] \not\models \psi_g(\lambda(p)) && (28)\\ & y[\cdot] \in \Sigma(x[0], u[\cdot]). && (29) \end{aligned}$$

The proper falsification engine to solve Problem 1 is implementation specific and depends on both the system dynamics and specification representation.

For black-box systems and systems exhibiting complex, hybrid, and non-linear dynamics, simulation-based falsification is the most practical method to prove that an assume-guarantee contract is satisfied. Most existing simulation-based falsification algorithms are sound but typically not complete. However, the failure to falsify a contract is evidence suggesting that the contract in fact holds. Simulation-based falsification tools are built into toolboxes `S-TaLiRo`[2] and `Breach`[8] for metric and signal temporal logic.

If the falsification algorithm is complete and no violating p, $x[0]$, and $u[\cdot]$ exist, then Σ satisfies (ϕ_a, ϕ_g). The examples in the next section use a component of the `BluSTL` toolbox [20] to translate bounded time temporal logic specifications (27) and (28) into mixed integer constraints for the optimization toolbox `YALMIP` [15].

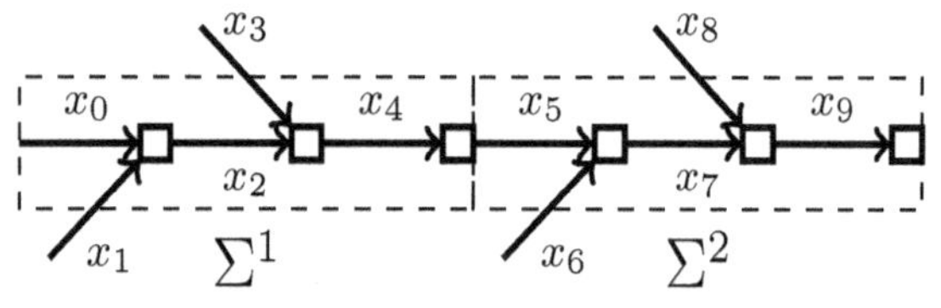

Figure 5: An example network with two on-ramps x_1, x_3. Dashed arrows are exogenous network links.

7. FREEWAY EXAMPLE

This section applies Theorems 1 and 2 to a freeway traffic example. Consider the two freeway segments depicted in Fig. 5, where the left segment has a main stretch of three links x_0, x_2, x_4 and two on-ramps x_1, x_3. The right segment has identical dynamics. We use the cell transmission model (CTM) [5][11], a macroscopic fluid-like model of freeway dynamics. Individual vehicles are not a component of this model. Each discrete time instant represents a five minute interval.

7.1 Freeway Dynamics

We first describe the dynamics for Σ^1, which are identical to the dynamics of Σ^2 besides a variable renaming, and subsequently describe how the interconnected networks resemble the small-gain interconnections (e.g. Figure 2) from previous sections.

Freeway segment Σ^1's state space $\mathcal{X}^1 \subset \mathbb{R}^5_{\geq 0}$ represents the average occupancy over the five minute period in each of the five links. We overload notation and refer to links and their occupancy values using the same variable. The upper bound on occupancy is encoded with a vector $x^{\max} = [40, 20, 40, 20, 40]$. The state update equations arise from conservation of mass:

$$\begin{aligned}
x_0[k+1] &= x_0[k] - f_0^{\text{out}}[k] + f_0^{\text{in}}[k] \\
x_1[k+1] &= x_1[k] - f_1^{\text{out}}[k] + f_1^{\text{in}}[k] \\
x_2[k+1] &= x_2[k] - f_2^{\text{out}}[k] + f_0^{\text{out}}[k] + f_1^{\text{out}}[k] \\
x_3[k+1] &= x_3[k] - f_3^{\text{out}}[k] + f_3^{\text{in}}[k] \\
x_4[k+1] &= x_4[k] - f_4^{\text{out}}[k] + f_2^{\text{out}}[k] + f_3^{\text{out}}[k]
\end{aligned}$$

where $f_i^{\text{out}}[k]$ and $f_i^{\text{out}}[k]$ respectively represent the flows exiting and entering link x_i at time k.

The flows into and out of a link are determined by *demand* and *supply.* A link's demand is the rate at which it would like to send vehicles to downstream links. The demand $d_i(x_i[k])$ that link x_i exhibits is a non-decreasing function

$$d_i(x_i[k]) = \min(c_i, x_i[k]) \tag{30}$$

where c_i is a saturation rate.The primary links have saturation rates $c_0 = c_2 = c_4 = 10$ and on-ramps have saturation rates $c_1 = c_3 = 5$. All links also exhibit a supply function

$$s(x_i[k]) = x_i^{\max} - x_i[k], \tag{31}$$

which is the rate of incoming vehicles that it can accept from upstream. A link's supply is partitioned among upstream links, with links x_2, x_4 allocating 80% of their supply to an upstream highway link and 20% to on-ramps. Link x_2's supply and demand functions are depicted in Figure 6. Congestion occurs when demand exceeds supply and the left

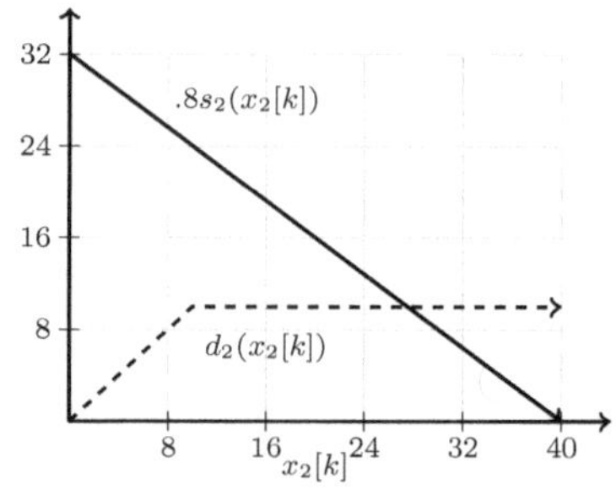

Figure 6: Supply (solid) that link x_2 provides to link x_0 and Demand (dashed) that link x_2 creates for link x_4

term in the minimization is active. The flows out of links $0, 1, 2, 3$ are the minimum between the supply available to them and their demand:

$$\begin{aligned}
f_0^{\text{out}}[k] &= \min\left(.8(40 - x_2[k]), 10, x_0[k]\right) \\
f_1^{\text{out}}[k] &= \min\left(.2(40 - x_2[k]), 5, x_1[k]\right) \\
f_2^{\text{out}}[k] &= \min\left(.8(40 - x_4[k]), 10, x_2[k]\right) \\
f_3^{\text{out}}[k] &= \min\left(.2(40 - x_4[k]), 5, x_3[k]\right)
\end{aligned}$$

7.2 Interconnection between Networks

Figure 7 summarizes the input and output variables for each network. Network Σ^1 has a vector of demands as its exogenous input $u^1_{ae} = (d^{\text{exog}}, d_1^{\text{on}}, d_3^{\text{on}})$ and the feedback input $u^1_{af} = (s_5)$ is the supply from downstream. Similarly, Σ^2 has exogenous input $u^2_{ae} = (s^{\text{exog}}, d_6^{\text{on}}, d_8^{\text{on}})$ and feedback input $u^2_{ae} = (d_4)$. The outputs can be identified in a similar manner.

With the notions of demand and supply in mind, we can now consider how both networks are affected by their interconnection and by exogenous environments. The flow f_4^{out} between Σ^1 and Σ^2 is determined by d_4 and s_5

$$f_4^{\text{out}}[k] = \min\left(.8(40 - x_5[k]), 10, x_4[k]\right).$$

Both systems experience an exogenous environment via the on ramp demands. The upstream system Σ^1 also experiences a demand d^{exog} for link x_0 and the downstream network Σ^2 experiences an exogenous supply for link x_9.

Link x_0 allocates 80% of its supply to the exogenous environment. The flow into x_0 is therefore

$$f_0^{\text{in}}[k] = \min(.8(40 - x_0[k]), d^{\text{exog}}).$$

The onramps x_i with $i \in \{1, 3, 6, 8\}$ allocate all supply to the environment so

$$f_i^{\text{in}}[k] = \min((20 - x_i[k]), d_i^{\text{exog}}).$$

Similarly, link x_9's outflow is governed by an exogenous environment so

$$f_9^{\text{out}}[k] = \min(.8s^{\text{exog}}, 10, x_9[k]).$$

7.3 Certifying Intermittent Congestion

Congestion is shown to be intermittent after the two segments are interconnected. Intermittency is encoded via "always" and "eventually" temporal operators augmented with

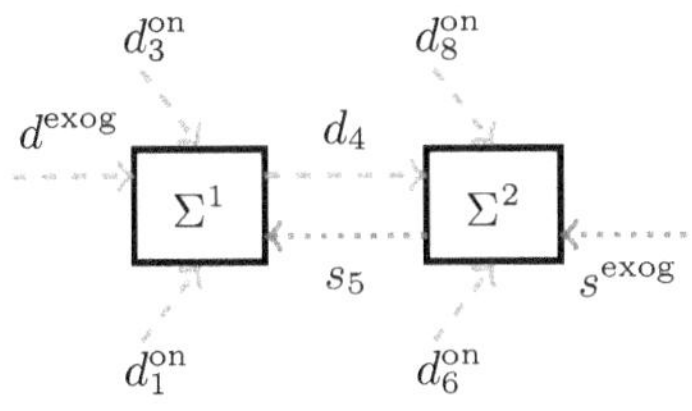

Figure 7: Although vehicular flow in Figure 5 is from left to right, the right network also affects the left network. Demand's influence (dashed lines) is directed forward while supply's influence (dotted lines) is directed backward.

intervals

$$\mathbf{G}_{[0,3]}\phi := \phi \wedge \mathbf{X}\phi \wedge \mathbf{XX}\phi \wedge \mathbf{XXX}\phi \quad (32)$$
$$\mathbf{F}_{[0,2]}\phi := \phi \vee \mathbf{X}\phi \vee \mathbf{XX}\phi. \quad (33)$$

For both systems, all onramp demands are limited to always be less than 3. That is,

$$\mathbf{G}(d_i^{on} \leq 3) \quad (34)$$

for all $i \in \{1, 3, 6, 8\}$. All links are assumed to have an initial occupancy less than 5, i.e., $\mathcal{X}_0 = \prod_{i=0,\ldots,4}[0, 5] \subset \mathcal{X}$.

From Figure 7, it's clear that the upstream network Σ^1 is subjected to an exogenous mainline demand d^{exog} and the supply availability from downstream network Σ^2. A static exogenous environment contract is imposed by assuming that the main line demand satisfies the assumption with no free parameters

$$\mathbf{G}_{[0,3]}\mathbf{F}_{[0,2]}(d^{exog} \leq 15). \quad (35)$$

How does the supply from Σ^2 affect the demand outputted by Σ^1? Via monotonicity of the network dynamics, a greater supply availability means that Σ^1 can expel vehicles quicker and will be able to lower the demand it outputs. This relationship is encoded in the parametric assume-guarantee contract below:

$$\phi_a^1 := \bigvee_{s \geq 0} \mathbf{G}_{[0,3]}\mathbf{F}_{[0,2]}(s_5(x_5) \geq 10 - s) \quad (36)$$
$$\phi_g^1 := \bigwedge_{s \geq 0} \Big(\mathbf{G}_{[0,3]}\mathbf{F}_{[0,2]}(s_5(x_5) \geq 10 - s) \quad (37)$$
$$\implies \mathbf{G}_{[0,3]}\mathbf{F}_{[0,2]}(d_4(x_4) \leq \lambda_1(s))\Big) \quad (38)$$
$$\lambda_1(s) := .9s + 4. \quad (39)$$

The falsification procedure encoded in Problem 1 failed to violate the assume-guarantee contract for any parameter $s \geq 0$ and hence Σ^1 satisfies the parametric contract (ϕ_a^1, ϕ_g^1).

Similarly the downstream network Σ^2 is subjected to the demand from x_4 and exogenous supply. The exogenous supply has a fixed assumption

$$\mathbf{G}_{[0,3]}\mathbf{F}_{[0,2]}(s^{exog} \geq 5). \quad (40)$$

It influences Σ_1 by outputting supply from x_5 and the contract is

$$\phi_a^2 := \bigvee_{d \geq 0} \mathbf{G}_{[0,3]}\mathbf{F}_{[0,2]}(d_4(x_4) \leq d) \quad (41)$$
$$\phi_g^2 := \bigwedge_{d \geq 0} \Big(\mathbf{G}_{[0,3]}\mathbf{F}_{[0,2]}(d_4(x_4) \leq d) \quad (42)$$
$$\implies \mathbf{G}_{[0,3]}\mathbf{F}_{[0,2]}(s_5(x_5) \geq 10 - \lambda_2(d))\Big) \quad (43)$$
$$\lambda_2(d) := .2d. \quad (44)$$

Again, Problem 1 failed to violate the contract and Σ^2 therefore satisfies the contract (ϕ_a^2, ϕ_g^2).

Each of the conditions for Theorem 1 have been proven to hold in this section.

1. The parametric contracts are satisfied for each network.
2. Guarantees from one network imply the feedback assumptions of the other network because they are of the same form. In other words, pairs (41), (38) and (36), (43) are identical parametric specifications.
3. The exogenous assumptions are satisfied via (34), (35), and (40).
4. Let $i = 2$. For a large enough $d \geq 0$, the feedback assumption $\psi_{af}^2(d) = \mathbf{G}_{[0,3]}\mathbf{F}_{[0,2]}(d_4(x_4) \leq d)$ is satisfied because d_4 has a maximum value of 10.

The composition of the parameter mapping functions λ_1, λ_2 is a contraction and hence converges in the limit to a fixed point $(d, s) = (4.878, .975)$. Thus, via Theorem 2 the following statement must also hold:

$$\mathbf{G}_{[0,3]}\mathbf{F}_{[0,2]}(d_4(x_4) \leq 4.878) \wedge \mathbf{G}_{[0,3]}\mathbf{F}_{[0,2]}(s_5(x_5) \geq 9.025).$$

8. CONCLUSION

This paper connects two formalisms for compositional reasoning in the CPS literature: small gain theorems and assume-guarantee contracts. We have incorporated continuous parameters into contracts and showed how to derive an analog of the small gain theorem with broader applicability. We showed that a fragment of parametrized linear temporal logic is Hausdorff continuous and can hence be levered by this small gain theorem, but richer fragments and analogous results for continuous time specifications may exist. Future work will also investigate applying the parametric assume-guarantee framework for additional variants of the small gain theorem (such as those involving input-to-state stability) and broader classes of input-output properties.

9. ACKNOWLEDGEMENTS

The authors would like to thank Shromona Ghosh for helpful discussions about assume-guarantee contracts.

10. REFERENCES

[1] M. Al Khatib, A. Girard, and T. Dang. Verification and synthesis of timing contracts for embedded controllers. In *Proceedings of the 19th International Conference on Hybrid Systems: Computation and Control*, pages 115–124. ACM, 2016.

[2] Y. Annpureddy, C. Liu, G. Fainekos, and S. Sankaranarayanan. S-taliro: A tool for temporal logic falsification for hybrid systems. In *International Conference on Tools and Algorithms for the Construction and Analysis of Systems*, pages 254–257. Springer, 2011.

[3] A. Benveniste, B. Caillaud, D. Nickovic, R. Passerone, J.-B. Raclet, P. Reinkemeier, A. Sangiovanni-Vincentelli, W. Damm, T. Henzinger, and K. Larsen. Contracts for systems design. 2012.

[4] R. Bloem, K. Chatterjee, T. A. Henzinger, and B. Jobstmann. Better quality in synthesis through quantitative objectives. In *International Conference on Computer Aided Verification*, pages 140–156. Springer, 2009.

[5] C. F. Daganzo. The cell transmission model: A Dynamic Representation of Highway Traffic Consistent with the Hydrodynamic Theory. *Transportation Research*, 28:269–287, 1994.

[6] E. Dallal and P. Tabuada. On compositional symbolic controller synthesis inspired by small-gain theorems. In *2015 54th IEEE Conference on Decision and Control (CDC)*, pages 6133–6138. IEEE, 2015.

[7] C. A. Desoer and M. Vidyasagar. *Feedback systems: input-output properties*, volume 55. Siam, 2009.

[8] A. Donzé. Breach, a toolbox for verification and parameter synthesis of hybrid systems. In *International Conference on Computer Aided Verification*, pages 167–170. Springer, 2010.

[9] A. Donzé and O. Maler. Robust satisfaction of temporal logic over real-valued signals. In *International Conference on Formal Modeling and Analysis of Timed Systems*, pages 92–106. Springer, 2010.

[10] G. E. Fainekos and G. J. Pappas. Robustness of temporal logic specifications for continuous-time signals. *Theoretical Computer Science*, 410(42):4262–4291, 2009.

[11] G. Gomes and R. Horowitz. Optimal freeway ramp metering using the asymmetric cell transmission model. *Transportation Research Part C: Emerging Technologies*, 14(4):244 – 262, 2006.

[12] X. Jin, A. Donzé, J. V. Deshmukh, and S. A. Seshia. Mining requirements from closed-loop control models. *IEEE Transactions on Computer-Aided Design of Integrated Circuits and Systems*, 34(11):1704–1717, 2015.

[13] E. S. Kim, M. Arcak, and S. A. Seshia. Compositional controller synthesis for vehicular traffic networks. In *2015 54th IEEE Conference on Decision and Control (CDC)*, pages 6165–6171. IEEE, 2015.

[14] M. Kwiatkowska, G. Norman, D. Parker, and H. Qu. Compositional probabilistic verification through multi-objective model checking. *Information and Computation*, 232:38–65, 2013.

[15] J. Lofberg. Yalmip: A toolbox for modeling and optimization in matlab. In *Computer Aided Control Systems Design, 2004 IEEE International Symposium on*, pages 284–289. IEEE, 2004.

[16] R. Majumdar, E. Render, and P. Tabuada. A theory of robust omega-regular software synthesis. *ACM Transactions on Embedded Computing Systems (TECS)*, 13(3):48, 2013.

[17] P. Nuzzo, A. L. Sangiovanni-Vincentelli, D. Bresolin, L. Geretti, and T. Villa. A platform-based design methodology with contracts and related tools for the design of cyber-physical systems. *Proceedings of the IEEE*, 103(11):2104–2132, 2015.

[18] P. Nuzzo, H. Xu, N. Ozay, J. B. Finn, A. L. Sangiovanni-Vincentelli, R. M. Murray, A. Donzé, and S. A. Seshia. A contract-based methodology for aircraft electric power system design. *IEEE Access*, 2:1–25, 2014.

[19] A. Pnueli. The temporal logic of programs. In *Foundations of Computer Science, 1977., 18th Annual Symposium on*, pages 46–57. IEEE, 1977.

[20] V. Raman, A. Donzé, D. Sadigh, R. M. Murray, and S. A. Seshia. Reactive synthesis from signal temporal logic specifications. In *Proceedings of the 18th International Conference on Hybrid Systems: Computation and Control*, pages 239–248. ACM, 2015.

[21] M. Rungger and M. Zamani. Compositional construction of approximate abstractions. In *Proceedings of the 18th International Conference on Hybrid Systems: Computation and Control*, pages 68–77. ACM, 2015.

[22] P. Tabuada, S. Y. Caliskan, M. Rungger, and R. Majumdar. Towards robustness for cyber-physical systems. *IEEE Transactions on Automatic Control*, 59(12):3151–3163, Dec 2014.

[23] D. C. Tarraf, A. Megretski, and M. A. Dahleh. A framework for robust stability of systems over finite alphabets. *IEEE Transactions on Automatic Control*, 53(5):1133–1146, June 2008.

Relaxed Decidability and the Robust Semantics of Metric Temporal Logic

Houssam Abbas
Electrical and Systems Engineering Department
The University of Pennsylvania
Philadelphia, Pennsylvania
habbas@seas.upenn.edu

Matthew O'Kelly
Electrical and Systems Engineering Department
The University of Pennsylvania
Philadelphia, Pennsylvania
mokelly@seas.upenn.edu

Rahul Mangharam
Electrical and Systems Engineering Department
The University of Pennsylvania
Philadelphia, Pennsylvania
rahulm@seas.upenn.edu

ABSTRACT

Relaxed notions of decidability widen the scope of automatic verification of hybrid systems. In quasi-decidability and δ-decidability, the fundamental compromise is that if we are willing to accept a slight error in the algorithm's answer, or a slight restriction on the class of problems we verify, then it is possible to obtain practically useful answers. This paper explores the connections between relaxed decidability and the robust semantics of Metric Temporal Logic formulas. It establishes a formal equivalence between the robustness degree of MTL specifications, and the imprecision parameter δ used in δ-decidability when it is used to verify MTL properties. We present an application of this result in the form of an algorithm that generates new constraints to the δ-decision procedure from falsification runs, which can speed up the verification run. We then establish new conditions under which robust testing, based on the robust semantics of MTL, is in fact a quasi-semidecision procedure. These results allow us to delimit what is possible with fast, robustness-based methods, accelerate (near-)exhaustive verification, and further bridge the gap between verification and simulation.

Keywords

Hybrid systems; robust semantics; falsification; metric temporal logic; δ-decidability; quasi-decidability

1. INTRODUCTION

The formal analysis of hybrid dynamical systems initially focused on decidability considerations. Studies such as [20, 4, 19] analyzed classes of hybrid systems for which questions like reachability could be decided. The commonly accepted lesson of these initial investigations was that most hybrid systems are undecidable, with the decidable class being rather special and placing strong limitations on what we can model and verify automatically.

Relaxed decidability. Partially as a result of this conclusion, two independent trends emerged, which we view as trying to bridge the gap between exhaustive verification (expensive, complete and sound) and testing (inexpensive, incomplete and sound).[1] See Fig. 1 (A)-(B). The first trend defined and applied *relaxed* notions of decidability to the analysis of hybrid systems [14, 8, 12, 28, 13, 17, 16, 18]. Broadly speaking, these works re-formulated the *safety* problem for hybrid systems as a first-order formula over real constraints: does there exist an initial point x_0 such that a system trajectory starting from x_0 reaches the unsafe set while respecting the system dynamics? In quasi-decidability [12, 28, 13], the (quasi-)decision procedure always returns a correct YES/NO answer to this question, except for 'pathological' cases on which it might run forever. The argument then is that such pathological cases are of little interest in practical system design. In δ-decidability [17, 16, 18], the (δ-complete) decision procedure always halts and returns either a correct NO answer (the formula is not true, i.e. the system is safe) or an approximate δ-YES answer (the formula may be false but a small δ-sized perturbation of it is true, i.e. the system is δ-close to being unsafe). The argument, then, is that a system which is δ-close to being unsafe should be, for all practical purposes, considered unsafe. Thus, this research thrust relaxes exhaustive verification to make it more widely applicable, at the cost of small errors in the answer or the arguably small likelihood of never getting an answer. These approaches were implemented in software tools (iSAT, dReach and HSolver).

Robustness-guided methods. Separately from the above efforts, the second line of research [9, 6, 21, 2] sought to put *falsification* (a.k.a. testing) on a more rigorous footing, thus bringing it closer to exhaustive verification. See Fig. 1 (C)-(D). This was done to leverage falsification's ability to handle any system, including black boxes, and any specification, not just safety. An additional benefit is that it only uses relatively inexpensive simulations. This enhancement to falsification was accomplished by defining a real-valued *robust satisfaction degree* of the formal specification expressed in Metric Temporal Logic (MTL). This robustness was used as an objective function to perform *robustness-guided falsification*: [1, 26, 2]. By minimizing the robustness over the set of initial conditions, we reach a system trajectory that violates the specification. It can also be used in *robust testing* [21], in which a finite number of simulations could cover the entire set of system behaviors. Thus, this approach provides stronger guarantees on the outcome of

[1]Other approaches exist, of course, but they are not in the scope of this paper.

HSCC'17, April 18-20, 2017, Pittsburgh, PA, USA

DOI: http://dx.doi.org/10.1145/3049797.3049813

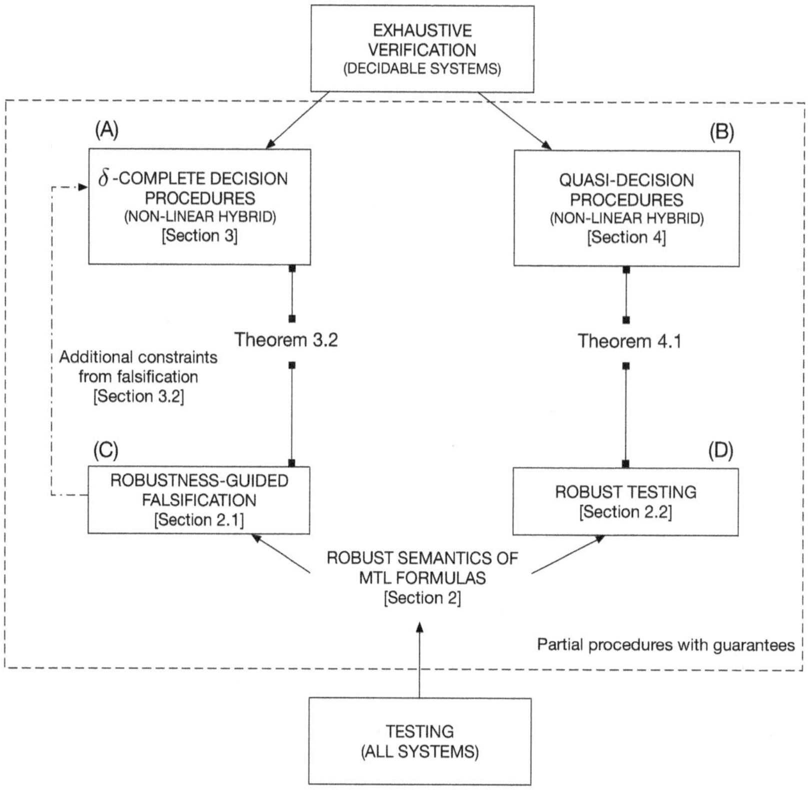

Figure 1: The rapprochement between formal verification and testing. Robustness-guided falsification is integrated with δ-complete decision procedures and Robust testing is a quasi-semidecision procedure.

testing and seeks better-performing falsification algorithms applicable to a broad class of problems.

While the connection between the relaxed decidability notions was previously observed [13], *the connection between the robust semantics and relaxed decidability has not been explored.* Notions of robustness are fundamental to both approaches, so it is tempting to study robustness-guided methods in the light of relaxed decidability. Our motivation is both theoretical and practical: we take testing as our starting point, and want to provide rigorous ways in which robustness-guided testing can accelerate relaxed decision procedures, and to delimit what is theoretically possible with robustness-guided methods.

Contributions. We establish a formal equivalence between the robustness degree of MTL specifications, and the imprecision parameter δ used in δ-decidability (Section 3). Informally, we find that δ-decidability is computing the robust semantics of the MTL formula and deciding whether it is negative (formula is False) or larger than $-\delta$ (formula is δ-True). We present an application of this connection by using the results of falsification to further constrain the operation of a δ-decidability tool (Section 3.3). Empirical evidence obtained using our approach demonsrates runtime savings for the δ-decider, which we expect will improve its scalability to larger systems. The paper then turns to the relation between robust testing and quasi-decidability. We establish a relation between the robust semantics of MTL and the notion of quasi-robustness. We then give new relaxed conditions under which Robust Testing terminates for (almost everywhere) robustly correct systems (Section 4). In the process, we delimit the class of MTL formulas for which there can be an arbitrary difference between the exact robustness degree of an MTL formula and the robust semantics used to approximate it (Section 4.1.2). The plan of the paper is given in Fig. 1.

This study opens the way to a principled integration of falsification and exhaustive verification, where inexpensive but robust simulations are *an integral part* of (relaxed) exhaustive verification algorithms, rather than an independent accessory in the verification process.

All proofs appear in the online technical report [3].

2. ROBUSTNESS OF MTL FORMULAS

A *falsification algorithm* searches a system's set of initial conditions $X_0 \subset \mathbb{R}^n$ for a point x_0 from which the system exhibits a trajectory that falsifies (i.e., violates) the system's specification. When the specification is expressed in Metric Temporal Logic (MTL) [25], then the *robustness degree* of the specification can be used to guide the search. We now define the robustness degree of an MTL formula and describe how it's approximated by the robust semantics of MTL formulas. The formal connections between these concepts and relaxed decidability are established in the next sections.

Notation. The word *signal* will refer to a function from some bounded time domain $\mathbb{T} \subset \mathbb{R}$ to the bounded state space $X \subset \mathbb{R}^n$. The set of all signals $\mathbf{x} : \mathbb{T} \to X$ is $X^{\mathbb{T}}$. Signals are denoted by the letters $\mathbf{x}, \mathbf{y}$, etc. The value of signal $\mathbf{x}$ at time t is x_t. All time intervals $I \subset \mathbb{R}$ that appear in what follows should be interpreted as meaning $I \cap \mathbb{T}$. Given $t \in \mathbb{R}$ and $I \subset \mathbb{R}$, $t +_{\mathbb{T}} I = \mathbb{T} \cap \{t + t' | t' \in I\}$. The symbols $\sqcup$ and $\sqcap$ denote the sup and inf opereators, respectively. A *trajectory* is a signal generated by a hybrid system. A trajectory starting from x_0 is denoted $\mathbf{y}_{x_0}$. $\mathcal{P}(X)$ is the set of all subset of X, and $\text{cl}(X)$ is its closure. The positive reals are $\mathbb{R}_+ := (0, \infty)$, and the negative reals are $\mathbb{R}_- = (-\infty, 0)$.

Let (A, d) be a metric space; that is, the distance function $d : A \times A \to \mathbb{R}_+$ is non-negative, symmetric, respects the triangle inequality and is 0 iff its arguments are equal. Let $Y \subset A$ be a subset of A, and let $\text{cl}(Y)$ denote its closure in the metric topology. Then we define:

$$\mathbf{dist}_d(x, Y) := \inf_{y \in \text{cl}(Y)} d(x, y) \quad (1)$$

$$\mathbf{depth}_d(x, Y) := \mathbf{dist}_d(x, A \setminus Y) \quad (2)$$

$$\mathbf{Dist}_d(x, Y) := \begin{cases} -\mathbf{dist}_d(x, Y), & x \notin Y \\ \mathbf{depth}_d(x, Y), & x \in Y \end{cases} \quad (3)$$

$$B_d(x, r) := \{y \in A \mid d(x, y) < r\} \quad (4)$$

For example, if $A = X$ is the state space and $d(a, b) = |a - b|$ is the Euclidian distance between points in X, then the above define, respectively, the distance of a point to a subset $Y \subset X$, the depth of a point in a set Y, the signed distance of point x to set Y (with positive value indicating the point a is in Y, and a negative value indicating otherwise), and the open ball of radius r centered on x. As another important example, $A = X^{\mathbb{T}}$ can be the signal space and $d(\mathbf{x}, \mathbf{y}) = \rho(\mathbf{x}, \mathbf{y}) := \sup_{t \in \mathbb{T}} |x_t - y_t|$ is the sup norm of the difference between the signals $\mathbf{x}$ and $\mathbf{y}$.

Let AP be a set of atomic propositions, and let φ be a formula in MTL$^+$, the set of MTL formulas in Negative Normal Form (so only atomic propositions can have a $\neg$ preceding them):

$$\varphi := \top | p | \neg p | \varphi_1 \vee \varphi_2 | \varphi_1 \wedge \varphi_2 | \varphi_1 \mathcal{U}_I \varphi_2 | \varphi_1 \mathcal{R}_I \varphi_2$$

Let $\mathcal{O} : AP \to \mathcal{P}(X)$ be an observation map for the atomic propositions. That is, for every $p \in AP$, $\mathcal{O}(p) = \{x \in X \mid x \models p\}$.

Assumption 2.1. *Unless otherwise indicated, signals are continuous-time. The set X is a bounded box in $\mathbb{R}^n$: $X = [a_1, b_1] \times \ldots \times [a_n, b_n]$, and is not included in any $\mathcal{O}(p)$. All formulas have a bounded horizon (all of their temporal intervals are bounded). Therefore, we may also assume that all trajectories have fininte length, that is no longer than the formula's horizon. When we need to compute the robustness (defined below) of a system trajectory, we assume a rigorous simulator is used, and a lower bound on the rigorous simulation's robustness is computed, as explained in [3, Section 6].*

Let $t \in \mathbb{T}$ be a time instant and φ be an MTL$^+$ formula. $\mathcal{L}_t(\varphi)$ is the set of signals in $X^{\mathbb{T}}$ that satisfy φ at time t, that is, $\mathcal{L}_t(\varphi) = \{\mathbf{x} \in X^{\mathbb{T}} \mid (\mathbf{x}, t) \models_{\mathcal{O}} \varphi\}$.

Definition 2.1. *[9] Define the distance $\rho : X^{\mathbb{T}} \times X^{\mathbb{T}} \to \mathbb{R}_+$ by $\rho(\mathbf{x}, \mathbf{y}) = \sup_{t \in \mathbb{T}} d(x_t, y_t)$. The* robustness degree *of signal $\mathbf{x}$ at time t relative to formula φ under observation $\mathcal{O}$ is $\mathbf{Dist}_\rho(\mathbf{x}, \mathcal{L}_t(\varphi))$.*

By definition, if for two signals $\mathbf{x}, \mathbf{y}$ it holds that $\rho(\mathbf{x}, \mathbf{y}) < |\mathbf{Dist}_\rho(\mathbf{x}, \mathcal{L}_t(\varphi))|$ then either both signals are in $\mathcal{L}_t(\varphi)$ or both are outside it, and so they both have the same truth value relative to φ. The robustness degree therefore defines a *level of perturbation* to $\mathbf{x}$ which will not change its truth value relative to φ. The perturbation is measured using the distance function ρ.

The robustness degree, in general, cannot be computed directly because the set $\mathcal{L}_t(\varphi)$ cannot be characterized. However, it can be conservatively approximated by the *robustness estimate*, defined using the following semantics of MTL formulas.

Definition 2.2 (Robust semantics [9])**.** *The* robust semantics *of φ are denoted by $[\![\varphi, \mathcal{O}]\!](\mathbf{x}, t)$ and are defined as*

$$\begin{aligned}
[\![\top, \mathcal{O}]\!](\mathbf{x}, t) &= +\infty \\
\forall p \in AP,\ [\![p, \mathcal{O}]\!](\mathbf{x}, t) &= \mathbf{Dist}_d(x_t, \mathcal{O}(p)) \\
[\![\neg\varphi, \mathcal{O}]\!](\mathbf{x}, t) &= -[\![\varphi, \mathcal{O}]\!](\mathbf{x}, t) \\
[\![\varphi_1 \vee \varphi_2, \mathcal{O}]\!](\mathbf{x}, t) &= [\![\varphi_1, \mathcal{O}]\!](\mathbf{x}, t) \sqcup [\![\varphi_2, \mathcal{O}]\!](\mathbf{x}, t) \\
[\![\varphi_1 \wedge \varphi_2, \mathcal{O}]\!](\mathbf{x}, t) &= [\![\varphi_1, \mathcal{O}]\!](\mathbf{x}, t) \sqcap [\![\varphi_2, \mathcal{O}]\!](\mathbf{x}, t) \\
[\![\varphi_1 \mathcal{U}_I \varphi_2, \mathcal{O}]\!](\mathbf{x}, t) &= \sqcup_{t' \in t +_{\mathbb{T}} I} \Big([\![\varphi_2, \mathcal{O}]\!](\mathbf{x}, t') \bigsqcap \\
&\quad \sqcap_{t'' \in [t, t')} [\![\varphi_1, \mathcal{O}]\!](\mathbf{x}, t'') \Big) \\
[\![\varphi_1 \mathcal{R}_I \varphi_2, \mathcal{O}]\!](\mathbf{x}, t) &= \sqcap_{t' \in t +_{\mathbb{T}} I} \Big([\![\varphi_2, \mathcal{O}]\!](\mathbf{x}, t') \bigsqcup \\
&\quad \sqcup_{t'' \in [t, t')} [\![\varphi_1, \mathcal{O}]\!](\mathbf{x}, t'') \Big)
\end{aligned}$$

The robustness estimate *of signal $\mathbf{x}$ relative to φ at time t under observation $\mathcal{O}$ is $[\![\varphi, \mathcal{O}]\!](\mathbf{x}, t)$.*

A *determistic* hybrid system produces a unique trajectory $\mathbf{y}_{x_0}$ from any initial point x_0. Therefore we will speak interchangeably of the robustness estimate of $\mathbf{y}_{x_0}$ and the robustness of the initial point x_0. The following establishes that the robustness estimate is a conservative bound on the robustness degree [9]

Theorem 2.1. *For any $\mathbf{x} \in X^{\mathbb{T}}$ and MTL$^+$ formula φ, the following hold*

1. $-\mathbf{dist}_\rho(\mathbf{x}, \mathcal{L}_t(\varphi)) \leq [\![\varphi, \mathcal{O}]\!](\mathbf{x}, t) \leq \mathbf{depth}_\rho(\mathbf{x}, \mathcal{L}_t(\varphi))$
2. *If $r = [\![\varphi, \mathcal{O}]\!](\mathbf{x}, t) < 0$ then $\mathbf{x}$ falsifies the spec φ, and if $r > 0$ then $\mathbf{x}$ satisfies φ. The case $r = 0$ is inconclusive.*
3. *Any signal in $B_\rho(\mathbf{x}, |r|)$ has the same truth value relative to φ as $\mathbf{x}$.*

2.1 Robustness-guided falsification

We now present two applications of the robust semantics, starting with robustness-guided falsification. Using Thm. 2.1, a *robustness-guided falsification* algorithm searches for falsifying trajectories by minimizing the robustness estimate over X_0, the set of initial conditons of the system.

$$\min_{x_0 \in X_0} [\![\varphi, \mathcal{O}]\!](\mathbf{y}_{x_0}, t)$$

where $\mathbf{y}_{x_0}$ is the system trajectory starting from x_0. If the found minimum is negative then this means the corresponding minimizer $\mathbf{y}^*_{x_0}$ falsifies φ. Falsification uses relatively fast simulations and only requires the ability to simulate the system.

2.2 Robust testing

A second application of the robust semantics is *robust testing* [10, 21]. It proceeds as shown in Algorithm 1: it iteratively samples the search space X_0 to yield a sequence of

Algorithm 1: Robust Testing

Data: An MTL formula φ, a system $\mathcal{H}$ with initial set $X_0 \subset \mathbb{R}^n$ and bisimulation $V : X \times X \to [0, \infty)$

1 Set $i = 0, X_r = X_0$;
`/* Sample while the balls have not yet covered` X_0 `*/`
2 **while** $X_r \neq \emptyset$ **do**
3 Sample x_i in the interior of X_r;
4 Compute $r_i = [\![\varphi, \mathcal{O}]\!](\mathbf{y}_{x_i}, t)$;
5 **if** $r_i < 0$ **then**
6 Return False ; `/* Found a falsifier */`
7 **else if** $r_i > 0$ **then**
`/* Compute a 'robustness ball'` B_i `around the initial point` x_i `*/`
8 Compute $c_i > 0$ s.t. $\forall z \in X_0$, $d(x_i, z) < c_i \implies d(\mathbf{y}_{x_i}(t), \mathbf{y}_z(t)) < r \forall t \in \mathbb{T}$;
9 Set $X_r = X_0 \setminus B_d(x_i; c_i)$
10 **else**
`/* No robustness ball - keep sampling */`
11 **end**
12 $i = i + 1$
13 **end**
14 Return True. `/* Covered` X_0 `with the balls` B_i `*/`

samples $x_0, x_1, \ldots$. If a new sample x_i yields a trajectory $\mathbf{y}_{x_i}$ with negative robustness $r_i < 0$, the algorithm returns False (Line 6). Otherwise, if $r_i > 0$, we know that any signal $\mathbf{x}$ within $B_\rho(\mathbf{y}_{x_i}, r_i)$ also satisfies φ. So we wish to exclude any points in X_0 that produce trajectories that stay in $B_\rho(\mathbf{y}_{x_i}; r_i)$ to avoid searching in them. We compute such a set of points $B_d(x_i; c_i)$ in Line 8, e.g., using bisimulations[2] [10]. The ball $B_d(x_i; c_i)$ is then excluded from X_0, and the sampling continues in the rest of the search space (Line 9). If X_0 is fully covered by the union of balls $\cup_i B_d(x_i; c_i)$ at some point, the algorithm halts and returns True. See Fig. 2.

Note that Robust Testing, as presented here, might not terminate. For example, if the sampler gets stuck sampling points of 0 robustness (Line 10), then it will run forever. Or, if the balls B_i become infinitesimally smaller, as shown in Fig. 2 (right), their union will never cover X_0.

Previous work has shown that Robust Testing terminates if the minimum robustness estimate of any system trajectory is *positive* [10, Thm. 21]. In essence, this guarantees that the '**if** $r_i > 0$' branch (Line 7) always executes, so every new sample reduces the residual search space X_r by a minimum amount r, $0 < r \leq r_i$. In Section 4 we establish a stronger result that extends the limits of what is achievable with Robust Testing.

3. ROBUSTNESS AND δ-DECIDABILITY

So-called δ-Complete Decision Procedures (δ-CDP) have been used to verify the safety of a large variety of hybrid systems. For examples, see the website of the tool dReach [23]. The approach to the problem is to write the reachability question

Do there exist initial conditions $x_0 \in X_0 \subset \mathbb{R}^n$ from which the system enters the unsafe set $U \subset \mathbb{R}^n$?

[2]Bisimulations are outside the scope of this paper. The reader is referred to [10] for details.

as a first-order formula over the reals. As an example, for a (non-hybrid) dynamical system $\dot{y}(t) = g(y(t, x_0))$ with $y(0, x_0) = x_0 \in X_0$ and bounded state-space X, the reachability question above is formulated as

$$\exists^{X_0} x_0 \exists^{[0,T]} t. \; f(y(t, x_0)) \geq 0$$

Here, the unsafe set is $U = \{u \in X \mid f(u) \geq 0\}$.

This is an example of the more general *bounded $\mathcal{L}_{\mathbb{R}_\mathcal{F}}$-sentence*. Let $\mathcal{F}$ be a set of Type 2 computable functions[3] which contains at least the constant 0, unary negation, addition and the absolute value. It is also closed under bounded minimization and maximization [22]. Let $\vec{v} = (v_1, \ldots, v_n)$ be a vector of variables. An $\mathcal{L}_{\mathbb{R}_\mathcal{F}}$-term f is either a variable or a computable function of a term: $f := v | g(f(\vec{v}))$ for some $g \in \mathcal{F}$. Let $Q_i \in \{\forall, \exists\}$. A bounded $\mathcal{L}_{\mathbb{R}_\mathcal{F}}$-sentence is

$$Q_1^{V_1} v_1 Q_2^{V_2} v_2 \ldots Q_n^{V_n} v_n \psi[f_i(\vec{v}) \geq 0, f_j(\vec{v}) > 0] \tag{5}$$

The constraint sets $V_\ell \subset \mathbb{R}$ are bounded intervals and the f_i, f_j's are $\mathcal{L}_{\mathbb{R}_\mathcal{F}}$-terms, with $i \in \{1, \ldots, k\}$ and $j \in \{k+1, \ldots, m\}$. ψ is a first-order, quantifier-free formula (a 'matrix') on the predicates $f_i \geq 0, f_j > 0$. See [17, 18].

Bounded $\mathcal{L}_{\mathbb{R}_\mathcal{F}}$ sentences have a notion of robustness that comes from relaxing or tightening the constraints in the matrix ψ.

Definition 3.1 (δ-variants and δ-robustness [17]). *Let $\delta \in \mathbb{Q}_+ \cup \{0\}$ and S be a bounded $\mathcal{L}_{\mathbb{R}_\mathcal{F}}$-sentence as in (5). The δ-weakening of S is obtained by replacing each atom $f_i(\vec{v}) \geq 0$ by $f_i(\vec{v}) \geq -\delta$ and $f_i(\vec{v}) > 0$ by $f_i(\vec{v}) > -\delta$:*

$$S^{-\delta} = Q_1^{V_1} v_1 Q_2^{V_2} v_2 \ldots Q_n^{V_n} v_n \psi[f_i(\vec{v}) \geq -\delta, f_j(\vec{v}) > -\delta]$$

The δ-strenghtening of S is analogously defined:

$$S^{+\delta} = Q_1^{V_1} v_1 Q_2^{V_2} v_2 \ldots Q_n^{V_n} v_n \psi[f_i(\vec{v}) \geq \delta, f_j(\vec{v}) > \delta]$$

We say S is robust to δ-weakening *if $S^{-\delta} \implies S$, and is* robust to δ-strenghtening *if $S \implies S^{+\delta}$.*

Because $S^{-\delta} \implies S$ is equivalent to $\neg S^{-\delta} \vee S$, if a sentence is robust to δ-weakening, this means that either it is true, or it is 'robustly' false, so that even a δ-relaxation of it won't make it true. Similarly for δ-strengthening. We refer to these notions as 'δ-robustness'.

3.1 Bounding δ for trajectories

We will now define a natural translation from an MTL formula φ to a bounded $\mathcal{L}_{\mathbb{R}_\mathcal{F}}$-formula $sen(\varphi)$. The translation allows us to connect the robustness degree of φ to the δ-robustness of $sen(\varphi)$.

In the following definition, given a boolean operator $\boxdot \in \{\vee, \wedge\}$ and two bounded $\mathcal{L}_{\mathbb{R}_\mathcal{F}}$ formulas S_1, S_2, we construct $S_1 \boxdot S_2$ in prenex normal form (i.e. all the quantifiers are pushed to the left and only a quantifier-free matrix ψ is used. New variable names are used to avoid conflicting quantifications on the same variable).

Definition 3.2. *Define the map*

$$sen : MTL^+ \times \mathcal{P}(Y)^{AP} \to (X^{\mathbb{T}} \times \mathbb{T} \to \mathcal{L}_{\mathbb{R}_\mathcal{F}} formulas)$$

$$sen(\varphi, \mathcal{O})(\mathbf{x}, t) = \mathcal{L}_{\mathbb{R}_\mathcal{F}} \; formula$$

[3]Intuitively, a function g is Type 2 computable if $g(x)$ can be computed with arbitrary precision given an arbitrarily precise approximation of x. See [22] or [17].

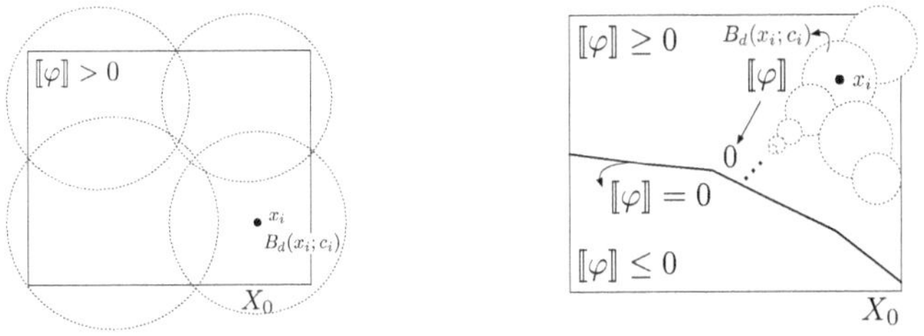

Figure 2: Robust testing terminates on robustly correct systems (left), but not necessarily on non-robust systems where the robustness vanishes gradually (right).

$$sen(\top, \mathcal{O})(\mathbf{x}, t) = 0 \geq 0$$

$$sen(p, \mathcal{O})(\mathbf{x}, t) = \begin{cases} \mathbf{Dist}_d(x_t, \mathcal{O}(p)) \geq 0 & , \mathcal{O}(p) \textit{ closed} \\ \mathbf{Dist}_d(x_t, \mathcal{O}(p)) > 0 & , \mathcal{O}(p) \textit{ open} \end{cases}$$

$$sen(\neg p, \mathcal{O})(\mathbf{x}, t), \begin{cases} -\mathbf{Dist}_d(x_t, \mathcal{O}(p)) \geq 0, & \mathcal{O}(p) \textit{ open} \\ -\mathbf{Dist}_d(x_t, \mathcal{O}(p)) > 0, & \mathcal{O}(p) \textit{ closed} \end{cases}$$

$$sen(\varphi_1 \vee \varphi_2, \mathcal{O})(\mathbf{x}, t) = sen(\varphi_1, \mathcal{O})(\mathbf{x}, t) \vee sen(\varphi_2, \mathcal{O})(\mathbf{x}, t)$$

$$sen(\varphi_1 \wedge \varphi_2, \mathcal{O})(\mathbf{x}, t) = sen(\varphi_1, \mathcal{O})(\mathbf{x}, t) \wedge sen(\varphi_2, \mathcal{O})(\mathbf{x}, t)$$

$$sen(\varphi_1 \mathcal{U}_I \varphi_2, \mathcal{O})(\mathbf{x}, t) = \exists^{t +_{\mathbb{T}} I} t' \forall^{(t,t')} t'' \; (sen(\varphi_1, \mathcal{O})(x, t'') \wedge sen(\varphi_2, \mathcal{O})(x, t'))$$

$$sen(\varphi_1 \mathcal{R}_I \varphi_2, \mathcal{O})(\mathbf{x}, t) = \forall^{t +_{\mathbb{T}} I} t' \exists^{(t,t')} t'' \; \big(sen(\varphi_1, \mathcal{O})(x, t'') \vee sen(\varphi_2, \mathcal{O})(x, t')\big)$$

where (recall) $t +_{\mathbb{T}} I := \mathbb{T} \cap (t + I)$ and all time intervals I are interpreted as $I \cap \mathbb{T}$.

E.g. if $\varphi = \Box_{[0,3]} \Diamond_{[1,2]} x > 5$ then $sen(\varphi, \mathcal{O})(\mathbf{x}, 0) = \forall^{[0,3]} t' \exists^{t'+[1,2]} t'' \; x_{t''} > 5$.

Lemma 3.1. *Consider a bounded-time MTL$^+$ formula φ and a signal $\mathbf{x}$. If every set $\mathcal{O}(p)$, $p \in AP$, is given by*

$$\mathcal{O}(p) = \{(y_1, \ldots, y_n) \in \mathbb{R}^n \mid y_i \in [u_i, v_i], 1 \leq i \leq n\}$$

where u_i, v_i are $\mathcal{L}_{\mathbb{R}_{\mathcal{F}}}$-terms that do not involve y_i, then it holds that $sen(\varphi, \mathcal{O})(\mathbf{x}, t)$ is a bounded $\mathcal{L}_{\mathbb{R}_{\mathcal{F}}}$ formula.

A simple special case of Lemma. 3.1 is when each $\mathcal{O}(p)$ is a box with constant endpoints, e.g. $\mathcal{O}(p) = \{(y_1, y_2) \in \mathbb{R}^2 \mid 1 \leq y_1 \leq 2, -3 \leq y_2 \leq -0.5\}$.

The following lemma about the boolean truth value of φ and its $\mathcal{L}_{\mathbb{R}_{\mathcal{F}}}$ translation is easily established by induction on the structure of φ:

Lemma 3.2. *Consider the MTL$^+$ formula φ, the signal $\mathbf{x} \in X^{\mathbb{T}}$, the observation map $\mathcal{O}$ and $t \in \mathbb{T}$. Then*

$$(\mathbf{x}, t) \models_{\mathcal{O}} \varphi \Leftrightarrow sen(\varphi, \mathcal{O})(\mathbf{x}, t) \textit{ is True} \tag{6}$$

The next lemma connects the robustness degree of φ and the robustness to δ-weakening/strengthening of $sen(\varphi)$.

Lemma 3.3. *Let $r = \mathbf{Dist}_\rho(\mathbf{x}, \mathcal{L}_t(\varphi))$. Under the hypothesis that $r \neq 0$, it holds that for any rational $0 \leq \delta < |r|$, $sen(\varphi, \mathcal{O})(\mathbf{x}, t)$ is both robust to δ-strengthening and robust to δ-weakening.*

If $r = 0$ is allowed, then φ merely implies $r \geq 0$, which doesn't leave enough 'room' for any δ-strengthening. Note that since $|[\![\varphi, \mathcal{O}]\!](\mathbf{x}, t)| \leq |\mathbf{Dist}_\rho(\mathbf{x}, \mathcal{L}_t(\varphi))|$, the result above holds also for all $\delta < |[\![\varphi, \mathcal{O}]\!](\mathbf{x}, t)|$.

3.2 Bounding δ for systems

We are now ready to lift the results of Section 3.1 to systems. We connect the minimum robustness of a *system* relative to an MTL spec to the δ-robustness of the corresponding $\mathcal{L}_{\mathbb{R}_{\mathcal{F}}}$-sentence. Let $\mathcal{H}$ be an ODE system. A *trajectory* of the system is a solution to its dynamical equations from some initial point. We will mostly be concerned with $\mathcal{L}_0$, the set of $\mathcal{H}$ trajectories with initial point chosen from the bounded set X_0 and of duration $T > 0$: $\mathcal{L}_0 = \{\mathbf{y}_{x_0} \mid x_0 \in X_0, \sup \mathrm{dom} y = T\}$. All ODE solution functions are assumed to be in $\mathcal{F}$.

Let $\varphi \in$ MTL$^+$. With abuse of notation, define the robustness degree and estimate of a system w.r.t. an MTL formula to be, respectively:

$$\begin{aligned} \mathbf{Dist}_\rho(\mathcal{L}_0, \mathcal{L}_t(\varphi)) &= \inf\{\mathbf{Dist}_\rho(\mathbf{x}, \mathcal{L}_t(\varphi)) \mid \mathbf{x} \in \mathcal{L}_0\} \\ [\![\varphi, \mathcal{O}]\!](\mathcal{L}_0, t) &= \inf\{[\![\varphi, \mathcal{O}]\!](\mathbf{x}, t) \mid \mathbf{x} \in \mathcal{L}_0\} \end{aligned} \tag{7}$$

When any of the quantities $\mathcal{O}, t, \mathcal{L}_0$ are clear from the context we may drop them from the notation. Define

$$ssen : MTL^+ \times \mathcal{P}(Y)^{AP} \to (\mathcal{P}(Y)^{AP} \times \mathbb{T} \to \text{bounded } \mathcal{L}_{\mathbb{R}_{\mathcal{F}}})$$

by

$$ssen(\varphi, \mathcal{O})(X_0, t) = \forall^{X_0} x_0 . sen(\varphi, \mathcal{O})(\mathbf{y}_{x_0}, t) \tag{8}$$

E.g. if $\varphi = \Box_{[0,3]} \Diamond_{[1,2]} x > 5$ and $X_0 = [-2, -1]$, then

$$ssen(\varphi, \mathcal{O})(X_0, 0) = \forall^{[-2,-1]} x_0 \; \forall^{[0,3]} t' \exists^{t'+[1,2]} t'' \; y(t'', x_0) > 5$$

For ease of reference later, we will define two flavors of δ-complete decision procedures [17]:

Definition 3.3. *Let B be a set of $\mathcal{L}_{\mathbb{R}_{\mathcal{F}}}$ formulas and $\delta \in \mathbb{Q}_+$. We say an algorithm A^- is an* optimistic δ-CDP *for B if for any formula S in B, A^- returns correctly one of these two answers:*

- *S is false*
- *$S^{-\delta}$ is true*

If the two cases overlap, either one is returned. We say an algorithm A^+ is a pessimistic δ-CDP *for B if for any $S \in \mathsf{B}$, A^+ returns correctly one of these two answers:*

- *S is true*
- *$S^{+\delta}$ is false*

If the two cases overlap, either one is returned.

Informally, if A^- returns δ-true, this means that the sentence $ssen(\varphi)$ may be false, but a small (δ-sized) relaxation of it makes it true. The main result of this section follows.

Theorem 3.1. *Consider the MTL$^+$ formula φ, the ODE system $\mathcal{H}$ with behavior $\mathcal{L}_0$, and the observation map $\mathcal{O}$. Let $r = \mathbf{Dist}_\rho(\mathcal{L}_0, \mathcal{L}_t(\varphi))$. Then it holds that:*

Table 1: Summary of Thm. 3.1

$A^+ \rightarrow$ $A^- \downarrow$	True	$(ssen(\varphi))^{+\delta}$ False
False	- - - -	$r \leq 0$
$(ssen(\varphi))^{-\delta}$ True	$r \geq 0$	$-\delta \leq r \leq \delta$

1. *If $r \neq 0$, then $ssen(\varphi)$ is robust to δ-strengthening and to δ-weakening for all $\delta < |r|$.*
2. *If a pessimistic A^+ returns $(ssen(\varphi))^{+\delta}$ False, then $r \leq \delta$.*
3. *If an optimistic A^- returns $(ssen(\varphi))^{-\delta}$ True, then $r \geq -\delta$.*

The last two results are summarized in Table 1. Each box indicates what we can infer about the system robustness, based on what is returned by A^+ and A^- when running on $ssen(\varphi)$.

This table asserts that *a δ-complete decision procedure can be used to bound the robustness degree.*

Thus we may consider that *any δ-CDP is actually a procedure for computing the robustness degree r of the system: it halts once it establishes either that $r \leq \delta$ (for a pessimistic procedure) or that $r \geq -\delta$ (for an optimistic procedure).*

3.3 Robustness-Guided Verification

There is a number of ways in which Thm. 3.1 can be exploited. The basic idea is that simulation provides system trajectories whose (MTL) robustness values are easily evaluated. These robustness values provide an upper bound on the δ with which the sentence $ssen(\varphi)$ is δ-robust. Therefore we may use them to guide a δ-CDP, either by suggesting choices of δ, areas of X_0 to be explored or ignored, or simulation times at which simulation gives way to verification. We present one such application here: we use robustness-guided falsification to accelerate a δ-CDP. The δ-decision problems for $\mathcal{L}_{\mathbb{R}_\mathcal{F}}$-sentences with ODEs are PSPACE-complete [17]. The practical runtimes of current tools can be exhorbitant (e.g., see the benhmarks for [24] for an idea of the runtimes), and they are sensitive to how the problem is encoded. Scaling these tools is therefore an important challenge. Due to current tool limiations, we restrict ourselves to safety specs in this section: $\varphi = \Box_{[0,T]}(\neg p)$. Let $\mathcal{H}$ be a system with initial set of conditions X_0. We ask a δ-CDP whether there exists a trajectory satisfying $\neg\varphi$:

$$\exists^{X_0} x_0 \exists^X x \exists^{[0,T]} t. x = y(t, x_0) \wedge \mathbf{Dist}_d(x_t, \mathcal{O}(p)) \geq 0 \quad (9)$$

Now if a trajectory $\mathbf{z}$ has robustness estimate $[\![\varphi, \mathcal{O}]\!](\mathbf{z}, t) = r > 0$, then $sen(\neg\varphi)(\mathbf{z})$ couldn't be δ-SAT for any $\delta < r$ by Lemma 3.3. But only δ-SAT initial conditions can be returned by an optimistic δ-CDP to indicate (δ)-unsafe behavior. Therefore, *we can use this robust trajectory to provide extra constraints to the δ-CDP, telling it to ignore such trajectories.*

Specifically, given a desired precision $\delta > 0$ and a trajectory $\mathbf{z}$ of robustness estimate $r = [\![\varphi, \mathcal{O}]\!](\mathbf{z}, t) > \delta$, we pass the following to the δ-CDP instead of (9):

$$\exists^{X_0} x_0 \, \exists^X x \, \exists^{[0,T]} t \, \exists^X x' \, \exists^{[0,T]} t'. \; x = y(t, x_0) \wedge x' = y(t', x_0) \wedge \underbrace{(|z_{t'} - x'| \geq r - \delta)}_{\rho(\mathbf{z}, \mathbf{y}_{x_0}) \geq r - \delta} \wedge \mathbf{Dist}_d(x_t, \mathcal{O}(p)) \geq 0 \quad (10)$$

Table 2: Falsification-Guided Verification: dReach running on an Intel(R) Core i7(R) 2.2GHz CPU and 16 GB memory

Benchmark	No constraint	With added constraint
Insulin	6secs	3secs
Afib1	5mins 27secs	2mins 3secs
Afib2	17mins 37secs	14mins 3secs

The extra constraint constrains the solver to look for those trajectories that are *not* robust to δ-weakening, i.e. it eliminates from consideration trajectories that are robustly false relative to $sen(\neg\varphi)$, and so robustly true relative to $sen(\varphi)$. Section 6 of [3] gives the detailed theoretical justification for why this works, and addresses the need for rigorous simulation.

Computational savings. The computational savings from adding this constraint can be substantial. dReach [23] implements a δ-CDP by integrating Interval Constraint Propagation with ODE solving. It uses a prune-and-split approach, where the prune step shrinks the constraint intervals [18]. By adding constraints to the formula, we are increasing the amount of pruning that is performed, and thus *reducing* the sizes of the sets that have to be propagated backward through the ODE dynamics at every iteration. Backward propagation is the most expensive step of the procedure, thus reducing its runtime can save substantial runtime.

Sample results. We did an initial exploration of these ideas using S-TaLiRo [5] to compute robustness of trajectories and dReach [23] to perform δ-complete reachability analysis. The implementation is crude, and we haven't attempted to optimize the choice of trajectories $\mathbf{z}$. Our goal is to show achievable savings on some simple benchmarks. Future work will optimize the approach in several ways.

We first ran this on a 3-dimensional ODE model of insulin processing by the body presented in [11]. The result is in Table 2. We also ran this on 4-dimensional hybrid models of atrial fibrillation (see [15]). Table 2 shows two examples of the obtained results (afib1 and afib2): in both cases, the added constraint caused a meaningful reduction in runtime. Note that these results were obtained with just *one* additional constraint. In general, we can add several constraints, coming from different trajectories returned by falsification, further pruning the search space.

Discussion. While promising, the above results are not conclusive. In general, the runtime savings will depend on the interplay between the components of the δ-CDP, in particular, how the new constraint affects the heuristics used by the SAT solver. The above results were obtained by adding a self-transition to each mode of the hybrid system, to capture the event $|z_{t'} - x'| > r - \delta$ from Eq. (10). These extra transitions could negatively affect the runtime and the overall savings will depend on how much is saved by adding the constraint. Future work will explore these issues in greater depth and seek more direct ways to encode the new constraint.

3.3.1 *Difference with robust testing.*

This approach has advantages over robust testing (Section 2.2). First, robust testing requires finding an approximate bisimulation of the system, which may not be possible for nonlinear systems. Secondly, computing a ball $B(x_i; c_i)$ using the bisimulation requires a costly bilevel optimization, whose solution may be very conservative depending on the particular bisimulation. The proposed approach also differs from simply removing B_i from X_0 and running dReach on $X \setminus B_i$. That's because the back-propagation step in dReach is more costly than forward simulation. By removing sets from X_0 we save runtime in forward propagation. By imposing an extra constraint we save runtime in backward propagation, achieving greater computational savings.

4. QUASI-SEMIDECISION PROCEDURES AND ROBUST TESTING

We now connect the robust semantics of MTL to quasi-semidecidability. This closes the loop on the relation between verification and testing by the means of relaxing decidability and robustifying testing. See Fig. 1 (B), (D).

Recall the Robust Testing algorithm Alg. 1. Robust Testing halts when it finds a falsifier to the MTL formula and returns False, or when X_0 has been covered by the balls $B_d(x_i; c_i) \equiv B_i$ and returns True. In both cases, the answer it returns is evidently correct. If neither of these things happens, then it will run forever.

Intuitively, robust testing might run forever on 'non-robust' instances of the problem: instances where the system has trajectories of vanishingly small positive robustness, leading to vanishingly small balls (Alg. 1). It might also run forever if the system can generate falsifying trajectories, since we have no deterministic guarantee, in general, that they will be sampled. This suggests that robust testing is a *quasi-semidecision procedure*.

Definition 4.1 (Quasi-(semi)decision procedure[13]). *A quasi-semidecision procedure P for some class B of formulas is an algorithm that returns True for any formula S in B which is True and robust, but might otherwise run forever.*

A quasi-decision procedure P for B is an algorithm that terminates and returns a correct answer for any robust formula S in B (whether it's true of false), but might otherwise run forever.

The notion of robustness used in Def. 4.1 refers to a distance function d_R *between formulas*, which we define for the class $\mathsf{B} = \mathcal{L}_{\mathbb{R}_\mathcal{F}}$. For a vector $x \in \mathbb{R}^n$, its norm is $|x| = \max\{|x_1|, |x_2|, \ldots, |x_n|\}$.

Definition 4.2 (Quasi-robustness[13]). *Two $\mathcal{L}_{\mathbb{R}_\mathcal{F}}$-sentences S and S' are said to have* the same structure *iff one can be obtained from the other by only exchanging terms. (I.e., they have the same Boolean and quantification structure, same bounds on quantified variables, and the same predicate symbols).*

Define the distance function $d_R(S, S')$ as follows: if S and S' have different structure then $d_R(S, S') = \infty$. Else let $\{f_i\}$ be the terms of S and $\{f_i'\}$ be the corresponding terms of S'. Their common domain Ω_i is given by the quantification of all variables. Then $d_R(S, S') = \max_i \|f_i - f_i'\|_\infty$, $\|f_i - f_i'\|_\infty := \sup_{\vec{v} \in \Omega_i} |f_i(\vec{v}) - f_i'(\vec{v})|$. A sentence S is ε-quasi-robust *if for any sentence S' that satisfies $d_R(S, S') < \varepsilon$, both S and S' have the same truth value.*

4.1 Robust testing as a quasi-semidecision procedure

The notion of quasi-robustness presented in Def. 4.2 is related to the robust semantics of MTL, as established in the following Lemma.

Lemma 4.1 (Quasi-robustness implies MTL$^+$ robustness). *Let φ be an MTL$^+$ formula and $\varepsilon \in \mathbb{R}_+$.*

$$ssen(\varphi, \mathcal{O})(X_0, t) \text{ is } \varepsilon\text{-quasi-robust and True} \implies [\![\varphi, \mathcal{O}]\!](\mathcal{L}_0, t) \geq \varepsilon$$

Lemma 4.1 is a one-sided result: it requires that $ssen(\varphi)$ be True. Even if $ssen(\varphi)$ is robustly false, this only implies that there exist trajectories that falsify the formula robustly, but says nothing about whether there exist trajectories that falsify it non-robustly. Thus we cannot bound $[\![\varphi, \mathcal{O}]\!](\mathcal{L}_0, \mathcal{L}_t(\varphi))$ from above away from zero.

When the robustness estimate of the system $[\![\varphi, \mathcal{O}]\!](\mathcal{L}_0, t)$ is positive, then X_0 can be covered with a finite number of balls by Robust Testing - see Fig. 2. Thus, from Lemma 4.1, it immediately follows that *Robust Testing is a quasi-semidecision procedure*: that is, it terminates and returns True if the system satisfies the spec and is ε-quasi-robust, but otherwise it might run forever. A similar theoretical result was proved for safety in [27].

We now generalize this result in two directions. First, we allow for 'small' sets of initial points that have zero robustness. Secondly, instead of requiring that the robustness estimate be positive, we only require that the robustness degree $\mathbf{Dist}_\rho(\mathcal{L}_0, t)$ be positive.

4.1.1 Almost-everywhere robust systems

For the first strengthening, we will need the sampler used in Line 3 of Alg. 1 to satisfy the following *coverage condition.*

(CC) *Let $Z \subset X_0$ have measure 0 in $\mathbb{R}^n$. Let $w_k \geq 0$ be the number of samples that belong to Z in the first k samples $x_0, x_1, \ldots, x_k$. Then*

$$\lim_{k \to \infty} \frac{w_k}{k} = 0$$

We call this a coverage criterion because it implies that the sampler will never get stuck in 'small' sets (of measure 0). For every w_k samples in a small set Z, the sampler will produce, in the long run, significantly more samples outside it. Any stochastic sampler, like Hit-and-Run, obeys (CC), since sets of measure 0 have probability 0. A deterministic sampler would have to be extremely unlucky to violate (CC). Note however that in higher dimensions, getting good coverage becomes harder. See [7] for a promising approach.

We now give the main result of this sub-section. It states that Robust Testing will terminate for a system even if it exhibits trajectories of 0 robustness, as long as there are only 'few' of them. We call this an *almost-everywhere robust system.*

Theorem 4.1. *Consider a hybrid system $\mathcal{H}$ with initial set X_0. Let $R_0 := \{x_0 \in X_0 \mid [\![\varphi, \mathcal{O}]\!](\mathbf{y}_{x_0}, t) = 0\}$ be the set of initial points of robustness 0, and set $R_1 = X_0 \setminus R_0$. If R_0 has measure 0 in $\mathbb{R}^n$, $\inf_{x_0 \in R_1} [\![\varphi, \mathcal{O}]\!](\mathbf{y}_{x_0}, t) := r_* > 0$, and the sampling strategy obeys the coverage criterion* (CC)*, then Robust Testing will terminate and return True.*

It is possible to bound the measure of R_0 rather than compute it exactly. For instance, if a region of X_0 is enclosed by sequences of $B(x_i; c_i)$ of vanishing radius, this can conservatively upper-bound the size of the set of zero robustness.

4.1.2 Robustness Degree Testing

The robustness estimate, which was used in Thm. 4.1, is a *lower* bound on the true robustness degree $\mathbf{Dist}_\rho(\mathcal{L}_0, \mathcal{L}_t(\varphi))$. Thus there may be systems that are indeed robust, in the sense that $\mathbf{Dist}_\rho(\mathcal{L}_0, \mathcal{L}_t(\varphi)) > 0$, but Robust Testing will not terminate for them because it looks at the system's robustness estimate, which could be 0. As an example of this phenomenon, consider the identically zero signal $\mathbf{x} \equiv 0$ and $\varphi = (x \geq 0 \vee x < 0)$, for which $\mathbf{Dist}_\rho(\mathbf{x}, 0) = \infty$ but $[\![\varphi, \mathcal{O}]\!](\mathbf{x}, 0) = 0$.

In this section, we give a technical condition under which this does not happen. Specifically, under this condition, a positive lower (negative upper) bound on the robustness degree implies a positive lower (negative upper) bound on the robustness estimate. As will be seen, the condition we give is not easy to check - we cannot presently think of an algorithm that might test it for a given system. Nonetheless, the theoretical interest of the link between robust testing and quasi-decidability is in its potential to suggest new ways to bridge the gap between verification and testing, *and to draw the limits of what can be done with robust testing and similar robustness-guided algorithms.* This is not affected by the hardness of this condition.

Lemma 4.2. *Consider a discrete-time system $\mathcal{H}$ with trajectory space $\mathcal{L}_0$, and let $t \in \mathbb{T}$ be a time instant. Consider the bounded-time MTL formula φ, and let S_φ be the set of all its sub-formulas. Given $L \subset X^{\mathbb{T}}$, $\overline{L} := X^{\mathbb{T}} \setminus L$. Define the set $\mathcal{D}_\varphi \subset X^{\mathbb{T}}$ as follows.*

- *For every $\psi_1 \vee \psi_2 \in \mathsf{S}_\varphi$ and $\psi_1 \wedge \psi_2 \in \mathsf{S}_\varphi$, $\mathcal{D}_\varphi$ contains $\mathcal{L}_t(\psi_i)$ and $\overline{\mathcal{L}_t(\psi_i)}$, $i = 1, 2$.*
- *for every $\psi_1 \mathcal{U}_I \psi_2 \in \mathsf{S}_\varphi$ and every $t' \in t+I$, $t'' \in (t, t')$, $\mathcal{D}_\varphi$ contains $\mathcal{L}_{t'}(\psi_2)$, $\mathcal{L}_{t''}(\psi_1)$, $\cap_{t'' \in (t,t')} \mathcal{L}_{t''}(\psi_1)$, and $\mathcal{L}_{t'}(\psi_2) \bigcap \cap_{t'' \in (t,t')} \mathcal{L}_{t''}(\psi_1)$.*

If

$$\text{for all } \mathbf{x} \in \mathcal{L}_0, \ \mathbf{x} \notin \bigcap_{A \in \mathcal{D}_\varphi} \mathrm{cl}(A) \tag{11}$$

then $\mathbf{Dist}_\rho(\mathcal{L}_0, t) > 0 \implies [\![\varphi, \mathcal{O}]\!](\mathcal{L}_0, t) > 0$.

The example we gave at the outset violates the Lemma's conditions since $\mathbf{x}$ is in the intersection of the closures $\mathrm{cl}(\mathcal{L}_0(x \geq 0))$ and $\mathrm{cl}(\mathcal{L}_0(x < 0))$. In fact, the Lemma establishes that *this is the prototypical example of this phenomenon:* namely, the only cases where we get $[\![\varphi, \mathcal{O}]\!](\mathbf{x}) = 0 < \mathbf{Dist}_\rho(\mathbf{x}, 0)$ is when $\mathbf{x}$ lives on the boundaries of all the sets $A \in \mathcal{D}_\varphi$.

Combining Lemma 4.2 and Thm. 4.1, we immediately get:

Theorem 4.2. *Let $\mathcal{H}$, R_0 and R_1 be as in Thm. 4.1. Assume the hypotheses of Lemma 4.2. If R_0 has measure 0 in $\mathbb{R}^n$, $\inf_{x_0 \in R_1} \mathbf{Dist}_\rho(\mathbf{y}_{x_0}, \mathcal{L}_t(\varphi)) > 0$, and the sampling strategy obeys the coverage criterion* (CC)*, then Robust Testing will terminate and return True.*

5. CONCLUSION

By exploring the connections between relaxed decidability and the robust semantics of MTL formulas, we improve near-exhausitve verification methods by the results of robust simulations, and delimit what is possible with robustness-guided testing. Future work will integrate robust simulations into a δ-complete decidability tool, to examine the achievable runtime savings on benchamrks of various sizes. In particular, we will explore the efficiency of different encodings of the additional constraints obtained from robust simulation. We will also pursue generalizations of Robust Testing in which a bisimulation is not needed, to tackle a broader range of systems which contain a mixture of robustly correct and robustly incorrect behavior.

6. REFERENCES

[1] H. Abbas and G. Fainekos. Linear hybrid system falsification through local search. In *Automated Technology for Verification and Analysis*, volume 6996 of *LNCS*, pages 503–510. Springer, 2011.

[2] H. Abbas, G. E. Fainekos, S. Sankaranarayanan, F. Ivancic, and A. Gupta. Probabilistic temporal logic falsification of cyber-physical systems. *ACM Transactions on Embedded Computing Systems*, 12(s2), May 2013.

[3] H. Abbas, M. O'Kelly, and R. Mangharam. Relaxed decidability and the robust semantics of metric temporal logic: Technical report. University of Pennsylvania Scholarly Commons, 2017.

[4] R. Alur, C. Courcoubetis, N. Halbwachs, T. A. Henzinger, P.-H. Ho, X. Nicollin, A. Olivero, J. Sifakis, and S. Yovine. The algorithmic analysis of hybrid systems. *Theoretical Computer Science*, 138(1):3–34, 1995.

[5] Y. S. R. Annapureddy, C. Liu, G. E. Fainekos, and S. Sankaranarayanan. S-taliro: A tool for temporal logic falsification for hybrid systems. In *Tools and algorithms for the construction and analysis of systems*, volume 6605 of *LNCS*, pages 254–257. Springer, 2011.

[6] A. Donze. Breach, a toolbox for verification and parameter synthesis of hybrid systems. In *Computer Aided Verification*, volume 6174 of *LNCS*, pages 167–170. Springer, 2010.

[7] T. Dreossi, T. Dang, A. Donze, J. Kapinski, X. Jin, and J. V. Deshmukh. A trajectory splicing approach to concretizing counterexamples for hybrid systems. In *NASA Symposium on Formal Methods*, 2015.

[8] A. Eggers, M. Fränzle, and C. Herde. *SAT Modulo ODE: A Direct SAT Approach to Hybrid Systems*, pages 171–185. Springer Berlin Heidelberg, Berlin, Heidelberg, 2008.

[9] G. Fainekos and G. Pappas. Robustness of temporal logic specifications for continuous-time signals. *Theoretical Computer Science*, 410(42):4262–4291, September 2009.

[10] G. E. Fainekos, A. Girard, and G. J. Pappas. Temporal logic verification using simulation. In E. Asarin and P. Bouyer, editors, *FORMATS*, volume 4202 of *LNCS*, pages 171–186. Springer, 2006.

[11] M. Fisher. A semiclosed-loop algorithm for the control of blood glucose levels in diabetics. *Biomedical Engineering, IEEE Transactions on*, 38(1):57–61, 1991.

[12] P. Franek, S. Ratschan, and P. Zgliczynski. *Satisfiability of Systems of Equations of Real Analytic Functions Is Quasi-decidable*, pages 315–326. Springer Berlin Heidelberg, Berlin, Heidelberg, 2011.

[13] P. Franek, S. Ratschan, and P. Zgliczynski. Quasi-decidability of a fragment of the first-order

theory of real numbers. *Journal of Automated Reasoning*, 57(2):157–185, 2016.
[14] M. Fränzle. Analysis of hybrid systems: An ounce of realism can save an infinity of states. In *Proceedings of the 13th International Workshop and 8th Annual Conference of the EACSL on Computer Science Logic (CSL)*, pages 126–140, London, UK, 1999. Springer-Verlag.
[15] S. Gao. Atrial fibrillation model. accessed 09/30/2016, 2016.
[16] S. Gao, J. Avigad, and E. M. Clarke. δ-complete decision procedures for satisfiability over the reals. In *Proceedings of the 6th International Joint Conference on Automated Reasoning*, IJCAR'12, pages 286–300, Berlin, Heidelberg, 2012. Springer-Verlag.
[17] S. Gao, J. Avigad, and E. M. Clarke. δ-decidability over the reals. In *Proceedings of the 2012 27th Annual IEEE/ACM Symposium on Logic in Computer Science*, LICS '12, pages 305–314, Washington, DC, USA, 2012. IEEE Computer Society.
[18] S. Gao, S. Kong, and E. M. Clarke. Satisfiability modulo ODEs. In *FMCAD*, pages 105–112, 2013.
[19] T. A. Henzinger. *The Theory of Hybrid Automata*, pages 265–292. Springer Berlin Heidelberg, Berlin, Heidelberg, 2000.
[20] T. A. Henzinger, P. W. Kopke, A. Puri, and P. Varaiya. What's decidable about hybrid automata? *Journal of Computer and System Sciences*, 57(1):94 – 124, 1998.
[21] A. A. Julius, G. Fainekos, M. Anand, I. Lee, and G. Pappas. Robust test generation and coverage for hybrid systems. In *Hybrid Systems: Computation and Control*, volume 4416 of *LNCS*, pages 329–342. Springer-Verlag Berlin Heidelberg, 2007.
[22] K.-I. Ko. *Complexity theory of real functions*. Birkhauser, 1991.
[23] S. Kong, S. Gao, W. Chen, and E. Clarke. *dReach: δ-Reachability Analysis for Hybrid Systems*, pages 200–205. Springer Berlin Heidelberg, Berlin, Heidelberg, 2015.
[24] S. Kong, S. Gao, W. Chen, and E. Clarke. dreach: delta-reachability analysis for hybrid systems. In C. Baier and C. Tinelli, editors, *TACAS*, volume 9035 of *Lecture Notes in Computer Science*. 2015.
[25] R. Koymans. Specifying real-time properties with metric temporal logic. *Real-Time Systems*, 2(4):255–299, 1990.
[26] T. Nghiem, S. Sankaranarayanan, G. Fainekos, F. Ivancic, A. Gupta, and G. Pappas. Monte-carlo techniques for falsification of temporal properties of non-linear hybrid systems. In *Hybrid Systems: Computation and Control*, 2010.
[27] S. Ratschan. *Safety Verification of Non-linear Hybrid Systems Is Quasi-Semidecidable*, pages 397–408. Springer Berlin Heidelberg, Berlin, Heidelberg, 2010.
[28] S. Ratschan. Safety verification of non-linear hybrid systems is quasi-decidable. *Formal Methods in System Design*, 44(1):71–90, 2014.

Sampling-based Approximate Optimal Control Under Temporal Logic Constraints

Jie Fu
Department of Electrical and Computer Engineering
Robotics Engineering Program
Worcester Polytechnic Institute
Worcester, MA, 01604
jfu2@wpi.edu

Ivan Papusha
Institute for Computational Engineering and Sciences
University of Texas at Austin
Austin, TX, USA
ipapusha@utexas.edu

Ufuk Topcu
Aerospace Engineering and Engineering Mechanics
University of Texas at Austin
Austin, TX, USA
utopcu@utexas.edu

ABSTRACT

We investigate a sampling-based method for optimal control of continuous-time and continuous-state (possibly nonlinear) systems under co-safe linear temporal logic specifications. We express the temporal logic specification as a deterministic, finite automaton (the specification automaton), and link the automaton's discrete transitions to the continuous system state as it passes through specified regions. The optimal hybrid controller is characterized by a set of coupled partial differential equations. Because these equations are difficult to solve exactly in practice in all cases, we propose instead a sampling based technique to solve for an approximate controller through approximate value iteration. We adopt model reference adaptive search—an importance sampling optimization algorithm—to determine the mixing weights of the approximate value function expressed in a finite basis. Under mild technical assumptions, the algorithm converges, with probability one, to an optimal weight that ensures the satisfaction of temporal logic constraints, while minimizing an upper bound for the optimal cost. We demonstrate the correctness and efficiency of the method through numerical experiments, including temporal logic planning for a linear system, and a nonlinear mobile robot.

Keywords

Approximate optimal control, formal methods, importance sampling, hybrid systems.

1. INTRODUCTION

In this work, we propose a novel sampling-based optimal control method for continuous-time and continuous-state nonlinear systems subject to a subclass of temporal logic constraints, i.e., co-safe Linear Temporal Logic (LTL) [15]. Co-safe LTL formulas are LTL formulas with satisfying traces that can be recognized by a deterministic finite automaton. Co-safe LTL is an expressive formal language that allows one to specify a variety of finite-time behaviors, including traditional reaching-a-goal, stability, obstacle avoidance, sequentially visiting regions of interest, and conditional reactive behaviors [21].

Typically, trajectory generation and control of continuous systems with formal specifications is performed using abstraction-based synthesis, for example, by computing a discrete transition system that abstracts or simulates the system dynamics, and then planning in the discrete state space. Abstraction-based synthesis methods have been studied extensively for continuous linear and nonlinear systems [12, 3, 5, 18, 2, 24, 27].

However, abstraction-based synthesis has several important limitations. Among these, we highlight three: first, because they rely on discretization, abstraction-based methods scale poorly with the dimension of the continuous state space; second, optimality is no longer guaranteed when a controller is synthesized with the discrete abstracted system; and third, depending on the specific abstraction method, it is possible that a control policy exists for the underlying continuous control system even when one does not appear to exist in the abstraction.

To address these concerns, the work [20] exploited the idea that continuous-time and continuous-state systems constrained by co-safe LTL specifications can be viewed as hybrid dynamical systems. The continuous state space is augmented with the discrete states of the specification automaton, derived from the co-safe LTL formula. Then, a hybrid feedback controller is obtained by solving or approximately solving the corresponding Hamilton–Jacobi–Bellman (HJB) equations for the hybrid value function. For linear systems, the approximate hybrid value function can be obtained by semidefinite programming. But for general nonlinear systems, the resulting optimization problem is semi-infinite [22], and difficult to solve.

We tackle the computational difficulty of this semi-infinite program in the optimal control synthesis for this class of hybrid systems by developing an importance sampling algorithm. The key idea is to regard the control problem as a problem of inference, from sampled trajectories, of a weight vector that defines an approximate value function in a given basis. For sample-efficient search through the weight parameter space, we use model reference adaptive search (MRAS) [9]. In our MRAS-inspired algorithm, specific policies are computed from the value function approximations. These weights are then ranked by the performance of their corre-

HSCC'17, April 18-20, 2017, Pittsburgh, PA, USA

DOI: http://dx.doi.org/10.1145/3049797.3049820

sponding controllers, and the best performing weights (elite samples) are used to improve the weight sampling distribution. The aim is to find a value function approximation that minimizes an upper bound on the total cost. Similar cross-entropy (CE) methods have been used for trajectory planning in the past [13, 19], with the goal of finding a sequence of motion primitives or a sequence of states for interpolation-based planning. In stochastic policy optimization [14], CE is also useful for computing linear feedback policies.

Under certain regularity assumptions, we show that our sampling method is probabilistically complete, i.e., it converges to the optimal value function approximation in a given basis as the sample size goes to infinity. To improve the sampling efficiency, we employ rank functions in the specification to guide the iterative update of the sampling distribution. Based on experimental studies, we show that our method can generate an initial feasible hybrid controller that satisfies the co-safe LTL specification, which is then continually improved as more computation time is permitted. However, when a limited number of samples is used for each iteration, the method may converge to local optima. In the last section, we discuss future extensions to address these problems and conclude the work.

2. PROBLEM DESCRIPTION

We consider a continuous-time and continuous-state dynamical system on $\mathbb{R}^n$. This system is given by

$$\dot{x} = f(x, u), \quad x(0) = x_0, \tag{1}$$

where $x(t) \in \mathcal{X} \subseteq \mathbb{R}^n$ and $u(t) \in \mathcal{U} \subseteq \mathbb{R}^m$ are the state and control signals at time t. For simplicity, we restrict f to be a Lipschitz continuous function of (x, u), and the control input u to be a piecewise right-continuous function of time, with finitely many discontinuities on any finite time interval. These conditions ensure the existence and uniqueness of solutions, and are meant to prevent Zeno behavior.

2.1 Co-safe Linear Temporal Logic

The system (1) is constrained to satisfy a specification on the discrete behavior obtained from its continuous trajectory. First, let $\mathcal{AP}$ be a finite set of atomic propositions, which are logical predicates that hold true when $x(t)$ is in a particular region of the state space $\mathcal{X}$. Then, define a labeling function $L : \mathcal{X} \to \Sigma$, which maps a continuous state $x \in \mathcal{X}$ to a finite set $\Sigma = 2^{\mathcal{AP}}$ of atomic propositions that evaluate to true at x. This function partitions the continuous space $\mathcal{X}$ into regions that share the same truth values in $\mathcal{AP}$. The labeling function also links the continuous system with its *discrete behavior*. In the following definition, $\phi(x_0, [0, T], u)$ refers to the trajectory of the continuous system with initial condition x_0 under the control input $u(t)$ over the time interval $[0, T]$.

Definition 1. *Let $t_0, t_1, \ldots, t_N$ be times, such that*

- $0 = t_0 < t_1 < \cdots < t_N = T$,
- $L(x(t)) = L(x(t_k))$, $t_k \leq t < t_{k+1}$, $k = 0, \ldots, N$,
- $L(x(t_k^-)) \neq L(x(t_k^+))$, $k = 0, \ldots, N$.

The discrete behavior, *denoted $\mathcal{B}(\phi(x_0, [0, T], u))$, is the discrete word $\sigma_0\sigma_1 \ldots \sigma_{N-1} \in \Sigma^*$, where $\sigma_k = L(x(t_k))$.*

In the scope of this paper, we consider a subclass of linear temporal logic (LTL) specifications called co-safe LTL. A co-safe LTL formula is an LTL formula such that every satisfying word has a *finite* good prefix[1] [15]. This subclass of LTL formulas can be used to express tasks that can be completed in a finite time horizon. Given a co-safe LTL specification φ over the set of atomic propositions $\mathcal{AP}$, there exists a corresponding deterministic finite-state automaton (DFA) $\mathcal{A}_\varphi = \langle Q, \Sigma, \delta, q_0, F \rangle$, where Q is a finite set of states (modes), $\Sigma = 2^{\mathcal{AP}}$ is a finite alphabet, $\delta : Q \times \Sigma \to Q$ is a *deterministic* transition function such that when the symbol $\sigma \in \Sigma$ is read at state q, the automaton makes a deterministic transition to state $\delta(q, \sigma) = q'$, $q_0 \in Q$ is the initial state, and $F \subseteq Q$ is a set of final, or *accepting* states. The transition function is extended to a sequence of symbols, or a *word* $w = \sigma_0\sigma_1 \ldots \in \Sigma^*$, in the usual way: $\delta(q, \sigma_0 v) = \delta(\delta(q, \sigma_0), v)$ for $\sigma_0 \in \Sigma$ and $v \in \Sigma^*$. We say that the finite word w satisfies φ if and only if $\delta(q_0, w) \in F$. The set of words satisfying φ is the *language* of the automaton $\mathcal{A}_\varphi$, denoted $\mathcal{L}(\mathcal{A}_\varphi)$.

The discrete behavior encodes the sequence of labels visited by the state as it moves along its continuous trajectory. Specifically, the atomic propositions are evaluated only at the times when the evaluation of an atomic proposition changes value, indicated by the sequence of discrete time-stamps $t_0, t_1, \ldots, t_N$. Thus a trajectory $\phi(x_0, [0, T], u)$ satisfies an LTL specification φ if and only if its discrete behavior is in the language $\mathcal{L}(\mathcal{A}_\varphi)$. The optimal control problem is formulated as follows.

Problem 1. *Consider the system* (1)*, a co-safe LTL specification φ, and a final state $x_f \in \mathcal{X}$. Design a control law u that minimizes the cost function*

$$J(x_0, u) = \int_0^T \ell(x(\tau), u(\tau))\, d\tau + \sum_{k=0}^{N} s(x(t_k), q(t_k^-), q(t_k^+)) \tag{2}$$

subject to the constraints that $\mathcal{B}(\phi(x_0, [0, T], u)) \in \mathcal{L}(\mathcal{A}_\varphi)$ and $x(T) = x_f$.

Here, $\ell : \mathcal{X} \times \mathcal{U} \to \mathbb{R}$ is a continuous loss function, and $s : \mathcal{X} \times Q \times Q \to \mathbb{R}$ is the cost to transition between two states of the automaton whenever such a transition is allowed. The final state $x(T) = x_f$ is also specified. Similar problems have been studied in prior work [7, 8, 28, 5, 27, 26, 11]. Recently, the work [20] showed that determining an optimal controller for continuous-time systems under co-safe LTL behavior constraints can be translated into an optimal hybrid control problem. For linear and polynomial systems, an approximate optimal controller can be obtained by a special formulation of semi-infinite programming problems. The novelty in this paper is the development of a sampling-based algorithm that handles both nonlinear dynamical constraints, and co-safe LTL specifications. The algorithm is based on MRAS, which is briefly described next.

2.2 Model Reference Adaptive Search (MRAS)

[1]For two given words $v, w \in \Sigma^*$, the word v is a prefix of w if and only if $w = vu$ for some $u \in \Sigma^*$. The word u is called the suffix of w.

MRAS [9] is a general sampling-based method for global optimization that aims to solve the following problem:

$$z^\star = \operatorname*{argmax}_{z \in Z} H(z),$$

where $Z \subseteq \mathbb{R}^n$ is the solution space and $H : \mathbb{R}^n \to \mathbb{R}$ is a real-valued function that is bounded from below. It assumes that the optimization problem has a unique maximum, i.e., $z^\star \in Z$, and $H(z) < H(z^\star)$ for all $z \neq z^\star$.

The key idea of MRAS is similar to cross-entropy (CE) optimization methods. First, we sample the solution space Z with a parameterized distribution. Then, we select samples with the highest objective values, termed "elite samples," and update the parameters of the sampling distribution to assign a higher probability mass to the elite samples. Assuming the neighborhood of the optimal solution $z^\star$ has a positive probability of being sampled, and H satisfies certain regularity conditions [9, §2], the parametrized distribution converges to a distribution concentrated around $z^\star$. The MRAS algorithm consists of the following key steps:

- Define a sequence of reference distributions $\{g_k(\cdot)\}$ that converges to a distribution centered on the optimal solution $z^\star$, for example,

  $$g_k(z) = \frac{H(z) g_{k-1}(z)}{\int_Z H(z') g_{k-1}(z') \nu(dz')}, \quad k = 1, 2, \ldots,$$

  where $\nu(\cdot)$ is the Lebesgue measure defined over Z.

- Define a parameterized family of distributions $\{p(\cdot, \theta) \mid \theta \in \Theta\}$ over Z, onto which the exact reference distributions $\{g_k(\cdot)\}$ will be projected.

- Generate a sequence of parameters $\{\theta_k\}$ by minimizing (over $\theta \in \Theta$) the Kullback–Leibler (KL) divergence between $g_k(\cdot)$ and $p(\cdot, \theta)$,

  $$D_{KL}(g_k, p(\cdot, \theta)) := \int_Z \ln \frac{g_k(z)}{p(z, \theta)} g_k(z) \nu(dz),$$

  at each step $k = 1, 2, \ldots$

The sample distributions $\{p(\cdot, \theta_k)\}$ are meant to be compact approximations of the reference distributions $\{g_k(\cdot)\}$ that converge to the same optimal solution. Note that the reference distributions $\{g_k(\cdot)\}$ are unknown beforehand, as the optimal solution is unknown. In order to represent the reference distributions $\{g_k(\cdot)\}$, MRAS uses estimation of distributions [6] from elite samples (similar to CE). Then, the MRAS algorithm computes the parameter that minimizes the KL divergence between the sampling distribution and the reference distribution. As shown in [9], MRAS has better convergence rates and stronger guarantees than CE over several benchmark examples.

3. HYBRID SYSTEM FORMULATION OF CONTROL SYSTEMS UNDER TEMPORAL LOGIC CONSTRAINTS

To apply MRAS in solving Problem 1, we follow the setting and notation of [20] to define a hybrid system from the control system dynamics and the temporal logic constraints. The state space of the hybrid system is the product of the continuous state space $\mathcal{X}$ and the discrete state space Q of the specification automaton $\mathcal{A}_\varphi$, which is obtained from the co-safe LTL specification φ with existing tools [4, 16]. This produces a hybrid system where each mode is governed by the same continuous vector field (1). Switching between different discrete modes occurs when the continuous state crosses a boundary between two labeled regions. Specifically, we consider the following product hybrid system:

Definition 2. *The product system $\mathcal{H} = \langle Q, \mathcal{X}, \Sigma, E, f, R, G \rangle$ is an internally forced hybrid system, where*

- *Q is the set of discrete states (modes) of $\mathcal{A}_\varphi$,*
- *$\mathcal{X} \subseteq \mathbb{R}^n$ is the set of continuous states,*
- *$\Sigma = 2^{\mathcal{AP}}$ is the power set of atomic propositions,*
- *$E \subseteq Q \times \Sigma \times Q$ is a set of discrete transitions, where $e = (q, \sigma, q') \in E$ if and only if $\delta(q,\sigma) = q'$,*
- *$f : \mathcal{X} \times \mathcal{U} \to \mathbb{R}^n$ is the continuous vector field given by (1),*
- *$R = \{R_q \mid q \in Q\}$ is a collection of regions, where*

  $$R_{q,\sigma} = \{x \in \mathcal{X} \mid (q, \sigma, q) \in E, \text{ and } L(x) = \sigma\}, \quad q \in Q, \sigma \in \Sigma,$$

  $$R_q = \bigcup_{\sigma \in \Sigma} R_{q,\sigma}, \quad q \in Q,$$

- *$G = \{G_e \mid e \in E\}$ is a collection of guards, where*

  $$G_e = \{x \in \partial R_{q,\sigma} \mid \delta(q, L(x)) = q'\},$$

  for each $e = (q, \sigma, q') \in E$.

Each invariant region R_q refers to the continuous states $x \in \mathcal{X}$ that are reachable while the automaton is in mode q. For each discrete mode q, the continuous state evolves inside R_q until it enters a guard region $G_{(q,\sigma,q')}$ and a discrete transition to mode q' is made.

We can solve the optimal control problem with dynamic programming by ensuring that the optimal value function is zero at every accepting state of the automaton. Let $V^\star : \mathcal{X} \times Q \to \mathbb{R}$ be the optimal cost-to-go in (2), with $V^\star(x_0, q_0)$ denoting the optimal objective value when starting at initial condition (x_0, q_0), subject to the discrete behavior specification and final condition $x(T) = x_f$ for a free terminal time T. The existance of the controller is assumed.

In this setting, the cost-to-go satisfies a collection of mixed continuous-discrete Hamilton–Jacobi–Bellman (HJB) equations,

$$0 = \min_{u \in \mathcal{U}} \left\{ \frac{\partial V^\star(x, q)}{\partial x} \cdot f(x, u) + \ell(x, u) \right\}, \quad \forall x \in R_q, \ \forall q \in Q, \tag{3}$$

$$V^\star(x, q) = \min_{q'} \left\{ V^\star(x, q') + s(x, q, q') \right\}, \quad \forall x \in G_e, \ \forall e = (q, \sigma, q') \in E, \tag{4}$$

$$0 = V^\star(x_f, q_f), \quad \forall q_f \in F. \tag{5}$$

Equation (3) says that $V^\star(x, q)$ is an optimal cost-to-go inside the regions where the label remains constant. The next equation (4) is a shortest-path equality that must hold at every continuous state x where discrete state transition to a different label can happen. Finally, the boundary equation (5) fixes the value function.

4. APPROXIMATE OPTIMAL CONTROL UNDER TEMPORAL LOGIC CONSTRAINTS

In this section, we show that by approximating the optimal value function $V^\star(x,q)$ at each state $q \in Q$ with a linear combination $\hat{V}(x,q)$ of pre-defined basis functions, we can formulate a semi-infinite programming problem over the weight parameters. This value function candidate minimizes an upper bound of the optimal total cost.

Assumption 1. *For each mode $q \in Q$, the optimal value function $V^\star(\cdot,q)$ is C^1-differentiable. Moreover, the optimal value function $V^\star(\cdot,q)$ is positive semidefinite. This is guaranteed by the condition $\ell(x,u) > 0$, for all $x \in \mathcal{X} \setminus \{x_f\}$ and $u \in \mathcal{U}$, and $s(x,q,q') > 0$, for all $x \in \mathcal{X}$, $q,q' \in Q$.*

Recall from the Weierstrass higher-order approximation theorem [25] that there exists a complete independent set of bases $\{\phi_i(x,q) \mid i = 1,\ldots,N_q\}$, such that the function $V^\star(x,q)$ is uniformly approximated as

$$V^\star(x,q) = \sum_{i=1}^{N_q} w_{i,q}\phi_{i,q}(x) + \sum_{i=N_q+1}^{\infty} w_{i,q}\phi_{i,q}(x), \text{ and}$$

$$\frac{\partial V^\star(x,q)}{\partial x} = \sum_{i=1}^{N_q} w_{i,q}\frac{\partial \phi_{i,q}(x)}{\partial x} + \sum_{i=N_q+1}^{\infty} w_{i,q}\frac{\partial \phi_{i,q}(x)}{\partial x},$$

for some weights $\{w_{i,q}\}$, where in both expressions, the last term converges uniformly to zero as $N_q \to \infty$.

Thus, it is justified to assume that for any state q, the optimal value function approximation $\hat{V}(x,q)$ in a given set $\{\phi_{i,q}(x)\}$ of bases is

$$\hat{V}(x,q) = \sum_{i=1}^{N_q} w_{i,q}\phi_{i,q}(x).$$

We write $\hat{V}(x,q)$ compactly as $\vec{w}_q^T\vec{\phi}_q(x)$ where

$$\vec{w}_q = [w_{1,q},\ldots,w_{N_q,q}]^T, \quad \vec{\phi}_q(x) = [\phi_{1,q}(x),\ldots,\phi_{N_q,q}(x)]^T.$$

With a slight abuse of notation, the overall piecewise continuous value function approximation is denoted $\hat{V} = \langle W,\Phi\rangle$ with $W = [\vec{w}_q]_{q\in Q}$ and $\Phi = [\vec{\phi}_q]_{q\in Q}$ and $\hat{V}(x,q) = \vec{w}_q^T\vec{\phi}_q(x)$, for all $x \in R_q$.

Given an approximate value function $\hat{V}$, we define a hybrid feedback control law $u : \mathcal{X} \times Q \to \mathcal{U}$ as

$$u(x,q) = \underset{a\in\mathcal{U}}{\operatorname{argmin}} \left\{ \frac{\partial \hat{V}(x,q)}{\partial x} \cdot f(x,a) + \ell(x,a) \right\}. \tag{6}$$

For simulation-based optimization, we minimize an upper bound for the optimal total cost, and define the optimal value function approximation as follows.

Definition 3. *The* projected optimal value function approximation *is given by an optimal $W^\star \in \mathcal{W}$ that solves*

$$\underset{W\in\mathcal{W}}{\textit{minimize}} \quad J(x_0,u) + \bar{J} \times (1 - 1_F(q_f)) \tag{7a}$$

$$\textit{subject to} \quad \hat{V} = \langle W,\Phi\rangle \tag{7b}$$

$$u(x,q) = \underset{a\in\mathcal{U}}{\operatorname{argmin}} \left\{ \frac{\partial \hat{V}(x,q)}{\partial x} \cdot f(x,a) + \ell(x,a) \right\}, \quad \forall x \in R_q,\ \forall q \in Q, \tag{7c}$$

$$\hat{V}(x,q) = \min_{q'} \{\hat{V}(x,q') + s(x,q,q')\}, \quad \forall x \in G_e,\ \forall e = (q,\sigma,q') \in E, \tag{7d}$$

$$\hat{V}(x_f,q_f) = 0,\ \forall q_f \in F \tag{7e}$$

$$\dot{x} = f(x,u),\ x(0) = x_0,$$
$$q(t_k^+) = \delta(q(t_k^-), L(x(t_k^+))), \quad \forall t_k \textit{ such that } L(x(t_k^-)) \neq L(x(t_k^+)), \tag{7f}$$

where $\bar{J} \in \mathbb{R}_+$ is a pre-defined large penalty for violating the specification.

The choice of $\bar{J}$ will be discussed in more detail in Section 4.2. Note that the decision variable W is implicit in the objective function and explicit in the controller u, on which the cost function is dependent.

We only consider value function approximations of the form $\hat{V} = \langle W,\Phi\rangle$ for a given set of bases Φ. For each value function approximation, the corresponding controller is fixed under constraint (7c). The optimal value function approximation is the one that minimizes the the actual cost $J(x_0,u)$ under that fixed controller within the constrained policy space. Slightly abusing notation, let us denote by $J(x_0;W)$ the cost generated by applying the controller u computed from the value function approximation $\langle W,\Phi\rangle$, and by $\hat{V}(x_0;W)$ the value function approximation $\langle W,\Phi\rangle$ evaluated at the initial state x_0.

4.1 Sampling-based control design

Previously, variants of gradient descent [17, 1] have been used to implement approximate value iteration. Local optima can be problematic when there is discontinuity in the value function for hybrid systems. Besides, finding a reasonable starting point within the weight space is also critical for the successful application of the gradient descent. We instead employ MRAS to solve (7). The idea is to sample the weight space $\mathcal{W}$ according to a parameterized distribution $p(\cdot,\theta)$ for parameter $\theta \in \Theta$. For each sampled weight, we simulate the run of the corresponding optimal controller using a model of the system for a finite time T. The finite time T is an estimated upper bound on the time it takes for the system to stabilize to x_f with a final bounded error, for any controller with which the closed-loop system satisfies the specification. By evaluating the sampled trajectory, we update θ to bias the sampling distribution towards promising weight parameters. With probability one, the distribution will converge to a parameter $\theta^\star$, and the distribution $p(\cdot,\theta^\star)$ concentrates on the solution $W^\star$ to the optimization problem (7).

First, we select a multivariate Gaussian distribution as the sample distribution. Recall that the probability density of a multivariate Gaussian distribution is given by

$$p(W;\theta) = \frac{1}{\sqrt{(2\pi)^N|\Sigma|}}\exp(-\frac{1}{2}(W-\mu)^T\Sigma^{-1}(W-\mu)),$$
$$\theta = (\mu,\Sigma), \quad \forall W \in \mathcal{W},$$

where μ is the mean vector, Σ is the covariance matrix, N is the dimension of weight vector $W \in \mathcal{W}$, and $|\Sigma|$ is the determinant of Σ.

Next, we iteratively update the mean and covariance of the sampling distribution until $p(\cdot,\theta_k)$ converges to a degenerate distribution with a vanishing covariance.

1) **Initialization**: Select an initial distribution over weight vectors $\mathcal{W}$, denoted $p(\cdot,\theta_0)$, for some $\theta_0 \in \Theta$. We specify a parameter $\rho \in (0,1]$, a small real $\varepsilon \in \mathbb{R}_+$ called an *improvement parameter*, an initial sample size N_0, a *smoothing coefficient* $\alpha \in (0,1]$, a strictly decreasing and positive function $S : \mathbb{R} \to \mathbb{R}_+$. Possible choices can be $S(x) = e^{-x}$ or $S(x) = \frac{1}{x}$ for x strictly positive (which is the case here because the total cost is always positive). Set $k := 1$ and go to step 2).

2) **Sampling**: At each iteration k, given the current distribution $p(\cdot,\theta_k)$, generate a set $\mathcal{SW}$ of N_k samples. For each $W \in \mathcal{SW}$ in the sample set, evaluate $J(x_0;W)$ by simulating the system model (1) with the approximate controller (6), where $\hat{V} = \langle W,\Phi\rangle$.

3) **Reject unsatisfiable policies**: Reject all weights for which the generated controllers do not satisfy the LTL formula. The remaining set of weights is denoted $\mathcal{SW}_{\mathsf{sat}}$.

4) **Select elite samples and threshold**: Order the set $\{J(x_0;W) \mid W \in \mathcal{SW}_{\mathsf{sat}}\}$ from largest (worst) to smallest (best) among the given samples,

$$J_{k,(0)} \geq \ldots \geq J_{k,(N_k)}.$$

Let κ be the estimated $(1-\rho)$-quantile of costs $J(\cdot;W)$, i.e., $\kappa = J_{k,\lceil(1-\rho)N_k\rceil}$.

- If $k = 0$, we introduce a threshold $\gamma := \kappa$.
- If $k \neq 0$, the following cases are further distinguished:
  - If $\kappa \leq \gamma - \varepsilon$, i.e., the estimated $(1-\rho)$-quantile of cost has been reduced by the amount ε from the last iteration, then update $\gamma := \kappa$, $N_{k+1} := N_k$, and go to step 5).
  - Otherwise, if $\kappa > \gamma - \varepsilon$, find the largest ρ', if it exists, such that the estimated $(1-\rho')$-quantile of cost $\kappa' = J_{k,\lceil(1-\rho')N_k\rceil}$ satisfies $\kappa' \leq \gamma - \varepsilon$. Then, update $\gamma := \kappa'$, and also the quantile $\rho := \rho'$. Set $N_{k+1} := N_0$ and go to step 5). If no such ρ' exists, increase the sample size by a factor of $(1+\alpha)$, $N_{k+1} = \lceil(1+\alpha)N_k\rceil$. Set $\theta_{k+1} := \theta_k$, $k := k+1$, and go to step 2).

5) **Parameter update**: Update parameters θ_{k+1} for iteration $k+1$ as follows. First, define a set $\mathcal{EW} = \{W \mid J(x_0;W) \leq \gamma, W \in \mathcal{SW}_{\mathsf{sat}}\}$ of *elite samples*. The samples in $\mathcal{EW}$ are *accepted* and samples not in $\mathcal{EW}$ are *rejected* during the parameter update defined next. Select the next parameter θ_{k+1} to maximize the weighted sum of probabilities of elite samples according to a weighting

$$\theta^\star_{k+1} = \operatorname*{argmax}_{\theta\in\Theta} \sum_{W\in\mathcal{EW}} \frac{S(J(x_0;W))^k}{p(W,\theta_k)} p(W,\theta) \quad (8)$$

that puts a higher weight on those weight vectors with the lowest costs. Since the optimal parameter $\theta^\star_{k+1}$ cannot be determined analytically, we use maximum likelihood estimate of the elite sample distribution $\theta^\star_{k+1} \approx (\mu_{k+1},\Sigma_{k+1})$, where

$$\mu_{k+1} = \frac{\mathbb{E}_{\theta_k}\left(\frac{S(J(x_0,W))^k}{p(W,\theta_k)}\right)I_{\mathcal{EW}}(W)\cdot W}{\mathbb{E}_{\theta_k}\left(\frac{S(J(x_0,W))^k}{p(W,\theta_k)}\right)I_{\mathcal{EW}}(W)} \approx \frac{\sum_{W\in\mathcal{SW}}\left(\frac{S(J(x_0,W))^k}{p(W,\theta_k)}\right)I_{\mathcal{EW}}(W)\cdot W}{\sum_{W\in\mathcal{SW}}\left(\frac{S(J(x_0,W))^k}{p(W,\theta_k)}\right)I_{\mathcal{EW}}(W)}, \quad (9)$$

and

$$\Sigma_{k+1} = \frac{\mathbb{E}_{\theta_k}\left(\frac{S(J(x_0,W))^k}{p(W,\theta_k)}\right)I_{\mathcal{EW}}(W)\cdot(W-\mu)(W-\mu)^T}{\mathbb{E}_{\theta_k}\left(\frac{S(J(x_0,W))^k}{p(W,\theta_k)}\right)I_{\mathcal{EW}}(W)} \approx \frac{\sum_{W\in\mathcal{SW}}\left(\frac{S(J(x_0,W))^k}{p(W,\theta_k)}\right)I_{\mathcal{EW}}(W)\cdot(W-\mu)(W-\mu)^T}{\sum_{W\in\mathcal{SW}}\frac{S(J(x_0;W))^k}{p(W,\theta_k)}I_{\mathcal{EW}}(W)}. \quad (10)$$

Note that we approximate $\mathbb{E}_{\theta_k} h(r)$ with its sample estimate, $\frac{1}{N_k}\sum_{W\in\mathcal{SW}} h(W)$ for $r \sim p(\cdot,\theta_k)$, and $I_{\mathcal{EW}} : W \to \{0,1\}$ is the indicator function that equals 1 if $W \in \mathcal{EW}$ and 0 otherwise.

6) **Smoothing update:** The actual parameter is smoothed with parameter $\lambda \in (0,1)$ as

$$\theta_{k+1} := \lambda\theta_k + (1-\lambda)\theta^\star_{k+1}. \quad (11)$$

7) **Stopping criterion:** Stop the iteration if the covariance matrixΣ_k becomes near singular, that is, the determinant ofΣ_k approaches 0. The reason for this choice of stopping criterion is given next.

In the algorithm, elite samples can be reused by including in the current sample $\mathcal{SW}$ at iteration k, denoted $\mathcal{SW}_k$, the set of elite samples from the previous iteration $\mathcal{EW}$, denoted $\mathcal{EW}_{k-1}$ for $k > 1$. The current set of elite samples is obtained from the ρ-quantile of $\mathcal{SW}_k \cup \mathcal{EW}_{k-1}$.

We show that the global convergence of the algorithm is ensured by the properties of MRAS under the following additional assumptions. Let $W^\star$ be the optimal weight parameterizing the projected optimal value function approximation.

Assumption 2. *For any given constant $\xi > J(x_0;W^\star)$, the set $\{W \mid J(x_0;W) \leq \xi\} \cap \mathcal{W}$ has a strictly positive Lebesgue measure.*

This condition ensures that any neighborhood of the optimal solution $W^\star$ will be sampled with a positive probability.

Assumption 3. *For any $\delta > 0$, we have $\inf_{W\in\mathcal{W}_\delta} J(x_0;W) > J(x_0;W^\star)$, where $W_\delta := \{W \mid \|W - W^\star\| \geq \delta\} \cap \mathcal{W}$.*

Theorem 1 (Adapted from Theorem 1 [9]). *Under assumptions 1–3, the algorithm converges (w.p.1) to*

$$\lim_{k\to\infty} \mu_k = W^\star \text{ and } \lim_{k\to\infty} \Sigma_k = 0_{n\times n},$$

provided that (8) is solved exactly.

Since our algorithm directly uses the multivariate Gaussian distribution, it would converge to the global optimal solution after finitely many iterations if it could be provided with an infinite number of samples. However, in practice, only finitely many samples can be used. In addition, the parameter update (8) is not solved exactly based on the entire set of elite samples. Instead, we provide a maximum likelihood estimation of θ for the next iteration using a finite number of elite samples. Similar to the CE method, the resulting algorithm may converge to local optimal solutions if the sample size is not sufficient. In general, the number of samples for each iteration is polynomial in the number of the decision variables [23], which, in this context, is the number of unknown weights.

It should be noted that the value function approximation computed with this sampling-based algorithm is not necessarily a control Lyapunov function. In fact, there is no guarantee ahead of time that the space of value function approximations in a given fixed bases contains a control Lyapunov function. In this case, this method performs approximate optimal feedback planning in the hybrid system instead of control design that stabilizes the system.

4.2 Rank-guided sample weighting

A direct implementation of the algorithm should enable the convergence to a global optimal weight given a chosen bases. However, for a high-dimensional weight vector space, it is not likely that many samples will satisfy the specifications in the first few iterations. As a consequence, we are left with limited information to update the sampling distribution and the resulting control policy.

To address this issue, we propose a rank-guided adaptive policy search, which incorporates an additional terminal cost associated with the rank of the specification state. This allows us to remove the rejection step, so that all sampled weight vectors will be associated with costs.

Definition 4. *The rank function* rank : $Q \to \mathbb{Z}_+$ *maps each specification state* $q \in Q$ *to a nonnegative integer and is defined recursively as*

$$\mathrm{rank}(q) = \begin{cases} 0, & \text{if } q \in F, \\ \min_{\sigma \in 2^{\mathcal{AP}}} \{1 + \mathrm{rank}(\delta(q,\sigma))\}, & \text{otherwise.} \end{cases}$$

It can be shown that given a set Q_k of states with rank k, the set of states Q_{k+1} with rank $k+1$ can be computed

$$Q_{k+1} = \{q \in Q \mid \forall 0 \leq i \leq k \text{ such that } q \notin Q_i \text{ and } \exists \sigma \in 2^{AP} \text{ such that } \delta(q,\sigma) \in Q_k\}.$$

In other words, Q_{k+1} contains a state which is not included in Q_i, for $i \leq k$, and can take a labeled transition to visit a state q' in Q_k.

Next, we redefine the terminal cost function related to the specification state $h : Q \to \mathbb{R}$ defined by

$$h(q) = \begin{cases} 0 & \text{if } q \in F, \\ \mathrm{rank}(q) \cdot c & \text{otherwise.} \end{cases}$$

where c is a constant. We must select a constant c at least as large as the the cost incurred when the system trajectory triggers a transition in the specification automaton. In practice, this cost is chosen based on an estimated upper bound and does not need to be precise.

In summary, we developed a sampling-based method to search for an optimal weight defining a value function approximation. The sample distribution is iteratively updated based on simulated runs that assign a higher probability to those sampled weights that produce controllers with the best performance. The method is probabilistically complete. That is, with infinite number of samples, the algorithm is ensured to converge to the optimal solution of (7). Furthermore, to address the sample scarcity caused by rejecting unsatisfying weights, we introduced a meta-heuristic using the rank function of the specification automaton. Instead of rejecting weights, the penalty associated with nonzero rank allows us to assign lower probabilities to those weights that do not generate correct controllers.

5. EXAMPLES

In this section, we illustrate the correctness and efficiency of the proposed method with two case studies. The first is an example linear system, and the second is a nonlinear system—a Dubins car. The experiments are carried out in Matlab on an Intel(R) Core(TM) i7 CPU with 16 GB RAM.

5.1 Linear system with halfspace labels

We consider the linear quadratic system on $\mathcal{X} = \mathbb{R}^2$ with the specific parameters

$$A = \begin{bmatrix} 2 & -2 \\ 1 & 0 \end{bmatrix}, \quad B = \begin{bmatrix} 1 \\ 1 \end{bmatrix}, Q = I, \quad R = 1, \quad \xi = 1,$$
$$x_0 = (0.5, 0.5), \quad x_f = (0, 0).$$

Let $\mathcal{AP} = \{a, b, c\}$ consist of atomic propositions that are true whenever the continuous state enters a specific region,

$$a : (x_1 \leq -1), \quad b : (-1 < x_1 \leq 1), \quad c : (x_1 > 1).$$

Note that each atomic proposition corresponds to a half space. Using $\mathcal{AP}$, we partition the state space into three regions $R_A = \{x \in \mathbb{R}^2 \mid x_1 \leq -1\}$, $R_B = \{x \in \mathbb{R}^2 \mid -1 < x_1 \leq 1\}$, and $R_C = \{x \in \mathbb{R}^2 \mid x_1 > 1\}$, with the following LTL specification

$$\varphi_1 = (A \to \diamond B) \wedge (C \to \diamond B) \wedge (\diamond A \vee \diamond C).$$

This specification ensures that either R_A or R_C must be reached, after which the system must eventually visit R_B. The automaton for this specification is shown in Fig. 1.

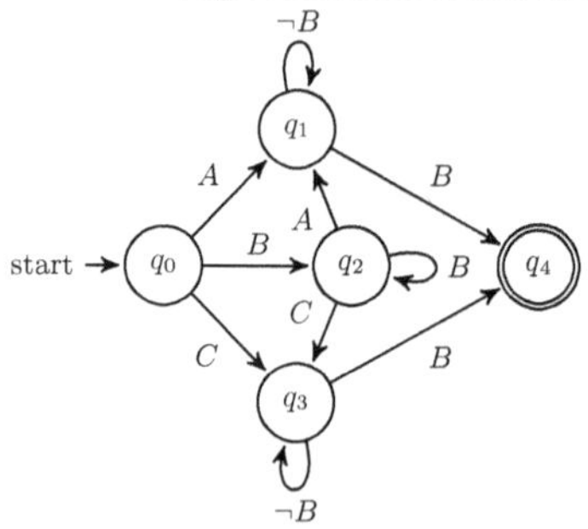

Figure 1: Automaton $\mathcal{A}_{\varphi_1}$ for $\varphi_1 = (A \to \diamond B) \wedge (C \to \diamond B) \wedge (\diamond A \vee \diamond C)$.

We consider value a function approximation with polynomial bases. The set of bases are $\{x_1^2, x_2^2, x_1x_2, x_1, x_2, 1\}$ for any specification state $q \in Q$. Thus, the total number of unknown weights is 30. Next, we employ the proposed algorithm to search for the approximate optimal weight vector $W^{\star}$. The following parameters are used: Initial sample size $N_0 = 100$, improvement parameter $\epsilon = 0.1$, smoothing parameter $\lambda = 0.2$, sample increment percentage $\alpha = 0.1$, and quantile parameter $\rho = 0.1$. The algorithm took 11 iterations to converge to the approximate optimal value function with the stopping criterion $\|\Sigma\| \leq 0.001$. The cost of the corresponding controller is 9.8384 with a terminal cost $100 \times \|x\|^2$ and a finite time horizon $T = 10$.

We test the controller for different initial states. As shown in Fig. 2b, a trajectory starting at $(0.5, 0.5)$ (near region R_C) visits R_C, then R_B and stabilizing to the origin. A trajectory starting at $(-0.5, -0.5)$ (near region R_A) visits R_A, then R_B in this order.

Remark. *When no terminal cost is considered, the approximate optimal controller can be obtained by convex optimization [20]. Using the proposed sampling-based method with sample size* 500 *for each iteration, the cost of the computed optimal controller is* 3.723. *The optimality can be improved by increasing sample size, which requires more computation. Overall, for linear quadratic systems with co-safe LTL specifications, the direct solution [20] is much more efficient. However, this solution does not apply to nonlinear systems, prompting the development of the sampling-based method.*

5.2 Dubins car system with obstacle

Given Dubins car dynamics $\dot{x} = u\cos(\theta)$, $\dot{y} = u\sin(\theta)$, and $\dot{\theta} = v$, where $x = (x, y, \theta) \in SE(2)$ is the state, and u and v are the inputs to the system (linear and angular velocities), we consider an LTL formula $\varphi_2 = \Diamond(\Diamond(A \wedge \Diamond B) \vee \Diamond(B \wedge \Diamond A) \wedge \Diamond C) \wedge \Box\neg\text{obs}$. The corresponding specification automaton is shown in Fig. 3. In this case, the system needs to traverse regions A and B in any order, and eventually reach C while avoiding collisions with a static obstacle. The running cost ℓ is the same as in the previous example, with terminal cost $100 \times \|(x, y) - (x_f, y_f)\|$. We define an additional cost $h(q) = 2 \times 10^3 \,\text{rank}(q)$, where $\text{rank}(q)$ is the minimum number of transitions required to reach an accepting state from $q(T)$, where the terminal time T is 50.

In Dubins car case, we select radial basis function (RBF) bases. An RBF is defined by

$$\phi(x) = \exp(-\|x - x_c\|^2 / 2\sigma^2),$$

where x_c is the center of the basis element, and σ is a free parameter. We define $\phi_{\text{rbf}} = [\phi_1, \ldots, \phi_N]^T$ where the ϕ_is are RBFs centered on a uniform grid in x-y coordinates with step sizes $\delta x = 5$ and $\delta y = 5$. The workspace is bounded $0 \leq x \leq 30$ and $0 \leq y \leq 30$. The free parameter σ of each RBF is 5. We also define the bases $\phi_\theta = [\sin(\theta), \cos(\theta)]^T$ such that for each state $q \in Q$, the vector of basic bases is $\phi_{\text{basic}} = [\phi_{\text{rbf}}^T, \phi_\theta^T]^T$.

Additional RBF bases are determined by picking their centers as the centers of disk regions A, B, C, and obs. For example, in the state q_2, since the region B has been visited, the center of region A is taken into the consideration, so the basis function with the respect to the state q_2 is: $\phi_2 = [\phi_{\text{basic}}^T, \phi_A^T, \phi_{\text{obs}}^T]^T$ where ϕ_A (resp. ϕ_{obs}) is an RBF with its center on the center of disk A (resp. obs) and an RBF parameter $\sigma = 5$. Finally, the total number of basis functions (weight parameters) is 530. For the sampling-based algorithm, the same set of parameters is used, except that the initial sample size is chosen to be 500. A smaller sample size leads to faster updates, but longer iterations.

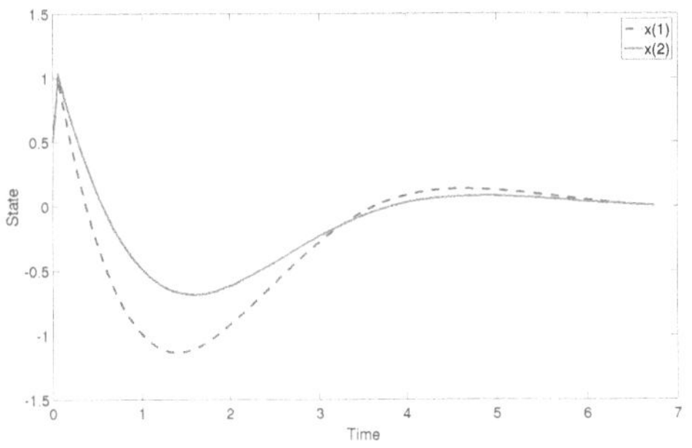

(a)

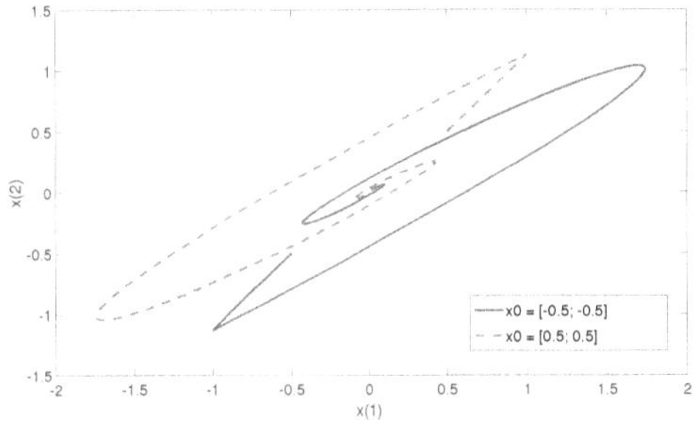

(b)

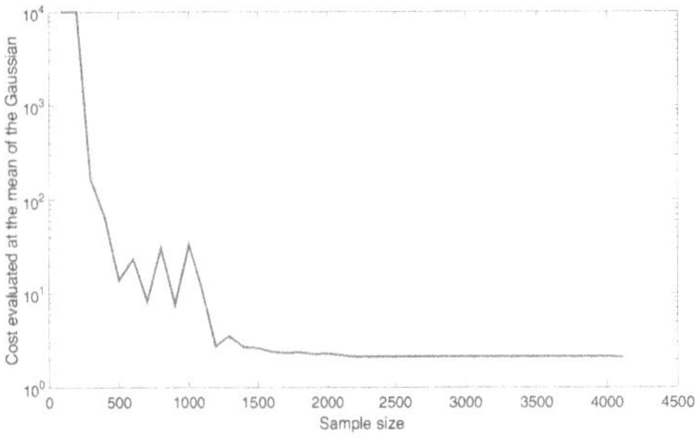

(c)

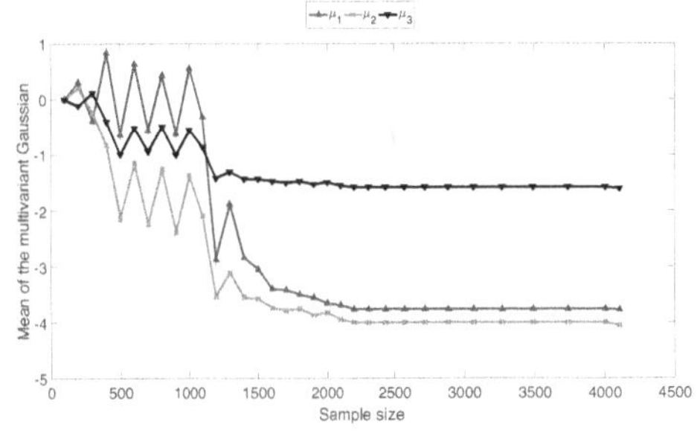

(d)

Figure 2: (a) The state trajectory for the linear system with $x_0 = (0.5, 0.5)$ calculated by the computed controller after the algorithm converges. (b) Approximate minimal cost trajectories satisfying the specification. The trajectories start with different initial states $x_0 = (-0.5, -0.5)$ and $x_0 = (0.5, 0.5)$ while the same controller is applied. (c) The cost over iterations. (d) The mean of the Gaussian distribution over iterations for the first three components in the mean vector.

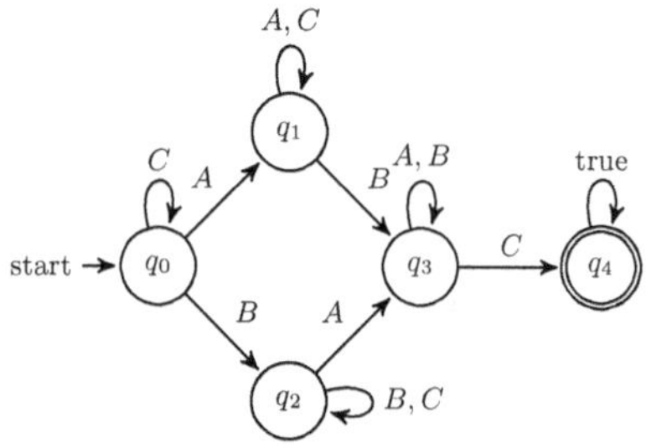

Figure 3: Automaton $\mathcal{A}_{\varphi_2}$ for $\varphi_2 = \Diamond(\Diamond(A \wedge \Diamond B) \vee \Diamond(B \wedge \Diamond A) \wedge \Diamond C) \wedge \Box\neg\text{obs}$. The self-loops with labels other than A, B, C, and obs are omitted.

Fig. 4a shows the system trajectories computed using the value function approximation parameterized by μ over 179 iterations. Each iteration takes 20 to 30 seconds and the algorithm converges to an optimal controller after 73 iterations, with the same stopping criterion as in the linear example. Interestingly, the algorithm quickly finds a control policy that satisfies the specification after 15 iterations. Figs. 4b and 4c show the x and y state trajectories with and without initial error. The solid lines are the state trajectories with small initial errors. Even with small initial errors, the controller ensures satisfaction of the temporal logic constraints. Finally, Fig. 4d shows the convergence of the total cost at each iteration. The x-axis is the iteration number k, while the y-axis is the total cost value of the mean μ_k. Note that the mean of the distribution upon convergence may not be optimal due to the finite sample size. As a consequence, when the algorithm terminates under the terminal condition $\|\Sigma_k\| \leq 0.005$, the distribution may converge to the sub-optimal solution.

6. CONCLUSION

In this work, we presented a sampling-based method for optimal control with co-safe LTL constraints. Through a hybrid system formulation, the objective is to solve a sequence of value functions over a hybrid state space, where the continuous component comes from the continuous-time and continuous-state dynamics of the system, and the discrete component comes from the specification automaton. By approximating the value functions with weighted combinations of pre-defined bases, we employ model reference adaptive search (MRAS)—a general sampling-based optimization method—to directly search over weight parameter space. The method often works in a near-anytime fashion: it quickly finds a hybrid controller that satisfies the temporal logic constraint, and improves the value function approximation by minimizing an upper bound on the actual value function as more computation time is permitted. The algorithm converges, with probability one, to an optimal value function approximation. This procedure does not rely on discretizing the time/state space.

Building on this result, we consider several further developments. At this stage, this approach is limited to a subset of LTL specifications that admit deterministic and finite (rather than Büchi) automaton representations. Extensions to the general class of LTL specifications that admit deterministic Büchi automaton are subjects of current work. We will also consider decomposition-based distributed sampling so that the algorithm scales to problems in a high-dimensional weight parameter space. We will further extend

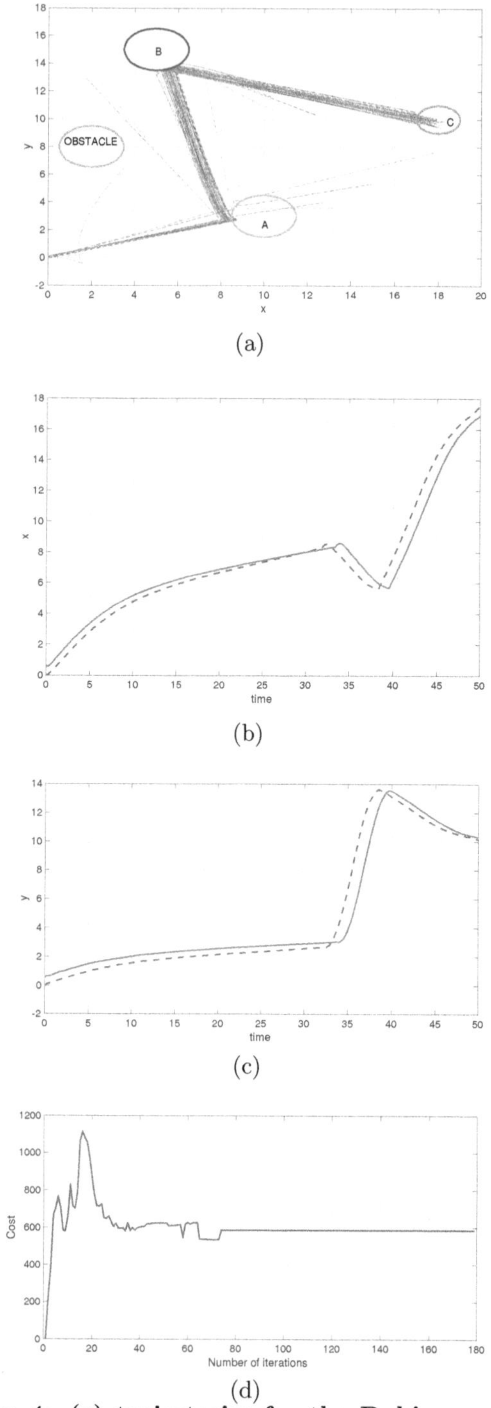

Figure 4: (a) trajectories for the Dubins car with the controller $u(x,q)$ computed from $\hat{V}(x;\mu)$ where μ is the mean of the Gaussian distribution over iterations. Dashed lines represent trajectories that do not satisfy the temporal logic constraints. (b–c) state trajectories of the Dubins car under the converged controller and errors in the initial states. (d) cost over iterations.

the proposed method as a building block in anytime optimal and provably correct decision making systems for nonlinear robotic systems. Finally, the sampling algorithm is highly parallelizable, suggesting the use of GPU-accelerated computing to speed up computations.

Acknowledgments

This work was supported in part by grants from AFRL #FA8650-15-C-2546, ONR #N00014-15-IP-00052, and NSF #1550212.

7. REFERENCES

[1] M. Abu-Khalaf and F. L. Lewis. Nearly optimal control laws for nonlinear systems with saturating actuators using a neural network HJB approach. *Automatica*, 41(5):779–791, 2005.

[2] R. Alur, T. A. Henzinger, G. Lafferriere, and G. J. Pappas. Discrete abstractions of hybrid systems. *Proceedings of the IEEE*, 88(7):971–984, July 2000.

[3] G. E. Fainekos, A. Girard, H. Kress-Gazit, and G. J. Pappas. Temporal logic motion planning for dynamic robots. *Automatica*, 45(2):343–352, 2009.

[4] P. Gastin and D. Oddoux. Fast LTL to Büchi automata translation. In G. Berry, H. Comon, and A. Finkel, editors, *International Conference on Computer Aided Verification (CAV'01)*, volume 2102 of *Lecture Notes in Computer Science*, pages 53–65, Paris, France, July 2001. Springer.

[5] L. C. G. J. M. Habets and C. Belta. Temporal logic control for piecewise-affine hybrid systems on polytopes. In *Proceedings of the 19th International Symposium on Mathematical Theory of Networks and Systems (MTNS)*, pages 195–202, July 2010.

[6] M. Hauschild and M. Pelikan. An introduction and survey of estimation of distribution algorithms. *Swarm and Evolutionary Computation*, 1(3):111–128, 2011.

[7] S. Hedlund and A. Rantzer. Optimal control of hybrid systems. In *IEEE Conference on Decision and Control (CDC)*, volume 4, pages 3972–3977, 1999.

[8] S. Hedlund and A. Rantzer. Convex dynamic programming for hybrid systems. *IEEE Transactions on Automatic Control*, 47(9):1536–1540, 2002.

[9] J. Hu, M. C. Fu, and S. I. Marcus. A model reference adaptive search method for global optimization. *Operations Research*, 55(3):549–568, 2007.

[10] M. Johansson and A. Rantzer. Computation of piecewise quadratic Lyapunov functions for hybrid systems. *IEEE Transactions on Automatic Control*, 43(4):555–559, Apr. 1998.

[11] N. Kariotoglou, S. Summers, T. Summers, M. Kamgarpour, and J. Lygeros. Approximate dynamic programming for stochastic reachability. In *European Control Conference (ECC)*, pages 584–589, July 2013.

[12] M. Kloetzer and C. Belta. A fully automated framework for control of linear systems from temporal logic specifications. *IEEE Transactions on Automatic Control*, 53(1):287–297, 2008.

[13] M. Kobilarov. Cross-entropy motion planning. *The International Journal of Robotics Research*, 31(7):855–871, 2012.

[14] M. Kobilarov. Sample complexity bounds for iterative stochastic policy optimization. In *Advances in Neural Information Processing Systems*, pages 3114–3122, 2015.

[15] O. Kupferman and M. Y. Vardi. Model checking of safety properties. *Formal Methods in System Design*, 19(3):291–314, Nov. 2001.

[16] T. Latvala. Efficient model checking of safety properties. In T. Ball and S. K. Rajamani, editors, *International SPIN Workshop on Model Checking of Software*, volume 2648 of *Lecture Notes in Computer Science*, pages 74–88. Springer, 2003.

[17] F. Lewis, S. Jagannathan, and A. Yesildirak. *Neural network control of robot manipulators and non-linear systems.* CRC Press, 1998.

[18] J. Liu and N. Ozay. Abstraction, discretization, and robustness in temporal logic control of dynamical systems. In *International Conference on Hybrid Systems: Computation and Control (HSCC)*, pages 293–302. ACM, 2014.

[19] S. C. Livingston, E. M. Wolff, and R. M. Murray. Cross-entropy temporal logic motion planning. In *International Conference on Hybrid Systems: Computation and Control*, pages 269–278. ACM, 2015.

[20] I. Papusha, J. Fu, U. Topcu, and R. M. Murray. Automata theory meets approximate dynamic programming: Optimal control with temporal logic constraints. In *IEEE Conference on Decision and Control (CDC)*, Dec. 2016.

[21] N. Piterman, A. Pnueli, and Y. Sa'ar. Synthesis of reactive (1) designs. In *International Workshop on Verification, Model Checking, and Abstract Interpretation*, pages 364–380. Springer, 2006.

[22] R. Reemtsen and J.-J. Rückmann. *Semi-infinite programming*, volume 25. Springer Science & Business Media, 1998.

[23] R. Y. Rubinstein and D. P. Kroese. *The cross-entropy method: a unified approach to combinatorial optimization, Monte-Carlo simulation and machine learning.* Springer Science & Business Media, 2013.

[24] S. L. Smith, J. Tumova, C. Belta, and D. Rus. Optimal path planning for surveilance with temporal-logic constraints. *International Journal of Robotics Research*, 30(14):1695–1708, Dec. 2011.

[25] K. Weierstrass. Über die analytische Darstellbarkheit sogenannter willhülicher Functionen einer reellen Veränderlichen. *Berliner Berichte*, 1885.

[26] E. M. Wolff, U. Topcu, and R. M. Murray. Automaton-guided controller synthesis for nonlinear systems with temporal logic. In *IEEE/RSJ International Conference on Intelligent Robots and Systems (IROS)*, pages 4332–4339, Nov. 2013.

[27] T. Wongpiromsarn, U. Topcu, and R. M. Murray. Receding horizon temporal logic planning. *IEEE Transactions on Automatic Control*, 57(11):2817–2830, Nov. 2012.

[28] X. Xu and P. J. Antsaklis. Optimal control of switched systems based on parameterization of the switching instants. *IEEE Transactions on Automatic Control*, 49(1):2–16, 2004.

Abnormal Data Classification Using Time-Frequency Temporal Logic

Luan Viet Nguyen
University of Texas at Arlington, USA

James Kapinski
Toyota Technical Center

Xiaoqing Jin
Toyota Technical Center

Jyotirmoy V. Deshmukh
Toyota Technical Center

Ken Butts
Toyota Technical Center

Taylor T. Johnson
Vanderbilt University, USA

ABSTRACT

We present a technique to investigate abnormal behaviors of signals in both time and frequency domains using an extension of time-frequency logic that uses the continuous wavelet transform. Abnormal signal behaviors such as unexpected oscillations, called *hunting* behavior, can be challenging to capture in the time domain; however, these behaviors can be naturally captured in the time-frequency domain. We introduce the concept of parametric time-frequency logic and propose a parameter synthesis approach that can be used to classify hunting behavior. We perform a comparative analysis between the proposed algorithm, an approach based on support vector machines using linear classification, and a method that infers a signal temporal logic formula as a data classifier. We present experimental results based on data from a hydrogen fuel cell vehicle application and electrocardiogram data extracted from the MIT-BIH Arrhythmia Database.

1. INTRODUCTION

For the last decade, signal temporal logic (STL) [11] has been successfully extended and applied in many domains such as exploring requirements for closed-loop control systems [8], identifying oscillatory behaviors of biology systems [5], and formalizing and recognizing music melodies [7]. Recently, Kapinski et al. introduced a new signal library template for constructing formal requirements of automotive control applications using STL [10]. These requirements involve various control signal behaviors such as settling time, overshoot, and steady state errors. Although most of such control signal behaviors can be characterized in the time domain, some abnormal signal behaviors such as *hunting* (undesirable oscillations) or *spikes* (abrupt, momentary jumps in signal values) are challenging to capture without frequency information. In most practical control systems, hunting behaviors are considered undesirable, or at least not ideal, and care is taken to minimize or eliminate the behavior. In signal processing, hunting behavior can manifest around sharp transitions, as a result of compression artifacts; this occurs, for example, in image processing, resulting in ghostly bands near edges, or in audio compression, resulting in forward echo problems. In circuit design, a hunting behavior can be the unwanted oscillation of an output current or voltage, which may cause a significant rise in power consumption, temperature, electromagnetic radiation, or settling time [9]. Although some hunting behaviors can be defined loosely as an oscillation around a given average and can be well captured using STL, some modulated hunting signals are challenging to detect using only time domain information [10]. Because hunting signals relate to oscillatory properties, it is appropriate to investigate them using time-frequency analysis.

The first attempt to introduce a specification formalism for both time and frequency properties of a signal, called time-frequency logic (TFL), was proposed by Donzé and his collaborators [7]. There, a signal is preprocessed using a Short-Time Fourier Transform (STFT) [4] to generate a spectral signal that represents the evolution of the STFT coefficients at some particular frequency over time. The time-frequency predicates and arithmetic expressions constructed from this spectral signal are added into an STL formula to yield a TFL formula. TFL was originally applied to music, though it can be easily extended to other application domains. A key limitation of the approach using the STFT is the inherent trade-off required between resolution in the time domain and resolution in the frequency domain; it is difficult or impossible to obtain satisfactory resolution in both time and frequency using the STFT for the analysis. Such limitations can be overcome using the continuous wavelet transform (CWT).

In the following, we extend the notion of TFL by using the CWT to specify and check time-frequency properties of signals. We introduce the concept of parametric time-frequency logic (PTFL) and use it to perform parameter synthesis for the purpose of classifying hunting behavior. Previous efforts have focused on data classification of time-series signals using STL [2, 3, 8], but identifying some abnormal behaviors such as hunting requires both time and frequency information [10]. Moreover, existing classification methods require an extensive amount of data, and the inferred classifier is often difficult for engineers to interpret. In contrast, our proposed method using PTFL can efficiently classify abnormal behaviors with an interpretable data classifier and requires less data than existing techniques. We note that although the below presentation is focused on one behavior type, it is straightforward to extend the work to detect other abnormal behaviors such as noise, spikes, or

HSCC '17, April 18–20, 2017, Pittsburgh, PA, USA.

DOI: http://dx.doi.org/10.1145/3049797.3049809

other anomalous behavior, in the time-frequency domain. We evaluate the proposed algorithm by comparing the performance against two existing classification techniques: a traditional machine learning technique using a support vector machine with a linear kernel, and a method that infers STL formulae as data classifiers [3]. To perform the evaluation, we use data sets from two different domains, the automotive and medical domains.

2. TIME-FREQUENCY LOGIC USING CWT

Although many control system behaviors can be naturally characterized in the time domain, there are some signal behaviors, such as hunting and spikes, that are challenging to capture without frequency information. This is especially true for non-stationary signals whose frequency components vary over time; for this class of signals, it is essential to analyze the signal properties in the time-frequency domain. STFT is a popular transformation that has been widely used in time-frequency analysis [4]. Using STFT to perform time-frequency analysis, a signal is partitioned into small segments (each segment is assumed to be stationary) whose lengths are equal to the width of a chosen window function. The window function is used to modulate the signal to emphasize the time instant associated with each segment. Unfortunately, the STSF provides a fixed time-frequency resolution so that it is not effective for signals that need to be analyzed with different time-frequency resolutions [14]. Moreover, it is difficult to choose a proper window function with an appropriate size that not only provides both desirable time and frequency resolutions but also does not violate the stationarity condition [14]. To overcome the limitation of the STFT, we use the CWT to analyze a signal in the time-frequency domain.

2.1 Continuous Wavelet Transform

The CWT of a signal $x(t)$ is formally defined as follows:

$$Wf(\zeta,\tau) = \int_{-\infty}^{+\infty} x(t)\psi^*_{\zeta,\tau}(t), \tag{1}$$

where $\psi^*_{\zeta,\tau}(t)$ is the complex conjugation of a basic wavelet function $\psi_{\zeta,\tau}(t)$ which is derived from a mother-wavelet function $\psi(t)$. This function has zero average in the time domain, i.e. $\int_{-\infty}^{+\infty}\psi(t)dt = 0$. Furthermore, a basic wavelet function $\psi_{\zeta,\tau}(t)$ can be written as:

$$\psi_{\zeta,\tau}(t) = \frac{1}{\sqrt{\zeta}}\psi\left(\frac{t-\tau}{\zeta}\right), \tag{2}$$

where $\zeta \in \mathbb{R}_{>0}$ is a scale parameter representing the width of the basic wavelet function, $\tau \in \mathbb{R}$ is a translation factor representing the location of the basic wavelet function, and $\frac{1}{\sqrt{\zeta}}$ is the energy normalization across different scales. Thus, the CWT maps an original signal to a function of ζ and τ that provides both time and frequency information. Note that the scale factor is inversely proportional to the frequency of a signal [14]. The CWT in Equation 1 measures the similarity between a basic wavelet function and a signal. Indeed, if a signal $x(t)$ has a frequency component f corresponding to a particular scale ζ of a wavelet function $\psi_{\zeta,\tau}(t)$, then the portion of $x(t)$ at some particular time interval where f exists will be similar to $\psi_{\zeta,\tau}(t)$. As a result, the CWT coefficients of $x(t)$ corresponding to f will be relatively large over this time interval. Moreover, the time-frequency energy density of the CWT is equivalent to the square norm of the CWT coefficients:

$$P_W f(\zeta,\tau) = |Wf(\zeta,\tau)|^2. \tag{3}$$

Time-frequency resolution. In contrast to the STFT, the CWT can either dilate or compress the window size of the wavelet function, and translate it along the time axis. The Heisenberg box [12] is a range of times and frequencies that indicates the accuracy of a time-frequency transformation. Although the area of the Heisenberg box does not change, the time and frequency resolutions can be varied depending on the value of ζ. As a result, the CWT can analyze all frequency components within a signal by considering appropriate scales of the mother-wavelet function. For instance, the CWT can use the wavelet function with a short duration and low scale for analyzing high frequency components, and vice versa. This advantage of the CWT allows us to efficiently analyze a signal that includes abnormal behaviors such as spikes and hunting.

2.2 Time-Frequency Logic

TFL is an extension of STL that can be used to specify both time and frequency properties of a signal [7]. In TFL, a signal predicate is defined over the signal representing the evolution of the STFT coefficient at a particular frequency over time. Given a pair (f,τ) of frequency and time, the STFT of a signal $x(t)$ is obtained by:

$$S_{f,\tau} = \int_{-\infty}^{+\infty} x(t)\psi_L(t-\tau)e^{-2i\pi f t}dt\,, \tag{4}$$

where $\psi_L(t)$ is a window function. A *spectral signal* $y(t) = |S_{f,t}|^2$ is the projection of the spectrogram of $x(t)$ on a particular frequency f. Such a signal can be incorporated in TFL formulae to form some interesting time-frequency specifications. We can see that a TFL formula is actually an STL formula in which the signal predicate is defined over $y(t)$ instead of $x(t)$. TFL has been used to formalize and recognize music melodies, where time-frequency requirements are simply specified as $\varphi \triangleq |S_{f_p,t}|^2 > \theta$, where f_p is the pitch frequency and θ is the STFT coefficient threshold [7]; however, the shortcomings of the STFT mentioned previously may reduce the ability of TFL to precisely specify and evaluate time-frequency properties of a signal. We extend TFL to use the CWT to obtain spectral signals from a given time-series signal. In effect, we construct a TFL formula based on the CWT coefficients of the spectral signals instead of the STFT coefficients. Because the CWT can appropriately use various scaling factors, ζ, to analyze all frequency components at different time intervals, it gives us an ability to study signals at flexible time-frequency resolutions.

Although the following presentation focuses on the classification of hunting behaviors, we note that the proposed approach using TFL and CWT can be used to capture other time-frequency specifications as well. For instance, consider the property: "*For some time in the future, the dominant frequency of the signal is ω for 5 time units, and the dominant frequency subsequently rises to twice of this value within 10-time units.*" Here, the *dominant frequency*, $f(t)$, of a signal $x(t)$ is defined as the frequency corresponding to the maximum magnitude frequency component of the signal at time t, as provided by a CWT. Such a time-frequency property can be written as a TFL formula, $\varphi \triangleq \Diamond(\Box_{[0,5]}(f = \omega) \wedge \Diamond_{[5,15]}(f = 2\omega))$. Then, the TFL formula φ can be evaluated as a normal STL formula using Breach[1] [6]. Consider another property such as "*At some time in the future the energy densities of the signal within a particular time inter-*

[1]Breach [6] is a tool that allows evaluation of STL and TFL formulae on signals.

val and a particular frequency bandwidth are always greater than some threshold value θ." This property can be specified as a TFL formula, $\phi \triangleq \Diamond\Box_{[t_1,t_2]}(z(f,t) > \theta)$, where $z(f,t)$ is a spectral signal that captures the minimum value of the CWT coefficients of a signal over some frequency bandwidth $[f_1, f_2]$.

Parametric Time-Frequency Logic. We introduce parametric time-frequency logic (PTFL), which is an extension of TFL where the parameters in TFL template formulae are symbolic parameters. Similar to the concept of parameter signal temporal logic (PSTL) introduced in [1], PTFL allows constants in intervals bounding the temporal operators and constant values in the predicates of PTFL formulae to be replaced with parameters.

The p parameters in a PTFL formula are classified into two sets:

(a) $\Upsilon = \{\tau_1, ..., \tau_{p_t}\}$ is a set of p_t *time* parameters occurring in the time intervals of the temporal operators, and

(b) $\Theta = \{\theta_1, ..., \theta_{p-p_t}\}$ is a set of $p - p_t$ *threshold* parameters occurring in the signal predicates.

For any fixed values of Υ and Θ, a PTFL formula $\varphi(\tau_1, \ldots, \tau_{p_t}, \theta_1, \ldots, \theta_{p-p_t})$ yields a TFL formula corresponding to the fixed values of the parameters. For instance, consider a PTFL formula $\varphi(\tau, \theta) \triangleq \Box_{[0,\tau]}(y(t) > \theta)$, where $y(t)$ is a spectral signal, τ and θ are time and threshold parameters, respectively. The formula $\varphi(5, 10)$ is defined as the TFL formula $\Box_{[0,5]}(y(t) > 10)$.

3. HUNTING CLASSIFICATION

In this section, we will describe three different approaches using PTFL and TFL to efficiently classify hunting behaviors in signals. Informally, a hunting behavior is an undesirable oscillation appearing within a signal over some time interval.

3.1 Parameter Synthesis Approach

We now propose a method to classify hunting behavior based on mining parameters of the following PTFL formula:

$$\varphi_h \triangleq \bigwedge_{i=1}^{m} \Diamond_{[0,\tau_i]}(Wf_i(t) > \theta_i). \quad (5)$$

Intuitively, this formula specifies that "*the energy densities of the given signal at particular frequencies are eventually greater than some threshold value*". Here, $Wf_i(t)$ is a spectral signal over time that captures the energy densities of the CWT of an original time-series signal $x(t)$ at a particular frequency $f_i \in F$. Note that F is a set of frequencies based on the scales of the CWT. Each spectral signal, $Wf_i(t)$, is the row vector of the matrix representing the energy densities of the CWT of $x(t)$; such a matrix is obtained using Equation 1 and Equation 3. Also, $\tau_i \in \Upsilon$ and $\theta_i \in \Theta$ denote a time and threshold parameter corresponding to each spectral signal $Wf_i(t)$. We note that the satisfaction value of the property φ_h monotonically increases in τ_i and decreases in θ_i. Because of monotonicity, we can exponentially reduce the search over the parameter space so that the synthesis procedure is efficient [8]. Figure 1 conceptually illustrates a spectral signal $Wf_i(t)$, and an instance of a hunting behavior that may occur within a signal. We say that a signal $x(t)$ contains hunting behavior if the property φ_h holds. Overall, the hunting classification problem can be written as follows.

- **Given** the following inputs:

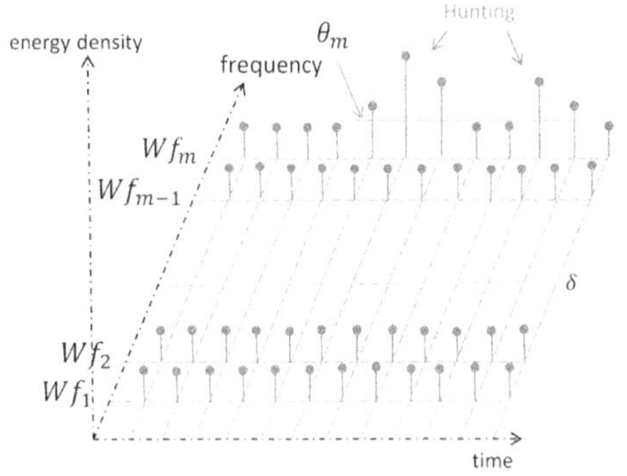

Figure 1: A sketch illustrates the hunting classification problem using time-frequency parameter synthesis. The set of spectral signals Wf_i is acquired from the CWT of an original time-series signal.

  - □ a set of labeled traces $\Psi \triangleq \{\Psi_\alpha, \Psi_\beta\}$, where Ψ_α and Ψ_β denote a set of training and testing traces, respectively. Moreover, we the notation $\Psi.B$ and $\Psi.G$ to respectively denote the set of traces with and without hunting behavior. Note that all traces in the training set exhibit hunting behavior, so that $\Psi_\alpha = \Psi_\alpha.B$
  - □ a cut-off frequency δ.
  - □ sets of parameters Υ, and Θ.
- **Find** values for Υ and Θ, such that:
  - □ $x_j(t) \models \varphi_h(\Upsilon, \Theta)$ for all $x_j(t) \in \Psi_\beta.B$.
  - □ $x_j(t) \not\models \varphi_h(\Upsilon, \Theta)$ for all $x_j(t) \in \Psi_\beta.G$.

We introduce the cut-off frequency δ to reduce the effort to exhaustively mine parameters over the entire time-frequency domain. It is essential for the control engineers to indicate that hunting behavior only occurs at some high-frequency region above δ.

Classification Algorithm. Next, we propose a heuristic to automatically obtain values for Υ and Θ that can be used to separate the hunting and non-hunting signals. An overview of the heuristic is described in Algorithm 1. The heuristic can be interpreted as follows.

Line 2 initializes a matrix Σ that represents the k m-dimensional spectral signals transformed from k original time-series signals in the training set using the CWT. We iterate over each trace in Ψ_α to construct sets of spectral signals $\{Wf_1(t), ..., Wf_m(t)\}$ using the CWT, and assign them to Σ. Next, we call the function TruncateParam to reduce the effort of exhaustively mining all parameters over the entire time-frequency domain. Here, Σ' represents the k n-dimensional $(n < m)$ matrix of Σ corresponding to the frequency range above δ. Next, we call the function HuntingParamSyn incorporated inside Breach to mine values for Υ and Θ. Then, we test the classifier with a given set of testing traces Ψ_β. The function Classifier checks the satisfaction of φ_h for each trace in Ψ_β, and returns the misclassification rate (MCR) value and the set of misclassified traces Ψ_m. The values of Υ, Θ and the set Ψ_m are then returned for further analysis. Furthermore, we can call EnhancedParam function to strengthen the values Υ and Θ and reduce the MCR value for the purpose of optimizing the classifier formula. Note that in the case studies, we do not use this function to evaluate the performance of the classifier to avoid the bias in our comparative analysis.

3.2 Decision Tree Approach

An approach based on decision trees to classify time series data using STL formulae was implemented in the tool

Algorithm 1 Hunting Classification Using Parameter Synthesis

```
function HuntingClassification(Ψ_α, Ψ_β, δ)
    Σ ← 0
    for each trace x_j(t) ∈ Ψ_α, j ≤ k
        Σ(j, :, :) ← Wf_1(t), ..., Wf_m(t) ← CWT(x_j(t))
    end for
    Σ' ← TruncateParam(δ, Σ)
    Υ, Θ ← HuntingParamSyn(Σ')
    MCR, Ψ_m ← Classifier(Υ, Θ, Ψ_β)
    return Υ, Θ, Ψ_m
end function
function EnhancedParam(Ψ_m, Ψ_α, Ψ_β, δ)
    if Ψ_m.B ≠ ∅ then
        Ψ'_α ← Ψ_α ∪ Ψ_m.B
        HuntingClassification(Ψ'_α, Ψ_β, δ)
    end if
end function
```

DT4STL [3]. That method uses a parameterized procedure to infer STL formulae from labeled data. Given a two-class training data and a set of PSTL templates, a decision tree for classification is recursively built such that each node of a tree is associated with a simple formula, selected from the given PSTL templates. The parameter synthesis is then conducted to find the STL formula that yields the best split for the data at each node. This technique can be used to automatically construct classifiers based on STL formula, but to achieve a low MCR value, the inferred STL formulae may be long and not easily interpretable by engineers. In this section, we apply this approach to classify hunting versus non-hunting signals. Instead of inferring an STL formula, we intend to infer a TFL formula as a data classifier. Thus, we transform original time series data into a collection of time-frequency data (spectral signals).

We assume that control engineers initially designate the frequency threshold separating hunting versus non-hunting behavior. A hunting behavior is specified as any oscillatory behavior occurring at frequencies above some specified cut-off frequency δ. Thus, the time-frequency profile of a hunting signal at some frequency component $f > \delta$ contains larger values for the CWT coefficients compared to those of non-hunting signals. So we define the spectral signal WThcoef based on the CWT coefficients of the signal in a high-frequency region such that:

$$\mathsf{WThcoef}(t) = \max_{\zeta \in [\frac{f_c}{T_s F_{max}}, \frac{f_c}{T_s \delta})} P_W f(\zeta, t), \tag{6}$$

where f_c is a center frequency associated with the mother-wavelet function, F_{max} is the maximum frequency that appears in the CWT, and T_s is the sampling period. We use such a spectral signal as an input for the DT4STL to infer a simple TFL formula. Note that in this scenario, the inferred TFL formula captures the non-hunting behavior of a signal.

3.3 Support Vector Machine Approach

Next, we present another approach that can solve the problem of hunting classification: linear classification using support vector machines (SVM) [15]. A linear SVM is a set of hyperplanes or decision boundaries that can correctly separate data into two classes. The general form of hyperplanes is $\langle w \cdot x \rangle + b = 0$, where w is a normal to the hyperplane, and $\frac{b}{||w||}$ is the perpendicular distance from the hyperplane to the origin. The sign of the linear discriminant function $f(x) \triangleq \langle w \cdot x \rangle + b$ determines on which side of the decision boundary the test data point is located. The distance from the decision boundary to the closest data point determines the *margin* of the linear classifier. Suppose that we have a set of n labeled training data $(x_i, c_i), ..., (x_n, c_n)$ where $x_i \in \mathbb{R}^d$ and $c_i \in \{1, -1\}$, the constrained optimization problem of linear classification using SVM is written as:

$$\begin{aligned} &\underset{w,b}{\text{minimize}} && \frac{1}{2}||w||^2 + C\sum_{i=1}^{n} \zeta_i \\ &\text{subject to} && c_i(\langle w \cdot x_i \rangle + b) \geq 1 - \zeta_i,\ i = 1, \ldots, n \\ &&& \zeta_i \geq 0. \end{aligned} \tag{7}$$

Here, ζ is a slack variable. If $0 < \zeta \leq 1$, the data point lies somewhere between the margin and the correct side of hyperplane, and the data point is misclassified if $\zeta > 1$. C is a regularization parameter that defines the trade-off between errors of the SVM on training data and margin maximization. A large value of C results in the low possibility of misclassified training data points, because the optimization in Equation 7 will choose a narrow margin hyperplane that correctly separates training data points as much as possible. In contrast, a small value of C will result in a large margin hyperplane, but it may yield a better result in terms of correctly separating testing data points. Due to space limitation, we will not discuss the formal optimization problem solved to obtain the SVM, but refer interested readers to [15]. In this work, instead of applying the linear SVM directly to original time series signals, we need to preprocess them to yield a corresponding set of time-frequency features. For each time-series signal $x(t)$, we collect a real-valued vector $W^{max} \triangleq [Wf_1^{max}, ..., Wf_m^{max}]$ such that each element $Wf_i^{max} \in W^{max}$ is the maximum value of a spectral signal $Wf_i(t)$. Such a vector will be used as a time-frequency feature to design the SVM.

4. CASE STUDIES

In this section, we evaluate the capabilities of three different methods to classify hunting behavior for two case studies. The first case study is based on data from an air compressor motor speed (ACMS) system in a fuel cell (FC) vehicle application. The second case study is based on electrocardiogram (ECG) data. In both examples, we apply the Morlet CWT [12] to the time-series signals.

4.1 ACMS Data

The ACMS system uses a compressor to regulate the air intake of a hydrogen FC vehicle. An FC stack uses a mixture of air and hydrogen to generate electrical power for the vehicle. Accurate control of the compressor which translates to control of the quantities of hydrogen and oxygen (air) is required to achieve good performance and proper operation from the FC stack. Also, the water balance (moisture level) within the stack needs to be carefully regulated, which requires regulation of the air pressure at the inlet of the stack. The task of the ACMS system is to regulate air flow and air pressure delivered to the inlet of the FC stack.

We consider ACMS data from an FC vehicle application. Specifics of the data, such as units and descriptions of the measured quantities are omitted here for proprietary reasons. The ACMS data are partitioned into a collection of traces that are 100 seconds in length and are labeled as either good (the trace does not exhibit hunting behavior) or bad (the trace does exhibit hunting behavior). The ACMS

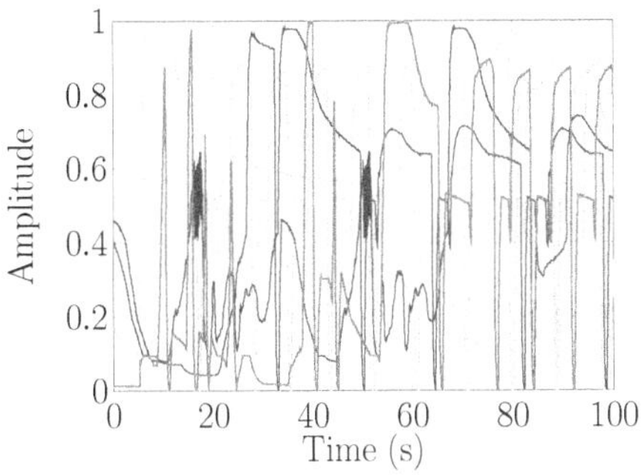

Figure 2: The classified testing data of the ACMS signals using parameter synthesis approach.

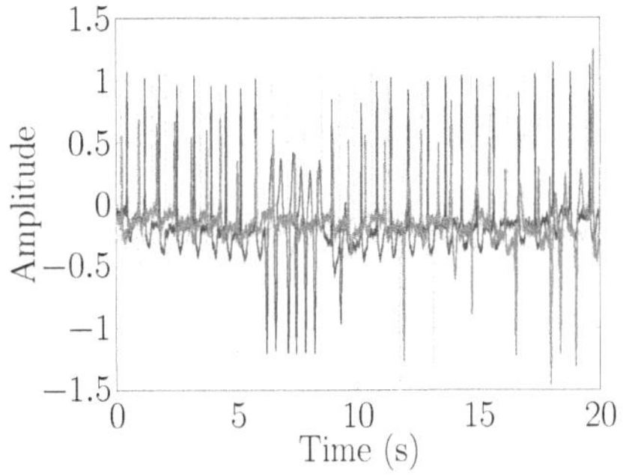

Figure 3: The classified testing data of the ECG signals using parameter synthesis approach.

data has a sampling period of 0.02 seconds. We note that the same training data is used for all of the evaluations, though the parameter synthesis approach only uses the bad traces. In this experiment, we use the training data including 50 total traces, in which 30 traces are labeled as good and the others are labeled as bad. We also use the same testing data including 10 good traces and 10 bad traces for all of the evaluations.

Parameter Synthesis. We now illustrate the performance of the classification heuristic shown in Algorithm 1 to classify hunting behavior for the ACMS signals. Because we do not know the frequency range where a hunting behavior may occur, we exhaustively mine all parameters $\tau_i \in \Upsilon$ and $\theta_i \in \Theta$. We choose the maximum frequency of the CWT as $F_{max} = 25$Hz. Here, the Algorithm 1 will search for the best $\theta_i \in [0, 1]$ and $\tau_i \in [0, 100]$ such that all spectral signals transformed from original time-series traces in the training data satisfy φ_h. We then use Breach with the optimized parameters of φ_h to classify good versus bad traces in the testing set.

Figure 2 shows the experimental results of classifying abnormal ACMS signals, using the function HuntingClassification. In the figure, we only show five representative signals in which good traces correctly classified are shown in green, and bad traces correctly classified are shown in blue. The one good trace that is misclassified is shown in red. The total running time of the classification process is approximately 3 minutes.

Decision Tree Approach. Next, we utilize the DT4STL toolbox to infer TFL formulae that can be used to classify hunting behavior for the ACMS data.

We preprocess the training data to yield the corresponding set of spectral signals WThcoef with $\delta = 15$Hz and $F_{max} = 25$Hz. We then run the DT4STL toolbox with this set of spectral signals using 2-fold cross-validation. As a result, we obtain the two following TFL formulae:

$$\varphi_{h1} \triangleq \Box_{[37.4,98.2)}(\mathsf{WThcoef} < 0.0435)$$

$$\varphi_{h2} \triangleq \Box_{[1.29,91.3)}(\mathsf{WThcoef} < 0.0394).$$

The procedure takes approximately 75 seconds to infer each formula. Using Breach, we then evaluate those formulae with the set of testing data. The formula φ_{h1} gives us all misclassified traces that are bad traces with the MCR value being equal to 25%. On the other hand, the formula φ_{h2} results in one misclassified trace, which is a bad trace.

SVM Approach. We apply the SVM method to classify normal versus abnormal ACMS data. We first transform all of the traces in the training data into sets of time-frequency features. Next, we run the linear SVM to learn the decision boundaries that separate data as either good or bad. Finally, we predict the testing data from the learned decision boundaries with different values of the SVM classifier margin C.

The MCR of the hunting classification for the ACMS data using SVM is 10% with $C = 10$ and reduces to 5% with $C = 100$. In this case, a larger value of C gives a better result for the classification. Moreover, the classification process takes only 0.393 seconds.

4.2 ECG Data

An electrocardiogram (ECG) test is a noninvasive procedure used to monitor the electrical activities of a heart via a collection of electrodes attached to the patient's skin. A doctor can read an ECG output signal to diagnose abnormal structure or function of the patient's heart. A normal ECG signal includes three signals: (a) the P wave representing the depolarization or contraction of the atrium (b) the QRS complex (the R wave) indicating the ventricular depolarization and (c) the T wave describing the ventricular repolarization. The distance between two consecutive R peaks is considered as a heartbeat. A healthy patient has a resting normal heartbeat (frequency) from 60 to 100 beats per minute (bpm).

In this paper, we focus on classifying the ECG signal that may contain a ventricular tachycardia (VT), a very fast heart rhythm arising in the ventricles that may cause a sudden heart failure. VT is defined as a sequence of three or more ventricular beats with the frequency varying from 110 to 250 bpm. Thus, a VT can be considered as a hunting behavior in an ECG signal. We conduct our classification approaches on the MIT-BIH Arrhythmia ECG Database. These data contain a variety of ECG signals collected from patients 23 to 89 years of age, including patients who experience ventricular arrhythmia [13]. We transform ECG signals 20 seconds in duration (provided at a sampling period of 0.0028 secs.) to spectral signals using the Morlet CWT. Here, the maximum frequency of the CWT is $F_{max} = 4.5$Hz ($\sim$ 270 bpm). For all of the evaluations, we use the same training data including 20 bad traces (the traces do contain a VT) and 40 good traces (the traces do not contain a VT), and the same testing data including 10 good traces and 10 bad traces.

Parameter Synthesis. In this scenario, we only mine the parameters for 20 bad traces in the training dataset. Here, we will search for the best $\theta_i \in [0, 5]$ and $\tau_i \in [0, 20]$. Figure 3 shows the experimental results of using the function HuntingClassification to classify abnormal ECG signals that contain VT. Here, we only show three signals for illustration. The approach results in one (5%) misclassified (red)

	PS	DT4STL	SVM
Interpretation of data classifier	○	△	×
Computation time	×	×	○
Bad behavior localization	○	○	×
Low misclassification rate	△	△	○

Table 1: The comparison between parameter synthesis (PS) using PTFL, DT4STL toolbox using TFL, and linear SVM in classifying abnormal signals, where ○, △, × respectively denote good, ok, bad.

trace, which is a bad trace. The total running time of the classification process is approximately 1 minute.

Decision Tree Approach. Next, we utilize the DT4STL toolbox to classify hunting behavior for the ECG data. We first preprocess the training data to yield the corresponding set of spectral signals WThcoef with $\delta = 1.5$Hz. Then, we run the DT4STL toolbox with this set of spectral signals using 2-fold cross-validation. As a result, we obtain two following TFL formulae:

$$\phi_{h1} \triangleq \Box_{[1.73,17.3)}(\mathsf{WThcoef} < 3.16)$$

$$\phi_{h2} \triangleq \Box_{[2.36,20)}(\mathsf{WThcoef} < 3.21).$$

The procedure takes approximately 105 seconds to infer each formula. We then use Breach to evaluate these formulae with a set of spectral data acquired from the CWT of 10 good traces and 10 bad traces in the testing data. The MCR values of using ϕ_{h1} and ϕ_{h2} to classify these data are both equal to 5% (but misclassified traces are different).

SVM Approach. Finally, we apply the SVM approach to classify hunting in the ECG data. Note that we use the same training and testing data used for the other methods. The hunting classification of the ECG data using an SVM results in a 5% MCR for all values of C (the one misclassified trace is a bad trace), and the classification procedure takes 0.3 seconds.

5. DISCUSSION

In this section, we discuss the trade-offs related to the three classification approaches presented above to classify normal versus abnormal signals. Table 1 shows an aggregate performance evaluation between the approaches in four different categories, including (a) the ability to interpret the structure and parameters used to define the classifier, (b) the computation time, (c) the capacity to localize where bad behavior occurs in a signal, and (d) the ability to correctly classify normal versus abnormal signals. Although the linear SVM can classify abnormal signals much faster and more accurately than the parameter synthesis and the decision tree approaches, the main drawback of this method is that it cannot reveal where the bad behavior occurs within a signal. We found that the decision tree approach can infer specifications that accurately classify data as either good or bad; however, it is not easy to interpret the inferred formula unless the user has some expertise about the input data. If a dataset is not homogeneous (i.e., both normal and abnormal signals are very different from each other), the DT4STL toolbox may infer a complicated formula that cannot be easily interpreted. The parameter synthesis using PTFL and the decision tree approach using TFL have similar performance except the former provides a clearer intuition about the classifier, as the temporal logic formula that results is usually simpler for the PTFL case. Overall, we conclude that a traditional machine learning technique such as the linear SVM is the best choice if the only goal is to classify data as either good or bad, and the most important thing is to select a proper feature on which to base the classification algorithm. Otherwise, if the designer additionally wishes to both understand the meaning of a data classifier and automatically localize where abnormal behaviors occur within a signal, we conclude that the parameter synthesis approach is the best option, as a simple temporal logic formula that defines the classifier results from the analysis.

6. ACKNOWLEDGMENTS

The material presented in this paper is based upon work supported by the National Science Foundation (NSF) under grant numbers CNS 1464311, EPCN 1509804, and SHF 1527398, the Air Force Research Laboratory (AFRL) through contract number FA8750-15-1-0105, and the Air Force Office of Scientific Research (AFOSR) under contract numbers FA9550-15-1-0258 and FA9550-16-1-0246. The U.S. government is authorized to reproduce and distribute reprints for Governmental purposes notwithstanding any copyright notation thereon. Any opinions, findings, and conclusions or recommendations expressed in this publication are those of the authors and do not necessarily reflect the views of AFRL, AFOSR, or NSF. The authors sincerely appreciate Jared Farnsworth and the Fuel Cell group at Toyota Technical Center for their help in obtaining and understanding the ACMS data.

7. REFERENCES

[1] E. Asarin, A. Donzé, O. Maler, and D. Nickovic. Parametric identification of temporal properties. In *Runtime Verification*, pages 147–160. Springer, 2011.

[2] E. Bartocci, L. Bortolussi, and G. Sanguinetti. Data-driven statistical learning of temporal logic properties. In *International Conference on Formal Modeling and Analysis of Timed Systems*, pages 23–37. Springer, 2014.

[3] G. Bombara, C.-I. Vasile, F. Penedo, H. Yasuoka, and C. Belta. A decision tree approach to data classification using signal temporal logic. In *Proceedings of the 19th international conference on Hybrid systems: computation and control*. ACM, 2016.

[4] L. Cohen. *Time-frequency analysis*, volume 299. Prentice hall, 1995.

[5] P. Dluhoš, L. Brim, and D. Šafránek. On expressing and monitoring oscillatory dynamics. *arXiv preprint arXiv:1208.3853*, 2012.

[6] A. Donzé. Breach, a toolbox for verification and parameter synthesis of hybrid systems. In *Computer Aided Verification*, pages 167–170. Springer, 2010.

[7] A. Donzé, O. Maler, E. Bartocci, D. Nickovic, R. Grosu, and S. Smolka. On temporal logic and signal processing. In *Automated Technology for Verification and Analysis*, pages 92–106. Springer, 2012.

[8] X. Jin, A. Donzé, J. V. Deshmukh, and S. A. Seshia. Mining requirements from closed-loop control models. *IEEE Transactions on Computer-Aided Design of Integrated Circuits and Systems*, 34(11):1704–1717, 2015.

[9] H. W. Johnson, M. Graham, et al. *High-speed digital design: a handbook of black magic*, volume 1. Prentice Hall Upper Saddle River, NJ, 1993.

[10] J. Kapinski, X. Jin, J. Deshmukh, A. Donze, T. Yamaguchi, H. Ito, T. Kaga, S. Kobuna, and S. Seshia. ST-Lib: A library for specifying and classifying model behaviors. 2016.

[11] O. Maler and D. Nickovic. Monitoring temporal properties of continuous signals. In *Formal Techniques, Modelling and Analysis of Timed and Fault-Tolerant Systems*, pages 152–166. Springer, 2004.

[12] S. Mallat. *A wavelet tour of signal processing*. Academic press, 1999.

[13] G. B. Moody and R. G. Mark. The impact of the mit-bih arrhythmia database. *IEEE Engineering in Medicine and Biology Magazine*, 20(3):45–50, 2001.

[14] R. Polikar. The wavelet tutorial. 1996.

[15] B. Scholkopf and A. J. Smola. *Learning with kernels: support vector machines, regularization, optimization, and beyond*. MIT press, 2001.

Piecewise–Differentiable Trajectory Outcomes in Mechanical Systems Subject to Unilateral Constraints

Andrew M. Pace
Univeristy of Washington
Seattle, WA, USA
apace2@uw.edu

Samuel A. Burden*
Univeristy of Washington
Seattle, WA, USA
sburden@uw.edu

ABSTRACT

We provide conditions under which trajectory outcomes in mechanical systems subject to unilateral constraints depend piecewise–differentiably on initial conditions, even as the sequence of constraint activations and deactivations varies. This builds on prior work that provided conditions ensuring existence, uniqueness, and continuity of trajectory outcomes, and extends previous differentiability results that applied only to fixed constraint (de)activation sequences. We discuss extensions of our result and implications for assessing stability and controllability.

Keywords

mechanical systems; stability; controllability

1. INTRODUCTION

To move through and interact with the world, terrestrial agents intermittently contact terrain and objects. The dynamics of this interaction are, to a first approximation, *hybrid*, with transitions between contact modes summarized by abrupt changes in system velocities [16]. Such phenomenological models are known in general to exhibit a range of pathologies that plague hybrid systems, including non–existence or non–uniqueness of trajectories [15, 34] [2, Sec. 5], or discontinuous dependence of trajectory outcomes on initial conditions (i.e. states and parameters) [28] [2, Sec. 7]; see Fig. 1 (*left*). Although instances of these pathologies can occur in physical systems [13], these occurrences are rare in everyday experience involving locomotion and manipulation with limbs. Our view is that these pathologies lie chiefly in the modeling formalism, and can be effectively removed by appropriately restricting the models under consideration without loss of relevance for many physical systems of interest.

*This material is based upon work supported by the U. S. Army Research Laboratory and the U. S. Army Research Office under contract/grant number W911NF-16-1-0158.

HSCC'17, April 18-20, 2017, Pittsburgh, PA, USA
© 2017 ACM. ISBN 978-1-4503-4590-3/17/04...$15.00
DOI: http://dx.doi.org/10.1145/3049797.3049807

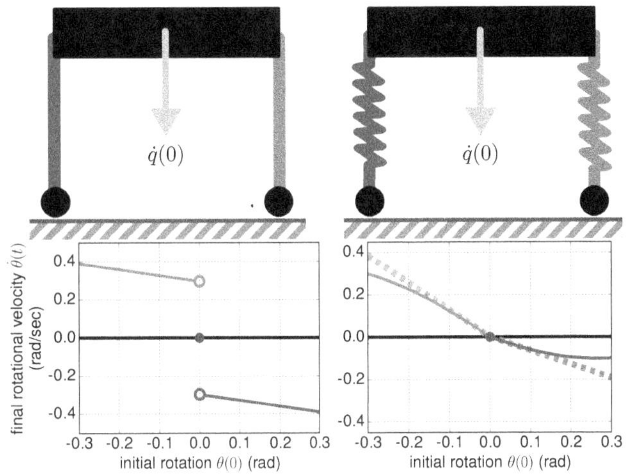

Figure 1: Trajectory outcomes in mechanical systems subject to unilateral constraints. (*left*) In general, trajectory outcomes depend discontinuously on initial conditions. In the pictured model for rigid–leg trotting (adapted from [28]), discontinuities arise when two legs touch down: if the legs impact simultaneously (corresponding to rotation $\theta(0) = 0$), then the post–impact rotational velocity is zero; if the left leg impacts before the right leg ($\theta(0) > 0$, blue) or vice–versa ($\theta(0) < 0$, red), then the post–impact rotational velocities are bounded away from zero. (*right*) In the pictured model for soft–leg trotting (adapted from [5] with the addition of a nonlinear damper coupling the body and limbs), trajectory outcomes (solid lines) are continuous and piecewise–differentiable at $\theta(0) = 0$ (dashed lines). These figures were generated using simulations of the depicted models; the sourcecode is available at https://bitbucket.org/apace2/2017hscc_figure1.

Specifically, this paper provides mathematical conditions on *mechanical* systems subject to *unilateral* constraints that ensure trajectory outcomes vary continuously and piecewise–differentiably with respect to initial conditions. Conditions that ensure continuity are known; see for instance Schatzman's work on the one–dimensional impact problem [32] or Ballard's seminal result [2, Thm. 20]. Furthermore, when the sequence of constraint activations and deactivations is held fixed, it has been known for some time that outcomes depend differentiably on initial conditions; see [1] for the earliest instance of this result we found in the English literature and [14, 11, 36, 6] for modern treatments. Our contribution is a proof that imposing an additional *admissibility* condition ensures continuous trajectory outcomes are *piecewise*–differentiable with respect to initial conditions, even as the sequence of constraint activations and deactivations varies; see Fig. 1 (*right*). The operative notion of piecewise–differentiability was originally developed by the nonsmooth analysis community to study structural stability of nonlinear programs [30], and has enabled a generalization of Calculus based on non–linear first–order approximations [33]. In the terminology of that community, we provide conditions that ensure the flow of a mechanical system subject to unilateral constraints is PC^r, and therefore possesses a piecewise–linear *Bouligand* (or *B*–)derivative.

As discussed in more detail in Sec. 6, we envision the existence and straightforward computability of the B–derivative of the flow to be useful in practice because it supports generalization of familiar control techniques to a class of hybrid systems with physical significance. In particular, building on related work that dealt with differential equations with discontinuous right–hand–sides [7, 4], the B–derivative can be used to assess stability, controllability, or optimality of trajectories in mechanical systems subject to unilateral constraints. As control of dynamic and dexterous robots increasingly relies on scalable algorithms for optimization and learning that presume the existence of first–order approximations (i.e. gradients or gradient–like objects) [26, 18, 22, 19], it is important to place application of such algorithms on a firm theoretical foundation. From a theoretical perspective, the results in this paper dovetail with recent advances in simulation of hybrid systems [5] in that one of the conditions necessary for the B–derivative to exist (namely, continuity of trajectory outcomes) is also requisite for convergence of numerical simulations. Taken together, these observations suggest that a unified analytical and computational framework for modeling and control of mechanical systems subject to unilateral constraints may be within reach.

1.1 Organization

We begin in Sec. 2 by specifying the class of dynamical systems under consideration, namely, *mechanical* systems subject to *unilateral* constraints. Sec. 3 summarizes the well–known fact that, when the contact mode sequence is fixed, trajectories vary differentiably with respect to initial conditions. In Sec. 4, we observe (as others have) that trajectories generally vary discontinuously with respect to initial conditions as the contact mode sequence varies, but provide a sufficient condition that is known to restore continuity. Sec. 5 leverages continuity to provide conditions under which trajectories vary piecewise–differentiably with respect to initial conditions across contact mode sequences, and Sec. 6 discusses extensions and implications for a systems theory for mechanical systems subject to unilateral constraints.

1.2 Relation to prior work

The technical content in Sec. 2, Sec. 3, and Sec. 4 appeared previously in the literature and is (more–or–less) well–known; we collate the results here in a sequence of technical Lemmas[1] to contextualize our contributions in Sec. 5.

2. MECHANICAL SYSTEMS SUBJECT TO UNILATERAL CONSTRAINTS

In this paper, we study the dynamics of a mechanical system with configuration coordinates $q \in Q = \mathbb{R}^d$ subject to (perfect, holonomic, scleronomic)[2] unilateral constraints $a(q) \geq 0$ specified by a differentiable function $a\colon Q \to \mathbb{R}^n$ where $d, n \in \mathbb{N}$ are finite. We are primarily interested in systems with $n > 1$ constraints, whence we regard the inequality $a(q) \geq 0$ as being enforced componentwise. Given any $J \subset \{1, \ldots, n\}$, and letting $|J|$ denote the number of elements in the set J, we let $a_J : Q \to \mathbb{R}^{|J|}$ denote the function obtained by selecting the component functions of a indexed by J, and we regard the equality $a_J(q) = 0$ as being enforced componentwise. It is well–known (see e.g. [2, Sec. 3] or [16, Sec. 2.4, 2.5]) that with $J = \{j \in \{1, \ldots, n\} : a_j(q) = 0\}$ the system's dynamics take the form

$$M(q)\ddot{q} = f(q, \dot{q}) + c(q, \dot{q})\dot{q} + Da_J(q)^\top \lambda_J(q, \dot{q}), \tag{1a}$$

$$\dot{q}^+ = \Delta_J(q, \dot{q}^-)\dot{q}^-, \tag{1b}$$

where $M\colon Q \to \mathbb{R}^{d\times d}$ specifies the mass matrix (or *inertia tensor*) for the mechanical system in the q coordinates, $f\colon TQ \to \mathbb{R}^d$ is termed the *effort map* [2] and specifies[3] the internal and applied forces, $c\colon TQ \to \mathbb{R}^{d\times d}$ denotes the *Coriolis matrix* determined[4] by M, $Da_J\colon Q \to \mathbb{R}^{|J|\times d}$ denotes the (Jacobian) derivative of the constraint function a_J with respect to the coordinates, $\lambda_J\colon TQ \to \mathbb{R}^{|J|}$ denotes the reaction forces generated in contact mode J to enforce the constraint $a_J(q) \geq 0$, $\Delta_J\colon TQ \to \mathbb{R}^{d\times d}$ specifies the collision restitution law that instantaneously resets velocities to ensure compatibility with the constraint $a_J(q) = 0$,

$$\Delta_J(q, \dot{q}) = I_d - (1 + \gamma(q, \dot{q}))M(q)^{-1}Da_J(q)^\top \Lambda_J(q) Da_J(q), \tag{2}$$

where I_d is the d–dimensional identity matrix, $\gamma\colon TQ \to [0, \infty)$ specifies the *coefficient of restitution*, $\dot{q}^+$ (resp. $\dot{q}^-$) denotes the right– (resp. left–)handed limits of the velocity vector with respect to time, and $\Lambda_J\colon Q \to R^{d\times d}$ is given by

$$\Lambda_J(q) = \left(Da_J(q)M(q)^{-1}Da_J(q)^\top\right)^{-1}. \tag{3}$$

Definition 1 (contact modes). *With* $A = \{q \in Q : a(q) \geq 0\}$ *denoting the set of* admissible *configurations, the constraint functions* $\{a_j\}_{j=1}^n$ *partition* A *into a finite collection*[5] $\{A_J\}_{J\in 2^n}$ *of* contact modes*:*

$$\forall J \in 2^n : A_J = \{q \in Q \mid a_J(q) = 0, \\ \forall i \notin J : a_i(q) > 0\}. \tag{4}$$

[1]For uniformity and clarity of exposition, we present previous results here as Lemmas regardless of the form in which they originally appeared.

[2]A constraint is: *perfect* if it only generates force in the direction normal to the constraint surface; *holonomic* if it varies with configuration but not velocity; *scleronomic* if it does not vary with time. We will discuss the inclusion of *imperfect*, *nonholonomic*, or *nonscleronomic* constraints in Sec. 6.

[3]We let $TQ = \mathbb{R}^d \times \mathbb{R}^d$ denote the *tangent bundle* of the configuration space Q; an element $(q, \dot{q}) \in TQ$ can be regarded as a pair containing a vector of generalized configurations $q \in \mathbb{R}^d$ and velocities $\dot{q} \in \mathbb{R}^d$; we write $\dot{q} \in T_qQ$.

[4]For each $\ell, m \in \{1, \ldots, d\}$ the (ℓ, m) entry $c_{\ell m}$ is determined from the entries of M via $c_{\ell m} = -\frac{1}{2}\sum_{k=1}^d (D_k M_{\ell m} + D_m M_{\ell k} - D_\ell M_{km})$.

[5]We let $2^n = \{J \subset \{1, \ldots, n\}\}$ denote the *power set* (i.e. the set containing all subsets) of $\{1, \ldots, n\}$.

We let $TA = \{(q,\dot q) \in TQ : q \in A\}$ *and* $TA_J = \{(q,\dot q) \in TQ : q \in A_J\}$ *for each* $J \in 2^n$.

REMARK 1. *In Def. 1 (contact modes),* $J = \{1,\ldots,n\}$ *indexes the maximally constrained contact mode and* $J = \emptyset$ *indexes the unconstrained contact mode. Since any velocity is allowable in the unconstrained mode, we adopt the convention* $\Delta_\emptyset(q,\dot q) = I_d$.

In the present paper, we will assume that appropriate conditions have been imposed to ensure trajectories of (1) exist on a region of interest in time and state.

ASSUMPTION 1 (EXISTENCE AND UNIQUENESS [2, THM. 10]). *There exists a flow for (1), that is, a function* $\phi : \mathcal{F} \to TA$ *where* $\mathcal{F} \subset [0,\infty)\times TA$ *is an open subset containing* $\{0\}\times TA$ *and for each* $(t,(q,\dot q)) \in \mathcal{F}$ *the restriction* $\phi|_{[0,t]\times\{(q,\dot q)\}} : [0,t] \to TQ$ *is the unique left-continuous trajectory for (1) initialized at* $(q,\dot q)$.

REMARK 2. *The problem of ensuring trajectories of (1) exist and are unique has been studied extensively; we refer the reader to [2, Thm. 10] for a specific result and [16] for a general discussion of this problem.*

Since we are concerned with differentiability properties of the flow, we assume the elements in (1) are differentiable.

ASSUMPTION 2 (C^r VECTOR FIELD AND RESET MAP [2, §3.4]). *The vector field (1a) and reset map (1b) are continuously differentiable to order* $r \in \mathbb{N}$.

REMARK 3. *If we restricted our attention to the continuous-time dynamics in (1), then Assump. 2 would suffice to provide the local existence and uniqueness of trajectories imposed by Assump. 1; as illustrated by [2, Ex. 2], Assump. 2 does not suffice when the vector field (1a) is coupled to the reset map (1b).*

3. DIFFERENTIABILITY WITHIN CONTACT MODE SEQUENCES

It is possible to satisfy Assump. 1 (existence and uniqueness of flow) under mild conditions that allow trajectories to exhibit phenomena such as *grazing* (wherein the trajectory activates a new constraint without undergoing impact) or *Zeno* (wherein the trajectory undergoes an infinite number of impacts in a finite time interval). In this and subsequent sections, where we seek to study differentiability properties of the flow, we will not be able to accommodate grazing or Zeno phenomena. Therefore we proceed to restrict the trajectories under consideration.

DEFINITION 2 (CONSTRAINT ACTIVATION/DEACTIVATION [8, CHPT. 2]). *The trajectory* $\phi^{(q,\dot q)}$ *initialized at* $(q,\dot q) \in TA_J \subset TQ$ activates constraints $I \in 2^n$ at time $t > 0$ *if (i) no constraint in* I *was active immediately before time* t *and (ii) all constraints in* I *become active at time* t*. Formally,*[6]

$$\exists \varepsilon > 0 : \; I \cap J = \emptyset, \; (i)\; \phi((t-\varepsilon,t),(q,\dot q)) \subset TA_J, \quad (ii)\; \phi(t,(q,\dot q)) \in TA_{I\cup J}. \tag{5}$$

We refer to t *as a* constraint activation time *for* $\phi^{(q,\dot q)}$. *Similarly, the trajectory* $\phi^{(q,\dot q)}$ deactivates constraints $I \in 2^n$ at time $t > 0$ *if (i) all constraints in* I *were active at time* t *and (ii) no constraint in* I *remains active immediately after time* t*. Formally,*

$$\exists \varepsilon > 0 : \; I \subset J, \; (i)\; \phi(t,(q,\dot q)) \in TA_J, \quad (ii)\; \phi((t,t+\varepsilon),(q,\dot q)) \subset TA_{J\setminus I}. \tag{6}$$

We refer to t *as a* constraint deactivation time *for* $\phi^{(q,\dot q)}$.

DEFINITION 3 (ADMISSIBLE ACTIVATION/DEACTIVATION). *A constraint activation time* $t > 0$ *for* $\phi^{(q,\dot q)}$ *is* admissible *if the constraint velocity*[7] *for all activated constraints* $I \in 2^n$ *is negative. Formally, with* $(\rho,\dot\rho^-) = \lim_{s\to t^-} \phi(s,(q,\dot q))$ *denoting the left-handed limit of the trajectory at time* t,

$$\forall i \in I : D_t\left[a_i \circ \phi\right](0,(\rho,\dot\rho^-)) = Da_i(\rho)\dot\rho^- < 0. \tag{7}$$

A constraint deactivation time $t > 0$ *for* $\phi^{(q,\dot q)}$ *is* admissible *if, for all deactivated constraints* $I \in 2^n$*: (i) the constraint velocity or constraint acceleration*[8] *is positive, or (ii) the time derivative of the contact force is negative. Formally, with* $(\rho,\dot\rho^+) = \lim_{s\to t^+} \phi(s,(q,\dot q))$ *denoting the right-handed limit of the trajectory at time* t*, for all* $i \in I$:

$$\begin{aligned} (i)\; & D_t\left[a_i \circ \phi\right](0,(\rho,\dot\rho^+)) > 0 \text{ or} \\ & D_t^2\left[a_i \circ \phi\right](0,(\rho,\dot\rho^+)) > 0, \\ \text{or } (ii)\; & D_t\left[\lambda_i \circ \phi\right](0,(\rho,\dot\rho^+)) < 0. \end{aligned} \tag{8}$$

REMARK 4. *The conditions for admissible constraint deactivation in case (i) of (8) can only arise at admissible constraint activation times; otherwise the trajectory is continuous, whence active constraint velocities and accelerations are zero.*

DEFINITION 4 (ADMISSIBLE TRAJECTORY). *A trajectory* $\phi^{(q,\dot q)}$ *is* admissible on $[0,t] \subset \mathbb{R}$ *if (i) it has a finite number of constraint activation (hence, deactivation) times on* $[0,t]$*, and (ii) every constraint activation and deactivation is admissible; otherwise the trajectory is* inadmissible.

REMARK 5 (ADMISSIBLE TRAJECTORIES). *The key property admissible trajectories possess that will be leveraged in what follows is: time-to-activation and time-to-deactivation are differentiable with respect to initial conditions; the same is not generally true of inadmissible trajectories.*

REMARK 6 (GRAZING IS NOT ADMISSIBLE). *The restriction in Def. 4 (admissible trajectory) that all constraint activation/deactivation times are admissible precludes admissibility of grazing.*

REMARK 7 (ZENO IS NOT ADMISSIBLE). *The restriction in Def. 4 (admissible trajectory) that a finite number of constraint activations occur on a compact time interval precludes admissibility of Zeno.*

[6] $\phi((t_1,t_2),(q,\dot q)) = \{\phi(t,(q,\dot q)) : t \in (t_1,t_2)\} \subset TQ$ denotes the *image* of $\phi^{(q,\dot q)}$ over the interval $(t_1,t_2) \subset [0,\infty)$.

[7] Formally, the *Lie derivative* [20, Prop. 12.32] of the constraint along the vector field specified by (1a). Although constraint functions are technically only functions of configuration $q \in Q$ and not the full state $(q,\dot q) \in TQ$, by a mild abuse of notation we allow ourselves to consider compositions $a \circ \phi$ rather than the formally correct $a \circ \pi_Q \circ \phi$ where $\pi_Q : TQ \to Q$ is the canonical projection.

[8] Formally, the second Lie derivative of the constraint along the vector field specified by (1a).

DEFINITION 5 (CONTACT MODE SEQUENCE [16, DEF. 4]). *The* contact mode sequence *associated with a trajectory* $\phi^{(q,\dot{q})}$ *that is admissible on* $[0,t] \subset \mathbb{R}$ *is the unique function*

$$\omega\colon \{0,\ldots,m\} \to 2^n \tag{9}$$

such that there exists a finite sequence of times $\{t_\ell\}_{\ell=0}^{m+1} \subset [0,t]$ *for which* $0 = t_0 < t_1 < \cdots < t_{m+1} = t$ *and*

$$\forall \ell \in \{0,\ldots,m\} : \phi((t_\ell, t_{\ell+1}), (q,\dot{q})) \subset TA_{\omega(\ell)}. \tag{10}$$

REMARK 8. *In Def. 8 (contact mode sequence), the sequence* ω *is easily seen to be unique by the admissibility of the trajectory; indeed, the associated time sequence consists of start, stop, and constraint activation/deactivation times. Note that successive modes in the sequence need not be related by set containment (i.e.* $\omega(\ell) \subset \omega(\ell+1)$ *or* $\omega(\ell) \supset \omega(\ell+1)$*) since, e.g., one constraint could activate and another deactivate at the same time instant as in Fig. 2. Thus,* ω *is not simply a discrete "counter" as in* hybrid time domains *[10, §3.2].*

ASSUMPTION 3 (INDEPENDENT CONSTRAINTS [2, §3.4]). *The constraints are independent:*

$$\forall J \in 2^n,\ q \in a_J^{-1}(0) : \{Da_j(q)\}_{j\in J} \subset T_q^*Q \quad \text{is linearly independent.} \tag{11}$$

REMARK 9. *Algebraically, Assump. 3 (independent constraints) implies that the constraint forces* λ_J *are well-defined, and that there are no more constraints than degrees-of-freedom,* $n \leq d$*. Geometrically, it implies for each* $J \in 2^n$ *that* $a_J^{-1}(0) \subset Q$ *is an embedded codimension-*$|J|$ *submanifold, and that the codimension-1 submanifolds* $\{a_j^{-1}(0)\}_{j\in J}$ *intersect transversally; this follows from [20, Thm. 5.12] since each* $a_J\colon Q \to \mathbb{R}$ *must be constant-rank on its zero section.*

We now state the well-known fact[9] that, if the contact mode sequence is fixed, then admissible trajectory outcomes are differentiable with respect to initial conditions.

LEMMA 1 (DIFFERENTIABILITY WITHIN MODE SEQ. [1]). *Under Assump. 1 (existence and uniqueness of flow), Assump. 2 (*C^r *vector field and reset map), and Assump. 3 (independent constraints), with* $\phi\colon [0,\infty) \times TA \to TA$ *denoting the flow, if* $\Sigma \subset TQ$ *is a* C^r *embedded submanifold such that all trajectories initialized in* $\Sigma \cap TA$

(i) are admissible on $[0,t] \subset \mathbb{R}$ *and*

(ii) have the same contact mode sequence,

then the restriction $\phi|_{\{t\}\times\Sigma}$ *is* C^r.

4. (DIS)CONTINUITY ACROSS CONTACT MODE SEQUENCES

As stated in Sec. 1, the point of this paper is to provide sufficient conditions that ensure trajectories of (1) vary differentiably as the contact mode sequence varies. A precondition for differentiability is continuity, whence in this section we consider what condition must be imposed to give rise to continuity in general. We begin in Sec. 4.1 by demonstrating that the transversality of constraints imposed by Assump. 3 (independent constraints) generally gives rise to discontinuity, then introduce an orthogonality condition in Sec. 4.2 that suffices to restore continuity.

[9]The result follows via a straightforward composition of smooth flows with smooth time–to–impact maps; we refer the interested reader to [6, App. A1] for details.

4.1 Discontinuity across contact mode sequences

Consider an unconstrained initial condition $(q,\dot{q}) \in TA_\emptyset \subset TQ$ that impacts (i.e. admissibly activates) exactly two constraints $i,j \in \{1,\ldots,n\}$ at time $t > 0$; with $(\rho,\dot{\rho}^-) = \phi(t,(q,\dot{q}))$ we have

$$a_{\{i,j\}}(\rho) = 0,\ Da_i(\rho)\dot{\rho}^- < 0,\ Da_j(\rho)\dot{\rho}^- < 0. \tag{12}$$

The pre–impact velocity $\dot{\rho}^-$ abruptly resets via (1b):

$$\dot{\rho}^+ = \Delta_{\{i,j\}}(\rho)\dot{\rho}^-. \tag{13}$$

As noted in Remark 9 (independent constraints), the constraint surfaces $a_i^{-1}(0)$, $a_j^{-1}(0)$ intersect transversally. Therefore given any $\varepsilon > 0$ it is possible to find $(q_i,\dot{q}_i)$ and $(q_j,\dot{q}_j)$ in the open ball of radius ε centered at $(q,\dot{q})$ such that the trajectory $\phi^{(q_i,\dot{q}_i)}$ impacts constraint i before constraint j and $\phi^{(q_j,\dot{q}_j)}$ impacts j before i. As $\varepsilon > 0$ tends toward zero, the time spent flowing according to (1a) tends toward zero, hence the post–impact velocities tend toward the twofold iteration of (1b):

$$\begin{aligned}\dot{\rho}_i^+ &= \Delta_{\{i,j\}}(\rho)\Delta_i(\rho)\dot{\rho}^-,\\ \dot{\rho}_j^+ &= \Delta_{\{i,j\}}(\rho)\Delta_j(\rho)\dot{\rho}^-.\end{aligned} \tag{14}$$

Recalling for all $J \in 2^n$ that $\Delta_J \in \mathbb{R}^{d\times d}$ is an orthogonal projection[10] onto the tangent plane of the codimension–$|J|$ submanifold $a_J^{-1}(0)$, observe that $\dot{\rho}_i^+ = \dot{\rho}^+ = \dot{\rho}_j^+$ if and only if $Da_i(\rho)$ is orthogonal to $Da_j(\rho)$. Therefore if constraints intersect transversally but non–orthogonally, outcomes from the dynamics in (1) vary discontinuously as the contact mode sequence varies.

REMARK 10 (DISCONTINUOUS LOCOMOTION OUTCOMES). *The analysis of a saggital-plane quadruped in [28] provides an instructive example of the behavioral consequences of transverse but non-orthogonal constraints in a model of legged locomotion. As summarized in [28, Table 2], the model possesses three distinct but nearby trot (or trot-like) gaits, corresponding to whether two legs impact simultaneously (as in (13)) or at different time instants (as in (14)); the trot that undergoes simultaneous impact is unstable due to discontinuous dependence of trajectory outcomes on initial conditions.*

4.2 Continuity across contact mode sequences

To preclude the discontinuous dependence on initial conditions exhibited in Sec. 4.1, we strengthen the *transversality* of constraints implied by Assump. 3 (independent constraints) by imposing *orthogonality* of constraints.

ASSUMPTION 4 (ORTHOGONAL CONSTRAINTS [2, THM. 20]). *Constraint surfaces intersect orthogonally:*

$$\forall i,j \in \{1,\ldots,n\},\ i \neq j,\ q \in a_i^{-1}(0) \cap a_j^{-1}(0) : \quad \langle Da_i(q), Da_j(q)\rangle_{M^{-1}} = 0. \tag{15}$$

REMARK 11. *Note that Assump. 4 (orthogonal constraints) is strictly stronger than Assump. 3 (independent constraints). Physically, the assumption can be interpreted as asserting that any two independent limbs that can undergo impact simultaneously must be inertially decoupled. This can be*

[10]relative to the inner product $\langle\cdot,\cdot\rangle_M$. For further discussion of orthogonal projection in constraint activation of mechanical systems, see [16, §1.3.4].

achieved in artifacts by introducing series compliance in a sufficient number of degrees–of–freedom.

Sec. 4.1 demonstrated that Assump. 4 (orthogonal constraints) is necessary in general to preclude discontinuous dependence on initial conditions. The following result demonstrates that this assumption is sufficient to ensure continuous dependence on initial conditions, even as the contact mode sequence varies.[11]

LEMMA 2 (CONTINUITY ACROSS MODE SEQ. [2, THM. 20]). *Under Assump. 1 (existence and uniqueness of flow), Assump. 2 (C^r vector field and reset map), and Assump. 4 (orthogonal constraints), with $\phi\colon [0,\infty) \times TA \to TA$ denoting the flow, if $t \in \mathbb{R}$ and $(p,\dot{p}) \in TA \subset TQ$ are such that t is not a constraint activation time for $(p,\dot{p})$, then ϕ is continuous at $(t,(p,\dot{p}))$.*

REMARK 12 (CONTINUITY ACROSS MODE SEQ.). *The preceding result implies that the flow ϕ is continuous almost everywhere in both time and state, without needing to restrict to admissible trajectories. Thus orthogonal constraints ensure the flow ϕ depends continuously on initial conditions, even along trajectories that exhibit grazing and Zeno phenomena.[12] For the reason described in Remark 5 (admissible trajectories), we will not be able to accommodate these phenomena when we study differentiability properties of trajectories in the next section.*

5. DIFFERENTIABILITY ACROSS CONTACT MODE SEQUENCES

We now provide conditions that ensure trajectories depend *differentiably* on initial conditions, even as the contact mode sequence varies. In general, the flow does not possess a classical Jacobian (alternately called *Fréchet* or *F–*)derivative, i.e. there does not exist a single linear map that provides a first–order approximation for the flow. Instead, under the admissibility conditions introduced in Sec. 3, we show that the flow admits a *piecewise*–linear first–order approximation termed[13] a *Bouligand* (or *B–*)derivative [33, Ch. 3.1]. Though perhaps unfamiliar, this derivative is nevertheless quite useful. Significantly, unlike functions that are merely directionally differentiable, B–differentiable functions admit generalizations of many techniques familiar from calculus, including the Chain Rule [33, Thm 3.1.1] (and hence Product and Quotient Rules [33, Cor. 3.1.1]), Fundamental Theorem of Calculus [33, Prop. 3.1.1], and Implicit Function Theorem [33, Thm. 4.2.3], and the B–derivative can be employed to implement scalable algorithms [17] for optimization or learning.

We proceed by showing that the flow is piecewise–differentiable in the sense defined in [33, Ch. 4.1] and recapitulated here; functions that are piecewise–differentiable in this sense are always B–differentiable [33, Prop. 4.1.3]. Let $r \in \mathbb{N} \cup \{\infty\}$ denote an order of differentiability[14] and $D \subset \mathbb{R}^m$ be open. A continuous function $\psi\colon D \to \mathbb{R}^\ell$ is called *piecewise–C^r* if the graph of ψ is everywhere locally covered by the graphs of a finite collection of functions that are r times continuously differentiable (C^r–functions).[15] Formally, for every $x \in D$ there must exist an open set $U \subset D$ containing x and a finite collection $\{\psi_\omega\colon U \to \mathbb{R}^\ell\}_{\omega\in\Omega}$ of C^r–functions such that for all $x \in U$ we have $\psi(x) \in \{\psi_\omega(x)\}_{\omega\in\Omega}$.

We now state and prove the main result of this paper: whenever the flow of a mechanical system subject to unilateral constraints is continuous and admissible, it is piecewise–C^r; see Fig. 2 for an illustration.

THEOREM 1 (PIECEWISE–DIFFERENTIABLE FLOW). *Under Assump. 1 (existence and uniqueness of flow), Assump. 2 (C^r vector field and reset map), and Assump. 4 (orthogonal constraints), with $\phi\colon [0,\infty) \times TA \to TA$ denoting the flow, if $t \in [0,\infty)$, $(p,\dot{p}) \in TA \subset TQ$, and $\Sigma \subset TQ$ is a C^r embedded submanifold containing $(p,\dot{p})$ such that*

(i) the trajectory $\phi^{(p,\dot{p})}$ activates and/or deactivates constraints at time $s \in (0,t)$,

(ii) $\phi^{(p,\dot{p})}$ has no other activation or deactivation times in $[0,t]$,

(iii) trajectories initialized in $\Sigma \cap TA$ are admissible on $[0,t]$, and

(iv) the set Ω of contact mode sequences for trajectories initialized in $\Sigma \cap TA$ is finite,

then the restriction $\phi|_{[0,\infty)\times\Sigma}$ is piecewise–C^r at $(t,(p,\dot{p}))$.

PROOF. We seek to show that the restriction $\phi|_{[0,\infty)\times\Sigma}$ is piecewise–C^r at $(t,(p,\dot{p}))$. We will proceed by constructing a finite set of r times continuously differentiable selection functions for ϕ on $[0,t]\times\Sigma$. In the example given in Fig. 2, there are two selection functions, one corresponding to a perturbation along $(v_r,\dot{v}_r)$, colored red, and the other along $(v_b,\dot{v}_b)$, colored blue. These selection functions will be indexed by a pair of functions (ω,η) where: $\omega\colon \{0,\ldots,m\} \to 2^n$ is a contact mode sequence, i.e. $\omega \in \Omega$; $\eta\colon \{0,\ldots,m-1\} \to \{1,\ldots,n\}$ indexes constraints that undergo admissible activation or deactivation[16] at the contact mode transition indexed by $\ell \in \{0,\ldots,m-1\}$. For instance, in Fig. 2 the index functions for the (de)activation sequence starting from $(v_r,\dot{v}_r)$, in red, are $\omega_r(0) = \{1\}, \omega_r(1) = \emptyset, \omega_r(2) = \{2\}$, $\eta_r(0) = 1, \eta_r(1) = 2$, and the index functions for the (de)activation sequence starting from $(v_b,\dot{v}_b)$, in blue, are

[11] We note for the interested reader that the result on continuity with respect to initial conditions in [25] is inapplicable along trajectories that simultaneously activate and/or deactivate more than one constraint; such trajectories do not satisfy hypotheses 4 and 5 of [25, Thm. III.2].

[12] We remark that [2, Thm. 20] implies the function ϕ is continuous everywhere with respect to the quotient metric defined in [5, Sec. III], whence the numerical simulation algorithm in [5, Sec. IV] is provably–convergent for all trajectories (even those that graze) up to the first occurrence of Zeno.

[13] This terminology was introduced, to the best of our knowledge, by Robinson [30].

[14] We let context specify whether $r = \infty$ indicates "mere" smoothness or the more stringent condition of analyticity.

[15] The definition of piecewise–C^r may at first appear unrelated to the intuition that a function ought to be piecewise–differentiable precisely if its "domain can be partitioned locally into a finite number of regions relative to which smoothness holds" [31, Section 1]. However, as shown in [31, Theorem 2], piecewise–C^r functions are always piecewise–differentiable in this intuitive sense.

[16] In light of Remark 4, we only consider deactivations of type (ii) in Def. 3 (admissible constraint activation/deactivation). In some systems, a deactivation of type (ii) may only arise following a (simultaneous) activation; it suffices to restrict to functions η that do not index such deactivations.

$\omega_b(0) = \{1\}, \omega_b(1) = \{1,2\}, \omega_b(2) = \{2\}, \eta_b(0) = 2, \eta_b(1) = 1$. Note that for each $\omega \in \Omega$ the set $H(\omega)$ of possible η's is finite; since the set Ω is finite by assumption, the set of pairs (ω, η) is finite.

Let $(\omega\colon \{0,\ldots,m\} \to 2^n) \in \Omega$ and $(\eta\colon \{0,\ldots,m-1\} \to \{1,\ldots,n\}) \in H(\omega)$ be as described above. Let $\mu\colon \{0,\ldots,m\} \to 2^n$ be defined as $\mu(k) = \bigcup_{i=0}^{k-1} \{\eta(i)\}$, where we adopt the convention that $\bigcup_{i=0}^{-1} \{i\} = \emptyset$; note that μ is uniquely determined by η.[17] For the sake of readability, we suppress dependence on η and ω until (22). Let $(\rho, \dot\rho^-) = \lim_{u \uparrow s} \phi(u, (p, \dot p))$. For all $k \in \{0,\ldots,m\}$ define $\dot\rho_k = \Delta_{\mu(k)}(\rho)\dot\rho^-$. There exists an open neighborhood $U_k \subset TQ$ containing $(\rho, \dot\rho_k)$ such that the vector field determined by (1a) at $\omega(k)$ admits a C^r extension to $F_k\colon U_k \to \mathbb{R}^{2d}$. (Note that for $k = m$ (resp. $k = 0$) the neighborhood U_k can be taken to additionally include $\phi((s,t],(p,\dot p))$ (resp. $\phi([0,s),(p,\dot p))$).)

By the Fundamental Theorem on Flows [20, Thm. 9.12], F_k determines a unique maximal flow $\phi_k\colon \mathcal{F}_k \to U_k$ over a maximal flow domain $\mathcal{F}_k \subset \mathbb{R} \times U_k$, which is an open set that contains $\{0\} \times U_k$, and the flow ϕ_ℓ is C^r. (Note that $(t - s, (\rho, \dot\rho_m)) \in \mathcal{F}_m$ and $(s, (p, \dot p)) \in \mathcal{F}_0$.)

If $\eta(\ell)$ indexes an admissible constraint activation (recall that $\ell \in \{0,\ldots,m-1\}$), then there exists a time-to-activation $\tau_\ell\colon U_\ell \to \mathbb{R}$ defined over an open set $U_\ell \subset TQ$ containing $(\rho, \dot\rho_\ell)$ such that

$$\forall (q,\dot q) \in U_\ell : a_{\eta(\ell)} \circ \phi_\ell(\tau_\ell(q,\dot q),(q,\dot q)) = 0. \quad (16)$$

If instead $\eta(\ell)$ indexes an admissible constraint deactivation, then there exists a time-to-deactivation $\tau_\ell\colon U_\ell \to \mathbb{R}$ defined over an open set $U_\ell \subset TQ$ containing $(\rho, \dot\rho_\ell)$ such that

$$\forall (q,\dot q) \in U_\ell : \lambda_{\eta(\ell)} \circ \phi_\ell(\tau_\ell(q,\dot q),(q,\dot q)) = 0. \quad (17)$$

In either case, τ_ℓ exists and is C^r by the Implicit Function Theorem [20, Thm. C.40] due to admissibility of trajectories initialized in Σ. (Note for $\ell = 0$ the neighborhood U_ℓ can be extended to include $\phi([0,s),(p,\dot p))$ using the semi-group property[18] of the flow ϕ_ℓ.) See Fig. 2 for an illustration of constraint activations and deactivations.

Let $\varphi_\ell\colon \mathbb{R} \times U_\ell \to \mathbb{R} \times U_\ell$ be defined for all $(u,(q,\dot q)) \in \mathbb{R} \times U_\ell$ by

$$\varphi_\ell(u,(q,\dot q)) = (u - \tau_\ell(q,\dot q), \phi_\ell(\tau_\ell(q,\dot q),(q,\dot q))). \quad (18)$$

The map φ_ℓ flows a state $(q, \dot q)$ using the vector field from contact mode $\omega(\ell)$ until constraint $\eta(\ell)$ undergoes admissible activation/deactivation, and deducts the time required from the given budget u. The total derivative of φ_ℓ at $(0,(\rho,\dot\rho_\ell))$ (see also [7, § 7.1.4]) is

$$D\varphi_\ell(0,(\rho,\dot\rho_\ell)) = \begin{bmatrix} 1 & \frac{1}{gf} g \\ 0 & I_{2d} - \frac{1}{gf} fg \end{bmatrix}, \quad (19)$$

where $f = F(\rho, \dot\rho_\ell)$ and $g = Dh_{\eta(\ell)}(\rho, \dot\rho_\ell)$ where $h_\ell\colon TQ \to \mathbb{R}$ is defined for all $(q,\dot q) \in TQ$ by $h_\ell(q,\dot q) = a_{\eta(\ell)}(q)$.

Let $\Gamma_\ell\colon \mathbb{R} \times TQ \to \mathbb{R} \times TQ$ be defined for all $(u,(q,\dot q)) \in \mathbb{R} \times TQ$ by

$$\Gamma_\ell(u,(q,\dot q)) = (u,(q,\Delta_{\mu(\ell)}(q)\dot q)). \quad (20)$$

The map Γ_ℓ resets velocities to be compatible with contact mode $\omega(\ell)$ while leaving positions and times unaffected. The total derivative of Γ_ℓ at $(u,(q,\dot q))$ is given by

$$D\Gamma_\ell(u,(q,\dot q)) = \begin{bmatrix} 1 & 0 & 0 \\ 0 & I_d & 0 \\ 0 & D_q(\Delta_{\mu(\ell)}(q)\dot q) & \Delta_{\mu(\ell)}(q) \end{bmatrix}. \quad (21)$$

For each $\omega \in \Omega$ and $\eta \in H(\omega)$ define ϕ_ω^η by the formal composition

$$\phi_\omega^\eta = \phi_m \circ \prod_{\ell=0}^{m-1} (\Gamma_{\ell+1} \circ \varphi_\ell). \quad (22)$$

We take as the domain of ϕ_ω^η the set

$$\mathcal{F}_\omega^\eta = (\phi_\omega^\eta)^{-1}(TQ) \subset \mathbb{R} \times TQ, \quad (23)$$

noting that $\mathcal{F}_\omega^\eta$ is (i) open since each function in the composition is continuous, and (ii) nonempty since $(t,(p,\dot p)) \in \mathcal{F}_\omega^\eta$. The map ϕ_ω^η flows states via a given contact mode sequence for a specified amount of time; note that some of the resulting "trajectories" are not physically realizable, as they may evaluate the flows $\{\phi_k\}_{k=0}^m$ in backward time. An example of such a physically unrealizable "trajectory" is illustrated in Fig. 2 by $\phi_{\eta_r}^{\omega_r}(t,(v_b,\dot v_b))$, which first flows forward in time via the extended vector field $F_{\{1\}}$ past the constraint surface $\{a_2(q) = 0\}$ until constraint 1 deactivates and then flows backwards in time until constraint 2 activates, ultimately terminating in $TA_{\{2\}}$.

With $\mathcal{F} = \bigcap \{\mathcal{F}_\omega^\eta : \omega \in \Omega, \eta \in H(\omega)\} \subset [0,\infty) \times TQ$, for any $(u,(q,\dot q)) \in \mathcal{F} \cap ([0,\infty) \times TA)$ with contact mode sequence $\omega \in \Omega$ and constraint sequence $\eta \in H(\omega)$, the trajectory outcome is obtained by applying ϕ_ω^η to $(u,(q,\dot q))$, i.e. $\phi(u,(q,\dot q)) = \phi_\omega^\eta(u,(q,\dot q))$. See Fig. 2 for an illustration of trajectories with different contact mode sequences.

The maps φ_ℓ, Γ_ℓ, and ϕ_ω^η are C^r on their domains since they are each obtained from a finite composition of C^r functions. Therefore the restriction[19] $\phi|_{[0,\infty)\times\Sigma}$ is a continuous selection of the finite collection of C^r functions

$$\{\phi_\omega^\eta : \omega \in \Omega, \eta \in H(\omega)\}$$

on the open neighborhood $\mathcal{F} \subset TQ$ containing $(t,(p,\dot p))$, i.e. $\phi|_{[0,\infty)\times\Sigma}$ is piecewise-C^r at $(t,(p,\dot p))$. See Fig. 2 for an illustration the piecewise-differentiability of trajectory outcomes arising from a transition between contact mode sequences.

Remark 13 (Satisfying Theorem hypotheses). *Models of animal or robot behaviors involving intermittent contact with terrain—walking, running, climbing, leaping, dancing, juggling, grasping—generally satisfy our hypotheses, so long as they possess sufficient compliance as in Fig. 1 (right).*

Remark 14 (Relaxing Theorem hypotheses). *Since the class of piecewise-differentiable functions is closed under finite composition, conditions (i) and (ii) in the preceding*

[17] η is not uniquely determined by ω due to the possibility of instantaneous activation/deactivation for the same constraint; consider for instance the bounce of an elastic ball [12, Ch. 2.4].

[18] $\phi_\ell(u+v,x) = \phi_\ell(u,\phi_\ell(v,x))$ whenever $(v,x),(u+v,x),(u,\phi_\ell(v,x)) \in \mathcal{F}_\ell$.

[19] As a technical aside, we remark that the domain of ϕ is confined to $[0,\infty) \times TA$, whence invoking the definition of piecewise-differentiability requires a continuous extension $\widetilde{\phi}$ of ϕ defined on a neighborhood of $(t,(p,\dot p))$ that is open relative to $[0,\infty) \times TQ$. One such extension is obtained by composing ϕ with a sufficiently differentiable retraction [20, Ch. 6] of TQ onto TA (such a retraction is guaranteed to exist locally by transversality of constraint surfaces).

Theorem can be readily relaxed to accommodate a finite number of constraint activation/deactivation times in the interval $(0,t)$. Conditions (iii) and (iv) are more difficult to relax since there are systems wherein trajectories initialized arbitrarily close to an admissible trajectory fail to be admissible themselves. As a familiar example, consider a 1 degree-of-freedom elastic impact oscillator [12, Ch. 2.4] (i.e. a bouncing ball): the stationary trajectory (initialized with $q, \dot{q} = 0$) is admissible for all time, but all nearby trajectories (initialized with $q \neq 0$ or $\dot{q} \neq 0$) exhibit the Zeno phenomenon. We will discuss further possible extensions in Sec. 6.1.1.

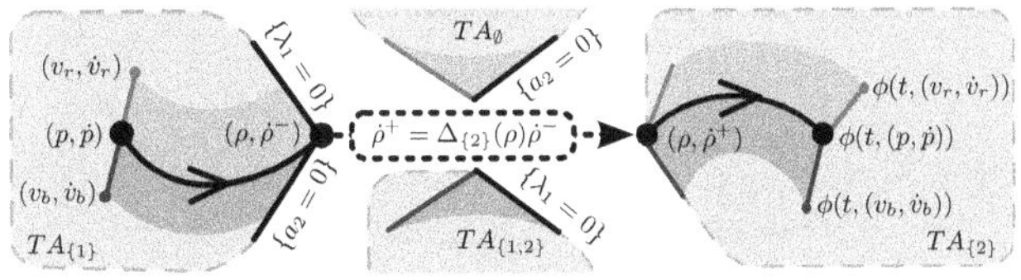

Figure 2: Illustration of trajectory undergoing simultaneous constraint activation and deactivation: the trajectory initialized at $(p, \dot{p}) \in TA_{\{1\}} \subset TQ$ flows via (1a) to a point $(\rho, \dot{\rho}^-) \in TA_{\{1\}}$ where both the constraint force λ_1 and constraint function a_2 are zero, instantaneously resets velocity via (1b) to $\dot{\rho}^+ = \Delta_{\{2\}}(\rho)\dot{\rho}^-$, then flows via (1a) to $\phi(t, (p, \dot{p})) \in TA_{\{2\}} \subset TQ$. Nearby trajectories undergo activation and deactivation at distinct times: trajectories initialized in the red region, e.g. $(v_r, \dot{v}_r)$, deactivate constraint 1 and flow through contact mode $TA_\emptyset$ before activating constraint 2—their contact mode sequence is $(\{1\}, \emptyset, \{2\})$—while trajectories initialized in the blue region, e.g. $(v_b, \dot{v}_b)$, activate 2 and flow through $TA_{\{1,2\}}$ before deactivating 1—their contact mode sequence is $(\{1\}, \{1,2\}, \{2\})$. Piecewise-differentiability of the trajectory outcome is illustrated by the fact that red outcomes lie along a different subspace than blue.

Under the hypotheses of the preceding Theorem, the continuous flow ϕ is piecewise-differentiable at a point $(t, (p, \dot{p})) \in [0, \infty) \times TA$, that is, near $(t, (p, \dot{p}))$ the graph of ϕ is has an open covering by the graphs of a finite collection $\{\phi_\omega^\eta : \omega \in \Omega, \eta \in H(\omega)\}$ of differentiable functions (termed selection functions). This implies in particular that there exists a continuous and piecewise-linear function

$$D\phi(t, (p, \dot{p})) : T_{(t,(p,\dot{p}))}([0, \infty) \times TA) \to T_{\phi(t,(p,\dot{p}))}A \quad (24)$$

(termed the Bouligand or B-derivative) that provides a first-order approximation for how trajectory outcomes vary with respect to initial conditions. Formally, for all $(u, (v, \dot{v})) \in T_{(t,(p,\dot{p}))}([0, \infty) \times TA)$, the vector $D\phi(t, (p, \dot{p}); u, (v, \dot{v})) \in \mathbb{R}^{2d}$ is the directional derivative of $\phi(t, (p, \dot{p}))$ in the $(u, (v, \dot{v}))$ direction:

$$\lim_{\alpha \downarrow 0} \frac{1}{\alpha} [(\phi(t + \alpha u, (p + \alpha v, \dot{p} + \alpha \dot{v})) - \phi(t, (p, \dot{p}))) - D\phi(t, (p, \dot{p}); u, (v, \dot{v}))] = 0. \quad (25)$$

Furthermore, this directional derivative is contained within the collection of directional derivatives of the selection functions. Formally, for all $(u, (v, \dot{v})) \in T_{(t,(p,\dot{p}))}([0, \infty) \times TA)$,

$$D\phi(t, (p, \dot{p}); u, (v, \dot{v})) \in \{D\phi_\omega^\eta(t, (p, \dot{p}); u, (v, \dot{v})) : \omega \in \Omega, \eta \in H(\omega)\}. \quad (26)$$

The selection functions are classically differentiable, whence their directional derivatives can be computed via matrix-vector multiplication between a classical (Jacobian/Fréchet) derivative matrix and the perturbation vector. Formally, for all $(u, (v, \dot{v})) \in T_{(t,(p,\dot{p}))}([0, \infty) \times TA)$, $\omega \in \Omega$, $\eta \in H(\omega)$,

$$D\phi_\omega^\eta(t, (p, \dot{p}); u, (v, \dot{v})) = D\phi_\omega^\eta(t, (p, \dot{p})) \begin{bmatrix} u \\ v \\ \dot{v} \end{bmatrix}, \quad (27)$$

where $D\phi_\omega^\eta(t, (p, \dot{p})) \in \mathbb{R}^{(2d)\times(1+2d)}$ is the classical derivative of the selection function ϕ_ω^η. The matrix $D\phi_\omega^\eta(t, (p, \dot{p}))$ can be obtained by applying the (classical) chain rule to the definition of ϕ_ω^η from (22).

6. DISCUSSION

We conclude by discussing possible routes (or obstacles) to extend our result, and implications for assessing stability and controllability.

6.1 Extending our result

6.1.1 Relaxing hypotheses

The hypotheses used to state Thm. 1 (piecewise differentiability across contact mode sequences) restrict either the systems or system trajectories under consideration; we will discuss the latter before addressing the former.

Trajectories we termed admissible exhibit neither *grazing* nor *Zeno* phenomena. Since grazing generally entails constraint activation times that are not even Lipschitz continuous with respect to initial conditions, the flow is not piecewise-C^r along grazing trajectories. This fact has been shown by others [8, Ex. 2.7], and is straightforward to see in an example. Indeed, consider the trajectory of a point mass moving vertically in a uniform gravitational field subject to a maximum height (i.e. ceiling) constraint. The grazing trajectory is a parabola, whence the time-to-activation function involves a square root of the initial position. Zeno trajectories, on the other hand, can exhibit differentiable trajectory outcomes following an accumulation of constraint activations (and, hence, deactivations); consider, for instance, the (stationary) outcome that follows the accumulation of impacts in a model of a bouncing ball [12, Ch. 2.4]. Thus we cannot at present draw any general conclusions regarding differentiability of the flow along Zeno trajectories, and speculate that it might be possible to recover piecewise-differentiability along such trajectories in the *completion* of the mechanical system [27, Sec. IV] after establishing continuity with respect to initial conditions in the intrinsic state-space metric [5, Sec. III].

The (so-called [2]) effort map f was not allowed to vary with the contact mode, while the dynamics in (1) vary with the contact mode $J \subset \{1, \ldots, n\}$ due to intermittent activation of unilateral constraints $a_J(q) \geq 0$. Contact-dependent effort can easily introduce nonexistence or nonuniqueness. Indeed, this phenomenon was investigated thoroughly by Carathéodory and, later, Filippov [9, Ch. 1]. For a specific example of the potential challenges in allowing contact-dependent forcing, note that the introduction of simple friction models into mechanical systems subject to unilateral constraints is known to produce pathologies including nonexistence and nonuniqueness of trajectories [34]. To generalize the preceding results to allow the above phenomena, one would need to provide conditions ensuring that trajectories (i) exist uniquely, (ii) depend continuously on initial conditions, and (iii) admit differentiable selection functions along trajectories of interest.

6.1.2 Including control inputs

We focused on autonomous dynamics in (1); however, parameterized control inputs can be incorporated through a standard state augmentation technique in such a way that Theorem 1 implies trajectory outcomes depend piecewise–differentiably on initial states and input parameters, even as the contact mode sequence varies.

Specifically, suppose (1a) is replaced with

$$M(q)\ddot{q} = \tilde{f}((q,\dot{q}),u) + c(q,\dot{q})\dot{q} + Da_J(q)^\top \tilde{\lambda}_J((q,\dot{q}),u), \tag{28a}$$

$$\dot{q}^+ = \widetilde{\Delta}_J((q,\dot{q}^-),u)\dot{q}^-, \tag{28b}$$

where $\tilde{f} \colon TQ \times U \to \mathbb{R}^d$ is an effort map that accepts a constant input parameter $u \in U = \mathbb{R}^m$, $\tilde{\lambda}_J \colon TQ \times U \to \mathbb{R}^{|J|}$ is the reaction force that results from applying effort $\tilde{f}(q,\dot{q},u)$ in contact mode J, and $\widetilde{\Delta}_J \colon TQ \times U \to \mathbb{R}^d$ is a reset map that accepts input parameter u as well. We interpret the vector u as parameterizing an open– or closed–loop input to the system; once initialized, u remains constant.[20] It is possible to generalize the proof of Thm. 1 (piecewise differentiability across contact mode sequences) to provide conditions under which there exists a continuous flow $\widetilde{\phi} : \widetilde{\mathfrak{F}} \to TA$ for (28) that is piecewise–differentiable with respect to initial conditions $(q,\dot{q}) \in TA$ and input parameters $u \in U$ over an open subset $\widetilde{\mathfrak{F}} \subset [0,\infty) \times TA \times U$ containing $\{0\} \times TA \times U$.

6.2 Assessing (in)stability of periodic orbits

In this section we consider the problem of assessing stability (or instability) of a periodic orbit in a mechanical system subject to unilateral constraints. Suppose $(\rho,\dot{\rho}) \in TA_\emptyset$ is an initial condition that lies on a *periodic orbit*, i.e. there exists $T > 0$ so that $\phi(T,(\rho,\dot{\rho})) = (\rho,\dot{\rho})$ and $\phi(t,(\rho,\dot{\rho})) \neq (\rho,\dot{\rho})$ for all $t \in (0,T)$. If the trajectory $\phi^{(\rho,\dot{\rho})}$ undergoes constraint activations and deactivations at isolated instants in time, then prior work has shown that ϕ is C^1 at $(T,(\rho,\dot{\rho}))$, and the classical derivative $D\phi(T,(\rho,\dot{\rho}))$ can be used to assess stability of the periodic orbit [1]. If instead the trajectory activates and/or deactivates some constraints simultaneously as in Fig. 3, then (so long as constraint activations/deactivations are admissible on and near $\phi^{(\rho,\dot{\rho})}$) the results of Sec. 5 ensure that ϕ is PC^1 at $(T,(\rho,\dot{\rho}))$ and the B–derivative $D\phi(T,(\rho,\dot{\rho}))$ is not generally given by a single linear map, whence classical tests for stability are not applicable. In what follows we generalize the classical techniques to use this B–derivative to assess stability (or instability) of the periodic orbit $\phi^{(\rho,\dot{\rho})}$.

[20]A control policy represented using a universal function approximator such as an artificial neural network [22, 19] provides an example of a parameterized closed–loop input, while a control signal represented using a finite truncation of an expansion in a chosen basis [26, 18] provides an example of a parameterized open-loop input.

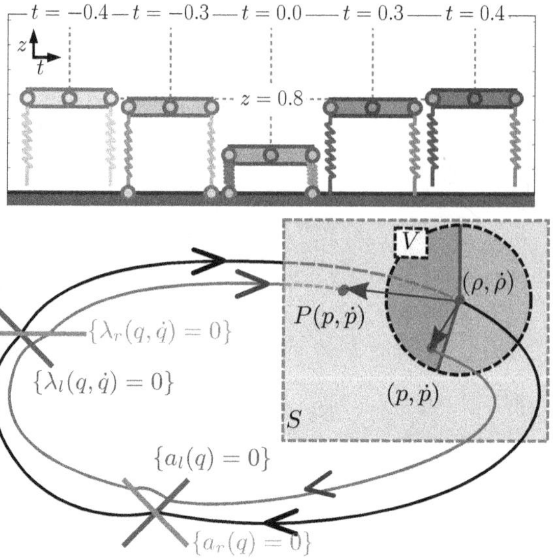

Figure 3: Illustration of a periodic orbit in the system depicted in Fig. 1(*right*) undergoing simultaneous activation (and, subsequently, simultaneous deactivation) of unilateral constraints. (*top*) Snapshots of the trajectory at apex ($t = \pm 0.4$), touchdown/liftoff ($t = \pm 0.3$), and nadir ($t = 0.0$). (*bottom*) Illustration of Poincaré map $P : V \to S$ over the apex section S, defined in Sec. 6.2; trajectories initialized in the open subset $V \subset S$ return to S. The set V is partitioned into regions where selection functions for the piecewise–C^r map P are active: initial conditions with $\theta > 0$, where the left leg constraint activates before the right, are colored blue; initial conditions with $\theta < 0$ are colored red. Along the trajectory generated by the fixed point $P(\rho,\dot{\rho}) = (\rho,\dot{\rho})$ (colored black), simultaneous constraint activation is indicated by the trajectory passing through the intersection of the constraint surfaces for the right ($\{a_r = 0\}$) and left ($\{a_l = 0\}$) legs; similarly for simultaneous deactivation through the intersection $\{\lambda_l = 0\} \cap \{\lambda_r = 0\}$. A nearby trajectory initialized at $(p,\dot{p}) \in V$ (colored blue) undergoes constraint activation and deactivation at distinct instants in time.

We start by constructing a Poincaré map for the periodic orbit $\phi^{(\rho,\dot{\rho})}$. Let $S \subset TQ$ be a Poincaré section for $\phi^{(\rho,\dot{\rho})}$ at $(\rho,\dot{\rho})$, i.e. a C^r embedded codimension–1 submanifold containing $(\rho,\dot{\rho})$ that is transverse to the vector field in (1a). For a concrete example we refer to the model in Fig. 3 where S is a Poincaré section about the apex and ρ the position vector with body height $z = 0.8$, rotation $\theta = 0$, and the legs oriented perpendicular to the body orientation. Given zero initial velocity, the orbit's period is $T \simeq 0.8$.

Since ϕ is continuous by Lem. 2 (continuity across contact mode sequences), there exists a *first–return time* $\tau \colon V \to (0,\infty)$ defined over an open neighborhood $V \subset S$ containing $(\rho,\dot{\rho})$ such that $\phi(\tau(q,\dot{q}),(q,\dot{q})) \in S$ for all $(q,\dot{q}) \in V$ and $\tau(\rho,\dot{\rho}) = T$; we let $P : V \to S$ be the Poincaré (or *first–return*) map defined by

$$\forall (q,\dot{q}) \in V \colon P(q,\dot{q}) = \phi(\tau(q,\dot{q}),(q,\dot{q})) \in S. \tag{29}$$

As an illustration, $(p, \dot{p}) \in V$ in Fig. 3(*bottom*) generates a trajectory initialized near $(\rho, \dot{\rho})$ that undergoes admissible constraint activations and deactivations at distinct instants in time, activating the left leg constraint before activating the right leg constraint, then deactivating both constraints in the same order. Since ϕ is PC^r and S is a C^r manifold we conclude that τ is PC^r [7, Thm. 10], whence P is PC^r. To assess exponential stability of $\phi^{(\rho,\dot{\rho})}$, it suffices to determine conditions under which the piecewise–linear map $DP(\rho, \dot{\rho})$ is exponentially contractive or expansive. This task is nontrivial since, as is well–known [3, Ex. 2.1], a piecewise–linear system constructed from stable subsystems may be unstable; similarly, a system constructed from unstable subsystems may be stable. We refer to [23, Sec. II-A] for a review of state–of–the-art methods for assessing stability of piecewise–linear systems, and provide an example test below.

Since P is PC^r, there exists a finite collection $\{P_\omega\}_{\omega\in\Omega}$ of C^r selection functions for P, and we assume the neighborhood V was chosen sufficiently small that $P_\omega : V \to S$ for each $\omega \in \Omega$. Let $R_\omega \subset V$ denote the region where the selection function P_ω is *active* (i.e. where $P|_{R_\omega} = P_\omega|_{R_\omega}$). The first order approximation for P_ω is given by the classical (Jacobian/Fréchet) derivative $DP_\omega : TV \to TS$, which can be calculated using the (classical) chain rule. If there is a norm $\|\cdot\| : \mathbb{R}^{2d-1} \to \mathbb{R}$ with respect to which $DP_\omega(\rho, \dot{\rho})$ is a contraction for all $\omega \in \Omega$ (i.e. for all $\omega \in \Omega$ the induced norm $\|DP_\omega(\rho, \dot{\rho})\| < 1$), then the periodic orbit $\phi^{(\rho,\dot{\rho})}$ is exponentially stable [7, Prop. 15]. (Note that it does not suffice to find a different norm $\|\cdot\|_\omega$ for each $\omega \in \Omega$ with respect to which $DP_\omega(\rho, \dot{\rho})$ is a contraction [3, Ex. 2.1].) If instead for some $\omega \in \Omega$ there exists an eigenvector ν for $DP_\omega(\rho, \dot{\rho})$ with eigenvalue λ such that $|\lambda| > 1$ and $\nu \in R_\omega$, then $(\rho, \dot{\rho})$ is exponentially unstable; this instability test is illustrated in Fig. 4.

6.3 Assessing controllability

In this section we consider the problem of assessing (*small–time, local* [35]) controllability along a trajectory in a mechanical system subject to unilateral constraints. The local control problem has been solved quite satisfactorily along trajectories in such systems that undergo constraint activation and deactivation at distinct instants in time for cases where the control input influences the discrete–time [24] or continuous–time [29] portions of (1). We concern ourselves here with the controlled dynamics in (28), and focus our attention on trajectories that activate and/or deactivate multiple constraints simultaneously since (to the best of our knowledge) this case has not previously been addressed in the literature.

Toward that end, let $\widetilde{\phi} : \widetilde{\mathfrak{F}} \to TA$ be the flow of (28) (a mechanical system subject to unilateral constraints with input parameter $u \in U = \mathbb{R}^m$), and let $\widetilde{\phi}^{((\rho,\dot{\rho}),\mu)}$ be a trajectory initialized at $(\rho, \dot{\rho}) \in TA$ with input parameter $\mu \in U$. If $\widetilde{\phi}$ were C^1 at $(t, (\rho, \dot{\rho}), \mu) \in \widetilde{\mathfrak{F}}$, then (small–time) local controllability about $\widetilde{\phi}^{((\rho,\dot{\rho}),\mu)}$ could be determined using an invertibility condition on the (Jacobian) matrix $D\widetilde{\phi}(t, (\rho, \dot{\rho}), \mu)$. Indeed, a straightforward application of the Implicit Function Theorem [20, Thm. C.40] shows that if the subblock $D_U\widetilde{\phi}(t, (\rho, \dot{\rho}), \mu)$, which transforms first–order variations in the input parameter u into the resulting first–order variations in the state $(q, \dot{q})$ at time t, is invertible, then (28) is (small–time) locally controllable along $\widetilde{\phi}^{((\rho,\dot{\rho}),\mu)}$ [21, Thm. 8].[21]

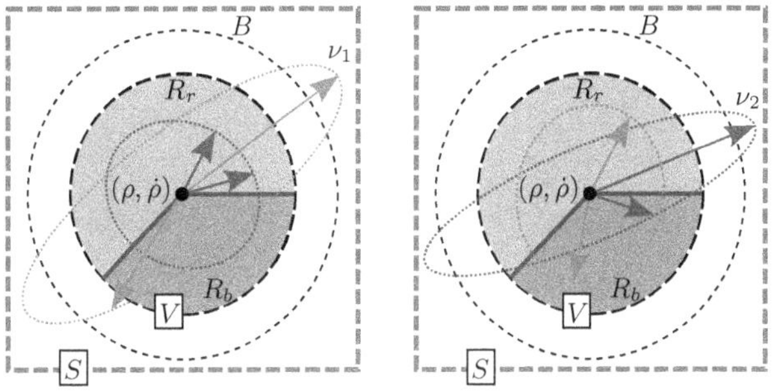

Figure 4: A Poincaré section S (outer grey box) and the neighborhood V (inner circle) containing $(\rho, \dot{\rho})$ over which the piecewise–differentiable Poincaré (or first–return) map $P : V \to S$ is defined. In this example: the set $\Omega = \{b, r\}$ indexes the colored (blue,red) region $R_\omega \subset V$ where the selection function P_ω is active for $\omega \in \Omega$; $B \subset S$ is the unit ball centered at $(\rho, \dot{\rho})$; dotted ellipses indicate unit balls transformed by the respective selection functions; and arrows indicate the principle axes of these ellipses. (*left*) P is exponentially unstable since the eigenvector ν_1 of DP_r has an eigenvalue $\lambda > 1$ and $\nu_1 \in R_r$. (*right*) The given instability check from Sec. 6.2 is inconclusive since there is no $\omega \in \Omega$ and eigenvector ν of DP_ω, for which $\nu \in R_\omega$ and $\|DP_\omega(\rho, \dot{\rho})\nu\| > 1$. Although the eigenvector v_2 of DP_b has eigenvalue $\lambda > 1$, v_2 is not active, i.e. $v_2 \notin R_b$.

In contrast to the preceding discussion, suppose now that $\widetilde{\phi}^{((\rho,\dot{\rho}),\mu)}$ undergoes simultaneous constraint activations in the time interval $(0, t) \subset [0, \infty)$. In this case $\widetilde{\phi}$ will not be C^1 at $(t, (\rho, \dot{\rho}), \mu)$, so the classical test for controllability is not applicable. If all constraint activations and deactivations are admissible for $\widetilde{\phi}^{((\rho,\dot{\rho}),\mu)}$ and nearby trajectories, then Thm. 1 (piecewise differentiability across contact mode sequences) implies that $\widetilde{\phi}$ is PC^r at $(t, (\rho, \dot{\rho}), \mu)$ and hence possesses a B–derivative $D\widetilde{\phi}(t, (\rho, \dot{\rho}), \mu)$, that is, a continuous and piecewise–linear first–order approximation. By analogy with the classical test [21, Thm. 8], a variant of the Implicit Function Theorem applicable to PC^r functions [33, Thm. 4.2.3] can be used to derive a sufficient condition for small–time local controllability along $\widetilde{\phi}^{((\rho,\dot{\rho}),\mu)}$: if the piecewise–linear function that transforms first–order variations in (an appropriately–chosen subspace of) input parameters u into the resulting first–order variations in the state $(q, \dot{q})$ at time t is a (piecewise–linear) homeomorphism, then (28) is (small–time) locally controllable along $\widetilde{\phi}^{((\rho,\dot{\rho}),\mu)}$.

7. REFERENCES

[1] M. A. Aizerman and F. R. Gantmacher. Determination of stability by linear approximation of a periodic solution of a system of differential equations with discontinuous right–hand sides. *The Quarterly Journal of Mechanics and Applied Mathematics*, 11(4):385–398, 1958.

[21] It will be useful in what follows to note that this invertibility condition is equivalent to the existence of a linear homeomorphism relating variations in (an appropriately–chosen subspace of) input parameters to variations in system states.

[2] P. Ballard. The dynamics of discrete mechanical systems with perfect unilateral constraints. *Archive for Rational Mechanics and Analysis*, 154(3):199–274, 2000.

[3] M. S. Branicky. Multiple Lyapunov functions and other analysis tools for switched and hybrid systems. *IEEE Transactions on Automatic Control*, 43(4):475–482, 1998.

[4] S. A. Burden. *A Hybrid Dynamical Systems Theory for Legged Locomotion*. PhD thesis, EECS Department, University of California, Berkeley, 2014.

[5] S. A. Burden, H. Gonzalez, R. Vasudevan, R. Bajcsy, and S. S. Sastry. Metrization and Simulation of Controlled Hybrid Systems. *IEEE Transactions on Automatic Control*, 60(9):2307–2320, 2015.

[6] S. A. Burden, S. Revzen, and S. S. Sastry. Model reduction near periodic orbits of hybrid dynamical systems. *IEEE Transactions on Automatic Control*, 60(10):2626–2639, 2015.

[7] S. A. Burden, S. S. Sastry, D. E. Koditschek, and S. Revzen. Event–selected vector field discontinuities yield piecewise–differentiable flows. *SIAM Journal on Applied Dynamical Systems*, 15(2):1227–1267, 2016.

[8] M. Di Bernardo, C. J. Budd, P. Kowalczyk, and A. R. Champneys. *Piecewise–smooth dynamical systems: theory and applications*. Springer, 2008.

[9] A. F. Filippov. *Differential equations with discontinuous righthand sides*. Springer, 1988.

[10] R. Goebel, J. Hespanha, A. R. Teel, C. Cai, and R. Sanfelice. Hybrid systems: Generalized solutions and robust stability. In *IFAC Symposium On Nonliear Control Systems*, pages 1–12, 2004.

[11] J. W. Grizzle, G. Abba, and F. Plestan. Asymptotically stable walking for biped robots: Analysis via systems with impulse effects. *IEEE Transactions on Automatic Control*, 46(1):51–64, 2002.

[12] J. Guckenheimer and P. Holmes. *Nonlinear oscillations, dynamical systems, and bifurcations of vector fields*. Springer, 1983.

[13] N. Hinrichs, M. Oestreich, and K. Popp. Dynamics of oscillators with impact and friction. *Chaos, Solitons & Fractals*, 8(4):535–558, 1997.

[14] I. A. Hiskens and M. A. Pai. Trajectory sensitivity analysis of hybrid systems. *IEEE Transactions on Circuits and Systems I: Fundamental Theory and Applications*, 47(2):204–220, 2000.

[15] Y. Hürmüzlü and D. B. Marghitu. Rigid body collisions of planar kinematic chains with multiple contact points. *The International Journal of Robotics Research*, 13(1):82–92, 1994.

[16] A. M. Johnson, S. A. Burden, and D. E. Koditschek. A hybrid systems model for simple manipulation and self–manipulation systems. *The International Journal of Robotics Research*, 35(11):1289–1327, 2016.

[17] K. C. Kiwiel. *Methods of descent for nondifferentiable optimization*. Springer, 1985.

[18] S. Kuindersma, R. Deits, M. Fallon, A. Valenzuela, H. Dai, F. Permenter, T. Koolen, P. Marion, and R. Tedrake. Optimization–based locomotion planning, estimation, and control design for the atlas humanoid robot. *Autonomous Robots*, pages 1–27, 2015.

[19] V. Kumar, E. Todorov, and S. Levine. Optimal control with learned local models: Application to dexterous manipulation. In *IEEE International Conference on Robotics and Automation (ICRA)*, pages 378–383, May 2016.

[20] J. M. Lee. *Introduction to smooth manifolds*. Springer–Verlag, 2012.

[21] A. U. Levin and K. S. Narendra. Control of nonlinear dynamical systems using neural networks: controllability and stabilization. *IEEE Transactions on Neural Networks*, 4(2):192–206, 1993.

[22] S. Levine, C. Finn, T. Darrell, and P. Abbeel. End–to–end training of deep visuomotor policies. *Journal of Machine Learning Research*, 17(1):1334–1373, 2016.

[23] H. Lin and P. J. Antsaklis. Stability and stabilizability of switched linear systems: A survey of recent results. *IEEE Transactions on Automatic Control*, 54(2):308–322, 2009.

[24] A. Long, T. Murphey, and K. Lynch. Optimal motion planning for a class of hybrid dynamical systems with impacts. In *IEEE International Conference on Robotics and Automation*, pages 4220–4226, 2011.

[25] J. Lygeros, K. H. Johansson, S. N. Simic, J. Zhang, and S. S. Sastry. Dynamical properties of hybrid automata. *IEEE Transactions on Automatic Control*, 48(1):2–17, Jan 2003.

[26] K. D. Mombaur, R. W. Longman, H. G. Bock, and J. P. Schlöder. Open–loop stable running. *Robotica*, 23(1):21–33, 2005.

[27] Y. Or and A. D. Ames. Stability and completion of Zeno equilibria in Lagrangian hybrid systems. *IEEE Transactions on Automatic Control*, 56(6):1322–1336, 2011.

[28] C. D. Remy, K. Buffinton, and R. Siegwart. Stability analysis of passive dynamic walking of quadrupeds. *The International Journal of Robotics Research*, 29(9):1173–1185, 2010.

[29] M. Rijnen, A. Saccon, and H. Nijmeijer. On optimal trajectory tracking for mechanical systems with unilateral constraints. In *IEEE Conference on Decision and Control*, pages 2561–2566, 2015.

[30] S. M. Robinson. Local structure of feasible sets in nonlinear programming, part iii: Stability and sensitivity. In *Nonlinear Analysis and Optimization*, volume 30 of *Mathematical Programming Studies*, pages 45–66. Springer Berlin Heidelberg, 1987.

[31] R. Rockafellar. A property of piecewise smooth functions. *Computational Optimization and Applications*, 25(1/3):247–250, 2003.

[32] M. Schatzman. Uniqueness and continuous dependence on data for one–dimensional impact problems. *Mathematical and Computer Modelling*, 28(4—8):1–18, 1998.

[33] S. Scholtes. *Introduction to piecewise differentiable equations*. Springer–Verlag, 2012.

[34] D. E. Stewart. Rigid–body dynamics with friction and impact. *SIAM Review*, 42(1):3–39, 2000.

[35] H. J. Sussmann. A General Theorem on Local Controllability. *SIAM Journal on Control and Optimization*, 25:158–194, 1987.

[36] E. D. Wendel and A. D. Ames. Rank deficiency and superstability of hybrid systems. *Nonlinear Analysis: Hybrid Systems*, 6(2):787–805, 2012.

Structural Analysis of Multi-Mode DAE Systems

Albert Benveniste
INRIA, Rennes, France
albert.benveniste@inria.fr

Benoît Caillaud
INRIA, Rennes, France
benoit.caillaud@inria.fr

Hilding Elmqvist
Mogram AB, Lund, Sweden
Hilding.Elmqvist@Mogram.net

Khalil Ghorbal
INRIA, Rennes, France
khalil.ghorbal@inria.fr

Martin Otter
DLR, Oberpfaffenhofen,
Germany
Martin.Otter@dlr.de

Marc Pouzet
ENS, Paris, France
marc.pouzet@ens.fr

ABSTRACT

Differential Algebraic Equation (DAE) systems constitute the mathematical model supporting physical modeling languages such as Modelica, VHDL-AMS, or Simscape. Unlike ODEs, they exhibit subtle issues because of their implicit *latent equations* and related *differentiation index*. Multi-mode DAE (mDAE) systems are much harder to deal with, not only because of their mode-dependent dynamics, but essentially because of the events and resets occurring at mode transitions. Unfortunately, the large literature devoted to the numerical analysis of DAEs does not cover the multi-mode case. It typically says nothing about mode changes. This lack of foundations cause numerous difficulties to the existing modeling tools. Some models are well handled, others are not, with no clear boundary between the two classes. In this paper we develop a comprehensive mathematical approach to the *structural analysis* of mDAE systems which properly extends the usual analysis of DAE systems. We define a constructive semantics based on nonstandard analysis and show how to produce execution schemes in a systematic way.

Keywords

Multi-mode systems, differential algebraic equations, DAE, differential index, structural analysis, operational semantics, nonstandard analysis

1. INTRODUCTION

Multi-mode DAE systems constitute the mathematical model supporting physical modeling languages such as Modelica. Multi-mode DAE models can be represented as systems of equations of the form

$$\begin{array}{ll} \text{if} & \gamma_j (\text{the } x_i \text{ and their derivatives}) \\ \text{do} & f_j (\text{the } x_i \text{ and their derivatives}) = 0 \end{array} \qquad (1)$$

where $x_1, \ldots, x_n$ denote the system variables, $\gamma_j(\ldots)$ is a predicate guarding the DAE $f_j(\ldots) = 0$. The meaning is

HSCC'17, April 18 - 20, 2017, Pittsburgh, PA, USA

© 2017 Copyright held by the owner/author(s). Publication rights licensed to ACM.
ISBN 978-1-4503-4590-3/17/04. . . $15.00

DOI: http://dx.doi.org/10.1145/3049797.3049806

that, if γ_j has the value true, then equation $f_j(\ldots) = 0$ has to hold, otherwise it is discarded. In particular, when all the predicates are the constant true, one obtains a *single-mode* DAE, that is a standard DAE defined by the set of equations $f_j(\ldots) = 0$. When the functions f_j have the special form $x'_j - g_j(x_1, \ldots, x_n)$, one recovers the usual Ordinary Differential Equations (ODE) system $x'_j = g_j(x_1, \ldots, x_n)$. DAEs are a strict generalization of ODEs, where the so-called *state variables* $x_1, \ldots, x_n$ are implicitly related to their time derivatives $x'_1, \ldots, x'_n$. Finally, our modeling framework is fully compositional, since systems of systems of equations of the form (1) are just systems of equations (with eventually additional constraints connecting the different state variables).

Solving numerically single-mode DAEs faces the well known issue of *differentiation index* [6], originating from the possible existence of so-called *latent constraints*. Informally, latent constraints in DAE systems are additional equations obtained from the original equations $f_j(\ldots) = 0$ by time differentiation, assuming the existence of smooth enough solutions for those extra equations to be well-defined. A DAE has differential index n if one or more equations must be differentiated n-times until the equations can be algebraically transformed to an ODE form with the x_i as states. In particular, ODEs are fully explicit differential equations and are therefore DAEs of index 0. In practice, systems with index greater than 1 are common (e.g., the DAE of a pendulum in Cartesian coordinates has index 3) and higher indexes are often encountered in common Modelica models. The *Structural Analysis* of DAE systems, such as the Pantelides algorithm [14], is an abstract lightweight graph-based analysis that constructively computes a "structural" differentiation index which can be formally related to the numerical differentiation index. Such structural analysis is often performed as a pre-processing step before calling numerical solvers.

Unlike single-mode DAE systems, however, no theory exists that supports the structural analysis of multi-mode DAE systems. The usual approach consists in performing the structural analysis for each mode. This, however, tells nothing about how mode changes could be handled. Even more so when mode changes occur in cascades.

Related Work: Multi-domain modeling languages that support DAEs such as Modelica or VHDL-AMS, but also proprietary languages such as Simscape have typically the restriction that the number of equations cannot change during simulation. Modeling tools have further restrictions, e.g. that the DAE index cannot change during simulation, or that impulses occurring due to mode switches are not supported. There are some proposals such as [11] that try to handle multi-mode DAEs by using source to source model transformations to bring the model in a form that is amenable to known structural analysis and index reduction techniques. The class of supported models is still however restricted, e.g., mode changes leading to impulses cannot be handled. On the other hand, there is a long tradition for mechanical systems to handle contact problems and friction which lead to mode changes, index changes and/or impulses. An overview of the actual state of the art is for example given in [15]. It is, however, not obvious how this domain-specific approach can be generalized.

To our knowledge, the only work addressing the structural analysis of multi-mode DAE systems is [13]. While this work contains interesting results regarding numerical techniques to detect chattering between modes, it assumes deterministic multi-mode systems where consistent resets are already known for each mode. Such assumptions do not hold in general, especially for a compositional framework where one wants to assemble pre-defined physical components. Besides, for complex systems, one often resorts to simulations to better understand resets and mode changes. In this work, we attempt to constructively build deterministic and causal execution schemes. In a sense, our analysis could be regarded as a pre-processing step to perform prior to simulating multi-mode DAE systems.

Contributions: In this paper, we consider systems of equations of the form (1) as a core framework for multi-mode DAE systems. This modeling framework is fully equational and compositional. We define a constructive (small-step) semantics for such framework by relying on nonstandard analysis [10, 1]. We handle in a unified way, discrete and possibly impulsive mode changes on one hand, and purely continuous evolution within one mode on the other hand. This makes it possible to formally define which systems a compiler should accept/refuse. We finally explain how to generate an execution scheme from the nonstandard constructive semantics. We illustrate the different steps of our analysis on a simple, yet challenging, example we explain next.

Detailed discussions and more examples are available in the companion technical report [2].

2. A SIMPLE CLUTCH

We consider a simple, idealized clutch involving two rotating shafts where no motor or brake are connected. The dynamics of each shaft i is modeled by $\omega_i' = f_i(\omega_i, \tau_i)$ for some functions f_i, where ω_i is the angular velocity, τ_i is the torque applied to the shaft i, and ω_i' denotes the time derivative of ω_i. Depending on the value of the input Boolean variable γ, the clutch is either engaged ($\gamma = \mathrm{T}$) or released ($\gamma = \mathrm{F}$). When the clutch is released, the two shafts rotate independently: no torque is applied to them ($\tau_i = 0$). When the clutch is engaged, it ensures a perfect join between the two shafts, forcing them to have the same angular velocity ($\omega_1 - \omega_2 = 0$) and opposite torques ($\tau_1 + \tau_2 = 0$). If the clutch is initially released, then at the instant of contact the relative speed of the two rotating shafts jumps to zero and, as a consequence, an impulse generally occurs on the torques. This idealized clutch model is not supported by the existing Modelica tools at the date of this writing—we later give explanations about what the difficulty is. The clutch model is summarized below.

$$\left\{\begin{array}{lll} & \omega_1' = f_1(\omega_1, \tau_1) & (e_1)\\ & \omega_2' = f_2(\omega_2, \tau_2) & (e_2)\\ \texttt{if } \gamma \texttt{ do} & \omega_1 - \omega_2 = 0 & (e_3)\\ \texttt{and} & \tau_1 + \tau_2 = 0 & (e_4)\\ \texttt{if not } \gamma \texttt{ do} & \tau_1 = 0 & (e_5)\\ \texttt{and} & \tau_2 = 0 & (e_6) \end{array}\right. \tag{2}$$

We first analyze separately the model for each mode of the clutch (Section 2.1). Then, we discuss the difficulties arising when handling mode changes (Section 2.2). Finally, we propose a global comprehensive analysis in Sections 2.3 and 2.4. For convenience, we recall basic notions of nonstandard analysis in Section 2.3.

2.1 Separate Analysis of Each Mode

In the released mode, when γ is false in System (2), the two shafts are independent and one obtains the following two independent ODEs for ω_1 and ω_2:

$$\begin{array}{llll} \omega_1' = f_1(\omega_1, \tau_1) & (e_1) & \tau_1 = 0 & (e_5)\\ \omega_2' = f_2(\omega_2, \tau_2) & (e_2) & \tau_2 = 0 & (e_6) \end{array} \tag{3}$$

In the engaged mode, however, γ holds true, and the two velocities and torques are algebraically related:

$$\begin{array}{llll} \omega_1' = f_1(\omega_1, \tau_1) & (e_1) & \omega_1 - \omega_2 = 0 & (e_3)\\ \omega_2' = f_2(\omega_2, \tau_2) & (e_2) & \tau_1 + \tau_2 = 0 & (e_4) \end{array} \tag{4}$$

Due to the additional constraints (e_3) and (e_4), System (4) is no longer an ODE, but rather a DAE. Notice in particular that the derivatives of the torques are not explicitly given and that the state variables ω_i have to satisfy the extra constraint (e_3) as long as the system evolves in that mode.

If one is able to uniquely determine the *leading variables* $(\omega_1', \omega_2', \tau_1, \tau_2)$ given a *consistent* value for the *state variables* (ω_1, ω_2), one could regard the DAE as an "extended ODE" [17] where an integration step is performed to update the current positions (ω_1, ω_2) using the computed values for their derivatives (ω_1', ω_2'). Here, by consistent values for (ω_1, ω_2) we mean a pair that satisfies (e_3).

It turns out that this does not work for System (4) as is. To intuitively explain what the problem is, we move to discrete time by applying an explicit first order Euler scheme with constant step size $\delta > 0$:

$$\begin{array}{llll} \omega_1^\bullet = \omega_1 + \delta \cdot f_1(\omega_1, \tau_1) & (e_1^\delta) & \omega_1 - \omega_2 = 0 & (e_3)\\ \omega_2^\bullet = \omega_2 + \delta \cdot f_2(\omega_2, \tau_2) & (e_2^\delta) & \tau_1 + \tau_2 = 0 & (e_4) \end{array} \tag{5}$$

where $\omega^\bullet(t) =_{\mathrm{def}} \omega(t+\delta)$ denotes the forward time shift operator by an amount of δ. Suppose we are given consistent initial values for ω_1 and ω_2 satisfying (e_3). Attempting to apply the Euler scheme (5) fails in that, generically, there is no unique values for the $\omega_i^\bullet$. Indeed, we have only three equations e_1^δ,e_2^δ, and e_4 for four unknowns, τ_1, τ_2, $\omega_1^\bullet$, and $\omega_2^\bullet$. However, since System (5) is time invariant, and assuming that the system remains in the engaged mode for at least δ seconds, there exists an additional *latent constraint* on the set of variables $(\omega_1, \omega_2, \tau_1, \tau_2, \omega_1^\bullet, \omega_2^\bullet)$, namely

$$\omega_1^\bullet - \omega_2^\bullet = 0 \qquad (e_3^\bullet) \tag{6}$$

obtained by shifting (e_3) forward. One can now use System (5) augmented with Eq. (6) to get an execution scheme for the engaged mode of the clutch (see Exec. Sch. 1 below).

Execution Scheme 1 System (5)+Eq. (6).

Require: consistent ω_1 and ω_2, i.e., satisfying (e_3).

1: `Solve` $\{e_1^\delta, e_2^\delta, e_3^\bullet, e_4\}$ $\triangleright$ 4 equations, 4 unknowns
2: $(\omega_1, \omega_2) \leftarrow (\omega_1^\bullet, \omega_2^\bullet)$ $\triangleright$ Update (ω_1, ω_2)
3: `Tick` $\triangleright$ Move to next discrete step

Since the new values of the state variables satisfy (6) by construction, the consistency condition is met at the next iteration step (should the system remains in the same mode). The implicit assumption behind Line 1 in Exec. Sch. 1 is that solving $\{e_1^\delta, e_2^\delta, e_3^\bullet, e_4\}$ always returns a unique set of values. In our example, this is true in a "generic" or "structural" sense,[1] because we are solving four algebraic equations involving four dependent variables.

Observe that the same analysis could be applied to the original continuous time dynamics (System (4)) by augmenting the latter with the following *latent differential equation*:

$$\omega_1' - \omega_2' = 0 \qquad (e_3') \tag{7}$$

obtained by differentiating (e_3)—since (e_3) holds at any instant, (e_3') follows as long as the solution is smooth enough for the derivatives ω_1' and ω_2' to be defined. The resulting execution scheme is given in Exec. Sch. 2 (compare with Exec. Sch. 1).

Execution Scheme 2 System (4)+Eq. (7).

Require: consistent ω_1 and ω_2, i.e., satisfying (e_3).

1: `Solve` $\{e_1, e_2, e_3', e_4\}$ $\triangleright$ 4 equations, 4 unknowns
2: `ODESolve` (ω_1, ω_2) $\triangleright$ Update (ω_1, ω_2)
3: `Tick` $\triangleright$ Move to next step

Line 1 is identical for the two schemes and is assumed to give a unique solution, generically. It fails if one omits the latent equation (e_3'). In Exec. Sch. 1, getting the next values for the ω_1 and ω_2 was straightforward. In Exec. Sch. 2, however, the derivatives (ω_1', ω_2') are first evaluated, and then used to update the state by using an ODE solver (here denoted by `ODESolve`). Note that, when considering an exact mathematical solution, if $\omega_1 - \omega_2 = 0$ holds initially and $\omega_1' - \omega_2' = 0$, then the linear constraint (e_3) will be satisfied for all positive time.

Exec. Sch. 2 is known in the literature as the method of *dummy derivatives* [12]. It requires adding the (smallest set of) latent equations needed for Line 1 of the execution scheme to become solvable and deterministic. The maximal amount of successive differentiation operations needed in obtaining all the latent equations is called the *differentiation index* [6], or simply the *index*. In Exec. Sch. 2, differentiating (e_3) once was sufficient. If, e.g., the second derivative of the state variables were involved in the system model, then, two successive differentiations would be needed. Observe that both execution schemes 1 and 2 rely on an algebraic equation system solver.

To conclude this section, we briefly discuss the initialization problem. Unlike ODE systems, the initialization problem is far from trivial for DAE systems, even more so when the state variables have to satisfy additional user-defined constraints. This is in fact often the case for multi-mode systems since the system has to start a new mode from a previously known state. For the clutch example, if one considers System (4) as a standalone DAE, the initialization is performed as indicated in Exec. Sch. 3.

Execution Scheme 3 Initialization of System (4)+Eq. (6).

1: $(\omega_1, \omega_2, \tau_1, \tau_2, \omega_1', \omega_2') \leftarrow$ `Solve`$\{e_1, e_2, e_3, e_3', e_4\}$ $\triangleright$ 5 equations, 6 unknowns

Observe that we have 6 unknowns and only 5 equations, so we are left with 1 degree of freedom—mathematically speaking, the set of all initial values for the 6-tuple of variables is a manifold of dimension 1. For example, one can freely fix the initial common rotation speed so that (e_3) is satisfied. Notice that the latent equation (e_3') is mandatory in order to determine the initial value of the torques τ_i.

2.2 Mode Transitions

In an attempt to reduce the full clutch model to the analysis of the DAE of each mode, one hopes that the handling of a mode change reduces to applying the initialization given in Exec. Sch. 3. If one was to treat resets at mode changes as initializations, it would mean that the clutch system is nondeterministic precisely because of the *extra* degree of freedom of Exec. Sch. 3. In contrast, the physics tells us that the state of the system should be entirely determined when the clutch is engaged after being released. This, therefore, comforts the intuition that resets at mode changes are not mere initializations.

If, however, one considers the known values of the state variables "immediately" before switching to the engaged mode, the system becomes over-determined as generically the equation (e_3) won't be satisfied. In this case, it is unclear what constraint should be relaxed and why.

This is precisely why this clutch model cannot be simulated as is with Modelica tools. A work around would be to compute and specify reset values by hand in the model. Such approach, however, impairs modularity since significant additional manual work is needed when building the clutch model from the two separate models for each mode.

We present next our approach to tackle such problems using nonstandard analysis.

2.3 Nonstandard Semantics

While the meaning of the clutch model in System (2) is fully clear when the system evolves continuously inside one of the two modes, the model does not say explicitly what happens at mode changes. We are in particular interested in two specific issues:

- (i) in case of discontinuous trajectories, what meaning one can give to the equations involving derivatives and what role those equations play in determining the discontinuity gap.
- (ii) if an event enables new constraints that make the system overdetermined, then what constraints one has to relax (and why) for the simulation to proceed.

To answer those questions, we use the *nonstandard analysis* [10] and in particular the nonstandard semantics of hybrid systems introduced in [1]. Nonstandard reals, a.k.a. hyperreals, denoted by $^\star\mathbb{R}$, extend the usual reals with *infinitesimals* and *infinite* numbers. A totally ordered field,

[1] See Section 3.1 for what is formally meant by "structural" in this context.

${}^\star\mathbb{R}$, could be constructed from the reals very much like $\mathbb{R}$ is constructed from the rationals using Cauchy sequences. A nonstandard real could be regarded as an infinite, not necessarily converging, sequence of real numbers. For instance, any real number a is a nonstandard real since it defines the sequence $\{a, a, a, \dots\}$. A hyperreal ε is said to be infinitesimal if $|\varepsilon| < r$ for all positive real numbers r. For instance, the sequences of $\{n^{-1}\}_{n\in\mathbb{N}^*}$ and $\{n^{-2}\}_{n\in\mathbb{N}^*}$ are (positive) infinitesimals.

Functions over the reals can be *internalized* as functions over the hyperreals by considering the constant sequence formed by the same function. If $x : t \mapsto x(t)$ denotes a function defined over $\mathbb{R}$, and $\partial = \{\partial_n\}$ denotes an infinitesimal then one defines ${}^\star x(t + \partial)$ as the infinite sequence formed by $x(t + \partial_n)$. To simplify the notations, we will simply write x instead of ${}^\star x$ whenever the distinction is clear from the context. We now formally define the immediate next value of a function we used earlier for the clutch example. Observe that such notion cannot be defined over the reals since bounded open sets do not have extrema over the reals.

DEFINITION 1 (FORWARD SHIFT). *Let x be a real valued function defined over $[t, s)$ for some $t, s \in \mathbb{R}$, $t < s$. Let ∂ denote a positive infinitesimal. We define $x^\bullet \in {}^\star\mathbb{R}$ as*

$$x^\bullet(t) =_{\text{def}} x(t + \partial) \ .$$

Observe that $t + \partial < s$ for any positive infinitesimal ∂ (by definition of the infinitesimals). Thus, for any positive infinitesimal ∂, one can find an equivalent positive infinitesimal such that almost all the elements of its sequence are in $[0, s - t)$.[2] Notice also that the definition of the forward shift is dependent on the infinitesimal ∂.

Solutions of multi-mode DAEs may be non differentiable and even non continuous at events of mode change. To give a meaning to the derivative x' at a point t of a function $x : t \mapsto x(t)$, we will define x' as the nonstandard difference quotient of x at t. For a fixed nonzero infinitesimal ε, the nonstandard difference quotient is formally defined as

$$\frac{x(t+\varepsilon) - x(t)}{\varepsilon} \ . \tag{8}$$

Such definition is motivated by the role the difference quotient plays in characterizing differentiable functions in the classical sense: a real (total) function f is differentiable at $a \in \mathbb{R}$ if and only if there exists a real number b such that

$$\frac{f(a+\varepsilon) - f(a)}{\varepsilon} \approx b$$

for all non zero infinitesimals ε (See for instance Proposition I.3.5 in [10]), where $u \approx v$ means that $u - v$ is infinitesimal.

In this paper, we restrict our attention to simulating the system when time moves forward. Thus, we consider that the system is at a known finite state and the goal of the simulation is to compute its next (in time) state, that is the next values of its state variables. This means that we can restrict our attention to right derivatives, and thus to positive infinitesimals in Eq. (8).

Substituting $x'(t)$ by the expression of Eq. (8), for a positive infinitesimal ∂, allows to extend the definition of the derivation operator even if x is non differentiable in the classical sense at t, in particular at events of modes change.

[2]We refer the reader to the companion report [2] for more details on the meaning of "equivalent" and "almost".

Notice that by doing so, one obtains a difference algebraic equations (dAE) system.[3]

Let us for instance examine the multi-mode dAE (mdAE) obtained from System (2) by replacing the ω_i' by their corresponding (positive) difference quotients for a fixed ∂:

$$\left\{\begin{array}{lll} & \frac{\omega_1^\bullet - \omega_1}{\partial} = f_1(\omega_1, \tau_1) & (e_1^\partial) \\ & \frac{\omega_2^\bullet - \omega_2}{\partial} = f_2(\omega_2, \tau_2) & (e_2^\partial) \\ \texttt{if } \gamma \ \texttt{do} & \omega_1 - \omega_2 = 0 & (e_3) \\ \quad\quad \texttt{and} & \tau_1 + \tau_2 = 0 & (e_4) \\ \texttt{if not } \gamma \ \texttt{do} & \tau_1 = 0 & (e_5) \\ \quad\quad \texttt{and} & \tau_2 = 0 & (e_6) \end{array}\right. \tag{9}$$

Following the reasoning of Section 2.1, one sees at once that within each mode, one obtains a discrete system very much like the explicit Euler scheme of Section 2.1, except that the step size is now infinitesimal and that the variables are all nonstandard reals. The crucial difference is that the nonstandard system will allow us to carefully analyze what happens at events of modes change. Recall that the state variables are ω_1, ω_2 whereas the leading variables are now γ, τ_1, τ_2, and $\omega_1^\bullet, \omega_2^\bullet$. Notice that we now add the guard γ to the set of leading variables. The rationale is that γ is an input variable and is not evaluated at the previous instant (unlike the state variables ω_1, ω_2). Since γ is a predicate, it must be evaluated first (causality principle).

Case 1. If γ=F, equations (e_1^∂), (e_2^∂), (e_5) and (e_6) are enabled, and can be evaluated, one at a time, in the following order: (e_5) sets τ_1 to 0; (e_6) sets τ_2 to 0; then (e_1^∂) is solved to compute $\omega_1^\bullet$; and finally (e_2^∂) is solved to compute $\omega_2^\bullet$.

Case 2. If γ=T, equations (e_3) and (e_4) become enabled with the notable difference that (e_3) involves the state variables ω_i (unlike (e_5) and (e_6) in the previous case where only the τ_i are involved). We discuss below the two possible subcases.

Case 2.1. If $\omega_1 - \omega_2 = 0$, then we are left with equations $(e_1^\partial), (e_2^\partial), (e_4)$ with dependent variables $\omega_1^\bullet, \omega_2^\bullet, \tau_1, \tau_2$, which brings us back to the underdetermined case we discussed about System (5): we add the latent equation $\omega_1' - \omega_2' = 0$, which, when transformed to its nonstandard form and simplified by (e_3), gives $\omega_1^\bullet - \omega_2^\bullet = 0$. Note that $\omega_1 - \omega_2 = 0$ provably holds if we were already in the same mode at the previous instant. Hence, this case gives the nonstandard version of the continuous evolution within the engaged mode.

Case 2.2. If $\omega_1 - \omega_2 \neq 0$, the system is overdetermined. A first idea would be to reject this model. This would be unfortunate as the original (standard) model seemed natural for the clutch. To overcome this issue, we defer the enabled equation (e_3) (which made the system overdetermined) to an immediate next instant $t + \partial$. This amounts to replacing the equation (e_3) by its forward shift $(e_3^\bullet) : \omega_1^\bullet - \omega_2^\bullet = 0$. By doing so, one hopes that the system recovers a consistent initial condition for the new mode in an infinitesimal time starting from its previous non consistent state.

The corresponding nonstandard execution scheme is summarized below (Exec. Sch. 4). We use the variable Δ to encode the *context*: that is the equations known to be satisfied by the state variables. At each tick, the context gets eventually updated to account for the equations that the new state satisfies. The procedure `Reset` solves the system

[3]Throughout this paper, we consistently use letters "D" and "d" to refer to "Differential" and "difference", respectively.

of equations in its argument to determine the reset values of the state variables (the computation is detailed next in Section 2.4). The procedure `Solve`, solves the (algebraic) system to determine the new values of the leading variables.

Execution Scheme 4 for Nonstandard System (9).

Require: ω_1 and ω_2.
if γ **then**
  if $e_3 \notin \Delta$ **then**
    $(\omega_1^\bullet, \omega_2^\bullet) \leftarrow$ `Reset` $\{e_1^\partial, e_2^\partial, e_3^\bullet, e_4\}$
    `Tick:` $\Delta \leftarrow \Delta \cup \{e_3\}$
  else
    $(\tau_1, \tau_2, \omega_1^\bullet, \omega_2^\bullet) \leftarrow$ `Solve` $\{e_1^\partial, e_2^\partial, e_3^\bullet, e_4\}$
    `Tick:` Δ unchanged
else
  $(\tau_1, \tau_2, \omega_1^\bullet, \omega_2^\bullet) \leftarrow$ `Solve` $\{e_1^\partial, e_2^\partial, e_5, e_6\}$
  `Tick:` $\Delta \leftarrow \Delta \setminus \{e_3\}$

Observe that Exec. Sch. 4 would work without changes if the guard γ was a predicate on the state variables ω_1, ω_2.

2.4 Standardization

Exec. Sch. 4 cannot be executed as is since it involves nonstandard reals. Thus, to recover executable code over the real numbers, a supplementary *standardization* step is needed. Recall that any finite nonstandard real can be written uniquely as a sum of a real number and an infinitesimal. For a finite nonstandard real x, we will denote by $\mathrm{st}(x) \in \mathbb{R}$ its real (or standard) part. The standardization procedure aims at recovering the standard parts of the leading variables from their nonstandard version. We distinguish two cases: continuous evolutions within each mode, assuming the sojourn time in each mode is not reduced to a single point, and discrete evolutions at events of mode change.

Standardization within continuous modes: If $x : t \mapsto x(t)$, $t \in [s, p)$, denotes the real continuous solution at a given mode, then, if it exists, such solution is in particular right differentiable for all t in $[s, p)$. Thus, for all $t \in [s, p)$, there exists a real number $x'(t) \in \mathbb{R}$ infinitely close to the difference quotient $(x^\bullet - x)/\partial$. In this case, we show that e_1^∂ and e_2^∂ standardize as e_1 and e_2 respectively. In addition, for the engaged mode, where the DAE has index 1, the pair $(e_3), (e_3^\bullet)$ standardizes as the pair $(e_3), (e_3')$. Thus, the (standard) latent equation (e_3') is recovered as expected.

Standardization at the instants of mode change: Suppose we have an event of mode change at time t, meaning that $\gamma(t) \neq \gamma({}^\bullet t)$.

For the clutch model, the transition $\gamma : \mathrm{T} \rightarrow \mathrm{F}$ does not result in an overdetermined system. Therefore, there is no need to compute any resets for this transition. Indeed, in this case, the standardization of the continuous released mode is sufficient. The transition $\gamma : \mathrm{F} \rightarrow \mathrm{T}$ is more involved. As established in Exec. Sch. 4, in order to compute the reset values, we use the system of 4 equations $\{e_1^\partial, e_2^\partial, e_3^\bullet, e_4\}$ to determine the leading variables $(\tau_1, \tau_2, \omega_1^\bullet, \omega_2^\bullet)$. In particular, from e_i^∂, we get

$$\frac{\omega_i^\bullet - \omega_i}{\partial} = f_i(\omega_i, \tau_i), \quad i = 1, 2. \tag{10}$$

Assuming $\omega_1 - \omega_2 \neq 0$, since $\omega_1^\bullet - \omega_2^\bullet = 0$ holds, the right difference quotient

$$\frac{(\omega_1^\bullet - \omega_2^\bullet) - (\omega_1 - \omega_2)}{\partial} = f_1(\omega_1, \tau_1) - f_2(\omega_2, \tau_2)$$

cannot be a finite nonstandard real because if it was, that would mean that the function $\omega_1 - \omega_2$ is right continuous which contradicts with the above assumption. Thus, the nonstandard real $f_1(\omega_1, \tau_1) - f_2(\omega_2, \tau_2)$ is necessarily not finite. However, we assumed continuous functions f_i and we started at a finite state (ω_1, ω_2). Thus, one of the torques τ_i is infinite at t. And because of equation (e_4), $\tau_1 + \tau_2 = 0$, both torques are in fact infinite. This informal *impulse analysis* can be formalized by abstracting variables by their *magnitude order* with respect to the infinitesimal ∂. For instance, the magnitude order of the finite hyperreals is zero, whereas the magnitude order of an infinite (or impulse) of the form $\partial^{-1} r$ for a finite non zero real number r is 1. (See Appendix A.1 for more details about the impulsive analysis).

It remains to compute the reset values for the state variables. To simplify our exposure, we assume that the f_i are linear in their arguments, i.e., f_i has the following form, where b_1 and b_2 are the inverse moments of inertia of the rotating masses and a_1 and a_2 are damping factors divided by the corresponding moment of inertia:

$$f_i(\omega_i, \tau_i) \quad = \quad a_i \omega_i + b_i \tau_i \ . \tag{11}$$

By symbolic manipulations, one finally gets

$$\mathrm{st}(\omega_i^\bullet) \quad = \quad \frac{b_2 \omega_1 + b_1 \omega_2}{b_1 + b_2}, \tag{12}$$

that is the weighted arithmetic mean of ω_1 and ω_2. Eq. (12) provides us with the reset values for the positions in the engaged mode, which is enough to restart the simulation in this mode. The actual impulsive values for the torques can be discarded. The above direct rewriting technique is limited to this linear case. We develop in Appendix A.2 a technique that applies whenever Taylor expansions are available for the functions f_i.

As a final observation, instead of computing the exact standard part of $\omega_i^\bullet$, one could instead attempt to approximate it by substituting ∂ with a small (but non infinitesimal) step size δ. It would then be interesting to study more in depth the numerical accuracy and convergence of such schemes. We leave this as a future work.

Figure 1 shows a simulation of the clutch model where the resets are explained above. One can see that the reset value is, as one may expect physically, between the two values of ω_1 and ω_2 when $\gamma : \mathrm{F} \rightarrow \mathrm{T}$ (at $t = 5$s), and that the transition is continuous at the second reset (at $t = 10$s).

3. STRUCTURAL ANALYSIS

The definition of an operational semantics of mDAE systems is a challenging problem. The root cause of this difficulty is that the classical structural analysis theory of DAE systems [6] does not apply because the set of active (or enabled) equations evolve over time when the system switches from one mode to another. In this section, we propose a novel approach to this problem, based on a formalization of the intuitions developed on the clutch example (Section 2).

As depicted in Figure 2, the method consists in several steps. The first step consists in transforming the mDAE system into a system of multi-mode difference Algebraic Equations (mdAE) using the nonstandard interpretation of

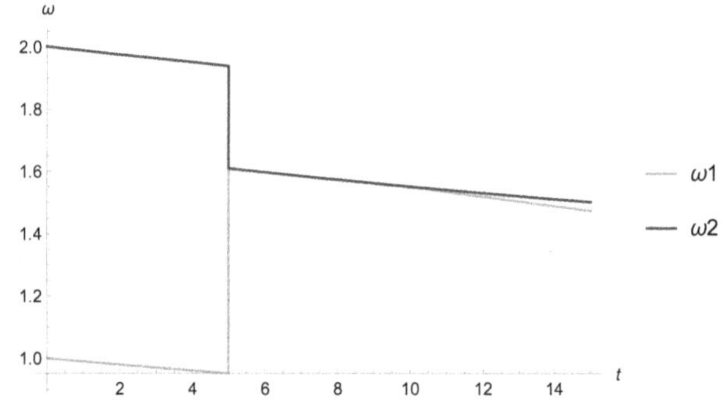

Figure 1: Simulation of the clutch model with resets. Mode change F → T occurs at $t = 5s$ and mode change T → F occurs at $t = 10s$.

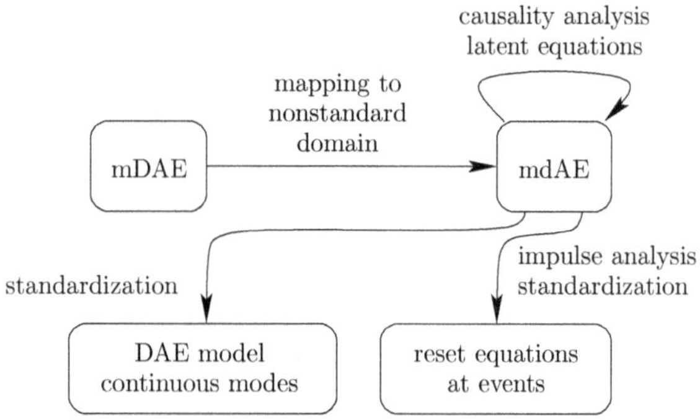

Figure 2: Structural analysis of mDAE systems.

the derivatives. The second step applies Algorithm 5 (See Section 3.3) to the mdAE system. The algorithm performs a structural analysis resulting in a new mdAE system where latent equations and a scheduling of blocks of equations are made explicit. The last steps are standardization steps, where the smooth dynamics in each mode, and the possibly discontinuous/impulsive state jumps occurring at mode changes are recovered from the latter mdAE system.

3.1 Structural Analysis of DAE Systems

As a background and to contrast the differences and the inherent difficulties of mDAEs, we first recall the structural analysis for DAE systems (single-mode) before extending it to the multi-mode case.

Consider a system of smooth algebraic equations with n equations and n dependent variables (unknowns) $y_1, \ldots, y_n$:

$$f_j(x_1, \ldots, x_m, y_1, \ldots, y_n) = 0, \quad j = 1, \ldots, n \tag{13}$$

rewritten as $F(X, Y) = 0$ where X and Y denote the vectors $(x_1, \ldots, x_m)$ and $(y_1, \ldots, y_n)$, respectively, and F is the vector $(f_1, \ldots, f_n)$. The Implicit Function Theorem (see, e.g., Theorem 10.2.2 in [7]) states that, if $(u, v) \in \mathbb{R}^{m+n}$ is a value for the pair (X, Y) such that $F(u, v) = 0$ and the Jacobian of F with respect to Y (denoted by $\nabla_Y F$) at (u, v) is nonsingular, then there exists, in an open neighborhood U of u, a unique set of functions G such that $v = G(u)$ and $F(w, G(w)) = 0$ for all $w \in U$. In words, Eq. (13) uniquely determines Y as a function of X, locally around u. Solving for Y, given F and a value u for X, requires forming $\nabla_Y F$ as well as inverting it.

Structural BTF decomposition: One could instead avoid forming $\nabla_Y F$ by focusing on its *structural* nonsingularity, which only exploits the incidence graph $\mathcal{G}_F$ of system F ($\mathcal{G}_F$ is the bipartite graph having $F \uplus Y$ as set of vertices and an edge (f, y) if and only if variable y occurs in function f). A square matrix is said to be *structurally nonsingular* if it remains almost everywhere[4] nonsingular when its nonzero coefficients vary over some neighborhood. It has been shown (see for instance [14, 12, 16, 17]) that the Jacobian $\nabla_Y F$ is structurally nonsingular if and only if there exists a bijective assignment $\psi : Y \mapsto F$ such that $(\psi(y), y)$ is an edge of $\mathcal{G}_F$ for every $y \in Y$. Having this bijection we turn $\mathcal{G}_F$ into a directed graph $\vec{\mathcal{G}}_F$ by fixing the orientation $z \to \psi(y) \to y$ for every $z \neq y$ such that $(\psi(y), z) \in \mathcal{G}_F$. The strongly connected components of $\vec{\mathcal{G}}_F$ are called the *blocks* of F and are independent from the particular choice for ψ. Blocks are partially ordered by the order induced by $\vec{\mathcal{G}}_F$. The set of blocks of F equipped with this partial order is called the (structural) *Block Triangular Form* (BTF) decomposition of F [8].

Index reduction: For DAE, determining the leading variables as functions of the state variables (assuming a consistent initial value) requires finding all the latent equations, until the augmented system becomes a *semi-explicit* DAE:

$$\begin{cases} X' = G(X, Y) \\ \;0 \;= F(X, Y) \end{cases} \text{with } \nabla_Y F \text{ nonsingular,} \tag{14}$$

so that the Implicit Function Theorem applies to F. The number of successive differentiations needed for getting this form is called the *differentiation index* [6] and the whole process is referred to as *index reduction.* Unlike ODEs, however, where the derivatives are explicitly given as functions of the state variables, simulating a semi-explicit DAE requires computing the Jacobian $\nabla_Y F$ and inverting it. Such computation will be performed eventually several times while searching for latent equations.

In practice, such brute force approach is ineffective and does not scale up. Tools handling DAE systems perform instead a *structural index* reduction, by exploiting the structural BTF decomposition of the involved Jacobians using the incidence graph of the system. The resulting procedure is called the *structural analysis* of DAE systems [14, 12, 17]. It may miss some numerical corner cases, but is computationally much more attractive than the full numerical approach. In the coming subsections we extend the structural analysis to multi-mode systems, by handling continuous modes and events with their resets as equal citizens.

3.2 Multi-Mode Systems

We now formally define the class of systems of multi-mode Differential/difference Algebraic Equations we are concerned with in this paper. Consider a finite set of variables X; for $x \in X$ and $m \in \mathbb{N}$, the m-differentiation and m-shift of x are denoted by $x^{(\prime m)}$ and $x^{(\bullet m)}$, respectively. Let $X^{(\prime m)}$ and $X^{(\bullet m)}$ denote the set of all $x^{(\prime m)}$ and $x^{(\bullet m)}$, for x ranging over the set X of variables. We define:

$$X^{(\prime)} =_{\text{def}} \bigcup_{m \in \mathbb{N}} X^{(\prime m)} \quad \text{and} \quad X^{(\bullet)} =_{\text{def}} \bigcup_{m \in \mathbb{N}} X^{(\bullet m)} \tag{15}$$

Definition 2. *A* mDAE *(*multi-mode DAE system*), resp.* mdAE *(*multi-mode dAE system*), s is a tuple of n*

[4]Outside a set of values of Lebesgue measure zero.

guarded equations:

$$\begin{array}{rcl} s & =_{\text{def}} & e_1, \ldots e_n \\ e_i & =_{\text{def}} & \texttt{if } \gamma_i \texttt{ do } f_i = 0 \end{array}$$

where: X is a finite set of variables; f_i is a smooth scalar function over $X^{(\prime)}$, resp. $X^{(\bullet)}$; γ_i is a predicate over $X^{(\prime)}$, resp. $X^{(\bullet)}$.

In a mDAE or mdAE, a *mode* is a valuation in $\{\mathrm{F}, \mathrm{T}\}$ of its guards $\gamma_i, i = 1, \ldots n$. In the guarded equation $(e_i) :=$ $(\texttt{if } \gamma_i \texttt{ do } f_i = 0)$, the equation $f_i = 0$ is enabled if and only if the guard γ_i holds. Otherwise the equation is disabled. Thus, a mode enables a subset of the equations $f_i = 0$ and disables the others.

A mDAE s_1 is transformed to an mdAE s_2 through the following syntactic transformation:

$$s_2 \quad =_{\text{def}} \quad s_1 \left[x' \text{ is replaced by } \frac{x^{\bullet} - x}{\partial} \right] \tag{16}$$

3.3 Constructive Semantics

The notion of constructive semantics was first introduced in the context of reactive synchronous programming languages [5, 3, 4], where it played an important role regarding causality and scheduling. Essentially, a constructive semantics for a discrete time dynamical system consists of:

1. A specification of the set of *atomic actions*, which are effective, non-interruptible, state transformation operations. Executing an atomic action is often referred to as performing a *micro-step*;
2. A specification of the correct scheduling of the set of micro-steps constituting a *reaction*, by which discrete time progresses, from the current instant to the next one.

The principle of a constructive semantics is to decompose a time step into a sequence of micro-steps. The effect of atomic actions is to propagate knowledge regarding the statuses (*not evaluated*, *evaluated*) and values of variables. For synchronous languages, atomic actions are restricted to either (i) the evaluation of a single equation, or (ii) control flow operations.

For mdAE systems, atomic actions comprise: (i) the evaluation of a guard; (ii) solving a block of numerical equations; (iii) equation management operations, for instance, adding a latent equation to a mdAE system.

Observe that solving systems of mixed logico-numerical equations, involving a combination of guards and numerical variables, is not considered as an atomic action. The constructive semantics presented in this Section, requires that the evaluation of a guard γ_i precedes the resolution of the equation body $f_i = 0$.

3.3.1 Abstract Domain, Statuses and Contexts

The structural analysis method is based on an abstract semantics, in which numerical values are ignored and no numerical computation actually takes place. Instead, the abstract semantics defines a computation as an evolving knowledge regarding the statuses of the guards, variables and equations of a mdAE, namely:

- A guard may be *not evaluated*, *evaluated to true* or *evaluated to false*;
- A variable may be *undefined*, or *defined*;
- An equation may be *not evaluated*, *disabled*, *enabled* but *not evaluated*, or *evaluated*.

Unlike mono-mode DAE, the set of equations describing the current status of an mDAE are mode related and evolve therefore dynamically. To capture this important fact, we tag as irrelevant all those equations that are not currently involved. Formally, the semantics defines computations in a partially ordered finite domain of values D:

$$D = \{\mathrm{I}, \mathrm{U}, \mathrm{F}, \mathrm{T}\} \quad \text{with} \quad \mathrm{I} < \mathrm{U} < \mathrm{F}, \mathrm{T} \tag{17}$$

The meaning of these values is as follows:

- The minimal element I is used to represent the fact that a variable, a guard, or an equation is irrelevant, that is not used to define the current status of the mdAE system.
- Value U means that a variable, guard or equation has not been evaluated yet. At the beginning of a time-step, only state variables are known, and all other variables are set to U, meaning that their numerical values are not known yet.
- Maximal element T has different meanings, depending on whether it applies to a variable, a guard or an equation. In the case of a variable, it means that the numerical value of the variable has been computed, whatever it could be. For a guard, it means that the guard has been evaluated to true. For an equation, it means that the equation has been solved.
- Maximal element F also has different meanings, depending on whether it applies to a guard or an equation. In the context of a guard, it means that the guard has been evaluated to false. When it applies to an equation, it means that the equation is disabled. Notice that this value does not apply to variables.

The constructive semantics defines the allowed micro-steps as a non-deterministic transition relation between abstract states, called *statuses*.

Definition 3 (Status). *The set V of* S-variables *is defined by*

$$V =_{\text{def}} \left\{ x^{(\bullet m)} \right\}_{x \in X, m \in \mathbb{N}} \cup \{\gamma_i\}_{i=1 \ldots n} \cup \left\{ e_i^{(\bullet m)} \right\}_{i=1 \ldots n, m \in \mathbb{N}}$$

A status σ is a valuation in D of the S-variables, that is a mapping $V \to D$. A status $\sigma : V \to D$ is said to be finite if it is almost everywhere equal to I. The set of statuses is partially ordered by the product order: $\sigma_1 \leq \sigma_2$ if and only if for all $v \in V$, $\sigma_1(v) \leq \sigma_2(v)$.

The partial order relation on statuses plays an important role to guarantee that knowledge increases at every micro-step of the semantics. This is ensured by the fact that the transition relation is strictly monotonous.

We define the incidence graph $\rho \subseteq V \times V$ of a mdAE system s as follows:

$$\begin{array}{rcl} \left(\gamma_i, x^{(\bullet m)}\right) \in \rho & \text{iff} & x^{(\bullet m)} \text{appears in } \gamma_i \\ \left(e_i^{(\bullet p)}, x^{(\bullet m)}\right) \in \rho & \text{iff} & x^{(\bullet m)} \text{ appears in } f_i^{(\bullet p)} \end{array}$$

Given a guard γ_i, $\rho(\gamma_i)$ is the set of variables $x^{(\bullet m)}$ appearing in γ_i. Given equation $e_i^{(\bullet p)}$, $\rho\left(e_i^{(\bullet p)}\right)$ is the set of variables $x^{(\bullet m)}$ appearing in $f_i^{(\bullet p)}$.

The constructive semantics follows a causality principle, namely that an equation can not be solved before its guard has been evaluated true. Similarly, a guard can not be evaluated before all its incident variables have been defined. This results in the following *coherence* property which is an invariant of the constructive semantics: A status σ is *coherent* if and only if the following properties hold:

$$\begin{aligned}\left(\gamma_i, x^{(\bullet m)}\right) \in \rho \text{ and } \sigma\left(x^{(\bullet m)}\right) \leq \text{U} &\Rightarrow \sigma(\gamma_i) \leq \text{U} \\ \left(e_i^{(\bullet p)}, x^{(\bullet m)}\right) \in \rho \text{ and } \sigma\left(x^{(\bullet m)}\right) \leq \text{U} &\Rightarrow \sigma\left(e_i^{(\bullet p)}\right) \leq \text{F} \\ \sigma(\gamma_i) \leq \text{U} &\Rightarrow \sigma\left(e_i^{(\bullet m)}\right) \leq \text{U}\end{aligned}$$

The constructive semantics must also take into account knowledge regarding the consistent initialization of the dAE system defined by the set of enabled equations in a given mode. This is the purpose of *contexts*, exemplified in Exec. Sch. 4 (Section 2). A *context*

$$\Delta \subseteq \left\{e_i^{(\bullet m)}\right\}_{i=1\ldots n, m\in\mathbb{N}}$$

is a set of equations. Given a context Δ, equation $e_i^{(\bullet m)} \in \Delta$ is assumed to be satisfied, as soon as its guard γ_i has been evaluated to true. In this case, the constructive semantics sets such an equation as being solved, without actually solving the equation. This means that the equation is treated as a redundant equation, that is known to be satisfied.

3.3.2 Constructive Semantics

Given a finite coherent initial status σ_0, and a finite context Δ, the *constructive semantics* of a mdAE system s is the set of the finite increasing sequences of statuses, called *runs*:

$$\sigma_0 < \sigma_1 < \cdots < \sigma_k < \sigma_{k+1} < \cdots < \sigma_K \qquad (18)$$

such that for every $k < K$, the pair (σ_k, σ_{k+1}) is a micro-step in the context Δ. A micro-step transforms status σ_k into status σ_{k+1} by updating the values of a bounded subset of S-variables, from U to T or F, or from I to U.

Enabled Sets, Shifting Degree and Leading Variables: Given a coherent status σ, $i = 1 \ldots n$, guard γ_i is *enabled in* σ if and only if for all $x^{(\bullet m)} \in \rho(\gamma_i)$, $\sigma\left(x^{(\bullet m)}\right) = \text{T}$. Given a coherent status σ, $i = 1 \ldots n$ and $m \in \mathbb{N}$, equation $e_i^{(\bullet m)}$ is *enabled in* σ if and only if $\sigma(\gamma_i) = \text{T}$. Denote by $En_\gamma(\sigma)$ the set of guards that are enabled in σ, and by $En_f(\sigma)$ the set of equations that are enabled in σ. Notice that for any finite status σ, these sets are finite. Denote by $Undef(\sigma) =_{\text{def}} \{v \in V | \sigma(v) \leq \text{U}\}$ the set of S-variables that are either irrelevant or undefined.

Define $d_\sigma^o(x)$, the *shifting degree* of x in σ, to be the least upper bound of the shifting degree m of all variables $x^{(\bullet m)}$ that are incident to an equation enabled in σ:

$$d_\sigma^o(x) =_{\text{def}} \sup \left\{ m \;\middle|\; \begin{array}{l} \exists i = 1 \ldots n, p \in \mathbb{N} \text{ s.t. } \\ e_i^{(\bullet p)} \in En_\gamma(\sigma) \text{ and } \\ x^{(\bullet m)} \in \rho\left(e_i^{(\bullet p)}\right) \end{array} \right\}$$

Notice that the shifting degree $d_\sigma^o(x) = -\infty$ if x is not incident to any enabled equation in σ. Furthermore, the shifting degrees in a finite status are bounded: given a finite status σ, there exists $N \in \mathbb{N}$ such that $d_\sigma^o(x) \leq N$ for all $x \in X$.

Given a status σ, the set of *leading variables* in status σ is the set of variables of maximal shifting degree that are incident to an enabled equation:

$$Ld(\sigma) =_{\text{def}} \left\{x^{(\bullet m)} \mid x \in X \text{ and } m = d_\sigma^o(x) \geq 0\right\}$$

DEFINITION 4. *A run $\sigma_0 < \ldots < \sigma_K$ is called* successful *if and only if in status σ_K is* successful, *that is all equations e_i have either the value* T *or* F *and no leading variable has the value* U. *The constructive semantics* succeeds *for an initial status σ_0 and context Δ if it has, for every mode, at least one successful run.*

When a run is successful, the system can proceed to the next time step, by executing a *Tick* micro-step, where, in a nutshell, time is advanced and defined variables are shifted. Algorithm 5 defines the computation of a micro-step from a given status σ and context Δ. To produce a run, Algorithm 5 should be iterated, until a *Tick* micro-step is performed. The different steps of the algorithm are explained below.

Algorithm 5 Computation of a Micro-Step

Require: a finite coherent status σ, and a finite context Δ
 return (updated) σ, Δ
1: **if** $Success(\sigma)$ **then**
2: $(\sigma, \Delta) \leftarrow Tick(\sigma)$
3: **else**
4: $F \leftarrow En_f(\sigma) \cap Undef(\sigma)$
5: **if exists** $B \in Blocks(F)$ **then**
6: $\sigma \leftarrow EvaluateBlock(B, \sigma)$
7: **else**
8: **if exists** $\gamma_i \in En_\gamma(\sigma) \cap Undef(\sigma)$ **then**
9: $\sigma(\gamma_i) \leftarrow$ T or F
10: $\sigma \leftarrow EvaluateRedundent(\gamma_i, \Delta, \sigma)$
11: **else**
12: **if exists** $e_i^{(\bullet m)} \in Overdetermined(F)$ **then**
13: $\sigma \leftarrow ForwardShift\left(e_i^{(\bullet m)}, \sigma\right)$
14: **else**
15: $L \leftarrow LatentEquations(F)$
16: **if** $L = \emptyset$ **then**
17: **fail**
18: **else**
19: $\sigma \leftarrow AddEquation(L, \sigma)$

The algorithm starts with a finite coherent status σ and a context Δ. The context Δ is the (possibly empty) set of equations known to be satisfied by the defined values in the current time-step. Notice that the context is updated at each *Tick*.

Line 1: Function $Success(\sigma)$ decides whether status σ is successful, according to Definition 4.

Line 2: If the status is deemed successful, a *Tick* micro-step is performed. This has the effect of shifting defined variables, and setting all other S-variables $v \in V$, either to U, if v is in the mdAE s, or I, otherwise. The new context is defined to be the set of equations that are known to be

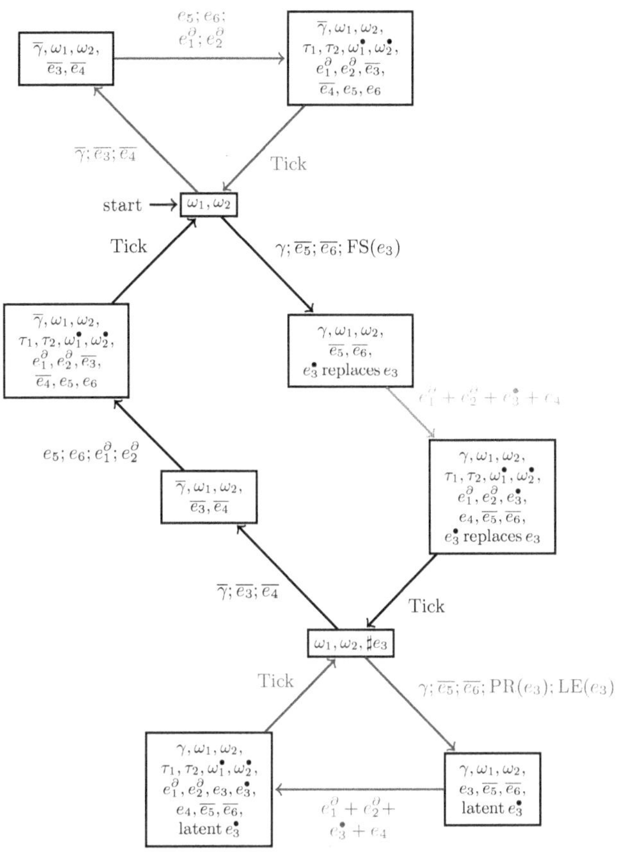

Figure 3: Constructive semantics of the Simple Clutch. Notations: For all statuses (shown in boxes), v (resp. $\overline{v}$) means $v = \text{T}$ (resp. $v = \text{F}$), and not mentioning v means $v = \text{U}$. $\sharp e$ means that e_f belongs to context Δ. FS(.) (resp. LE(.); resp. PR(.)) refers to line 13, forward shift (resp. 15, latent equation; resp. 10, redundent equations) of Algorithm 5. Blue (resp. black) transitions belong to a continuous-time (resp. discrete-time) dynamics. The red transition is impulsive. A semicolon is the sequential composition of micro-steps, and the $+$ sign denotes blocks of equations.

satisfied. Formally $Tick(\sigma) =_{\text{def}} (\sigma', \Delta')$, where:

$$\begin{array}{rcl}\sigma'(\gamma_i) & = & \text{U} \\ \sigma'\left(x^{(\bullet m)}\right) & = & \textbf{if } \sigma\left(x^{(\bullet m+1)}\right) = \text{T} \textbf{ then } \text{T} \\ & & \textbf{else if } x^{(\bullet m)} \text{ is a variable of mdAE } s \\ & & \textbf{then } \text{U} \textbf{ else } \text{I} \\ \sigma'\left(e^{(\bullet m)}\right) & = & \textbf{if } e^{(\bullet m)} \text{ is a variable of } s \textbf{ then } \text{U} \textbf{ else } \text{I} \\ \Delta' & = & \left\{ e_i^{(\bullet m)} \;\middle|\; \begin{array}{l} \exists j = 1 \ldots n, f_j \text{ is} \\ \text{syntactically identical to } f_i \\ \text{and } \sigma\left(e_j^{(\bullet m+1)}\right) = \text{T} \end{array} \right\}\end{array}$$

The system F is formed Line 4 by the enabled guarded equations in the status σ that are still undefined. By applying the procedure BTF (Section 3.1) to F one gets three distinct sets: $B_{\mathfrak{ns}}$, $B_{\mathfrak{o}}$, and $B_{\mathfrak{u}}$, the enabled, overdetermined, and underdetermined blocks, respectively. We further apply a post processing step to the standard BTF: for the overdetermined subsystem, we select a maximum square triangular submatrix and append it to $B_{\mathfrak{ns}}$ to obtain $Blocks(F)$ (Line 5).

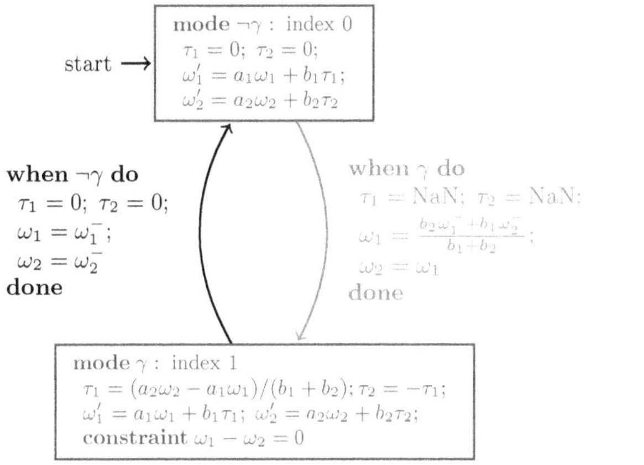

Figure 4: Standardization of the clutch's constructive semantics. Blocks have been standardized and then symbolically pivoted. x^- is the previous value of state variable x, which is the left limit of x when exiting a mode. Continuous-time dynamics are colored blue; non-impulsive (resp. impulsive) state-jumps are colored black (resp. red). The dynamics in mode $\neg\gamma$ is defined by an ODE system, while in mode γ, it is defined by an over-determined index-1 DAE system consisting of an ODE system coupled to an algebraic constraint. In the transition from mode $\neg\gamma$ to mode γ, variables τ_1 and τ_2 are impulsive, and their standardization is undefined. This explains why they are set to NaN (Not a Number).

Function *Overdetermined* (Line 12) returns what is left in $B_{\mathfrak{o}}$. For instance, for the system $F := \{f_1(x_1){=}0, f_2(x_1){=}0\}$, BTF gives $B_{\mathfrak{u}} = B_{\mathfrak{ns}} = \emptyset$ and $B_{\mathfrak{o}} = \{f_1{=}0, f_2{=}0\}$. We match arbitrarily either f_1 or f_2 to x_1. We therefore get $Blocks(F) = \{f_1{=}0\}$, and $Overdetermined(F) = \{f_2{=}0\}$. The impact of the different possible choices on the simulation of the system is left as a future work.

The procedure $\sigma' =_{\text{def}} EvaluateBlock(B, \sigma)$ (Line 6) updates the status σ to reflect that the undefined variables and equations involved in B becomes defined. Formally, for all $e_i^{(\bullet p)} \in B$, $\sigma'(e_i^{(\bullet p)}) = \text{T}$ and for all $v \in \rho\left(e_i^{(\bullet p)}\right)$, $\sigma'(v) = \text{T}$.

Line 8 selects one enabled but undefined guard γ_i, and evaluates it to T or F (Line 9). Both cases must be explored, and an implementation will fork two child Micro-Step procedures to explore the graph of all possible runs. Such implementation details are out of scope for this paper.

In Line 10, the context Δ is used to update the status σ. For the freshly evaluated guard γ_i, all its corresponding equations $e_i^{(\bullet m)}$ belonging to the context Δ are set to evaluated (T). Equations $e_i^{(\bullet m)} \notin \Delta$ remain unchanged.

Line 13: The algorithm attempts to relax an overdetermined system F by shifting one blocking (overdetermined) equation at a time.

Definition 5 (Structural Forward Shift). *The* forward shift *of equation* $e_i^{(\bullet m)} =_{\text{def}}$ `if` γ_i `do` $f_i^{(\bullet m)} = 0$, *is defined by* $e_i^{(\bullet m+1)} =_{\text{def}}$ `if` γ_i `do` $f_i^{(\bullet m+1)} = 0$ *where* $f_i^{(\bullet k)}$ *amounts to shifting forward k-times the arguments of* f_i. *Notice that only the body of the equation is shifted, not its guard.*

Line 15: Exhibiting latent equations is a classical task since we are just dealing with a dAE (difference Algebraic

Equation) system. We can, e.g., use the Pantelides algorithm [14] or the Σ-method of [17], which also identifies when the index is infinite. Indeed, the algorithm rejects models with infinite structural index (Lines 16 and 17). Intuitively, this problem occurs when exhibiting latent equations results in introducing at least as many extra variables as new equations making the perfect matching problem unsolvable in finitely many steps.

Line 19: The procedure *AddEquation* extends the support of the status σ with the finitely many extra latent equations in L such that the newly obtained status is coherent and $\sigma(v) > \imath$ for all $v \in L$.

Properties of the Constructive Semantics: Algorithm 5 is iterated in order to generate all possible runs, corresponding to the different modes of the system. This is done until all reachable pairs (σ, Δ) of statuses and contexts have been explored. As a result, we obtain the Constructive Semantics in the form of a graph **CS** having as nodes the different encountered status-context pairs and as edges the micro-steps. Elementary cycles of **CS** capture runs with stationary valuations of the guards and define the continuous dynamics in each mode. Other runs capture mode changes and their reset actions, we call them *reset runs*. Elementary cycles of **CS** containing at least two reset runs and having stationary assignments of the guards correspond to an execution looping forever, in an attempt to handle a mode change: a model exhibiting this situation is rejected—see [2] for a simple example.

In Figure 3, we depict the graph **CS** produced for the clutch example and Figure 4 shows the effective code resulting from the standardization of **CS**.

4. CONCLUSION

We propose a formal approach for the structural analysis of multi-mode DAE systems that extends and adapts the dummy derivatives method of [12]. We further complement our analysis with a standardization step leading, when successful, to execution schemes that could be used for numerical simulations. The use of nonstandard analysis was essential in defining an operational semantics when discrete events occur. We see our work as a generalization of adequate formalizations where only ODEs are involved [9].

We identified several interesting avenues for future work. In particular, we plan to work on generic standardization techniques to handle a larger class of problems. This is a crucial step for our structural analysis to be useful in practice. The exact computation of standard finite solutions has the advantage of giving exact reset maps at events of mode changes. It, however, requires symbolic manipulations and could therefore be computationally expensive. A viable and relatively cheaper approach would be to use numerical approximations where the infinitesimals are substituted by small real numbers. In this case, one has to rely on sufficient conditions to prove the existence of the standard solutions and to study further the accuracy and the effect of their numerical approximations on subsequent computations. We are also currently implementing Algorithm 5 to assess its performance on real case studies. The prototype will help us studying the confluence of local nondeterministic choices when handling overdetermined modes and, more importantly, their effect on the overall simulation.

5. REFERENCES

[1] A. Benveniste, T. Bourke, B. Caillaud, and M. Pouzet. Nonstandard semantics of hybrid systems modelers. *J. Comput. Syst. Sci.*, 78(3):877–910, 2012.

[2] A. Benveniste, B. Caillaud, H. Elmqvist, K. Ghorbal, M. Otter, and M. Pouzet. Structural Analysis of Multi-Mode DAE Systems. Research Report RR-8933, Inria, Feb. 2017.

[3] A. Benveniste, B. Caillaud, and P. L. Guernic. Compositionality in dataflow synchronous languages: Specification and distributed code generation. *Inf. Comput.*, 163(1):125–171, 2000.

[4] A. Benveniste, P. Caspi, S. A. Edwards, N. Halbwachs, P. L. Guernic, and R. de Simone. The synchronous languages 12 years later. *Proceedings of the IEEE*, 91(1):64–83, 2003.

[5] G. Berry. Constructive semantics of Esterel: From theory to practice (abstract). In *AMAST '96: Proceedings of the 5th International Conference on Algebraic Methodology and Software Technology*, page 225, London, UK, 1996. Springer-Verlag.

[6] S. L. Campbell and C. W. Gear. The index of general nonlinear DAEs. *Numer. Math.*, 72:173–196, 1995.

[7] J. Dieudonné. *Fondements de l'analyse moderne.* Gauthier-Villars, 1965.

[8] I. S. Duff, A. M. Erisman, and J. K. Reid. *Direct Methods for Sparse Matrices.* Numerical Mathematics and Scientific Computation. Oxford University Press, 1986.

[9] E. A. Lee. Constructive models of discrete and continuous physical phenomena. *IEEE Access*, 2:797–821, 2014.

[10] T. Lindstrøm. An invitation to nonstandard analysis. In N. Cutland, editor, *Nonstandard Analysis and its Applications*, pages 1–105. Cambridge Univ. Press, 1988.

[11] S.-E. Mattsson, M. Otter, and H. Elmqvist. Multi-Mode DAE Systems with Varying Index. In H. Elmqvist and P. Fritzson, editors, *Proc. of the 11th Int. Modelica Conference*, Versailles, France, Sept. 2015. Modelica Association.

[12] S. E. Mattsson and G. Söderlind. Index reduction in Differential-Algebraic Equations using dummy derivatives. *Siam J. Sci. Comput.*, 14(3):677–692, 1993.

[13] V. Mehrmann and L. Wunderlich. Hybrid systems of differential-algebraic equations – analysis and numerical solution. *Journal of Process Control*, 19(8):1218 – 1228, 2009. Special Section on Hybrid Systems: Modeling, Simulation and Optimization.

[14] C. Pantelides. The consistent initialization of differential-algebraic systems. *SIAM J. Sci. Stat. Comput.*, 9(2):213–231, 1988.

[15] F. Pfeiffer. On non-smooth multibody dynamics. *Proceedings of the Institution of Mechanical Engineers, Part K: Journal of Multi-body Dynamics*, 226(2):147–177, 2012.

[16] A. Pothen and C. Fan. Computing the block triangular form of a sparse matrix. *ACM Trans. Math. Softw.*, 16(4):303–324, 1990.

[17] J. D. Pryce. A simple structural analysis method for DAEs. *BIT*, 41(2):364–394, 2001.

APPENDIX

A. STANDARDIZATION

We mechanize below the manual reasoning performed in Section 2 for a larger class of continuous functions.

A.1 Impulse Analysis

The impulse analysis consists in abstracting hyperreals with their magnitude order (or simply "order") compared to the infinitesimal ∂. The order of the hyperreal x, denoted by $[x]$, is defined as the integer $n \in \mathbb{Z}$, if it exists, such that the standard part of $x.\partial^n$ is a nonzero finite real number. By convention, the order of 0 is $-\infty$.

For instance, the order of any nonzero real number, seen as a hyperreal, is 0. Multiplying x by ∂^m, for some integer m shifts $[x]$ by $-m$: $[x.\partial^m] := -m + [x]$. The order for a monomial function is given by $[x_1^{r_1} \cdots x_n^{r_n}] = \sum_{i=1}^n r_i[x_i]$. For a multivariate polynomial function, the order is the maximum of the orders of all its monomials with highest total degree, and, for a rational function $\frac{P}{Q}$, the order is $[P] - [Q]$. For instance, the order of a linear function $f(x_1, \ldots, x_n)$ is

$$[f(x_1, \ldots, x_n)] = \max_{i \in [1,\ldots,n]} [x_i] \ . \tag{19}$$

whereas the order of $f(x_1, x_2) := x_1 + x_1 x_2 + x_2^2$ is $\max\{[x_1] + [x_2], 2[x_2]\}$. We leave the general case for continuous functions as a future work.

We develop below the impulse analysis for the two transitions $\gamma : \text{T} \rightarrow \text{F}$ and $\gamma : \text{F} \rightarrow \text{T}$ of System (9) assuming linear f_i as in Eq. (11).

Mode change $\gamma : \text{T} \rightarrow \text{F}$*:* Recall that when γ goes from T to F, we obtain a system of 4 equations $(e_1^\partial, e_2^\partial, e_5, e_6)$ for 4 unknowns $(\tau_1, \tau_2, \omega_1^\bullet, \omega_2^\bullet)$ and we assume that the state variables ω_1 and ω_2 are known and finite. Thus, $[\omega_i] \leq 0$ (we use an inequality to take into account the special case $\omega_i = 0$, in which case the order would be $-\infty$). This yields the following abstraction ($i = 1, 2$):

$$\left\{ \begin{array}{rcll} [\omega_i^\bullet - \omega_i] & = & -1 + [f_i] & ([e_i^\partial]) \\ [\tau_1] & = & -\infty & ([e_5]) \\ [\tau_2] & = & -\infty & ([e_6]) \end{array} \right. \tag{20}$$

In (20), since f_i, $i = 1, 2$, are linear, $[f_i] = \max\{[\omega_i], [\tau_i]\}$ (cf. Eq. (19)), and therefore, $[f_i] \leq [\omega_i] \leq 0$. We are interested in the order of the difference $\omega_i^\bullet - \omega_i$, regarded as a single hyperreal. Eq. (20) thus gives $[\omega_i^\bullet - \omega_i] = -1 + [f_i] \leq -1 + [\omega_i] \leq -1$ and we conclude that the transition is continuous in ω_i.

Mode change $\gamma : \text{F} \rightarrow \text{T}$*:* Similar to the previous case, we also assume that the values of ω_i are known and are finite from the previous step. Thus $[\omega_i] \leq 0$. When γ becomes T, the new state may not satisfy $\omega_1 - \omega_2 = 0$, since $(eq_3^\bullet)$ was not active in previous mode ($\gamma = \text{F}$).

We eliminate, in the system of Line 3 in Exec. Sch. 4, $(eq_3^\bullet)$ and (eq_4) by setting $\omega^\bullet =_{\text{def}} \omega_1^\bullet = \omega_2^\bullet$ and $\tau =_{\text{def}} \tau_1 = -\tau_2$, which yields

$$\left\{ \begin{array}{ll} \omega^\bullet - \omega_1 = \partial.f_1(\omega_1, \tau) & (eq_1^\partial) \\ \omega^\bullet - \omega_2 = \partial.f_2(\omega_2, \tau) & (eq_2^\partial) \end{array} \right. \tag{21}$$

Using (19), the impulse analysis for the simplified system yields, for $i = 1, 2$:

$$[\omega^\bullet - \omega_i] = -1 + \max\{[\omega_i], [\tau]\}$$

At this point, two cases can occur: if $[\tau] \leq 0$, then $[\omega^\bullet - \omega_i] \leq -1$ for $i = 1, 2$, which is not possible since it would require $\omega_1 = \omega_2$, which does not hold in general. Thus, $[\tau] \geq 1$ and τ is impulsive. This implies $[\omega^\bullet - \omega_i] \geq 0$, expressing impulsive torques and discontinuous angular velocities.

A.2 Computation of Resets

In this section we mechanize the computation of the resets. We replace the manual rewriting used in Section 2.4 by a calculus on formal power series. In (21), we now regard the leading variables $\omega^\bullet, \tau$, as formal power series in the variable ∂^{-1}. The support of these series is determined by the impulse analysis developed in Appendix A.1:

$$\begin{array}{rcl} \omega^\bullet & = & \sum_{k=0}^{\infty} \omega_k^\bullet \, \partial^k \\ \tau & = & \partial^{-1} \sum_{k=0}^{\infty} \tau_k \, \partial^k \end{array} \tag{22}$$

where all coefficients $\omega_k^\bullet, \tau_k$ are finite. Using this expansion and the linearity of the f_i, (21) becomes

$$\sum_{k=0}^{\infty} \omega_k^\bullet \, \partial^k - \omega_1 = \partial. \left(a_1\omega_1 + b_1 \left(\partial^{-1} \sum_{k=0}^{\infty} \tau_k \, \partial^k \right) \right)$$
$$\sum_{k=0}^{\infty} \omega_k^\bullet \, \partial^k - \omega_2 = \partial. \left(a_2\omega_2 - b_2 \left(\partial^{-1} \sum_{k=0}^{\infty} \tau_k \, \partial^k \right) \right)$$

We standardize this system by keeping only the dominant terms:

$$\left\{ \begin{array}{rcl} \omega_0^\bullet - \omega_1 & = & b_1\tau_0 \\ \omega_0^\bullet - \omega_2 & = & -b_2\tau_0 \end{array} \right. \tag{23}$$

It remains to solve this system for the standard variables (coefficients) $\omega_0^\bullet, \tau_0$). Thus,

$$\omega_0^\bullet = \frac{b_2\omega_1 + b_1\omega_2}{b_1 + b_2} \tag{24}$$

and our analysis is complete.

Dividing the value τ_0 for the solution of (23) by the actual (non infinitesimal) step size δ used, yields an estimate of the Dirac impulse for the torque, integrated over the time interval of length δ. It would be interesting to study the accuracy of this estimate.

Bipedal Robotic Running with DURUS-2D: Bridging the Gap between Theory and Experiment *

Wen-Loong Ma
California Institute of Technology
Pasadena, CA
wma@caltech.edu

Shishir Kolathaya
California Institute of Technology
Pasadena, CA
sny@caltech.edu

Eric R. Ambrose
California Institute of Technology
Pasadena, CA
eambrose@caltech.edu

Christian M. Hubicki
Georgia Institute of Technology
Atlanta, GA
chubicki6@gatech.edu

Aaron D. Ames
California Institute of Technology
Pasadena, CA
ames@cds.caltech.edu

ABSTRACT

Bipedal robotic running remains a challenging benchmark in the field of control and robotics because of its highly dynamic nature and necessarily underactuated hybrid dynamics. Previous results have achieved bipedal running experimentally with a combination of theoretical results and heuristic application thereof. In particular, formal analysis of the hybrid system stability is given based on a theoretical model, but due to the gap between theoretical concepts and experimental reality, extensive tuning is necessary to achieve experimental success. In this paper, we present a formal approach to bridge this gap, starting from theoretical gait generation to a provably stable control implementation, resulting in bipedal robotic running. We first use a large-scale optimization to generate an energy-efficient running gait, subject to hybrid zero dynamics conditions and feasibility constraints which incorporate practical limitations of the robot model based on physical conditions. The stability of the gait is formally guaranteed in the hybrid system model with an input to state stability (ISS) based control law. This implementation improves the stability under practical control limitations of the system. Finally, the methodology is experimentally realized on the planar spring-legged bipedal robot, DURUS-2D, resulting in sustainable running at 1.75 m/s. The paper, therefore, presents a formal method that takes the first step toward bridging the gap between theory and experiment.

*This research is supported by NSF CPS Grant CNS-1239055 and NRI Grant IIS-1526519.

HSCC'17, April 18-20, 2017, Pittsburgh, PA, USA
© 2017 ACM. ISBN 978-1-4503-4590-3/17/04... $15.00
DOI: http://dx.doi.org/10.1145/3049797.3049823

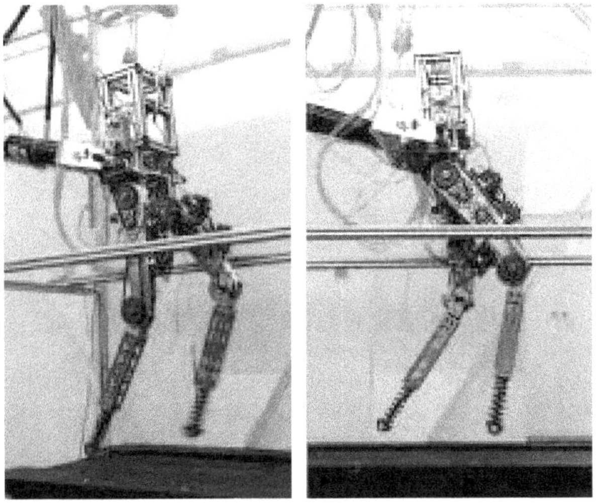

Figure 1: The spring-legged planar running biped, DURUS-2D, during take off (left) and while airborne (right).

CCS Concepts

•Theory of computation → Numeric approximation algorithms; Convex optimization; •Computer systems organization → Robotic control; •Applied computing → *Physical sciences and engineering;*

Keywords

Bipedal running; multi-domain hybrid systems; hybrid zero dynamics; nonlinear programming; input to state stability.

1. INTRODUCTION

The task of controlling bipedal robot is often a precarious balance between maintaining formal stability guarantees and expanding control capabilities. This duality has been present since the genesis of bipedal control. Beginning in the 1960's, Zero Moment Point [29] methods were the original foundation of formal biped control, but its validity required significant restrictions on the dynamics of the robot (fully-actuated flat-footed contact). In contrast, the

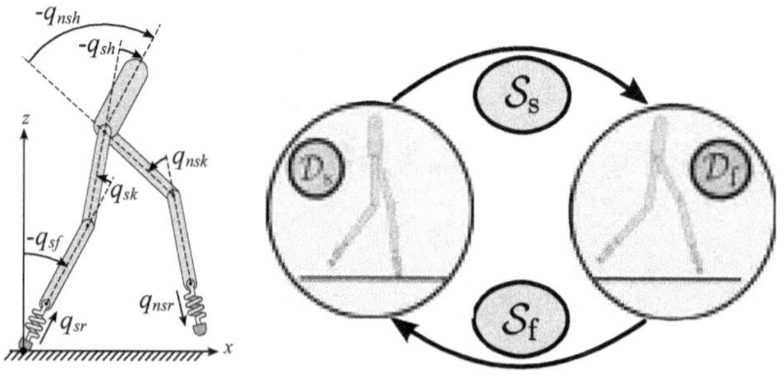

(a) (b)

Figure 2: (a) The model of DURUS-2D with two linear springs; (b) The directed cycle structure of the multi-domain hybrid system model for DURUS-2D running.

Raibert hoppers [22] exhibited agile bounces and flips that remain impressive today. But their control was built without the *a priori* confidence of formal methods. Research over the following decades has considerably narrowed this formality gap, with formal approaches rising to the challenge of underactuation [18, 21, 27, 12] and highly dynamic robots incorporating formal analysis in their control [7, 24].

Bipedal robotic running, despite the 30 years that have passed since the Raibert's hopper, remains an extremely difficult control problem. Very few control methodologies have been presented that lead to experimental success with prominent aerial phases [28, 22, 27]. With an eye toward viewing bipedal running as a hybrid dynamical system: an alternating sequence of stance and flight domains with instantaneous impacts in between, the notion of hybrid zero dynamics (HZD) was used in [10, 5, 19].

HZD operates on a principle of dimensional reduction, aimed at simplifying the numerous degrees of freedom present in legged machines, while also allowing for underactuation. This framework was used to enable bipedal running on MABEL [27], a pivotal demonstration showing the intersection of theory and experiment. However, on top of the HZD framework used on MABEL, there are also important expert-driven adjustments to the implementation, like tuning of control loops, adding feedforward trajectories, and on-line parameter update routines. One way to interpret this is: the gap between the assumed model and the experimental testbed necessitated modifications in the control implementation that is needed to realize stable robotic running. Similar modifications have been used previously for robotic walking implementations [20, 26, 14]. We seek to further reduce the need for this expert adjustment with formal stabilizing controllers.

There are two main central principles underlying our approach: a) gait synthesis via an optimization method, b) controller design that yields formal guarantees of robustness. We use a direct collocation based optimization method coupled with HZD constraints to generate running gaits on the spring-legged robot, DURUS-2D (Fig. 1). This nonlinear programming is notably fast, capable of generating a feasible running gait within a minute that satisfies all physical limitations of the running dynamics. However, the resulting gait that was built upon an ideal model and precise sensing cannot guarantee experimental realization. Unlike theoretical simulation, where most variables are either measurable or exclusively solvable, real world experiments suffer from a wide array of uncertainties. Indeed, uncertainties like unmodeled dynamics, nonlinear stiffness properties, damping effects and actuators, poor signal to noise ratio, and even deformations due to impacts are often observed. Therefore, we not only seek a fast optimization approach that yields feasible solutions under the assumed model, but also seek a controller formally guaranteeing robustness under real-world constraints. In this paper, we use the notion of *input to state stability* (ISS) that captures the practical limitations of the actuator inputs in an elegant manner. Specifically we address the *phase* based uncertainty that are typically a high deterrence in tracking parameterized functions. Similar problems involving inaccurate phase determinations were solved in [16], where pure time based parameterizations were used. But this paper will construct time+state based parameterizations to yield stronger stability conditions. Note that, in order to realize running, a variety of uncertainties need to be considered. So we will use the solutions from [15, 6] to account for the remaining uncertainties.

The paper is structured as follows. Section 2 introduces the HZD framework in the context of running, and the direct collocation based optimization method to generate running gaits (outputs). Next, Section 3 introduces a state+time based controller for driving these outputs to zero. By using the notion of ISS criterion for hybrid systems, we establish ultimate boundedness and also realize robust variants of the controller [16]. Finally in Section 4, 5, an experimental implementation is explained in detail, together with some simulated results where similar uncertainty was added to the model. The result is a stable, sustainable and agile running on DURUS-2D at 1.75 m/s, with a notable ground clearance and 60% aerial phase. We believe that this successful hardware implementation, which matches simulation results, indicates an important step toward bridging the gap between theory and experiment.

2. HZD GAIT GENERATION

In this section, we will introduce the hybrid model of the bipedal running robot, DURUS-2D (Fig. 1). This is the planar version of the three-dimensional DURUS humanoid robot designed and built by SRI International with the objective of achieving dynamic multi-domain underactuated locomotion [13, 9] with special emphasis on energy efficiency. But in the context of running, we will take our first step by investigating the characteristics of 2D robots.

2.1 Hybrid Model of Running

Model Configuration. As shown in Fig. 2a, the configuration space $\mathbb{Q} \subset \mathbb{R}^n$, $n = 9$, of DURUS-2D is defined as $q = (sf_x, sf_z, \theta_{sf}, r_{sp}, \theta_{sk}, \theta_{sh}, \theta_{nsh}, \theta_{nsk}, r_{nsp})^T \in \mathbb{Q}$, where sf_x and sf_z are the positions of the end points of the stance foot along x and z directions, r_{sp}, r_{nsp} are the deflections of the springs on stance and nonstance legs, $\theta_\square$ are the joint angles of the stance foot, stance knee, stance hip, nonstance hip and nonstance knee. In addition, the control inputs are defined as $u = (u_{sk}, u_{sh}, u_{nsh}, u_{nsk})^T \in \mathbb{R}^k$, $k = 4$, which represent the torque applied at knee and hip joints.

Hybrid System Model. Bipedal robotic running is represented by a special class of hybrid systems: systems with impulse effects. They can be represented by a tuple:

$$\mathscr{H} = (\mathcal{D}, S, \mathcal{U}, \Delta, \mathcal{FG}).$$

Here, $\mathcal{D} = \{\mathcal{D}_\mathrm{s}, \mathcal{D}_\mathrm{f}\}$ is the set of domains which are the sets of possible states assumed by the robot. For running, we have the stance domain $\mathcal{D}_{\mathrm{s}}$, where only stance foot is on the ground; and the flight domain $\mathcal{D}_{\mathrm{f}}$, where both feet are swinging in the air (see Fig. 2b). The set of guards $S = \{S_{\mathrm{s}}, S_{\mathrm{f}}\}$ represent the switching surfaces, which are states of the robot at transition. Possible guards are the transition from stance to flight domain: S_{s}, and the transition from flight to stance domain: S_{f}. Besides, $\mathcal{U}$ is the set of admissible inputs, Δ is the set of switching functions, called impact maps and finally $\mathcal{FG}$ is the set of fields yielding the continuous dynamics. A mathematical representation of the hybrid system in terms of output dynamics will be given in Section 3.3.

Continuous Dynamics. The Equation of Motion (EOM) over a continuous domain $\mathcal{D}_v$, $v \in \{\mathrm{s},\mathrm{f}\}$, is determined by the Euler-Lagrange equation and holonomic constraints [11]:

$$\begin{aligned} D(q)\ddot{q} + H(q,\dot{q}) &= Bu + J_v^T(q)F_v, \\ J_v(q)\ddot{q} + \dot{J}_v(q,\dot{q})\dot{q} &= 0, \end{aligned} \tag{1}$$

where $D(q) \in \mathbb{R}^{n\times n}$ is the inertia matrix, $H(q,\dot{q}) \in \mathbb{R}^n$ contains the Coriolis-centrifugal and gravity terms, $B \in \mathbb{R}^{n\times k}$ is the actuation distribution matrix, $J_v(q) \in \mathbb{R}^{n\times m}$ is the Jacobian of the holonomic constraints $\Gamma_v(q)$, and $F_v \in \mathbb{R}^m$ is a *wrench* containing the constraint forces or moments, which can be explicitly solved as a function of system states and inputs. The holonomic constraints for each domain are defined as

$$\begin{aligned} \Gamma_{\mathrm{s}}(q) &= \left(sf_x, sf_z, r_{nsp}\right)^T \\ \Gamma_{\mathrm{f}}(q) &= \left(r_{sp}, r_{nsp}\right)^T, \end{aligned} \tag{2}$$

meaning, the stance foot must remain on the ground during the stance domain, and stance and nonstance springs must be locked during the flight domain. More details about constrained dynamics can be found in [11]. Further, by defining $x = (q,\dot{q}) \in \mathbb{R}^{2n}$, the EOM can be converted to an affine control system:

$$\dot{x} = f_v(x) + g_v(x)u. \tag{3}$$

Discrete Dynamics. Because of the landing impact at the end of flight domain $\mathcal{S}_{\mathrm{f}}$, and the hard stop to prevent stance spring from further oscillation at the end of stance domain $\mathcal{S}_{\mathrm{s}}$, discrete dynamics are considered (see Fig. 2b). The discrete dynamics are determined by changes in the contact points of the system, for which only the velocity terms are affected through the plastic impacts by imposing the holonomic constraints of the subsequent domain. And the roles of the "stance" and "nonstance" legs are simultaneously swapped. Similar dynamics were detailed for walking in [4].

2.2 HZD control Framework

Virtual Constraints (Outputs). Any applicable state-based feedback controllers that have been applied on the control system, yield a closed-loop hybrid system [5]. This can be done by defining a set of outputs and applying feedback controllers to drive them to zero. In other words, we define the outputs (also often refereed to as the virtual constraints [20]) of the system on a domain $\mathcal{D}_v$, $v \in \{\mathrm{s},\mathrm{f}\}$ as

$$y_v(q) = y^a(q) - y_v^d(\tau_v), \tag{4}$$

where $y^a : \mathbb{Q} \to \mathbb{R}^k$ is the actual output of the system. Here, it is chosen as the four actuated joint angles:

$$y^a(q) = \begin{bmatrix} \theta_{sk} & \theta_{sh} & \theta_{nsh} & \theta_{nsk} \end{bmatrix}. \tag{5}$$

And $y_v^d : \mathbb{R}_{\geq 0} \to \mathbb{R}^k$ is the desired output represented by a set of 5th order Bézier curves $y_v^d = \mathcal{B}(\alpha_v, \tau_v)$ (the parameters α_v are solved by an optimization in Section 2.3). The *phase variable* τ_v is used to modulates the desired outputs y_v^d. Normally, in order to make the outputs purely state based, we can have the phase variable $\tau_v : \mathbb{Q} \to \mathbb{R}_{\geq 0}$, purely a function of the robot configuration:

$$\tau_v(q) = \frac{\theta_{sf} - p_v^+}{p_v^- - p_v^+}, \tag{6}$$

with p_v^-, p_v^+ the initial and final position of θ_{sf} for $\mathcal{D}_v$. Although, it must be noted that state based modulation has implementation difficulties due to noisy sensing of under-actuated degrees of freedom of DURUS-2D. This motivates the use of a time based phase variable $\tau_v : \mathbb{R}_{\geq 0} \to \mathbb{R}_{\geq 0}$,

$$\tau_v(t) = \textstyle\sum_{i=0}^{5} p_i t^i,$$

where p_i is a set of power series polynomial coefficients obtained by a curve fitting from $\tau_v(q)$ w.r.t. time. This has desirable stability properties under sensory perturbations, which will be discussed in Section 3.

State-Based Feedback Controller. To drive the virtual constraints (outputs) $y_v \to 0$ exponentially for each domain $\mathcal{D}_v$, we utilize the feedback linearization control law [3]:

$$u_v = \left(\mathcal{L}_g\mathcal{L}_f y_v\right)^{-1}\left(-\mathcal{L}_f^2 y_v + \mu_v\right), \tag{7}$$

with $\mathcal{L}$ the Lie derivative. Applying this control law yields the output dynamics $\ddot{y}_v = \mu_v$. Further, by picking μ_v as

$$\mu_v = -\frac{2}{\varepsilon}\dot{y}_v - \frac{1}{\varepsilon^2}y_v, \quad 0 < \varepsilon < 1, \tag{8}$$

the virtual constraints will converge to zero exponentially at the rate $1/\varepsilon > 0$. Since the number of virtual constraints is less than the degrees of freedom of the robot, the uncontrolled states evolve according to the *zero dynamics.* In other words, we have a set of states defined by the vector: $\eta_v = [y_v, \dot{y}_v]^T \in \mathbb{R}^{2k}$, that are controllable, and the set of states defined by z_v, that are uncontrollable and normal to η_v for each domain $\mathcal{D}_v$. We can then reformulate (1) to the following form:

$$\begin{aligned} \dot{\eta}_v &= \underbrace{\begin{bmatrix} 0_{k\times k} & 1_{k\times k} \\ 0_{k\times k} & 0_{k\times k} \end{bmatrix}}_{F} \eta_v + \underbrace{\begin{bmatrix} 0_{k\times k} \\ 1_{k\times k} \end{bmatrix}}_{G} \mu_v \\ \dot{z}_v &= \Psi_v(\eta_v, z_v), \end{aligned} \tag{9}$$

where Ψ_v is assumed Lipschitz continuous. The convergence of the outputs η_v can be shown in terms of Lyapunov functions: $V_\varepsilon(\eta_v) = \eta_v^T P_\varepsilon \eta_v$, where P_ε is the solution to the *continuous time algebraic Riccati equation* (CARE) (see [3]). By choosing $\mu_v(\eta)$ from (8), we have $\dot{V}_\varepsilon \leq -\frac{\gamma}{\varepsilon}V_\varepsilon$ with γ the constant obtained from the CARE. Note that in order to make DURUS-2D run experimentally, a time-based feedback controller is ultimately deployed, which will be explained in Section 3.

Hybrid Zero Dynamics. Given the control law (8), the controllable states η_v are driven exponentially to zero. In other words, the control law (7) renders the *zero dynamics surface* exponentially stable and invariant over both continuous domains [5]. However, due to the impact dynamics at the end of each domain, the invariance of the zero dynamics surface is not guaranteed. Therefore, the goal is to find a set of parameters $\alpha = \{\alpha_{\mathrm{s}}, \alpha_{\mathrm{f}}\}$, which defines the desired outputs (4), to ensure there exists a periodic orbit and the zero dynamics surface

$$Z_v = \{(q,\dot{q}) \in \mathcal{D}_v : y_v(q) = 0, \dot{y}_v(q,\dot{q}) = 0\}, \quad v \in \{\mathrm{s},\mathrm{f}\},$$

is invariant through impacts, i.e., hybrid invariant. Mathematically, hybrid invariance is represented as

$$\begin{aligned} \Delta(Z_{\mathrm{s}} \cap S_{\mathrm{s}}) &\subset Z_{\mathrm{f}}, \\ \Delta(Z_{\mathrm{f}} \cap S_{\mathrm{f}}) &\subset Z_{\mathrm{s}}. \end{aligned} \tag{10}$$

The process of finding α is often formulated as a nonlinear constrained optimization problem subject to the multi-domain hybrid system model. Details about the construction of HZD on walking robots can be found in [5].

2.3 Direct Collocated Gait Optimization

Once a hybrid control model is defined, a periodic running gait that can be implemented on DURUS-2D is needed. For this purpose, an optimization algorithm is utilized to determine the parameters α that guarantee HZD. Traditionally, *direct shooting methods* based nonlinear programming (NLP) is often used in bipedal walking [23, 5, 26, 30] and even planar running [31, 27]. However, its key methodology—numerical integration—has made it computationally expensive to solve for a running gait, due to the multiple degrees of underactuation involved in the multi-domain hybrid system. Therefore a *direct collocation method* based NLP is used under the HZD framework. Previously, this method has been applied to the humanoid DURUS to successfully achieve walking [12]. And an extensive study about this NLP on simulated 3D running is detailed in [17].

Essentially, we discretized each continuous domain $\mathcal{D}_v$ based on time t_v^i, where $i = 1, 2...N$ is defined as the grid index. Let x^i and $\dot{x}^i$ be the approximate states and its derivative at node i, the *defect constraints* at each odd node are defined as

$$\begin{aligned} &\dot{x}^i - 3(x^{i+1} - x^{i-1})/2\Delta t_v^i + (\dot{x}^{i-1} + \dot{x}^{i+1})/4 = 0, \\ &x^i - (x^{i+1} - x^{i-1})/2\Delta t_v^i + \Delta t_v^i(\dot{x}^{i-1} + \dot{x}^{i+1})/8 = 0, \end{aligned}$$

where $\Delta t_v^i = t_v^{i+1} - t_v^{i-1}$. Plus, $x^i, \dot{x}^i$ need to satisfy the dynamical constraints $\dot{x}^i = f_v(x^i) + g_v(x^i)u^i$, where u^i is exclusively solved by (7). In summary, the nonlinear dynamics are treated as an equality constraint with the use of implicit Runge-Kutta methods and *defect variables.* This modification also allows the analytical Jacobians of all optimization constraints to be pre-computed, which dramatically scales down the computation cost. This can also significantly increase the possibilities of finding a feasible solution to the nonlinear system.

Finally, the direct collocation based, constrained optimization can be stated as:

$$\mathcal{Z}^* = \underset{\mathcal{Z}}{\operatorname{argmin}} \sum_{v=\{\mathrm{s},\mathrm{f}\}} \mathrm{J}_v(\mathcal{Z}_v) \tag{11}$$

$$\text{s.t} \quad \mathcal{Z}_{\min} \leq \mathcal{Z}_v \leq \mathcal{Z}_{\max}, \tag{12}$$

$$\mathbf{C}_{\min} \leq \mathbf{C}(\mathcal{Z}_v) \leq \mathbf{C}_{\max}, \tag{13}$$

where $\mathcal{Z}_v$ is the set of all unknowns including the parameters α that define the running gait, $\mathrm{J}_v(\mathcal{Z}_v)$ is the objective function which minimizes the torque inputs. And $\mathbf{C}(\mathcal{Z})$ is a collection of necessary constraints, such as HZD constraints in (10). A major difference between walking and running, the foot clearance constraint for the flight domain, needs to be enforced on both feet to ensure the robot is in the air. More details about constructing other physical and geometric constraints can be found at [17]. By utilizing this NLP, we are able to generate a HZD running gait within 43 s from a initial guess at $\mathbf{0}$, whereas a direct shooting method could require hours of computation [31].

3. TIME BASED FEEDBACK

By using the feedback control law given by (7), (8), it can be shown that with sufficiently small ε, the output dynamics are exponentially driven to zero. In fact, [3] shows that by picking a *rapidly exponentially stable control Lyapunov function* (RES-CLF), locally exponentially stable hybrid periodic orbits can be realized. However in reality, due to the difficulty in estimating the phase variable (6) (which is a function of the unactuated degrees of freedom), a better controller is required that is less susceptible to the noisy state estimation. Motivated by the time based implementation of the tracking controller in [16], the goal of this section is to construct a controller that uses a time based instead of state based desired trajectory for robotic running.

3.1 Input to State Stability

Feedback Linearization for Time Based Outputs. For the ease of notations, we will omit the domain representations (the subscripts v) in this section. If the state based desired relative degree two outputs are functions of q, $y^d : \mathbb{Q} \to \mathbb{R}^k$, then the time based desired outputs are functions of time $y^{t,d} : \mathbb{R}_{\geq 0} \to \mathbb{R}^k$. We thus have the time based output representation as follows:

$$y^t(t,q) = y^a(q) - y^{t,d}(\tau(t)). \tag{14}$$

Similar to the construction of state based controller (7), we would drive $y^t \to 0$ exponentially. Therefore, the feedback controller that linearizes the time based output is given as

$$u_t = \left(\mathcal{L}_g \mathcal{L}_f y^a\right)^{-1} \left(-\mathcal{L}_f^2 y^a + \ddot{y}^{t,d} + \mu_t\right), \tag{15}$$

where μ_t is the linear feedback applied after the feedback linearization. We can either pick μ_t via a simple PD law

$$\mu_t = -\frac{2}{\varepsilon}\dot{y}^t - \frac{1}{\varepsilon^2}y^t, \tag{16}$$

for some $0 < \varepsilon < 1$, or via an optimal control law through *control Lyapunov functions* (CLFs). Nevertheless, using the time based feedback linearizing controller (15) reduces the nonlinear system (3) to the normal form

$$\begin{aligned} \dot{\eta}_t &= \underbrace{\begin{bmatrix} 0_{k\times k} & 1_{k\times k} \\ 0_{k\times k} & 0_{k\times k} \end{bmatrix}}_{F} \eta_t + \underbrace{\begin{bmatrix} 0_{k\times k} \\ 1_{k\times k} \end{bmatrix}}_{G} \mu_t \\ \dot{z}_t &= \Psi_t(\eta_t, z_t), \end{aligned} \tag{17}$$

which is similar to (9), but with the use of time based outputs: $\eta_t = [y^t, \dot{y}^t]^T \in \mathbb{R}^{2k}$. Note that the zero dynamics coordinates z_t, evolve based on time due to the dependency on η_t. Accordingly, if the time based transverse dynamics η_t are 0, we have the zero dynamics $\dot{z}_t = \Psi_t(0, z_t)$. Convergence of the time based outputs can be ensured by picking an appropriate time based control law (16). But this controller does not necessarily ensure the convergence of the state based outputs. We are interested in the stability of the state based transverse dynamics (η), given that the time based control law is implemented on the robot.

State based vs. time based control laws. Given the controller (16) that could drive the time based outputs $\eta_t \to 0$, we will study the evolution of the state based outputs η in (9). By the assumption of Theorem 1 in [3], the controller yields an exponentially stable periodic orbit for hybrid dynamics. Therefore, we will obtain conditions for the stability of this hybrid periodic orbit when a time based control law is applied. Picking the input (15) on the dynamics of state based output y, we have

$$\ddot{y} = \mathcal{L}_f^2 y + \mathcal{L}_g \mathcal{L}_f y u_t, \tag{18}$$

$$\ddot{y} = \underbrace{\mathcal{L}_f^2 y + \mathcal{L}_g \mathcal{L}_f y u}_{=:\mu} + \underbrace{\mathcal{L}_g \mathcal{L}_f y (u_t - u)}_{=:d}, \tag{19}$$

$$\ddot{y} = \mu + d, \tag{20}$$

where $d = \mathcal{L}_g\mathcal{L}_f y (\mathcal{L}_g\mathcal{L}_f y^a)^{-1}(-\mathcal{L}_f^2 y^a + \ddot{y}^{t,d} + \mu_t) - \mu + \mathcal{L}_f^2 y$, is obtained by substituting for u_t, u from (7), (15). An alternative interpretation of (18) is that, the stabilizing control input $\mu(\eta)$ (which is state based) should have been applied, but instead, the time based input $\mu + d$ was applied to the state based output dynamics of y. Applying a time based feedback control law completely eliminated the dependency on the noisy phase variable $\tau(q)$, but the consequence is the appearance of the disturbance input d. The expression for d can be further simplified to

$$d(t, q, \dot{q}, \ddot{q}, \mu_t, \mu) = (\mu_t - \mu) + (\ddot{y}^{t,d} - \ddot{y}^d). \tag{21}$$

We know that, $y^d = y^d(\tau(q))$ (for bipedal robots), and it can be observed that d becomes small by minimizing the error $\ddot{y}^{t,d}(\tau(t)) - \ddot{y}^d(\tau(q))$. Therefore d can be termed *time-phase uncertainty*, or just *phase uncertainty.*

In the context of linear systems, it is important to have bounded state based output dynamics if d is bounded. Of course, the time based outputs $\eta_t \to 0$. Denote the supremum of the uncertainty over time as $\|d\|_\infty$, we can easily establish that a bounded d results in bounded outputs $y, \dot{y}$ (or just η), for the continuous dynamics. However, due to the impact dynamics that are not just nonlinear, but also extremely destabilizing (the noisy impacts can be observed in the video [1]), output boundedness cannot be guaranteed for the hybrid dynamics. This motivates using the notion of input to state stability to establish boundedness on the state based outputs for bipedal robotic running on DURUS-2D.

Going back to (18), we can substitute this formulation in (9), which results in the following representation:

$$\dot{\eta} = F\eta + G\mu + Gd,$$
$$\dot{z} = \Psi(\eta, z). \tag{22}$$

As mentioned before, we are free to pick $\mu(\eta)$ (say (8)), since the actual control input applied is time based $\mu_t(\eta_t)$ (from (36)) which is implicit in d. From the point of view of the state based outputs η, we have the following representation dynamics of the Lyapunov function:

$$\dot{V}_\varepsilon = \eta^T(F^T P_\varepsilon + P_\varepsilon F)\eta + 2\eta^T P_\varepsilon G\mu + 2\eta^T P_\varepsilon G d, \tag{23}$$

obtained by substituting (22) for η. Using the linear feedback law $\mu(\eta)$ from (8), the following is obtained:

$$\dot{V}_\varepsilon \leq -\frac{\gamma}{\varepsilon} V_\varepsilon + 2\eta^T P_\varepsilon G d. \tag{24}$$

It should be noted that even though the time based controller leads to convergence of time based outputs $y^t \to 0$, equation (24) extends it to state based outputs y that are driven exponentially to an ultimate bound. And this ultimate exponential bound is explicitly derived from d, which is established via the notion of *input to state stability* (ISS).

Input to State Stability. We will first introduce the basic definitions and results related to ISS for a general nonlinear system and then focus on the hybrid running dynamics (see [25] for a detail survey on ISS). Assume we have a general nonlinear system, represented in the following fashion:

$$\dot{x} = f(x, d), \tag{25}$$

with x taking values in Euclidean space $\mathbb{R}^n$, the input $d \in \mathbb{R}^m$ for some positive integers n, m. The mapping $f : \mathbb{R}^n \times \mathbb{R}^m \to \mathbb{R}^n$ is considered Lipschitz continuous and $f(0,0) = 0$. It can be seen that the input considered here is d. Therefore, the construction is such that a stabilizing controller $u(x)$ has been applied (such as (7)). Any deviation from this stabilizing controller can be viewed as $u(x) + d$, with d being a new disturbance input. In the example of the linearized system (22), a suitable stabilizing controller $\mu(\eta)$ is applied and the effect of the disturbance input d is analyzed. We assume that d takes values in the space of all Lebesgue measurable functions: $\|d\|_\infty = \text{ess.sup}_{t\geq 0}\|d(t)\| < \infty$, which can be denoted as $d \in \mathbb{L}^\infty$.

Class $\mathcal{K}_\infty$ and $\mathcal{KL}$ functions. A class $\mathcal{K}_\infty$ function is a function $\alpha : \mathbb{R}_{\geq 0} \to \mathbb{R}_{\geq 0}$ which is continuous, strictly increasing, unbounded, and satisfies $\alpha(0) = 0$. And a class $\mathcal{KL}$ function is a function $\beta : \mathbb{R}_{\geq 0} \times \mathbb{R}_{\geq 0} \to \mathbb{R}_{\geq 0}$ such that $\beta(r, .) \in \mathcal{K}_\infty$ for each t and $\beta(., t) \to 0$ as $t \to \infty$.

We can now define ISS for the system (25).

Definition 1. *The system (25) is input to state stable (ISS) if there exists $\beta \in \mathcal{KL}$, $\iota \in \mathcal{K}_\infty$ such that*

$$|x(t, x_0)| \leq \beta(|x_0|, t) + \iota(\|d\|_\infty), \qquad \forall x_0, \forall t \geq 0, \tag{26}$$

and considered locally ISS, if the inequality (26) is valid for an open ball of radius r, $x_0 \in \mathbb{B}_r(0)$.

Definition 2. *The system (25) is exponentially input to state stable (e-ISS) if there exists $\beta \in \mathcal{KL}$, $\iota \in \mathcal{K}_\infty$ and a positive constant $\lambda > 0$ such that*

$$|x(t, x_0)| \leq \beta(|x_0|, t)e^{-\lambda t} + \iota(\|d\|_\infty), \qquad \forall x_0, \forall t \geq 0, \tag{27}$$

and considered locally e-ISS, if the inequality (27) is valid for an open ball of radius r, $x_0 \in B_r(0)$.

ISS-Lyapunov functions. We can develop Lyapunov functions that satisfy the ISS conditions and achieve the stability property.

Definition 3. *A smooth function $V : \mathbb{R}^n \to \mathbb{R}_{\geq 0}$ is an ISS-Lyapunov function for (25) if there exist functions $\underline{\alpha}$, $\bar{\alpha}$, α, $\iota \in \mathcal{K}_\infty$ such that*

$$\underline{\alpha}(|x|) \leq V(x) \leq \bar{\alpha}(|x|)$$
$$\dot{V}(x, d) \leq -\alpha(|x|) \quad \text{for} |x| \geq \iota(\|d\|_\infty). \tag{28}$$

The following lemma establishes the relationship between the ISS-Lyapunov function and the ISS of (25).

Lemma 1. *The system (25) is ISS if and only if it admits a smooth ISS-Lyapunov function.*

Proof of Lemma 1 was given in [25]. In fact the inequality condition can be made stricter by using the exponential estimate:

$$\dot{V}(x,d) \leq -cV(x) + \iota(\|d\|_\infty), \qquad \forall x, d. \tag{29}$$

which is then called the e-ISS Lyapunov function.

3.2 Phase Uncertainty to State Stability

We can now define the notion of *phase to state stability* (PSS). Without loss of generality, we denote $(\eta, z) = (\eta_v, z_v)$, and the subscript v will be specified when a specific domain (s or f) is considered.

Definition 4. *Assume a ball of radius r centered at the origin. The system given by (22) is locally* ***phase to η stable****, if there exists $\beta \in \mathcal{KL}$, $\iota \in \mathcal{K}_\infty$ such that*

$$|\eta(t)| \leq \beta(|\eta(0)|, t) + \iota(\|d\|_\infty), \forall \eta(0) \in \mathbb{B}_r(0), \forall t \geq 0, \tag{30}$$

and it is locally PSS if

$$|(\eta(t), z(t))| \leq \beta(|(\eta(0), z(0))|, t) + \iota(\|d\|_\infty),$$
$$\forall \eta(0) \in \mathbb{B}_r(0), \forall t \geq 0.$$

Based on the asymptotic gain and zero stability property of the system (22) w.r.t. the *phase uncertainty* d, we have the following lemma.

Lemma 2. *Given the controller $\mu(\eta)$ in (8), the system (22) is phase to η stable.*

PROOF. Based on the constructions of the Lyapunov function V_ε, we have the dynamics of the from (24):

$$\begin{aligned}\dot{V}_\varepsilon &\leq -\frac{\gamma}{\varepsilon}V_\varepsilon + 2\eta^T P_\varepsilon G d \\ &\leq -\frac{\gamma}{\varepsilon}V_\varepsilon + 2|\eta|\|P_\varepsilon\|\|d\|_\infty \\ &\leq -\frac{\gamma}{2\varepsilon}V_\varepsilon \qquad \text{for} \quad |\eta| \geq \frac{4c_2}{\gamma c_1 \varepsilon}\|d\|_\infty,\end{aligned} \tag{31}$$

which is thus an ISS-Lyapunov function (28). □

We can also realize exponentially ultimate boundedness of the entire dynamics by appending a state based linear feedback law to the time based feedback controller (16)

$$u_T = u_t + \bar{\mu}, \tag{32}$$

which results in the following output dynamics in the place of (18):

$$\ddot{y} = \mu + d + \mathcal{L}_g\mathcal{L}_f y\bar{\mu}. \tag{33}$$

$\mathcal{L}_g\mathcal{L}_f y$ can be explicitly computed as $\mathcal{L}_g\mathcal{L}_f y = \mathcal{J}D^{-1}B$, where D and B are obtained from (1), and $\mathcal{J} = \partial y/\partial q$ is the Jacobian of the outputs. Since D is invertible, it can be easily shown that $\mathcal{J}D^{-1}B$ is invertible. By applying (32), system (22) will have an extra input $\bar{\mu}$ that yields:

$$\begin{aligned}\dot{\eta} &= F\eta + G\mu + Gd + G\mathcal{J}D^{-1}B\bar{\mu} \\ \dot{z} &= \Psi(\eta, z),\end{aligned} \tag{34}$$

then (24) gets reformulated as

$$\dot{V}_\varepsilon \leq -\frac{\gamma}{\varepsilon}V_\varepsilon + 2\eta^T P_\varepsilon G d + 2\eta^T P_\varepsilon G\mathcal{J}D^{-1}B\bar{\mu}. \tag{35}$$

By picking a control law for the auxiliary input

$$\bar{\mu} = -\frac{1}{2\bar{\varepsilon}}(\mathcal{J}D^{-1}B)^{-1}G^T P_\varepsilon \eta, \tag{36}$$

we have the following simplification of (35):

$$\dot{V}_\varepsilon \leq -\frac{\gamma}{\varepsilon}V_\varepsilon + 2\eta^T P_\varepsilon G d - \frac{1}{\bar{\varepsilon}}\eta^T P_\varepsilon G G^T P_\varepsilon \eta. \tag{37}$$

Therefore, by defining the semi-definite function $\bar{V}_\varepsilon(\eta) = \eta^T P_\varepsilon G G^T P_\varepsilon \eta$, we can pick $\bar{\varepsilon}$ small enough to cancel the effect of *phase uncertainty* on the dynamics. Lemma 2 can now be redefined to obtain exponential ultimate boundedness for the new control input (32).

Lemma 3. *Given the controllers $\mu(\eta)$ in (8), and $\bar{\mu}(\eta)$ in (36), the system (34) is exponentially phase to η stable w.r.t. the input disturbance $d \in \mathbb{L}^\infty$.*

PROOF. We again pick the derivative of the Lyapunov function V_ε resulting in

$$\begin{aligned}\dot{V}_\varepsilon &\leq -\frac{\gamma}{\varepsilon}V_\varepsilon - \frac{1}{\bar{\varepsilon}}\eta^T P_\varepsilon G G^T P_\varepsilon \eta + 2\eta^T P_\varepsilon G d \\ &\leq -\frac{\gamma}{\varepsilon}V_\varepsilon \qquad \text{for} \quad |\eta| \geq \frac{2\bar{\varepsilon}c_2}{c_1^2\varepsilon^2}\|d\|_\infty,\end{aligned} \tag{38}$$

which satisfies the exponential estimate (29). □

Now Lemma 3 can be extended to include the uncontrolled states z given that they are stable. Let $Y \subset \mathbb{R}^{2k}$, $Z \subset \mathbb{R}^{2(n-k)}$, $\phi_t(\eta, z)$ be the flow of (34) with the initial condition $(\eta, z) \in Y \times Z$. And let the flow ϕ_t be periodic with period $T_* > 0$ and a fixed point (η^*, z^*) if $\phi_{T_*}(\eta^*, z^*) = (\eta^*, z^*)$. Associated with the periodic flow is the periodic orbit

$$\mathcal{O} = \{\phi_t(\eta^*, z^*) \in Y \times Z : 0 \leq t \leq T_*\}.$$

Similarly, we denote the flow of the zero dynamics given by (34) by $\phi_t|_z$ and for a periodic flow we denote the corresponding periodic orbit by $\mathcal{O}_z = \mathcal{O}|_z$. Due to the invariance of the zero dynamics, we have the mapping $\mathcal{O} = \iota_0(\mathcal{O}_z)$, where $\iota_0 : Z \to Y \times Z$ is the canonical embedding. For any (η, z), we can denote the distance from $\mathcal{O}$ as $\|(\eta, z)\|_\mathcal{O}$. We now have the following theorem to establish *phase to state stability* of $\mathcal{O}$.

Theorem 1. *Assume that the periodic orbit $\mathcal{O}_z \subset Z$ is exponentially stable in the zero dynamics. Given the controllers $\mu(\eta)$ in (8), $\bar{\mu}(\eta)$ in (36) applied on (34), that render the outputs exponential phase to η stable, then the periodic orbit $\mathcal{O}$ obtained from the canonical embedding is exponentially phase to state stable.*

PROOF SKETCH. By the converse Lyapunov theorems, we can construct a quadratic Lyapunov function for the zero dynamics, $V_z(z)$ that satisfies the exponential inequality constraint:

$$\begin{aligned}&c_4\|z\|^2_{\mathcal{O}_z} \leq V_z \leq c_5\|z\|^2_{\mathcal{O}_z}, \\ &\frac{\partial V_z}{\partial z}\Psi(0, z) \leq -c_6 V_z, \qquad \left|\frac{\partial V_z}{\partial z}\right| \leq c_7\|z\|_{\mathcal{O}_z},\end{aligned} \tag{39}$$

where $\|z\|_{\mathcal{O}_z} = \|(0, z)\|_\mathcal{O}$. Consider the following Lyapunov candidate for the full order dynamics: $V_c(\eta, z) = \sigma V_z(z) + V_\varepsilon(\eta)$. This Lyapunov function is quadratic and satisfies the boundedness properties. Taking the derivative

$$\begin{aligned}\dot{V}_c &\leq -\sigma\frac{\partial V_z}{\partial z}\Psi(\eta, z) + \sigma\frac{\partial V_z}{\partial z}(\Psi(\eta, z) - \Psi(0, z)) + \dot{V}_\varepsilon, \\ &\leq -\sigma c_6 V_z + \sigma c_7 L_q\|z\|_{\mathcal{O}_z}\|\eta\| - \frac{\gamma}{\varepsilon}V_\varepsilon, \text{ for } |\eta| \geq \frac{2\bar{\varepsilon}c_2}{c_1^2\varepsilon^2}\|d\|_\infty,\end{aligned}$$

where the bounds on η are obtained from (38). By picking a suitable σ, we can render $\dot{V}_\varepsilon$ negative definite. □

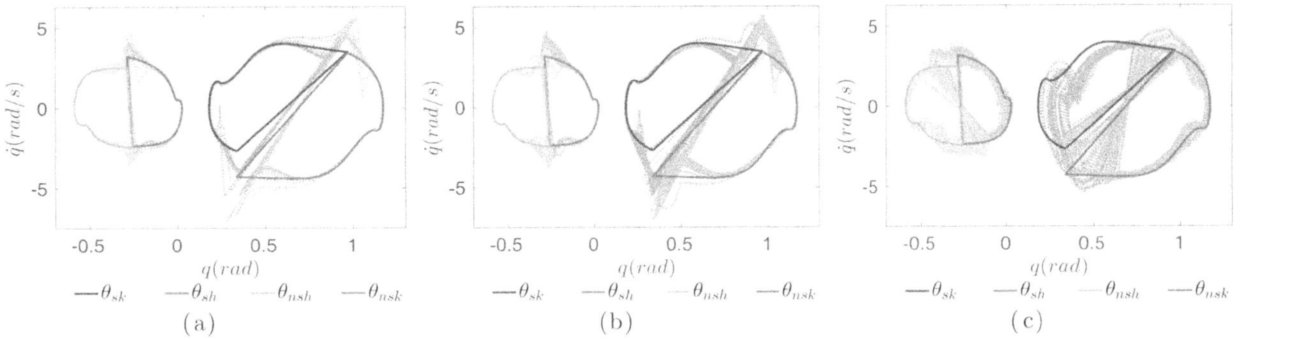

Figure 3: Limit cycles of (a) simulation where time based IO + state based PD controller was applied for 100 steps; (b) Simulation where white noise was added to $\tau_v(q)$; (c) Experimental data. Note the solid lines are the designated gait.

3.3 PSS for Hybrid Dynamics

In this part, we can extend the stability properties for hybrid systems. The subscripts v will be reintroduced to distinguish the domain representations. Here, we define the two-domain hybrid system that represents running dynamics of the robot in the following manner:

$$\mathscr{H} = \begin{cases} \dot{\eta}_v = F\eta_v + G\mu_v + G\mathcal{J}D^{-1}B\bar{\mu}_v + Gd \\ \dot{z}_v = \Psi_v(\eta_v, z_v), \quad \text{if}(\eta_v, z_v) \in \mathcal{D}_v \backslash S_v \\ \eta_{\mathrm{f}}^+ = \Delta_\eta(\eta_{\mathrm{s}}^-, z_{\mathrm{s}}^-) \\ z_{\mathrm{f}}^+ = \Delta_z(\eta_{\mathrm{s}}^-, z_{\mathrm{s}}^-), \quad \text{if}(\eta_{\mathrm{s}}^-, z_{\mathrm{s}}^-) \in S_{\mathrm{s}} \\ \eta_{\mathrm{s}}^+ = \Delta_\eta(\eta_{\mathrm{f}}^-, z_{\mathrm{f}}^-) \\ z_{\mathrm{s}}^+ = \Delta_z(\eta_{\mathrm{f}}^-, z_{\mathrm{f}}^-), \quad \text{if}(\eta_{\mathrm{f}}^-, z_{\mathrm{f}}^-) \in S_{\mathrm{f}} \end{cases} \tag{40}$$

where $\eta = \{\eta_{\mathrm{s}}, \eta_{\mathrm{f}}\}$, $z = \{z_{\mathrm{s}}, z_{\mathrm{f}}\}$, $\mathcal{D}_v$ are the domains and S_v are the switching surfaces given by

$$\mathcal{D}_{\mathrm{s}} = \{(\eta_{\mathrm{s}}, z_{\mathrm{s}}) \in Y \times Z : h_{nsf} > 0, h_{sf} = 0\},$$
$$S_{\mathrm{s}} = \{(\eta_{\mathrm{s}}, z_{\mathrm{s}}) \in Y \times Z : h_{nsf} > 0, h_{sf} = 0, \dot{h}_{sf} \geq 0\},$$
$$\mathcal{D}_{\mathrm{f}} = \{(\eta_{\mathrm{f}}, z_{\mathrm{f}}) \in Y \times Z : h_{nsf} \geq 0, h_{sf} > 0\},$$
$$S_{\mathrm{f}} = \{(\eta_{\mathrm{f}}, z_{\mathrm{f}}) \in Y \times Z : h_{nsf} = 0, h_{sf} > 0, \dot{h}_{nsf} < 0\},$$

with $h_{sf}, h_{nsf} : Y \times Z \to \mathbb{R}$ the heights of the stance and nonstance foot respectively. The reset map $\Delta(\eta_v, z_v) = (\Delta_\eta(\eta_v, z_v), \Delta_z(\eta_v, z_v))$ represents the discrete dynamics of the system. For the robot, it represents the impact dynamics of the system when it switches from flight to stance phase and vice versa. Plastic impacts are assumed.

In order to obtain bounds on the output dynamics for hybrid periodic orbits, it is assumed that $\mathscr{H}$ has hybrid zero dynamics for state based control law given by (7) and (8). More specifically we assume that $\Delta_\eta(0, z_v) = 0$, so that the surface Z is invariant through the discrete dynamics. The hybrid zero dynamics can be described as

$$\mathscr{H}|_Z = \begin{cases} \dot{z}_v = \Psi(0, z_v) & \text{if } z_v \in Z \backslash (S_{\mathrm{s}} \cup S_{\mathrm{f}}) \\ z_{\mathrm{f}}^+ = \Delta_z(0, z_{\mathrm{s}}^-) & \text{if } z_{\mathrm{s}}^- \in (S_{\mathrm{s}} \cap Z) \\ z_{\mathrm{s}}^+ = \Delta_z(0, z_{\mathrm{f}}^-) & \text{if } z_{\mathrm{f}}^- \in (S_{\mathrm{f}} \cap Z). \end{cases} \tag{41}$$

Let $\phi_t(\eta, z)$ be the hybrid flow of (22) with the initial condition (η, z), t be the time, which is typically the time taken to pass through all domains. Since we are considering a two-domain hybrid system, if $(\eta, z) \in S_{\mathrm{f}}$, then $\phi_t(\eta, z) = \phi^{\mathrm{f}}_{t_1} \circ \Delta \circ \phi^{\mathrm{s}}_{t_2}(\Delta(\eta, z))$, and $t = t_1 + t_2$. The flow ϕ_t is periodic with period $T > 0$, and a fixed point $\phi_T(\eta^*, z^*) = (\eta^*, z^*)$. For the period T, T_1, T_2 are the impact times in the two domains such that $T_1 + T_2 = T$. Associated with the periodic flow is the periodic orbit $\mathcal{O} = \{\phi^{\mathrm{s}}_{t_1}(\Delta(\eta^*, z^*)) \cup \phi^{\mathrm{f}}_{t_2} \circ \Delta \circ \phi^{\mathrm{s}}_{T_1}(\Delta(\eta^*, z^*)) : 0 \leq t_1 \leq T_1, 0 \leq t_2 \leq T_2\}$. Similarly, we denote the flow of the zero dynamics $\dot{z} = \Psi(0, z)$ by $\phi_T|_z$ and for a periodic flow we denote the corresponding periodic orbit by $\mathcal{O}_z \subset Z$. The periodic orbit in Z corresponds to a periodic orbit for the full order dynamics, $\mathcal{O} = \iota_0(\mathcal{O}_z)$, through the canonical embedding $\iota_0(z) = (0, z)$.

Main Theorem. We can now introduce the main theorem of the paper. Similar to the continuous dynamics, it is assumed that the periodic orbit $\mathcal{O}_z$ is exponentially stable in the hybrid zero dynamics.

Theorem 2. *Let $\mathcal{O}_z$ be an exponentially stable periodic orbit of the hybrid zero dynamics $\mathscr{H}|_Z$ transverse to $S \cap Z$. Given the controllers $\mu_v(\eta_v)$ in (8), $\bar{\mu}_v(\eta_v)$ in (36), and given $r > 0$ such that $(\eta, z) \in \mathbb{B}_r(0, 0)$, then there exists $\delta_d > 0$ such that $\forall \; \|d\|_\infty < \delta_d$ the periodic orbit $\mathcal{O}$ is phase to state stable.*

Proof sketch. A sketch of the proof is provided here due to space limits. We shall use most of the concepts from [3]. Proof is also similar to that provided for parameter uncertainty in [15]. The key idea is to establish the boundedness of states for a bounded phase uncertainty d. We just need to realize a discrete time Lyapunov function for a Poincaré map that satisfies the conditions of an ISS-Lyapunov function. Note that for a small enough $\varepsilon > 0$, and $\|d\|_\infty = 0$, the full order periodic orbit $\mathcal{O}$ is exponentially stable. For $\|(\eta, z)\|_{\mathcal{O}} \geq \iota(\|d\|_\infty)$, we know that with sufficiently small $\bar{\varepsilon}$ in (36) we can retain the original convergence rate as indicated by (38). Thus, for the continuous dynamics, $\dot{V}_\varepsilon \leq -\frac{\gamma}{\varepsilon} V_\varepsilon$ for $\|(\eta, z)\|_{\mathcal{O}}$ sufficiently large. With this inequality, all of the formulations from equations (61) to (67) in [3] can be used. In other words, the periodic orbit $\mathcal{O}$ is exponentially converging till the ultimate bound, meaning the periodic orbit $\mathcal{O}$ is exponentially phase to state stable. □

Theorem 2 has powerful implications, due to the elimination of the noisy phase variable estimation. This elimination has its effect on tracking, which yields lower errors than that for the noisy phase based modulation. The time based phase modulation is a smooth and better candidate to replicate the unknown actual phase of the robot. This methodology can be easily extended to all kinds of additive uncertainties observed in hybrid systems in general. See [15] for analysis on parameter uncertainty.

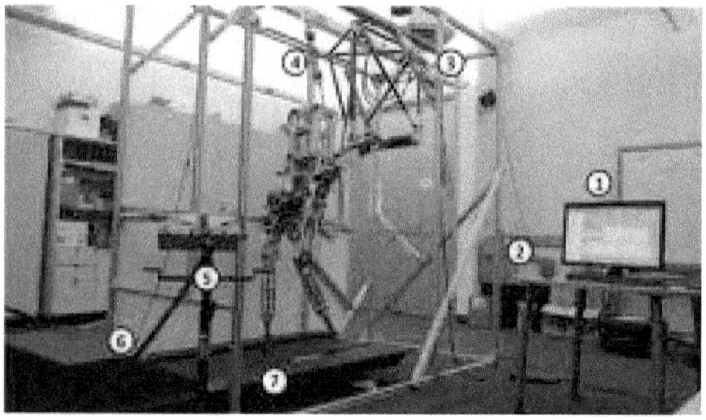

Figure 4: Experimental setup for DURUS-2D running: 1) Control station computer, 2) Emergency stop, 3) Four LiPo batteries, 4) Tripping harness, 5) Treadmill control panel, 6) Encoder Wheel to measure treadmill speed, 7) Treadmill.

4. EXPERIMENTAL IMPLEMENTATION

With the optimal running gait generated (Section 2.3) and time dependent RES-CLF controller defined (Section 3.3), we achieved sustainable robotic running. The goal of this section is to describe the experimental setup and the control methods adopted to realize stable running on DURUS-2D.

DURUS-2D Hardware. A popular approach for robotic running is to utilize the *spring-loaded inverted pendulum* (SLIP) model [8, 24], where the presence of springs allows for storing energy during high speed impacts thereby improving energy efficiency and torque performance. The previous version of DURUS-2D [9], had rigid carbon fiber calves, unlike the current version which has a linear spring at the end of each aluminum calf. The spring has a stiffness of 20 000 N/m and a damping constant of 100 N s/m. In addition, a 11.5 kg torso is installed to resemble the human weight distribution. The positions and velocities of the torso, knee and hip joints are measured by the attached incremental encoders. Further, the actuated joints, knees and hips, are powered by BLDC motors via cycloidal gear reduction, that provides a maximum continuous torque of 200 N m. With the new legs, DURUS-2D weights 41.7 kg. Other details about the electrical and software system can be found in [9].

Experimental Setup. As shown in Fig. 4, DURUS-2D is mounted on a carbon fiber boom structure which is attached to a cage frame via a fixed one dimensional track. This setup is used to isolate the lateral motions, leaving DURUS-2D to move freely in the sagittal plane. Moreover, the treadmill speed is measured by an encoder wheel and fed to the robot as an environment feedback.

Switching logic. Guard condition is used to switch the controller to the subsequent domain (stance or flight). In simulation, the guard condition is triggered when non-stance spring returns to the neutral position for stance domain, i.e., $r_{sp} = 0$. And when the nonstance foot lands on the ground, i.e., $nsf_z = 0$, the flight domain ends. However, due to a lack of effective sensing mechanism, we developed a time+state based switching logic for experiments. For a particular domain $\mathcal{D}_v$, the maximum value of time t_v^{max} and phase variable τ_v^{max} can be obtained from the gait design process. Then the guard condition is triggered when $t > 1.2t_v^{max}$. But if $t < 1.2t_v^{max}$, the guard will be triggered if $\tau_v(q) > \tau_v^{max}$. This way, the controller can respond to the feedback similarly to simulation while allowing for sensing noise of the phase variable.

Experimental Controller. Motivated by the results on ISS properties of PD controlled robotic systems in [6], we can replace the time based IO with a time based PD control law, and claim that the resulting system still retains desirable stability properties. For a robot like DURUS-2D , the inertia of the motor (proportional to the square of the gear ratio) coupled with relatively light legs results in stronger ISS conditions for model based uncertainty (see [15, 6]). We therefore pick a time+state based PD control law as follows

$$u_E = -K_p^t y_v^t - K_d^t \dot{y}_v^t - K_p y_v - K_d \dot{y}_v, \tag{42}$$

where K_p^t, K_d^t, K_p, K_d are constant gain matrices with appropriately tuned values.

5. RESULTS

We first validate the proposed control law in simulation. As explained in Section 2, a HZD running gait was first generated that meets all physical limitations, which assumed a feedback linearization controller (7). Then we utilized the time based feedback linearization + state based PD control law given by (32) (see Section 3) in simulation, stable trajectory tracking is achieved that is ultimately bounded to the periodic orbit (see Fig. 7b for the evolution of virtual constraints, i.e., output errors, for 100 steps, and Fig. 3a for phase portrait that is also bounded around the desired gait) when the phase uncertainty is bounded (Fig. 7a). However, in experiments, noisy sensing often occurs around impact dynamics. Therefore to simulate an unideal case, we added a noise signal with amplitude 0.1 to $\tau_s(q)$ before and after impacts (see Fig. 7c). By applying the same controller, ultimate boundless was also achieved (see Fig. 7d and Fig. 3b) and a stable bipedal running is accomplished. The running tiles are shown in Fig. 5. These simulated results, as a proof of concept, aligned with Theorem 2 in Section 3.3.

In reality, neither state based phase measurements $\tau_v(q)$, nor time based phase calculation $\tau_v(t)$ is capable of producing successful bipedal running (watch [2] for the failed running when pure time based controller was used). However, by applying a variant of time + state based feedback as shown by (42), a sustainable running on DURUS-2D is immediately shown in real world experiments. Multiple views in [1] show that the running is repeatable for over 150 steps. The phase portrait for 30 steps are shown in Fig. 3c, and the output errors are shown in Fig. 7f, both of which have shown ultimate boundedness. Further, the time based and state based phase variables are shown in Fig. 7e. Experimental running tiles are compared to simulation at Fig. 5. The most distinguishable feature of running, foot clearance, is shown in Fig. 6, with the maximum clearance 13 cm, and the flight domain takes 60% of one step. The average running speed is 1.75 m/s, and the measured average mechanical cost of transport (MCOT) for 100 steps is 0.5287.

6. CONCLUSIONS

The high degrees of underactuation coupled with rapid switching behaviors between two domains (stance and flight) make bipedal running an important problem, both from a theoretical and experimental standpoint. The success of the demonstrated results serves two important purposes: 1) The reliability and efficiency of the direct collocation based tra-

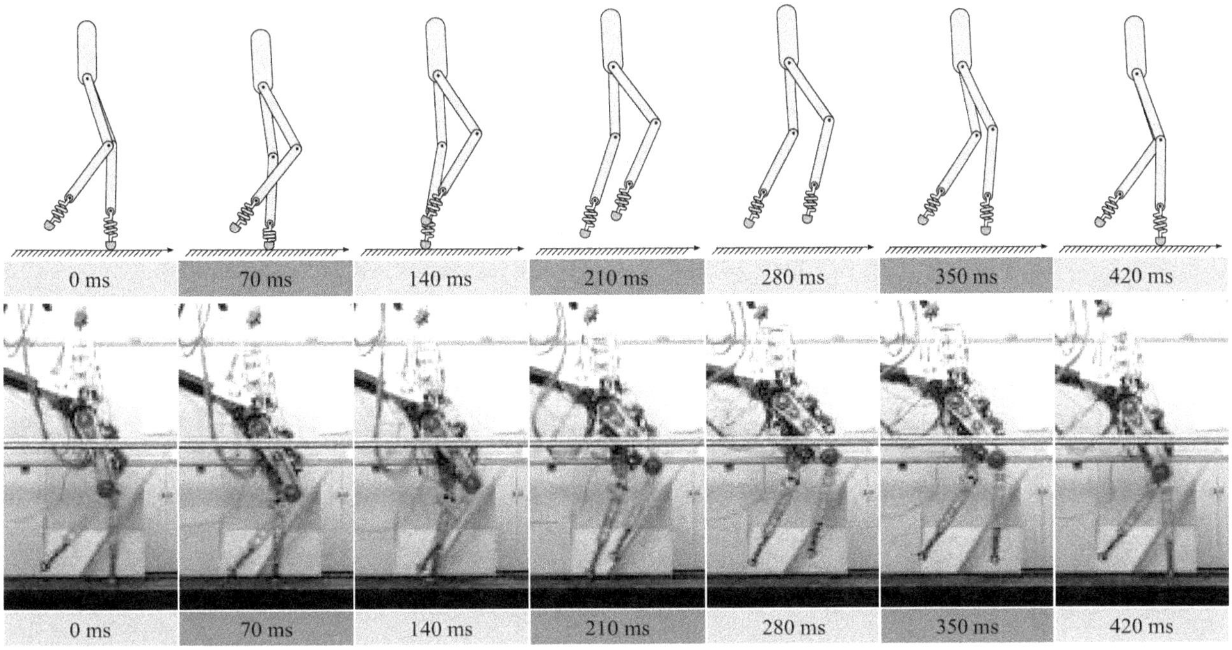

Figure 5: Running tiles of simulation (top) vs. experiment (bottom) for one step.

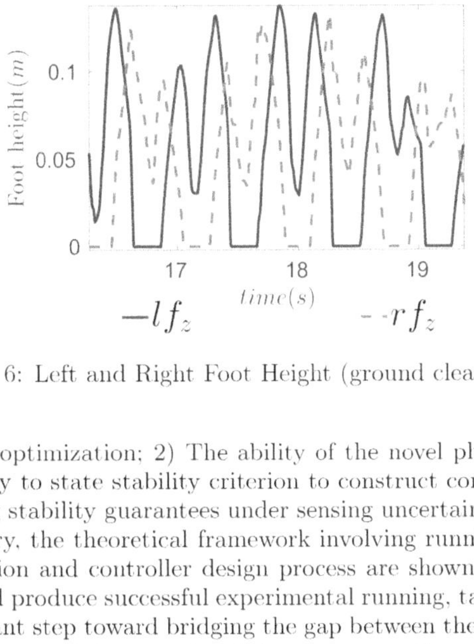

Figure 6: Left and Right Foot Height (ground clearance).

jectory optimization; 2) The ability of the novel phase uncertainty to state stability criterion to construct controllers yielding stability guarantees under sensing uncertainties. In summary, the theoretical framework involving running gait generation and controller design process are shown to predict and produce successful experimental running, taking an important step toward bridging the gap between theory and experiment. Future work will involve expanding on these techniques to realize 3D running.

7. REFERENCES

[1] Bipedal robotic running of DURUS-2D. https://youtu.be/6k9_tf4ctk4.

[2] Failed time based running. https://youtu.be/2Stq0Q1bEFk.

[3] A. Ames, K. Galloway, K. Sreenath, and J. Grizzle. Rapidly exponentially stabilizing control lyapunov functions and hybrid zero dynamics. *Automatic Control, IEEE Transactions on*, 59(4):876–891, 2014.

[4] A. D. Ames. Human-inspired control of bipedal robots via control lyapunov functions and quadratic programs. In *Proceedings of the 16th international conference on Hybrid systems: computation and control*, pages 31–32. ACM, 2013.

[5] A. D. Ames. Human-inspired control of bipedal walking robots. *IEEE Transactions on Automatic Control*, 59(5):1115–1130, May 2014.

[6] D. Angeli. Input-to-state stability of pd-controlled robotic systems. *Automatica*, 35(7):1285 – 1290, 1999.

[7] P. A. Bhounsule, J. Cortell, A. Grewal, B. Hendriksen, J. D. Karssen, C. Paul, and A. Ruina. Low-bandwidth reflex-based control for lower power walking: 65 km on a single battery charge. *The International Journal of Robotics Research*, 33(10):1305–1321, 2014.

[8] R. Blickhan. The spring–mass model for running and hopping. *Journal of Biomechanics*, 22(11):1217–1227.

[9] E. Cousineau and A. D. Ames. Realizing underactuated bipedal walking with torque controllers via the ideal model resolved motion method. In *Robotics and Automation (ICRA), IEEE International Conference on*, pages 5747–5753, May 2015.

[10] J. W. Grizzle, G. Abba, and F. Plestan. Asymptotically Stable Walking for Biped Robots: Analysis via Systems with Impulse Effects. *IEEE Trans. on Automatic Control*, 46(1):51–64, Jan. 2001.

[11] J. W. Grizzle, C. Chevallereau, R. W. Sinnet, and A. D. Ames. Models, feedback control, and open problems of 3D bipedal robotic walking. *Automatica*, 50(8):1955 – 1988, 2014.

[12] A. Hereid, E. Cousineau, C. Hubicki, and A. D. Ames. 3D dynamic walking with underactuated humanoid robots: A direct collocation framework for optimizing hybrid zero dynamics. In *IEEE International Conference on Robotics and Automation*, 2016.

[13] A. Hereid, C. M. Hubicki, E. A. Cousineau, J. W. Hurst, and A. D. Ames. Hybrid zero dynamics based

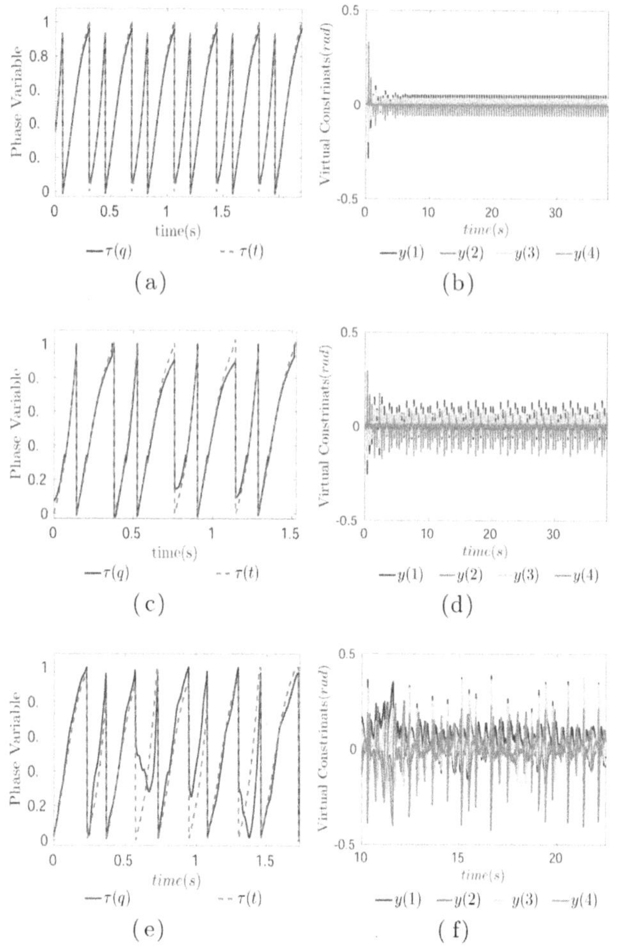

Figure 7: The left column is the phase variables which are used to calculate time and state based outputs: $y^{d,t}(t) = y_v^d(\tau_v(t))$, $y^d(q) = y_v^d(\tau_v(q))$, the right column is output errors (virtual constraints) showing ultimate boundedness. (a, b, c, d) are from two simulations with controller given by (32). And (c, d) has a sinusoidal disturbance with 10% amplitude added to $\tau_v(q)$; (e, f) are from experiments.

multiple shooting optimization with applications to robotic walking. In *Robotics and Automation (ICRA), IEEE International Conference on*, 2015.

[14] S. Kolathaya and A. D. Ames. Achieving bipedal locomotion on rough terrain through human-inspired control. In *Safety, Security, and Rescue Robotics (SSRR), IEEE International Symposium on*, 2012.

[15] S. Kolathaya and D. A. Ames. Parameter to state stability of control lyapunov functions for hybrid system models of robots. In *Nonlinear Analysis Hybrid Systems*. Elsevier, 2016.

[16] S. Kolathaya, A. Hereid, and A. D. Ames. Time dependent control lyapunov functions and hybrid zero dynamics for stable robotic locomotion. In *American Control Conference (ACC)*. IEEE, 2016.

[17] W. Ma, A. Hereid, C. Hubicki, and A. D. Ames. Efficient hzd gait generation for three-dimensional underactuated humanoid running. In *2016 IEEE International Conference on Intelligent Robots and Systems (IROS)*, Korea, 2016.

[18] I. R. Manchester, U. Mettin, F. Iida, and R. Tedrake. Stable dynamic walking over uneven terrain. *The International Journal of Robotics Research*, 30(3):265–279, Jan. 2011.

[19] A. E. Martin, D. C. Post, and J. P. Schmiedeler. Design and experimental implementation of a hybrid zero dynamics-based controller for planar bipeds with curved feet. *The International Journal of Robotics Research*, 33(7):988–1005, 2014.

[20] B. Morris and J. Grizzle. Hybrid invariant manifolds in systems with impulse effects with application to periodic locomotion in bipedal robots. *IEEE Transactions on Automatic Control*, 54(8):1751–1764.

[21] H. Park, K. Sreenath, A. Ramezani, and J. W. Grizzle. Switching control design for accommodating large step-down disturbances in bipedal robot walking. In *IEEE/RSJ International Conference on Robotics and Automation (ICRA)*, pages 45–50. Ieee, May 2012.

[22] M. Raibert. *Legged robots that balance*, volume 3. MIT press Cambridge, MA, 1986.

[23] A. V. Rao. A survey of numerical methods for optimal control. *Advances in the Astronautical Sciences*, 2009.

[24] S. Rezazadeh, C. M. Hubicki, M. Jones, A. Peekema, J. Van Why, A. Abate, and J. Hurst. Spring-mass walking with ATRIAS in 3D: Robust gait control spanning zero to 4.3 kph on a heavily underactuated bipedal robot. In *Proceedings of the ASME 2015 Dynamic Systems and Control Conference*, 2015.

[25] E. D. Sontag. Input to state stability: Basic concepts and results. In *Nonlinear and optimal control theory*, pages 163–220. Springer, 2008.

[26] K. Sreenath, H. Park, I. Poulakakis, and J. W. Grizzle. A compliant hybrid zero dynamics controller for stable, efficient and fast bipedal walking on MABEL. *The International Journal of Robotics Research*, 30(9):1170–1193, 2011.

[27] K. Sreenath, H.-W. Park, I. Poulakakis, and J. Grizzle. Embedding active force control within the compliant hybrid zero dynamics to achieve stable, fast running on MABEL. *The International Journal of Robotics Research*, 32(3):324–345, Mar. 2013.

[28] T. Tamada, W. Ikarashi, D. Yoneyama, K. Tanaka, Y. Yamakawa, T. Senoo, and M. Ishikawa. High-speed bipedal robot running using high-speed visual feedback. In *2014 IEEE-RAS International Conference on Humanoid Robots*, pages 140–145, Nov 2014.

[29] M. Vukobratovic and B. Borovac. Zero-moment point? thirty five years of its life. *International Journal of Humanoid Robotics*, 1(1):157–173, 2004.

[30] H. Zhao, A. Hereid, W. l. Ma, and A. D. Ames. Multi-contact bipedal robotic locomotion. *Robotica*, FirstView:1–35, 2 2016.

[31] H. Zhao, S. Yadukumar, and A. Ames. Bipedal robotic running with partial hybrid zero dynamics and human-inspired optimization. In *IEEE/RSJ International Conference on Intelligent Robots and Systems (IROS)*, pages 1821–1827, Oct 2012.

Author Index

www.ingramcontent.com/pod-product-compliance
Lightning Source LLC
LaVergne TN
LVHW060137070326
832902LV00018B/2833